The Penguin Dictionary of
British Place Names

Adrian Room

PENGUIN BOOKS

PENGUIN BOOKS

Published by the Penguin Group
Penguin Books Ltd, 80 Strand, London WC2R 0RL, England
Penguin Putnam Inc., 375 Hudson Street, New York, New York 10014, USA
Penguin Books Australia Ltd, 250 Camberwell Road, Camberwell, Victoria 3124, Australia
Penguin Books Canada Ltd, 10 Alcorn Avenue, Toronto, Ontario, Canada M4V 3B2
Penguin Books India (P) Ltd, 11, Community Centre, Panchsheel Park, New Delhi – 110 017, India
Penguin Books (NZ) Ltd, Cnr Rosedale and Airborne Roads, Albany, Auckland, New Zealand
Penguin Books (South Africa) (Pty) Ltd, 24 Sturdee Avenue, Rosebank 2196, South Africa

Penguin Books Ltd, Registered Offices: 80 Strand, London WC2R 0RL, England

www.penguin.com

First published 2003
2

This book was produced using Librios® authoring & content management technology
Printed in England by Clays Ltd, St Ives plc

Always it is the names that work the most powerful magic, and nowhere more so than in Britain ... They tell us not only where we want to go but where we have come from; clues to our past and the forces that have shaped the land we live in.

Brian Jackman in the *Sunday Times Magazine*, 24 January 1988

PENGUIN REFERENCE

The Penguin Dictionary of British Place Names

Adrian Room is the author of several books on the origin of words and names, including *A Concise Dictionary of Modern Place-Names in Great Britain and Ireland* (1983), *A Dictionary of Irish Place-Names* (1986), *Dictionary of Place-Names in the British Isles* (1988) and *Placenames of the World* (1997). He also wrote the sections on Irish, Welsh and Scottish place names for *The Oxford Names Companion* (2002). He is a Fellow of the Royal Geographical Society and a member of the English Place-Name Society, Scottish Place-Name Society and American Name Society.

Contents

Abbreviations

c	century
c.	*circa* ('about')
cp.	compare
DB	Domesday Book, 1086
EPNS	English Place-Name Society
LGBC	Local Government Boundary Commission
ME	Middle English
OC	Old Cornish
OE	Old English
OF	Old French
OI	Old Irish
OS	Old Scandinavian
OW	Old Welsh

Abbreviated County, Unitary Authority and London Borough Names

Aberdeens *Aberdeenshire (distinct from Aberdeen)*
Argyll & Bute *Argyll and Bute*
Barking & Dag *Barking and Dagenham*
Bath & NE Somerset *Bath and North East Somerset*
Beds *Bedfordshire*
Blackburn with Dar *Blackburn with Darwen*
Borders *Scottish Borders*
Bracknell F *Bracknell Forest*
Brighton & Hove *Brighton and Hove*
Bucks *Buckinghamshire*
Cambs *Cambridgeshire*
Carm *Carmarthenshire*
Clack *Clackmannanshire*
Denb *Denbighshire*
Derbys *Derbyshire (distinct from Derby)*
Dumfries & Gall *Dumfries and Galloway*
E Ayrs *East Ayrshire*
E Dunbartons *East Dunbartonshire*
E Lothian *East Lothian*
E Renfrews *East Renfrewshire*
E Sussex *East Sussex*
E Yorks *East Riding of Yorkshire*
Flints *Flintshire*
Glos *Gloucestershire*
Hammersmith & Ful *Hammersmith and Fulham*
Hants *Hampshire*
Herefords *Herefordshire*
Herts *Hertfordshire*
Hull *Kingston upon Hull*
IoW *Isle of Wight*
Kensington & Chel *Kensington and Chelsea*
Kingston *Kingston upon Thames*
Lancs *Lancashire*
Leics *Leicestershire (distinct from Leicester)*
Lincs *Lincolnshire*
Milton K *Milton Keynes*
Mon *Monmouthshire*
M Tydfil *Merthyr Tydfil*

N Ayrs *North Ayrshire*
Neath PT *Neath Port Talbot*
NE Lincs *North East Lincolnshire*
Newcastle *Newcastle upon Tyne*
N Lanarks *North Lanarkshire*
N Lincs *North Lincolnshire*
Northants *Northamptonshire*
Northd *Northumberland*
Notts *Nottinghamshire (distinct from Nottingham)*
N Somerset *North Somerset*
N Tyneside *North Tyneside*
N Yorks *North Yorkshire*
Oxon *Oxfordshire*
Pemb *Pembrokeshire*
Perth & Kin *Perth and Kinross*
Redcar & Clev *Redcar and Cleveland*
Renfrews *Renfrewshire*
Rhondda CT *Rhondda Cynon Taff*
Richmond *Richmond upon Thames*
S Ayrs *South Ayrshire*
Scilly *Isles of Scilly*
S Glos *South Gloucestershire*
S Lanarks *South Lanarkshire*
Staffs *Staffordshire*
Stockton *Stockton-on-Tees*
Stoke *Stoke-on-Trent*
S Tyneside *South Tyneside*
Vale of Glam *Vale of Glamorgan*
Waltham F *Waltham Forest*
Warwicks *Warwickshire*
W Berks *West Berkshire*
W Dunbartons *West Dunbartonshire*
Westminster *City of Westminster*
Wilts *Wiltshire*
Windsor & Maid *Windsor and Maidenhead*
W Isles *Western Isles*
W Lothian *West Lothian*
Worcs *Worcestershire*
Wrekin *Telford and Wrekin*
W Sussex *West Sussex*

Introduction

1. The world of place names

Place names are everywhere, in the literal sense of the word. They serve as directional markers and as locational statements: 'I am going to London tomorrow', 'We went to Cornwall last year', 'She used to live in Leeds', 'Do you like Dundee?', 'He showed us his photos of Snowdonia'. The average Briton carries a sizeable mental portfolio of well-known names such as these, and can usually readily associate them with their location, as well as their actual or reputed attributes. 'London' is not just a city in the southeast of England but the capital of the United Kingdom. 'Cornwall' is not just a county in the southwest of England but a place of summer holidays, with a beautiful coastline. 'Dundee' is not merely a city in eastern Scotland but a place noted for its cake and its marmalade. 'Snowdonia' is not simply a mountainous region of northwest Wales, but another holiday region with attractive views.

Names of small or unfamiliar places will fail to carry such associations, except to those who know them on a local basis: 'I am going to Linton tomorrow', 'We went to Sandhead last year', 'She used to live in Ledsham', 'Do you like Devonside?', 'He showed us his photos of Northop'. But purely as place names, such names are as valid and meaningful as those of familiar places and regions.

Meaningful? Or meaningless? What does 'London' mean? What does 'Dundee' mean? Or 'Linton'? Or 'Northop'? We become so familiar with place names that we are able to make general deductions about the place itself from its name, often correctly. A name ending in '-ton', for example, we expect to be that of an inhabited place such as a town or village. We do not expect it to be that of a river, or a mountain, or some other natural feature. A name ending in '-bury', '-borough' or '-brough' is also usually that of a town, sometimes an important one, such as *Newbury* or *Scarborough* or *Middlesbrough*, while a place ending in '-chester' or '-caster' or '-cester' is often an ancient town or city, such as *Winchester* or *Doncaster* or *Leicester*.

When it comes to the meaning of names such as *Tring* or *Troon* or *Tenby*, however, we are often left guessing. *Newcastle* is straightforward enough. But *Wigan*? *Windsor*? Place names are notoriously susceptible to explanations of the romantic or 'storybook' type, and there are thus those who will assure you that *Edinburgh* is named after King Edwin, or that *Coventry* arose around a convent. There is nothing new in this. Bailey's *Universal Etymological English Dictionary* of 1721 offers some place-name origins that were regarded as genuine in their day but that are now seen as fantastic. Thus the name of *Amersham* is said to mean 'a Village fenced from the Violence of the Winds with a Row of Oaks', while *Buxton* is so called 'by Reason of the Plenty of Beeches growing there'. *Hatfield* is named 'from the hot sandy Soil of the Ground' (i.e. as if 'hot field'), and *Maidenhead* is 'so called upon the Account of their superstitious adoring the Head of a certain British Maid, one of the 11,000 Companions of St Ursula'. *Maidstone*, on the other hand, is supposedly named after the river Medway, on which it stands, while *Thanet* takes its name from Greek *thanatos*, 'death', 'because it killeth Serpents that are brought into it'. (This last fiction was first proposed by the Latin grammarian Solinus in the third century AD.) Linguistic expertise has moved on since then, however, and we can now propose a proper meaning for many of the names in Britain, if usually a much more prosaic one.

And that is where the present dictionary comes in, its aim being to give the origins of over 10,000 names of places in Great Britain by 'cracking' the information that each of them holds. The names are those of cities, towns and villages, of urban districts and suburbs, of counties and unitary authorities, and of rivers, lakes, hills, mountains, forests, islands and other natural features. English names (meaning names in England) predominate over those in Scotland and Wales, simply because more is known about them. But this imbalance should not detract from the overall representation of name types. Nor does it diminish the incidental information provided, such as the meanings of the many surnames that derive from place names, names such as Bickford, Churchill, Dymock, Hackforth, Lupton, Mumby, Scargill and Wickham, originally borne by those who came from these places.

2. *The chronology of place names*

The language of place names is intimately linked with the history of their country. Britain has seen a series of invasions over the centuries that have introduced a variety of languages, each spoken by the people who actually gave the names in the first place. It is usual to divide place names by language types into (a) *pre-Celtic*, existing before the Celts came to the British Isles from Europe in the fourth century BC; (b) *Celtic*, given by the Celts once they had settled; (c) *Latin*, given by the Romans, who came to Britain with Julius Caesar in 55 BC and stayed until the fifth century AD; (d) *Old English*, given by the Anglo-Saxons, who invaded Britain from the fifth century AD; (e) *Scandinavian*, given by the Vikings, who came to Britain in the ninth century; (f) *Norman French*, given by the Normans, who invaded England under William the Conqueror in 1066 (as every schoolboy once knew); and (g) *Modern English*, as names given in more recent times by the descendants of this mixture of peoples.

From a purely linguistic point of view, three different language groups are involved here, beginning with Celtic and proceeding through Romance (Latin, then Norman French) to Germanic (Anglo-Saxon, then Scandinavian, then finally modern English).

Celtic names, represented in their most familiar form today by most place names in Wales and Scotland, are by definition the oldest in Britain, except for those deemed to be pre-Celtic. They are mainly found as names of natural objects, such as rivers and hills, but there are also Celtic names of inhabited places and of regions. Examples include the rivers *Avon*, *Clyde*, *Forth* and *Severn*, and the modern counties of *Devon*, *Kent* and *Lothian*. *Glasgow* and *York* both have Celtic names. Most Scottish Celtic names are Gaelic in origin, while those in Wales are, predictably, Welsh. But many Celtic names in England derive from British, as the form of Celtic spoken by the 'Ancient' Britons of southern Britain. Such names include

Dover, *Penrith* and the first word of *Lytchett Matravers*. (The language name 'British' is avoided in this book, however, to avoid confusion with modern 'British English', and the Celtic words in such names are usually explained in terms of their modern Welsh equivalents. Similarly, the Britons who spoke the language are usually specified as 'Ancient'.)

Latin names are nothing like as widespread as might be supposed, given four centuries of Roman occupation. But this is because the Romans were in Britain as military occupiers, not as settlers. Many names now generally said to be Latin in origin, whether in their Roman or modern form, are in fact based on existing Celtic words or names. Thus *Camulodunum*, the Roman name of Colchester, is based on the name of the Celtic war god Camulos, while *Lindum* (Lincoln) is based on a Celtic word related to modern Welsh *llyn*, 'lake'. But modern *Lincoln* also preserves Latin *colonia*, 'colony', so is closer to an original Latin name. (Some towns and cities have preserved their Roman names in modern street and building names, so that *Chester* has a Deva Link, *Cirencester* a Corinium Gate, *Colchester* a Camulodunum Way, *Gloucester* a Glevum Shopping Centre, *Lincoln* a Lindum Avenue and *St Albans* a Verulam Industrial Estate.) Entirely original Latin names are few, one noted example being *Pontefract*, from Latin *ponte fracto*, '(at the) broken bridge'. Latin *castrum*, 'camp', through Old English, gave the '-chester' and '-caster' names already mentioned. Many of these have a Celtic river name for their first part, such as *Doncaster* on the Don, *Lancaster* on the Lune, and *Exeter* on the Exe. But *Manchester*, *Winchester* and *Dorchester* (in both Dorset and Oxfordshire) are based on other Celtic or even pre-Celtic sources. In more recent times, Latin has become familiar from the *Magna* ('great') and *Parva* ('little') in a number of compound names, and a Latin genitive plural will also be readily recognized in the second word of names such as *Whitchurch Canonicorum*, *Ashby Puerorum* and *Toller Porcorum*.

Old English names are everywhere in England, with many spilling over into eastern Wales and southern Scotland. These are the names that are most familiar, with endings such as '-ton' (and '-ington'), '-ham' or '-don'. Many Old English names comprise a personal name and an Old English word, such as *Caston*, 'Catt's farmstead', *Hersham*, 'Hæferic's homestead', or *Stopsley*, 'Stoppa's woodland clearing'. But both parts of an Old English name can equally represent ordinary words, such as *Brockworth*, 'enclosure by the brook', *Dipton*, 'deep valley', or *Plumstead*, 'place where plum trees grow'. Sometimes a river name is involved, such as *Bruton*, 'farmstead on the river Brue', *Lugwardine*, 'enclosure on the river Lugg', or *Lydford*, 'ford over the river Lyd'. In some such cases, the river name may no longer be in use, and the river known by another name. Thus the river at *Smallburgh*, Norfolk, is now the Ant, but the name of the village means 'hill by the river Smale'.

Old English as a language is the forerunner of modern English, and some of its vocabulary words have remained unchanged over the centuries. Place names containing *calf*, *ford*, *lamb* and *sand*, for example, have these words in their present sense, as do those with *ēast*, *north* and *west*. Old English *sūth*, 'south', is still recognizable in sense, and not too different from modern English are *blæc*, 'black', *cumb*, 'coomb', *fearn*, 'fern', *geat*, 'gate', *grēne*, 'green', *mōr*, 'moor', and *wæter*, 'water', among others. Given such leeway, Old English (OE) *tūn*, 'farmstead', 'estate', can be seen as the ancestor of modern *town*, *dūn*, 'hill', of *down*, and *feld* of *field* (though meaning 'open country'). But these two last words point to a potential pitfall in the interpretation of place names, since a name that is now '-ton' may have originally been a '-don'. Thus *Seckington* means 'Secca's hill', not 'Secca's farmstead', while *Ilmington* is 'hill growing with elm trees', not 'farmstead where elm trees grow'. Similarly, names ending in '-ham' can represent either OE *hām*, 'homestead', or *hamm*, 'enclosure', 'riverside meadow'. Sometimes it is hard to say which of the two applies, so that *Hailsham* could mean either 'Hægel's homestead' or 'Hægel's enclosure'. In such cases, even a physical examination of the site may not determine the actual origin, either because the original feature has been lost or because both could equally apply. A place by a low hill may have been named for the original farmstead (*tūn*) or for the hill (*dūn*) where it stood, and a place by a river may take its name from the original homestead (*hām*) or from the riverside land (*hamm*) where it arose.

OE *burh*, 'fortified place', gave the many '-bury' or '-borough' names that exist, usually through OE *byrig*, the dative form of this word. 'Fortified place' is a catch-all term that can apply to anything from an ancient hill fort or Roman fortification on the one hand to a fortified manor house, town or borough on the other. *Bunbury* is 'Būna's stronghold', but *Bushbury* is 'bishop's fortified manor'. Another common OE word is *lēah* (modern English *lea*), meaning either 'wood' or 'clearing', and often found as the '-ley' of such names as *Burley*, 'woodland clearing by a fortified place', or *Hailey*, 'clearing where hay is made'. (The apparent disparity between 'wood' and 'clearing' can be resolved if one thinks of a sense development: 'wood', 'part of a wood', 'clearing in a wood'.) OE *stōw* in such names as *Burstow* has a general sense 'place' that can often be more specifically rendered 'assembly place' or 'holy place'. For *Hibaldstow* it clearly means the latter, as the personal name is that of St Higebald, but for *Spurstow* it is 'assembly place'. (The first part of the name is OE *spor*, 'trackway'.) Names ending in '-ey' or '-y' often have OE *ēg*, 'island', such as *Hincksey*, 'island of the stallion', or *Sandy*, 'sandy island'. 'Island' in such names does not usually have its modern sense but denotes a raised area of land in marshes or by a river. Finally, names ending in '-den' or '-don' may take this from OE *denu*, 'valley' (modern English *dene* or *dean*), so that *Calmsden* is 'Calumund's valley', and *Sawdon* is 'valley where willow trees grow'. Sometimes an OE word can have a range of meanings, and the appropriate one needs to be selected or proposed. An example is *wīc*, which can mean anything from a Romano-British settlement to a dairy farm to an industrial village. (The word itself is a borrowing of Latin *vicus*, 'group of dwellings'.) A specialized sense is 'saltworks', as for *Droitwich* and *Nantwich*.

Many names ending in '-ington' begin with a personal name and have an overall sense that means 'estate associated with So-and-So'. *Ilsington* thus means 'estate associated with Ielfstān'. In this name, 'Ils-' represents the OE personal name, '-ing-' is a connective particle meaning 'associated with' or 'named after', and '-ton' is OE *tūn*, 'estate'. (Such names were formerly interpreted as 'Ielfstān's estate', but it is wrong to assume a direct ownership, and the tie between the estate and the named person is looser than that. Hence, 'associated with'.) Names ending in '-ingham', on the other hand, often mean 'homestead of So-and-So's people', so that *Empingham* means 'homestead of Empa's people'. Here 'Emp-' represents the OE personal name, '-ing-' means 'of the people of', and '-ham' is OE *hām*, 'homestead'. Linguistically, this sort of '-ing-' represents OE *-inga-*, the genitive form of the plural suffix *-ingas*, 'people', found as the final '-ing' in such names as *Fulking*, '(settlement of) Folca's people', or *Pickering*, '(settlement of) 'Pīcer's people'. The 'people' in such names can be understood either as members of the (extended) family of the named person or else his followers.

Scandinavian names are most clearly seen in northern and eastern England. The Vikings who gave the names came chiefly from Denmark and Norway, the Danes settling mainly in northern and eastern England, in the region known historically as the Danelaw, and the Norwegians mainly in the northwest of England. The languages they respectively spoke, Old Danish and Old Norse, were very similar, and in this book are referred to jointly as Old Scandinavian (OS). Names ending in '-by' are invariably of Viking origin, OS *bý* being the equivalent of OE *tūn* and so meaning 'farmstead', 'village'. (The word is the source of the first part of modern English *bylaw*.) Many such names have a Scandinavian personal name for their first part, such as *Corby*, 'Kori's farmstead', or *Spilsby*, 'Spillir's farmstead'. But as with corresponding OE names, two standard OS words may be involved, as for *Crosby*, 'village with crosses', or *Derby*, 'farmstead where deer are kept'. Other common OS words in place names are *á*, 'river', *askr*, 'ash tree', *dalr*, 'valley', *ēy*, 'island' (Scottish *Sanday*, 'sandy island', corresponds to OE *Sandy* above), *kirkja*, 'church' (modern Scottish *kirk*), and *thveit*, 'clearing'. Many of these have their linguistically related counterparts, so that OS *á* shares the Germanic source of OE *ēa*, *askr* of *æsc*, *dalr* of *dæl* (modern English *dale*) and *kirkja* of *cirice* (modern English *church*).

Norman French names are most readily represented in the distinctive 'double-barrelled' names of central and southern England in which one 'barrel' is the name of a manor and the other that of the Norman family who possessed it. Examples are legion, and paradoxically are often regarded as the most tyically 'English'. *Kingston Bagpuize, Leighton Buzzard* and *Stansted Mountfitchet* are just three. In many such cases, the family name serves to distinguish the manor name from an identical name nearby. Thus *Hampton Poyle*, Oxfordshire, was held by the de la Puile family, as distinct from nearby *Hampton Gay*, held by the de Gay family, while *Sampford Arundel*, Somerset, was held by Roger Arundel, his name distinguishing this Sampford from *Sampford Brett*, held by the Bret family. (The last two are 15 miles apart, so that 'nearby' can be a relative term.) Other than these distinctive names, there are only a few names of entirely Norman origin. They include *Belper, Devizes, Malpas, Montacute* and *Richmond*, at least two of which still have a recognizably French appearance. Typical Old French (OF) words behind these and similar names are *beau*, 'beautiful', and *mont*, 'hill'.

Modern English names need not necessarily look modern. *Newcastle* and *Portsmouth*, for example, have modern-looking and transparently meaningful names but in fact date back several centuries. On the other hand, names such as *Camberley, Craven Arms, Coalville, Devonport, Glenrothes, Grantown-on-Spey, Helensburgh, Leverburgh, Maryport, Nelson, Newhaven, Peterhead, Peterlee, Pimlico, Portmeirion, Princetown, Southport, Southsea, Telford, Tunbridge Wells* and *Waterlooville* are all recent, and date from the sixteenth century or later. *Morecambe* also qualifies as a modern name, although based on an old Celtic name for the estuary of the river Lune recorded by Ptolemy in the second century AD. Names devised for the new administrative regions created in the local government reorganization of 1974 are some of the most recent, and include *Castle Point* and *Wychavon*.

Distinctive among modern names are the river names that arose as a so-called 'back formation' from a place on the river in question. Thus the *Arun* gets its name from *Arundel*, the *Chelmer* from *Chelmsford*, the *Mole* from *Molesey*, the *Rom* from *Romford*, and the *Wandle* from *Wandsworth*. Many such rivers had earlier original names which were replaced by the new names from the sixteenth century.

The renaming of towns or villages is not common in Britain, but *Enham Alamein*, earlier *Knight's Enham*, is a noted example. Names that have added modern English words in recent times include *Royal Cheltenham Spa* and *Royal Tunbridge Wells* (already a modern name), and seaside resorts such as *Frinton-on-Sea* and *Ogmore-by-Sea*. The maritime additions are mainly made as a commercial lure.

3. Personal and family names

Personal names are most obviously present in Old English and Old Scandinavian names, while family names, as mentioned, are best seen in Norman French names. Names of Anglo-Saxons were often meaningful, but sometimes had a random sense. Common words found in OE personal names include *ælf*, 'elf' (as in the Ælfhere who gave the name of *Alfreton*), *beorht*, 'bright' (Beorhthelm in *Brighton*), *ēad*, 'riches' (Ēadhelm in *Edenbridge*), *here*, 'army' (Baldhere in *Balderstone*), *lēof*, 'beloved' (Lēofhere in *Loversall*), *mund*, 'protection' (Hēahmund in *Heckmondwike*), *ōs*, 'god' (Ōsmund in *Osmaston*), *wulf*, 'wolf' (Ecgwulf in *Eglingham*), and *wynn*, 'joy' (Cēolwynn in *Chelington*). This last is a female name, and in such compound names, the second element was a gender indicator. The *gifu*, 'gift', of Gōdgifu, who gave the name of *Goodwood*, is another such female indicator. (Her name is more familiar today in the form Godiva.) Yet another is *burh*, 'fortified place', as for Sæburh, who gave the name of *Sebergham*. Many of the OE names in place names are short forms of compound names, however, or short names in their own right. An example of the former is the Guma who gave the name of *Gomshall*, his name being short for Gumbeorht or some similar name. The latter often originated as meaningful nicknames, so that in some cases it is difficult to say whether the place name contains a personal name (as nickname) or the actual word that gave that nickname, and that describes the place. For example, the place name *Hauxley* could mean either 'Hafoc's mound' or 'mound where hawks are seen', from OE *hafoc*, 'hawk', and *Catsfield* could mean either 'Catt's open land' or 'open land where wildcats are seen' (OE *catt*, 'wildcat'). Old Scandinavian personal names are similar, so that *Enderby*, meaning 'Eindrithi's farmstead', has an OS personal name made up of *ein*, 'one', and *ræthi*, 'ruler', while the Skarthi who gave the name of *Scarborough* had a nickname meaning 'hare-lipped'. In *Catesby*, 'Káti's farmstead', the OS personal name represents *káti*, 'boy'.

Norman family names in place names such as *Sutton Courtenay* often represent the name of the place in France from which they had come. Thus the Conyers family who held the manor at *Hutton Conyers* came from *Coignières* or *Cogners*, the de Pinkeny family who gave the name of *Moreton Pinkney* came from (French *de*, 'of') *Picquigny*, the Punchardon family who held the manor at *Heaton Punchardon* came from a place in Normandy called *Pontchardon*, literally 'thistle bridge', and *Huish Champflower* took the second word of its name from the Champflur family, who came from a place in Normandy called *Champfleury*, 'field of flowers'. But as with Old English and Scandinavian names, some Norman family names arose as nicknames. The manor at *Berwick Bassett* was held by the Basset family, whose name means 'of low stature' (OF *basset*), while the name of the Toner family who held the manor at *Turners Puddle* originated as a nickname meaning 'thunder' (French *tonnerre*).

4. Place names and church dedications

Names beginning *St* usually contain the name of the saint to whom the local parish church is dedicated. Thus *St Albans* commemorates St Alban, *St Andrews* St Andrew, *St David's* St David, *St Helens* St Helen, *St Leonards* St Leonard, *St Neots* St Neot and *St Pancras* St Pancras. In some cases, the church may now be dedicated to a different saint or never have been dedicated to the named saint in the first place. At *Marstow*, Herefordshire, the church is now dedicated to St Matthew, but it was earlier dedicated to St Martin, and the name derives from this dedication. At *St Ives*, Cambridgeshire, the parish church is dedicated to All Saints, although the place name commemorates St Ive, whose bones were discovered here, while at *St Briavels*, Gloucestershire, the church is dedicated to St Mary the Virgin, not the Welsh saint Briavel. The parish church at *St Austell*, Cornwall, is dedicated to the Holy Trinity, but in many smaller Cornish places the place name matches or reflects the church dedication, as at *St Blazey*, *St Columb Major*, *St Erth*, *St Ives*, *St Just in Roseland*, *St Ruan* and *St Tudy*.

   In the Scilly Isles, three of the five inhabited islands bear saints' names, although that of *St Agnes* is a red herring, and the name is not that of the saint but of Scandinavian origin. Even so, by popular association, the parish church on the island is dedicated to St Agnes. This is a phenonemon found elsewhere in Britain, where the resemblance of an original place name to the name of a saint has led to the dedication of the church to that saint. A noted example is *Boston*, Lincolnshire, where the famous 'Boston Stump' is dedicated to St Botolph. Yet the place derives its name from an Anglo-Saxon called Bōtwulf, not the seventh-century missionary Botolph. The same saint appears in church dedications at *Bossall* and *Botesdale*, but these two names respectively mean 'Bōtsige's corner of land' and 'Bōtwulf's valley', again with the names of Anglo-Saxons. Further such misassociations are found for St Bridget at *Bridgerule* ('Ruald's place at the bridge'), St Ebba at *Ebchester* ('Ebba's Roman fort'), St Mark at *Marks Gate* ('de Merc's estate at the gate'), St Martin at *Martinhoe* ('hill spur of Matta's people'), St Michael at *Mickleham* ('large homestead') and at *Mitcheldean* ('large place in the valley'), and St Peter at *Petersham* ('Peohtrīc's homestead'). As may be seen, in some cases the original name did not even contain a personal name to begin with. In others there is a more understandable link between a familiar personal name and that of the particular saint. Thus *Patrington* and *Patterdale*, with churches dedicated to St Patrick, derive their names from quite a different Patrick, while *Margaret Marsh*, with a church dedicated to St Margaret, takes its name from that of an abbess of Shaftesbury Abbey, and *Maryport*, with St Mary's church, is named after the wife of Humphrey Senhouse, who founded the town in the eighteenth century. At *Catherington*, Hants, the church is now dedicated to All Saints, but was earlier dedicated to St Catherine. The name in fact means 'farmstead of the people living by Cadeir', from the name of a hill, or else 'farmstead of Cattor's people', after an Anglo-Saxon.

   Without careful consideration of the early forms of a given place name, it can be difficult to determine if such a misassociation is actually valid. There are thus many places with churches dedicated to St Mary whose names appear to suggest that of the saint, such as *Marholm*, *Marlston*, *Marshchapel*, *Marshfield*, *Marske* and *Marston*. But this particular dedication is so common that the link may be simply coincidental. On the other hand, *Sinfin*, Derby, with St Stephen's church, was recorded in the thirteenth century as *Sidefen*, a form that may have led to the adoption of this particular saint. And just as *Petersham* is named after the Anglo-Saxon Peohtrīc, not St Peter, it is possible that *Petersfield*, with a church dedicated to this saint, may have originally had a name of similar origin.

5. Welsh place names

As visitors to Wales are immediately aware, or as anyone scanning a map of Wales can straightaway see, the place names of Wales are mostly Welsh. As such, in many cases they can be directly translated into English to give a meaningful topographical description. Thus *Cwm-bach* is 'little valley', *Pen-y-foel* is 'top of the bare hill', and *Rhydd-ddu* is 'black ford'. Even names of well-known places can often be reliably interpreted in this way. *Maesteg* is thus 'fair field' and *Penrhyndeudraeth* 'promontory with two beaches'. But there are also a fair proportion of English names, such as *Bridgend*, *Haverfordwest*, *Newport* and *Welshpool*, and a noticeable representation of Scandinavian names, such as *Fishguard*, *Milford Haven* and *Swansea*. In fact most of the islands off the Welsh coast have Scandinavian names, from *Anglesey* in the northwest to *Skokholm* in the southwest, witnesses to the maritime encroachments of the Vikings in this part of Britain.

Most major places with English names in Wales have a Welsh name, especially in official writing, which may or may not be the equivalent of the English. Thus *Bridgend* is *Pen-y-Bont ar Ogwr*, 'end of the bridge over the Ogwr', *Cowbridge* is *Y Bont-Faen*, 'the stone bridge', *Knighton* is *Trefyclo*, 'farm by the dyke', *Newport* is *Casnewydd-ar-Wysg*, 'new castle on the Usk', and *Welshpool* is *Y Trallwng*, 'the very wet quagmire'. Some apparently English (or Scandinavian) names are actually Welsh, so that *Tenby* is *Dinbych-y-pysgod*, 'little fort of the fish', while *Barmouth* is a tangle of Welsh *aber*, 'river mouth', English *mouth*, and the Welsh name of the river *Mawdd* (now the *Mawddach*). *Prestatyn* looks Welsh, but is really a form of English *Preston*, while *Hwlffordd*, the Welsh name of *Haverfordwest*, is a phonetic rendering of the English (less the *-west*). *Rhyl* is a blend of Welsh *yr*, 'the', and English *hill*.

Common Welsh prefixes are *aber*, 'river mouth', as for *Aberaeron*, *Abergavenny*, *Abertillery* and *Aberystwyth*, and *llan*, 'church', as for *Llanberis*, *Llandudno*, *Llanelli* and *Llantrisant*. The *aber* names usually (but not always) contain the name of the river at whose mouth the place in question lies, while the *llan* names often give the name of the saint to whom the local church is dedicated. Many such saints are obscure in origin, and only known from their place names. Elsewhere, Welsh words such as *coed*, 'wood', *cwm*, 'valley', *llyn*, 'lake', *mynydd*, 'mountain', *pen*, 'top' or 'end', and *tre* or *tref*, 'farm' or 'village', are regularly met.

Distinctive in Wales are the names of settlements that have grown up around Nonconformist chapels. Such names are usually of biblical places, such as *Bethel*,

Bethesda, Carmel, Hebron and *Salem*. There is even a *Bethlehem* and a *Sodom*, the latter probably originating as a wilful nickname. Most such names originated in the nineteenth century. Wales is popularly famous, however, not for chapel names but for the so-called 'longest place name in Britain', known in its more concise form as *Llanfair Pwllgwyngyll*.

6. Scottish place names

Just as the majority of place names in Wales are Welsh in origin, so most of the names in Scotland are Gaelic. In the southern half of Scotland many names are English, such as *Hawick, Falkirk, Motherwell, Prestwick, Saltcoats* and *Selkirk*, while Scandinavian *kirkja*, 'church', is found in such names as *Kirkcudbright* and *Kirkoswald*. These represent a Gaelic word order, however, with the personal name (saint's name) following the generic word, unlike *Felixkirk* and *Oswaldkirk* in England. In the north of Scotland, *Kirkwall* in Orkney and *Lerwick* in Shetland testify to a Scandinavian presence, as do *Stornoway* in the Hebrides and *Wick* in mainland Scotland.

Gaelic words frequently found in place names include *beinn*, 'mountain', as in *Ben Nevis, caol*, 'strait', as in *Kyle of Lochalsh, cill*, 'church', as in *Kilmarnock, gleann*, 'valley', as in *Glencoe, inbhir*, 'river mouth', as in *Inverness, loch*, 'lake', as in *Loch Lomond*, and *srath*, 'valley', as in *Strathclyde*. Pictish *pett*, 'portion', is found in such names as *Pitlochry* and *Pittenweem*, while Old Welsh *aber*, 'river mouth', corresponding to the *aber* of Welsh names, is seen in *Aberdeen* and *Aberfoyle*, where it relates to (but is of earlier origin than) Gaelic *inbhir*. As with Welsh names, the main part of an *aber* name is usually that of the river at whose mouth the town stands, although there are exceptions, and it is Old Aberdeen that stands at the mouth of the Don, not modern Aberdeen, which is on the Dee.

The official promotion of Gaelic names in Scotland is nothing like as general as it is for Welsh names in Wales, although in the Western Isles (na h-Eileanan an Iar), where Gaelic is the first language of many islanders, the roadside place names are in Gaelic, so that *Stornoway*, although not itself of Gaelic origin, is there officially known as *Steornabhagh*.

7. Place names and their sources

To determine the origin and meaning of a place name, it is obviously necessary to go back as far as possible to find the earliest forms. Some of the very earliest records of British place names are to be found in Ptolemy's *Geographia* of the second century AD, where *Eborakon* is modern York, *Katouraktonion* is *Catterick*, and *Lindon* is modern *Lincoln*. But the first actual interpreter of British place names was the Venerable Bede, who gives many correct meanings in his *Historia Ecclesiastica Gentis Anglorum*, completed in 731. He thus writes that *Bamburgh* is 'called after a former queen named Bebba', that *Ely* 'derives its name from the vast quantity of eels that are caught in the marshes', that *Rendlesham* means 'Rendil's House', that *Selsey* 'means the seal's island', that *Hreutford*, now *Redbridge* (Hants), means 'the Ford of Reeds', and that *Whithorn* 'is commonly known as *Candida Casa*, the White

House'. (These English versions of the Latin are from Leo Sherley-Price's translation, revised by R. E. Latham, published by Penguin in 1968.) Bede's original Latin description of *Derwent Water* is quoted in the present dictionary, as is a fuller version of his explanation of the name *Ely*.

The fullest historical record of English (and a few Welsh) place names is to be found in the *Domesday Book*, a written record of the survey of land holdings in England, carried out for William the Conqueror during 1086. The entire country was covered, except for the extreme north (modern Northumberland, Durham and Cumbria), which at the time was not yet firmly under Norman control. (An unexplained omission was the two main cities of the realm, London and Winchester, the latter then being the capital.) The wealth of information for each of the 13,400 or so named places, including numbers of peasantry, ploughs, ploughlands and some categories of livestock, as well as details of rents, tax and manorial values, was written in clerical Latin, with many words stylized or abbreviated. The record for each place was noted locally and then eventually returned to a central 'editorial office' at Winchester, where the final version was written by a single scribe.

Not surprisingly, some place names were transcribed erroneously, not least because Norman scribes were working in a language that was not only foreign but that belonged to a different language group (Germanic) from their own (Romance). Thus the Domesday Book record for *Sinfin*, mentioned above, is *Sedenefeld*, as if the name ended in OE *feld*, 'open land', not *fenn*, 'fen'. Other faulty or at any rate suspect transcriptions include *Berlescoma* for modern *Burlescombe*, *Craohy* for *Cranham*, *Dondeme* for *Dundon*, *Grentevorde* for *Greatworth*, *Hemegretham* for *Hengrave*, *Guldelsmere* for *Ingoldmells*, *Ledlinghe* for *Leavening*, *Molesham* for *Molesey*, *Pochelac* for *Pockley*, and *Stamphotne* for *Starbotton*. Some transcriptions bear little resemblance to the current name. Thus *Hadleigh* in the DB record is *Leam*, and *Trowbridge* is *Straburg*. In the former, the clerk has corrupted the second part of the name while omitting the first part altogether. In the latter, he appears to have taken the first part of the name as beginning *Str-*, not *Tr-*, and the second part as OE *burh*, 'fortified place', not *brycg*, 'bridge'. Norman clerks could also have problems with consonant clusters, either spacing or prefixing letters with vowels or omitting them. Thus modern *Stradbroke* is DB *Statebroc*, *Streat* is *Estrat*, and *Stubbs* is *Istop*. On the other hand, *Stincteford* for modern *Stinsford* is acceptable, given the name's origin in *stint* and *ford*, as is *Stocheslage* for *Stokesley*, *Straford* for *Strefford*, and *Sulgrave* for *Sulgrave*. This last name has thus retained its DB form letter for letter to the present day. A complete translation of *Domesday Book* was published by Penguin in 2002.

8. The arrangement of entries

Each entry contains information as follows: (a) the place name itself; (b) a description of the place, such as 'town', 'village', 'district', etc., with its location by county or unitary authority; (c) the meaning of the name; (d) the language(s) of origin and generic word(s) behind the name; and (e) a historical record or records of the name. Appropriate supplementary information is often provided between (d) and (e). To say a little about each of these:

(a) The place name is in its generally accepted and familiar form, as one or more words. Thus although the 'main' name of *Black Callerton* is *Callerton*, it will be found under *Black*, not *Callerton*, as in some dictionaries and gazetteers. This means that names beginning *East*, *West*, etc., or *Great*, *Little*, etc., will be found under those words, giving *East Halton*, not *Halton, East*, and *Great Bookham* not *Bookham, Great*. The name chosen for the main entry in such cases is usually the one that is the better known of the two (or more), but either way there will almost always be a cross-reference from the other name(s) to the prime one, as from *West Halton* to *East Halton* and *Little Bookham* to *Great Bookham*. In a few cases, where major places are involved, there will be separate entries for each place, even where the 'main' name is of identical origin. Thus *East Kilbride* and *West Kilbride* have their respective entries. (The same applies more obviously for certain names with an identical first word, such as *Chipping Campden*, *Chipping Norton*, *Chipping Ongar* and *Chipping Sodbury*.) For lesser places, cross-references are provided for a run of compound names with an identical first word. Thus *Winterborne Clenston*, *Winterborne Houghton*, *Winterborne Stickland*, *Winterborne Tomson* and *Winterborne Whitchurch* are all cross-referred to *Winterborne Zelstone*. But where there is only a single entry under the first word, there is no cross-reference. Thus *Lydiard Millicent* and *Lydiard Tregoze* are both dealt with under the former name. In a few cases, cross-references for local names containing a common word are made to a prominent natural feature. *Great Malvern*, *Little Malvern*, *West Malvern*, *Malvern Wells* and *Malvern Link* are all thus cross-referred to *Malvern Hills*. Roman names of places, in bold italic, are cross-referred to the modern equivalent name or location. Thus ***Aballava***, the very first entry, cross-refers to BURGH-BY-SANDS, and ***Nidum*** to NEATH.

Names of places in Wales with English and Welsh forms are usually given under their English form with a cross-reference from the Welsh. Thus *Knighton* is dealt with under its English name, with a cross-reference from *Trefyclo*, and *Denbigh* is cross-referred from *Dinbych*. Such a 'nationalistic' approach is adopted here since the English form is likely to be more familiar to the general reader. In fact many such traditional forms are now anyway in official use, and unitary authorities in Wales include *Anglesey* (not *Môn*), *Caerphilly* (not *Caerffili*), *Swansea* (not *Abertawe*) and *Wrexham* (not *Wrecsam*).

River names are subsumed as far as possible into the name of an inhabited place, so that *Thames* is treated under *Thames Ditton*, and *Severn* under *Severn Stoke*. In cases where a river name is not the first word in the name of an inhabited place, it is cross-referred, such as *Humber* to *Humberston* and *Don* to *Doncaster*. It is also cross-referred where it is the last word, so that *Wye* refers to *Ross-on-Wye*.

(b) Most places are described as 'town' or 'village'. For a small village or inhabited place, 'hamlet' is also used. 'District' is normally used for a distinct part of a large town or city, such as *Radford*, a district of Nottingham, or *Dagenham*, a district of Barking and Dagenham. 'Region' is normally used for a defined area outside a town or city, such as *Rannoch Moor* in Highland, or the *New Forest* in Hampshire. 'Suburb' is used of an outlying district of a town or city, and where the town name is identical to that of its unitary authority, it is not repeated. Thus *Kirk Sandall* is a suburb of Doncaster in the unitary authority of Doncaster.

As the dictionary contains the names of district councils, the term 'council district' is used for the administrative district in a county where that council exercises its authority. Thus *Castle Morpeth* is a council district of Northumberland, and *Hart* is a council district in Hampshire. Unitary authorities, by definition, have no district councils, as there is only one 'all-purpose' local government authority. From the place-name point of view, the reorganization of local government in the 1990s has produced some anomalies. Thus the original counties of *Herefordshire* and *Worcestershire* were combined in 1974 as the new county of *Hereford and Worcester*. In 1998 the two component regions were restored to their original areas, but while *Worcestershire* regained county status, *Herefordshire* became a unitary authority. This means that a 'shire' name is not now necessarily that of a county. The disparity is particularly apparent in Wales, where there are solely unitary authorities, not counties, despite such familiar county names as *Denbighshire*, *Flintshire* and *Monmouthshire*. There are also unitary authorities alone in Scotland, although many, such as *Aberdeenshire*, *Clackmannanshire* and *Fife*, similarly preserve historic county names.

In England, the 'new' 1974 counties of *Avon*, *Cleveland* and *Humberside* have now been replaced by unitary authorities with different names, while the name of the 'old' county of *Berkshire* survives only in the unitary authority of *West Berkshire*. Further victims of the reorganization are the counties of *Rutland* and the *Isle of Wight*, now also unitary authorities. It was in fact the latter's county council that proposed the creation of a single all-purpose authority for the island. The Local Government Boundary Commission supported the change on the grounds that the Isle of Wight was unique, both because it was an island and because of its small size and population, and that this uniqueness implied that a local government structure different from that on the mainland might be appropriate (*People and Places: Local Government Boundary Commission for England Report No. 550*, 1988). The most obvious unitary authority names are now those of major towns and cities, such as *Bradford*, *Doncaster* and *Sheffield*.

Changes in regional government have also had their impact on London. In 1986 the Greater London Council (GLC) was abolished, leaving no central authority for Greater London. Instead, local powers and responsibilities devolved on thirty-two borough councils, and these are the locations used for places in the dictionary, as *Camberwell* in Southwark. The boroughs themselves, however, are located in 'Greater London'. In the event this is not the administrative anachronism it seems, as in 2000 a Greater London Authority was appointed on the lines of the old GLC, embracing the borough councils as before.

The name of the given county or unitary authority is often given in abbreviated form, as *Lincs* for the county of *Lincolnshire* or *E Yorks* for the unitary authority formally known as *East Riding of Yorkshire*.

(c) The meaning is given in a concise but readily assimilable form, with bracketed words used to clarify or amplify the sense where necessary, especially for a name that is now that of an inhabited place but which originated as that of a natural feature. Thus the village of *Hackness* in North Yorkshire has a name that primarily refers to the site where the place arose. The meaning is thus '(place at the) hook-shaped headland'. Without examining a large-scale map or visiting the location in question, it is not always possible to say whether a place 'at' or 'by' such a feature is near it or actually in or on it. One can perhaps assume that a place said to be 'by' a woodland clearing or corner of land may have originated in it, then developed outside it. But a place 'by' a hill could have arisen on it or near it, in the former case perhaps as a defensive site, in the latter as a naturally protective one. Hills are good sites for forts and lookouts but they also provide a haven from the enemy or shelter from the weather.

It can be difficult to choose an appropriate verb for a name referring to a wild living creature. The formula 'are seen' is usually adopted, meaning that the creature in question inhabits, frequents, haunts or is otherwise found in the place mentioned. Thus *Harewood* means 'wood where hares are seen', and *Warkleigh*, 'wood or clearing where spiders are seen'. In some cases the creature is unwelcome, such as *Wormley*, 'woodland clearing swarming with snakes', and here the verb can be more precise. In other instances the creature is likely to be heard rather than seen. *Cuckfield* is thus 'open land where cuckoos are heard'. But 'are seen' covers most names arising from a visual awareness that a particular animal, bird or insect is or has been present at the location concerned.

The meaning of a name as given is the most likely known. In some cases it is certain that the interpretation is correct. In others it is more tentative. In others again more than one interpretation is possible, and an alternative will be offered in the supplementary information. In a few cases it is difficult to give any actual meaning, and here the frustrating formula 'meaning uncertain' will appear.

(d) The language of origin, in abbreviated form (see p. ix), is followed by the generic word or element that gave all or part of the name. Where a personal name is given in the meaning, it is not repeated here. It can be assumed that in England the personal name itself is that of an Anglo-Saxon male unless otherwise indicated in the supplementary information. Some personal names that resemble modern female names are thus actually those of men, such as the Anna who gave the name of *Amble* or the Hilda behind *Hillingdon*. Most non-OE personal names will be Scandinavian. But where a manorial name is involved, the personal or family name is usually Norman, as mentioned, and in many cases preceded by *de*, 'of', followed by the name of the place from which the person or family had come. Thus *Abberton* means 'Ēadburh's farmstead', with an OE personal name, *Hackthorpe* means 'Haki's outlying farmstead', with a Scandinavian personal name, and at *Aspley Guise* the Norman family of de Gyse, who held the manor in the thirteenth century, came from Guise in France.

In some cases a related or equivalent modern English word or even foreign word is given following the meaning of an OE or OS word as an aid to comprehension. Thus modern English *grit* evolved from OE *grēot* in the name of *Cretingham*, and modern German *Schlucht*, 'ravine', is related to OE *slōhtre* in the name of *Upper Slaughter*. Modern English *field* is regularly added to OE *feld* as a reminder of the origin of the word, which is thus not from *felled*, as some suppose, as if referring to a place where trees have been cleared.

It should be pointed out that some of the generic words or elements given for place names have been recorded only in the names themselves and not in the language generally. They are thus postulated or hypothetical, but none the less usually have a definable meaning. Examples are OE *ric*, 'raised strip of land', for *Chatteris*, or OS *fili*, 'planks', for *Filby*. The same applies for many personal names, which have been deduced from the place name itself or from knowledge of attested names. Examples here are the Ceacca who gave the name of *Checkendon* or the Loca behind *Lockington*.

(e) The historical forms of the name are given with year or century of record, but Domesday Book forms, as stated above, are simply preceded by 'DB', meaning 1086. This last entry item is sometimes followed by the words 'SO ALSO' and an identical name elsewhere, as for *Halstead*, Essex, which has 'SO ALSO: *Halstead*, Kent, Leics'. This means that the Kent and Leicestershire Halsteads have a name of identical origin to the Essex one, though not (except coincidentally) identical historical forms.

Supplementary information given between (d) and (e) may typically identify the owner of a manorial name and the date when the manor was held, or explain the geographical relationship between two (or more) places that share a basic name, or give the meaning of a river name, if known. Many river names are ancient, and their meaning and even language of origin are often uncertain or unknown. If a place had a Roman name, it will similarly be treated here. Cross-references to relevant other names may also be given. Where a name involves a distinctive natural feature or an ancient fortification, the latter is often identified, even where this may involve identical names with identical meanings. Thus, the name of *Brough* means 'fortification' in Cumbria, Derbyshire, East Yorkshire and Nottinghamshire, but these places are entered separately so that the fortification in question can be identified. Similarly, *Stretton* means 'farmstead on a Roman road', but five Strettons are entered individually so that the Roman road in question can be identified. For a place with a 'ford' name, the river in question will often also be identified, as *Hainford* on the river Bure. In this respect it should be noted that 'ford' names rarely evolve from that of the local river.

Sometimes the supplementary information is more discursive, or is presented in the form of a literary diversion, such as the doggerel quoted for *Birmingham* or the popular etymology for *Bristol*. But such departures from the norm are restricted in number, as space for such indulgences is limited.

9. The sweeping scene

The dictionary entries in their individual and collective form present a broad picture of ancient and modern England, Scotland and Wales. The English names, in particular, offer an evocative but authentic depiction of life in medieval England, and of the natural world that so often dominated it. Here alders, aspens, beavers, bucks, ferns, hawks, horses, oaks, snakes, swans, wildcats, willows and wolves are to be found among the banks, fords, groves, hills, islands, meadows, pools, ridges, rivers, streams, valleys and woodland clearings. Here are barns, bridges, churches, cottages, crosses, enclosures, estates, farms, halls, hamlets, homesteads, houses, manors, mills, monasteries, paths, roads and villages inhabited, owned or used by abbots, armies, huntsmen, kings, lords, maidens, monks, peasants and tribes. Here there is a neglected clearing (*Netley*) and there a muddy shelter for animals (*Horsell*). There was a holy valley at *Hellidon* and an enclosure belonging to Weorca at *Warkworth*. The whole presents a colourful kaleidoscope of a way of life long gone but still today exercising a powerful hold on the half-romanticized, half-nostalgic collective memory of the English.

Place names in Celtic countries can be equally evocative. *Cromarty* is thus a crooked place by the sea, and *Radnor* a place by a red bank. Priests operated salt-pans at *Prestonpans*, and there was a prayer house in the wood at *Betws-y-coed*.

This Introduction deals with just some of the aspects of place names, and it is left for the entries themselves, like the component pieces of a jigsaw puzzle, to form a fuller and more detailed picture of their historical, geographical and linguistic background.

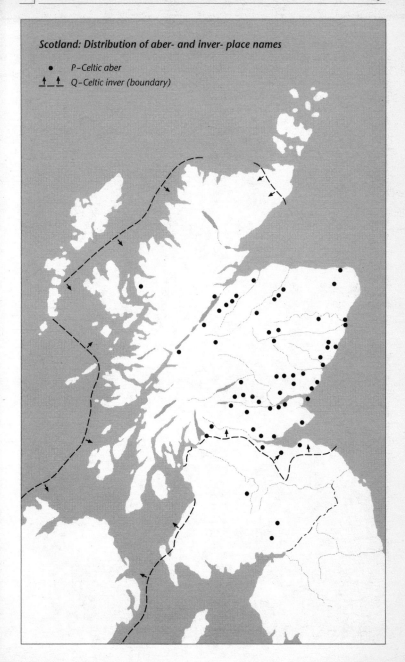

Scotland: Distribution of aber- and inver- place names

- *P–Celtic aber*
- *Q–Celtic inver (boundary)*

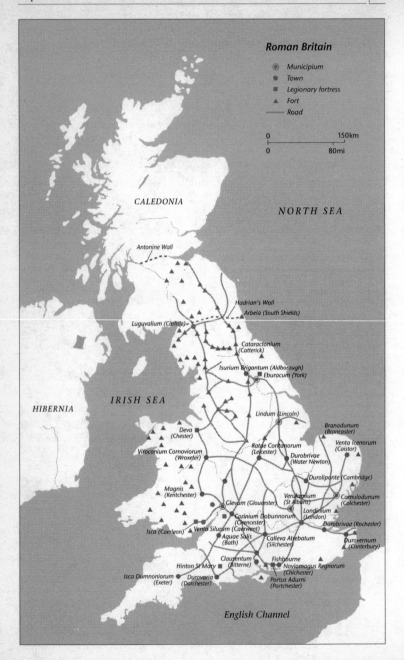

Roman Britain

- ⊚ Municipium
- ● Town
- ■ Legionary fortress
- ▲ Fort
- — Road

0 _____ 150km
0 _____ 80mi

CALEDONIA

NORTH SEA

Antonine Wall

Hadrian's Wall
Arbeia (South Shields)

Luguvalium (Carlisle)

Cataractonium
(Catterick)

Isurium Brigantum (Aldborough)
Eburacum (York)

HIBERNIA

IRISH SEA

Lindum (Lincoln)

Branodunum
(Brancaster)

Venta Icenorum
(Caistor)

Deva
(Chester)

Viroconium Cornoviorum
(Wroxeter)

Ratae Coritanorum
(Leicester)

Durobrivae
(Water Newton)

Durolipunte (Cambridge)

Magnis
(Kentchester)

Glevum (Gloucester)

Verulamium
(St Albans)

Camulodunum
(Colchester)

Londinium
(London)

Isca (Caerleon)

Corinium Dobunnorum
(Crencester)

Venta Siluram (Caerwent)

Aquae Sulis
(Bath)

Calleva Atrebatum
(Silchester)

Durobrivae (Rochester)

Durovernum
(Canterbury)

Isca Dumnoniorum
(Exeter)

Hinton St Mary

Durovaria
(Dorchester)

Clausentum
(Bitterne)

Fishbourne

Noviomagus Regnorum
(Chichester)

Portus Adurni
(Portchester)

English Channel

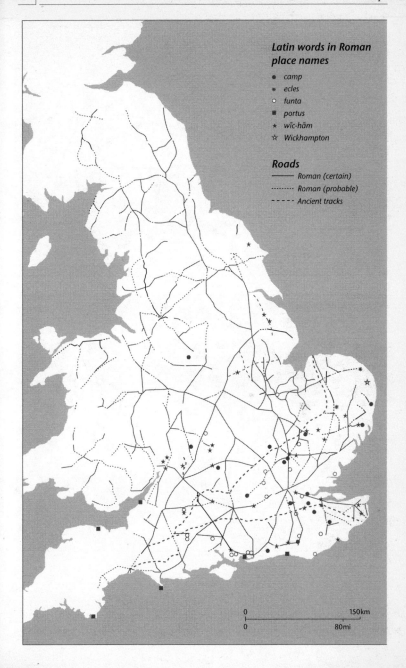

Latin words in Roman place names

- • camp
- ✳ ecles
- ○ funta
- ■ portus
- ★ wīc-hām
- ☆ Wickhampton

Roads

——— Roman (certain)
·········· Roman (probable)
– – – Ancient tracks

0 ——— 150km
0 ——— 80mi

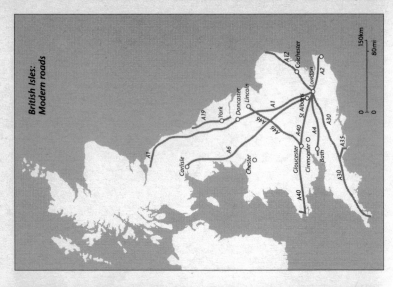

**British Isles:
Modern roads**

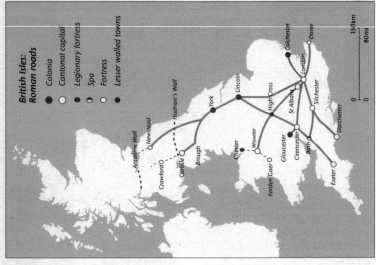

**British Isles:
Roman roads**

- ● Colonia
- ○ Cantonal capital
- ● Legionary fortress
- ◑ Spa
- ○ Fortress
- ● Lesser walled towns

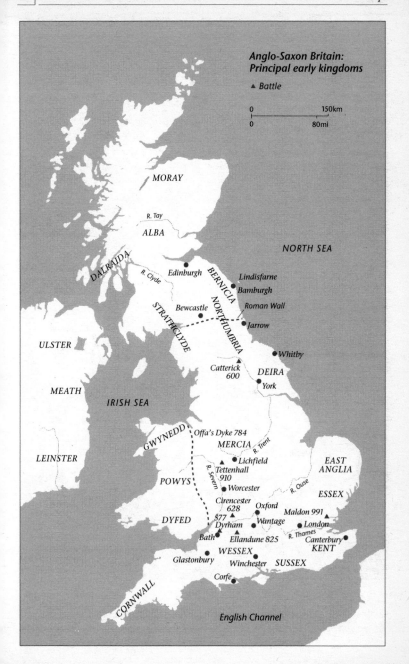

Anglo-Saxon Britain:
Principal early kingdoms

▲ Battle

0   150km
0   80mi

MORAY

ALBA

R. Tay

NORTH SEA

DALRIADA

R. Clyde

Edinburgh

BERNICIA

Lindisfarne

Bamburgh

Roman Wall

STRATHCLYDE

Bewcastle

NORTHUMBRIA

Jarrow

ULSTER

Whitby

MEATH

IRISH SEA

Catterick
600

DEIRA

York

LEINSTER

GWYNEDD

Offa's Dyke 784

MERCIA

R. Trent

EAST
ANGLIA

POWYS

Tettenhall
910

Lichfield

R. Severn

Worcester

ESSEX

R. Ouse

DYFED

Cirencester
628

577

Dyrham

Oxford

Wantage

Maldon 991

London

Bath

Ellandune 825

R. Thames

Canterbury

Glastonbury

WESSEX

Winchester

KENT

SUSSEX

Corfe

CORNWALL

English Channel

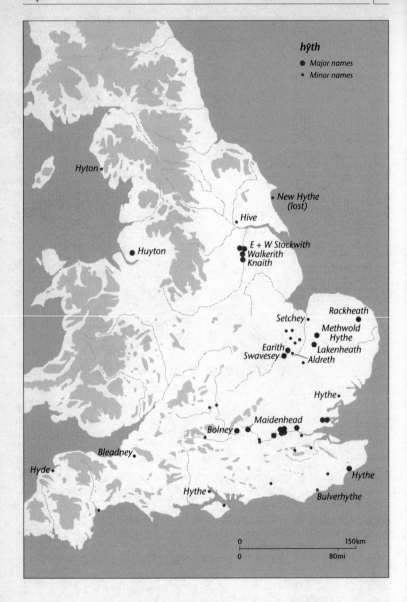

England: Place names containing Old English *hȳth*

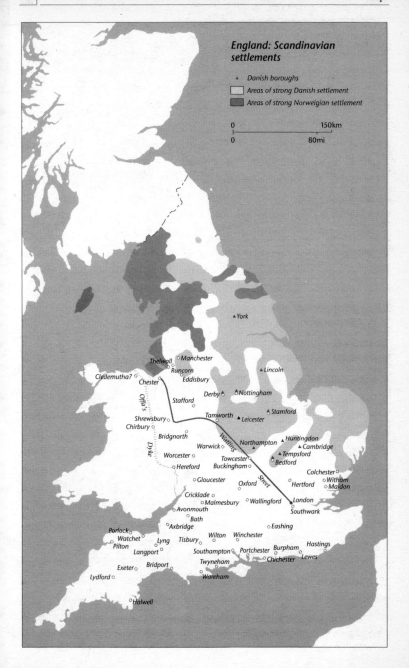

England: Scandinavian settlements

▲ Danish boroughs

Areas of strong Danish settlement

Areas of strong Norweigian settlement

0   150km

0   80mi

▲ York

Thelwall   ○ Manchester

Runcorn

Cledemutha?   Eddisbury

Chester

Offa's

Stafford

Derby ○   ▲ Nottingham

Shrewsbury ○   Tamworth   ▲ Stamford

Chirbury ○   ○ Leicester

Dyke

Bridgnorth

Warwick ○   Northampton   ▲ Huntingdon

Worcester ○   ▲ Cambridge

Towcester   ▲ Tempsford

Hereford   Buckingham ○   Bedford

Street

Gloucester ○   Oxford ○   Colchester ○

Hertford   ○ Witham

Cricklade ○   Maldon

Malmesbury ○   Wallingford   London

Avonmouth   Southwark

Bath

Porlock ○   Axbridge ○   Eashing

Watchet ○   Wilton ○   Winchester

Pilton   Lyng   Tisbury ○   Hastings

Langport ○   Southampton ○   Portchester   Burpham ○

Twyneham   Chichester ○   Lewes

Exeter ○   Bridport

Lydford ○   Wareham

○ Halwell

Lincoln ▲

Watling

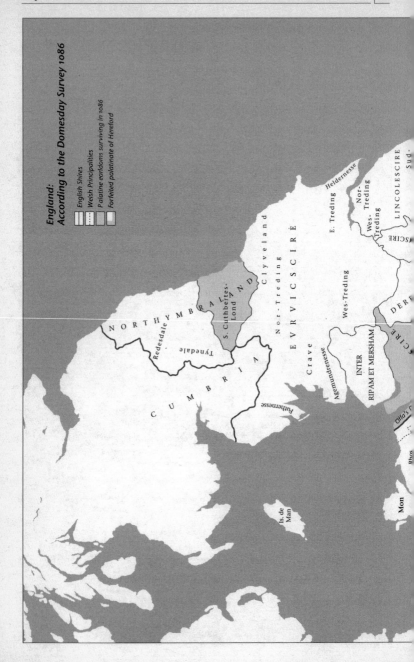

England:
According to the Domesday Survey 1086

English Shires
Welsh Principalities
Palatine earldoms surviving in 1086
Forfeited palatinate of Hereford

NORTHYMBRALOND

Redesdale

Tynedale

S. Cuthbertes-Lond

CUMBRIA

Clyveland

Ruttlenesse

Nor-Treding

EVRVICSCIRÈ

Crave

Agemundrenesse

Wes-Treding

INTER RIPAM ET MERSHAM

Is. de Man

Heldernesse

E. Treding

Nor-Treding

Wes-Treding

LINCOLESCIRE

Sud-

DERE

Offa's

SCIRE

Rhos

Mon

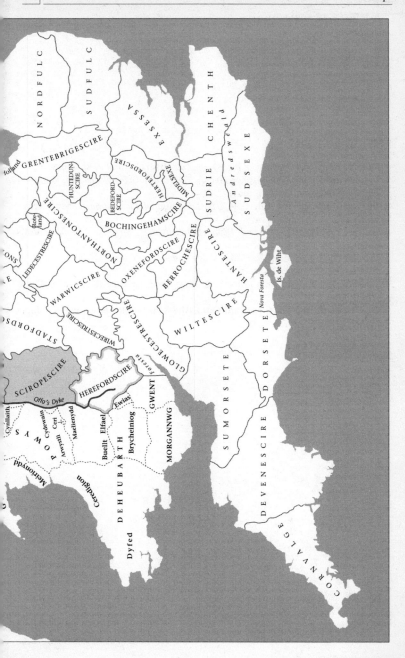

Map Sources

1. Simon Taylor (ed.), *The Uses of Place-Names* (Scottish Cultural Press, 1998).
2. Juliet Gardiner and Neil Wenborn (eds.), *The History Today Companion to British History* (Collins and Brown, 1995).
3. Margaret Gelling and Ann Cole, *The Landscape of Place-Names* (Shaun Tyas, 2000).
4. Stephen and Hazel Usherwood, *History from Familiar Things: Place Names* (Ginn, 1969).
5. Gardiner and Wenborn, *The History Today Companion to British History*.
6. Taylor, *The Uses of Place-Names*.
7. Margaret Gelling, *Signposts to the Past: Place-Names and the History of England* (Phillimore, 1988).
8. R. F. Treharne and Harold Fullard (eds.), *Muir's Historical Atlas* (George Philip, 1963).

The first and best resource for detailed information about English place names is the series of volumes published by the English Place-Name Society (EPNS). The Society was founded in 1923 to carry out a survey of English place names, county by county, and by the end of the twentieth century had covered the pre-1974 counties of Bedfordshire, Berkshire, Buckinghamshire, Cambridgeshire, Cheshire, Cumberland, Derbyshire, Devon, Dorset, Essex, Gloucestershire, Hertfordshire, Huntingdonshire, Middlesex (apart from the City of London), Northamptonshire, Oxfordshire, Rutland, Surrey, Sussex, Warwickshire, Westmorland, Wiltshire, Worcestershire and Yorkshire, with ongoing volumes on Leicestershire, Lincolnshire, Norfolk, Shropshire and Staffordshire, and a separate volume of Cornish place-name elements. Two volumes published in 1956 were similarly devoted to the words or elements found in English place names, and the first of a paperback series, *The Vocabulary of English Place-Names*, was issued in 1997. The twenty-first century opened with the publication of Part 6 of the Lincolnshire series as Volume 77 overall. There are thus as yet no volumes for Cornwall, Durham, Hampshire, Herefordshire, Kent, Lancashire, Northumberland, Somerset or Suffolk. The early volumes are generally less reliable and less detailed than the most recent, but even so contain valuable information, especially historical forms, not readily available elsewhere. The EPNS also issues an annual *Journal* with supplementary material and commentary. Many libraries hold a full set of the volumes to date.

General dictionaries of place names in the British Isles include John Field, *Place-Names of Great Britain and Ireland* (David & Charles, 1980), and Adrian Room, *Dictionary of Place-Names in the British Isles* (Bloomsbury, 1988). The latter is supplemented by a more specialist work, *Modern Place-Names in Great Britain and Ireland* (Oxford University Press, 1983). Similarly restricted, but with detailed and accessible entries, is W. F. H. Nicolaisen, Margaret Gelling and Melville Richards, *The Names of Towns and Cities in Britain* (Batsford, 1970). A lively and readable overview of the subject is provided by Fred McDonald and Julia Cresswell, *The Guinness Book of British Place Names* (Guinness, 1993), and a reliable and accessible overview is offered in John Field, *Discovering Place-names* (Shire Publications, 1994), No. 102 in the 'Discovering' series. Special mention should be made of two other authorities: A. L. F. Rivet and Colin Smith, *The Place-Names of Roman Britain* (Batsford, 1979), and Edmund McClure, *British Place-Names in Their Historical Setting* (EP Publishing, 1972, first published by SPCK, 1910). Despite its dated style and a number of erroneous etymologies (as we now know with hindsight), the latter was a genuine pioneering work. Thus, McClure's conjecture that *Faversham* is 'a case of the survival of the Latin *Faber*, = Smith, in a thoroughly Latinized district such as Kent must have been' has since been entirely validated.

Long the standard single-volume source for English place names alone, Eilert Ekwall, *The Concise Oxford Dictionary of English Place-Names* (Oxford University Press,

4th edition, 1960), has now been effectively superseded by A. D. Mills, *A Dictionary of English Place-Names* (Oxford University Press, new edition, 1998).

Dictionaries of place names in individual English counties include O. J. Padel, *Cornish Place-Names* (Alison Hodge, 1988), Richard Coates, *The Place-Names of Hampshire* (Batsford, 1989), and Kenneth Cameron, *A Dictionary of Lincolnshire Place-Names* (EPNS, 1998). This last is the first in a series of popular volumes issued by the EPNS. Dictionaries of London place names include John Field, *Place-Names of Greater London* (Batsford, 1980), worthily succeeded by A. D. Mills, *London Place Names* (Oxford University Press, 2001). Two dictionaries dealing with counties not yet covered by the EPNS are Judith Glover, *The Place Names of Kent* (Batsford, 1976), and David Mills (no relation to A. D.), *The Place Names of Lancashire* (Batsford, 1976). A. D. Mills, *The Place-Names of the Isle of Wight* (Paul Watkins, 1996), also deserves mention here. Dictionaries of place names in other counties exist. Some of them are reliable enough, although there are also the few that should never have seen the light of day.

Two discursive but systematic studies that no student or lover of English place names should be without are Kenneth Cameron, *English Place Names* (Batsford, new edition, 1996), and Margaret Gelling and Ann Cole, *The Landscape of Place-Names* (Shaun Tyas, 2000). The latter is an important and eminently readable account of the way place names relate to and derive from natural features.

Those interested in the creation of new counties in 1974 in the reorganization of local government should peruse the *Local Government Boundary Commission for England Report No. 1* (HMSO, 1972) and, in particular, the same body's *Report No. 2* (HMSO, 1973), where the new district names are proposed. The latter publication quotes the guidelines for the creation of new names set forth in a letter of 21 December 1972 to the LGBC from the Secretary of State for the Environment (Geoffrey Ripon):

(a) local wishes should be followed as far as possible and there should be a strong presumption in favour of a name generally acceptable within the area;

(b) the name should be relevant to the geographical, historical or traditional background of the district concerned;

(c) the names should be simple and straightforward; hybrid, concocted or double-barrelled names are best avoided;

(d) districts in the same county should not have names so similar as to give rise to confusion between them; and

(e) the implications should be considered if the name suggested for the district is already in use at parish level.

Almost all the proposed district names were in fact adopted, even the hybrid ones, although Norfolk's romantic-sounding *Pastonacres*, named after the hamlet of *Paston*, home of the well-to-do Paston family and their famous fifteenth-century Paston Letters, settled as prosaic *North Norfolk*.

The pronunciation of English place names has long been a subject of popular interest, and there are guides and other publications that still purport to give the 'correct' pronunciation of certain names, so that *Cirencester* is 'Sisister' and *Hunstanton* 'Hunston'. Local pronunciations can in fact be helpful in determining the origin or meaning of a name, and are often quoted in their historical or current forms in the EPNS volumes mentioned above. A useful reference source in this respect is Klaus Forster, *A Pronouncing Dictionary of English Place-Names* (Routledge & Kegan Paul, 1981), which gives the phonetic forms of around 12,000 names of places in England.

Dictionaries of Scottish and Welsh place names are rather thin on the ground, although a helpful guide to the respective Gaelic, Scandinavian and Welsh words behind names in Scotland and Wales will be found in the Ordnance Survey's 2000 edition of their booklet *Place names on maps of Scotland and Wales*, first published in 1968. Two fairly comprehensive dictionaries of Scottish names, although uneven in content and reliability, are James B. Johnson, *Place-Names of Scotland* (S. R. Publishers, 1970, a reprint of the 3rd edition of the original, 1934), and Mike Darton, *The Dictionary of Place Names in Scotland* (Dobby, new edition, 1994), while mainly discursive accounts are W. F. H. Nicolaisen, *Scottish Place-Names* (John Donald, 2001), and David Dorward, *Scotland's Place-Names* (Mercat Press, 1995). A reasonably reliable listing of the Gaelic forms of Scottish names is printed at the end of Edward Dwelly, *The Illustrated Gaelic–English Dictionary* (Gairm Publications, 12th edition, 2001).

Dictionaries or studies of Welsh place names are few. Those that exist are mostly either paperback listings of the literal meanings of Welsh names or more substantial, academic surveys of restricted geographical areas. One of the better and more detailed paperbacks, though far from comprehensive, is Hywel Wyn Owen, *A Pocket Guide: The Place-Names of Wales* (University of Wales Press/The Western Mail, 1998). Listings of the official forms of Welsh names will be found in Melville Richards, *Welsh Administrative and Territorial Units* (University of Wales Press, 1969), and Elwyn Davies, ed., *A Gazetteer of Welsh Place-Names* (University of Wales Press, 1975).

Readers seeking further place-name information are recommended to consult Jeffrey Spittal and John Field, *A Reader's Guide to the Place-Names of the United Kingdom* (Paul Watkins, 1990), subtitled *A Bibliography of Publications (1920–89) on the Place-Names of Great Britain and Northern Ireland, The Isle of Man, and The Channel Islands.*

Dictionary of British Place Names

A

Aballava. See BURGH-BY-SANDS.

Abbas Combe (village, Somerset): 'abbess's (estate in the) valley'. OE *cumb*, 'valley'. The manor here was held early by the Abbess of Shaftesbury Abbey. The first word of the name represents Latin *abbatisse*, a genitive form of *abbatissa*, 'abbess'. DB *Cumbe*, 1327 *Coumbe Abbatisse*.

Abberley (village, Worcs): 'Ēadbeald's woodland clearing'. OE *lēah*, 'wood', 'clearing'. DB *Edboldelege*.

Abberton (village, Essex): 'Ēadburh's farmstead'. OE *tūn*, 'farmstead', 'estate'. The personal name is that of a woman. DB *Edburgetuna*.

Abberton (village, Worcs): 'estate associated with Ēadbeorht'. OE *-ing-*, 'associated with', + *tūn*, 'farmstead', 'estate'. 972 *Eadbrihtincgtun*, DB *Edbretintune*.

Abbess Roding. See RODINGS.

Abbey Dore (village, Herefords): 'abbey by the (river) Dore'. The reference is the former Cistercian abbey here. The river has a Celtic name meaning simply 'waters' (cp. DOVER). 1147 *Dore*.

Abbey Hulton (district of Stoke-on-Trent, Stoke): 'farmstead on a hill with an abbey'. OE *hyll*, 'hill', + *tūn*, 'farmstead'. The first word of the name refers to the Cistercian abbey founded here in 1223. 1235 *Hulton*.

Abbeystead (hamlet, Lancs): 'site of the abbey'. ME *abbeye*, 'abbey', + *stede*, 'site', 'place'. The reference is to the former Cistercian abbey of Wyresdale here. It was founded in the late 12C but closed soon after when the monks moved to Ireland. 1323 *Abbey*.

Abbey Town (village, Cumbria): 'estate by the abbey'. The name refers to the former abbey of Holme Cultram here. 1649 *Abbey Towne*.

Abbots Bickington (village, Devon): 'abbot's estate associated with Beocca'. OE *-ing-*, 'associated with', + *tūn*, 'farmstead', 'estate'. The

manor here was held early by Hartland Abbey. DB *Bicatona*, 1580 *Abbots Bekenton*.

Abbots Bromley (town, Staffs): 'woodland clearing where broom grows belonging to the abbey'. OE *brōm*, 'broom', + *lēah*, 'wood'. The manor here was held early by Burton Abbey. 1002 *Bromleage*, 1304 *Bromleigh Abbatis*.

Abbotsbury (village, Dorset): 'fortified house of the abbot'. OE *abbod*, 'abbot', + *burh*, 'fortified place', 'manor'. The reference is to early possession of the place by the Abbot of Glastonbury. 946 *Abbedesburie*, DB *Abedesberie*.

Abbotsford (mansion, Borders): '(place of the) abbot's ford'. The mansion was built by Sir Walter Scott in 1816–23 and so named because it was on land owned by the Abbot of Melrose by a ford over the river Tweed.

Abbotsham (village, Devon): 'abbot's enclosure'. OE *abbod*, 'abbot', + *hamm*, 'enclosure'. The manor here was held early by the Abbot of Tavistock. DB *Hama*, 1238 *Abbudesham*.

Abbotskerswell (village, Devon): 'abbot's (estate by the) spring where watercress grows'. OE *cærse*, 'cress', + *wella*, 'spring', 'stream'. The Abbot of Tavistock held the manor early here. 956 *Cærswylle*, DB *Carsuella*, 1285 *Karswill Abbatis*, 1675 *Abbots Keswell*, 1868 *Abbotskerswell*, or *Abbot's Carswell*.

Abbots Langley (town, Herts): 'long wood or clearing belonging to the abbey'. OE *lang*, 'long', + *lēah*, 'wood', 'clearing'. The manor here was held early by the Abbot of St Albans. Cp. KINGS LANGLEY. *c*.1060 *Langalege*, DB *Langelai*, 1263 *Abbotes Langele*.

Abbots Leigh (village, N Somerset): 'abbot's (estate in the) woodland clearing'. OE *lēah*, 'wood', 'clearing'. The manor here was held early by the Abbot of St Augustine's, Bristol. DB *Lege*.

Abbots Lench. See ROUS LENCH.

Abbots Morton (village, Worcs): 'abbot's farmstead in marshland'. OE *mōr*, 'moor', 'marsh', + *tūn*, 'farmstead'. The manor here was held by the Abbot of Evesham, whose title distinguishes this Morton from *Morton Underhill*, 3 miles away, under the hills of Inkberrow. 708 *Mortun*, 1418 *Abbotes Morton*.

Abbots Salford. See SALFORD PRIORS.

Abbotts Ann (village, Hants): 'abbot's (estate on the river) Ann'. The estate was an early possession of Hyde Abbey at Winchester. The river, now the Anton, gave the name of ANDOVER. The DB form of the name below may have suggested the name ANNA VALLEY. 901 *Anne*, DB *Anna*, *c*.1270 *Anne Abbatis*.

Abdon (village, Shropshire): 'Abba's farmstead'. OE *tūn*, 'farmstead', 'estate'. DB *Abetune*.

Aberaeron (town, Ceredigion): 'mouth of the (river) Aeron'. OW *aber*, 'river mouth'. The river's name means 'battle', referring to the goddess of war said to live in its waters. 1184 *ad ostium Ayron*.

Aberafan. See ABERAVON.

Aberavon (district of Port Talbot, Neath PT): 'mouth of the (river) Afan'. OW *aber*, 'river mouth'. The river probably derives its name from a personal name. The Welsh form of the name is *Aberafan*, but the name of the English *Avon* (see AVONMOUTH) and Welsh *afon*, 'river', have resulted in the present spelling. *c*.1400 *Abberauyn*, 1548 *Aberavan*.

Aberdare (town, Rhondda CT): 'mouth of the (river) Dâr'. OW *aber*, 'river mouth'. The river's name probably means 'oak', referring to the trees that grew here. 1203 *Aberdar*.

Aberdaugleddau. See MILFORD HAVEN.

Aberdeen (city, Aberdeen): 'mouth of the (river) Don'. Celtic *aber*, 'river mouth'. The river is named after Devona, a Celtic goddess. Modern Aberdeen is at the mouth of the Dee, but the name relates to Old Aberdeen, to the north, at the mouth of the Don. *c*.1187 *Aberdon*, *c*.1214 *Aberden*.

Aberdour (town, Fife): 'mouth of the (river) Dour'. Celtic *aber*, 'river mouth'. The river's name means simply 'waters'. 1226 *Abirdaur*.

Aberdovey. See ABERDYFI.

Aberdyfi (town, Gwynedd): 'mouth of the (river) Dyfi'. OW *aber*, 'river mouth'. The river's name probably means 'black', 'dark'. 12C *Aberdewi*, 14C *aber dyfi*.

Aberfeldy (town, Perth & Kin): 'confluence of Peallaidh'. Celtic *aber*, 'river mouth', 'confluence'. Peallaidh is the name of a water sprite said to haunt the place where the Moness Burn enters the Tay.

Aberford (village, Leeds): 'Ēadburh's ford'. OE *ford*, 'ford'. The personal name is that of a woman. The ford carried the Great North Road (now bypassed here by the A1) across Cock Beck. 1176 *Ædburford*.

Aberfoyle (village, Stirling): 'confluence of the streams'. Celtic *aber*, 'river mouth', 'confluence', + Gaelic *poll*, genitive *phuill*, 'pool'. The two headstreams of the river Forth unite near here, and are joined by the river Foyle. 1481 *Abirfull*.

Abergafenni. See ABERGAVENNY.

Abergavenny (town, Mon): 'mouth of the (river) Gafenni'. OW *aber*, 'river mouth'. The river's name probably means 'the smith' (modern Welsh *gof*, 'blacksmith'), referring to the ironworks exploited here by the Romans, whose fort was accordingly *Gobannium*, from the same Celtic source. The current name is more correctly spelt *Abergafenni*, while the actual Welsh name of the town is *Y Fenni*, from Welsh *y*, 'the', and a shortened form of *Gafenni*. The first form of the name below is that of the river. 4C *Gobannio*, 1175 *Abergavenni*.

Abergele (town, Conwy): 'mouth of the (river) Gele'. OW *aber*, 'river mouth'. The river's name means 'blade', 'spear' (OW *gelau*), referring to its straight course. 9C *Opergelei*, 1257 *Abergele*.

Abergwaun. See FISHGUARD.

Aberhonddu. See BRECON.

Aberlour (town, Moray): 'confluence of the (river) Lour'. Celtic *aber*, 'river mouth'. The name of the Lour Burn means 'talkative', as if a 'babbling brook'. The town's formal name is *Charlestown of Aberlour*, after Charles Grant, who laid the original village out in 1812.

Abermo. See BARMOUTH.

Abernethy (town, Perth & Kin): 'confluence of the (river) Nethy'. Celtic *aber*, 'river mouth', 'confluence'. The river's name means 'pure' (Celtic *nectona*). The Nethy is a tributary of the Tay. *c*.970 *Aburnethige*.

Aberpennar. See MOUNTAIN ASH.

Aberporth (resort town, Ceredigion): 'estuary in the bay'. OW *aber*, 'river mouth', 'estuary', + *porth*, 'bay', 'port', 'harbour'. The bay is the one into which the river Hoddni flows. Its own name means 'quiet', 'pleasant' (modern Welsh *hawdd*, 'easy'). Cp. BRECON. 1284 *Aberporth*.

Abersoch (resort town, Gwynedd): 'mouth of the (river) Soch'. OW *aber*, 'river mouth'. The river has a Celtic name meaning 'nosing one' (Irish *soc*, 'nose', 'muzzle', modern Welsh *hwch*, 'sow'), referring to the way it 'roots' its course through the land. Cp. AMMANFORD. 1350 *Absogh*, 1598 *Avon Soch*.

Abertawe. See SWANSEA.

Aberteifi. See CARDIGAN.

Aberteleri. See ABERTILLERY.

Abertillery (town, Blaenau Gwent): 'confluence of the (river) Teleri'. OW *aber*, 'river mouth', 'confluence'. The Teleri, its own name from a personal name, joins the Ebwy Fach here. The Welsh spelling of the name is *Abertyleri* or *Aberteleri*. 1332 *Teleri*, 1779 *Aber-Tilery*.

Abertyleri. See ABERTILLERY.

Aberystwyth (resort town, Ceredigion): 'mouth of the (river) Ystwyth'. OW *aber*, 'river mouth'. The river's name means 'curved', 'winding' (OW *ystwyth*). Modern Aberystwyth is at the mouth of the Rheidol, but the name relates to the Ystwyth, to the south, where a Norman castle was built in 1110. A second castle was built on the present site in 1211, and the town grew up around it, retaining the name of the earlier site. 1232 *Aberestuuth*, 14C *aber ystwyth*, 1868 *Aberystwith, or Aberrheidol*.

Abingdon (town, Oxon): '(place by) Æbba's or Æbbe's hill'. OE *dūn*, 'hill'. Abingdon is on level ground by the Thames, and the 'hill' must have been the higher ground to the north. The personal names are respectively those of a man and a woman. 968 *Abbandune*, DB *Abbendone*.

Abinger Hammer (village, Surrey): 'foundry at the enclosure of Abba's people'. OE *-inga-*, 'of the people of', + *worth*, 'enclosure', + modern English *hammer*, 'foundry'. The second word of the name refers to an iron foundry here, recorded in 1600 as *The Hammer Mill*. The first word could also mean simply 'enclosure at Abba's place' (OE *-ing*, 'place belonging to', + *worth*). The DB form of the name below is corrupt. DB *Abinceborne*, 1191 *Abingewurd*.

Abington Pigotts. See GREAT ABINGTON.

Ab Kettleby (village, Leics): 'Abba's (estate at) Ketil's village'. OS *bý*, 'farmstead', 'village'. The place was originally *Kettleby*, with a Scandinavian personal name, before Abba held the manor here in the 13C. DB *Chetelbi*, 1236 *Abeketleby*.

Ablington (village, Glos): 'estate associated with Ēadbeald'. OE *-ing-*, 'associated with', + *tūn*, 'farmstead', 'estate'. 855 *Eadbaldingtun*.

Aboyne (town, Aberdeens): '(place by the river) Aboyne'. The river's name means 'river of the white cow' (Gaelic *abh*, 'river', + *bo*, 'cow', + *fionn*, 'white'). Aboyne is actually on the Dee but takes its name from the small stream to the north. Its formal name is *Charleston of Aboyne*, after Charles Gordon, 1st Earl of Aboyne (d.1681), who erected a burgh of barony here in 1670. 1260 *Obyne*.

Abram (town, Wigan): 'Ēadburh's homestead or enclosure'. OE *hām*, 'homestead', or *hamm*, 'enclosure'. The personal name is that of a woman. late 12C *Adburgham*.

Abridge (village, Essex): 'Ǣffa's bridge'. OE *brycg*, 'bridge'. The bridge in question would have been over the river Roding here. 1203 *Affebrigg*.

Abson (hamlet, S Glos): 'abbot's manor'. OE *abbod*, 'abbot', + *tūn*, 'farmstead', 'manor'. The manor here was held early by Glastonbury Abbey. c.1150 *Abbedeston*.

Abthorpe (village, Northants): 'Abba's outlying farmstead'. OE *throp* or OS *thorp*, 'outlying farmstead', 'secondary settlement'. 1190 *Abetrop*.

Acaster Malbis (village, York): 'Malbis's (estate at) fortification on the river'. OS *á*, 'river', + OE *ceaster*, 'fortification'. The Malbis family held lands here, their name distinguishing this Acaster from ACASTER SELBY, 3 miles further south down the river Ouse. DB *Acastre*, 1252 *Acaster Malebisse*.

Acaster Selby (village, N Yorks): 'fortification on the river belonging to Selby'. OS *á*, 'river', + OE *ceaster*, 'fortification'. Lands here were held by SELBY Abbey, its name distinguishing this Acaster from ACASTER MALBIS, York, 3 miles further north up the river Ouse. DB *Acastre*, 1285 *Acastre Seleby*.

Accrington (town, Lancs): 'farmstead where acorns are stored'. OE *æcern*, 'acorn', + *tūn*, 'farmstead'. The original settlement was on the edge of Rossendale Forest, from where acorns would have been gathered to feed pigs. 12C *Akarinton*.

Acharacle (village, Highland): 'Torquil's ford'. Gaelic *àth*, 'ford'. The personal name is Scandinavian. The ford here would have been over the river Shiel.

Achnashellach Forest (forest, Highland): 'forest by the field of the willows'. Gaelic *achadh*, 'field', + *na*, 'of the', + *seileach*, 'willow' (related modern English *sallow*). 1543 *Auchnashellicht*.

Achray Forest (forest, Stirling): 'forest by the shaking ford'. Gaelic *àth*, 'ford', + *crathaidh*, 'shaking'. The 'shaking ford' is a quagmire here. 1791 *Achray*.

Acklam (village, N Yorks): '(place by the) oak woods or clearings'. OE *āc*, 'oak', + *lēah*, 'wood', 'clearing'. The second part of the name represents OE *lēagum*, the dative plural form of *lēah*. DB *Aclun*. SO ALSO: *Acklam*, Middlesbrough.

Acklington (village, Northd): 'estate associated with Ēadlāc'. OE *-ing-*, 'associated with', + *tūn*, 'farmstead', 'estate'. 1177 *Eclinton*.

Ackton (hamlet, Wakefield): 'farmstead where oak trees grow'. OS *eik*, 'oak', + OE *tūn*, 'farmstead'. The DB form of the name below has omitted the *c*. DB *Aitone*, *c.*1166 *Aicton*.

Ackworth. See HIGH ACKWORTH.

Acle (town, Norfolk): '(place by the) oak wood'. OE *āc*, 'oak', + *lēah*, 'wood', 'clearing'. DB *Acle*.

Acocks Green (district, Birmingham): 'Acock's green'. The district arose around a green that belonged to Richard Acock here in the 17C.

Acol (village, Kent): '(place by the) oak wood'. OE *āc*, 'oak', + *holt*, 'wood'. 1270 *Acholt*.

Acomb (village, Northd): '(place by the) oak trees'. OE *āc*, 'oak'. The name represents OE *ācum*, the dative plural form of *āc*. 1268 *Akum*. SO ALSO: *Acomb*, York.

Aconbury (village, Herefords): 'old fort where squirrels are seen'. OE *ācweorna*, 'squirrel' (from *āc*, 'oak'), + *burh*, 'fortified place'. The 'old fort' is represented by the remains of a Roman camp on nearby Aconbury Hill. 1213 *Akornebir*, 1868 *Aconbury, or Acornbury*.

Acton (hamlet, Dorset): 'farmstead where young sheep are reared'. OE *tacca*, 'young sheep', + *tūn*, 'farmstead', 'village'. The *t-* of *tacca* was dropped in the 16C when it became confused with the *-t* of preceding *at*. DB *Tacatone*.

Acton (district, Ealing): 'farmstead by the oaks'. OE *āc*, 'oak', + *tūn*, 'farmstead', 'village'. The name is reflected in that of *Old Oak Common*, just west of Wormwood Scrubs. 1181 *Acton*, 1211 *Aketon*.

Acton (village, Suffolk): 'Aca's farmstead'. OE *tūn*, 'farmstead'. *c.*995 *Acantun*, DB *Achetuna*.

Acton Beauchamp (village, Herefords): 'Beauchamp's farmstead by the oak tree'. OE *āc*, 'oak', + *tūn*, 'farmstead'. The Beauchamp family held the manor here from the 12C. 727 *Aactune*.

Acton Burnell (village, Shropshire): 'Burnell's farmstead by the oak tree'. OE *āc*, 'oak', + *tūn*, 'farmstead', 'village'. The Burnell family held the manor here from the 12C, their name distinguishing the village from nearby *Acton Pigott*, held by the Picot family. DB *Actune*, 1199 *Akton Burnell*.

Acton Pigott. See ACTON BURNELL.

Acton Round (village, Shropshire): 'round-shaped farmstead by the oak tree'. OE *āc*, 'oak', + *tūn*, 'farmstead', 'village', + ME *rond*, 'round'. The manor here was held early by the earls of Arundel, and the second word of the name may have evolved from this, with *Arundel* seen as containing *round*. There is no natural circular feature here, nor has there ever been a round church, as is sometimes claimed. DB *Achetune*, 1284 *Acton la Runde*.

Acton Scott (village, Shropshire): 'Scot's farmstead by the oak trees'. OE *āc*, 'oak', + *tūn*, 'farmstead'. The Scot family held the manor here in the 13C. DB *Actune*, 1289 *Scottes Acton*.

Acton Trussell (village, Staffs): 'Trussell's farmstead by the oak trees'. OE *āc*, 'oak', + *tūn*, 'farmstead'. The Trussell family owned land here in the 14C. DB *Actone*, 1481 *Acton Trussel*.

Acton Turville (village, S Glos): 'Turville's (estate in) Acca's village'. OE *tūn*, 'farmstead', 'village'. The Turville family held the manor here in the 13C. DB *Achetone*, 1284 *Acton Torvile*.

Ad Ansam. See HIGHAM.

Adbaston (village, Staffs): 'Ēadbald's farmstead'. OE *tūn*, 'farmstead', 'village'. DB *Edboldestone*.

Adber (hamlet, Dorset): 'Ēata's grove'. OE *bearu*, 'grove'. 956 *Eatan beares*, DB *Ateberie*.

Adderbury (village, Oxon): 'Ēadburh's stronghold'. OE *burh*, 'fortified place'. The personal name is that of a woman, popularly identified as the 7C saint Edburga (Ēadburh) of Bicester, said to be a daughter of Penda, king of Mercia. The village properly combines the townships of *East Adderbury* and *West Adderbury*. *c.*950 *Eadburggebyrig*, DB *Edburgberie*.

Adderley (village, Shropshire): 'Althrȳth's woodland clearing'. OE *lēah*, 'wood', 'clearing'. The personal name is that of a woman. DB *Eldredelei*.

Adderstone (hamlet, Northd): 'Ēadrēd's farmstead'. OE *tūn*, 'farmstead', 'village'. 1233 *Edredeston*.

Addingham (village, Bradford): 'homestead associated with Adda'. OE *-ing-*, 'associated with', + *hām*, 'homestead'. *c.*972 *Haddincham*, DB *Odingehem*.

Addington (district, Croydon): 'estate associated with Eadda or Æddi'. OE *-ing-*, 'associated with', + *tūn*, 'farmstead', 'estate'. DB *Eddintone*. SO ALSO: *Addington*, Bucks, Kent.

Addiscombe (district, Croydon): 'Æddi's enclosed land'. OE *camp*, 'enclosed piece of land'. The same man may have given the name of ADDINGTON. 1229 *Edescamp*.

Addlestone (suburban district, Surrey): 'Ættel's valley'. OE *denu*, 'valley'. Addlestone lies on the stream known as The Bourne, a tributary of the Thames. 1241 *Attelesdene*.

Addlethorpe (hamlet, Lincs): 'Eardwulf's outlying farmstead'. OS *thorp*, 'outlying farmstead'. The settlement may have been dependent on Ingoldmells. DB *Arduluetorp*.

Adel (district, Leeds): 'dirty place'. OE *adela*, 'liquid filth' (modern English *addle*). DB *Adele*.

Adisham (village, Kent): 'Ēad's or Eddi's homestead'. OE *hām*, 'homestead', 'village'. 616 *Adesham*, DB *Edesham*.

Adlestrop (village, Glos): 'Tætel's outlying farmstead'. OE *throp*, 'dependent farmstead'. The initial *T-* of the personal name disappeared in the 14C when it became confused with the *-t* of the preceding word *at*, as happened with ELSTREE. The DB form of the name below has omitted the *l* of the personal name. 714 *Titlestrop*, DB *Tedestrop*.

Adlingfleet (village, Yorks): 'water channel of the prince'. OE *ætheling*, 'prince', 'nobleman', + *flēot*, 'water channel', 'stream'. The village stands on the bank of the old river Don. DB *Adelingesfluet*.

Adlington (town, Lancs): 'estate associated with Ēadwulf'. OE *-ing-*, 'associated with', + *tūn*, 'farmstead', 'estate'. *c*.1190 *Edeluinton*. SO ALSO: *Adlington*, Cheshire.

Admaston (hamlet, Staffs): 'Ēadmund's farmstead'. OE *tūn*, 'farmstead', 'village'. 1176 *Ædmundeston*.

Admington (village, Warwicks): 'estate associated with Æthelhelm'. OE *-ing-*, 'associated with', + *tūn*, 'farmstead', 'estate'. DB *Edelmintone*.

Adstone (village, Northants): 'Ættin's farmstead'. OE *tūn*, 'farmstead', 'village'. DB *Atenestone*.

Adur (river). See SHOREHAM-BY-SEA.

Adventurers' Fen (fenland, Cambs). The name alludes to the adventurers (in modern terms venture capitalists) who invested their money in the reclamation of the fenland here to create the present BEDFORD LEVEL. As such, they were distinct from the undertakers, who undertook the actual draining. 1717 *Adventure land*.

Adwell (hamlet, Oxon): '(place by) Eadda's spring'. OE *wella*, 'spring', 'stream'. DB *Advelle*.

Adwick le Street (town, Doncaster): 'Adda's dairy farm on a Roman road'. OE *wīc*, 'dwelling', 'specialized farm', + *strǣt*, 'Roman road' (modern English *street*). Adwick le Street is on the Roman road from Doncaster to Tadcaster. The second part of the name distinguishes the town from the village of *Adwick upon Dearne*, 6 miles to the southwest on the river Dearne (for the river name, see BOLTON UPON DEARNE). DB *Adeuuic*.

Afan (river). See ABERAVON.

Affpuddle (village, Dorset): 'Æffa's estate on the (river) Piddle'. For the river name, see PUDDLETOWN. DB *Affapidele*.

Agglethorpe (hamlet, N Yorks): 'Ācwulf's outlying farmstead'. OS *thorp*, 'outlying farmstead'. DB *Aculestorp*.

Aikton (hamlet, Cumbria): 'farmstead by the oak tree'. OS *eik*, 'oak', + OE *tūn*, 'farmstead'. *c*.1200 *Aictun*.

Ailsa Craig (island, S Ayrs): 'fairy rock'. Gaelic *aillse*, 'fairy', + *creag*, 'rock'. The rocky island is associated in legend with tales of fairies or ghosts.

Ailsworth (village, Peterborough): 'Ægel's enclosure'. OE *worth*, 'enclosure'. 948 *Ægeleswurth*, DB *Eglesworde*.

Ainderby Steeple (village, N Yorks): 'Eindrithi's village with a steeple'. OS *bý*, 'farmstead', 'village', + OE *stēpel*, 'steeple', 'church tower'. The personal name is Scandinavian. The second word of the name distinguishes this village from *Ainderby Myres*, on miry ground nearby, and from *Ainderby Quernhow*, 7 miles to the south, named from a nearby hill (with a name meaning 'mill hill'). DB *Eindrebi*, 1316 *Aynderby wyth Stepil*.

Ainsdale (district of Southport, Sefton): 'Einulfr's valley'. OS *dalr*, 'valley'. The personal name is Scandinavian. DB *Einuluesdel*.

Ainstable (village, Cumbria): '(place on the) slope where bracken grows'. OS *einstapi*, 'bracken', + *hlíth*, 'slope'. *c*.1210 *Ainstapillith*.

Ainsworth (district, Bury): 'Ægen's enclosure'. OE *worth*, 'enclosure'. *c*.1200 *Haineswrthe*.

Aintree (district, Sefton): '(place by the) solitary tree'. OS *einn*, 'one', + *tré*, 'tree'. At one time there would have been an isolated tree here. *c*.1220 *Ayntre*.

Airdrie (town, N Lanarks): '(place on the) high slope'. Gaelic *àrd*, 'high', + *ruighe*, 'slope'. The reference would be to the western spur of the Pentland Hills on which the original settlement developed. 1584 *Airdrie*.

Aire (river). See AIRMYN.

Airmyn (village, E Yorks): 'mouth of the (river) Aire'. OS *mynni*, 'mouth'. The river's name may represent OS *eyjar*, 'islands', but more likely is of Celtic or pre-Celtic origin meaning 'strongly flowing'. The Aire flows into the Ouse here. DB *Ermenie*.

Airton (village, N Yorks): 'farmstead on the (river) Aire'. OE *tūn*, 'farmstead'. For the river name, see AIRMYN. DB *Airtone*.

Aisholt (hamlet, Somerset): 'ash-tree wood'. OE *æsc*, 'ash', + *holt*, 'wood'. Nearby is *Lower Aisholt*. 854 *Æscholt*.

Aiskew (village, N Yorks): '(place by the) oak wood'. OS *eik*, 'oak', + *skógr*, 'wood'. The DB form of the name below is garbled. DB *Echescol*, 1235 *Aykescogh*.

Aislaby (hamlet, N Yorks): 'Áslákr's farmstead'. OS *bý*, 'farmstead', 'village'. This is Aislaby near Pickering. Aislaby near Whitby has a name meaning 'Ásulfr's farmstead'. The personal name in each case is Scandinavian. DB *Aslachesbi*.

Akeld (hamlet, Northd): '(place on the) slope where oak trees grow'. OE *āc*, 'oak', + *helde*, 'slope'. 1169 *Achelda*.

Akeley (village, Bucks): '(place by the) oak wood or clearing'. OE *ācen*, 'growing with oaks', + *lēah*, 'wood', 'clearing'. DB *Achelei*.

Akeman Street (Roman road, England): 'Roman road associated with Acemann'. OE *strǣt*, 'Roman road' (modern English *street*). The road ran from Bath to St Albans, and an alternative name for BATH in Anglo-Saxon times was *Acemannes ceastre* (OE *ceaster*, 'Roman station'), after the same man. (His name was popularly understood to mean 'Ache-man', as if personifying Bath's medicinal waters.) It is possible, however, that no personal name is involved, and that 'Ake-' represents the Roman name of Bath, *Aquae Sulis*, while '-man-' represents a Celtic word meaning 'place' (modern Welsh *man*). The overall meaning of Akeman Street would thus be simply 'Bath road'. In more recent times the name Akeman Street has also been given to the Roman road from Arrington, on Ermine Street, to Cambridge, Ely, and Denver, Norfolk. 12C *Accemannestrete*.

Akenham (village, Suffolk): 'Aca's homestead'. OE *hām*, 'homestead', 'village'. DB *Acheham*.

Alauna. See (1) ALCESTER, (2) MARYPORT.

Alberbury (village, Shropshire): 'Aluburh's manor house'. OE *burh*, 'fortified place', 'manor'. The personal name is that of a woman. DB *Alberberie*.

Albert Village (village, Leics). The village arose in the 19C as a coal-mining settlement and was named after Prince Albert (1819–61), consort of Queen Victoria.

Albion (ancient name of Britain): 'the world'. The name is of Celtic origin, and has been popularly associated with Latin *albus*, 'white', supposedly referring to the white cliffs of Dover. But recent scholarship prefers a meaning 'the land', 'the world', given by the country's own inhabitants, from a word related to modern (but obsolete) Welsh *elfydd*, 'world', 'land'. The name also means 'Scotland', as distinct from 'Pictland', and is found in the latter half of the name of BREADALBANE. Hence also *Alba* as the modern Gaelic name of Scotland.

Albourne (village, W Sussex): '(place by the) stream where alders grow'. OE *alor*, 'alder', + *burna*, 'stream'. Albourne lies on a tributary of the river Adur. 1177 *Aleburn*.

Albrighton (village, Shropshire): 'Ēadbeorht's farmstead'. OE *tūn*, 'farmstead', 'village'. This Albrighton, north of Shrewsbury, has a name of different origin to that of ALBRIGHTON in the east of the county. DB *Etbritone*.

Albrighton (village, Shropshire): 'Æthelbeorht's farmstead'. OE *tūn*, 'farmstead', 'village'. This Albrighton, near Shifnal, has a name of different origin from that of ALBRIGHTON near Shrewsbury. DB *Albricstone*.

Alburgh (village, Norfolk): '(place by the) old hill'. OE *eald*, 'old', + *beorg*, 'mound', 'hill'. The name could also mean 'Alda's hill'. DB *Aldeberga*.

Albury (village, Herts): 'old stronghold'. OE *eald*, 'old', + *burh*, 'fortified place'. There are no signs of any fortification here now. DB *Eldeberie*.

Albury (village, Surrey): 'old stronghold'. OE *eald*, 'old', + *burh*, 'fortified place'. The 'old stronghold' may be the Romano-British settlement on Farley Heath to the south. 1062 *Ealdeburi*, DB *Eldeberie*.

Alby Hill (hamlet, Norfolk): 'Áli's farmstead'. OS *bý*, 'farmstead', 'village'. The personal name is Scandinavian. The place later became associated with a nearby hill. DB *Alebei*.

Alcester (town, Warwicks): 'Roman town on the (river) Alne'. OE *ceaster*, 'Roman station'. The river has a Celtic name, perhaps meaning 'shining one', seen also in *Alauna*, the name of the Roman town here, on Icknield Street. 1138 *Alencestre*.

Alchester (Roman town, Oxon): 'Roman town (called) Alauna'. OE *ceaster*, 'Roman town'. The Roman town, in Wendlebury, has a name identical to that of ALCESTER, Warwicks. *c.*1160 *Alencestr.*

Alciston (village, E Sussex): 'Ælfsige's or Ealhsige's farmstead'. OE *tūn*, 'farmstead', 'village'. DB *Alsistone.*

Alconbury (village, Cambs): 'Ealhmund's stronghold'. OE *burh*, 'fortified place'. The DB form of the name below has corrupted the personal name. DB *Acumesberie*, 12C *Alcmundesberia.*

Aldborough (village, N Yorks): 'old stronghold'. OE *eald*, 'old', + *burh*, 'fortified place'. The 'old stronghold' here is the Roman fort of *Isurium Brigantum*. The first word of this relates to the river *Ure* here (see JERVAULX ABBEY). The second word names the *Brigantes*, the most populous tribe in Roman Britain, whose capital this was. DB *Burg*, 1145 *Aldeburg*. SO ALSO: *Aldborough*, Norfolk.

Aldbourne (village, Wilts): 'stream associated with Ealda'. OE *-ing-*, 'associated with', + *burna*, 'stream'. The original *-ing-* has disappeared from the name. *c.*970 *Ealdincburnan*, DB *Aldeborne.*

Aldbrough (village, E Yorks): 'old stronghold'. OE *eald*, 'old', + *burh*, 'fortified place'. There is no trace of any stronghold here now. DB *Aldenburg.*

Aldbrough (village, N Yorks): 'old stronghold'. OE *eald*, 'old', + *burh*, 'fortified place'. Aldbrough is by Watling Street and there are a number of old entrenchments here, the most prominent being Scots Dyke, a long earthwork extending for several miles to the north. The second part of the DB form of the name below is corrupt. DB *Aldeburne*, 1247 *Aldeburg.*

Aldbury (village, Herts): 'old stronghold'. OE *eald*, 'old', + *burh*, 'fortified place'. There is no sign of a fort here now. DB *Aldeberie.*

Aldeburgh (resort town, Suffolk): 'old stronghold'. OE *eald*, 'old', + *burh*, 'stronghold'. The river Alde here gets its name from that of the town. DB *Aldeburc*, 1868 *Aldeburgh, or Aldborough.*

Aldeby (village, Norfolk): 'old stronghold'. OE *eald*, 'old', + *burh*, 'fortified place'. An 'old' stronghold is a disused one. OE *burh* was later replaced by OS *bý*, 'farmstead'. DB *Aldebury*, *c.*1180 *Aldeby.*

Aldenham (village, Herts): 'old homestead'. OE *eald*, 'old', + *hām*, 'homestead'. The name could also mean 'Ealda's homestead'. If the former, 'Alden-' represents OE *ealdan*, the dative form of *eald*. If the latter, it represents *Ealdan*,

the genitive form of the personal name. 785 *Ældenham*, DB *Eldeham.*

Alderbury (village, Wilts): 'Æthelwaru's stronghold'. OE *burh*, 'fortified place'. The personal name is that of a woman. 972 *Æthelware byrig*, DB *Alwarberie.*

Alderford (village, Norfolk): '(place by the) ford where alders grow'. OE *alor*, 'alder', + *ford*, 'ford'. The river here is the Wensum. 1163 *Alraforda.*

Alderholt (village, Dorset): '(place by the) alder wood'. OE *alor*, 'alder', + *holt*, 'wood'. 1285 *Alreholt.*

Alderley (village, Glos): 'woodland clearing where alders grow'. OE *alor*, 'alder', + *lēah*, 'wood', 'clearing'. DB *Alrelie.*

Alderley Edge (town, Cheshire): '(settlement by) Alderley Edge'. The town arose in the 19C and took its name from the nearby escarpment *Alderley Edge* (OE *ecg*, 'edge'), itself named after the village of *Alderley* to the south (see NETHER ALDERLEY). The first form of the name below relates to the ridge, the second to the town. 14C *le Hegge*, 1860 *Alderley Edge.*

Aldermaston (village, W Berks): 'farmstead of the nobleman'. OE *ealdormann*, 'man of high rank' (modern English *alderman*), + *tūn*, 'farmstead'. DB *Ældremanestone.*

Alderminster (village, Warwicks): 'farmstead of the nobleman'. OE *ealdormann*, 'man of high rank' (modern English *alderman*), + *tūn*, 'farmstead'. Cp. ALDERMASTON. 1167 *Aldermanneston.*

Aldersbrook (district, Redbridge): '(place by the) brook where alders grow'. ME *alder*, 'alder', + *broke*, 'brook'. The brook in question is a tributary of the river Roding. 1535 *Aldersbroke.*

Aldershot (town, Hants): 'corner of land where alders grow'. OE *alor*, 'alder', + *scēat*, 'corner of land'. The 'corner of land' is probably the part of Hampshire that projects into Surrey here. 1171 *Halreshet*, 1248 *Alreshete*, 1868 *Aldershott.*

Alderton (village, Glos): 'estate associated with Ealdhere'. OE *-ing-*, 'associated with', + *tūn*, 'farmstead', 'estate'. DB *Aldritone*. SO ALSO: *Alderton*, Northants, Wilts.

Alderton (village, Suffolk): 'farmstead where alders grow'. OE *alor*, 'alder', + *tūn*, 'farmstead'. DB *Alretuna*. SO ALSO: *Alderton*, Shropshire.

Alderwasley (village, Derbys): 'clearing by the alluvial land where alders grow'. OE *alor*, 'alder', + *wæsse*, 'alluvial land', + *lēah*, 'wood', 'clearing'. The stream that flows past Alderwasley Hall here must have been liable to flood. 1251 *Alrewaseleg.*

Aldfield (village, N Yorks): '(place in) old open country'. OE *ald*, 'old', + *feld*, 'open country' (modern English *field*). 'Old' open country is land that has been long used. DB *Aldefeld*.

Aldford (village, Cheshire): '(place by the) old ford'. OE *eald*, 'old', + *ford*, 'ford'. An 'old' ford is one formerly used, here the one near Iron Bridge where the Roman road from Chester to Wroxeter crossed the river Dee. It was superseded by the ford at Aldford Bridge. 1153 *Aldefordia*.

Aldham (village, Essex): 'old homestead'. OE *eald*, 'old', + *hām*, 'homestead'. The name could also mean 'Ealda's homestead'. DB *Aldeham*. SO ALSO: *Aldham*, Suffolk.

Aldingbourne (village, W Sussex): '(place by the) stream associated with Ealda'. OE *-ing-*, 'associated with', + *burna*, 'stream'. *c.*880 *Ealdingburnan*, DB *Aldingeborne*.

Aldingham (coastal hamlet, Cumbria): 'homestead of Alda's people'. OE *-inga-*, 'of the people of', + *hām*, 'homestead'. DB *Aldingham*.

Aldington (village, Kent): 'estate associated with Ealda'. OE *-ing-*, 'associated with', + *tūn*, 'farmstead', 'estate'. DB *Aldintone*. SO ALSO: *Aldington*, Worcs.

Aldon (hamlet, Shropshire): '(place by the) hill with a spring'. OE *æwell*, 'spring', + *dūn*, 'hill'. The hamlet lies just below the tip of a hill above a headstream ('spring') of a tributary of the river Onny. DB *Alledone*.

Aldridge (town, Walsall): 'farm among the alders'. OE *alor*, 'alder', + *wīc*, 'dwelling', 'farm'. DB *Alrewic*.

Aldringham (village, Suffolk): 'homestead of Aldhere's people'. OE *-inga-*, 'of the people of', + *hām*, 'homestead'. DB *Alrincham*.

Aldrington (district of Hove, Brighton & Hove): 'estate associated with Ealdhere'. OE *-ing-*, 'associated with', + *tūn*, 'farmstead', 'estate'. The name could also mean 'estate of Ealdhere's people' (OE *-inga-*, 'of the people of', + *tūn*). DB *Eldretune*.

Aldsworth (village, Glos): 'Ald's enclosure'. OE *worth*, 'enclosure'. 1004 *Ealdeswyrthe*, DB *Aldeswrde*.

Aldwark (hamlet, Derbys): '(place by the) old fortification'. OE *ald*, 'old', + *weorc*, 'building', 'fortification' (modern English *work*). The reference would be to a Roman or earlier fortification. Aldwark is close to the Roman road known as The Street and to the ancient route called Portway. 1140 *Aldwerk*. SO ALSO: *Aldwark*, N Yorks.

Aldwick (district of Bognor Regis, W Sussex): 'old dwelling'. OE *eald*, 'old', + *wīc*, 'dwelling'.

The name could also mean 'Ealda's dwelling'. 1235 *Aldewyc*.

Aldwincle (village, Northants): '(place by) Ealda's river bend'. OE *wincel*, 'corner', 'bend'. There is a big bend in the river Nene here. DB *Eldewincle*.

Aldworth (village, W Berks): 'old enclosure'. OE *eald*, 'old', + *worth*, 'enclosure'. The name could also mean 'Ealda's enclosure'. The DB form of the name below has a second *l* for *d*. DB *Elleorde*.

Alexandria (town, W Dunbartons): '(place of) Alexander'. The town arose in the mid-18C when bleaching and dyeing works were built here and the name was given in *c.*1760 for Alexander Smollett (d.1799), the local MP for Bonhill. Cp. RENTON.

Alfold (village, Surrey): 'old fold'. OE *eald*, 'old', + *fald*, 'fold', 'enclosure'. 1227 *Alfold*.

Alford (town, Aberdeens): '(place by the) high ford'. Gaelic *àth*, 'ford', + *àrd*, 'high'. The river here is the Don. But the terrain is flat, not elevated, and the second part of the name may have another origin. *c.*1200 *Afford*, 1654 *Afurd*.

Alford (town, Lincs): '(place by the) old ford'. OE *ald*, 'old', + *ford*, 'ford'. The original road over the stream that runs through the town was probably Roman origin. DB *Alforde*.

Alford (village, Somerset): '(place by) Ealdgȳth's ford'. OE *ford*, 'ford'. The personal name is that of a woman. The river here is the Brue. DB *Aldedeford*.

Alfreton (town, Derbys): 'Ælfhere's farmstead'. OE *tūn*, 'farmstead', 'village'. The DB form of the name below has miscopied *f* as *s*. DB *Elstretune*, 12C *Alferton*.

Alfrick (village, Worcs): 'Ealhrǣd's dairy farm'. OE *wīc*, 'dwelling', 'specialized farm'. Early 13C *Alcredeswike*.

Alfriston (village, E Sussex): 'Ælfrīc's farmstead'. OE *tūn*, 'farmstead', 'village'. DB *Alvricestone*.

Algarkirk (village, Lincs): 'Ælfgār's church'. OE *cirice*, 'church'. The OE word was subsequently replaced by the equivalent OS *kirkja* to give the present '-kirk'. The DB form of the name below records the personal name alone. DB *Alfgare*, 1194 *Algarescherche*, 1212 *Algarekirke*.

Alhampton (village, Somerset): 'estate on the (river) Alham'. OE *tūn*, 'farmstead', 'estate'. The river has a Celtic name of uncertain meaning. DB *Alentona*.

Alice Holt Forest (wooded region, Hants): 'Ælfsige's wood'. OE *holt*, 'wood'. 1167 *Alsiholt*, 1168 *Alfsiholt*, 1190 *Alsieholt*.

Alkborough (village, N Lincs): 'Alca's hill'. OE *beorg*, 'hill'. DB *Alchebarge*, 12C *Alchebarua*.

Alkerton (village, Oxon): 'estate associated with Ealhhere'. OE *-ing-*, 'associated with', + *tūn*, 'farmstead', 'estate'. DB *Alcrintone*.

Alkham (village, Kent): 'temple homestead'. OE *ealh*, 'temple', + *hām*, 'homestead'. A 'temple homestead' is either one in a sheltered place or one used as a sanctuary. *c*.1100 *Ealhham*.

Alkington (hamlet, Shropshire): 'estate associated with Ealha'. OE *-ing-*, 'associated with', + *tūn*, 'farmstead', 'estate'. DB *Alchetune*, 1256 *Alkinton*.

Alkmonton (hamlet, Derbys): 'Ealhmund's farmstead'. OE *tūn*, 'farmstead', 'village'. DB *Alchementune*.

All Cannings. See BISHOPS CANNINGS.

Allendale Town (town, Northd): 'settlement in the valley of the (river) Allen'. OE *tūn*, 'settlement', + OS *dalr*, 'valley'. The river's name, of uncertain meaning, is Celtic or pre-Celtic. 1245 *Alewenton*.

Allenheads (village, Northd): '(place by the) source of the (river) Allen'. OE *hēafod*, 'head'. The river has a Celtic or pre-Celtic name of uncertain origin. 1868 *Allenheads, or Allonhead*.

Allensmore (village, Herefords): 'Alain's marshy ground'. OE *mōr*, 'moor', 'marsh'. The personal name is Old French. DB *More*, 1220 *Aleinesmor*.

Allenton (district, Derby): 'Allen's town'. The district is named after a Mr Allen, builder of the houses here in the late 19C.

Aller (village, Somerset): '(place by the) alder tree'. OE *alor*, 'alder'. DB *Alre*.

Allerdale (council district, Cumbria): 'valley of the (river) Ellen'. OS *dalr*, 'valley'. The name of the river is of uncertain origin. The original barony of Allerdale became the ward of *Allerdale-below-Derwent*, one of the five wards of Cumberland. Cp. COPELAND FOREST. 11C *Alnerdall*, 1268 *Aldersdale*.

Allerford (village, Somerset): '(place at the) ford where alders grow'. OE *alor*, 'alder', + *ford*, 'ford'. The form of the name below is that of Allerford near Minehead. DB *Alresford*.

Allerston (village, N Yorks): 'Ælfhere's stone'. OE *stān*, 'stone'. The name presumably refers to a boundary stone here. DB *Alurestan*.

Allerthorpe (village, E Yorks): 'Ælfweard's or Alfvarthr's outlying farmstead'. OS *thorp*, 'outlying farmstead'. The personal names are respectively OE and Scandinavian. DB *Aluuarestorp*.

Allerton (district, Liverpool): 'farmstead where alders grow'. OE *alor*, 'alder', + *tūn*, 'farmstead'. DB *Alretune*. SO ALSO: *Allerton*, Bradford.

Allerton Bywater (district, Leeds): 'farmstead where alders grow by the water'. OE *alor*, 'alder', + *tūn*, 'farmstead'. The second word of the name refers to the location of the place on the river Aire. DB *Alretune*, 1430 *Allerton by ye water*.

Allerton Mauleverer (hamlet, N Yorks): 'Mauleverer's (estate at) Allerton's farmstead'. OE *tūn*, 'farmstead'. The Mauleverer family held Allerton from the 12C to the 18C. DB *Aluertone*, 1231 *Aluerton Mauleuerer*.

Allesley (district, Coventry): 'Ælle's woodland clearing'. OE *lēah*, 'wood', 'clearing'. 1176 *Alleslega*.

Allestree (suburb of Derby): 'Æthelheard's tree'. OE *trēow*, 'tree'. DB *Adelardestre*.

Allexton (village, Leics): 'Æthellāc's farmstead'. OE *tūn*, 'farmstead', 'village'. DB *Adelachestone*.

Allhallows (resort village, Medway): '(place with) All Saints church'. The first word of the first two forms of the name below represents OE *hōh*, 'spur of land', and *Hoo* was the name of the hundred here. Allhallows arose on high ground amid marshes by the Thames estuary. 1285 *Ho All Hallows*, 1896 *Hoo Allhallows*, 1966 *Allhallows-on-Sea*.

Allington (district of Maidstone, Kent): 'farmstead associated with Ælla or Ælle'. OE *-ing-*, 'associated with', + *tūn*, 'farmstead'. DB *Elentun*.

Allington (village, Lincs): 'farmstead of the princes'. OE *ætheling*, 'prince', + *tūn*, 'farmstead'. DB *Adelingetone*.

Allington (village, Wilts): 'farmstead associated with Ealda'. OE *-ing-*, 'associated with', + *tūn*, 'farmstead'. This is Allington near Amesbury. Allington near Devizes has a name of the same origin as ALLINGTON, Lincs. 1178 *Aldintona*.

Allithwaite (village, Cumbria): 'Eilífr's clearing'. OS *thveit*, 'clearing'. The personal name is Scandinavian. *c*.1170 *Hailiuethait*.

Alloa (town, Clack): 'rocky plain'. Gaelic *all-mhagh*. The town lies on level ground north of the river Forth. Cp. ALLOWAY, ALVA. 1357 *Alveth*.

Allonby (resort village, Cumbria): 'Alein's farmstead'. OS *bý*, 'farmstead', 'village'. The personal name is Old French. 1262 *Alayneby*.

Alloway (village, S Ayrs): '(place on a) rocky plain'. Gaelic *allmhagh*. The village, now effectively a southern suburb of Ayr, lies on level ground on the lower course of the river Doon. 1324 *Auleway*.

All Saints South Elmham. See NORTH ELM-HAM.

All Stretton. See CHURCH STRETTON.

Allt Melyd. See MELIDEN.

Allweston (village, Dorset): 'Ælfflæd's or Ælf-gifu's farmstead'. OE *tūn*, 'farmstead', 'village'. The personal names are those of women. 1214 *Alfeston*.

Almeley (village, Herefords): '(place by the) elm wood or clearing'. OE *elm*, 'elm', + *lēah*, 'wood', 'clearing'. DB *Elmelie*.

Almer (hamlet, Dorset): '(place by the) pool where eels are caught'. OE *ǣl*, 'eel', + *mere*, 'pool'. The pool in question is on the river Winterborne nearby. 943 *Elmere*.

Almington (hamlet, Staffs): 'Alhmund's farmstead'. OE *tūn*, 'farmstead', 'village'. DB *Almentone*.

Almondbury (district of Huddersfield, Kirklees): 'stronghold of the whole community'. OS *almenn*, 'all men', + OE *burh*, 'fortified place'. The first half of the name represents OS *almanna*, the genitive plural form of *almenn*. DB *Almaneberie*.

Almondsbury (village, S Glos): 'Æthelmōd's or Æthelmund's stronghold'. OE *burh*, 'fortified place'. The 'stronghold' may be the Roman camp site to the southwest of the village. DB *Almodesberie*.

Alne (village, N Yorks): meaning uncertain. The name is Celtic in origin. *c*.1050 *Alna*, DB *Alne*.

Alness (town, Highland): '(place on the river) Alness'. The river name is of pre-Celtic origin and uncertain meaning. 1226 *Alenes*.

Alnham (hamlet, Northd): 'homestead on the (river) Aln'. OE *hām*, 'homestead'. For the river name, see ALNMOUTH. 1228 *Alneham*.

Alnmouth (resort town, Northd): 'mouth of the (river) Aln'. OE *mūtha*, 'mouth'. The river has a Celtic name of uncertain origin. 1201 *Alnemuth*.

Alnwick (town, Northd): 'farm on the (river) Aln'. OE *wīc*, 'farm'. The river enters the sea at ALNMOUTH. 1178 *Alnewich*.

Alperton (district, Brent): 'estate associated with Ealhbeorht'. OE *-ing-*, 'associated with', + *tūn*, 'farmstead', 'estate'. 1199 *Alprinton*.

Alphamstone (village, Essex): 'Ælfhelm's farmstead'. OE *tūn*, 'farmstead', 'village'. DB *Alfelmestuna*.

Alpheton (village, Suffolk): 'Ælfflæd's or Æthelflæd's farmstead'. OE *tūn*, 'farmstead'. The personal names are those of women. 1204 *Alfledeston*.

Alphington (district of Exeter, Devon): 'estate associated with Ælf'. OE *-ing-*, 'associated with', + *tūn*, 'farmstead', 'estate'. Cp. WEST ALVINGTON. *c*.1060 *Alfintune*, DB *Alfintone*.

Alport (village, Derbys): 'old town'. OE *eald*, 'old', + *port*, 'town'. The name implies a long-inhabited settlement. 12C *Aldeport*.

Alpraham (village, Cheshire): 'Alhburh's homestead'. OE *hām*, 'homestead', 'village'. The personal name is that of a woman. DB *Alburgham*.

Alresford (village, Essex): '(place by) Ægel's ford'. OE *ford*, 'ford'. There was no *r* in the original name. *c*.1000 *Ælesford*, DB *Eilesforda*.

Alresford (town, Hants): '(place by the) ford where alders grow'. OE *alor*, 'alder', + *ford*, 'ford'. The town is properly known as *New Alresford*, as distinct from *Old Alresford*, a village to the north. The river Alre here takes its name from that of the town. DB *Alresforde*, 13C *Nova Villa de Alresford*.

Alrewas (village, Staffs): 'alluvial land where alders grow'. OE *alor*, 'alder', + *wæsse*, 'alluvial land' (related modern English *wash*). Alrewas lies by the confluence of the river Tame with the Trent. 942 *Alrewasse*, DB *Alrewas*.

Alsager (town, Cheshire): 'Ælle's plot of land'. OE *æcer*, 'cultivated land' (modern English *acre*). The DB form of the name below is corrupt. DB *Eleacier*, 13C *Allesacher*.

Alsh, Loch. See KYLE OF LOCHALSH.

Alsop en le Dale (village, Derbys): 'Ælle's valley in the valley'. OE *hop*, 'valley', + OF *en le*, 'in the', + OE *dæl*, 'valley'. The second part of the name was added when the sense of OE *hop* was no longer understood. (A *hop* is a remote valley, as distinct from a *dæl*, which is a main valley.) DB *Elleshope*, 1535 *Alsope in le dale*.

Alston (town, Cumbria): 'Halfdan's farmstead'. OE *tūn*, 'farmstead'. The personal name is Scandinavian, and OE *tūn* replaced earlier equivalent OS *bý*. 1164 *Aldeneby*, 1209 *Aldeneston*.

Alstone (village, Glos): 'Ælfsige's farmstead'. OE *tūn*, 'farmstead', 'village'. 969 *Ælfsigestun*.

Alstonefield (village, Staffs): 'Ælfstān's open country'. OE *feld*, 'open land' (modern English *field*). The DB form of the name below has garbled the personal name. DB *Ænestanefelt*, 1179 *Alfstanesfeld*.

Altarnun (village, Cornwall): 'altar of St Nonn'. Cornish *alter*, 'altar'. Nonn is said to have been the mother of the Welsh St David. *c.*1100 *Altrenune*, 1868 *Altarnun, or Alternon*.

Altcar. See GREAT ALTCAR.

Altham (village, Lancs): 'river meadow where swans are seen'. OE *elfitu*, 'swan', + *hamm*, 'river meadow'. The village is near the river Calder. *c.*1150 *Elvetham*.

Althorne (village, Essex): '(place by the) burnt thorn bush'. OE *æled*, 'burnt', + *thorn*, 'thorn bush'. 1198 *Aledhorn*.

Althorp (country house, Northants): 'Olla's outlying farmstead'. OS *thorp*, 'outlying farmstead'. DB *Olletorp*, 1208 *Olethorp*.

Alton (village, Derbys): 'old farmstead'. OE *ald*, 'old', + *tūn*, 'farmstead'. 1296 *Alton*.

Alton (town, Hants): 'farmstead at the river source'. OE *æwiell*, 'river source', + *tūn*, 'farmstead'. The town is near the source of the river Wey. DB *Aultone*.

Alton (village, Staffs): 'Ælfa's farmstead'. OE *tūn*, 'farmstead'. DB *Elvetone*.

Alton Priors (village, Wilts): 'farmstead at the river source of the priory'. OE *æwiell*, 'river source', + *tūn*, 'farmstead'. Alton Priors was held by the priory of St Swithin's, Winchester. The addition distinguishes the village from nearby *Alton Barnes*, where the manor was held by the Berners family. 825 *Aweltun*, DB *Auuiltone*, 1199 *Aulton Prioris*.

Altrincham (town, Trafford): 'homestead of Aldhere's people'. OE *-inga-*, 'of the people of', + *hām*, 'homestead'. The name could also mean 'homestead associated with Aldhere' (OE *-ing*, 'place associated with', + *hām*). The soft *g* of *-ing* gave the '-ch-' of the present name. 1290 *Aldringeham*.

Alum Bay (bay, IoW). The bay is so called from the large amount of alum quarried from the rocks here from the 16C. 1769 *Allum Bay*.

Alva (town, Clack): '(place on the) rocky plain'. Gaelic *allmhagh*, 'rocky plain'. The town lies at the base of the Ochill Hills. 1489 *Alweth*.

Alvanley (village, Cheshire): 'Ælfweald's woodland clearing'. OE *lēah*, 'wood', 'clearing'. DB *Elveldelie*.

Alvaston (district, Derby): 'Æthelwald's or Ælfwald's farmstead'. OE *tūn*, 'farmstead', 'village'. *c.*1002 *Alewaldestune*, DB *Alewoldestune*.

Alvechurch (village, Worcs): 'Ælfgȳth's church'. OE *cirice*, 'church'. The personal name is that of a woman. The DB form of the name below has rendered its *f* and *th* as *v*. 10C *Ælfgythe cyrcan*, DB *Alvievecherche*.

Alvecote (hamlet, Warwicks): 'Afa's cottage'. OE *cot*, 'cottage'. *c.*1160 *Avecote*.

Alvediston (village, Wilts): 'Ælfgeat's farmstead'. OE *tūn*, 'farmstead', 'village'. 1165 *Alfwieteston*.

Alveley (village, Shropshire): 'Ælfgȳth's woodland clearing'. OE *lēah*, 'wood', 'clearing'. The personal name is that of a woman. DB *Alvidelege*.

Alverdiscott (hamlet, Devon): 'Elfrēd's cottage'. OE *cot*, 'cottage'. DB *Alveredescota*.

Alverstoke (district of Gosport, Hants): 'Ælfwaru's or Æthelwaru's outlying farmstead'. OE *stoc*, 'outlying farmstead', 'secondary settlement'. Both personal names are of women. 938 *Stoce*, DB *Alwarestoch*.

Alverstone (village, IoW): 'Elfrēd's farmstead'. OE *tūn*, 'farmstead'. DB *Alvrestone*.

Alverton (hamlet, Notts): 'estate associated with Ælfhere'. OE *-ing-*, 'associated with', + *tūn*, 'farmstead', 'estate'. DB *Aluriton*.

Alvescot (village, Oxon): 'Ælfhēah's cottage'. OE *cot*, 'cottage'. DB *Elfegescote*.

Alveston (village, S Glos): 'Ælfwīg's stone'. OE *stān*, 'stone'. The reference is probably to a boundary stone here. DB *Alwestan*.

Alveston (village, Warwicks): 'Ēanwulf's farmstead'. OE *tūn*, 'farmstead', 'village'. 966 *Eanulfestun*, DB *Alvestone*.

Alvingham (village, Lincs): 'homestead of Ælf's people'. OE *-inga-*, 'of the people of', + *hām*, 'homestead'. DB *Aluingeham*.

Alvington (village, Glos): 'estate associated with Ælf'. OE *-ing-*, 'associated with', + *tūn*, 'farmstead', 'estate'. 1220 *Eluinton*.

Alwalton (village, Cambs): 'estate associated with Æthelwald'. OE *-ing-*, 'associated with', + *tūn*, 'farmstead', 'estate'. The *-ing-* has disappeared from the name. 955 *Æthelwoldingtun*, DB *Alwoltune*.

Alwinton (village, Northd): 'farmstead on the (river) Alwin'. OE *tūn*, 'farmstead', 'village'. The river has a Celtic or pre-Celtic name of uncertain meaning. 1242 *Alwenton*.

Alwoodley (district, Leeds): 'Æthelwald's woodland clearing'. OE *lēah*, 'wood', 'clearing'. DB *Aluuoldelei*, 1166 *Adelwaldesleia*.

Alyth (town, Perth & Kin): 'rocky place'. Gaelic *eileach*, 'mound', 'bank', 'rock'. The name alludes to nearby Alyth Hill. *c*.1249 *Alicht*, 1327 *Alyth*.

Ambergate (village, Derbys): '(place with a) gate by the (river) Amber'. The name is recent, and refers to a tollgate here. For the river name, see AMBER VALLEY. 1836 *Ambergate*.

Amberley (village, W Sussex): 'woodland clearing where yellowhammers are seen'. OE *amer*, 'yellowhammer', 'bunting', + *lēah*, 'wood', 'clearing'. 957 *Amberle*, DB *Ambrelie*. SO ALSO: *Amberley*, Glos.

Amber Valley (council district, Derbys): 'valley of the (river) Amber'. The river has a pre-Celtic name of uncertain meaning.

Amble (coastal town, Northd): 'Amma's or Anna's promontory'. OE *bile*, 'promontory' (modern English *bill*). 1204 *Ambell*, 1256 *Anebell*.

Amblecote (district of Stourbridge, Dudley): 'Æmela's cottage'. OE *cot*, 'cottage'. DB *Elmelecote*.

Ambleside (town, Cumbria): 'summer pasture by the river sandbank'. OS *á*, 'river', + *melr*, 'sandbank', + *sǣtr*, 'summer pasture'. The name illustrates the rural practice of transhumance, whereby flocks are transferred to mountain or hill pastures in the summer. The alternative form of the second name below relates to the Stock Ghyll stream here. The town lies below the waterfall known as Stockghyll Force. *c*.1095 *Ameleseta*, 1868 *Ambleside, or Ambleside-above-and-below-Stock*.

Ambleston (village, Pemb): 'Amelot's farm'. OE *tūn*, 'farm'. The equivalent Welsh name is *Treamlod* (Welsh *tre*, 'farm'). 1230 *Amleston*.

Ambrosden (village, Oxon): 'Ambre's hill'. OE *dūn*, 'hill'. The name could also mean 'hill where yellowhammers are seen' (OE *amer*, 'yellowhammer', 'bunting', + *dūn*). DB *Ambresdone*.

Amersham (town, Bucks): 'Ealhmund's homestead'. OE *hām*, 'homestead', 'village'. 1066 *Agmodesham*, DB *Elmodesham*.

Amesbury (town, Wilts): 'Ambre's stronghold'. OE *burh*, 'fortified place'. The 'stronghold' is the nearby Iron Age hill fort known as Vespasian's Camp. The name has inspired various fictions. 'Its name is derived, according to some authorities, from Ambrosius, a Roman and a descendant of Constantine, who became the sovereign of Britain; but according to others, from Ambrius, or Ambrosius, a British monk, the founder of a large monastery, which was destroyed by the Saxons; but both derivations are purely conjectural' (*The National Gazetteer of Great Britain and Ireland*, 1868). *c*.880

Ambresbyrig, DB *Ambresberie*, 1868 *Amesbury, or Ambresbury*.

Amington (hamlet, Staffs): 'estate associated with Earma'. OE *-ing-*, 'associated with', + *tūn*, 'farmstead', 'estate'. The DB form of the name below is corrupt. DB *Ermendone*, 1150 *Aminton*.

Amlwch (village and port, Anglesey): '(place) near the swamp'. Welsh *am*, 'by', 'near', + *llwch*, 'swamp', 'pool'. The 'swamp' was presumably the bay here that became a proper harbour when the copper mines of nearby Parys Mountain were exploited in the 18C. 1254 *Anulc*, 1352 *Amelogh*.

Ammanford (town, Carm): 'ford over the (river) Aman'. OE *ford*, 'ford'. The river's name derives from Welsh *banw*, 'pig', meaning a river that 'roots' its way through the ground. The Welsh name of Ammanford is *Rhydaman* (Welsh *rhyd*, 'ford'). 1541 *Amman*.

Amotherby (village, N Yorks): 'Eymundr's farmstead'. OS *bý*, 'farmstead', 'village'. The personal name is Scandinavian. DB *Aimundrebi*.

Ampleforth (village, N Yorks): 'ford where dock grows'. OE *ampre*, 'dock', 'sorrel', + *ford*, 'ford'. The ford would have been over a stream here, a tributary of the river Rye. DB *Ampreforde*.

Ampney Crucis (village, Glos): '(church) of the Holy Rood by the Ampney Brook'. The river name means 'Amma's stream' (OE *ēa*, 'river', 'stream'). The second word of the name (Latin *crucis*, 'of the cross') distinguishes this village from nearby *Ampney St Mary* and *Ampney St Peter*, named for the dedications of their churches, and from *Down Ampney*, downstream from the others. DB *Omenie*, 1287 *Ameneye Sancte Crucis*.

Ampthill (town, Beds): '(place by the) anthill'. OE *ǣmette*, 'ant' (modern English dialect *emmet*), + *hyll*, 'hill'. Ants would have been regularly in evidence here. DB *Ammetelle*.

Ampton (village, Suffolk): 'Amma's farmstead'. OE *tūn*, 'farmstead', 'village'. DB *Hametuna*.

Amwell. See GREAT AMWELL.

Amwythig. See SHREWSBURY.

Ancaster (village, Lincs): 'Roman fort associated with Anna'. OE *cæster*, 'Roman station'. The Roman encampment near here was *Causennis*, a name of obscure origin. 12C *Anecastre*.

Ancroft (hamlet, Northd): 'isolated enclosure'. OE *āna*, 'lonely', + *croft*, 'enclosure'. 1195 *Anecroft*.

Anderitum. See PEVENSEY.

Andover (town, Hants): '(place by the) ash tree waters'. The name is Celtic. 'An-' represents the name of the river Ann (now the Anton), meaning 'ash tree', while '-dover', meaning 'waters', is related to the name of DOVER. The 'waters' are the Anton itself and a stream that joins it here. 955 *Andeferas*, DB *Andovere*.

Andoversford (village, Glos): '(place by) Anna's ford'. OE *ford*, 'ford'. The ford would have been over the river Isborne here. The name appears to have been influenced by that of ANDOVER. 759 *Onnan ford*.

Anerley (district, Bromley): 'lonely place'. The name, Scottish English for 'lonely', was that of a house here in the 19C owned by a Scotsman, William Sanderson, who offered land to the railway company on condition the name be used for their station, which opened in 1839. Further development followed. 1904 *Anerley*.

Anfield (district, Liverpool): 'sloping piece of ground'. ME *hange*, 'slope', + OE *feld*, 'open land' (modern English *field*). The district appears to have arisen around a house called Anfield House, itself named for the ground nearby. 1642 *Hongfield*.

Angersleigh (hamlet, Somerset): 'Aunger's (estate in the) woodland clearing'. OE *lēah*, 'wood', 'clearing'. The Aunger family held the manor here in the 13C. DB *Lega*, 1354 *Aungerlegh*.

Anglesey (island, Anglesey): 'Ongull's island'. OS *ey*, 'island'. The personal name is Scandinavian. The name is often popularly interpreted as 'island of the Angles' (who gave the name of ENGLAND). The Welsh name of Anglesey is *Môn*, 'hill', 'mountain', referring to Holyhead Mountain. The Roman name, from the same Celtic source, was *Mona*. Cp. CAERNARFON. 815 *ynys uon*, 1098 *Anglesege*, 13C *Ongulsey*, 1868 *Anglesey*, or *Anglesea*.

Angmering (suburb of Littlehampton, W Sussex): '(settlement of) Angenmǣr's people'. OE *-ingas*, 'people of'. The name has 'spread' to the nearby coastal resort of *Angmering-on-Sea*. c.880 *Angemæringum*, DB *Angemare*.

Angram (hamlet, N Yorks): '(place at the) pastures'. OE *anger*, 'pasture', 'grassland'. The name represents OE *angrum*, the dative plural form of *anger*. The form of the name below applies to Angram near Tadcaster, but Angram near Muker has a name of identical origin. 13C *Angrum*.

Angus (unitary authority, E Scotland): '(place of) Angus'. The district is named for Angus, 8C king of the Picts, whose own name (Gaelic *Aonghas*) means 'sole choice'. 12C *Enegus*.

Anlaby (suburb of Hull, E Yorks): 'Óláfr's farmstead'. OS *bý*, 'farmstead', 'village'. The personal name is Scandinavian. The DB form of the name below is garbled. DB *Unlouebi*, 1203 *Anlauebi*.

Anmer (village, Norfolk): '(place by the) pool where ducks are seen'. OE *æned*, 'duck', + *mere*, 'pool'. The DB form of the name below has omitted a syllable. DB *Anemere*, 1291 *Anedemere*.

Annan (town, Dumfries & Gall): '(place by the) water'. The name is that of the river here, its own name early Celtic in origin. The last three forms of the name below have added a word meaning 'valley', respectively Welsh *ystrad*, Gaelic *srath* and OS *dalr*. 7C *Anava*, 1304 *Anand*, 1124 *Estrahanent*, 1152 *Stratanant*, 1179 *Annandesdale*.

Anna Valley (district of Andover, Hants): 'valley of the (river) Ann'. The name is recent, but refers to the former name of the river Anton, which gave the name of ANDOVER. 1908 *Vale of Anna*. See also ABBOTTS ANN.

Annesley Woodhouse (village, Notts): 'Ān's woodland clearing by the woodland hamlet'. OE *lēah*, 'wood', 'clearing', + *wudu*, 'wood', + *hūs*, 'house'. The main name could also mean 'woodland clearing with a hermitage' (OE *ānsetl*, 'hermitage', literally 'solitary settlement', + *lēah*). The ancient parish of *Annesley* here came to comprise the four hamlets of *Annesley*, *Woodhouse*, *Wandesley* and *Felley*. DB *Aneslei*, c.1190 *Anseleia*, 13C *Annesley Wodehouse*.

Annfield Plain (town, Durham). The town arose only in the 19C but the first word of its name is much older, meaning 'Ann's open country' (OE *feld*, modern English *field*). The second word is said to refer to the 'planes' or slopes where wagons were hauled up during construction of the Stanhope and Tyne Railway in 1834. The name is first recorded c.1865. 1893 *Annfield Plain*.

Ansdell (district of Lytham St Anne's, Lancs). The district is named after the painter Richard Ansdell (1815–85), who built a large house here called 'Star Hills'.

Ansford (village, Somerset): 'ford associated with Ealhmund'. OE *ford*, 'ford'. Ansford lies near the river Brue. DB *Almundesford*, 1868 *Almsford, or Ansford*.

Ansley (village, Warwicks): 'woodland clearing with a hermitage'. OE *ānsetl*, 'hermitage' (literally 'solitary settlement'), + *lēah*, 'wood', 'clearing'. DB *Hanslei*, 1235 *Anesteleye*.

Anslow (village, Staffs): 'Ēanswīth's woodland clearing'. OE *lēah*, 'wood', 'clearing'. The personal name is that of a woman. 1012 *Eansythelege*.

Anstey (village, Leics): '(place by the) single track'. OE *ān*, 'one', + *stīg*, 'path', 'track'. The name can mean either 'single path', meaning a stretch of road used by lesser routes that converge on it at either end, or '(route) on a steep track' (OE *an*, 'on', + *stīg*, 'climbing path'). Here the former sense is appropriate. DB *Anstige*.

Anstruther (resort and port, Fife): '(place by) the little stream'. Gaelic *an*, 'the', + *sruthair*, 'little stream'. The mouth of the 'little stream' effectively divides the town into two distinct parts, *Anstruther Easter* and *Anstruther Wester*. *c.*1205 *Anestrothir*.

Ansty (village, Warwicks): '(place by the) ascent'. OE *ānstīg* (see ANSTEY). The village stands on a hill reached by roads ascending from the southeast and southwest. DB *Anestie*. SO ALSO: *Ansty*, Wilts.

Anthorn (hamlet, Cumbria): '(place by the) solitary thorn bush'. OS *einn*, 'one', + *thorn*, 'thorn bush'. Cp. AINTREE. 1279 *Eynthorn*.

Antingham (village, Norfolk): 'homestead of Anta's people'. OE *-inga-*, 'of the people of', + *hām*, 'homestead'. DB *Antingham*.

Antonine Wall (Roman fortification, Scotland): 'wall of Antoninus'. The wall from the Forth to the Clyde was built in AD 142 for the Roman emperor Antoninus Pius. Hence its name.

Antony (village, Cornwall): 'Anna's or Anta's farmstead'. OE *tūn*, 'farmstead'. The form of the name has probably been influenced by the personal name Anthony. DB *Antone*.

Apethorpe (village, Northants): 'Api's outlying farmstead'. OS *thorp*, 'secondary settlement', 'outlying farmstead'. The DB form of the name below has garbled the Scandinavian personal name. DB *Patorp*, 1162 *Apetorp*.

Appin (mountainous region, Highland): 'abbey land'. Gaelic *apainn*, 'abbey lands'. Land here was owned by Lismore Abbey in medieval times.

Appleby (town, Cumbria): 'farmstead where apple trees grow'. OE *æppel* or OS *epli*, 'apple', + OS *bý*, 'farmstead', 'village'. The town is also known as *Appleby-in-Westmorland*, after its historic county, to distinguish it from other places of the same name. 1130 *Aplebi*. SO ALSO: *Appleby*, N Lincs.

Appleby Magna (village, Leics): 'greater farmstead where apple trees grow'. OE *æppel* or OS *epli*, 'apple', + OS *bý*, 'farmstead'. The second word of the name, Latin for 'great', distin-

guishes this Appleby from nearby *Appleby Parva* (Latin *parva*, 'small'). 1002 *Æppelby*, DB *Aplebi*.

Applecross (coastal village, Highland): 'mouth of the (river) Crosan'. Celtic *aber*, 'river mouth'. The river name means 'little cross', from Gaelic *cros*, 'cross' and the diminutive suffix *-an*. The village is on Applecross Bay south of the mouth of the river Applecross. *c.*1080 *Aporcrosan*.

Appledore (village, Devon): '(place by the) apple tree'. OE *apuldor*, 'apple tree'. 1335 *le Apildore*. SO ALSO: *Appledore*, Kent.

Appledram. See APULDRAM.

Appleton (village, Oxon): 'farmstead where apples grow'. OE *æppel*, 'apple', + *tūn*, 'farmstead'. 942 *Æppeltune*, DB *Apletune*. SO ALSO: *Appleton*, Halton.

Appleton-le-Moors (village, N Yorks): 'farmstead where apples grow by the moors'. OE *æppel*, 'apple', + *tūn*, 'farmstead'. The village lies on the southern edge of the North York Moors. The addition to the name distinguishes this Appleton from APPLETON-LE-STREET, 8 miles to the south. DB *Apeltun*.

Appleton-le-Street (village, N Yorks): 'farmstead where apples grow on the road'. OE *æppel*, 'apple', + *tūn*, 'farmstead'. A Roman road probably ran between Malton and Hovingham here, on the route now followed by the B1257. The addition to the name distinguishes this Appleton from APPLETON-LE-MOORS, 8 miles to the north. DB *Apletun*.

Appleton Roebuck (village, N Yorks): 'Rabuk's farmstead where apples grow'. OE *æppel*, 'apple', + *tūn*, 'farmstead'. The Rabuk family held the manor here in the 14C, their name distinguishing the village from NUN APPLETON, 2 miles to the south. *c.*972 *Æppeltune*, 1664 *Appleton Roebucke*.

Appleton Wiske (village, N Yorks): 'farmstead where apples grow by the (river) Wiske'. OE *æppel*, 'apple', + *tūn*, 'farmstead'. The river name represents OE *wisc*, 'marshy meadow'. DB *Apeltona*.

Appletreewick (village, N Yorks): 'farm by the apple trees'. OE *æppel*, 'apple', + *trēow*, 'tree', + *wīc*, 'dwelling', 'farm'. DB *Apletrewic*.

Appley Bridge (hamlet, Lancs): '(place at the) bridge by the apple-tree wood or clearing'. OE *æppel*, 'apple', + *lēah*, 'wood', 'clearing'. The bridge in question is over the river Douglas and the Leeds and Liverpool Canal here. 13C *Appelleie*.

Apuldram (village, W Sussex): 'homestead or enclosure where apple trees grow'. OE *apuldor*, 'apple tree', + *hām*, 'homestead', or *hamm*, 'enclosure'. The name is still sometimes found in the alternative form *Appledram*. 12C *Apeldreham*, 1868 *Appledram*.

Aquae Arnemetiae. See BUXTON.

Aquae Sulis. See BATH.

Aqualate Mere (lake, Staffs): 'stream where oak trees grow'. OE *āc*, 'oak', + *gelād*, 'watercourse'. The name was originally that of a place here, not of the lake ('mere'). An association with Latin *aqua*, 'water', and *aquila*, 'eagle', has inevitably led to various fanciful interpretations. 1227 *Aguilade*.

Arberth. See NARBERTH.

Arborfield (village, Wokingham): 'Hereburh's open land'. OE *feld*, 'open land' (modern English *field*). The personal name is that of a woman. *c*.1190 *Edburgefeld*, 1222 *Erburgefeld*.

Arbroath (town and port, Angus): 'mouth of the (river) Brothock'. Celtic *aber*, 'river mouth'. The river's name comes from Gaelic *brothach*, 'boiling', 'seething'. Robert Southey's poem *The Inchcape Rock* (1802) preserves the medieval form of the town's name:

And then they knew the perilous rock,
And blest the Abbot of Aberbrothok.

1178 *Aberbrothok*, 1868 *Arbroath, or Aberbrothwick*.

Ardeley (village, Herts): 'Earda's woodland clearing'. OE *lēah*, 'wood', 'clearing'. 939 *Eardeleage*, DB *Erdelei*.

Arden. See HENLEY-IN-ARDEN.

Ardingly (village, W Sussex): 'woodland clearing of Earda's people'. OE *-inga-*, 'of the people of', + *lēah*, 'wood', 'clearing'. Early 12C *Erdingelega*.

Ardington (village, Oxon): 'estate associated with Earda'. OE *-ing-*, 'associated with', + *tūn*, 'farmstead', 'estate'. DB *Ardintone*.

Ardleigh (village, Essex): 'woodland clearing with a dwelling place'. OE *eard*, 'native place', 'dwelling place', + *lēah*, 'wood', 'clearing'. The DB form of the name below is corrupt. DB *Erleiam*, 12C *Ardlega*.

Ardley (village, Oxon): 'Eardwulf's woodland clearing'. OE *lēah*, 'wood', 'clearing'. 995 *Eardulfes lea*, DB *Ardulveslie*.

Ardnamurchan (peninsula, Highland): 'height of the otters'. Gaelic *àrd*, 'height', + *na*, 'of the', + *muir*, 'sea', + *chon*, genitive plural of *cù*, 'dog'. The first form of the name below seems to suggest a final element *chol*, 'sin', with 'sea sins' implying piracy. *c*.700 *Art Muirchol*, 1309 *Ardnamurchin*.

Ardrishaig (town, Argyll & Bute): 'height of the brambles'. Gaelic *àrd*, 'height', + *dris*, 'bramble'.

Ardrossan (town and port, N Ayrs): 'height of the little headland'. Gaelic *àrd*, 'height', + *ros*, 'headland', + *-an*, diminutive suffix. The 'little headland' is the lower land on which Saltcoats now stands to the east of the town. *c*.1320 *Ardrossane*.

Ardsley (district, Barnsley): 'Eorēd's or Ēanrēd's woodland clearing'. OE *lēah*, 'wood', 'clearing'. 12C *Erdeslaia*.

Ardsley East (village, Leeds): 'Eorēd's or Ēanrēd's mound'. OE *hlāw*, 'mound'. The village is also known as *East Ardsley*, the first word distinguishing it from nearby *West Ardsley*. DB *Erdeslawe*.

Areley Kings (hamlet, Worcs): 'royal (estate by the) wood or clearing where eagles are seen'. OE *earn*, 'eagle', + *lēah*, 'wood', 'clearing'. The estate here was part of the royal manor of Martley. Areley Kings was at one time also known as *Nether Arley*, the first word distinguishing it from UPPER ARLEY, 7 miles to the north. *c*.1138 *Erneleia*, 1405 *Kyngges Arley*.

Argyll (region, Argyll & Bute): 'coastland of the Gaels'. Gaelic *oirthir Ghaideal* (*oirthir*, 'coastland', + *Ghaidel*, 'Gael'). The 'Gaels' were originally an Irish race who entered this region through Kintyre and settled in what was then Celtic territory. *c*.970 *Arregaithel*, 1292, *Argail*.

Ariconium. See WESTON UNDER PENYARD.

Arkendale (village, N Yorks): 'Eorcna's or Eorcon's valley'. OE *denu*, 'valley'. OE *denu* was replaced from the 14C by equivalent OS *dalr*. DB *Arghendene*, 1301 *Erkendale*.

Arkesden (village, Essex): 'Arnkel's valley'. OE *denu*, 'valley'. The personal name is Scandinavian. DB *Archesdana*.

Arkholme (village, Lancs): '(place by the) hill pastures'. OS *erg*, 'shieling', 'hill pasture'. The name represents OS *ergum*, the dative plural form of *erg*, but has been influenced by OS *holmr*, 'island'. DB *Ergune*.

Arkley (district, Barnet): 'woodland clearing where arks are made'. OE *arc*, 'ark', 'chest', + *lēah*, 'wood', 'clearing'. The first part of the name is also found in the surname Arkwright, 'maker of arks'. The first two forms of the name below have added OE *land*, 'cultivated land'. 1332 *Arkleyslond*, 1436 *Arcleylond*, 1547 *Arkeley*.

Arksey (suburb of Doncaster): 'Arnkel's island'. OE *ēg*, 'island'. The personal name is Scandinavian. The 'island' is raised ground in marshland here near the river Don. DB *Archeseia*.

Arkwright Town (village, Derbys). The name is that of the family of Sir Richard Arkwright (1732–92), inventor of the spinning frame, who bought the manor of Sutton here in 1824.

Arlecdon (village, Cumbria): '(place in the) valley of the stream where eagles are seen'. OE *earn*, 'eagle', + *lacu*, 'stream' (related modern English *lake*), + *denu*, 'valley'. This interpretation has been challenged by some on the grounds that it does not fit early forms of the name. c.1130 *Arlauchdene*.

Arlesey (village, Beds): 'Ælfrīc's island'. OE *ēg*, 'island'. The 'island' here is well-watered land. DB *Alricheseia*, 1868 *Arlsey*.

Arleston (suburb of Wellington, Wrekin): 'Eardwulf's farmstead'. OE *tūn*, 'farmstead', 'estate'. c.1138 *Erdulfest*.

Arley (hamlet, Cheshire): '(place by the) grey wood'. OE *hār*, 'grey' (modern English *hoar*), + *lēah*, 'wood'. The name could also mean '(place by the) wood on a boundary' (OE *hār*, 'boundary', + *lēah*). In the latter case, the reference would be to Arley's location on the boundary between the hundreds of Bochelau and Tunendune. 1340 *Arlegh*.

Arley (village, Warwicks): 'wood or clearing where eagles are seen'. OE *earn*, 'eagle', + *lēah*, 'wood', 'clearing'. 1001 *Earnlege*, DB *Arlei*.

Arlingham (village, Glos): 'homestead or enclosure of Eorla's people'. OE *-inga-*, 'of the people of', + *hām*, 'homestead', or *hamm*, 'enclosure'. DB *Erlingeham*.

Arlington (hamlet, Devon): 'estate associated with Ælffrith'. OE *-ing-*, 'associated with', + *tūn*, 'farmstead', 'estate'. DB *Alferdintona*.

Arlington (village, E Sussex): 'estate associated with Eorla'. OE *-ing-*, 'associated with', + *tūn*, 'farmstead', 'estate'. DB *Erlington*.

Armadale (town, W Lothian). The town arose in the mid-19C and takes its name from its former owner, William Honeyman, Lord Armadale, who took his title from *Armadale*, Highland, itself meaning 'elongated valley' (OS *armr*, 'arm', + *dalr*, 'valley').

Armathwaite (village, Cumbria): '(place by the) clearing of the hermit'. ME *ermite* (modern English *hermit*), + OS *thveit*, 'clearing'. 1212 *Ermitethwait*.

Arminghall (village, Norfolk): 'corner of land of Ambre's or Ēanmǣr's people'. OE *-inga-*, 'of

the people of', + *halh*, 'nook', 'corner of land'. DB *Hameringahala*.

Armitage (village, Staffs): '(place at the) hermitage'. ME *ermitage*, 'hermitage'. 1520 *Armytage*.

Armley (district, Leeds): 'Earma's woodland clearing'. OE *lēah*, 'wood', 'clearing'. DB *Ermelai*.

Armthorpe (suburb of Doncaster): 'Earnwulf's or Arnulfr's outlying farmstead'. OS *thorp*, 'outlying farmstead'. The personal names are respectively OE and Scandinavian. DB *Ernulfestorp*.

Arncliffe (village, N Yorks): '(place by the) cliff where eagles are seen'. OE *earn*, 'eagle', + *clif*, 'cliff'. The cliff in question is Arnberg Scar, south of the village. DB *Arneclif*.

Arne (hamlet, Dorset): 'building'. OE *ærn*, 'house', 'building'. The name could also mean '(place by the) tumuli', from OE *hær*, 'heap of stones', 'tumulus', in the dative plural form *harum*. The reference would be to the two tumuli on Arne Hill nearby. 1268 *Arne*.

Arnesby (village, Leics): 'Iarund's or Erendi's farmstead'. OS *bý*, 'farmstead', 'village'. The personal names are Scandinavian. DB *Erendesbi*.

Arnold (town, Notts): 'corner of land where eagles are seen'. OE *earn*, 'eagle', + *halh*, 'nook', 'corner of land'. The 'corner of land' may have been the valley of the stream here, where eagles nested. DB *Ernehale*. SO ALSO: *Arnold*, E Yorks.

Arnside (town, Cumbria): 'Earnwulf's or Arnulfr's headland'. OE *hēafod*, 'headland'. The headland would have been a feature on the estuary of the river Kent here. The personal names are respectively OE and Scandinavian. 1184 *Harnolvesheuet*.

Arram (village, E Yorks): '(place by) hill pastures'. OS *erg*, 'shieling', 'summer pasture'. The name represents OS *ergum*, the dative plural form of *erg*. DB *Argun*.

Arrathorne (hamlet, N Yorks): '(place at the) thorn bush by the hill pasture'. OS *erg*, 'shieling', 'hill pasture', + *thorn*, 'thorn bush'. 13C *Ergthorn*.

Arreton (village, IoW): 'estate associated with Ēadhere'. OE *-ing-*, 'associated with', + *tūn*, 'farmstead', 'estate'. c.880 *Eaderingtune*, DB *Adrintone*.

Arrington. See ERMINE STREET.

Arrow (village, Warwicks): '(place on the river) Arrow'. The river has a Celtic or pre-Celtic name meaning simply 'stream'. The *n* in the first form of the name below represents a miscopied *u*. 710 *Arne*, DB *Arue*.

Arthington (village, Leeds): 'estate associated with Earda'. OE -*ing*-, 'associated with', + *tūn*, 'farmstead', 'estate'. DB *Hardinctone*.

Arthingworth (village, Northants): 'enclosure associated with Earna'. OE -*ing*-, 'associated with', + *worth*, 'enclosure'. DB *Arningvorde*.

Arundel (town, W Sussex): 'valley where horehound grows'. OE *hārhūne*, 'horehound', + *dell*, 'valley'. Horehound is a plant of the mint family with a traditional use in medicine. Local legend derives the town's name from Arondel (French *hirondelle*, '(swift as a) swallow'), the horse of the legendary hero Bevis of Hampton, and a swallow is depicted on the town's coat of arms. Another tale explains it as 'Arun dale', referring to the valley of the river *Arun*, although its own name (now also that of the local council district) comes from that of the town. It was originally the Tarrant, a name of the same origin as the Trent (see STOKE-ON-TRENT), preserved in Tarrant Street here. DB *Harundel*.

Ascot (town, Windsor & Maid): 'eastern cottage'. OE *ēast*, 'east', + *cot*, 'cottage'. The place may have been 'east' with regard to *Easthampstead*, 'homestead by the gate' (OE *geat*, 'gate', + *hām-stede*, 'homestead'). 1177 *Estcota*.

Ascott under Wychwood (village, Oxon): 'eastern cottages near (the forest of) Wychwood'. OE *ēast*, 'eastern', + *cot*, 'cottage'. For the forest name, see SHIPTON UNDER WYCHWOOD. 1220 *Estcot*.

Asenby (village, N Yorks): 'Eysteinn's farmstead'. OS *bý*, 'farmstead', 'village'. The personal name is Scandinavian. DB *Æstanesbi*.

Asfordby (village, Leics): 'Ásfrøthr's or Ásfrithr's farmstead'. OS *bý*, 'farmstead', 'village'. The personal names are Scandinavian. DB *Osferdebie*.

Asgarby (hamlet, Lincs): 'Ásgeirr's farmstead'. OS *bý*, 'farmstead'. The personal name is Scandinavian. The form of the name below is for Asgarby near Sleaford, but Asgarby near Spilsby has a name of identical origin. 1201 *Asegarby*.

Ash (village, Kent): '(place by the) ash tree'. OE *æsc*, 'ash'. The form of the name below is for Ash near Sandwich. *c*.1100 *Æsce*. SO ALSO: *Ash*, Surrey.

Ashbocking (hamlet, Suffolk): 'de Bocking's (estate by the) ash tree'. OE *æsc*, 'ash'. The de Bocking family held the manor here in the 14C. DB *Assa*, 1411 *Bokkynge Assh*.

Ashbourne (town, Derbys): 'stream where ash trees grow'. OE *æsc*, 'ash', + *burna*, 'stream'. Henmore Brook here was originally known as the Ashbourne, and this gave the name of the town. DB *Esseburne*.

Ashbrittle (village, Somerset): 'Bretel's (estate by the) ash tree'. OE *æsc*, 'ash'. One Bretel held the manor here in 1086. DB *Aisse*, 1212 *Esse Britel*.

Ashburnham (hamlet, W Sussex): 'meadow by the stream where ash trees grow'. OE *æsc*, 'ash', + *burna*, 'stream', + *hamm*, 'meadow'. The river here is the Ashburn. DB *Esseborne*, 12C *Esburneham*.

Ashburton (town, Devon): 'farmstead by the stream where ash trees grow'. OE *æsc*, 'ash', + *burna*, 'stream', + *tūn*, 'farmstead'. The river Yeo here was formerly the Ashbourne. DB *Essebretone*.

Ashbury (village, Oxon): 'stronghold where ash trees grow'. OE *æsc*, 'ash', + *burh*, 'fortified place'. The stronghold in question is the nearby hill fort known as Alfred's Castle. The first part of the DB form of the name below is corrupt. DB *Eissesberie*, 1187 *Æsseberia*.

Ashby cum Fenby (village, NE Lincs): 'Aski's farmstead with Fenby'. OS *bý*, 'farmstead', 'village'. The personal name is Scandinavian. Ashby now forms a single village with (Latin *cum*) Fenby, 'farmstead in a fen' (OE *fenn*, 'fen', + OS *bý*). DB *Aschebi*, *Fendebi*, 1594 *Ashbye cum fenbye*.

Ashby de la Launde (village, Lincs): 'de la Launde's farmstead where ash trees grow'. OS *askr*, 'ash', + *bý*, 'farmstead'. The manor here was held in the 14C by William de la Laund. DB *Aschebi*.

Ashby de la Zouch (town, Leics): 'de la Zuche's farmstead where ash trees grow'. OE *æsc* or OS *askr*, 'ash', + OS *bý*, 'farmstead'. The manor here was held in the 13C by Roger de la Zuche. DB *Ascebi*, 1241 *Esseby la Zusche*.

Ashby Folville (village, Leics): 'de Foleuilla's farmstead where ash trees grow'. OE *æsc* or OS *askr*, 'ash', + OS *bý*, 'farmstead', 'village'. The de Foleuilla family held the manor here in the 12C. DB *Aschi*.

Ashby Puerorum (village, Lincs): 'farmstead of the boys where ash trees grow'. OE *æsc* or OS *askr*, 'ash', + OS *bý*, 'farmstead', 'village', + Latin *puerorum*, 'of the boys'. The manor here was appropriated in the 13C for the support of the choristers of Lincoln Cathedral. DB *Aschebi*.

Ashby St Ledgers (village, Northants): 'farmstead where ash trees grow with St Leger's church'. OE *æsc* or OS *askr*, 'ash', + OS *bý*, 'farmstead'. It seems likely that OS *bý* replaced original OE *tūn*. Leger was a 7C Bishop of Autun. DB

*Ascebi, c.*1230 *Esseby Sancti Leodegarii,* 1868 *Ashby St. Legers.*

Ashby St Mary (village, Norfolk): 'farmstead where ash trees grow with St Mary's church'. OE *æsc* or OS *askr*, 'ash', + OS *bý*, 'farmstead', 'village'. Ashby St Mary or *Ashby-near-Norwich*, 7 miles southeast of Norwich, is distinguished by its church dedication from *Ashby-with-Oby*, or simply *Ashby*, 11 miles northeast of Norwich (but also with a church dedicated to St Mary). DB *Ascebei.*

Ashchurch (village, Glos): 'church by the ash tree'. OE *æsc*, 'ash', + *cirice*, 'church'. 1287 *Asschirche.*

Ashcombe (village, Devon): '(place in the) valley where ash trees grow'. OE *æsc*, 'ash', + *cumb*, 'valley'. DB *Aissecome.*

Ashcott (village, Somerset): 'cottage where ash trees grow'. OE *æsc*, 'ash', + *cot*, 'cottage'. DB *Aissecote.*

Ashdon (village, Essex): 'hill overgrown with ash trees'. OE *æscen*, 'growing with ash trees', + *dūn*, 'hill'. *c.*1036 *Æstchendune,* DB *Ascenduna.*

Ashdown Forest (heathland region, E Sussex): 'hill overgrown with ash trees'. OE *æscen*, 'growing with ash trees', + *dūn*, 'hill'. Most of the ancient forest's ash trees have now disappeared, but some remain in the triangle formed by Uckfield, East Grinstead and Tunbridge Wells. 1207 *Essendon.*

Asheldham (village, Essex): 'Æschild's homestead'. OE *hām*, 'homestead', 'village'. The personal name is that of a woman. *c.*1130 *Assildeham.*

Ashen (village, Essex): '(place by the) ash trees'. OE *æsc*, 'ash'. The name represents the dative plural form of OE *æsc* in the phrase *æt thǣm æscum*, 'at the ashes'. DB *Asce,* 1344 *Asshen.*

Ashendon (village, Bucks): 'hill overgrown with ash trees'. OE *æscen*, 'growing with ashes', + *dūn*, 'hill'. Cp. ASHDON. DB *Assedune.*

Ashfield (council district, Notts): 'open land where ash trees grow'. OE *æsc*, 'ash', + *feld*, 'open land' (modern English *field*). The old name has been revived for that of the modern district. 1216 *Esfeld.* SO ALSO: *Ashfield,* Suffolk.

Ashford (village, Devon): '(place by the) ford where ash trees grow'. OE *æsc*, 'ash', + *ford*, 'ford'. The ford must have been over the estuary of the river Taw here, west of Barnstaple. DB *Aiseforda.*

Ashford (town, Kent): 'ford by a clump of ash trees'. OE *æsc*, 'ash', + *-et*, 'clump of', + *ford*, 'ford'. The ford would probably have been over the East Stour here. DB *Essetesford.*

Ashford (residential district, Surrey): 'Eccel's ford'. OE *ford*, 'ford'. The first part of the name may be Ecel, a former name of the river Ash here. As a personal name it could be of Celtic origin, not OE (cp. CHERTSEY), and may even be that of Echel, a legendary Welsh hero. 969 *Ecelesford,* DB *Exeforde.*

Ashford Bowdler (village, Shropshire): 'de Boulers' (estate by the) ford where ash trees grow'. OE *æsc*, 'ash', + *ford*, 'ford'. The river here is the Teme. The manor was held early by the de Boulers family, their name distinguishing this Ashford from nearby *Ashford Carbonel*, held by the Carbunel family. DB *Esseford,* 1255 *Asford Budlers.*

Ashford Carbonel. See ASHFORD BOWDLER.

Ashford in the Water (village, Derbys): '(place by the) ford where ash trees grow in the water'. OE *æsc*, 'ash', + *ford*, 'ford'. The second part of the name, added only in the 17C, alludes to the location of the village on the river Wye, which here follows a meandering course. 926 *Æscforda,* DB *Aisseford,* 1697 *Ashford in the watter.*

Ashill (village, Norfolk): 'ash-tree wood'. OE *æsc*, 'ash', + *lēah*, 'wood'. DB *Asscelea.*

Ashill (village, Somerset): '(place by the) hill where ash trees grow'. OE *æsc*, 'ash', + *hyll*, 'hill'. DB *Aisselle.*

Ashingdon (district of Rochford, Essex): '(place by the) hill where asses are kept'. OE *assa*, 'ass', + *dūn*, 'hill'. The name could also mean '(place by) Assa's hill', but not 'hill where ash trees grow', *pace* the author of the 11C *Encomium Emmae* ('In Praise of Emma'), who tells of a fight '*in Aesceneduno loco quod nos Latini montem fraxinorum possumus interpretari*' ('in Ashingdon, a place that we Latin writers can translate as hill of ashes'). The DB form of the name below has added an initial *N-*. 1016 *Assandun,* DB *Nesenduna.*

Ashington (town, Northd): 'valley where ash trees grow'. OE *æscen*, 'ash trees', + *denu*, 'valley'. The valley would have been that of the river Wansbeck, to the south of the town. 1205 *Essenden.*

Ashington (village, W Sussex): 'farmstead of Æsc's people'. OE *-inga-*, 'of the people of', + *tūn*, 'farmstead'. 1073 *Essingetona.*

Ashleworth (village, Glos): 'Æscel's enclosure'. OE *worth*, 'enclosure'. DB *Escelesuuorde*.

Ashley (village, Cambs): '(place by the) ash tree wood or clearing'. OE *æsc*, 'ash', + *lēah*, 'wood', 'clearing'. DB *Esselie*. SO ALSO: *Ashley*, Cheshire, Devon, Hants (near Lymington, near Winchester), Northants, Staffs.

Ashley Green (village, Bucks): '(place by the) ash tree wood or clearing'. OE *æsc*, 'ash', + *lēah*, 'wood', 'clearing'. The village became associated with its green. 1227 *Essleie*, 1468 *Assheley grene*.

Ashmanhaugh (hamlet, Norfolk): 'Æscmann's enclosure'. OE *haga*, 'enclosure' (related modern English *hedge*). The first part of the name could also represent OE *æsc-mann*, 'pirate' (from *æsc*, 'Viking ship' (made of ashwood), + *mann*, 'man'). 1153 *Asmanhawe*.

Ashmore (village, Dorset): '(place by the) pool where ash trees grow'. OE *æsc*, 'ash', + *mere*, 'pool'. The 'pool' is the duck pond in the centre of this hill-top village. DB *Aisemare*.

Ashover (village, Derbys): '(place by the) ridge where ash trees grow'. OE *æsc*, 'ash', + *ofer*, 'ridge'. DB *Essovre*.

Ashow (village, Warwicks): 'hill spur of the ash tree'. OE *æsc*, 'ash', + *hōh*, 'hill spur'. There is a steep hill here. The name could also mean 'Æsc's hill spur'. The DB form of the name below is corrupt. DB *Asceshot*, 12C *Essesho*.

Ashperton (village, Herefords): 'Æscbeorht's or Æscbeorn's farmstead'. OE *tūn*, 'farmstead', 'village'. The DB form of the name below is corrupt. DB *Spertune*. 1144 *Aspretonia*.

Ashprington (village, Devon): 'estate associated with Æscbeorht or Æscbeorn'. OE *-ing-*, 'associated with', + *tūn*, 'farmstead', 'estate'. DB *Aisbertone*.

Ash Priors (village, Somerset): 'prior's (estate by the) ash tree'. OE *æsc*, 'ash'. The manor here was held early by the Prior of Taunton. 1065 *Æsce*, 1263 *Esse Prior*.

Ashreigney (village, Devon): 'de Regny's (estate by the) ash tree'. OE *æsc*, 'ash'. The de Regny family held the manor here in the 13C. DB *Aissa*, 1238 *Esshereingni*.

Ashtead (residential district, Surrey): 'place where ash trees grow'. OE *æsc*, 'ash', + *stede*, 'place'. The district is still relatively well wooded. DB *Stede*, *c.*1150 *Estede*.

Ashton (village, Northants): 'farmstead where ash trees grow'. OE *æsc*, 'ash', + *tūn*, 'farmstead'. This is Ashton near Oundle. DB *Ascetone*. SO ALSO: *Ashton*, Cheshire, Herefords.

Ashton (village, Northants): '(place by the) ash trees'. OE *æsc*, 'ash'. The name represents OE *æscum*, the dative plural form of *æsc*. This is Ashton near Towcester. DB *Asce*, 1296 *Asshen*.

Ashton-in-Makerfield (town, Wigan): 'farmstead where ash trees grow in Makerfield'. OE *æsc*, 'ash', + *tūn*, 'farmstead'. The district name means 'open land with ruins', from a Celtic word meaning 'wall', 'ruin', related to Latin *maceria*, 'masonry', and OE *feld*, 'open land' (modern English *field*). The ruins in question may have been those of the dilapidated Roman fort at Wigan, 4 miles away. 1212 *Eston*.

Ashton Keynes. See SOMERFORD KEYNES.

Ashton under Hill (village, Worcs): 'farmstead where ash trees grow below the hill'. OE *æsc*, 'ash', + *tūn*, 'farmstead'. The hill in question is nearby Bredon Hill. 991 *Æsctun*, DB *Essetone*, 1544 *Assheton Underhill*.

Ashton-under-Lyne (town, Tameside): 'farmstead where ash trees grow by Lyne'. OE *æsc*, 'ash', + *tūn*, 'farmstead'. The district name is Celtic in origin and means 'region of elms'. Cp. NEWCASTLE-UNDER-LYME. *c.*1160 *Haistune*, 1305 *Assheton under Lyme*.

Ashton upon Mersey (suburb of Sale, Trafford): 'farmstead where ash trees grow on the (river) Mersey'. OE *æsc*, 'ash', + *tūn*, 'farmstead'. Ashton stands on the south bank of the MERSEY, the river name distinguishing it from ASHTON-UNDER-LYNE, 12 miles to the north-east. *c.*1284 *Ashton*.

Ashurst (village, Kent): 'wooded hill growing with ash trees'. OE *æsc*, 'ash', + *hyrst*, 'wooded hill'. *c.*1100 *Aeischerste*.

Ashwater (village, Devon): 'Walter's (estate by the) ash trees'. OE *æsc*, 'ash'. The manor here was held in the 13C by one Walter. DB *Aissa*, 1270 *Esse Valteri*.

Ashwell (village, Herts): '(place by the) spring where ash trees grow'. OE *æsc*, 'ash', + *wella*, 'spring', 'stream'. DB *Asceuuelle*. SO ALSO *Ashwell*, Rutland.

Ashwellthorpe (village, Norfolk): 'outlying hamlet belonging to Ashwell'. OS *thorp*, 'outlying farmstead'. The village originally belonged to nearby *Ashwell*, its name as ASHWELL. *c.*1066 *Aescewelle*, *Thorp*.

Ashwick (village, Somerset): 'dwelling where ash trees grow'. OE *æsc*, 'ash', + *wīc*, 'dwelling', 'specialized farm'. DB *Escewiche*.

Askam in Furness (village, Cumbria): '(place by the) ash trees in Furness'. OS *askr*, 'ash'. The name represents OS *askum*, the dative plural

form of *askr*. For the district name, see BARROW
IN FURNESS. 1535 *Askeham*.

Askern (town, Doncaster): 'house near the
ash tree'. OS *askr*, 'ash', + OE *ærn*, 'house'. *c.*1170
Askern.

Askham (village, Cumbria): '(place by the) ash
trees'. OS *askr*, 'ash'. The name represents OS
askum, the dative plural form of *askr*. 1232
Askum.

Askham (village, Notts): 'homestead or enclosure where ash trees grow'. OE *æsc*, 'ash', + *hām*,
'homestead', or *hamm*, 'enclosure'. OE *æsc* has
been replaced in the name by equivalent OS
askr. DB *Ascam*.

Askham Bryan (village, York): 'Brian's homestead or enclosure where ash trees grow'. OE *æsc*,
'ash', + *hām*, 'homestead', or *hamm*, 'enclosure'.
The manor here was held early by one Brian,
whose name distinguishes the village from
nearby *Askham Richard*, where it was held by
one Richard. DB *Ascham*, 1285 *Ascam Bryan*.

Askham Richard. See ASKHAM BRYAN.

Askrigg (village, N Yorks): '(place by the) ridge
where ash trees grow'. OS *askr*, 'ash', + OE *ric*,
'ridge'. DB *Ascric*.

Askwith (village, N Yorks): 'wood where ash
trees grow'. OS *askr*, 'ash', + *vithr*, 'wood'. DB
Ascvid.

Aslackby (village, Lincs): 'Áslákr's farmstead'.
OS *bý*, 'farmstead', 'village'. The personal name
is Scandinavian. DB *Aslachebi*.

Aslacton (village, Norfolk): 'Áslákr's farmstead'. OE *tūn*, 'farmstead', 'village'. The personal name is Scandinavian. DB *Aslactuna*.

Aslockton (village, Notts): 'Áslákr's farmstead'. OE *tūn*, 'farmstead', 'village'. The personal name is Scandinavian. DB *Aslachetune*.

Aspatria (town, Cumbria): '(place by) St
Patrick's ash tree'. OS *askr*, 'ash'. Patrick is a
Celtic name, and the order of elements in the
name is Celtic, with the personal name following the common noun. *c.*1160 *Aspatric*.

Aspenden (village, Herts): '(place in the) valley where aspens grow'. OE *æspe*, 'aspen', + *denu*,
'valley'. DB *Absesdene*.

Aspley Guise (village, Beds): 'de Gyse's (estate
by the) clearing where aspens grow'. OE *æspe*,
'aspen', + *lēah*, 'wood', 'clearing'. The de Gyse
family held the manor here in the 13C. 969
Æpslea, DB *Aspeleia*, 1363 *Aspeleye Gyse*.

Aspull (town, Wigan): 'hill where aspens grow'.
OE *æspe*, 'aspen', + *hyll*, 'hill'. Aspull stands on

high land northeast of Wigan, but there are few
aspens here today. 1212 *Aspul*.

Asselby (village, E Yorks): 'Áskell's farmstead'.
OS *bý*, 'farmstead', 'village'. The personal name
is Scandinavian. DB *Aschilebi*.

Assington (village, Suffolk): 'estate associated
with Asa'. OE *-ing-*, 'associated with', + *tūn*,
'farmstead', 'estate'. DB *Asetona*, 1175 *Assintona*.

Astbury (village, Cheshire): 'eastern stronghold'. OE *ēast*, 'eastern', + *burh*, 'fortified place',
'manor'. 1093 *Astbury*.

Asthall (village, Oxon): 'eastern corner of
land'. OE *ēast*, 'eastern', + *halh*, 'nook', 'corner of
land'. DB *Esthale*.

Astley (village, Shropshire): '(place by the)
eastern clearing'. OE *ēast*, 'eastern', + *lēah*,
'wood', 'clearing'. The clearing was probably
'east' in relation to Albrighton. DB *Hesleie*. SO
ALSO: *Astley*, Warwicks, Worcs.

Astley Abbotts (village, Shropshire): 'abbot's
(estate by the) eastern wood or clearing'. OE *ēast*,
'eastern', + *lēah*, 'wood', 'clearing'. The clearing
was 'east' with regard to Morville. The manor
here was held early by Shrewsbury Abbey.
*c.*1090 *Estleia*, late 13C *Astleye Abbatis*.

Aston (district, Birmingham): 'eastern farmstead'. OE *ēast*, 'eastern', + *tūn*, 'farmstead'. The
farm was probably so called as it lay to the east
of Birmingham, although William Dugdale, in
The Antiquities of Warwickshire (1656), when it
was still in Warwickshire, says it is so called as
lying 'eastwards from Wedgbury [i.e. Wednes-
bury] in Staffordshire, a town of some note in
the Saxons time'. DB *Estone*. SO ALSO: *Aston*,
Rotherham.

Aston Blank. See COLD ASTON.

Aston Botterell. See ASTON EYRE.

Aston Cantlow (village, Warwicks): 'de Cantilupe's eastern farmstead'. OE *ēast*, 'eastern', +
tūn, 'farmstead', 'estate'. The de Cantilupe family held the manor here in the 13C. The farmstead was probably 'east' with regard to Alcester.
DB *Estone*, 1273 *Aston Cantelou*.

Aston Clinton (village, Bucks): 'de Clinton's
eastern farmstead'. OE *ēast*, 'eastern', + *tūn*,
'farmstead', 'estate'. The de Clinton family held
the manor here in the 12C. The farmstead was
'east' with regard to nearby WESTON TURVILLE. DB
Estone, 1237 *Aston Clinton*.

Aston Eyre (village, Shropshire): 'Fitz Aer's
eastern farmstead'. OE *ēast*, 'eastern', + *tūn*,
'farmstead', 'estate'. The Fitz Aer family held
land here in the 13C, their name distinguishing
this Aston from *Aston Botterell*, 7 miles to the

south, held by William Boterell. DB *Estone*, 1284 *Aston Aer*.

Aston Fields (district of Bromsgrove, Worcs): 'eastern farmstead with fields'. OE *ēast*, 'eastern', + *tūn*, 'farmstead'. The farmstead was 'east' with regard to Bromsgrove. The second word of the name distinguishes this Aston from others. 767 *Eastun*, DB *Estone*, 1649 *Aston Fields*.

Aston Ingham (village, Herefords): 'Ingan's eastern farmstead'. OE *ēast*, 'eastern', + *tūn*, 'farmstead'. The Ingan family held the manor here in the 13C. DB *Estune*, 1242 *Estun Ingan*.

Aston le Walls (village, Northants): 'eastern farmstead by the walls'. OE *ēast*, 'eastern', + *tūn*, 'farmstead'. The 'walls' are probably the irregular entrenchments here. The farmstead was 'east' with regard to Upper and Lower Boddington, to the northwest. DB *Estone*.

Aston on Clun (village, Shropshire): 'farmstead where ash trees grow on the (river) Clun'. OE *æsc*, 'ash', + *tūn*, 'farmstead'. For the river name, see CLUN. 1291 *Assheston*.

Aston Rowant (village, Oxon): 'Rowald's eastern farmstead'. OE *ēast*, 'eastern', + *tūn*, 'farmstead', 'estate'. Rowald de Eston held the manor here in 1236. DB *Estone*, 1318 *Aston Roaud*.

Aston Somerville (village, Worcs): 'Somerville's eastern farmstead'. OE *ēast*, 'eastern', + *tūn*, 'farmstead', 'estate'. The Somerville family held the manor here from the 13C. DB *Estune*, 1285 *Eston Somervill*.

Aston Subedge. See WESTON-SUB-EDGE.

Aston upon Trent (village, Derbys): 'eastern farmstead on the (river) Trent'. OE *ēast*, 'eastern', + *tūn*, 'farmstead'. The river name (see STOKE-ON-TRENT) distinguishes this Aston from nearby *Weston upon Trent*. DB *Estune*.

Astwood (village, Milton K): '(place by the) eastern wood'. OE *ēast*, 'eastern', + *wudu*, 'wood'. The village stands on what was formerly the eastern border of Buckinghamshire. 1151 *Estwode*. SO ALSO: *Astwood*, Worcs.

Atcham (village, Shropshire): 'homestead of Etti's or Ēata's people'. OE *-inga-*, 'of the people of', + *hām*, 'homestead'. The name could also mean 'homestead at the place associated with Etti or Ēata' (OE *-ing*, 'place associated with'), and the final part of the name could be OE *hamm*, 'land in a river bend'. Atcham lies at the confluence of the Tern and the Severn. Either way, the original *-inga-* or *-ing* has disappeared. DB *Atingeham*, 1868 *Atcham, or Attingham*.

Atch Lench. See ROUS LENCH.

Athelhampton (hamlet, Dorset): 'Æthelhelm's farmstead'. OE *tūn*, 'farmstead'. As can be seen from the early forms of the name below, Athelhampton was originally named after the river *Piddle* that gave the name of nearby PUDDLETOWN. DB *Pidele*, 1285 *Pidle Athelamston*, 1868 *Admiston, or Athelampton*.

Athelington (village, Suffolk): 'farmstead of the princes'. OE *ætheling*, 'prince', 'lord', + *tūn*, 'farmstead', 'village'. 1219 *Alinggeton*.

Athelney (village, Somerset): 'island of the princes'. OE *ætheling*, 'prince', 'lord', + *ēg*, 'island'. The name implies that members of a noble Anglo-Saxon family lived here. The 'island' is dry land amid marshes. 878 *Æthelingaeigge*, DB *Adelingi*.

Atherington (village, Devon): 'estate associated with Ēadhere or Ethelhere'. OE *-ing-*, 'associated with', + *tūn*, 'farmstead', 'estate'. 1272 *Hadrintone*.

Atherstone (town, Warwicks): 'Æthelrēd's farmstead'. OE *tūn*, 'farmstead'. DB *Aderestone*, 1221 *Atheredestone*.

Atherstone on Stour (village, Warwicks): 'Ēadrīc's farmstead on the (river) Stour'. OE *tūn*, 'farmstead', 'village'. The addition of the river name (see STOURBRIDGE) distinguishes the village from ATHERSTONE. 710 *Eadrichestone*, DB *Edricestone*.

Atherton (town, Wigan): 'Æthelhere's farmstead'. OE *tūn*, 'farmstead'. 1212 *Aderton*.

Atholl. See BLAIR ATHOLL.

Atlow (village, Derbys): 'Eatta's burial mound'. OE *hlāw*, 'mound'. DB *Etelawe*.

Attenborough (district of Beeston, Notts): 'stronghold associated with Adda or Æddi'. OE *-ing-*, 'associated with', + *burh*, 'fortified place'. 12C *Adinburcha*.

Atterby (hamlet, Lincs): 'Ēadrēd's farmstead'. OS *bý*, 'farmstead', 'village'. 1185 *Adredeb*.

Attleborough (town, Norfolk): 'Ætla's stronghold'. OE *burh*, 'stronghold'. Attleborough is only 15 miles from ATTLEBRIDGE, and it is possible the same man is named. DB *Atleburc*.

Attleborough (district of Nuneaton, Warwicks): 'Ætla's hill'. OE *beorg*, 'hill', 'mound'. 12C *Atteleberga*.

Attlebridge (village, Norfolk): 'Ætla's bridge'. OE *brycg*, 'bridge'. The bridge would have been over the river Wensum here. DB *Atlebruge*.

Atwick (village, E Yorks): 'Atta's dairy farm'. OE *-ing-*, 'associated with', + *wīc*, 'dwelling', 'dairy farm'. 12C *Attingwik*.

Atworth (village, Wilts): 'Atta's enclosure'. OE *worth*, 'enclosure'. 1001 *Attenwrthe*.

Auburn (deserted village, E Yorks): '(place by the) stream where eels are found'. OE *ǣl*, 'eel', + *burna*, 'stream'. The village was gradually washed away by the sea from the 18C. DB *Eleburne*, 1731 *Awburn*.

Auchinleck (town, E Ayrs): 'field of the flat stones'. Gaelic *achadh*, 'field', + *leac*, 'flat stone', 'slab of rock'. 1239 *Auechinlec*.

Auchterarder (town, Perth & Kin): 'upland of high water'. Gaelic *uachdar*, 'upper', + *àrd*, 'high', + *dobhar*, 'water'. The town lies on high ground to the north of the Ochill Hills on the river Ruthven. *c*.1200 *Vchterardouere*.

Auchtermuchty (town, Fife): 'upland of the pig place'. Gaelic *uachdar*, 'upper', + *muccatu*, 'pig place'. Pigs must have been reared here at one time. *c*.1210 *Vchtermuckethin*.

Auckley (village, Doncaster): 'Alca's or Alha's woodland clearing'. OE *lēah*, 'wood', 'clearing'. DB *Alchelie*.

Audenshaw (town, Tameside): 'Aldwine's copse'. OE *sceaga*, 'copse'. *c*.1200 *Aldwynshawe*.

Audlem (village, Cheshire): '(place in the) old (part of) Lyme'. OE *ald*, 'old'. The name could also mean 'Alda's (part of) Lyme'. The district name is Celtic in origin and means 'region of elm trees'. Audlem is 12 miles west of NEWCASTLE-UNDER-LYME. DB *Aldelime*.

Audley (village, Staffs): 'Aldgȳth's woodland clearing'. OE *lēah*, 'wood', 'clearing'. The personal name is that of a woman. DB *Aldidelege*.

Audley End (mansion, Essex): 'Audley's estate'. The name is that of Sir Thomas Audley (1488–1544), granted an estate here by Henry VIII after the dissolution of the monasteries in 1539. 1555 *Audleyend*.

Aughton (village, E Yorks): 'farmstead where oak trees grow'. OE *āc*, 'oak', + *tūn*, 'farmstead'. DB *Actun*. SO ALSO: *Aughton*, Lancs (near Lancaster, near Ormskirk), Rotherham.

Aultbea (village, Highland): '(place by the) stream where birch trees grow'. Gaelic *allt*, 'stream', + *beithe*, 'birch'.

Ault Hucknall (hamlet, Derbys): 'Hucca's corner of land on a height'. OE *halh*, 'nook', 'corner of land'. The first word of the name (OF *haut*, 'high') distinguishes this Hucknall from *Hucknall Torkard* (now simply HUCKNALL), Notts, 11 miles to the south. 1291 *Hokenhale*, 1535 *Haulte Huknall*.

Aust (village, S Glos): '(place of) Augustus'. The name is of Latin origin and may refer to the crossing of the river Severn used here by the Roman Second Legion, the *Legio II Augusta*, named for the Emperor Augustus. The origin could also lie in the Roman personal name *Augustinus*. 794 *Austan*.

Austerfield (village, Doncaster): 'open land with a sheepfold'. OE *eowestre*, 'sheepfold', + *feld*, 'open land' (modern English *field*). *c*.715 *Eostrefeld*, DB *Oustrefeld*.

Austrey (village, Warwicks): 'Ealdwulf's tree'. OE *trēow*, 'tree'. 958 *Alduluestreow*, DB *Aldulvestreu*.

Austwick (village, N Yorks): 'eastern dairy farm'. OS *austr*, 'eastern', + OE *wīc*, 'dwelling', 'specialized farm'. The place is probably 'east' with regard to Clapham. DB *Ousteuuic*.

Avebury (village, Wilts): 'Afa's stronghold'. OE *burh*, 'stronghold'. The 'stronghold' is probably the Bronze Age burial ground here rather than a defensive site. DB *Aureberie*.

Aveley (town, Thurrock): 'Ælfgȳth's woodland clearing'. OE *lēah*, 'clearing'. The personal name is that of a woman. DB *Aluitheleam*.

Avening (village, Glos): '(settlement of the) people living by the (river) Avon'. OE *-ingas*, 'dwellers at', 'people living by'. The stream that flows through Avening must at one time have been known as the *Avon* (see AVONMOUTH). 896 *Æfeningum*, DB *Aveninge*.

Averham (village, Notts): '(place by the) floods'. OE *ēgor*, 'flood', 'high tide' (perhaps related to modern English *eagre*, 'bore'). Averham is on the river Trent, and the reference is to the Trent bore. The name represents OE *ēgrum*, the dative plural form of *ēgor*. DB *Aigrun*.

Aveton Gifford (village, Devon): 'Giffard's farmstead on the (river) Avon'. OE *tūn*, 'farmstead'. Walter Giffard held the manor here in the 13C, his name apparently distinguishing this village from BLACKAWTON, 8 miles to the east. The Avon here has a name of the same origin as that at AVONMOUTH. DB *Avetone*, 1276 *Aveton Giffard*.

Aviemore (village, Highland): '(place by the) big hill face'. Gaelic *aghaid*, 'hill face', + *mór*, 'big'.

Avington (hamlet, W Berks): 'estate associated with Afa'. OE *-ing-*, 'associated with', + *tūn*, 'farmstead', 'estate'. DB *Avintone*.

Avon (river). See AVONMOUTH.

Avon Dassett (village, Warwicks): '(place by the) fold or shelter for deer on the (river) Avon'. OE *dēor*, 'deer', + *set*, 'fold', or *cēte*, 'shelter'. The river name (see AVONMOUTH) distinguishes this place from nearby *Burton Dassett* (OE *burh-tūn*, 'fortified farmstead'). DB *Dercetone*, 1185 *Afnedereceth*.

Avonmouth (port, Bristol): 'mouth of the (river) Avon'. OE *mūtha*, 'mouth'. The river has a Celtic name meaning simply 'river' (modern Welsh *afon*). There are many rivers named Avon in Britain. This one, often distinguished as the Bristol or Lower Avon, gave the name of the former modern county of *Avon*. 10C *Afenemuthan*.

Awe, Loch (loch, Argyll & Bute): 'loch of the (river) Awe'. Gaelic *loch*, 'lake'. The river name is a Gaelic variant of *Avon* (see AVONMOUTH). Loch Awe discharges by the river Awe to Loch Etive. 700 *Aba*.

Awliscombe (village, Devon): '(place in the) valley by a fork in the river'. OE *āwel*, 'fork', + *cumb*, 'valley'. Awliscombe stands on a stream that runs into the river Otter nearby. DB *Aulescome*.

Awre (village, Glos): '(place by the) alder tree'. OE *alor*, 'alder'. DB *Avre*.

Awsworth (village, Notts): 'Eald's enclosure'. OE *worth*, 'enclosure'. 1001 *Ealdeswyrthe*, DB *Eldesvorde*.

Axbridge (village, Somerset): '(place by the) bridge over the (river) Axe'. OE *brycg*, 'bridge'. For the river name, see AXMINSTER. 10C *Axanbrycg*.

Axe (river). See AXMINSTER.

Axholme, Isle of (region, N Lincs): 'island of Haxey'. OS *holmr*, 'island'. 'Island' here means an area of raised ground in marshland. Axholme is bounded by the rivers Trent, Torne and Idle. The first part of the name derives from the village of *Haxey*, 'Hákr's island' (OS *ey*, 'island'), with a Scandinavian personal name, where 'island' has the same sense. *c.*1115 *Haxeholm*, 1135 *Axiholm*.

Axminster (town, Devon): 'monastery by the (river) Axe'. OE *mynster*, 'monastery', 'large church'. The river's name is Celtic, meaning simply 'river', 'water'. 9C *Ascanmynster*, DB *Aixeministra*.

Axmouth (resort town, Devon): 'mouth of the (river) Axe'. OE *mūtha*, 'mouth'. The town is on the same river as AXMINSTER. (It is now a mile from the sea but the estuary is known to have silted up.) The DB form of the name below may have resulted from a mishearing rather than a miscopying. *c.*880 *Axanmuthan*, DB *Alsemuda*.

Aycliffe. See NEWTON AYCLIFFE.

Aylburton (village, Glos): 'Æthelbeorht's farmstead'. OE *tūn*, 'farmstead', 'village'. 12C *Ailbricton*.

Ayle (hamlet, Northd): '(place on the) Ayle Burn'. The river name is of Celtic origin and uncertain meaning. 1347 *Alne*.

Aylesbeare (village, Devon): 'Ægel's grove'. OE *bearu*, 'grove'. DB *Ailesberga*.

Aylesbury (town, Bucks): 'Ægel's stronghold'. OE *burh*, 'stronghold'. There must have been an Anglo-Saxon fort here at some time. *Aylesbury Vale* is now the name of the local council district, the valley being that of the river Thame. late 9C *Ægelesburg*, DB *Eilesberia*.

Aylesby (village, NE Lincs): 'Áli's farmstead'. OS *bý*, 'farmstead', 'village'. The personal name is Scandinavian. DB *Alesbi*.

Aylesford (village, Kent): 'Ægel's ford'. OE *ford*, 'ford'. The ford would have been over the Medway here. 10C *Æglesforda*, DB *Ailesford*.

Aylesham (village, Kent): 'Ægel's homestead or enclosure'. OE *hām*, 'homestead', or *hamm*, 'enclosure'. 1367 *Elisham*.

Aylestone (district, Leicester): 'Ægel's farmstead'. OE *tūn*, 'farmstead', 'village'. DB *Ailestone*.

Aylmerton (village, Norfolk): 'Æthelmǣr's farmstead'. OE *tūn*, 'farmstead', 'village'. DB *Almartune*.

Aylsham (town, Norfolk): 'Ægel's homestead'. OE *hām*, 'homestead', 'village'. DB *Ailesham*.

Aylton (hamlet, Herefords): 'Æthelgifu's farmstead'. OE *tūn*, 'farmstead', 'village'. The personal name is that of a woman. 1138 *Aileuetona*.

Aymestrey (village, Herefords): 'Æthelmund's tree'. OE *trēow*, 'tree'. DB *Elmodestreu*.

Aynho (village, Northants): 'Æga's hill spur'. OE *hōh*, 'hill spur'. The village stands on a prominent hill. DB *Aienho*.

Ayot St Lawrence (village, Herts): '(place by) Æga's gap with St Lawrence's church'. OE *geat*, 'pass', 'gap' (modern English *gate*). The 'gap' is probably the lower land between this village and *Ayot St Peter*. The church dedications distinguish the two places, which are 2 miles apart. *c.*1060 *Aiegete*, DB *Aiete*, 1367 *Ayot Laurence*.

Ayr (town and resort, S Ayrs): '(mouth of the river) Ayr'. The Celtic river name means simply 'river'. The town was formerly known as *Inverayr*, but the 'mouth' element was later dropped. 1177 *Ar*.

Aysgarth (village, N Yorks): 'open place where oak trees grow'. OS *eiki*, 'oak', + *skarth*, 'gap', 'open place'. Aysgarth was in the centre of the Forest of Wensleydale. DB *Echescard*.

Ayston (hamlet, Rutland): 'Æthelstān's farmstead'. OE *tūn*, 'farmstead', 'village'. 1046 *Æthelstanestun*.

Aythorpe Roding. See RODINGS.

Azerley (hamlet, N Yorks): 'Atsurr's woodland clearing'. OE *lēah*, 'wood', 'clearing'. The personal name is Scandinavian. DB *Asserle*.

B

Babbacombe (district of Torquay, Torbay): 'Babba's valley'. OE *cumb*, 'valley'. The ground at Babbacombe slopes quite steeply down to the shore. *c.*1200 *Babbecumbe*.

Babcary (village, Somerset): 'Babba's (estate on the river) Cary'. For the river name, see CASTLE CARY. DB *Babba Cari*.

Babergh (council district, Suffolk): 'Babba's mound'. OE *berg*, 'hill', 'mound'. The name was originally that of a hundred here.

Babraham (village, Cambs): 'Beaduburh's homestead'. OE *hām*, 'homestead', 'village'. The personal name is that of a woman. DB *Badburgham*.

Babworth (hamlet, Notts): 'Babba's enclosure'. OE *worth*, 'enclosure'. DB *Baburde*.

Backford (village, Cheshire): '(place at a) ford by a ridge'. OE *bæc*, 'ridge' (modern English *back*), + *ford*, 'ford'. The village lies on a low hill at the end of a ridge, and the ford in question would have been over Backford Brook below it. 1150 *Bacfort*.

Backwell (village, N Somerset): '(place by a) spring by the ridge'. OE *bæc*, 'ridge' (modern English *back*), + *wella*, 'spring', 'stream'. The name refers to a nearby high ridge. The DB form of the name below is somewhat garbled. DB *Bacoile*, 1202 *Bacwell*.

Baconsthorpe (village, Norfolk): 'Bacon's outlying farmstead'. OS *thorp*, 'outlying farmstead'. Bacon is a Norman surname. DB *Baconstorp*.

Bacton (village, Norfolk): 'Bacca's farmstead'. OE *tūn*, 'farmstead'. DB *Baketuna*. SO ALSO: *Bacton*, Herefords, Suffolk.

Bacup (town, Lancs): '(place in a) valley by a ridge'. OE *bæc*, 'ridge' (modern English *back*), + *hop*, 'enclosed valley'. The town is in the valley of the river Irwell with higher ground to the west. The first form of the name below begins with OE *fūl*, 'foul', 'muddy'. *c.*1200 *Fulebachope*, 1324 *Bacop*.

Badbury (village, Swindon): 'Badda's stronghold'. OE *burh*, 'fortified place'. The 'stronghold' is nearby Liddington Castle, an Iron Age fort on Liddington Hill, which was formerly known as Badbury Hill. 955 *Baddeburi*.

Badbury Rings (Iron Age fort, Dorset): 'Badda's stronghold'. OE *burh*, 'fortified place'. The 'rings' are the circular ramparts on the hill fort. The Roman settlement nearby was *Vindocladia*, a Celtic name meaning '(place with) white ditches', referring to defences cut in the chalk here. 901 *Baddanbyrig*.

Badby (village, Northants): 'Badda's stronghold'. OE *burh*, 'fortified place'. OE *burh* was replaced at an early date with the equivalent OS *bý*. 944 *Baddanbyrig*, DB *Badebi*.

Baddeley Green (district of Stoke-on-Trent, Stoke): 'Badda's woodland clearing'. OE *lēah*, 'wood', 'clearing'. Baddeley became associated with its village green. 1227 *Baddilige*.

Baddesley Ensor (village, Warwicks): 'de Edneshoure's (estate at) Bæddi's woodland clearing'. OE *lēah*, 'wood', 'clearing'. The de Edneshoure family (from EDENSOR) held the manor here in the 13C, their name distinguishing this Baddesley from *Baddesley Clinton*, 17 miles to the south, where the manor was held by the Clinton family. DB *Bedeslei*, 1327 *Baddesley Endeshouer*.

Baddow. See GREAT BADDOW.

Badenoch (region, Highland): 'submerged land'. Gaelic *bàithteanach*, from *bàithte*, 'drowned'. The region lies to the south of the river Spey, which is liable to flood. 1229 *Badenach*.

Badger (village, Shropshire): '(place by) Bæcg's ridge top'. OE *ofer*, 'flat-topped ridge'. DB *Beghesovre*.

Badgeworth (village, Glos): 'Bæcga's enclosure'. OE *worth*, 'enclosure'. 862 *Beganwurthan*, DB *Beiewrda*.

Badgworth (village, Somerset): 'Bæcga's enclosure'. OE *worth*, 'enclosure'. DB *Bagewerre*.

Badingham (village, Suffolk): 'homestead associated with Bēada'. OE *-ing-*, 'associated with', + *hām*, 'homestead'. DB *Badincham*.

Badlesmere (village, Kent): 'Bæddel's pool'. OE *mere*, 'pool'. DB *Badelesmere*.

Badminton (village, S Glos): 'estate associated with Baduhelm'. OE *-ing-*, 'associated with', + *tūn*, 'farmstead', 'estate'. The village is properly *Great Badminton*, as distinct from *Little Badminton* to the north across Badminton Park. The *M*- of the DB form of the name below was probably due to a mishearing. 972 *Badimyncgtun*, DB *Madmintune*.

Badsey (village, Worcs): 'Bæddi's island'. OE *ēg*, 'island'. The 'island' here is well-watered land. Badsey stands at the junction of three streams. 709 *Baddeseia*, DB *Badesei*.

Badsworth (village, Wakefield): 'Bæddi's enclosure'. OE *worth*, 'enclosure'. DB *Badesuuorde*.

Badwell Ash (village, Suffolk): 'Bada's spring near Ashfield'. OE *wella*, 'spring', 'stream'. The second word of the name refers to nearby GREAT ASHFIELD. 1254 *Badewell*, 13C *Badewelle Asfelde*.

Bae Colwyn. See COLWYN BAY.

Bagby (village, N Yorks): 'Baggi's farmstead'. OS *bý*, 'farmstead', 'village'. The personal name is Scandinavian. DB *Baghebi*.

Bag Enderby. See MAVIS ENDERBY.

Bagendon (village, Glos): 'valley of Bæcga's people'. OE *-inga-*, 'of the people of', + *denu*, 'valley'. The valley in question is that of the river Churn. The DB form of the name below is corrupt. DB *Benwedene*, 1220 *Baggingeden*, 1868 *Badgington, or Bagendon*.

Baginton (village, Warwicks): 'estate associated with Badeca'. OE *-ing-*, 'associated with', + *tūn*, 'estate'. DB *Badechitone*.

Baglan (town, Neath PT): '(church of) St Baglan'. Baglan, about whom little is known, is the saint to whom the now disused church here was dedicated. 1199 *Bagelan*.

Bagnall (village, Staffs): 'Badeca's corner of land'. OE *halh*, 'nook', 'corner of land'. 1273 *Badegenhall*.

Bagshot (town, Surrey): 'corner of land where badgers are seen'. OE *bagga*, 'badger', + *scēat*, 'corner of land'. 1164 *Bagsheta*.

Bagthorpe (hamlet, Norfolk): 'Bakki's or Bacca's outlying farmstead'. OS *thorp*, 'outlying farmstead'. The personal names are respectively Scandinavian and OE. DB *Bachestorp*.

Bagworth (village, Leics): 'Bæcga's enclosure'. OE *worth*, 'enclosure'. DB *Bageworde*.

Baildon (district, Bradford): '(place by the) rounded hill'. OE *bǣgel*, 'bend', + *dūn*, 'hill'. The hill in question is the great round one nearby called Baildon Hill. *c.*1030 *Bægeltune*, DB *Beldune*.

Bainbridge (village, N Yorks): '(place by the) bridge over the (river) Bain'. OE *brycg*, 'bridge'. The river name derives from OS *beinn*, 'direct', 'short'. 1218 *Bainebrigg*.

Bainton (village, E Yorks): 'estate associated with Bæga'. OE *-ing-*, 'associated with', + *tūn*, 'estate'. DB *Bagentone*.

Bainton (village, Peterborough): 'estate associated with Bada'. OE *-ing-*, 'associated with', + *tūn*, 'farmstead', 'estate'. *c.*980 *Badingtun*.

Bakewell (town, Derbys): '(place by) Badeca's spring'. OE *wella*, 'spring', 'stream'. The warm springs here are well known. 949 *Badecanwelle*, DB *Badequella*.

Bala (town, Gwynedd): '(place by the) outlet'. Welsh *bala*, 'outlet'. The town is at the point where the river Dee leaves Bala Lake. The Welsh name of the lake is *Llyn Tegid*, 'Tegid's lake', with a personal name. 1331 *la Bala*, 1582 *the Bala*.

Balcombe (village, W Sussex): 'Bealda's valley'. OE *cumb*, 'valley'. Balcombe lies on a ridge between two valleys and the name must refer to the valley below. The absence of *d* in early forms of the name, however, casts doubt on the interpretation of 'Bal-' as a personal name, and an origin in OE *bealu*, 'evil', 'calamity' (modern English *bale*), has also been proposed, referring to some memorable unpleasant happening here. Late 11C *Balecumba*, 1279 *Baldecombe*, 1284 *Baldcomb*.

Baldersby (village, N Yorks): 'Baldhere's farmstead'. OS *bý*, 'farmstead', 'village'. DB *Baldrebi*.

Balderstone (village, Lancs): 'Baldhere's farmstead'. OE *tūn*, 'farmstead'. 1323 *Baldreston*.

Balderton (district of Newark-on-Trent, Notts): 'Baldhere's farmstead'. OE *tūn*, 'farmstead'. DB *Baldretune*.

Baldock (town, Herts): 'Baghdad'. The town was founded in the 12C by the Knights Templars, who called it *Baldac*, the OF form for the Arabian city of Baghdad, now the capital of Iraq. Templar Avenue, Baldock, is a reminder of the town's origin. *c.*1140 *Baldoce*.

Bale (village, Norfolk): 'woodland clearing with a bathing place'. OE *bæth*, 'bath', + *lēah*, 'wood', 'clearing'. The bathing place would have been a pool created from springs here. DB *Bathele*, 1868 *Bale, or Batheley*.

Balerno (village, Edinburgh): 'homestead of the sloe tree'. Gaelic *baile*, 'homestead', + *airneach*, 'sloe tree'. 1280 *Belhernoch*.

Balham (district, Wandsworth): 'rounded enclosure'. OE *bealg*, 'rounded', + *hamm*, 'enclosure'. The reference would be to the land between the two arms of Falcon Brook. 957 *Bælgenham*, DB *Belgeham*.

Balkholme (hamlet, E Yorks): 'island with a low ridge'. OE *balca*, 'balk', 'ridge', + OS *holmr*, 'island'. The name could also mean 'Balki's island', with a Scandinavian personal name. The 'island' is raised ground in former fenland. 1199 *Balcholm*.

Ballachulish (village, Highland): 'homestead of the strait'. Gaelic *baile*, 'homestead', + *caolas*, 'strait' (genitive *chaolais*). The village is at the point where Loch Leven narrows as it flows into Loch Linnhe.

Ballantrae (village and port, S Ayrs): 'village on the shore'. Gaelic *baile*, 'village', + *traigh*, 'shore'.

Ballater (town, Aberdeens): '(place by the) water pass'. Gaelic *bealach*, 'pass', + *dobhar*, 'water'. The name originally applied to the pass where the Ballater Burn flows through the mountains here. 1704 *Balader*, 1716 *Ballader*.

Ballingham (village, Herefords): 'homestead of Badela's people'. OE *-inga-*, 'of the people of', + *hām*, 'homestead'. The name could also mean 'homestead at the place associated with Badela' (OE *-ing*, 'place associated with', + *hām*). In either case the '-ham' could represent OE *hamm*, 'enclosure', 'land in a river bend'. Ballingham lies in a loop of the river Wye. 1215 *Badelingeham*.

Balmoral (mansion, Aberdeens): 'homestead in the big clearing'. Gaelic *baile*, 'homestead', + *mór*, 'big', + Celtic *ial*, 'open space'. 1451 *Bouchmorale*.

Balne (hamlet, N Yorks): 'bathing place'. Latin *balneum*, 'bath', 'bathing place'. The bathing place in question must have been one of the pools or streams here. The name later gave that of the surrounding district. 12C *Balne*.

Balsall (village, Solihull): 'Bælli's corner of land'. OE *halh*, 'nook', 'corner of land'. 1185 *Beleshale*.

Balsham (village, Cambs): 'Bælli's homestead'. OE *hām*, 'homestead', 'village'. 974 *Bellesham*, DB *Belesham*.

Balterley (hamlet, Staffs): 'Baldthrȳth's woodland clearing'. OE *lēah*, 'wood', 'clearing'. The personal name is that of a woman. 1002 *Baltrytheleag*, DB *Baltredelege*.

Baltonsborough (village, Somerset): 'Bealdhūn's hill'. OE *beorg*, 'mound', 'hill'. 744 *Balteresberghe*, DB *Baltunesberge*.

Bamber Bridge (town, Lancs): '(place by the) bridge made of tree trunks'. OE *bēam*, 'tree trunk', 'timber beam', + *brycg*, 'bridge'. The bridge in question was over the river Lostock here. The form of the name below comes from an undated medieval document. *Bymbrig*.

Bamburgh (village, Northd): 'Bebbe's stronghold'. OE *burh*, 'stronghold'. Bebbe was the wife of Æthelfrith, king of Northumbria, who ruled from 593 to 617. *c.*710 *Bebbanburge*.

Bamford (village, Derbys): '(place by the) tree-trunk ford'. OE *bēam*, 'tree trunk', 'beam', + *ford*, 'ford'. A 'tree-trunk ford' is either one marked by a wooden post or one with a wooden footbridge. DB *Banford*.

Bampton (town, Devon): 'farmstead of the dwellers by the pool'. OE *bæth*, 'pool' (modern English *bath*), + *hǣme*, 'dwellers' (related modern English *home*), + *tūn*, 'farmstead'. The pool in question would have been in the river Batherm here, itself taking its name from the town. DB *Badentone*.

Bampton (village, Oxon): 'farmstead made of beams'. OE *bēam*, 'beam', 'tree', + *tūn*, 'farmstead'. 1069 *Bemtun*, DB *Bentone*. SO ALSO: *Bampton*, Cumbria.

Banbury (town, Oxon): 'Bana's stronghold'. OE *burh*, 'stronghold'. The 'stronghold' could have been an Iron Age fort, although none is known here. DB *Banesberie*.

Banchory (town, Aberdeens): 'place of the peaks'. Gaelic *beannachar*, 'mountainous', from *beann*, 'mountain' (modern English *ben*). Banchory is in a valley surrounded by hills and mountains.

Banff (town, Aberdeens): '(place on the river) Banff'. The river name, from Gaelic *banbh*, 'piglet', was probably a nickname for the present river Deveron, which would have been seen as 'rooting' its way to the coast. According to another theory, the name represents *Banbha*, an early name for Ireland imported to Scotland by colonists. *c.*1150 *Banb*.

Bangor (city, Gwynedd): '(place protected by a) wattled fence'. Welsh *bangor*, 'plaited cross-bar strengthening the top of a wattled fence'. The reference is probably to the original wattled construction of the monastery here, founded in 525 by St Deiniol (cp. DEINIOLEN), or to the fence that enclosed it. 634 *Benchoer*.

Bangor Is-coed. See BANGOR ON DEE.

Bangor on Dee (village, Wrexham): '(place of the people of) Bangor on (the river) Dee'. The monastery here is said to have been founded by St Deiniol, the founder of BANGOR, with the river name (see CHESTER) added for distinction from that town. The Welsh name of the village is *Bangor Is-coed*, the addition being a local parish name meaning 'below the wood'. The third form of the name below is Latin for 'Bangor of the monks'. 8C *Bancor*, 1277 *Bangor*, 1607 *Bangor monachorum*.

Banham (village, Norfolk): 'homestead or enclosure where beans are grown'. OE *bēan*, 'bean', + *hām*, 'homestead', or *hamm*, 'enclosure'. DB *Benham*.

Bannau Brycheiniog. See BRECON BEACONS.

Banningham (village, Norfolk): 'homestead of Bana's people'. OE *-inga-*, 'of the people of', + *hām*, 'homestead', 'village'. DB *Banincham*.

Bannockburn (village, Stirling): '(place on the) Bannock Burn'. OE *burna*, 'stream'. The name derives from a Celtic word related to modern Welsh *bannog*, 'peaked', 'horned', referring to the hill from which the stream flows. 1314 *Bannockburn*, 1654 *Bannokburne*.

Bannovalium. See (1) CAISTOR, (2) HORNCASTLE.

Banstead (town, Surrey): 'place where beans are grown'. OE *bēan*, 'bean', + *stede*, 'place'. DB *Benestede*.

Banwell (village, N Somerset): '(place by the) killer spring'. OE *bana*, 'killer', 'poison' (modern English *bane*), + *wella*, 'spring', 'stream'. The name may allude to a contaminated spring here. 904 *Bananwylle*, DB *Banwelle*.

Bapchild (village, Kent): '(place by) Bacca's spring'. OE *celde*, 'spring'. 696 *Baccancelde*.

Barby (village, Northants): 'farmstead on the hill'. OS *berg*, 'hill', + *bý*, 'farmstead', 'village'. Barby stands on a hill. DB *Berchebi*.

Barcheston (village, Warwicks): 'Beadurīc's farmstead'. OE *tūn*, 'farmstead'. DB *Berricestone*.

Barcombe (village, E Sussex): 'enclosed piece of land used for barley'. OE *bere*, 'barley', + *camp*, 'enclosed land' (modern English *camp*). The DB form of the name below has apparently taken OE *camp* as *hām*, 'homestead'. DB *Bercham*, 12C *Berecampe*.

Barden (hamlet, N Yorks): '(place in the) valley where barley is grown'. OE *beren*, 'growing with barley', + *denu*, 'valley'. DB *Bernedan*.

Bardfield Saling. See GREAT BARDFIELD.

Bardney (village, Lincs): 'Bearda's island'. OE *ēg*, 'island'. The 'island' here is raised ground by the river Witham. 731 *Beardaneu*, DB *Bardenai*.

Bardsea (resort village, Cumbria): 'Beornrǣd's island'. OE *ēg* or OS *ey*, 'island'. The 'island' is the raised site on which Bardsea stands overlooking Morecambe Bay. DB *Berretseige*.

Bardsey (village, Leeds): 'Beornrǣd's island'. OE *ēg*, 'island'. The 'island' is the area of higher ground here on which the village stands. DB *Berdesei*.

Bardsey Island (island, Gwynedd): 'Bardr's island'. OS *ey*, 'island'. The personal name is Scandinavian, as for other islands off the Welsh coast. Bardsey's Welsh name is *Ynys Enlli*, supposedly after a legendary giant, Benlli, but popularly translated as 'island of currents' (Welsh *ynys*, 'island', + *lli*, 'flood', 'current'). 'The tides dominate Bardsey; the race through the sound always affects boats seeking the island' (*The Shell Guide to Wales*, 1969).

Bardsley (district, Oldham): 'Beornrǣd's woodland clearing'. OE *lēah*, 'wood', 'clearing'. 1422 *Berdesley*.

Bardwell (village, Suffolk): 'Bearda's spring'. OE *wella*, 'spring', 'stream'. DB *Berdeuuella*.

Barford (village, Warwicks): '(place by the) barley ford'. OE *bere*, 'barley', + *ford*, 'ford'. A 'barley ford' is one used at harvest time. The river here is the Avon. DB *Bereforde*. SO ALSO: *Barford*, Norfolk.

Barford St John (village, Oxon): '(place by the) barley ford with St John's church'. OE *bere*, 'barley', + *ford*, 'ford'. See BARFORD. The church dedication distinguishes this Barford from nearby *Barford St Michael*. DB *Bereford*, 1299 *Bereford Sancti Johannis*.

Barford St Martin (village, Wilts): '(place by the) barley ford with St Martin's church'. OE *bere*, 'barley', + *ford*, 'ford'. See BARFORD. The river here is the Nadder. The second part of the name refers to the dedication of the church. DB *Bereford*, 1304 *Berevord St Martin*.

Barford St Michael. See BARFORD ST JOHN.

Barfrestone (hamlet, Kent): 'Beornfrith's farmstead'. OE *tūn*, 'farmstead'. DB *Berfrestone*.

Bargoed (town, Caerphilly): '(place at the) boundary'. Welsh *bargod*, 'border', 'boundary'. The name is that of the river here, which apparently marked off the land at Brithdir from other land in the commote (subdivision of a cantred or hundred) of Senghennydd uwch Caeach. In more recent times it formed the boundary between the counties of Gwent and Mid Glamorgan.

Barham (village, Kent): 'Beora's homestead'. OE *hām*, 'homestead', 'village'. *799 Bioraham*, DB *Berham*.

Barham (village, Suffolk): 'homestead or enclosure on a hill'. OE *beorg*, 'hill', + *hām*, 'homestead', or *hamm*, 'enclosure'. DB *Bercham*. SO ALSO: *Barham*, Cambs.

Barkby (village, Leics): 'Bọrkr's or Barki's farmstead'. OS *bý*, 'farmstead', 'village'. The personal names are Scandinavian. DB *Barchebi*.

Barkestone (village, Leics): 'Barkr's or Bọrkr's farmstead'. OE *tūn*, 'farmstead'. The personal names are Scandinavian. The village is also known as *Barkestone-le-Vale*, for its location in the Vale of Belvoir, for distinction from BARKSTON, Lincs, 11 miles to the northeast. DB *Barchestone*.

Barking (town, Barking & Dag): '(settlement of) Berica's people'. OE *-ingas*, 'people of'. Barking and Dagenham form a single Greater London borough. *731 Berecingum*, DB *Berchinges*. SO ALSO: *Barking*, Suffolk.

Barkingside (district, Redbridge): '(place) beside Barking'. ME *side*, 'side', 'land alongside'. Barkingside is to the north of BARKING. *1538 Barkingside*.

Barkisland (village, Calderdale): 'Barkr's cultivated land'. OS *land*, 'tract of land'. The personal name is Scandinavian. *1246 Barkesland*.

Barkston (village, Lincs): 'Barkr's or Bọrkr's farmstead'. OE *tūn*, 'farmstead'. The personal names are Scandinavian. DB *Barchestune*.

Barkston Ash (village, N Yorks): 'Barkr's or Bọrkr's farmstead with an ash tree'. OE *tūn*, 'farmstead', + *æsc*, 'ash'. The personal names are Scandinavian. The village has been regularly known as *Barkston*, but is now usually *Barkston Ash*, the name of the local wapentake. *c.1030 Barcestune*, DB *Barchestun*, *1893 Barkston Ash, or Barkston*.

Barkway (village, Herts): 'birch-tree way'. OE *beorc*, 'birch', + *weg*, 'way'. The name implies a track or path lined with birches. DB *Bercheuuei*.

Barlaston (village, Staffs): 'Beornwulf's farmstead'. OE *tūn*, 'farmstead'. *1002 Beorelfestun*, DB *Bernulvestone*.

Barlavington (hamlet, W Sussex): 'estate associated with Beornlāf'. OE *-ing-*, 'associated with', + *tūn*, 'farmstead', 'estate'. DB *Berleventone*.

Barlborough (village, Derbys): 'stronghold by the wood where boars are seen'. OE *bār*, 'boar', + *lēah*, 'wood', 'clearing', + *burh*, 'fortified place'. *c.1002 Barleburh*, DB *Barleburg*.

Barlby (village, N Yorks): 'Beardwulf's or Bardulf's farmstead'. OS *bý*, 'farmstead', 'village'. The first personal name is OE, the second Old German. DB *Bardulbi*.

Barlestone (village, Leics): 'Beornwulf's or Berwulf's farmstead'. OE *tūn*, 'farmstead'. DB *Berulvestone*.

Barley (village, Herts): 'Beora's woodland clearing'. OE *lēah*, 'wood', 'clearing'. *c.1050 Beranlei*, DB *Berlai*.

Barley (village, Lancs): 'woodland clearing where boars are seen'. OE *bār*, 'boar', + *lēah*, 'wood', 'clearing'. The name could also mean 'woodland clearing where barley is grown' (OE *bere*, 'barley', + *lēah*). *1324 Bayrlegh*.

Barleythorpe (village, Rutland): 'le Bolour's outlying farmstead'. OS *thorp*, 'outlying farmstead'. John le Bolour was here in 1200, his name later becoming associated with *barley*. *1203 Bolaresthorp*.

Barling (village, Essex): '(settlement of) Bærla's people'. OE *-ingas*, 'people of'. *998 Bærlingum*, DB *Berlinga*.

Barlow (village, Derbys): 'woodland clearing where boars are seen'. OE *bār*, 'boar', + *lēah*, 'wood', 'clearing'. The name could also mean 'woodland clearing where barley is grown' (OE *bere*, 'barley', + *lēah*). DB *Barleie*.

Barlow (village, N Yorks): 'woodland clearing with a barn'. OE *bere-ærn* (from *bere*, 'barley', + *ærn*, 'building'), + *lēah*, 'wood', 'clearing'. The name could also mean 'woodland clearing where barley is grown' (OE *beren*, 'growing with barley', + *lēah*). *c.1030 Bernlege*, DB *Berlai*.

Barmby Moor (village, E Yorks): 'Barni's or Bjarni's farmstead on the moor'. OS *bý*, 'farmstead'. The personal names are Scandinavian. The second word of the name, referring to Spaldingmoor here, distinguishes this Barmby from *Barmby on the Marsh*, 15 miles to the south. DB *Barnebi*, *1371 Berneby in the More*, *1868 Barmby-on-the-Moor*.

Barmer (hamlet, Norfolk): '(place by the) pool where bears are seen'. OE *bera*, 'bear', + *mere*, 'pool'. The name could also mean '(place by) Bera's pool'. The DB form of the name below has *n* for *r*. DB *Benemara*, *1202 Beremere*.

Barming. See EAST BARMING.

Barmouth (resort town, Gwynedd): 'mouth of the (river) Mawddach'. OW *aber*, 'mouth'. The town is on the river Mawddach, originally known as the *Mawdd*, probably from a personal name. The estuary of the Mawdd was thus *Aber-mawdd*, which in modern Welsh became *Abermo* and *Y Bermo*. (In the latter, the *A-* of *Abermo* was taken as *y*, 'the'.) The English modification of *Abermawdd* turned out as modern *Barmouth*, influenced by *mouth*. 1410 *Abermowth*.

Barmston (village, E Yorks): 'Beorn's farmstead'. OE *tūn*, 'farmstead'. DB *Benestone*.

Barnack (village, Peterborough): '(place at the) oak tree of the warriors'. OE *beorn*, 'warrior', + *āc*, 'oak'. Celticists prefer to relate the name to that of the historic kingdom of *Bernicia* in Northumbria, itself of tribal origin and meaning '(people of the mountain) passes'. *c.*980 *Beornican*, DB *Bernac*.

Barnacle (hamlet, Warwicks): 'wooded slope by a barn'. OE *bere-ærn*, 'barn' (from *bere*, 'barley', + *ærn*, 'building'), + *hangra*, 'wooded slope'. The *r* of *hangra* became *l* under Norman influence, as for SALISBURY, and the name then acquired its present form by popular association. DB *Bernhangre*.

Barnard Castle (town, Durham): 'Bernard's castle'. Bernard was a baron here in the 12C. Barnard Castle is known locally as 'Barney'. 1200 *Castellum Bernardi*.

Barnardiston (hamlet, Suffolk): 'Beornheard's farmstead'. OE *tūn*, 'farmstead'. 1194 *Bernardeston*.

Barnby (village, Suffolk): 'farmstead of the children'. OS *barn*, 'child', + *bý*, 'farmstead'. The name implies a farmstead held jointly by a number of descendants. The name could also mean 'Barni's or Bjarni's farmstead', with a Scandinavian personal name. DB *Barnebei*.

Barnby Dun (village, Doncaster): 'Bjarni's farmstead on the (river) Don'. OS *bý*, 'farmstead'. The personal name is Scandinavian. The river name (see DONCASTER) was added to distinguish this Barnby from BARNBY MOOR, Notts, 17 miles to the south. DB *Barnebi*, 1285 *Barneby super Don*.

Barnby Moor (village, Notts): 'Barni's farmstead on the moor'. OS *bý*, 'farmstead'. The personal name is Scandinavian. The second word of the name distinguishes this Barnby from BARNBY DUN, Doncaster, 17 miles to the north. DB *Barnebi*.

Barnehurst (district, Bexley): 'Barne's wooded hill'. ME *hurst*, 'wooded hill'. The district name comes from that of the station here, itself so called because built on land owned by a Colonel Barne. 1905 *Barnehurst*.

Barnes (district, Richmond): '(place by the) barns'. OE *bere-ærn*, 'barn' (from *bere*, 'barley', + *ærn*, 'building'). There may have been one barn here originally, as suggested by the DB form of the name below. DB *Berne*, 1222 *Bernes*.

Barnet (borough, Greater London): 'land cleared by burning'. OE *bærnet*, 'burning'. The name would originally have been applied to woodlands cleared by burning, in an area between the present A1000 and A111. Nearby are *Chipping Barnet* (OE *cīeping*, 'market'), *East Barnet*, *Friern Barnet* (ME *freren*, 'of the brethren', from the Knights of St John of Jerusalem who held it) and *New Barnet*. Chipping Barnet has also been known as *High Barnet* since the 17C, although the two names are now separately marked on maps. *c.*1070 *Barneto*.

Barnetby le Wold (village, N Lincs): 'Beornnōth's or Beornede's farmstead in the Wolds'. OS *bý*, 'farmstead', 'village'. The second part of the name refers to the location of the village in the Lincolnshire WOLDS. DB *Bernedebi*.

Barney (village, Norfolk): 'Bera's island'. OE *ēg*, 'island'. The 'island' would be dry ground in marshland here. The DB form of the name below has *l* for *n*. DB *Berlei*, 1198 *Bernei*.

Barnham (village, Suffolk): 'homestead of the warrior'. OE *beorn*, 'warrior', + *hām*, 'homestead'. The name could also mean 'Beorn's homestead'. The village is sometimes known as *Barnham St Gregory*, after its church dedication, for distinction from BARNHAM BROOM, Norfolk, 23 miles to the northeast. *c.*1000 *Byornham*, DB *Bernham*.

Barnham (village, W Sussex): 'Beorna's homestead or enclosure'. OE *hām*, 'homestead', or *hamm*, 'enclosure'. The name could also mean 'homestead or enclosure of the warriors' (OE *beorn*, 'warrior', + *hām* or *hamm*). DB *Berneham*.

Barnham Broom (village, Norfolk): 'homestead of the warrior by broom'. OE *beorn*, 'warrior', + *hām*, 'homestead', + *brōm*, 'broom'. The name could also mean 'Beorn's homestead'. The second word of the name distinguishes this Barnham from BARNHAM, Suffolk, 23 miles to the southwest. DB *Bernham*.

Barningham (village, Suffolk): 'homestead of Beorn's people'. OE *-inga-*, 'of the people of', + *hām*, 'homestead', 'village'. DB *Bernincham*. SO ALSO: *Barningham*, Durham.

Barnoldby le Beck (village, NE Lincs): 'Bjǫrnulfr's farmstead on the stream'. OS *bý*, 'farmstead', 'village', + *bekkr*, 'stream'. The personal name is Scandinavian. DB *Bernulfbi*.

Barnoldswick (town, Lancs): 'Beornwulf's or Bjǫrnulfr's farm'. OE *wīc*, 'dwelling', 'dairy farm'. The personal names are respectively OE and Scandinavian. DB *Bernulfesuuic*.

Barnsbury (district, Islington): 'de Berners' manor'. OE *burh*, 'fortified place', 'manor'. The de Berners family held land in Islington in the 13C. 1406 *Bernersbury*.

Barnsley (town, Barnsley): 'Beorn's woodland clearing'. OE *lēah*, 'wood', 'clearing'. DB *Berneslai*.

Barnsley (village, Glos): 'Beornmōd's woodland clearing'. OE *lēah*, 'wood', 'clearing'. *c*.802 *Bearmodeslea*, DB *Bernesleis*.

Barnstaple (town, Devon): 'post or pillar of the battleaxe'. OE *bearde*, 'battleaxe', + *stapol*, 'post'. The allusion is to an early Saxon assembly place involving a brandishing of weapons, like the Viking *vápnatak* (English *wapentake*, literally 'weapon take'). The abbreviated name *Barum* (like *Sarum* for SALISBURY) was formerly found on milestones nearby. late IOC *Beardastapol*, DB *Barnestaple*.

Barnston (village, Essex): 'Beorn's farmstead'. OE *tūn*, 'farmstead'. DB *Bernestuna*.

Barnston (village, Wirral): 'Beornwulf's farmstead'. OE *tūn*, 'farmstead'. DB *Bernestone*.

Barnton (suburb of Northwich, Cheshire): 'Beornthrȳth's farmstead'. OE *tūn*, 'farmstead'. The personal name is that of a woman. DB *Bertintune*, 1313 *Bertherton*, 1319 *Berneton*.

Barnwell All Saints (village, Northants): '(place by) Beorna's spring with All Saints church'. OE *wella*, 'spring', 'stream'. The main name could also mean 'spring of the warriors' (OE *beorn*, 'warrior', + *wella*). The church dedication distinguishes this village from nearby *Barnwell St Andrew*. *c*.980 *Byrnewilla*, DB *Bernewelle*.

Barnwood (district of Gloucester, Glos): 'wood of the warriors'. OE *beorn*, 'warrior', + *wudu*, 'wood'. Other possible meanings are 'Beorna's wood' or 'wood with a barn' (OE *bere-ærn*, 'barn', from *bere*, 'barley', + *ærn*, 'building'). DB *Berneuude*.

Barra (island, W Isles): 'hilly island'. The first part of the name represents a Celtic word related to Gaelic *barr*, 'hill'. The second is OS *ey*, 'island'. The name is popularly associated with that of St Finbar, 6C Irish Bishop of Cork, regarded as a patron of the island. *c*.1090 *Barru*, *c*.1200 *Barey*.

Barrasford (village, Northd): '(place at the) ford by a grove'. OE *bearu*, 'grove', + *ford*, 'ford'.

The first part of the name represents OE *bearwes*, the genitive form of *bearu*. 1242 *Barwisford*.

Barrhead (town, E Renfrews): 'head headland'. Gaelic *barr*, 'top', 'head', + modern English *head*. The town lies on Levern Water at the foot of lofty moorland. The name is really tautologous, and the Gaelic word must have been added when the Gaelic original was no longer understood.

Barri, Y. See BARRY.

Barrington (village, Cambs): 'Bāra's farmstead'. OE *tūn*, 'farmstead'. The genitive ending *-n* on the personal name gave the '-ing-' of the present name. DB *Barentone*.

Barrington (village, Somerset): 'estate associated with Bāra'. OE *-ing-*, 'associated with', + *tūn*, 'farmstead', 'estate'. DB *Barintone*.

Barriper (village, Cornwall): 'beautiful retreat'. OF *beau*, 'beautiful', + *repaire*, 'retreat'. Cp. BELPER. 1397 *Beaurepere*.

Barrow (hamlet, Rutland): '(place by the) burial mound'. OE *beorg*, 'hill', 'burial mound'. The reference is to a tumulus nearby. 1197 *Berc*.

Barrowby (village, Lincs): 'farmstead on the hill'. OS *berg*, 'hill', + *bý*, 'farmstead'. DB *Bergebi*.

Barrowden (village, Rutland): '(place by the) hill with burial mounds'. OE *beorg*, 'burial mound', + *dūn*, 'hill'. The barrows in question were on the ridge here overlooking the river Welland. DB *Berchedone*.

Barrowford (town, Lancs): '(place at the) ford by the grove'. OE *bearu*, 'grove', + *ford*, 'ford'. Barrowford stands on the Pendle Water, its name distinguishing it from nearby *Higherford*, further up the river, and *Lowerford*, below it (but both above Barrowford). 1296 *Barouforde*.

Barrow Gurney (village, N Somerset): 'de Gurnai's (estate by the) wood'. OE *bearu*, 'grove', 'wood'. Nigel de Gurnai held the manor here in 1086. DB *Berue*, 1283 *Barwe Gurnay*.

Barrow-in-Furness (town, Cumbria): 'promontory island in Furness'. Celtic *barr*, 'headland', + OS *ey*, 'island'. Barrow was originally an island, but is now part of the mainland. The island now known as Piel Island was originally *Futh* (OS *futh*, 'buttock'), so called because of the 'cleavage' that runs across it. The district name *Furness* thus refers to the headland (OS *nes*) opposite this island. 1190 *Barrai*; *c*.1150 *Fuththernessa*.

Barrow upon Humber (village, N Lincs): '(place by the) wood on the (river) Humber'. OE *bearu*, 'grove', 'wood'. For the river name, see HUMBERSTON. 731 *Ad Baruae*, DB *Barewe*.

Barrow upon Soar (village, Leics): '(place by the) wood on the (river) Soar'. OE *bearu*, 'grove', 'wood'. The river name is Celtic or pre-Celtic and may mean 'flowing one'. DB *Barhou*.

Barrow upon Trent (village, Derbys): '(place by the) wood on the (river) Trent'. OE *bearu*, 'grove', 'wood'. For the river name, see STOKE-ON-TRENT. DB *Barewe*.

Barry (town, Vale of Glam): '(place of the) hill'. OW *barr*, 'hill'. The name properly refers to Barry Island. The Welsh name of the town is *Y Barri* (Welsh *y*, 'the'). *c.*1190 *Barri*.

Barsby (hamlet, Leics): 'Barn's farmstead'. OS *bý*, 'farmstead', 'village'. The personal name is Scandinavian. The first part of the name could also represent OS *barn*, 'child', giving a sense 'farmstead of the young heir'. DB *Barnesbi*.

Barsham (village, Suffolk): 'Bār's homestead'. OE *hām*, 'homestead', 'village'. DB *Barsham*.

Barston (village, Solihull): 'Beorhtstān's farmstead'. OE *tūn*, 'farmstead', 'estate'. DB *Bertanestone*, 1185 *Berestanestone*.

Bartestree (village, Herefords): 'Beorhtwald's tree'. OE *trēow*, 'tree'. DB *Bertoldestreu*.

Barthomley (village, Cheshire): 'woodland clearing at Brightham'. OE *lēah*, 'wood', 'clearing'. The first part of the name seems to represent a name *Brightham*, in which 'Bright-' is either OE *beorht*, 'bright', or the first part of a personal name beginning *Beorht-* (as for BRIGHTON), and '-ham' is OE *hamm* or *homm*, 'enclosure'. The DB form of the name below is garbled. DB *Bertemeleu*, 13C *Bertamelegh*.

Bartlow (village, Cambs): '(place by the) mounds where birch trees grow'. OE *beorc*, 'birch', + *hlāw*, 'mound'. The 'mounds' are the famous Roman barrows of the Bartlow Hills nearby. 1232 *Berkelawe*.

Barton (village, Cambs): 'barley farm'. OE *bere-tūn* (from *bere*, 'barley', + *tūn*, 'farm'). The OE term denoted an outlying grange where corn was stored. 1060 *Barton*, DB *Bertone*. SO ALSO: *Barton*, Devon, Glos, Lancs.

Barton Bendish (village, Norfolk): 'barley farm inside the ditch'. OE *bere-tūn* (from *bere*, 'barley', + *tūn*, 'farm'), + *binnan*, 'inside', + *dīc*, 'ditch'. The second word of the name refers to Devil's Dyke here, built as a boundary for the local hundred. DB *Bertuna*, 1249 *Berton Binnedich*.

Barton in Fabis (village, Notts): 'barley farm where beans are grown'. OE *bere-tūn* (from *bere*, 'barley', + *tūn*, 'farm'), + Latin *in fabis*, 'in the beans'. Cp. BARTON IN THE BEANS. DB *Bartone*, 1388 *Barton in le Benes*.

Barton in the Beans (village, Leics): 'barley farm where beans are grown'. OE *bere-tūn* (from *bere*, 'barley', + *tūn*, 'farmstead'). Cp. BARTON IN FABIS. DB *Bartone*.

Barton-le-Clay (village, Beds): 'barley farm on clay soil'. OE *bere-tūn* (from *bere*, 'barley', + *tūn*, 'farm'), + OF *le*, 'the', + modern English *clay*. An alternative name is *Barton-in-the-Clay*. DB *Bertone*, 1535 *Barton-in-the-Clay*, *c.*1560 *Barton-le-Clay*, 1868 *Barton-in-the-Clay, or Barton-le-Clay*.

Barton-le-Street (village, N Yorks): 'barley farm on the Roman road'. OE *bere-tūn* (from *bere*, 'barley', + *tūn*, 'farm'), + *strǣt*, 'Roman road' (modern English *street*). A Roman road probably ran between Malton and Hovingham here, on the route now followed by the B1257. Cp. APPLETON-LE-STREET. The second part of the name distinguishes this Barton from BARTON-LE-WILLOWS, 7½ miles to the south. DB *Bartun*.

Barton-le-Willows (village, N Yorks): 'barley farm by the willow trees'. OE *bere-tūn* (from *bere*, 'barley', + *tūn*, 'farmstead'). The second part of the name distinguishes this Barton from BARTON-LE-STREET, 7½ miles to the north. DB *Bartun*.

Barton Mills (village, Suffolk): 'barley farm with mills'. OE *bere-tūn* (from *bere*, 'barley', + *tūn*, 'farmstead'). The mills were by the river Lark here. The first word of the second form of the name below is Latin *parva*, 'little'. DB *Bertona*, 1254 *Parva Bertone*, 1868 *Barton-Mills, or Little Barton*.

Barton on Sea (resort district of Lymington, Hants): 'estate associated with Beorma by the sea'. OE *-ing-*, 'associated with', + *tūn*, 'farmstead', 'estate': The second part of the name may have been added to match that of nearby MILFORD ON SEA. DB *Bermintune*.

Barton-on-the-Heath (village, Warwicks): 'barley farm on the heath'. OE *bere-tūn* (from *bere*, 'barley', + *tūn*, 'farmstead'). The second part of the name distinguishes this Barton from *Barton*, 13 miles to the northwest. DB *Bertone*.

Barton Seagrave (village, Northants): 'de Segrave's barley farm'. OE *bere-tūn* (from *bere*, 'barley', + *tūn*, 'farm'). The de Segrave family held the manor here in the 13C. DB *Bertone*, 1321 *Barton Segrave*.

Barton Stacey (village, Hants): 'de Saci's barley farm'. OE *bere-tūn* (from *bere*, 'barley', + *tūn*, 'farm'). The de Saci family held the manor here in the 12C. Their name has been corrupted in the present name. *c.*1000 *Bertune*, DB *Bertune*, 1302 *Berton Sacy*.

Barton Turf (hamlet, Norfolk): 'barley farm with turf'. OE *bere-tūn* (from *bere*, 'barley', + *tūn*, 'farm'). The second word of the name presumably denotes that good turf was cut here. DB *Bertuna*, 1394 *Berton Turfe*.

Barton-under-Needwood (village, Staffs): 'barley farm near Needwood'. OE *bere-tūn* (from *bere*, 'barley', + *tūn*, 'farm'). The second part of the name refers to Needwood Forest (see NEEDWOOD). 942 *Barton*, DB *Bertone*.

Barton-upon-Humber (town, N Lincs): 'outlying grange on the (river) Humber'. OE *bere-tūn* (from *bere*, 'barley', + *tūn*, 'farm'). Barton was probably an outlying grange of Barrow upon Humber, 3 miles to the west. For the river name, see HUMBERSTON. DB *Bertone*.

Barwell (village, Leics): '(place by the) stream where boars come'. OE *bār*, 'boar', + *wella*, 'spring', 'stream'. DB *Barewelle*.

Barwick (village, Somerset): 'barley farm'. OE *bere-wīc* (from *bere*, 'barley', + *wīc*, 'specialized farm'). 1219 *Berewyk*.

Barwick in Elmet (village, Leeds): 'barley farm in Elmet'. OE *bere-wīc* (from *bere*, 'barley', + *wīc*, 'specialized farm'). The district name, of uncertain origin, was recorded in the 7C as *Elmed*. DB *Bereuuith*.

Baschurch (village, Shropshire): 'Bassa's church'. OE *cirice*, 'church'. DB *Bascherche*.

Basford (district, Nottingham): '(place by) Basa's ford'. OE *ford*, 'ford'. The district is divided into *Old Basford* and *New Basford*, the latter as a southern extension of the original Basford. DB *Baseford*.

Bashall Eaves (hamlet, Lancs): '(place on the) ridge by the shelf at the edge of a wood'. OE *bæc*, 'ridge' (modern English *back*), + *scelf*, 'shelf', 'ledge', + *efes*, 'edge (of a wood)' (modern English *eaves*). The ridge in question is a narrow tongue of land extending between two brooks from Backridge (also named after it) to Bashall Town, a large farm situated on a shelf formed by the broadening of the ridge at its western end. The wood referred to is the Forest of Bowland. DB *Bacschelf*.

Basildon (town, Essex): '(place by) Beorhtel's hill'. OE *dūn*, 'hill'. The DB form of the name below has omitted the *t* of the personal name. DB *Berlesduna*, 1194 *Bertlesdon*, 1868 *Basildon, or Bassildon*.

Basildon (village, W Berks): '(place in) Bæssel's valley'. OE *denu*, 'valley'. *c*.690 *Bestlesforda*, DB *Bastedene*.

Basingstoke (town, Hants): 'outlying farmstead of Basa's people'. OE *-inga-*, 'of the people of', + *stoc*, 'outlying place', 'dependent settlement'. The original settlement here would have depended on nearby *Old Basing*. The council district name *Basingstoke and Deane* includes the hamlet of *Deane*, west of Basingstoke, its own name meaning '(place in the) valley' (OE *denu*), the valley being that of the river Test. 990 *Basingastoc*, DB *Basingestoches*.

Baslow (village, Derbys): 'Bassa's burial mound'. OE *hlāw*, 'mound', 'hill'. DB *Basselau*.

Bassenthwaite (lake, Cumbria): 'Bastun's clearing'. OS *thveit*, 'clearing', 'meadow'. The personal name is a ME surname or family name. The lake is properly *Bassenthwaite Lake*, as the only lake in the Lake District to have 'lake' in its name. *c*.1175 *Bastunthuait*, *c*.1220 *Bastunwater*.

Bassetlaw (council district, Notts): 'hill of the dwellers on land cleared by burning'. OE *bærnet*, 'burning' (cp. BARNET), + *sǣte*, 'dwellers' (cp. DORSET), + *hlāw*, 'mound', 'hill'. The name was originally that of a wapentake here. DB *Bernesedelaue*.

Bassingbourn (village, Cambs): '(place by the) stream of Bassa's people'. OE *-inga-*, 'of the people of', + *burna*, 'stream'. DB *Basingborne*.

Bassingthorpe (hamlet, Lincs): 'Basewin's outlying farmstead'. OS *thorp*, 'outlying farmstead'. The original settlement here probably depended on Westby or Bitchfield. DB *Torp*, 1202 *Basewinttorp*.

Baston (village, Lincs): 'Bak's farmstead'. OE *tūn*, 'farmstead'. The personal name is Scandinavian. DB *Bacstune*.

Bastwick (village, Norfolk): 'building where bast is stored'. OE *bæst*, 'bast', + *wīc*, 'building', 'specialized farm'. Bast is lime-tree bark used for ropemaking. 1044 *Bastwic*, DB *Bastuuic*.

Batcombe (village, Dorset): '(place in) Bata's valley'. OE *cumb*, 'valley'. 1201 *Batecumbe*. SO ALSO: *Batcombe*, Somerset.

Bath (city, Bath & NE Somerset): '(place at the Roman) baths'. OE *bæth*, 'bath'. The Roman baths are famous, and the Roman station here was *Aquae Sulis*, 'waters of Sulis', referring to a pagan goddess. The uniqueness of the place has generated a rich and romantic history: 'The name of the city is obviously derived from its medicinal springs, the efficacy of which has been celebrated from remote antiquity. It is stated to have been a British town prior to the Roman invasion and to have been named *Caer Badon*, or "the place of baths," from an accidental discovery of the medicinal properties of its waters by Bladud, son of Lud Hudibras, king of Britain, who, according to the fabulous histories of those times, having been banished from court on account of leprosy, came to this place, and being cured of that disease by using the waters, is said, after his accession to the throne, to have built a palace here, and to have encouraged the resort of persons affected with cutaneous disorders. So favourably was this fable received even till the eighteenth century, that his statue was erected in the king's bath, with an inscription to that effect, in 1699. The researches of modern historians, however, have induced them to reject this tradition, as entirely destitute of support, and to ascribe the foundation of the city to the Romans, in the reign of Claudius' (Samuel Lewis, *A Topographical Dictionary of England*, 1840). The first form of the name below represents the dative plural form of OE *bæth*. See also AKEMAN STREET. 796 *Bathum*, DB *Bade*.

Bathampton (village, Bath & NE Somerset): 'home farm near Bath'. OE *hām-tūn*, 'homestead' (from *hām*, 'homestead', + *tūn*, 'farmstead'). The name of nearby BATH was added to distinguish this *Hampton* from others. 956 *Hamtun*, DB *Hantone*.

Bathealton (village, Somerset): 'Beaduhelm's farmstead'. OE *tūn*, 'farmstead'. DB *Badeheltone*.

Batheaston (village, Bath & NE Somerset): 'eastern farmstead near Bath'. OE *ēast*, 'eastern', +*tūn*, 'farmstead'. The name of nearby BATH distinguishes this *Easton* from others. DB *Estone*, 1258 *Batheneston*.

Bathford (village, Bath & NE Somerset): '(place at the) ford near Bath'. OE *ford*, 'ford'. The name of nearby BATH distinguishes this ford (on the river Avon) from others. 957 *Forda*, DB *Forde*, 1575 *Bathford*.

Bathgate (town, W Lothian): '(place by the) boar wood'. The name comes from Celtic words related to modern Welsh *baedd*, 'boar', and *coed*, 'wood'. *c*.1160 *Batket*.

Bathley (village, Notts): 'woodland clearing with bathing places'. OE *bæth*, 'bath', 'pool', + *lēah*, 'wood', 'clearing'. The springs here would have been used for bathing. DB *Badeleie*.

Bathpool (village, Cornwall): 'pool with a bathing place'. OE *bæth*, 'bath', + *pōl*, 'pool'. The reference is to a bathing place in the river Lynher nearby. 1474 *Bathpole*.

Batley (town, Kirklees): 'Bata's woodland clearing'. OE *lēah*, 'wood', 'clearing'. This part of the former West Riding of Yorkshire must have been heavily wooded at one time, as there are many '-ley' names in the vicinity. Cp. ILKLEY, MORLEY, OTLEY. DB *Bathelie*.

Batsford (village, Glos): 'Bæcci's hill slope'. OE *ōra*, 'hill slope'. The slope in question is the steep hillside here. The second half of the name is thus misleading, and there is no ford here. 727 *Bæccesore*, DB *Beceshore*.

Battersby (village, N Yorks): 'Bọthvarr's farmstead'. OS *bý*, 'farmstead', 'village'. The personal name is Scandinavian. DB *Badresbi*.

Battersea (district, Wandsworth): 'Beadurīc's island'. OE *ēg*, 'island'. The 'island' would have been higher land in marshland by the Thames here. Spellings of the name with *P-*, like that of the DB form below, have led to a false association with St Patrick, while the name is still popularly explained as 'Peter's island', from the adjacent Abbey of St Peter, Westminster. 11C *Badrices ege*, DB *Patricesy*.

Battisford (hamlet, Suffolk): '(place by) Bætti's ford'. OE *ford*, 'ford'. DB *Betesfort*.

Battle (town, E Sussex): '(place of the) battle'. OF *bataille*, 'battle'. The abbey here was founded by William the Conqueror to commemorate his victory at the Battle of Hastings (1066), which thus took place 6 miles from Hastings itself. The old name of the hill on which the battle was fought is *Senlac*, 'sandy stream' (OE *sand*, 'sand', + *lacu*, 'stream'). This name was long popularly given the derivation in William Camden's *Britannia* (1586), which describes Battle as a town 'wherein there is a place called by a French word *sangue lac*, of the bloud there shed, which by nature of the ground seemeth after raine to wax red'. The small stream here does in fact run red after heavy rain. DB *La Batailge*.

Battlefield (hamlet, Shropshire): '(place at the) battlefield'. OF *bataille*, 'battle'. A college of secular canons was founded here to commemorate the Battle of Shrewsbury (1403). The battle itself was probably fought in a location called *Hayteley*, 'heathy clearing' (OE *hǣthiht*, 'heathy', + *lēah*, 'clearing'), a name not found independently but first in 1406 as *Hayteleyfeld*, the *-feld* meaning 'field' (i.e. of battle). The first part of this was then popularly associated with *battle* to give the present name. 1410 *Bateleyfield*, 1419 *Batelfeld*.

Battlesbridge (village, Essex): 'Bataille's (estate at the) bridge'. OE *brycg*, 'bridge'. The Bataille family held the manor in the 14C here near the head of the river Crouch estuary. 1351 *Batailesbregge*.

Baumber (village, Lincs): 'Badda's stronghold'. OE *burh*, 'fortified place'. DB *Badeburg*.

Baunton (village, Glos): 'estate associated with Balda'. OE *-ing-*, 'associated with', + *tūn*, 'farmstead', 'estate'. DB *Baudintone*.

Baverstock (village, Wilts): 'Babba's outlying farmstead'. OE *stoc*, 'outlying farmstead'. 968 *Babbanstoc*, DB *Babestoche*.

Bawburgh (village, Norfolk): 'Bēawa's stronghold'. OE *burh*, 'fortified place'. DB *Bauenburc*.

Bawdeswell (village, Norfolk): 'Baldhere's spring'. OE *wella*, 'spring', 'stream'. DB *Baldereswella*.

Bawdrip (village, Somerset): 'place where badgers are trapped'. OE *bagga*, 'badger', + *træppe*, 'trap'. DB *Bagetrepe*.

Bawdsey (village, Suffolk): 'Baldhere's island'. OE *ēg*, 'island'. The 'island' is the raised land on which the village stands near the coast. DB *Baldereseia*.

Bawtry (town, Doncaster): '(place by the) ball tree'. OE *ball*, 'ball', + *trēow*, 'tree'. A 'ball tree' is a tree rounded like a ball. 1199 *Baltry*.

Baxenden (village, Lancs): '(place in the) valley where bakestones are found'. OE *bæc-stān* (from *bacan*, 'to bake', + *stān*, 'stone'), + *denu*, 'valley'. Bakestones are flat stones on which cakes are baked. The final part of the form of the name below represents OE *clōh*, 'ravine'. 1194 *Bastanedenecloch*.

Baxterley (village, Warwicks): 'woodland clearing of the baker'. OE *bæcestre*, 'baker', + *lēah*, 'wood', 'clearing'. The OE word for 'baker' (which gave the modern surname Baxter) is properly feminine, but was adopted early for men. *c.*1170 *Basterleia*.

Baycliff (coastal village, Cumbria): '(place on the) cliff where beacons are lit'. OE *bēl*, 'fire', + *clif*, 'cliff'. Baycliff stands above Morecambe Bay. 1212 *Belleclive*.

Baydon (village, Wilts): '(place by the) hill where berries grow'. OE *beg*, 'berry', + *dūn*, 'hill'. 1146 *Beidona*.

Bayford (village, Herts): '(place by) Bæga's ford'. OE *ford*, 'ford'. DB *Begesford*, *c.*1090 *Begeford*.

Baylham (village, Suffolk): 'homestead or enclosure at the river bend'. OE *bēgel*, 'bend', + *hām*, 'homestead', or *hamm*, 'enclosure'. The river here is the Gipping. DB *Beleham*.

Bayston Hill (village, Shropshire): 'hill by Bayston'. OE *hyll*, 'hill'. The village takes its name from the hill near *Bayston*, 'Bēage's or Bæga's stone' (OE *stān*, 'stone'), the first personal name being that of a woman. The 'stone' is a nearby rock outcrop. 1301 *Beystaneshull*.

Bayswater (district, Westminster): 'watering place for horses'. ME *bayard*, 'bay horse', + *watering*, 'watering place'. The name could equally have come from the family name Bayard, itself from the ME word. The 'watering place' would have been the river Westbourne, dammed up in 1730 to form the Serpentine in Hyde Park. 1380 *Bayards Watering Place*, 1659 *Bayeswater*.

Bayton (village, Worcs): 'Bēage's or Bæga's farmstead'. OE *tūn*, 'farmstead'. The personal names are respectively those of a woman and a man. DB *Betune*.

Beachampton (village, Bucks): 'home farm by a stream'. OE *bece*, 'stream', + *hām-tūn*, 'home farm' (*hām*, 'homestead', + *tūn*, 'farmstead'). The stream in question runs through the middle of the village. DB *Bechentone*.

Beachley (hamlet, Glos): 'Betti's woodland clearing'. OE *lēah*, 'wood', 'clearing'. 12C *Beteslega*.

Beachy Head (headland, E Sussex): 'beautiful headland'. OF *beau*, 'beautiful', + *chef*, 'head'. The name refers to the headland's striking appearance as one approaches the English coast from France. English *head* was added when *chef* in the original was no longer understood. 1279 *Beuchef*.

Beaconsfield (town, Bucks): 'open land by a beacon'. OE *bēacen*, 'beacon', + *feld*, 'open land' (modern English *field*). The original 'beacon' may have been a signal fire on Beacon Hill at Penn, some 3 miles from Beaconsfield. 1184 *Bekenesfelde*.

Beadlam (hamlet, N Yorks): '(place at the) buildings'. OE *bōthl*, 'building'. The name represents OE *bōthlum*, the dative plural form of *bōthl*. DB *Bodlum*.

Beadnell (resort village, Northd): 'Bēda's corner of land'. OE *halh*, 'nook', 'corner of land'. 1161 *Bedehal*.

Beaford (village, Devon): '(place by the) ford plagued with gadflies'. OE *bēaw*, 'gadfly', + *ford*, 'ford'. The gadflies doubtless worried the cattle crossing Beaford Brook here. The DB form of the name below is corrupt. DB *Baverdone*, 1242 *Beuford*.

Beal (hamlet, Northd): '(place by the) hill where bees are kept'. OE *bēo*, 'bee', + *hyll*, 'hill'. 1208 *Behil*.

Beal (village, N Yorks): 'corner of land in a river bend'. OE *bēag*, 'circle', + *halh*, 'nook', 'corner of land'. The reference is probably to the land to the north of Beal across the river Aire, which is a virtual oval island between the Aire to the south and the Old Eye to the north. DB *Begale*.

Beaminster (town, Dorset): 'Bebbe's large church'. OE *mynster*, 'large church', 'monastery'. The original 'large church' was probably on the site of the present 15C parish church. The personal name is that of a woman. 862 *Bebingmynster*, DB *Beiminstre*.

Beamish (village, Durham): 'beautiful mansion'. OF *beau*, 'beautiful', + *mes*, 'mansion'. 1288 *Bewmys*.

Beamsley (village, N Yorks): 'pasture by the valley bottom'. OE *bethme*, 'valley bottom', + *lēah*, 'clearing', 'pasture'. DB *Bedmesleia*, 1185 *Bethmesleia*.

Beanley (hamlet, Northd): 'clearing where beans are grown'. OE *bēan*, 'bean', + *lēah*, 'wood', 'clearing'. *c*.1150 *Benelega*.

Bearley (village, Warwicks): 'woodland clearing by a fortified place'. OE *burh*, 'fortified place', + *lēah*, 'wood', 'clearing'. DB *Burlei*.

Bearpark (village, Durham): 'beautiful retreat'. OF *beau*, 'beautiful', + *repaire*, 'retreat' (modern English *repair*, 'haunt', 'resort'). 1267 *Beaurepeyr*.

Bearsden (town, E Dunbartons): 'valley where wild boars are seen'. OE *bār*, 'boar', + *denu*, 'valley'.

Bearsted (suburb of Maidstone, Kent): 'homestead on a hill'. OE *beorg*, 'hill', + *hām-stede* (see HAMPSTEAD). 695 *Berghamstyde*.

Bearstone (hamlet, Shropshire): 'Bæghard's farmstead'. OE *tūn*, 'farmstead', 'estate'. DB *Bardestune*.

Beauchamp Roding. See RODINGS.

Beauchief (district, Sheffield): 'beautiful headland'. OF *beau*, 'beautiful', + *chef*, 'headland', 'hill spur'. 12C *Beuchef*.

Beaudesert (hamlet, Warwicks): 'beautiful wasteland'. OF *beau*, 'beautiful', + *desert*, 'wasteland', 'desert'. The name was that of the Norman castle here. 1141 *Castellum de Bello Deserto*.

Beaufort (town, Blaenau Gwent). The name is that of the Duke of Beaufort, the 18C landowner. The Welsh name of the town is *Cendl*, from the surname of Edward Kendall, the ironmaster who was granted a lease of the site by the duke in 1780.

Beaulieu (village, Hants): 'beautiful place'. OF *beau*, 'beautiful', + *lieu*, 'place'. The site is still attractive, at the head of the river Beaulieu estuary. Cp. BEAULY. The first form of the name below is the Latin equivalent, with added *Regis*, 'of the king'. 1205 *Bellus Locus Regis*, *c*.1300 *Beulu*.

Beauly (town, Highland): 'beautiful place'. OF *beau*, 'beautiful', + *lieu*, 'place'. The town is in a picturesque setting on the river of the same name. Cp. BEAULIEU. The Latin form of the name below means 'priory of the lovely spot'. 1230 *Prioratus de bello loco*.

Beaumaris (resort town, Anglesey): 'beautiful marsh'. OF *beau*, 'beautiful', + *marais*, 'marsh'. The site is not noticeably attractive, and Edward I is said to have given the name to tempt English settlers to his new castle and fortified town. The Welsh form of the name is *Biwmares*. 1284 *Bello Marisco*.

Beaumont (village, Cumbria): '(place on a) beautiful hill'. OF *beau*, 'beautiful', + *mont*, 'Beaumont, a town so named of the fair hill on which it stands from whence every way lies a goodly prospect' (J. Denton, *An Accompt of the most considerable Estates and Families in the County of Cumberland*, edited by R.S. Ferguson, 1887). *c*.1240 *Beumund*.

Beaumont (village, Essex): '(place on a) beautiful hill'. OF *beau*, 'beautiful', + *mont*, 'hill'. The original name of the place was *Fulepet*, '(place in the) foul pit' (OE *fūl* 'foul', + *pytt*, 'pit', 'hollow'), but this unpleasant OE name was replaced by the present pleasant OF one. DB *Fulepet*, 12C *Bealmont*.

Beausale (village, Warwicks): 'Bēaw's corner of land'. OE *halh*, 'nook', 'corner of land'. The DB form of the name below is corrupt. DB *Beoshelle*, 12C *Beausala*.

Beauworth (hamlet, Hants): 'enclosure where bees are kept'. OE *bēo*, 'bee', + *worth*, 'enclosure'. 1208 *Beworda*.

Beaworthy (village, Devon): 'Bēage's or Bæga's enclosure'. OE *worth*, 'enclosure'. The personal names are respectively those of a woman and a man. DB *Begeurde*.

Bebington (town, Wirral): 'estate associated with Bebbe or Bebba'. OE *-ing-*, 'associated with', + *tūn*, 'estate'. The personal names are respectively those of a woman and a man. *c*.1100 *Bebinton*.

Bebside (hamlet, Northd): 'Bibba's projecting piece of land'. OE *scēat*, 'projecting piece of land'. 1198 *Bibeshet*.

Beccles (town, Suffolk): 'pasture by a stream'. OE *bece*, 'stream', + *lǣs*, 'pasture', 'meadowland'. The 'stream' is probably a tributary of the river Waveney to the west of the town. Celticists prefer a meaning 'little court', however, from words related to modern Welsh *bach*, 'little', and *llys*, 'court'. DB *Becles*, 1157 *Beclis*.

Becconsall (village, Lancs): 'Bekan's burial mound'. os *haugr*, 'mound'. The personal name is Old Irish. 1208 *Bekaneshou*.

Beckbury (village, Shropshire): 'Becca's manor house'. OE *burh*, 'fortified place', 'manor'. DB *Becheberie*.

Beckenham (town, Bromley): 'Beohha's homestead or enclosure'. OE *hām*, 'homestead', or *hamm*, 'enclosure'. The first form of the name below contains OE *gemǣre*, 'boundary'. 973 *Beohha hammes gemǣru*, DB *Bacheham*.

Beckford (village, Worcs): '(place by) Becca's ford'. OE *ford*, 'ford'. The ford in question was probably over the Carrant Brook here. 803 *Beccanford*, DB *Beceford*.

Beckhampton (village, Wilts): 'home farm by the ridge'. OE *bæc*, 'ridge' (modern English *back*), + *hām-tūn*, 'homestead' (from *hām*, 'homestead', + *tūn*, 'farmstead'). The ridge in question is probably the long, narrow one to the west of the village. DB *Bachentune*.

Beckingham (village, Lincs): 'homestead of Becca's people'. OE *-inga-*, 'of the people of', + *hām*, 'homestead'. 1177 *Bekingeham*. SO ALSO: *Beckingham*, Notts.

Beckington (village, Somerset): 'estate associated with Becca'. OE *-ing-*, 'associated with', + *tūn*, 'farmstead', 'estate'. DB *Bechintone*.

Beckley (village, Oxon): 'Becca's woodland clearing'. OE *lēah*, 'wood', 'clearing'. 1005 *Beccalege*, DB *Bechelie*.

Beckton (district, Newham): 'Beck's town'. The name is that of Simon Adams Beck, governor of the Gas, Light and Coke Company by the Thames here in 1869.

Becontree (district, Barking & Dag): 'Beohha's tree'. OE *trēow*, 'tree'. The 'tree' would have served as the assembly point for the hundred (in what is now Becontree Heath). The DB form of the name below is garbled. DB *Beuentreu*, 12C *Begintre*.

Bedale (town, N Yorks): 'Bēda's corner of land'. OE *halh*, 'nook', 'corner of land'. The 'corner of land' is in a bend of Bedale Beck here. DB *Bedale*.

Bedburn (hamlet, Durham): '(place by) Bēda's stream'. OE *burna*, 'stream'. 1291 *Bedburn*.

Beddgelert (village, Gwynedd): 'Celert's grave'. Welsh *bedd*, 'grave'. Local legend derives the personal name from Gelert, a hound slain by its master, Prince Llewellyn, when he thought it had killed his baby son, although it had actually killed a wolf that threatened the child. The poignant tale was popularized in the 18C, when a commemorative stone was erected on the supposed site of the dog's grave. 1281 *Bedkelert*.

Beddingham (village, E Sussex): 'promontory of Bēada's people'. OE *-inga-*, 'of the people of', + *hamm*, 'enclosure', 'promontory'. Beddingham lies on a low, narrow promontory by a tributary of the river Ouse. c.800 *Beadyngham*, DB *Bedingeham*.

Beddington (district, Sutton): 'estate associated with Beadda'. OE *-ing-*, 'associated with', + *tūn*, 'farmstead', 'estate'. 901 *Beaddinctun*, DB *Beddintone*.

Bedfield (village, Suffolk): 'Bēda's open land'. OE *feld*, 'open land' (modern English *field*). The DB form of the name below has an extraneous *r*. DB *Berdefelda*, 12C *Bedefeld*.

Bedford (town, Beds): '(place by) Bīeda's ford'. OE *ford*, 'ford'. The ford would have been an important crossing of the river Ouse here. 880 *Bedanford*, DB *Bedeford*.

Bedford Level (fenland region, Cambs/Peterborough). In 1631 Francis Russell, 4th Earl of Bedford (1593–1641), undertook to drain the extensive fenland area here, now comprising the *North Level* between the rivers Welland and Nene, *Middle Level*, between the Nene and the New Bedford River, and *South Level*, between the New Bedford River and Brandon. *Level* means simply 'level stretch of land'. 1632 *the Great Level of the Fens*, 1661 *Bedford levell*.

Bedford Park (district, Ealing). The district was built as a garden suburb in the 1870s and named to commemorate the dukes of Bedford, who had a residence here in the 17C.

Bedfordshire (county, S central England): 'district based on Bedford'. OE *scīr*, 'shire', 'district'. See BEDFORD. 11C *Bedanfordscir*.

Bedhampton (district of Havant, Hants): 'farmstead of the dwellers where beet is grown'. OE *bēte*, 'beet', + *hǣme*, 'inhabitants', 'dwellers' (related modern English *home*), + *tūn*, 'farmstead'. DB *Betametone*.

Bedingfield (village, Suffolk): 'open land of Bēda's people'. OE *-inga-*, 'of the people of', + *feld*, 'open land' (modern English *field*). DB *Bedingefelda*.

Bedlington (town, Northd): 'estate associated with Bēdla or Bētla'. OE *-ing-*, 'associated with', + *tūn*, 'estate'. c.1050 *Bedlingtun*.

Bednall (village, Staffs): 'Bēda's corner of land'. OE *halh*, 'nook', 'corner of land'. DB *Bedehala*.

Bedruthan Steps (beach, Cornwall). The sandy beach is reached by steps down from the farm of *Bedruthan*, 'Rudhynn's dwelling' (Cornish *bod*, 'dwelling'). 1335 *Bodruthyn*, 1851 *Bodrothan Steps*.

Bedstone (village, Shropshire): 'Bedgēat's farmstead'. OE *tūn*, 'farmstead', 'estate'. DB *Betietetune*.

Bedwas (town, Caerphilly): 'grove of birch trees'. Welsh *bedwos*, 'birch grove'. c.1102 *Bedewas*.

Bedworth (town, Warwicks): 'Bēda's enclosure'. OE *worth*, 'enclosure'. William Dugdale has a fair interpretation in *The Antiquities of Warwickshire* (1656): 'As for the name therof, I conceive it did originally proceed from one that possest it in the Saxons time, whose name was *Bede*; the late sillable *worth*, signifying a habitation. In Domesday-book it is written *Bedeword*, the *d* wanting a stroke through it, which with the Saxons stood for *th*'. DB *Bedeword*.

Bedwyn (village, Wilts): 'place where bindweed grows'. OE *bedwinde*, 'bindweed', 'convolvulus'. The name may really be that of the stream here, from Celtic words related to modern Welsh *bedw*, 'birch', and *gwyn*, 'white', but it is more likely the stream took its name from that of the village. It is properly *Great Bedwyn*, for distinction from nearby *Little Bedwyn*. 778 *Bedewinde*, DB *Bedvinde*.

Beeby (hamlet, Leics): 'farmstead where bees are kept'. OE *bēo*, 'bee', + OS *bý*, 'farmstead', 'village'. DB *Bebi*.

Beechingstoke (village, Wilts): 'outlying farmstead where bitches are kept'. OE *bicce*, 'bitch', + *stoc*, 'outlying farmstead'. The hounds would have been used for breeding as well as hunting. 941 *Stoke*, DB *Bichenestoch*.

Beedon (village, W Berks): '(place at the) tub-shaped valley'. OE *byden*, 'vessel', 'tub', 'hollow'. The reference is to the deep, narrow valley below the village. 965 *Bydene*, DB *Bedene*.

Beeford (village, E Yorks): '(place) by the ford'. OE *bī*, 'by', + *ford*, 'ford'. The name could also mean '(place by the) ford where bees are kept' (OE *bēo*, 'bee', + *ford*). DB *Biuuorde*.

Beeley (village, Derbys): 'Bēage's or Bēga's woodland clearing'. OE *lēah*, 'wood', 'clearing'. Bēage is a woman's name, Bēga a man's. DB *Begelie*.

Beelsby (village, NE Lincs): 'Beli's farmstead'. OS *bý*, 'farmstead', 'village'. The personal name is Scandinavian. DB *Belesbi*.

Beer (resort village, Devon): '(place by the) grove'. OE *bearu*, 'grove', 'wood'. DB *Bera*.

Beer Crocombe (village, Somerset): 'Craucombe's (estate by the) grove'. OE *bearu*, 'grove'. The first word of the name could also represent OE *bǣr*, 'woodland pasture'. The Craucombe family held the manor here in the 13C. DB *Bere*.

Beer Hackett (village, Dorset): 'Haket's (estate by the) grove'. OE *bearu*, 'grove'. The first word of the name could also represent OE *bǣr*, 'woodland pasture'. One Haket held the manor here in the 12C. 1176 *Bera*, 1362 *Berhaket*.

Beeston (hamlet, Cheshire): 'rock where trading is done'. OE *byge*, 'traffic', 'commerce' (related modern English *buy*), + *stān*, 'stone', 'rock'. The name implies that the crag on which Beeston Castle stands was at one time an active commercial centre. DB *Buistane*.

Beeston (town, Notts): 'farmstead where bents grow'. OE *bēos*, 'bent grass', 'rough grass', + *tūn*, 'farmstead'. Bents have a practical use for pasture and thatching. DB *Bestune*. SO ALSO: *Beeston*, Beds, Leeds, Norfolk.

Beetham (village, Cumbria): '(place by the) embankments'. OS *beth*, 'embankment', 'river bank'. The name represents *bjothum*, the dative plural form of the OS word. The reference is to the built-up banks of the river Beela here, whose own name is based on the same word. DB *Biedun*.

Beetley (village, Norfolk): 'clearing where beet is grown'. OE *bēte*, 'beet', + *lēah*, 'wood', 'clearing'. DB *Betellea*.

Begbroke (village, Oxon): '(place by) Becca's brook'. OE *brōc*, 'brook'. DB *Bechebroc*.

Beggearn Huish. See HUISH CHAMPFLOWER.

Beighton (village, Norfolk): 'Bēage's or Bǣga's farmstead'. OE *tūn*, 'farmstead'. The first personal name is that of a woman, the second of a man. DB *Begetuna*.

Beighton (district, Sheffield): 'farmstead by the stream'. OE *bece*, 'stream', + *tūn*, 'farmstead'. c.1002 *Bectune*.

Beith (town, N Ayrs): '(place of) birches'. Gaelic *beith*, 'birch'. Cp. COWDENBEATH.

Belaugh (village, Norfolk): 'enclosure where the dead are cremated'. OE *bēl*, 'fire', 'funeral pyre', + *haga*, 'enclosure' (related modern English *hedge*). DB *Belaga*.

Belbroughton (village, Worcs): 'farmstead on the brook (called) Bell'. OE *brōc*, 'brook', + *tūn*, 'farmstead'. *Bell* and *Broughton* were originally two separate names. *Bell* is the former name of the brook here, perhaps meaning 'henbane' (OE *beolone*). The name survives in *Bell Hall*, *Bell Heath*, *Bell End* and *Bell Mill*, places through which the brook passes before it reaches Belbroughton. *Bell* had early forms 817 *Beolne*, DB *Bellem*, while *Broughton* had 817 *Broctun*, DB *Brocton*. They are merged as now in 1292 *Bellebrocton*.

Belchamp Otten (village, Essex): 'Otto's homestead with a beamed roof'. OE *belc*, 'beam' (related modern English *baulk*), + *hām*, 'homestead'. The manor here was held by one Otto, whose name distinguishes this village from nearby *Belchamp St Paul*, belonging to St Paul's Cathedral, London, and *Belchamp Walter*, held by one Walter. *c*.940 *Bylcham*, DB *Belcham*, 1256 *Belcham Otes*.

Belford (village, Northd): 'ford by the bell hill'. OE *belle*, 'bell', + *ford*, 'ford'. A 'bell hill' is a hill shaped like a bell. The ford is over a small stream that joins the Elwick Burn about a mile from the town. 1242 *Beleford*.

Belgravia (district, Westminster): '(place of) Belgrave'. *Belgrave*, an estate in Cheshire, was the property of the dukes of Westminster, who owned much of what is now Belgravia. The Cheshire place was originally *Merdegrave*, 'grove of martens' (OE *mearth*, 'marten'), but the name was taken to derive from French *merde*, 'dung', and for reasons of propriety changed to *Belgrave*, as if meaning 'beautiful grove' (French *bel*, 'beautiful'). The London district was developed from the 1820s.

Belle Isle (island, Cumbria): 'beautiful island'. French *belle*, 'beautiful', + *isle*, 'island'. The Windermere island was purchased in 1781 by Isabella Curwen, who may in part have named it punningly after her own first name. It was earlier known simply as *The Island*, as the largest in the lake, or as *The Holme* (OS *holmr*, 'island').

Bellerby (village, N Yorks): 'Belgr's farmstead'. OS *bý*, 'farmstead', 'village'. The personal name is Scandinavian. DB *Belgebi*.

Bellingham (district, Lewisham): 'homestead of Bera's people'. OE *-inga-*, 'of the people of', + *hām*, 'homestead'. The *r* of the personal name has become *l*, as with SALISBURY. 998 *Beringaham*, 1198 *Belingeham*.

Bellingham (town, Northd): 'homestead of the dwellers at the bell hill'. OE *belle*, 'bell', + *-inga-*, 'of the dwellers at', + *hām*, 'homestead'. A 'bell hill' is a hill shaped like a bell. Cp. BELFORD. The name could also mean 'homestead at the bell hill' (OE *-ing*, 'place characterized by'). 1254 *Bellingham*.

Belmesthorpe (hamlet, Rutland): 'Beornhelm's outlying farmstead'. OS *thorp*, 'outlying farmstead'. *c*.1050 *Beolmesthorp*, DB *Belmestorp*.

Belmont (village, Blackburn with Dar): 'beautiful hill'. OF *bel*, 'beautiful', + *mont*, 'hill'. 1212 *Belmunt*.

Belmont (district, Sutton): 'beautiful hill'. The name, of the same ultimate origin as BELMONT, Blackburn with Dar, was applied arbitrarily in the early 19C to a district formerly known as *Little Hell*.

Belper (town, Derbys): 'beautiful retreat'. OF *beau*, 'beautiful', + *repaire*, 'retreat' (modern English *repair*, 'haunt', 'resort'). The Norman barons sometimes gave grand names to their country seats. 1231 *Beurepeir*.

Belsay (village, Northd): 'Bil's hill spur'. OE *hōh*, 'hill spur'. 1163 *Bilesho*.

Belstead (village, Suffolk): 'place in a glade'. OE *bel*, 'glade' (literally 'interval'), + *stede*, 'place'. The name could also mean 'place of a funeral pyre' (OE *bēl*, 'fire', + *stede*). DB *Belesteda*.

Belstone (village, Devon): (place at the) bell-shaped stone'. OE *belle*, 'bell', + *stān*, 'stone'. According to Sabine Baring-Gould's *Devon* (1907) in the *Little Guide Series*: 'The bellstone was a remarkably fine logan rock that rolled like a ship in a gale ... It has been thrown down and broken up by quarrymen'. The DB form of the name below has *m* for *n*. DB *Bellestam*, 1167 *Bellestan*.

Belton (village, Lincs): 'farmstead on dry ground in marshland'. OE *bel*, 'dry ground in fen', + *tūn*, 'farmstead', 'village'. DB *Beltone*. SO ALSO: *Belton*, N Lincs.

Belton (village, Norfolk): 'farmstead in a glade'. OE *bel*, 'glade' (literally 'interval'), + *tūn*, 'farmstead'. The same source could give a meaning 'farmstead on dry ground in marshland'. The name could also mean 'farmstead near a beacon' (OE *bēl*, 'fire', + *tūn*) or, from the same source, 'farmstead near a funeral pyre'. DB *Beletuna*. SO ALSO: *Belton*, Leics, Rutland.

Belvedere (district, Bexley): 'beautiful view'. OF *bel*, 'beautiful', + *vedeir*, 'view'. Cp. BELVOIR. The 'beautiful view' is the one from Lessness Heath, where a mansion named 'Belvedere' was built in *c*.1740 to enjoy the prospect over the Thames.

Belvoir (hamlet, Leics): '(place with a) beautiful view'. OF *bel*, 'beautiful', + *vedeir*, 'view'. The hamlet is noted for Belvoir Castle, which stands on a hill on the south side of the Vale of Belvoir, over which it commands a panoramic prospect. 1130 *Belveder*.

Bembridge (resort town, IoW): '(place lying) inside the bridge'. OE *binnan*, 'within', + *brycg*, 'bridge'. 'Inside the bridge' means this side of it. The town is on a peninsula that at one time must have been reached by a bridge across the entrance to what is now Bembridge Harbour. 1316 *Bynnebrygg*.

Bemerton (district of Salisbury, Wilts): 'farmstead of the trumpeters'. OE *bȳmere*, 'trumpeter', + *tūn*, 'farmstead'. This is the traditional (and unlikely) explanation of the name, but the 'trumpeter' may actually be a bird, as the OE word is related to modern English *boomer*, a name for the bittern. The sense would then be 'farmstead where bitterns are heard'. DB *Bimertone*.

Bempton (village, E Yorks): 'farmstead made of beams'. OE *bēam*, 'tree trunk', 'timber beam', + *tūn*, 'farmstead'. DB *Bentone*.

Benacre (hamlet, Suffolk): 'cultivated land where beans are grown'. OE *bēan*, 'bean', + *æcer*, 'cultivated land' (modern English *acre*). DB *Benagra*.

Benbecula (island, W Isles): 'hill of the fords'. Gaelic *beinn-na-fhaodla*, 'hill of the fords'. The island has many lochs and streams, and fords would have been common. 1449 *Beanbeacla*.

Ben Cruachan (mountain, Argyll & Bute): 'mountain of the stacks'. Gaelic *beinn*, 'mountain', + *cruach*, 'pile', 'stack'. The name refers to the mountain's rugged appearance, with peaks of different heights. *c.*1375 *Crechanben*.

Benefield. See UPPER BENEFIELD.

Benenden (village, Kent): 'woodland pasture associated with Bionna'. OE *-ing-*, 'associated with', + *denn*, 'woodland pasture'. The name denotes a place where pigs could feed on acorns. 993 *Bingdene*, DB *Benindene*.

Benfleet. See SOUTH BENFLEET.

Bengeo (district of Hertford, Herts): 'hill spur of the dwellers by the (river) Beane'. OE *-ingas*, 'dwellers at', + *hōh*, 'hill spur'. The river has a pre-English name of uncertain meaning. DB *Belingehou*, 1378 *Bengeho*.

Benhall Green (village, Suffolk): 'corner of land where beans are grown'. OE *bēanen*, 'growing with beans', + *halh*, 'nook', 'corner of land'. Benhall later became associated with its village green. DB *Benenhala*.

Benhilton (district, Sutton): 'hill where beans grow'. OE *bēan*, 'bean', + *hyll*, 'hill'. The final '-ton' is a later addition, perhaps from SUTTON, as if 'Benhill in Sutton'. 1392 *Benhull*.

Beningbrough (hamlet, N Yorks): 'stronghold associated with Beonna'. OE *-ing-*, 'associated with', + *burh*, 'fortified place'. DB *Benniburg*.

Benington (village, Herts): 'farmstead by the (river) Beane'. OE *-ing-*, 'associated with', + *tūn*, 'farmstead'. For the river name, see BENGEO. DB *Benintone*.

Benington (village, Lincs): 'farmstead associated with Beonna'. OE *-ing-*, 'associated with', + *tūn*, 'farmstead'. 12C *Benigtun*.

Benllech (resort village, Anglesey): '(place by the) head of the stone'. Welsh *pen*, 'head', 'top', + *llech*, 'flat stone'. The reference is to the flat capstone of a cromlech, which gave the name of a farm here, *Tyddyn y Benllech* ('cottage of the capstone'). The farm then gave the name of the 18C village.

Ben Lomond. See LOMOND.

Ben More (mountain, Stirling): 'big mountain'. Gaelic *beinn*, 'mountain', + *mór*, 'big'. The mountain is the highest in this part of the Grampians. The name is also found elsewhere.

Bennacott (hamlet, Cornwall): 'Bynna's cottage'. OE *cot*, 'cottage'. 1201 *Bennacote*, 1302 *Bunacote*.

Ben Nevis (mountain, Highland): 'mountain by the (river) Nevis'. Gaelic *beinn*, 'mountain'. The river's name means 'spiteful' (Gaelic *nemess*), alluding to its evil reputation in Gaelic folklore. The form of the name below refers to its valley. 16C *Gleann Nibheis*.

Ben Rhydding (district of Ilkley, Bradford): 'Ben's clearing'. OE *rydding*, 'clearing'. The name is first recorded on an Ordnance Survey map of 1858 and caught on when the place developed as an inland health resort. It was formerly known as *Wheatley*, 'clearing where wheat is grown' (OE *hwǣte*, 'wheat', + *lēah*, 'clearing').

Benson (village, Oxon): 'estate associated with Benesa'. OE *-ing-*, 'associated with', + *tūn*, 'farmstead', 'estate'. *c.*900 *Bænesingtun*, DB *Besintone*, 1868 *Bensington, or Benson*.

Benthall (hamlet, Shropshire): 'corner of land where bents grow'. OE *beonet*, 'bent', + *halh*, 'nook', 'corner of land'. 12C *Benethala*.

Bentley (district, Doncaster): 'woodland clearing where bents grow'. OE *beonet*, 'bent', + *lēah*, 'wood', 'clearing'. DB *Benedleia*. SO ALSO: *Bentley*, E Yorks, Hants.

Ben Vorlich (mountain, Argyll & Bute): 'mountain of the sea bag'. Gaelic *beinn*, 'mountain', + *murbhlag* (from *mur*, 'sea', + *lag*, 'bag'). A 'sea bag' is a sea inlet shaped like a sack, as here at the head of Loch Lomond. *Ben Vorlich*, Perth & Kin, south of Loch Earn, has a name of the same origin.

Benwell (district of Newcastle upon Tyne, Newcastle): '(place) within the wall'. OE *binnan*, 'within', + *wall*, 'wall'. Benwell lies between Hadrian's Wall and the river Tyne, west of Newcastle city centre. The Roman fort here was *Condercum*, a name of Celtic origin meaning '(place with a) wide view'. *c.*1050 *Bynnewalle*.

Benwick (village, Cambs): 'farm where beans are grown'. OE *bēan*, 'bean', + *wīc*, 'specialized farm'. The first part of the name could also represent OE *bēam*, 'tree trunk', in which case the meaning would be 'farm by a tree trunk'. 1221 *Beymwich*.

Beoley (village, Worcs): 'wood or clearing where bees swarm'. OE *bēo*, 'bee', + *lēah*, 'wood', 'clearing'. 972 *Beoleah*, DB *Beolege*.

Bepton (village, W Sussex): 'estate associated with Bebbe or Bebba'. OE *-ing-*, 'associated with', + *tūn*, 'farmstead', 'estate'. The personal names are respectively those of a woman and a man. The original *-ing-* has disappeared from the name. DB *Babintone*.

Berden (village, Essex): 'valley with a woodland pasture'. OE *bær*, 'woodland pasture', + *denu*, 'valley'. DB *Berdane*.

Bere Alston (town, Devon): 'Ælfhelm's farmstead belonging to Bere'. OE *tūn*, 'farmstead'. *Bere* is Bere Ferrers, 'de Ferers' woodland pasture' (from William de Ferers, who held the manor here in the 13C), 2½ miles to the south. 1339 *Alphameston*, *c.*1450 *Berealmiston*.

Bere Ferrers. See BERE ALSTON.

Bere Regis (village, Dorset): 'royal wood'. OE *bearu*, 'grove', + Latin *regis*, 'of the king'. Bere was a royal manor in Norman times, while the wood was a royal forest. DB *Bere*, 1264 *Kyngesbyre*.

Berkeley (village, Glos): 'birch wood or clearing'. OE *beorc*, 'birch', + *lēah*, 'wood', 'clearing'. 824 *Berclea*, DB *Berchelai*.

Berkhamsted (town, Herts): 'homestead by a hill'. OE *beorg*, 'hill', + *hām-stede*, 'homestead'. Berkhamsted lies in a gap of the Chiltern Hills. The town was at one time known as *Great Berkhamsted* for distinction from LITTLE BERKHAMSTED, 19 miles to the east, where the name has a different origin. 10C *Beorhthanstædæ*, DB *Berchehamstede*, 1580 *Great Barkhamstead*.

Berkley (village, Somerset): 'birch wood or clearing'. OE *beorc*, 'birch', + *lēah*, 'wood', 'clearing'. DB *Berchelei*.

Berkshire (historic county, central S England): 'district of the hilly place'. The first part of the name derives from a Celtic word related to modern Irish *barr*, 'hill'. The second is OE *scīr*, 'shire', 'district'. A hill named *Berroc*, recorded in the 9C, was probably one near Hungerford. The county name is unusual in not deriving from that of a town (as *Lincolnshire* from *Lincoln*, *Wiltshire* from *Wilton*, etc.). It is now represented by the unitary authority of *West Berkshire*. 893 *Berrocscire*.

Berkswell (village, Solihull): 'Beorcol's spring'. OE *wella*, 'spring', 'stream'. William Dugdale, in *The Antiquities of Warwickshire* (1656), writes of the village 'having that denomination (as I guess) from the large spring which boileth up on the south side of the Churchyard'. DB *Berchewelle*.

Bermo, Y. See BARMOUTH.

Bermondsey (district, Southwark): 'Beornmund's island'. OE *ēg*, 'island'. The 'island' is the area of higher dry ground beside the lower marshy bank of the Thames here. The first form of the name below has *V-* in error for *B-*. *c.*712 *Vermundesei*, DB *Bermundesye*.

Berners Roding. See RODINGS.

Berrick Salome (village, Oxon): 'de Suleham's (estate at the) barley farm'. OE *bere-wīc* (see BERWICK-UPON-TWEED). The OE word later had the meaning 'outlying part of an estate' and this could apply here. The de Suleham family held the manor early here, as they did at BRITWELL SALOME, 3 miles to the east. DB *Berewiche*, 1571 *Berwick Sullame*.

Berrier (hamlet, Cumbria): 'shieling on a hill'. OS *berg*, 'hill', + *erg*, 'shieling', 'pasture'. 1166 *Berghgerge*.

Berrington (hamlet, Northd): '(place by the) hill with a fort'. OE *burh*, 'fortified place', + *dūn*, 'hill'. The 'fort' is an old camp nearby. 1208 *Berigdon*.

Berrington (hamlet, Shropshire): 'farmstead with a fort'. OE *burh*, 'fortified place', + *tūn*, 'farmstead'. The '-ing-' of the name represents the ending of OE *byrig*, the dative form of *burh*. DB *Beritune*.

Berrow (resort village, Somerset): '(place by the) mounds'. OE *beorg*, 'hill', 'mound'. The 'mounds' are the sand dunes here by the Bristol Channel. 973 *Burgh*, 1196 *Berges*.

Berrow Green (hamlet, Worcs): '(place by the) mound'. OE *beorg*, 'hill', 'mound'. Berrow later became associated with its green. 1275 *Berga*.

Berrylands (district, Kingston): 'tract of arable land by a hill'. OE *beorg*, 'hill', + *land*, 'arable land'. The name was originally that of a farm here. 1241 *La Bergh*, 1439 *Le Berowe*.

Berrynarbor (village, Devon): 'Nerebert's (place at the) fortification'. OE *burh*, 'fortified place'. The original fortification here was probably on the site where the medieval castle was built. The Nerebert family held the manor here in the 13C. The personal name has been misdivided in the last two forms of the name below. *c.*1150 *Biria*, 1244 *Bery Narberd*, 1394 *Byry in Arberd*, 1868 *Berryn-Arbor*.

Berry Pomeroy (village, Devon): 'de Pomerei's (estate by the) fortification'. OE *burh*, 'fortified place'. The original fortification was probably on the site where the (now ruined) 13C castle was built. The de Pomerei family held the manor here in the 11C. DB *Beri*, 1281 *Bury Pomery*.

Berwick Bassett (village, Wilts): 'Basset's barley farm'. OE *bere-wīc* (see BERWICK-UPON-TWEED). The Basset family held the manor here in the 13C. 1168 *Berwicha*, 1321 *Berewykbasset*.

Berwick St James. See BERWICK ST LEONARD.

Berwick St John. See BERWICK ST LEONARD.

Berwick St Leonard (village, Wilts): 'barley farm with St Leonard's church'. OE *bere-wīc* (see BERWICK-UPON-TWEED). The church dedication distinguishes the village from *Berwick St John*, 7 miles to the southeast, and *Berwick St James*, 10 miles to the northeast. 12C *Berewica*, 1291 *Berewyk Sancti Leonardi*.

Berwick-upon-Tweed (town, Northd): 'barley farm on the (river) Tweed'. OE *bere-wīc* (from *bere*, 'barley', + *wīc*, 'specialized farm'). A 'barley farm' was a farm outlying from a more important place, such as a manor. The river name, of Celtic origin and perhaps meaning 'powerful one', was added to distinguish this Berwick from NORTH BERWICK, E Lothian, 35 miles to the northwest. 1167 *Berewich*, 1229 *Berewicum super Twedam*.

Besford (village, Worcs): 'Betti's ford'. OE *ford*, 'ford'. The ford would have been over the river Avon here. The DB form of the name below has omitted the second part of the personal name. 972 *Bettesford*, DB *Beford*.

Bessacarr (district, Doncaster): 'cultivated plot where bents grow'. OE *bēos*, 'bent grass', 'rough grass', + *æcer*, 'plot of land' (modern English *acre*). 1182 *Beseacra*.

Bessels Leigh (hamlet, Oxon): 'Besyles' (estate by the) woodland clearing'. OE *lēah*, 'wood', 'clearing'. The Besyles family held the manor here in the 15C. DB *Leie*, 1538 *Bessilles Lee*.

Bessingham (village, Norfolk): 'homestead of Basa's people'. OE *-inga-*, 'of the people of', + *hām*, 'homestead'. DB *Basingeham*.

Besthorpe (village, Notts): 'Bøsi's outlying farmstead'. OS *thorp*, 'outlying farmstead'. The personal name is Scandinavian. The name could also mean 'outlying farmstead where bents grow' (OE *bēos*, 'bent grass', + *thorp*). 1147 *Bestorp*. SO ALSO: *Besthorpe*, Norfolk.

Beswick (village, E Yorks): 'Bøsi's or Bessi's dairy farm'. OE *wīc*, 'dwelling', 'dairy farm'. The personal names are Scandinavian. DB *Basewic*.

Betchworth (village, Surrey): 'Becci's enclosure'. OE *worth*, 'enclosure'. DB *Becesworde*.

Bethersden (village, Kent): 'Beadurīc's woodland pasture'. OE *denn*, 'woodland pasture'. *c.*1100 *Baedericesdaenne*.

Bethesda (town, Gwynedd). The town arose in the 19C around a Welsh Nonconformist chapel built in 1820 that was named after the biblical pool where Jesus healed the sick (John 5:1–9). There are other places of the name in Wales.

Bethnal Green (district, Tower Hamlets): 'Blītha's corner of land'. OE *halh*, 'nook', 'corner of land'. The original settlement later became associated with its village green. 13C *Blithehale*, 1443 *Blethenalegrene*.

Betley (village, Staffs): 'Bette's woodland clearing'. OE *lēah*, 'wood', 'clearing'. The personal name is that of a woman. DB *Betelege*.

Bettiscombe (village, Dorset): 'Betti's valley'. OE *cumb*, 'valley'. 1129 *Bethescomme*.

Betton Abbots (hamlet, Shropshire): 'farmstead of the abbot where beech trees grow'. OE *bēce*, 'beech', + *tūn*, 'farmstead'. The manor here was held early by Shrewsbury Abbey. The second word of the name distinguishes this Betton from nearby *Betton Strange*, held in the 12C by Hamon le Strange. DB *Betune*, 1271 *Bettone Abbatis*.

Bettws-y-Crwyn (hamlet, Shropshire): 'chapel by the pigsty'. Welsh *betws*, 'chapel', + *y*, 'the', + *crowyn*, 'sty', 'shed'. 1256 *Betteus*, 1811 *Bettws y Crewin*.

Bettyhill (village, Highland): 'Betty's hill'. The settlement here was set up in *c.*1820 to house crofters evicted from Strathnaver during the Highland Clearances and named in honour of Elizabeth, Countess of Sutherland and Marchioness of Stafford (1765–1839).

Betws-y-Coed (town, Conwy): 'chapel in the wood'. Welsh *betws*, 'chapel', + *y*, 'the', + *coed*, 'wood'. Welsh *betws* is borrowed from OE *bed-hūs*, 'oratory', literally 'prayer house'. 1254 *Betus*, 1727 *Bettws y Coed*.

Bevercotes (hamlet, Notts): 'beavers' dwellings'. OE *beofor*, 'beaver', + *cot*, 'cottage', 'shelter'. The name denotes a place where beavers have built their nests. 1165 *Beurecote*.

Beverley (town, E Yorks): '(place by the) beaver lodge'. Formerly regarded as OE, the name is now believed to be of Celtic origin, from words related to OC *befer*, 'beaver', and obsolete modern Welsh *llech*, 'covert', the latter later being confused with OE *lēah*, 'wood' (cp. BEWERLEY). *c.*1025 *Beferlic*, DB *Bevreli*.

Beverston (village, Glos): 'Beofor's stone'. OE *stān*, 'stone'. The reference is probably to a boundary stone here. DB *Beurestane*.

Bewaldeth (hamlet, Cumbria): 'Aldgȳth's homestead'. OS *bú*, 'homestead', 'estate'. The order of the two parts of the name is Celtic, with the woman's personal name following the common noun. 1255 *Bualdith*.

Bewcastle (village, Cumbria): 'Roman fort with shelters'. OS *búth*, 'shelter' (modern English *booth*), + OE *ceaster*, 'Roman station'. The name implies that materials from the former Roman fort here were used to build shelters for sheep or shepherds. The fort itself was *Fanum Cocidi*, 'temple of Cocidius', after the war god of the Celts. 12C *Bothecastre*.

Bewdley (town, Worcs): 'beautiful place'. OF *beau*, 'beautiful', + *lieu*, 'place'. Bewdley lies on the river Severn and is described in Philemon Holland's translation (1610) of William Camden's *Britannia* (1586) as 'worthily so called for the Beautifull site thereof'. Cp. BEAULIEU. 1275 *Beuleu*.

Bewerley (village, N Yorks): 'woodland clearing where beavers are seen'. OE *beofor*, 'beaver', + *lēah*, 'wood', 'clearing'. DB *Beurelie*.

Bewholme (village, E Yorks): '(place by the) river bends'. OE *bēag*, 'ring', 'circle', or OS *bjúgr*, 'river bend'. The name represents either OE *bēagum* or OS *bjúgum*, the respective dative plural forms of *bēag* and *bjúgr*. There are several streams with winding courses round the village. DB *Begun*.

Bewley Castle (ruined castle, Cumbria): 'beautiful place'. OF *beau*, 'beautiful', + *lieu*, 'place'. The castle, near Appleby, was built in the 13C as a residence of the bishops of Carlisle. Hugh, Abbot of BEAULIEU, Hants, became Bishop of Carlisle in 1218 and so probably gave the name of the abbey to this place. The form of the name below is the Latin equivalent. 1250 *Bellum locum*.

Bexhill (resort town, E Sussex): 'wood where box trees grow'. OE *byxe*, 'box', + *lēah*, 'wood', 'clearing'. The misleading '-hill' arose from spellings such as that in the DB form of the name below. The town, which evolved only in the late 19C, is also known for touristic reasons as *Bexhill-on-Sea*. Cp. BEXLEY. 772 *Bixlea*, DB *Bexelei*.

Bexley (borough, Greater London): 'wood where box trees grow'. OE *byxe*, 'box', + *lēah*, 'wood', 'clearing'. 814 *Byxlea*.

Bexleyheath (district, Bexley): 'heath by Bexley'. Remnants of the original heath here still exist to the north of BEXLEY. The present district developed from the early 19C. 1805 *Bexley New Town*, 1876 *Bexley Heath*.

Bexwell (village, Norfolk): '(place by) Bēac's spring'. OE *wella*, 'spring', 'stream'. DB *Bekeswella*.

Beyton (village, Suffolk): 'Bēage's or Bæga's farmstead'. OE *tūn*, 'farmstead'. Bēage is a woman's name, Bæga a man's. DB *Begatona*.

Bibury (village, Glos): 'Bēage's stronghold'. OE *burh*, 'fortified place', 'manor house'. The personal name is that of the daughter of Earl Leppa, to whom land here was granted by the Bishop of Worcester in the 8C. 8C *Beaganbyrig*, DB *Begeberie*.

Bicester (town, Oxon): 'Beorna's fort'. OE *ceaster*, 'Roman station', 'old fort'. The name could also mean 'fort of the warriors', from OE *beorn*, 'nobleman', 'warrior', + *ceaster*. DB *Bernecestre*.

Bickenhall (village, Somerset): 'Bica's hall'. OE *heall*, 'hall'. The first part of the name represents *Bican*, the genitive form of the OE personal name. DB *Bichehalle*.

Bickenhill (village, Solihull): '(place by the) hill with a point'. OE *bica*, 'projection', + *hyll*, 'hill'. DB *Bichehelle*, 1202 *Bikenhulle*.

Bicker (village, Lincs): '(place) by the marsh'. OE *bī*, 'by', + OS *kjarr*, 'marsh'. Bicker is on the edge of fenland. DB *Bichere*.

Bickerstaffe (village, Lancs): 'landing place of the beekeepers'. OE *bīcere*, 'beekeeper', + *stæth*, 'landing place'. The nature of the landing place is uncertain, as Bickerstaffe is not on a river. There may have been a marsh settlement here, with communication made by dugout. Late 12C *Bikerstad*.

Bickerton (hamlet, Cheshire): 'farmstead of the beekeepers'. OE *bīcere*, 'beekeeper', + *tūn*, 'farmstead'. DB *Bicretone*. SO ALSO: *Bickerton*, N Yorks.

Bickford (hamlet, Staffs): '(place by) Bica's ford'. OE *ford*, 'ford'. DB *Bigeford*.

Bickington (village, Devon): 'estate associated with Beocca'. OE *-ing-*, 'associated with', + *tūn*, 'farmstead', 'estate'. The form of the name below relates to Bickington near Ashburton, but Bickington as a suburb of Barnstaple has a name of identical origin. 1107 *Bechintona*.

Bickleigh (village, Devon): 'woodland clearing by a pointed hill'. OE *bica*, 'pointed hill', + *lēah*, 'wood', 'clearing'. The form of the name below relates to Bickleigh near Plymouth, but Bickleigh near Tiverton has a name of identical origin. DB *Bicheleia*.

Bickley (district, Bromley): 'woodland clearing by a pointed hill'. OE *bica*, 'pointed hill', + *lēah*, 'wood', 'clearing'. The original 'pointed hill' may have been that of Goshill Wood. A meaning 'Bica's woodland clearing' has also been proposed. 1279 *Byckeleye*.

Bickley Moss (village, Cheshire): 'woodland clearing by a pointed hill'. OE *bica*, 'pointed hill', + *lēah*, 'wood', 'clearing'. The village later became associated with the nearby peat bog (OE *mos*, 'moss', 'marsh'). DB *Bichelei*.

Bicknacre (village, Essex): 'Bica's cultivated land'. OE *æcer*, 'plot of arable land' (modern English *acre*). 1186 *Bikenacher*.

Bicknoller (village, Somerset): 'Bica's alder tree'. OE *alor*, 'alder'. 'Bickn-' represents *Bican*, the genitive form of the OE personal name. 1291 *Bykenalre*.

Bicknor (hamlet, Kent): '(place on the) slope below the pointed hill'. OE *bica*, 'bill', 'beak', + *ōra*, 'slope'. 1186 *Bikenora*.

Bicton (hamlet, Shropshire): '(place by the) hill with beaks'. OE *bica*, 'bill', 'beak', + *dūn*, 'hill'. Bicton lies in the 'dip' of a long hill with pointed peaks to north and south. DB *Bichetone*.

Bidborough (village, Kent): 'Bitta's hill'. OE *beorg*, 'mound', 'hill'. *c*.1100 *Bitteberga*.

Biddenden (village, Kent): 'woodland pasture associated with Bida'. OE *-ing-*, 'associated with', + *denn*, 'woodland pasture'. 993 *Bidingden*.

Biddestone (village, Wilts): 'Bīedin's or Bīede's farmstead'. OE *tūn*, 'farmstead'. DB *Bedestone*, 1187 *Bedeneston*.

Biddisham (village, Somerset): 'Biddi's homestead or enclosure'. OE *hām*, 'homestead', or *hamm*, 'enclosure'. 1065 *Biddesham*.

Biddlesden (hamlet, Bucks): 'valley with a building'. OE *bythle*, 'building', + *denu*, 'valley'. The name could also mean 'Byttel's valley'. The DB form of the name below is corrupt. DB *Betesdene*, 12C *Bethlesdena*.

Biddlestone (hamlet, Northd): 'valley with a building'. OE *bythle*, 'building', + *denu*, 'valley'. 1242 *Bidlisden*.

Biddulph (town, Staffs): '(place) by the quarry'. OE *bī*, 'by', + *dylf*, 'pit', 'quarry', literally 'diggings' (related modern English *delve*). Stone quarries still exist locally. DB *Bidolf*.

Bideford (town, Devon): '(place by the) ford over the river Byd'. OE *ēa*, 'river', + *ford*, 'ford'. The stream's name is Celtic and of unknown meaning. The river here is the Torridge, and the stream would probably have been a tributary. DB *Bedeford*.

Bidford-on-Avon (village, Warwicks): '(place by the) ford over the river Byd'. OE *ēa*, 'river', + *ford*, 'ford'. The river name, identical to the one behind BIDEFORD, may have originally been that of a tributary of the Avon (see AVON-MOUTH). The first part of the name could also represent OE *byden*, 'tub', 'deep place'. 710 *Budiford*, DB *Bedeford*.

Bidston (district of Birkenhead, Wirral): 'rocky hill with a building'. OE *bythle*, 'building', + *stān*, 'stone', 'rock'. The reference is to Bidston Hill, the steep rocky hill on which Bidston stands. 1260 *Budeston*, 1286 *Budestan*.

Bierley (district, Bradford): 'woodland clearing by the stronghold'. OE *burh*, 'fortified place', + *lēah*, 'wood', 'clearing'. DB *Birle*.

Bierton (village, Bucks): 'farmstead by the stronghold'. OE *byrh-tūn* (from *burh*, 'fortified place', + *tūn*, 'farmstead'). The 'stronghold' would have been nearby AYLESBURY. DB *Bortone*.

Bigbury (resort town, Devon): 'Bica's stronghold'. OE *burh*, 'stronghold'. The town is also known as *Bigbury-on-Sea* to distinguish it from the village of *Bigbury*, 2 miles to the north. DB *Bicheberie*.

Bigby (village, Lincs): 'Bekki's farmstead'. OS *bý*, 'farmstead', 'village'. The personal name is Scandinavian. DB *Bechebi*.

Biggar (town, S Lanarks): '(place by the) barley plot'. OS *bygg*, 'barley', + *geiri*, 'triangular plot of land' (modern English *gore*). Viking names are not uncommon in SE Scotland. 1170 *Bigir*.

Biggin Hill (district, Bromley): 'hill by a building'. ME *bigging*, 'building', + *hull*, 'hill'. The hill in question lies behind the nickname 'Biggin on the Bump' for the World War I aerodrome here. 1499 *Byggunhull*.

Biggleswade (town, Beds): 'Biccel's ford'. OE *wæd*, 'ford' (modern English *wade*). The town is on the river Ivel. The initial *P-* for *B-* in the DB form of the name below may be either a miscopying or the result of a mishearing. DB *Pichelesuuade*, 1132 *Bicheleswada*.

Bignor (village, W Sussex): 'Bicga's hill brow'. OE *yfer*, 'hill brow'. DB *Bigenevre*.

Bilborough (district, Nottingham): 'Bila's or Billa's stronghold'. OE *burh*, 'fortified place'. DB *Bileburch*.

Bilbrook (district of Codsall, Staffs): '(place by the) brook where watercress grows'. OE *billere*, 'water plants', + *brōc*, 'brook'. DB *Bilrebroch*.

Bilbrough (village, N Yorks): 'Bila's or Billa's stronghold'. OE *burh*, 'fortified place'. The DB form of the name below has *M-* for *B-*, probably through a mishearing. DB *Mileburg*, 1167 *Billeburc*.

Bildeston (village, Suffolk): 'Bildr's farmstead'. OE *tūn*, 'farmstead'. The personal name is Scandinavian. The first part of the name could also represent OS *bildr*, 'angle', referring to a hill or promontory here. DB *Bilestuna*.

Billericay (town, Essex): 'dyehouse'. Medieval Latin *bellerica*, 'dyehouse', 'tanhouse'. The meaning of the name had long proved elusive and was determined only in 1983. 1291 *Byllyrica*.

Billesdon (village, Leics): 'Bill's hill'. OE *dūn*, 'hill'. The first part of the name could also represent OE *bill*, 'sword', referring to a pointed hill. DB *Billesdone*.

Billesley (village, Warwicks): 'Bill's woodland clearing'. OE *lēah*, 'wood', 'clearing'. The first part of the name could also represent OE *bill*, 'sword', referring to a pointed hill. 704 *Billeslæh*, DB *Billeslei*.

Billingborough (village, Lincs): 'stronghold of Bill's or Billa's people'. OE *-inga-*, 'of the people of', + *burh*, 'fortified place'. DB *Billingeburg*.

Billinge (town, St Helens): '(place by the) hill'. OE *billing*, 'hill', 'sharp ridge' (from *bill*, 'sword'). The name properly applies to nearby Billinge Hill. 1202 *Billing*.

Billingham (town, Stockton): 'village on the hill'. OE *billing*, 'hill', 'ridge', + *hām*, 'homestead', 'village'. The hill in question is the low one overlooking Billingham Beck on which St Cuthbert's church stands. *c.*1040 *Billingham*.

Billinghay (village, Lincs): 'island of Bill's or Billa's people'. OE *-inga-*, 'of the people of', + *ēg*, 'island'. The 'island' is raised ground in fenland. DB *Belingei*.

Billingley (village, Barnsley): 'woodland clearing of Bill's or Billa's people'. OE *-inga-*, 'of the people of', + *lēah*, 'wood', 'clearing'. DB *Bilingeleia*.

Billingshurst (town, W Sussex): 'Billing's wooded hill'. OE *hyrst*, 'wooded hill'. The first part of the name could also derive from OE *billing*, 'hill' (cp. BILLINGE), although this would produce a tautology. 1202 *Bellingesherst*.

Billingsley (village, Shropshire): 'woodland clearing by Billing'. OE *lēah*, 'wood', 'clearing'. *Billing* is the name of a nearby hill meaning simply 'hill', 'sharp ridge' (OE *bill*, 'sword'). 11C *Billingesle*.

Billington (village, Lancs): '(place by the) hill with a steep ridge'. OE *billing*, 'hill', 'steep ridge', + *dūn*, 'hill'. The reference is to the long ridge to the southeast of the village. 1196 *Billingduna*.

Billockby (hamlet, Norfolk): 'Bithil-Áki's farmstead'. OS *bý*, 'farmstead', 'village'. The personal name (meaning 'Áki the wooer') is Scandinavian. DB *Bithlakebei*.

Bilsington (village, Kent): 'Bilswīth's farmstead'. OE *tūn*, 'farmstead'. The personal name is that of a woman. DB *Bilsvitone*.

Bilsthorpe (village, Notts): 'Bildr's outlying farmstead'. OS *thorp*, 'outlying farmstead'. The personal name is Scandinavian. The first part of the name could also represent OS *bildr*, 'angle', referring to a hill or promontory here. DB *Bildestorp*.

Bilston (district, Wolverhampton): 'farmstead of the dwellers at the sharp ridge'. OE *bill*, 'sharp ridge' (literally 'sword'), + *sǣte*, 'dwellers', 'settlers', + *tūn*, 'farmstead'. The 'sharp ridge' could be the nearby hill. 996 *Bilsetnatun*, DB *Billestune*.

Bilstone (hamlet, Leics): 'Bildr's farmstead'. OE *tūn*, 'farmstead'. The personal name is Scandinavian. The name could also mean 'farmstead at the angle' (OS *bildr*, 'angle'), referring to a hill here. DB *Bildestone*.

Bilton (district of Hull, E Yorks): 'Bill's or Billa's farmstead'. OE *tūn*, 'farmstead'. DB *Billetone*. SO ALSO: *Bilton*, Northd, N Yorks.

Bilton (village, Warwicks): 'farmstead where henbane grows'. OE *beolone*, 'henbane', + *tūn*, 'farmstead'. DB *Beltone*.

Binbrook (village, Lincs): '(place by) Bynna's brook'. OE *brōc*, 'brook'. DB *Binnibroc*.

Binchester (hamlet, Durham): '(settlement) within the Roman fort'. OE *binnan*, 'within', + *ceaster*, 'Roman camp'. The name of the Roman fort here was *Vinovia*, of uncertain meaning. *c.*1040 *Bynceastre*.

Bincombe (village, Dorset): '(place in the) valley where beans are grown'. OE *bēan*, 'bean', + *cumb*, 'valley'. 987 *Beuncumbe*, DB *Beincome*.

Binegar (village, Somerset): 'Bēage's wooded slope'. OE *hangra*, 'wooded slope'. The personal name is that of a woman. The name could also mean 'wooded slope where berries grow' (OE *begen*, 'growing with berries', + *hangra*). The village is situated at the southeastern end of the Mendip Hills. 1065 *Begenhangra*.

Binfield (village, Bracknell F): 'open land where bents grow'. OE *beonet*, 'bent', + *feld*, 'open land' (modern English *field*). *c*.1160 *Benetfeld*.

Bingfield (hamlet, Northd): 'open land of Bynna's people'. OE *-inga-*, 'of the people of', + *feld*, 'open land' (modern English *field*). The first part of the name could also represent OE *bing*, 'hollow'. 1181 *Bingefeld*.

Bingham (village, Notts): 'homestead of Bynna's people'. OE *-inga-*, 'of the people of', + *hām*, 'homestead'. The first part of the name could also represent OE *bing*, 'hollow'. Bingham lies in the Vale of Belvoir. DB *Bingheham*.

Bingley (town, Bradford): 'woodland clearing of Bynna's people'. OE *-inga-*, 'of the people of', + *lēah*, 'wood', 'clearing'. DB *Bingelei*.

Binham (village, Norfolk): 'Bynna's homestead or enclosure'. OE *hām*, 'homestead', or *hamm*, 'enclosure'. DB *Binneham*.

Binley (district, Coventry): 'island by a ridge'. OE *bile*, 'ridge', + *ēg*, 'island'. The 'island' would have been raised land by the river Sowe here. DB *Bilnei*.

Binsey (village, Oxon): 'Byni's island'. The 'island' is raised ground by the river Thames here. 1122 *Beneseye*.

Binstead (district of Ryde, IoW): 'place where beans are grown'. OE *bēan*, 'bean', + *stede*, 'place'. DB *Benestede*.

Binton (village, Warwicks): 'estate associated with Bynna'. OE *-ing-*, 'associated with', + *tūn*, 'farmstead', 'estate'. The original *-ing-* has disappeared from the name. *c*.1005 *Bynningtun*, DB *Beninton*.

Bintree (village, Norfolk): 'Bynna's tree'. OE *trēow*, 'tree'. DB *Binnetre*.

Birch (village, Essex): '(place on) land newly broken up for cultivation'. OE *bryce*, 'breaking'. DB *Briciam*.

Bircham Newton. See GREAT BIRCHAM.

Bircham Tofts. See GREAT BIRCHAM.

Birchanger (village, Essex): 'wooded slope growing with birch trees'. OE *birce*, 'birch', + *hangra*, 'wooded slope'. The DB form of the name below has *l* for *r*. DB *Bilichangra*, 12C *Birichangre*.

Bircher (hamlet, Herefords): '(place by the) ridge where birch trees grow'. OE *birce*, 'birch', + *ofer*, 'ridge'. 1212 *Burchoure*.

Birchington (district of Margate, Kent): 'farmstead where birch trees grow'. OE *bircen*, 'birches', + *tūn*, 'farmstead'. 1240 *Birchenton*.

Birchover (village, Derbys): 'ridge where birch trees grow'. OE *birce*, 'birch', + *ofer*, 'ridge'. The first part of the DB form of the name below is garbled. DB *Barcovere*, 1226 *Birchoure*.

Birdbrook (village, Essex): '(place by the) brook where birds are seen'. OE *bridd*, 'bird', + *brōc*, 'brook'. DB *Bridebroc*.

Birdham (village, W Sussex): 'homestead or enclosure where birds are seen'. OE *bridd*, 'bird', + *hām*, 'homestead', or *hamm*, 'enclosure'. 683 *Bridham*, DB *Brideham*.

Birdlip (village, Glos): 'steep place where birds are seen'. OE *bridd*, 'bird', + *hlēp*, 'steep place' (modern English *leap*). The village stands at the top of a steep hill on the edge of the Cotswolds. 1221 *Bridelepe*.

Birdsall (village, N Yorks): 'Bridd's corner of land'. OE *halh*, 'nook', 'corner of land'. DB *Brideshala*.

Birkby (hamlet, N Yorks): 'farmstead of the Britons'. OS *Bretar*, '(Ancient) Britons', + *bý*, 'farmstead', 'village'. The name implies that men of British descent accompanied Viking settlers here. DB *Bretebi*.

Birkdale (district of Southport, Sefton): '(place in the) valley where birch trees grow'. OS *birki*, 'birch', + *dalr*, 'valley'. *c*.1200 *Birkedale*.

Birkenhead (town and port, Wirral): 'headland where birch trees grow'. OE *birce*, 'birch', + *hēafod*, 'headland'. It is uncertain which headland is meant, but it may have been Bidston Hill (see BIDSTON). The '-k-' of the name is due to Scandinavian influence. *c*.1200 *Bircheveth*, 1294 *Birchinheuid*.

Birkenshaw (suburb of Bradford, Kirklees): 'copse where birch trees grow'. OE *birce*, 'birch', + *sceaga*, 'wood', 'copse'. The '-k-' of the name is due to Scandinavian influence. 1274 *Birkenschawe*.

Birkin (village, N Yorks): '(place) growing with birch trees'. OE *bircen*, 'place overgrown with birches'. The '-k-' of the name is due to Scandinavian influence. *c*.1030 *Byrcene*, DB *Berchine*.

Birley (village, Herefords): 'woodland clearing by a stronghold'. OE *burh*, 'fortified place', + *lēah*, 'wood', 'clearing'. DB *Burlei*.

Birling (village, Kent): '(settlement of) Bærla's people'. OE *-ingas*, 'people of'. 788 *Boerlingas*, DB *Berlinge*. SO ALSO: *Birling*, Northd.

Birlingham (village, Worcs): 'land in a river bend of Byrla's people'. OE *-inga-*, 'of the people of', + *hamm*, 'enclosure', 'land in a river bend'. The village lies in a great bend of the river Avon. 972 *Byrlingahamm*, DB *Berlingeham*.

Birmingham (city, Birmingham): 'homestead of Beorma's people'. OE *-inga-*, 'of the people of', + *hām*, 'homestead'. A variant is 'homestead at the place associated with Beorma' (OE *-ing*, 'place associated with'). English colloquial *Brummagem*, meaning 'cheap and showy', represents a 17C dialect pronunciation, itself doubtless aided through association with the *Bromwich* of nearby CASTLE BROM-WICH and WEST BROMWICH. The origin of the name became a subject of popular speculation on the rise of Birmingham as an industrial centre in the late 18C. The opening lines of John Collins' *A Poetical History of Birmingham* (1796) typify the spirit: 'Of Birmingham's name, tho' a deal has been said, / Yet a little, we doubt, to the purpose, / As when "hocus pocus" was jargon'd instead / Of the Catholic text "*hoc est corpus*." / For it, doubtless, for ages was Bromwicham called, / But historians, their readers to bam [i.e. hoax], / Have Brom, Wich, and Ham so corrupted and maul'd, / That their strictures have all proved a flam [i.e. deceit]. / That Brom implies Broom none will dare to deny, / And that Wich means a Village or Farm; / Or a Slope, or a Saltwork, the last may imply, / And to read Ham for Town is no harm. / But when jumbled together, like stones in a bag, / To make it a Broom-sloping town, / Credulity's pace at such juggling must flag, / And the critic indignant will frown. / Tis so much like the Gazetteer's riddle-my-ree, / Who, untwisting Antiquity's cable, / Makes Barnstaple's town with its name to agree, / Take its rise from a Barn and a Stable.' DB *Bermingeham*.

Birstall (district, Kirklees): 'site of a fort'. OE *byrh-stall* (from *byrh*, genitive singular of *burh*, 'fortified place', + *stall*, 'site'). 12C *Birstale*.

Birstall (district, Leicester): 'site of a fort'. OE *burh*, 'fortified place', + *stall*, 'stall', 'site'. DB *Burstelle*.

Birstwith (village, N Yorks): 'farmstead'. OS *bȳjar-stathr* (from *bȳjar*, genitive of *bȳ*, 'farmstead', + *stathr*, 'place'). The name implies a

farm built on the site of a former farmstead. DB *Beristade*.

Birtley (town, Gateshead): '(place in the) bright clearing'. OE *beorht*, 'bright', + *lēah*, 'wood', 'clearing'. 1183 *Britleia*.

Bisbrooke (village, Rutland): '(place by) Bitel's or Byttel's brook'. OE *brōc*, 'brook'. The name could also mean '(place by the) stream full of water beetles' (OE *bitel*, 'beetle', + *brōc*). DB *Bitlesbroch*.

Bisham (village, Windsor & Maid): 'Byssel's enclosure'. OE *hamm*, 'enclosure'. Cp. MED-MENHAM. DB *Bistesham*, 1199 *Bistlesham*.

Bishampton (village, Worcs): 'Bisa's homestead'. OE *hām-tūn* (from *hām*, 'homestead', + *tūn*, 'farmstead'). DB *Bisantune*.

Bishop Auckland (town, Durham): 'bishop's (estate by the) cliff on the (river) Clyde'. The second word of the name represents a Celtic word meaning 'cliff' related to modern Welsh *allt*, 'hillside', and the Celtic river name *Clyde* (see CLYDEBANK), originally that of the Gaunless here. The present spelling of the name arose because the Vikings associated it with OS *auk-land*, 'additional land'. The first word, referring to the bishops of Durham who had their residence here from the 12C, distinguishes the town from the nearby villages of *St Helen Auck-land*, so called from the dedication of its church, and *West Auckland*, to the west. c.1040 *Alclit*, 1202 *Auclent*, 1254 *Aucland*.

Bishop Burton (village, E Yorks): 'bishop's fortified farmstead'. OE *burh-tūn* (from *burh*, 'fortified place', + *tūn*, 'farmstead'). The manor here was held early by the Archbishop of York, whose title distinguishes this Burton from nearby *Cherry Burton*, where cherry trees grew. Cp. BURTON AGNES. DB *Burton*, 1376 *Bisshop-burton*.

Bishop Monkton. See NUN MONKTON.

Bishop Norton (village, Lincs): 'bishop's northern farmstead'. OE *north*, 'northern', + *tūn*, 'farmstead'. The manor here was held early by Lincoln Cathedral. The farmstead may have been regarded as 'north' in relation to Glentham. DB *Nortune*, 1346 *Byschop Norton*.

Bishop Rock (rock, Scilly). The rock, at the southwestern extremity of the Scilly Isles, is presumably so called from its fancied resemblance to a bishop rather than from any ecclesiastical ownership. The first form of the name below represents the original Cornish (*men*, 'stone', + *an*, 'the', + *escop*, 'bishop'). This was then translated into English and gave the later names, the added words referring to the surrounding smaller rocks. 1302 *Maenenescop*, 1564 *The byshop and hys clerks*, 1779 *Bishop and His Clerks*.

Bishopsbourne   (village, Kent): 'bishop's (estate on the river) Bourne'. The river here now is the Little Stour, but earlier it was the *Bourne* (OE *burna*, 'stream'). The manor here was held early by the Archbishop of Canterbury. 799 *Burnan*, DB *Burnes*, 11C *Biscopesburne*.

Bishops Cannings   (village, Wilts): 'bishop's (estate at the settlement of) Cana's people'. OE -*ingas*, 'people of'. The first word of the name, referring to the early possession of the manor by the Bishop of Salisbury, distinguishes the village from nearby *All Cannings* (OE *eald*, 'old'). DB *Caninge*, 1314 *Bisshopescanyngges*.

Bishop's Castle   (town, Shropshire): 'bishop's castle'. The town takes its name from the castle built here in *c*.1127 by the Bishop of Hereford. The first form of the name below is the Latin equivalent. 1255 *Castrum Episcopi*, 1282 *Bisshopescastel*.

Bishop's Caundle   (village, Dorset): 'bishop's (estate in) Caundle'. *Caundle*, of uncertain meaning, may have been a name for the chain of hills here. The manor at Bishop's Caundle was held early by the Bishop of Salisbury, whose title distinguishes the village from *Purse Caundle*, 3 miles to the north, where the manor was held by the Purse family, and from *Stourton Caundle*, between the two, where the manor was held by the lords Staunton from the 15C until 1727. DB *Candel*, 1294 *Caundel Bishops*.

Bishop's Cleeve   (village, Glos): 'bishop's (estate by the) cliff'. OE *clif*, 'cliff', 'bank'. The 'cliff' is nearby Cleeve Hill, below which the village stands. Cp. CLEEVE HILL. The manor was held early by the Bishop of Worcester. 8C *Clife*, DB *Clive*, 1284 *Bissopes Clive*.

Bishop's Frome   (village, Herefords): 'bishop's (estate on the river) Frome'. The manor here was held by the Bishop of Hereford, whose title distinguishes the village from nearby *Castle Frome*, where there was a Norman castle, from *Canon Frome*, 3 miles to the south, held by the canons of Llanthony, and from *Prior's Frome*, 8 miles to the southwest, belonging to Hereford Priory. The river name has the same origin as that for FROME. The second part of the second form of the name below represents OF *eveske*, 'bishop'. DB *Frome*, 1252 *Frume al Evesk*.

Bishop's Hull   (suburb of Taunton, Somerset): 'bishop's (estate by the) hill'. OE *hyll*. The manor here was held early by the bishops of Winchester. 1033 *Hylle*, DB *Hilla*, 1327 *Hulle Episcopi*.

Bishops Itchington. See LONG ITCHINGTON.

Bishop's Lydeard   (village, Somerset): 'bishop's (estate by the) grey ridge'. The second word of the name is of Celtic origin, as for LYDIARD MILLICENT. The first word, referring to the early possession of the manor by the Bishop of Wells, distinguishes the village from *Lydeard St Lawrence*, 6 miles to the northwest, named for the dedication of its church. 854 *Lidegeard*, DB *Lediart*.

Bishop's Nympton. See KING'S NYMPTON.

Bishop's Offley. See HIGH OFFLEY.

Bishop's Stortford   (town, Herts): 'bishop's (estate at the) ford by the tongues of land'. OE *steort*, 'tail', 'tongue of land', + *ford*, 'ford'. The 'tongues of land' would have been between streams, with a ford needed to cross them. The manor was held early by the Bishop of London. The river Stort here derives its name from that of the town. DB *Storteford*, 1587 *Bysshops Stortford*.

Bishop's Tachbrook   (village, Warwicks): 'bishop's (estate by the) boundary brook'. OE *tæcels*, 'thing that points out' (related modern English *teach*), + *brōc*, 'brook'. The stream on which the village stands formed the boundary between the dioceses of Lichfield and Worcester. The manor here was held by the Bishop of Chester in 1086. 1033 *Tæcelesbroc*, DB *Tacesbroc*, 1511 *Bishops Tachebroke*.

Bishop's Tawton   (village, Devon): 'bishop's village on the (river) Taw'. OE *tūn*, 'farmstead', 'village'. The river has a Celtic name perhaps meaning 'strong one' or 'silent one'. The first word, alluding to the possession of the place by the Bishop of Exeter in 1086, distinguishes this Tawton from *North Tawton* and *South Tawton*, some 20 miles to the south. DB *Tautona*, 1284 *Tautone Episcopi*.

Bishopsteignton   (village, Devon): 'bishop's manor on the (river) Teign'. OE *tūn*, 'manor'. The Bishop of Exeter held the manor here in 1086. Cp. KINGSTEIGNTON. For the river name, see TEIGNMOUTH. DB *Taintona*, 1341 *Teynton Bishops*.

Bishopstone   (village, Bucks): 'bishop's estate'. OE *biscop*, 'bishop', + *tūn*, 'farmstead', 'estate'. The manor here was held (briefly) by the Bishop of Bayeux, France. 1227 *Bissopeston*.

Bishopstone   (village, E Sussex): 'bishop's estate'. OE *biscop*, 'bishop', + *tūn*, 'farmstead', 'estate'. The manor here was held early by the Bishop of Chichester. DB *Biscopestone*.

Bishopstone   (village, Swindon): 'bishop's estate'. OE *biscop*, 'bishop', + *tūn*, 'farmstead', 'estate'. The manor here was held early by the Bishop of Salisbury. 1186 *Bissopeston*.

Bishopstone (village, Wilts): 'bishop's estate'. OE *biscop*, 'bishop', + *tūn*, 'farmstead', 'estate'. The manor here was held early by the Bishop of Winchester. 1166 *Bissopeston*.

Bishopstrow (village, Wilts): 'bishop's tree'. OE *biscop*, 'bishop', + *trēow*, 'tree'. According to local legend St Aldhelm preached here, and when he placed his pastoral staff in the ground it generated a host of ash trees, so that the place was known as *ad Episcopi arbores*, 'at the Bishop's trees'. The church here is dedicated to St Aldhelm. DB *Biscopestreu*.

Bishop's Waltham (town, Hants): 'bishop's homestead in a forest'. OE *weald*, 'forest', + *hām*, 'homestead'. The royal woodland domain was held early by the bishops of Winchester. DB *Waltham*.

Bishopsworth (district, Bristol): 'bishop's enclosure'. OE *biscop*, 'bishop', + *worth*, 'enclosure'. DB *Biscopewrde*.

Bishop Thornton (village, N Yorks): 'bishop's farmstead where thorn bushes grow'. OE *thorn*, 'thorn bush', + *tūn*, 'farmstead'. The manor here was held early by the Archbishop of York. *c.*1030 *Thorntune*, DB *Torentune*.

Bishopthorpe (village, York): 'bishop's outlying hamlet'. OE *biscop*, 'bishop', + OS *thorp*, 'outlying farmstead', 'secondary settlement'. The manor here was held by the Archbishop of York. DB *Torp*, 1275 *Biscupthorp*.

Bishopton (village, Darlington): 'bishop's estate'. OE *biscop*, 'bishop', + *tūn*, 'farmstead', 'estate'. The estate here was held by the Bishop of Durham. 1104 *Biscoptun*.

Bishop Wilton (village, E Yorks): 'bishop's village where willow trees grow'. OE *wilig*, 'willow', + *tūn*, 'farmstead', 'village'. The manor here was held early by the Archbishop of York. DB *Wiltone*.

Bisley (village, Glos): 'Bisa's woodland clearing'. OE *lēah*, 'wood', 'clearing'. 986 *Bislege*, DB *Biselege*.

Bisley (village, Surrey): 'Byssa's woodland clearing'. OE *lēah*, 'wood', 'clearing'. 933 *Busseleghe*.

Bispham (resort district, Blackpool): 'bishop's estate'. OE *biscop*, 'bishop', + *hām*, 'homestead', 'estate'. The reference is to a manor held by a bishop. DB *Biscopham*.

Bittadon (hamlet, Devon): 'Beotta's valley'. OE *denu*, 'valley'. The DB form of the name below has *d* for *t*. DB *Bedendône*, 1205 *Bettenden*.

Bittering (hamlet, Norfolk): '(settlement of) Beorhthere's people'. OE *-ingas*, 'people of'. DB *Britringa*.

Bitterley (village, Shropshire): 'butter pasture'. OE *butere*, 'butter', + *lēah*, 'clearing', 'pasture'. A 'butter pasture' is one with good grazing. DB *Buterlie*.

Bitterne (district, Southampton): 'house near a bend'. OE *byht*, 'bend' (modern English *bight*), + *ærn*, 'building'. The bend in question was presumably one in the river Itchen here. *c.*1090 *Byterne*.

Bitteswell (village, Leics): '(place by the) stream in a broad valley'. OE *bytm*, 'broad valley' (related modern English *bottom*), + *wella*, 'spring', 'stream'. DB *Betmeswelle*.

Bitton (village, S Glos): 'farmstead on the (river) Boyd'. OE *tūn*, 'farmstead'. The river has a Celtic name of uncertain meaning. DB *Betune*.

Biwmares. See BEAUMARIS.

Bix (village, Oxon): '(place by the) wood where box trees grow'. OE *byxe*, 'box grove'. DB *Bixa*.

Blaby (village, Leics): 'Blár's farmstead'. OS *bý*, 'farmstead', 'village'. The Scandinavian personal name means 'dark one' (literally 'dark blue'). The DB form of the name below has *b* miscopied as *d*. DB *Bladi*, 1175 *Blabi*.

Blackawton (village, Devon): 'Afa's farmstead on dark soil'. OE *blæc*, 'black', 'dark', + *tūn*, 'farmstead'. The adjectival addition apparently distinguishes this village from AVETON GIFFORD, 8 miles to the west, although that main name has a different origin. DB *Auetone*, 1281 *Blakeauetone*.

Black Bourton (village, Oxon): 'fortified farmstead of the (clergy in) black'. OE *burh-tūn*, 'fortified farmstead'. The first word of the name probably refers to the black habits of the canons of Osney Abbey, who held lands here. DB *Burtone*.

Blackburn (town, Blackburn with Dar): '(place by the) dark stream'. OE *blæc*, 'black', 'dark', + *burna*, 'stream'. The stream here is now called the Blackwater. DB *Blacheburne*.

Black Callerton (hamlet, Newcastle): 'dark-coloured hill where calves graze'. OE *blæc*, 'black', 'dark', + *calf*, 'calf', + *dūn*, 'hill'. The first part of the main name represents OE *calfra*, the genitive plural form of *calf*. The first word of the name distinguishes this Callerton from nearby *High Callerton*, now a suburb of Ponteland, Northd. 1212 *Calverdona*.

Black Country, The (region, central England). The region roughly between Birmingham and Wolverhampton came to be so called from the early 19C when the towns were blackened and grimed by the murk of the collieries, blast furnaces and foundries set up during the Industrial Revolution following exploitation of the South Staffordshire coalfield. Ironically, the name is now used in the touristic promotion of 'industrial heritage'.

Blackford (village, Somerset): '(place by the) dark ford'. OE *blæc*, 'black', 'dark', + *ford*, 'ford'. The form of the name below is for Blackford near Wedmore, but Blackford near Wincanton has a name of identical origin. 1227 *Blacford*.

Blackfordby (village, Leics): 'farmstead by the dark ford'. OE *blæc*, 'black', 'dark', + *ford*, 'ford', + OS *bȳ*, 'farmstead'. *c*.1125 *Blakefordebi*.

Blackgang (village, IoW): '(place by the) dark path'. OE *blæc*, 'black', 'dark', + *gang*, 'path', 'track'. The village stands above the coast and Blackgang Chine, the path being at the bottom of the latter. 1781 *Blackgang*.

Blackheath (district, Lewisham): 'dark heathland'. OE *blæc*, 'black', 'dark', + *hæth*, 'heath'. The reference is to the dark-coloured soil of the heathland. The form of the name below includes OE *feld*, 'open land' (modern English *field*). 1166 *Blachehedfeld*.

Black Heddon. See HEDDON-ON-THE-WALL.

Blackley (district, Manchester): 'dark wood or clearing'. OE *blæc*, 'black', 'dark', + *lēah*, 'wood', 'clearing'. 1282 *Blakeley*.

Blackmoor Vale (region, Dorset/Somerset): 'valley by Blackmore'. The fertile stretch of country takes its name from the former manor of *Blackmore*, whose location is preserved in *Blackmore Cottages*, Wootton Glanville, Dorset. The name itself means 'dark marshland' (cp. BLACKMORE). 1212 *Blakemore*.

Blackmore (village, Essex): '(place by) dark marshland'. OE *blæc*, 'black', + *mōr*, 'marshland', 'moor'. 1213 *Blakemore*.

Black Mountains (hill range, Powys): 'dark mountains'. The hills are so called because they appear dark when viewed from the east or south. Their Welsh name, *Y Mynyddoedd Duon*, has the same sense.

Black Notley. See WHITE NOTLEY.

Blackpool (resort town, Blackpool): '(place by the) dark pool'. OE *blæc*, 'black', 'dark', + *pull*, 'pool'. The original settlement here arose by the peaty-coloured pool that drained Marton Mere into Spen Dyke and so into the sea. *c*.1260 *Pul*, 1602 *Blackpoole*.

Blackrod (town, Wigan): '(place by the) dark clearing'. OE *blæc*, 'black', 'dark', + *rodu*, 'clearing'. The clearing would have been 'dark' because of its dense trees and bushes. The '-rod' of the name is the '-royd' in MYTHOLMROYD and in places that gave the surnames Ackroyd ('oak clearing') and Murgatroyd ('Margaret's clearing'). *c*.1189 *Blacherode*.

Blackthorn (village, Oxon): '(place by the) blackthorn'. OE *blæc-thorn*. 1190 *Blaketorn*.

Blacktoft (village, E Yorks): 'dark-coloured homestead'. OE *blæc*, 'black', + OS *toft*, 'homestead'. *c*.1160 *Blaketofte*.

Black Torrington. See TORRINGTON.

Blackwater (village, Hants): '(place by the river) Blackwater'. The river has a name meaning 'dark water' (OE *blæc*, 'black', + *wæter*, 'water'). 1298 *Blakwatere*.

Blackwell (hamlet, Derbys): '(place with a) dark-coloured spring'. OE *blæc*, 'black', 'dark', + *wella*, 'spring', 'stream'. The spring in question is opposite the church. DB *Blachewelle*. SO ALSO: *Blackwell*, Darlington, Warwicks.

Blackwood (town, Caerphilly): '(place by the) dark wood'. The Welsh name of the town is *Coed-duon* (Welsh *coed*, 'wood', + *duon*, plural of *du*, 'black'). 1833 *Coed-dduon*, 1856 *Blackwood*.

Blacon (district of Chester, Cheshire): '(place by a) dark-coloured hill'. OE *blæc*, 'black', 'dark', + *cnoll*, 'hill'. The reference is to the headland known as Blacon Point. The DB form of the name below has *n* miscopied as *h*. DB *Blachehol*, 1093 *Blachenol*.

Bladon (village, Oxon): '(place on the river) Bladon'. The river here is now the *Evenlode* (see EVENLODE), but earlier it was known as the *Bladon*, a name of uncertain origin. Cp. BLEDINGTON. DB *Blade*.

Blaenafon. See BLAENAVON.

Blaenau Ffestiniog (town, Gwynedd): 'uplands of Ffestiniog'. Welsh *blaenau*, plural of *blaen*, 'upland', 'height'. *Ffestiniog*, a village 3 miles to the south, has a name meaning 'defensive (place)', from Welsh *ffestiniog* (related modern English *fast*, 'firm', 'secure'). The town is a 19C industrial development. Ffestiniog was recorded in *c*.1420 as *Festynyok*.

Blaenavon (town, Torfaen): 'headstream of the river'. Welsh *blaen*, 'height', 'headstream', + *afon*, 'river'. The river is the Sychan, which flows from Blaen Sychan nearby. The Welsh form of the name is *Blaenafon*. 1532 *Blaen Avon*, 1868 *Blaen-Avon, or Avon*.

Blagdon (village, N Somerset): '(place by the) dark-coloured hill'. OE *blæc*, 'black', 'dark', + *dūn*, 'hill'. DB *Blachedone*. SO ALSO: *Blagdon*, Devon, Somerset.

Blaina (village, Blaenau Gwent): '(place in) uplands'. Welsh *blaenau*, plural of *blaen*, 'upland', 'height'. The present name is a poor representation of the Welsh original. Cp. BLAENAU FFESTINIOG.

Blair Atholl (village, Perth & Kin): 'plain in Atholl'. Gaelic *blàr*, 'plain'. The second word of the name means 'Ireland again', from Gaelic *ath*, 'again', + *Fótla*, a poetic name for Ireland, linked with the name of Fodla, an Irish goddess. Atholl is thus essentially 'New Ireland', and was so named by the Gaels (the original 'Scots') when they came from Ireland to settle in this part of Scotland in the 5C. *c*.970 *Athochlach*, *c*.1050 *Athfoithle*.

Blairgowrie (town, Perth & Kin): 'plain in Gowrie'. Gaelic *blàr*, 'plain'. The second word of the name means '(territory of) Gabran', after a 6C Gaelic king, and was given to distinguish this place from BLAIR ATHOLL. 13C *Blare*, 1604 *Blair in Gowrie*.

Blaisdon (village, Glos): 'Blæcci's hill'. OE *dūn*, 'hill'. 1186 *Blechedon*.

Blakemere (village, Herefords): '(place by the) dark-coloured pool'. OE *blæc*, 'black', 'dark', + *mere*, 'pool'. The pool in question would have been in the river Wye here. 1249 *Blakemere*, 1868 *Blakemere, or Blackmoor*.

Blakeney (coastal village, Norfolk): 'dark island'. OE *blæc*, 'black', 'dark', + *ēg*, 'island'. The 'island' would have been dry ground in marshland. 1242 *Blakenye*. SO ALSO: *Blakeney*, Glos.

Blakenhall (hamlet, Cheshire): '(place by the) dark corner of land'. OE *blæc*, 'black', 'dark', + *halh*, 'nook', 'corner of land'. The hamlet lies in a valley. DB *Blachenhale*.

Blakesley (village, Northants): 'Blæcwulf's woodland clearing'. OE *lēah*, 'wood', 'clearing'. DB *Blaculveslei*.

Blanchland (village, Northd): 'white woodland glade'. OF *blanche*, 'white', + *launde*, 'wooded heath' (modern English *lawn*). 1165 *Blanchelande*.

Blandford (town, Dorset): '(place by the) ford where gudgeon are seen'. OE *blæge*, 'blay', 'gudgeon', + *ford*, 'ford'. The river here is the Stour. The town was formally *Blandford Forum*, the second word being Latin *forum*, 'market', added to distinguish this Blandford from nearby *Blandford St Mary*, named from the dedi-

cation of its church. DB *Blaneford*, 1297 *Blaneford Forum*.

Blankney (village, Lincs): 'Blanca's island'. OE *ēg*, 'island'. The 'island' is raised ground in fenland. The DB form of the name below has omitted the *n* of the personal name. DB *Blachene*, 1157 *Blancaneia*.

Blantyre (town, S Lanarks): 'edge land'. The first part of the name is of uncertain origin. It may be related to Welsh *blaen*, 'front', 'top' (cp. BLAENAVON). The second part is probably Gaelic *tir*, 'land'. 'Edge land' would denote territory at the foot of higher ground, as would suit Blantyre.

Blaston (village, Leics): 'Blēath's farmstead'. OE *tūn*, 'farmstead'. DB *Bladestone*.

Blatherwycke (village, Northants): 'farm where bladder plants grow'. OE *blædre*, 'bladder', + *wīc*, 'dwelling', 'specialized farm'. 'Bladder plants' are those such as bladder campion that have a swollen, bladder-like calyx. DB *Blarewiche*.

Blawith (hamlet, Cumbria): '(place by the) dark wood'. OS *blár*, 'dark', + *vithr*, 'wood'. 1276 *Blawit*.

Blaxhall (village, Suffolk): 'Blæc's corner of land'. OE *halh*, 'nook', 'corner of land'. DB *Blaccheshala*.

Blaxton (village, Doncaster): '(place by the) black stone'. OE *blæc*, 'black', + *stān*, 'stone'. The stone presumably marked the border between the former West Riding of Yorkshire and Nottinghamshire. 1213 *Blactson*.

Blaydon (town, Gateshead): '(place by the) black hill'. OS *blár*, 'dark', 'cheerless', + OE *dūn*, 'hill'. There is no hill near Blaydon, and the name may have originally applied to the small stream 2 miles away now known as Barlow Burn, which may originally have been called Blaydon Burn. 1340 *Bladon*.

Bleadon (village, N Somerset): '(place by the) coloured hill'. OE *blēo*, 'coloured', 'variegated' (related modern English *blue*), + *dūn*, 'hill'. The name implies a hill with rocky outcrops standing out against a background of green grass. The hill in question is Bleadon Hill. 956 *Bleodun*, DB *Bledone*.

Blean (village, Kent): '(place in the) rough ground'. OE *blēa*, 'rough ground'. The DB form of the name below is corrupt. 774 *Blean*, DB *Blehem*.

Bleasby (village, Notts): 'Blesi's farmstead'. OS *bý*, 'farmstead', 'village'. The first form of the name below shows that OS *bý* replaced earlier OE *tūn* in the same sense. The personal name is Scandinavian. 956 *Blisetune*, 1268 *Blesby*.

Bledington (village, Glos): 'farmstead on the (river) Bladon'. OE *tūn*, 'farmstead'. The river *Evenlode* (see EVENLODE) here was earlier known as the *Bladon* (see BLADON). DB *Bladintun*.

Bledlow (village, Bucks): 'Bledda's burial mound'. OE *hlāw*, 'mound', 'hill'. 10C *Bleddanhlæw*, DB *Bledelai*.

Blencogo (village, Cumbria): '(place by the) summit where cuckoos are heard'. The name is Celtic in origin, from words related to modern Welsh *blaen*, 'point', 'end', and *cog* (plural *cogau*), 'cuckoo'. *c.*1190 *Blencoggou*.

Blennerhasset (hamlet, Cumbria): '(place on a) summit with a summer pasture where hay is stored'. There are four parts to this name. The first is Celtic, from a word related to modern Welsh *blaen*, 'summit'. The second is of uncertain origin. (It is probably also Celtic, and may relate to modern Welsh *tre*, 'farm'.) The third and fourth are OS *hey*, 'hay', and *sǽtr*, 'shieling'. 1188 *Blennerheiseta*.

Bletchingdon (village, Oxon): 'Blecci's hill'. OE *dūn*, 'hill'. DB *Blecesdone*.

Bletchingley (village, Surrey): 'woodland clearing of Blæcca's people'. OE *-inga-*, 'of the people of', + *lēah*, 'wood', 'clearing'. DB *Blachingelei*.

Bletchley (town, Milton K): 'Blæcca's or Blecci's woodland clearing'. OE *lēah*, 'wood', 'clearing'. Bletchley is near Whaddon Chase, a former hunting forest and a heavily wooded area. 12C *Blechelai*.

Bletsoe (village, Beds): 'Blecci's hill spur'. OE *hōh*, 'hill spur'. DB *Blechesho*.

Blewbury (village, Oxon): 'hill fort with coloured soil'. OE *blēo*, 'coloured', 'variegated' (related modern English *blue*), + *burh*, 'fortified place'. The prehistoric fort referred to is the one on nearby Blewburton Hill. The DB form of the name below is corrupt. 944 *Bleobyrig*, DB *Blidberia*.

Blickling (village, Norfolk): '(settlement of) Blicla's people'. OE *-ingas*, 'people of'. DB *Blikelinges*.

Blidworth (village, Notts): 'Blītha's enclosure', OE *worth*, 'enclosure'. DB *Blideworde*.

Blindcrake (village, Cumbria): '(place by the) rock summit'. The name is Celtic, from words related to modern Welsh *blaen*, 'summit', and *craig*, 'rock'. 12C *Blenecreyc*.

Blisland (village, Cornwall): '(place with an) estate'. OE *land*, 'tract of land', 'estate'. The first part of the name is of uncertain origin. 1284 *Bleselonde*.

Blisworth (village, Northants): 'Blīth's enclosure'. OE *worth*, 'enclosure'. DB *Blidesworde*.

Blithbury (hamlet, Staffs): 'stronghold on the (river) Blythe'. OE *burh*, 'fortified place'. The river name has the same origin as that for BLYTH, Northd. 1200 *Blidebire*.

Blockley (village, Glos): 'Blocca's woodland clearing'. OE *lēah*, 'wood', 'clearing'. 855 *Bloccanleah*, DB *Blochelei*.

Blofield (village, Norfolk): 'exposed open country'. OE *blāw*, 'blast of wind' (modern English *blow*), + *feld*, 'open land' (modern English *field*). DB *Blafelda*.

Blo' Norton (village, Norfolk): 'bleak northern farmstead'. ME *blo*, 'bleak' (modern English *blow*), + OE *north*, 'northern', + *tūn*, 'farmstead'. DB *Nortuna*, 1291 *Blonorton*.

Bloomsbury (district, Camden): 'de Blemund's manor'. OE *burh*, 'stronghold', 'manor'. The de Blemund family held the manor here in the 13C. 1291 *Blemondesberi*.

Blore (hamlet, Staffs): '(place on the) hill'. OE *blōr*, 'blister', 'swelling'. Blore is in an exposed site, and an association with modern English *blore*, 'violent gust of wind', is also possible. DB *Blora*.

Bloxham (village, Oxon): 'Blocc's homestead'. OE *hām*, 'homestead', 'village'. DB *Blochesham*.

Bloxwich (district, Walsall): 'Blocc's dairy farm'. OE *wīc*, 'dwelling', 'specialized farm'. DB *Blocheswic*.

Bloxworth (village, Dorset): 'Blocc's enclosure'. OE *worth*, 'enclosure'. 987 *Blacewyrthe*, DB *Blocheshorde*.

Blubberhouses (village, N Yorks): 'houses by the bubbling spring'. ME *bluber*, 'foaming', 'bubbling', + OE *hūs*, 'house'. There are several springs locally. The second part of the form of the name below represents OE *hūsum*, the dative plural form of *hūs*. 1172 *Bluberhusum*.

Blundeston (village, Suffolk): 'Blunt's farmstead'. OE *tūn*, 'farmstead'. 1203 *Blundeston*.

Blunsdon St Andrew. See BROAD BLUNSDON.

Bluntisham (village, Cambs): 'Blunt's homestead or enclosure'. OE *hām*, 'homestead', or *hamm*, 'enclosure'. DB *Bluntesham*.

Blyborough (hamlet, Lincs): 'Blītha's fortified place'. OE *burh*, 'fortified place'. DB *Bliburg*.

Blyford (hamlet, Suffolk): '(place by the) ford over the (river) Blyth'. The river name has the same origin as that for BLYTH, Northd. The first form of the name below has *tl* for *d* as a copying error. *c.*1060 *Blitleford*, DB *Blideforda*.

Blymhill (village, Staffs): 'hill where plum trees grow'. OE *plȳme*, 'plum tree', + *dūn*, 'hill'. The DB form of the name below is corrupt. DB *Brumhelle*, 1167 *Blumehil*.

Blyth (resort town and port, Northd): '(place on the river) Blyth'. The river derives its name from OE *blīthe*, 'gentle', 'pleasant' (modern English *blithe*). *Blyth Valley* is now the name of the local council district. 1130 *Blida*.

Blyth (village, Notts): '(place on the river) Blyth'. The river here now is the Ryton. Its former name has the same origin as that for BLYTH, Northd. DB *Blide*.

Blythburgh (village, Suffolk): 'stronghold on the (river) Blyth'. OE *burh*, 'fortified place'. The river name has the same origin as that for BLYTH, Northd. DB *Blideburh*.

Blyton (village, Lincs): 'Blītha's farmstead'. OE *tūn*, 'farmstead'. DB *Blitone*.

Boarhunt (village, Hants): '(place by the) spring at the stronghold'. OE *burh*, 'fortified place', + *funta*, 'spring' (related modern English *fount*). The spring in question is at Offwell Farm. 10C *Byrhfunt*, DB *Borehunte*.

Boarstall (hamlet, Bucks): 'site of a stronghold'. OE *burh-stall* (from *burh*, 'fortified place', + *stall*, 'site', 'stall'). 1158 *Burchestala*.

Boat of Garten (village, Highland): 'ferry by (the river) Garten'. The English name translates Gaelic *Coit Ghairtean*. The ferry formerly crossed the river Spey here near the point where it is joined by the river Garten, whose name means 'cornfield' (Gaelic *gairtean*, from *gart*, 'standing corn').

Bobbington (village, Staffs): 'estate associated with Bubba'. OE *-ing-*, 'associated with', + *tūn*, 'farmstead', 'estate'. DB *Bubintone*.

Bocking (district of Braintree, Essex): '(settlement of) Bocca's people'. OE *-ingas*, 'people of'. The name could also mean simply 'Bocca's place' (OE *-ing*, 'place belonging to'). c.995 *Boccinges*, DB *Bochinges*.

Boddington (village, Glos): 'estate associated with Bōta'. OE *-ing-*, 'associated with', + *tūn*, 'farmstead', 'estate'. DB *Botingtune*.

Bodenham (village, Herefords): 'Boda's homestead or enclosure'. OE *hām*, 'homestead', or *hamm*, 'enclosure'. Bodenham is on the river Lugg, so that 'enclosure' is best understood as 'riverside land'. DB *Bodeham*.

Bodenham (village, Wilts): 'Bōta's homestead or enclosure'. OE *hām*, 'homestead', or *hamm*, 'enclosure'. 1249 *Boteham*.

Bodham Street (village, Norfolk): 'Boda's homestead or enclosure'. OE *hām*, 'homestead', or *hamm*, 'enclosure'. The second word of the name implies a settlement on the road here. DB *Bodenham*.

Bodiam (village, E Sussex): 'Boda's enclosure'. OE *hamm*, 'enclosure', 'riverside land'. Bodiam lies by the river Rother. DB *Bodeham*.

Bodicote (village, Oxon): 'cottage associated with Boda'. OE *-ing-*, 'associated with', + *cot*, 'cottage'. DB *Bodicote*.

Bodmin (town, Cornwall): 'dwelling by churchland'. OC *bod*, 'house', 'dwelling', + *meneghi*, 'churchland' (related to *managh*, 'monk'). King Athelstan is said to have founded a monastery here in the 10C. c.975 *Bodmine*.

Bognor Regis (resort town, W Sussex): 'Bucge's shore'. OE *ōra*, 'shore', 'landing place'. The personal name is that of a woman. Latin *regis*, 'of the king', was added to the original name following the convalescence of George V at nearby Aldwick in 1929. The present town began to develop in the late 18C, when Sir Richard Hotham bought land with the aim of developing a resort to rival Brighton. He named his enterprise *Hothampton*, but the name fell out of favour after his death. He is commemorated, however, in Hotham Park, the town's main public park. c.975 *Bucganora*.

Bolam (village, Durham): '(place by the) tree trunks'. OE *bola* or OS *bolr*, 'tree trunk'. The name represents OE or OS *bolum*, the dative plural form of *bola* and *bolr*. 1317 *Bolom*. SO ALSO: *Bolam*, Northd.

Boldon (town, S Tyneside): '(place by the) rounded hill'. OE *bol*, 'rounded hill', + *dūn*, 'hill'. The hill in question is the one near West Boldon, the site of the original settlement. c.1170 *Boldun*.

Boldron (hamlet, Durham): 'clearing where bulls are kept'. OS *boli*, 'bull', + *rúm*, 'clearing'. c.1180 *Bolrum*.

Bole (village, Notts): '(place by the) tree trunks'. OE *bola* or OS *bolr*, 'tree trunk'. The name represents *bolum*, the dative plural form of the OE or OS word. Cp. BOLAM. DB *Bolun*.

Bolingey (village, Cornwall): 'mill house'. Cornish *melin*, 'mill', + *chi*, 'house'. 1566 *Velingey*, 1650 *Melinge*.

Bollington (town, Cheshire): 'farmstead on the (river) Bollin'. OE *tūn*, 'farmstead'. The town is actually on the Dean, but named after the nearby *Bollin*, a name of uncertain origin. 1270 *Bolynton*.

Bolney (village, W Sussex): 'Bola's island'. OE *ēg*, 'island'. Bolney lies on an 'island' surrounded by well-watered land. 1263 *Bolneye*.

Bolsover (town, Derbys): 'Boll's or Bull's ridge'. OE *ofer*, 'slope', 'ridge'. The 'ridge' is a hillside spur to the east of the town. The DB form of the name below has *e* for *o*. DB *Belesovre*, 12C *Bolesoura*.

Bolstone (hamlet, Herefords): 'Bola's stone'. OE *stān*, 'stone'. The reference is probably to a boundary stone here. 1193 *Boleston*, 1868 *Boulstone, or Bolston*.

Boltby (village, N Yorks): 'Boltr's or Bolti's farmstead'. OS *bý*, 'farmstead', 'village'. The personal names are Scandinavian. DB *Boltebi*.

Bolton (town, Bolton): 'settlement with buildings'. OE *bōthl-tūn* (from *bōthl*, 'building', + *tūn*, 'settlement', 'village'). A 'settlement with buildings' was the main part of a settlement, as distinct from outlying farms. 1185 *Boelton*.

Bolton Abbey (hamlet, N Yorks): 'settlement with buildings by the abbey'. OE *bōthl-tūn* (see BOLTON). An Augustinian priory was founded here in the 12C and its ruins were later popularly referred to as 'the abbey'. DB *Bodeltone*, 1586 *Bolton Abbey*.

Bolton-by-Bowland (village, Lancs): 'settlement with buildings by Bowland'. OE *bōthl-tūn* (see BOLTON). The second part of the name denotes the location of the village on the edge of the Forest of BOWLAND. DB *Bodeltone*.

Bolton-le-Sands (town, Lancs): 'settlement with buildings on the sands'. OE *bōthl-tūn* (see BOLTON), + OF *le*, 'the', + OE *sand*, 'sand'. The town is near the coast of Morecambe Bay. DB *Bodeltone*.

Bolton-on-Swale (village, N Yorks): 'settlement with buildings on the (river) Swale'. OE *bōthl-tūn* (see BOLTON). For the river name, see BROMPTON-ON-SWALE. DB *Boletone*.

Bolton Percy (village, N Yorks): 'de Percy's settlement with buildings'. OE *bōthl-tūn* (see BOLTON). The manor here was held by the de Percy family from 1086. DB *Bodeltune*, 1305 *Bolton Percy*.

Bolton upon Dearne (town, Barnsley): 'settlement with buildings on the (river) Dearne'. OE *bōthl-tūn* (see BOLTON). The river name may represent OE *derne*, 'hidden', but could be Celtic in origin. DB *Bodeltone*.

Bolventor (village, Cornwall): '(place of the) bold venture'. The name dates only from the 19C, and refers to the 'bold venture' in attempting to found a farming community here in the middle of Bodmin Moor. 1844 *Boldventure*.

Bonby (village, N Lincs): 'farmstead of the peasant farmers'. OS *bóndi*, 'peasant farmer', + *bý*, 'farmstead', 'village'. DB *Bundebi*.

Bonchurch (village, IoW): 'Bona's church'. OE *cirice*, 'church'. The personal name is thought to be a short form of (St) Boniface, to whom the church here is dedicated. Nearby *Boniface Down* has been so named since at least the 13C. DB *Bonecerce*.

Bondleigh (village, Devon): 'Bola's woodland clearing'. OE *lēah*, 'wood', 'clearing'. The DB form of the name below is corrupt. DB *Bolenei*, 1205 *Bonlege*.

Bonehill (suburb of Tamworth, Staffs): '(place by the) hill where bulls graze'. OE *bula*, 'bull', + *hyll*, 'hill'. The first part of the name represents OE *bulena*, the genitive plural form of *bula*. 1230 *Bolenhull*.

Bo'ness (town, Falkirk): 'promontory of Borrowstoun'. OE *næss*, 'promontory'. The town's full name is *Borrowstounness*. *Borrowstoun* is 'Beornweard's farm' (OE *tūn*, 'farm'). The name might have become 'Bernardston' but was understood as *burrowstown*, a Scots word meaning 'municipality' (as if 'borough-town'). *c*.1335 *Berwardeston*, 1494 *Nes*, 1532 *Burnstounnes*, 1868 *Borrowstownness, or Bo'ness*.

Bonhill (town, W Dunbartons): 'house by the stream'. Gaelic *bot an uillt* (from *bot*, 'house', + *an*, 'the', + *uillt*, genitive of *allt*, 'stream'). The stream in question would presumably have run into the river Leven here. 1225 *Buchlul*, *c*.1270 *Buthelulle*, *c*.1320 *Buchnwl*.

Boningale (village, Shropshire): 'corner of land associated with Bola'. OE *-ing-*, 'associated with', + *halh*, 'nook', 'corner of land'. 12C *Bolynghale*.

Bonnington (village, Kent): 'estate associated with Buna'. OE *-ing-*, 'associated with', + *tūn*, 'farmstead', 'estate'. DB *Bonintone*.

Bonnybridge (town, Falkirk): '(place by the) bridge over the Bonny Water'. The river name, recorded in 1682 as *aquae de Boine*, is said to derive from modern Scottish English *bonny*, 'beautiful', although river names are rarely modern English. The town itself is recent in origin.

Bonnyrigg (town, Midlothian): '(place by the) bannock-shaped ridge'. The name was originally that of a field or area of land, describing its shape, although *bannock* has come to be influenced by *bonny*. In 1929 Bonnyrigg was united with the adjoining town of Lasswade, so that the burgh is *Bonnyrigg and Lasswade*. The latter name means '(place by the) pasture ford' (OE *lǣswe*, genitive of *lǣs*, 'pasture', + *wæd*, 'ford'). The ford would have been over the river North Esk. 1148 *Laswade*, c.1150 *Lesswade*.

Bonsall (village, Derbys): 'Bunt's corner of land'. OE *halh*, 'nook', 'corner of land'. The first part of the name could also be a bird name related to modern English *bunting*. DB *Bunteshale*.

Bont-Faen, Y. See COWBRIDGE.

Bonvilston (village, Vale of Glam): 'de Bonville's farm'. OE *tūn*, 'farm'. The de Bonville family held land here from the 12C and Simon de Bonville gave the Welsh name of the village, *Tresimwn*, 'Simon's farm' (Welsh *tref*, 'farm'). c.1160 *Boleuilston*, c.1206 *Bonevillestun*.

Bookham. See GREAT BOOKHAM.

Booth (village, E Yorks): '(place of) Boothby'. The village takes its name from a person who originally came from one of the nearby places called *Boothby*, 'farmstead with shelters' (OS *bōth*, 'shelter', + *bý*, 'farmstead'). In 1550 it was thus known as *Botheby*. *Boothferry Bridge* here over the river Ouse takes its name from *Boothferry*, 'ferry at Booth' (OS *ferja*, 'ferry'). 1651 *Booth's Ferry*.

Boothby Graffoe (village, Lincs): 'farmstead with shelters in Graffoe'. OS *bōth*, 'booth', + *bý*, 'farmstead'. The district name, that of the wapentake in which Boothby is situated, probably means 'grove on a hill spur' (OE *grāf*, 'grove', + *hōh*, 'hillspur'), but the site of this has not been identified. It distinguishes this Boothby from *Boothby Pagnell*, 18 miles to the south, where the Paynel family held the manor in the 14C. DB *Bodebi*.

Boothferry. See BOOTH.

Bootle (town, Sefton): 'building'. OE *bōtl*. The OE word was used for a special building of some kind, not necessarily a residence. The DB form of the name below has an extraneous *l*. DB *Boltelai*. SO ALSO: *Bootle*, Cumbria.

Boraston (village, Shropshire): 'eastern farmstead by the fort'. OE *burh*, 'fortified place', + *ēast*, 'eastern', + *tūn*, 'farmstead'. 1188 *Bureston*, 1256 *Buraston*.

Borden (village, Kent): 'valley or woodland pasture by a hill'. OE *bor*, 'hill', + *denu*, 'valley', or *denn*, 'woodland pasture'. 1177 *Bordena*.

Bordley (hamlet, N Yorks): 'woodland clearing where boards are obtained'. OE *bord*, 'board', + *lēah*, 'wood', 'clearing'. The DB form of the name below has omitted *d*. DB *Borelaie*, c.1140 *Bordeleia*.

Bordon (village, Hants): 'Burdun's valley'. OE *denu*, 'valley'. The Burdun family were here in the 13C. c.1230 *Burdunesdene*.

Boreham (village, Essex): 'homestead or enclosure by a hill'. OE *bor*, 'hill', + *hām*, 'homestead', or *hamm*, 'enclosure'. c.1045 *Borham*.

Borehamwood (residential district, Herts): '(place by the) wood near the homestead or enclosure by a hill'. OE *bor*, 'hill', + *hām*, 'homestead', or *hamm*, 'enclosure', + *wudu*, 'wood'. The name is that of the wood itself. 1188 *Borham*, 13C *Burhamwode*, 1868 *Boreham Wood*.

Borley (hamlet, Essex): 'woodland clearing where wild boars are seen'. OE *bār*, 'boar', + *lēah*, 'wood', 'clearing'. DB *Barlea*.

Borough, The (district, Southwark): 'borough'. OE *burh*, 'fortified place', 'borough'. The district was so named from its suburban status, as against the City of London just across the Thames to the north. 1559 *Southwarke borow*.

Boroughbridge: (town, N Yorks): '(place at the) bridge by the stronghold'. OE *burh*, 'stronghold', + *brycg*, 'bridge'. The bridge took the Great North Road (now bypassed by the A1(M)) over the river Ure here, while the 'stronghold' was nearby ALDBOROUGH. 1220 *Burbrigg*.

Borough Green (village, Kent): 'manor'. OE *burh*, 'manor', 'borough'. The reference may be to the manor (borough) of Wrotham. But the name could also mean '(place by the) hill' (OE *beorg*, 'mound', 'hill'). The place later became associated with its village green. 1575 *Borrowe Grene*.

Borrowash (suburb of Derby, Derbys): '(place by the) ash tree near the fortified place'. OE *burh*, 'fortified place', + *æsc*, 'ash'. c.1200 *Burg*, 1272 *Burysasch*.

Borrowby (village, N Yorks): 'farmstead on a hill'. OS *berg*, 'hill', + *bý*, 'farmstead', 'village'. This is Borrowby near Thirsk, but Borrowby near Staithes has a name of identical origin. DB *Bergebi*.

Borrowdale (river valley, Cumbria): 'valley of the (river) Borrow'. OS *dalr*, 'valley'. The valley is actually that of the river Derwent, whose upper reach was named *Borrow*, 'river by a fort' (OS *borg*, 'fort', genitive *borgar* + *á*, 'river'). There was probably a Romano-British hill fort at the site now called Castle Crag. c.1170 *Borgordale*.

Borstal (district of Rochester, Medway): 'place of safety'. OE *borg*, 'security', + *steall*, 'place', 'stall'. The name implies a place where refuge could be sought when fleeing in battle, here between the Maidstone Road (the present

B2097) and the river Medway. *Borstal* later became a dialect word for a steep and narrow path up a hill, in which one could 'lose' oneself. DB *Borcstele*.

Borth-y-gest (resort village, Gwynedd): 'harbour of the paunch'. Welsh *porth*, 'port', 'harbour', + *y*, 'the', + *cest*, 'belly', 'paunch'. The village takes its name from the nearby mountain Moel y Gest ('bare hill of the paunch'), so named for its shape. 1748 *Gest harbour*.

Borwick (village, Lancs): 'barley farm'. OE *berewīc* (see BERWICK-UPON-TWEED). DB *Bereuuic*.

Bosbury (village, Herefords): 'Bōsa's stronghold'. OE *burh*, 'fortified place'. DB *Boseberge*, *c.*1118 *Bosanbirig*.

Boscastle (coastal village, Cornwall): 'Boterel's castle'. OF *castel*, 'castle'. William de Botereus held the castle here in the early 14C. Little remains of it now. 1302 *Boterelescastel*.

Boscobel House (country house, Shropshire): '(place in the) beautiful wood'. Italian *bosco*, 'wood', + *bello*, 'beautiful'. The house was built in *c.*1606. 1707 *Baskabell*, 1784 *Boscobel*.

Boscombe (district, Bournemouth): 'Bōsa's valley'. OE *cumb*, 'valley'. The first part of the name could also represent OE *bors*, a word for some kind of spiky or bristly plant (related modern English *burr*), although the *r* of this has disappeared. 1273 *Boscumbe*. SO ALSO: *Boscombe*, Wilts.

Bosham (resort town, W Sussex): 'Bōsa's promontory'. OE *hamm*, 'enclosure', 'promontory'. Bosham lies on a promontory in an arm of Chichester Harbour. 731 *Bosanham*, DB *Boseham*.

Bosherston (village, Pemb): 'Bosher's farm'. OE *tūn*, 'farm'. The Bosher family held the manor here in the 13C. The village was originally *Stackpole Bosher*, the manorial name distinguishing it from *Stackpole Elidor*, an alternative name for CHERITON, 2 miles to the northeast. 1291 *Stakep' bosser*, 1594 *Bosherston (alias Stacpoll Bosher)*.

Bosley (village, Cheshire): 'Bōsa's or Bōt's woodland clearing'. OE *lēah*, 'wood', 'clearing'. DB *Boselega*.

Bossall (hamlet, N Yorks): 'Bōt's or Bōtsige's corner of land'. OE *halh*, 'nook', 'corner of land'. DB *Bosciale*.

Bossiney (village, Cornwall): 'Kyni's dwelling'. OC *bod*, 'dwelling'. The *K-* of the Cornish personal name appears to have changed to *s* under Norman influence. DB *Botcinnii*, 1291 *Boscini*.

Bostock Green (hamlet, Cheshire): 'Bōta's outlying farmstead'. OE *stoc*, 'outlying farmstead'. The village later became associated with its green. DB *Botestoch*.

Boston (town, Lincs): 'Bōtwulf's stone'. OE *stān*, 'stone'. Botwulf is popularly identified with the 7C missionary St Botolph, to whom the parish church (the 'Boston Stump') is dedicated. The 'stone' would have marked a boundary or a place of assembly. 1130 *Botuluestan*.

Boston Spa (village, Leeds): 'Boston's (place with a) spa'. 'This village is of recent origin, the first house having been built in 1753. Owing to the discovery, in 1744, of a saline spring in the vicinity, it has now become a place of fashionable resort' (Samuel Lewis, *A Topographical Dictionary of England*, 1840). The discoverer of the spring was John Shires, who lived in Thorp Arch across the river Wharfe, and the name *Thorp Arch* was in use for Boston until at least the 19C. The original village perhaps took its name from a family called Boston (from BOSTON). 1799 *Bostongate*, 1822 *Boston*, 1868 *Boston, or Thorpe Arch*.

Boswinger (village, Cornwall): 'Gwengor's house'. OC *bod*, 'house', 'dwelling'. 1301 *Boswengar*.

Botallack (village, Cornwall): 'steep-browed dwelling'. OC *bod*, 'house', 'dwelling', + *talek* 'steep-browed' (from *tal*, 'brow', + adjectival suffix *-ek*). The village stands near a cliff. 1262 *Botalec*.

Botesdale (village, Suffolk): 'Bōtwulf's valley'. OE *dæl*, 'valley'. 1275 *Botholuesdal*.

Bothal (village, Northd): 'Bōta's corner of land'. OE *halh*, 'nook', 'corner of land'. 12C *Bothala*.

Bothamsall (village, Notts): '(place on a) shelf by a broad river valley'. OE *bothm*, 'broad river valley', + *scelf*, 'shelf'. The village lies on a long level bank overlooking the broad valley between the rivers Meden and Maun. DB *Bodmescel*.

Bothel (village, Cumbria): 'special dwelling'. OE *bōthl*, 'special house'. *c.*1125 *Bothle*.

Bothenhampton (village, Dorset): 'home farm in a valley'. OE *bothm*, 'valley', + *hām-tūn*, 'home farm' (from *hām*, 'homestead', + *tūn*, 'farmstead'). 1268 *Bothehamton*.

Bothwell (town, S Lanarks): 'shelter by the stream'. ME *bothe*, 'hut', 'shelter' (modern English *booth*), + OE *wella*, 'spring', 'stream'. *c.*1242 *Botheuill*, *c.*1300 *Bothvile*.

Botley (village, Bucks): 'Botta's woodland clearing'. OE *lēah*, 'wood', 'clearing'. 1167 *Bottlea*.

Botley (town, Hants): 'Bōta's woodland clearing'. OE *lēah*, 'wood', 'clearing'. The name could also mean 'woodland clearing where timber is obtained', from OE *bōt*, 'right of a tenant to take timber' (modern English *boot* in 'to boot'). DB *Botelie*.

Botley (suburb of Oxford, Oxon): 'Bōta's woodland clearing'. OE *lēah*, 'wood', 'clearing'. The name could also mean 'woodland clearing where timber is obtained', from OE *bōt*, 'right of a tenant to take timber' (modern English *boot* in 'to boot'). 12C *Boteleam*.

Botolph Claydon. See STEEPLE CLAYDON.

Botolphs (village, W Sussex): 'St Botolph's (church)'. The church here is dedicated to St Botolph. 1288 *Sanctus Botulphus*.

Bottesford (village, Leics): '(place at the) ford by the building'. OE *bōtl*, 'house', 'building', + *ford*, 'ford'. The ford would have been over the river Devon here. DB *Botesford*, 1868 *Bottesford, or Botsworth*. SO ALSO: *Bottesford*, N Lincs.

Bottisham (village, Cambs): 'Boduc's homestead or enclosure'. OE *hām*, 'homestead', or *hamm*, 'enclosure'. 1060 *Bodekesham*, DB *Bodicchesham*.

Boughton (village, Notts): 'Bucca's farmstead'. OE *tūn*, 'farmstead'. The name could also mean 'farmstead where bucks or he-goats are kept' (OE *bucc*, 'buck', 'male deer', or *bucca*, 'he-goat', + *tūn*). DB *Buchetone*. SO ALSO: *Boughton*, Northants.

Boughton Monchelsea (village, Kent): 'de Montchensie's farmstead held by charter'. OE *bōc*, 'book', 'charter', + *tūn*, 'farmstead'. The de Montchensie family held the manor here in the 13C. Their name distinguishes this Boughton from *Boughton Malherbe*, 7 miles to the east, where the manor was held early by the Malherbe family, and from *Boughton Aluph*, 17 miles to the east, where one Aluf held the manor in the 13C. The DB form of the name below has *c* miscopied as *l*. DB *Boltone*, 1278 *Bocton Monchansy*.

Boulge (hamlet, Suffolk): 'uncultivated land where heather grows'. OF *bouge*, 'heath'. DB *Bulges*, 1254 *Bulge*.

Boulmer (coastal village, Northd): '(place by the) pond where bulls come'. OE *bula*, 'bull', + *mere*, 'pond'. 1161 *Bulemer*.

Bourn (village, Cambs): '(place at the) stream'. OE *burna*, 'stream'. The name refers to the Bourn Brook here, a tributary of the river Cam. DB *Brune*.

Bourne (town, Lincs): '(place at the) stream'. OS *brunnr*, 'spring', 'stream'. The name probably comes from *brunnum*, the dative plural form of the OS word. Bourne is near the source of a stream, named the Bourne Eau after it. (The second word of this is OE *ēa*, 'river', 'stream', influenced by French *eau*, 'water'.) DB *Brune*.

Bourne End (residential district, Bucks): 'end of the stream'. OE *burna*, 'stream', + *ende*, 'end'. The 'stream' is the river Wye, which meets the Thames here. 1236 *Burnend*.

Bournemouth (resort town, Dorset): 'mouth of the stream'. OE *burna*, 'stream', + *mūtha*, 'mouth'. The 'stream' is the river Bourne, which enters the sea here. The town arose only in the 19C. 1407 *La Bournemowthe*.

Bournville (district, Birmingham): 'town on the (river) Bourne'. French *ville*, 'town'. The name is that of the model estate built here in 1879 by George Cadbury for employees at the chocolate factory. The river name is from OE *burna*, 'stream'.

Bourton (village, Dorset): 'farmstead by a fortified place'. OE *burh*, 'fortified place', + *tūn*, 'farmstead'. 1212 *Bureton*.

Bourton on Dunsmore (village, Warwicks): 'fortified farmstead on Dunsmore'. OE *burh-tūn* (from *burh*, 'fortified place', + *tūn*, 'farmstead'). The district name (see CLIFTON UPON DUNSMORE) distinguishes this village from BURTON HASTINGS, 13 miles to the north. DB *Bortone*.

Bourton-on-the-Water (town, Glos): 'farm by a fortification on the water'. OE *burh-tūn* (from *burh*, 'fortified place', + *tūn*, 'farmstead'). The 'fortification' is the adjoining large hill fort known as Salmonsbury. The 'water' is the river Windrush, which flows through the town beside the main street. The second part of the name distinguishes this Bourton from *Bourton-on-the-Hill*, 7 miles to the north. 714 *Burchtun*, DB *Bortune*, 1575 *Bourton super aquam*.

Bovey Tracey (town, Devon): 'de Tracy's (estate by the river) Bovey'. The pre-English river name is of unknown meaning. Eva de Tracy held the manor here in the early 13C, and her name distinguishes this Bovey from *North Bovey*, 6 miles to the northwest. DB *Bovi*, 1276 *Bovy Tracy*, 1868 *Bovey-Tracey, or South Bovey*.

Bovingdon (village, Herts): 'hill associated with Bōfa'. OE *-ing-*, 'associated with', + *dūn*, 'hill'. The 'hill' is the high location (albeit in a slight hollow) where Bovingdon lies. *c.*1200 *Bovyndon*.

Bovington Camp (military camp, Dorset): 'camp at the estate associated with Bōfa'. OE

-*ing*-, 'associated with', + *tūn*, 'farmstead', 'estate'. DB *Bovintone*.

Bow (village, Devon): '(place by the) arched bridge'. OE *boga*, 'bow', 'arch'. The bridge in question would have been over the river Yeo here, formerly known as the *Nymet* (see NYMET ROWLAND). Hence the first two forms of the name below (the DB one being corrupt). The name is preserved in the nearby village of *Nymet Tracey*, which seems to have served as an alternative name for Bow itself. DB *Limet*, 1270 *Nymetboghe*, 1281 *la Bogh*, 1868 *Bow, or Nymet Tracey*.

Bow (district, Tower Hamlets): '(place by the) arched bridge'. OE *boga*, 'bow', 'arch'. The bridge in question was built in the 12C over the river Lea here. Local lore tells how Queen Matilda (1080–1118), wife of Henry I, ordered it to be built in the shape of her bow after floods held her up while hunting. The original name of Bow was *Stratford*, later called *Stratford atte Bow* (ME *atte*, 'at the') for distinction from nearby STRATFORD, on the east side of the river in what was then Essex. 1177 *Stratford*, 1279 *Stratford atte Bowe*, 1868 *Bow, or Stratford-Bow*.

Bow Brickhill. See GREAT BRICKHILL.

Bowdon (town, Trafford): '(place by the) curved hill'. OE *boga*, 'bow', 'bend', + *dūn*, 'hill'. The hill in question is the one known as Bowdon Downs, which curves sharply here. DB *Bogedone*.

Bowerchalke. See BROAD CHALKE.

Bowers Gifford (village, Essex): 'Giffard's (estate at the) cottages'. OE *būr*, 'cottage', 'dwelling' (modern English *bower*). The Giffard family held the manor here in the 13C. 1065 *Bure*, DB *Bura*, 1315 *Buresgiffard*.

Bowes (town, Durham): '(place by the) bends'. OE *boga* or OS *bogi*, 'bow', 'bend'. The 'bends' are those in the river Greta. The Roman fort here was *Lavatris*, a name of Celtic origin perhaps meaning '(place of the) river bed', referring to the Greta. 1148 *Bogas*.

Bowland (moorland region, Lancs): 'district of the bend'. OE *boga*, 'bow', 'bend', + *land*, 'land'. Much of the Forest of Bowland lies in bends of the river Ribble. 1102 *Boelanda*.

Bowley (hamlet, Herefords): 'Bola's woodland clearing'. OE *lēah*, 'wood', 'clearing'. The name could also mean 'woodland clearing with tree trunks' (OE *bola*, 'tree trunk', + *lēah*). DB *Bolelei*.

Bowling (district, Bradford): 'place by the hollow'. OE *bolla*, 'bowl', 'hollow', + -*ing*, 'place characterized by'. The name refers to the wide hollow lying between West Bowling and Bowling Park. DB *Bollinc*.

Bowness-on-Solway (village, Cumbria): '(place by the) rounded headland on the Solway'. OE *boga* or OS *bogi*, 'bow', 'bend', + OE *næss* or OS *nes*, 'headland'. The second part of the name (see SOLWAY FIRTH) distinguishes this Bowness from BOWNESS-ON-WINDERMERE, 45 miles to the south. *c*.1225 *Bounes*, 1868 *Bowness, or Boulness*.

Bowness-on-Windermere (hamlet, Cumbria): 'headland where bulls are pastured by (Lake) Windermere'. OE *bula*, 'bull', + *næss*, 'headland'. The location of the place on Lake WINDERMERE distinguishes it from BOWNESS-ON-SOLWAY at the opposite end of the county. (They were formerly in Westmorland and Cumberland respectively.) Describing Bowness in *A Six Months Tour through the North of England* (1770), Arthur Young wrote: 'I am sensible ... of misspelt names; but many of the places I mention are not to be found in maps, I am obliged, therefore, to write from the ear'. He accordingly spelt the name *Bonus*. 1282 *Bulnes*.

Bowsden (hamlet, Northd): 'Boll's hill'. OE *dūn*, 'hill'. 1195 *Bolesdon*.

Bowthorpe (district of Norwich, Norfolk): 'Búi's outlying farmstead'. OS *thorp*, 'outlying farmstead'. The personal name is Scandinavian. DB *Boethorp*.

Box (village, Wilts): '(place by the) box tree'. OE *box*, 'box'. 1144 *Bocza*. SO ALSO: *Box*, Glos.

Boxford (village, Suffolk): '(place by the) ford where box trees grow'. OE *box*, 'box', + *ford*, 'ford'. The ford in question is over the river Box here, itself taking its name from the village. 12C *Boxford*.

Boxgrove (village, W Sussex): 'box tree grove'. OE *box*, 'box', + *grāf*, 'grove'. DB *Bosgrave*.

Box Hill (hill, Surrey): 'hill where box trees grow'. OE *box*, 'box'. The name has not been recorded earlier than 1629 and may originally have been that of a farm here.

Boxley (village, Kent): 'wood or clearing where box trees grow'. OE *box*, 'box', + *lēah*, 'wood', 'clearing'. The DB form of the name below has *s* for *x*. DB *Boseleu*, *c*.1100 *Boxlea*.

Boxted (hamlet, Essex): 'place where beech trees grow'. OE *bōc*, 'beech', + *stede*, 'place'. DB *Bocstede*.

Boxted (village, Suffolk): 'place where beech trees grow'. OE *bōc*, 'beech', + *stede*, 'place'. The name could also mean 'place where box trees grow' (OE *box*, 'box', + *stede*). The DB form of the name below has *c* miscopied as *e*. DB *Boesteda*, 1154 *Bocstede*.

Boxworth (village, Cambs): 'Bucc's enclosure'. OE *worth*, 'enclosure'. DB *Bochesuuorde*.

Boylestone (village, Derbys): 'farmstead by the rounded hill'. OE *boga*, 'bow', 'bend', + *hyll*, 'hill', + *tūn*, 'farmstead'. DB *Boilestun*.

Boynton (village, E Yorks): 'estate associated with Bōfa'. OE *-ing-*, 'associated with', + *tūn*, 'farmstead', 'estate'. DB *Bouintone*.

Boyton (village, Wilts): 'Boia's farmstead'. OE *tūn*, 'farmstead'. The name could also mean 'farmstead of the servants' (OE *boia*, 'boy', 'servant', + *tūn*). DB *Boientone*. SO ALSO: *Boyton*, Cornwall, Suffolk.

Bozeat (village, Northants): '(place by) Bōsa's gap'. OE *geat*, 'gate', 'gap'. DB *Bosiete*.

Brabourne (village, Kent): '(place by the) broad stream'. OE *brād*, 'broad', + *burna*, 'stream'. The 'broad stream' is the East Stour, which flows near the village. Cp. BRADBOURNE. *c.*860 *Bradanburna*, DB *Bradeburne*.

Bracebridge (district of Lincoln, Lincs): '(place by the) brushwood bridge'. OE *brǣsc*, 'brushwood', + *brycg*, 'bridge', 'causeway'. The name seems to imply a bridge or causeway made of brushwood or small branches, in this case over the river Witham. DB *Brachebrige*.

Bracewell (hamlet, Lancs): 'Breithr's spring'. OE *wella*, 'spring', 'stream'. The personal name is Scandinavian. DB *Braisuelle*.

Brackenfield (hamlet, Derbys): 'clearing where bracken grows'. OS *brækni*, 'bracken', + *thveit*, 'clearing'. The second OS word has been replaced by OE *feld*, 'open land' (modern English *field*). 1269 *Brachentheyt*.

Bracklesham Bay (resort village, W Sussex). The resort takes its name from the bay here, itself named after the farm of *Bracklesham*, 'Braccol's homestead' (OE *hām*, 'homestead'). 945 *Brakelesham*, 1635 *Bragglesham*, 1893 *Bracklesham Bay*.

Brackley (town, Northants): 'Bracca's woodland clearing'. OE *lēah*, 'wood', 'clearing'. DB *Brachelai*.

Bracknell (town, Bracknell F): 'Bracca's corner of land'. OE *halh*, 'nook', 'corner of land'. The *n* in the name represents the genitive ending of the personal name (as in the form of the name below). 942 *Braccan heal*.

Bracon Ash (village, Norfolk): '(place amid) bracken'. OS *brækni* or OE *brǣcen*, 'bracken'. The second word of the name is a later addition

referring to a prominent ash tree here. 1175 *Brachene*.

Bradbourne (village, Derbys): '(place by the) broad stream'. OE *brād*, 'broad', + *burna*, 'stream'. The name is that of the stream near which the village is situated. Cp. BRABOURNE. DB *Bradeburne*.

Bradden (village, Northants): '(place in the) broad valley'. OE *brād*, 'broad', + *denu*, 'valley'. DB *Bradene*.

Bradenham (village, Bucks): 'broad homestead or enclosure'. OE *brād*, 'broad', + *hām*, 'homestead', or *hamm*, 'enclosure'. DB *Bradeham*. SO ALSO: *Bradenham*, Norfolk.

Bradenstoke (village, Wilts): 'settlement dependent on Braydon forest'. OE *stoc*, 'dependent settlement'. The forest has a pre-English name of uncertain meaning. DB *Bradenestoche*.

Bradfield (village, W Berks): 'broad stretch of open land'. OE *brād*, 'broad', + *feld*, 'open land' (modern English *field*). 990 *Bradanfelda*, DB *Bradefelt*. SO ALSO: *Bradfield*, Essex, Norfolk.

Bradfield Combust (village, Suffolk): 'burnt (place at the) broad stretch of open land'. OE *brād*, 'broad', + *feld*, 'open land' (modern English *field*), + ME *combust*, 'burnt'. The second word of the name alludes to the burning down of the hall here during the riots of 1327. The addition distinguishes this Bradfield from nearby *Bradfield St Clare*, so named from the Seyncler family who held the manor early here, their name giving the dedication of the church to St Clare, and from *Bradfield St George*, 2½ miles to the northeast, so named from its church dedication. DB *Bradefelda*, 1868 *Bradfield-Combust, or Burnt Bradfield*.

Bradford (city, Bradford): '(place at the) broad ford'. OE *brād*, 'broad', + *ford*, 'ford'. The original 'broad ford' would have been over Bradford Beck in the centre of the present town. DB *Bradeford*.

Bradford Abbas (village, Dorset): 'abbot's (estate by the) broad ford'. OE *brād*, 'broad', + *ford*, 'ford', + Latin *abbas*, 'abbot'. The ford would have been over the river Yeo here, where the manor was held early by Sherborne Abbey. 933 *Bradanforda*, DB *Bradeford*, 1386 *Braddeford Abbatis*.

Bradford-on-Avon (town, Wilts): '(place at the) broad ford on the (river) Avon'. OE *brād*, 'broad', + *ford*, 'ford'. For the river name, see AVONMOUTH. *c.*900 *Bradanforde be Afne*, DB *Bradeford*.

Bradford Peverell (village, Dorset): 'Peverel's (estate by the) broad ford'. OE *brād*, 'broad', + *ford*, 'ford'. The ford in question would have been over the river Frome here. The manor was held in the 13C by the Peverel family. DB *Bradeford*, 1244 *Bradeford Peuerel*.

Brading (village, IoW): '(settlement of the) dwellers by the hillside'. OE *brerd*, 'hillside', + *-ingas*, 'dwellers at'. Brading lies at the foot of Brading Down, the hillside in question. 683 *Brerdinges*, DB *Berardinz*.

Bradley (village, Derbys): '(place in the) broad clearing'. OE *brād*, 'broad', + *lēah*, 'wood', 'clearing'. DB *Braidelei*.

Bradley in the Moors (village, Staffs): '(place by the) wood where boards are obtained'. OE *bred*, 'board', 'plank', + *lēah*, 'wood'. The second part of the name distinguishes the village from *Bradley*, 19 miles to the southwest, where the name is as for BRADLEY. DB *Bretlei*.

Bradmore (village, Notts): '(place by the) broad pool'. OE *brād*, 'broad', + *mere*, 'pool'. The 'pool' in question would have been the area of marshy land to the west of the village, now long drained. DB *Brademere*.

Bradninch (town, Devon): '(place at the) broad ash tree'. OE *brād*, 'broad', + *æsc*, 'ash'. The second part of the name could equally be OE *āc*, 'oak tree'. The middle '-n-' represents the ending of *brādan*, the dative form of *brād*. DB *Bradenese*.

Bradpole (village, Dorset): '(place by the) broad pool'. OE *brād*, 'broad', + *pōl*, 'pool'. DB *Bratepolle*.

Bradshaw (suburb of Bolton): '(place by the) broad wood'. OE *brād*, 'broad', + *sceaga*, 'wood', 'copse'. 1246 *Bradeshaghe*.

Bradstone (hamlet, Devon): '(place by the) broad stone'. OE *brād*, 'broad', + *stān*, 'stone'. The reference is perhaps to an ancient stone by the church. *c.*970 *Bradan stane*, DB *Bradestana*.

Bradwell (village, Derbys): '(place at the) broad stream'. OE *brād*, 'broad', + *wella*, 'spring', 'stream'. The stream in question is Bradwell Brook here. DB *Bradewelle*. SO ALSO: *Bradwell*, Essex, Milton K, Norfolk, Staffs.

Bradwell-on-Sea (village, Essex): '(place at the) broad stream by the sea'. OE *brād*, 'broad', + *wella*, 'spring', 'stream'. The village is also known as *Bradwell juxta Mare*, the latter two words being Latin for 'near the sea'. (Bradwell is not actually '-on-Sea' but 2 miles from it.) The addition distinguishes this Bradwell from *Bradwell-juxta-Coggeshall* (see COGGESHALL), 15 miles to the northwest, which 'derives its name

... from a copious spring to the north of the hall, from which issues a stream powerful enough to turn a mill near its source' (Samuel Lewis, *A Topographical Dictionary of England*, 1840). The Roman fort of *Othona* near Bradwell-on-Sea has a name of uncertain origin. 1194 *Bradewella*, 1552 *Bradwell nexte the See*.

Bradwell Waterside (village, Essex): '(place at the) broad stream beside the water'. OE *brād*, 'broad', + *wella*, 'spring', 'stream'. The second word refers to the location of the village by the estuary of the river Blackwater, distinguishing it from nearby BRADWELL-ON-SEA. It was formerly *Bradwell Quay* and originally *Hackfleet*, '(place on the) creek with the angular bend' (OE *haca*, 'hook', + *flēot*, 'creek'). DB *Hacflet*.

Bradworthy (village, Devon): 'broad enclosure'. OE *brād*, 'broad', + *worthign* or *worthig*, 'enclosure'. The DB form of the name below has omitted the *d* of *brād*. DB *Brawardine*, 1175 *Bradewurtha*.

Braemar (village, Aberdeens): 'upper part of Marr'. Gaelic *braigh*, 'upper'. The district name ultimately represents a personal name. 1560 *the Bray of Marre*.

Brafferton (village, N Yorks): 'farmstead by the broad ford'. OE *brād*, 'broad', + *ford*, 'ford', + *tūn*, 'farmstead'. The river here is the Swale. DB *Bradfortune*. SO ALSO: *Brafferton*, Darlington.

Brafield-on-the-Green. See COLD BRAYFIELD.

Brailsford (village, Derbys): '(place by the) ford near a burial place'. OE *brægels*, 'burial place', + *ford*, 'ford'. The first part of the name could also be of Celtic origin and mean 'hill court' (modern Welsh *bre*, 'hill', and *llys*, 'court'). No burial place is known, but the village lies on the slopes of a prominent hill, which suits the second sense. DB *Brailesford*.

Braintree (town, Essex): 'Branca's tree'. OE *trēow*, 'tree'. The tree would either have been a natural prominent one or a 'built' tree in the form of a cross. Either could have served as an assembly point. DB *Branchetreu*.

Braiseworth (hamlet, Suffolk): 'enclosure plagued with gadflies'. OE *brīosa*, 'gadfly', + *worth*, 'enclosure'. The name could also mean 'Brīosa's enclosure'. DB *Briseworde*.

Braithwaite (village, Cumbria): '(place by the) broad clearing'. OS *breithr*, 'broad', + *thveit*, 'clearing'. *c.*1160 *Braithait*. SO ALSO: *Braithwaite*, Doncaster.

Braithwell (village, Doncaster): '(place by the) broad stream'. OE *brād*, 'broad', + *wella*, 'spring', 'stream'. OE *brād* was replaced in the name by equivalent OS *breithr*. DB *Bradewelle*.

Bramber (village, W Sussex): '(place by the) bramble thicket'. OE *brēmer*, 'bramble thicket'. 956 *Bremre*, DB *Brembre*.

Bramcote (district of Beeston, Notts): 'cottage where broom grows'. OE *brōm*, 'broom', + *cot*, 'cottage'. The DB form of the name below is corrupt. DB *Brunecote*, c.1156 *Bramcote*.

Bramdean (village, Hants): 'valley where broom grows'. OE *brōm*, 'broom', + *denu*, 'valley'. 824 *Bromdene*, DB *Brondene*.

Bramerton (village, Norfolk): 'farmstead by the bramble thicket'. OE *brēmer*, 'bramble thicket', + *tūn*, 'farmstead'. DB *Brambretuna*.

Bramfield (village, Herts): '(place on) burnt open land'. OE *brænde*, 'burnt', + *feld*, 'open land' (modern English *field*). The name denotes an area of land cleared by burning. The DB form of the name below has *ll* for *lt* (or *ld*). DB *Brandefelle*, 12C *Brantefelt*.

Bramfield (village, Suffolk): 'open land where broom grows'. OE *brōm*, 'broom', + *feld*, 'open land' (modern English *field*). The DB form of the name below is corrupt. DB *Brunfelda*, 1166 *Bramfeld*.

Bramford (village, Suffolk): '(place by the) ford where broom grows'. OE *brōm*, 'broom', + *ford*, 'ford'. The ford would have been over the river Gipping here. 1040 *Bromford*, DB *Branfort*.

Bramhall (town, Stockport): 'corner of land where broom grows'. OE *brōm*, 'broom', + *halh*, 'nook', 'corner of land'. DB *Bramale*.

Bramham (village, Leeds): 'homestead or enclosure where broom grows'. OE *brōm*, 'broom', + *hām*, 'homestead', or *hamm*, 'enclosure'. DB *Brameham*.

Bramhope (suburb of Leeds): 'valley where broom grows'. OE *brōm*, 'broom', + *hop*, 'valley'. DB *Bramhop*.

Bramley (village, Hants): 'woodland clearing where broom grows'. OE *brōm*, 'broom', + *lēah*, 'wood', 'clearing'. DB *Brumelai*. SO ALSO: *Bramley*, Rotherham, Surrey.

Brampford Speke (village, Devon): 'Espec's (estate by the) ford where broom grows'. OE *brōm*, 'broom', + *ford*, 'ford'. The village is on the river Exe. The manor here was held in the 12C by the Espec family. DB *Branfort*, 1275 *Bramford Spec*.

Brampton (town, Cumbria): 'farmstead where broom grows'. OE *brōm*, 'broom', + *tūn*, 'farmstead'. 1169 *Brampton*. SO ALSO: *Brampton*, Cambs.

Brampton Bryan (village, Herefords): 'Brian's farmstead where broom grows'. OE *brōm*, 'broom', + *tūn*, 'farmstead'. One Brian held the manor here in the 12C. DB *Brantune*, 1275 *Bramptone Brian*.

Bramshall (village, Staffs): '(place on the) shelf of land where broom grows'. OE *brōm*, 'broom', + *scelf*, 'shelf'. The 'shelf' is a large hill here with a flat, wide summit. The DB form of the name below is corrupt. DB *Branselle*, 1327 *Bromschulf*.

Bramshill House (mansion, Hants): '(place on the) hill where broom grows'. OE *brōm*, 'broom', + *hyll*, 'hill'. DB *Bromeselle*.

Brancaster (village, Norfolk): 'Roman station at Branodunum'. OE *ceaster*, 'Roman camp'. *Branodunum* is a name of Celtic origin meaning 'fort of the raven' (related modern Welsh *brân*, 'raven', + *dinas*, 'city'). c.960 *Bramcestria*, DB *Broncestra*.

Brancepeth (village, Durham): 'Brandr's path'. OE *pæth*, 'path', 'road'. The personal name is Scandinavian. Folk etymology has produced a local tale: 'The name of this place is supposed to be a corruption of *Brawn's path*, in allusion to the number of wild boars that formerly infested the district' (Samuel Lewis, *A Topographical Dictionary of England*, 1840). c.1170 *Brantespethe*.

Brandesburton (village, E Yorks): 'Brandr's fortified farmstead'. OE *burh-tūn* (from *burh*, 'fortified place', + *tūn*, 'farmstead'). The personal name is Scandinavian. DB *Brantisburtone*.

Brandeston (village, Suffolk): 'Brant's farmstead'. OE *tūn*, 'farmstead'. DB *Brantestona*.

Brandiston (village, Norfolk): 'Brant's farmstead'. OE *tūn*, 'farmstead'. DB *Brantestuna*.

Brandon (town, Durham): 'hill where broom grows'. OE *brōm*, 'broom', + *dūn*, 'hill'. c.1190 *Bromdune*. SO ALSO: *Brandon*, Northd, Warwicks.

Brandon (village, Lincs): 'hill by the (river) Brant'. OE *dūn*, 'hill'. The river's name means 'deep one' (OE *brant*, 'steep', 'deep'). 1060 *Branthon*, DB *Brandune*.

Brandon (town, Suffolk): 'hill where broom grows'. OE *brōm*, 'broom', + *dūn*, 'hill'. DB *Brandona*, 11C *Bromdun*.

Brandsby (village, N Yorks): 'Brandr's farmstead'. OS *bý*, 'farmstead'. The personal name is Scandinavian. DB *Branzbi*.

Branksome (district, Poole). The name arose in the 19C from a house here called *Branksome Tower*, itself apparently named for the setting of

Sir Walter Scott's *The Lay of the Last Minstrel* (1805) ('The feast was over in Branksome tower').

Branodunum. See BRANCASTER.

Branogenium. See LEINTWARDINE.

Branscombe (village, Devon): 'Branoc's valley'. OE *cumb*, 'valley'. The personal name is Celtic. 9C *Branecescumbe*, DB *Branchescome*.

Bransford (village, Worcs): '(place at the) ford by the hill'. OE *brægen*, 'hill' (modern English *brain*), + *ford*, 'ford'. The ford would have been over the river Teme here. 963 *Bregnesford*, DB *Bradnesford*.

Bransgore (village, Hants): '(place with the) triangular piece of land'. ME *gore*, 'triangular plot of ground'. The first part of the name is of uncertain origin and no early forms exist. The second form of the name below is corrupt. 1759 *Bransgoer*, 1817 *Bransgrove*.

Branston (village, Leics): 'Brant's farmstead'. OE *tūn*, 'farmstead'. DB *Brantestone*. SO ALSO: *Branston*, Staffs.

Branston (village, Lincs): 'Brandr's farmstead'. OE *tūn*, 'farmstead'. The personal name is Scandinavian. DB *Branztune*.

Branstone (hamlet, IoW): 'Brandr's farmstead'. OE *tūn*, 'farmstead'. The personal name is Scandinavian. DB *Brandestone*.

Brant Broughton (village, Lincs): 'burnt (place by the) farmstead near a fortification'. ME *brende*, 'burnt', + OE *burh-tūn*, 'farmstead near a fortified place'. The village must have been burnt down in the 13C. One might have expected 'Brent' for the first word, but the spelling has presumably been influenced by the river Brant on which the village lies. DB *Burtune*, 1250 *Brendebrocton*.

Brantham (village, Suffolk): 'Branta's homestead or enclosure'. OE *hām*, 'homestead', or *hamm*, 'enclosure'. DB *Brantham*.

Branthwaite (village, Cumbria): 'clearing where broom grows'. OE *brōm*, 'broom', + OS *thveit*, 'clearing'. 1210 *Bromthweit*.

Brantingham (village, E Yorks): 'homestead of Brant's people'. OE *-inga-*, 'of the people of', + *hām*, 'homestead'. The name could also mean 'homestead of the dwellers on the steep slopes' (OE *brant*, 'steep', + *-inga-*, 'of the dwellers at', + *hām*). Brantingham is located in very steep country at the southern end of the Yorkshire Wolds. DB *Brentingeham*.

Branton (village, Doncaster): 'farmstead where broom grows'. OE *brōm*, 'broom', + *tūn*, 'farmstead'. DB *Brantune*.

Branton (hamlet, Northd): 'farmstead overgrown with broom'. OE *brēmen*, 'overgrown with broom', + *tūn*, 'farmstead'. *c*.1150 *Bremetona*.

Branxton (village, Northd): 'Branoc's farmstead'. OE *tūn*, 'farmstead'. The personal name is Celtic. 1195 *Brankeston*.

Brassington (village, Derbys): 'estate associated with Brandsige'. OE *-ing-*, 'associated with', + *tūn*, 'farmstead', 'estate'. DB *Branzinctun*.

Brasted (village, Kent): 'broad place'. OE *brād*, 'broad', + *stede*, 'place'. The DB form of the name below is somewhat garbled. DB *Briestede*, *c*.1100 *Bradestede*.

Bratton (village, Wilts): 'farmstead by newly cultivated ground'. OE *brǣc*, 'newly cultivated (literally, broken) ground', + *tūn*, 'farmstead'. 1177 *Bratton*.

Bratton (hamlet, Wrekin): 'farmstead by a brook'. OE *brōc*, 'brook', + *tūn*, 'farmstead'. Bratton lies by a tributary of the river Tern. DB *Brochetone*.

Bratton Clovelly. See BRATTON FLEMING.

Bratton Fleming (village, Devon): 'farmstead by newly cultivated ground'. OE *brǣc*, 'newly cultivated (literally, broken) ground', + *tūn*, 'farmstead'. The manor here was held in the 13C by the Flemeng family, their name distinguishing this Bratton from *Bratton Clovelly*, 32 miles to the southwest, where it was held by the de Clavill family. The name of the latter village was probably influenced by CLOVELLY, 23 miles to the northwest. DB *Bratona*.

Bratton Seymour (village, Somerset): 'Saint Maur's farmstead by a brook'. OE *brōc*, 'brook', + *tūn*, 'farmstead'. The Saint Maur family held the manor here in the early 15C. DB *Broctune*.

Braughing (village, Herts): '(settlement of) Breahha's people'. OE *-ingas*, 'people of'. 825 *Breahingas*, DB *Brachinges*.

Braunston (village, Northants): 'Brant's farmstead'. OE *tūn*, 'farmstead'. 956 *Brantestun*, DB *Brandestone*. SO ALSO: *Braunston*, Rutland (also known as *Braunston-in-Rutland* for distinction from BRANSTON, Leics, BRAUNSTON, Northants, and BRAUNSTONE, Leicester).

Braunstone (district, Leicester): 'Brant's farmstead'. OE *tūn*, 'farmstead'. DB *Brantestone*.

Braunton (town, Devon): 'farmstead where broom grows'. OE *brōm*, 'broom', + *tūn*, 'farmstead'. DB *Brantona*.

Brawby (village, N Yorks): 'Bragi's farmstead'. OS *bȳ*, 'farmstead', 'village'. The personal name is Scandinavian. DB *Bragebi*.

Bray (village, Windsor & Maid): 'marshy place'. OF *braye*, 'marsh'. The village lies by the Thames. DB *Brai*.

Braybrooke (village, Northants): '(place by the) broad brook'. OE *brād*, 'broad', + *brōc*, 'brook'. The Braybrooke is normally a small stream, but after heavy rain can deepen and widen. DB *Bradebroc*.

Bray Shop (village, Cornwall): 'Bray's workshop'. The name is first recorded in the 18C. 1728 *Bray's Shop*.

Brayton (village, N Yorks): 'broad farmstead'. OS *breithr*, 'broad', + OE *tūn*, 'farmstead'. The name could also mean 'Breithi's farmstead', with a Scandinavian personal name. *c.*1030 *Breithe-tun*, DB *Bretone*.

Breadalbane (mountainous district, Stirling/Perth & Kin): 'upper part of Alban'. Gaelic *bràghad*, 'neck', 'upper part'. *Alban* is essentially the same name as ALBION. Breadalbane is in the heart of the Grampians to the south of Loch Tay. *c.*1600 *Bredalban*.

Breadsall (village, Derbys): 'Brægd's corner of land'. OE *halh*, 'nook', 'corner of land'. 1002 *Brægdeshale*, DB *Braideshale*.

Breadstone (hamlet, Glos): '(place by the) broad stone'. OE *brād*, 'broad', + *stān*, 'stone'. The first form of the name below has *l* for *n*. 1236 *Bradelestan*, 1273 *Bradeneston*.

Breage (village, Cornwall): '(church of) St Breage'. The church here is dedicated to Breage, said to have been born in Ireland and to have come to Cornwall with other local saints. The form of the name below has added Cornish *eglos*, 'church'. *c.*1170 *Egglosbrec*.

Breamore (village, Hants): 'marshland where broom grows'. OE *brōm*, 'broom', + *mōr*, 'moor', 'marshy ground'. Breamore lies on the river Avon and is surrounded by ponds. DB *Brumore*.

Brean (coastal village, Somerset): '(place by the) hill'. The name is of Celtic origin from a word related to modern Welsh *bre*, 'hill', referring to nearby Brean Down, a lofty promontory. The dedication of the church here to St Bridget may have been suggested by the name. DB *Brien*.

Brearton (village, N Yorks): 'farmstead among the briars'. OE *brēr*, 'briar', + *tūn*, 'farmstead'. DB *Braretone*.

Breaston (suburb of Long Eaton, Derbys): 'Brægd's farmstead'. OE *tūn*, 'farmstead'. DB *Braidestune*.

Brechin (town, Angus): '(place of) Brychan'. The same Celtic personal name occurs for BRECON. *c.*1145 *Brechin*.

Breckland (region, Norfolk): 'broken land'. Modern English dialect *breck* + modern English *land*. The name, now that of the local council district, dates only from the 19C and refers to land that has been 'broken' for cultivation.

Breckles (hamlet, Norfolk): 'meadow by newly cultivated land'. OE *brēc*, 'land broken up for cultivation', + *lǣs*, 'meadow'. DB *Brecchles*.

Brecknock. See BRECON.

Brecon (town, Powys): '(place of) Brychan'. Brychan is the name of a 5C prince. The Welsh name of Brecon is *Aberhonddu*, 'mouth of the (river) Honddu', from OW *aber*, 'mouth', and a river name meaning 'pleasant' (modern Welsh *hawdd*, 'easy'). In the variant form of the name *Brecknock*, '-ock' represents the Welsh 'territorial' suffix *-iog*. 1100 *Brecheniauc*.

Brecon Beacons (mountain range, Pemb/Powys): 'beacons by Brecon'. The mountains near BRECON are 'beacons' as they were used for signal fires in medieval times. Their Welsh name is *Bannau Brycheiniog*, 'peaks of Brycheiniog' ('territory of Brychan').

Bredbury (town, Stockport): 'fortification built of planks'. OE *bred*, 'board', 'plank', + *burh*, 'fortified place'. DB *Bretberie*.

Brede (village, E Sussex): 'broad stretch of land'. OE *brǣdu*, 'breadth', 'broad stretch of land'. The reference must be to the broad valley here known as Brede Level. 1161 *Brade*.

Bredfield (village, Suffolk): 'broad stretch of open land'. OE *brǣdu*, 'breadth', + *feld*, 'open land' (modern English *field*). DB *Bredefelda*.

Bredgar (village, Kent): 'broad triangular plot of land'. OE *brād*, 'broad', + *gāra*, 'triangular piece of land' (modern English *gore*). *c.*1100 *Bradegare*.

Bredhurst (village, Kent): 'wooded hill where boards are obtained'. OE *bred*, 'board', + *hyrst*, 'wooded hill'. 1240 *Bredehurst*.

Bredon (village, Worcs): '(place by the) hill Bre'. OE *dūn*, 'hill'. The name of the hill itself represents a Celtic word related to modern Welsh *bre*, 'hill'. Cp. BREEDON ON THE HILL; BRILL. 772 *Breodun*.

Bredon's Norton (village, Worcs): 'northern farmstead near Bredon'. OE *north*, 'northern', + *tūn*, 'farmstead'. The village is 1½ miles north of BREDON. DB *Nortune*, 1320 *Northton in Bredon*, 1868 *Norton-by-Bredon*.

Bredwardine (village, Herefords): 'enclosure with planks'. OE *bred*, 'board', 'plank', + *worthign*, 'enclosure'. The first part of the name could also represent OE *brǣdu*, 'broad stretch of land'. The DB form of the name below is garbled. DB *Brocheurdie*, late 12C *Bredewerthin*.

Breedon on the Hill (village, Leics): '(place on) the hill Bre on the hill'. OE *dūn*, 'hill'. The original (Celtic) name of the hill on which the church stands here actually means 'hill' (see BREDON). The OE word for 'hill' was added to this when it was no longer understood, and modern English *hill* was further added when *Breedon* in turn was no longer meaningful. The name thus has 'hill' three times. Cp. PENDLE HILL. 731 *Briudun*.

Breighton (village, E Yorks): 'bright farmstead'. OE *beorht*, 'bright', + *tūn*, 'farmstead'. The name could also mean 'Beorhta's farmstead'. DB *Bricstune*.

Bremenium. See ROCHESTER (Northd).

Bremetenacum Veteranorum. See RIBCHESTER.

Bremhill (village, Wilts): '(place by the) bramble thicket'. OE *brēmel*, 'bramble thicket'. The DB form of the name below omits the final *l*. 937 *Bremel*, DB *Breme*.

Brenchley (village, Kent): 'Brænci's woodland clearing'. OE *lēah*, 'wood', 'clearing'. Celticists see the personal name as Brenci, a Cornish name with a literal meaning 'raven hound' (OC *bran*, 'raven', 'crow', + *ci*, 'hound'). *c*.1100 *Braencesli*, 1185 *Brencheslega*, 1242 *Brenchesle*.

Brendon (village, Devon): 'hill where broom grows'. OE *brōm*, 'broom', + *dūn*, 'hill'. DB *Brandone*.

Brent (borough, Greater London): '(place on the river) Brent'. See BRENTFORD. The borough of Brent was created in 1965.

Brent Eleigh (village, Suffolk): 'burnt (place at) Illa's woodland clearing'. ME *brende*, 'burnt', + OE *lēah*, 'wood', 'clearing'. The first word of the name distinguishes the village from nearby *Monks Eleigh*, held by the monks of St Paul's, London. *c*.995 *Illanlege*, DB *Illeleia*, 1312 *Brendeylleye*, 1868 *Brent Eleigh, or Ely Brent*.

Brentford (district, Hounslow): '(place by the) ford over the (river) Brent'. OE *ford*, 'ford'. The river name is Celtic, meaning 'holy one'. The ford in question was probably near the junction of London Road (the present A315) and Commerce Road. 705 *Breguntford*.

Brent Knoll (village, Somerset): 'high place by a hilltop'. The first word of the name is of Celtic origin, related to modern Welsh *bre*, 'hill'. The second is OE *cnoll*, 'hilltop', 'knoll', referring to the hill here so named in the form of a truncated cone rising from a ridge. The addition distinguishes this Brent from nearby *East Brent*. Brent

Knoll is still sometimes known as *South Brent*. 1289 *Brenteknol*.

Brent Pelham (village, Herts): 'burnt (estate at) Pēola's homestead'. OE *bærned*, 'burnt', + *hām*, 'homestead', 'village'. The first word of the name distinguishes this Pelham from *Furneux Pelham*, 2 miles to the south, held by the de Fornellis family in the 13C, and *Stocking Pelham*, 2 miles to the southeast (OE *stoccen*, 'made of logs' or 'by the tree stumps'). DB *Peleham*, 1230 *Barndepelham*.

Brent Tor. See NORTH BRENTOR.

Brentwood (town, Essex): '(place by the) burnt wood'. OE *berned*, 'burnt', + *wudu*, 'wood'. An area of woodland in the old Forest of Essex was destroyed by fire. The first form of the name below is the Latin equivalent. 1176 *Boscus arsus*, 1274 *Brendewode*.

Brenzett (village, Kent): 'burnt fold'. OE *berned*, 'burnt', + *set*, 'fold', 'stable'. DB *Brensete*.

Brereton (suburb of Rugeley, Staffs): '(place on the) hill where briars grow'. OE *brēr*, 'briar', + *dūn*, 'hill'. 1279 *Breredon*.

Brereton Green (village, Cheshire): 'farmstead among the briars'. OE *brēr*, 'briar', + *tūn*, 'farmstead'. Brereton was later distinguished by its village green. The DB form of the name below has omitted a syllable. DB *Bretone*, *c*.1100 *Brereton*.

Bressay (island, Shetland): 'breast island'. OS *brjóst*, 'breast', + *ey*, 'island'. The name would refer to the island's shape. 1654 *Bressa*.

Bressingham (village, Norfolk): 'homestead of Brīosa's people'. OE *-inga-*, 'of the people of', + *hām*, 'homestead'. DB *Bresingaham*.

Bretby (village, Derbys): 'farmstead of the Britons'. OS *Bretar*, '(Ancient) Britons', + *bý*, 'farmstead'. The Britons would presumably have accompanied the Scandinavians in this settlement. DB *Bretbi*.

Bretford (village, Warwicks): '(place by the) ford with planks'. OE *bred*, 'board', 'plank', + *ford*, 'ford'. The river here is the Avon. Early 11C *Bretford*.

Bretforton (village, Worcs): 'farmstead near the plank ford'. OE *bred*, 'board', 'plank', + *ford*, 'ford', + *tūn*, 'farmstead'. A 'plank ford' is one provided with planks as an aid to crossing. 709 *Bretfertona*, DB *Bratfortune*.

Bretherton (village, Lancs): 'farmstead of the brothers'. OE *brōthor* or OS *bróthir*, 'brother', + OE *tūn*, 'farmstead'. The 'brothers' are presumably monks or friars. 1190 *Bretherton*.

Brettenham (village, Suffolk): 'Bretta's or Beorhta's homestead'. OE *hām*, 'homestead', 'village'. The river Brett that rises nearby takes its name from the village. DB *Bretenhama*. SO ALSO; *Brettenham*, Norfolk.

Brewood (village, Staffs): 'wood by (the hill) Bre'. OE *wudu*, 'wood'. The hill has a Celtic name related to modern Welsh *bre*, 'hill'. DB *Breude*.

Briantspuddle (village, Dorset): 'Brian's (estate on the river) Piddle'. For the river name, see PUDDLETOWN. One Brian held the manor here in the 14C. DB *Pidele*, 1465 *Brianis Pedille*, 1868 *Bryant's-Puddle*.

Bricklehampton (village, Worcs): 'estate associated with Beorhthelm'. OE *-ing-*, 'associated with', + *tūn*, 'farmstead', 'estate'. DB *Bricstelmestune*.

Bridekirk (village, Cumbria): 'church of St Bride'. OS *kirkja*, 'church'. St Bride is the Irish saint also known as St Bridget (Brigid), to whom the church here is dedicated. *c.*1210 *Bridekirke*.

Bridestowe (village, Devon): 'holy place of St Bride'. OE *stōw*, 'holy place'. The church here is dedicated to the Irish saint also known as St Bridget (Brigid). DB *Bridestou*.

Bridford (village, Devon): '(place by the) brides' ford'. OE *brȳd*, 'bride', + *ford*, 'ford'. A 'brides' ford' is one that is shallow and easy to cross, here over a tributary of the Teign. DB *Brideforda*.

Bridge (village, Kent): '(place by the) bridge'. OE *brycg*, 'bridge'. The river here is the Little Stour. DB *Brige*.

Bridge Hewick. See COPT HEWICK.

Bridgend (town, Bridgend): '(place at the) end of the bridge'. OE *brycg*, 'bridge', + *ende*, 'end'. A Norman castle is said to have protected the crossing here over the river Ogmore. The Welsh name of Bridgend is *Pen-y-bont ar Ogwr*, 'head of the bridge on the Ogmore'. For the river name, see OGMORE. 1535 *Byrge End*.

Bridge of Allan (town, Stirling): 'bridge over the (river) Allan'. The town is by the Strath Allan, or valley of the Allan Water, whose own name is Celtic, perhaps meaning 'holy one'.

Bridge of Weir (town, Renfrews): 'bridge by the weir'. The weir in question is on the river Gryfe.

Bridgerule (village, Devon): 'Ruald's (estate by the) bridge'. OE *brycg*, 'bridge'. The Scandinavian personal name is that of the tenant of the manor here in 1086. The bridge is over the Tamar. DB *Brige*, 1238 *Briggeroald*.

Bridge Sollers (village, Herefords): 'de Solers' (estate by the) bridge'. OE *brycg*, 'bridge'. The bridge in question would have been over the river Wye. The de Solers family held the manor here in the 12C. DB *Bricge*, 1291 *Bruges Solers*.

Bridge Trafford. See MICKLE TRAFFORD.

Bridgewater Canal (canal, Halton/Warrington). Francis Egerton, 3rd Duke of Bridgewater (1736–1803), financed the construction of the canal from 1759 to 1765. The dukes took their title from BRIDGWATER.

Bridgham (village, Norfolk): 'homestead or enclosure by a bridge'. OE *brycg*, 'bridge', + *hām*, 'homestead', or *hamm*, 'enclosure'. The bridge in question would have been over the river Thet here. *c.*1050 *Brugeham*.

Bridgnorth (town, Shropshire): '(place at the) northern bridge'. OE *brycg*, 'bridge', + *north*, 'northern'. The bridge over the river Severn here is said to be so called as it was to the north of an earlier bridge at QUATFORD. But there is no record of a bridge at Quatford, and Bridgnorth may be named in contrast to some other place with *Bridge* in its name, such as BRIDGWATER, Somerset. 1156 *Brug*, 1282 *Brugg Norht*.

Bridgwater (town, Somerset): '(place at) Walter's bridge'. OE *brycg*. The Norman owner of the bridge over the river Parrett here was Walter de Dowai. DB *Brugie*, 1194 *Brigewaltier*.

Bridlington (resort town, E Yorks): 'estate associated with Berhtel'. OE *-ing-*, 'associated with', + *tūn*, 'farmstead', 'estate'. DB *Bretlinton*, 1651 *Burlington*, 1868 *Bridlington, or Burlington*.

Bridport (town, Dorset): 'Bredy port'. OE *port*, 'harbour', 'market town'. *Bredy* is the name of a former borough here, itself named after the river *Bride*, whose Celtic name means 'gushing one'. Bridport is actually on the river Brit, named after it. DB *Brideport*.

Bridstow (village, Herefords): 'St Bride's holy place'. OE *stōw*, 'holy place'. St Bride is the Irish saint Bridget, to whom the church here is dedicated. 1277 *Bridestowe*.

Brierfield (town, Lancs): 'field of briars'. The name dates only from the 19C and was probably influenced by nearby *Briercliffe* ('bank where briars grow'), recorded in 1193 as *Brerecleve*.

Brierley (village, Barnsley): 'woodland clearing where briars grow'. OE *brēr*, 'briar', + *lēah*, 'wood', 'clearing'. The first part of the name below is corrupt. DB *Breselai*, 1194 *Brerelay*.

Brierley Hill (district, Dudley): 'hill of the clearing where briars grow'. OE *brēr*, 'briar', + *lēah*, 'wood', 'clearing'. The name of the hill was adopted for that of the town. 14C *Brereley*.

Brigg (town, N Lincs): '(place at the) bridge'. OE *brycg*, 'bridge'. *Glanford*, the first word of the form of the name below, means 'ford where people gather for games' (OE *glēam*, 'revelry', + *ford*, 'ford'). The name was adopted for the local administrative district of the former county of Humberside and is preserved in Glanford Road in Brigg itself. The river here is the Ancholme. 1235 *Glanford Brigg*.

Brigham (village, Cumbria): 'homestead or enclosure by a bridge'. OE *brycg*, 'bridge', + *hām*, 'homestead', or *hamm*, 'enclosure'. The bridge in question would have been over the Ellerbeck here. *c.*1175 *Briggham*.

Brigham (hamlet, E Yorks): 'homestead or enclosure by a bridge'. OE *brycg*, 'bridge', + *hām*, 'homestead', or *hamm*, 'enclosure'. The bridge in question would probably have been at the point where Frodingham Bridge now crosses Frodingham Beck. The DB form of the name below is corrupt. DB *Bringeham*, 12C *Brigham*.

Brighouse (town, Calderdale): 'houses by the bridge'. OE *brycg*, 'bridge', + *hūs*, 'house'. The town arose on an old crossing of the river Calder here. 1240 *Brighuses*.

Brighstone (village, IoW): 'Beorhtwīg's farmstead'. OE *tūn*, 'farmstead'. 1212 *Brihtwiston*.

Brighthampton (hamlet, Oxon): 'Beorhthelm's farmstead'. OE *tūn*, 'farmstead'. The name is of identical origin to that of BRIGHTON. 984 *Byrhtelmingtun*, DB *Bristelmestone*.

Brightling (village, E Sussex): '(settlement of) Beorhtel's people'. OE *-ingas*, 'people of'. 1016 *Byrhtlingan*, DB *Brislinga*.

Brightlingsea (town, Essex): 'Beorhtrīc's island'. OE *ēg*, 'island'. The town is on the estuary of the river Colne and is essentially an island in the accepted sense, surrounded on all sides but the northeast by the river and its branches. DB *Brictriceseia*.

Brighton (resort city, Brighton & Hove): 'Beorhthelm's farmstead'. OE *tūn*, 'farmstead'. The present form of the name was not regularly current until the 19C. DB *Bristelmestune*, 1840 *Brighthelmstone ... now, by contraction, generally Brighton*, 1868 *Brighton, or Brighthelmston*.

Brighton (hamlet, Cornwall). The hamlet is presumably named after the Sussex resort, although it is not on the coast. Cp. NEW BRIGHTON. *Brighton* 1888.

Brightwell (village, Oxon): '(place by the) bright spring'. OE *beorht*, 'bright', + *wella*, 'spring', 'stream'. The spring in question produced the many streams near the village.

Brightwell is formally coupled (via Latin *cum*, 'with') with nearby SOTWELL. 854 *Beorhtawille*, DB *Bricsteuuelle*. SO ALSO: *Brightwell*, Suffolk.

Brightwell Baldwin (village, Oxon): 'Baldwin's (estate by the) bright spring'. OE *beorht*, 'bright', 'clear', + *wella*, 'spring', 'stream'. The manor here was granted in the 14C to Sir Baldwin de Bereford, whose name distinguishes the place from BRIGHTWELL, 5 miles to the southwest. 887 *Berhtanwellan*, DB *Britewelle*.

Brignall (village, Durham): 'corner of land of Brȳni's people'. OE *-inga-*, 'of the people of', + *halh*, 'nook', 'corner of land'. DB *Bringenhale*.

Brigsley (village, NE Lincs): 'woodland clearing by a bridge'. OE *brycg*, 'bridge', + *lēah*, 'wood', 'clearing'. The bridge in question would probably have been over the present Waithe Beck. DB *Brigeslai*.

Brigstock (village, Northants): 'outlying farm by a bridge'. OE *brycg*, 'bridge', + *stoc*, 'outlying farmstead'. DB *Bricstoc*.

Brill (village, Bucks): '(place by the) hill (called) Bre'. OE *hyll*, 'hill', was added to a Celtic word meaning 'hill' (modern Welsh *bre*) when the latter lost its original meaning. Cp. BREEDON ON THE HILL. The DB form of the name below has an extraneous *n*. 1072 *Bruhella*, DB *Brunhelle*.

Brilley (village, Herefords): 'woodland clearing where broom grows'. OE *brōm*, 'broom', + *lēah*, 'wood', 'clearing'. 1219 *Brunlege*.

Brimfield (village, Herefords): 'open land where broom grows'. OE *brōm*, 'broom', + *feld*, 'open land' (modern English *field*). DB *Bromefeld*.

Brimington (suburb of Staveley, Derbys): 'estate associated with Brēme'. OE *-ing-*, 'associated with', + *tūn*, 'farmstead', 'estate'. DB *Brimintune*.

Brimpsfield (village, Glos): 'Brēme's open land'. OE *feld*, 'open land' (modern English *field*). DB *Brimesfelde*.

Brimsdown (district, Enfield): 'Gryme's down'. ME *doun*, 'down'. The 'down' would have been raised ground in marshland here by the river Lea. The first letter of the surname has changed. 1420 *Grymesdown*, 1610 *Brymesdowne*.

Brimstage (hamlet, Wirral): '(place by) Brūna's river bank'. OE *stæth*, 'landing place', 'river bank'. The OE word could not mean 'landing stage' here as Brimstage is inland on a small stream. 13C *Brunestathe*.

Brindle (village, Lancs): '(place at the) hill by a stream'. OE *burna*, 'stream', + *hyll*, 'hill'. The stream in question is Lostock Brook, which rises here. 1206 *Burnhull*.

Brineton (hamlet, Staffs): 'estate associated with Brȳni'. OE *-ing-*, 'associated with', + *tūn*, 'farmstead', 'estate'. DB *Brunitone*.

Bringhurst (village, Leics): 'wooded hill of Brȳni's people'. OE *-inga-*, 'of the people of', + *hyrst*, 'wooded hill'. 1188 *Bruninghyrst*.

Brington. See GREAT BRINGTON.

Briningham (village, Norfolk): 'homestead of Brȳni's people'. OE *-inga-*, 'of the people of', + *hām*, 'homestead'. DB *Bruningaham*.

Brinkley (village, Cambs): 'Brynca's woodland clearing'. OE *lēah*, 'wood', 'clearing'. Late 12C *Brinkelai*.

Brinklow (village, Warwicks): 'Brynca's burial mound'. OE *hlāw*, 'mound', 'hill'. The name could also mean 'burial mound on the brink of a hill' (OE *brince*, 'brink', + *hlāw*). William Dugdale writes in *The Antiquities of Warwickshire* (1656): 'This place hath its name doubtless from that eminent *Tumulus*, whereon the Keep, or Watch-tower of the Castle, which long ago was there, did stand; but whether it was because that this little hill, by our ancients termed a *low* stood upon the edge or *brink* of the natural ascent, overtopping the rest of the country thereabouts ... 'tis hard to say'. *c.*1155 *Brinckelawe*.

Brinkworth (village, Wilts): 'Brynca's enclosure'. OE *worth*, 'enclosure'. 1065 *Brinkewrtha*, DB *Brenchewrde*.

Brinscall (village, Lancs): '(place by the) burnt huts'. ME *brende*, 'burnt', + OS *skáli*, 'shieling', 'hut'. *c.*1200 *Brendescoles*.

Brinsley (village, Notts): 'Brūn's woodland clearing'. OE *lēah*, 'wood', 'clearing'. DB *Brunesleia*.

Brinsop (hamlet, Herefords): 'Brūn's or Brȳni's valley'. OE *hop*, 'valley'. DB *Hope*, *c.*1130 *Bruneshopa*.

Brinsworth (village, Rotherham): '(place by) Brȳni's ford'. OE *ford*, 'ford'. The present form of the name with *-worth* instead of the original *-ford* is first recorded only in the 19C. DB *Brinesford*.

Brinton (village, Norfolk): 'estate associated with Brȳni'. OE *-ing-*, 'associated with', + *tūn*, 'farmstead', 'estate'. DB *Bruntuna*.

Brisley (village, Norfolk): 'woodland clearing full of gadflies'. OE *brīosa*, 'gadfly', + *lēah*, 'wood', 'clearing'. *c.*1105 *Bruselea*.

Brislington (district, Bristol): 'Beorhthelm's farmstead'. OE *tūn*, 'farmstead'. The name has an identical origin to that of BRIGHTON. 1199 *Brihthelmeston*.

Bristol (city, Bristol): 'assembly place by the bridge'. OE *brycg*, 'bridge', + *stōw*, 'assembly place'. The original 'assembly place' may have been where Bristol Bridge is now, across the Floating Harbour. The final *-l* of the name is due to Norman French influence. The colloquial ME form of the name was *Bristow*, surviving as a surname. The name has been popularly interpreted as 'bright place': 'BRISTOL, more truly *Bright-stow*, that is, *illustrious* or *bright dwelling*, answers its name in many respects: *bright* in the situation thereof, conspicuous on the rising of a hill; *bright*, in the buildings, fair and firm; *bright* in the streets, so cleanly kept, as if scoured ... but chiefly *bright* for the inhabitants thereof, having bred so many eminent persons' (Thomas Fuller, *The Worthies of England*, 1662). 11C *Brycg stowe*, DB *Bristou*, 1290 *Brestol*.

Briston (village, Norfolk): 'farmstead by a landslip'. OE *byrst*, 'landslip' (related modern English *burst*), + *tūn*, 'farmstead'. Burston is in a pass on the upper reaches of the river Bure. DB *Burstuna*.

Britannia (suburb of Bacup, Lancs). The settlement arose in the 19C and took its name from an inn here.

Britannia Bridge (railway bridge, Gwynedd). The tubular bridge across the Menai Strait was designed by Robert Stephenson and opened in 1850. The centre tower was built on the Britannia Rock and the bridge took its name from it.

Britford (village, Wilts): '(place at the) ford of the Britons'. OE *Bryt*, '(Ancient) Briton', + *ford*, 'ford'. The river here is the Avon. 826 *Brutford*, DB *Bredford*, 1868 *Britford, or Burford*.

British Legion Village. See ROYAL BRITISH LEGION VILLAGE.

Briton Ferry (town, Neath PT): 'ferry at the farm by the bridge'. OE *brycg*, 'bridge', + *tūn*, 'farm', + modern English *ferry*. Nothing is known of a bridge over the river Neath here, but a ferry was recorded in the 16C. The Welsh name of the town is *Llansawel*, 'church of St Sawel' (Welsh *llan*, 'church'). The church at *Llansawel*, Carm, is dedicated to the same 6C saint, whose name is the equivalent of English Samuel. 1201 *Brigeton*, 1315 *Brytton*, 1536 *Britan Ferry caullid in Walsche Llanisauel*.

Britwell Salome (village, Oxon): 'de Suleham's (estate by the) spring of the Britons'. OE

Bryt, '(Ancient) Briton', + *wella*, 'spring', 'stream'. The de Suleham family held the manor here in the 13C. Cp. BERRICK SALOME. DB *Brutwelle*, 1320 *Brutewell Solham*.

Brixham (resort town, Devon): 'Brioc's homestead or enclosure'. OE *hām*, 'homestead', or *hamm*, 'enclosure'. The personal name is Celtic. The DB form of the name below is corrupt. DB *Briseham*, 1205 *Brikesham*.

Brixton (village, Devon): 'Brioc's farmstead'. OE *tūn*, 'farmstead'. The personal name is Celtic. The DB form of the name below is corrupt. DB *Brisetona*, 1200 *Brikeston*.

Brixton (district, Lambeth): 'Beorhtsige's stone'. OE *stān*, 'stone'. The 'stone' would probably have marked the assembly place of a hundred. 1062 *Brixges stan*, DB *Brixiestan*.

Brixton Deverill. See KINGSTON DEVERILL.

Brixworth (village, Northants): 'Beorhtel's or Bricel's enclosure'. OE *worth*, 'enclosure'. DB *Briclesworde*.

Brize Norton (village, Oxon): 'le Brun's northern farmstead'. OE *north*, 'northern', + *tūn*, 'farmstead', 'village'. William le Brun held land here in 1200. Brize Norton church is dedicated to St Britius, whose name may have been suggested by that of the village. DB *Nortone*, c.1266 *Northone Brun*.

Broad Blunsdon (village, Swindon): 'great (place by) Blunt's hill'. OE *dūn*, 'hill'. The first word of the name (OE *brād*, 'broad', 'great') distinguishes the village from nearby *Blunsdon St Andrew*, named after the dedication of its church. DB *Bluntesdone*, 1234 *Bradebluntesdon*.

Broad Campden. See CHIPPING CAMPDEN.

Broad Chalke (village, Wilts): 'great (place on the) chalk'. OE *brād*, 'broad', 'great', + *cealc*, 'chalk'. The first word of the name distinguishes the village from nearby *Bowerchalke* (OE *būra*, 'of the peasants', or *burh*, 'fortified place', + *cealc*). 955 *Ceolcum*, DB *Chelche*, 1380 *Brode Chalk*.

Broad Clyst (village, Devon): 'large (estate on the river) Clyst'. OE *brād*, 'broad', 'large'. For the river name, see CLYST HONITON. The first two forms of the name below mean 'farmstead on the Clyst' (OE *tūn*, 'farmstead'). DB *Clistone*, c.1100 *Clistun*, 1372 *Brodeclyste*.

Broad Colney. See LONDON COLNEY.

Broadford (village, Highland): 'broad ford'. The name of Skye's main village translates Gaelic *an t-ath leathan*, 'the broad ford', referring to the ford over the river here, now itself called the Broadford.

Broad Haven (coastal village, Pemb): '(place with a) wide harbour'. The first word of the name distinguishes the village from nearby LITTLE HAVEN. 1578 *Brode Hauen*.

Broadhembury (village, Devon): 'great high fortified place'. OE *brād*, 'broad', 'great', + *hēah*, 'high', + *burh*, 'fortified place'. The 'high fortified place' is the nearby Iron Age earthwork known as Hembury Fort. Broadhembury is 'great' for distinction from *Payhembury* to the south, where one Pǣga held the manor in or before the 13C. DB *Hanberia*, 1273 *Brodehembyri*.

Broadhempston (village, Devon): 'large (place called) Hǣme's or Hemme's farmstead'. OE *brād*, 'broad', 'large', + *tūn*, 'farmstead'. The first part of the name distinguishes this Hempston from *Littlehempston*, 2½ miles to the southeast. DB *Hamistone*, 1362 *Brodehempstone*.

Broad Hinton (village, Wilts): 'great high farmstead'. OE *brād*, 'broad', 'great', + *hēah*, 'high', + *tūn*, 'farmstead'. The first word distinguishes this Hinton from *Hinton Parva* or (less commonly) *Little Hinton*, Swindon, 9 miles to the northeast, where the name means 'farmstead belonging to a religious community' (OE *hīwan*, 'household (of monks)', genitive *hīgna*, + *tūn*). The manor here was held by the monks of Winchester. Cp. GREAT HINTON. DB *Hentone*, 1319 *Brodehenton*.

Broadland (council district, Norfolk): 'land of the Broads'. The region, northeast of Norwich, contains the Norfolk BROADS. The name dates only from the 19C.

Broad Marston. See LONG MARSTON.

Broadmayne (village, Dorset): 'great (place by the) stones'. OE *brād*, 'broad', 'great'. The second part of the name is of Celtic origin, related to modern Welsh *maen*, 'stone'. The reference would be to the many large sarsen stones nearby. The first part of the name distinguishes the village from nearby *Littlemayne*. DB *Maine*, 1202 *Brademaene*.

Broads, The (series of lakes, Norfolk): 'broad (waters)'. The name refers to the wider waters of the lakes by comparison with the 'narrows' of the rivers. The Broads are also known as the *Norfolk Broads*. See also OULTON BROAD. 1659 *Broades*.

Broadstairs (resort town, Kent): 'broad stairway'. OE *brād*, 'broad', + *stǣger*, 'stair'. A 'broad stairway' was cut in the cliff face here in the early 15C to give access to the sea. The fiction that the town was originally *Bradstow*, as if meaning 'broad place', is perpetuated in the central street Bradstow Way and in the name of Bradstow School. 1435 *Brodsteyr*.

Broadstone (district, Poole). The name is recent, and perhaps refers to stepping stones across the Blackwater stream here. Broadstone Farm was built in 1840 and a railway station in 1872, successively named *New Poole Junction, New Poole Junction and Broadstone, Broadstone and New Poole Junction* and finally *Broadstone*.

Broad Town (village, Wilts): 'large farmstead'. OE *brād*, 'broad', + *tūn*, 'farmstead'. The farm was 'large' by comparison with former nearby *Little Town*, now represented by *Littletown Farmhouse*. 12C *Bradetun*.

Broadwas (village, Worcs): 'broad stretch of alluvial land'. OE *brād*, 'broad', + *wæsse*, 'alluvial land' (related modern English *wash*). The name refers to a meandering river, here the Teme, that floods and drains quickly. The DB form of the name below has added OE *hām*, 'homestead'. 779 *Bradeuuesse*, DB *Bradewesham*.

Broadwater (district of Worthing, W Sussex): '(place at the) broad stream'. OE *brād*, 'broad', + *wæter*, 'water', 'stream'. The name implies a stream liable to flood, in this case probably the one between Worthing and Lancing. DB *Bradewatre*.

Broadway (town, Worcs): '(place at the) broad way'. OE *brād*, 'broad', + *weg*, 'way'. The 'broad way' is not the town's wide main road (the present A44) but the minor road running up to the village of Snowshill. 972 *Bradanuuege*, DB *Bradeweia*. SO ALSO: *Broadway*, Somerset.

Broadwell (village, Oxon): '(place by the) broad spring'. OE *brād*, 'broad', + *wella*, 'spring', 'stream'. The spring in question rises near Broadwell Manor. DB *Bradewelle*, 1868 *Broadwell, or Bradle*. SO ALSO: *Broadwell*, Glos, Warwicks.

Broadwey (village, Dorset): 'broad (place by the) river) Wey'. OE *brād*, 'broad'. For the river name, see WEYMOUTH. The first part of the name may refer to the width of the river here or to the extent of the manor. DB *Wai*, 1243 *Brode Way*, 1664 *Brodway*, 1868 *Broadway*.

Broadwindsor (village, Dorset): 'great (place by the) river bank with a windlass'. OE *brād*, 'broad', + *windels*, 'windlass', + *ōra*, 'bank'. Cp. WINDSOR. Broadwindsor is 'great' by comparison with nearby *Littlewindsor*. DB *Windesore*, 1324 *Brodewyndesore*, 1868 *Broadwinsor*.

Broadwoodkelly (village, Devon): 'de Kelly's (estate by the) broad wood'. OE *brād*, 'broad', + *wudu*, 'wood'. The de Kelly family held the manor here in the 13C, their name distinguishing this place from BROADWOODWIDGER, 17

miles to the southwest. The DB form of the name below has *h* for *w*. DB *Bradehoda*, 1261 *Brawode Kelly*.

Broadwoodwidger (village, Devon): 'Wyger's (estate by the) broad wood'. OE *brād*, 'broad', + *wudu*, 'wood'. The Wyger family held the manor here in the 13C, their name distinguishing this place from BROADWOODKELLY, 17 miles to the northeast. DB *Bradewode*, 1310 *Brodwode Wyger*.

Brobury (hamlet, Herefords): 'stronghold by a brook'. OE *brōc*, 'brook', + *burh*, 'fortified place', 'manor'. DB *Brocheberie*.

***Brocavum*.** See BROUGHAM.

Brockdish (village, Norfolk): 'pasture by the brook'. OE *brōc*, 'brook', + *edisc*, 'enclosure', 'pasture'. The DB form of the name below has *c* miscopied as *e*. DB *Brodise*, c.1095 *Brochedisc*.

Brockenhurst (town, Hants): 'Broca's wooded hill'. OE *hyrst*, 'wooded hill'. The first part of the name could also be OE *brocen*, 'broken', meaning land broken up by streams. The name is popularly explained as 'badgers' hill', as if from OE *brocc*, 'badger'. The DB form of the name below is corrupt. DB *Broceste*, 1158 *Brocheherst*.

Brockford Street (hamlet, Suffolk): '(place by the) ford over the brook'. OE *brōc*, 'brook', + *ford*, 'ford'. The second word of the name, referring to the hamlet's location on the Roman road from Colchester to Caistor St Edmund, distinguishes this Brockford from nearby *Brockford Green*. DB *Brocfort*.

Brockhall (village, Northants): '(place by the) badger sett'. OE *brocc-hol* (from *brocc*, 'badger', + *hol*, 'hole'). DB *Brocole*.

Brockham (village, Surrey): 'river meadow by the brook'. OE *brōc*, 'brook', + *hamm*, 'river meadow'. The first part of the name could also represent OE *brocc*, 'badger'. 1241 *Brocham*.

Brockhampton (hamlet, Herefords): 'homestead by the brook'. OE *brōc*, 'brook', + *hām-tūn*, 'homestead' (from *hām*, 'homestead', + *tūn*, 'farmstead'). 1251 *Brockampton*. SO ALSO: *Brockhampton*, Glos.

Brocklesby (village, Lincs): 'Bróklauss's farmstead'. OS *bý*, 'farmstead', 'village'. The personal name is Scandinavian. DB *Brochelesbi*.

Brockley (district, Lewisham): 'Broca's woodland clearing'. OE *lēah*, 'wood', 'clearing'. The name could also mean 'wood or clearing where badgers are seen' (OE *brocc*, 'badger', + *lēah*). 1182 *Brocele*.

Brockley (village, N Somerset): 'Broca's woodland clearing'. OE *lēah*, 'wood', 'clearing'. The name could also mean 'wood or clearing where badgers are seen' (OE *brocc*, 'badger', + *lēah*). DB *Brochelie*.

Brockton (village, Shropshire): 'farmstead by a brook'. OE *brōc*, 'brook', + *tūn*, 'farmstead'. There are six Brocktons in Shropshire, two of them now in Wrekin (one the present BRAT-TON). The form of the name below relates to the Brockton southwest of Much Wenlock, where the 'brook' is a small tributary of the river Corve. DB *Broctune*.

Brockworth (town, Glos): 'enclosure by the brook'. OE *brōc*, 'brook', + *worthign*, 'enclosure'. The brook in question is Horsbere Brook. DB *Brocowardinge*.

Brocton (village, Staffs): 'farmstead by a brook'. OE *brōc*, 'brook', + *tūn*, 'farmstead'. The brook in question is Oldacre Brook. DB *Broctone*.

Brodick (resort town, N Ayrs): '(place by the) broad bay'. OS *breithr*, 'broad', + *vík*, 'bay'. The Isle of Arran town is on the bay of the same name. 1306 *Brathwik*, 1450 *Bradewik*.

Brodsworth (village, Doncaster): 'Broddr's or Brord's enclosure'. OE *worth*, 'enclosure'. The personal names are respectively Scandinavian and OE. DB *Brodesworde*.

Brokenborough (village, Wilts): '(place by the) broken barrow'. OE *brocen*, 'broken', + *beorg*, 'hill', 'barrow'. The reference is probably to a local tumulus that had been broken into. 956 *Brokene beregge*, DB *Brocheneberge*.

Bromborough (district of Bebington, Wirral): 'Brūna's stronghold'. OE *burh*, 'fortified place'. Bromborough may have been the site of the battle of *Brunanburh* (937), in which the English under King Athelstan defeated an invading army of Norsemen from Ireland. Early 12C *Brunburg*, 1155 *Brumburh*, 1260 *Broneburgh*.

Brome (village, Suffolk): 'place where broom grows'. OE *brōm*, 'broom'. DB *Brom*.

Bromeswell (village, Suffolk): '(place on) rising ground where broom grows'. OE *brōm*, 'broom', + *swelle*, 'swelling'. DB *Bromeswella*.

Bromfield (village, Cumbria): '(place on) brown open land'. OE *brūn*, 'brown', + *feld*, 'open land' (modern English *field*). The first part of the name could also represent OE *brōm*, 'broom', giving a meaning 'open land where broom grows'. *c*.1125 *Brounefeld*.

Bromfield (village, Shropshire): 'open land where broom grows'. OE *brōm*, 'broom', + *feld*, 'open land' (modern English *field*). 1061 *Bromfelde*, DB *Brunfelde*.

Bromham (village, Wilts): 'homestead or enclosure where broom grows'. OE *brōm*, 'broom', + *hām*, 'homestead', or *hamm*, 'enclosure'. DB *Bromham*. SO ALSO: *Bromham*, Beds.

Bromley (borough, Greater London): 'woodland clearing where broom grows'. OE *brōm*, 'broom', + *lēah*, 'wood', 'clearing'. 862 *Bromleag*, DB *Bronlei*. SO ALSO: *Bromley*, Herts.

Bromley (district, Tower Hamlets): 'woodland clearing where brambles grow'. OE *bræmbel*, 'bramble', + *lēah*, 'wood', 'clearing'. The district is also known as *Bromley-by-Bow*, from its proximity to BOW, for distinction from what is now the borough of BROMLEY, some 8 miles to the south. *c*.1000 *Bræmbelege*, 1274 *Bromlegh*.

Bro Morgannwg. See GLAMORGAN.

Brompton (village, N Yorks): 'farmstead where broom grows'. OE *brōm*, 'broom', + *tūn*, 'farmstead'. The form of the name below is for Brompton near Scarborough, but the Brompton that is now a suburb of Northallerton has a name of identical origin. DB *Bruntun*.

Brompton-on-Swale (village, N Yorks): 'farmstead where broom grows on the (river) Swale'. OE *brōm*, 'broom', + *tūn*, 'farmstead'. The river name has an identical origin to that of the Swale at SWALECLIFFE. DB *Brunton*.

Brompton Ralph (village, Somerset): 'Ralph's farmstead by Brendon'. OE *tūn*, 'farmstead'. The first half of the first word of the name represents the nearby *Brendon* Hills (OE *brūn*, 'brown', + *dūn*, 'hill'). The manor here was held early by one Ralph, his name distinguishing this Brompton from *Brompton Regis*, 9 miles to the west, where the manor was held by the king (Latin *regis*, 'of the king'). DB *Burnetone*, 1274 *Brompton Radulphi*.

Brompton Regis. See BROMPTON RALPH.

Bromsberrow (hamlet, Glos): 'Brēme's hill'. OE *beorg*, 'hill'. The name could also mean 'hill where broom grows' (OE *brōm*, 'broom', + *beorg*). Perhaps the latter is more likely. DB *Brunmeberge*.

Bromsgrove (town, Worcs): 'Brēme's grove or copse'. OE *græfe*, 'grove', or *grāf*, 'copse'. 804 *Bremesgrefan*, DB *Bremesgrave*.

Bromyard (town, Herefords): 'enclosure where broom grows'. OE *brōm*, 'broom', + *geard*, 'enclosure' (modern English *yard*). *c*.840 *Bromgeard*, DB *Bromgerde*.

Brondesbury (district, Brent): 'Brand's manor'. OE *burh*, 'fortified place', 'manor'. 1254 *Bronnesburie*.

Brook (village, IoW): '(place by the) brook'. OE *brōc*, 'brook'. The name refers to the small stream that flows into the sea at Brook Bay nearby. DB *Broc*.

Brook (village, Kent): '(place by the) brook'. OE *brōc*, 'brook'. The brook in question is a tributary of the river Stour. 11C *Broca*.

Brooke (hamlet, Rutland): '(place by the) brook'. OE *brōc*, 'brook'. The 'brook' is the upper reaches of the river Gwash here. 1176 *Broc*. SO ALSO: *Brooke*, Norfolk.

Brookland (village, Kent): 'cultivated land by a brook'. OE *brōc*, 'brook', + *land*, 'cultivated land'. Brookland lies on the edge of the Romney Marshes. 1262 *Broklande*.

Brook Street (suburb of Brentwood, Essex): '(place by the) brook on the street'. OE *brōc*, 'brook'. The brook in question is Weald Brook, which south of Brook Street becomes the river Ingrebourne. The 'street' is the Roman road to Colchester (the present A1023). 1479 *Brokestreete*.

Brookthorpe (village, Glos): 'outlying farmstead by a brook'. OE *brōc*, 'brook', + *throp*, 'outlying farmstead', 'dependent settlement'. The DB form of the name below has *s* for *c*. DB *Brostorp*, 12C *Brocthrop*, 1868 *Brockthrop, or Brookthrop*.

Brookwood (village, Surrey): 'wood by a brook'. OE *brōc*, 'brook', + *wudu*, 'wood'. 1225 *Brocwude*.

Broom (village, Beds): 'place where broom grows'. OE *brōm*, 'broom'. DB *Brume*. SO ALSO: *Broom*, Warwicks.

Broome (village, Worcs): 'place where broom grows'. OE *brōm*, 'broom'. 1169 *Brom*. SO ALSO: *Broome*, Norfolk.

Broomfield (suburb of Chelmsford, Essex): 'open land where broom grows'. OE *brōm*, 'broom', + *feld*, 'open land' (modern English *field*). DB *Brumfeldam*.

Broomfleet (village, E Yorks): 'Brūngār's stretch of river'. OE *flēot*, 'stream'. The river in question is the Humber. 1150 *Brungareflet*.

Brora (coastal village, Highland): '(place by the) river of the bridge'. OS *brúar*, genitive of *brú*, 'bridge', + *á*, 'river'. The bridge, at the mouth of the Brora, was for long the only one in Sutherland. The first part of the form of the name below represents Gaelic *srath*, 'valley'. 1499 *Strabroray*.

Broseley (town, Shropshire): 'woodland clearing of the guardian of the fort'. OE *burhweard*, 'guardian of the fort' (from OE *burh*,

'fortified place', + *weard*, 'guardian', 'ward'), + *lēah*, 'wood', 'clearing'. The name could also mean 'Burgweard's woodland clearing'. 1177 *Burewardeslega*.

Brotherton (village, N Yorks): 'farmstead of the brother'. OE *brōthor*, 'brother', + *tūn*, 'farmstead'. The name could also mean 'Bróthir's farmstead', with a Scandinavian personal name. *c*.1030 *Brothertun*.

Brotton (town, Redcar & Clev): 'farmstead by a brook'. OE *brōc*, 'brook', + *tūn*, 'farmstead'. DB *Broctune*.

Brough (village, Cumbria): 'stronghold'. OE *burh*, 'fortified place'. The stronghold in question was the Roman fort of *Verteris* (perhaps meaning 'summit') on which a medieval castle was later built. 1174 *Burc*, 1198 *Burgus*, 1228 *Burgh*, 1594 *Brough*.

Brough (hamlet, Derbys): 'stronghold'. OE *burh*, 'fortified place'. The 'stronghold' was the Roman fort of *Navio* here, taking its name from the river Noe. Its own name, of Celtic origin, means 'fast-flowing'. This Brough is also known as *Brough-on-Noe*, for distinction from the others. 1195 *Burc*.

Brough (hamlet, E Yorks): 'stronghold'. OE *burh*, 'fortified place'. The 'stronghold' here was the Roman town of *Petuaria*, a Celtic name meaning 'fourth (part)' (modern Welsh *pedwar*, 'four'), referring to a division of the Parisii. This Brough, where Ermine Street crossed the Humber by ferry from Lincolnshire on its way north to York, is also known for distinction as *Brough-on-Humber*. *c*.1200 *Burg*, 1868 *Brough, or Brough Ferry*.

Brough (hamlet, Notts): 'stronghold'. OE *burh*, 'fortified place'. The 'stronghold' here on the Fosse Way was the Roman settlement of *Crococalana*, a Celtic name apparently meaning 'settlement by the tumulus'. 1525 *Burgh*.

Brougham (hamlet, Cumbria): 'homestead by the stronghold'. OE *burh*, 'fortified place', + *hām*, 'homestead'. The 'stronghold' here was the Roman fort of *Brocavum*. Its Celtic name perhaps means 'heathery place' (modern Welsh *grug*, 'heather'), although 'place where badgers are seen' (modern Welsh *broch*, 'badger') has also been suggested. 1130 *Bruham*.

Brough Sowerby. See TEMPLE SOWERBY.

Broughton (village, Flints): 'farmstead by the brook'. OE *brōc*, 'brook', + *tūn*, 'farmstead'. The stream here is itself called the Broughton Brook. The Welsh name of the village is *Brychdyn*, a form of the English. DB *Brochetune*.

Broughton (village, Northants): 'fortified farmstead'. OE *burh-tūn* (from *burh*, 'fortified place', + *tūn*, 'farmstead'). DB *Burtone*.

Broughton (village, N Lincs): 'farmstead by a hill'. OE *beorg*, 'hill', + *tūn*, 'farmstead'. The village is on a slope that ascends to the ridge along which Ermine Street runs. DB *Bertone*. SO ALSO: *Broughton*, Hants.

Broughton Astley (village, Leics): 'de Estle's farmstead by a brook'. OE *brōc*, 'brook', + *tūn*, 'farmstead'. The de Estle family held the manor here in the 13C. DB *Broctone*, 1423 *Broghton Astley*.

Broughton Gifford (village, Wilts): 'Giffard's farmstead by the brook'. OE *brōc*, 'brook', + *tūn*, 'farmstead'. The Giffard family held the manor here in the 13C. 1001 *Broctun*, DB *Broctone*, 1288 *Brocton Giffard*.

Broughton Hackett (village, Worcs): 'Hackett's farm by the brook'. OE *brōc*, 'brook', + *tūn*, 'farmstead'. The Hackett family held the manor here in the 12C. 972 *Broctun*, DB *Broctune*, 1275 *Broctone Haket*.

Broughton in Furness (village, Cumbria): 'farm by the brook in Furness'. OE *brōc*, 'brook', + *tūn*, 'farmstead'. For the district name, see BARROW-IN-FURNESS. 1196 *Brocton*.

Broughton Poggs (village, Oxon): 'Pugeys' farm by the brook'. OE *brōc*, 'brook', + *tūn*, 'farmstead'. The Pugeys family held land early here. DB *Brotone*, 1526 *Broughton Pouges*.

Brown Candover. See PRESTON CANDOVER.

Brownhills (town, Walsall): '(place by the) brown hills'. The name is recent. 1868 *Brownhills*.

Brownsea Island (island, Dorset): 'Brūnoc's island'. OE *ēg*, 'island'. Modern *island* was added when the presence of the original OE word was forgotten. 1241 *Brunkeseye*.

Brown Willy (hill, Cornwall): 'hill of swallows'. Cornish *bronn*, 'breast', 'hill', + *gwennol*, 'swallow'. Cornish *gwennol* is here in the plural (*gwennili*, 'swallows'). 1239 *Brunwenely*, 1576 *Brounwellye hill*.

Broxbourne (district of Hoddesdon, Herts): '(place by the) stream where badgers are seen'. OE *brocc*, 'badger', + *burna*, 'stream'. DB *Brochesborne*.

Broxburn (town, W Lothian): '(place by the) stream where badgers are seen'. OE *brocc*, 'badger', + *burna*, 'stream'. 1638 *Broxburne*.

Broxted (village, Essex): 'hill where badgers are seen'. OE *brocc*, 'badger', + *hēafod*, 'head', 'hill'. The name could also mean 'hill resembling a badger's head'. c.1050 *Brocheseued*, DB *Brocchesheuot*.

Broxton (village, Cheshire): 'village by the burial place'. OE *burgæsn*, 'burial place' (related modern English *bury*), + *tūn*, 'farmstead', 'village'. The interpretation of the name is doubtful, and the '-ton' is first recorded only in the 13C. DB *Brosse*, 1260 *Brocton*.

Broxtowe (council district, Notts): 'Brōcwulf's place'. OE *stōw*, 'place', 'assembly place'. The name is that of a former wapentake here. Its meeting place was probably at the site of the present Broxtowe Hall in Bilborough, now a district of Nottingham. DB *Brochelestou*.

Bruisyard (village, Suffolk): 'peasants' enclosure'. OE *būr*, 'peasant' (related modern English *boor*), + *geard*, 'enclosure' (modern English *yard*). DB *Buresiart*.

Brumby (district of Scunthorpe, N Lincs): 'Brúni's farmstead'. OS *bȳ*, 'farmstead'. The personal name is Scandinavian. The first part of the name could also represent OS *brunnr*, 'spring'. DB *Brunebi*.

Brundall (village, Norfolk): 'corner of land where broom grows'. OE *brōmede*, 'broomy', + *halh*, 'nook', 'corner of land'. DB *Brundala*.

Brundish (village, Suffolk): 'pasture by a stream'. OE *burna*, 'stream', + *edisc*, 'pasture'. 1177 *Burnedich*.

Brunton (hamlet, Northd): 'farmstead by a stream'. OE *burna*, 'stream', + *tūn*, 'farmstead'. 1242 *Burneton*.

Brushford (village, Devon): '(place at the) ford by the bridge'. OE *brycg*, 'bridge', + *ford*, 'ford'. The river here is the Taw. DB *Brigeford*.

Brushford (village, Somerset): '(place at the) ford by the bridge'. OE *brycg*, 'bridge', + *ford*, 'ford'. The river here is the Barle, a tributary of the Exe. DB *Brigeford*.

Bruton (town, Somerset): 'farmstead on the (river) Brue'. OE *tūn*, 'farmstead'. The river has a Celtic name meaning 'brisk'. DB *Briwetone*.

Bryanston (village, Dorset): 'Brian's estate'. OE *tūn*, 'farmstead', 'estate'. The manor here was held by Brian de Insula in the 13C and the place itself was originally called *Blaneford*, from nearby BLANDFORD. DB *Blaneford*, 1268 *Brianeston*.

Brychdyn. See BROUGHTON (Flints).

Bryher (island, Scilly): '(place of) hills'. Cornish *bre*, 'hill', + *-yer*, plural suffix. Bryher would at one time have been the hilliest part of the single island of Scilly. 'The island is really a series of low granite hills, sloping gently to the sea on the eastern side, but more steeply and rugged on the Atlantic side' (*The Shell Book of the Islands of Britain*, 1981). 1319 *Braer*.

Brympton (hamlet, Somerset): 'farmstead where broom grows'. OE *brōm*, 'broom', + *tūn*, 'farmstead'. DB *Brunetone*, 1264 *Brimpton*, 1331 *Bromton*, 1868 *Brimpton*.

Brynbuga. See USK.

Bryn-mawr (town, Blaenau Gwent): '(place on the) big hill'. Welsh *bryn*, 'hill', + *mawr*, 'big'. The name is very common in Wales. Until the early 19C Bryn-mawr was known as *Gwaunhelygen*, 'moorland of the willow tree' (Welsh *gwaun*, 'moorland', + *helygen*, 'willow tree'). 1832 *Bryn-mawr*.

Bubbenhall (village, Warwicks): 'Bubba's hill'. OE *hyll*, 'hill'. The DB form of the name has *a* for *u*. DB *Bubenhalle*, 1211 *Bubenhull*.

Bubwith (village, E Yorks): 'Bubba's wood'. OS *vithr*, 'wood'. The OS word may have replaced an earlier OE *wīc*, 'dwelling'. 1066 *Bobewyth*, DB *Bubvid*.

Buchan (region, Aberdeens): 'place of cows'. OW *buwch*, 'cow'. *c.*1150 *Buchan*.

Buckden (village, Cambs): 'Bucge's valley'. OE *denu*, 'valley'. The personal name is that of a woman. DB *Bugedene*.

Buckden (village, N Yorks): 'valley where bucks are seen'. OE *bucc*, 'buck' (male deer), + *denu*, 'valley'. 12C *Buckeden*.

Buckerell (village, Devon): meaning uncertain. The second part of the name may be related to that of CHICKERELL and similar names. 1165 *Bucherel*.

Buckfastleigh (town, Devon): 'wood or clearing near Buckfast'. OE *lēah*, 'wood', 'clearing'. *Buckfast*, a village to the north, has a name meaning 'place of shelter for bucks' (OE *bucc*, 'buck', 'male deer', + *fæsten*, 'stronghold'). 13C *Leghe Bucfestre*.

Buckhaven (town and port, Fife): 'harbour where bucks are seen'. OE *bucc*, 'buck', + *hæfen*, 'harbour', 'haven'. 1605 *Buckheven*, 1618 *Buckhevin*.

Buckhorn Weston (village, Dorset): 'Bouker's (estate at the) western farmstead'. OE *west*, 'western', + *tūn*, 'farmstead', 'village'. The farm may have been 'west' with regard to Gillingham. A man named (or nicknamed) Bouker held the manor early here. DB *Westone*, 1275 *Boukeresweston*.

Buckhurst Hill (residential district, Essex): 'wooded hill where beech trees grow'. OE *bōc*, 'beech', + *hyrst*, 'wooded hill'. An alternative name *Goldhurst* was recorded in the 15C, presumably referring to the autumn colouring of the beech leaves. 1135 *Bocherst*.

Buckie (resort town, Moray): '(place of) bucks'. Gaelic *boc*, 'buck', 'male deer'. The name was originally that of the stream here, the Burn of Buckie. 1362 *Buky*.

Buckingham (town, Bucks): 'river bend of Bucca's people'. OE *-inga-*, 'of the people of', + *hamm*, 'enclosure', 'land in a river bend'. Buckingham lies in a bend of the river Ouse. Early 10C *Buccingahamme*, DB *Bochingeham*.

Buckinghamshire (county, S central England): 'district based on Buckingham'. OE *scīr*, 'shire', 'district'. See BUCKINGHAM. 11C *Buccingahamscir*.

Buckland (village, Surrey): 'charter land'. OE *bōc-land* (from *bōc*, 'beech', 'book', + *land*, 'land'). The name refers to an estate having certain rights and privileges created by written royal decree. DB *Bochelant*.

Buckland Brewer (village, Devon): 'Briwerre's (estate on) charter land'. OE *bōc-land* (see BUCKLAND). The manor here was held in the 13C by the Briwerre family, whose name distinguishes the village from *Buckland Filleigh*, 9 miles to the southeast, where it was held by the de Fyleleye family. DB *Bochelanda*, 1290 *Boclande Bruere*.

Buckland Dinham (village, Somerset): 'de Dinan's (estate on) charter land'. OE *bōc-land* (see BUCKLAND). The de Dinan family held the manor here in the 13C. 951 *Boclande*, DB *Bochelande*, 1329 *Bokelonddynham*.

Buckland Filleigh. See BUCKLAND BREWER.

Buckland in the Moor. See EGG BUCKLAND.

Buckland Monachorum. See EGG BUCKLAND.

Buckland Newton (village, Dorset): 'charter land near Sturminster Newton'. OE *bōc-land* (see BUCKLAND). The village lies 8 miles southwest of STURMINSTER NEWTON (originally known as *Newton*). The alternative last form of the name below refers to Glastonbury Abbey, who held the manor here. 941 *Boclonde*, DB *Bochelande*, 1576 *Newton Buckland*, 1868 *Buckland-Newton*, or *Buckland Abbas*.

Bucklebury (village, W Berks): 'Burghild's stronghold'. OE *burh*, 'fortified place'. The personal name is that of a woman. DB *Borgeldeberie*.

Bucklers Hard (village, Hants): 'Buckler's hard'. A 'hard' is a firm landing place, in this case on the river Beaulieu. The Buckler family are recorded here in 1664. 1789 *Bucklers Hard*.

Bucklesham (village, Suffolk): 'Buccel's homestead'. OE *hām*, 'homestead', 'village'. DB *Bukelesham*.

Buckley (town, Flints): 'wood of the bucks'. OE *bucc*, 'buck', 'male deer', + *lēah*, 'wood', 'clearing'. The Welsh form of the name is *Bwcle*. 1294 *Bokkeley*, 1301 *Bukkelee*.

Buckminster (village, Leics): 'Bucca's large church'. OE *mynster*, 'minster', 'large church'. DB *Bucheminstre*.

Bucknall (district of Stoke-on-Trent, Stoke): 'Bucca's corner of land'. OE *halh*, 'nook', 'corner of land'. The name could also mean 'corner of land where he-goats graze' (OE *bucca*, 'he-goat', + *halh*). DB *Bucenhole*. SO ALSO: *Bucknall*, Lincs.

Bucknell (village, Oxon): 'Bucca's hill'. OE *hyll*, 'hill'. The name could also mean 'hill where he-goats graze' (OE *bucca*, 'he-goat', + *hyll*). DB *Buchehelle*. SO ALSO: *Bucknell*, Shropshire.

Buckton (hamlet, E Yorks): 'Bucca's farmstead'. OE *tūn*, 'farmstead'. The name could also mean 'farmstead where bucks or he-goats are kept' (OE *bucc*, 'buck', 'male deer', or *bucca*, 'he-goat', + *tūn*). DB *Bochetone*. SO ALSO: *Buckton*, Herefords, Northd.

Budbrooke (village, Warwicks): '(place by) Budda's brook'. OE *brōc*, 'brook'. DB *Budebroc*.

Budby (hamlet, Notts): 'Butti's farmstead'. OS *bý*, 'farmstead', 'village'. The personal name is Scandinavian. DB *Butebi*.

Bude (resort town, Cornwall): '(place on the river) Bude'. The origin of the river name is uncertain. A meaning 'dirty' has been suggested. 1400 *Bude*.

Budle (coastal hamlet, Northd): 'special building'. OE *bōthl*, 'special building'. 1166 *Bolda*.

Budleigh Salterton (resort town, Devon): 'building where salt is made near Budleigh'. OE *salt-ærn* (from *salt*, 'salt', + *ærn*, 'house', 'building'). The nearby village of *East Budleigh* has a basic name meaning 'Budda's woodland clearing' (OE *lēah*, 'wood', 'clearing'). 1210 *Saltre*, 1405 *Salterne in the manor of Buddeleghe*.

Budock Water (village, Cornwall): 'St Budoc's church by the water'. The village arose in the 19C on a stream ('water') by the church, which is dedicated to Budoc, as at ST BUDEAUX. 1884 *Budockwater*.

Buerton (village, Cheshire): 'enclosure belonging to a fortified place'. OE *byrh-tūn* (from *burh*, 'fortified place', + *tūn*, 'farmstead', 'enclosure'). The nature of the 'fortified place' is uncertain. DB *Burtune*.

Bugbrooke (village, Northants): '(place by) Bucca's brook'. OE *brōc*, 'brook'. DB *Buchebroc*.

Bugle (village, Cornwall). The village grew up in the 19C round the inn of the same name, which was built in *c.*1840 and apparently named in honour of a local bugler. 1888 *Bugle*, 1893 *Carnrosemary, ... locally called Bugle*.

Bugthorpe (village, E Yorks): 'Buggi's outlying farmstead'. OS *thorp*, 'outlying farmstead'. The personal name is Scandinavian. DB *Bugetorp*.

Buildwas (village, Shropshire): '(place on) alluvial land'. OE *wæsse*, 'alluvial land'. The first part of the name is of uncertain origin. It may represent an OE word related to modern English *bold*, referring to surging water. Buildwas overlooks a stretch of the river Severn that meanders over a flood plain, in which land can be dry and suitable for grazing one day and a lake the next. DB *Beldewas*.

Builth Wells (town, Powys): 'cow pasture with springs'. Welsh *bu*, 'cow', + *gellt* (later *gwellt*), 'pasture'. The second word of the name was added in the 19C when chalybeate springs were discovered here. The town's Welsh name is *Llanfair-ym-Muallt*, 'St Mary's church in Buallt' (Welsh *llan*, 'church', + *Mair*, 'Mary', + *yn*, 'in'). *Buallt* gave English *Builth*. 10C *Buelt*.

Bulford (village, Wilts): '(place by the) ford where ragged robin grows'. OE *bulut*, 'ragged robin', + *ford*, 'ford'. The ford in question would have been over one of the streams into which the river Avon is divided here. 12C *Bultesford*.

Bulkeley (village, Cheshire): 'pasture where bullocks graze'. OE *bulluc*, 'bullock', + *lēah*, 'clearing', 'pasture'. 1170 *Bulceleia*.

Bulkington (village, Warwicks): 'estate associated with Bulca'. OE *-ing-*, 'associated with', + *tūn*, 'farmstead', 'estate'. DB *Bochintone*. SO ALSO: *Bulkington*, Wilts.

Bulkworthy (village, Devon): 'Bulca's enclosure'. OE *worth*, 'enclosure'. DB *Buchesworde*.

Bulley (hamlet, Glos): 'woodland clearing where bulls graze'. OE *bula*, 'bull', + *lēah*, 'wood', 'clearing'. DB *Bulelege*.

Bullinghope. See LOWER BULLINGHAM.

Bulmer (village, Essex): '(place by the) pool where bulls come'. OE *bula*, 'bull', + *mere*, 'pool'. DB *Bulenemera*. SO ALSO: *Bulmer*, N Yorks.

Bulphan (village, Thurrock): '(place in the) fen with a fortified place'. OE *burh*, 'fortified place', + *fenn*, 'fen'. The *r* of *burh* became *l* under Norman influence, as for SALISBURY. DB *Bulgeuen*.

Bulverhythe (coastal suburb of Hastings, E Sussex): 'landing place of the town dwellers'. OE *burh-ware* (from *burh*, 'fortified place', 'town', + *-ware*, 'dwellers'), + *hȳth*, 'landing place'. The 'town dwellers' in question are those of Hastings. 12C *Bulwareheda*.

Bulwell (district, Nottingham): '(place by) Bula's spring'. OE *wella*, 'spring', 'stream'. The name could also mean '(place by the) spring where bulls drink' (OE *bula*, 'bull', + *wella*). DB *Buleuuelle*.

Bulwick (village, Northants): 'farm where bulls are kept'. OE *bula*, 'bull', + *wīc*, 'farm'. 1162 *Bulewic*.

Bunbury (village, Cheshire): 'Būna's stronghold'. OE *burh*, 'fortified place'. The name is popularly associated with St Boniface, to whom the church here is dedicated. The DB form below has *l* for *n* in the personal name. DB *Boleberie*, 12C *Bonebury*.

Bungay (town, Suffolk): 'island of Būna's people'. OE *-inga-*, 'of the people of', + *ēg*, 'island'. The 'island' is land in a loop of the river Waveney here. DB *Bunghea*.

Bunny (village, Notts): 'island where reeds grow'. OE *bune*, 'reed', + *ēg*, 'island'. The 'island' here is dry ground in marshland, the latter lying to the west of the village. DB *Bonei*.

Buntingford (town, Herts): '(place by the) ford where buntings are seen'. ME *bunting + ford*. The ford would have been over the river Rib here. 1185 *Buntingeford*.

Bunwell (hamlet, Norfolk): '(place by the) stream where reeds grow'. OE *bune*, 'reed', + *wella*, 'spring', 'stream'. 1198 *Bunewell*.

Burbage (district of Buxton, Derbys): 'stream by a fortified place'. OE *burh*, 'fortified place', + *bece*, 'stream'. The second part of the name could also represent OE *bæc*, 'ridge' (modern English *back*). 1417 *Burbache*.

Burbage (suburb of Hinckley, Leics): 'ridge by a fortified place'. OE *burh*, 'fortified place', + *bæc*, 'ridge' (modern English *back*). The 'ridge' is the hill on which Burbage lies. 1043 *Burhbeca*, DB *Burbece*.

Burbage (village, Wilts): 'stream by a fortified place'. OE *burh*, 'fortified place', + *bece*, 'stream'. A meaning 'ridge by a fortified place' (OE *bæc*, 'ridge') is also possible, referring to nearby Easton Hill. The 'fortified place' would be the (traces of the) ancient earthwork known as Godsbury, to the south. 961 *Burhbece*, DB *Burbetce*.

Burcombe (village, Wilts): 'Brȳda's valley'. OE *cumb*, 'valley'. 937 *Brydancumb*, DB *Bredecumbe*.

Burdale (hamlet, N Yorks): 'house made of planks'. OE *bred*, 'board', 'plank', + *hall*, 'hall', 'house'. DB *Bredhalle*.

Bures (village, Essex): '(place at the) dwellings'. OE *būr*, 'cottage', 'dwelling' (modern English *bower*). DB *Bura*, 1198 *Bures*.

Burford (town, Oxon): '(place at the) ford by the fortified place'. OE *burh*, 'fortified place', + *ford*, 'ford'. The town is in a hilly location (a natural 'fortified place') on the river Windrush. DB *Bureford*. SO ALSO: *Burford*, Shropshire.

Burgess Hill (town, W Sussex): '(place by) Burgeys' hill'. A family named Burgeys was here in the 13C. 1597 *Burges Hill*.

Burgh (village, Suffolk): 'fortification'. OE *burh*, 'fortified place'. The bank on which the church was built is thought to have been the site of a Roman encampment. DB *Burc*.

Burgh-by-Sands (village, Cumbria): 'fortification by the sands'. OE *burh*, 'fortified place'. The village, on Hadrian's Wall, is on sandy soil on the site of an old Roman fort called *Aballava*, '(place of) apples', a Celtic name related to the *Avalon* of Arthurian legend. *c.*1180 *Burch*, 1292 *Burg en le Sandes*.

Burgh Castle (village, Norfolk): 'castle at the fortified place'. OE *burh*, 'fortified place'. The 'fortified place' is the Roman fort *Gariannum*, whose name is essentially that of the river Yare here, near YARMOUTH, while the castle is the Norman one built on its site. DB *Burch*, 1281 *Borough-Castell*.

Burghclere. See KINGSCLERE.

Burghfield (village, W Berks): '(place on the) open land by the hill'. OE *beorg*, 'hill', + *feld*, 'open land' (modern English *field*). Burghfield lies on the lower slopes of a raised area. DB *Borgefel*.

Burghill (village, Herefords): '(place by the) hill with a fort'. OE *burh*, 'fortified place', + *hyll*, 'hill'. The 'fort' is the square encampment on nearby Burghill itself. DB *Burgelle*.

Burgh le Marsh (village, Lincs): 'fortified place in the marshland'. OE *burh*, 'fortified place'. The second part of the name distinguishes the village from *Burgh on Bain*, some 22 miles to the north (with river name as for BAINBRIDGE). DB *Burg*, 1275 *Burgo in Marisco*, 1868 *Burgh-in-the-Marsh*.

Burgh on Bain. See BURGH LE MARSH.

Burgh St Margaret (village, Norfolk): 'fortified place with St Margaret's church'. OE *burh*, 'fortified place'. The church dedication distinguishes this Burgh from *Burgh St Peter*, 14 miles to the south. The 'fortified place' may have been a Roman coastal defence, but if so its location is unknown. DB *Burh*, 1286 *Burgo Sancte Margarete*.

Burghwallis (village, Doncaster): 'Waleys' (estate at the) fortified manor'. OE *burh*, 'fortified place'. The Waleys family held the manor here from the 12C. DB *Burg*, 1283 *Burghwaleys*.

Buriton (village, Hants): 'farmstead by the fortified place'. OE *burh*, 'fortified place', + *tūn*, 'farmstead'. The 'fortified place' is the Iron Age earthwork on nearby Butser Hill. 1227 *Buriton*.

Burlawn (village, Cornwall): 'Lowen's house'. OC *bod*, 'house', 'dwelling'. The name could in theory also mean 'happy house' (OC *bod* + *lowen*, 'happy') but the personal name is more likely. 1243 *Bodolowen*.

Burlescombe (hamlet, Devon): 'Burgweald's valley'. OE *cumb*, 'valley'. The DB form of the name below has contracted the personal name. DB *Berlescoma*, 12C *Burewoldescumbe*.

Burleston (hamlet, Dorset): 'Burdel's farmstead'. OE *tūn*, 'farmstead'. 934 *Bordelestone*.

Burley (village, Rutland): 'woodland clearing by (or belonging to) a fortified place'. OE *burh*, 'fortified place', + *lēah*, 'wood', 'clearing'. The 'fortified place' was probably nearby Hambleton. DB *Burgelai*. SO ALSO: *Burley*, Hants, Leeds.

Burleydam (village, Cheshire): 'woodland clearing of the peasants with a dam'. OE *būr*, 'peasant' (related modern English *boor*), + *lēah*, 'wood', 'clearing', + ME *damme*, 'dam'. The latter part of the name refers to an old mill dam here. *c*.1130 *Burley*, 1643 *Burleydam*.

Burley in Wharfedale (village, Bradford): 'woodland clearing by (or belonging to) a fortified place in the valley of the (river) Wharfe'. OE *burh*, 'fortified place', + *lēah*, 'wood', 'clearing', + OS *dalr*, 'valley'. The river has a Celtic name meaning 'winding one'. The precise location of the 'fortified place' is unknown. *c*.972 *Burhleg*, DB *Burghelai*.

Burmington (village, Warwicks): 'estate associated with Beornmund or Beorma'. OE *-ing-*, 'associated with', + *tūn*, 'farmstead', 'estate'. The DB form of the name below has *d* for *m*. DB *Burdintone*, late 12C *Burminton*.

Burn (village, N Yorks): 'place cleared by burning'. OE *bryne*, 'burning'. *c*.1030 *Byrne*.

Burnaston (village, Derby): 'Brūnwulf's or Brynjólfr's farmstead'. OE *tūn*, 'farmstead'. The personal names are respectively OE and Scandinavian. DB *Burnulfestune*.

Burnby (village, E Yorks): 'farmstead by a stream'. OS *brunnr*, 'spring', 'stream', + *bý*, 'farmstead', 'village'. DB *Brunebi*.

Burneside (village, Cumbria): 'Brūnwulf's or Brunulf's hill'. OE *hēafod*, 'headland', 'hill'. The hill in question is the one near the confluence of the rivers Kent and Sprint by Burnside Hall. The personal names are respectively OE and Old German. *c*.1180 *Brunoluesheued*.

Burneston (village, N Yorks): 'Brýningr's farmstead'. OE *tūn*, 'farmstead'. The personal name is Scandinavian. Cp. BURNISTON. DB *Brennigston*.

Burnett (hamlet, Bath & NE Somerset): 'land cleared by burning'. OE *bærnet*, 'burning'. DB *Bernet*.

Burnham Beeches (region of woodland, Bucks): 'beech trees by Burnham'. The village of *Burnham* here has a name meaning 'homestead by a stream' (OE *burna*, 'stream', + *hām*, 'homestead', 'village'). DB *Burneham*.

Burnham Deepdale. See BURNHAM MARKET.

Burnham Market (village, Norfolk): 'village by a stream with a market'. OE *burna*, 'stream', + *hām*, 'homestead', 'village'. The second word of the name distinguishes the village from other Burnhams in this part of northern Norfolk: *Burnham Deepdale*, 'deep valley' (OE *dēop*, 'deep', + *dæl*, 'valley'), *Burnham Norton*, 'northern farmstead' (OE *north*, 'northern', + *tūn*, 'farmstead'), *Burnham Overy*, 'over the river' (OE *ofer*, 'over', + *ēa*, 'river'), and *Burnham Thorpe*, 'outlying farmstead' (OS *thorp*, 'outlying farmstead'). Burnham Overy is divided into *Burnham Overy Staithe* (OE *stæth*, 'landing place'), on a creek of the river Burn, and *Burnham Overy Town*, across the river. Burnham Market was also known as *Burnham Westgate* ('western gate'). DB *Bruneham*.

Burnham Norton. See BURNHAM MARKET.

Burnham-on-Crouch (town, Essex): 'village by a stream on the (river) Crouch'. OE *burna*, 'stream', + *hām*, 'homestead'. The 'stream' in question is to the north of the town, which lies on the estuary of the Crouch. The river appears to derive its name from a place called (or based on) *Crouch*, itself from OE *crūc*, 'cross'. DB *Burneham*.

Burnham-on-Sea (resort town, Somerset): 'enclosure by a stream by the sea'. OE *burna*, 'stream', + *hamm*, 'enclosure'. The 'stream' is the river Brue here. The latter part of the name is a recent addition designed as a touristic lure rather than to distinguish from another Burnham. *c*.880 *Burnhamm*, DB *Burneham*.

Burnham Overy. See BURNHAM MARKET.

Burnhams, The. See BURNHAM MARKET.

Burnham Thorpe. See BURNHAM MARKET.

Burniston (village, N Yorks): 'Brýningr's farmstead'. OE *tūn*, 'farmstead'. The personal name is Scandinavian. Cp. BURNESTON. DB *Brinniston*.

Burnley (town, Lancs): 'woodland clearing by the (river) Brun'. OE *lēah*, 'wood', 'clearing'. The river name means either 'brown' (OE *brūn*) or simply 'river' (OE *burna*, 'stream'). 1124 *Brunlaia*.

Burnsall (village, N Yorks): 'Brýni's corner of land'. OE *halh*, 'nook', 'corner of land'. DB *Brineshale*.

Burntisland (coastal town, Fife): 'burnt island'. OE *brende*, 'burnt', + modern English *island*. A 'burnt island' is one where buildings were destroyed by fire or where land was cleared for cultivation by burning. The burning in this case is said to have been of fishermen's huts on a small island east of the present harbour. *c*.1600 *Bruntisland*.

Burnt Oak (district, Barnet): '(place by the) burnt oak'. The name was originally that of a field here on the parish boundary, itself so called from a burnt oak tree (perhaps struck by lightning) that served as a landmark. 1754 *Burnt Oak Close*.

Burpham (district of Guildford, Surrey): 'homestead by the stronghold'. OE *burh*, 'fortified place', + *hām*, 'homestead'. The 'stronghold' may have guarded the river Wey here. DB *Borham*.

Burpham (village, W Sussex): 'homestead by the stronghold'. OE *burh*, 'fortified place', + *hām*, 'homestead'. The 'stronghold' was probably the ancient earthwork here, which may have guarded the river Arun. *c*.920 *Burhham*, DB *Bercheham*.

Burradon (hamlet, Northd): 'hill with a fort'. OE *burh*, 'fortified place', + *dūn*, 'hill'. early 13C *Burhedon*. SO ALSO: *Burradon*, N Tyneside.

Burrill (hamlet, N Yorks): 'hill with a fort'. OE *burh*, 'fortified place', + *hyll*, 'hill'. DB *Borel*.

Burringham (village, N Lincs): 'estate of Burgrēd's or Burgrīc's people'. OE *-inga-*, 'of the people of', + *hām*, 'homestead', 'estate'. 1199 *Burringham*.

Burrington (village, Devon): 'estate associated with Beorn'. OE *-ing-*, 'associated with', + *tūn*, 'farmstead', 'estate'. DB *Bernintone*.

Burrington (village, Herefords): 'farmstead by a fortified place'. OE *burh*, 'fortified place', + *tūn*, 'farmstead'. The first part of the name represents OE *byrig*, the genitive (or dative) form of *burh*. DB *Boritune*.

Burrington (village, N Somerset): 'farmstead by a fortified place'. OE *burh*, 'fortified place', + *tūn*, 'farmstead'. Cp. BURRINGTON (Herefords). 12C *Buringtune*.

Burrough Green (village, Cambs): 'fortified place'. OE *burh*, 'fortified place'. The remains of an ancient earthwork may still be seen here in Park Wood as those of the original 'fortified place'. The village subsequently became associated with its green. *c*.1045 *Burg*, DB *Burch*, 1571 *Boroughegrene*.

Burrough on the Hill (village, Leics): 'fortified place on the hill'. OE *burh*, 'fortified place'. The hill here has the remains of an extensive Iron Age camp. DB *Burg*.

Burrow Bridge (village, Somerset): '(place) at the hill with a bridge'. OE *beorg*, 'hill'. The bridge was over the river Parrett here. The form of the name below means 'at the hill'. 1065 *Æt tham Beorge*.

Burry Port (town and port, Carm): 'port of the sand dune'. Modern English dialect *burry*, 'burrow', + modern English *port*. The town is named for the 'burrows' (sand dunes) that lie to the west.

Burscough (village, Lancs): 'wood by the fort'. OE *burh*, 'fortified place', + OS *skógr*, 'wood'. *c*.1190 *Burscogh*.

Burshill (hamlet, E Yorks): '(place by the) hill with a landslip'. OE *byrst*, 'landslip' (related modern English *burst*), + *hyll*, 'hill'. 12C *Bristehil*.

Bursledon (village, Hants): '(place by the) hill associated with Beorhtsige'. OE *-ing-*, 'associated with', + *dūn*, 'hill'. *c*.1170 *Brixendona*.

Burslem (town, Stoke): 'Burgweard's (estate in) Lyme (Forest)'. The first part of the name could also mean 'keeper of the fort' (OE *burhweard*, from *burh*, 'fort', + *weard*, 'keeper'). *Lyme Forest* has a Celtic name meaning 'region of elms'. Cp. ASHTON-UNDER-LYNE. The DB form of the name below has garbled the personal name. DB *Barcardeslim*, 1242 *Borewardeslyme*.

Burstall (village, Suffolk): 'site of a stronghold'. OE *burh-stall* (from *burh*, 'fortified place', + *stall*, 'stall', 'site'). DB *Burgestala*.

Burstock (village, Dorset): 'Burgwynn's or Burgwine's outlying farmstead'. OE *stoc*, 'outlying farmstead'. The personal names are respectively those of a woman and a man. DB *Burewinestoch*.

Burston (village, Norfolk): 'farmstead by a landslip'. OE *byrst*, 'landslip' (related modern English *burst*), + *tūn*, 'farmstead'. Cp. BRISTON. DB *Borstuna*.

Burston (hamlet, Staffs): 'Burgwine's or Burgwulf's farmstead'. OE *tūn*, 'farmstead'. DB *Burouestone*.

Burstow (village, Surrey): 'place by a stronghold'. OE *burh*, 'fortified place', + *stōw*, 'place'. 12C *Burestou*.

Burstwick (village, E Yorks): 'Bursti's farm'. OE *wīc*, 'dwelling', 'farm'. The personal name is Scandinavian. DB *Brostewic*.

Burton (village, Cheshire): 'farmstead near a fortification'. OE *burh*, 'fortified place', + *tūn*, 'farmstead'. The reference is to the Iron Age fort at Burton Point here on the Wirral peninsula. 1152 *Burton*.

Burton Agnes (village, E Yorks): 'Agnes's fortified farmstead'. OE *burh-tūn* (from *burh*, 'fortified place', + *tūn*, 'farmstead'). The manor here was held in the late 12C by Agnes de Percy. Her name distinguishes this Burton from *Burton Fleming* (or *North Burton*), 6 miles to the north, where the manor was held by the Fleming family, *Burton Constable*, 19 miles to the south, held in the 12C by the constables of Richmond Castle, and *Burton Pidsea*, 22 miles to the south, near a pool in the marsh (OE *pide*, 'marsh', + *sǣ*, 'pool'). See also BISHOP BURTON. DB *Bortona*, 1231 *Burton Agneys*.

Burton Bradstock (village, Dorset): 'farmstead on the (river) Bride belonging to Bradenstoke'. OE *tūn*, 'farmstead'. For the river name, see BRIDPORT. The manor here was held in the 13C by the Abbey of BRADENSTOKE. DB *Bridetone*.

Burton Constable. See BURTON AGNES.

Burton Dassett. See AVON DASSETT.

Burton Fleming. See BURTON AGNES.

Burton Hastings (village, Warwicks): 'de Hasteng's fortified farmstead'. OE *burh-tūn* (from *burh*, 'fortified place', + *tūn*, 'farmstead'). William Dugdale comments on the main name in *The Antiquities of Warwickshire* (1656): 'From the old English word *burh* and *burgh* (as I guess) signifying, with the Saxons, not only a place fortified with some warlike rampier [i.e. rampart] or wall, but that which had a kind of fence or enclosure about it'. The de Hasteng family held the manor here in the 13C. 1002 *Burhtun*, DB *Bortone*, 1313 *Burugton de Hastings*.

Burton Joyce (suburb of Nottingham, Notts): 'de Jorz's farmstead of the fortified place'. OE *byrh-tūn* (from *byrh*, genitive of *burh*, 'fortified place', + *tūn*, 'farmstead'). The de Jorz family held the manor here in the 13C. DB *Bertune*, 1327 *Birton Jorce*.

Burton Latimer (town, Northants): 'le Latimer's fortified farmstead'. OE *burh-tūn* (from *burh*, 'fortified place', + *tūn*, 'farmstead'). The le Latimer family held the manor here in the 13C, their name distinguishing this Burton from nearby *Burton Wold*. DB *Burtone*, 1482 *Burton Latymer*.

Burton Lazars (village, Leics): 'fortified farmstead with St Lazarus' hospital'. OE *burh-tūn* (from *burh*, 'fortified place', + *tūn*, 'farmstead'). The hospital of St Lazarus for lepers was founded here in 1135, its name alluding to the biblical Lazarus, a beggar covered in sores (Luke 16:20). DB *Burtone*.

Burton Leonard (village, N Yorks): 'fortified farmstead with St Leonard's church'. OE *burh-tūn* (from *burh*, 'fortified place', + *tūn*, 'farmstead'). The church here was formerly dedicated to St Helen, but is now, and was presumably earlier, dedicated to St Leonard. DB *Burtone*, 1276 *Burton Leonard*.

Burton Pidsea. See BURTON AGNES.

Burton Salmon (village, N Yorks): 'Salamone's (estate at the) farmstead of the Britons'. OE *Brettas*, '(Ancient) Britons', + *tūn*, 'farmstead'. One Salamone held lands here in the 13C. c.1160 *Brettona*, 1516 *Burton Salamon*.

Burton upon Stather (village, N Lincs): 'farmstead of the fortified place by the landing places'. OE *byrh-tūn* (from *byrh*, genitive of *burh*, 'fortified place', + *tūn*, 'farmstead'), + OS *stǫthvar*, plural of *stǫth*, 'landing place'. The landing places in question would have been on the river Trent. The location of the fortified place is unknown. DB *Burtone*, 1201 *Burton-stathel*.

Burton upon Trent (town, Staffs): 'farmstead of the fortified place on the (river) Trent'. OE *byrh-tūn* (from *byrh*, genitive of *burh*, 'fortified place', + *tūn*, 'farmstead'). For the river name, see STOKE-ON-TRENT. 1002 *Byrtun*, DB *Bertone*, 1234 *Burton super Trente*.

Burtonwood (town, Warrington): 'wood by the fortified farmstead'. OE *burh-tūn* (from *burh*, 'fortified place', + *tūn*, 'farmstead'), + *wudu*, 'wood'. The site of the original 'fortified farmstead' is uncertain. 1228 *Burtoneswod*.

Burwardsley (village, Cheshire): 'woodland clearing of the guardian of the stronghold'. OE *burh-weard*, 'fort keeper' (from *burh*, 'fortified place', + *weard*, 'watch'), + *lēah*, 'wood', 'clearing'. The name could also mean 'Burgweard's woodland clearing'. DB *Burwardeslei*.

Burwarton (village, Shropshire): 'Burgweard's farmstead'. OE *tūn*, 'farmstead'. The first part of the name could also represent OE *burhweard*, 'fort keeper'. The DB form of the name below is corrupt. DB *Burertone*, 1194 *Burwardton*.

Burwash (village, E Sussex): '(place by the) ploughed field by the fort'. OE *burh*, 'fortified place', + *ersc*, 'ploughed field'. The precise nature of the 'fort' here is uncertain. 12C *Burhercse*.

Burwell (village, Cambs): '(place by the) spring by the fort'. OE *burh*, 'fortified place', + *wella*, 'spring', 'stream'. There was a Norman castle here, itself probably built on the site of an earlier earthwork. This would have been the original 'fort'. 1060 *Burcwell*, DB *Buruuella*. SO ALSO: *Burwell*, Lincs.

Bury (town, Bury): '(place by the) stronghold'. OE *burh*, 'stronghold', 'fortified place'. The name represents OE *byrig*, the dative of *burh*. 1194 *Biri*. SO ALSO: *Bury*, Cambs, W Sussex.

Bury St Edmunds (town, Suffolk): 'town associated with St Edmund'. OE *burh*, 'stronghold', 'manor', 'town'. St Edmund, 9C king of East Anglia, was buried here. The main name represents OE *byrig*, the dative of *burh*. The form of the name below gave *St Edmundsbury* for the local council district, and the town itself is in the diocese of St Edmundsbury and Ipswich. 1038 *Sancte Eadmundes Byrig*.

Burythorpe (village, N Yorks): 'Bjǫrg's outlying farmstead'. OS *thorp*, 'outlying farmstead'. The Scandinavian personal name is that of a woman. DB *Bergetorp*.

Bushbury (district, Wolverhampton): 'bishop's fortified manor'. OE *biscop*, 'bishop', + *burh*, 'fortified place', 'manor'. The identity of the bishop in question is unknown. 996 *Byscopesbyri*, DB *Biscopesberie*.

Bushey (town, Herts): 'enclosure by a thicket'. OE *bysce*, 'thicket', + *hæg*, 'enclosure'. The name could also mean 'enclosure hedged with box trees' (OE *byxe*, 'box', + *hæg*). DB *Bissei*.

Bushley (village, Worcs): 'woodland clearing with bushes'. OE *bysce*, 'bush', + *lēah*, 'wood', 'clearing'. The name could also mean 'Byssa's woodland clearing'. DB *Biselege*.

Butcombe (village, N Somerset): 'Buda's valley'. OE *cumb*, 'valley'. *c*.1000 *Budancumb*, DB *Budicome*.

Bute (island, Argyll & Bute): '(island of) fire'. Gaelic *bód*, 'fire'. The reference may be to signal fires here. 1093 *Bot*, 1292 *Boot*.

Butleigh (village, Somerset): 'Budeca's woodland clearing'. OE *lēah*, 'wood', 'clearing'. 725 *Budecalech*, DB *Boduchelei*.

Butlers Marston (village, Warwicks): 'Boteler's farmstead by a marsh'. OE *mersc*, 'marsh', + *tūn*, 'farmstead'. The manor here was held in the 12C by the Boteler family. DB *Merstone*, 1176 *Merston le Motiler*.

Butley (village, Suffolk): 'Butta's woodland clearing'. OE *lēah*, 'wood', 'clearing'. DB *Butelea*.

Butterleigh (village, Devon): '(place by the) clearing with rich pasture'. OE *butere*, 'butter', + *lēah*, 'wood', 'clearing'. A rich pasture will produce good butter. DB *Buterlei*.

Buttermere (lake, Cumbria): 'butter lake'. OE *butere*, 'butter', + *mere*, 'lake', 'pool'. A 'butter lake' is one surrounded by rich pastures. 1230 *Butermere*, 1343 *Water of Buttermere*. SO ALSO: *Buttermere*, Wilts.

Butterton (village, Staffs): '(place on the) hill with rich pasture'. OE *butere*, 'butter', + *dūn*, 'hill'. The form of the name below relates to Butterton near Leek. 1200 *Buterdon*.

Butterwick (village, N Yorks): 'dairy farm where butter is made'. OE *butere*, 'butter', + *wīc*, 'specialized farm'. The form of the name below is for Butterwick near Malton, in the fertile valley of the river Rye, but Butterwick near Driffield has a name of identical origin. DB *Butruic*. SO ALSO: *Butterwick*, Durham, Lincs.

Buxhall (village, Suffolk): 'Bucc's corner of land'. OE *halh*, 'nook', 'corner of land'. *c*.995 *Bucyshealæ*, DB *Buckeshala*.

Buxted (village, E Sussex): 'place where beech trees grow'. OE *bōc*, 'beech', + *stede*, 'place'. The trees could also be box trees (OE *box*). 1199 *Boxted*.

Buxton (town, Derbys): '(place at the) rocking stones'. OE *būg-stān* (from *būgan*, 'to bend', + *stān*, 'stone'). There must have been rocking stones (logan stones) near here, but their location is unknown. The Roman spa at Buxton was *Aquae Arnemetiae*, 'waters of Arnemetia', the latter being a goddess with a Celtic name meaning 'before the sacred grove'. *c*.1100 *Buchestanes*.

Buxton (village, Norfolk): 'Bucc's farmstead'. OE *tūn*, 'farmstead'. DB *Bukestuna*.

Bwcle. See BUCKLEY.

Byers Green (village, Durham): '(place by the) cowsheds'. OE *bȳre*, 'byre', 'cowshed'. The village later became associated with its green. 1345 *Bires*.

Byfield (village, Northants): '(place) by open country'. OE *bī*, 'by', + *feld*, 'open land' (modern English *field*). DB *Bifelde*.

Byfleet (residential district, Surrey): '(place) by the stream'. OE *bī*, 'by', + *flēot*, 'stream'. The 'stream' here would be the river Wey. As a compound word, OE *bī-flēot* could also denote a small area of land cut off by a stream as it changes course. 933 *Biflete*, DB *Biflet*.

Byford (village, Herefords): '(place at the) ford by the river bend'. OE *byge*, 'bend', + *ford*, 'ford'. Byford lies by a former ferry crossing on the river Wye. DB *Buiford*.

Bygrave (village, Herts): '(place) by the trench'. OE *bī*, 'by', + *grafa*, 'pit', 'trench'. The name could also mean '(place) by the grove' (OE *grāfa*). 973 *Bigravan*, DB *Bigrave*.

Bythorn (village, Cambs): '(place) by the thorn bush'. OE *bī*, 'by', + *thyrne*, 'thorn bush'. The DB form of the name below has omitted the *th*. *c*.960 *Bitherna*, DB *Bierne*.

Byton (village, Herefords): 'farmstead by the river bend'. OE *byge*, 'bend', + *tūn*, 'farmstead'. Byton is on the river Lugg. DB *Boitune*.

Bywell (hamlet, Northd): '(place at the) spring by the river bend'. OE *byge*, 'bend', + *wella*, 'spring', 'stream'. Bywell lies in a bend of the river Tyne. 1104 *Biguell*, 1195 *Biewell*.

Byworth (village, W Sussex): 'Bēaga's or Bǣga's enclosure'. OE *worth*, 'enclosure'. The personal names are those of a woman and a man respectively. 1279 *Begworth*.

Cabourne (village, Lincs): '(place by the) stream where jackdaws are seen'. OE *cā*, 'jackdaw', + *burna*, 'stream'. The stream has now almost dried up. DB *Caburne*.

Cadbury (village, Devon): 'Cada's fortified place'. OE *burh*, 'fortified place'. The stronghold in question is the Iron Age fort here known as Cadbury Castle. The extensive Iron Age camp of this name in Somerset has a name of identical origin. DB *Cadebirie*.

Caddington (village, Beds): '(place by) Cada's hill'. OE *dūn*, 'hill'. The '-ing-' represents the genitive ending of the personal name (*Cadan*). *c.*1000 *Caddandun*, DB *Cadendone*.

Cadeby (village, Doncaster): 'Káti's farmstead'. OS *bý*, 'farmstead', 'village'. The personal name is Scandinavian. DB *Catebi*. SO ALSO: *Cadeby*, Leics.

Cadeleigh (village, Devon): 'Cada's woodland clearing'. OE *lēah*, 'wood', 'clearing'. Cadeleigh is only 2 miles from CADBURY, and it seems likely the same man gave both names. DB *Cadelie*.

Cader Idris (mountain, Gwynedd): 'seat of Idris'. OW *cadeir*, 'seat' (from Latin *cathedra*, 'chair'). The mountain, named after a legendary giant and magician, marks the boundary between the old kingdoms of Gwynedd and Powys.

Cadgwith (coastal village, Cornwall): '(harbour by a) thicket'. Cornish *caswydh*, 'thicket'. The first two forms of the name below have Cornish *porth*, 'harbour'. 1358 *Porthcaswith*, 1699 *Por Cadgwith*, 1748 *Cadgewith*.

Cadishead (district, Salford): 'fold by Cada's stream'. OE *wælla*, 'stream', + *set*, 'fold' (for animals). 1212 *Cadewalesate*.

Cadnam (village, Hants): 'Cada's homestead or enclosure'. OE *hām*, 'homestead', or *hamm*, 'enclosure'. 1272 *Cadenham*.

Cadney (village, N Lincs): 'Cada's island'. OE *ēg*, 'island'. The 'island' is the raised piece of ground on which the village lies by the river Ancholme. DB *Catenai*.

Cadoxton (district of Barry, Vale of Glam): 'Cadog's farmstead'. OE *tūn*, 'farmstead'. The parish church here is dedicated to St Cadog, 6C founder of the church at Llancarfan, 6 miles west of Cadoxton, whose Welsh name is *Tregatwg*, 'Cadog's farm'. 1254 *Caddokeston*, 1535 *Cadoxston*.

Caenby (village, Lincs): 'Kafni's farmstead'. OS *bý*, 'farmstead', 'village'. The personal name is Scandinavian. DB *Couenebi*.

Caerdydd. See CARDIFF.

Caerffili. See CAERPHILLY.

Caerfyrddin. See CARMARTHEN.

Caergwrle (village, Flints): 'fort by the clearing where cranes are seen'. Welsh *caer*, 'fort', + OE *corn*, 'crane', + *lēah*, 'wood', 'clearing'. The 'fort' was a Roman station here. The second part of the name is entirely English and corresponds to the village of CORLEY, Warwicks. 1327 *Caergorlei*.

Caergybi. See HOLYHEAD.

Caerleon (town, Newport): 'fort of the legion'. Welsh *caer*, 'fort', + Latin *legionis*, 'of the legion'. The allusion is to the Second Legion, stationed here after moving from *Glevum* (Gloucester). The name of the Roman fort was *Isca Legionis*, 'Isca of the legion', from the river Usk here. The town's Welsh name is *Caerllion-ar-Wysg*, 'Caerleon on the Usk'. For the river name, see USK. *c.*150 *castra Legionis*, DB *Caerleion*.

Caerllion-ar-Wysg. See CAERLEON.

Caernarfon (town, Gwynedd): 'fort in Arfon'. Welsh *caer*, 'fort', + *yn*, 'in'. Arfon was a cantref (hundred) here, so called because it was *ar Fôn*, 'opposite Môn', this being the Welsh name of ANGLESEY. Caernarfon stands at the mouth of the river Seiont, a Celtic name meaning 'strong one' that gave *Segontium* as the name of the

Roman fort here. 1191 *Kairarvon*, 1258 *Kaer yn Arvon*.

Caerphilly (town, Caerphilly): 'Ffili's fort'. Welsh *caer*, 'fort'. The identity of Ffili is unknown. The Welsh form of the name is *Caerffili*, but this has not been officially adopted, even for the modern unitary authority. 1271 *Kaerfili*, 1314 *Kaerphilly*.

Caersws (village, Powys): 'Swys's fort'. Welsh *caer*, 'fort'. Swys is said to have been a local queen. The name is formally *Caerswŝs*, but is now generally found without the circumflex. 14C *Caerswys*.

Caerwent (village, Mon): 'fort of Gwent'. Welsh *caer*, 'fort'. The Roman fort here was *Venta Silurum*, 'market of the Silures', the tribe who had their capital here, with *Venta* related to GWENT itself. *c*.800 *Cair Guent*.

Caesaromagus. See CHELMSFORD.

Cainscross (suburb of Stroud, Glos): 'Cain's cross'. The name is not recorded earlier than 1776 (as *Cain's Cross*) and may refer to a person surnamed Cain and to crossroads here.

Cairngorm (mountains, Moray): 'blue rocky hill'. Gaelic *carn*, 'rocky hill', 'pile of rocks' (modern English *cairn*), + *gorm*, 'blue'. The mountains (popularly pluralized as 'the Cairngorms') are named for their highest peak, *Cairn Gorm*.

Caister-on-Sea (resort town, Norfolk): 'Roman camp by the sea'. OE *cæster*, 'Roman camp'. The name of the Roman town here is not known. The latter part of the name is a recent addition. DB *Castra*.

Caistor (town, Lincs): 'Roman camp'. OE *cæster*, 'Roman camp'. The Roman town may have been *Bannovalium*, 'strong horn' (cp. HORNCASTLE), referring to the spur of the Wolds here. DB *Castre*.

Caistor St Edmund (village, Norfolk): 'St Edmund's (estate by the) Roman camp'. OE *cæster*, 'Roman camp'. The manor here was held early by the Abbey of Bury St Edmunds. The Roman town was *Venta Icenorum*, 'market of the Iceni'. *c*.1025 *Castre*, DB *Castrum*, 1254 *Castre Sancti Eadmundi*.

Caistron (hamlet, Northd): '(place at the) thorn bush by the fen'. ME *kers*, 'fen' (modern Scottish English *carse*), + OS *thyrnir*, 'thorn bush'. Caistron is in a moorland district on the river Coquet. *c*.1160 *Cers*, 1202 *Kerstirn*.

Caithness (region, Highland): 'promontory of the Cats'. OS *nes*, 'headland', 'promontory'. It is not known why the early Celtic tribe here were called 'cats'. *c*.970 *Kathenessia*.

Calbourne (village, IoW): '(place by the) stream where cole or cabbage grows'. OE *cawel*, 'cole', + *burna*, 'stream'. The reference would be to seakale or sea cabbage. The first part of the name could also represent a Celtic river name *Cawel*, of uncertain meaning. 826 *Cawelburne*, DB *Cavborne*.

Calcaria. See TADCASTER.

Caldbeck (village, Cumbria): '(place by the) cold stream'. OS *kaldr*, 'cold', + *bekkr*, 'stream'. The 'cold stream' itself is the Caldew ('cold water'). 11C *Caldebek*.

Caldbergh (hamlet, N Yorks): '(place on the) cold hill'. OS *kaldr*, 'cold', + *berg*, 'hill'. DB *Calderber*.

Caldecote (village, Cambs): 'cold shelter'. OE *cald*, 'cold', + *cot*, 'cottage', 'shelter'. A 'cold shelter' is an exposed one for humans or animals. DB *Caldecote*. SO ALSO: *Caldecote*, Herts, Northants.

Caldecott (village, Rutland): 'cold shelter'. OE *cald*, 'cold', + *cot*, 'cottage', 'shelter'. Here the 'cold shelter' could have been for travellers on the Roman road that is part of Ermine Street. DB *Caldecote*. SO ALSO: *Caldecott*, Northants.

Calder Bridge (village, Cumbria): '(place with a) bridge over the (river) Calder'. For the river name, see CALDERDALE. 1178 *Calder*.

Calderdale (valley, Calderdale): 'valley of the (river) Calder'. OS *dalr*, 'valley'. The river has a Celtic name meaning 'rapid stream'.

Caldicot (town, Mon): 'cold shelter'. OE *cald*, 'cold', + *cot*, 'cottage', 'shelter'. This 'cold shelter' would have been exposed to winds blowing off the Severn estuary. DB *Caldecote*, 1286 *Caldicote*.

Caldwell (village, N Yorks): '(place by the) cold spring'. OE *cald*, 'cold', + *wella*, 'spring', 'stream'. The 16C antiquary John Leland says that Caldwell 'is so caullid from a lattle font or spryng, by the ruines of the old place, and so rennith into a beke halfe a quarter of a mile off'. DB *Caldeuuella*.

Caldy (hamlet, Wirral): 'cold island'. OE *cald*, 'cold', + *ēg*, 'island'. The name may have originally referred to Hilbre Island, off the coast of West Kirby. But the DB form of the name below reveals an earlier meaning 'cold backside' (OE *cald* + *ears*, 'arse'), as the name of the rounded hill on which Caldy lies. DB *Calders*, 1182 *Caldei*.

Caldy Island (island, Pemb): 'cold island'. OS *kald*, 'cold', + *ey*, 'island'. The island is exposed to southwesterly winds and gales. Its Welsh name is *Ynys Bŷr*, 'Pŷr's island', after a 6C saint who founded a religious community here. Cp. MANORBIER. *c*.1120 *Caldea*.

Caledonian Canal (canal, Highland): 'canal in Caledonia'. *Caledonia*, the Roman name for northern Britain, comes from the *Caledonii*, 'hard ones', 'tough men' (modern Welsh *caled*, 'hard'), the Celtic tribe who originally inhabited just a part of the Highlands. Construction of the canal began in 1803.

Calke (village, Derbys): '(place on) limestone'. OE *calc*, 'limestone' (related modern English *chalk*). 1132 *Calc*.

Callaly (hamlet, Northd): 'clearing where calves graze'. OE *calf*, 'calf', + *lēah*, 'wood', 'clearing'. The first part of the name represents OE *calfra*, the genitive plural form of *calf*. 1161 *Calualea*.

Callander (town, Stirling): '(place by the) turbulent stream'. The town takes its name from an old Celtic name for the river here, now the Teith. 1504 *Kalentare*.

Calleva Atrebatum. See SILCHESTER.

Callington (town, Cornwall): 'farmstead by the bare hill'. OE *calu*, 'bare hill', + *tūn*, 'farmstead'. The 'bare hill' is Kit Hill ('kite hill'), which dominates the town. DB *Calwetone*.

Callow (village, Herefords): '(place on the) bare hill'. OE *calu*, 'bare hill'. The name represents OE *calwe*, the dative form of *calu*. 1180 *Calua*.

Calmsden (hamlet, Glos): 'Calumund's valley'. OE *denu*, 'valley'. 852 *Kalemundesdene*.

Calne (town, Wilts): '(place by the river) Calne'. The river here, now the Marden Brook, had an earlier pre-English name of uncertain meaning. Cp. COLNE. DB *Calne*.

Calow (village, Derbys): '(place by the) bare corner of land'. OE *calu*, 'bare', + *halh*, 'nook', 'corner of land'. The name could also mean 'corner of land by a bare hill', with *calu* understood as 'bare hill'. DB *Calehale*.

Calshot (coastal hamlet, Hants): '(place by the) spit of land'. OE *ord*, 'point of land'. The first part of the name is of uncertain origin. It may represent OE *cǣlic*, 'cup', 'chalice', referring to some natural feature here. The second part of the first form of the name below represents OE *ōra*, 'shore'. 980 *Celcesoran*, 1011 *Celceshord*, 1347 *Calchesorde*, 1579 *Calshot*.

Calstock (town, Cornwall): 'outlying farm (of some place)'. OE *stoc*, 'outlying farm', 'secondary settlement'. The 'Cal-' of the name represents the primary settlement. It may be a short form of CALLINGTON, 4 miles away. DB *Kalestoc*.

Calthorpe (village, Norfolk): 'Kali's outlying farmstead'. OS *thorp*, 'outlying farmstead'. The personal name is Scandinavian. 1044 *Calethorp*, DB *Caletorp*.

Calton (hamlet, N Yorks): 'farm where calves are reared'. OE *calf*, 'calf', + *tūn*, 'farmstead'. DB *Caltun*. SO ALSO: *Calton*, Staffs.

Calver (village, Derbys): 'ridge where calves graze'. OE *calf*, 'calf', + *ofer*, 'ridge', 'slope'. The village is on a steepish slope above the river Derwent. DB *Calvoure*.

Calverhall (village, Shropshire): 'corner of land where calves graze'. OE *calf*, 'calf', + *halh*, 'nook', 'corner of land'. The first half of the name represents OE *calfra*, the genitive plural form of *calf*. DB *Cavrahalle*, 1256 *Caluerhale*.

Calverleigh (hamlet, Devon): 'clearing in the bare wood'. OE *calu*, 'bald', 'bare', + *wudu*, 'wood', + *lēah*, 'clearing'. The DB form of the name below is garbled. DB *Calodelie*, 1194 *Calewudelega*.

Calverley (district, Leeds): 'clearing where calves are pastured'. OE *calf*, 'calf', + *lēah*, 'wood', 'clearing'. The first part of the name represents OE *calfra*, the genitive plural form of *calf*. DB *Caverleia*.

Calverton (village, Milton K): 'farm where calves are reared'. OE *calf*, 'calf', + *tūn*, 'farmstead'. The first part of the name represents OE *calfra*, the genitive plural form of *calf*. DB *Calvretone*. SO ALSO: *Calverton*, Notts.

Cam (village, Glos): '(place on the river) Cam'. The river has a Celtic name meaning 'crooked one' (modern Welsh *cam*, 'crooked', 'bent'). DB *Camma*.

Cam (river). See CAMBRIDGE (Cambs).

Cambeak (headland, Cornwall): 'comb beak'. The name is English, not Cornish, and denotes a sharply crested promontory. 1789 *Cambeak*.

Camber (resort town, E Sussex): 'enclosed space'. OF *cambre*, 'room' (modern English *chamber*). The name apparently refers to the restricted harbour here before the silting up of the Rother estuary. 1375 *Camere*, 1397 *Portus Camera*, 1442 *Caumbre*.

Camberley (town, Surrey): The settlement here was originally named *Cambridge Town* in 1862 after George William Frederick Charles, 2nd Duke of Cambridge (1819–1904), commander-in-chief of the British army. The name was postally confused with that of CAMBRIDGE, however, and was altered as now in 1877 when the railway station opened. The '-ley' mirrors local names such as FRIMLEY and YATELEY.

Camberwell (district, Southwark): '(place by the) spring'. OE *wella*, 'spring', 'stream'. The first part of the name is of uncertain origin but may represent the personal name Cantbeorht or Cantmær. DB *Cambrewelle*.

Camblesforth (village, N Yorks): '(place by the) ford associated with Camel'. OE *ford*, 'ford'. The actual site of the ford is uncertain, and there is no identifiable river here. DB *Camelesforde*.

Cambo (village, Northd): 'hill spur by a ridge'. OE *camb*, 'ridge', 'crest' (modern English *comb*), + *hōh*, 'hill spur'. 1230 *Camho*.

Cambois (coastal hamlet, Northd): 'crooked place'. The name is Celtic in origin, from a word related to modern Welsh *cam*, 'crooked', and originally referring to the bay here. *c*.1050 *Cammes*.

Camborne (town, Cornwall): '(place by the) crooked hill'. Cornish *camm*, 'crooked', + *bronn*, 'breast', 'hill'. The 'crooked hill' is Camborne Beacon, which overlooks the town. 1182 *Camberon*.

Cambrian Mountains (mountains, Wales): 'mountains of Cambria'. *Cambria*, the Roman name for Wales, came from the people's name for themselves, modern Welsh *Cymry*. Cp. CUMBRIA.

Cambridge (city, Cambs): '(place by the) bridge over the (river) Granta'. OE *brycg*, 'bridge'. The river also gave the name of GRANTCHESTER, but here 'Grant-' finally became 'Cam-' under Norman influence. (The Granta is now better known as the Cam, named after the town.) The original name of Cambridge, as in the first form of the name below, comprised the river name and OE *ceaster*, 'Roman fort', the Roman town itself being *Duroliponte*, perhaps meaning 'walled town on the marshy river'. *c*.730 *Grantacaestir*, *c*.745 *Grontabricc*, DB *Cantebrigie*.

Cambridge (village, Glos): 'bridge over the (river) Cam'. OE *brycg*, 'bridge'. For the river name, see CAM. 1200 *Cambrigga*.

Cambridgeshire (county, E England): 'district based on Cambridge'. OE *scīr*, 'shire', 'district'. See CAMBRIDGE (Cambs). 11C *Grantabrycgscir*.

Cambuslang (town, S Lanarks): 'river bend of the ship'. Gaelic *camas*, 'bend', + *long*, 'ship'. The town is on the river Clyde. 1296 *Camboslanc*.

Camden Town (district, Camden). The district was named in 1795 after Charles Pratt, 1st Earl Camden (1714–94), who came into possession of the manor of Kentish Town here through his marriage in 1749 to Elizabeth Jeffrys, daughter of Nicholas Jeffrys of Brecknock

Priory. His title came from Camden Place, Chislehurst, itself named after the antiquary William Camden (1551–1623). 1822 *Camden Town*.

Camelford (town, Cornwall): 'ford over the (river) Camel'. OE *ford*, 'ford'. The river has a Celtic name probably meaning 'crooked one' (Cornish *camm*, 'crooked'). 13C *Camelford*.

Camerton (village, Bath & NE Somerset): 'farmstead on Cam Brook'. OE *tūn*, 'farmstead', 'estate'. The river name, earlier *Cameler*, is of Celtic origin meaning 'crooked' (modern Welsh *cam*, 'crooked', 'bent'). 954 *Camelartone*, DB *Camelertone*.

Camerton (village, Cumbria): '(place with a) farmstead'. OE *tūn*, 'farmstead', 'estate'. The first part of the name is of uncertain origin. It may represent a personal name. *c*.1150 *Camerton*.

Cammeringham (village, Lincs): 'homestead of Cantmær's people'. OE *-inga-*, 'of the people of', + *hām*, 'homestead'. The DB form of the name below has *l* for *r* as in SALISBURY. DB *Camelingeham*, *c*.1115 *Cameryngham*.

Campbeltown (town, Argyll & Bute): 'Campbell's town'. Archibald Campbell, Earl of Argyle, was granted the site here in 1667 for the erection of a burgh of barony to be named after him.

Campsall (village, Doncaster): 'Cam's corner of land'. OE *halh*, 'nook', 'corner of land'. The first part of the name could also represent a Celtic word meaning 'crooked' (modern Welsh *cam*), alluding to some natural feature here. The corner of land would be the small valley of Stream Dike below the village. The DB form of the name below is corrupt. DB *Cansale*, 12C *Camshale*.

Campsey Ash (village, Suffolk): 'island with an enclosure near Ash'. OE *camp*, 'enclosed piece of land', + *ēg*, 'island'. The 'island' is dry ground in marshland here. *Ash*, '(place by the) ash tree' (OE *æsc*, 'ash'), was originally a separate place. DB *Campeseia*.

Campsie Fells (hill range, Stirling): 'hills of Campsie'. OS *fjall*, 'hill' (modern English *fell*). The range is named from the single hill *Campsie*, 'crooked fairy mountain' (Gaelic *cam*, 'crooked', + *sith*, 'fairy').

Camulodunum. See COLCHESTER.

Canewdon (village, Essex): 'hill of Cana's people'. OE *-inga-*, 'of the people of', + *dūn*, 'hill'. The DB form of the name below has *r* for *n*. DB *Carenduna*, 1181 *Canuedon*.

Canford Magna (village, Poole): 'greater (place by) Cana's ford'. OE *ford*, 'ford'. The river here is the Stour. The second word of the name (Latin *magna*, 'great') distinguishes the village from nearby *Little Canford*. The DB form of the name below has garbled the personal name. DB *Cheneford*, 1195 *Kaneford*, 1612 *Greate Canford*, 1868 *Great Canford, or Canford Magna*.

Cann (hamlet, Dorset): '(place by the) hollow'. OE *canne*, 'can', 'cup'. Cann lies in a steep-sided valley. 12C *Canna*.

Cannington (village, Somerset): 'estate by (the) Quantock (Hills)'. OE *tūn*, 'estate', 'village'. The village lies east of the QUANTOCK HILLS. *c*.880 *Cantuctun*, DB *Cantoctona*.

Canning Town (district, Newham). The name is probably that of Sir Samuel Canning, of the India Rubber, Gutta Percha and Telegraph Works Company here in the 19C. 1868 *Canning New Town*.

Cannock (town, Staffs): '(place by the) small hill'. OE *cnocc*, 'hillock'. The 'small hill' that gave the town's name is probably Shoal Hill, to the west of Cannock. It also gave the name of *Cannock Chase*, a former royal hunting enclosure, now the name of the local council district. The DB form of the name below has *c* as *t* by way of a scribal flourish. DB *Chenet*, 12C *Canoc*.

Canonbury (district, Islington): 'manor of the canons'. ME *canoun*, 'canon', + *bury*, 'manor'. The Augustinian canons of St Bartholomew's, Smithfield, were granted land here in the 13C. 1373 *Canonesbury*.

Canon Frome. See BISHOP'S FROME.

Canonium. See KELVEDON.

Canon Pyon. See KING'S PYON.

Canons Ashby (village, Northants): 'canons' farmstead where ash trees grow'. ME *canoun*, 'canon', + OE *æsc* or OS *askr*, 'ash', + OS *bý*, 'farmstead', 'village'. The first word of the name, referring to the priory founded here in the 12C, distinguishes this Ashby from ASHBY ST LEDGERS, 12 miles to the north. DB *Ascebi*, 13C *Essheby Canons*.

Canonstown (village, Cornwall): 'canon's town'. The village arose in the 19C and is named after a local landowner, Canon John Rogers (1778–1856). 1839 *Canons Town*.

Canovium. See CONWY.

Canterbury (city, Kent): 'stronghold of the people of Kent'. OE *-ware*, 'dwellers', + *burh*, 'fortified place'. 'Cant-' represents modern KENT. The Roman city here was *Durovernum Cantiacorum*, 'walled fort by the alder swamp of the Cantiaci'. *c*.900 *Cantwaraburg*, DB *Canterburie*.

Cantium. See KENT.

Cantley (village, Doncaster): 'Canta's woodland clearing'. OE *lēah*, 'wood', 'clearing'. DB *Canteleia*. SO ALSO: *Cantley*, Norfolk.

Cantlop (hamlet, Shropshire): 'enclosed place'. OE *hop*, 'enclosed place'. The first part of the name is of uncertain meaning. DB *Cantelop*.

Canvey Island (island, Essex): 'island of Cana's people'. OE *-inga-*, 'of the people of', + *ēg*, 'island'. Canvey Island is a proper island in the Thames Estuary, separated from the mainland on the north side by creeks. The second word of the name is strictly speaking tautologous. 1255 *Canveye*.

Canwick (village, Lincs): 'Cana's dairy farm'. OE *wīc*, 'dwelling', 'dairy farm'. DB *Canewic*.

Canworthy Water (village, Cornwall): 'enclosure at Carn by the water'. OE *worthig*, 'enclosure'. The location of *Carn* (Cornish *carn*, 'rock') is uncertain. The 'water' is the river Ottery here. 1699 *Kennery bridg*, 1748 *Kenworthy Water*.

Cape Cornwall (headland, Cornwall). The cape lies to the west of St Just. 1699 *Cap Cornwall*.

Capel (village, Surrey): '(place with a) chapel'. ME *capel*, 'chapel'. The village was a former chapelry of Dorking. 1190 *Capella*.

Capel Curig (village, Conwy): 'Curig's chapel'. Welsh *capel*, 'chapel'. Curig was the son of Ilid, a 7C saint, and the church here is dedicated to him. 1536 *Capel Kiryg*, 1578 *Capel Kerig*.

Capel-le-Ferne (village, Kent): 'chapel at the ferny place'. ME *capel*, 'chapel', + OE *ferne*, 'ferny place'. 1377 *Cepel ate Verne*.

Capel St Andrew. See CAPEL ST MARY.

Capel St Mary (village, Suffolk): 'St Mary's chapel'. ME *capel*, 'chapel'. The chapel (now church) dedication distinguishes the village from *Capel St Andrew*, 18 miles to the northeast. 1254 *Capeles*.

Capenhurst (village, Cheshire): 'wooded hill at a lookout place'. OE *cape*, 'lookout place', + *hyrst*, 'wooded hill'. There is not much of a hill here, in the middle of the Wirral peninsula, and the 'lookout place' may have been some kind of raised structure from which an all-round watch could be kept. The DB form of the name below is corrupt. DB *Capeles*, 13C *Capenhurst*.

Capernwray (hamlet, Lancs): 'merchant's corner of land'. OS *kaup-mathr*, 'merchant' (from *kaup*, 'trade', + *mathr*, 'man'), + *vrá*, 'nook', 'corner of land'. The first part of the name represents OS *kaup-manna*, the genitive plural form of *kaup-mathr*. *c*.1200 *Coupmanwra*.

Cape Wrath (headland, Highland): 'turning point'. OS *hvarf*, 'corner', 'bend' (related modern English *wharf*). The cape marks the point where ships would alter course to follow the coast. 1583 *Wraith*.

Capheaton. See KIRKHEATON (Northd).

Caradon Hill (hill, Cornwall): 'tor hill'. Cornish *carn*, 'pile of rocks' (related modern English *cairn*), + OE *dūn*, 'hill'. The hill took its name from the nearby village of *Caradon*, itself named after it, and now giving the name of the local council district. The full name thus effectively has 'hill' three times. Cp. PENDLE HILL. DB *Carnetone*, c.1160 *Carnedune*.

Carbis Bay (suburb of St Ives, Cornwall). The place arose as a village in the 19C and took its name from the bay here. This in turn was named from a farm called *Carbis* (OC *carr-bons*, 'causeway', literally 'cart bridge'). 1884 *Carbis Bay*.

Carbrooke (village, Norfolk): '(place by the) stream in the marsh'. OS *kjarr*, 'marsh', + OE *brōc*, 'brook'. The first part of the name could also represent a former Celtic name for the stream here. DB *Cherebroc*.

Carburton (hamlet, Notts): '(special) farmstead'. OE *tūn*, 'farmstead', 'village'. The first part of the name is obscure in origin and meaning. DB *Carbertone*.

Car Colston (village, Notts): 'Kolr's farmstead with a church'. OE *tūn*, 'farmstead'. The personal name is Scandinavian. The first word (OS *kirkja*, 'church') distinguishes this Colston from *Colston Bassett*, 6 miles to the south, where the manor was held by the Basset family in the 12C. DB *Colestone*, 1242 *Kyrcoluiston*.

Carcroft (village, Doncaster): 'enclosure by the marsh'. OS *kjarr*, 'marsh', + OE *croft*, 'enclosure'. 12C *Kercroft*.

Cardenden (village, Fife): 'hollow by Carden'. OE *denu*, 'valley', 'hollow'. *Carden* is a name of Celtic origin meaning 'thicket' (modern Welsh *cardden*). 14C *Cardenane*, 1516 *Cardwane*.

Cardeston (hamlet, Shropshire): 'Card's farmstead'. OE *tūn*, 'farmstead', 'estate'. DB *Cartistune*.

Cardiff (city, Cardiff): 'fort on the (river) Taf'. Welsh *caer*, 'fort'. The river has a name of Celtic origin meaning simply 'water' (modern Welsh *dwfr*). The city's name is an anglicization of Welsh *Caerdydd*, itself properly *Caer-Dyf*. Cp. LLANDAFF. 1106 *Kairdif*, 1566 *o gaer dydd*, 1698 *Caer Didd*.

Cardigan (town, Ceredigion): 'Ceredig's land'. The name is an anglicization of CEREDIGION. The Welsh name of Cardigan is *Aberteifi*, 'mouth of

the (river) Teifi' (Welsh *aber*, 'mouth'). The meaning of the river name is uncertain. 1194 *Kerdigan*.

Cardington (village, Beds): 'estate associated with Cærda'. OE *-ing-*, 'associated with', + *tūn*, 'farmstead', 'estate'. The DB form of the name below is corrupt. DB *Chernetone*, c.1190 *Kerdinton*.

Cardington (village, Shropshire): 'estate associated with Card'. OE *-ing-*, 'associated with', + *tūn*, 'farmstead', 'estate'. DB *Cardintune*.

Cardinham (village, Cornwall): 'fort'. Cornish *ker*, 'fort', + *dinan*, 'fort'. Both parts of the name mean 'fort', but presumably the original name was *Dinan*, with *ker* added subsequently. The reference is probably to Bury Castle, an Iron Age hill fort nearby. c.1180 *Cardinan*.

Cardurnock (hamlet, Cumbria): 'pebbly fortification'. The name is Celtic in origin, from words related to modern Welsh *caer*, 'fort', and *dwrnog*, 'knoblike'. The reference is probably to the cobblestones of the former fort here. 13C *Cardrunnock*.

Cargo (village, Cumbria): '(place on the) rocky hill'. The first part of the name is Celtic in origin, from a word related to modern Welsh *carreg*, 'rock'. The second part represents OS *haugr*, 'hill'. The village stands on a long hill above marshland. c.1178 *Cargaou*.

Cargreen (village, Cornwall): '(place by the) rock where seals are seen'. Cornish *carrek*, 'rock', + *reun*, 'seal'. Cargreen lies on the estuary of the river Tamar. Late 11C *Carrecron*.

Carham (hamlet, Northd): '(place by the) rocks'. OE *carr*, 'rock'. The name represents OE *carrum*, the dative plural form of *carr*. c.1050 *Carrum*.

Carhampton (village, Somerset): 'farm at the place by the rocks'. OE *carr*, 'rock', + *tūn*, 'farmstead'. The first part of the name represents OE *carrum*, the dative plural form of *carr*. 9C *Carrum*, DB *Carentone*.

Carharrack (village, Cornwall): 'fort of the high place'. Cornish *ker*, 'fort', + *ardhek* (from *ardh*, 'height', + adjectival suffix *-ek*). 1408 *Cararthek*.

Carisbrooke (village, IoW): '(place by the) Cary brook'. OE *brōc*, 'brook', 'stream'. The Celtic name of the brook was presumably at one time that of the present Lukely Brook. Its meaning is uncertain, but it may be the same as that of the river Cary that gave the name of CASTLE CARY. 12C *Caresbroc*.

Cark (village, Cumbria): '(place by the) rock'. The name comes from a Celtic word related to modern Welsh *carreg*, 'stone'. 1491 *Karke*.

Carleton (village, Wakefield): 'farmstead of the freemen'. OS *karl*, 'freeman', 'peasant', + OE *tūn*, 'farmstead', 'estate'. Cp. CARLTON. DB *Carlentone*. SO ALSO: *Carleton*, Cumbria.

Carleton Forehoe (village, Norfolk): 'farmstead of the freemen by the Forehoe Hills'. OS *karl*, 'freeman', + OE *tūn*, 'farmstead', 'estate'. The hill name, meaning 'four hills' (OE *fēower*, 'four', + OS *haugr*, 'hill'), distinguishes the village from CARLETON RODE, 8 miles to the south. 'The distinguishing appellation is derived from four hills, supposed to have been artificially constructed, on one of which the court for the hundred [of Forehoe] was anciently held' (Samuel Lewis, *A Topographical Dictionary of England*, 1840). DB *Carletuna*, 1268 *Karleton Fourhowe*.

Carleton Rode (village, Norfolk): 'de Rode's (estate at the) farmstead of the freemen'. OS *karl*, 'freeman', + OE *tūn*, 'farmstead', 'estate'. The de Rode family held the manor here in the 14C, their name distinguishing this Carleton from CARLETON FOREHOE, 8 miles to the north. DB *Carletuna*, 1201 *Carleton Rode*.

Carlingcott (hamlet, Bath & NE Somerset): 'cottage associated with Cridela'. OE *-ing-*, 'associated with', + *cot*, 'cottage'. DB *Credelincote*.

Carlisle (city, Cumbria): 'fortified town of Luguvalos'. Celtic *cair*, 'fort'. The Roman fort here was *Luguvalium*, from the Celtic personal name Luguvalos, meaning 'strong as Lugus', the name of a Celtic god. (The same god's name appears in *Lugudunum*, 'fort of Lugus', the Roman name of Lyon, France.) The present form of the name is due to Norman influence. The Latin second form of the name below means 'Luel, which is now called Carleol'. 4C *Luguvalio*, *c*.1106 *Luel, quod nunc Carleol appellatur*.

Carlton (town, Notts): 'farmstead of the freemen'. OS *karl*, 'freeman', 'peasant', + OE *tūn*, 'farmstead', 'estate'. The name is mainly northern equivalent of southern CHARLTON. 1182 *Karleton*. SO ALSO: *Carlton*, Beds, N Yorks (near Snaith).

Carlton Curlieu (village, Leics): 'de Curly's (estate at the) farmstead of the freemen'. OS *karl*, 'freeman', 'peasant', + OE *tūn*, 'farmstead'. The de Curly family held the manor here in the 13C. DB *Carletone*, 1273 *Carleton Curly*.

Carlton Husthwaite. See CARLTON MINIOTT.

Carlton in Lindrick (village, Notts): 'farmstead of the freemen in Lindrick'. OS *karl*, 'free-

man', 'peasant', + OE *tūn*, 'farmstead'. The district name means 'strip of land where lime trees grow' (OE *lind*, 'lime', + *ric*, 'raised strip of land'). DB *Carletone*, 1212 *Carleton in Lindric*.

Carlton Miniott (village, N Yorks): 'Miniott's (estate at the) farmstead of the freemen'. OS *karl*, 'freeman', 'peasant', + OE *tūn*, 'farmstead'. The Miniott family held land here in the 14C. Their name distinguishes this Carlton from *Carlton Husthwaite*, 7½ miles to the southeast, near HUSTHWAITE. DB *Carletun*, 1579 *Carleton Mynyott*.

Carlton-on-Trent (village, Notts): 'farmstead of the freemen on the (river) Trent'. OS *karl*, 'freeman', 'peasant', + OE *tūn*, 'farmstead'. The addition of the river name (see STOKE-ON-TRENT) distinguishes this Carlton from nearby *Little Carlton* (formerly *South Carlton*). DB *Carletune*.

Carluke (town, S Lanarks): meaning uncertain. An origin in Gaelic *càrr na luig*, 'rock by the hollow', has been proposed. 1304 *Carlug*, *c*.1320 *Cerneluke*.

Carlyon Bay (resort village, Cornwall): 'fort with the flat stones'. Cornish *ker*, 'fort', + *legh*, 'flat stone', 'slab'. The second part of the name represents Cornish *leghyon*, the plural form of *legh*. The name passed to the bay here, then to the village by it.

Carmarthen (town, Carm): 'fort at Moridunum'. Welsh *caer*, 'fort'. The Roman city here was *Moridunum*, 'fort by the sea', from Celtic words related to modern Welsh *môr*, 'sea', and *dinas*, 'fort'. *Moridunum* developed into *Myrddin*, taken as a personal name (and itself giving the name of the legendary magician Merlin). The Welsh name of Carmarthen is thus *Caerfyrddin*. 1130 *Cair Mirdin*.

Carmel (village, Gwynedd): '(place of) Carmel'. The village adopted the name of the Welsh Nonconformist chapel here, itself named (aptly, given its Snowdonia setting) after the biblical Mount Carmel (1 Kings 18:19, etc.).

Carnaby (village, E Yorks): 'Kærandi's or Keyrandi's farmstead'. OS *bý*, 'farmstead', 'village'. The personal names are Scandinavian. DB *Cherendebi*.

Carnarvon. See CAERNARFON.

Carnforth (town, Lancs): 'ford where cranes are seen'. OE *cran*, 'crane', + *ford*, 'ford'. Cp. CRANFORD. The ford would have been over the river Keer near here. DB *Chreneforde*.

Carnon Downs (village, Cornwall): '(place on the) downs by Carnon'. The village arose in the late 19C or early 20C on moorland belonging to the group of farms called *Carnon*, 'little rock' (Cornish *carn*, 'rock', + diminutive ending -*ynn*) or 'rocky place' (Cornish *carn* + -*an*, 'place of'). 1569 *Carnon*.

Carnoustie (resort town, Angus): meaning uncertain. The first part of the name may represent Gaelic *cathair*, 'fort', *càrr*, 'rock', or *carn*, 'cairn'. The second part has not been satisfactorily explained. 1493 *Donaldus Carnusy*.

Carpenders Park (district of Watford, Herts): 'Carpenter's park'. One Simon le Carpenter is recorded as living here in the 14C. 1556 *Carpenters hill*.

Carperby (village, N Yorks): 'Cairpre's farmstead'. OS *bý*, 'farmstead', 'village'. The personal name is Old Irish. DB *Chirprebi*.

Carrick Roads (estuary, Cornwall): 'roads of the rock'. Cornish *carrek*, 'rock', + modern English *road*, 'roadstead'. The rock referred to is the one now called Black Rock at the entrance to the estuary of the river Fal. The name gave *Carrick* as that of the local council district. c.1540 *Caryk Rood*.

Carrington (district, Nottingham). The district is named after the banker Robert Smith, 1st Baron Carrington (1752–1838), born in Nottingham, who owned land here north of the city centre.

Carrington (village, Trafford): 'estate associated with Cāra'. OE -*ing*-, 'associated with', + *tūn*, 'farmstead', 'estate'. The first part of the name could also represent OE *caring*, 'tending', 'herding' (modern English *caring*), or *cǣring*, 'river bend'. Carrington is on the Mersey. 12C *Carrintona*.

Carshalton (district, Sutton): 'farm by the spring where cress grows'. OE *cærse*, 'cress', + *ǣwiell*, 'well', 'spring', + *tūn*, 'farm'. The 'spring' is one of the sources of the river Wandle. Watercress has been grown here since medieval times. The DB form of the name below is the equivalent of ALTON (Hants). DB *Aultone*, 1235 *Cresaulton*.

Carsington (village, Derbys): 'farmstead where cress grows'. OE *cærsen*, 'growing with cress', + *tūn*, 'farmstead'. Cp. CASSINGTON. DB *Ghersintune*.

Carstairs (village, S Lanarks): 'Tarres' castle'. ME *castel*, 'castle'. The identity of Tarres is unknown. 1170 *Casteltarres*.

Carterton (town, Oxon): 'Carter's town'. The town was founded in 1901 by William Carter, director of the firm of Homesteads Ltd, who purchased land on the Duke of Marlborough's

estate here and sold it off in allotments as a smallholding colony.

Carthew (village, Cornwall): 'black fort'. Cornish *ker*, 'fort', + *du*, 'black'. 1327 *Carduf*.

Cartington (hamlet, Northd): 'hill associated with Certa'. OE -*ing*-, 'associated with', + *dūn*, 'hill'. 1220 *Cretenden*.

Cartmel (village, Cumbria): 'sandbank by rough stony ground'. OS *kartr*, 'stony ground', + *melr*, 'sandbank'. Cartmel is on elevated ground above Morecambe Bay. 12C *Cartmel*.

Cary Fitzpaine. See CASTLE CARY.

Cas-Gwent. See CHEPSTOW.

Caslai. See HAYSCASTLE.

Casllwchwr. See LOUGHOR.

Casmael. See PUNCHESTON.

Casnewydd-ar-Wysg. See NEWPORT (Newport).

Cassington (village, Oxon): 'farmstead where cress grows'. OE *cærsen*, 'growing with cress', + *tūn*, 'farmstead'. Cp. CARSINGTON. DB *Cersetone*, 12C *Kersinton*.

Cassop (village, Durham): '(place in the) valley of the stream where wildcats are seen'. OE *catt*, 'wildcat', + *ēa*, 'stream', 'river', + *hop*, 'valley'. The reference is to one of the side valleys to the north or south of the village. The form of the name below applies to the hamlet now known as *Old Cassop*, as distinct from the nearby colliery village of *New Cassop* (later *Cassop Colliery*, then just *Cassop*). 1183 *Cazehope*.

Castellhaidd. See HAYSCASTLE.

Castell-Nedd. See NEATH.

Castellnewydd Emlyn. See NEWCASTLE EMLYN.

Casterton (village, Cumbria): 'farmstead by the Roman fort'. OE *cæster*, 'Roman fort', + *tūn*, 'farmstead'. No Roman fort has actually been found here, but the village lies near the Roman road from Ribchester to the north. DB *Castretune*.

Castle Acre (village, Norfolk): 'newly cultivated land with a castle'. OF *castel*, 'castle', + OE *æcer*, 'plot of cultivated land' (modern English *acre*). The first word refers to the former Norman castle here and distinguishes this Acre from the nearby village of *West Acre* and hamlet of *South Acre*. DB *Acre*, 1235 *Castelacr*.

Castle-an-Dinas (hill fort, Cornwall): 'fort at Dennis'. Cornish *castell*, 'fort'. *Dennis*, now the name of a nearby farm, means 'hill fort' (Cornish *dinas*). It must have earlier been known as *An Dinas*, 'the hill fort'. 1478 *Dynas*, c.1504 *Castel an dynas*.

Castle Ashby (village, Northants): 'farmstead where ash trees grow with a castle'. ME *castel*, 'castle', + OS *askr*, 'ash', + *bý*, 'farmstead'. The first word, referring to the former castle here, distinguishes this Ashby from MEARS ASHBY, 5 miles to the north. DB *Asebi*, 1361 *Castel Assheby*.

Castlebay (coastal town, W Isles): '(town by) Castle Bay'. The bay on the island of Barra takes its name from Kiessimul Castle, built on a rocky outcrop in the water. The town arose in the 19C as a fishing port.

Castle Bolton (village, N Yorks): 'settlement with a special building by a castle'. OE *bōthl-tūn* (from *bōthl*, 'building', + *tūn*, 'farmstead', 'settlement'). The first word of the name refers to the castle built here in 1379. DB *Bodelton*.

Castle Bromwich (suburb of Birmingham, Solihull): 'farm where broom grows with a castle'. ME *castel* + OE *brōm*, 'broom', + *wīc*, 'specialized farm'. The first word refers to the former Norman motte-and-bailey castle here and distinguishes this Bromwich from WEST BROMWICH, 10 miles to the west. 1168 *Bramewice*, 13C *Castelbromwic*.

Castle Bytham (village, Lincs): 'homestead in the broad valley with a castle'. ME *castel*, 'castle', + OE *bythme*, 'broad valley', + *hām*, 'homestead'. The first word, referring to the former Norman castle here, distinguishes this place from nearby *Little Bytham*. c.1067 *Bytham*, DB *Bitham*, 1219 *castellum de Biham*.

Castle Camps. See SHUDY CAMPS.

Castle Carrock (village, Cumbria): 'fortified castle'. The name is Celtic, from words related to modern Welsh *castell*, 'castle', and *caerog*, 'fortified' (from *caer*, 'fort'). An old entrenchment on the summit of Carrock Fell here is said to mark the site of the original castle. c.1165 *Castelcairoc*.

Castle Cary (town, Somerset): '(place by the river) Cary with a castle'. ME *castel*, 'castle'. The river has a Celtic name perhaps meaning 'pleasant one'. The Norman castle has not survived. The first word of the name distinguishes the town from BABCARY, 6 miles to the southwest, and also from *Cary Fitzpaine*, 8 miles to the west, where the Fitz Payn family held the manor in the 13C. DB *Cari*, 1237 *Castelkary*.

Castle Combe (village, Wilts): '(place in the) valley with a castle'. ME *castel*, 'castle', + OE *cumb*, 'valley'. The village stands in a winding valley of the By Brook. The Norman castle has not survived. DB *Come*, 1270 *Castelcumbe*.

Castle Donington (village, Leics): 'estate associated with Dunn with a castle'. ME *castel*, 'castle', + OE *-ing-*, 'associated with', + *tūn*, 'farmstead',

'estate'. The first word of the name, referring to a former Norman castle here, distinguishes this Donington from *Donington le Heath*, originally on heathland, 10 miles to the south. DB *Dunintone*, 1428 *Castel Donyngton*.

Castle Douglas (town, Dumfries & Gall): 'Douglas's castle'. The castle is nearby Threave Castle. In 1789 Sir William Douglas bought the village of Carlingwerk here and developed it into a burgh of barony.

Castle Eaton (village, Swindon): 'farmstead by a river with a castle'. ME *castel*, 'castle', + OE *ēa*, 'river', + *tūn*, 'farmstead'. The river here is the Thames, but the whereabouts of any castle is unknown. DB *Ettone*, 1469 *Castel Eton*.

Castle Eden (village, Durham): '(place with a) castle on Castle Eden Burn'. *Eden* is a Celtic river name meaning simply 'water'. The 'castle' is the 18C mansion here known earlier as Castle Eden Hall and Castle Eden Castle but now as The Castle. c.1050 *Iodene*.

Castleford (town, Wakefield): 'ford by the Roman fort'. OE *cæster*, 'Roman fort', + *ford*, 'ford'. The ford took Ermine Street over the river Aire here. The Roman station was *Lagentium*, a name of uncertain meaning. Late 11C *Ceaster forda*.

Castle Frome. See BISHOP'S FROME.

Castle Gresley. See CHURCH GRESLEY.

Castle Heaton (hamlet, Northd): 'high farmstead with a castle'. OE *hēah*, 'high', + *tūn*, 'farmstead'. There is no actual castle here, and the first word of the name presumably refers to a medieval hall. 1183 *Heton*.

Castle Hedingham. See SIBLE HEDINGHAM.

Castle Howard (mansion, N Yorks): 'Howard's castle'. The original 'castle' here was the mansion called Hinderskelfe Castle. *Hinderskelfe* means 'Hildr's shelf' (OS *skjalf*, 'shelf'), with a Scandinavian woman's name, the 'shelf' being the small plateau to the west. The house burned down in 1693 and Charles Howard, 3rd Earl of Carlisle (1674–1738), built Castle Howard in the 1730s to replace it. 'The name is gradually displacing the name Hinderskelfe, which is now only the name of the township' (A. H. Smith, *The Place-Names of the North Riding of Yorkshire*, 1928).

Castle Levington. See KIRKLEVINGTON.

Castlemartin (village, Pemb): 'fort by St Martin's church'. ME *castel*, 'castle', 'fort'. The former fort here, whose remains are still visible, was named after nearby St Martin's church (now dedicated to St Michael). 1290 *Castro Sancti Martini*, 1341 *Castlemartin*.

Castle Morpeth (council district, Northd). The name combines those of the two former wards of *Castle*, which included NEWCASTLE UPON TYNE and MORPETH.

Castlemorton (village, Worcs): 'farmstead in the marshy ground with a castle'. ME *castel*, 'castle', + OE *mōr*, 'moor', 'marsh', + *tūn*, 'farmstead'. 'Near the church is a moat surrounding a mound, supposed [i.e. believed] to be the site of an ancient castle' (*The National Gazetteer of Great Britain and Ireland*, 1868). 1235 *Mortun*, 1346 *Castell Morton*.

Castle Point (council district, Essex). The name was devised for the administrative district set up in 1974 with reference to two prominent local features: Hadleigh *Castle*, the ruined Norman castle at Hadleigh, and Canvey *Point*, the headland at the eastern end of Canvey Island. The name exists elsewhere for a headland with a castle, as *Castle Point*, Northd, on which Dunstanburgh Castle stands.

Castle Rising (village, Norfolk): '(settlement of the) dwellers in the brushwood with a castle'. ME *castel*, 'castle', + OE *hrīs*, 'brushwood', + *-ingas*, 'dwellers at'. The original name could also mean '(settlement of) Risa's people' (OE *-ingas*, 'people of'). Remains of a Norman castle are here. DB *Risinga*, 1254 *Castel Risinge*.

Castleton (village, Derbys): 'farmstead by a castle'. OE *castel*, 'castle', + *tūn*, 'farmstead', 'village'. The name alludes to the ruined Peveril Castle nearby. 13C *Castelton*.

Castleton (village, N Yorks): 'farmstead by a castle'. OE *castel*, 'castle', + *tūn*, 'farmstead', 'village'. The name refers to (the remains of medieval) Danby Castle nearby. 1577 *Castleton*.

Castleton (district, Rochdale): 'farmstead by a castle'. 'Here was formerly a castle of very ancient date, some vestiges of which remain' (*The National Gazetteer of Great Britain and Ireland*, 1868). 1246 *Castelton*.

Castley (village, N Yorks): '(place at the) wood or clearing by the heap of stones'. OE *ceastel*, 'heap', + *lēah*, 'wood', 'clearing'. The 'heap of stones' would be the remains of an ancient fort here. DB *Castelai*.

Caston (village, Norfolk): 'Catt's or Káti's farmstead'. OE *tūn*, 'farmstead', 'estate'. The personal names are respectively OE and Scandinavian. DB *Catestuna*.

Castor (district, Peterborough): 'Roman fort'. OE *cæster*, 'Roman camp'. The Roman town here on Ermine Street by the river Nene was *Durobrivae*, 'walled town with a bridge'. Cp. ROCHESTER (Medway). The first form of the name below refers to St Kyneburga, daughter of Penda, king of Mercia, who is said to have founded a monastery here in the 7C. (Castor church is dedicated to her.) 948 *Kyneburga cæstre*, DB *Castre*.

Castra Exploratorum. See NETHERBY.

Cas-wis. See WISTON.

Cataractonium. See CATTERICK.

Catcleugh (hamlet, Northd): '(place in the) deep valley where wildcats are seen'. OE *catt*, 'wildcat', + *clōh*, 'ravine'. Catcleugh, now associated with its reservoir, lies in upper Redesdale. 1279 *Cattechlow*.

Catcott (village, Somerset): 'Cada's cottage'. OE *cot*, 'cottage'. DB *Cadicote*.

Caterham (town, Surrey): 'homestead or enclosure by Cadeir'. OE *hām*, 'homestead', or *hamm*, 'enclosure'. The hill called *Cadeir*, which has not been identified, has a Celtic name meaning 'chair' (as for CADER IDRIS). The name could also mean 'Catta's homestead or enclosure'. 1179 *Catheham*.

Catesby (village, Northants): 'Kátr's or Káti's farmstead'. OS *bý*, 'farmstead', 'village'. The personal names are Scandinavian. The parish of Catesby contains the hamlets of *Upper Catesby* and *Lower Catesby*. DB *Catesbi*.

Catfield (village, Norfolk): 'open land where wildcats are seen'. OE *catt*, 'wildcat', + *feld*, 'open land' (modern English *field*). The name could also mean 'Káti's field', with a Scandinavian personal name. DB *Catefelda*.

Catford (district, Lewisham): 'ford where wildcats are seen'. OE *catt*, 'cat', + *ford*, 'ford'. At one time wildcats would have been seen in the woodland by the river Ravensbourne here. 1254 *Catford*.

Cathays (district, Cardiff): 'enclosure where wildcats are seen'. OE *catt*, 'wildcat', + *haga*, 'enclosure'. 1699 *Catt Hays*.

Catherine-de-Barnes (district, Solihull): 'Ketelbern's (estate)'. The name probably comes from Ketelbern of Longdon, who founded the 12C priory of Henwood nearby. It was then applied to the heath here. The present form of the name is due to French influence. 1602 *Katherine barnes heath*.

Catherington (village, Hants): 'farmstead of the people living by Cadeir'. OE *-inga-*, 'of the people at', + *tūn*, 'farmstead'. *Cadeir* is the name of a nearby hill, from a Celtic word related to modern Welsh *cadair*, 'chair' (cp. CADER IDRIS). The name could also mean 'farmstead of Cattor's people' with a personal name. The name gave the dedication of the church here (earlier All Saints) to St Catherine. *c.*1015 *Cateringatune*.

Catherston Leweston (village, Dorset). OE *tūn*, 'farmstead', 'estate'. Originally two separate estates: *Catherston*, owned by the Charteray family, and *Leweston*, owned by the Lester family. 1268 *Chartreston*, 1316 *Lesterton*.

Catmose, Vale of (region, Rutland): 'valley of the marsh where wildcats are seen'. ME *vale*, 'valley', + OE *catt*, 'wildcat', + *mos*, 'marsh'. 1576 *Val of Catmouse*.

Caton (village, Lancs): 'Káti's farmstead'. OE *tūn*, 'farmstead', 'village'. The personal name is Scandinavian. DB *Catun*.

Catsfield (village, E Sussex): 'Catt's open land'. OE *feld*, 'open land' (modern English *field*). The name could also mean 'open land where wildcats are seen' (OE *catt*, 'wildcat'). The DB form of the name below has *d* for *tt*. DB *Cedesfeld*, 12C *Cattesfeld*.

Catshill (village, Worcs): 'Catt's hill'. OE *hyll*, 'hill'. The name could also mean 'hill where wildcats are seen' (OE *catt*, 'cat', + *hyll*). 1199 *Catteshull*.

Cattal (village, N Yorks): 'corner of land where wildcats are seen'. OE *catt*, 'wildcat', + *halh*, 'nook', 'corner of land'. The corner of land in question would probably have been in a nearby loop of the river Nidd. DB *Catale*.

Cattawade (village, Suffolk): '(place by the river) crossing where wildcats are seen'. OE *catt*, 'wildcat', + *gewæd*, 'ford', 'crossing place'. Cattawade is at the head of the river Stour estuary, and the crossing would have been over tidal water. 1247 *Cattiwad*.

Catterall (village, Lancs): '(place by the) cat's tail'. OS *kattar-hali*, 'cat's tail'. The reference would be to the shape of some feature here. The name could also mean '(place by the) corner of land' (OE *halh*, 'nook', 'corner of land'), with a first element of obscure origin. DB *Catrehala*.

Catterick (village, N Yorks): '(place by the) waterfall'. Latin *cataracta*, 'waterfall' (modern English *cataract*). The reference would be to the rapids on the river Swale here. But this may be a misinterpretation of an earlier Celtic name meaning '(place of) battle ramparts', from Celtic *catu-*, 'battle' (modern Welsh *cad*), and *ratis*, 'rampart'. The Roman town at Catterick was *Cataractonium*. *c.*150 *Katouraktonion*, DB *Catrice*.

Catterlen (hamlet, Cumbria): '(place by a) hill'. The first part of the name is Celtic in origin, from a word related to modern Welsh

cadair, 'chair', as for CADER IDRIS. The second part is of uncertain origin. The hill in question is presumably one of the two to the west of the hamlet. 1158 *Kaderleng*.

Catterton (hamlet, N Yorks): 'farmstead by a hill'. OE *tūn*, 'farmstead'. The first part of the name is Celtic in origin, from a word related to modern Welsh *cadair*, 'chair', as for CADER IDRIS. There is a slight hill here. DB *Cadretune*.

Catthorpe (village, Leics): 'le Cat's outlying farmstead'. OS *thorp*, 'outlying farmstead'. The le Cat family held the manor early here, their name distinguishing this Thorpe from COUNTESTHORPE, 11 miles to the north. DB *Torp*, 1276 *Torpkat*.

Cattishall (hamlet, Suffolk): 'Catt's corner of land'. OE *halh*, 'nook', 'corner of land'. The name could also mean 'corner of land where wildcats are seen' (OE *catt*, 'wildcat', + *halh*). 1187 *Catteshale*.

Cattistock (village, Dorset): 'Catt's outlying farmstead'. OE *stoc*, 'outlying farm', 'secondary settlement'. A man or family called Catt held the manor here in the 13C. DB *Stoche*, 1288 *Cattestok*.

Catton (village, Northd): '(place in the) valley where wildcats are seen'. OE *catt*, 'wildcat', + *denu*, 'valley'. 1229 *Catteden*.

Catton (village, N Yorks): 'Catta's or Káti's farmstead'. OE *tūn*, 'farmstead'. The personal names are respectively OE and Scandinavian. DB *Catune*. SO ALSO: *Catton*, Norfolk.

Catwick (village, E Yorks): 'dairy farm associated with Catta'. OE *-ing-*, 'associated with', + *wīc*, 'dwelling', 'dairy farm'. DB *Catingewuic*.

Catworth (village, Cambs): 'Catt's or Catta's enclosure'. OE *worth*, 'enclosure'. 10C *Catteswyrth*, DB *Cateuuorde*.

Caunton (village, Notts): 'Calnōth's farmstead'. OE *tūn*, 'farmstead'. DB *Calnestune*.

Causey Park (hamlet, Northd): '(place on an) embankment'. ME *cauce*, 'embankment', 'raised way' (related modern English *causeway*). Causey Park is on a road built over moorland. 1242 *La Chauce*.

Cavendish (village, Suffolk): 'Cāfna's enclosure'. OE *edisc*, 'enclosure', 'enclosed park'. DB *Kauanadisc*.

Cavenham (village, Suffolk): 'Cāfna's homestead or enclosure'. OE *hām*, 'homestead', or *hamm*, 'enclosure'. The DB form of the name below has garbled the personal name. DB *Kanauaham*.

Caversfield (village, Oxon): 'Cāfhere's open land'. OE *feld*, 'open land' (modern English *field*). DB *Cavrefelle*.

Caversham (district, Reading): 'Cāfhere's homestead or enclosure'. OE *hām*, 'homestead', or *hamm*, 'enclosure'. Caversham is by the Thames. DB *Caueresham*.

Caverswall (village, Staffs): 'Cāfhere's spring'. OE *wella*, 'spring', 'stream'. DB *Cavreswelle*.

Cavil (hamlet, E Yorks): 'open land where jackdaws are seen'. OE *cā*, 'jackdaw', + *feld*, 'open land' (modern English *field*). 959 *Cafeld*, DB *Cheuede*.

Cawood (village, N Yorks): 'wood where jackdaws are seen'. OE *cā*, 'jackdaw', + *wudu*, 'wood'. 963 *Kawuda*.

Cawsand (coastal village, Cornwall): 'sandy beach of (the) Cow'. The name may come from a rock by the beach here called 'Cow' from its shape. Cp. COWES. 1405 *Couyssond*.

Cawston (village, Norfolk): 'Kalfr's farmstead'. OE *tūn*, 'farmstead', 'village'. The personal name is Scandinavian. DB *Caustuna*.

Cawthorne (village, Barnsley): '(place by) cold thorn bush'. OE *cald*, 'cold', + *thorn*, 'thorn bush'. The name implies an exposed site. DB *Caltorne*.

Cawton (hamlet, N Yorks): 'farm where calves are reared'. OE *calf*, 'calf', + *tūn*, 'farmstead'. DB *Caluetun*.

Caxton (village, Cambs): 'Kakkr's farmstead'. OE *tūn*, 'farmstead'. The personal name is Scandinavian. The DB form of the name below is corrupt. DB *Caustone*, c.1150 *Kakestune*.

Caynham (village, Shropshire): 'Cǣga's homestead or enclosure'. OE *hām*, 'homestead', or *hamm*, 'enclosure'. DB *Caiham*, 1255 *Cainham*.

Caythorpe (village, Lincs): 'Káti's outlying farmstead'. OS *thorp*, 'outlying farmstead', 'secondary settlement'. The personal name is Scandinavian. DB *Catorp*. SO ALSO: *Caythorpe*, Notts.

Cayton (village, N Yorks): 'Cǣga's farmstead'. OE *tūn*, 'farmstead'. DB *Caitun*.

Ceinewydd. See NEW QUAY.

Cemaes Bay (village resort, Anglesey): '(place by) Cemaes Bay'. The bay takes its name from the village, originally simply *Cemaes*, '(place of) bends' (Welsh *cemais*, plural of *camas*, 'bend', 'inlet'. The 'bends' may be those in the coastline here or those in the river Wygyr before it reaches the beach. The spelling of the name may have been influenced by Welsh *maes*, 'field'. 1291 *Kemmeys*.

Cendl. See BEAUFORT.

Ceredigion (unitary authority, W Wales): 'Ceredig's land'. Ceredig was one of the sons of Cunedda, who gave the name of Gwynedd. His name is followed by the Welsh territorial suffix *-ion*. Ceredigion itself gave the name of CARDIGAN. 12C *Cereticiaun*.

Cerne Abbas (village, Dorset): '(place by the river) Cerne belonging to the abbey'. Latin *abbas*, 'abbot'. The river has a Celtic name meaning 'heap of stones' (related English *cairn*). DB *Cernel*, 1288 *Cerne Abbatis*.

Chaceley (village, Glos): '(place by the) wood'. The first part of the name is of Celtic origin, from a word related to modern Welsh *coed*, 'wood'. The tautological second part represents OE *lēah*, 'wood', 'clearing'. 972 *Ceatewesleah*.

Chacewater (village, Cornwall): 'chase by the water'. The 'chase' is a former hunting ground here, and the 'water' the stream nearby. 1613 *Chasewater*.

Chadderton (town, Oldham): 'farmstead at Cadeir'. OE *tūn*, 'farmstead'. The hill *Cadeir* has a Celtic name meaning 'chair' (as for CADER IDRIS). The hill itself is probably the one in Royton known as Hanging Chadder. c.1200 *Chaderton*.

Chaddesden (district, Derby): 'Ceadd's valley'. OE *denu*, 'valley'. DB *Cedesdene*.

Chaddesley Corbett (village, Worcs): 'Corbet's (estate) by the wood at Cadair'. OE *lēah*, 'wood', 'clearing'. *Cadair* is the Celtic name of a hill here meaning 'chair', as for CADER IDRIS. The Corbet family held the manor here in the 12C. 816 *Ceadresleahge*, DB *Cedeslai*.

Chadlington (village, Oxon): 'estate associated with Ceadela'. OE *-ing-*, 'associated with', + *tūn*, 'farmstead', 'estate'. DB *Cedelintone*.

Chadshunt (hamlet, Warwicks): '(place by) Ceadel's spring'. OE *funta*, 'spring'. 949 *Ceadeles funtan*, DB *Cedeleshunte*.

Chadwell (hamlet, Leics): '(place by the) cold spring'. OE *ceald*, 'cold', + *wella*, 'spring', 'stream'. DB *Caldeuuelle*.

Chadwell Heath (district, Barking & Dag): '(place by the) cold spring'. OE *ceald*, 'cold', + *wella*, 'spring', 'stream'. The original village later became associated with its heath. 1254 *Chaudewell*, 1609 *Chaldwell heth*.

Chadwell St Mary (village, Thurrock): '(place by the) cold spring with St Mary's church'. OE *ceald*, 'cold', + *wella*, 'spring', 'stream'. The spring in question is St Chad's Well, just south of the church, the saint's name being suggested by the place name. The recent addition of the church dedication distinguishes this Chadwell from CHADWELL HEATH, Barking & Dag, 13 miles to the northwest. DB *Celdeuuella*.

Chaffcombe (village, Somerset): 'Ceaffa's valley'. OE *cumb*, 'valley'. DB *Caffecome*.

Chagford (town, Devon): '(place by the) ford where chag grows'. OE *ceacga*, 'chag', + *ford*, 'ford'. 'Chag' is a dialect word for broom or gorse. The river here is the Teign. DB *Chageford*.

Chailey (village, E Sussex): '(place by the) clearing where chag grows'. OE *ceacga*, 'chag', + *lēah*, 'wood', 'clearing'. 'Chag' is a dialect word for broom or gorse. 11C *Cheagele*.

Chalbury (hamlet, Dorset): 'fortified place associated with Cēol'. OE *burh*, 'fortified place'. The 'fortified place' is the ancient hill fort here. 946 *Cheoles burge*.

Chaldon (village, Surrey): 'hill where calves graze'. OE *cealf*, 'calf', + *dūn*, 'hill'. DB *Calvedone*.

Chaldon Herring (village, Dorset): 'Harang's (estate by the) hill where calves graze'. OE *cealf*, 'calf', + *dūn*, 'hill'. The Harang family held the manor here in the 12C. Their name distinguishes this Chaldon from nearby *Chaldon Boys*, where the manor was held by the de Bosco family. Chaldon Herring is also known as *East Chaldon*, and Chaldon Boys invariably as *West Chaldon*. DB *Celvedune*, 1243 *Chaluedon Hareng*.

Chale (village, IoW): '(place by the) ravine'. OE *ceole*, 'throat'. The name refers to the famous Blackgang Chine nearby. See BLACKGANG. DB *Cela*.

Chalfont St Giles (village, Bucks): '(place by the) spring where calves drink with St Giles's church'. OE *cealf*, 'calf', + *funta*, 'spring'. The church dedication was added to distinguish this Chalfont from CHALFONT ST PETER, 2 miles to the southeast. DB *Celfunte*, 1237 *Chalfund Sancti Egidii*.

Chalfont St Peter (town, Bucks): '(place by the) spring where calves drink with St Peter's church'. OE *cealf*, 'calf', + *funta*, 'spring'. The church dedication was added to distinguish this Chalfont from CHALFONT ST GILES, 2 miles to the northwest. DB *Celfunte*, 1237 *Chalfhunte Sancti Petri*.

Chalford (village, Glos): '(place by the) chalk ford'. OE *cealc*, 'chalk', 'limestone', + *ford*, 'ford'. The village lies on oolite (limestone) beds and the river here is the Frome. *c*.1250 *Chalforde*. SO ALSO: *Chalford*, Oxon.

Chalgrove (village, Oxon): '(place by the) chalk pit'. OE *cealc*, 'chalk', + *græf*, 'pit' (modern English *grave*). DB *Celgrave*.

Chalk Farm (district, Camden): 'farm by the cold cottages'. OE *ceald*, 'cold', + *cot*, 'cottage'. The association with 'chalk' is misleading, and the '-k' represents the *c-* of *cot*. The main name is thus identical in meaning to CALDICOT. 1253 *Chaldecote*, *c*.1400 *Caldecote*, 1593 *Chalcot*, 1746 *Chalk*.

Challacombe (village, Devon): '(place in the) cold valley'. OE *ceald*, 'cold', + *cumb*, 'valley'. The form of the name below applies to Challacombe near Lynton. DB *Celdecomba*.

Chalton (village, Hants): 'farmstead on chalk'. OE *cealc*, 'chalk', + *tūn*, 'farmstead'. Chalton lies on the chalk downs. 1015 *Cealctun*, DB *Ceptune*.

Chalvey (district, Slough): 'island where calves are kept'. OE *cealf*, 'calf', + *ēg*, 'island'. Chalvey is almost surrounded by streams. 1227 *Chalfheye*.

Chalvington (village, E Sussex): 'estate associated with Cealf'. OE *-ing-*, 'associated with', + *tūn*, 'farmstead', 'estate'. DB *Calvintone*.

Chanctonbury Ring (Iron Age fort, W Sussex): 'circle (of stones) at the fortification by Chancton'. OE *burh*, 'fortified place'. The ancient earthwork is near *Chancton*, 'farmstead of Ceawa's people' (OE *-inga-*, 'of the people of', + *tūn*, 'farmstead'). The site of the encampment is ringed with beech trees planted in the 18C, but these did not give the second word of the name. 1351 *Changebury*.

Chandler's Ford (suburb of Eastleigh, Hants): 'Sēarnægel's ford'. OE *ford*, 'ford'. The personal name has apparently been assimilated to that of the Chaundler family, here from the 14C. The ford took a Roman road over Monks Brook. 909 *Searnægles Ford*, 1280 *Sarnayylesford*, 1759 *Chandlers Ford*.

Chapel Allerton (district, Leeds): 'village where alders grow with a chapel'. OE *alor*, 'alder', + *tūn*, 'farmstead', 'village'. The first word of the name distinguishes this Allerton from nearby *Moor Allerton*, formerly on the moor. Contracted forms of these two names respectively gave the Leeds district names *Chapeltown* and *Moortown*. DB *Alretun*, 1360 *Chapel Allerton*.

Chapel Allerton (village, Somerset): 'Ælfweard's farmstead with a chapel'. OE *tūn*, 'farmstead'. The first word of the name distinguishes the village from nearby *Stone Allerton*, with a boundary stone. DB *Alwarditone*.

Chapel Amble (village, Cornwall): '(part of) Amble with a chapel'. *Amble* apparently derives from Cornish *ammal*, 'edge', 'boundary', referring to its location near the boundary of the hundred of Trigg. The first form of the name below means 'Amble church' (Cornish *eglos*, 'church'). 1284 *Amaleglos*, 1664 *Chaple Amble*.

Chapel Brampton (village, Northants): 'village where broom grows with a chapel'. OE *brōm*, 'broom', + *tūn*, 'farmstead'. The first word of the name distinguishes the village from nearby *Church Brampton*. There is no chapel here now. DB *Brantone*.

Chapel Chorlton (village, Staffs): 'farmstead of the freemen with a chapel'. OE *ceorl*, 'freeman', 'peasant' (modern English *churl*), + *tūn*, 'farmstead'. The first word of the name distinguishes the village from nearby *Hill Chorlton*. DB *Cerletone*.

Chapel Cleeve. See OLD CLEEVE.

Chapel-en-le-Frith (town, Derbys): 'chapel in the sparse woodland'. ME *chapele*, 'chapel', + OF *en le*, 'in the', + OE *fyrhth*, 'woodland'. The chapel of St Thomas Becket was built here in the 13C. 1272 *Capella de le Frith*.

Chapel Haddlesey (village, N Yorks): '(place by a) marshy pool in heathland with a chapel'. OE *hathel*, 'heathland', + *sǽ*, 'sea', 'marshland'. The first word of the name distinguishes the village from nearby *West Haddlesey*. c.1030 *Hathelsæe*, 1605 *Chappel Haddlesey*.

Chapel Island (island, Cumbria). The island in the estuary of the river Leven takes its name from the chapel here used by travellers across the Leven Sands, guided by monks from Cartmel or Conishead.

Chapel St Leonards (resort village, Lincs): 'St Leonard's chapel'. The chapel dedicated to St Leonard here originally belonged to the nearby village of Mumby. 1503 *the chapell of seint Leonard in Mumby*, 1556 *Mumby Chapell*, 1896 *Mumby Chapel, or Chapel*.

Chapeltown (suburb of Sheffield): 'settlement by the chapel'. ME *chapel*, 'chapel'. The medieval chapel here was a chapel of ease to Ecclesfield. 13C *Le Chapel*, 1707 *Chappeltown*.

Chapeltown (Leeds). See CHAPEL ALLERTON (Leeds).

Chapmanslade (village, Wilts): '(place in the) valley of the merchants'. OE *cēap-mann*, 'merchant' (from *cēap*, 'trade', + *mann*, 'man'), + *slæd*, 'valley'. The valley in question must be one of the small ones at the end of the ridge along which the village lies. 1245 *Chepmanesled*.

Chard (town, Somerset): 'house in rough ground'. OE *ceart*, 'rough ground', + *ærn*, 'house', 'building'. The second part of the name subsequently disappeared. 1065 *Cerdren*, DB *Cerdre*.

Chardstock (village, Devon): 'secondary settlement belonging to Chard'. OE *stoc*, 'outlying farmstead', 'secondary settlement'. Chardstock is 3 miles from CHARD. DB *Cerdestoche*.

Charfield (village, S Glos): 'open land with a rough surface'. OE *ceart*, 'rough ground', + *feld*, 'open land' (modern English *field*). The name could also mean 'open land by a bending road' (OE *cearr*, 'bend', + *feld*). DB *Cirvelde*.

Charing (town, Kent): '(place at the) bend'. OE *cerring*, 'bend in a road'. The name could also mean 'place associated with Ceorra' (OE *-ing*, 'place associated with'). 799 *Ciorrincg*, DB *Cheringes*.

Charing Cross (district, Westminster): 'bend with a cross'. OE *cerring*, 'bend in a road'. The bend in question may have been that in the Thames here or, more likely, one in the old main road from London to the west, a former Roman road. The cross was the 'Queen Eleanor cross' erected here in the 14C (with a 19C equivalent in the forecourt of Charing Cross station), resulting in a popular etymology for the name in French *chère reine*, 'dear queen'. c.1000 *Cyrring*, 1360 *La Charryngcros*.

Charlbury (town, Oxon): 'fortified place associated with Ceorl'. OE *-ing-*, 'associated with', + *burh*, 'fortified place'. The *-ing-* of the original name has disappeared. c.1000 *Ceorlingburh*.

Charlecote (village, Warwicks): 'cottages of the freemen'. OE *ceorl*, 'freeman', 'peasant' (modern English *churl*), + *cot*, 'cottage'. DB *Cerlecote*.

Charles (hamlet, Devon): 'court among rocks'. Cornish *carn*, 'rock', + *lys*, 'court'. The DB form of the name below is corrupt. DB *Carmes*, 1244 *Charles*.

Charleston of Aboyne. See ABOYNE.

Charlestown (coastal suburb of St Austell, Cornwall): 'Charles's town'. The port was founded in 1791 to serve the china-clay industry by Charles Rashleigh (1747–1825) and named after him. Its earlier Cornish name was *Polmear* ('great harbour'), surviving in Polmear Island, at the entrance to the harbour. See also PORTHPEAN. 1800 *Charles-Town*.

Charlestown of Aberlour. See ABERLOUR.

Charlesworth (village, Derbys): 'Ceafl's enclosure'. OE *worth*, 'enclosure'. The first part of the name could also represent OE *ceafl*, literally 'jaw', referring to a ravine or valley here. The name has probably been influenced by that of nearby *Charlestown*. The DB form of the name below is corrupt. DB *Cheuenwrde*, 1286 *Chauelisworth*.

Charlinch (hamlet, Somerset): 'Cēolrēd's ridge'. OE *hlinc*, 'ridge'. DB *Cerdeslinc*.

Charlotteville (district of Guildford, Surrey). French *ville*, 'town'. The district, south of Mount Alvernia Hospital and St Luke's Hospital, was laid out in 1892 on behalf of a local doctor, Thomas Sells, who named it after his wife Charlotte. He also named a number of streets here after medical men, such as Addison Road, Harvey Road, Jenner Road and Bright Hill.

Charlton (district, Greenwich): 'farmstead of the freemen'. OE *ceorl*, 'freeman', 'peasant' (modern English *churl*), + *tūn*, 'farmstead'. Cp. CARLTON. DB *Cerletone*. SO ALSO: *Charlton*, Hants.

Charlton (former district, Surrey): 'estate associated with Cēolrēd'. OE *-ing-*, 'associated with', + *tūn*, 'farmstead', 'estate'. The name of the district is preserved in Charlton Road, to the east of Queen Mary Reservoir. DB *Cerdentone*.

Charlton (village, Wilts): 'farmstead of the freemen'. OE *ceorl*, 'freeman', 'peasant' (modern English *churl*), + *tūn*, 'farmstead'. Cp. CARLTON. The forms of the name below relate to Charlton near Malmesbury, but Charlton near Upavon and Charlton near Salisbury have names of identical origin. 10C *Ceorlatunæ*, DB *Cerletone*.

Charlton Abbots. See CHARLTON KINGS.

Charlton Adam (village, Somerset): 'fitz Adam's (estate at the) farmstead of the freemen'. OE *ceorl*, 'freeman', 'peasant' (modern English *churl*), + *tūn*, 'farmstead'. The fitz Adam family held the manor here in the 13C, their name distinguishing this Charlton from nearby CHARLTON MACKRELL. DB *Cerletune*, 13C *Cherleton Adam*.

Charlton Horethorne (village, Somerset): 'farmstead of the freemen in Horethorne'. OE *ceorl*, 'freeman', 'peasant' (modern English *churl*), + *tūn*, 'farmstead'. *Horethorne* is the name of the hundred here, meaning 'grey thorn bush' (OE *hār*, 'grey', + *thyrne*, 'thorn bush'). The addition distinguishes this Charlton from CHARLTON MUSGROVE, 5 miles to the northeast. *c.*950 *Ceorlatun*.

Charlton Kings (town, Glos): 'king's (estate at the) farmstead of the freemen'. OE *ceorl*, 'free-

man', 'peasant' (modern English *churl*), + *tūn*, 'farmstead'. The second word of the name, denoting that the place was an ancient royal demesne, distinguishes it from *Charlton Abbots*, 4 miles to the northeast, which was held by Winchcomb Abbey. 1160 *Cherletone*, 1245 *Kynges Cherleton*, 1868 *King's Charlton*.

Charlton Mackrell (village, Somerset): 'Makerel's (estate at the) farmstead of the freemen'. OE *ceorl*, 'freeman', 'peasant' (modern English *churl*), + *tūn*, 'farmstead'. The Makerel family held the manor here, their name distinguishing this Charlton from nearby CHARLTON ADAM and also from CHARLTON HORETHORNE, 10 miles to the southeast. DB *Cerletune*, 1243 *Cherletun Makerel*.

Charlton Marshall (village, Dorset): 'Mareschal's (estate at the) farmstead of the freemen'. OE *ceorl*, 'freeman', 'peasant' (modern English *churl*), + *tūn*, 'farmstead'. The Mareschal family, who also gave their name to *Sturminster Marshall* (see STURMINSTER NEWTON), held the manor here in the 13C. DB *Cerletone*, 1288 *Cherleton Marescal*.

Charlton Musgrove (village, Somerset): 'Mucegros's (estate at the) farmstead of the freemen'. OE *ceorl*, 'freeman', 'peasant' (modern English *churl*), + *tūn*, 'farmstead'. The Mucegros family held the manor here in the 13C, their name distinguishing this Charlton from CHARLTON HORETHORNE, 5 miles to the southwest. DB *Cerletone*, 1225 *Cherleton Mucegros*.

Charlton-on-Otmoor (village, Oxon): 'farmstead of the freemen on Otmoor'. OE *ceorl*, 'freeman', 'peasant' (modern English *churl*), + *tūn*, 'farmstead'. The second part of the name distinguishes this Charlton from others by locating it on *Ot Moor*, 'Otta's marshy ground' (OE *mōr*, 'moor', 'marshy ground'). DB *Cerlentone*, 1314 *Cherleton upon Ottemour*, 1868 *Charlton-upon-Otmoor*.

Charlwood (village, Surrey): 'wood of the freemen'. OE *ceorl*, 'freeman', 'peasant', + *wudu*, 'wood'. 12C *Cherlewde*.

Charminster (village, Dorset): 'church on the (river) Cerne'. OE *mynster*, 'monastery', 'church'. The Cerne also flows through CERNE ABBAS. DB *Cerminstre*.

Charmouth (resort town, Dorset): 'mouth of the (river) Char'. OE *mūtha*, 'mouth'. The river's name is identical with that of the Cerne of CERNE ABBAS. DB *Cernemude*.

Charndon (village, Bucks): '(place by the) hill (called) Carn'. OE *dūn*, 'hill'. The first part of the name represents a Celtic hill name meaning 'place of stones' (modern Welsh *carn*, 'cairn'). The DB form of the name below is corrupt. DB *Credendune*, 1227 *Charendone*.

Charney Bassett (village, Oxon): 'Basses' island on the (river) Cern'. OE *ēg*, 'island'. The river name, of Celtic origin and identical to that behind CERNE ABBAS, is a former name of a tributary of the river Ock, while the 'island' is the ground on which the village lies amid streams. The second word names a family called Bass or Basses (later corrupted to Bassett) who probably held the manor here. 821 *Ceornei*, DB *Cernei*, 1833 *Charney Basses*.

Charnock Richard (village, Lancs): 'Richard's (estate by the) cairn'. The first word of the name is of Celtic origin and related to modern Welsh *carn*, 'cairn', 'heap of stones'. The second word names one Richard who held the manor here in the 13C. 1194 *Chernoch*, 1288 *Chernok Richard*.

Charnwood Forest (region, Leics): 'wood in rocky country'. Celtic *carn*, 'rocky region' (modern English *cairn*), + OE *wudu*, 'wood'. The modern name, which gave *Charnwood* as that of the local council district, is essentially a tautology. 1129 *Cernewoda*.

Charsfield (village, Suffolk): '(place on) open land by the (river) Char'. OE *feld*, 'open land' (modern English *field*). The first part of the name represents a former Celtic river name for the Potsford Brook here, a tributary of the river Deben. The name itself perhaps means 'pleasant stream' (related to modern Welsh *caru*, 'to love'). Ronald Blythe's study *Akenfield: Portrait of an English Village* (1969) was essentially based on Charsfield. DB *Ceresfelda*.

Charterhouse (hamlet, Somerset): 'house of Carthusian monks'. OF *chartrouse*, 'Carthusian house'. The present name evolved by popular association with English *charter* and *house*. 1243 *Chartuse*.

Charterville Allotments (district of Minster Lovell, Oxon). 'It was here that [the Chartist leader] Feargus O'Connor in 1847 tried to carry his land scheme into effect, and it was divided into nearly 100 small holdings' (*Cassell's Gazetteer of Great Britain and Ireland*, 1893). See also HERONSGATE.

Chartham (village, Kent): 'homestead on rough ground'. OE *cert*, 'rough ground', + *hām*, 'homestead'. *c.*871 *Certham*, DB *Certeham*.

Charwelton (village, Northants): 'farmstead on the (river) Cherwell'. OE *tūn*, 'farmstead'. The river name, now adopted for an Oxfordshire council district, means 'winding stream'

(OE *cearr*, 'turn', 'bend', + *wella*, 'stream'), referring to its meandering course. DB *Cerweltone*.

Chastleton (village, Oxon): 'farmstead by a ruined camp'. OE *ceastel*, 'ruined camp' (from *ceas*, 'heap'), + *tūn*, 'farmstead'. The reference is to a prehistoric camp nearby. 777 *Ceastelton*, DB *Cestitone*.

Chatburn (village, Lancs): 'Ceatta's stream'. OE *burna*, 'stream'. The stream in question is Heys Brook, which flows into the river Ribble nearby. 1242 *Chatteburn*.

Chatcull (hamlet, Staffs): 'Ceatta's kiln'. OE *cyln*, 'kiln'. The reference is probably to a limekiln here. The DB form of the name below is corrupt. DB *Ceteruille*, 1199 *Chatculne*.

Chatham (town, Medway): 'settlement by a wood'. The first part of the name comes from a Celtic word related to modern Welsh *coed*, 'wood'. The second is OE *hām*, 'homestead', 'village'. 880 *Cetham*, DB *Ceteham*.

Chatsworth (mansion, Derbys): 'Ceatt's enclosed settlement'. OE *worth*, 'enclosure'. DB *Chetesuorde*, 1276 *Chattesworth*.

Chattenden (hamlet, Medway): 'Ceatta's hill'. OE *dūn*, 'hill'. *c.*1100 *Chatendune*.

Chatteris (town, Cambs): 'Ceatta's raised strip of land'. OE *ric*, 'narrow ridge'. The first part of the name could also mean 'wood', from a Celtic word related to modern Welsh *coed*. 974 *Cæateric*, DB *Cietriz*.

Chattisham (village, Suffolk): 'Ceatt's homestead or enclosure'. OE *hām*, 'homestead', or *hamm*, 'enclosure'. DB *Cetessam*.

Chatton (village, Northd): 'Ceatta's farmstead'. OE *tūn*, 'farmstead'. 1178 *Chetton*.

Chawleigh (village, Devon): 'clearing where calves graze'. OE *cealf*, 'calf', + *lēah*, 'wood', 'clearing'. DB *Calvelie*.

Chawton (village, Hants): 'farmstead on chalk'. OE *cealc*, 'chalk', + *tūn*, 'farmstead'. The name could also mean 'farmstead where calves are reared' (OE *cealf*, 'calf', + *tūn*). DB *Celtone*.

Cheadle (town, Staffs): '(place by the) wood'. The first part of the name comes from a Celtic word meaning 'wood' related to modern Welsh *coed*. The second part represents OE *lēah*, 'wood', added to the Celtic word when the latter was no longer understood. DB *Celle*.

Cheadle (town, Stockport): '(place by the) wood'. The name has the same origin as CHEADLE, Staffs. DB *Cedde*, *c.*1165 *Chedle*.

Cheadle Hulme (district, Stockport): 'island belonging to Cheadle'. OS *holmr*, 'island', 'river meadow'. The 'island' is the higher ground on which Cheadle Hulme lies by comparison with the main part of CHEADLE. 12C *Hulm*.

Cheam (district, Croydon): 'homestead by the tree stumps'. OE *ceg*, 'tree stump', + *hām*, 'homestead', 'village'. 967 *Cegham*, DB *Ceiham*.

Chearsley (village, Bucks): 'Cēolrēd's wood or clearing'. OE *lēah*, 'wood', 'clearing'. DB *Cerdeslai*.

Chebsey (village, Staffs): 'Cebbi's island'. OE *ēg*, 'island'. The 'island' is raised ground by the river Sow here. DB *Cebbesio*.

Checkendon (village, Oxon): 'Ceacca's valley'. OE *denu*, 'valley'. The name could also mean 'valley by the hill' (OE *ceacce*, 'lump', 'hill', + *denu*). DB *Cecadene*.

Checkley (hamlet, Cheshire): 'Ceaddica's wood or clearing'. OE *lēah*, 'wood', 'clearing'. 1252 *Chackileg*.

Checkley (hamlet, Herefords): 'Ceacca's wood or clearing'. OE *lēah*, 'wood', 'clearing'. The name could also mean 'wood or clearing by a hill' (OE *ceacce*, 'lump', + *lēah*). 1195 *Chakkeleya*. SO ALSO: *Checkley*, Staffs.

Chedburgh (village, Suffolk): 'Cedda's hill'. OE *beorg*, 'hill'. DB *Cedeberia*.

Cheddar (town, Somerset): '(place by the) ravine'. OE *cēodor*, 'ravine' (from *cēod*, 'bag', 'pouch'). The ravine is that of Cheddar Gorge here. c.880 *Ceodre*, DB *Cedre*.

Cheddington (village, Bucks): '(place by) Cetta's hill'. OE *dūn*, 'hill'. DB *Cetendone*.

Cheddleton (village, Staffs): 'farmstead in a valley'. OE *cetel*, 'valley' (modern English *kettle*), + *tūn*, 'farmstead'. DB *Celtetone*, 1201 *Chetilton*.

Cheddon Fitzpaine (village, Somerset): 'Fitzpaine's (estate in the) wooded valley'. The first word of the name apparently combines a Celtic word for 'wood', related to modern Welsh *coed*, with OE *denu*, 'valley'. The Fitzpaine family held the manor here in the 13C. DB *Succedene*, 1182 *Chedene*.

Chedgrave (village, Norfolk): 'Ceatta's pit'. OE *græf*, 'pit', 'trench' (modern English *grave*). The river Chet here takes its name from that of the village. DB *Scatagraua*, 1165 *Chategrave*.

Chedington (village, Dorset): 'estate associated with Cedd or Cedda'. OE *-ing-*, 'associated with', + *tūn*, 'farmstead', 'estate'. 1194 *Chedinton*.

Chediston (village, Suffolk): '(place by) Cedd's stone'. OE *stān*, 'stone'. The reference is probably to a boundary stone here. DB *Cedestan*.

Chedworth (village, Glos): 'Cedda's enclosure'. OE *worth*, 'enclosure'. The first form of the name below has a garbled second element. 962 *Ceddanwryde*, DB *Cedeorde*.

Chedzoy (village, Somerset): 'Cedd's island'. OE *ēg*, 'island'. The 'island' is dry ground in marshland. 729 *Chedesie*.

Cheetham (district, Manchester): 'homestead by the wood'. OE *hām*, 'homestead', 'village'. The first part of the name is of Celtic origin, from a word related to modern Welsh *coed*, 'wood'. It had probably lost its original meaning when OE *hām* was added. Cp. CHEETWOOD. Late 12C *Cheteham*.

Cheetwood (district, Manchester). Cheetwood is near CHEETHAM, and OE *wudu*, 'wood', was added to the same original Celtic name when its own meaning of 'wood' had been forgotten. 1489 *Chetewode*.

Cheldon (hamlet, Devon): 'Ceadela's hill'. OE *dūn*, 'hill'. DB *Chadeledona*.

Chelford (village, Cheshire): 'Cēola's ford'. OE *ford*, 'ford'. The first part of the name could also represent OE *ceole*, 'throat', referring to a local gorge. DB *Celeford*.

Chellaston (district, Derby): 'Cēolheard's farmstead'. OE *tūn*, 'farmstead'. DB *Celerdestune*.

Chell Heath (district of Stoke-on-Trent, Stoke): 'Cēola's wood'. OE *lēah*, 'wood', 'clearing'. The second word of the name distinguishes this Chell from neighbouring *Great Chell* and *Little Chell*. 1227 *Chelle*.

Chellington (village, Beds): 'Cēolwynn's farmstead'. OE *tūn*, 'farmstead'. The personal name is that of a woman. 1219 *Chelewentone*.

Chelmarsh (village, Shropshire): '(place by the) marsh marked out with poles'. OE *cegel*, 'pole', + *mersc*, 'marsh'. There is no marsh here now. DB *Celmeres*.

Chelmondiston (village, Suffolk): 'Cēolmund's farmstead'. OE *tūn*, 'farmstead'. 1174 *Chelmundeston*.

Chelmorton (village, Derbys): 'Cēolmǣr's hill'. OE *dūn*, 'hill'. 12C *Chelmerdon*.

Chelmsford (city, Essex): 'Cēolmǣr's ford'. OE *ford*, 'ford'. The ford would have been over the river Chelmer, whose own name comes from that of the town. The Roman name of Chelmsford was *Caesaromagus*, 'Caesar's market place', unusually combining a Latin imperial name with a Celtic word (related Irish *machaire*, 'plain'). DB *Celmeresfort*.

Chelsea (district, Kensington & Chel): 'landing place for chalk'. OE *cealc*, 'chalk', + *hȳth*, 'landing place'. Chalk would have been shipped to this point on the Thames, then unloaded and transported for use elsewhere. The first part of the name could also mean 'chalice', 'cup' (OE *cælic*), referring to some topographical feature. 789 *Celchyth*, DB *Chelchede*.

Chelsfield (village, Bromley): 'Cēol's open land'. OE *feld*, 'open land' (modern English *field*). DB *Cillesfelle*.

Chelsworth (village, Suffolk): 'enclosure of the freeman'. OE *ceorl*, 'freeman' (modern English *churl*), + *worth*, 'enclosure'. The name could also mean 'Ceorl's enclosure'. 962 *Ceorleswyrthe*, DB *Cerleswrda*.

Cheltenham (town, Glos): 'river meadow by Celte'. OE *hamm*, 'enclosure', 'river meadow'. *Celte* is an OE or Celtic name meaning 'hill slope' that perhaps applied to nearby Cleeve Hill. Cp. CHILTERN HILLS. The first part of the name could also be the personal name Celta. The river Chelt here is named after the town. The DB form of the name below has *n* for *l*. 803 *Celtanhomme*, DB *Chinteneham*.

Chelveston (village, Northants): 'Cēolwulf's farmstead'. OE *tūn*, 'farmstead'. DB *Celuestone*.

Chelvey (hamlet, N Somerset): 'farm where calves are reared'. OE *cealf*, 'calf', + *wīc*, 'specialized farm'. DB *Calviche*.

Chelwood (village, Bath & NE Somerset): 'Cēola's enclosure'. OE *worth*, 'enclosure'. DB *Celeworde*.

Cheney Longville (hamlet, Shropshire): 'de Cheyny's (estate on the) long stretch of open land'. OE *lang*, 'long', + *feld*, 'open land' (modern English *field*). Roger de Cheyny held land here in 1315. DB *Languefelle*, 1421 *Longefelde Cheyne*.

Chenies (village, Bucks): 'Cheyne's (estate)'. The Cheyne family held the manor here in the 13C. Their name was added to an earlier name, now disappeared, that meant 'Isa's homestead', from OE *hām-stede*, 'homestead'. (Neighbouring LATIMER had an identical original name.) 12C *Isenhamstede*, 13C *Ysenamstud Cheyne*, 1536 *Cheynes*.

Chepstow (town, Mon): 'market place'. OE *cēap*, 'market', + *stōw*, 'place'. The Welsh name of Chepstow is *Cas-Gwent*, 'castle in Gwent'. See GWENT. The first form of the name below is unexplained. 1224 *Strigull*, 1308 *Chepstowe*, 1338 *Chapestowe*.

Chequers (country house, Bucks): '(place of) Scaccario'. The house, properly Chequers Court, arose on the site of a 13C building owned

by Laurence de Scaccario, whose surname means 'officer of the exchequer'. A shortening of the latter English word gave the present name.

Cherhill (village, Wilts): 'place of regular resort'. The name is perhaps of Celtic origin from a word related to modern Welsh *cyrchu*, 'to go to', 'to resort', 'to repair', the second syllable representing an adjectival suffix. 1155 *Ciriel*, 1207 *Chyriel*, 1275 *Churiel*.

Cherington (village, Glos): 'village with a church'. OE *cirice*, 'church', + *tūn*, 'farmstead', 'village'. DB *Cerintone*. SO ALSO: *Cherington*, Warwicks.

Cheriton (village, Hants): 'village with a church'. OE *cirice*, 'church', + *tūn*, 'farmstead', 'village'. The presence of a tumulus nearby suggests that the first part of the name could equally represent a Celtic word related to modern Welsh *crug*, 'hillock', 'tumulus'. 1167 *Cherinton*. SO ALSO: *Cheriton*, Devon.

Cheriton (hamlet, Pemb): 'village with a church'. OE *cirice*, 'church', + *tūn*, 'farmstead', 'village'. Cheriton is also known as *Stackpole Elidor*, 'Elidir's (estate by the) pool near the rock'. OS *stakkr*, 'stack', 'rock', + *pollr*, 'pool'. The original settlement was probably near or even at BOSHERSTON, originally known as *Stackpole Bosher*, and the rock in question is probably the prominent one known as Stack Rock at the entrance to Broad Haven, not far from the Bosherston mere ('pool') that runs down to the seashore. One Elidir held the manor here in the 13C. 1813 *Cheriton*.

Cheriton Fitzpaine (village, Devon): 'Fitzpayn's (estate at the) village with a church'. OE *cirice*, 'church', + *tūn*, 'farmstead', 'village'. The manor here was held in the 13C by the Fitzpayn family, their name distinguishing this Cheriton from *Cheriton Bishop*, 10 miles to the southwest, where the Bishop of Exeter was granted land in the 13C. DB *Cerintone*, 1335 *Cheriton Fitz Payn*.

Cherrington (village, Wrekin): 'estate associated with Ceorra'. OE *-ing-*, 'associated with', + *tūn*, 'farmstead', 'estate'. The name could also mean 'settlement by a river bend' (OE *cerring*, 'bend', + *tūn*). The village lies in a bend of the river Meese. DB *Cerlintone*, 1230 *Cherington*.

Cherry Burton. See BISHOP BURTON.

Cherry Hinton (district of Cambridge, Cambs): 'farmstead belonging to a religous community with cherry trees'. ME *chiri*, 'cherry tree', + OE *hīwan*, 'household (of monks)', + *tūn*, 'farmstead'. The 'Hin-' of Hinton represents OE *hīgna*, the genitive form of the plural noun *hīwan*. The first word of the name refers to the cherry trees formerly here. DB *Hintone*, 1576 *Cheryhynton*.

Cherry Willingham (village, Lincs): 'homestead of Willa's people where cherry trees grow'. OE -*inga*-, 'of the people of', + *hām*, 'homestead'. The first word of the name (ME *chiri*, 'cherry tree') distinguishes the village from SOUTH WILLINGHAM, 13 miles to the northeast. DB *Wilingeham*, 1386 *Chyry Wylynham*.

Chertsey (town, Surrey): 'Cerot's island'. OE *ēg*, 'island'. The 'island' was probably not in the Thames here but the higher ground where the town stands. The personal name is Celtic. The first form of the name below represents Latin *Ceroti insula*, 'island of Cerotus'. 731 *Cerotaesei*, DB *Certesy*.

Cherwell (river). See CHARWELTON.

Cheselbourne (village, Dorset): '(place by the) gravelly stream'. OE *cisel*, 'gravel', + *burna*, 'stream'. 869 *Chiselburne*, DB *Ceseburne*.

Chesham (town, Bucks): 'river meadow by a heap of stones'. OE *ceastel*, 'heap of stones' (related modern English *castle*), + *hamm*, 'river meadow'. The 'heap of stones' was a circle of boulders on which the church was built. The river here is the Chess, which takes its name from that of the town. 1012 *Cæstæleshamme*, DB *Cestreham*.

Chesham Bois (suburb of Amersham, Bucks): 'de Bois' (estate at) Chesham'. The de Bois family held the manor here near CHESHAM in the 13C. 1339 *Chesham Boys*.

Cheshire (county, NW England): 'district based on Chester'. OE *scīr*, 'shire', 'district'. See CHESTER. DB *Cestre Scire*.

Cheshunt (town, Herts): 'spring by the Roman fort'. OE *ceaster*, 'Roman camp', + *funta*, 'spring'. No actual Roman settlement is known at Cheshunt, but the town is on Ermine Street. DB *Cestrehunt*.

Chesil Bank (shingle bank, Dorset): 'bank of shingle'. OE *cisel*, 'shingle'. An alternative name for the bank, stretching from Abbotsbury to the Isle of Portland, is *Chesil Beach*. c.1540 *Chisille bank*.

Cheslyn Hay (suburb of Cannock, Staffs): '(place by the) coffin ridge with an enclosure'. OE *cest*, 'coffin', + *hlinc*, 'ridge', + *hæg*, 'enclosure'. A 'coffin ridge' is one where a coffin was found. The former village was earlier known as *Wyrley Bank* (see GREAT WYRLEY). 1236 *Haya de Chistlin*.

Chessington (district, Kingston): 'Cissa's hill'. OE *dūn*, 'hill'. Chessington is on high ground. DB *Cisendone*.

Chester (city, Cheshire): 'Roman city'. OE *ceaster*, 'Roman camp'. The first form of the name below comes from the river Dee. Its own name, of Celtic origin and meaning 'goddess', gave that of the Roman town of *Deva* here. The second name below means 'Roman city of the legions' (Latin *legionum*, 'of the legions', + OE *ceaster*). Cp. CAERLEON. The city name is unusual in retaining simply its '-chester' after losing the first element (unlike DORCHESTER, MANCHESTER, WINCHESTER, etc). c.150 *Deoua*, 735 *Legacæstir*, DB *Cestre*.

Chesterblade (village, Somerset): '(place on a) ledge by an old fort'. OE *ceaster*, 'Roman camp', + OE *blæd*, 'blade' (here, 'ledge'). The 'old fort' is evident as traces of an earthwork an small hill nearby. 1065 *Cesterbled*.

Chesterfield (town, Derbys): 'open land near a Roman fort'. OE *ceaster*, 'Roman camp', + *feld*, 'open land' (modern English *field*). The name of the Roman town here is unknown. 955 *Cesterfelda*, DB *Cestrefeld*.

Chesterford. See GREAT CHESTERFORD.

Chesterholm (hamlet, Northd): 'island by a Roman fort'. OE *ceaster*, 'Roman camp', + OS *holmr*, 'island'. The 'island' is raised ground in marshland here. The Roman fort here was *Vindolanda*, perhaps meaning 'bright moorland', from Celtic words related to modern Welsh *gwyn*, 'white', and *llan*, 'church' (earlier 'enclosure').

Chester-le-Street (town, Durham): 'Roman fort on the Roman road'. OE *ceaster*, 'Roman camp', + OF *le*, 'the', + OE *strǣt*, 'Roman road' (modern English *street*). The town is on the Roman road between Durham and Newcastle upon Tyne. The second part of the name was given to distinguish this Chester from CHESTER. The Roman town here was *Concangis*, perhaps meaning '(place of the) horse people'. c.1160 *Cestra*, 1400 *Cestria in Strata*.

Chesterton (suburb of Cambridge, Cambs): 'village by a Roman fort'. OE *ceaster*, 'Roman camp', + *tūn*, 'farmstead', 'village'. The Roman camp in question was to the north of the river Cam at CAMBRIDGE. DB *Cestretone*. SO ALSO: *Chesterton*, Staffs.

Chesterton (village, Cambs): 'village by a Roman fort'. OE *ceaster*, 'Roman camp', + *tūn*, 'farmstead', 'village'. The Roman town here near Ermine Street on the river Nene was

Durobrivae, 'walled town with a bridge'. Cp. CASTOR. DB *Cestretone*.

Chesterton (hamlet, Warwicks): 'village by a Roman fort'. OE *ceaster*, 'Roman camp', + *tūn*, 'farmstead', 'village'. The place lies about a mile from the Fosse Way, where there is the site of a Roman building. 1043 *Cestretune*, DB *Cestretone*.

Cheswardine (village, Shropshire): 'enclosed settlement where cheese is made'. OE *cēse*, 'cheese', + *worthign*, 'enclosure'. DB *Ciseworde*, 1160 *Chesewordin*.

Cheswick (hamlet, Northd): 'farm where cheese is made'. OE *cēse*, 'cheese', + *wīc*, 'specialized farm'. Cp. CHISWICK, KESWICK. 1208 *Chesewic*.

Chetnole (village, Dorset): 'Ceatta's hilltop'. OE *cnoll*, 'hilltop' (modern English *knoll*). 1242 *Chetenoll*.

Chettle (village, Dorset): '(place in a) deep valley'. OE *ceotel*, 'deep valley' (related modern English *kettle*). Chettle is in a valley surrounded by hills. DB *Ceotel*.

Chetton (village, Shropshire): 'estate associated with Ceatta'. OE *-ing-*, 'associated with', + *tūn*, 'farmstead', 'estate'. DB *Catinton*, 1210 *Chetintone*.

Chetwode (hamlet, Bucks): '(place by the) wood'. The first part of the name is Celtic, related to modern Welsh *coed*, 'wood'. The second part represents OE *wudu*, 'wood', added to the first when its meaning was no longer understood. 949 *Cetwuda*, DB *Ceteode*.

Chetwynd Aston (village, Wrekin): 'de Chetwynd's eastern farmstead'. OE *ēast*, 'eastern', + *tūn*, 'farmstead', 'estate'. The de Chetwynd family, from *Chetwynd*, 'Ceatta's winding ascent' (OE *gewind*, 'winding ascent'), 3 miles to the northwest, held land here in the 13C, their name distinguishing this Aston from nearby *Church Aston*, named for its chapel. 1155 *Estona*, 1619 *Greate Aston alias Chetwynde Aston*, 1868 *Chetwynd Aston, or Field Aston*.

Cheveley (village, Cambs): 'wood full of fallen twigs'. OE *ceaf*, 'chaff', 'fallen twigs', + *lēah*, 'wood'. *c*.1000 *Cæafle*, DB *Chauelai*.

Chevening (hamlet, Kent): '(settlement of the) dwellers by the ridge'. OE *-ingas*, 'dwellers at'. The first part of the name is Celtic in origin, from a word related to modern Welsh *cefn*, 'back', 'ridge'. Chevening lies on the southern slope of a pronounced ridge. 1199 *Chivening*.

Cheviot Hills (hill range, Northd/Borders): meaning uncertain. The pre-English name is that of the single mountain here called *The Cheviot*. Celticists favour a meaning 'ridge',

from a root word related to modern Welsh *cefn* in this sense. 1181 *Chiuiet*.

Chew Magna (village, Bath & NE Somerset): 'greater (place on the river) Chew'. The river has a Celtic name of uncertain origin. The second word of the name is Latin *magna*, 'great', contrasting the village with nearby CHEW STOKE. 1065 *Ciw*, DB *Chiwe*, 1868 *Chew Magna, or Bishop's Chew*.

Chew Stoke (village, Bath & NE Somerset): 'secondary settlement belonging to Chew'. OE *stoc*, 'secondary settlement'. *Chew* is nearby CHEW MAGNA. DB *Stoche*.

Chewton Mendip (village, Bath & NE Somerset): 'estate on the (river) Chew by the Mendip Hills'. OE *tūn*, 'farmstead', 'estate'. For the river name, see CHEW MAGNA. The village lies below the slopes of the MENDIP HILLS. *c*.880 *Ciwtun*, DB *Ciwetune*, 1313 *Cheuton by Menedep*.

Chicheley (village, Milton K): 'Cicca's wood'. OE *lēah*, 'wood', 'clearing'. DB *Cicelai*.

Chichester (city, W Sussex): 'Cissa's Roman town'. OE *ceaster*, 'Roman camp'. Cissa is traditionally identified as the third son of Ælle (d.*c*.514), first king of the South Saxons. The first part of the name could also mean 'gravelly place' (OE *cisse*). The Roman city here was *Noviomagus*, 'new market', as for CRAYFORD. 895 *Cisseceastre*, DB *Cicestre*.

Chickerell (village, Dorset): meaning uncertain. This name has so far defied plausible explanation. DB *Cicherelle*.

Chicklade (village, Wilts): '(place at the) gate by the wood'. The first part of the name is Celtic in origin and related to modern Welsh *coed*, 'wood'. The second is either OE *hlid*, 'gate', or an identical word meaning 'slope'. *c*.912 *Cytlid*.

Chiddingfold (village, Surrey): 'fold of Ciddel's or Cidda's people'. OE *-inga-*, 'of the people of', + *fald*, 'fold'. The first form of the name below is corrupt. 1130 *Chedelingefelt*, 12C *Chidingefaud*.

Chiddingly (hamlet, E Sussex): 'wood or clearing of Citta's people'. OE *-inga-*, 'of the people of', + *lēah*, 'wood', 'clearing'. The DB form of the name below is garbled. DB *Cetelingei*, *c*.1230 *Chitingeleghe*.

Chiddingstone (village, Kent): 'stone associated with Cidd or Cidda'. OE *-ing-*, 'associated with', + *stān*, 'stone'. The stone in question was probably a boundary marker here. *c*.1110 *Cidingstane*.

Chideock (village, Dorset): 'wooded place'. The name derives from a Celtic source related to modern Welsh *coed*, 'wood'. The river Chid here derives its name from that of the village. DB *Cidihoc*.

Chidham (village, W Sussex): 'peninsula by the bay'. OE *cēod*, 'bag', 'bay', + *hamm*, 'enclosure', 'peninsula'. 'This parish constitutes a peninsula, formed by Bosham creek on the east, Thorney channel on the west, and Chichester harbour on the south' (Samuel Lewis, *A Topographical Dictionary of England*, 1840). 1193 *Chedeham*.

Chieveley (village, W Berks): 'Cifa's wood or clearing'. OE *lēah*, 'wood', 'clearing'. 951 *Cifanlea*, DB *Civelei*.

Chignall Smealy (hamlet, Essex): 'Cicca's corner of land by the smooth clearing'. OE *halh*, 'nook', 'corner of land', + *smēthe*, 'smooth', + *lēah*, 'clearing'. The second word of the name distinguishes the place from nearby *Chignall St James*, named from the dedication of its church. DB *Cingehala*, 1279 *Chigehale Smetheleye*.

Chigwell (town, Essex): '(place by) Cicca's spring'. OE *wella*, 'spring', 'stream'. DB *Cingheuuella*, 1187 *Chiggewell*.

Chilcombe (hamlet, Dorset): '(place in a) valley by Cilte'. OE *cumb*, 'valley'. *Cilte* is the OE or Celtic name of a hill slope here meaning simply 'hill slope', as for the CHILTERN HILLS. DB *Ciltecombe*.

Chilcompton (village, Somerset): 'valley farmstead of the young men'. OE *cild*, 'child', 'young man', + *cumb*, 'valley', + *tūn*, 'farmstead', 'village'. DB *Comtuna*, 1227 *Childecumpton*.

Chilcote (village, Leics): 'cottage of the young men'. OE *cild*, 'child', 'young man', + *cot*, 'cottage'. DB *Cildecote*.

Childer Thornton (village, Cheshire): 'young men's (estate at the) farmstead where thorn bushes grow'. OE *thorn*, 'thorn bush', + *tūn*, 'farmstead'. The first word of the name represents the genitive plural of *cild*, 'child', 'young man', referring to the young monks of St Werburgh's Abbey, Chester, which held the manor here in the 13C. *c*.1210 *Thorinthun*, 1288 *Childrethornton*.

Child Okeford (village, Dorset): 'noble-born son's (estate by the) ford where oaks grow'. OE *cild*, 'child', 'young man', + *āc*, 'oak', + *ford*, 'ford'. The first word of the name, referring to an early owner of the manor here, distinguishes this village from nearby *Okeford Fitzpaine*, where the manor was held by the Fitz Payn family from the 13C. (See also SHILLINGSTONE.) The ford may have been where the road from Child

Okeford crosses the river Stour at Hayward Bridge. DB *Acford*, 1227 *Childacford*.

Childrey (village, Oxon): '(place by the) Childrey Brook'. The river name means 'Cilla's or Cille's stream' (OE *rīth*, 'stream'), the personal names being respectively those of a man and a woman. The first part of the name could also represent OE *cille*, 'spring (in a gully)'. 950 *Cillarithe*, DB *Celrea*.

Child's Ercall. See HIGH ERCALL.

Child's Hill (district, Barnet): 'Child's hill'. One Richard Child is recorded here in the 14C. 1593 *Childes Hill*, 1822 *Child's Hill*.

Childswickham (village, Worcs): 'young man's lodge in the meadow'. OE *cild*, 'child', 'young man'. The second part of the name is apparently of Celtic origin from words related to modern Welsh *gwig*, 'lodge', 'wood', and *gwaun*, 'moor', 'meadow'. 706 *Childeswicwon*, DB *Wicvene*.

Childwall (district, Liverpool): '(place by the) spring where young people gather'. OE *cild*, 'child', 'young man', + *wella*, 'spring', 'stream'. DB *Cildeuuelle*.

Chilfrome (village, Dorset): '(estate of the) young men on the (river) Frome'. OE *cild*, 'child', 'young man'. For the river name, see FROME. DB *Frome*, 1206 *Childefrome*.

Chilgrove (hamlet, W Sussex): 'grove in a gorge'. OE *ceole*, 'throat', 'gorge', + *grāf*, 'grove'. The 'gorge' would be the deep valley here. The name could also mean 'Cēola's grove'. 1200 *Chelegrave*.

Chilham (village, Kent): 'Cilla's or Cille's homestead'. OE *hām*, 'homestead', 'village'. The personal names are respectively those of a man and a woman. The first part of the name could also represent OE *cille*, 'spring' (a variant of *ceole*, 'throat', 'gorge'), giving a sense 'homestead by the spring'. DB *Cilleham*.

Chillerton (village, IoW): 'enclosed farmstead in a valley'. OE *ceole*, 'throat', 'valley', + *geard*, 'enclosure', + *tūn*, 'farmstead'. The name could also mean 'Cēolheard's farmstead'. DB *Celertune*.

Chillesford (village, Suffolk): '(place by the) gravel ford'. OE *ceosol*, 'gravel', + *ford*, 'ford'. Chillesford is at the head of the estuary of the river Butley. DB *Cesefortda*, 1211 *Chiselford*.

Chillingham (village, Northd): 'homestead of Ceofel's people'. OE *-inga-*, 'of the people of', + *hām*, 'homestead'. 1187 *Cheulingeham*.

Chillington (village, Devon): 'estate associated with Ceadela'. OE -*ing*-, 'associated with', + *tūn*, 'farmstead', 'estate'. DB *Cedelintone*.

Chillington (village, Somerset): 'Cēola's farmstead'. OE *tūn*, 'farmstead'. 1261 *Cheleton*.

Chilmark (village, Wilts): 'boundary mark in the form of a pole'. OE *cigel*, 'pole', + *mearc*, 'mark'. 984 *Cigelmerc*, DB *Chilmerc*.

Chilson (village, Oxon): 'farmstead of the young man'. OE *cild*, 'child', 'young man', + *tūn*, 'farmstead'. *c.*1200 *Cildestuna*.

Chiltern Hills (hill range, Bucks/Oxon): 'hill slope'. OE or Celtic *celte*, *cilte*, 'hill slope'. The OE or Celtic word probably also gave the names of CHELTENHAM and CHILTHORNE DOMER, while *Chiltern* is now the name of the local council district. 1009 *Ciltern*.

Chilthorne Domer (village, Somerset): 'Dummere's (estate on the) hill slope'. The first word of the name is possibly a derivative of an OE or Celtic word *celte*, *cilte*, 'hill slope', as for the CHILTERN HILLS. The second word names the Dummere family, who held the manor here in the 13C. DB *Cilterne*, 1280 *Chilterne Dunmere*.

Chilton (village, Bucks): 'farm of the young men'. OE *cild*, 'child', 'young man', + *tūn*, 'farmstead'. DB *Ciltone*. SO ALSO: *Chilton*, Durham, Oxon.

Chilton Candover. See PRESTON CANDOVER.

Chilton Cantelo (village, Somerset): 'Cantelu's (estate at the) farm of the young men'. OE *cild*, 'child', 'young man', + *tūn*, 'farmstead'. The Cantelu family held the manor here in the 13C. 1201 *Childeton*, 1361 *Chiltone Cauntilo*.

Chilton Foliat (village, Wilts): 'Foliot's (estate at the) farm of the young men'. OE *cild*, 'child', 'young man', + *tūn*, 'farmstead'. The Foliot family held the manor here in the 13C. DB *Cilletone*, 1221 *Chilton Foliot*.

Chilton Polden (village, Somerset): 'farmstead on chalk by the Polden Hills'. OE *cealc*, 'chalk', + *tūn*, 'farmstead'. The second word of the name refers to the nearby *Polden Hills*, whose own name probably comes from OE *dūn*, 'hill', added to an earlier Celtic name meaning 'cow pasture' (related to the first word of BUILTH WELLS). The hill name distinguishes this Chilton from CHILTON TRINITY, 5 miles to the west. DB *Ceptone*, 1303 *Chauton*, 1868 *Chilton-upon-Polden*.

Chilton Street (village, Suffolk): 'farm of the young men'. OE *cild*, 'child', 'young man', + *tūn*, 'farmstead'. The second word of the name prob-ably denotes a village that straggles along a road. 1254 *Chilton*.

Chilton Trinity (village, Somerset): 'farm of the young men with Holy Trinity church'. OE *cild*, 'child', 'young man', + *tūn*, 'farmstead'. The church dedication distinguishes this Chilton from CHILTON POLDEN, 5 miles to the east. DB *Cildetone*, 1431 *Chilton Sancte Trinitatis*.

Chilvers Coton (district of Nuneaton, Warwicks): 'Cēolfrith's cottages'. OE *cot*, 'cottage' (ME plural *coten*). The second part of the DB form of the name below represents OE *stoc*, 'outlying hamlet'. DB *Celverdestoche*, 1185 *Chelverdescote*.

Chilwell (district of Beeston, Notts): 'spring where young people gather'. OE *cild*, 'child', + *wella*, 'spring', 'stream'. Several small streams rise near Chilwell, and one of these would have been a favourite meeting place for young people on summer evenings. Cp. CLERKENWELL. DB *Chideuuelle*.

Chilworth (village, Hants): 'Cēola's enclosure'. OE *worth*, 'enclosure'. DB *Celeorde*. SO ALSO: *Chilworth*, Surrey.

Chimney (hamlet, Oxon): 'Ceomma's island'. OE *ēg*, 'island'. The 'island' here is dry ground in marshland. 1069 *Ceommanyg*.

Chingford (town, Waltham F): '(place by the) shingle ford'. OE *cingel*, 'shingle', + *ford*, 'ford'. The ford in question was probably over the river Lea here. The DB form of the name below has omitted *l*. DB *Cingefort*, *c.*1243 *Chingelford*.

Chinley (village, Derbys): 'wood or clearing in a deep valley'. OE *cinu*, 'deep valley' (modern English *chine*), + *lēah*, 'wood', 'clearing'. 1285 *Chynleye*.

Chinnor (village, Oxon): 'Ceonna's slope'. OE *ōra*, 'hill slope', 'flat-topped hill'. The slope in question descends from the Chilterns here. DB *Chennore*.

Chipnall (hamlet, Shropshire): 'Cippa's knoll'. OE *cnoll*, 'knoll'. The name could also mean 'knoll where logs are obtained' (OE *cipp*, 'log', + *cnoll*). DB *Ceppacanole*, *c.*1250 *Chippeknol*.

Chippenham (village, Cambs): 'Cippa's homestead'. OE *hām*, 'homestead', 'village'. DB *Chipeham*.

Chippenham (town, Wilts): 'Cippa's enclosure'. OE *hamm*, 'enclosure', 'water meadow'. The 'enclosure' would have been land in the bend of the river Avon here. *c.*900 *Cippan-hamme*, DB *Chipehame*.

Chipperfield (village, Herts): 'open land where merchants meet'. OE *cēapere*, 'merchant', 'trader' (related modern English *cheap*), + *feld*, 'open land' (modern English *field*). 1375 *Chiperfeld*.

Chipping (village, Lancs): '(place with a) market'. OE *cēping*, 'market'. 1203 *Chippin*.

Chipping Barnet. See BARNET.

Chipping Campden (town, Glos): 'valley with enclosures with a market'. OE *cēping*, 'market', + OE *camp*, 'camp', 'enclosure', + *denu*, 'valley'. The first word of the name distinguishes this Campden from nearby *Broad Campden*, 'broad valley with enclosures' (OE *brād*, 'broad'). DB *Campedene*, 1287 *Chepyng Campedene*.

Chipping Norton (town, Oxon): 'northern farmstead with a market'. OE *cēping*, 'market', + *north*, 'northern', + *tūn*, 'farmstead'. The first word of the name distinguishes this Norton from nearby *Over Norton*, 'higher northern farmstead' (OE *uferra*, 'higher'). DB *Nortone*, 1224 *Chepingnorthona*.

Chipping Ongar (town, Essex): 'pastureland with a market'. OE *cēping*, 'market', + *anger*, 'grassland', 'pasture'. The first word of the name distinguishes this Ongar from nearby *High Ongar*, 'high pastureland' (OE *hēah*, 'high'). 1045 *Aungre*, DB *Angra*, 1314 *Chepyngaungre*.

Chipping Sodbury (town, S Glos): 'Soppa's fortified place with a market'. OE *cēping*, 'market'. The 'fortified place' (OE *burh*) is the Roman camp near the village of *Old Sodbury*, 2 miles to the east, called 'old' as Chipping Sodbury was the 'new' market town, while 1 mile north of Old Sodbury, formerly also known as *Sodbury Magna* (Latin *magna*, 'great'), is the village of *Little Sodbury*, so called in contrast. 972 *Soppanbyrig*, DB *Sopeberie*, 1269 *Cheping Sobbyri*.

Chipping Warden (village, Northants): 'lookout hill with a market'. OE *cēping*, 'market', + *weard*, 'watch' (modern English *ward*), + *dūn*, 'hill'. The hill in question is Warden Hill, to the east of the village. DB *Waredone*, 1389 *Chepyng Wardoun*.

Chipstead (village, Surrey): 'market place'. OE *cēap-stede* (from *cēap*, 'market', + *stede*, 'place'). The DB form of the name below has *C-* miscopied as *T-*. DB *Tepestede*, 1100 *Chepstede*. SO ALSO: *Chipstead*, Kent.

Chirbury (village, Shropshire): 'fortified place with a church'. OE *cirice*, 'church', + *burh*, 'fortified place'. The whereabouts of the 'fortified place' in question is unknown. mid-11C *Cyricbyrig*, DB *Cireberie*.

Chirk (town, Wrexham): '(place on the river) Ceiriog'. The town's name is an anglicized form of that of the river, whose Celtic name means something like 'favoured one'. The town's Welsh name is *Y Waun*, 'the moorland' (Welsh *gwaun*, 'moor'), referring to the moorland near Chirk Castle. 1295 *Chirk*, 1309 *Cheyrk*.

Chirton (village, Wilts): 'village with a church'. OE *cirice*, 'church', + *tūn*, 'farmstead', 'village'. DB *Ceritone*, 1221 *Chiritun*, 1868 *Cherrington, Chirton, or Churton*.

Chisbury (hamlet, Wilts): 'fortified place associated with Cissa'. OE *burh*, 'fortified place'. There is an ancient earthwork here. Early 10C *Cissanbyrig*, DB *Cheseberie*.

Chiselborough (village, Somerset): '(place by the) gravel hill'. OE *cisel*, 'gravel', + *beorg*, 'hill'. DB *Ceoselbergon*.

Chiseldon (village, Swindon): '(place in the) gravel valley'. OE *cisel*, 'gravel', + *denu*, 'valley'. *c*.880 *Cyseldene*, DB *Chiseldene*.

Chislehampton (hamlet, Oxon): 'high farm on gravel'. OE *cisel*, 'gravel', + *hēah*, 'high', + *tūn*, 'farm'. DB *Hentone*, 1147 *Chiselentona*.

Chislehurst (district, Bromley): 'gravelly wooded hill'. OE *cisel*, 'gravel', + *hyrst*, 'wooded hill'. 973 *Cyselhyrst*.

Chislet (village, Kent): '(place by the) chestnut wood'. OE *cistelet*, 'chestnut copse' (from OE *cist*, 'chestnut'). The name could perhaps also derive from a combination of OE *cist*, 'container', and *gelǣt*, 'water conduit'. 605 *Cistelet*, DB *Cistelet*.

Chiswick (district, Hounslow): 'farm where cheese is made'. OE *cīese*, 'cheese', + *wīc*, 'dwelling', 'specialized farm'. Cp. KESWICK. *c*.1000 *Ceswican*.

Chisworth (village, Derbys): 'Cissa's enclosure'. OE *worth*, 'enclosure'. DB *Chisewrde*.

Chithurst (hamlet, W Sussex): 'Citta's wooded hill'. OE *hyrst*, 'wooded hill'. The first part of the name could also represent a Celtic word related to modern Welsh *coed*, 'wood', despite the apparent tautology. The DB form of the name below has *C-* miscopied as *T-*. DB *Titesherste*, 1279 *Chyteherst*.

Chitterne (village, Wilts): '(place by the) wood'. It is generally held that the first part of this name derives from a Celtic word related to modern Welsh *coed*, 'wood'. The second part was long believed to represent OE *ærn*, 'building', 'house', giving an overall sense 'house in the wood'. Celticists hold, however, that although the final part of the name does actually mean 'dwelling', 'homestead', it in fact represents a Celtic word related to modern Welsh *tref*, 'home', 'town', and Cornish *tre*, 'farmstead', 'hamlet'. Early forms of the name seem to support this origin, which thus gives a sense 'woodland settlement', although the downs around Chitterne on Salisbury Plain are now devoid of trees. Chitterne was formerly *Chitterne All Saints*, from the dedication of its church, as distinct from the neighbouring parish of *Chitterne St Mary*, which has long had no church. DB *Chetre*, 1167 *Chettra*, 1232 *Chittra*, 1268 *Chytterne*, 1868 *Chiltern All Saints*, or *Chittern All Saints*.

Chittlehamholt (village, Devon): 'wood of the valley dwellers'. OE *cietel*, 'valley' (modern English *kettle*), + *hǣme*, 'dwellers' (related modern English *home*), + *holt*, 'wood'. 1288 *Chitelhamholt*.

Chittlehampton (village, Devon): 'farmstead of the valley dwellers'. OE *cietel*, 'valley' (modern English *kettle*), + *hǣme*, 'dwellers' (related modern English *home*), + *tūn*, 'farmstead'. DB *Citremetona*, 1176 *Chitelhamtone*.

Chittoe (village, Wilts): '(place by the) wood'. As for CHITTERNE, the first part of this name derives from a Celtic word related to modern Welsh *coed*, 'wood'. The second part is probably related to modern Welsh *tew*, 'thick', 'fat', giving an overall sense '(place by the) thick wood'. 1167 *Chetewe*.

Chivelstone (hamlet, Devon): 'Ceofel's farmstead'. OE *tūn*, 'farmstead'. DB *Cheueletona*.

Chobham (village, Surrey): 'Ceabba's homestead or enclosure'. OE *hām*, 'homestead', or *hamm*, 'enclosure'. DB *Cebeham*.

Cholderton (village, Wilts): 'estate associated with Cēolhere or Cēolrēd'. OE *-ing-*, 'associated with', + *tūn*, 'farmstead', 'estate'. DB *Celdretone*.

Chollerton (village, Northd): 'Cēolferth's farmstead'. OE *tūn*, 'farmstead'. c.1175 *Choluerton*.

Cholmondeley Castle (mansion, Cheshire): 'Cēolmund's woodland clearing'. OE *lēah*, 'wood', 'clearing'. The mansion dates from the 18C. DB *Calmundelei*, c.1200 *Chelmundeleia*.

Cholsey (village, Oxon): 'Cēol's island'. OE *ēg*, 'island'. The 'island' is land by the river Thames here. c.895 *Ceolesig*, DB *Celsei*.

Cholstrey (hamlet, Herefords): 'Ceorl's tree'. OE *trēow*, 'tree'. The first part of the name could also represent OE *ceorl*, 'freeman', 'peasant' (modern English *churl*). DB *Cerlestreu*.

Choppington (village, Northd): 'estate associated with Ceabba'. OE *-ing-*, 'associated with', + *tūn*, 'farmstead', 'estate'. c.1050 *Cebbington*.

Chopwell (village, Gateshead): '(place by the) spring where trading is carried on'. OE *cēap*, 'trade', 'market' (modern English *cheap*), + *wella*, 'spring', 'stream'. c.1155 *Cheppwell*.

Chorley (town, Lancs): 'clearing of the peasants'. OE *ceorl*, 'freeman', 'peasant' (modern English *churl*), + *lēah*, 'wood', 'clearing'. 1246 *Cherleg*. SO ALSO: *Chorley*, Cheshire, Staffs.

Chorleywood (town, Herts): 'wood by the clearing of the peasants'. OE *ceorl*, 'freeman', 'peasant', + *lēah*, 'wood', 'clearing', + modern English *wood*. Cp. CHORLEY. 1278 *Cherle*, 1524 *Charlewoode*, 1868 *Chorley Wood*.

Chorlton (hamlet, Cheshire): 'farmstead of the peasants'. OE *ceorl*, 'freeman', 'peasant' (modern English *churl*), + *tūn*, 'farmstead'. DB *Cerletune*.

Chorlton-cum-Hardy (district, Manchester): 'Cēolfrith's farmstead with the hard island'. OE *tūn*, 'farmstead', + Latin *cum*, 'with', + OE *heard*, 'hard', + *ēg*, 'island'. The name unites two formerly distinct villages. A 'hard island' would be raised ground that is hard to till. 1243 *Cholreton*, 1555 *Hardey*.

Chrishall (village, Essex): 'corner of land dedicated to Christ'. OE *Crist*, 'Christ', + *halh*, 'nook', 'corner of land'. The precise import of this name is uncertain. DB *Cristeshala*.

Christchurch (town, Dorset): 'church of Christ'. OE *Crist*, 'Christ', + *cirice*, 'church'. The name relates to the dedication of the priory church. The place was earlier known as *Twynham*, '(place) between the rivers' (OE *betwēonan*, 'between', + *ēa*, 'river'), preserved in the name of Twynham comprehensive school here. Cp. TWINEHAM. The town lies between the rivers Stour and Avon. c.1125 *Christecerce*.

Christchurch (district, Newport): 'church of Christ'. The name relates to the original dedication of the parish church. The Welsh name of Christchurch is *Eglwys y Drindod*, 'Church of the Trinity', relating to a later dedication, while the present dedication is to St Mary. 1290 *Christi Ecclesia*, 1291 *Christeschurche*.

Christian Malford (village, Wilts): '(place by the) ford by a cross'. OE *cristel-mǣl*, 'cross' (from *Crist*, 'Christ', + *mǣl*, 'cross'), + *ford*, 'ford'. The river here is the Avon. The name has been misdivided and assimilated to modern *Christian*. 937 *Cristemaleford*, DB *Cristemeleford*, 1574 *Cristine Malford*.

Christleton (suburb of Chester, Cheshire): 'farmstead of the Christians'. OE *Cristen*, 'Christian', + *tūn*, 'farmstead'. See also ROWTON (Cheshire). DB *Cristetone*, 12C *Cristentune*.

Christmas Common (hamlet, Oxon): '(place by) holly bushes'. *Christmas tree* is a dialect name for holly. The village later became associated with its green or common. Early 18C *a village called Christmas*, early 18C *Christmas Green*.

Christon (village, N Somerset): 'farmstead by the hill'. The first part of the name is Celtic, from a word related to modern Welsh *crug*, 'hillock'. The second part is OE *tūn*, 'farmstead'. 1197 *Crucheston*.

Christow (village, Devon): 'Christian place'. OE *Cristen*, 'Christian', + *stōw*, 'place'. The place must have earned the name through some special Christian association. 1244 *Cristinestowe*.

Chudleigh (town, Devon): 'Ciedda's clearing'. OE *lēah*, 'wood', 'clearing'. The name could also mean 'clearing in a hollow' (OE *cēod*, 'hollow', + *lēah*). c.1150 *Ceddelegam*.

Chulmleigh (town, Devon): 'Cēolmund's clearing'. OE *lēah*, 'wood', 'clearing'. DB *Chalmonleuga*.

Church (town, Lancs): '(place by the) church'. OE *cirice*, 'church'. The church in question stood either on or near the site of the present St James's church, which is locally called 'Church Kirk'. 1202 *Chirche*, 1868 *Church-Kirk*.

Churcham (village, Glos): '(place by) river meadow with a church'. OE *cirice*, 'church', + *hamm*, 'river meadow'. The first part of the name was added to distinguish this place from nearby HIGHNAM. DB *Hamme*, 1200 *Churchehamme*.

Church Aston. See CHETWYND ASTON.

Church Brampton. See CHAPEL BRAMPTON.

Church Broughton (village, Derbys): 'village by a brook with a church'. OE *brōc*, 'brook', + *tūn*, 'farmstead', 'village'. DB *Broctune*, 1327 *Chirchebroghtone*.

Churchdown (suburb of Gloucester, Glos): '(place at the) hill'. The first part of the name represents a Celtic word related to modern Welsh *crug*, 'hill'. The second part is OE *dūn*, also meaning 'hill', added to the Celtic word when it was no longer understood. The hill in question, which happens to have an ancient church on it, is *Churchdown Hill*, which thus has 'hill' three times. Cp. PENDLE HILL. DB *Circesdune*, 1868 *Churchdown, or Choren*.

Church Eaton (village, Staffs): 'farmstead on an island with a church'. OE *ēg*, 'island', + *tūn*, 'farmstead'. The 'island' here is land partly surrounded by water. The first word of the name distinguishes this Eaton from nearby *Wood Eaton*, by a wood. DB *Eitone*, 1261 *Church Eyton*.

Church Fenton (village, N Yorks): 'farmstead in the fen with a church'. OE *fenn*, 'fen', + *tūn*, 'farmstead'. The first word of the name distinguishes the village from nearby *Little Fenton*. 963 *Fentune*, DB *Fentun*, 1338 *Kirkfenton*.

Church Gresley (village, Derbys): '(place by the) woodland clearing with a church'. OE *lēah*, 'wood', 'clearing'. The first part of the main name is of uncertain origin. It may represent OE *grēosn*, 'gravel'. The first word of the name distinguishes the village from nearby *Castle Gresley*, where there was formerly a castle. c.1125 *Gresele*, 1363 *Churchegreseleye*.

Church Hanborough (village, Oxon): 'Hagena's or Hana's hill with a church'. OE *beorg*, 'hill'. The first word of the name distinguishes this village from nearby *Long Hanborough*, named for its length. DB *Haneberge*.

Church Honeybourne. See HONEYBOURNE.

Churchill (village, N Somerset): '(place by the) hill with a church'. OE *cirice*, 'church' + *hyll*, 'hill'. 1201 *Cherchille*. SO ALSO: *Churchill*, Oxon, Worcs (near Worcester).

Churchill (village, Devon): '(place by the) hill with a tumulus'. The first part of the name derives from a Celtic word related to modern Welsh *crug*, 'hillock'. This was subsequently associated with OE *cirice*, 'church', to give the present form of the name. The second part of the name is OE *hyll*, 'hill'. The form of the name below relates to Churchill near Barnstaple. DB *Cercelle*. SO ALSO: *Churchill*, Worcs (near Kidderminster).

Church Knowle (village, Dorset): '(place by the) hill top with a church'. OE *cirice*, 'church', + *cnoll*, 'hilltop'. The reference is to Knowle Hill here. DB *Cnolle*, 1346 *Churchecnolle*.

Church Langton (village, Leics): 'long village with a church'. OE *lang*, 'long', + *tūn*, 'farmstead', 'estate'. The first word of the name distinguishes this Langton from nearby *East Langton*. DB *Langetone*, 1316 *Chirch Langeton*.

Church Lawford (village, Warwicks): '(place by) Lealla's ford with a church'. OE *ford*, 'ford'. The first word of the name distinguishes this Lawford from nearby *Long Lawford*, a straggling village, and *Little Lawford*, a small one. DB *Lelleford*, 1235 *Chirche Lalleford*.

Church Lench. See ROUS LENCH.

Church Minshull (village, Cheshire): 'Monn's shelf (of land) with a church'. OE *scelf*, 'shelf'. The village lies on a broad shelving terrain. The first word of the name distinguishes this Minshull from nearby *Minshull Vernon*, where the manor was held in the 13C by the de Vernon family. The DB form of the name below is corrupt. DB *Maneshale*, late 13C *Chirchemunsulf*.

Churchover (village, Warwicks): 'church (by the river) Wavre'. The second part of the name represents a former name for the river Swift here meaning 'winding stream' (OE *wæfre*, 'wandering one'). OE *cirice*, 'church', was added subsequently. DB *Wavre*, 12C *Chirchewavre*.

Church Preen (village, Shropshire): '(place by a) brooch-shaped feature with a church'. OE *prēon*, 'brooch', 'pin'. The identity of the feature so described is uncertain. The first word of the name distinguishes the village from nearby *Holt Preen*, now known as *Holt* ('wood'). DB *Prene*, 1256 *Chircheprene*.

Churchstanton (village, Somerset): 'farmstead on stony ground with a church'. OE *cirice*, 'church', + *stān*, 'stone', + *tūn*, 'farmstead'. The first part of the name was added to distinguish this *Stanton* from WHITESTAUNTON, 6 miles to the southeast. DB *Stantone*, 13C *Cheristontone*.

Churchstow (village, Devon): 'place with a church'. OE *cirice*, 'church', + *stōw*, 'place'. 1242 *Churechestowe*.

Church Stretton (town, Shropshire): 'village on a Roman road with a church'. OE *strǣt*, 'Roman road' (modern English *street*), + *tūn*, 'farmstead', 'village'. The town is on the stretch of Roman road between Leintwardine and Wroxeter. The first word of the name was added subsequently to distinguish this Stretton from nearby *All Stretton*, to the north, named from an early owner called Alfred, and *Little Stretton*, to the south. DB *Stratune*, 1262 *Chirich Stretton*.

Churston Ferrers (village, Torbay): 'de Fereris' (estate at the) village with a church'. OE *cirice*, 'church', + *tūn*, 'farmstead', 'village'. The de Fereris family held the manor here in the early 14C. DB *Cercitona*, 1345 *Churcheton Ferers*.

Churt (village, Surrey): '(place on) rough ground'. OE *cert*, 'rough ground'. 685 *Cert*.

Churton (village, Cheshire): 'village with a church'. OE *cirice*, 'church', + *tūn*, 'farmstead', 'village'. 12C *Churton*.

Churwell (village, Leeds): '(place by the) spring of the freemen'. OE *ceorl*, 'freeman', 'peasant' (modern English *churl*), + *wella*, 'spring', 'stream'. 1226 *Cherlewell*.

Chute. See UPPER CHUTE.

Chysauster (ancient village, Cornwall): 'Sylvester's cottage'. Cornish *chi*, 'cottage'. The name was originally that of a farm here. 1302 *Chisalwester*.

Cilgerran (village, Pemb): 'Cerran's corner of land'. Welsh *cil*, 'nook', 'corner of land'. 1165 *Kilgerran*, 1166 *Chilgerran*.

Cilgeti. See KILGETTY.

Cinderford (town, Glos): 'ford of cinders'. OE *sinder*, 'cinder', + *ford*, 'ford'. The ford over the stream here would have been built up with cinders or slag from the local ironworks. 1258 *Sinderford*.

Cinque Ports (coastal towns, E Sussex/Kent): OF *cink porz*, Latin *quinque portus*, 'five ports'. The name is that of the five English Channel ports Hastings, Dover, Sandwich, Romney and Hythe, which from at least the 12C combined for defence. 1191 *de quinque portibus*, 1297 *the sink pors*.

Cirencester (town, Glos): 'Roman camp of Corinium'. OE *ceaster*, 'Roman camp'. The name of the Roman town of *Corinium* here is of Celtic origin but uncertain meaning. (The name has been adopted for Corinium Gate and the Corinium Museum here, as well as for the Corinium Business Park near Cinderford.) The river Churn here took its name from the same source. Cp. NORTH CERNEY. *c*.150 *Korinion*, *c*.900 *Cirenceaster*, DB *Cirecestre*.

Cissbury Ring (Iron Age fort, W Sussex): 'Cissa's fort'. OE *burh*, 'fortified place'. The association with Cissa (see CHICHESTER) is apparently an artificial one introduced in the 16C by antiquarians. 1477 *Byry*, *c*.1588 *Sieberie hille*, 1610 *Sissabury*, 1724 *Cissbury*.

Clackmannan (town, Clack): 'stone of Manau'. Welsh *clog*, 'stone'. Manau is the name of the district here. The 'stone' is a glacial rock preserved in the middle of the town next to the Town Cross. 1147 *Clacmanan*.

Clacton-on-Sea (resort town, Essex): 'estate associated with Clacc by the sea'. OE *-ing-*, 'associated with', + *tūn*, 'farmstead', 'estate'. The second part of the name was added to distinguish this Clacton from *Great Clacton*, now a district of Clacton itself, and the village of *Little Clacton* to the north, and also more generally to serve as a commercial lure. *c*.1000 *Claccingtune*, DB *Clachintune*.

Claines (hamlet, Worcs): '(place on the) clay headland'. OE *clǣg*, 'clay', + *næss*, 'headland'. The church stands on a slight headland projecting into marshland here. 11C *Cleinesse*.

Clandon. See EAST CLANDON.

Clanfield (village, Oxon): '(place by) clean open land'. OE *clǣne*, 'clean', + *feld*, 'open land' (modern English *field*). 'Clean' land is land cleared of weeds or other unwanted growth. The DB form of the name below has *h* for *l*. DB *Chenefelde*, 1196 *Clenefeld*. SO ALSO: *Clanfield*, Hants.

Clapham (district, Lambeth): 'homestead near a hill'. OE *clopp*, 'hill' (modern English *clump*), + *hām*, 'homestead'. Clapham is on rising ground south of the Thames. *c.*880 *Cloppaham*, DB *Clopeham*. SO ALSO: *Clapham*, Beds, W Sussex.

Clapham (village, N Yorks): 'homestead or enclosure by the noisy stream'. OE *clæpe*, 'noisy' (modern English *clap*), + *hām*, 'homestead', or *hamm*, 'enclosure'. The 'noisy stream' is Clapham Beck. DB *Clapeham*.

Clapton (village, Somerset): 'farmstead by a hill'. OE *clopp*, 'hill', + *tūn*, 'farmstead', 'village'. The form of the name below relates to Clapton near Crewkerne. 1243 *Clopton*.

Clapton in Gordano (village, N Somerset): 'village by a hill in Gordano'. OE *clopp*, 'hill', + *tūn*, 'farmstead', 'village'. For the district name, see EASTON-IN-GORDANO. The DB form of the name below has omitted the *p*. DB *Clotune*, 1225 *Clopton*.

Clapton-on-the-Hill (village, Glos): 'village on a hill'. OE *clopp*, 'hill', + *tūn*, 'farmstead', 'village'. As the extended name tautologically indicates, the village lies on a prominent hill. 1171 *Clopton*.

Clarborough (village, Notts): 'fortified place where clover grows'. OE *clǣfre*, 'clover', + *burh*, 'fortified place'. The name implies an old fortification overgrown with clover. DB *Claureburg*.

Clare (town, Suffolk): '(place on the river) Clare'. The town is on the river Stour, but this must have had an earlier name of Celtic origin perhaps meaning 'bright stream' (modern Welsh *claer*, 'bright'). DB *Clara*.

Clarendon Park (park, Wilts): 'hill where clover grows'. OE *clǣfre*, 'clover', + *dūn*, 'hill'. This interpretation is disputed by some on the grounds that *f* is missing from early forms of the name. Cp. CLAVERDON. The origin may instead lie in a former Celtic name for the river Bourne here. 1072 *Clarendun*.

Clas-ar-Wy. See GLASBURY.

Clatterford (hamlet, IoW): '(place by the) ford with loose stones'. OE *clater*, 'loose stones' (related modern English *clatter*), + *ford*, 'ford'. The ford in question would have been over Lukely Brook here. *c.*1150 *Claterford*.

Clatworthy (hamlet, Somerset): 'enclosure where burdock grows'. OE *clāte*, 'burdock', +

worth, 'enclosure'. OE *worth* was later replaced by *worthig*, identical in meaning. DB *Clateurde*, 1243 *Clatewurthy*.

Claughton (village, Lancs): 'village by a hill'. OE *clacc*, 'hill', + *tūn*, 'farmstead', 'village'. The form of the name below relates to Claughton near Lancaster, but Claughton near Garstang has a name of identical meaning. DB *Clactun*.

Claverdon (village, Warwicks): '(place by the) hill where clover grows'. OE *clǣfre*, 'clover', + *dūn*, 'hill'. The DB form of the name below has *n* for *r*. DB *Clavendone*, 1123 *Claverdona*.

Claverham (village, N Somerset): 'homestead or enclosure where clover grows'. OE *clǣfre*, 'clover', + *hām*, 'homestead', or *hamm*, 'enclosure'. DB *Claveham*.

Clavering (village, Essex): 'place where clover grows'. OE *clǣfre*, 'clover', + *-ing*, 'place characterized by'. *c.*1000 *Clǣfring*, DB *Clauelinga*.

Claverley (village, Shropshire): 'clearing where clover grows'. OE *clǣfre*, 'clover', + *lēah*, 'wood', 'clearing'. DB *Claverlege*.

Claverton (village, Bath & NE Somerset): 'farmstead by the ford where burdock grows'. OE *clāte*, 'burdock', + *ford*, 'ford', + *tūn*, 'farmstead'. The river here is the Avon. *c.*1000 *Clatfordtun*, DB *Claftertone*.

Clawdd Offa. See OFFA'S DYKE.

Clawton (village, Devon): 'farmstead at the tongue of land'. OE *clawu*, 'tongue of land' (modern English *claw*), + *tūn*, 'farmstead'. Clawton stands on a tongue of land between streams. The river Claw here takes its name from that of the village. DB *Clavetone*.

Claxby (village, Lincs): 'Klakkr's farmstead'. OS *bý*, 'farmstead', 'village'. The personal name is Scandinavian. The forms of the name below relate to Claxby near Market Rasen, but Claxby near Alford has a name of identical origin. 1066 *Cleaxbyg*, DB *Clachesbi*.

Claxton (village, N Yorks): 'farmstead on a hill'. OE *clacc*, 'hill', + *tūn*, 'farmstead'. The name could also mean 'Klakkr's farmstead', with a Scandinavian personal name. The DB form of the name below has OS *thorp*, 'outlying farmstead', subsequently replaced by OE *tūn*. DB *Claxtorp*, 1176 *Clakeston*.

Claybrooke Magna (village, Leics): 'greater (place by the) clayey brook'. OE *clǣg*, 'clay', + *brōc*, 'brook'. The second word of the name (Latin *magna*, 'great') distinguishes the village from nearby *Claybrooke Parva* (Latin *parva*, 'little'). DB *Claibroc*.

Clay Coton (village, Northants): 'cottages in the clayey district'. OE *clǣg*, 'clay', + *cot*, 'cottage'. The second word of the name represents either OE *cotum* (the dative plural form of *cot*) or ME *coten* (the plural form). 12C *Cotes*, 1284 *Cleycotes*.

Clay Cross (town, Derbys): '(place by the) clayey crossing'. The name is recent, and could derive from a local family called Clay. The civil parish here was named *Clay Lane* until it was extended in 1935, when *Clay Cross* became the name of both the civil parish and the village, as it then was. 1734 *Clay Cross*, 1868 *Claycross, or Claylane*.

Claydon (village, Suffolk): '(place by the) clayey hill'. OE *clǣgig*, 'clayey', + *dūn*, 'hill'. DB *Clainduna*. SO ALSO: *Claydon*, Oxon.

Claydons, The. See STEEPLE CLAYDON.

Clayhanger (village, Devon): '(place on a) clayey wooded slope'. OE *clǣg*, 'clay', + *hangra*, 'wooded slope'. The village lies on a steepish slope. DB *Clehangra*. SO ALSO: *Clayhanger*, Walsall.

Clayhidon (hamlet, Devon): 'clayey (place on the) hill where hay is made'. OE *clǣg*, 'clay', + *hīeg*, 'hay', + *dūn*, 'hill'. DB *Hidone*, 1485 *Cleyhidon*.

Claypole (village, Lincs): '(place by the) clayey pool'. OE *clǣg*, 'clay', + *pōl*, 'pool'. The pool in question is in the river Witham here. DB *Claipol*.

Clayton (village, Doncaster): 'farmstead on clayey soil'. OE *clǣg*, 'clay', + *tūn*, 'farmstead'. 'Soil clay and loam, overlying clay' (*Cassell's Gazetteer of Great Britain and Ireland*, 1895). Clayton was formerly known as *Clayton in the Clay* for distinction from *Clayton West*, Kirklees, 13 miles to the west. DB *Claitone*. SO ALSO: *Clayton*, Bradford, Staffs.

Clayton (village, W Sussex): 'farmstead on clayey soil'. OE *clǣg*, 'clay', + *tūn*, 'farmstead'. 'Soil loam and sand, overlying mould, clay, and sand' (*Cassell's Gazetteer of Great Britain and Ireland*, 1895). DB *Claitune*.

Clayton-le-Moors (town, Lancs): 'farmstead on clayey soil on the moorland'. OE *clǣg*, 'clay', + *tūn*, 'farmstead', + OF *le*, 'the', + OE *mōr*, 'moor'. The 'moorland' is the high ground between Accrington and Great Harwood. 1243 *Cleyton*, 1284 *Clayton super Moras*.

Clayton West. See CLAYTON (Doncaster).

Clayworth (village, Notts): 'enclosure on the claw-shaped hill'. OE *clawu*, 'claw', + *worth*, 'enclosure'. Clayworth stands on a low, curving hill that projects slightly into the flat region alongside the river Idle, and this is the 'claw'. DB *Clauorde*.

Cleadon (village, S Tyneside): 'hill of the cliffs'. OE *clif*, 'cliff', + *dūn*, 'hill'. Cp. CLEVEDON. The reference is probably to the hill northwest of the village, although Cleadon is not far from the sea coast, where there are actual cliffs. 1183 *Clyvedon*.

Clearwell (village, Glos): '(place by the) stream where clover grows'. OE *clāfre*, 'clover', + *wella*, 'spring', 'stream'. c.1282 *Clouerwalle*.

Cleasby (village, N Yorks): 'Kleppr's or Kleiss's farmstead'. OS *bý*, 'farmstead', 'village'. The personal names are Scandinavian. DB *Clesbi*.

Cleatlam (village, Durham): '(place by the) clearings where burdock grows'. OE *clǣte*, 'burdock', + *lēah*, 'wood', 'clearing'. The second part of the name represents OE *lēaum*, the dative plural form of *lēah*. The first form of the name below has OE *-ingas*, 'dwellers at'. c.1050 *Cletlinga*, 1271 *Cletlum*.

Cleator (village, Cumbria): 'hill pasture where burdock grows'. OE *clǣte*, 'burdock', + OS *erg*, 'hill pasture'. A 'hill pasture' would have been a smallish dairy settlement used only in summer months. c.1200 *Cletergh*.

Cleckheaton (town, Kirklees): 'high farmstead by a hill'. OS *klakkr*, 'hill', + OE *hēah*, 'high', + *tūn*, 'farmstead'. The hill in question is the round peaked one above Cleckheaton. The first part of the name distinguishes the town from KIRKHEATON, 5 miles to the south. DB *Hetun*, 1285 *Claketon*.

Clee St Margaret (village, Shropshire): '(village near) Clee Hill with St Margaret's church'. *Clee Hill* takes its name from OE *clēo*, 'rounded hill'. Cp. CLEOBURY MORTIMER. The church dedication distinguishes the village from *Cleeton St Mary*, 'village near Clee Hill with St Mary's church' (OE *tūn*, 'farmstead', 'village'), 5 miles to the southeast. DB *Cleie*, 1285 *Clye Sancte Margarete*.

Cleethorpes (resort town, NE Lincs): 'hamlets near Clee'. OS *thorp*, 'outlying farm', 'hamlet'. The town takes its name from what is now the district of Grimsby called *Old Clee* (OE *clǣg*, 'clay'), referring to the clayey soil here. The hamlets themselves were probably Hole, Itterby and Thrunscoe. 1406 *Thorpe*, 1552 *Clethorpe*, 1558 *Clethorpes*.

Cleeve (village, N Somerset): '(place by the) cliff'. OE *clif*, 'cliff', 'bank'. 1243 *Clive*.

Cleeve Hill (village, Glos): '(place by) Cleeve Hill'. OE *clif*, 'cliff', 'bank'. The village is named for *Cleeve Hill* here, the steep hill near *Cleeve Cloud*, where *Cloud* represents OE *clūd*, '(rocky) hill' (modern English *cloud*). Cp. BISHOP'S CLEEVE. 1564 *Clevehill*.

Cleeve Prior (village, Worcs): 'prior's (estate by the) cliff'. OE *clif*, 'cliff', 'bank'. The village lies on a conspicuous ridge near the river Avon. The second word of the name refers to the early possession of the manor by the Prior of Worcester. DB *Clive*, 1291 *Clyve Prior*, 1868 *Prior's Cleeve*.

Clehonger (village, Herefords): '(place on the) clayey wooded slope'. OE *clǣg*, 'clay', + *hangra*, 'wooded slope'. Cp. CLAYHANGER. DB *Cleunge*.

Clench (hamlet, Wilts): '(place by the) hill'. OE *clenc*, 'hill' (related modern English *clench*). Clench lies near a big rounded hill. 1289 *Clenche*.

Clenchwarton (village, Norfolk): 'farmstead of the dwellers by the hill'. OE *clenc*, 'hill' (related modern English *clench*), + *-ware*, 'dwellers', + *tūn*, 'farmstead'. The DB form of the name below is garbled. DB *Ecleuuartuna*, 1196 *Clenchewarton*.

Clent (village, Worcs): '(place by the) rocky hill'. OE *clent*, 'rock'. DB *Clent*.

Cleobury Mortimer (village, Shropshire): 'Mortemer's fortified place by Clee Hill'. OE *burh*, 'fortified place'. For the hill name, see CLEE ST MARGARET. The Mortemer family held the manor here in the 11C, their name distinguishing this Cleobury from *Cleobury North*, 7 miles to the north. DB *Cleberie*, 1272 *Clebury Mortimer*.

Clerkenwell (district, Islington): 'spring where students gather'. ME *clerc*, 'student' (modern English *clerk*), + OE *wella*, 'well', 'spring'. The first part of the name represents ME *clercen*, the plural of *clerc*. Students would doubtless gather at the spring on summer evenings. The site of the spring in question is now covered by Farringdon Road. *c.*1150 *Clerkenwell*.

Clevancy (hamlet, Wilts): 'de Wancy's (estate by the) cliff'. OE *clif*, 'cliff', 'bank'. The de Wancy family held the manor here in the 13C. DB *Clive*, 1231 *Clif Wauncy*.

Clevedon (resort town, N Somerset): '(place on the) hill of the cliffs'. OE *clif*, 'cliff', + *dūn*, 'hill'. Clevedon has a number of hills, and the cliffs behind the town are quite high. DB *Clivedon*.

Cleveland (hilly region, N Yorks): 'hilly district'. OE *clif*, 'cliff', + *land*, 'land'. 'One glance at the map will show the appropriateness of the name' (A. H. Smith, *The Place-Names of the North Riding of Yorkshire*, 1928). The name was adopted

for the modern county of Cleveland (1974–96). *c.*1110 *Clivelanda*.

Cleveleys (coastal town, Lancs): 'Cleveley's (estate)'. The name is recorded only in the 19C and apparently derives from a family here named Cleveley. They may have originally come from the location now marked by *Cleveley Bank Farm*, 4 miles northeast of Garstang, the name itself meaning 'woodland clearing by a cliff' (OE *clif*, 'cliff', + *lēah*, 'wood', 'clearing'). 1868 *Cleveleys*.

Clewer (hamlet, Somerset): '(place of the) dwellers on the (river) bank'. OE *clif*, 'cliff', 'bank', + *-ware*, 'dwellers'. Clewer is on the river Axe. DB *Cliveware*.

Cley-next-the-Sea (village, Norfolk): 'clayey place by the sea'. OE *clǣg*, 'clay'. Cley is on clayey soil by some marshes near the low-lying coast. The latter part of the name was added for distinguishing or commercial purposes. DB *Claia*.

Cliburn (village, Cumbria): '(place by the) stream by the cliff'. OE *clif*, 'cliff', 'bank', + *burna*, 'stream'. The 'stream' is the river Leith here, and the 'cliff' one of the scars alongside it, or the hillside on which the village stands. *c.*1140 *Clibbrun*.

Cliddesden (village, Hants): 'valley of the rocky hill'. OE *clȳde*, 'lump', 'rock', + *denu*, 'valley'. The 'rocky hill' in question may be nearby Farleigh Hill. The DB form of the name below has *r* for *d*. DB *Cleresden*, 1194 *Cledesdene*.

Cliffe (village, Medway): '(place by the) cliff'. OE *clif*, 'cliff'. The 'cliff' here is actually a low bank at the end of a chalk range. The village is also known as *Cliffe-at-Hoo* (OE *hōh*, 'spur of land'). 10C *Cliua*, DB *Clive*.

Cliffe (village, N Yorks): '(place by the) cliff'. OE *clif*, 'cliff'. The 'cliff' here may have been the bank of the river Ouse before the latter was diverted to the southwest. DB *Clive*.

Clifford (village, Herefords): '(place by the) ford by a bank'. OE *clif*, 'bank', 'cliff', + *ford*, 'ford'. Clifford is on the river Wye. DB *Cliford*.

Clifford (village, Leeds): '(place by the) ford by a bank'. OE *clif*, 'bank', 'cliff', + *ford*, 'ford'. The ford in question crossed Carr Beck where the bridge now takes Windmill Road over it. DB *Cliford*.

Clifford Chambers (village, Warwicks): 'chamberlain's (estate by the) ford by a bank'. OE *clif*, 'bank', 'cliff', + *ford*, 'ford'. The river here is the Avon. The second word (ME *chamberere*, 'chamberlain') relates to the chamberlain of St Peter's, Gloucester, who was given the manor

here in 1099. 922 *Clifforda*, DB *Clifort*, 1388
Chaumberesclifford.

Clifftown (coastal district of Southend-on-
Sea, Southend): 'town by the cliffs'. The district
developed as a residential area east of WEST-
CLIFF-ON-SEA in the 1830s. 'The old village [of
Southend] consists principally of an irregular
line of houses facing the sea, but a terrace and a
new village called Clifton have recently been
added' (*The National Gazetteer of Great Britain
and Ireland*, 1868).

Clifton (district, Bristol): 'farmstead on a
bank'. OE *clif*, 'bank', 'cliff', + *tūn*, 'farmstead'.
The 'bank' is the steep hill above the Avon
Gorge to the west of the city centre. The DB form
of the name below has *s* for *f*. DB *Clistone*. SO
ALSO: *Clifton*, Derbys, Oxon.

Clifton (village, Cumbria): 'farmstead by a
cliff'. OE *clif*, 'cliff', + *tūn*, 'farmstead'. The village stands above two prominent cliffs that
overlook the river Lowther. 1204 *Clifton*.

Clifton (suburb of West Bridgford, Nottingham): 'farmstead by a bank'. OE *clif*, 'bank',
'cliff', + *tūn*, 'farmstead'. The bank in question is
the steep slope above the river Trent here. DB
Cliftone.

Clifton Campville (village, Staffs): 'de Camvill's farmstead on a bank'. OE *clif*, 'bank', 'cliff',
+ *tūn*, 'farmstead'. The de Camvill family held
the manor here in the 13C. 942 *Clyfton*, DB
Cliftune.

Clifton Hampden (village, Oxon): 'Hampden's village on a cliff'. OE *clif*, 'cliff', + *tūn*,
'farmstead', 'village'. The 'cliff' is the rock outcrop on which the village church stands. The
second word of the name is first recorded only
in 1836 and apparently relates to a family called
Hampden. 1146 *Cliftona*.

Clifton Reynes (village, Milton K): 'de Reynes' farmstead on a bank'. OE *clif*, 'bank', 'cliff',
+ *tūn*, 'farmstead'. The de Reynes family held
the manor here in the early 14C. DB *Cliftone*,
1383 *Clyfton Reynes*.

Clifton upon Dunsmore (village, Warwicks): 'farmstead on a bank on Dunsmore'. OE
clif, 'bank', 'cliff', + *tūn*, 'farmstead'. As noted by
William Dugdale in *The Antiquities of Warwickshire* (1656), Clifton 'standeth upon the top of
an indifferent hill ... having its name from the
scituation; *Cliffe*, with the Saxons, signifying
not only a rocky place, but any shelving
ground'. The district name *Dunsmore* means
'Dunn's moor' (OE *mōr*). DB *Cliptone*, 1306
Clifton super Donesmore.

Clifton upon Teme (village, Worcs): 'farmstead on a bank on the (river) Teme'. OE *clif*,
'bank', 'cliff', + *tūn*, 'farmstead'. For the river
name, see TENBURY WELLS. The village stands
on high ground overlooking the Teme. The DB
form of the name below has *f* miscopied as *s*. 934
Cliftun ultra Tamedam, DB *Clistune*.

Cliftonville (district of Margate, Kent). The
district, at the foot of chalk cliffs, took its name
from the 19C Cliftonville Hotel here, its own
name referring to its location on Clifton Street.

Climping (village, W Sussex): '(settlement of)
Climp's people'. OE *-ingas*, 'people of'. The DB
form of the name below is corrupt. DB *Clepinges*,
1228 *Clympinges*.

Clint (village, N Yorks): '(place on a) steep
bank'. OS *klint*, 'rocky cliff'. The village is high
up a steep bank overlooking the river Nidd. 1208
Clint.

Clippesby (hamlet, Norfolk): 'Klyppr's or
Klippr's farmstead'. OS *bý*, 'farmstead', 'village'.
The personal name in its variant forms is Scan-
dinavian. DB *Clepesbei*.

Clipsham (village, Rutland): 'Cylp's village'.
OE *hām*, 'homestead', 'village', 'estate'. 1203
Kilpesham.

Clipston (village, Northants): 'Klyppr's or
Klippr's farmstead'. OE *tūn*, 'farmstead'. The
personal name is Scandinavian. DB *Clipestune*.
SO ALSO: *Clipston*, Notts.

Clipstone (village, Notts): 'Klyppr's or Klippr's
farmstead'. OE *tūn*, 'farmstead'. The personal
name is Scandinavian. DB *Clipestune*.

Clitheroe (town, Lancs): '(place on the) hill
with loose stones'. OE *clȳder*, 'loose stones', +
hōh 'spur', or OS *haugr*, 'hill'. The 'loose stones'
are the crumbling limestone on which the 12C
castle here was built. 1102 *Cliderhou*.

Clive (village, Shropshire): '(place by the) cliff'.
OE *clif*, 'cliff', 'bank'. The 'cliff' in question is the
fairly steep slope on the side of nearby Grinshill
Hill. 1255 *Clive*.

Cliveden (country house, Bucks): 'valley by
the cliffs'. OE *clif*, 'cliff', 'hill slope', + *denu*, 'valley'. The 'cliff' here is an escarpment by the
Thames. 1195 *Cliueden*.

Clodock (hamlet, Herefords): '(church of) St
Clydog'. The church here is dedicated to Cly-
dog, said to be of the family of the Welsh prince
Brychan (see BRECON). *c*.1150 *Ecclesia Sancti
Clitauci*.

Clophill (village, Beds): '(place on the) lumpy
hill'. OE *clopp*, 'lump', + *hyll*, 'hill'. DB *Clopelle*.

Clopton (hamlet, Suffolk): 'farmstead by a hill'. OE *clopp*, 'lump', 'hill', + *tūn*, 'farmstead'. DB *Cloptuna*.

Clothall (hamlet, Herts): 'corner of land where burdock grows'. OE *clāte*, 'burdock', + *healh*, 'nook', 'corner of land'. *c*.1060 *Clatheala*, DB *Cladhele*.

Clotton (hamlet, Cheshire): 'farmstead in a valley'. OE *clōh*, 'valley', + *tūn*, 'farmstead'. DB *Clotone*.

Cloud, The (hill, Cheshire/Staffs): 'the rocky hill'. OE *clūd*, 'mass of rock' (modern English *cloud*). The name is that of a prominent hill on the county boundary.

Cloughton (village, N Yorks): 'farmstead in a valley'. OE *clōh*, 'valley', + *tūn*, 'farmstead'. DB *Cloctune*.

Clovelly (coastal village, Devon): 'earthworks associated with Fele'. Cornish *cleath*, 'dyke', 'bank'. The 'earthworks' would be those of the nearby Iron Age fort known as Clovelly Dykes. An alternative interpretation is 'cleft of Velly', from OE *clof*, 'cleft', and *Velly*, the name of a nearby hill, whose own name may mean 'felly' (OE *felg*). The semicircular shape of the hill suggests a felly (outer rim of a wheel), with Clovelly in a 'cleft' or V-shaped indentation in it. In the first interpretation, Fele is a personal name. DB *Cloveleia*, 1296 *Clofely*.

Clowne (town, Derbys): '(place on the river) Clowne'. The river, which rises nearby, has a name identical in origin to that of the *Clun* (see CLUN). DB *Clune*.

Clun (village, Shropshire): '(place on the river) Clun'. The river has a pre-English name of uncertain meaning. DB *Clune*.

Clunbury (village, Shropshire): 'fortified place on the (river) Clun'. OE *burh*, 'fortified place'. For the river name, see CLUN. The 'fortified place' was probably a manor house rather than an actual fort. DB *Cluneberie*.

Clungunford (village, Shropshire): 'Gunward's (estate on the river) Clun'. For the river name, see CLUN. Gunward held the manor here in the 11C, his name later being taken as a place name in *-ford*. DB *Clone*, 1242 *Cloune Goneford*.

Clunton (village, Shropshire): 'farmstead on the (river) Clun'. OE *tūn*, 'farmstead'. For the river name, see CLUN. The DB form of the name below has omitted the *n*. DB *Clutone*, 12C *Cluntune*.

Clutton (village, Cheshire): 'farmstead by a hill'. OE *clūd*, 'hill' (modern English *cloud*), +

tūn, 'farmstead', 'village'. DB *Clutone*. SO ALSO: *Clutton*, Bath & NE Somerset.

Clwyd (historic county, N Wales): '(district of the river) Clwyd'. The river has a name meaning 'hurdle' (Welsh *clwyd*), perhaps originally referring to a place on it where there was a ford or causeway made out of hurdles. 1191 *Cloid fluvium*.

Clydach (town, Swansea): '(place on the river) Clydach'. The river derives its name from the same Celtic source as that of the Clyde (see CLYDEBANK). 1208 *Cleudach*.

Clyde (river). See CLYDEBANK.

Clydebank (town, W Dunbartons): '(place on the) bank of the (river) Clyde'. The town arose from the shipyard built here in the 1870s. The river has a Celtic name meaning 'cleansing one'.

Clyffe Pypard (village, Wilts): 'Pipard's (estate at the) cliff'. OE *clif*, 'cliff', 'bank'. Richard Pipard held the manor here in the 13C. An earlier form of the name was *Pepper Cleeve*, as in the local rhyme: 'White Cleeve, Pepper Cleeve, Cleeve and Cleveancy, / Lyneham and lousy Clack, Cris Mavord and Dauntsey'. ('Cleveancy' is CLEVANCY, and 'Cris Mavord' CHRISTIAN MALFORD.) 983 *æt Clife*, DB *Clive*, 1291 *Clive Pipard*.

Clyst Honiton (village, Devon): 'farmstead on the (river) Clyst belonging to a religious community'. OE *hīwan* 'household (of monks)', 'religious community', + *tūn*, 'farmstead'. (The 'Honi-' of the name represents OE *hīgna*, the genitive form of the plural noun *hīwan*.) The community in question is Exeter Cathedral. The river has a Celtic name probably related to modern Welsh *clust*, 'ear', here in the sense 'sea inlet', 'river reach', referring to the salt-water inlet of the Clyst at its broad mouth, which opens onto the estuary of the Exe. The proximity of the place to HONITON led to the assimilation of its name to that of the town. There are a whole cluster of Clysts to the northeast of Exeter, others being *Clyst St George*, *Clyst St Lawrence* and *Clyst St Mary*, named after their church dedications, *Clyst Hydon*, where the manor was held by the de Hidune family in the 13C, and *Clyst William*, near the source of the river (OE *æwylm*, 'source'). See also BROAD CLYST, SOWTON. *c*.1100 *Hinatune*, 1281 *Clysthynetone*.

Coalbrookdale (village, Wrekin): 'valley of the (river) Coalbrook'. Modern English *dale* was added to the river's name, which means 'cold brook' (OE *cald*, 'cold', + *brōc*, 'brook'). The first part of the name has been influenced by the former coalfield here. 1250 *Caldebrok*, 1756 *Coalbrooke Dale*, 1868 *Colebrookdale*.

Coalbrookvale. See NANTYGLO.

Coaley (village, Glos): 'clearing with a shelter'. OE *cofa*, 'chamber', 'shelter' (modern English *cove*), + *lēah*, 'wood', 'clearing'. DB *Couelege*.

Coalport (village, Wrekin): 'coal port'. The village arose by the river Severn in the 1790s as a port for coal transported via the newly constructed Shropshire Canal, which enters the river here. The name echoes that of COALBROOKDALE further up the same river, although that name does not contain 'coal'.

Coalville (town, Leics): 'coal town'. Modern English *coal* + French *ville*, 'town'. The coal-mining town arose from a colliery settlement that grew up around Coalville House here in the 1820s.

Coatbridge (town, N Lanarks): '(place by the) bridge at Coats'. The latter name means '(place with) cottages' (OE *cot*, 'shelter'), referring to the cottages by the Monkland Canal here. 1584 *Coittis*.

Coate (village, Wilts): 'cottages'. OE *cot*, 'cottage', 'hut'. 1255 *Cotes*.

Coates (village, Glos): 'cottages'. OE *cot*, 'cottage', 'hut'. 1175 *Cota*. SO ALSO: *Coates*, Cambs, Notts.

Coatham (coastal hamlet, Redcar & Clev): '(place by the) cottages'. OE *cot*, 'cottage', 'hut'. The name represents OE *cotum*, the dative plural form of *cot*. 1123 *Cotum*.

Coatham Mundeville (hamlet, Darlington): 'de Amundevilla's (estate at the) cottages'. OE *cot*, 'cottage', 'hut'. Cp. COATHAM. The de Amundevilla family held the manor here in the 13C. 12C *Cotum*, 1344 *Cotum Maundevill*.

Coberley (village, Glos): 'Cūthbeorht's wood or clearing'. OE *lēah*, 'wood', 'clearing'. DB *Culberlege*.

Cobham (village, Kent): 'Cobba's enclosure or homestead'. OE *hamm*, 'enclosure', or *hām*, 'homestead'. The first form of the name below contains OE *mearc*, 'boundary'. 939 *Cobba hammes mearce*, 1197 *Cobbeham*.

Cobham (town, Surrey): 'Cofa's homestead or enclosure'. OE *hām*, 'homestead', or *hamm*, 'enclosure'. The first part of the name could also represent OE *cofa*, 'hut', 'shelter' (modern English *cove*). DB *Covenham*.

Cockayne Hatley (village, Beds): 'Cockayne's (estate at the) woodland clearing by the hill'. OE *hætt*, 'hill' (modern English *hat*), + *lēah*, 'wood', 'clearing'. The Cockayne family held the manor

here in the 15C. c.960 *Hattenleia*, 1576 *Cocking Hatley*.

Cockenzie (town, N Ayrs): meaning unknown. A personal name may be involved. 1590 *Cowkany*.

Cockerham (village, Lancs): 'homestead or enclosure on the (river) Cocker'. OE *hām*, 'homestead', or *hamm*, 'enclosure'. The river name (identical with that of the Cocker at COCKERMOUTH) is presumably a former name for the present river Lud. DB *Cocreham*.

Cockermouth (town, Cumbria): 'mouth of the (river) Cocker'. OE *mūtha*, 'mouth'. The town lies at the confluence of the rivers Cocker and Derwent. The Cocker has a Celtic name meaning 'crooked'. c.1150 *Cokyrmoth*.

Cockfield (village, Durham): 'open land where cockbirds are seen'. OE *cocc*, 'cock', + *feld*, 'open land' (modern English *field*). The name could also mean 'Cocca's open land'. 1223 *Kokefeld*.

Cockfield (village, Suffolk): 'Cohha's open land'. OE *feld*, 'open land' (modern English *field*). 10C *Cochanfelde*.

Cockfosters (district, Barnet): '(house of the) chief forester'. modern English *cock*, 'chief', + obsolete *foster*, 'forester'. The settlement arose at the edge of Enfield Chase, a former hunting ground. 1524 *Cokfosters*.

Cocking (village, W Sussex): '(place of the) dwellers at the hillock'. OE *cocc*, 'hillock', + *-ingas*, 'dwellers at'. The first part of the name could also represent the personal name Cocc. DB *Cochinges*.

Cockington (district of Torquay, Torbay): 'estate associated with Cocc'. OE *-ing-*, 'associated with', + *tūn*, 'farmstead', 'estate'. DB *Cochintone*.

Cockley Cley (village, Norfolk): 'Cockley's (estate on) clayey soil'. OE *clæg*, 'clay'. The first word of the name could also represent a local name meaning 'wood where woodcock are seen' (OE *cocc*, 'cockbird', 'woodcock', + *lēah*, 'wood', 'clearing'). DB *Cleia*, 1324 *Coclikleye*.

Cockshutt (village, Shropshire): 'cockshoot'. OE *cocc-scīete*, 'cockshoot' (from *cocc*, 'woodcock', + *scīete*, 'shoot'). A 'cockshoot' is a woodland glade where nets are stretched to catch any woodcock that might 'shoot' (dart) through it. 1270 *La Cockesete*.

Cockthorpe (hamlet, Norfolk): 'Cocke's (estate at the) outlying farmstead'. OS *thorp*, 'outlying farmstead'. The name could also mean 'outlying farmstead where cocks are reared' (OE *cocc*, 'cock', + OS *thorp*). DB *Torp*, 1254 *Coketorp*.

Coddenham (village, Suffolk): 'Codda's homestead or enclosure'. OE *hām*, 'homestead', or *hamm*, 'enclosure'. The '-en-' represents the genitive ending of the personal name. DB *Codenham*.

Coddington (village, Cheshire): 'estate associated with Cotta'. OE *-ing-*, 'associated with', + *tūn*, 'farmstead', 'estate'. DB *Cotintone*. SO ALSO: *Coddington*, Herefords, Notts.

Codford St Mary (village, Wilts): '(place at) Codda's ford with St Mary's church'. OE *ford*, 'ford'. The church dedication distinguishes this Codford from nearby *Codford St Peter*. The ford would have been over the river Wylye here. 901 *Codan ford*, DB *Coteford*, 1291 *Codeford Sancte Marie*.

Codicote (village, Herts): 'cottages associated with Cūthhere'. OE *-ing-*, 'associated with', + *cot*, 'cottage'. 1002 *Cutheringcoton*, DB *Codicote*.

Codnor (village, Derbys): 'Codda's ridge'. OE *ofer*, 'ridge'. DB *Cotenoure*.

Codrington (hamlet, S Glos): 'estate associated with Cūthhere'. OE *-ing-*, 'associated with', + *hām*, 'homestead', 'estate'. 12C *Cuderintuna*.

Codsall (suburb of Wolverhampton, Staffs): 'Cōd's corner of land'. OE *halh*, 'nook', 'corner of land'. DB *Codeshale*.

Coed-duon. See BLACKWOOD.

Coffinswell (village, Devon): 'Coffin's (estate by the) spring'. OE *wella*, 'spring', 'stream'. The Coffin family held the manor here in the 12C. DB *Willa*, 1249 *Coffineswell*.

Cofton Hackett (village, Worcs): 'Haket's farmstead with a hut'. OE *cofa*, 'hut', 'shelter' (modern English *cove*), + *tūn*, 'farmstead'. The Haket family held the manor here in the 12C. The DB form of the name below has miscopied *f* as *s*. 8C *Coftune*, DB *Costune*, 1431 *Corfton Hakett*.

Cogges (hamlet, Oxon): '(place among) hills'. OE *cogg*, 'hill' (modern English *cog*). Cogges Hill is nearby. DB *Coges*.

Coggeshall (village, Essex): 'Cogg's corner of land'. OE *halh*, 'nook', 'corner of land'. DB *Cogheshala*.

Colaton Raleigh. See COLLATON ST MARY.

Colburn (village, N Yorks): '(place by the) cool stream'. OE *cōl*, 'cool', + *burna*, 'stream'. The 'cool stream' in question is Colburn Beck, which enters the river Swale nearby. The DB form of the name below has *r* for *l*. DB *Corburne*, 1198 *Coleburn*.

Colby (village, Cumbria): 'Kolli's farmstead'. OS *bý*, 'farmstead', 'village'. The personal name is Scandinavian. The name could also mean 'farmstead on a hill' (OS *kollr*, 'hill', + *bý*). DB *Collebi*.

Colby (village, Norfolk): 'Koli's farmstead'. OS *bý*, 'farmstead', 'village'. The personal name is Scandinavian. DB *Colebei*.

Colchester (town, Essex): 'Roman town on the (river) Colne'. OE *ceaster*, 'Roman camp'. The river's name is pre-English and of uncertain meaning. The first part of the town's name could also derive from Latin *colonia*, 'colony' (cp. LINCOLN). The Roman camp here was *Camulodunum*, 'fort of Camulos', from the Celtic war god. The name is popularly associated with Old King Cole of the nursery rhyme, as recounted by the 12C chronicler Robert of Gloucester: 'Cole was a noble mon. & gret poer adde an honde. Erle he was of colchestre. here in thisse londe. & Colchestre after is name. icluped is ich under stonde.' ('Cole was a nobleman and had great power in his hands. He was earl of Colchester here in this land, and Colchester is named after him, I understand.') Early 10C *Colneceastre*, DB *Colecestra*.

Cold Ashby (village, Northants): 'cold farmstead where ash trees grow'. OE *cald*, 'cold', + *æsc*, 'ash', + OS *bý*, 'farmstead'. A 'cold' farmstead is an exposed one. DB *Essebi*, c.1150 *Caldessebi*.

Cold Ashton (village, S Glos): 'cold farmstead by the ash tree'. OE *cald*, 'cold', + *æsc*, 'ash', + *tūn*, 'farmstead'. The place was in a 'cold' location, 'much exposed to the violence of the winds' (Samuel Rudder, *A New History of Gloucestershire*, 1779). 931 *Æsctun*, DB *Escetone*, 1287 *Cold Aston*.

Cold Aston (village, Glos): 'cold eastern farmstead'. OE *cald*, 'cold', + *ēast*, 'eastern', + *tūn*, 'farmstead'. An eastern farmstead is likely to be 'cold' or exposed to the east wind. The village is alternatively known as *Aston Blank*, the second word perhaps representing OF *blanc*, 'white', 'bare', referring to its scant vegetation. 716 *Eastunæ*, DB *Estone*, 1590 *Colde Aston*, 1685 *Aston Blanc*, 1868 *Aston Blank, or Cold Aston*.

Cold Brayfield (village, Milton K): 'cold (place on) open land by higher ground'. OE *bragen*, 'higher ground' (related modern English *brain*), + *feld*, 'open land' (modern English *field*). The first word of the name distinguishes the village from *Brafield-on-the-Green*, Northants, 8 miles to the northwest, where the name has an identical meaning. The respective additions are first recorded only in the 16C. 967 *Bragenfelda*.

Cold Hanworth (hamlet, Lincs): 'cold (place called) Hana's enclosure'. OE *worth*, 'enclosure'. The place was presumably 'cold' (OE *cald*) from its exposed location. DB *Haneurde*, 1322 *Calthaneworth*.

Cold Hatton. See HIGH HATTON.

Cold Higham (village, Northants): 'cold high homestead'. OE *cald*, 'cold', + *hēah*, 'high', + *hām*, 'homestead'. The village stands on a high and exposed site. DB *Hecham*, 1541 *Colehigham*.

Cold Kirby (village, N Yorks): 'Kærir's bleak farmstead'. OS *bý*, 'farmstead'. The personal name is Scandinavian. The first word of the name distinguishes this Kirby from KIRBY KNOWLE, 4 miles to the northwest. DB *Carebi*.

Coldridge (village, Devon): 'ridge where charcoal is made'. OE *col*, 'coal', 'charcoal', + *hrycg*, 'ridge'. DB *Colrige*, 1868 *Coleridge, or Coldridge*.

Coldstream (town, Borders): '(place on the) cold stream'. The town is on the river Tweed, but the smaller Leet Water, which joins it here, may have been the original 'cold stream'. *c*.1178 *Kaldestrem, c*.1207 *Caldestream*, 1290 *Coldstreme*.

Coldwaltham. See UPWALTHAM.

Cole (village, Somerset): '(place on the river) Cole'. The former name of the stream here is pre-English and of uncertain meaning. 1212 *Colna*.

Colebatch (hamlet, Shropshire): 'Cola's (valley with a) stream'. OE *bece*, 'stream'. The first part of the name could also represent OE *col*, 'charcoal'. 1176 *Colebech*.

Colebrooke (village, Devon): '(place by the) cool brook'. OE *cōl*, 'cool', + *brōc*, 'brook'. 12C *Colebroc*.

Coleby (village, N Lincs): 'Koli's farmstead'. OS *bý*, 'farmstead', 'village'. The personal name is Scandinavian. DB *Colebi*.

Coleford (town, Glos): '(place by the) coal ford'. OE *col*, 'coal', 'charcoal', + *ford*, 'ford'. The name refers to a small stream here across which charcoal (rather than coal) could be carried. 1282 *Coleforde*.

Coleford (village, Somerset): '(place by the) coal ford'. OE *col*, 'coal', 'charcoal', + *ford*, 'ford'. The name refers to the river Mells here, across which coal or charcoal could be carried. 1234 *Culeford*.

Colehill (village, Dorset): '(place by the) hill where charcoal is made'. OE *col*, 'charcoal', + *hyll*, 'hill'. The first part of the name could also

represent OE *coll*, 'hill', giving a simple sense '(place by the) hill', with *hyll* added when this was no longer understood. 1431 *Colhulle*.

Colemere (village, Shropshire): '(place by) Cūla's pool'. OE *mere*, 'pool'. DB *Colesmere*.

Coleorton (hamlet, Leics): 'higher farmstead (at the place of) coal'. OE *uferra*, 'higher', + *tūn*, 'farmstead'. The first part of the name refers to coal mining here, near COALVILLE. DB *Ovretone*, 1571 *Cole Orton*.

Colerne (village, Wilts): 'building where charcoal is made or kept'. OE *col*, 'coal', 'charcoal', + *ærn*, 'building'. DB *Colerne*.

Colesbourne (village, Glos): '(place by) Col's or Coll's stream'. The stream in question is the headwater of the river Churn. Until recently the name was spelt *Colesborne*. 9C *Colesburnan*, DB *Colesborne*, 1868 *Colesborne*.

Coleshill (village, Bucks): '(place by the) hill'. OE *coll*, 'hill', + *hyll*, 'hill'. The second part of the name was added to explain the first when it was no longer understood. The name could also mean 'Coll's hill'. The earlier name of the village in medieval times was *Stoke* (OE *stoc*, 'secondary settlement'). 1175 *Stoke*, 1224 *Stokke*, 1507 *Coleshyll*.

Coleshill (village, Oxon): '(place by the) hill'. OE *coll*, 'hill', + *hyll*, 'hill'. The second part of the name was added to explain the first when it was no longer understood. The name could also mean 'Coll's hill'. Either way, the river Cole here took its name from the village. 10C *Colleshylle*, DB *Coleselle*.

Coleshill (town, Warwicks): 'hill on the (river) Cole'. OE *hyll*, 'hill'. The river has a Celtic name meaning '(river of) hazels' (related to modern Welsh *collen*). 799 *Colleshyl*, DB *Coleshelle*.

Colkirk (village, Norfolk): 'Cola's or Koli's church'. OS *kirkja*, 'church'. The personal names are respectively OE and Scandinavian. DB *Colechirca*.

Coll (island, Argyll & Bute): '(place of) hazels'. Gaelic *coll*, 'hazel'. An alternative origin from OS *kollr*, 'bald head' (i.e. 'barren place'), has also been proposed.

Collaton St Mary (village, Torbay): 'Cola's farmstead with St Mary's church'. OE *tūn*, 'farmstead'. The church dedication distinguishes this village from *Colaton Raleigh*, 22 miles to the northeast, where the manor was held in the 13C by the de Ralegh family. 1261 *Coletone*.

Collingbourne Ducis (village, Wilts): 'duke's (estate by the) stream of Col's or Cola's people'. OE *-inga-*, 'of the people of', + *burna*, 'stream'.

The dukes of Lancaster held the manor here, their title (Latin *ducis*, 'of the duke') distinguishing the village from nearby *Collingbourne Kingston* (OE *cyning*, 'king', + *tūn*, 'estate'), held by the king. 903 *Colengaburnam*, DB *Colingeburne*.

Collingham (village, Notts): 'homestead of Col's or Cola's people'. OE *-inga-*, 'of the people of', + *hām*, 'homestead', 'village'. The two villages of *North Collingham* and *South Collingham* are continuous and are usually known jointly by this name. DB *Colingeham*. SO ALSO: *Collingham*, Leeds.

Collington (hamlet, Herefords): 'estate associated with Col or Cola'. OE *-ing-*, 'associated with', + *tūn*, 'farmstead', 'estate'. DB *Colintune*.

Collyweston (village, Northants): 'Colin's western farmstead'. OE *west*, 'western', + *tūn*, 'farmstead'. Nicholas de Segrave held the manor here in the 13C. (Colin is a pet form of Nicholas.) The village is 'west' with respect to EASTON ON THE HILL. DB *Westone*, 1309 *Colynweston*, 1868 *Colleyweston*.

Colnbrook (hamlet, Bucks): '(place by the) cool brook'. OE *cōl*, 'cool', + *brōc*, 'brook'. The name could also mean '(place by the) brook near the (river) Colne'. The stream called the Colne Brook here flows south parallel with the Colne to enter the Thames. 1107 *Colebroc*.

Colne (town, Lancs): '(place by the river) Colne'. The river has a pre-English name of uncertain meaning. The same name gave that of CALNE. 1124 *Calna*.

Colne (river). See COLCHESTER.

Colne Engaine (village, Essex): 'Engayne's (estate by the river) Colne'. For the river name, see COLCHESTER. The Engayne family held the manor here in medieval times, their name distinguishing this village from nearby *Earls Colne*, held by the earls of Oxford, *Wakes Colne*, held by the Wake family, and *White Colne*, held in 1086 by Dimidius Blancus, whose surname means 'white'. *c.*950 *Colne*, DB *Colun*, 1254 *Colum Engayne*.

Colney (village, Norfolk): 'Cola's island'. OE *ēg*, 'island'. The 'island' is raised ground by the river Yare here. DB *Coleneia*.

Colney Hatch (district, Barnet): 'Colney's hatch'. OE *hæcc*, 'hatchgate'. The name refers to a former gateway into Enfield Chase here, apparently owned by a family called Colney. 1492 *Colnehatche*.

Coln St Aldwyns (village, Glos): '(village on the river) Coln with St Athelwine's church'. The river has a pre-English name of uncertain meaning. The church dedication (now to St John the Baptist) distinguishes this village from *Coln St Dennis*, 6 miles to the northwest, with a church dedicated to St Denis of Paris, and nearby *Coln Rogers*, where the manor was held in the 11C by Roger of Gloucester. 962 *Cungle*, DB *Colne*, 12C *Culna Sancti Aylwini*.

Colonsay (island, Argyll & Bute): 'Kolbein's island'. OS *ey*, 'island'. The personal name is Scandinavian. 14C *Coluynsay*.

Colsterdale (hamlet, N Yorks): 'valley of the charcoal burners'. OE *colestre*, 'charcoal burner', + OE *dæl* or OS *dalr*, 'valley'. 1301 *Colserdale*.

Colsterworth (village, Lincs): 'enclosure of the charcoal burners'. OE *colestre*, 'charcoal burner', + *worth*, 'enclosure'. DB *Colsteuorde*.

Colston Bassett. See CAR COLSTON.

Coltishall (village, Norfolk): 'Cohhede's or Coccede's corner of land'. OE *halh*, 'nook', 'corner of land'. DB *Coketeshala*.

Colton (hamlet, Cumbria): 'farmstead on the (river) Cole'. OE *tūn*, 'farmstead'. The river name is Celtic in origin and of uncertain meaning. The stream is now known as Colton Beck. 1202 *Coleton*.

Colton (village, Norfolk): 'Cola's or Koli's farmstead'. OE *tūn*, 'farmstead'. The personal names are respectively OE and Scandinavian. DB *Coletuna*. SO ALSO: *Colton*, N Yorks.

Colton (village, Staffs): 'Cola's farmstead'. OE *tūn*, 'farmstead'. DB *Coltone*.

Colwall (village, Herefords): '(place by the) cool stream'. OE *cōl*, 'cool', + *wella*, 'spring', 'stream'. DB *Colewelle*.

Colwell (village, Northd): '(place by the) cool stream'. OE *cōl*, 'cool', + *wella*, 'spring', 'stream'. 1236 *Colewel*.

Colwich (village, Staffs): 'building where charcoal is made or kept'. OE *col*, 'coal', 'charcoal', + *wīc*, 'building', 'dwelling'. 1240 *Colewich*.

Colworth (village, W Sussex): 'Cola's enclosure'. OE *worth*, 'enclosure'. 10C *Coleworth*.

Colwyn Bay (resort town, Conwy): '(place on the) bay of the (river) Colwyn'. The river's name derives from Welsh *colwyn*, 'puppy', alluding to its small size. The name of the town added 'Bay' in the 19C partly to be distinguished from the nearby village of *Colwyn* (now *Old Colwyn*), partly to denote its seaside status. The town's Welsh name is *Bae Colwyn* (Welsh *bae*, 'bay'). 1334 *Coloyne*.

Colyford (village, Devon): '(place by the) ford over the (river) Coly'. OE *ford*, 'ford'. For the river name, see COLYTON. 1244 *Culyford*.

Colyton (town, Devon): 'farmstead by the (river) Coly'. OE *tūn*, 'farmstead'. The river has a Celtic name perhaps meaning 'narrow'. 946 *Culintona*, DB *Colitone*.

Combe (village, Oxon): '(place in the) valley'. OE *cumb*, 'valley'. The village was moved to its present hillside site from the nearby valley of the river Evenlode in the 14C. DB *Cumbe*.

Combe Florey (village, Somerset): 'de Flury's (estate in the) valley'. OE *cumb*, 'valley'. The de Flury family held the manor here in the 12C. 12C *Cumba*, 1291 *Cumbeflori*.

Combe Hay (village, Bath & NE Somerset): 'de Haweie's (estate in the) valley'. OE *cumb*. The de Haweie family held the manor here in the 13C. DB *Come*, 1249 *Cumbehawya*.

Combeinteignhead (village, Devon): '(place in the) valley in Tenhide'. OE *cumb*, 'valley'. The name of the district means 'ten hides' (OE *tēn*, 'ten', + *hīd*, 'hide'), denoting its extent. Cp. STOKEINTEIGNHEAD. The spelling has been influenced by the name of the nearby river Teign (see TEIGNMOUTH). DB *Comba*, 1227 *Cumbe in Tenhide*, 1868 *Combe-in-Teignhead*.

Combe Martin (village, Devon): 'Martin's (estate in the) valley'. OE *cumb*, 'valley'. Robert, the son of Martin, held the manor here in 1133. DB *Comba*, 1265 *Combe Martini*, 1868 *Combmartin*.

Combe Raleigh (village, Devon): 'de Ralegh's (estate in the) valley'. OE *cumb*, 'valley'. The de Ralegh family held the manor here in the 13C. 1237 *Cumba*, 1383 *Comberalegh*.

Comberbach (village, Cheshire): '(place by the) stream of the Britons'. OE *bece*, 'stream'. The first part of the name, referring to the (Ancient) Britons who lived here, is related to modern Welsh *Cymry*, 'the Welsh'. 12C *Combrebeche*.

Comberford (hamlet, Staffs): '(place by the) ford of the Britons'. The first part of the name is as for COMBERBACH. The second is OE *ford*, 'ford'. The river here is the Tame. 1187 *Cumbreford*.

Comberton (village, Cambs): 'Cumbra's farmstead'. OE *tūn*, 'farmstead'. DB *Cumbertone*.

Combe St Nicholas (village, Somerset): '(estate of) St Nicholas (in the) valley'. OE *cumb*, 'valley'. The manor here was held by the priory of St Nicholas, Exeter, and the church is dedicated to St Nicholas. DB *Cumbe*.

Combrook (village, Warwicks): '(place by the) brook in a valley'. OE *cumb*, 'valley', + *brōc*, 'brook'. The brook in question is the stream that flows down the valley of Compton Verney and passes the village. 1217 *Cumbroc*.

Combs (village, Suffolk): '(place by the) ridges'. OE *camb*, 'ridge'. The name may originally have been that of a region here, referring to the series of low ridges that run up to the river Gipping. DB *Cambas*.

Commondale (village, N Yorks): 'Colman's valley'. OS *dalr*, 'valley'. The personal name is Old Irish. 1272 *Colemandale*.

Compton (village, Surrey): 'farmstead in a valley'. OE *cumb*, 'valley', + *tūn*, 'farmstead', 'village'. The 'valley' is the slight depression in which the village lies, below the Hogs Back. DB *Contone*. SO ALSO: *Compton*, Hants, W Berks.

Compton Abbas (village, Dorset): 'abbess's farmstead in a valley'. OE *cumb*, 'valley', + *tūn*, 'farmstead', 'village', + Latin *abbatisse*, 'of the abbess'. The manor here was held early by Shaftesbury Abbey. The hamlet of *Compton Abbas* near Maiden Newton, with a name meaning 'abbot's farmstead in a valley' (it belonged to Milton Abbey), is now called *West Compton* for purposes of distinction. 956 *Cumtune*, DB *Cuntone*, 1293 *Cumpton Abbatisse*.

Compton Abdale (village, Glos): 'Apdale's farmstead in a valley'. OE *cumb*, 'valley', + *tūn*, 'farmstead', 'village'. The manor here was apparently held by a family called Apdale. DB *Contone*, 1504 *Apdale Compton*.

Compton Bassett (village, Wilts): 'Basset's farmstead in a valley'. OE *cumb*, 'valley', + *tūn*, 'farmstead', 'village'. The Basset family held the manor here in the 13C. DB *Contone*, 1228 *Cumptone Basset*.

Compton Beauchamp (village, Oxon): 'Beauchamp's farmstead in a valley'. OE *cumb*, 'valley', + *tūn*, 'farmstead', 'village'. The Beauchamp family held the manor here in the 13C. 955 *Cumtune*, DB *Contone*, 1236 *Cumton Beucamp*.

Compton Bishop (village, Somerset): 'bishop's farmstead in a valley'. OE *cumb*, 'valley', + *tūn*, 'farmstead', 'village'. The manor here was held early by the Bishop of Bath and Wells. The second word of the second form of the name below is Latin *episcopi*, 'of the bishop'. 1067 *Cumbtune*, 1332 *Compton Episcopi*.

Compton Chamberlayne (village, Wilts): 'Chamberlain's farmstead in a valley'. OE *cumb*, 'valley', + *tūn*, 'farmstead', 'village'. The Chamberlain family held the manor here from the 13C. DB *Contone*, 1316 *Compton Chamberleyne*.

Compton Dando (village, Bath & NE Somerset): 'de Auno's or Dauno's farmstead in a valley'. OE *cumb*, 'valley', + *tūn*, 'farmstead', 'village'. The de Auno or Dauno family held the manor here in the 12C. DB *Contone*, 1256 *Cumton Daunon*.

Compton Martin (village, Bath & NE Somerset): 'Martin's farmstead in a valley'. OE *cumb*, 'valley', + *tūn*, 'farmstead', 'village'. The son of one Martin de Tours held the manor here in the early 12C. DB *Comtone*, 1228 *Cumpton Martin*.

Compton Pauncefoot (village, Somerset): 'Pauncefote's farmstead in a valley'. OE *cumb*, 'valley', + *tūn*, 'farmstead', 'village'. The manor here was held by the Pauncefote family. DB *Cuntone*, 1291 *Cumpton Paunceuot*.

Compton Valence (village, Dorset): 'de Valencia's farmstead in a valley'. OE *cumb*, 'valley', + *tūn*, 'farmstead', 'village'. The manor here was held in the 13C by William de Valencia, Earl of Pembroke. DB *Contone*, 1280 *Compton Valance*.

Compton Wynyates (hamlet, Warwicks): 'farmstead in a valley with a windy pass'. OE *cumb*, 'valley', + *tūn*, 'farmstead', 'estate', + *wind-geat*, 'windy pass' (*wind*, 'wind', + *geat*, 'gate', 'pass'). The hamlet lies in a valley or hollow surrounded by low hills. DB *Contone*, 1242 *Cumpton Wincate*, 1868 *Compton Wyniates*, or *Compton-in-the-Hole*.

Comrie (village, Perth & Kin): '(place at the) confluence'. Gaelic *comar*, 'confluence'. The village stands at the junction of Glen Artney (valley of the Ruchill Water), Glen Lednock (valley of the river Lednock) and Strathearn (valley of the river Earn). 1268 *Comry*.

Conanby. See CONISBROUGH.

Concangis. See CHESTER-LE-STREET.

Condate. See NORTHWICH.

Condercum. See BENWELL.

Conderton (village, Worcs): 'farmstead of the Kent dwellers'. OE *Cantware*, 'Kent dwellers', + *tūn*, 'farmstead'. Cp. CANTERBURY. The settlement here must have been established by migrants from Kent. 875 *Cantuaretun*, 1201 *Canterton*.

Condicote (village, Glos): 'cottage associated with Cunda'. OE *-ing-*, 'associated with', + *cot*, 'cottage'. *c*.1052 *Cundicotan*, DB *Condicote*.

Condover (village, Shropshire): '(place by the) flat-topped ridge by Cound Brook'. OE *ofer*, 'flat-topped ridge'. There is a slight ridge here. For the river name, see COUND. DB *Conedoure*.

Coneysthorpe (village, N Yorks): 'king's farmstead'. OS *konungr*, 'king', + *thorp*, 'farmstead'. DB *Coningestorp*.

Coney Weston (village, Suffolk): 'royal estate'. OS *konungr*, 'king', + OE *tūn*, 'farmstead', 'manor', 'estate'. The suggestion of 'west' is misleading, and the name overall is essentially the equivalent of *Kingston*. Cp. CONGERSTONE, CONISTONE. DB *Cunegestuna*.

Congerstone (village, Leics): 'king's manor'. OS *konungr*, 'king', + OE *tūn*, 'farmstead', 'manor'. DB *Cuningestone*.

Congham (village, Norfolk): 'homestead by the round-topped hill'. OE *cung*, 'steep round hill', + *hām*, 'homestead', 'village'. DB *Congheham*.

Congleton (town, Cheshire): 'farmstead at the round-topped hill'. OE *cung*, 'steep round hill', + *hyll*, 'hill', + *tūn*, 'farmstead'. It is not certain which of the hills here is the one in question. The DB form of the name below has omitted the first *n*. DB *Cogeltone*, 13C *Congulton*.

Congresbury (village, N Somerset): 'fortified place associated with (St) Congar'. OE *burh*, 'fortified place', 'manor'. The 6C Welsh saint Congar is said to be buried here. 9C *Cungresbyri*, DB *Cungresberie*.

Coningsby (village, Lincs): 'king's village'. OS *konungr*, 'king', + *bý*, 'village'. DB *Cuningesbi*.

Conington (village, Cambs): 'king's manor'. OS *konungr*, 'king', + OE *tūn*, 'manor', 'estate'. The forms of the name below are for Conington near Sawtry, but Conington near St Ives has a name of identical origin. 10C *Cunningtune*, DB *Cunitone*.

Conisbrough (town, Doncaster): 'king's fortification'. OS *konungr*, 'king', + OE *burh*, 'fortified place'. Conisbrough was one of a series of forts along the valley of the river Don, the fort itself probably being on Castle Hill here. The 12C chronicler Geoffrey of Monmouth referred to Conisbrough as '*oppidum Kaerconan quod nunc Cuningeburg appellatur*' ('the town Kaerconan which is now called Conisbrough'), with *Kaerconan* since popularly taken to mean 'Conan's town'. (The name was really Geoffrey's misinterpretation of *Cuningesburh*.) This name was adopted for *Conanby*, a housing estate to the west of Conisbrough. *c*.1003 *Cunugesburh*, DB *Coningesburg*.

Conisholme (village, Lincs): 'island of the king'. OS *konungr*, 'king', + *holmr*, 'island'. The 'island' is raised ground in marshland here. 1195 *Cuninggesholm*.

Coniston (village, Cumbria): 'king's manor'. os *konungr*, 'king', + OE *tūn*, 'farmstead', 'estate', 'manor'. 12C *Coningeston*. SO ALSO: *Coniston*, E Yorks.

Coniston Cold (village, N Yorks): 'bleak royal manor'. os *konungr*, 'king', + OE *tūn*, 'farmstead', 'estate', 'manor', + OE *cald*, 'cold'. The second word of the name, referring to the village's exposed situation, distinguishes it from CONISTONE, 9 miles to the northeast. DB *Cuningestone*, 1202 *Calde Cuningeston*, 1868 *Cold Coniston*.

Conistone (village, N Yorks): 'king's manor'. os *konungr*, 'king', + OE *tūn*, 'farmstead', 'estate', 'manor'. DB *Cunestune*.

Connah's Quay (town and port, Flints): 'Connah's quay'. The identity of Connah is uncertain. He may have been the local innkeeper. The actual pier here was known in the 19C as the New Quay. 1791 *Connas Quay*.

Cononley (village, N Yorks): '(place by the) wood or clearing'. OE *lēah*, 'wood', 'clearing'. The origin of the first part of the name is uncertain. It may represent an old Celtic river name or an Old Irish personal name. DB *Cutnelai*, 12C *Conanlia*.

Consett (town, Durham): 'headland of Conek'. OE *hēafod*, 'headland'. The hill name *Conek* is from a Celtic (or pre-Celtic) word meaning simply 'hill' (modern Welsh *cnwc*, 'hillock'). Consett lies on a prominent hill. 1183 *Conekesheued*, 1385 *Conkeshed*.

Constable Burton (village, N Yorks): 'fortified farmstead of the constable'. OE *burh-tūn* (from *burh*, 'fortified place', + *tūn*, 'farmstead'). The manor here was held in the 12C by the constables of Richmond Castle. DB *Bortone*, 1301 *Burton Constable*.

Constantine (village, Cornwall): '(church of) St Constantine'. The church here is dedicated to the little-known saint Constantine, commemorated as a 'king and martyr'. DB *Sanctus Constantinus*, 1441 *Costentyn*.

Conwy (resort town, Conwy): '(place on the river) Conwy'. The river name, of Celtic origin and meaning 'reedy one', gave the name of *Canovium*, the Roman town at Caerhun, 4 miles to the south. Conwy was formerly known as *Aberconwy* (Welsh *aber*, 'mouth'), and the anglicized form *Conway* was long current for the town. 12C *Conguoy*, 12C *Aberconuy*, 1698 *Conway als. Aberconway*, 1868 *Conway, or Conwy*.

Cooden (resort district of Bexhill, E Sussex): '(settlement of) Cōda's people'. OE *-ingas*, 'peo-ple of'. The name is now familiar for *Cooden Beach*. 1291 *Codinges*.

Cookbury (village, Devon) 'Cuca's fortification'. OE *burh*, 'fortified place'. 1242 *Cukebyr*.

Cookham (village, Windsor & Maid): 'cook village'. OE *cōc*, 'cook', + *hām*, 'village'. The name implies a village noted for its cooks. The first part of the name could also be 'hill' (OE *cōc*), perhaps referring to Cookham Rise, to the west. 798 *Coccham*, DB *Cocheham*.

Cookhill (village, Worcs): '(place on the) hill'. OE *cōc*, 'hill', + *hyll*, 'hill'. The second part of the name was added to the first when the latter was no longer understood. 1156 *Cochilla*.

Cookley (hamlet, Suffolk): 'Cuca's wood or clearing'. OE *lēah*, 'wood', 'clearing'. The name could also mean 'wood or clearing where the cuckoo is heard' (OE *cucu*, 'cuckoo', + *lēah*). DB *Cokelei*, late 12C *Kukeleia*.

Cookley (village, Worcs): '(place by) Cūlna's cliff'. OE *clif*, 'cliff'. The 'cliff' is above the river Stour here. 964 *Culnan clif*, 11C *Culleclive*.

Cooling (village, Medway): '(settlement of) Cūl's or Cūla's people'. OE *-ingas*, 'people of'. 808 *Culingas*, DB *Colinges*.

Coombe Bissett (village, Wilts): 'Biset's (estate in the) valley'. OE *cumb*, 'valley'. The Biset family held the manor here in the 12C. DB *Come*, 1288 *Coumbe Byset*.

Coombe Keynes (village, Dorset): 'de Cahaignes' (estate in the) valley'. OE *cumb*, 'valley'. The de Cahaignes family held the manor here in the 12C. DB *Cume*, 1299 *Combe Kaynes*.

Copdock (village, Suffolk): '(place by the) lopped oak tree'. OE *copped*, 'polled', 'lopped' (from *copp*, 'top'), + *āc*, 'oak'. A 'lopped' oak is one with its top removed. 1195 *Coppedoc*.

Copeland Forest (region of fells, Cumbria): 'purchased land'. os *kaupa-land* (from *kaupa*, 'to buy', + *land*, 'land'). See COUPLAND. *Copeland*, now the name of the local council district, was originally that of the barony here that later became the ward of *Allerdale-above-Derwent* (cp. ALLERDALE). c.1282 *foreste de Coupland*.

Copford Green (village, Essex): '(place by) Coppa's ford'. OE *ford*, 'ford'. The river here is the Roman. The village later became associated with its green. 995 *Coppanforda*, DB *Copeforda*.

Copmanthorpe (village, York): 'outlying farmstead of the merchants'. os *kaup-mathr*, 'merchant' (from *kaup*, 'trade', + *mathr*, 'man'), + *thorp*, 'outlying farmstead'. The first part of the name represents OS *kaup-manna*, the genitive plural form of *kaup-mathr*. DB *Copeman Torp*.

Coppenhall (village, Staffs): 'Coppa's corner of land'. OE *halh*, 'nook', 'corner of land'. DB *Copehale*.

Copplestone (village, Devon): '(place by the) peaked stone'. OE *copel*, 'crest', 'peak', + *stān*, 'stone'. The reference is to the standing stone here, which may have originally been a boundary stone. Copplestone lies at the meeting point of three parishes. 974 *Copelan stan*.

Coppull (village, Lancs): '(place by the) hill with a peak'. OE *copp*, 'peak', + *hyll*, 'hill'. The name is something of a mystery, as the region here is flat. 1218 *Cophill*.

Copt Hewick (village, N Yorks): 'high dairy farm with a peak'. OE *copped*, 'having a peak', + *hēah*, 'high', + *wīc*, 'dairy farm'. The village stands on a hill. The first word of the name distinguishes it from nearby *Bridge Hewick*, with a bridge taking the road to Ripon (now the B6265) over the river Ure. DB *Heawic*, 1208 *Coppedehaiwic*.

Coquet (river). See COQUETDALE.

Coquetdale (region, Northd): 'valley of the (river) Coquet'. OE *dæl*, 'valley'. The river takes its name from *Cockwooddale*, 'Cockwood valley', where *Cockwood*, the name of a former forest here, means 'wood where woodcock are seen' (OE *cocc*, 'cockbird', 'woodcock', + *wudu*, 'wood'). *c*.1160 *Cokedale*.

Corbridge (town, Northd): 'bridge near Corchester'. OE *brycg*, 'bridge'. *Corchester* is the local name for the nearby Roman town of *Corstopitum*, whose own name is of Celtic origin but unknown meaning. *c*.1050 *Corebricg*.

Corby (town, Northants): 'Kori's village'. OS *bý*, 'village'. The personal name is Scandinavian. DB *Corbei*.

Corby Glen (village, Lincs): 'Kori's village on the (river) Glen'. OS *bý*, 'village'. The personal name is Scandinavian. The river name, of Celtic origin and meaning 'clean one', was added to the original village name in 1959 for distinction from CORBY, Northants, 25 miles to the south. DB *Corbi*.

Coreley (hamlet, Shropshire): 'woodland clearing where cranes are seen'. OE *corn*, 'crane', + *lēah*, 'wood', 'clearing'. DB *Cornelie*.

Corfe (village, Somerset): '(place by the) pass'. OE *corf*, 'pass', 'gap'. Corfe is situated by a pass in a steep ridge. 1243 *Corf*.

Corfe Castle (village, Dorset): '(place in a) pass with a castle'. OE *corf*, 'cutting', 'pass'. Corfe Castle, with its Norman castle, lies in a gap of the Purbeck Hills. The second word of the name distinguishes the village from CORFE MULLEN, 11 miles to the north. 955 *Corf*, 1302 *Corffe Castell*.

Corfe Mullen (village, Dorset): '(place in a) pass with a mill'. OE *corf*, 'cutting', 'pass', + OF *molin*, 'mill'. Corfe Mullen lies between two hills. The second word of the name, referring to a valuable mill here, distinguishes the village from CORFE CASTLE, 11 miles to the south. DB *Corf*, 1176 *Corf le Mulin*.

Corfton (village, Shropshire): 'settlement by the (river) Corve'. OE *tūn*, 'farmstead', 'village'. The river name derives from OE *corf*, 'valley', 'pass'. DB *Cortune*, 1222 *Corfton*.

Corhampton (village, Hants): 'estate where grain is produced'. OE *corn*, 'grain', 'corn', + *hām-tūn*, 'home farm', 'estate'. 1201 *Cornhamton*.

Corinium. See CIRENCESTER.

Corley (village, Warwicks): '(place by the) clearing where cranes are seen'. OE *corn*, 'crane', + *lēah*, 'wood', 'clearing'. DB *Cornelie*.

Corney (hamlet, Cumbria): 'island where cranes are seen'. OE *corn*, 'crane', + *ēg*, 'island'. The 'island' here is the long promontory on which Corney stands amid wet land. 12C *Corneia*.

Cornforth (village, Durham): '(place by the) ford where cranes are seen'. OE *corn*, 'crane', + *ford*, 'ford'. 1116 *Corneford*.

Cornhill-on-Tweed (village, Northd): 'corner of land where cranes are seen by the (river) Tweed'. OE *corn*, 'crane', + *halh*, 'nook', 'corner of land'. For the river name, see BERWICK-UPON-TWEED. 12C *Cornehale*.

Cornwall (county, SW England): '(territory of the) Cornovii Britons'. OE *walh*, '(Ancient) Briton', 'foreigner'. The name of the Cornovii is of Celtic origin and means 'horn people' (modern Welsh and Irish *corn*, 'horn'), referring to the long peninsula that is Cornwall, the 'horn' of Britain. The Cornish name of Cornwall is *Kernow*, of the same origin. *c*.705 *Cornubia*, 891 *Cornwalas*, DB *Cornualia*.

Cornwell (hamlet, Oxon): '(place by the) stream where cranes are seen'. OE *corn*, 'crane', + *wella*, 'spring', 'stream'. DB *Cornewelle*.

Cornwood (village, Devon): 'wood where cranes are seen'. OE *corn*, 'crane', + *wudu*, 'wood'. The DB form of the name below has miscopied *u* as *h*. DB *Cornehuda*.

Cornworthy (village, Devon): 'enclosure where cranes are seen'. OE *corn*, 'crane', +

worthig, 'enclosure'. The name could also mean 'enclosure where corn is grown' (OE *corn*, 'corn', + *worthig*). DB *Corneorda*.

Corpusty (village, Norfolk): '(place by the) path where ravens are seen'. OS *korpr*, 'raven', + *stígr*, 'path'. The name could also mean '(place by) Korpr's path', with a Scandinavian personal name. DB *Corpestih*.

Corringham (village, Lincs): 'homestead of Cora's people'. OE *-inga-*, 'of the people of', + *hām*, 'homestead'. DB *Coringeham*.

Corringham (town, Thurrock): 'homestead of Curra's people'. OE *-inga-*, 'of the people of', + *hām*, 'homestead'. DB *Currincham*.

Corscombe (village, Dorset): '(place in the) valley of the road in the pass'. OE *corf*, 'pass', + *weg*, 'way', 'road', + *cumb*, 'valley'. As with CROS-COMBE, Somerset, early forms of the name do not support this reading, and its origin and meaning are open to doubt. 1014 *Corigescumb*, DB *Coriescumbe*.

Corsham (town, Wilts): 'Cosa's or Cossa's homestead'. OE *hām*, 'homestead', 'village'. The *r* probably entered under Norman influence, and the name might otherwise have been identical with that of COSHAM. 1001 *Coseham*, DB *Cosseham*, 1868 *Corsham, or Corsham Regis*.

Corsley (village, Wilts): 'wood or clearing by the marsh'. The first part of the name is Celtic, from a word related to modern Welsh *cors*, 'bog', 'swamp'. The second part is OE *lēah*, 'wood', 'clearing'. DB *Corselie*.

Corston (village, Bath & NE Somerset): 'farmstead on Gauze Brook'. OE *tūn*, 'farmstead', 'estate'. The river name is of Celtic origin and means 'swamp', 'bog' (modern Welsh *cors*). Cp. CORSLEY. 941 *Corsantune*, DB *Corstune*.

Corstorphine (district, Edinburgh): 'Thorfinn's crossing'. OS *kros*, 'cross'. The name relates to the crossing of a water barrier here. The personal name is Scandinavian. *c*.1140 *Crostorfin*.

Corton (resort village, Suffolk): 'Kári's farmstead'. OE *tūn*, 'farmstead'. The personal name is Scandinavian. DB *Karetuna*.

Corton Denham (village, Somerset): 'de Dinan's farmstead by a pass'. OE *corf*, 'pass', 'gap', + *tūn*, 'farmstead', 'village'. The village, where the de Dinan family held the manor in the 13C, lies by a pass in a steep ridge. DB *Corfetone*.

Corwen (town, Denb): 'sanctuary stone'. Welsh *côr*, 'sanctuary', + *maen*, 'stone'. The

church in Corwen has a reputedly ancient stone called Carreg-y-Big ('pointed stone') built into the porch, and this may be the 'sanctuary stone'. The first part of the name could also mean 'small' (Welsh *cor*). 1254 *Corvaen*, 14C *Korvaen*, 1443 *Corwen*.

Coryton (hamlet, Devon): 'farmstead on the (river) Curi'. OE *tūn*, 'farmstead'. The former name of the river Lyd here is pre-English and of uncertain origin. *c*.970 *Curitun*, DB *Coriton*.

Coryton (town, Thurrock): 'Cory's town'. The name is modern, and derives from the oil refinery established here in 1922 by Messrs Cory Brothers & Co.

Cosby (village, Leics): 'Cossa's farmstead'. OS *bý*, 'farmstead', 'village'. DB *Cossebi*.

Coseley (district, Dudley): 'clearing of the charcoal burners'. OE *colestre*, 'charcoal burner' (from *col*, 'coal', 'charcoal'), + *lēah*, 'clearing'. 1357 *Colseley*.

Cosgrove (village, Northants): 'Cōf's grove'. OE *grāf*, 'grove'. DB *Covesgrave*.

Cosham (town, Portsmouth): 'Cossa's homestead or enclosure'. OE *hām*, 'homestead', or *hamm*, 'enclosure'. Cp. CORSHAM. DB *Cosseham*.

Cossall (village, Notts): 'Cott's corner of land'. OE *halh*, 'nook', 'corner of land'. DB *Coteshale*.

Cossington (village, Leics): 'estate associated with Cosa or Cusa'. OE *-ing-*, 'associated with', + *tūn*, 'farmstead', 'estate'. DB *Cosintone*. SO ALSO: *Cossington*, Somerset.

Costessy (village, Norfolk): 'Cost's island'. OE *ēg*, 'island'. The 'island' would be dry ground by the river Wensum here. The personal name could be OE or Scandinavian. DB *Costeseia*, 1868 *Cossey, or Costessy*.

Costock (village, Notts): 'outlying farmstead of Cort's people'. OE *-inga-*, 'of the people of', + *stoc*, 'outlying farmstead'. The original *-inga-* has disappeared. DB *Cortingestoche*, 1868 *Cortlingstock, or Costock*.

Coston (hamlet, Leics): 'Kátr's farmstead'. OE *tūn*, 'farmstead'. The personal name is Scandinavian. DB *Castone*.

Cotehele House (manor house, Cornwall): 'house by the wood on an estuary'. Cornish *coes* (earlier *cuit*), 'wood', + *heyl*, 'estuary'. The house stands on a well-wooded site by the Tamar estuary. *c*.1286 *Cotehulle*, 1305 *Cotehele*.

Cotes (hamlet, Leics): 'cottages'. OE *cot*, 'cottage'. 12C *Cothes*. SO ALSO: *Cotes*, Staffs.

Cotesbach (village, Leics): '(place by) Cott's stream'. OE *bece* or *bæce*, 'stream'. The OE words imply a stream in a valley. DB *Cotesbece*.

Cotgrave (village, Notts): 'Cotta's grove'. OE *grāf*, 'grove'. The DB form of the name below has a miscopied *C-* as *G-*. DB *Godegrave*, 1094 *Cotegrava*.

Cotham (village, Notts): '(place at the) cottages'. OE *cot*, 'cottage'. The name represents OE *cotum*, the dative plural form of *cot*. DB *Cotune*.

Cothelstone (hamlet, Somerset): 'Cūthwulf's farmstead'. OE *tūn*, 'farmstead'. 1327 *Cothelestone*.

Cotherstone (village, Durham): 'Cūthhere's farmstead'. OE *tūn*, 'farmstead'. The place has been popularly linked with St Cuthbert, to whom the church here is dedicated. DB *Codrestune*.

Cotleigh (village, Devon): 'Cotta's clearing'. OE *lēah*, 'wood', 'clearing'. DB *Coteleia*.

Coton (village, Cambs): '(place at the) cottages'. OE *cot*, 'cottage'. The name represents OE *cotum*, the dative plural form of *cot*. DB *Cotis*. SO ALSO: *Coton*, Northants, Staffs (near Stone).

Coton Clanford (hamlet, Staffs): '(place at the) cottages by Clanford'. OE *cot*, 'cottage'. *Clanford* is the name of a local place in nearby Seighford meaning 'clean ford' (OE *clǣne*, 'clean', + *ford*, 'ford'). Coton Clanford itself stands on Clanford Brook. DB *Cote*.

Coton in the Elms (village, Derbys): '(place at the) cottages in the elms'. OE *cot*, 'cottage'. The main name represents OE *cotum*, the dative plural form of *cot*. The second part of the name refers to the abundance of elms here. DB *Cotune*, 1868 *Coton-in-the-Elms*.

Cotswolds (hill range, Glos): 'Cōd's high forest'. OE *wald*, 'woodland', 'high forest'. See WOLDS. The name would have originally applied to a particular part of the range, then spread to the whole region. 12C *Codesuualt*.

Cottam (hamlet, E Yorks): '(place by the) cottages'. OE *cot*, 'cottage'. The name represents OE *cotum*, the dative plural form of *cot*. DB *Cottun*. SO ALSO: *Cottam*, Lancs, Notts.

Cottenham (village, Cambs): 'Cotta's homestead'. OE *hām*, 'homestead', 'village'. 948 *Cotenham*, DB *Coteham*.

Cottered (village, Herts): '(place by the) stream'. OE *rīth*, 'stream'. The first part of the name is of uncertain origin. OE *cōd*, 'fish spawn', has been suggested, but it seems unlikely that the small stream here would have been described in terms of its fish spawn. The DB

form of the name below is corrupt. DB *Chodrei*, 1220 *Codreth*.

Cotterstock (village, Northants): 'dairy farm'. OE *corther-stoc* (from *corther*, 'troop', 'band', + *stoc*, 'place'). DB *Codestoche*, 12C *Cotherstoke*.

Cottesbrooke (village, Northants): '(place by) Cott's brook'. OE *brōc*, 'brook'. DB *Cotesbroc*.

Cottesmore (village, Rutland): 'Cott's moor'. OE *mōr*, 'moor'. c.976 *Cottesmore*, DB *Cotesmore*.

Cottingham (town, E Yorks): 'homestead of Cott's or Cotta's people'. OE *-inga-*, 'of the people of', + *hām*, 'homestead'. DB *Cotingeham*. SO ALSO: *Cottingham*, Northants.

Cottisford (hamlet, Oxon): '(place by) Cott's ford'. OE *ford*, 'ford'. DB *Cotesforde*.

Cotwalton (hamlet, Staffs): 'farmstead by Cotta's wood'. OE *wald*, 'wood', + *tūn*, 'farmstead'. The name could also mean 'farmstead by Cotta's stream' (OE *wælla*, 'stream', + *tūn*). 1002 *Cotewaltun*, DB *Cotewoldestune*.

Coughton (village, Warwicks): 'farmstead by the hillock'. OE *cocc*, 'hillock', + *tūn*, 'farmstead'. DB *Coctune*.

Coulsdon (district, Croydon): 'Cūthræd's hill'. OE *dūn*, 'hill'. Celticists prefer to derive the first part of the name from a word related to modern Welsh *côl*, 'bosom' (apparently from Latin *culleus*, 'leather bag', 'sack for holding liquids'), so that the sense is '(place at the) hill (called) Cull', itself so named from its rounded shape. The hill in question lies to the south of the town. DB *Colesdone*.

Coulston (village, Wilts): 'Cufel's farmstead'. OE *tūn*, 'farmstead'. The village is formally *East Coulston* but has been known by the main name alone after subsuming the adjacent *West Coulston*. DB *Covelestone*.

Coulton (hamlet, N Yorks): 'farmstead where charcoal is made'. OE *col*, 'charcoal', + *tūn*, 'farmstead'. DB *Coltune*.

Cound (hamlet, Shropshire): '(place on the) Cound Brook'. The river name is Celtic in origin with an uncertain meaning. DB *Cuneet*.

Coundon (village, Durham): '(place by the) hill where cows are pastured'. OE *cū*, 'cow', + *dūn*, 'hill'. The first part of the name represents OE *cūna*, the genitive plural form of *cū*. 1196 *Cundun*.

Countess Wear (district of Exeter, Devon): '(place by the) countess's weir'. The name refers to Isabella de Fortibus, Countess of Devon, who held the manor of Topsham in the 13C. She is said to have built a weir over the river Exe here to spite the trade of the city of Exeter after being offended by its citizens over some minor incident.

Countesthorpe (village, Leics): 'outlying settlement held by a countess'. ME *contesse*, 'countess', + OS *thorp*, 'secondary settlement', 'outlying hamlet'. 1209 *Torp*, 1242 *Cuntastorp*.

Countisbury (hamlet, Devon): 'fortified place at Cunet'. OE *burh*, 'fortified place'. *Cunet* is a Celtic hill name of uncertain meaning. DB *Contesberie*.

Coupar Angus (town, Perth & Kin): 'community in Angus'. Gaelic *comh-phàirt*, 'community'. The first word of the name is of conjectural origin, but the second locates this place in ANGUS, as distinct from CUPAR in Fife.

Coupland (hamlet, Northd): 'purchased land'. OS *kaupa-land* (from *kaupa*, 'to buy', + *land*, 'land'). The OS term applied to land that had been bought, as distinct from *óthals-jorth*, land that was acquired by customary law. 1242 *Coupland*.

Cove (village, Devon): '(place by the) shelter'. OE *cofa*, 'shelter' (modern English *cove*). 1242 *La Kove*. SO ALSO: *Cove*, Hants.

Covehithe. See NORTH COVE.

Coven (village, Staffs): '(place by the) shelters'. OE *cofa*, 'shelter'. The 'shelters' here are recesses in the steep hillside. The name represents OE *cofum*, the dative plural form of *cofa*. DB *Cove*.

Coveney (village, Cambs): 'Cofa's island'. OE *ēg*, 'island'. The name could also mean 'island in the bay' (OE *cofa*, 'cove', 'bay'). Coveney, in the Bedford Level, was at one time a real island, perhaps in a bay now represented by the West Fen. c.1060 *Coueneia*.

Covenham St Mary (village, Lincs): 'Cofa's homestead with St Mary's church'. OE *hām*, 'homestead'. The basic name could also mean 'homestead with a shelter' (OE *cofa*, 'hut', 'shelter', + *hām*). The church dedication distinguishes this Covenham from nearby *Covenham St Bartholomew*. DB *Covenham*.

Coventry (city, Coventry): 'Cofa's tree'. OE *trēow*, 'tree'. The tree would have had some special function or significance. The popular derivation of the name from *convent*, still found in some modern guidebooks, has its own spurious pedigree: '[It] took its name of Coventry from the convent round which it gathered' (Mandell Creighton, *The Story of Some English Shires*, 1897). 1043 *Couentre*, DB *Couentreu*.

Coverack (coastal village, Cornwall): '(place on the river) Coverack'. The name was no doubt originally that of the stream that emerges at the

cove here. Its meaning is unknown. The form of the name below has added Cornish *porth*, 'cove', 'harbour'. 1262 *Porthcovrec*.

Coverham (hamlet, N Yorks): 'homestead on the (river) Cover'. OE *hām*, 'homestead', 'village'. The river name is Celtic in origin but of uncertain meaning. DB *Covreham*.

Cowbit (village, Lincs): '(place by the) river bend where cows are pastured'. OE *cū*, 'cow', + *byht*, 'bend' (modern English *bight*). The village lies in a bend of the river Welland. 1267 *Coubiht*.

Cowbridge (town, Vale of Glam): '(place by the) cattle bridge'. OE *cū*, 'cow', + *brycg*, 'bridge'. The bridge would have been used by cows on their way to market. The Welsh name of Cowbridge is *Y Bont-Faen*, 'the stone bridge', referring to another bridge nearby. 1263 *Coubrugge*, c.1500 *Bontvaen*.

Cowden (village, Kent): 'pasture for cows'. OE *cū*, 'cow', + *denn*, 'pasture'. c.1100 *Cudena*.

Cowdenbeath (town, Fife): 'Cowden's (place in the) birch trees'. Gaelic *beith*, 'birch'. 1626 *terris de Baithe-Moubray alias Cowdounes-baithe*.

Cowes (resort town, IoW): '(place by the) Cows'. OE *cū*, 'cow'. The name refers to two former sandbanks in the Medina estuary here, recorded in 1413 as *Estcowe* and *Westcowe*, and known jointly as 'The Cows' from their fancied resemblance to this animal. The names were then transferred to the two settlements either side of the estuary, *East Cowes* and *West Cowes*, the latter becoming the Cowes of today.

Cowesby (village, N Yorks): 'Kausi's farmstead'. OS *bý*, 'farmstead', 'village'. The personal name is Scandinavian. DB *Cahosbi*.

Cowfold (village, W Sussex): 'enclosure for cows'. OE *cū*, 'cow', + *fald*, 'fold', 'pen'. 1232 *Coufaud*.

Cow Honeybourne. See HONEYBOURNE.

Cowley (village, Glos): '(place in the) clearing where cows are pastured'. OE *cū*, 'cow', + *lēah*, 'wood', 'clearing'. DB *Kulege*.

Cowley (district, Hillingdon): 'Cofa's clearing'. OE *lēah*, 'wood', 'clearing'. 959 *Cofenlea*, DB *Covelie*.

Cowley (district of Oxford, Oxon): 'Cofa's or Cufa's clearing'. OE *lēah*, 'wood', 'clearing'. 1004 *Couelea*, DB *Covelie*.

Cowling (hamlet, N Yorks). The hamlet, near Bedale, was originally *Thornton*, 'farmstead where thorn bushes grow' (OE *thorn*, 'thorn bush', + *tūn*, 'farmstead'). It then became *Thornton Colling*, from a person or family called Colling who owned land here. The first word of the name was then dropped. DB *Torneton*, 1202 *Thornton Colling*, 1400 *Collyng*, 1572 *Cowling*.

Cowling (village, N Yorks): 'place by a hill'. OE *coll*, 'hill', + *-ing*, 'place characterized by'. This is Cowling near Colne, where the hill in question is Cowling Hill. DB *Collinghe*.

Cowlinge (village, Suffolk): 'place associated with Cūl or Cūla'. OE *-ing*, 'place associated with'. DB *Culinge*.

Cowpen Bewley (district, Stockton): '(place by the) coops belonging to Bewley'. OE *cūpe*, 'coop', 'basket'. The first word of the name represents OE *cūpum*, the dative plural form of *cūpe*, referring to baskets for catching fish in the streams of the Tees estuary. The second word names the manor of *Bewley*, 'beautiful place' (cp. BEWLEY CASTLE). *c*.1150 *Cupum*.

Cowplain (district of Waterlooville, Hants): '(forest) plain where cows are pastured'. The name is modern. 1859 *Cow-plain*.

Coxhoe (village, Durham): 'Cocc's hill spur'. OE *hōh*, 'hill spur'. The spur in question is the high ground to the east of the village where the former Coxhoe Hall stood (the birthplace of Elizabeth Barrett Browning). 1277 *Cokeshow*.

Coxley (village, Somerset): 'cook's wood or clearing'. OE *cōc*, 'cook', + *lēah*, 'wood', 'clearing'. The wife of a cook in the royal household is recorded as holding lands here in 1086. 1207 *Cokesleg*.

Coxwell. See GREAT COXWELL.

Coxwold (village, N Yorks): 'woodland where cuckoos are heard'. OE *cucu*, 'cuckoo', + *wald*, 'woodland', 'forest'. The first form of the name below is apparently irregular. 758 *Cuhawalda*, DB *Cucualt*, 1154 *Cukewald*.

Crackenthorpe (village, Cumbria): 'Krakandi's outlying farmstead'. OS *thorp*, 'outlying farmstead'. The personal name is Scandinavian. The name could also mean 'outlying farmstead where crows are seen' (OE *crāca*, 'crow', genitive plural *crācena*, + OS *thorp*). late 12C *Cracantorp*.

Crackington Haven (resort village, Cornwall): 'harbour at Crackington'. OE *hæfen*, 'harbour'. *Crackington*, the name of a nearby manor, means 'farmstead at Crak' (OE *tūn*, 'farmstead'), with *Crak* from Cornish *crag*, 'sandstone'. *c*.1170 *Cracumtona*, 1358 *Crakamphavene*, 1813 *Crackington Horn*.

Cracoe (village, N Yorks): '(place on the) hill spur where ravens are seen'. OS *krāka*, 'raven', + OE *hōh*, 'hill spur'. The second part of the name could also represent OS *haugr*, 'hill'. 12C *Crakehou*.

Cradley (village, Herefords): 'Creoda's woodland clearing'. OE *lēah*, 'wood', 'clearing'. DB *Credelaie*.

Crafthole (village, Cornwall): 'hill with an enclosure'. OE *croft*, 'enclosure', + *hyll*, 'hill'. The first form of the name below has added OE *burh*, 'fortified place', 'borough'. 1314 *Croftilberwe*, 1348 *Crofthol*.

Crail (resort town, Fife): 'rocky place'. Gaelic *carr*, 'rock', + *all*, 'rock'. The two Gaelic words have blended in the name and refer to the craggy coast here and the Carr Rocks off it. *c*.1150 *Cherel*, 1153 *Caraile*.

Crambe (village, N Yorks): '(place by the) river bends'. OE *cramb*, 'crook', 'bend'. The name represents OE *crambum*, the dative plural form of *cramb*. The village lies by a winding stretch of the river Derwent. DB *Crambom*.

Cramlington (town, Northd): 'farmstead of the people at the spring where cranes are seen'. OE *cran*, 'crane', + *wella*, 'spring', + *-inga-*, 'of the dwellers at', + *tūn*, 'farmstead'. Cp. CRANWELL. *c*.1130 *Cramlingtuna*.

Cranage (village, Cheshire): '(place by the) boggy stream where crows are seen'. OE *crāwe*, 'crow', + *lǣc*, 'bog', 'stream'. The '-n-' of the name comes from OE *crāwena*, the genitive plural form of *crāwe*. The DB form of the name below is corrupt. DB *Croeneche*, 12C *Cranlach*.

Cranborne (village, Dorset): '(place by the) stream where cranes are seen'. OE *cran*, 'crane', + *burna*, 'stream'. The stream here is the Crane, named after the village, which also gave the name of *Cranborne Chase* (ME *chace*, 'area of unenclosed land reserved for hunting'). DB *Creneburne*.

Cranbrook (town, Kent): '(place by the) brook where cranes are seen'. OE *cran*, 'crane', + *brōc*, 'brook'. A nearby stream, the Crane Brook, takes its name from that of the town. 11C *Cranebroca*.

Cranford (district, Hounslow): '(place by the) ford where cranes are seen'. OE *cran*, 'crane', + *ford*, 'ford'. The ford was where the Bath Road (now the A4) crosses the river Crane here, itself named after the settlement. DB *Cranforde*.

Cranford St Andrew (village, Northants): '(place by the) ford where cranes are seen with St Andrew's church'. OE *cran*, 'crane', + *ford*, 'ford'. The church dedication distinguishes this Cranford from nearby *Cranford St John*. DB *Craneford*, 1254 *Craneford Sancti Andree*.

Cranham (village, Glos): 'enclosure where cranes are seen'. OE *cran*, 'crane', + *hamm*, 'enclosure', 'river meadow'. 12C *Craneham*.

Cranleigh (town, Surrey): 'woodland clearing where cranes are seen'. OE *cran*, 'crane', + *lēah*, 'wood', 'clearing'. Until relatively recently the name was spelt *Cranley*, and the present spelling was adopted, in an age of handwritten addresses, to avoid postal confusion with CRAWLEY. 1166 *Cranlea*, 1840 *Cranley*, 1895 *Cranley, or Cranleigh*.

Cranoe (village, Leics): '(place on the) spur of land where crows are seen'. OE *crāwe*, 'crow', + *hōh*, 'hill spur'. The first part of the name represents OE *crāwena*, the genitive plural form of *crāwe*. DB *Craweho*.

Cransley. See GREAT CRANSLEY.

Cranswick. See HUTTON CRANSWICK.

Crantock (village, Cornwall): '(church of) St Carantoc'. The church here is dedicated to Carantoc, a saint said to be of Welsh origin. DB *Sanctus Carentoch*.

Cranwell (village, Lincs): 'spring where cranes are seen'. OE *cran*, 'crane', + *wella*, 'spring', 'stream'. There are springs to the south of the village. DB *Craneuuelle*.

Cranwich (hamlet, Norfolk): 'marshy meadow where cranes are seen'. OE *cran*, 'crane', + *wisc*, 'marshy meadow'. DB *Cranewisse*.

Cranworth (village, Norfolk): 'enclosure where cranes are seen'. OE *cran*, 'crane', + *worth*, 'enclosure'. DB *Cranaworda*.

Craster (coastal village, Northd): 'old fortification where crows are seen'. OE *crāwe*, 'crow', + *ceaster*, 'Roman fort', 'old fortification'. 1242 *Craucestre*.

Craswall (hamlet, Herefords): '(place by the) stream where watercress grows'. OE *cærse*, 'cress', + *wella*, 'spring', 'stream'. 1231 *Cressewell*.

Cratfield (village, Suffolk): 'Cræta's open land'. OE *feld*, 'open land' (modern English *field*). DB *Cratafelda*.

Crathorne (village, N Yorks): '(place by the) thorn bush in a corner of land'. OS *krá*, 'nook', 'corner of land', + *thorn*, 'thorn bush'. DB *Cratorne*.

Craven. See CRAVEN ARMS.

Craven Arms (town, Shropshire). The town arose in the 19C and takes its name from an inn here, itself named after the earls of Craven, who held the manor of Stokesay in the 17C. The earls took their title from *Craven*, a district in the former West Riding of Yorkshire, with a Celtic name meaning 'place of garlic' (modern Welsh *craf*) that is now that of the local council district.

Crawcrook (village, Gateshead): 'bend where crows are seen'. OE *crāwe*, 'crow', + OS *krókr* or OE *crōc*, 'crook', 'bend'. The reference may be to a bend in the road by the river Tyne here. 1130 *Crawecroca*.

Crawford (village, S Lanarks): 'ford where crows are seen'. OE *crāwe*, 'crow', + *ford*, 'ford'. The river here is the Clyde. *c*.1150 *Crauford*.

Crawley (town, W Sussex): 'wood or clearing where crows are seen'. OE *crāwe*, 'crow', + *lēah*, 'wood', 'clearing'. 1203 *Crauleia*. SO ALSO: *Crawley*, Hants, Oxon.

Crawshawbooth (village, Lancs): '(place by the) copse where crows are seen with a cowhouse'. OE *crāwe*, 'crow', + *sceaga*, 'wood', 'copse', + OS *bōth*, 'cowhouse', 'herdsman's hut' (modern English *booth*). 1324 *Croweshagh*, 1507 *Crawshaboth*.

Crayford (district, Bexley): 'ford over the (river) Cray'. OE *ford*, 'ford'. The river has a Celtic name meaning 'fresh', 'clean' (modern Welsh *crai*). The ford in question was at the point where Crayford High Street now branches off from Crayford Road (which itself follows the course of Watling Street). It is unusual for *ford* to be added to a river name. The Roman settlement here was *Noviomagus*, 'new market', as for CHICHESTER. 1199 *Creiford*.

Crayke (village, N Yorks): '(place by the) rock'. The name comes from a Celtic word related to modern Welsh *craig*, 'rock'. Cp. CRICK. The castle at Crayke was built on a very steep rock. 10C *Creic*, DB *Creic*.

Crays, The. See ST MARY CRAY.

Creacombe (hamlet, Devon): '(place in the) valley where crows are seen'. OE *crāwe*, 'crow', + *cumb*, 'valley'. DB *Crawecome*.

Creaton (village, Northants): 'farmstead by the rock'. The first part of the name is of Celtic origin from a word related to modern Welsh *craig*, 'rock'. The second part is OE *tūn*, 'farmstead'. Creaton stands on a high ridge, and this is presumably the 'rock' in question. Cp. CRICK. DB *Cretone*.

Credenhill (village, Herefords): 'Creoda's hill'. OE *hyll*, 'hill'. DB *Cradenhille*.

Crediton (town, Devon): 'estate on the (river) Creedy'. OE *tūn*, 'farmstead', 'estate'. The river has a Celtic name perhaps meaning 'weakly flowing one' (modern Welsh *cryddu*, 'to shrink'), comparing it to the full-flowing Yeo, which it joins southeast of Crediton. 930 *Cridiantune*, DB *Chritetona*.

Creech St Michael (village, Somerset): '(place by the) hill with St Michael's church'. The main name comes from a Celtic word related to modern Welsh *crug*, 'hillock'. The hill in question is *Creech Barrow Hill*, a name whose second and third words are really redundant (cp. PENDLE HILL). The second part of the name distinguishes this village from nearby *Creech Heathfield*. DB *Crice*.

Creekmouth (district, Barking & Dag): 'mouth of the creek'. ME *creke*, 'inlet', 'stream', + OE *mūtha*, 'mouth'. Creekmouth, on the Thames, is at the mouth of the river Roding, known here as Barking Creek. The first word of the name below is based on OE *flēot*, 'estuary', 'inlet', 'creek'. 1323 *Fletesmouthe de Berkingge*.

Creeting St Mary (village, Suffolk): '(settlement of) Crǣta's people with St Mary's church'. OE *-ingas*, 'people of'. The church dedication distinguishes the village from nearby *Creeting St Peter*. DB *Cratingas*, 1254 *Creting Sancte Marie*.

Cressage (village, Shropshire): '(place by) Christ's oak tree'. OE *Crist*, 'Christ', + *āc*, 'oak'. 'The name is said to be a corruption of Christ's Oak, and in the neighbourhood is an old oak called the Lady Oak, hollow, and having a younger tree inside it' (*Cassell's Gazetteer of Great Britain and Ireland*, 1895). The church here is Christ Church. DB *Cristesache*.

Cressing (village, Essex): 'place where watercress grows'. OE *cœrsing* (from *cœrse*, 'cress'). Cressing is on a tributary of the river Blackwater. 1136 *Cressyng*.

Cresswell (village, Staffs): '(place by the) spring where cress grows'. OE *cœrse*, 'cress', + *wella*, 'spring', 'stream'. DB *Cressvale*. SO ALSO: *Cresswell*, Northd.

Creswell (village, Derbys): '(place by the) spring where cress grows'. OE *cœrse*, 'cress', + *wella*, 'spring', 'stream'. 1176 *Cressewella*.

Cretingham (village, Suffolk): 'homestead of the dwellers in a gravelly district'. OE *grēot*, 'gravel' (modern English *grit*), + *-inga-*, 'of the dwellers at', + *hām*, 'homestead'. DB *Gretingaham*.

Crewe (town, Cheshire): '(place by the) fish trap'. The name is Celtic in origin, from a word related to modern Welsh *cryw*, 'creel', 'weir'. The word came to mean 'stepping stones', probably because such stones were laid along a wickerwork fence that had itself been laid over a river to trap fish. This is perhaps the best sense here, referring to stepping stones over a local stream. The modern railway town of Crewe took its name from the railway station *Crewe* built in 1837 at Woodnets Green. DB *Creu*.

Crewe-by-Farndon (village, Cheshire): '(place by the) fish trap'. The name has the same origin as that of CREWE, from which it is distinguished by its proximity to FARNDON. The form of the name below has OE *hall*, 'hall', 'manor house'. DB *Creuhalle*.

Crewkerne (town, Somerset): 'building by the hill'. The first part of the name represents a Celtic word related to modern Welsh *crug*, 'hillock'. The second part is OE *œrn*, 'building'. Crewkerne lies in a hollow, and one of the surrounding hills would have been the particular hill mentioned. The second part of the name could, however, be simply a Celtic suffix. 9C *Crucern*, DB *Cruche*.

Criccieth (town, Gwynedd): 'mound of the captives'. Welsh *crug*, 'hill', 'mound', + *caith*, 'captives'. The name refers to the Norman castle here, build in 1230 on a headland ('mound') to the south of the town. The preferred Welsh spelling of the name is *Cricieth*. 1273 *Crukeith*.

Crich (village, Derbys): '(place by a) hill'. The name represents a Celtic word related to modern Welsh *crug*, 'hill', 'mound' (as for CRICCIETH). 1009 *Cryc*, DB *Crice*.

Cricieth. See CRICCIETH.

Crick (village, Northants): '(place by a) rock'. The name derives from a Celtic word related to modern Welsh *craig*, 'rock'. The 'rock' is presumably the small limestone hillock on which the village lies. Cp. CRAYKE. DB *Crec*.

Crickadarn (village, Powys): '(place by the) strong mound'. Welsh *crug*, 'mound', + *cadarn*, 'strong', 'secure'. The Welsh form of the name is *Crucadarn*, which over the years became misleadingly associated with *cerrig*, 'stones' (plural of *carreg*), and *craig*, 'rock'. 1550 *Kruc kadarn*, 1566 *Crucadarne*, 1578 *Crickadarne*, 1727 *Crickadarn*, 1868 *Crickadarn, or Cerrigcadarn*.

Cricket St Thomas (estate, Somerset): '(place by a) little mound with St Thomas's church'. The main part of the name represents a Celtic word related to modern Welsh *crug*, 'mound', with the OF diminutive suffix *-ette*. This originally applied to the smaller *Cricket Malherbe* nearby, where the Malherbe family held the manor in the 13C. DB *Cruche*, 1291 *Cruk Thomas*.

Crickhowell (village, Powys): 'Hywel's mound'. Welsh *crug*, 'hill', 'mound'. The 'mound' is the Iron Age fort to the north of the village, locally known as Crug Hywel or Table Mountain. The identity of Hywel is unknown. The Welsh form of the name is *Crucywel*. 1263 *Crichoel*, 1281 *Crukhowell*.

Cricklade (village, Wilts): 'river crossing by the rock or hill'. The first part of the name represents a Celtic word related to modern Welsh *craig*, 'rock', or possibly *crug*, 'hill'. The second part is OE *gelād*, 'crossing'. The river here is the Thames. The hill in question would probably have been nearby Horsey Down. 10C *Cracgelade*, DB *Crichelade*.

Cricklewood (district, Brent): 'crickled wood'. ME *crikeled*, 'crickled', + *wode*, 'wood'. A 'crickled' wood is one with a 'crimped' or indented edge. English *crickle* is a dialect word related to *crinkle*. 1294 *Le Crikeldwode*.

Cridling Stubbs. See WALDEN STUBBS.

Crieff (resort town, Perth & Kin): '(place among the) trees'. Gaelic *craobh*, 'tree'. (no date) *Craiobh*.

Crigglestone (village, Wakefield): 'farmstead by Crik Hill'. OE *tūn*, 'farmstead'. *Crik* was the name of a hill here, from a Celtic word related to modern Welsh *crug*, 'hillock'. OE *hyll*, 'hill', was added to this when its meaning was no longer understood. The hill in question is probably the one now known as Crigglestone Cliff, on which Crigglestone itself stands overlooking the river Calder. DB *Crigestone*.

Crimplesham (village, Norfolk): 'Crympel's homestead'. OE *hām*, 'homestead'. The DB form of the name below has omitted the *m* of the personal name. DB *Crepelesham*, 1200 *Crimplesham*.

Cringleford (village, Norfolk): '(place at the) ford by the round hill'. OS *kringla*, 'circle', + OE *ford*, 'ford'. The river here is the Yare. DB *Kringelforda*.

Crococalana. See BROUGH (Notts).

Croft (village, Leics): '(place with a) machine'. OE *cræft*, 'machine', 'engine' (modern English *craft*). The reference may be to some kind of mill here, by the river Soar. The DB form of the name below is corrupt. 836 *Craeft*, DB *Crebre*.

Croft (village, Lincs): '(place by the) enclosure'. OE *croft*, 'small enclosed field'. DB *Croft*.

Crofton (village, Wakefield): 'farmstead with an enclosure'. OE *croft*, 'croft', 'enclosure', + *tūn*, 'farmstead'. The DB form of the name below has prefixed an extraneous *S-*. DB *Scroftune*, 12C *Croftona*.

Croglin (village, Cumbria): '(place by the) torrent with a bend in it'. OE *crōc*, 'bend', + *hlynn*, 'torrent'. The village lies by a big bend in the river known as Croglin Water. *c.*1140 *Crokelyn*.

Cromarty (town, Highland): 'crooked (place by the) sea'. Old Gaelic *crumb*, 'crooked', + OI *bath*, 'sea'. The coastline here at the entrance to Cromarty Firth is very irregular. The former county of Cromarty, named after the town, was incorporated into ROSS to give the county of Ross and Cromarty. 1264 *Crumbathyn*.

Cromer (resort town, Norfolk): '(place by the) lake where crows are seen'. OE *crāwe*, 'crow', + *mere*, 'lake'. The lake in question would have been some distance inland from the sea. 13C *Crowemere*.

Cromford (village, Derbys): '(place at the) ford by the river bend'. OE *crumbe*, 'bend', + *ford*, 'ford'. The bridge over the river Derwent at Cromford, which is probably close to the site of the original ford, is near a right-angled bend in the river. DB *Crunforde*.

Cromhall (village, S Glos): 'corner of land in the river bend'. OE *crumbe*, 'crook', + *halh*, 'nook', 'corner of land'. The stream at Cromhall has a sharp bend. DB *Cromhal*.

Crompton (district, Oldham): 'farmstead in a bend'. OE *crumb*, 'crooked', + *tūn*, 'farmstead', 'estate'. The bend would have been in a stream here. 1246 *Crompton*.

Cromwell (village, Notts): '(place by the) crooked stream'. OE *crumb*, 'crooked', + *wella*, 'stream'. The 'crooked stream' is the big bend in the small tributary of the river Trent here. DB *Crunwelle*.

Crondall (village, Hants): '(place at the) chalk pits'. OE *crundel*, 'pit' (literally 'crooked diggings'). *c.*880 *Crundellan*, DB *Crundele*.

Cronton (village, Knowsley): 'farmstead at the place with a corner of land'. OE *crōh*, 'corner', + *-ing*, 'place characterized by', + *tūn*, 'farmstead'. 1242 *Crohinton*.

Crook (village, Cumbria): 'land in a bend'. OS *krókr* or OE *crōc*, 'crook', 'bend'. The name implies a secluded corner of land, as that occupied by Crook Hall here. 12C *Croke*.

Crook (town, Durham): '(place) in a bend'. OE *crōc*, 'crook', 'bend'. Crook lies in a nook of hillside at the far end of Brancepeth parish. 1301 *Crok*.

Cropredy (village, Oxon): 'Croppa's little stream'. OE *rīthig*, 'little stream'. The first part of the name could also represent OE *cropp*, 'hump', 'rounded hill', giving a sense 'little stream by a hill'. The hill in question would be on the ridge to the west of the village, where the 'little stream' rises. The second part of the DB form of the name below is garbled. DB *Cropelie*, c.1275 *Croprithi*.

Cropston (village, Leics): 'Cropp's or Kroppr's farmstead'. OE *tūn*, 'farmstead'. The personal names are respectively OE and Scandinavian. The name could also mean 'farmstead on a hill' (OE *cropp*, 'hill', + *tūn*). 12C *Cropeston*.

Cropthorne (village, Worcs): '(place at the) thorn bush by a hill'. OE *cropp*, 'hump', 'rounded hill', + *thorn*, 'thorn bush'. 8C *Croppethorne*, DB *Cropetorn*.

Cropton (village, N Yorks): 'farmstead by a hill'. OE *cropp*, 'hill', + *tūn*, 'farmstead'. DB *Croptune*.

Cropwell Butler (village, Notts): 'Butler's (estate by the) rounded hill'. OE *cropp*, 'hump', + *hyll*, 'hill'. The hill in question is nearby Hoe Hill. The manor here was held in the 12C by the Butler family, their name distinguishing the village from nearby *Cropwell Bishop*, held by the Archbishop of York. DB *Crophille*, 1265 *Croppill Boteiller*.

Crosby (district of Scunthorpe, N Lincs): 'Kroppr's farmstead'. OS *bý*, 'farmstead', 'village'. The personal name is Scandinavian. This interpretation assumes that the DB form of the name below is correct. If not, the meaning could be 'village (marked) with crosses' (OS *kross*, 'cross', + *bý*). DB *Cropesbi*, 12C *Crochesbi*.

Crosby (town, Sefton): 'village with crosses'. OS *krossa-bý* (from OS *kross*, 'cross', + *bý*, 'farmstead', 'village'). *Little Crosby*, to the north, has 'an ancient [Viking] stone cross in the centre of the village, another in the wall of Crosby Hall Park, and a third in a wood in the park' (*Cassell's Gazetteer of Great Britain and Ireland*, 1895). DB *Crosebi*. SO ALSO: *Crosby*, Cumbria.

Crosby Ravensworth (village, Cumbria): 'Rafnsvartr's farmstead with crosses'. OS *krossa-bý* (from OS *kross*, 'cross', + *bý*, 'farmstead', 'village'). The manor here was held in the 12C by one Rafnsvartr, whose Scandinavian name distinguishes this Crosby from *Crosby Garrett*, 8 miles to the southeast, where the manor was held early by one Garrett (or a family of this name). 12C *Crosseby Raveneswart*.

Croscombe (village, Somerset): '(place in the) valley of the road in the pass'. OE *corf*, 'pass', + *weg*, 'way', 'road', + *cumb*, 'valley'. This is the traditional origin of the name, although it is unlikely that *corf* + *weges* (the genitive form of *weg*) would have been reduced to *Correges* in the first form of the name below. 705 *Correges cumb*, DB *Coriscoma*.

Crosscanonby (hamlet, Cumbria): 'canons' (estate at the) village with crosses'. OS *krossa-bý* (from *kross*, 'cross', + *bý*, 'farmstead', 'village'). The first word of the name was added when lands here were given to the canons of Carlisle. 1285 *Crosseby Canoun*, 1535 *Crosbycannonby*, 1777 *Cross-Canonby*.

Crossens (district, Sefton): 'headland with crosses'. OS *kross*, 'cross', + *nes*, 'headland', 'promontory'. Crossens lies on a promontory at the mouth of the river Ribble. c.1250 *Crossenes*.

Cross Fell (mountain, Cumbria). The mountain was originally known as *Fiends Fell* (OE *fēond*, 'fiend', 'devil', + OS *fjall*, 'hill', 'fell'), referring to the notorious 'helm wind' that blows down from here. A Christian cross was erected to banish this evil force and *Cross* was accordingly substituted for *Fiend*. 1340 *Fendesfeld*, 1608 *Cross Fell*.

Cross in Hand (village, E Sussex). According to local legend, the place was a meeting point for Crusaders on their way to Rye for embarkation to the Holy Land, an event marked by an inn sign here depicting a hand holding a quartered standard. 1547 (*via*) *cruce manus*, 1597 *Crosse in Hand*.

Crosthwaite (hamlet, Cumbria): '(place in a) clearing with a cross'. OS *kross*, 'cross', + *thveit*, 'clearing'. Cp. CROSTWICK. 12C *Crosthwait*.

Croston (village, Lancs): 'village with a cross'. OE *cros*, 'cross', + *tūn*, 'farmstead', 'village'. Part of the market cross still remains. 1094 *Croston*.

Crostwick (hamlet, Norfolk): '(place in a) clearing with a cross'. OS *kross*, 'cross', + *thveit*, 'clearing'. The cross in question may have marked a boundary or been set up for devotional purposes. Cp. CROSTHWAITE. The name has been influenced by OE *wīc*, 'dwelling', 'dairy farm'. DB *Crostueit*.

Crostwight (hamlet, Norfolk): '(place in a) clearing with a cross'. OS *kross*, 'cross', + *thveit*, 'clearing'. The name is identical to that of CROSTWICK. DB *Crostwit*.

Crouch (river). See BURNHAM-ON-CROUCH.

Crouch End (district, Haringey): 'district by a cross'. ME *crouch*, 'cross', + *ende*, 'end', 'district of an estate'. There would probably have been a crucifix by a crossroads here at some time, giving the two senses of 'cross'. 1553 *Crutche Ende*.

Croughton (village, Northants): 'farmstead on the fork of land'. OE *creowel*, 'fork', + *tūn*, 'farmstead', 'village'. Croughton lies between two streams. DB *Creveltone*.

Crowan (village, Cornwall): 'church of St Cravenna'. The church here is dedicated to Cravenna, said to have come to Cornwall from Ireland. The form of the name below has Cornish *eglos*, 'church'. *c*.1170 *Eggloscrauuen*.

Crowborough (town, E Sussex): 'hill where crows are seen'. OE *crāwe*, 'crow', + *beorg*, 'hill', 'mound'. Crowborough is on an elevated site to the east of Ashdown Forest. In the form of the name below, the scribe has miscopied *u* as *n*. 1292 *Cranbergh*.

Crowcombe (village, Somerset): 'valley where crows are seen'. OE *crāwe*, 'crow', + *cumb*, 'valley'. 10C *Crawancumb*, DB *Crawecumbe*.

Crowfield (village, Suffolk): 'open country near the corner of land'. OE *crōh*, 'nook', 'corner of land', + *feld*, 'open land' (modern English *field*). DB *Crofelda*.

Crowhurst (village, E Sussex): 'wooded hill near the corner of land'. OE *crōh*, 'nook', 'corner of land', + *hyrst*, 'wooded hill'. 772 *Croghyrste*, DB *Croherst*.

Crowhurst (hamlet, Surrey): 'wooded hill where crows are seen'. OE *crāwe*, 'crow', + *hyrst*, 'wooded hill'. 12C *Crouhurst*.

Crowland (town, Lincs): 'estate at the bend'. OE *crūw*, 'bend', + *land*, 'land', 'estate'. There would have formerly been a bend in the river Welland here, now lost through land reclamation. 8C *Cruwland*, DB *Croiland*.

Crowlas (village, Cornwall): '(place by the) ford with a weir'. Cornish *crew*, 'weir', + *rys*, 'ford'. The village stands at a stream crossing. 1327 *Croures*, 1361 *Croulys*.

Crowle (village, N Lincs): '(place by the river) Crowle'. The river name means 'winding one' (OE *crull*, related modern English *curl*), although the river itself no longer exists following draining. DB *Crule*.

Crowle (village, Worcs): 'woodland clearing by the corner'. OE *crōh*, 'bend', 'corner', + *lēah*, 'wood', 'clearing'. 9C *Crohlea*, DB *Croelai*.

Crowmarsh Gifford (village, Oxon): 'Gifard's (estate at the) marsh where crows are seen'. OE *crāwe*, 'crow', + *mersc*, 'marsh'. The manor was held in 1086 by one Gifard. DB *Cravmares*, 1316 *Crowmershe Giffard*.

Crownthorpe (village, Norfolk): '(particular) outlying farmstead'. OS *thorp*, 'outlying farmstead'. The first part of the name is of uncertain origin. It may represent a personal name. DB *Cronkethor*.

Crowthorne (town, Wokingham): 'thorn tree where crows are seen'. The name originally referred to an isolated tree here. The town arose only in the 19C following the arrival of Wellington College (1859) and Broadmoor Asylum (now Broadmoor Hospital) (1863). 1607 *Crowthorne*.

Croxall (hamlet, Staffs): 'Krókr's corner of land'. OE *halh*, 'nook', 'corner of land'. The personal name is Scandinavian. The first part of the name could also represent OE *crōc*, 'bend' (related modern English *crook*), giving a sense 'corner of land near a bend'. 942 *Crokeshalle*, DB *Crocheshalle*.

Croxdale (village, Durham): 'Krókr's projecting piece of land'. OE *tægl*, 'tail'. The personal name is Scandinavian. 1195 *Crokesteil*.

Croxden (hamlet, Staffs): 'Krókr's valley'. OE *denu*, 'valley'. The personal name is Scandinavian. The first part of the name could alternatively represent OE *crōc*, 'bend', as for CROXALL. DB *Crochesdene*.

Croxley Green (hamlet, Herts): 'Krókr's woodland clearing'. OE *lēah*, 'wood', 'clearing'. The personal name is Scandinavian. Croxley later became associated with its green. 1166 *Crokesleya*.

Croxton (village, N Lincs): 'Krókr's farmstead'. OE *tūn*, 'farmstead'. The personal name is Scandinavian. The name implies that an Anglo-Saxon settlement here was taken over by the Danes. DB *Crochestune*. SO ALSO: *Croxton*, Cambs, Staffs.

Croxton Kerrial (village, Leics): 'Kyriel's (estate at) Krókr's farmstead'. OE *tūn*, 'farmstead'. The personal name in the main name is Scandinavian. The Kyriel family held the manor here in the 13C. DB *Crohtone*, 1247 *Croxton Kyriel*.

Croyde (village, Devon): '(place by the) headland'. OE *cryde*, 'headland'. The name is traditionally said to refer to the nearby promontory called Croyde Hoe, the latter word representing OE *hōh*, 'hill spur', which appears in the two forms of the name below (corruptly in the DB form). It may actually be of Celtic origin, however, from a word related to modern Welsh *crud*, 'cradle', referring to Croyde's location in a trough-like valley. DB *Crideholda*, 1242 *Crideho*.

Croydon (village, Cambs): '(place in the) valley where crows are seen'. OE *crāwe*, 'crow', + *denu*, 'valley'. DB *Crauuedene*.

Croydon (borough, Greater London): 'valley where wild saffron grows'. OE *croh*, 'saffron' (related modern English *crocus*), + *denu*, 'valley'. Saffron was formerly used for dyeing and pharmaceutical purposes. The valley here is that of the river Wandle. 809 *Crogedene*, DB *Croindene*.

Crucadarn. See CRICKADARN.

Crucywel. See CRICKHOWELL.

Crudgington (village, Wrekin): 'farmstead by a tumulus-shaped hill'. The first part of the name is Celtic, from a word related to modern Welsh *crug*, 'hillock'. The second part represents OE *hyll*, 'hill', added when the meaning of this had been forgotten. The third part is OE *tūn*, 'farmstead'. The hill in question is probably one of the small ones to the east of the village. The DB form of the name below has omitted the *l* of *hyll*. DB *Crugetone*, 12C *Crugelton*.

Crudwell (village, Wilts): 'Creoda's spring'. OE *wella*, 'spring', 'stream'. 9C *Croddewelle*, DB *Credvelle*.

Cruwys Morchard. See MORCHARD BISHOP.

Cubbington (village, Warwicks): 'estate associated with Cubba'. OE *-ing-*, 'associated with', + *tūn*, 'farmstead', 'estate'. DB *Cobintone*.

Cubert (village, Cornwall): 'church of St Cuthbert'. The church here is dedicated to the 7C English saint Cuthbert, Bishop of Lindisfarne. 1269 *Sanctus Cubertus*.

Cubitt Town (district, Tower Hamlets). The name is that of William Cubitt (1791–1863), Lord Mayor of London, who laid out the district here on the Isle of Dogs in the 1840s and 1850s to house workers at the nearby shipyards and docks.

Cublington (village, Bucks): 'estate associated with Cubbel'. OE *-ing-*, 'associated with', + *tūn*, 'farmstead', 'estate'. The DB form of the name below has OE *cot*, 'cottage', for *tūn*. DB *Coblincote*, 12C *Cubelintone*.

Cuckfield (town, W Sussex): 'open land where cuckoos are heard'. OE *cucu*, 'cuckoo', + *feld*, 'open land' (modern English *field*). The 'open land' would have been an unforested stretch in mainly wooded country. *c*.1095 *Kukefeld*.

Cucklington (village, Somerset): 'estate associated with Cucol or Cucola'. OE *-ing-*, 'associated with', + *tūn*, 'farmstead', 'estate'. The DB form of the name below has corrupted the personal name. DB *Cocintone*, 1212 *Cukelingeton*.

Cuddesdon (village, Oxon): 'Cūthen's hill'. OE *dūn*, 'hill'. 956 *Cuthenesdune*, DB *Codesdone*.

Cuddington (village, Bucks): 'estate associated with Cudda'. OE *-ing-*, 'associated with', + *tūn*, 'farmstead', 'estate'. 12C *Cudintuna*. SO ALSO: *Cuddington*, Cheshire.

Cudham (village, Bromley): 'Cuda's homestead'. OE *hām*, 'homestead', 'village'. DB *Codeham*.

Cudworth (town, Barnsley): 'Cūtha's enclosure'. OE *worth*, 'enclosure'. 12C *Cutheworthe*.

Cudworth (village, Somerset): 'Cuda's enclosure'. OE *worth*, 'enclosure'. DB *Cudeworde*.

Cuffley (residential district, Herts): 'Cuffa's woodland clearing'. OE *lēah*, 'wood', 'clearing'. 1255 *Kuffele*.

Culcheth (town, Warrington): '(place by the) narrow wood'. The name is Celtic in origin, from words related to modern Welsh *cul*, 'narrow', and *coed*, 'wood'. 1201 *Culchet*.

Culford (village, Suffolk): '(place at) Cūla's ford'. OE *ford*, 'ford'. The river here is the Lark. DB *Culeforda*.

Culgaith (village, Cumbria): '(place by the) narrow wood'. The name has an identical Celtic origin to that of CULCHETH. 12C *Culgait*.

Culham (village, Oxon): 'Cūla's river meadow'. OE *hamm*, 'river meadow'. Culham lies in a bend of the river Thames. 821 *Culanhom*.

Cullercoats (coastal village, N Tyneside): '(place by the) dovecotes'. OE *culfre*, 'dove', + *cot*, 'cottage'. *c*.1600 *Culvercoats*.

Cullingworth (village, Bradford): 'enclosure of Cūla's people'. OE *-inga-*, 'of the people of', + *worth*, 'enclosure'. DB *Colingauuorde*.

Cullompton (town, Devon): 'farmstead on the (river) Culm'. OE *tūn*, 'farmstead'. The river has a Celtic name traditionally said to mean 'winding stream' (modern Welsh *clwm*, 'knot'), but the Culm is not noticeably winding and the name may actually represent a Celtic word meaning 'dove' (modern Welsh *colomen*, from Latin *columba*), referring to the river's slow and gentle current. The DB form of the name below has omitted the '-ton'. *c*.880 *Columtune*, DB *Colump*.

Culmington (village, Shropshire): 'estate associated with Cūthhelm'. OE *-ing-*, 'associated with', + *tūn*, 'farmstead', 'estate'. The DB form of the name below has omitted the *l* of the personal name. DB *Comintone*, 1197 *Culminton*.

Culmstock (village, Devon): 'outlying farmstead on the (river) Culm'. OE *stoc*, 'outlying farmstead'. Culmstock is on the same river as CULLOMPTON. 938 *Culmstocc*, DB *Culmestoche*.

Culross (town, Fife): 'ridge of the promontory'. Gaelic *cùl*, 'ridge', + *ros*, 'promontory'. 12C *Culenross*.

Cults (district, Aberdeen): '(place by the) woods'. Gaelic *coillte*, 'woods'. An English plural *s* has been added to the Gaelic word. 1450 *Qhylt*, 1456 *Cuyltis*.

Culworth (village, Northants): 'Cūla's enclosure'. OE *worth*, 'enclosure'. DB *Culeorde*.

Cumberland. See CUMBRIA.

Cumbernauld (town, N Lanarks): '(place at the) confluence'. Gaelic *comar-an-allt*, 'meeting of the streams'. A stream still flows through the original village of Cumbernauld, now a New Town, to join another nearby. c.1295 *Cumbrenald*, 1417 *Cumyrnald*.

Cumbrae (island, N Ayrs): 'island of the Cymry'. OS *ey*, 'island'. The islands of *Great Cumbrae* and *Little Cumbrae* are named after the Welsh (Cumbrian) inhabitants of southern Scotland, *Cymry* being the name of the Welsh for themselves (see WALES). Cp. CUMBRIA. 1264 *Cumberays*.

Cumbria (county, NW England): 'territory of the Cymry'. The Cymry (Welsh), or Cumbrian Britons, inhabited an area of northwest England that extended as far as southern Scotland. Their territory was *Cumbria*, and this Latinized name was resurrected in 1974 for the new county that was made largely from the former counties of *Cumberland* ('land of the Cymry') and *Westmorland*. Cp. CUMBRAE. It is still sometimes supposed that Cumbria is so called from its many valleys (OE *cumb*, Welsh *cwm*), if only because of names such as CUMREW, CUMWHINTON and CUMWHITTON that begin thus. In the words of the Cumberland poet Robert Anderson (1770–1833): 'There's Cum-whitton, Cum-whinton, Cum-ranton, / Cum-rangan, Cum-rew, and Cum-catch, / And mony mair "Cums" i' the county / But nin wi' Cum-divock can match.' 8C *Cumbria*, 945 *Cumbra land*.

Cummersdale (village, Cumbria): 'valley of the Cymry'. OE *Cumbre*, 'Cymry', + OS *dalr*, 'valley'. The Cymry (Welsh) were the Cumbrian Britons who inhabited this part of England and who gave the name of the present county of CUMBRIA. 1227 *Cumbredal*.

Cumnock (town, E Ayrs): meaning uncertain. The name has never been satisfactorily explained. 1297 *Comnocke*, 1298 *Comenok*, 1300 *Cumnock*.

Cumnor (village, Oxon): 'Cuma's hill slope'. OE *ōra*, 'hill slope'. The ground gradually rises here. 931 *Cumanoran*, DB *Comenore*.

Cumrew (village, Cumbria): '(place in the) valley by the hill slope'. The name is Celtic in origin, from words related to modern Welsh *cwm*, 'valley', and *rhiw*, 'hill', 'slope'. The hill slope in question is Cumrew Fell. c.1200 *Cumreu*.

Cumwhinton (village, Cumbria): '(place in) Quintin's valley'. The first part of the name is as for CUMWHITTON. The second part represents the OF personal name. Cumwhinton and Cumwhitton are barely 4 miles apart, and it is likely that one name influenced the other. c.1155 *Cumquintina*.

Cumwhitton (village, Cumbria): '(place in a) valley by Whittington'. The first part of the name is Celtic in origin and related to modern Welsh *cwm*, 'valley'. The rest is an OE name meaning 'estate associated with Hwīta' (OE *-ing-*, 'associated with', + *tūn*, 'farmstead', 'estate'). 1278 *Cumwyditon*.

Cundall (village, N Yorks): '(place in a) valley'. The name is said to have been originally OE *cumb*, 'valley', to which OS *dalr*, 'valley', was added when the former word was no longer understood. This interpretation is disputed by some, however, on the grounds that there is no actual valley here. A meaning 'hollow of the cows' (OE *cūna-dœl*, from *cūna*, genitive plural of *cū*, 'cow', + *dœl*, 'hollow') has thus also been proposed. DB *Cundel*.

Cunetio. See MILDENHALL (Wilts).

Cupar (town, Fife): meaning uncertain. The name is probably of pre-Celtic origin. Cp. COUPAR ANGUS. 1183 *Cupre*, 1294 *Coper*.

Curbridge (village, Oxon): '(place by) Creoda's bridge'. OE *brycg*, 'bridge'. 956 *Crydan brigce*.

Curdworth (village, Warwicks): 'Creoda's enclosure'. OE *worth*, 'enclosure'. DB *Credeworde*.

Curland (village, Somerset): 'cultivated land belonging to Curry'. OE *land*, 'cultivated land'. *Curry* is CURRY RIVEL, or one of the other places to the northeast with this river name. 1252 *Curiland*.

Currie (district, Edinburgh): '(place) in the marshland'. Gaelic *currach*, 'bog', 'marsh'. The name represents the locative form of the Gaelic original. Currie is on the Water of Leith. 1210 *Curey*, 1213 *Curry*, 1246 *Curri*.

Curry Rivel (village, Somerset): 'Revel's (estate on the river) Curry'. The river name, formerly that of a stream here, is of pre-English origin and uncertain meaning. The manor here was held from the late 12C by the Revel family, whose name distinguishes the village from *Curry Mallet*, 5 miles to the southwest, where it was held by the Malet family, and *North Curry*, to the north of Curry Mallet. 9C *Curig*, DB *Curi*, 1225 *Curry Revel*.

Cusop (village, Herefords): '(place in the) valley'. OE *hop*, 'enclosed valley'. Cusop is on the

Welsh border, and the first part of the name may represent a Celtic stream name related to modern Welsh *cyw*, 'young bird', 'chick'. DB *Cheweshope*.

Cutsdean (village, Glos): 'Cōd's farmstead'. OE *tūn*, 'farmstead'. The name could also mean 'Cōd's valley' (OE *denu*, 'valley'). There seem to have been two distinct forms of the name, one with *tūn* denoting the farmstead, and one with *denu* denoting the valley in which it lay. 10C *Codestune*, DB *Codestune*, 12C *Cottesdena*.

Cuxham (village, Oxon): 'Cuc's river meadow'. OE *hamm*, 'enclosure', 'riverside land'. 995 *Cuces hamm*, DB *Cuchesham*.

Cuxton (village, Medway): 'Cucola's stone'. OE *stān*, 'stone'. The stone in question was probably a boundary marker. 880 *Cucolanstan*, DB *Coclestane*.

Cuxwold (village, Lincs): '(place by) high woodland where cuckoos are heard'. OE *cucu*, 'cuckoo', + *wald*, 'high woodland'. The name could also mean 'Cuca's high woodland'. The village lies in a depression surrounded by higher open land. DB *Cucuwalt*.

Cwmafan (town, Neath PT): 'valley of the (river) Afan'. Welsh *cwm*, 'valley'. The river Afan flows through the town to enter the sea at ABER-AVON.

Cwmbran (town, Newport): 'valley of the (river) Brân'. Welsh *cwm*, 'valley'. The river has a Celtic name meaning 'raven' (Welsh *brân*), referring to its dark waters. The town (properly *Cwmbrân*) did not come into being until 1949, when it was developed as a New Town. The form of the name below refers to the valley. 1707 *Cwmbran*.

Cydweli. See KIDWELLY.

D

Dacorum (council district, Herts): '(hundred) of the Danes'. The name represents Latin *Dacorum*, genitive plural of *Daci*, 'Dacians', a name used in medieval times for the Danes. The name itself referred to a hundred on the English side of the Danelaw boundary, i.e. one in an Anglo-Saxon region but having a Danish overlord. The western boundary of the Danelaw was Watling Street, which runs through the western portion of Hertfordshire, with Dacorum to the west of it. DB *Danais*, 1196 *de hundredo Dacorum*.

Dacre (village, Cumbria): '(place on the) Dacre Beck'. The river name is of Celtic origin meaning 'trickling one' (related to modern Welsh *deigr*, 'tear'). *c*.1125 *Dacor*.

Dacre (hamlet, N Yorks): '(place on the river) Dacre'. The name, originally that of the stream here, a tributary of the Nidd, is of Celtic origin and means 'trickling one' as for DACRE, Cumbria. DB *Dacre*.

Dadlington (village, Leics): 'estate associated with Dæddel'. OE *-ing-*, 'associated with', + *tūn*, 'farmstead', 'estate'. *c*.1190 *Dadelintona*.

Dagenham (district, Barking & Dag): 'Dæcca's homestead'. OE *hām*, 'homestead', 'village'. *c*.690 *Dæccanhaam*.

Daglingworth (village, Glos): 'enclosure of Dæggel's or Dæccel's people'. OE *-inga-*, 'of the people of', + *worth*, 'enclosure'. The name could also mean 'enclosure associated with Dæggel or Dæccel' (OE *-ing-*, 'associated with', + *worth*). *c*.1150 *Daglingworth*.

Dagnall (village, Bucks): 'Dægga's corner of land'. OE *healh*, 'nook', 'corner of land'. 1196 *Dagenhale*.

Dalbeattie (town, Dumfries & Gall): 'field by the birch trees'. Gaelic *dail*, 'field', + *beith*, 'birch'. 1469 *Dalbaty*.

Dalby (hamlet, N Yorks): 'farmstead in a valley'. OS *dalr*, 'valley', + *bý*, 'farmstead', 'village'. DB *Dalbi*.

Dalby (Leics). See GREAT DALBY.

Dale (hamlet, Derbys): '(place in a) valley'. OE *dæl*, 'valley'. The remains of Dale Abbey nearby lie in the valley known as *Deepdale*. Late 12C *La Dale*.

Dalham (village, Suffolk): 'homestead in a valley'. OE *dæl*, 'valley', + *hām*, 'homestead', 'village'. DB *Dalham*.

Dalkeith (town, Midlothian): 'field by a wood'. The name is Celtic, from words related to modern Welsh *dôl*, 'meadow', and *coed*, 'wood'. The area around Dalkeith is still well wooded. 1144 *Dolchet*.

Dallas (village, Moray): 'homestead by a meadow'. The name represents Celtic words related to modern Welsh *dôl*, 'meadow', and *gwas*, 'abode'. 1232 *Dolays*.

Dallinghoo (village, Suffolk): 'hill spur of Dalla's people'. OE *-inga-*, 'of the people of', + *hōh*, 'hill spur'. DB *Dallingahou*.

Dallington (village, E Sussex): 'estate associated with Dalla'. OE *-ing-*, 'associated with', + *tūn*, 'farmstead', 'estate'. DB *Dalintone*.

Dalry (town, N Ayrs): 'meadow of heather'. Gaelic *dail*, 'meadow', + *fraoch*, genitive *fhraoich*, 'heather'. The name is also explained as 'king's meadow', from Gaelic *dail an rìgh*, 'meadow of the king'. 1315 *Dalry*.

Dalston (village, Cumbria): 'Dall's farmstead'. OE *tūn*, 'farmstead'. 1187 *Daleston*.

Dalston (district, Hackney): 'Dēorlāf's farmstead'. OE *tūn*, 'farmstead'. Cp. DARLASTON. 1294 *Derleston*.

Dalton (hamlet, Cumbria): 'farmstead in a valley'. OE *dæl*, 'valley', + *tūn*, 'farmstead'. The valley in question may be the small one between Dalton Park Wood and Dalton Hall. DB *Dalton*. SO ALSO: *Dalton*, Northd (near Hexham, near Stamfordham), N Yorks (near Thirsk).

Dalton (suburb of Rotherham): 'farmstead in a valley'. OE *dæl*, 'valley', + *tūn*, 'farmstead'. The valley is that of Dalton Brook, which flows into the river Don nearby. To the south of Dalton are *Dalton Parva* (Latin *parva*, 'little') and *Dalton Magna* (Latin *magna*, 'great'). DB *Daltone*.

Dalton (Lancs). See UP HOLLAND.

Dalton-in-Furness (town, Cumbria): 'farmstead in a valley in Furness'. OE *dæl*, 'valley', + *tūn*, 'farmstead', 'village'. For the district name, see BARROW-IN-FURNESS. DB *Daltune*, 1332 *Dalton in Fournais*.

Dalton-le-Dale (village, Durham): 'farmstead in a valley in a valley'. OE *dæl*, 'valley', + *tūn*, 'farmstead', 'village', + *dæl*, 'valley'. 'The village lies a mile from the sea, scattered along the side of a small brook, & almost hid in a deep, romantic dell' (Robert Surtees, *The History and Antiquities of the County Palatine of Durham*, 1816). The tautological addition to the name distinguishes this Dalton from DALTON-ON-TEES, 27 miles to the south. 8C *Daltun*.

Dalton-on-Tees (village, N Yorks): 'farmstead in a valley on the (river) Tees'. OE *dæl*, 'valley', + *tūn*, 'farmstead', 'village'. The addition of the river name (see TEESDALE) distinguishes this Dalton from DALTON-LE-DALE, 27 miles to the north. 1204 *Dalton*, 1221 *Dalton super Tese*, 1868 *Dalton-upon-Tees*.

Dalwhinnie (village, Highland): 'valley of the champions'. Gaelic *dail*, 'valley', + *cuingid*, 'champion'. The reference is apparently to some memorable contest.

Dalwood (village, Devon): '(place by the) wood in a valley'. OE *dæl*, 'valley', + *wudu*, 'wood'. There is not much woodland here now. 1195 *Dalewude*.

Damerham (village, Hants): 'enclosure of the judges'. OE *dōmere*, 'judge' (related modern English *doom*, *deem*), + *hamm*, 'enclosure', 'river meadow'. The precise significance of the name is uncertain. The DB form of the name below has *b* for *m*. c.880 *Domra hamme*, DB *Dobreham*.

Danbury (village, Essex): 'stronghold of Dene's people'. OE *-inga-*, 'of the people of', + *burh*, 'fortified place'. The 'stronghold' is evident in traces of an ancient camp on nearby Danbury Hill. The original *-inga-* has disappeared. DB *Danengeberiam*.

Danby (village, N Yorks): 'village of the Danes'. OS *Danir*, 'Danes' (genitive plural *Dana*), + *bý*, 'farmstead', 'village'. DB *Danebi*.

Danby Wiske (village, N Yorks): 'village of the Danes on the (river) Wiske'. OS *Danir*, 'Danes' (genitive plural *Dana*), + *bý*, 'farmstead', 'village'. For the river name, see APPLETON WISKE. DB *Danebi*, 13C *Daneby super Wiske*.

Danehill (village, E Sussex): 'hill by the woodland pasture'. OE *denn*, 'woodland pasture', + *hyll*, 'hill'. 1279 *Denne*, 1437 *Denhill*.

Danum. See DONCASTER.

Darcy Lever. See LITTLE LEVER.

Darenth (village, Kent): '(settlement on the river) Darent'. The river has a Celtic name meaning 'river where oak trees grow'. Cp. DARTFORD. 10C *Daerintan*, DB *Tarent*.

Daresbury (village, Halton): 'Dēor's stronghold'. OE *burh*, 'fortified place'. 12C *Deresbiria*.

Darfield (town, Barnsley): 'open land where deer are seen'. OE *dēor*, 'deer', + *feld*, 'open land' (modern English *field*). OE *dēor* also meant 'animal', so the name could equally mean 'open land where wild animals are seen'. DB *Dereuueld*.

Darite (village, Cornwall): origin uncertain. The name may derive from a family name. 1506 *Daryet*.

Darlaston (district, Walsall): 'Dēorlāf's farmstead'. OE *tūn*, 'farmstead'. 1262 *Derlaveston*.

Darley Dale (village, Derbys): '(village in the) valley of the woodland clearing where deer are seen'. OE *dēor*, 'deer', 'wild animal', + *lēah*, 'wood', 'clearing'. The name, originally that of a hamlet in the parish of Darley, is now used both for the village and for the stretch of the Derwent valley between Rowsley and Darley Bridge where it lies. DB *Dereleie*.

Darlington (town, Darlington): 'estate associated with Dēornōth'. OE *-ing-*, 'associated with', + *tūn*, 'farmstead', 'estate'. The *r* of the personal name became *l* under Norman influence. Cp. SALISBURY. c.1009 *Dearthingtun*.

Darlton (village, Notts): 'Dēorlufu's farmstead'. OE *tūn*, 'farmstead'. The personal name is that of a woman. DB *Derluuetun*.

Darrington (village, Wakefield): 'estate associated with Dēornōth'. OE *-ing-*, 'associated with', + *tūn*, 'farmstead', 'estate'. DB *Darnintone*.

Darsham (village, Suffolk): 'Dēor's homestead'. OE *hām*, 'homestead', 'village'. DB *Dersham*.

Dart (river). See DARTMOUTH.

Dartford (town, Kent): 'ford over the (river) Darent'. OE *ford*, 'ford'. For the river name, see DARENTH. As with CRAYFORD, it is unusual for a ford to be named after the river it crosses. DB *Tarentefort*.

Dartington (village, Devon): 'farmstead on the (river) Dart'. OE -ing-, 'associated with', + tūn, 'farmstead'. For the river name, see DART-MOUTH. DB Dertrintona.

Dartmoor (upland region, Devon): 'moor in the valley of the (river) Dart'. OE mōr, 'moor'. The Dart rises on the moor and flows southeast to enter the sea at DARTMOUTH. 1182 Dertemora.

Dartmouth (port and resort, Devon): 'mouth of the (river) Dart'. OE mūtha, 'mouth'. The Dart has a name of identical origin to that of the Darent at DARENTH. 11C Dertamuthan.

Darton (town, Barnsley): 'deer park'. OE dēor-tūn (from dēor, 'deer', + tūn, 'farmstead', 'enclosure'). DB Dertun.

Darwen (town, Blackburn with Dar): '(estate on the river) Darwen'. Like the Derwent (see DERWENT WATER), the Darwen has a Celtic name meaning 'river where oak trees grow'. 1208 Derewent.

Datchet (town, Windsor & Maid): meaning uncertain. The name is probably Celtic in origin, with the second part representing a word related to modern Welsh coed, 'wood'. 10C Decet, DB Daceta.

Datchworth (village, Herts): 'Dæcca's enclosure'. OE worth, 'enclosure'. 969 Decewrthe, DB Daceuuorde.

Dauntsey (village, Wilts): 'Dōmgeat's island'. OE ēg, 'island'. The 'island' is well-watered land by the river Avon here. 850 Dometesig, DB Dantesie.

Davenham (village, Cheshire): 'homestead on the (river) Dane'. OE hām, 'homestead'. The river has a Celtic name meaning 'trickling one'. DB Deveneham.

Daventry (town, Northants): 'Dafa's tree'. OE trēow, 'tree'. The 'tree' may have been a cross or a crucifix. Local legend gives the name a different origin, quoted in John Bridges, History and Antiquities of Northamptonshire (1791): 'The common people have a tradition that it was built by the Danes, and had thence the name Danetre, as it is now pronounced ... this name is very probably supposed to be a compound of the British Dwy Avon Tre, the town of the two Avons [i.e. rivers, from its location between the Leam and the Nene]. From this fanciful conceit, however, hath been taken the device of the town cryer, who bears upon his badge the effigies of a Dane cutting down a tree'. DB Daventrei, 1868 Daventry, or Daintree.

Davidson's Mains (district, Edinburgh): 'Davidson's home farm'. The name is that of William Davidson, who acquired the home farm ('mains') of the Muirhouse estate here in 1776. Mains is related to demesne and domain.

Davidstow (village, Cornwall): 'St David's holy place'. OE stōw, 'holy place'. The church here is dedicated to the patron saint of Wales (and at nearby ALTARNUN to his mother). 1269 Sanctus David.

Dawley (town, Wrekin): 'woodland clearing associated with Dealla'. OE -ing-, 'associated with', + lēah, 'wood', 'clearing'. DB Dalelie, c.1200 Dalilea.

Dawlish (resort town, Devon): '(place on the) Dawlish Water'. The river has a name of Celtic origin meaning 'dark stream' (related modern Welsh du, 'black', and glais, 'stream'). DB Douelis.

Daylesford (hamlet, Glos): 'Dægel's ford'. OE ford, 'ford'. The DB form of the name below has garbled the personal name. 718 Dæglesford, DB Eilesford.

Deal (resort town, Kent): '(place) at the valley'. OE dæl, 'valley'. There is no valley here now, but a former hollow may have disappeared through changes in local topography. The first part of the DB form of the name below represents Latin ad, 'at'. DB Addelam, 1158 Dela.

Dean. See FOREST OF DEAN.

Deane. See BASINGSTOKE.

Dean Prior (village, Devon): 'prior's (estate in a) valley'. OE denu, 'valley'. The manor here belonged to Plympton Priory in the 11C. The second word distinguishes the village from Dean, to the north. DB Denu, 1415 Dene Pryour.

Dearham (suburb of Maryport, Cumbria): 'homestead or enclosure where deer are kept'. OE dēor, 'deer', + hām, 'homestead', or hamm, 'enclosure'. c.1160 Derham.

Debach (hamlet, Suffolk): '(place in the) valley of the deep river'. OE dēop, 'deep', + bece, 'valley'. There is no 'deep river' here, but Debach stands on a tributary of the Deben, whose name means 'deep one' (see DEBENHAM). The second part of the name could also represent OE bæc, 'ridge' (modern English back). DB Depebecs.

Debden (village, Essex): '(place in the) deep valley'. OE dēop, 'deep', + denu, 'valley'. DB Deppedana.

Debenham (village, Suffolk): 'homestead by the (river) Deben'. OE hām, 'homestead'. The river's name (pronounced 'Deeben') means 'deep one' (OE dēop, 'deep'). DB Depbenham.

Deddington (village, Oxon): 'estate associated with Dæda'. OE -ing-, 'associated with', +

tūn, 'farmstead', 'estate'. 1050 *Dædintun*, DB *Dadintone*.

Dedham (village, Essex): 'Dydda's homestead'. OE *hām*, 'homestead', 'village'. The DB form of the name below has a miscopying of *d* as *l*. DB *Delham*, 1166 *Dedham*.

Dee (river). See CHESTER.

Deene (village, Northants): '(place in the) valley'. OE *denu*, 'valley'. The village lies in the valley of the Willow Brook. 1065 *Den*, DB *Dene*.

Deenethorpe (village, Northants): 'secondary settlement dependent on Deene'. OS *thorp*, 'outlying farmstead', 'secondary settlement'. Deenethorpe is nearly a mile south of DEENE. 1169 *Denetorp*.

Deepdale (hamlet, Cumbria): '(place in the) deep valley'. OE *dēop*, 'deep', + *dæl*, 'valley'. The valley is that of Deepdale Beck. 1433 *Depedale*.

Deeping Gate (village, Peterborough): '(place on the) road to Deeping'. OS *gata*, 'road'. The village lies on the road that leads across the river Welland to MARKET DEEPING. 1390 *Depynggate*.

Deeping St James. See MARKET DEEPING.

Deeping St Nicholas. See MARKET DEEPING.

Deerhurst (village, Glos): 'wooded hill where deer are seen'. OE *dēor*, 'deer', + *hyrst*, 'wooded hill'. The hill in question is the one behind the village. The DB form of the name below has omitted the *r* of *hyrst*. 804 *Deorhyrst*, DB *Derheste*.

Defford (village, Worcs): '(place by the) deep ford'. OE *dēop*, 'deep', + *ford*, 'ford'. Cp. DEPTFORD. Defford is on the river Avon. 972 *Deopanforda*, DB *Depeford*.

Deganwy (district of Llandudno, Conwy): '(place of the) Decantae'. The name is that of an (Ancient) British tribe who occupied this region of north Wales. The meaning of their name is uncertain, but it may be 'noble ones', related indirectly to English *decorous* and *decent*. The Latin form of the name below means 'stronghold of the Decantae'. 812 *Arx Decantorum*, 1191 *Dugannu*, 1254 *Diganwy*.

Deighton (village, York): 'farmstead surrounded by a ditch'. OE *dīc*, 'ditch', + *tūn*, 'farmstead'. The DB form of the name below has *s* for *c*. DB *Distone*, 1176 *Dicton*. SO ALSO: *Deighton*, N Yorks.

Deiniolen (village, Gwynedd): '(church of) St Deiniolen'. The village was originally called *Ebeneser*, from the name of the Welsh Nonconformist chapel here, itself from the biblical place where the Israelites were defeated by the Philistines (1 Samuel 4:1). (The name is Hebrew

for 'stone of help'.) In the early 20C the present name was adopted from the parish name *Llanddeiniolen* (Welsh *llan*, 'church'). Deiniolen ('little Deiniol') was the son of Deiniol of Bangor, whom he succeeded as abbot.

Delabole (village, Cornwall): 'Deli with a pit'. Cornish *pol*, 'pit'. *Deli* is the name of a Cornish manor, perhaps meaning 'leaves' (Cornish *deyl*). The 'pit' is the great slate quarry here. DB *Deliou*, 1284 *Delyou Bol*.

Delamere (village, Cheshire). The village takes its name from the ancient *Delamere Forest* here, its own name meaning 'forest of the lake' (OF *forest*, 'forest', + *de la*, 'of the', + OE *mere*, 'lake'). The lake in question is probably Blakemere, near Eddisbury. 13C *foresta de la Mare*.

Delph. See NEW DELPH.

Demelza (hamlet, Cornwall): 'Maeldaf's fort'. Cornish *dyn*, 'fort'. The name became familiar after its adoption by Winston Graham for an urchin servant girl in his historical *Poldark* novels, subsequently televised. 'I was looking for a name for a thin dark waif when I saw the signpost. Twenty years later I went on a pilgrimage there, and found one neglected farm, two brothers who said they had farmed there since 1705 and a tiny medieval chapel' (Winston Graham, interview in *The Times*, 7 May 2002).

Denbigh (town, Denb): 'little fortress'. Welsh *din*, 'fortress', + *bach*, 'little'. The 'little fortress' would have stood where the the ruins of the 12C castle now lie. The Welsh form of the name is *Dinbych*. Cp. TENBY. 1269 *Dinbych*.

Denbury (village, Devon): 'fortification of the Devon people'. OE *Defnas* (see DEVON), + *burh*, 'fortified place'. The fortification in question is the earthwork here known as Denbury Camp. DB *Deveneberie*.

Denby (village, Derbys): 'farmstead of the Danes'. OE *Dene*, 'Danes', + OS *bý*, 'farmstead', 'village'. DB *Denebi*.

Denby Dale (town, Kirklees): 'farmstead of the Danes in a valley'. OE *Dene*, 'Danes', + OS *bý*, 'farmstead', + OE *dæl*, 'valley'. The name contrasts with the nearby villages of *Lower Denby* and *Upper Denby*. DB *Denebi*.

Denford (village, Northants): '(place by the) ford in a valley'. OE *denu*, 'valley', + *ford*, 'ford'. DB *Deneforde*.

Dengie (village, Essex): 'island associated with Dene'. OE *-ing-*, 'associated with', + *ēg*, 'island'. The name could also mean 'island associated with Dene's people' (OE *-inga-*, 'of the people of', + *ēg*). The 'island' is raised ground by Dengie Marshes here. *c.*707 *Deningei*, DB *Deneseia*.

Denham (village, Bucks): 'homestead in a valley'. OE *denu*, 'valley', + *hām*, 'homestead', 'village'. 1066 *Deneham*, DB *Daneham*.

Denholme (village, Bradford): 'water meadow in the valley'. OE *denu*, 'valley + OS *holmr*, 'water meadow'. 1252 *Denholme*.

Dennington (village, Suffolk): 'Denegifu's farmstead'. OE *tūn*, 'farmstead'. The personal name is that of a woman. DB *Dingifetuna*.

Denny (town, Falkirk): 'island valley'. OE *denu*, 'valley', + *ēg*, 'island'. The 'island' here is raised ground by the river Carron. 1510 *Litill Dany*.

Denston (village, Suffolk): 'Deneheard's farmstead'. OE *tūn*, 'farmstead'. DB *Danerdestuna*.

Denstone (village, Staffs): 'Dene's farmstead'. OE *tūn*, 'farmstead'. DB *Denestone*.

Dent (town, Cumbria): '(place on the river) Dent'. The river name, of unknown origin and meaning, appears to be a former name of the Dee here. 1202 *Denet*.

Denton (village, Northants): 'estate associated with Dodda'. OE *-ing-*, 'associated with', + *tūn*, 'farmstead', 'estate'. Denton was formerly *Little Doddington*, by contrast with GREAT DODDINGTON, 5 miles to the northeast. DB *Dodintone*, 1371 *Little Denynton*, 1563 *Dodington al. Deynton*.

Denton (town, Tameside): 'farmstead in a valley'. OE *denu*, 'valley', + *tūn*, 'farmstead', 'village'. Denton is in the valley of the river Tame. *c.*1220 *Denton*. SO ALSO: *Denton*, Cambs, Darlington, E Sussex, Kent (near Dover), Lincs, Norfolk, N Yorks, Oxon.

Denver (village, Norfolk): 'passage of the Danes'. OE *Dene*, 'Danes', + *fær*, 'passage'. Denver lies close to a Roman road that crossed the river Ouse here on its route to the east coast. The name refers to this crossing as used for traffic with Denmark before the arrival of the Vikings. The DB form of the name below has corrupted the second part. DB *Danefella*, 1200 *Denever*.

Denwick (hamlet, Northd): 'dairy farm in a valley'. OE *denu*, 'valley', + *wīc*, 'dwelling', 'dairy farm'. 1242 *Denwyc*.

Deopham (village, Norfolk): 'homestead by the deep place'. OE *dēop*, 'deep', + *hām*, 'homestead', 'village'. The 'deep place' is probably the nearby lake known as Sea Mere. DB *Depham*, 1868 *Deopham, or Deepham*.

Depden (hamlet, Suffolk): '(place in the) deep valley'. OE *dēop*, 'deep', + *denu*, 'valley'. DB *Depdana*.

Deptford (district, Lewisham): '(place by the) deep ford'. OE *dēop*, 'deep', + *ford*, 'ford'. The 'deep ford' would have been across the river Ravensbourne here, probably at the point where Deptford Bridge (the modern A2) is now. 1293 *Depeforde*. SO ALSO: *Deptford*, Wilts.

Derby (city, Derby): 'farmstead where deer are kept'. OS *djúr*, 'deer', + *bý*, 'farmstead', 'village'. The original name of the settlement was *Northworthy*, 'northern enclosure' (OE *north*, 'northern', + *worthig*, 'enclosure'), recorded in *c.*1000 as *Northworthige*. The corresponding 'southern enclosure' has not been identified. The Danes gave the present name, which is one of the few recorded examples of the replacement of an English place name by a Scandinavian. 10C *Deoraby*, DB *Derby*.

Derbyshire (county, central England): 'district based on Derby'. OE *scīr*, 'shire', 'district'. See DERBY. 11C *Deorbyscire*.

Derbyshire Dales (council district, Derbys). The district, formerly known as *West Derbyshire*, includes many hills and dales (and 'dale' names such as ALSOP EN LE DALE) and has DOVE DALE as its (and the county's) western boundary.

Dereham. See EAST DEREHAM.

Derrington (village, Staffs): 'estate associated with Dodda or Dudda'. OE *-ing-*, 'associated with', + *tūn*, 'farmstead', 'estate'. DB *Dodintone*.

Dersingham. See SANDRINGHAM.

Derventio. See (1) DERWENT WATER, (2) MALTON, (3) PAPCASTLE.

Derwent (river). See DERWENT WATER.

Derwentside (council district, Durham): '(region) beside the (river) Derwent'. The district takes its name from the river Derwent that forms its (and the county's) northern border. (This is not the same Derwent as that of DERWENT WATER but its name means the same.)

Derwent Water (lake, Cumbria): 'lake of the (river) Derwent'. The lake is formed by the Derwent southwest of Keswick. The river has a Celtic name meaning 'river where oak trees grow' (related modern Welsh *derwen*, 'oak'). The Romans knew the Derwent as *Derventio*, as mentioned in Bede's *History of the English Church and People* (completed 731): '*insula stagni illius pergrandis, de quo Deruuentionis fluuii primordia erumpunt*' ('an island in the great lake [Derwent Water] which is the source of the river Derwent'). *c.*1240 *Derewentwatre*, 1552 *Darwentwater*.

Desborough (town, Northants): 'Dēor's stronghold'. OE *burh*, 'fortified place'. The *r* of the personal name has been dropped by the process known as dissimilation, i.e. it has come to be represented by the *r* of *burh*. DB *Dereburg*, 1166 *Deresburc*, 1197 *Desburc*.

Desford (village, Leics): '(place by) Dēor's ford'. OE *ford*, 'ford'. DB *Deresford*.

Detchant (hamlet, Northd): '(place at the) end of the ditch'. OE *dīc*, 'ditch', 'dyke', + *ende*, 'end'. 1166 *Dichende*.

Dethick (hamlet, Derbys): '(place by the) death oak'. OE *dēath*, 'death', + *āc*, 'oak'. A 'death oak' was one on which criminals were hanged. 1154 *Dethec*.

Detling (village, Kent): '(settlement of) Dyttel's people'. OE *-ingas*, 'people of'. 11C *Detlinges*.

Deva. See CHESTER.

Deverills, The. See KINGSTON DEVERILL.

Devil's Dyke (ancient earthwork, W Sussex). The steep declivity ('dyke') on the South Downs lies below an Iron Age fort said to be the work of the devil. 'There is a tradition that Satan, beholding the numerous churches in the weald of Sussex, determined to make a channel and admit the sea, swamping the whole tract. But as he was working by night an old woman saw him from her cottage window, and held up a candle to find out his design; Satan, seeing the light, thought it was sunrise, and disappeared, being afterwards ashamed to return' (*Cassell's Gazetteer of Great Britain and Ireland*, 1895).

Devizes (town, Wilts): '(place on the) boundaries'. OF *devise*, 'boundary' (related modern English *division*). The town is at the boundary of two hundreds, that of Potterne (held by the king) and that of Cannings (held by the Bishop of Salisbury), and the boundaries of the two passed through the former Norman castle. Both the full and short form of the name are found with English *the* or the French equivalent, in the former case no doubt suggested by the association of sound between *De-* and *the*. 1152 *Divises*, 1381 *Les Divyses*, 1480 *The Vyse*, 1675 *the Devizes*, 1868 *Devizes, or The Vies*.

Devon (county, SW England): '(territory of the) Devonians'. The Devonians (OE *Defnas*) were earlier known by the Celtic name of *Dumnonii*, meaning either 'deep ones', referring to their mining, or 'worshippers of (the god) Dumnonos', whose name may mean 'mysterious one'. See also EXETER. The alternative name *Devonshire* has OE *scīr*, 'shire', 'district'. Late 9C *Defena, Defenascir*.

Devonport (district, Plymouth): 'Devon port'. The district was originally known as *Plymouth Dock* where it arose around the dockyard established here in the 17C. When the docks were enlarged in the 1820s, the name was changed to Devonport, implying a future as a leading British port. 'Till 1824 the town was called Plymouth Dock, or more usually "Dock," and the inhabitants "Dockers"' (*The National Gazetteer of Great Britain and Ireland*, 1868).

Devonshire. See DEVON.

Devoran (village, Cornwall): '(place by the) waters'. Cornish *devryon* (plural of *devr-*, a variant of *dowr*, 'water'). The village is located at the point where three streams merge into Restronguet Creek. 1275 *Dephryon*.

Dewlish (village, Dorset): '(place on the river) Dewlish'. The earlier name of the stream here, now known as Devil's Brook, is of Celtic origin and means 'dark stream', as for DAWLISH. The DB form of the name below is corrupt. DB *Devenis*.

Dewsbury (town, Kirklees): 'Dewi's stronghold'. OE *burh*, 'fortified place'. The OW personal name is the equivalent of English David. The stronghold in question was on the north side of the river Calder here, but no trace of it now remains. DB *Deusberia*.

Dibden (village, Hants): '(place by the) deep valley'. OE *dēop*, 'deep', + *denu*, 'valley'. There is hardly a valley here in the normal sense, let alone a deep one, and the first part of the name may refer to a point of deep water in nearby Southampton Water. DB *Depedene*.

Dibden Purlieu (village, Hants): '(place by) Dibden on the edge of the forest'. ME *purlewe*, 'purlieu'. The village is near DIBDEN on the edge of the New Forest. 'Purlieu' here applies to a tract of land that has been removed from the forest but that is still partly subject to forest laws. 1486 *Dibden in purlieu*.

Dicker, The. See LOWER DICKER.

Dickleburgh (village, Norfolk): 'Dicel's or Dicla's stronghold'. OE *burh*, 'fortified place'. DB *Dicclesburc*.

Didbrook (hamlet, Glos): '(place by) Dydda's brook'. OE *brōc*, 'brook'. 1248 *Duddebrok*.

Didcot (town, Oxon): 'Dudda's cottage'. OE *cot*, 'cottage', 'hut'. 1206 *Dudecota*.

Diddlebury (village, Shropshire): 'Dudela's manor'. OE *burh*, 'fortified place', 'manor'. c.1090 *Dodeleberia*.

Didley (hamlet, Herefords): 'Dodda's or Dudda's woodland clearing'. OE *lēah*, 'wood', 'clearing'. DB *Dodelegie*.

Didmarton (village, Glos): 'Dydda's boundary farmstead'. OE *mǣre*, 'boundary', + *tūn*, 'farmstead'. The name could also mean 'farmstead by Didda's pool' (OE *mere*, 'pool'). There are still pools near Didmarton. See also TORMARTON. 972 *Dydimeretune*, DB *Dedmertone*.

Didsbury (district, Manchester): 'Dyddi's stronghold'. OE *burh*, 'fortified place'. 1246 *Dedesbiry*.

Digby (village, Lincs): 'farmstead by the ditch'. OS *dík*, 'ditch', 'dyke', + *bý*, 'farmstead', 'village'. The ditch in question was probably a drainage channel here. DB *Dicbi*.

Dilham (village, Norfolk): 'homestead or enclosure where dill grows'. OE *dile*, 'dill', + *hām*, 'homestead', or *hamm*, 'enclosure'. DB *Dilham*.

Dilhorne (village, Staffs): 'building by a pit'. OE *dylf*, 'pit', 'quarry' (related modern English *delve*), + *ærn*, 'house', 'building'. DB *Dulverne*.

Dilston (hamlet, Northd): 'farmstead on Devil's Water'. OE *tūn*, 'farmstead'. The stream here called *Devil's Water* has a name popularly associated with the devil but actually of Celtic origin meaning 'dark stream' (related modern Welsh *du*, 'black', + *glais*, 'stream'). Cp. DOUGLAS. 1172 *Deuelestune*, 1868 *Dilston, or Devilstone*.

Dilton Marsh (village, Wilts): 'Dulla's farmstead in marshland'. OE *tūn*, 'farmstead'. The original village of Dilton is now known as *Old Dilton*, to the south, while Dilton Marsh is the larger and more recent settlement. 1190 *Dulinton*, 1638 *Dilton le Marsh*.

Dilwyn (village, Herefords): '(settlement by the) secret places'. OE *dīgle*, 'concealment', 'secret place'. The name represents OE *dīglum*, the dative plural form of *dīgle*. The reference would be to an isolated place. DB *Dilven*.

Dinas Powis (district of Penarth, Vale of Glam): 'fort of Powis'. Welsh *dinas*, 'fortified place'. The name is that of a former hundred here. The second word of the name apparently has the same origin as that of POWYS. 1187 *Dinaspowis*, c.1262 *Dinas Powis*.

Dinbych. See DENBIGH.

Dinbych-y-pysgod. See TENBY.

Dinder (village, Somerset): '(place by the) hill with a fort'. The name is Celtic, from words related to modern Welsh *dinas*, 'fort', and *bre*, 'hill'. 1174 *Dinre*.

Dinedor (village, Herefords): '(place by the) hill with a fort'. The name is Celtic, as for DINDER. The 'hill with a fort' is nearby Dinedor Hill, with the remains of a Roman camp. DB *Dunre*.

Dingley (village, Northants): 'woodland clearing with dells'. ME *dingle*, 'dell', 'hollow', + OE *lēah*, 'wood', 'clearing'. The terrain is uneven here. DB *Dinglei*.

Dingwall (town, Highland): 'field of the assembly'. OS *thing-vǫllr* (from *thing*, 'assembly', + *vǫllr*, 'field'). The assembly was the Scandinavian 'parliament', or periodical gathering of free men to administer justice and discuss public affairs. This took place in the designated field. The OS word also gave *Tynwald*, the name of the parliament of the Isle of Man, and *Thingvellir*, Iceland, the ancient place of assembly of the Althing, the Icelandic parliament. See also THINGWALL. 1227 *Dingwell*.

Dinnington (town, Rotherham): 'estate associated with Dunna'. OE *-ing-*, 'associated with', + *tūn*, 'farmstead', 'estate'. DB *Dunintone*. SO ALSO: *Dinnington*, Newcastle.

Dinnington (village, Somerset): 'estate associated with Dynne'. OE *-ing-*, 'associated with', + *tūn*, 'farmstead', 'estate'. DB *Dinnitone*.

Dinorwic. See PORT DINORWIC.

Dinton (village, Wilts): 'estate associated with Dunna'. OE *-ing-*, 'associated with', + *tūn*, 'farmstead', 'estate'. The *-ing-* has disappeared from the name, unlike identical DINNINGTON, Rotherham. The DB form of the name below may have resulted from a mishearing. DB *Domnitone*, 12C *Dunyngtun*. SO ALSO: *Dinton*, Bucks.

Diptford (village, Devon): '(place by the) deep ford'. OE *dēop*, 'deep', + *ford*, 'ford'. The ford in question would have been over the river Avon here. Cp. DEPTFORD. DB *Depeforde*.

Diserth. See DYSERTH.

Diseworth (village, Leics): 'Digoth's enclosure'. OE *worth*, 'enclosure'. c.972 *Digtheswyrthe*, DB *Diwort*.

Dishforth (village, N Yorks): '(place by the) ford across a ditch'. OE *dīc*, 'ditch', 'dyke', + *ford*, 'ford'. DB *Disforde*.

Disley (town, Cheshire): 'clearing by a mound'. OE *dystels*, 'mound', 'heap', + *lēah*, 'wood', 'clearing'. The first part of the name was long thought to represent a personal name, but the origin given here is now generally accepted. The alternative second form of the name below relates to nearby *Stanley Hall*, its name as for STANLEY. c.1251 *Destesleg*, 1868 *Disley, or Distley-Stanley*.

Diss (town, Norfolk): '(place by the) ditch'. OE *dīc*, 'ditch', 'dyke'. There must have been an ancient ditch or dyke somewhere here. DB *Dice*.

Distington (hamlet, Cumbria): '(place with a) farmstead'. OE *tūn*, 'farmstead', 'estate'. The first part of the name is of uncertain origin. It may represent a personal name. *c.*1230 *Dustinton*.

Ditchampton (hamlet, Wilts): 'farmstead of the dwellers by the dyke'. OE *dīc*, 'ditch', 'dyke', + *hǣme*, 'dwellers' (related modern English *home*), + *tūn*, 'farmstead'. The 'dyke' is the nearby ancient earthwork known as Grim's Ditch, which runs north through Grovely Wood. 1045 *Dichæmatune*, DB *Dicehantone*.

Ditcheat (village, Somerset): '(place by the) gap in the dyke'. OE *dīc*, 'dyke', + *geat*, 'gap' (modern English *gate*). The 'dyke' is the nearby Fosse Way. 842 *Dichesgate*, DB *Dicesget*.

Ditchingham (village, Norfolk): 'homestead of the dwellers by a dyke'. OE *dīc*, 'ditch', 'dyke', + *-inga-*, 'of the dwellers at', + *hām*, 'homestead'. The name could also mean 'homestead of Dica's or Dīca's people' (OE *-inga-*, 'of the people of', + *hām*). DB *Dicingaham*.

Ditchling (village, E Sussex): '(settlement of) Dīcel's people'. OE *-ingas*, 'people of'. 765 *Dicelinga*, DB *Dicelinges*.

Dittisham (village, Devon): 'Dyddi's enclosure'. OE *hamm*, 'enclosure'. The sense of OE *hamm* here is more precisely 'cultivated area of land on the edge of moorland', referring to Dittisham's location near the southeastern edge of Dartmoor. DB *Didasham*.

Ditton (district of Runcorn, Halton): 'farmstead by a ditch'. OE *dīc*, 'ditch', 'dyke', + *tūn*, 'farmstead'. The reference is probably to a drainage ditch in this low-lying area near the river Mersey. 1194 *Ditton*. SO ALSO: *Ditton*, Kent.

Ditton Priors (village, Shropshire): 'prior's (estate at the) settlement associated with Dodda or Dudda'. OE *-ing-*, 'associated with', + *tūn*, 'farmstead', 'village'. The manor here was held by Wenlock Priory. DB *Dodintone*, 1346 *Dodyton Prioris*.

Dobcross (village, Oldham): '(place by the) cross associated with Dobbe'. The 'cross' may have been an actual cross or a crossroads. Dobbe is either a pet form of Robert or a surname. 1662 *Dobcrosse*.

Dobwalls (village, Cornwall): 'Dobb's walls'. Dobb is a surname (now more usually Dobbe), and the walls are apparently those of a ruined building here. The name has been popularly associated with that of the nearby hamlet of *Doublebois*, but the names are not doublets and the latter means 'double wood' (OF *double*, 'double', + *bois*, 'wood'). 1607 *Dobwalls*.

Docking (village, Norfolk): 'place where docks grow'. OE *docce*, 'dock', + *-ing*, 'place characterized by'. *c.*1035 *Doccynge*, DB *Dochinga*.

Docklow (village, Herefords): '(place by the) hill where docks grow'. OE *docce*, 'dock', + *hlāw*, 'mound', 'hill'. 1291 *Dockelawe*.

Doddinghurst (village, Essex): 'wooded hill of Dudda's or Dodda's people'. OE *-inga-*, 'of the people of', + *hyrst*, 'wooded hill'. The DB form of the name below is corrupt. DB *Doddenhenc*, 1218 *Duddingeherst*.

Doddington (village, Cambs): 'estate associated with Dudda or Dodda'. OE *-ing-*, 'associated with', + *tūn*, 'farmstead', 'estate'. The first form of the name below has an extraneous *n*. *c.*975 *Dundington*, DB *Dodinton*. SO ALSO: *Doddington*, Kent, Lincs, Northd, Shropshire.

Doddiscombsleigh (village, Devon): 'Doddescumb's (estate at the) woodland clearing'. OE *lēah*, 'wood', 'clearing'. The Doddescumb family held the manor here in the 13C. DB *Leuga*, 1309 *Doddescumbeleghe*.

Dodford (village, Northants): '(place by) Dodda's ford'. OE *ford*, 'ford'. 944 *Doddanford*, DB *Dodeforde*.

Dodington (hamlet, S Glos): 'estate associated with Dudda or Dodda'. OE *-ing-*, 'associated with', + *tūn*, 'farmstead', 'estate'. DB *Dodintone*.

Dodleston (village, Cheshire): 'Dodel's farmstead'. OE *tūn*, 'farmstead'. The DB form of the name below has omitted the *l* of the personal name. DB *Dodestune*, 1153 *Dodleston*.

Dodworth (town, Barnsley): 'Dodd's or Dodda's enclosure'. OE *worth*, 'enclosure'. DB *Doddesuuorde*.

Dolgarrog (village, Conwy): 'water meadows of the fast-flowing stream'. Welsh *dôl*, 'water meadow', + *carrog*, 'torrent'. The meadows in question lie between the rivers Conwy, Afon Porth-llwyd and Afon Ddu. There is a waterfall on the nearby river Dulyn. 1534 *Dolgarrog*.

Dolgellau (town, Gwynedd): 'water meadow of cells'. Welsh *dôl*, 'water meadow', + *cell*, 'cell' (plural *cellau*). Dolgellau lies at the confluence of the rivers Wnion and Aran. The 'cells' were presumably monastic cells. 1254 *Dolkelew*, 1338 *Dolgethly*.

Dollar (town, Clack): '(place by the) ploughed field'. Celtic *dol*, 'field', + *ar*, 'arable land'. The interpretation of the name is conjectural. 1461 *Doler*.

Dollis Hill (district, Brent): 'Dalley's hill'. The name is that of a family apparently called Dalley, recorded as being here in the 16C. The first form of the name below is corrupt. 1593 *Daleson Hill*, 1612 *Dalleys Hill*.

Dolphinholme (hamlet, Lancs): 'Dolgfinnr's island'. OS *holmr*, 'island'. The personal name is Scandinavian. The 'island' would have been land by the river Wyre here. 1591 *Dolphineholme*.

Dolton (village, Devon): meaning uncertain. The second part of the name is OE *tūn*, 'farmstead'. The first part is of obscure origin. A meaning 'open land where doves are seen' has been suggested (OE *dūfe*, 'dove', + *feld*, 'open land'). Dolton is not far from DOWLAND, with a similar name. DB *Duueltone*.

Don (river). See DONCASTER.

Doncaster (town, Doncaster): 'Roman fort on the (river) Don'. OE *ceaster*, 'Roman fort'. The river has a Celtic name meaning simply 'water', 'river'. The Roman town here was *Danum*, after the river. The river name has its European relations in the *Danube* (German *Donau*), French *Rhône* (Latin *Rhodanus*), and Russian *Don* and *Dnieper*. 1002 *Doneceastre*, DB *Donecastre*.

Donhead St Mary (village, Wilts): '(place at the) end of the down with St Mary's church'. OE *dūn*, 'hill', 'down', + *hēafod*, 'head', 'end'. The church dedication distinguishes the village from nearby *Donhead St Andrew*. 871 *Dunheved*, DB *Duneheve*, 1298 *Donheved Sancte Marie*.

Donington (village, Lincs): 'estate associated with Dunn'. OE *-ing-*, 'associated with', + *tūn*, 'farmstead', 'estate'. DB *Duninctune*.

Donington le Heath. See CASTLE DONINGTON.

Donisthorpe (village, Leics): 'Durand's outlying farmstead'. OS *thorp*, 'outlying farmstead'. The personal name is Old French. DB *Durandestorp*.

Donnington (suburb of Newbury, W Berks): 'estate associated with Dunn'. OE *-ing-*, 'associated with', + *tūn*, 'farmstead', 'estate'. The first DB form of the name below is corrupt, perhaps as the result of a mishearing. DB *Deritone*, DB *Dunintona*. SO ALSO: *Donnington*, Glos, Shropshire, Wrekin.

Donnington (hamlet, W Sussex): 'Dunnuca's farmstead'. OE *tūn*, 'farmstead'. The DB form of the name below has *D*- misread or miscopied as *Cl*-. 966 *Dunketone*, DB *Cloninctune*.

Donyatt (village, Somerset): 'Dunna's gate'. OE *geat*, 'gate', 'gap'. 8C *Duunegete*, DB *Doniet*.

Dorchester (town, Dorset): 'Roman town of Durnovaria'. OE *ceaster*, 'Roman fort'. The Roman name *Durnovaria* is based on a Celtic word meaning 'fist' (modern Welsh *dwrn*), perhaps referring to fist-sized pebbles here or even to fist fights (as a form of boxing). Cp. DORNOCH. The name gave that of DORSET. The middle element of the first form of the name below represents OE *-ware*, 'dwellers'. 864 *Dornwaraceaster*, DB *Dorecestre*.

Dorchester (village, Oxon): 'Roman town of Dorcic'. OE *ceaster*, 'Roman fort'. The origin of *Dorcic* is uncertain. It is a Celtic name, with the first part meaning 'walled town' and the second apparently meaning 'meat' (modern Welsh *cig*) in the transferred sense 'breast', referring to a local rounded hill. The actual name of the Roman station here is unknown. It was not *Dorocina*, as stated in some sources ('The Romans founded the town of Dorocina'. *The New Shell Guide to England*, 1981). 731 *Dorciccaestræ*, DB *Dorchecestre*.

Dordon (village, Warwicks): 'hill where deer are seen'. OE *dēor*, 'deer', + *dūn*, 'hill'. OE *dēor* also meant 'animal', so the name could equally mean 'hill where wild animals are seen'. 13C *Derdon*.

Dore (district, Sheffield): '(place at the) door'. OE *dor*, 'door', 'gate'. The 'door' is the pass in which the town is located, on the former boundary between the kingdoms of Northumbria and Mercia and subsequently between Derbyshire and the West Riding of Yorkshire. Dore was transferred to the city of Sheffield in 1934. DB *Dore*.

Dorking (town, Surrey): '(settlement of) Deorc's people'. OE *-ingas*, 'people of'. DB *Dorchinges*.

Dormanstown (suburb of Redcar, Redcar & Clev). The settlement was built in 1918 for steelworkers at the firm of Dorman Long, founded in 1876 by Arthur John Dorman and Albert Long.

Dormington (village, Herefords): 'estate associated with Dēormōd or Dēormund'. OE *-ing-*, 'associated with', + *tūn*, 'farmstead', 'estate'. 1216 *Dorminton*.

Dorney (village, Bucks): 'island where bumble bees are seen'. OE *dora* (genitive plural *dorena*) 'bumble bee', + *ēg*, 'island'. Dorney is bounded on two sides by the Thames, and this is the 'island'. DB *Dornei*.

Dornoch (town, Highland): 'place of fist-stones'. Gaelic *dornach*, from *dorn*, 'fist'. The 'fist-stones' may have been pebbles used for throwing as missiles. 1145 *Durnach*.

Dorrington (village, Shropshire): 'estate associated with Doda' OE -*ing*-, 'associated with', + *tūn*, 'farmstead', 'estate'. 1198 *Dodinton*.

Dorset (county, S England): '(territory of the) people around Dorn'. OE *sǣte*, 'dwellers', 'settlers'. *Dorn* is a short form of *Dornwaraceaster*, an early name of DORCHESTER. The alternative name *Dorsetshire* has OE *scīr*, 'shire', 'district'. 9C *Dornsǣtum, Dorseteschire*.

Dorsington (village, Warwicks): 'estate associated with Dēorsige'. OE -*ing*-, 'associated with', + *tūn*, 'farmstead', 'estate'. DB *Dorsintune*.

Dorstone (village, Herefords): 'estate associated with Dēorsige'. OE -*ing*-, 'associated with', + *tūn*, 'farmstead', 'estate'. The DB form of the name below has garbled the personal name. DB *Dodintune, c.*1138 *Dorsington*.

Dorton (village, Bucks): 'farmstead at the narrow pass'. OE *dor*, 'door', + *tūn*, 'farmstead', 'village'. The village stands at the entrance to a narrow pass between hills, now traversed by the railway. DB *Dortone*.

Doublebois. See DOBWALLS.

Doughton (hamlet, Glos): 'farmstead where ducks are kept'. OE *dūce*, 'duck', + *tūn*, 'farmstead'. 775 *Ductune*.

Douglas (town, S Lanarks): '(place on the) Douglas Water'. The river has a Celtic name meaning 'black water' (Gaelic *dubh*, 'black', + *glais*, 'stream'). The name is found elsewhere with this meaning (including the capital of the Isle of Man). *c.*1150 *Duuelglas*.

Doulting (village, Somerset): '(place on the river) Doulting'. The former name of the river Sheppey here is probably of Celtic origin but unknown meaning. 725 *Dulting*, DB *Doltin*.

Dove (river). See DOVE DALE.

Dovecot (district, Liverpool). The name comes from the former Dovecot House in Pilch Lane here, demolished in the 18C and originally so called for its dovecote.

Dove Dale (valley, Staffs/Derbys): 'valley of the (river) Dove'. OS *dalr*, 'valley'. The river has a Celtic name meaning 'black', 'dark', referring to the colour of the water. 1269 *Duvesdale*.

Dovenby (village, Cumbria): 'Dufan's farmstead'. OS *bȳ*, 'farmstead', 'village'. The personal name is Old Irish. 1230 *Duuaneby*.

Dover (town and port, Kent): '(place on the river) Dour'. The river has a Celtic name meaning simply 'waters' (modern Welsh *dwfr*, 'water'). The Roman town here was *Dubris*, of the same origin. *c.*700 *Dofras*, DB *Dovere*.

Dovercourt (resort district of Harwich, Essex): 'enclosed farmyard by the (river) Dover'. OE *cort*, 'short plot of ground', 'piece of land cut off' (related modern English *court*). Dovercourt is actually at the mouth of the Stour, so *Dover* must have been the name of the stream to the north. It is of Celtic origin and means 'waters' (cp. DOVER). The DB form of the name below is garbled. *c.*1000 *Douorcortae*, DB *Druurecurt*.

Doverdale (village, Worcs): '(place in the) valley of the (river) Dover'. OE *dæl*, 'valley'. The stream here, now known in succession as Dordale Brook, Elmley Brook and Hadley Brook, had an original name of Celtic origin meaning simply 'waters'. Cp. DOVER. (*Dordale* is a form of *Doverdale*.) The DB form of the name below has garbled this. 706 *Douerdale*, DB *Lunvredele*.

Doveridge (village, Derbys): '(place by the) bridge over the (river) Dove'. OE *brycg*, 'bridge'. For the river name, see DOVE DALE. DB *Dubrige*, 1252 *Duvebruge*.

Dovey (river). See ABERDOVEY.

Dowdeswell (hamlet, Glos): '(place by) Dogod's spring'. OE *wella*, 'spring', 'stream'. A number of springs unite here to form the river Chelt. Dowdeswell Reservoir is also here. 8C *Dogodeswellan*, DB *Dodesuuelle*.

Dowlais (district of Merthyr Tydfil, M Tydfil): '(place by the) black stream'. Welsh *du*, 'black', + *glais*, 'stream', 'brook'. The name refers to the colour of the waters or the bed of the stream. Cp. BLACKBURN.

Dowland (hamlet, Devon): meaning uncertain. The second part of the name is OE *land*, 'estate'. The first part is of obscure origin. A meaning 'open country where doves are seen' has been suggested (OE *dūfe*, 'dove', + *feld*, 'open land'). Cp. DOLTON. DB *Duuelande*.

Dowlish Wake (village, Somerset): 'Wake's (estate by the river) Dowlish'. The stream here has a Celtic name meaning 'dark stream' (cp. DAWLISH). The Wake family held the manor here in the 12C, their name distinguishing the village from nearby *Dowlish Ford*. DB *Duuelis*, 1243 *Duueliz Wak*.

Down Ampney. See AMPNEY CRUCIS.

Downderry (resort village, Cornwall): meaning uncertain. The name may have originated as that of a field or plot of land, and may be connected with the song refrain 'derry derry down'. 1699 *Downderry*.

Downend (district of Mangotsfield, S Glos): '(place at the) end of the down'. OE *dūn*, 'hill'. 1573 *Downe ende*.

Downgate (village, Cornwall): 'gate to the downs'. Downgate arose in the 19C on the edge of Hingston Downs. 1840 *Downgate*.

Downham (village, Cambs): 'homestead by a hill'. OE *dūn*, 'hill', + *hām*, 'homestead'. The Post Office has adopted the name *Little Downham* for the village to avoid confusion with DOWNHAM MARKET, Norfolk, 14 miles to the northeast. DB *Duneham*.

Downham (village, Essex): 'homestead by a hill'. OE *dūn*, 'hill', + *hām*, 'homestead'. 1168 *Dunham*.

Downham (village, Lancs): '(place at the) hills'. OE *dūn*, 'hill'. The name represents OE *dūnum*, the dative plural form of *dūn*. The village is on the slope of a ridge with several hills nearby. 1194 *Dunum*. SO ALSO: *Downham*, Northd.

Downham Market (town, Norfolk): 'homestead by a hill with a market'. OE *dūn*, 'hill', + *hām*, 'homestead', + ME *market*. There was a market here as early as the 11C. DB *Dunham*, 1130 *Mercatus de Dunham*.

Down Hatherley (village, Glos): 'downstream (place by the) clearing where hawthorn grows'. OE *dūne*, 'lower downstream', + *haguthorn*, 'hawthorn', + *lēah*, 'wood', 'clearing'. The first word of the name contrasts with that of *Up Hatherley*, now a suburb of Cheltenham, further upstream (OE *upp*). The places are 3 miles apart on the Hatherley Brook. DB *Atherlai*, 1273 *Dunheytherleye*.

Downhead (village, Somerset): '(place at the) end of the down'. OE *dūn*, 'down', 'hill', + *hēafod*, 'head', 'end'. Both this Downhead, near Shepton Mallet, and the smaller Downhead, near Sparkford, are situated on flat ground at the lower point of a narrow ridge. 851 *Duneafd*, DB *Dunehefde*.

Downholme (village, N Yorks): '(place at the) hills'. OE *dūn*, 'hill'. The name represents OE *dūnum*, the dative plural form of *dūn*. DB *Dune*, 12C *Dunum*, 1868 *Downholme, or Downham*.

Down St Mary (village, Devon): '(place at the) hill with St Mary's church'. OE *dūn*, 'hill'. DB *Done*, 1297 *Dune St Mary*.

Downton (village, Wilts): 'farmstead by the hill'. OE *dūn*, 'hill', + *tūn*, 'farmstead'. 672 *Duntun*, DB *Duntone*.

Downton on the Rock (village, Herefords): 'farmstead by the hill on the rock'. OE *dūn*, 'hill', + *tūn*, 'farmstead'. 'The soil is shallow, on a substratum of rock' (*The National Gazetteer of Great Britain and Ireland*, 1868). The second part of the name distinguishes the village from *Downton*, Shropshire, 8 miles to the northeast. DB *Duntune*.

Dowsby (village, Lincs): 'Dúsi's farmstead'. OS *bý*, 'farmstead', 'village'. The personal name is Scandinavian. DB *Dusebi*.

Doxey (district of Stafford, Staffs): 'Docc's island'. OE *ēg*, 'island'. The 'island' is raised ground beside Doxey Marshes here, through which flows the river Sow. DB *Dochesig*.

Doynton (village, S Glos): 'estate associated with Dydda'. OE *-ing-*, 'associated with', + *tūn*, 'farmstead', 'estate'. DB *Didintone*.

Dragonby (village, N Lincs). The village lies 2 miles north of Scunthorpe and was founded in *c*.1912 on land owned by the Elwes family for newly arrived Roman Catholic steelworkers in the town. The original street of houses was named by Lady Winefride Elwes, wife of Gervase Henry Elwes (1866–1921), after *The Dragon*, the local name of a rock ridge resembling the outline of a dragon. The '-by' of the name accords with other OS names in the region, such as Risby, Roxby, Normanby, Thealby.

Drake's Island (island, Plymouth). The small island in Plymouth Sound was earlier *St Nicholas Island*, from a chapel on it dedicated to St Nicholas. From the late 16C it was associated with Sir Francis Drake (*c*.1540–96), who knew the island as a boy and who anchored the *Golden Hind* off it in 1580 on returning from his circumnavigation of the globe. 1396 *isle of St Nicholas*.

Draughton (village, Northants): 'farmstead with a portage'. OS *drag*, 'portage' (relate modern English *drag*, *draw*), + OE *tūn*, 'farmstead'. Draughton lies on the slope of a hill, and the portage would have been a 'chute' here for dragging down timber and the like. DB *Dractone*. SO ALSO: *Draughton*, N Yorks.

Drax (village, N Yorks): '(place by the) portages'. OS *drag*, 'portage' (related modern English *drag*, *draw*). Drax is on the Ouse, north of the Aire, and there must have been a portage, or place for dragging boats overland, between the two rivers. DB *Drac*, 11C *Drachs*.

Draycott (village, Somerset): 'building where drays are kept'. OE *dræg*, 'dray', 'sledge', + *cot*, 'cottage'. DB *Draicote*. SO ALSO: *Draycott*, Derbys.

Draycott in the Clay (village, Staffs): 'building where drays are kept in the clayey district'. OE *dræg*, 'dray', 'sledge', + *cot*, 'cottage', + *clǣg*, 'clay'. The second part of the name distinguishes the village from *Draycott in the Moors*, 13 miles to the northwest. DB *Draicote*.

Drayton (village, Oxon): 'estate where sledges are used'. OE *dræg*, 'dray', 'sledge', + *tūn*, 'farmstead', 'estate'. There is still marshy ground between Drayton and Abingdon, and the use of sledges here would have been appropriate. The same sense probably applies for Drayton near Banbury. 958 *Draitune*, DB *Draitone*. SO ALSO: *Drayton*, Norfolk, Somerset (near Langport).

Drayton Bassett (village, Staffs): 'Basset's estate by a portage'. OE *dræg*, 'portage' (related modern English *drag*, *draw*), + *tūn*, 'farmstead', 'estate'. Drayton Bassett is near the river Tame. The Basset family held the manor here in the 12C. DB *Draitone*, 1301 *Drayton Basset*.

Drayton Beauchamp. See DRAYTON PARSLOW.

Drayton Parslow (village, Bucks): 'Passelewe's estate where sledges are used'. OE *dræg*, 'dray', 'sledge', + *tūn*, 'farmstead', 'estate'. The manor here was held in the 11C by the Passelewe family, whose name distinguishes this Drayton from *Drayton Beauchamp*, 13 miles to the south, where it was held in the 13C by the Beauchamp family. DB *Draitone*, 1254 *Drayton Passelewe*.

Drayton St Leonard (village, Oxon): 'estate where sledges are used with St Leonard's church'. OE *dræg*, 'dray', 'sledge', + *tūn*, 'farmstead', 'estate'. The church dedication distinguishes the village from DRAYTON, 8 miles to the west. 1146 *Drætona*.

Drenewydd, Y. See NEWTOWN (Powys).

Drewsteignton (village, Devon): 'Drew's farmstead on the (river) Teign'. OE *tūn*, 'farmstead', 'village'. One Drew held the manor here in the 13C. For the river name, see TEIGNMOUTH. DB *Taintone*, 1275 *Teynton Drue*.

Driffield (town, E Yorks): 'dirty or stubbly open land'. OE *drit*, 'dirt', or *drīf*, 'stubble', + *feld*, 'open land' (modern English *field*). The town was formerly known as *Great Driffield*, for distinction from *Little Driffield*, immediately west of it, but the first word was dropped in the late 20C when there was concern in the town that business was suffering because of the difficulty of finding the name in geographical indexes under 'D'. DB *Drifeld*. SO ALSO: *Driffield*, Glos.

Drift Reservoir (reservoir, Cornwall): The reservoir, constructed in 1961, takes its name from the nearby hamlets of *Higher Drift* and *Lower Drift*, the basic name representing Cornish *an tre*, 'the village', but with the loss of *an* and an added *-t*. 1302 *Dref*, 1748 *Drift*.

Drigg (village, Cumbria): '(place by the) portage'. OS *dræg*, 'portage'. The name denotes a place where boats were dragged overland, in this case probably between the sea and the river Irt. 12C *Dreg*.

Drighlington (village, Leeds): 'estate associated with Dryhtel or Dyrhtla'. OE *-ing-*, 'associated with', + *tūn*, 'farmstead', 'estate'. The DB form of the name below has garbled the personal name. DB *Dreslingtone*, 1202 *Drichtlington*.

Drimpton (village, Dorset): 'Drēama's farmstead'. OE *tūn*, 'farmstead'. 1244 *Dremeton*.

Drinkstone (village, Suffolk): 'Drengr's farmstead'. OE *tūn*, 'farmstead'. The personal name is Scandinavian. c.1050 *Drincestune*, DB *Drencestuna*.

Drointon (hamlet, Staffs): 'farmstead of the free tenants'. OS *drengr*, 'young man', 'free tenant', + OE *tūn*, 'farmstead'. The DB form of the name below has omitted *n*. DB *Dregetone*, 1199 *Drengeton*.

Droitwich (town, Worcs): 'dirty salt works'. OE *drit*, 'dirt', + *wīc*, 'dwelling', 'specialized settlement'. The Roman station here was called *Salinae*, showing that the salt works were long established. They were 'dirty' because they were muddy. The first part of the name was long said to derive from OF *droit*, 'right', 'due', referring to the rights of Anglo-Saxon kings to levy dues at the saltpans. But early forms of the name clearly refute this interpretation. DB *Wich*, 1347 *Drihtwych*.

Dronfield (town, Derbys): 'open land plagued with drones'. OE *drān*, 'drone', + *feld*, 'open land' (modern English *field*). The 'drones' would have been wild male honeybees. DB *Dranefeld*.

Droxford (village, Hants): 'ford at the dry place'. OE *drocen*, 'dry place', + *ford*, 'ford'. The ford would have been over the small stream here. 826 *Drocenesforda*, DB *Drocheneford*.

Droylsden (district, Manchester): 'valley of the dry stream'. OE *drȳge*, 'dry', 'dried up', + *wella*, 'stream', + *denu*, 'valley'. This seems a likely origin of the name, although the middle element is open to dispute. A 'dry' stream is one that dries up in summer. c.1250 *Drilisden*.

Druidston (hamlet, Pemb): 'Drew's farm'. OE *tūn*, 'farmstead'. The present form of the name arose by popular association with a supposed Druidical stone formerly here. 1393 *Drewyston*.

Drumnadrochit (village, Highland): '(place by the) ridge of the bridge'. Gaelic *druim*, 'ridge', + *na*, 'of the', + *drochaid*, 'bridge'. The bridge in question is over the river Enrick, which flows east to enter Loch Ness.

Dryburgh (village, Borders): 'dry fortress'. OE *drȳge*, 'dry', + *burh*, 'fortified place'. The name must refer to a dried-up stream here at one time. *c*.1160 *Drieburh*.

Dry Drayton (village, Cambs): 'farmstead on a slope in a dry region'. OE *drȳge*, 'dry', + *dræg*, 'portage', 'slope used for dragging loads down', + *tūn*, 'farmstead'. The 'slope' would have been the nearby hill, while the village is 'dry' by contrast with FEN DRAYTON, as noted by the 18C Cambridge antiquary William Cole: 'Drye-Drayton, so called *not* from the *Drynesse* of the *Soile*, but for that it *standeth* in the *Upland* and Champion [i.e. champaign] Countrie, thereby to *distinguish* it from the other *Drayton*, which *taketh* Appellation from the *Fenne*'. DB *Draitone*, 1218 *Driedraiton*.

Dubris. See DOVER.

Duckington (hamlet, Cheshire): 'estate associated with Ducca'. OE *-ing-*, 'associated with', + *tūn*, 'farmstead', 'estate'. DB *Dochintone*.

Ducklington (village, Oxon): 'estate associated with Ducel'. OE *-ing-*, 'associated with', + *tūn*, 'farmstead', 'estate'. 958 *Duclingtun*, DB *Dochelintone*.

Duddington (village, Northants): 'estate associated with Dudda'. OE *-ing-*, 'associated with', + *tūn*, 'farmstead', 'estate'. DB *Dodintone*.

Duddo (hamlet, Northd): 'Dudda's hill spur'. OE *hōh*, 'hill spur'. 1208 *Dudehou*.

Dudley (town, Dudley): 'Dudda's woodland clearing'. OE *lēah*, 'wood', 'clearing'. Dudley is one of many '-ley' names locally, testifying to the importance of timber in the local iron and steel industry. DB *Dudelei*.

Duffield (village, Derbys): 'open land where doves are seen'. OE *dūfe*, 'dove', + *feld*, 'open land' (modern English *field*). The DB form of the name below is corrupt. DB *Duvelle*, 12C *Duffeld*.

Dufftown (town, Moray): 'Duff's town'. The name is that of James Duff, 4th Earl of Fife (1776–1857), who founded the town in 1817.

Dufton (village, Cumbria): 'farmstead where doves are kept'. OE *dūfe*, 'dove', + *tūn*, 'farmstead'. 1256 *Dufton*.

Duggleby (village, N Yorks): 'Dubgall's or Dubgilla's farmstead'. OS *bý*, 'farmstead', 'village'. The personal names are Old Irish. DB *Difgelibi*.

Dukeries, The (region, Notts): '(region of) ducal estates'. The estates so compositely named originally belonged to four ducal fami-

lies: Duke of Newcastle (Clumber Park), Duke of Portland (Welbeck Abbey), Duke of Norfolk (Worksop Manor) and Duke of Kingston (Thoresby Hall). The name dates from the 19C.

Dukestown (district of Tredegar, Blaenau Gwent): 'duke's town'. The township arose in the 19C around the Duke's Pit coalmine, opened on land owned by the Duke of BEAUFORT.

Dukinfield (town, Tameside): 'open land where ducks are seen'. OE *dūce*, 'duck', + *feld*, 'open land' (modern English *field*). The ducks are more likely to have been wild than domestic. 12C *Dokenfeld*.

Dullingham (village, Cambs): 'homestead of Dulla's people'. OE *-inga-*, 'of the people of', + *hām*, 'homestead'. *c*.1045 *Dullingham*, DB *Dullingeham*.

Duloe (village, Cornwall): '(place by) two pools'. Cornish *dew*, 'two', + *logh*, 'pool'. The village is located between the two rivers Looe, whose name means 'pool'. Cp. LOOE. 1283 *Dulo*.

Dulverton (town, Somerset): 'farmstead by the hidden ford'. OE *dīegel*, 'hidden', + *ford*, 'ford', + *tūn*, 'farmstead'. A 'hidden' ford is one not easily located, as here on the river Barle on the edge of Exmoor. DB *Dolvertune*.

Dulwich (district, Southwark): 'marshy meadow where dill grows'. OE *dile*, 'dill', + *wisc*, 'marshy meadow'. The herb dill has long been cultivated for medicinal use. Parts of Dulwich are still low-lying, with many ponds and lakes. 967 *Dilwihs*.

Dumbarton (town, W Dunbartons): 'fort of the Britons'. Gaelic *dùn*, 'fort', 'stronghold'. The name was applied by the neighbouring Gaels to the stronghold occupied by the (Ancient) Britons from the 5C. The Britons themselves called their fortress *Alclut*, 'rock of the Clyde'. Cp. BISHOP AUCKLAND. The historic county of *Dunbartonshire* took its name from that of the town but with *m* changed to *n* in modern times. *c*.1290 *Dumbrethan*.

Dumbleton (village, Glos): 'farmstead by a shady glen'. OE *dumbel*, 'hollow', 'shady dell', + *tūn*, 'farmstead'. The 'shady glen' in question could be the valley that runs up from the village into the hillside between The Park and Dumbleton Hill. The DB form of the name below is corrupt. 995 *Dumbeltun*, DB *Dubentune*.

Dumfries (town, Dumfries & Gall): 'woodland stronghold'. Gaelic *dùn*, 'fort', 'stronghold', + *preas*, 'copse', 'thicket'. The original 'woodland stronghold' probably stood in the centre of the town, in the part now known as Mid Steeple. *c*.1183 *Dunfres*.

Dummer (village, Hants): '(place by a) pond on a hill'. OE *dūn*, 'hill', + *mere*, 'pond'. There is a small pond by the village, which is on a hilltop. DB *Dunmere*.

Dumnonium Promontorium. See LIZARD.

Dunbar (resort town, E Lothian): 'fort on the height'. Gaelic *dùn*, 'fort', 'stronghold', + *barr*, 'height'. The 'height' where the original fort stood is the rocky headland where the ruins of Dunbar Castle lie. 709 *Dynbaer*.

Dunbartonshire. See DUMBARTON.

Dunblane (town, Stirling): 'Blaan's hill'. Gaelic *dùn*, 'hill', 'fort'. Blaan was a 6C bishop who had a monastery here on the site where the cathedral now stands. *c.*1200 *Dumblann*.

Duncansby Head (headland, Highland): 'headland by Donald's farm'. OS *bý*, 'farm'. *c.*1225 *Dungalsbaer*.

Dunchurch (village, Warwicks): 'Dunn's church'. OE *cirice*, 'church'. The DB form of the name below is corrupt. DB *Donecerce, c.*1150 *Duneschirche*.

Duncton (village, W Sussex): 'Dunnuca's farmstead'. OE *tūn*, 'farmstead'. DB *Donechitone*.

Dundee (city, Dundee): 'Daig's fort'. Gaelic *dùn*, 'fort', 'stronghold'. The 'fort' would have been where Dundee Castle formerly stood, by the present High Street. It is not known who Daig was. *c.*1180 *Dunde*.

Dundraw (hamlet, Cumbria): '(place by the) slope of the ridge'. The first part of the name is Celtic in origin, from a word related to modern Welsh *trum*, 'ridge'. The second part is OS *drag*, 'slope'. The form of the name below has added OS *hryggr*, 'ridge'. 1194 *Drumdrahhrigg*.

Dundry (village, N Somerset): '(place by a) hill where loads are dragged down'. OE *dūn*, 'hill', + *dræg*, 'portage'. 'slope used for dragging down loads'. The village lies on the slope of a long ridge known as Dundry Hill. 1065 *Dundreg*.

Dunfermline (town, Fife): meaning uncertain. The first element of the name is undoubtedly Gaelic *dùn*, 'hill', but the rest is unexplained. 11C *Dumfermelyn*, 1124 *Dumferlin*.

Dungeness (headland, Kent): 'headland by Denge Marsh'. OE *næss*, 'headland'. Denge Marsh may have a name meaning 'marsh of the valley district' (OE *denu*, 'valley', + *gē*, 'district', + *mersc*, 'marsh'). But there is no obvious valley here, and the first part of the name may mean 'manured land', from OE *dyncge* (Kentish *dencge*), 'dung', 'manure'. 1335 *Dengenesse*.

Dunham (village, Notts): 'homestead on a hill'. OE *dūn*, 'hill', + *hām*, 'homestead'. The village is also known as *Dunham on Trent*. (For the river name, see STOKE-ON-TRENT.) DB *Duneham*.

Dunham-on-the-Hill (village, Cheshire): 'village on a hill'. OE *dūn*, 'hill', + *hām*, 'homestead', 'village'. The tautologous second part of the name distinguishes this Dunham from DUNHAM TOWN, Trafford, 19 miles to the northeast. DB *Doneham*, 1534 *Dunham on the Hill*.

Dunhampton (village, Worcs): 'home farm by the hill'. OE *dūn*, 'hill', + *hām-tūn* (from *hām*, 'homestead', + *tūn*, 'farmstead'). 1222 *Dunhampton*.

Dunham Town (village, Trafford): 'village by the hill'. OE *dūn*, 'hill', + *hām*, 'homestead', 'village'. The hill in question is the one known as Bowdon Downs (which gave the name of BOWDON). The second word of the name distinguishes this Dunham from DUNHAM-ON-THE-HILL, Cheshire, 19 miles to the southwest. DB *Doneham*, 1841 *Dunham Town*.

Dunkeld (town, Perth & Kin): 'fort of the Caledonians'. Gaelic *dùn*, 'fort'. The 'Caledonians' are the Picts who occupied this region. 10C *Duncalden*.

Dunkery Beacon (hill, Somerset): 'fort of rocks'. The name is Celtic, from words related to modern Welsh *dinas*, 'fort' (here influenced by OE *dūn*, 'hill'), and *craig*, 'rock'. The hill is a 'beacon' as it was used for signal fires in medieval times. 1298 *Dunnecray*.

Dunkeswell (village, Devon): 'Duduc's or Dunnuc's spring'. OE *wella*, 'spring', 'stream'. The DB form of the name below has garbled the personal name. DB *Doducheswelle*, 1219 *Dunekeswell*.

Dunkeswick (village, N Yorks): 'lower farm where cheese is made'. OE *dūne*, 'lower', + *cēse*, 'cheese', + *wīc*, 'specialized farm'. This Keswick lies lower in the valley of the river Wharfe than EAST KESWICK, Leeds, south of the river. DB *Chesuic*.

Dunkirk (village, Kent): '(settlement named after) Dunkerque'. The name is a transfer of that of *Dunkerque*, France, an English possession for a time in the 17C. Its own name means 'church on the (sand) dunes' (Middle Dutch *dune*, 'dune', + *kerke*, 'church'). 1790 *Dunkirk*, 1868 *Dunkirk, or Dunkirk-Ville*.

Dunmow (town, Essex): 'meadow on a hill'. OE *dūn*, 'hill', + *māwe*, 'meadow'. The town is properly *Great Dunmow*, as distinct from nearby *Little Dunmow*. 951 *Dunemowe*, DB *Dommawa*.

Dunnet Head. See THURSO.

Dunnington (hamlet, E Yorks): 'estate associated with Dudda'. OE *-ing-*, 'associated with', + *tūn*, 'farmstead', 'estate'. DB *Dodintone*.

Dunnington (village, York): 'estate associated with Dunna'. OE *-ing-*, 'associated with', + *tūn*, 'farmstead'. 'estate'. DB *Donniton*.

Dunnockshaw (village, Lancs): '(place by the) wood where sparrows are seen'. OE *dunnoc*, 'sparrow' (modern English *dunnock*), + *sceaga*, 'wood', 'copse'. 1296 *Dunnockschae*.

Dunoon (town, Argyll & Bute): 'fort of the river'. Gaelic *dùn*, 'fort', + *abh*, 'river'. The fort in question would have stood where the castle remains now lie. The river is the Clyde. *c.*1240 *Dunnon*, 1270 *Dunhoven*.

Duns (town, Borders): '(place by the) hills'. OE *dūn*, 'hill'. The most obvious of the hills here is Duns Law, with the town at its foot.

Dunsfold (village, Surrey): 'Dunt's fold'. OE *fald*, 'fold', 'small enclosure'. 1259 *Duntesfaude*.

Dunsford (village, Devon): 'Dunn's ford'. OE *ford*, 'ford'. The river here is the Teign. DB *Dunnesforda*.

Dunsley (hamlet, N Yorks): 'Dunn's woodland clearing'. OE *lēah*, 'wood', 'clearing'. DB *Dunesle*.

Dunstable (town, Beds): 'Dunna's post'. OE *stapol*, 'post', 'pillar'. The 'post' was perhaps a boundary mark on the estate of the named man. The Roman settlement here was *Durocobrivis*, a name of Celtic origin probably meaning 'fort with a bridge-like structure'. (It cannot actually mean 'bridge', as for *Durobrivae* at CASTOR, as there is no bridge and no river at Dunstable.) Bailey's *Universal Etymological English Dictionary* (1721) says that the name is 'of Dunus, a Robber in the Time of King Henry I, who made it dangerous for Travellers, by his continual Robberies'. The time is right, but not the origin. 1123 *Dunestaple*.

Dunstall (hamlet, Staffs): 'farm site'. OE *tūnstall* (see TUNSTALL). 13C *Tunstall*.

Dunster (village, Somerset): 'Dunn's tor'. OE *torr*, 'tor', 'craggy hilltop'. The 'tor' is probably the nearby hill on which the 11C castle stands. DB *Torre*, 1138 *Dunestore*.

Duns Tew. See GREAT TEW.

Dunston (village, Lincs): 'Dunn's farmstead'. OE *tūn*, 'farmstead'. DB *Dunestune*. SO ALSO: *Dunston*, Norfolk, Staffs.

Dunterton (hamlet, Devon): 'farmstead at Dunter'. OE *tūn*, 'farmstead'. *Dunter* is an old Celtic name meaning literally 'fort village', from words related to modern Welsh *dinas*, 'fort', and *tref*, 'home'. The fort in question is

the ancient castle here by the river Tamar. DB *Dondritone*.

Duntisbourne Rouse (village, Glos): 'le Rous's (estate by) Dunt's stream'. OE *burna*, 'stream'. The le Rous family held the manor here in medieval times, their name distinguishing the village from nearby *Duntisbourne Abbots*, owned by the Abbot of St Peter's Abbey, Gloucester, and *Duntisbourne Leer*, owned by the Abbey of Lire, Normandy. DB *Duntesborne*, 1287 *Duntesbourn Rus*.

Duntish (hamlet, Dorset): 'pasture on a hill'. OE *dūn*, 'hill', + *etisc*, 'pasture'. 1249 *Dunhethis*.

Dunton (village, Beds): 'farmstead on a hill'. OE *dūn*, 'hill', + *tūn*, 'farmstead'. DB *Donitone*.

Dunton (village, Bucks): 'estate associated with Dudda or Dodda'. OE *-ing-*, 'associated with', + *tūn*, 'farmstead', 'estate'. DB *Dodintone*.

Dunton (hamlet, Norfolk): 'farmstead on a hill'. OE *dūn*, 'hill', + *tūn*, 'farmstead'. DB *Dontuna*.

Dunton Bassett (village, Leics): 'Basset's farmstead on a hill'. OE *dūn*, 'hill', + *tūn*, 'farmstead'. The Basset family held the manor here in the 13C. DB *Donitone*, 1418 *Dunton Basset*.

Dunton Green (suburb of Sevenoaks, Kent): 'estate associated with Dunn or Dunna'. OE *-ing-*, 'associated with', + *tūn*, 'farmstead', 'estate'. The village was later associated with its green. The original *-ing-* has disappeared from the name. 1244 *Dunington*.

Dunwich (coastal village, Suffolk): '(place by) deep water'. The name is ultimately Celtic in origin (modern Welsh *dwfn*, Irish *domhain*, 'deep'). Much of the former thriving port here was destroyed by erosion of the cliffs. The '-wich' of the name apparently evolved from the second syllable of the Celtic original and was taken to be OE *wīc*, 'harbour', 'trading centre'. 731 *Domnoc*, DB *Duneuuic*.

Durdle Door (coastal rock arch, Dorset): 'pierced opening'. OE *thyrelod*, 'pierced', + *duru*, 'door', 'opening'. Durdle Door is a rocky arch with a hole ('door') that has been cut out ('pierced') by the sea. There are no early records of the name, but the above origin seems likely. 1811 *Dirdale Door*.

Durham (city, Durham): 'island with a hill'. OE *dūn*, 'hill', + OS *holmr*, 'island'. The 'island with a hill' is the rocky site on which Durham stands in a loop of the river Wear. (See MONKWEARMOUTH for a possible meaning of the river name and its relevance to Durham.) The *n* of the original name became *r* under Norman influence. The county of Durham came into existence comparatively late, because it was long a palatinate (1071–1836) under the jurisdiction of the Bishop of Durham. There has thus never been a 'Durhamshire', and the county name is the same as that of the city (and traditionally differentiated from it as *County Durham* or *Co. Durham*). *c.*1000 *Dunholm*.

Durleigh (village, Somerset): 'wood or clearing where deer are seen'. OE *dēor*, 'deer', + *lēah*, 'wood', 'clearing'. DB *Derlege*.

Durnford. See GREAT DURNFORD.

Durnovaria. See DORCHESTER (Dorset).

Durobrivae. See (1) CASTOR, (2) CHESTERTON (Cambs), (3) ROCHESTER (Medway).

Durocobrivis. See DUNSTABLE.

Durocornovium. See WANBOROUGH.

Duroliponte. See CAMBRIDGE (Cambs).

Durovernum Cantiacorum. See CANTERBURY.

Durovigutum. See GODMANCHESTER.

Durrington (village, Wilts): 'estate associated with Dēora'. OE *-ing-*, 'associated with', + *tūn*, 'farmstead', 'estate'. *Durrington Walls*, as the name of the local telephone exchange, refers to a large 'henge' nearby in the form of an earth ring. DB *Derintone*. SO ALSO: *Durrington*, W Sussex.

Dursley (town, Glos): 'Dēorsige's woodland clearing'. OE *lēah*, 'wood', 'clearing'. DB *Dersilege*.

Durston (village, Somerset): 'Dēor's farmstead'. OE *tūn*, 'farmstead'. DB *Derstona*.

Durweston (village, Dorset): 'Dēorwine's farmstead'. OE *tūn*, 'farmstead'. DB *Derwinestone*.

Duston (district of Northampton, Northants): 'farmstead on a mound'. OE *dus*, 'mound', + *tūn*, 'farmstead'. The name could also mean 'dusty farmstead' (OE *dūst*, 'dust', + *tūn*), referring to the dusty soil. The name applies historically to

Old Duston, in the south of the district, not *New Duston*, in the northwest of the city. DB *Dustone*.

Dutton (village, Cheshire): 'farmstead by a hill'. OE *dūn*, 'hill', + *tūn*, 'farmstead'. DB *Duntune*.

Duxford (village, Cambs): 'Duc's enclosure'. OE *worth*, 'enclosure'. *c.*950 *Dukeswrthe*, DB *Dochesuuorde*.

Dwygyfylchi (district of Penmaenmawr, Conwy): '(place by) two circular forts'. Welsh *dwy*, 'two', + *cyfylchi*, 'circular fort'. There are several fortifications on the surrounding hills here.

Dyfed (historic county, SW Wales): '(district of the) Demetae'. The pre-Roman people of this name inhabited the part of Wales corresponding to modern Pembrokeshire. The origin of their name is unknown but they are mentioned by Ptolemy in the 2C AD.

Dymchurch (coastal town, Kent): 'church of the judge'. OE *dēma*, 'judge' (related modern English *deem*, *doom*), + *cirice*, 'church'. *c.*1100 *Deman circe*.

Dymock (village, Glos): 'fort of pigs'. The name is probably of Celtic origin, from words related to modern Welsh *din*, 'fort', and *moch*, 'pigs'. The pigs in question would presumably have fed in the woods around Dymock. The name is thus a Celtic equivalent of SWINTON. DB *Dimoch*.

Dyrham (village, S Glos): 'enclosed valley where deer are seen'. OE *dēor*, 'deer', + *hamm*, 'enclosed land'. A special sense of *hamm* was 'valley bottom hemmed in by higher ground', as exactly at Dyrham Park, where there are still deer to be seen in the grounds. 950 *Deorhamme*, DB *Dirham*.

Dyserth (village, Denb): 'hermitage'. Welsh *diserth*, 'hermit's cell' (from Latin *desertum*, 'retreat'). The Welsh form of the name is *Diserth*. DB *Dissard*, 1320 *Dyssart*.

E

Eagle (village, Lincs): 'wood where oak trees grow'. OE *āc*, 'oak', + *lēah*, 'wood', 'clearing'. The OE word for 'oak' has been replaced by *eik*, the OS equivalent, to give the present form of the name, which has apparently been further influenced by the name of the bird. Cp. ACLE. DB *Aycle*.

Eaglesfield (village, Cumbria): 'open land by a church'. The first part of the name is a Celtic word for 'church' corresponding to modern Welsh *eglwys*. Cp. ECCLES. The second part is OE *feld*, 'open land' (modern English *field*). *c.*1170 *Eglesfeld*.

Eakring (village, Notts): '(place by the) circle of oak trees'. OS *eik*, 'oak', + *hringr*, 'ring'. DB *Ecringhe*.

Ealing (borough, Greater London): '(settlement of) Gilla's people'. OE *-ingas*, 'people of'. *c.*698 *Gillingas*.

Eamont Bridge (village, Cumbria): '(place by the) bridge over the (river) Eamont'. OE *brycg*, 'bridge'. The river name means 'river junction' (OE *ēa-mōt*, from *ēa*, 'river', + *mōt*, 'meeting'), referring to the confluence of the river Lowther with the Eamont itself. The present form of the name evolved from OS *á-mót* as the equivalent of this. 11C *Eamotum*, 1362 *Amotbrig*.

Earby (town, Lancs): 'upper farmstead'. OS *efri*, 'upper', + *bȳ*, 'farmstead'. The name could also mean 'Jofurr's farmstead', with a Scandinavian personal name. DB *Eurebi*.

Eardington (village, Shropshire): 'estate associated with Earda'. OE *-ing-*, 'associated with', + *tūn*, 'farmstead', 'estate'. *c.*1030 *Eardigtun*, DB *Ardintone*.

Eardisland (village, Herefords): 'nobleman's estate in Leon'. OE *eorl*, 'earl', 'nobleman'. The '-land' represents *Leon*, the Celtic district name, seen also in LEOMINSTER. DB *Lene*, 1230 *Erleslen*.

Eardisley (village, Herefords): 'Ægheard's woodland clearing'. OE *lēah*, 'wood', 'clearing'. DB *Herdeslege*.

Eardiston (village, Worcs): 'Eardwulf's farmstead'. OE *tūn*, 'farmstead'. *c.*957 *Eardulfestun*, DB *Ardolvestone*.

Earith (village, Cambs): 'gravelly landing place'. OE *ēar*, 'gravel' (related modern English *earth*), + *hȳth*, 'landing place'. Earith is on the river Ouse. The origin of the name is identical to that of ERITH. 1244 *Herheth*.

Earle (hamlet, Northd): 'hill with an enclosure'. OE *geard*, 'enclosure' (modern English *yard*), + *hyll*, 'hill'. 1242 *Yherdhill*.

Earlestown (district of Newton-le-Willows, St Helens). The settlement developed in the 1820s round railway workshops here and was named after Sir Hardman Earle, director of the Liverpool and Manchester Railway Company.

Earley (suburb of Reading, Wokingham): 'wood or clearing where eagles are seen'. OE *earn*, 'eagle', + *lēah*, 'wood', 'clearing'. 8C *Earneleagh*, DB *Herlei*.

Earlham (district of Norwich, Norfolk): 'homestead of a nobleman'. OE *eorl*, 'nobleman' (modern English *earl*), + *hām*, 'homestead'. DB *Erlham*.

Earls Barton (village, Northants): 'earl's barley farm'. OE *bere-tūn* (from *bere*, 'barley', + *tūn*, 'farmstead'). David, Earl of Huntingdon held the manor here in the 12C. DB *Bartone*, 1261 *Erlesbarton*.

Earls Colne. See COLNE ENGAINE.

Earls Court (district, Hammersmith & Ful): 'earl's court'. The name is that of a manor house ('court') formerly here owned by the earls of Oxford until the 16C. The district grew up around the house, which was not demolished until 1886. 1593 *Earles Court*, 1654 *Erls Cort*, 1868 *Earl's Court*.

Earl's Croome (village, Worcs): 'earl's (estate by the river) Croome'. The river name, originally that of the stream here, is Celtic in origin and means 'winding one' (modern Welsh *crwm*, 'crooked'). The manor was held early by the earls of Warwick. 10C *Cromman*, DB *Crumbe*, 1495 *Erlescrombe*.

Earlsfield (district, Wandsworth): 'earl's field'. The earls Spencer held land here in the 18C and 19C.

Earlsheaton. See KIRKHEATON (Kirklees).

Earl Shilton (suburb of Hinckley, Leics): 'earl's farmstead on a shelf'. OE *scylfe*, 'shelf', + *tūn*, 'farmstead'. A 'shelf' is an area of noticeably flat or level ground. The manor here was held early by the earls of Leicester. DB *Sceltone*.

Earl Soham (village, Suffolk): 'earl's homestead by a pool'. OE *sǣ*, 'pool' (modern English *sea*), + *hām*, 'homestead'. The manor here was held early by the Earl of Norfolk, whose title distinguishes this Soham from nearby *Monk Soham*, held by the monks of Bury St Edmunds. DB *Saham*.

Earl Sterndale (village, Derbys): 'earl's (estate in the) valley with rocky ground'. OE *stǣner*, 'stony ground' (from *stān*, 'stone'), + *dæl*, 'valley'. The manor here was held in the 13C by the Earl of Derby, whose title distinguishes the village from *King Sterndale*, 3 miles to the north, where it was held by the king. The first form of the name below is corrupt. 1244 *Stenredile*, 1251 *Sternedale*, 1330 *Erlisstenerdale*.

Earlston (town, Borders): 'Earcil's hill'. OE *dūn*, 'hill'. Earlston is in Lauderdale surrounded by hills. c.1144 *Erchildun*, c.1180 *Ercildune*, 1868 *Earlston*, or *Ercildon*.

Earl Stonham (village, Suffolk): 'earl's (estate at the) homestead by a stone'. OE *stān*, 'stone', + *hām*, 'homestead'. The basic name could also mean 'homestead on stony ground'. The manor here was held in the 13C by Earl Roger Bigod, whose title distinguishes the village from nearby *Little Stonham* and *Stonham Aspal*, the latter held by the de Aspale family. c.1040 *Stonham*, DB *Stanham*.

Earnley (village, W Sussex): 'wood or clearing where eagles are seen'. OE *earn*, 'eagle', + *lēah*, 'wood', 'clearing'. 8C *Earneleagh*.

Earsdon (suburb of Whitley Bay, N Tyneside): 'Ēanrǣd's or Ēorǣd's hill'. OE *dūn*, 'hill'. 1233 *Erdesdon*.

Earsham (village, Norfolk): 'Ēanhere's homestead'. OE *hām*, 'homestead', 'village'. DB *Ersam*.

Earswick (hamlet, York): 'Æthelrīc's farm'. OE *wīc*, 'dwelling', 'farmstead'. The DB form of the

name below has garbled the personal name. DB *Edresuuic*, 13C *Ethericewyk*.

Eartham (village, W Sussex): 'homestead or enclosure with ploughed land'. OE *erth*, 'ploughed land' (related modern English *earth*), + *hām*, 'homestead', or *hamm*, 'enclosure'. The first form of the name below has *t* miscopied as *c*. 12C *Ercheham*, 1279 *Ertham*.

Easby (hamlet, N Yorks): 'Ēsi's farmstead'. OS *bý*, 'farmstead', 'village'. The personal name is Scandinavian. The form of the name below is for Easby near Great Ayton. DB *Esebi*.

Easebourne (village, W Sussex): '(place by) Ēsa's stream'. OE *burna*, 'stream'. DB *Eseburne*.

Easenhall (village, Warwicks): 'Ēsa's hill'. OE *hyll*, 'hill'. 1221 *Esenhull*.

Eashing (village, Surrey): '(settlement of) Æsc's people'. OE *-ingas*, 'people of'. The name could also mean '(settlement of the) dwellers by the ash tree' (OE *æsc*, 'ash', + *-ingas*, 'dwellers at'). Late 9C *Æscengum*, 1272 *Essinge*.

Easington (town, Durham): 'estate associated with Ēsa'. OE *-ing-*, 'associated with', + *tūn*, 'farmstead', 'estate'. c.1050 *Esingtun*. SO ALSO: *Easington*, Bucks, E Yorks, Redcar & Clev.

Easington (hamlet, Northd): 'farmstead on the (river) Yese'. OE *tūn*, 'farmstead'. The first part of the name is probably a former name of the stream here, itself related to the name of the *Ouse* (see OUSEFLEET). 1242 *Yesington*.

Easington (hamlet, Oxon): 'Ēsa's hill'. OE *dūn*, 'hill'. This is Easington near Chalgrove. DB *Esidone*.

Easingwold (town, N Yorks): 'high forestland of Ēsa's people'. OE *-inga-*, 'of the people of', + *wald*, 'woodland', 'high forest'. See WOLDS. Easingwold is on the western side of the Howardian Hills in the Vale of York. DB *Eisincewald*.

East Adderbury (village, Oxon): 'eastern (place called) Ēadburh's stronghold'. OE *burh*, 'fortified place'. The personal name is that of a woman. The first word of the name distinguishes the village from nearby *West Adderbury*. c.950 *Eadburggebyrig*, DB *Edburgberie*.

East Allington (village, Devon): 'eastern farmstead associated with Ælla or Ælle'. OE *-ing-*, 'associated with', + *tūn*, 'farmstead'. The first word of the name distinguishes the village from the hamlet of *South Allington*, 8 miles to the south. DB *Alintone*.

East Anstey (village, Devon): 'eastern (place with a) single track'. OE *ānstīg* (see ANSTEY). The first word of the name distinguishes the village from nearby *West Anstey*. The track in each case may have led to the summit of the hill on which the respective churches stand. DB *Anestiga*.

East Appleton (hamlet, N Yorks): 'eastern farmstead where apples grow'. OE *æppel-tūn* (from *æppel*, 'apple', + *tūn*, 'farmstead'). The first word of the name distinguishes the place from nearby *West Appleton*. DB *Apelton*.

East Ashling (village, W Sussex): 'eastern (settlement of) Æscla's people'. OE *-ingas*, 'people of'. The first word of the name distinguishes the village from nearby *West Ashling*. 1185 *Estlinges*.

East Ayton. See WEST AYTON.

East Bagborough. See WEST BAGBOROUGH.

East Barkwith (village, Lincs): 'eastern (place called) Barki's enclosure'. OE *worth*, 'enclosure'. The personal name is Scandinavian. The village is 'east' with regard to the hamlet of *West Barkwith*. DB *Barcuurde*.

East Barming (village, Kent): 'eastern (place)'. The meaning of the main name is uncertain. The first word distinguishes the village from nearby *West Barming*. DB *Bermelinge*.

East Barnet. See BARNET.

East Barsham (village, Norfolk): 'eastern (place called) Bār's homestead'. OE *hām*, 'homestead', 'village'. The village is 'east' with regard to the hamlets of *West Barsham* and *South Barsham*. DB *Barseham*.

East Barton. See GREAT BARTON.

East Beckham (village, Norfolk): 'eastern (place called) Becca's homestead'. OE *hām*, 'homestead', 'village'. The first word of the name distinguishes the village from nearby *West Beckham*. DB *Beccheham*.

East Bedfont (district, Hounslow): 'eastern spring (provided) with a drinking vessel'. OE *byden*, 'tub', 'cask', + *funta*, 'spring'. East Bedfont is on the Roman road from London to Silchester, and travellers would have been able to replenish their water supplies here. The first word of the name distinguishes this Bedfont from nearby *West Bedfont*, Surrey. DB *Bedefunt*.

East Bergholt (village, Suffolk): 'eastern wood by a hill'. OE *beorg*, 'hill', + *holt*, 'wood'. The village is 'east' with regard to *West Bergholt*, Essex, 9 miles to the southwest. DB *Bercolt*.

East Bilney (village, Norfolk): 'eastern island near a ridge'. OE *bile*, 'beak', 'ridge', + *ēg*, 'island'. The name could also mean 'Billa's island'. The 'island' would have been raised ground in marshland here. The first interpretation of the name above is rejected by some on the grounds that OE *bile* did not form a genitive in *-n* (to give the *n* of the name). The first word of the name

distinguishes this Bilney from *West Bilney*, 16 miles to the west. 1254 *Billneye*.

East Blatchington (suburb of Newhaven, E Sussex): 'eastern estate associated with Blæcca'. OE *-ing-*, 'associated with', + *tūn*, 'farmstead', 'estate'. The first word of the name distinguishes this Blatchington from *West Blatchington*, W Sussex, 14 miles to the west, now a district of Hove. 1169 *Blechinton*.

Eastbourne (resort town, E Sussex): '(place at the) eastern stream'. OE *ēast*, 'eastern', + *burna*, 'stream' (modern northern English *burn*). The first part of the name was apparently added to distinguish the town from WESTBOURNE, W Sussex, almost 60 miles to the west. The stream in question is the one that rises near St Mary's Church, in the old part of the town, and that flows (now covered) to the sea, crossing the present Bourne Street. DB *Burne*, 1310 *Estbourne*, 1868 *East Bourne*.

East Brent. See BRENT KNOLL.

East Bridgford. See WEST BRIDGFORD.

East Budleigh. See BUDLEIGH SALTERTON.

Eastbury (village, W Berks): 'eastern manor'. OE *ēast*, 'eastern', + *burh*, 'fortified place', 'manor'. The manor was probably regarded as 'east' in relation to Bockhampton. *c.*1090 *Eastbury*.

East Butterwick (village, N Lincs): 'eastern dairy farm where butter is made'. OE *butere*, 'butter', + *wīc*, 'dairy farm'. The first word of the name distinguishes the village from *West Butterwick*, on the opposite bank of the river Trent. DB *Butreuuic*.

East Carlton (village, Northants): 'eastern farmstead of the peasants'. OS *karl*, 'freeman', 'peasant', + OE *tūn*, 'farmstead', 'estate'. The place is probably 'east' with regard to CARLTON CURLIEU, Leics, 10 miles to the northwest. DB *Carlintone*.

East Chaldon. See CHALDON HERRING.

East Challow (village, Oxon): 'eastern (place called) Ceawa's tumulus'. OE *hlǣw*, 'tumulus', 'mound'. The village is 'east' with regard to *West Challow*. The DB form of the name below is corrupt. 947 *Ceawanhlǣwe*, DB *Ceveslane*.

East Charleton (village, Devon): 'eastern farmstead of the freemen'. OE *ceorl*, 'freeman', 'peasant' (modern English *churl*), + *tūn*, 'farmstead'. The first word of the name distinguishes this Charleton from nearby *West Charleton*. DB *Cherletone*.

East Chelborough (hamlet, Dorset): 'eastern (place called) Cēola's hill'. OE *beorg*, 'hill'. The first part of the main name could also represent OE *ceole*, 'throat', 'gorge', or *cealc*, 'chalk'. The first word of the name distinguishes the hamlet from nearby *West Chelborough*. DB *Celberge*.

East Chiltington. See WEST CHILTINGTON.

East Chinnock (village, Somerset): 'eastern (place in the) valley'. OE *cinu*, 'deep valley' (modern English *chine*). The name could also be that of a hill here and of Celtic origin. The village is 'east' with regard to *West Chinnock*. *c.*950 *Cinnuc*, DB *Cinioch*.

East Chisenbury (village, Wilts): 'eastern stronghold of the dwellers on the gravel'. OE *cis*, 'gravel', + *-inga-*, 'of the dwellers at', + *burh*, 'stronghold'. The first half of the main name could also represent OE *cising*, 'gravelly place'. The subsoil is gravelly here, and the 'stronghold' would be Chisenbury Camp, an old earthwork not far off. The first word of the name distinguishes the village from nearby *West Chisenbury*. DB *Chesigeberie*, 1202 *Chisingburi*.

Eastchurch (village, Kent): 'eastern church'. OE *ēast*, 'eastern', + *cirice*, 'church'. The village lies on the eastern side of the Isle of Sheppey. *c.*1100 *Eastcyrce*.

East Clandon (village, Surrey): 'eastern (place by the) clean hill'. OE *clǣne*, 'clean', + *dūn*, 'hill'. A 'clean' hill is one free from weeds or other unwanted growth. The first word of the name distinguishes the village from nearby *West Clandon*. DB *Clanedun*.

East Claydon. See STEEPLE CLAYDON.

East Coker (village, Somerset): 'eastern (place by the river) Coker'. The former name of the stream here is of Celtic origin and means 'winding one'. The village is 'east' with regard to *West Coker*. North of East Coker is *North Coker*. DB *Cocre*.

East Cottingwith (village, E Yorks): 'eastern dairy farm associated with Cott or Cotta'. OE *-ing-*, 'associated with', + *wīc*, 'dairy farm' (replaced by OS *vithr*, 'wood'). The first word of the name distinguishes the village from *West Cottingwith*, N Yorks, across the river Derwent. The DB form of the name below is corrupt. DB *Coteuuid*, 1195 *Cotingwic*.

East Coulston. See COULSTON.

East Cowton (village, N Yorks): 'eastern dairy farm'. OE *cū*, 'cow', + *tūn*, 'farmstead'. The first word of the name distinguishes the village from nearby *North Cowton* and *South Cowton*. DB *Cudtone*.

East Cranmore. See WEST CRANMORE.

Eastdean (village, E Sussex): '(place in the) eastern valley'. OE *ēast*, 'eastern', + *denu*, 'valley'. The village is 'east' with regard to *Westdean*, 2 miles to the northwest. DB *Esdene*.

East Dean (village, W Sussex): '(place in the) eastern valley'. OE *ēast*, 'eastern', + *denu*, 'valley'. The village is 'east' with regard to *West Dean*, 3 miles to the west. 8C *Dene*, 1150 *Estdena*.

East Dean (Hants). See WEST DEAN.

East Dereham (town, Norfolk): 'eastern enclosure for deer'. OE *dēor*, 'deer', + *hamm*, 'enclosure'. Cp. DYRHAM. The first word distinguishes this Dereham from *West Dereham*, 22 miles to the southwest. DB *Derham*, 1428 *Estderham*.

East Down. See WEST DOWN.

East Drayton (village, Notts): 'eastern farmstead by a portage'. OE *dræg*, 'portage' (related modern English *drag*, *draw*), + *tūn*, 'farmstead'. The 'portage' would have been a 'chute' nearby where timber or other materials could be dragged down. East Drayton is on a road that rises quite steeply to the west. The first word of the name distinguishes the village from *West Drayton*, 4 miles to the west. DB *Draitone*, 1276 *Est Draiton*.

Eastergate (village, W Sussex): '(place at the) more easterly gap'. OE *ēasterra*, 'more easterly', + *geat*, 'gap' (modern English *gate*). The village is 'more easterly' with regard to nearby *Westergate*. DB *Gate*, 1263 *Estergat*.

Easterton (village, Wilts): 'more easterly farmstead'. OE *ēasterra*, 'more easterly', + *tūn*, 'farmstead'. The village is 'more easterly' with regard to nearby Market Lavington. 1348 *Esterton*.

East Farleigh (village, Kent): 'eastern woodland clearing where ferns grow'. OE *fearn*, 'fern', + *lēah*, 'wood', 'clearing'. The village is 'east' with regard to *West Farleigh*. 9C *Fearnlege*, DB *Ferlaga*.

East Farndon (village, Northants): 'eastern hill where ferns grow'. OE *fearn*, 'fern', + *dūn*, 'hill'. The village is 'east' with respect to the hamlet of *West Farndon*. DB *Ferendone*.

East Garston (village, W Berks): 'Esgar's estate'. OE *tūn*, 'farmstead', 'estate'. The personal name is Scandinavian. The present form of the name arose by way of folk etymology, and there is no 'West Garston'. 1180 *Esgareston*, 1535 *Est Garston*.

East Grafton (village, Wilts): 'eastern farmstead by a grove'. OE *grāf*, 'grove', + *tūn*, 'farmstead'. The village is 'east' with regard to *West Grafton*. DB *Graftone*.

East Grimstead (village, Wilts): 'eastern green place'. OE *grēne*, 'green', + *stede*, 'place'. Cp. EAST GRINSTEAD. The first word of the name distinguishes the village from nearby *West Grimstead*. DB *Gremestede*.

East Grinstead (town, W Sussex): 'eastern green place'. OE *grēne*, 'green', + *stede*, 'place', A 'green place' is a pasture for grazing. The first word of the name distinguishes the town from the village of *West Grinstead*, 19 miles to the southwest. 1121 *Grenesteda*, 1271 *Estgrenested*.

East Guldeford (village, E Sussex). The place takes its name from the Guldeford family, from GUILDFORD, here in the early 16C, and it lies east of that town. An entry for the year 1505 in the register of Richard Fitzjames, Bishop of London, notes that 'the church of New Guldeford, within the brook commonly called Guldeford Innyng, now reclaimed from the sea and made dry land by Richard Guldeford, Kt., having been newly built at his expense', was consecrated by the bishop and made into a parish church. 1517 *Est Guldeford*.

East Haddon. See WEST HADDON.

East Hagbourne (village, Oxon): 'eastern (place by) Hacca's stream'. OE *burna*, 'stream'. The village is east of *West Hagbourne*. c.895 *Haccaburna*, DB *Hacheborne*.

East Halton (village, N Lincs): 'eastern farmstead in a corner of land'. OE *halh*, 'nook', 'corner of land', + *tūn*, 'farmstead'. The first word of the name distinguishes this Halton from *West Halton*, 15 miles to the west. DB *Haltune*.

Eastham (district of Bebington, Wirral): 'eastern homestead or enclosure'. OE *ēast*, 'eastern', + *hām*, 'homestead', or *hamm*, 'enclosure'. Eastham is in the east of the Wirral peninsula. DB *Estham*.

East Ham (town, Newham): 'eastern riverside land'. OE *hamm*, 'enclosure', 'river meadow'. East Ham is in an angle formed by the rivers Thames and Roding. The first word of the name distinguishes this place from nearby WEST HAM. 958 *Hamme*, DB *Hame*, 1206 *Estham*.

East Hampnett. See WESTHAMPNETT.

East Hanney (village, Oxon): 'eastern island where cockbirds are seen'. OE *hana*, 'cockbird' (related modern English *hen*), + *ēg*, 'island'. The 'island' here is land between streams. The village is 'east' with regard to *West Hanney*. 956 *Hannige*, DB *Hannei*.

East Hanningfield (village, Essex): 'eastern open land of Hana's people'. OE *-inga-*, 'of the people of', + *feld*, 'open land' (modern English *field*). The first word of the name distinguishes the village from *South Hanningfield*, 3 miles to the southwest, and *West Hanningfield*, 3 miles to

the west. c.1036 *Hamningefelde*, DB *Haningefelda*.

East Harling (village, Norfolk): 'eastern (settlement of) Herela's people'. OE *-ingas*, 'people of'. The basic name could also mean 'Herela's place' (OE *-ing*, 'place belonging to'). The village is 'east' with regard to the much smaller *West Harling*. *Middle Harling* lies between them. c.1060 *Herlinge*, DB *Herlinga*.

East Harlsey (village, N Yorks): 'eastern (place called) Herel's island'. OE *ēg*, 'island'. The 'island' is dry ground in marshland here. The first word of the name distinguishes the village from nearby (and much smaller) *West Harlsey*. DB *Herlesege*.

East Harnham. See WEST HARNHAM.

East Harptree. See WEST HARPTREE.

East Hatley. See HATLEY ST GEORGE.

East Hauxwell (village, N Yorks): 'eastern (place at the) stream where hawks are seen'. OE *hafoc*, 'hawk', + *wella*, 'spring', 'stream'. The first part of the name could also represent the personal name Hafoc. The first word of the name contrasts the village with nearby much smaller *West Hauxwell*. DB *Hauocheswelle*.

East Hendred (village, Oxon): 'eastern (place on a) stream where henbirds are seen'. OE *henn*, 'hen', + *rīth*, 'stream'. The village is 'east' with respect to *West Hendred*. 956 *Hennarith*, DB *Henret*.

East Herrington (district, Sunderland): 'eastern estate associated with Here'. OE *-ing-*, 'associated with', + *tūn*, 'farmstead', 'estate'. The district is 'east' by comparison with *West Herrington*. There are also *Middle Herrington*, between the two, and *New Herrington*, the whole area being often referred to as simply *Herrington*. 1196 *Erinton*.

East Heslerton. See WEST HESLERTON.

East Hoathly (village, E Sussex): 'eastern woodland clearing where heather grows'. OE *hāth*, 'heather', + *lēah*, 'wood', 'clearing'. The name contrasts with that of *West Hoathly*, W Sussex, 15 miles to the northwest. 1286 *Hodlegh*.

East Holme (hamlet, Dorset): 'eastern (place by the) holly tree'. OE *holegn*, 'holly'. The first word of the name contrasts the place with nearby *West Holme*. DB *Holne*, 1288 *Estholn*.

Easthope (village, Shropshire): 'eastern enclosed valley'. OE *ēast*, 'eastern', + *hop*, 'enclosed valley'. The valley is 'east' in relation to a number of other places with names ending in *hop*. The DB form of the name below has omitted the vowels of *ēast*. 901 *Easthope*, DB *Stope*.

East Horndon. See HORNDON ON THE HILL.

Easthorpe (hamlet, Essex): 'eastern outlying farmstead'. OE *ēast*, 'eastern', + OS *thorp*, 'outlying farmstead'. Easthorpe lies east of the river Blackwater. DB *Estorp*.

East Horrington (village, Somerset): 'eastern (place by the) horn-shaped hill'. OE *horning*, 'horn-shaped hill', + *dūn*, 'hill'. The main name could also mean 'hill of the dwellers on the horn-shaped piece of land' (OE *horn*, 'horn', + *-inga-*, 'of the dwellers at', + *dūn*). The first word of the name distinguishes the village from nearby *West Horrington*. 1065 *Hornningdun*.

East Horsley (village, Surrey): 'eastern clearing where horses are pastured'. OE *hors*, 'horse', + *lēah*, 'wood', 'clearing'. The first word of the name distinguishes the village from nearby *West Horsley*. 9C *Horsalæge*, DB *Horslei*.

Easthouses (village, Midlothian): 'eastern house'. OE *ēast*, 'eastern', + *hūs*, 'house'. The plural *-s* is a recent development. 1241 *Esthus*, 1345 *Esthouse*, 1590 *Eisthousis*.

East Ilsley (village, W Berks): 'eastern (place called) Hild's woodland clearing'. OE *lēah*, 'wood', 'clearing'. The name contrasts with that of *West Ilsley*, to the northwest. DB *Hildeslei*.

Eastington (village, Glos): 'Ēadstān's farmstead'. OE *tūn*, 'farmstead'. This is Eastington near Stroud. Eastington near Northleach is 'east' of that village. 1220 *Esteueneston*.

East Keal (village, Lincs): 'eastern (place by the) ridge'. OS *eystri* or OE *ēasterra*, 'more easterly', + OS *kjǫlr*, 'ridge' (modern English *keel*). The first word of the name distinguishes the village from *West Keal*. DB *Estrecale*.

East Keswick (village, Leeds): 'eastern farm where cheese is made'. OE *cēse*, 'cheese', + *wīc*, 'specialized farm'. This Keswick is 'east' in relation to DUNKESWICK, N Yorks, across the river Wharfe. DB *Chesuic*.

East Kilbride (town, S Lanarks): 'eastern (place by) St Brigid's church'. Gaelic *cill*, 'church'. The first word distinguishes the town from WEST KILBRIDE. 1180 *Kellebride*.

East Knapton. See WEST KNAPTON.

East Knighton. See WEST KNIGHTON.

East Knoyle (village, Wilts): 'eastern (place at the) knuckle-shaped hill'. OE *cnugel*, 'knuckle'. The village is 'east' by contrast with *West Knoyle*, to the northwest. 948 *Knugel*, DB *Chenvel*.

East Kyloe (hamlet, Northd): 'eastern pasture for cows'. OE *cū*, 'cow', + *lēah*, 'clearing', 'pasture'. The first word of the name distinguishes this Kyloe from nearby *West Kyloe*. 1195 *Culeia*.

East Lambrook (village, Somerset): 'eastern (place by the) boundary brook'. OE *land*, 'cultivated land', 'estate', + *brōc*, 'brook'. The first word of the name distinguishes the village from nearby *West Lambrook*, while between the two is *Mid Lambrook*. 1065 *Landbroc*.

East Langton. See CHURCH LANGTON.

East Lavant (village, W Sussex): 'eastern farmstead on the (river) Lavant'. OE *tūn*, 'farmstead'. The river name is of Celtic origin and means 'gliding one'. The 'farmstead' element has disappeared from the name, now distinguished from those of nearby *Mid Lavant* and the former *West Lavant*, the latter perhaps originally on the site now occupied by Lavant House. DB *Loventone*, 1227 *Lavent*.

East Lavington. See WEST LAVINGTON (W Sussex).

East Layton (village, N Yorks): 'eastern enclosure where leeks are grown'. OE *lēac-tūn* (from *lēac*, 'leek', + *tūn*, 'enclosure'). The first word of the name distinguishes the village from nearby *West Layton*. DB *Latton*.

Eastleach (parish, Glos): 'eastern (place) on the (river) Leach'. OE *ēast*, 'eastern'. The parish is 'east' with regard to NORTHLEACH (see for the river name). It is divided into the villages of *Eastleach Martin* and *Eastleach Turville*, either side of the river, the former named from the dedication of its church to St Martin, the latter from the de Turville family, who held the manor in the 13C. 862 *Lecche*, DB *Lecce*.

East Leake (village, Notts): 'eastern (place by the) stream'. OS *lœkr*, 'stream'. The village is east of *West Leake*, and both are on the same stream, a tributary of the river Soar. DB *Lecche*.

Eastleigh (town, Hants): 'eastern wood or clearing'. OE *ēast*, 'eastern', + *lēah*, 'wood', 'clearing'. The name could also mean '(place) east of the wood'. The town arose only in the 19C. 932 *East lea*, DB *Estleie*.

Eastleigh (Devon). See WESTLEIGH.

East Lexham (village, Norfolk): 'eastern homestead of the physician'. OE *lǣce*, 'physician' (modern English *leech*), + *hām*, 'homestead', 'village'. The first word of the name distinguishes the village from nearby *West Lexham*. DB *Lecesham*.

East Lilling. See WEST LILLING.

Eastling (village, Kent): '(settlement of) Ēsla's people'. OE *-ingas*, 'people of'. DB *Eslinges*.

East Linton (town, E Lothian): 'eastern flax enclosure'. OE *līn*, 'flax' (related modern English *linen*), + *tūn*, 'enclosure', 'village'. 'East' was added to the original name to distinguish this place from *West Linton*, now a village southwest of Penicuik. 1127 *Lintun*.

East Lockinge (hamlet, Oxon): 'eastern (place on the) Lockinge Brook'. The name of the stream means 'playful one' (OE *lāc*, 'play', + *-ing*, 'stream characterized by'). The first word of the name distinguishes the hamlet from nearby *West Lockinge*. 868 *Lacinge*, DB *Lachinges*, 1327 *Estloking*.

East Lulworth (village, Dorset): 'eastern (place called) Lulla's enclosure'. OE *worth*, 'enclosure'. The first word of the name distinguishes this Lulworth from the coastal village of *West Lulworth*, 3 miles to the west, above the circular bay known as *Lulworth Cove*. DB *Lulvorde*.

East Lydford (village, Somerset): 'eastern (place by the) ford over the noisy stream'. OE *hlȳde*, 'loud one', + *ford*, 'ford'. The first word of the name distinguishes the village from nearby *West Lydford*. DB *Lideford*.

East Malling. See WEST MALLING.

East Marden (village, W Sussex): 'eastern (place by the) boundary hill'. OE *gemǣre*, 'boundary', + *dūn*, 'hill'. The village lies on the South Downs near the county border with Hampshire. The first word of the name distinguishes it from nearby *North Marden* and *Up Marden*, with *West Marden* further west. DB *Meredone*.

East Markham (village, Notts): 'eastern homestead on a boundary'. OE *mearc*, 'boundary' (modern English *mark*), + *hām*, 'homestead', 'village'. The first word of the name distinguishes the village from nearby *West Markham*. It is uncertain which boundary is referred to. DB *Marcham*, 1192 *Estmarcham*.

East Meon. See WEST MEON.

East Molesey (residential district, Surrey): 'eastern (place called) Mūl's island'. OE *ēg*, 'island'. The 'island' is an area of raised land beside the river Mole, which takes its own name from Molesey. (The river was earlier known as the Emele. See ELMBRIDGE.) The first word of the name distinguishes this Molesey from neighbouring *West Molesey*. The Mole itself, rising in West Sussex, flows mostly north through Surrey to enter the Thames at East Molesey. Hence *Mole Valley* as the name of the local council district. The DB form of the name below is corrupt. 672 *Muleseg*, DB *Molesham*.

East Ness (hamlet, N Yorks): 'eastern (place by the) headland'. OE *næss*, 'promontory'. Both this place and nearby *West Ness* take their names from the eastern end of a ridge of land between the river Rye and Hole Beck. DB *Nesse*.

Eastnor (village, Herefords): '(place to the) east of the ridge'. OE *ēastan*, 'east of', + *ofer*, 'ridge'. DB *Astenofre*.

Eastoft (village, N Lincs): 'homestead where ash trees grow'. OS *eski*, 'ash', + *toft*, 'homestead'. *c*.1170 *Eschetoft*.

East Ogwell (village, Devon): 'eastern (place by) Wocga's spring'. OE *wella*, 'spring', 'stream'. The first word of the name distinguishes this Ogwell from the nearby hamlet of *West Ogwell*. 956 *Wogganwylle*, DB *Wogewille*.

Easton (village, Cambs): 'eastern farmstead'. OE *ēast*, 'eastern', + *tūn*, 'farmstead', 'village'. The farm was probably 'east' with regard to Old Weston. DB *Estone*. SO ALSO: *Easton*, Cumbria (near Netherby), Hants, IoW, Lincs, Norfolk, Suffolk.

Easton Grey (village, Wilts): 'de Grey's eastern village'. OE *ēast*, 'eastern', + *tūn*, 'farmstead', 'village'. John de Grey is recorded as holding the manor here in 1243. DB *Estone*, 1281 *Eston Grey*.

Easton-in-Gordano (town, N Somerset): 'eastern village in Gordano'. OE *ēast*, 'eastern', + *tūn*, 'farmstead', 'village'. The district name probably meaning 'filthy valley' (OE *gor*, 'dirt', 'dung', + *denu*, 'valley'). DB *Estone*, 1293 *Eston in Gordon*.

Easton Maudit (village, Northants): 'Mauduit's eastern farmstead. OE *ēast*, 'eastern', + *tūn*, 'farmstead', 'village'. The farm may have been 'eastern' with regard to Denton and Whiston. The manor here was held in the 12C by the Mauduit family. DB *Estone*, 1298 *Estonemaudeut*.

Easton on the Hill (village, Northants): 'eastern farmstead on a hill'. OE *ēast*, 'eastern', + *tūn*, 'farmstead', 'village'. The village is 'east' with regard to COLLYWESTON. The second part of the name refers to the location of the village on the brow of a hill. DB *Estone*.

Easton Royal (village, Wilts): 'royal eastern farmstead'. OE *ēast*, 'eastern', + *tūn*, 'farmstead', + OF *roial*, 'royal'. The farmstead, 'east' of Milton, is on the edge of the old royal forest of Savernake. DB *Estone*, 1868 *Easton, or Easton Royal*.

East Orchard. See WEST ORCHARD.

East Ord (village, Northd): 'eastern (place by the) projecting ridge'. OE *ord*, 'point of land'. The name probably refers to the long ridge on which nearby *Middle Ord* lies, with *West Ord* to the west. 1196 *Horde*.

East Pennard. See WEST PENNARD.

East Poringland (village, Norfolk): 'eastern cultivated land of the Porringas'. OE *land*, 'cultivated land'. The tribal name consists of an uncertain personal name with OE *-ingas*, 'people of'. The first word of the name distinguishes the village from nearby *West Poringland*. DB *Porringalanda*.

East Portlemouth (village, Devon): 'eastern (place on the) harbour estuary'. Cornish *porth*, 'harbour', + OE *mūtha*, 'mouth'. The main name could also mean 'mouth of the harbour stream' (OE *port*, 'harbour', + *wella*, 'stream', + *mūtha*). The first word of the name distinguishes the village from the much smaller *West Portlemouth*, south of Malborough, across the Kingsbridge Estuary. The DB form of the name below lacks a *t*. DB *Porlamuta*, 1308 *Porthelemuthe*.

East Preston (coastal town, W Sussex): 'eastern farmstead of the priests'. OE *prēost*, 'priest', + *tūn*, 'farmstead'. The first word of the name distinguishes this place from *West Preston*, now a district of Rustington. DB *Prestetune*, 1327 *Est Preston*.

East Putford (village, Devon): 'eastern (place called) Putta's ford'. OE *ford*, 'ford'. The name could also mean '(place by the) ford where hawks are seen' (OE *putta*, 'hawk', + *ford*). The first word of the name distinguishes the village from nearby *West Putford*. Both are on the river Torridge. DB *Potiforda*.

East Quantoxhead (village, Somerset): 'eastern place (at the) head of the Quantock Hills'. OE *hēafod*, 'head', 'end of a ridge'. The village lies east of *West Quantoxhead*, at the northern end of the QUANTOCK HILLS. DB *Cantocheve*.

East Rainton (village, Sunderland): 'eastern estate associated with Rægen or Regna'. OE *-ing-*, 'associated with', + *tūn*, 'farmstead', 'estate'. The first word of the name distinguishes this Rainton from nearby *West Rainton*, Durham. Between the two is *Middle Rainton*. *c.*1170 *Reiningtone*.

East Ravendale (village, NE Lincs): 'eastern (place in the) valley where ravens are seen'. OS *hrafn*, 'raven', + *dalr*, 'dale'. The first word of the name distinguishes the village from nearby *West Ravendale*. DB *Ravenedal*.

East Raynham (village, Norfolk): 'eastern (place called) Regna's homestead'. OE *hām*, 'homestead', 'village'. The village is east of *West Raynham*, with *South Raynham* to the south. DB *Reineham*.

East Retford. See RETFORD.

East Riding (unitary authority, Yorkshire). Yorkshire was long divided administratively into *East Riding*, *North Riding* and *West Riding*, in which *Riding* represents OS *thrithjungr*, 'third part', from *thrithi*, 'third', the initial *th-* having blended with the final *-t* of OE *ēast*, 'eastern', and *west*, 'western', and the *-th* of *north*, 'northern'. The name disappeared with the reorganization of local government in 1974 but *East Riding of Yorkshire* was reinstated in 1996 as a unitary authority. DB *Estreding*, *Nortreding*, *Westreding*.

Eastrington (village, E Yorks): 'farmstead of the dwellers to the east'. OE *ēastor*, 'eastern', + *-inga-*, 'of the dwellers at', + *tūn*, 'farmstead'. The reference is probably to those living east of Howden. 959 *Eastringatun*, DB *Estrincton*.

East Rounton (village, N Yorks): 'eastern farmstead enclosed with poles'. OE *hrung*, 'rung', 'pole', + *tūn*, 'farmstead'. The first word of the name distinguishes the village from nearby *West Rounton*. DB *Rontun*, *c.*1130 *Rungtune*.

East Rudham (village, Norfolk): 'eastern (place called) Rudda's homestead'. OE *hām*, 'homestead', 'village'. The village lies east of nearby *West Rudham*. DB *Rudeham*.

East Runton. See WEST RUNTON.

East Ruston (village, Norfolk): 'eastern farmstead among brushwood'. OE *hrīs*, 'brushwood', + *tūn*, 'farmstead'. There is no 'West Ruston', but the first word of the name contrasts the village with *Sco Ruston* (OS *skógr*, 'wood'), 6 miles to the southwest. DB *Ristuna*, 1361 *Estriston*.

Eastry (village, Kent): 'eastern district'. OE *ēastor*, 'eastern', + *gē*, 'district'. The second OE word is rare in place names but is also found in ELY and SURREY. Eastry is in the east of the county. 9C *Eastorege*, DB *Estrei*.

East Scrafton. See WEST SCRAFTON.

East Sheen. See RICHMOND UPON THAMES.

East Somerton. See WINTERTON-ON-SEA.

East Stockwith. See WEST STOCKWITH.

East Stour. See WEST STOUR.

East Stourmouth (village, Kent): 'eastern (place at the) mouth of the (river) Stour'. OE *mūtha*, 'mouth'. For the river name, see STOURBRIDGE. East Stourmouth and nearby *West Stourmouth* are near the point (at Plucks Gutter Bridge) where the Great and Little Stour join to form the Stour (which formerly entered the sea strait known as Wantsum Channel here). Late 11C *Sturmutha*.

East Studdal (village, Kent): 'eastern (place in the) forest where a herd of horses is kept'. OE *stōd*, 'stud', + *weald*, 'forest' (cp. WEALD). The first word of the name distinguishes the village from former nearby *West Studdal*, now represented by the hamlet of *Studdal* (but with *West Studdal Farm* to the northwest). 1240 *Stodwalde*.

East Sutton. See SUTTON VALENCE.

East Thirston (hamlet, Northd): 'eastern (place called) Thræsfrith's farmstead'. OE *tūn*, 'farmstead', 'village'. The first word of the name distinguishes the place from nearby *West Thirston*. 1242 *Thrasfriston*.

East Tisted (village, Hants): 'eastern place where young goats are kept'. OE *ticce*, 'kid', + *stede*, 'place'. The first word of the name distinguishes the village from *West Tisted*, 4 miles to the southwest. 932 *Ticcesstede*, DB *Tistede*.

East Tytherton (village, Wilts): 'eastern estate associated with Tydre'. OE *-ing-*, 'associated with', + *tūn*, 'farmstead', 'estate'. The first word of the name distinguishes the village from nearby *West Tytherton*, also known as *Tytherton Lucas*, after the Lucas family who held the manor here in the 13C. DB *Tedrintone*.

East Walton. See WEST WALTON.

Eastwell (village, Leics): '(place by the) eastern stream'. OE *ēast*, 'eastern', + *wella*, 'spring', 'stream'. DB *Estwelle*.

East Wellow. See WEST WELLOW.

Eastwick (village, Herts): 'eastern dairy farm'. OE *ēast*, 'eastern', + *wīc*, 'dwelling', 'dairy farm'. DB *Esteuuiche*.

East Wickham. See WEST WICKHAM.

East Williamston (village, Pemb): 'eastern (place called) William's farm'. OE *tūn*, 'farm'. The first word of the name distinguishes the village from nearby smaller *West Williamston*. 1541 *Williamston*.

East Winch (village, Norfolk): 'eastern farmstead with meadowland'. OE *winn*, 'meadowland', + *wīc*, 'farmstead'. The first word of the name distinguishes the village from *West Winch*, 3 miles to the west. DB *Estwinic*.

East Wittering. See WEST WITTERING.

East Witton (village, N Yorks): 'eastern farmstead by a wood'. OE *widu*, 'wood', + *tūn*, 'farmstead'. The first word of the name distinguishes the village from *West Witton*, 6 miles to the west. DB *Witun*.

Eastwood (town, Notts): 'eastern clearing'. OE *ēast*, 'east', + OS *thveit*, 'clearing', 'meadow'. It is not certain where the 'western clearing' was. The name may simply designate Eastwood as lying east of the river Erewash. The DB form of the name below has mistaken OS *thveit* for OE *wīc*, 'settlement'. The same word gave the present equally misleading '-wood'. DB *Estewic*, 1165 *Estweit*.

Eastwood (district of Southend-on-Sea, Southend): 'eastern wood'. OE *ēast*, 'eastern', + *wudu*, 'wood'. Eastwood was originally part of the royal forest here that lay to the east of Rayleigh. DB *Estuuda*.

East Worlington (hamlet, Devon): 'eastern estate associated with Wulfrēd'. OE *-ing-*, 'associated with', + *tūn*, 'farmstead', 'estate'. The first word of the name distinguishes this Worlington from nearby *West Worlington*. DB *Ulvredintone*.

East Wretham (village, Norfolk): 'eastern homestead where crosswort grows'. OE *wrætt*, 'crosswort' (a medicinal plant), + *hām*, 'homestead'. Corresponding *West Wretham* is now part of the same village. DB *Wretham*.

Eathorpe (village, Warwicks): 'outlying farmstead on the river'. OE *ēa*, 'river', + OS *thorp*, 'outlying farmstead'. As noted by William Dugdale in *The Antiquities of Warwickshire* (1656), the village 'hath its name from the situation thereof near the River; *Ea* in our old English signifying water, and *thorpe* a village or hamlet'. Eathorpe lies in a bend of the river Itchen. 1232 *Ethorpe*.

Eaton (village, Cheshire): 'farmstead by a river'. OE *ēa*, 'river', + *tūn*, 'farmstead'. The river here (near Congleton) is the Dane. *c*.1262 *Yeiton*. SO ALSO: *Eaton*, Norfolk, Notts, Shropshire (near Bishop's Castle, near Ticklerton).

Eaton (village, Cheshire): 'farmstead on an island'. OE *ēg*, 'island', + *tūn*, 'farmstead'. The 'island' is the raised ground between two streams near Tarporley on which the village stands. 1240 *Eyton*. SO ALSO: *Eaton*, Leics.

Eaton Bishop (village, Herefords): 'bishop's farmstead by the river'. OE *ēa*, 'river', + *tūn*, 'farmstead'. The manor here was held by the Bishop of Hereford. The village lies near the river Wye. The second word of the second form of the name below is Latin *episcopi*, 'of the bishop'. DB *Etune*, 1316 *Eton Episcopi*.

Eaton Bray (village, Beds): 'Bray's farmstead on an island'. OE *ēg*, 'island', + *tūn*, 'farmstead'. The Bray family held the manor here in the 15C. The village stands on an 'island' of raised ground amid many streams. DB *Eitone*.

Eaton Constantine (village, Shropshire): 'de Constentin's farmstead by a river'. OE *ēa*, 'river', + *tūn*, 'farmstead'. The de Constentin family held the manor here in the 13C. The nearby river is the Severn. DB *Etune*, 1285 *Eton Costentyn*.

Eaton Socon (village, Cambs): 'farmstead by a river with a soke'. OE *ēa*, 'river', + *tūn*, 'farmstead', + *sōcn*, 'soke'. The village was a soke, holding a right of local jurisdiction, in the 13C. DB *Etone*, 1247 *Soka de Eton*, 1645 *Eaton cum Soca*.

Ebberston (village, N Yorks): 'Ēadbeorht's farmstead'. OE *tūn*, 'farmstead'. DB *Edbriztune*.

Ebbesbourne Wake (village, Wilts): 'Wake's (estate by) Ebbel's stream'. OE *burna*, 'stream'. The Wake family held the manor here in the 12C. 826 *Eblesburna*, DB *Eblesborne*, 1249 *Ebbeleburn Wak*.

Ebbw Vale (town, Blaenau Gwent): 'valley of the (river) Ebwy'. The river name means 'horse' (Welsh *ebol*, 'colt'), perhaps because horses regularly drank or forded the river here. It was originally known as *Ebwydd* (1180, *Eboth*), and the second part of this could mean 'anger' (Welsh *gŵyth*) or 'wild' (Welsh *gŵydd*), so that 'angry horse' or 'wild horse' would denote a turbulent current. The Welsh name of Ebbw Vale is *Glynebwy* (Welsh *glyn*, 'valley'). The town arose around the ironworks set up in 1786 at the farm at *Pen-y-cae* ('top of the field'). The current name was created in the 19C.

Ebchester (village, Durham): 'Ebba's or Ebbe's Roman fort'. OE *ceaster*, 'Roman fort'. The Roman fort of *Vindomora* ('bright waters') was here on the river Derwent. The church here is dedicated to the 7C saint Ebbe, but her name was suggested by that of the (male) Anglo-Saxon Ebba. 1230 *Ebbecestr*.

Eboracum. See YORK.

Ebrington (village, Glos): 'Ēadbeorht's farmstead'. OE *tūn*, 'farmstead'. The church here is dedicated to St Edburga (Ēadburh) (see ADDERBURY), but her name was suggested by that of the (male) Anglo-Saxon Ēadbeorht. The DB form of the name below is garbled. DB *Bristentune*, 1155 *Edbrihttona*.

Ebudae. See HEBRIDES.

Ecclefechan (town, Dumfries & Gall): 'St Fechin's church'. The first part of the name is Celtic in origin (see ECCLES). Fechin was a 7C Irish abbot. 1303 *Eglesfeghan*.

Eccles (town, Salford): 'church'. The name, denoting an ancient (Romano-British) Christian church, represents a Celtic word related to modern Welsh *eglwys* and Cornish *eglos* (also English *ecclesiastic* and French *église*) that ultimately derives from Greek *ekklēsia*, 'assembly', 'church'. *c*.1200 *Eccles*. SO ALSO: *Eccles*, Kent.

Ecclesfield (district, Sheffield): 'open land by a church'. The first part of the name is Celtic in origin (see ECCLES). The second is OE *feld*, 'open land' (modern English *field*). DB *Eclesfeld*.

Eccleshall (village, Staffs): 'corner of land by a church'. The first part of the name is Celtic in origin (see ECCLES). The second is OE *halh*, 'nook', 'corner of land'. The second part of the DB form of the name below is corrupt. DB *Ecleshelle*, 1227 *Eccleshale*.

Eccleston (town, Lancs): 'farmstead by a church'. The first part of the name is Celtic in origin (see ECCLES). The second is OE *tūn*, 'farmstead'. 1094 *Aycleton*. SO ALSO: *Eccleston*, Cheshire, St Helens.

Eckington (village, Worcs): 'estate associated with Ecca'. OE -*ing*-, 'associated with', + *tūn*, 'farmstead', 'estate'. 972 *Eccyncgtun*, DB *Aichintune*. SO ALSO: *Eckington*, Derbys.

Ecton (village, Northants): 'Ecca's farmstead'. OE *tūn*, 'farmstead'. DB *Echentone*.

Edale (village, Derbys): 'valley with an island'. OE *ēg*, 'island', + *dæl*, 'valley'. The 'island' here is well-watered land by the Grinds Brook, a tributary of the river Noe, whose valley is here known as the *Vale of Edale*. DB *Aidele*.

Edburton (hamlet, W Sussex): 'Ēadburh's farmstead'. OE *tūn*, 'farmstead'. The personal name is that of a woman. 12C *Eadburgeton*.

Eddystone Rocks (reef, Cornwall): 'eddy stone'. The reef, famous for its successive lighthouses and notorious for its former shipwrecks, is named for the sea currents that eddy round it. 1405 *Ediston*.

Eden (river). See EDENHALL.

Edenbridge (town, Kent): 'Ēadhelm's bridge'. OE *brycg*, 'bridge'. The river Eden here is named after the town. *c*.1100 *Eadelmesbregge*.

Edenfield (village, Lancs): 'open land by the island farmstead'. OE *ēg*, 'island', + *tūn*, 'farmstead', + *feld*, 'open land' (modern English *field*). The 'island' would have been well-watered land here. 1324 *Aytounfeld*, 1868 *Edenfield, or Enfield*.

Edenhall (village, Cumbria): 'corner of land by the (river) Eden'. OE *halh*, 'nook', 'corner of land'. The river has a Celtic name, adopted for the local council district, meaning simply 'water'. 1159 *Edenhal*.

Edenham (village, Lincs): 'Ēada's homestead'. OE *hām*, 'homestead', 'village'. DB *Edeneham*.

Edensor (village, Derbys): 'Ēadin's sloping bank'. OE *ofer*, 'bank', 'ridge'. The village lies on the steepish bank of the river Derwent. DB *Edensoure*.

Edgbaston (district, Birmingham): 'Ecgbald's farmstead'. OE *tūn*, 'farmstead'. The DB form of the name below has miscopied the first part of the personal name. DB *Celboldeston*, 1184 *Egbaldeston*.

Edgcott (village, Bucks): 'cottage made of oak'. OE *æcen*, 'oaken', + *cot*, 'cottage'. DB *Achecote*.

Edgefield (village, Norfolk): 'open land by an enclosure'. OE *edisc*, 'enclosure', 'enclosed park', + *feld*, 'open land' (modern English *field*). DB *Edisfelda*.

Edge Green (hamlet, Cheshire): '(place by the) edge'. OE *ecg*, 'edge'. The 'edge' is nearby Edge Scar. The village later became associated with its green. DB *Eghe*.

Edge Hill (escarpment, Warwicks): 'hill with an edge'. OE *ecg*, 'edge'. The long narrow ridge has a very steep edge or slope. *c.*1250 *le Hegge*, 1656 *Edge hill*.

Edgmond (village, Wrekin): '(place by) Ecgmund's hill'. OE *dūn*, 'hill'. The final syllable of the original name was dropped to give the present form (which might otherwise have been 'Edgmonden'.) The hill in question is the large raised area to the west of the village. The DB form of the name below has *d* for *g* in the personal name. DB *Edmendune*, 1155 *Egmundun*.

Edgton (village, Shropshire): 'Ecga's hill'. OE *dūn*, 'hill'. DB *Egedune*.

Edgware (district, Barnet): 'Ecgi's weir'. OE *wer*, 'weir'. The 'weir' would have been a fishing enclosure here, probably at the point where Edgware Brook is crossed by the High Street (now the A5, and following the course of Watling Street). *c.*975 *Ægces wer*.

Edgworth (village, Blackburn with Dar): 'enclosure on an edge'. OE *ecg*, 'edge', + *worth*, 'enclosure'. The 'edge' would have been a hillside. 1212 *Eggewrthe*.

Edinburgh (city, Edinburgh): 'fortification at Eidyn'. OE *burh*, 'fortified place'. The name is often said to mean 'Edwin's fort', after Edwin, king of Northumbria from 617 to 633. But *Eidyn* (a name of uncertain origin and meaning) is recorded before his time. *c.*600 *Eidyn*, 1126 *Edenburge*.

Edingale (village, Staffs): 'corner of land of Ēadin's people'. OE *-inga-*, 'of the people of', + *halh*, 'nook', 'corner of land'. DB *Ednunghale*.

Edingley (village, Notts): 'woodland clearing associated with Eddi'. OE *-ing-*, 'associated with', + *lēah*, 'wood', 'clearing'. *c.*1180 *Eddyngleia*.

Edingthorpe (village, Norfolk): 'Ēadgȳth's outlying farmstead'. OS *thorp*, 'outlying farmstead'. The personal name is that of a woman. The second form of the name below has *n* for *u*. 1177 *Ædidestorp*, 1198 *Edinestorp*.

Edington (village, Somerset): 'Ēadwine's or Ēadwynn's farmstead'. OE *tūn*, 'farmstead'. The personal names are respectively those of a man and a woman. DB *Eduuintone*.

Edington (village, Wilts): '(place by the) bare hill'. OE *ēthe*, 'bare', 'barren', + *dūn*, 'hill'. OE *ēthe* has been recorded only once. Edington lies just below the chalk downs at the edge of Salisbury Plain. The name could also mean 'Etha's hill'. Late 9C *Ethandune*, DB *Edendone*.

Edith Weston (village, Rutland): 'Edith's western estate'. OE *west*, 'western', + *tūn*, 'farmstead', 'estate'. Edith Weston was a royal estate and part of the dower lands of Queen Edith (d.1075), wife of Edward the Confessor. The estate was west of the royal manor of Ketton. 1114 *Weston*, 1275 *Weston Edith*.

Edlesborough (village, Bucks): 'Ēadwulf's hill'. OE *beorg*, 'hill'. The hill in question is the rounded one on which the medieval parish church stands. The DB form of the name below has corrupted the personal name. DB *Eddinberge*, 1163 *Eduluesberga*.

Edlingham (village, Northd): 'homestead of Ēadwulf's people'. OE *-inga-*, 'of the people of', + *hām*, 'homestead'. The name could also mean 'homestead at Ēadwulf's place' (OE *-ing*, 'place belonging to'). *c.*1050 *Eadwulfincham*.

Edlington. See NEW EDLINGTON.

Edmondsham (village, Dorset): 'Ēadmōd's or Ēadmund's homestead or enclosure'. OE *hām*, 'homestead', or *hamm*, 'enclosure'. DB *Amedesham*.

Edmondthorpe (village, Leics): 'Ēadmǣr's outlying farmstead'. OS *thorp*, 'outlying farmstead'. DB *Edmerestorp*.

Edmonton (town, Enfield): 'Ēadhelm's farmstead'. OE *tūn*, 'farmstead'. DB *Adelmetone*.

Edstaston (hamlet, Shropshire): 'Ēadstān's farmstead'. OE *tūn*, 'farmstead'. The DB form of the name below has omitted the first part of the personal name. DB *Stanestune*, 1256 *Edestaneston*.

Edvin Loach (hamlet, Herefords): 'de Loges' (estate by) Gedda's marshland'. OE *fenn*, 'fen', 'marshland'. The de Loges family had a holding here in the 13C. DB *Gedeuen*, 1242 *Yedefen Loges*.

Edwalton (suburb of West Bridgford, Notts): 'Ēadweald's farmstead'. OE *tūn*, 'farmstead'. DB *Edvvoltone*.

Edwardstone (hamlet, Suffolk): 'Ēadweard's farmstead'. OE *tūn*, 'farmstead'. DB *Eduardestuna*.

Edwinstowe (village, Notts): 'St Ēadwine's holy place'. OE *stōw*, 'holy place'. There is a chapel here dedicated to St Edwin, but this may have simply derived from the original name.

The parish church is dedicated to St Mary. DB *Edenestou*.

Effingham (village, Surrey): 'homestead of Effa's people'. OE *-inga-*, 'of the people of', + *hām*, 'homestead'. The DB form of the name below has *p* for *ff*. DB *Epingeham*, 1180 *Effingeham*.

Egerton (village, Kent): 'estate associated with Ecgheard'. OE *-ing-*, 'associated with', + *tūn*, 'farmstead', 'estate'. The first form of the name below has garbled the personal name. *c.*1100 *Eardingtun*, 1203 *Egarditon*.

Egerton Green (hamlet, Cheshire): 'Ecghere's farmstead'. OE *tūn*, 'farmstead'. The village later became associated with its green. 1259 *Eggerton*.

Eggardon Hill (hill, Dorset): 'Eohhere's hill'. OE *dūn*, 'hill'. The meaning 'hill' was already present in the name before the second word was added. 1084 *Giochresdone*.

Egg Buckland (district, Plymouth): 'Heca's charter land'. OE *bōc-land* (see BUCKLAND). One Heca held the manor here in 1086, his name distinguishing this Buckland from *Buckland Monachorum*, 7 miles to the north, where an abbey was founded in 1278 (Latin *monachorum*, 'of the monks'), and *Buckland in the Moor*, 17 miles to the northeast, on the edge of DARTMOOR. DB *Bochelanda*, 1221 *Eckebokelond*.

Egginton (village, Derbys): 'estate associated with Ecga'. OE *-ing-*, 'associated with', + *tūn*, 'farmstead', 'estate'. 1012 *Ecgintune*, DB *Eghintune*.

Egglescliffe (suburb of Stockton-on-Tees, Stockton): 'cliff by the church'. The first part of the name is of Celtic origin, as for ECCLES. The second is OE *clif*, 'cliff', 'bank'. There would have been a Celtic Christian church or community here. Until recently the name was spelt *Eaglescliffe*, preserved in that of a nearby smaller suburb. 1085 *Eggasclif*, 1868 *Eaglescliffe*, 1895 *Egglescliffe*, or *Eaglescliffe*.

Eggleston (village, Durham): 'Ecgwulf's farmstead'. OE *tūn*, 'farmstead'. 1196 *Egleston*.

Egham (town, Surrey): 'Ecga's homestead'. OE *hām*, 'homestead', 'village'. DB *Egeham*.

Egleton (village, Rutland): 'Ecgwulf's farmstead'. OE *tūn*, 'farmstead'. 1218 *Egoluestun*.

Eglingham (village, Northd): 'homestead of Ecgwulf's people'. OE *-inga-*, 'of the people of', + *hām*, 'homestead'. The name could also mean 'homestead at Ecgwulf's place' (OE *-ing*, 'place belonging to', + *hām*). *c.*1050 *Ecgwulfincham*.

Egloshayle (village, Cornwall): 'church on an estuary'. Cornish *eglos*, 'church', + *heyl*, 'estu-

ary'. The estuary is that of the river Camel. 1166 *Egloshail*.

Egloskerry (village, Cornwall): 'church of St Keri'. Cornish *eglos*, 'church'. The church here is dedicated to the female saint Keri, about whom little is known. *c.*1145 *Egloskery*.

Eglwys Lwyd, Yr. See LUDCHURCH.

Eglwys y Drindod. See CHRISTCHURCH (Newport).

Egmanton (village, Notts): 'Ecgmund's farmstead'. OE *tūn*, 'farmstead'. DB *Agemuntone*.

Egremont (town, Cumbria): 'sharp-pointed hill'. OF *aigre*, 'sharp', + *mont*, 'hill'. The name is Norman in origin. There is no obvious 'sharp-pointed hill' here, but the name could refer to the old castle site, or even have been suggested by that of the river Ehen here (see ENNERDALE WATER). *c.*1125 *Egremont*.

Egton (village, N Yorks): 'Ecga's farmstead'. OE *tūn*, 'farmstead'. DB *Egetune*.

Egton Bridge (village, N Yorks): '(place at the) bridge by Egton'. The village is adjacent to EGTON and takes its name from the railway bridge over the river Esk here.

Eigg (island, Highland): '(island with a) notch'. Gaelic *eag*, 'nick', 'notch'. The name of the island in the Inner Hebrides probably refers to the 'rift' between the high plateau to the north and the rocky moorland to the south. 1654 *Egg*.

Eilean Siar. See WESTERN ISLES.

Elberton (hamlet, S Glos): 'Æthelbeorht's farmstead'. OE *tūn*, 'farmstead'. The DB form of the name below has garbled the personal name. DB *Eldbertone*, 1186 *Albricton*.

Eldersfield (village, Worcs): 'open land where elder trees grow'. OE *elle*, 'elder', + *feld*, 'open land' (modern English *field*). The name could also mean 'Ealdhere's open land'. The first part of the DB form of the name below has omitted the *l*. 972 *Yldresfeld*, DB *Edresfelle*.

Eldwick (district, Bradford): 'Helgi's dairy farm'. OE *wīc*, 'dwelling', 'specialized farm'. The personal name is Scandinavian. DB *Helguic*.

Elford (village, Staffs): '(place by the) ford where elder trees grow'. OE *elle*, 'elder', + *ford*, 'ford'. The name could also mean 'Ella's ford'. The ford in either case would have been over the river Tame. 1002 *Elleford*, DB *Eleford*. SO ALSO: *Elford*, Northd.

Elgin (town, Moray): 'little Ireland'. The name derives from *Elg*, one of the early Gaelic names for Ireland, with the diminutive suffix *-in*. Such a name would have been given by Scots who commemorated their mother country in a 'home from home'. Cp. GLENELG. 1136 *Elgin*.

Elham (village, Kent): 'enclosure where eels are found'. OE *ǽl*, 'eel', + *hamm*, 'enclosure', 'river meadow'. Elham (pronounced 'Eelham') lies on the Nail Bourne. DB *Alham*.

Elie (resort town, Fife): '(place of the) tomb'. Gaelic *ealadh*, 'tomb', 'grave'. The name is said to refer to an old cemetery here. 1491 *Elye*, *c.*1600 *The Alie*.

Eling (village, Hants): '(settlement of) Ēadla's or Ethel's people'. OE *-ingas*, 'people of'. DB *Edlinges*.

Elkesley (village, Notts): 'Ēalāc's woodland clearing'. OE *lēah*, 'wood', 'clearing'. DB *Elchesleie*.

Elkstone (village, Glos): 'Ēalāc's stone'. OE *stān*, 'stone'. The 'stone' would probably have marked a boundary of some kind. DB *Elchestane*.

Elland (town, Calderdale): '(place on the) riverside land'. OE *ēa-land* (from *ēa*, 'river', + *land*, 'land'). The land in question was probably a tract that had recently been cultivated. Elland lies on the south bank of the river Calder. DB *Elant*.

Ellastone (village, Staffs): 'Ēadlāc's farmstead'. OE *tūn*, 'farmstead'. DB *Edelachestone*.

Ellenhall (village, Staffs): 'corner of land associated with Ælle or Ella'. OE *-ing-*, 'associated with', + *halh*, 'nook', 'corner of land'. The DB form of the name below suggests an alternative earlier meaning 'corner of land where flax is grown' (OE *līn*, 'flax', + *halh*), with OE *ēa*, 'river', prefixed subsequently. Ellenhall is by Gamesley Brook. DB *Linehalle*, *c.*1200 *Ælinhale*.

Ellerbeck (hamlet, N Yorks): '(place by the) stream where alders grow'. OS *elri*, 'alder', + *bekr*, 'stream'. DB *Elrebec*.

Ellerby (hamlet, N Yorks): 'Ælfweard's farmstead'. OS *bý*, 'farmstead', 'village'. DB *Elwordebi*.

Ellerdine Heath (hamlet, Wrekin): 'Ella's enclosure'. OE *worthign*, 'enclosure'. The place later became associated with its heath. DB *Elleurdine*.

Ellerker (village, E Yorks): '(place by the) marsh where alders grow'. OS *elri*, 'alder', + *kjarr*, 'marsh'. DB *Alrecher*.

Ellerton (village, E Yorks): 'farmstead by the alders'. OS *elri*, 'alder', + OE *tūn*, 'farmstead'. DB *Elreton*.

Ellesborough (village, Bucks): '(place by the) hill where asses are pastured'. OE *esol*, 'ass', + *beorg*, 'hill'. The DB form of the name below has

n for *l*, and *Eselborough* became *Ellesborough* in the 15C. DB *Esenberge*, 1195 *Eselbergh*.

Ellesmere (town, Shropshire): 'Elli's lake'. OE *mere*, 'lake', 'pool'. The lake of the name is the one to the east of the town known as The Mere. See also ELLESMERE PORT. The DB form of the name below has mistranscribed the 'lake' element. DB *Ellesmeles*, 1177 *Ellismera*.

Ellesmere Port (town and port, Cheshire): 'Ellesmere port'. As described by the local historian George Ormerod in his *History of Cheshire* (1819), the town was originally 'a petty port, [named] from the termination of the Dee and Mersey branch of the Ellesmere Canal [i.e. the Shropshire Union Canal, from ELLESMERE], and its connection with the estuary of the latter river, taking place at this point'. The town evolved as a major industrial centre following the opening of the Manchester Ship Canal in 1894.

Ellingham (hamlet, Hants): 'homestead of Æthel's people'. OE *-inga-*, 'of the people of', + *hām*, 'homestead'. DB *Adelingeham*.

Ellingham (village, Norfolk): 'homestead of Ella's people'. OE *-inga-*, 'of the people of', + *hām*, 'homestead'. The name could also mean 'homestead at Ella's place' (OE *-ing*, 'place belonging to', + *hām*). DB *Elincham*. SO ALSO: *Ellingham*, Northd.

Ellingstring (village, N Yorks): 'watercourse at the place where eels are caught'. OE *ǽl* or *ēl*, 'eel', + *-ing*, 'place characterized by', + OS *strengr*, 'watercourse'. The name could also mean 'watercourse at the place associated with Ella or Eli' (OE *-ing*, 'place associated with'). 1198 *Elingestrengge*.

Ellington (village, Northd): 'farmstead at the place where eels are found'. OE *ǽl* or *ēl*, 'eel', + *-ing*, 'place characterized by', + *tūn*, 'farmstead'. The name could also mean 'farmstead associated with Ella or Eli' (OE *-ing-*, 'associated with', + *tūn*). Ellington lies on a small stream. 1166 *Elingtona*. SO ALSO: *Ellington*, Cambs.

Ellistown (hamlet, Leics). The mining settlement, near COALVILLE, was named after local colliery owner Joseph Joel Ellis, whose wife cut the first turf with a silver spade inscribed: 'The first sod turned on the Ellistown new colliery site, by Mrs. J. J. Ellis, July 2, 1873' (*Colliery Guardian*, 11 July 1873).

Ellon (town, Aberdeens): '(place on the) island'. Gaelic *eilean*, 'island'. The source of the name is uncertain but the interpretation given here suits the town's location on the river Ythan. *c.*1150 *Eilan*.

Ellough (hamlet, Suffolk): '(place by the) heathen temple'. OS *elgr*, 'heathen temple'. DB *Elga*.

Elloughton (village, E Yorks): 'hill with a heathen temple'. OS *elgr*, 'heathen temple', + OE *dūn*, 'hill'. The name could also mean 'Helgi's hill', with a Scandinavian personal name. DB *Elgendon*.

Elm (village, Cambs): '(place at the) elm tree'. OE *elm*, 'elm'. 1OC *Elm*.

Elmbridge (council district, Surrey): 'bridge over the (river) Emele'. The name is that of a former hundred here, from a bridge over the river now known as the Mole (see EAST MOLESEY). The bridge in question probably took the London road (the present A244) across the river between Esher and Hersham, at the point where Albany Bridge crosses the Mole today. DB *Amelebrige*.

Elmbridge (hamlet, Worcs): '(place by the) ridge where elm trees grow'. OE *elm*, 'elm', + *hrycg*, 'ridge'. DB *Elmerige*.

Elmdon (village, Essex): '(place by the) hill where elm trees grow'. OE *elmen*, 'growing with elms', + *dūn*, 'hill'. DB *Elmenduna*.

Elmdon (village, Solihull): '(place by the) hill of the elm trees'. OE *elm*, 'elm', + *dūn*, 'hill'. DB *Elmedone*.

Elmesthorpe (village, Leics): 'Æthelmǣr's outlying farmstead'. OS *thorp*, 'outlying farmstead'. 1207 *Ailmerestorp*.

Elmley Castle (village, Worcs): '(place at the) elm wood or clearing with a castle'. OE *elm*, 'elm', + *lēah*, 'wood', 'clearing'. The second word of the name, referring to the former medieval castle nearby, distinguishes this Elmley from *Elmley Lovett*, 30 miles to the northwest, where the Lovett family held land in the 13C. 780 *Elmlege*, 1327 *Castel Elmeleye*.

Elmore (village, Glos): '(place by the) river bank or ridge where elm trees grow'. OE *elm*, 'elm', + *ōfer*, 'river bank', or *ofer*, 'ridge'. Elmore lies on the river Severn, and a low ridge here may have served as a landmark for river traffic. 1176 *Elmour*.

Elmsett (village, Suffolk): '(settlement of the) dwellers among the elm trees'. OE *elme*, 'elm grove', + *sǣte*, 'dwellers'. *c.*995 *Ylmesæton*, DB *Elmeseta*.

Elmstead Market (village, Essex): 'place where elm trees grow with a market'. OE *elmen*, 'growing with elms', + *stede*, 'place', + ME *merket*, 'market'. There was an important early market here. DB *Elmesteda*, 1475 *Elmested Market*.

Elmsted (hamlet, Kent): ' homestead by the elm trees'. OE *elm*, 'elm', + *hām-stede* (see HAMPSTEAD). 811 *Elmanstede*.

Elmstone Harwicke (hamlet, Glos): 'Alhmund's stone near Harwicke'. OE *stān*, 'stone'. The name relates to a boundary stone here. The second word of the name refers to nearby HARWICKE. DB *Almundestan*.

Elmswell (village, Suffolk): '(place by the) stream where elm trees grow'. OE *elm*, 'elm', + *wella*, 'spring', 'stream'. DB *Elmeswella*.

Elmton (village, Derbys): 'farmstead where elm trees grow'. OE *elm*, 'elm', + *tūn*, 'farmstead'. DB *Helmetune*.

Elsdon (village, Northd): 'Elli's valley'. OE *denu*, 'valley'. 1226 *Eledene*.

Elsenham (village, Essex): 'Elesa's homestead'. OE *hām*, 'homestead', 'village'. DB *Elsenham*.

Elsfield (village, Oxon): 'Elesa's open land'. OE *feld*, 'open land' (modern English *field*). DB *Esefelde*, *c.*1130 *Elsefeld*.

Elsham (village, N Lincs): 'Elli's homestead'. OE *hām*, 'homestead', 'village'. DB *Elesham*.

Elsing (village, Norfolk): '(settlement of) Elesa's people'. OE *-ingas*, 'people of'. DB *Helsinga*.

Elslack (village, N Yorks): '(place by) Elli's stream'. OE *lacu*, 'stream'. The stream in question is the one now known as Elslack Beck. DB *Eleslac*.

Elstead (village, Surrey): 'place where elder trees grow'. OE *elle*, 'elder', + *stede*, 'place'. 1128 *Helestede*.

Elsted (village, W Sussex): 'place where elder trees grow'. OE *elle*, 'elder', + *stede*, 'place'. The first part of the DB form of the name below is corrupt. DB *Halestede*, 1180 *Ellesteda*.

Elston (village, Notts): 'Eiláfr's farmstead'. OE *tūn*, 'farmstead'. The personal name is Scandinavian. DB *Elvestune*.

Elstow (village, Beds): 'Ællen's assembly place'. OE *stōw*, 'assembly place'. DB *Elnestou*.

Elstree (village, Herts): 'Tīdwulf's tree'. OE *trēow*, 'tree'. The tree would have marked an important boundary here, at a point where four parishes met. The *T-* of the personal name disappeared in the 13C when it was confused with the *-t* of preceding OE *æt*, 'at'. 785 *Tithulfes treow*, 1188 *Tidulvestre*, 1320 *Idelestre*, 1598 *Elstre*, 1868 *Elstree*, *or Idlestree*.

Elstronwick (village, E Yorks): 'Ælfstān's dairy farm'. OE *wīc*, 'dwelling', 'specialized farm'. The DB form of the name below has garbled the personal name. DB *Asteneuuic*, *c.*1265 *Elstanwik*.

Elswick (village, Lancs): 'Æthelsige's dairy farm'. OE *wīc*, 'dwelling', 'specialized farm'. DB *Edelesuuic*.

Elswick (district, Newcastle): 'Ælfsige's dairy farm'. OE *wīc*, 'dwelling', 'specialized farm'. 1204 *Alsiswic*.

Elsworth (village, Cambs): 'Elli's enclosure'. OE *worth*, 'enclosure'. 974 *Eleswurth*, DB *Elesuuorde*.

Elterwater (village, Cumbria): '(place by the) lake where swans are seen'. OS *elptr*, 'swan', + OE *wæter*, 'water', 'lake'. The lake in question is nearby Elter Water. *c.*1160 *Heltrewatra*.

Eltham (district, Greenwich): 'Elta's village'. OE *hām*, 'homestead', 'village'. The name could also mean 'village where swans are seen' (OE *elfitu*, 'swan', + *hām*). DB *Elteham*.

Eltisley (village, Cambs): 'Elti's woodland clearing'. OE *lēah*, 'wood', 'clearing'. The DB form of the name below is garbled. DB *Hecteslei*, 1228 *Eltesle*.

Elton (village, Cambs): 'farmstead of the princes'. OE *ætheling*, 'prince', + *tūn*, 'farmstead'. The name could also mean 'farmstead associated with Æthel' (OE *-ing-*, 'associated with', + *tūn*). 10C *Æthelingtun*, DB *Adelintune*.

Elton (village, Cheshire): 'farmstead where eels are found'. OE *æl*, 'eel', + *tūn*, 'farmstead'. Elton lies on a low peninsula in marshland not far from the Mersey estuary. DB *Eltone*. SO ALSO: *Elton*, Derbys, Stockton.

Elton (village, Notts): 'Ella's farmstead'. OE *tūn*, 'farmstead'. The DB form of the name below has garbled the personal name. DB *Ailetone*, 1088 *Elleton*. SO ALSO: *Elton*, Herefords.

Elvaston (village, Derbys): 'Æthelweald's farmstead'. OE *tūn*, 'farmstead'. DB *Ælwoldestune*.

Elveden (village, Suffolk): '(place in the) valley where swans are seen'. OE *elfitu*, 'swan', + *denu*, 'valley'. DB *Eluedena*, 1868 *Elveden, or Elden*.

Elvington (village, York): 'Ælfwine's or Ælfwynn's farmstead'. OE *tūn*, 'farmstead'. The first personal name is that of a man, the second that of a woman. DB *Aluuintone*.

Elwick (village, Hartlepool): 'Ægla's or Ella's dairy farm'. OE *wīc*, 'dwelling', 'dairy farm'. *c.*1150 *Ailewic*.

Elwick (hamlet, Northd): 'Ella's dairy farm'. OE *wīc*, 'dwelling', 'dairy farm'. 12C *Ellewich*.

Elworthy (hamlet, Somerset): 'Ella's enclosure'. OE *worth*, 'enclosure'. OE *worth* was subsequently replaced by *worthig*, of identical meaning. DB *Elwrde*.

Ely (city, Cambs): 'district where eels are found'. OE *æl*, 'eel', + *gē*, 'district'. Eels have long been caught in the fens here. The 'district' would have been an administrative region of Anglo-Saxon England, before the division into counties. The first form of the name below is from Bede's *A History of the English Church and People* (completed 731): '*Est autem Elge ... regio ... in similitudinem insulae uel paludibus, ut diximus, circumdata uel aquis, unde et a copia anguillarum quae in eisdem paludibus capiuntur nomen accepit*' ('Ely is also ... a region ... resembling an island surrounded by water and marshes, as we have said, and it takes its name from the vast quantity of eels that are caught in the same marshes'). 731 *Elge*, DB *Elyg*.

Emberton (village, Milton K): 'Ēanbeorht's farmstead'. OE *tūn*, 'farmstead'. DB *Ambretone*, 1227 *Emberdestone*.

Embleton (village, Cumbria): 'Ēanbald's farmstead'. OE *tūn*, 'farmstead'. 1195 *Emelton*.

Embleton (village, Northd): 'hill full of caterpillars'. OE *emel*, 'caterpillar', + *dūn*, 'hill'. The name could also mean 'Æmele's hill'. 1212 *Emlesdone*.

Emborough (hamlet, Somerset): '(place by the) level hill'. OE *emn*, 'even', 'level', + *beorg*, 'mound', 'hill'. The hill in question has only a slight curve. The first part of the DB form of the name below is garbled. DB *Amelberge*, 1200 *Emeneberge*.

Embsay (village, N Yorks): 'Embe's enclosure'. OE *hæg*, 'enclosure' (related modern English *hedge*). DB *Embesie*.

Emley (village, Kirklees): 'Emma's woodland clearing'. OE *lēah*, 'wood', 'clearing'. DB *Ameleia*.

Emmington (hamlet, Oxon): 'estate associated with Eama'. OE *-ing-*, 'associated with', + *tūn*, 'farmstead', 'estate'. DB *Amintone*.

Emneth (village, Norfolk): 'Ēana's river confluence'. OE *mȳthe*, 'confluence of rivers'. The name could also mean 'Ēana's meadow' (OE *mǣth*, 'mowing grass'). 1170 *Anemetha*.

Empingham (village, Rutland): 'homestead of Empa's people'. OE *-inga-*, 'of the people of', + *hām*, 'homestead'. The DB form of the name below has omitted the *m* of the personal name. DB *Epingeham*, 12C *Empingeham*.

Emsworth (town, Hants): 'Æmele's enclosure'. OE *worth*, 'enclosure'. Emsworth is on the river Ems, whose name comes from that of the town. 1224 *Emeleswurth*.

Enborne (village, W Berks): '(place on the) stream where ducks are seen'. OE *ened*, 'duck', +

burna, 'stream'. The stream in question is not the river Enborne, to the south, which took its name from the village, but the stream that flows into the river Kennet here. The DB form of the name below owes its A- to French influence. DB *Aneborne*, 1220 *Enedburn*.

Enderby (village, Leics): 'Eindrithi's farmstead'. OS *bý*, 'farmstead', 'village'. The personal name is Scandinavian. DB *Endrebie*.

Endon (village, Staffs): 'Eana's hill'. OE *dūn*, 'hill'. The name could also mean 'hill where lambs are reared' (OE *ēan*, 'lamb', + *dūn*). DB *Enedun*.

Enfield (borough, Greater London): 'Eana's open land'. OE *feld*, 'open land' (modern English *field*). The name could also mean 'open land where lambs are reared', from OE *ēan*, 'lamb'. The 'open land' would have a been large clearing in the woodland area that became Enfield Chase. DB *Enefelde*.

Enford (village, Wilts): '(place by the) ford where ducks are seen'. OE *ened*, 'duck', + *ford*, 'ford'. The river here is the Avon. 934 *Enedford*, DB *Enedforde*.

England (country, central and S Britain): 'land of the Angles'. OE *Engle*, 'Angles', + *land*, 'land'. The Angles came from Angeln ('angle of land') in Schleswig, northern Germany. England could equally have been named after the Saxons, who came to Britain with the Angles in the 5C. (Hence *Sassenach* as a Scots term for an Englishman, and Welsh *Saesneg*, 'English'.) *c*.890 *Englaland*.

Englefield (village, W Berks): 'open land of the Angles'. OE *Engle*, 'Angles', + *feld*, 'open land' (modern English *field*). The name indicates that a group of Angles held land here in West Saxon territory. *c*.900 *Englafelda*, DB *Englefel*.

English Bicknor (village, Glos): 'English ridge with a point'. OE *bica*, 'point', + *ofer*, 'flat-topped ridge'. The first word of the name indicates the location of the village on the English side of the river Wye, as distinct from *Welsh Bicknor*, on the Welsh side (though not actually in Wales). DB *Bicanofre*, 1248 *Englise Bykenore*.

Englishcombe (village, Bath & NE Somerset): 'Ingel's or Ingweald's valley'. OE *cumb*, 'valley'. DB *Ingeliscuma*.

English Frankton (hamlet, Shropshire): 'English (place called) Franca's farmstead'. OE *tūn*, 'farmstead', 'village'. The first word of the name distinguishes this Frankton from *Welsh Frankton*, 5 miles nearer the Welsh border. DB *Franchetone*, 1577 *Englyshe Frankton*.

Enham Alamein (village, Hants): 'homestead where lambs are reared'. OE *ēan*, 'lamb', + *hām*, 'homestead'. The village was originally named *Knight's Enham*, from the knight's fee held here by Matthew de Columbers in the 13C. A rehabilitation centre for ex-servicemen was set up here after World War I and re-endowed after World War II by the Egyptian government in gratitude for the defeat of the German army at El Alamein (1942), when the name was changed as now. The DB form of the name below is corrupt. early 11C *Eanham*, DB *Etham*, 1389 *Knyghtesenham*.

Enmore (village, Somerset): '(place by the) pool where ducks are seen'. OE *ened*, 'duck', + *mere*, 'pool'. DB *Animere*.

Ennerdale Water (lake, Cumbria): 'lake of Anundr's valley'. OS *dalr*, 'valley'. The Scandinavian personal name was later replaced by that of the river Ehen here. Its own name (recorded in *c*.1125 as *Egre*) is of uncertain origin. *c*.1135 *Anenderdale*, 1321 *Eghnerdale*.

Enstone (village, Oxon): 'Enna's stone'. OE *stān*, 'stone'. The stone in question would have probably been a boundary marker. DB *Henestan*.

Enville (village, Staffs): 'smooth open country'. OE *efn*, 'even', 'smooth', + *feld*, 'open land' (modern English *field*). DB *Efnefeld*.

Epidium Promontorium. See KINTYRE.

Epperstone (village, Notts): 'Eorphere's farmstead'. OE *tūn*, 'farmstead'. DB *Eprestone*.

Epping (town, Essex): '(settlement of the) people of the lookout'. OE *yppe*, 'raised place' (related modern English *up*), + *-ingas*, 'dwellers at'. The lookout in question may have been the ancient hill fort known as Ambresbury Banks in *Epping Forest*, a name now adopted for the local council district. DB *Eppinges*.

Eppleby (village, N Yorks): 'farmstead where apple trees grow'. OE *epli* or OS *epli*, 'apple tree', + *bý*, 'farmstead'. DB *Aplebi*.

Epsom (town, Surrey): 'Ebbe's or Ebbi's homestead'. OE *hām*, 'homestead', 'village'. The DB form of the name below may have resulted from a mishearing. *c*.973 *Ebbesham*, DB *Evesham*.

Epwell (village, Oxon): '(place by) Eoppa's spring'. OE *wella*, 'spring', 'stream'. 956 *Eoppan wyllan*.

Epworth (town, N Lincs): 'Eoppa's enclosure'. OE *worth*, 'enclosure'. DB *Epeurde*.

Erdington (district, Birmingham): 'estate associated with Earda'. OE *-ing-*, 'associated with', + *tūn*, 'farmstead', 'estate'. The DB form of the name below has an extraneous H-. DB *Hardintone*.

Erewash (council district, Derbys): '(district of the river) Erewash'. The river, forming the eastern boundary of the district and of Derbyshire itself, has a name meaning 'wandering stream' (OE *irre*, 'wandering', + *wisce*, 'marshy meadow', 'stream'). The second part of the name later became associated with *Wash* as a river name. *c.*1145 *Irewys*.

Eridge Green (village, E Sussex): '(place by the) ridge where eagles are seen'. OE *earn*, 'eagle', + *hrycg*, 'ridge'. Eridge later became associated with its village green. 1202 *Ernerigg*.

Eriskay (island, W Isles): 'Erikr's island'. OS *ey*, 'island'. The personal name is Scandinavian. A meaning 'island of the goblin' has also been proposed, from Gaelic *uruisg*, 'brownie'. 1549 *Eriskeray*.

Eriswell (village, Suffolk): 'Here's spring'. OE *wella*, 'spring', 'stream'. DB *Hereswella*.

Erith (district, Bexley): 'gravelly landing place'. OE *ēar*, 'gravel' (related modern English *earth*), + *hȳth*, 'landing place'. Erith is on the south bank of the Thames. *c.*960 *Earhyth*, DB *Erhede*.

Erlestoke (village, Wilts): 'outlying farmstead of the nobleman'. OE *eorl*, 'nobleman', 'earl', + *stoc*, 'outlying farmstead'. It is just possible the earl in question was Earl Harold, recorded as having held Melksham, 10 miles away. 12C *Erlestoke*, 1868 *Earl Stoke*.

Ermine Street (Roman road, England): 'Roman road of Earna's people'. OE *-inga-*, 'of the people of', + *strǣt*, 'Roman road' (modern English *street*). Ermine Street ran from London to the Humber, but the name may have originally applied to the stretch near *Arrington*, Cambs, whose name means 'farmstead of Earna's people' (OE *tūn*, 'farmstead'). Another Ermine Street ran from Gloucester to Silchester, and both remain major routes today. 955 *Earningas strǣt*.

Ermington (village, Devon): 'estate associated with Earma'. OE *-ing-*, 'associated with', + *tūn*, 'farmstead', 'estate'. The river Erme here took its name from that of the village. DB *Ermentona*.

Erpingham (village, Norfolk): 'homestead of Eorp's people'. OE *-inga-*, 'of the people of', + *hām*, 'homestead'. DB *Erpingaham*.

Erskine (town, Renfrews): meaning uncertain. The name may be Celtic, from words related to modern Welsh *ir*, 'green', and *esgyn*, 'to ascend', suggesting a grassy slope. This would suit the site, but early forms of the name are inconsistent. 1225 *Erskin*, 1227 *Yrskin*, 1262 *Ireskin*, *c.*1300 *Harskin*.

Erwarton (village, Suffolk): 'Eoforweard's farmstead'. OE *tūn*, 'farmstead'. DB *Eurewardestuna*.

Eryholme (village, N Yorks): '(place at the) summer pastures'. OS *erg*, 'shieling', 'summer pasture'. The name represents OS *ergum*, the dative plural form of *erg*. DB *Argun*.

Eryri. See SNOWDON.

Escomb (hamlet, Durham): '(place by the) enclosed pastures'. OE *edisc*, 'enclosure'. The name represents the OE word in a dative plural form. 10C *Ediscum*.

Escrick (village, N Yorks): 'strip of land where ash trees grow'. OS *eski*, 'ash', + OE *ric*, 'raised strip of land'. The DB form of the name below is garbled. DB *Ascri*, 1169 *Eskrik*.

Esh (village, Durham): '(place by the) ash tree'. OE *æsc*, 'ash'. 12C *Esse*.

Esher (town, Surrey): 'district of ash trees'. OE *æsc*, 'ash', + *scearu*, 'district', 'share'. The DB form of the name below is garbled. 1005 *Æscæron*, DB *Aissele*.

Eshott (hamlet, Northd): 'corner of land growing with ash trees'. OE *æsc*, 'ash', + *scēat*, 'corner of land'. The name could also mean '(place by the) clump of ash trees' (OE *æscet*, 'clump of ashes'). 1187 *Esseta*.

Eshton (hamlet, N Yorks): 'farmstead by the ash tree'. OE *æsc*, 'ash', + *tūn*, 'farmstead'. DB *Estune*.

Esk (river). See ESKDALE GREEN.

Eskdale Green (village, Cumbria): '(place in the) valley of the (river) Esk'. OS *dalr*, 'valley'. The river has a Celtic name meaning simply 'water'. Eskdale later became associated with its village green. 1294 *Eskedal*.

Esprick (hamlet, Lancs): '(place by the) slope where ash trees grow'. OS *eski*, 'ash', + *brekka*, 'slope'. *c.*1210 *Eskebrec*.

Essendine (village, Rutland): '(place in) Ēsa's valley'. OE *denu*, 'valley'. The second part of the DB form of the name below erroneously implies OE *dūn*, 'hill'. DB *Esindone*, 1222 *Essenden*.

Essendon (village, Herts): 'valley of Ēsla's people'. OE *-inga-*, 'of the people of', + *denu*, 'valley'. 11C *Eslingadene*.

Essex (county, E England): '(territory of the) East Saxons'. OE *ēast*, 'east', + *Seaxe*, 'Saxons'. The Saxons also gave the names of MIDDLESEX, SUSSEX and WESSEX. Late 9C *East Seaxe*, DB *Exsessa*.

Essington (village, Staffs): 'farmstead of Esne's people'. OE *-inga-*, 'of the people of', + *tūn*, 'farmstead'. 996 *Esingetun*, DB *Eseningetone*.

Eston (town, Redcar & Clev): 'eastern village'. OE *ēast*, 'eastern', + *tūn*, 'farmstead', 'village'. Eston is in the eastern part of the parish of Ormesby. DB *Astun*.

Etal (village, Northd): 'corner of land used for grazing'. OE *ete*, 'grazing', + *halh*, 'nook', 'corner of land'. The name could also mean 'Ēata's corner of land'. 1232 *Ethale*.

Etchilhampton (village, Wilts): 'farmstead of the dwellers at the hill where oak trees grow'. OE *āc*, 'oak', + *hyll*, 'hill', + *hǣme*, 'dwellers' (related modern English *home*), + *tūn*, 'farmstead'. The village lies at the foot of a small hill. The name is often abbreviated locally to *Etchil*. DB *Echesatingetone*, 1196 *Ehelhamton*.

Etchingham (village, E Sussex): 'homestead or enclosure of Ecci's people'. OE *-inga-*, 'of the people of', + *hām*, 'homestead', or *hamm*, 'enclosure'. 1158 *Hechingeham*.

Etive, Loch (loch, Argyll & Bute): 'Eite's loch'. Gaelic *loch*, 'lake'. Eite is the name of a goddess of the loch, meaning 'horrid one'.

Eton (town, Windsor & Maid): 'farmstead by the river'. OE *ēa*, 'river', + *tūn*, 'farmstead'. Eton lies by the Thames. DB *Ettone*.

Etruria (district, Stoke). Josiah Wedgwood (1730–95), founder in 1769 of the famous pottery here, built a house called Etruria Hall, and this gave the name of the town that grew up around it. The house was itself named for Etruria (modern Tuscany, Italy), famous for its pottery.

Ettington (village, Warwicks): '(place by) Ēata's hill'. OE *dūn*, 'hill'. The '-ing-' represents the genitive ending of the personal name (*Ēatan*). An alternative meaning may be 'hill used for grazing', 'pasture', + *dūn*). DB *Etendone*, 1868 *Eatington*.

Etton (village, Peterborough): 'Ēata's farmstead'. OE *tūn*, 'farmstead'. 1125 *Ettona*. SO ALSO: *Etton*, E Yorks.

Ettrick Forest (moorland region, Borders): 'forest of the Ettrick Water'. The forest takes its name from the river that flows through it. Its own name is of uncertain meaning. An origin in Gaelic *eadar*, 'division', has been proposed. *c*.1235 *Ethric*.

Etwall (village, Derbys): '(place by) Ēata's stream'. OE *wella*, 'spring', 'stream'. DB *Etewelle*.

Euston (village, Suffolk): 'Efe's farmstead'. OE *tūn*, 'farmstead'. London's Euston Road, Square and Station take their name from the earls of Euston, who owned land there. DB *Euestuna*.

Euxton (village, Lancs): 'Æfic's farmstead'. OE *tūn*, 'farmstead'. 1187 *Eueceston*.

Evanton (village, Highland): 'Evan's village'. The name is that of Evan Fraser of Balconie, who founded the village in the early 19C.

Evenley (village, Northants): '(place at the) level woodland clearing'. OE *efen*, 'even', 'level', + *lēah*, 'wood', 'clearing'. The DB form of the name below has omitted the *n*. DB *Evelaia*, 1147 *Euenlai*.

Evenlode (village, Glos): '(place by) Eowla's river crossing'. OE *gelād*, 'river crossing'. The river Evenlode here takes its name from the village. It was earlier known as the *Bladon* (see BLADON). 772 *Euulangelade*, DB *Eunilade*.

Evenwood (village, Durham): '(place by) level woodland'. OE *efen*, 'even', 'level', + *wudu*, 'wood'. *c*.1050 *Efenwuda*.

Evercreech (village, Somerset): '(place by the) hill'. The second part of the name represents a Celtic word related to modern Welsh *crug*, 'hillock'. The first part may represent OE *eofor*, 'boar', or may more likely be the Celtic name of some unidentified plant or tree (perhaps a yew). 1065 *Evorcric*, DB *Evrecriz*.

Everdon. See GREAT EVERDON.

Everingham (village, E Yorks): 'homestead of Eofor's people'. OE *-inga-*, 'of the people of', + *hām*, 'homestead'. *c*.972 *Yferingaham*, DB *Evringham*.

Everleigh (village, Wilts): 'wood or clearing where wild boars are seen'. OE *eofor*, 'boar', + *lēah*, 'wood', 'clearing'. 704 *Eburleagh*, 1868 *Everleigh, or Everley*.

Everley (hamlet, N Yorks): 'wood or clearing where wild boars are seen'. OE *eofor*, 'boar', + *lēah*, 'wood', 'clearing'. DB *Eurelai*.

Evershot (village, Dorset): 'corner of land where wild boars are seen'. OE *eofor*, 'boar', + *scēat*, 'corner of land'. The initial *T-* in the first form of the name below may represent the final letter of preceding OE *æt*, 'at'. 1202 *Teversict*, 1286 *Evershet*.

Eversley (village, Hants): 'wood or clearing where wild boars are seen'. OE *eofor*, 'boar', + *lēah*, 'wood', 'clearing'. The first part of the name could equally represent the personal name Eofor. *c*.1050 *Evereslea*, DB *Evreslei*.

Everton (district, Liverpool): 'farmstead where wild boars are seen'. OE *eofor*, 'wild boar', + *tūn*, 'farmstead'. 1094 *Evretona*. SO ALSO: *Everton*, Beds, Notts.

Evesham (town, Worcs): 'Ēof's land in a river bend'. OE *hamm*, 'enclosure', 'land in a river bend'. Evesham lies in a great bend of the river Avon. 709 *Eveshomme*, DB *Evesham*.

Evington (district, Leicester): 'estate associated with Eafa'. OE *-ing-*, 'associated with', + *tūn*, 'farmstead', 'estate'. DB *Avintone*.

Ewell (town, Surrey): '(place at the) river source'. OE *ǣwell*, 'river source' (from *ēa*, 'river', + *wella*, 'spring', 'source'). The stream called the Hogsmill River rises at Ewell. The DB form of the name below is corrupt. 933 *Euuelle*, DB *Etwelle*.

Ewell Minnis. See TEMPLE EWELL.

Ewelme (village, Oxon): '(place at the) river source'. OE *ǣwylm*, 'river source'. The 'river source' is a nearby spring that until recently was used to grow watercress. DB *Auuilme*.

Ewen (village, Glos): '(place at the) river source'. OE *ǣwylm*, 'river source'. The 'river source' is probably the nearby spring known as Thames Head, the source of the Thames. 931 *Awilme*.

Ewerby (village, Lincs): 'Ivar's farmstead'. OS *bý*, 'farmstead', 'village'. The personal name is Scandinavian. DB *Ieresbi*.

Ewhurst (village, Surrey): 'wooded hill where yew trees grow'. OE *īw*, 'yew', + *hyrst*, 'wooded hill'. 1179 *Iuherst*.

Ewyas Harold (village, Herefords): 'Harold's sheep district'. The basic name is Celtic in origin, from a word related to modern Welsh *ewig*, 'hind'. A nobleman called Harold held the manor here in the 11C, and his name distinguished the village from the former *Ewyas Lacy* (now called *Longtown*), 4 miles to the west, where the manor was held by Roger de Laci. *c*.1150 *Euwias*, 1176 *Euuiasharold*.

Exbourne (village, Devon): '(place by the) stream where cuckoos are heard'. OE *gēac*, 'cuckoo', + *burna*, 'stream'. The name could also mean '(place by) Gēac's stream'. The first part of the DB form of the name below is corrupt. DB *Hechesburne*, 1242 *Yekesburne*.

Exe (river). See EXETER.

Exelby (village, N Yorks): 'Eskil's farmstead'. OS *bý*, 'farmstead', 'village'. The personal name is Scandinavian. DB *Aschilebi*.

Exeter (city, Devon): 'Roman town on the (river) Exe'. OE *ceaster*, 'Roman town'. The river has a Celtic name meaning simply 'water'. The Roman station here was *Isca Dumnoniorum*, the first word of this representing the river name, the second being that of the people who gave the name of DEVON. The city's present name has 'smoothed' from the original. *c*.900 *Exanceaster*, DB *Execestre*.

Exford (village, Somerset): '(place at the) ford over the (river) Exe'. OE *ford*, 'ford'. For the river name, see EXETER. The DB form below probably

resulted from the Norman clerk's attempt to render the awkward river name. DB *Aisseford*, 1243 *Exeford*.

Exminster (village, Devon): 'monastery by the (river) Exe'. OE *mynster*, 'monastery'. For the river name, see EXETER. *c*.880 *Exanmynster*, DB *Esseminstre*.

Exmoor (upland area, Somerset/Devon): 'moorland on the (river) Exe'. OE *mōr*, 'moor'. The Exe (see EXETER) rises here. 1204 *Exemora*.

Exmouth (resort town, Devon): 'mouth of the (river) Exe'. OE *mūtha*, 'mouth'. The Exe (see EXETER) enters the sea here. *c*.1025 *Exanmutha*.

Exning (village, Suffolk): '(settlement of) Gyxen's people'. OE *-ingas*, 'people of'. The DB form of the name below is corrupt. DB *Essellinge*, 1158 *Exningis*.

Exton (village, Devon): 'farmstead on the (river) Exe'. OE *tūn*, 'farmstead'. Exton is on the estuary of the Exe (see EXETER) 4 miles north of Exmouth. 1242 *Exton*.

Exton (village, Rutland): 'farmstead where oxen are kept'. OE *oxa*, 'ox', + *tūn*, 'farmstead'. DB *Exentune*.

Eyam (village, Derbys): '(place) at the islands'. OE *ēg*, 'island'. The name represents OE *ēgum*, the dative plural of *ēg*. The 'islands' are the pieces of land between the streams here known as Jumber Brook and Hollow Brook. DB *Aiune*.

Eydon (village, Northants): '(place by) Æga's hill'. OE *dūn*, 'hill'. DB *Egedone*.

Eye (suburb of Peterborough): '(place on the) island'. OE *ēg*, 'island'. John Bridges, in *History and Antiquities of Northamptonshire* (1791), describes Eye as 'situate on a rising ground, and before the draining of the fen, in winter time surrounded by water'. 10C *Ege*. SO ALSO: *Eye*, Herefords.

Eye (town, Suffolk): '(place on the) island'. OE *ēg*, 'island'. The 'island' here is an area of higher ground among a network of streams. DB *Eia*.

Eyemouth (town, Borders): 'mouth of the Eye Water'. OE *mūtha*, 'mouth'. The river has a name meaning simply 'river' (OE *ēa*). 1250 *Aymouthe*.

Eyeworth (village, Beds): 'island enclosure'. OE *ēg*, 'island', + *worth*, 'enclosure'. The village lies amid streams. The DB form of the name below is corrupt. DB *Aisseuuorde*, 1202 *Eywrth*.

Eyke (village, Suffolk): '(place at the) oak tree'. OS *eik*, 'oak'. 1185 *Eik*.

Eynesbury (district of St Neots, Cambs): 'Ēanwulf's stronghold'. OE *burh*, 'fortified place'. *c*.1000 *Eanulfesbyrig*, DB *Einuluesberie*.

Eynsford (village, Kent): '(place at) Ægen's ford'. OE *ford*, 'ford'. The river here is the Darent. *c.*960 *Æinesford*.

Eynsham (town, Oxon): 'Ægen's enclosure'. OE *hamm*, 'enclosure', 'river meadow'. Eynsham is on the Thames, with the Evenlode nearby. 864 *Egenes homme*, DB *Eglesham*.

Eype (village, Dorset): 'steep place'. OE *gēap*, 'steep'. The place in question may be a nearby hill. Eype is near the coast. 1365 *Yepe*.

Eythorne (village, Kent): 'Hēahgȳth's thorn bush'. OE *thorn*, 'thorn bush'. The personal name is that of a woman. 9C *Heagythethorne*.

Eyton upon the Weald Moors (village, Wrekin): 'island farmstead in the uncultivated marshland'. OE *ēg*, 'island', + *tūn*, 'farmstead', + *wilde*, 'wild', 'uncultivated', + *mōr*, 'moor', 'marsh'. The 'island' would have been raised ground in marshland. OE *wilde* has become confused with *weald* ('forest'). DB *Etone*, 1344 *Eyton super le Wildmore*, 1868 *Eyton-upon-the-Wild-Moors*.

F

Faceby (village, N Yorks): 'Feitr's farmstead'. os *bý*, 'farmstead', 'village'. The personal name is Scandinavian. DB *Feizbi*.

Fadmoor (hamlet, N Yorks): 'Fadda's moor'. OE *mōr*, 'moor'. DB *Fademora*.

Failsworth (town, Oldham): 'fenced enclosure'. OE *fēgels*, 'fence', + *worth*, 'enclosure'. OE *worth* often occurs with a word denoting a particular type of enclosure. Cp. LETCHWORTH. 1212 *Fayleswrthe*.

Fairburn (village, N Yorks): '(place by the) stream where ferns grow'. OE *fearn*, 'fern', + *burna*, 'stream'. The stream in question flows into the river Aire. *c*.1030 *Farenburne*, DB *Fareburne*.

Fairford (town, Glos): '(place by the) fair ford'. OE *fæger*, 'fair', + *ford*, 'ford'. A 'fair' ford is a clean or clear one, as distinct from a foul or dirty one, as at FULFORD. Fairford is on the river Coln. 862 *Fagranforda*, DB *Fareforde*.

Fair Isle (island, Shetland): 'island of sheep'. OS *faar*, 'sheep', + *ey*, 'island'. Fair Isle is noted for its knitwear, made from local wool. The *Faeroe Islands*, north of Shetland, have a name of identical origin. 1350 *Fároy*.

Fairlie (resort town, N Ayrs): '(place by the) fair wood'. OE *fæger*, 'fair', 'pleasant', + *lēah*, 'wood', 'clearing'.

Fairlight (village, E Sussex): 'woodland clearing where ferns grow'. OE *fearn*, 'fern', + *lēah*, 'wood', 'clearing'. The second part of the name may have resulted from the location of the village below Fairlight Down, a suitable place for a beacon to be lit. *c*.1175 *Farleghe*, 1673 *Fairelight*.

Fairlop (district of Hainault, Redbridge): '(place by the) lopped tree with a fair'. The name derives from a famous oak tree here under which a fair was held in the 18C. The tree, felled in 1820, stood on the site of the present Fairlop Oak playing field. 1738 *Fair Lop Tree*, 1805 *Fairlop Oak*.

Fairstead (hamlet, Essex): 'pleasant place'. OE *fæger*, 'fair', 'pleasant', + *stede*, 'place'. DB *Fairstedam*.

Fakenham (town, Norfolk): 'Facca's homestead'. OE *hām*, 'homestead', 'village'. DB *Fachenham*.

Faldingworth (village, Lincs): 'enclosure of Falda's people'. OE *-inga-*, 'of the people of', + *worth*, 'enclosure'. The name could also mean 'enclosure where animals are placed in folds' (OE *falding*, 'the placing of animals in folds'). DB *Faldingeurde*.

Falfield (village, S Glos): '(place by the) fallow-coloured open land'. OE *fealu*, 'fallow', + *feld*, 'open land' (modern English *field*). 1227 *Falefeld*.

Fali, Y. See VALLEY.

Falkenham (village, Suffolk): 'Falta's homestead'. OE *hām*, 'homestead'. The *t* of the personal name was misread as *c*, and this gave the *k* of the present name. DB *Faltenham*, 1254 *Falcenham*.

Falkirk (town, Falkirk): '(place with a) speckled church'. OE *fāg*, 'speckled', 'variegated', + *cirice*, 'church'. A 'speckled' church is one with mottled stone. The first three forms of the name below, respectively Gaelic, Latin and OF, have the same meaning. 1065 *Egglesbreth*, 1166 *varia capella*, 1253 *Varie Capelle*, 1298 *Faukirke*.

Falkland (town, Fife): 'folkland'. OE *folc*, 'folk', 'people', + *land*, 'land'. 'Folkland' would be land held according to folkright, i.e. common law. But the forms of the name below cast some doubt on this origin. 1128 *Falleland*, 1160 *Falecklen*.

Fallowfield (district, Manchester): 'fallow-coloured open land'. OE *fealu*, 'fallow', + *feld*, 'open land' (modern English *field*). The name could also mean 'fallow land', referring to newly cultivated land (OE *fealg*, 'ploughed land'). 1317 *Fallufeld*.

Falmer (village, E Sussex): '(place by the) fallow-coloured pool'. OE *fealu*, 'fallow', + *mere*, 'pool'. The pool is still here. DB *Falemere*.

Falmouth (town and port, Cornwall): 'mouth of the (river) Fal'. OE *mūtha*, 'mouth'. The meaning of the river name is uncertain. It may be pre-Celtic in origin. 1235 *Falemuth*.

Fangdale Beck (hamlet, N Yorks): '(place by the) stream in the valley used for fishing'. OS *fang*, 'fishing', + *dalr*, 'valley', + *bekkr*, 'stream'. 12C *Fangedala*.

Fangfoss (village, E Yorks): '(place by the) ditch used for fishing'. OS *fang*, 'fishing', + OE *foss*, 'ditch'. The DB form of the name below has an extraneous *r*. DB *Frangefos*, 12C *Fangefosse*.

Fanum Cocidi. See BEWCASTLE.

Farcet (village, Cambs): 'bull's hill'. OE *fearr*, 'bull', + *hēafod*, 'headland', 'hill'. The name probably denotes a hill where bulls were kept rather than one where the head of a sacrificed bull was displayed or one that resembled a bull's head in outline. 10C *Faresheued*.

Fareham (town, Hants): 'homestead where ferns grow'. OE *fearn*, 'fern', + *hām*, 'homestead'. *c.*970 *Fearnham*, DB *Fernham*.

Farewell (hamlet, Staffs): '(place by the) pleasant stream'. OE *fæger*, 'fair', 'pleasant', + *wella*, 'spring', 'stream'. 1200 *Fagerwell*.

Faringdon (town, Oxon): '(place by the) fern-covered hill'. OE *fearn*, 'fern', + *dūn*, 'hill'. The hill in question lies to the east of the town. See also LITTLE FARINGDON. *c.*971 *Færndunæ*, DB *Ferendone*.

Farington (hamlet, Lancs): 'farmstead where ferns grow'. OE *fearn*, 'fern', + *tūn*, 'farmstead'. 1149 *Farinton*.

Farleigh Hungerford (village, Somerset): 'Hungerford's (estate in the) woodland clearing where ferns grow'. OE *fearn*, 'fern', + *lēah*, 'wood', 'clearing'. The Hungerford family held the manor here in the 14C, their name distinguishing this Farleigh from MONKTON FARLEIGH, Wilts, 5 miles to the north. 987 *Fearnlæh*, DB *Ferlege*, 1404 *Farlegh Hungerford*.

Farleton (hamlet, Cumbria): 'Færela's or Faraldr's farmstead'. OE *tūn*, 'farmstead'. The personal names are respectively OE and Scandinavian. DB *Farelton*.

Farley (village, Wilts): 'woodland clearing where ferns grow'. OE *fearn*, 'fern', + *lēah*, 'wood', 'clearing'. DB *Farlege*. SO ALSO: *Farley*, Staffs.

Farlington (village, N Yorks): 'estate associated with Færela'. OE *-ing-*, 'associated with', + *tūn*, 'farmstead', 'estate'. DB *Ferlintun*.

Farlow (hamlet, Shropshire): '(place by the) fern-covered mound'. OE *fearn*, 'fern', + *hlāw*, 'mound', 'hill'. When the present church was built in 1858 a seated skeleton was found in a mound. DB *Ferlau*, 1222 *Farnlawe*.

Farmborough (village, Bath & NE Somerset): '(place by the) hill growing with ferns'. OE *fearn*, 'fern', + *beorg*, 'mound', 'hill'. The second *n* of the first form of the name below is extraneous. 901 *Fearnberngas*, DB *Ferenberge*.

Farmington (village, Glos): 'farmstead by the pool where thorn bushes grow'. OE *thorn*, 'thorn bush', + *mere*, 'pool', + *tūn*, 'farmstead'. The pool in question may have been at nearby Bittam Copse. The DB form of the name below has *r* and the original OE *th* later became *f*. DB *Tormentone*, 1182 *Tormerton*.

Farnborough (town, Hants): 'hill covered with ferns'. OE *fearn*, 'fern', + *beorg*, 'hill'. The hill in question may be the lowish one with Farnborough Park at its southern end. DB *Ferneberga*. SO ALSO: *Farnborough*, Bromley, W Berks.

Farnborough (village, Warwicks): 'hill covered with ferns'. OE *fearn*, 'fern', + *beorg*, 'hill'. William Dugdale, in *The Antiquities of Warwickshire* (1656), says that Farnborough probably 'had at first that name from the naturall disposition of the soil to bear *Ferne*, the later syllable *Berge* signifying in our old English a little Hill, as we see the ground, whereon the town stands, is'. *c.*1015 *Feornebeorh*, DB *Ferneberge*.

Farndon (village, Cheshire): 'hill growing with ferns'. OE *fearn*, 'fern', + *dūn*, 'hill'. The 14C chronicler Ranulph Higden says in his Latin *Polychronicon* that Edward the Elder, king of England, died (in 924) at FARINGDON, Oxon: '*Rex Edwardus obiit apud Farnedoun xii milliaribus ab Oxonia ad occidentem distantem*' ('King Edward died at Faringdon, 12 miles west of Oxford'). The *Dictionary of National Biography* says he died at EAST FARNDON, Northants. The true place of his death, as stated by Frank Stenton in *Anglo-Saxon England* (3rd edition, 1971), was almost certainly Farndon, Cheshire. The DB form of the name below has apparently taken OE *dūn* as *tūn*, 'farmstead'. 924 *Fearndune*, DB *Ferentone*.

Farndon (village, Notts): 'hill growing with ferns'. OE *fearn*, 'fern', + *dūn*, 'hill'. DB *Farendune*.

Farne Islands (island group, Northd): 'fern islands'. OE *fearn*, 'fern'. This traditional explanation of the name is now generally rejected in favour of a Celtic origin, with a meaning '(islands of the) domain', referring to LINDISFARNE, some 6 miles away. *c.*700 *Farne*.

Farnham (town, Surrey): 'river meadow where ferns grow'. OE *fearn*, 'fern', + *hamm*, 'enclosure', 'river meadow'. Farnham is on the river Wey. *c*.686 *Fernham*, DB *Ferneham*. SO ALSO: *Farnham*, Dorset, Essex, N Yorks, Suffolk.

Farnham Royal (suburb of Slough, Bucks): 'royal homestead where ferns grow'. OE *fearn*, 'fern', + *hām*, 'homestead', + OF *roial*, 'royal'. The second word of the name refers to the holding of the place by the grand serjeanty, a form of tenure conditional on rendering some personal service to the king. DB *Ferneham*, 1477 *Fernham Riall*.

Farningham (village, Kent): 'homestead of the dwellers among the ferns'. OE *fearn*, 'fern', + *-inga-*, 'of the dwellers at', + *hām*, 'homestead'. DB *Ferningeham*.

Farnley (district, Leeds): 'woodland clearing where ferns grow'. OE *fearn*, 'fern', + *lēah*, 'wood', 'clearing'. *New Farnley* is a southern extension of Farnley. DB *Fernelei*. SO ALSO: *Farnley*, N Yorks.

Farnley Tyas (village, Kirklees): 'le Tyeis' (estate at the) woodland clearing where ferns grow'. OE *fearn*, 'fern', + *lēah*, 'wood', 'clearing'. The le Tyeis family held land here in the 13C. The DB form of the name below has omitted the *n*. DB *Fereleia*, 1322 *Farnley Tyas*.

Farnsfield (village, Notts): 'open land where ferns grow'. OE *fearn*, 'fern', + *feld*, 'open land' (modern English *field*). 958 *Fearnesfeld*, DB *Farnesfeld*.

Farnworth (town, Bolton): 'enclosure where ferns grow'. OE *fearn*, 'fern', + *worth*, 'enclosure'. 1185 *Farnewurd*. SO ALSO: *Farnworth*, Halton.

Farringdon (village, Devon): '(place by the) fern-covered hill'. OE *fearn*, 'fern', + *dūn*, 'hill'. DB *Ferhendone*.

Farrington Gurney (village, Bath & NE Somerset): 'de Gurnay's farmstead where ferns grow'. OE *fearn*, 'fern', + *tūn*, 'farmstead'. The de Gurnay family held the manor here in the 13C. DB *Ferentone*.

Far Sawrey (village, Cumbria): 'farther (place with) muddy grounds'. OS *saurr* (plural *saurar*), 'sour ground', 'mud'. The first word contrasts the village with *Near Sawrey*, to the west. 1336 *Sourer*.

Farsley (district, Leeds): 'clearing where heifers are kept'. OE *fers*, 'heifer', + *lēah*, 'wood', 'clearing'. DB *Ferselleia*.

Farthinghoe (village, Northants): 'hill spur of the dwellers among the ferns'. OE *fearn*, 'fern', + *-inga-*, 'of the dwellers at', + *hōh*, 'hill spur'. DB *Ferningeho*.

Farthingstone (village, Northants): 'Farthegn's farmstead'. OE *tūn*, 'farmstead'. The personal name is Scandinavian. DB *Fordinestone*.

Farway (village, Devon): '(place by the) dangerous way'. OE *fǣr*, 'danger' (modern English *fear*), + *weg*, 'way'. Several roads make steep descents to reach the village. DB *Farewei*.

Fauldhouse (village, W Lothian): 'house on fallow land'. OE *falh*, 'fallow land', + *hūs*, 'house'. The name became wrongly associated with Scottish English *fauld*, 'fold'. 1523 *Fawlhous*, *c*.1540 *Falhous*, 1559 *Faldhous*.

Faulkbourne (hamlet, Essex): '(place by the) stream where falcons are seen'. OE *falca*, 'falcon', + *burna*, 'stream'. DB *Falcheburna*.

Faulkland (village, Somerset): 'folkland'. OE *folc-land* (from *folc*, 'folk', + *land*, 'land'). 'Folkland' is land held by folkright, i.e. by the common law or right of the people, as distinct from 'bookland' (OE *bōc-land*), land held by charter (see BUCKLAND). 1243 *Foukelande*.

Faversham (town, Kent): 'village of the smith'. OE *fæfer*, 'smith' (from Latin *faber*), + *hām*, 'homestead', 'village'. Metal workings are believed to have existed locally since Roman times. 811 *Fefresham*, DB *Faversham*.

Fawkham Green (village, Kent): 'Fealcna's homestead'. OE *hām*, 'homestead', 'village'. The village later became associated with its green. The DB form of the name below is corrupt. 10C *Fealcnaham*, DB *Fachesham*.

Fawler (village, Oxon): '(place with a) variegated floor'. OE *fāg*, 'variegated', + *flōr*, 'floor'. The 'variegated floor' is a Roman tessellated pavement here. 1205 *Fauflor*.

Fawley (village, Bucks): 'fallow-coloured woodland clearing'. OE *fealu*, 'fallow', + *lēah*, 'wood', 'clearing'. The name could also mean 'clearing with arable land' (OE *fealg*, 'ploughed land', + *lēah*). DB *Falelie*.

Fawley (village, Hants): 'fallow-coloured woodland clearing'. OE *fealu*, 'fallow', + *lēah*, 'wood', 'clearing'. The name could also mean 'clearing with arable land' (OE *fealg*, 'ploughed land', + *lēah*). DB *Falelei*.

Fawley (village, W Berks): 'wood where fallow deer are seen'. OE *fealu*, 'fallow (deer)', + *lēah*, 'wood'. DB *Faleslei*.

Fawley Chapel (hamlet, Herefords): 'woodland clearing where hay is made'. OE *fǣlethe*, 'hay', + *lēah*, 'wood', 'clearing'. The place was later associated with a chapel of ease here by the river Wye. 1142 *Falileiam*.

Faxfleet (hamlet, E Yorks): '(place by) Faxi's stream'. OE *flēot*, 'stream'. The personal name is Scandinavian. The name could also mean '(place by the) stream near which coarse grass grows' (OE *feax*, 'hair', 'coarse grass', + *flēot*). 1190 *Faxflete*.

Fazakerley (district, Liverpool): 'woodland clearing by the borderland'. OE *fæs*, 'fringe', 'border', + *æcer*, 'plot of cultivated land' (modern English *acre*), + *lēah*, 'forest', 'clearing'. 1325 *Fasacrelegh*.

Fazeley (village, Staffs): 'clearing where bulls are kept'. OE *fearr*, 'bull', + *lēah*, 'wood', 'clearing'. *c.*1142 *Faresleia*.

Fearby (village, N Yorks): '(particular) farmstead'. OS *bȳ*, 'farmstead', 'village'. The first part of the name is of uncertain origin. It may represent OE *fether* or OS *fjǫthr*, 'feather', referring to a place where flocks of birds were seen. DB *Federbi*.

Fearnhead (district, Warrington): '(place on the) hill where ferns grow'. OE *fearn*, 'fern', + *hēafod*, 'hill'. 1292 *Ferneheued*.

Featherstone (village, Staffs): '(place at the) four stones'. OE *feother-*, 'four', + *stān*, 'stan'. The reference is to a tetralith, as at FOUR-STONES, Northd. No trace of this survives. 10C *Feotherstan*, DB *Ferdestan*. SO ALSO: *Featherstone*, Wakefield.

Feckenham (village, Worcs): 'Fecca's water meadow'. OE *hamm*, 'enclosure', 'river meadow'. Feckenham is surrounded by streams. 804 *Feccanhom*, DB *Fecheham*.

Feering (village, Essex): '(settlement of) Fēra's people'. OE *-ingas*, 'people of'. DB *Feringas*.

Feetham (village, N Yorks): '(place in the) riverside meadows'. OS *fit*, 'meadow'. The name represents OS *fitjum*, the dative plural form of *fit*. 1242 *Fytun*.

Felbridge (suburb of East Grinstead, Surrey): '(place at the) bridge by open land'. OE *feld*, 'open land' (modern English *field*), + *brycg*, 'bridge'. The bridge would have been over Felbridge Water, separating Surrey from Sussex, and the 'open land' would have been part of the Weald. 12C *Feltbruge*.

Felbrigg (village, Norfolk): '(place by the) plank bridge'. OS *fjǫl*, 'plank', + OE *brycg*, 'bridge'. DB *Felebruge*.

Felinheli, Y. See PORT DINORWIC.

Felixkirk (village, N Yorks): 'St Felix's church'. OS *kirkja*, 'church'. It is uncertain to which Felix the church is dedicated here. 13C *Felicekirke*, 1868 *Feliskirk, or Felix-Kirk*.

Felixstowe (resort town and port, Suffolk): 'Filica's holy place'. OE *stōw*, 'place', 'holy place'. The personal name later became associated with St Felix (d.647), the first bishop of East Anglia, though none of the three churches here is dedicated to him. 1254 *Filchestou*, 1868 *Felixstow, or Felstow*.

Felkirk (hamlet, Wakefield): 'church made of planks'. OS *fjǫl*, 'board', 'plank', + *kirkja*, 'church'. *c.*1130 *Felechirche*.

Felling (town, Gateshead): 'woodland clearing'. OE *felling*, 'a felling of trees'. The town is still known locally as 'the Felling', as in the children's rhyme: 'Two lovely black eyes! / Oh, what a surprise! / Only for sellin "Scotch hares" in the Fellin, / Two lovely black eyes!' *c.*1220 *Fellyng*.

Felmersham (village, Beds): 'river meadow by a fallow-coloured pool'. OE *fealu*, 'fallow', + *mere*, 'pool', + *hamm*, 'enclosure', 'river meadow'. The name could also mean 'Feolomær's river meadow'. Felmersham lies in a bend of the river Ouse. DB *Falmeresham*.

Felmingham (village, Norfolk): 'homestead of Feolma's people'. OE *-inga-*, 'of the people of', + *hām*, 'homestead'. DB *Felmincham*.

Felpham (resort district of Bognor Regis, W Sussex): 'enclosure with fallow land'. OE *felh*, 'fallow land', + *hamm*, 'enclosure'. *c.*880 *Felhhamm*, DB *Falcheham*.

Felsham (village, Suffolk): 'Fæle's homestead'. OE *hām*, 'homestead', 'village'. DB *Fealsham*.

Felsted (village, Essex): 'place in open land'. OE *feld*, 'open land' (modern English *field*), + *stede*, 'place', 'site'. DB *Felstede*.

Feltham (district, Hounslow): 'homestead where mullein grows'. OE *felte*, 'mullein', + *hām*, 'homestead'. Mullein is the tall, yellow-flowered, woolly plant known popularly as Aaron's rod. The name could also mean 'homestead on open land' (OE *feld*, 'open land', + *hām*). 969 *Feltham*, DB *Felteham*.

Felthorpe (village, Norfolk): 'Fæla's outlying farmstead'. OS *thorp*, 'outlying farmstead'. DB *Felethorp*.

Felton (village, Northd): 'farmstead in open country'. OE *feld*, 'open land' (modern English *field*), + *tūn*, 'farmstead', 'village'. 1167 *Feltona*. SO ALSO: *Felton*, Herefords.

Felton Butler. See WEST FELTON.

Feltwell (village, Norfolk): '(place by the) spring where mullein grows'. OE *felte*, 'mullein', + *wella*, 'spring', 'stream'. DB *Feltuuella*.

Fen Ditton (village, Cambs): 'farmstead by a dyke in fenland'. OE *fenn*, 'fen', + *dīc*, 'ditch', 'dyke', + *tūn*, 'farmstead'. The dyke in question is Fleam Dyke here. The first word of the name distinguishes this village from the hamlet of *Woodditton*, 'farmstead by a dyke in woodland' (OE *wudu*, 'wood'), 11 miles to the east, where the dyke is the Devil's Dyke. *c*.975 *Dictunæ*, 1286 *Fen Dytton*.

Fen Drayton (village, Cambs): 'farmstead by a portage in marshland'. OE *fenn*, 'marshland', + *dræg*, 'portage' (related modern English *drag*, *draw*), + *tūn*, 'farmstead'. It is unclear where the portage would have been here, and there is no slope where loads would have been dragged down. The first word distinguishes the village from DRY DRAYTON, 5 miles to the southeast. 1012 *Drægtun*, DB *Draitone*, 1188 *Fendreiton*.

Fenham (coastal hamlet, Northd): '(place in the) fens'. OE *fenn*, 'fen'. The name represents OE *fennum*, the dative plural form of *fenn*. *c*.1085 *Fennum*.

Feniton (village, Devon): 'farmstead by Vine Water'. OE *tūn*, 'farmstead'. The river name is of Celtic origin and means 'boundary stream' (modern Welsh *ffin*, 'boundary', 'limit', from Latin *finis*, 'end'). The stream, a tributary of the Otter, forms the boundary of the parish of Ottery here. DB *Finetone*.

Fenland (council district, Cambs): 'land of fens'. The district occupies the northeast of the county, as part of *The Fens*, the low-lying region of former marshland in eastern England that was mostly drained for agricultural purposes from the 17C. (See BEDFORD LEVEL.) The name (or word) dates from at least the 11C and derives from OE *fenn*, 'marsh', 'mud'.

Fenni, Y. See ABERGAVENNY.

Fenny Bentley (village, Derbys): 'marshy woodland clearing where bents grow'. OE *fennig*, 'marshy', + *beonet*, 'bent grass', + *lēah*, 'wood', 'clearing'. DB *Benedlege*, 1272 *Fennibenetlegh*.

Fenny Compton (village, Warwicks): 'muddy farmstead in a valley'. OE *fennig*, 'muddy', 'marshy', + *cumb*, 'valley', + *tūn*, 'farmstead'. The village lies below Compton Hill, from which water drains. DB *Contone*, 1221 *Fennicumpton*.

Fenny Drayton (village, Leics): 'marshy farmstead by a portage'. OE *fennig*, 'muddy', 'marshy', + *dræg*, 'portage' (related modern English *drag*, *draw*), + *tūn*, 'farmstead'. The village is on the river Anker. DB *Draitone*, 1465 *Fenedrayton*.

Fenny Stratford (district of Bletchley, Milton K): 'marshy (place at a) ford on a Roman road'. OE *fennig*, 'marshy', + *strǣt*, 'Roman road' (modern English *street*), + *ford*, 'ford'. Fenny Stratford lies on Watling Street, the first word of its name distinguishing it from STONY STRATFORD, 10 miles to the northwest on the same Roman road. The river here is the Ouzel. 1252 *Fenni Stratford*.

Fenstanton (village, Cambs): 'farmstead on stony ground in marshland'. OE *fenn*, 'fen', 'marshy ground', + *stān*, 'stone', + *tūn*, 'farmstead'. The first part of the name distinguishes this Stanton from *Longstanton*, 'long farmstead on stony ground', 6 miles to the southeast. 1012 *Stantun*, DB *Stantone*, 1260 *Fenstanton*.

Fenton (town, Stoke): 'farmstead in marshland'. OE *fenn*, 'fen', 'marshland', + *tūn*, 'farmstead', 'village'. DB *Fentone*. SO ALSO: *Fenton*, Cambs, Lincs (near Claypole, near Torksey).

Fenwick (hamlet, Northd): 'dairy farm in fenland'. OE *fenn*, 'fen', + *wīc*, 'dwelling', 'dairy farm'. The form of the name below is for Fenwick near Stamfordham, but Fenwick near Belford has a name of identical origin. 1242 *Fenwic*.

Feock (village, Cornwall): '(church of) St Fioc'. The church here is dedicated to Fioc, about whom nothing is known. The form of the name below has Cornish *lann*, 'church site'. *c*.1165 *Lanfioc*.

Ferndown (suburb of Bournemouth, Dorset): '(place on the) fern-covered down'. OE *fierne*, 'ferny place', + *dūn*, 'down', 'hill'. The first part of the name, which originally stood alone, could also represent OE *fergen*, 'wooded hill'. 1321 *Fyrne*.

Fernham (village, Oxon): '(place by the) river meadow where ferns grow'. OE *fearn*, 'fern', + *hamm*, 'enclosure', 'river meadow'. The village lies near the source of the river Ock, 2 miles south of the hill that gave the name of FARINGDON. 9C *Fernham*.

Fernhurst (village, W Sussex): '(place by the) fern-covered wooded hill'. OE *fearn*, 'fern', + *hyrst*, 'wooded hill'. *c*.1200 *Fernherst*.

Fernilee (hamlet, Derbys): 'woodland clearing where ferns grow'. OE *fearn*, 'fern', + *lēah*, 'wood', 'clearing'. 12C *Ferneley*.

Ferrensby (village, N Yorks): 'farmstead of the Faeroese'. OS *færeyingr*, 'Faeroese' (person from the Faeroe Islands), + *bý*, 'farmstead', 'village'. The DB form of the name below has omitted a syllable. DB *Feresbi*, 13C *Feringesby*.

Ferring (coastal town, W Sussex): '(settlement of) Fēra's people'. OE -*ingas*, 'people of'. 765 *Ferring*, DB *Feringes*.

Ferrybridge (district of Knottingley, Wakefield): '(place at the) bridge by the ferry'. OS *ferja*, 'ferry', + OE *brycg*, 'bridge'. The first bridge over the river Aire here was built in the late 12C at the point where an earlier ferry took the traffic of the Great North Road across. See also FERRYHILL. DB *Ferie*, 1198 *Ferybrig*.

Ferry Fryston. See MONK FRYSTON.

Ferryhill (town, Durham): '(place by the) wooded hill'. OE *fergen*, 'wooded hill', + *hyll*, 'hill'. The tautologous *hyll* was probably added to distinguish this place from FERRYBRIDGE, Wakefield, since both places were originally simply *Ferry* and both were on the Great North Road. 10C *Feregenne*, c.1125 *Ferie*, 1316 *Ferye on the Hill*.

Fersfield (village, Norfolk): 'open land where heifers graze'. OE *fers*, 'heifer', + *feld*, 'open land' (modern English *field*). The DB form of the name below has apparently taken the second part as OE *wella*, 'spring', 'stream'. c.1035 *Fersafeld*, DB *Ferseuella*.

Fetcham (residential district, Surrey): 'Fecca's homestead'. OE *hām*, 'homestead', 'village'. 10C *Fecham*, DB *Feceham*.

Fettercairn (village, Aberdeens): '(place on a) slope by a thicket'. Gaelic *faithir*, 'slope', + Celtic *carden*, 'thicket'. c.970 *Fotherkern*, c.1350 *Fettercairn*.

Fewston (village, N Yorks): 'Fótr's farmstead'. OE *tūn*, 'farmstead'. The personal name is Scandinavian. DB *Fostune*.

Ffestiniog. See BLAENAU FFESTINIOG.

Fflint, Y. See FLINT.

Fforest Fawr (region of moorland hills, Powys): 'great forest'. Welsh *fforest*, 'forest', + *mawr*, 'big', 'great'. Welsh *mawr* has mutated to *fawr* following the feminine noun *fforest*.

Fiddington (village, Somerset): 'estate associated with Fita'. OE -*ing*-, 'associated with', + *tūn*, 'farmstead', 'estate'. DB *Fitintone*. SO ALSO: *Fiddington*, Glos.

Fiddleford (village, Dorset): '(place by) Fitela's ford'. OE *ford*, 'ford'. 1244 *Fitelford*.

Field Dalling. See WOOD DALLING.

Fife (unitary authority, SE Scotland): '(territory of) Fib'. The name of the historic Pictish kingdom and former county is traditionally derived from Fib, one of the seven sons of Cruithe, legendary father of the Picts. But the personal name dates later than the territory associated with it, so some earlier name must be involved. c.1150 *Fib*, 1165 *Fif*.

Fifehead Magdalen (village, Dorset): '(estate of) five hides with (St Mary) Magdalen's church'. OE *fíf*, 'five', + *hīd*, 'hide'. Cp. FIFIELD. The church dedication distinguishes this Fifehead from *Fifehead Neville*, 7 miles to the south, and *Fifehead St Quintin*, nearby, where the manors were held respectively by the de Nevill and St Quintin families in the 13C. DB *Fifhide*, 1388 *Fifyde Maudaleyne*.

Fifield (village, Oxon): '(estate of) five hides'. OE *fíf*, 'five', + *hīd*, 'hide'. A hide was about 40 acres, regarded as enough to support a peasant family, and the estate here was assessed in DB at five hides. DB *Fifhide*. SO ALSO: *Fifield*, Windsor & Maid.

Fifield Bavant (village, Wilts): 'de Bavant's (estate of) five hides'. OE *fíf*, 'five', + *hīd*, 'hide'. Cp. FIFIELD. The de Bavant family held the manor here from the 14C. DB *Fifhide*, 1436 *Fiffehyde Beaufaunt*.

Figheldean (village, Wilts): 'Fygla's valley'. OE *denu*, 'valley'. The DB form of the name below has an extraneous *s*. DB *Fisgledene*, 1227 *Figelden*.

Filby (village, Norfolk): 'Fili's or Fila's farmstead'. OS *bý*, 'farmstead', 'village'. The first personal name is Scandinavian, the second OE. The first part of the name could also represent OS *fili*, 'planks', perhaps referring to a wooden footbridge over marshland here in the Norfolk Broads. DB *Filebey*.

Filey (resort town, N Yorks): 'five clearings'. OE *fíf*, 'five', + *lēah*, 'wood', 'clearing'. An alternative meaning is 'promontory like a sea monster' (OE *fífel*, 'sea monster', + *ēg*, 'island', 'promontory'), referring to Filey Brigg, a ridge of rock projecting half a mile into the sea. The DB form of the name below has a garbled second part. DB *Fiuelac*, 12C *Fivelai*.

Filkins (village, Oxon): '(settlement of) Filica's people'. OE -*ingas*, 'people of'. 12C *Filching*.

Filleigh (village, Devon): 'woodland clearing where hay is made'. OE *filethe*, 'hay', + *lēah*, 'wood', 'clearing'. DB *Filelei*.

Fillingham (village, Lincs): 'homestead of Fygla's people'. OE -*inga*-, 'of the people of', + *hām*, 'homestead'. DB *Figelingeham*.

Fillongley (village, Warwicks): 'woodland clearing of Fygla's people'. OE -*inga*-, 'of the people of', + *lēah*, 'wood', 'clearing'. DB *Filingelei*.

Filton (district of Bristol, S Glos): 'farm where hay is made'. OE *filethe*, 'hay', + *tūn*, 'farmstead', 'estate'. 1187 *Filton*.

Fimber (village, E Yorks): '(place at a) pool by a wood pile'. OE *fin*, 'wood pile', + *mere*, 'pool'. The pool is not natural but has been cut into a hollow here. 12C *Fymmara*.

Finchale Priory (ruined priory, Durham): 'priory in the river bend where finches are seen'. OE *finc*, 'finch', + *halh*, 'nook', 'corner of land'. The ruins of the 12C priory lie in a bend of the river Wear. The 13C monk Reginald of Durham repeats an old account of the name: '*Finchale locus dicitur qui quondam diebus antiquis a rege Finc dicto sic vocari putabatur*' ('This place is called Finchale and was thought to have been so named in former times after a king called Finc'). *c.*1100 *Finchale*.

Fincham (village, Norfolk): 'homestead or enclosure where finches are seen'. OE *finc*, 'finch', + *hām*, 'homestead', or *hamm*, 'enclosure'. DB *Pincham*.

Finchampstead (village, Wokingham): 'homestead where finches are seen'. OE *finc*, 'finch', + *hām-stede* (see HAMPSTEAD). DB *Finchamestede*.

Finchingfield (village, Essex): 'open land of Finc's people'. OE *-inga-*, 'of the people of', + *feld*, 'open land' (modern English *field*). DB *Fincingefelda*.

Finchley (district, Barnet): 'woodland clearing where finches are seen'. OE *finc*, 'finch', + *lēah*, 'wood', 'clearing'. *c.*1208 *Finchelee*.

Findern (village, Derbys): origin uncertain. No satisfactory origin has been proposed for this name. DB *Findre*.

Findhorn (village, Moray): '(place on the river) Findhorn'. The river has a Celtic name meaning 'white Isarona' (Gaelic *fionn*, 'white'), referring to the goddess believed to dwell in its waters.

Findon (village, W Sussex): 'hill with a heap of wood'. OE *fin*, 'wood pile', + *dūn*, 'hill'. The hill in question is presumably the rising ground behind Findon church. DB *Findune*.

Finedon (town, Northants): 'valley where assemblies meet'. OE *thing*, 'assembly', 'meeting', + *denu*, 'valley'. DB *Tingdene*.

Fingal's Cave (island cave, Argyll & Bute). Fingal is the legendary Irish giant Fionn Mac Cumhail. The Gaelic name of the Staffa cave is *An Uamh Binn*, 'the melodious cave', referring to the eerie sound made by the sea among the basalt pillars.

Fingest (village, Bucks): 'wooded hill where the assembly is held'. OE *thing*, 'assembly', 'meeting', + *hyrst*, 'wooded hill'. The assembly in question was probably the shire court that gave the name of nearby SKIRMETT. 12C *Tingeherst*.

Finghall (village, N Yorks): 'corner of land of Fīn's people'. OE *-inga-*, 'of the people of', + *halh*, 'nook', 'corner of land'. The DB form of the name below is corrupt. DB *Finegala*, 1157 *Finyngale*.

Finglesham (hamlet, Kent): 'homestead of the prince'. OE *thengel*, 'prince', + *hām*, 'homestead', 'village'. The name could also mean 'Thengel's homestead'. The DB form of the name below is garbled. 832 *Thenglesham*, DB *Flengvessam*.

Fingringhoe (village, Essex): 'hill spur of the dwellers on the finger-shaped hill'. OE *finger*, 'finger', + *-inga-*, 'of the dwellers at', + *hōh*, 'hill spur'. The reference is to the broad finger of land between Roman River and Geeton Creek. 10C *Fingringaho*.

Finmere (village, Oxon): '(place by the) pool where woodpeckers are seen'. OE *fina*, 'woodpecker', + *mere*, 'pool'. DB *Finemere*.

Finningham (village, Suffolk): 'homestead of Fīn's people'. OE *-inga-*, 'of the people of', + *hām*, 'homestead'. DB *Finingaham*.

Finningley (village, Doncaster): 'woodland clearing of the fen dwellers'. OE *fenn*, 'fen', + *-inga-*, 'of the dwellers at', + *lēah*, 'wood', 'clearing'. The DB form of the name below has omitted the *n* of *-inga-*. DB *Feniglei*, 1175 *Feningelay*.

Finsbury (district, Islington): 'Finn's manor'. ME *bury*, 'manor' (from OE *byrig*, dative of *burh*, 'fortified place'). The personal name is Scandinavian. 1235 *Finesbire*.

Finsbury Park (district, Haringey/Islington). The park here was opened in 1857 and so named as it was designated for the use of the inhabitants of the old parliamentary borough of FINSBURY, although this is some 3 miles to the south.

Finsthwaite (hamlet, Cumbria): 'Finn's clearing'. OS *thveit*, 'clearing'. The personal name is Scandinavian. 1336 *Fynnesthwayt*.

Finstock (village, Oxon): 'outlying farmstead where woodpeckers are seen'. OE *fina*, 'woodpecker', + *stoc*, 'outlying farmstead'. 12C *Finestochia*.

Firbeck (village, Rotherham): '(place by the) woodland stream'. OE *fyrhth*, 'woodland', + OS *bekkr*, 'stream'. Firbeck lies on the edge of a forest area. 12C *Fritebec*.

Firle Beacon. See WEST FIRLE.

Firth of Forth (sea inlet, Fife/E Lothian): 'estuary of the (river) Forth'. ME *firth* (from OS *fjorthr*, 'fjord', 'arm of the sea'). The river has a Celtic name meaning 'silent one' (modern Welsh *byddar*, 'deaf'). The form of the river name (*c.970 Forthin*) has probably been influenced by 'Firth' itself.

Fishbourne (village, W Sussex): '(place by the) stream where fish are caught'. OE *fisc*, 'fish', + *burna*, 'stream'. The village is properly *New Fishbourne*, or formerly *East Fishbourne*, as distinct from nearby *Old Fishbourne*, or formerly *West Fishbourne*. DB *Fiseborne*.

Fisherton de la Mere (hamlet, Wilts): 'de la Mere's (estate at the) farmstead of the fishermen'. OE *fiscere*, 'fisherman', + *tūn*, 'farmstead'. The de la Mere family held the manor here by the river Wylye in the 14C. Their name distinguishes this Fisherton from the former *Fisherton Anger*, now absorbed into Salisbury, where the son of one Aucher (later misread as Ancher) held the manor in the 13C. (Fisherton Street in the city led to it and is named after it.) DB *Fisertone*.

Fishguard (town and port, Pemb): 'fish yard'. OS *fiskr*, 'fish', + *garthr*, 'yard'. A 'fish yard' is an enclosure for catching fish or for keeping them in when caught. The Welsh name of Fishguard is *Abergwaun*, 'mouth of the (river) Gwaun' (OW *aber*, 'river mouth'.) The river name means 'marsh', 'moor' (Welsh *gwaun*). 1200 *Fissigart*, 1210 *Fissegard, id est, Aber gweun*.

Fishlake (village, Doncaster): '(place by the) stream where fish are caught'. OE *fisc*, 'fish', + *lacu*, 'stream' (related modern English *lake*). DB *Fiscelac*.

Fiskerton (village, Notts): 'farmstead of the fishermen'. OE *fiscere*, 'fisherman', + *tūn*, 'farmstead', 'village'. OE *fiscere* was replaced in the name by equivalent OS *fiskari*. The village, on the river Trent, is still a favourite spot for anglers. 956 *Fiscertune*, DB *Fiscartune*. SO ALSO: *Fiskerton*, Lincs.

Fittleton (village, Wilts): 'Fitela's farmstead'. OE *tūn*, 'farmstead'. DB *Viteletone*.

Fittleworth (village, W Sussex): 'Fitela's enclosure'. OE *worth*, 'enclosure'. 1168 *Fitelwurtha*.

Fitz (hamlet, Shropshire): 'Fitt's hill spur'. OE *hōh*, 'hill spur'. The second part of the original name has disappeared. The DB form of the name below has garbled the personal name. DB *Witesot*, 1194 *Fittesho*, 1255 *Fittes*.

Fitzhead (village, Somerset): '(estate of) five hides'. OE *fīf*, 'five', + *hīd*, 'hide'. Cp. FIFIELD. The name appears to have been influenced by that of nearby *Fitzroy*. 1065 *Fifhida*.

Fivehead (village, Somerset): '(estate of) five hides'. OE *fīf*, 'five', + *hīd*, 'hide'. Cp. FIFIELD. DB *Fifhide*.

Fladbury (village, Worcs): 'Flǣde's stronghold'. OE *burh*, 'fortified place', 'manor house'. The personal name is that of a woman. Late 7C *Fledanburg*, DB *Fledebirie*.

Flagg (village, Derbys): 'place where turfs are cut'. OS *flag*, 'turf'. The DB form of the name below represents OS *flagum*, the dative plural form of *flag*. DB *Flagun*.

Flamborough (village, E Yorks): 'Fleinn's stronghold'. OE *burh*, 'fortified place'. The personal name is Scandinavian. The headland *Flamborough Head* 2 miles to the east is named from the village and first recorded in the 14C. The name has been popularly associated with English *flame*, supposedly referring to a beacon lit here to guide ships in the North Sea. DB *Flaneburg*.

Flamstead (village, Herts): 'place of refuge'. OE *flēam*, 'flight' (related modern English *flee*), + *stede*, 'place', 'site'. The manor here, near the Bedfordshire border, was held on condition that it provided protection for travellers. 990 *Fleamstede*, DB *Flamestede*.

Flasby (hamlet, N Yorks): 'Flatr's farmstead'. OS *bý*, 'farmstead', 'village'. The personal name is Scandinavian. DB *Flatebi*.

Flash (village, Staffs): '(place by the) marshy ground'. OS *flask*, 'marshy place', 'pool'.

Flaunden (village, Herts): '(place in the) valley where there are flagstones'. OE *flage*, 'flagstone', + *denu*, 'valley'. 13C *Flawenden*.

Flawborough (village, Notts): '(place on the) hill with stones'. OE *flōh*, 'stone chip', + *beorg*, 'hill'. The DB form of the name below has *d* for *h*. DB *Flodberge*, 12C *Flouberge*.

Flawith (hamlet, N Yorks): '(place by the) ford of the witch'. OS *flagth*, 'female troll', 'witch', + *vath*, 'ford'. The first part of the name could also represent OS *flatha*, 'flat meadow', or OE *fleathe*, 'water lily'. *c.*1190 *Flathwayth*.

Flax Bourton (village, N Somerset): 'farmstead by the hill where flax is grown'. OE *fleax*, 'flax', + *beorg*, 'hill', + *tūn*, 'farmstead'. 1276 *Bricton*.

Flaxby (village, N Yorks): 'Flatr's farmstead'. OS *bý*, 'farmstead', 'village'. The personal name is Scandinavian. DB *Flatesbi*.

Flaxley (hamlet, Glos): 'clearing where flax is grown'. OE *fleax*, 'flax', + *lēah*, 'clearing'. 1163 *Flaxlea*.

Flaxton (village, N Yorks): 'farmstead where flax is grown'. OE *fleax*, 'flax', + *tūn*, 'farmstead'. DB *Flaxtune*, 1868 *Flaxton-on-the-Moor*.

Fleckney (village, Leics): 'Flecca's well-watered land'. OE *ēg*, 'island'. DB *Flechenie*.

Flecknoe (village, Warwicks): 'Flecca's hill spur'. OE *hōh*, 'hill spur'. There is a prominent spur of land here. DB *Flechenho*.

Fleet (town, Hants): '(place at the) pool'. OE *flēot*, 'pool', 'creek'. The town takes its name from the large natural lake here called Fleet Pond. 1313 *Flete*.

Fleetwood (town and port, Lancs): 'Until 1836 this place was merely a rabbit warren, when Sir P. H. Fleetwood, Bart., commenced the foundation of a future town, and by his energy and enterprise has succeeded in making it a flourishing watering-place and bonding port' (*The National Gazetteer of Great Britain and Ireland*, 1868). Peter Hesketh Fleetwood (1801–66), MP for Preston, was born Peter Hesketh but added his mother's maiden name as his surname in 1831. He based his new town on his estate at Rossall Hall, now Rossall School.

Flempton (village, Suffolk): 'farmstead of the Flemings'. OE *Fleming*, 'Fleming' (person from Flanders), + *tūn*, 'farmstead'. DB *Flemingtuna*.

Fletching (village, E Sussex): '(settlement of) Flecci's people'. OE *-ingas*, 'people of'. DB *Flescinges*.

Fletton. See OLD FLETTON.

Flexbury (district of Bude, Cornwall): 'hill where flax grows'. OE *fleax*, 'flax', + *beorg*, 'mound', 'hill'. The 'hill' may have been a former tumulus here. 1201 *Flexberi*.

Flimby (coastal village, Cumbria): 'farmstead of the Flemings'. OS *Flémingr*, 'Fleming' (person from Flanders), + *bý*, 'farmstead', 'village'. 12C *Flemyngeby*.

Flint (town, Flints): '(place of) hard rock'. ME *flint*, 'hard rock' (modern English *flint*). The name refers to the stone platform here on which Flint Castle was built in 1277. The town's Welsh name is *Y Fflint* ('the Flint'), after the English. The first form of the name below is the French equivalent. 1277 *Le Chaylou*, 1300 *le Fflynt*.

Flintham (village, Notts): 'Flinta's homestead or enclosure'. OE *hām*, 'homestead', or *hamm*, 'enclosure'. DB *Flintham*.

Flitcham (village, Norfolk): 'homestead where flitches are made'. OE *flicce*, 'flitch' (of bacon), + *hām*, 'homestead', 'village'. DB *Flicham*.

Flitton (village, Beds): meaning uncertain. Early forms of the name suggest that the second part does not represent OE *tūn*, 'farmstead'. The DB form below may be corrupt. *c.*985 *Flittan*, DB *Flichtham*.

Flitwick (village, Beds): '(place with a) dairy farm'. OE *wīc*, 'dwelling', 'dairy farm'. The first part of the name is of obscure origin. DB *Flicteuuiche*.

Flixborough (village, N Lincs): 'Flík's fortified place'. OE *burh*, 'fortified place'. The personal name is Scandinavian. DB *Flichesburg*.

Flixton (village, N Yorks): 'Flík's farmstead'. OE *tūn*, 'farmstead', 'village'. The personal name is Scandinavian (and garbled in the DB form below). DB *Fleustone*, 12C *Flixtona*. SO ALSO: *Flixton*, Suffolk, Trafford.

Flockton (village, Kirklees): 'Flóki's farmstead'. OE *tūn*, 'farmstead'. The personal name is Scandinavian. DB *Flochetone*.

Flodden (hamlet, Northd): '(place by the) hill with (stone) slabs'. OE *flōh*, 'slab', + *dūn*, 'hill'. The Battle of Flodden Field (1513) was really fought at Branxton, 2 miles away. 1517 *Floddoun*.

Flookburgh (village, Cumbria): 'Flóki's stronghold'. OE *burh*, 'fortified place'. The personal name is Scandinavian. 1246 *Flokeburg*.

Flordon (village, Norfolk): '(place by the) hill with a floor'. OE *flōre*, 'floor', + *dūn*, 'hill'. The 'floor' was perhaps some kind of paving here. DB *Florenduna*.

Flore (village, Northants): '(place by the) floor'. OE *flōr*, 'floor'. The 'floor' is probably a now lost Roman tessellated pavement here. DB *Flore*.

Flotterton (hamlet, Northd): 'farmstead by the road liable to flood'. OE *flot*, 'flood', + *weg*, 'way', 'road', + *tūn*, 'farmstead'. Flotterton lies near the river Coquet. 12C *Flotweyton*.

Flowton (hamlet, Suffolk): 'Flóki's farmstead'. OE *tūn*, 'farmstead'. The personal name is Scandinavian. DB *Flochetuna*.

Flushing (coastal village, Cornwall). The village was named in the 17C after the port of Flushing (Vliessingen) in Holland, probably because it was founded by Dutch settlers. 1698 *Flushing*.

Flyford Flavell (village, Worcs). This is a complex name with a devious history. The first word is the original, comprising a first part of uncertain origin (perhaps a personal name) and a second part that was formerly thought to have represented OE *fyrhth*, 'sparse woodland', but that is now also regarded as of uncertain origin. It was subsequently assimilated to the more familiar OE *ford*, 'ford'. The second word is a Normanized form of the same name, added to distinguish this Flyford (Flavell) from nearby GRAFTON FLYFORD. 10C *Fleferth*, 1190 *Flavel*, 1420 *Fleford*, 16C *Fleford Flavell*.

Fobbing (village, Thurrock): '(settlement of) Fobba's people'. OE *-ingas*, 'people of'. The name could also mean simply 'Fobba's place' (OE *-ing*, 'place belonging to'). DB *Phobinge*.

Fochabers (town, Moray): 'lake marsh'. Gaelic *fothach*, 'lake', + *abor*, 'marsh'. The town lies in a valley on the river Spey. The final *-s* is a later English addition. 1124 *Fochoper*, 1238 *Fochabyr*, 1514 *Fochabris*.

Fockerby (village, N Lincs): 'Folcward's farmstead'. OS *bȳ*, 'farmstead', 'village'. The personal name is Old German. 12C *Fulcwardby*.

Foggathorpe (village, E Yorks): 'Folcward's outlying farmstead'. OS *thorp*, 'outlying farmstead'. The personal name is Old German. DB *Fulcartorp*.

Foleshill (district, Coventry): 'hill of the people'. OE *folc*, 'folk', 'people', + *hyll*, 'hill'. The reference would be to a place of communal activity. But the meaning could equally be 'Folc's hill'. The DB form of the name below has omitted *l* from the first part. DB *Focheshelle*, 12C *Folkeshulla*.

Folke (village, Dorset): '(land held by the) people'. OE *folc*, 'folk', 'people'. 1244 *Folk*.

Folkestone (town and port, Kent): 'Folca's stone'. OE *stān*, 'stone'. The stone in question would have marked the meeting place of the hundred here. c.647 *Folcanstan*, DB *Fulchestan*.

Folkingham (village, Lincs): 'homestead of Folca's people'. OE *-inga-*, 'of the people of', + *hām*, 'homestead'. DB *Folchingeham*, 1868 *Falkingham*, 1895 *Folkingham, or Falkingham*.

Folkington (hamlet, E Sussex): 'estate associated with Folca'. OE *-ing-*, 'associated with', + *tūn*, 'farmstead', 'estate'. The DB form of the name below has omitted the *l* of the personal name. DB *Fochintone*, c.1150 *Folkintone*.

Folkton (village, N Yorks): 'Folki's or Folca's farmstead'. OE *tūn*, 'farmstead'. The personal names are respectively Scandinavian and OE. DB *Fulcheton*.

Follifoot (village, N Yorks): '(place of) horse fighting'. OE *fola*, 'foal', + *feoht*, 'fight'. The name alludes to a Viking sport in which stallions fought each other when aroused by the sight and smell of tethered mares nearby. 12C *Pholifet*.

Fonthill Bishop (village, Wilts): 'bishop's (estate by the river) Fonthill'. The first word apparently represents a Celtic river name meaning 'stream in fertile upland'. The second word refers to the Bishop of Winchester, who held the manor early here. His title distinguishes this Fonthill from nearby *Fonthill Gifford*, where the manor was held in 1086 by the Gifard family. 901 *Funtial*, DB *Fontel*, 1291 *Fontel Episcopi*, 1868 *Bishop's Fonthill*.

Fontmell Magna (village, Dorset): 'greater (place by) Fontmell Brook'. The river name is of Celtic origin and means 'spring by the bare hill'. The second word (Latin *magna*, 'great') distinguishes the village from *Fontmell Parva* (Latin *parva*, 'little'), 5 miles to the southwest. 877 *Funtemel*, DB *Fontemale*, 1391 *Magnam Funtemell*.

Foolow (hamlet, Derbys): '(place on the) hill where birds are seen'. OE *fugol*, 'bird' (modern English *fowl*), + *hlāw*, 'hill'. 1269 *Foulowe*.

Foots Cray. See ST MARY CRAY.

Forcett (hamlet, N Yorks): 'fold by a ford'. OE *ford*, 'ford', + *set*, 'stable', 'fold'. DB *Forset*.

Ford (village, Northd): '(place by the) ford'. OE *ford*, 'ford'. The river here is the Till. 1224 *Forda*. SO ALSO: *Ford*, Shropshire.

Ford (village, W Sussex): '(place by the) fords'. OE *ford*, 'ford'. Early forms of the name show that more than one ford was involved. There may have been two fords over the river Arun here, or one over the Arun and another over Binsted Brook, its tributary. c.1194 *Fordes*.

Fordham (village, Cambs): 'homestead by a ford'. OE *ford*, 'ford', + *hām*, 'homestead', 'village'. 10C *Fordham*, DB *Fordeham*. SO ALSO: *Fordham*, Essex.

Fordham (village, Norfolk): 'homestead by a ford'. OE *ford*, 'ford', + *hām*, 'homestead', 'village'. The river here is the Wissey. DB *Fordham*.

Fordingbridge (town, Hants): 'bridge of the people living by the ford'. OE *ford*, 'ford', + *-inga-*, 'of the dwellers at', + *brycg*, 'bridge'. The bridge and ford would have been over the river Avon here, the former being built to replace the latter. DB *Fordingebrige*.

Fordon (hamlet, E Yorks): '(place) before the hill'. OE *fore*, 'before', + *dūn*, 'hill'. Fordon lies at the foot of a steep hill. DB *Fordun*.

Fordwich (village, Kent): 'trading settlement at the ford'. OE *ford*, 'ford', + *wīc*, 'specialized farm', 'trading settlement'. The river here is the Great Ouse. The DB form of the name below has omitted the *d*. 675 *Fordeuuicum*, DB *Forewic*.

Forebridge (district of Stafford, Staffs): '(place by the) bridge before the town'. OE *fore*, 'before', + *brycg*, 'bridge'. A road over a tributary of the river Sow here enters Stafford from the south-east. 1221 *Forebrigge*.

Foremark (hamlet, Derbys): '(place by the) old fort'. OS *forn*, 'old', + *verk*, 'work', 'fort'. Some raised earth workings nearby are probably the site of the original 'old fort'. DB *Fornewerche*.

Forest Gate (district, Newham). The district arose around a former gate in Woodgrange Road that prevented cattle from straying from the forest onto the main road here. The gate was removed in 1883.

Forest Heath (council district, Suffolk): '(district of) forest and heath'. The district occupies the northwest of the county in a region that includes much of Thetford Forest Park and the downs and heaths around Newmarket. It also includes *Lakenheath*, but its name means 'landing place of the people living by streams' (OE *lacu*, 'stream', + *-inga-*, 'of the people of', + *hȳth*, 'landing place').

Forest Hill (village, Oxon): '(place by the) hill with a ridge'. OE *forst*, 'ridge', + *hyll*, 'hill'. The first part of the name has been assimilated to *forest*. The DB form of the name below is corrupt. DB *Fostel*, 1122 *Forsthulle*.

Forest of Dean (wooded region, Glos): 'forest of the valley'. OE *denu*, 'valley'. The main valley that gave the name of the region, between the rivers Severn and Wye, is that of Cannop Brook, which enters the Severn at Lydney. 12C *foresta de Dene*.

Forest Row (village, E Sussex): 'row (of houses) in the forest'. ME *forest*, 'forest', + *row*, 'row'. The forest in question is Ashdown Forest. 1467 *Forstrowe*.

Forfar (town, Angus): 'slope on a ridge'. Gaelic *fothair*, 'terraced slope', + *fàire*, 'ridge'. The second part of the name may mean 'watching' (Gaelic *faire*), giving a sense 'slope of the lookout'. But Forfar is on level ground, and the only possible place for a 'lookout' would be the nearby Hill of Finhaven. *c*.1200 *Forfare*.

Formby (town, Sefton): 'Forni's farmstead'. OS *bý*, 'farmstead'. The personal name is Scandinavian. The name could also mean 'old farmstead' (OS *forn*, 'old'). DB *Fornebei*.

Forncett St Mary (village, Norfolk): 'Forni's dwelling with St Mary's church'. OE *set*, 'dwelling', 'fold'. The personal name is Scandinavian. The church dedication distinguishes the village from nearby *Forncett St Peter*. DB *Fornesetta*.

Fornham All Saints (village, Suffolk): 'village where trout are caught, with All Saints church'. OE *forne*, 'trout', + *hām*, 'homestead', 'village'. The river here is the Lark. The church dedication distinguishes the village from nearby *Fornham St Martin* and *Fornham St Genevieve*. DB *Fornham*, 1254 *Fornham Omnium Sanctorum*.

Forres (town, Moray): '(place) below a copse'. Gaelic *fo*, 'below', 'under', + *ras*, 'shrub', 'underwood'. *c*.1195 *Forais*.

Forsbrook (village, Staffs): '(place by) Fótr's brook'. OE *brōc*, 'brook'. The *t* of the Scandinavian personal name has disappeared. DB *Fotesbroc*.

Forston (hamlet, Dorset): 'Forsard's estate'. ME *toun*, 'estate'. The Forsard family held land here from the early 13C. 1236 *Fosardeston*.

Fort Augustus (village, Highland). The village grew up around the garrison enlarged here by General Wade in the 1730s and named after William Augustus, Duke of Cumberland (1721–65).

Forth (river). See FIRTH OF FORTH.

Forthampton (village, Glos): 'estate associated with Forthhelm'. OE *-ing-*, 'associated with', + *tūn*, 'farmstead', 'estate'. The potential '-ington' of the name has become '-hampton'. DB *Forhelmentone*.

Forton (hamlet, Shropshire): 'farmstead by a ford'. OE *ford*, 'ford', + *tūn*, 'farmstead', 'village'. The river here is the Severn. The DB form of the name below is corrupt. DB *Fordune*, 1240 *Forton*. SO ALSO: *Forton*, Hants, Lancs.

Forton (village, Staffs): 'farmstead by a ford'. OE *ford*, 'ford', + *tūn*, 'farmstead', 'village'. The river here is the Meece. 1198 *Forton*.

Fortrose (town, Highland): '(place) beneath the headland'. Gaelic *foter*, 'lower', + *ros*, 'headland'. Fortrose is on the Inner Moray Firth below the village of Rosemarkie ('headland of the horse stream'). 1455 *Forterose*.

Fortuneswell (town, Dorset). The name is modern, and alludes either to a lucky well or spring or to one in which fortunes could be told. 1608 *Fortunes Well*.

Fort William (town, Highland). The fortress here was originally built in 1655 then rebuilt in 1690 as a garrison and named after the reigning monarch, William III.

Fosse Way (Roman road, England): '(Roman) road with a ditch'. OE *foss*, 'ditch' (from Latin *fossa*). The ancient trackway adapted by the Romans for a road from Devon to Lincoln, and still a major route today, had a prominent ditch on either side. Hence the name. 956 *strata publica de Fosse*.

Foston (hamlet, Derbys): 'Fótr's farmstead'. OE *tūn*, 'farmstead', 'village'. The DB form of the name below means 'Farulfr's farmstead', and the present name may have originally been that of a separate settlement nearby. The personal name for each is Scandinavian. DB *Farulveston*, 12C *Fostun*. SO ALSO: *Foston*, N Yorks.

Foston (village, Lincs): 'Fótr's farmstead'. OE *tūn*, 'farmstead', 'village'. The personal name is Scandinavian. DB *Foztun*.

Foston on the Wolds (village, E Yorks): 'Fótr's farmstead on the Wolds'. OE *tūn*, 'farmstead', 'village'. The personal name is Scandinavian. The second part of the name refers to the Yorkshire WOLDS. DB *Fodstone*, 1609 *Foston on le Wolde*.

Fotherby (village, Lincs): 'Fótr's farmstead'. OS *bý*, 'farmstead', 'village'. The personal name is Scandinavian. DB *Fodrebi*.

Fotheringhay (village, Northants): 'island used for grazing'. OE *fodring*, 'grazing' (related modern English *fodder*), + *ēg*, 'island'. The 'island' would have been well-watered land here, with the river Nene to the south and Willow Brook to the north. DB *Fodringeia*.

Foula (island, Shetland): 'bird island'. OS *fugl*, 'bird' (related modern English *fowl*), + *ey*, 'island'. Foula is noted for its sea birds. Cp. FOULNESS.

Foulden (village, Norfolk): '(place by the) hill where birds are seen'. OE *fugol*, 'bird' (modern English *fowl*), + *dūn*, 'hill'. DB *Fugalduna*.

Foulness (island, Essex): 'bird promontory'. OE *fugol*, 'bird' (modern English *fowl*), + *næss*, 'headland', 'promontory'. The island, originally a promontory, is noted for its wildfowl. 1215 *Fughelnesse*.

Foulridge (village, Lancs): '(place by the) ridge where foals graze'. OE *fola*, 'foal', + *hrycg*, 'ridge'. The name may have originally applied to nearby Pasture Hill. 1219 *Folric*.

Foulsham (village, Norfolk): 'Fugol's homestead'. OE *hām*, 'homestead'. DB *Folsham*.

Fountains Abbey (abbey remains, N Yorks): 'abbey by the springs'. OF *fontein*, 'fountain', 'spring'. The name refers to the six springs within the 12C abbey site. 1275 *Fonteyns*.

Four Elms (village, Kent): '(place by the) four elms'. The name is recent, and was presumably adopted from a field name or other local name here northwest of Edenbridge. 1892 *Four Elms*.

Fourstones (village, Northd): '(place by) four stones'. OE *fēower*, 'four', + *stān*, 'stone'. The name refers to a tetralith here, as a group of three upright stones capped by a lintel. 1236 *Fourstanys*.

Fovant (village, Wilts): '(place by) Fobba's spring'. OE *funta*, 'spring'. The DB form of the name below has garbled the personal name. 901 *Fobbefunte*, DB *Febefonte*.

Fowey (resort town and port, Cornwall): '(place on the river) Fowey'. The river has a Cornish name meaning '(river of) beeches' (Cornish *faw*, 'beeches'). The '-ey' represents the Cornish name-forming suffix *-i* found mainly in river names. c.1223 *Fawi*.

Fowlmere (village, Cambs): '(place by the) lake where birds are seen'. OE *fugol*, 'bird' (modern English *fowl*), + *mere*, 'lake'. There is no actual lake here now. DB *Fuglemære*, 1868 *Foulmire, or Fulmer*.

Fownhope (village, Herefords): '(place in the) multicoloured valley'. OE *fāg*, 'variegated', + *hop*, 'small valley'. DB *Hope*, 1242 *Faghehope*.

Foxearth (village, Essex): '(place by the) fox's earth'. The DB form of the name below has *earth* to mean 'fox's hole' almost 500 years before the earliest example in the *Oxford English Dictionary* ('If you … put the Terryer into an earth where foxes be', George Gascoigne, *The Noble Arte of Venerie*, 1575). DB *Focsearde*.

Foxholes (village, N Yorks): '(place by) fox's holes'. OE *fox-hol* (from *fox*, 'fox', + *hol*, 'hole'). There must have been some fox earths here. DB *Foxhole*.

Foxley (hamlet, Wilts): 'woodland clearing where foxes are seen'. OE *fox*, 'fox', + *lēah*, 'wood', 'clearing'. DB *Foxelege*. SO ALSO: *Foxley*, Norfolk.

Foxt (village, Staffs): '(place by the) fox's den'. OE *fox*, 'fox', + *wist*, 'dwelling'. 1176 *Foxwiss*.

Foxton (hamlet, Durham): '(place in the) valley where foxes are seen'. OE *fox*, 'fox', + *denu*, 'valley'. c.1170 *Foxedene*.

Foxton (village, Leics): 'farmstead where foxes are seen'. OE *fox*, 'fox', + *tūn*, 'farmstead'. DB *Foxtone*. SO ALSO: *Foxton*, Cambs.

Foy (village, Herefords): '(church of) St Moi'. The church here is dedicated to St Moi. Foy is not far from the Welsh border. Hence the form of the name below, with Welsh *llan*, 'church'. The second word is the personal name prefixed with Welsh *dy*, 'thy', as a term of affection. *c*.1150 *Lann Timoi*.

Fraddon (village, Cornwall): 'place of streams'. Cornish *fros* (earlier *frod*), 'stream', + *-an*, 'place of'. 1321 *Frodan*.

Fradswell (village, Staffs): '(place by) Frōd's spring'. OE *wella*, 'spring', 'stream'. DB *Frodeswelle*.

Fraisthorpe (hamlet, E Yorks): 'Freistingr's or Freysteinn's outlying farmstead'. OS *thorp*, 'outlying farmstead'. The personal names are Scandinavian. DB *Frestintorp*.

Framfield (village, E Sussex): 'Frema's or Fremi's open land'. OE *feld*, 'open land' (modern English *field*). The second part of the DB form of the name below is garbled. DB *Framelle*, 1257 *Fremefeld*.

Framingham Earl (village, Norfolk): 'earl's (estate at the) homestead of Fram's people'. OE *-inga-*, 'of the people of', + *hām*, 'homestead'. The manor here was held early by the Earl of Norfolk, whose title distinguishes the village from nearby *Framingham Pigot*, held by the Picot family. The second word of the second form of the name below is Latin *comitis*, 'of the earl'. DB *Framingaham*, 1254 *Framelingham Comitis*.

Framlingham (town, Suffolk): 'homestead of Framela's people'. OE *-inga-*, 'of the people of', + *hām*, 'homestead'. DB *Framelingaham*.

Frampton (village, Dorset): 'farmstead on the (river) Frome'. OE *tūn*, 'farmstead'. The Dorset river Frome has a name of the same origin as the Somerset one (see FROME). DB *Frantone*.

Frampton (village, Lincs): 'Fráni's farmstead'. OE *tūn*, 'farmstead'. The personal name is Scandinavian. DB *Franetone*.

Frampton Cotterell (suburb of Chipping Sodbury, S Glos): 'Cotel's village by the (river) Frome'. OE *tūn*, 'farmstead', 'village'. The Cotel family held the manor here in the 12C, their name distinguishing this Frampton from *Frampton Mansell*, Glos, 23 miles to the northeast, where the Maunsel family held the manor in the 13C, and *Frampton on Severn*, Glos, 17 miles to the north. This river Frome has a name of the same origin as the Somerset one (see FROME). DB *Frantone*, 1257 *Frampton Cotell*.

Framsden (village, Suffolk): 'Fram's valley'. OE *denu*, 'valley'. DB *Framesdena*.

Framwellgate Moor (suburb of Durham): 'street by the strongly flowing spring'. OE *fram*, 'strong', 'vigorous', + *wella*, 'spring', 'stream', + OS *gata*, 'street'. The place became associated with moorland here by the river Wear. 1352 *Framwelgat*.

Franche (district of Kidderminster, Worcs): '(place by) Frēa's ash tree'. OE *æsc*, 'ash'. DB *Frenesse*.

Frankby (village, Wirral): 'Frenchman's farmstead'. OE *Franca*, 'Frenchman', + OS *bý*, 'farmstead'. The first part of the name could also represent the Scandinavian personal name Franki. 13C *Frankeby*.

Frankley (village, Worcs): 'Franca's woodland clearing'. OE *lēah*, 'wood', 'clearing'. DB *Franchelie*.

Frankton (village, Warwicks): 'Franca's farmstead'. OE *tūn*, 'farmstead', 'village'. DB *Franchetone*.

Frant (village, E Sussex): 'place overgrown with ferns'. OE *fiernthe* (from *fearn*, 'fern'). 956 *Fyrnthan*.

Fraserburgh (town and port, Aberdeens): 'Fraser's chartered town'. OE *burh*, 'fortified place', 'borough'. Alexander Fraser, 7th Laird of Philorth, was granted a charter to raise the town of Faithlie into a burgh of barony here in 1546. 1597 *The toun and burghe of Faythlie, now callit Fraserburghe*.

Frating Green (hamlet, Essex): '(settlement of) Frǣta's people'. OE *-ingas*, 'people of'. The name could also mean simply 'Frǣte's place' (OE *-ing*, 'place belonging to'). The village later became associated with its green. *c*.1060 *Fretinge*, DB *Fratinga*.

Fratton (district, Portsmouth): 'estate associated with Frōda'. OE *-ing-*, 'associated with', + *tūn*, 'farmstead', 'estate'. The *-ing-* of the original name disappeared in the 17C. 982 *Frodingtune*, DB *Frodinton*.

Freathy (village, Cornwall): origin uncertain. The name may derive from a surname that is perhaps a variant of Friday. 1286 *Vridie*.

Freckenham (village, Suffolk): 'Freca's homestead'. OE *hām*, 'homestead', 'village'. The '-en-' represents the genitive ending of the personal name. 895 *Frekeham*, DB *Frakenaham*.

Freckleton (village, Lancs): 'Frecla's farmstead'. OE *tūn*, 'farmstead'. DB *Frecheltun*.

Freeby (village, Leics): 'Fræthi's farmstead'. OS *bý*, 'farmstead', 'village'. The personal name is Scandinavian. DB *Fredebi*.

Freefolk (hamlet, Hants): '(place of the) free folk'. OE *frēo*, 'free', + *folc*, 'folk'. The precise sense of the name is uncertain. Freefolk is the only village name in England ending in '-folk'. DB *Frigefolc*.

Freethorpe (village, Norfolk): 'Fræthi's outlying farmstead'. OS *thorp*, 'outlying farmstead'. The personal name is Scandinavian. DB *Frietorp*.

Freiston (village, Lincs): 'farmstead of the Frisians'. OE *Frisa*, 'Frisian', + *tūn*, 'farmstead', 'village'. DB *Fristune*.

Fremington (village, Devon): 'estate associated with Fremi or Frema'. OE *-ing-*, 'associated with', + *tūn*, 'farmstead', 'estate'. DB *Framintone*.

Frenchay (suburb of Bristol, S Glos): '(place by the) wood on the (river) Frome'. OE *sceaga*, 'wood', 'copse'. The river has a name identical with the one behind FROME. 1248 *Fromshawe*, 1607 *Frenchay*.

Frensham (village, Surrey): 'Fremi's homestead'. OE *hām*, 'homestead', 'village'. 10C *Fermesham*.

Freshfield (district of Formby, Sefton). The former village here, originally called Church Mere, was gradually covered by sand from the mid-18C to the mid-19C. A Mr Fresh is said to have then reclaimed the land by laying topsoil over the sand. When the site was used for further building, the new settlement was named Freshfield after him.

Freshford (village, Bath & NE Somerset): 'ford over a freshwater stream'. OE *fersc*, 'fresh', + *ford*, 'ford'. Freshford is usually contrasted with SALT-FORD, 8 miles to the northwest, both places being on the same river Avon. OE *fersc* is used as a noun here. *c.*1000 *Ferscesford*.

Freshwater (resort town, IoW): '(place on the river) Freshwater'. The name presumably applies to the fresh water in one of the streams that flow into the Yar (see YARMOUTH) here (OE *fersc*, 'fresh', + *wæter*, 'water'), as distinct from the salt water of the Yar itself, which is tidal as far as Freshwater. DB *Frescewatre*.

Fressingfield (village, Suffolk): 'open land of Frīsa's people'. OE *-inga-*, 'of the people of', + *feld*, 'open land' (modern English *field*). The personal name (or nickname) means 'Frisian'. The DB form of the name below is corrupt. DB *Fessefelda*, 1185 *Frisingefeld*.

Freston (village, Suffolk): 'farmstead of the Frisian'. OE *Frīsa*, 'Frisian', + *tūn*, 'farmstead', 'village'. 1001 *Fresantun*, DB *Fresetuna*.

Fridaythorpe (village, E Yorks): 'Frīgedæg's outlying farmstead'. OS *thorp*, 'outlying farmstead'. DB *Fridagstorp*.

Friern Barnet. See BARNET.

Frilford (village, Oxon): '(place by) Frithela's ford'. OE *ford*, 'ford'. The ford in question may have been where a Roman road crosses the stream known as Osse Ditch here. DB *Frieliford*.

Frimley (town, Surrey): 'Frema's woodland clearing'. OE *lēah*, 'wood', 'clearing'. 1203 *Fremle*.

Frindsbury (district of Rochester, Medway): 'Frēond's stronghold'. OE *burh*, 'fortified place'. 764 *Freondesberiam*, DB *Frandesberie*.

Fring (hamlet, Norfolk): '(settlement of) Frēa's people'. OE *-ingas*, 'people of'. DB *Frainghes*.

Fringford (village, Oxon): '(place by the) ford of Fēra's people'. OE *-inga-*, 'of the people of', + *ford*, 'ford'. DB *Feringeford*.

Frinton-on-Sea (resort town, Essex): 'Fritha's farmstead by the sea'. OE *tūn*, 'farmstead'. The name could also mean 'protected farmstead' (OE *frithen*, 'safeguarded', from *frith*, 'peace'). The latter part of the name is a recent commercial addition. DB *Frientuna*.

Frisby on the Wreake (village, Leics): 'farmstead of the Frisians on the (river) Wreake'. OS *Frísir*, 'Frisians', + *bý*, 'farmstead'. The river name is Scandinavian in origin and means 'winding one'. The main name alludes to an isolated settlement of Frisians among Danes. DB *Frisebie*.

Friskney (village, Lincs): '(place by the) river with fresh water'. OE *fresc*, 'fresh', + *ēa*, 'river'. The '-sk-' of the name is due to Scandinavian influence. DB *Frischenei*.

Friston (village, E Sussex): 'Frēo's farmstead'. OE *tūn*, 'farmstead'. 1200 *Friston*.

Friston (village, Suffolk): 'farmstead of the Frisians'. OE *Frisa*, 'Frisian', + *tūn*, 'farmstead', 'village'. DB *Frisetuna*.

Frithelstock (village, Devon): 'Frithulāc's outlying farmstead'. OE *stoc*, 'outlying farmstead'. DB *Fredeletestoc*.

Frithville (village, Lincs): 'village by sparse woodland'. OE *fyrhth*, 'wood', 'land overgrown with brushwood', + French *ville*, 'village', 'town'. The second part of the name was added when the settlement was formed into a township by Act of Parliament in 1812 following drainage of a large area of Wildmore Fen and in the East and West Fens. 1331 *Le Frith*, 1868 *Frith-Ville, or West Fen*.

Frittenden (village, Kent): 'woodland pasture associated with Frith'. OE *-ing-*, 'associated with', + *denn*, 'woodland pasture'. 9C *Friththingden*.

Fritton (village, Norfolk): 'Frithi's farmstead'. OE *tūn*, 'farmstead'. The personal name is Scandinavian. The name could also mean 'farmstead offering safety' (OE *frith*, 'refuge', 'protection'). The form of the name below relates to Fritton near Gorleston, but Fritton near Morningthorpe has a name of identical origin. DB *Fridetuna*.

Fritwell (village, Oxon): '(place by the) spring used for divination'. OE *freht*, 'augury', + *wella*, 'spring'. The interpretation is problematic as early forms of the name lack the necessary *h*. DB *Fertwelle*.

Frizington (hamlet, Cumbria): 'estate of Frīsa's people'. OE *-inga-*, 'of the people of', + *tūn*, 'farmstead', 'estate'. The personal name means 'Frisian'. *c.*1160 *Frisingaton*.

Frocester (village, Glos): 'Roman station on the (river) Frome'. OE *ceaster*, 'Roman station'. This river Frome has a name of the same origin as that behind FROME. DB *Frowecestre*.

Frodesley (village, Shropshire): 'Frōd's woodland clearing'. OE *lēah*, 'wood', 'clearing'. DB *Frodeslege*.

Frodingham (district of Scunthorpe, N Lincs): 'homestead of Frōda's people'. OE *-inga-*, 'of the people of', + *hām*, 'homestead'. 12C *Frodingham*.

Frodsham (town, Cheshire): 'Frōd's homestead or promontory'. OE *hām*, 'homestead', or *hamm*, 'promontory'. OE *hamm* could mean 'promontory extending into marshland', and this suits the site of Frodsham, on the river Weaver near the point where it joins the Mersey. DB *Frotesham*.

Froggatt (village, Derbys): 'cottage where frogs are seen'. OE *frogga*, 'frog', + *cot*, 'cottage'. The village is on low-lying land near the river Derwent. 1225 *Froggecot*.

Frogmore (village, Devon): '(place by the) pool where frogs are seen'. OE *frogga*, 'frog', + *mere*, 'pool'. 1522 *Froggemere*.

Frome (town, Somerset): '(place on the river) Frome'. The river has a Celtic name meaning 'fair', 'fine', 'brisk' (related modern Welsh *ffraw*). 8C *Froom*.

Frome St Quintin (village, Dorset): 'St Quintin's (estate on the river) Frome'. The Dorset river Frome has a name of the same origin as the Somerset one (see FROME). The St Quintin family held the manor here in the 13C, their name distinguishing the estate from others on the same river. The first form of the name below has 'Little' used earlier for the same purpose. DB *Litelfrome*, 1288 *Fromequintin*.

Frostenden (hamlet, Suffolk): '(place in the) valley where frogs are seen'. OE *frosc*, 'frog', + *denu*, 'valley'. DB *Froxedena*.

Frosterley (village, Durham): 'woodland clearing of the forester'. ME *forester*, 'forester', + OE *lēah*, 'wood', 'clearing'. 1239 *Forsterlegh*.

Froxfield (village, Wilts): 'open land where frogs are seen'. OE *frosc*, 'frog', + *feld*, 'open land' (modern English *field*). 9C *Forscanfeld*.

Fryerning (village, Essex): 'Ing of the brethren'. ME *frere*, 'friar', 'brother'. *Ing* was the name of a manor here, itself from a tribal name meaning 'people of the district' (OE *gē*, 'district', + *-ingas*, 'people of'). The first part of the name refers to its possession by the Knights Hospitallers in the 12C. Cp. INGATESTONE, MARGARETTING. DB *Inga*, 1469 *Friering*.

Fryton (hamlet, N Yorks): 'farmstead offering shelter'. OE *frith*, 'refuge', 'protection', + *tūn*, 'farmstead'. The name could also mean 'Frithi's farmstead', with a Scandinavian personal name. DB *Frideton*.

Fulbeck (village, Lincs): '(place by the) dirty stream'. OE *fūl*, 'dirty' (modern English *foul*), + OS *bekkr*, 'stream'. DB *Fulebec*.

Fulbourn (village, Cambs): '(place by the) stream where wild birds are seen'. OE *fugol*, 'bird' (modern English *fowl*), + *burna*, 'stream'. *c.*1050 *Fuulburne*, DB *Fuleberne*.

Fulbrook (village, Oxon): '(place by the) dirty brook'. OE *fūl*, 'dirty' (modern English *foul*), + *broc*, 'brook'. DB *Fulebroc*.

Fulford (district, York): '(place by the) dirty ford'. OE *fūl*, 'dirty' (modern English *foul*), + *ford*, 'ford'. The name denotes a river crossing with muddy water, as distinct from one with clear water, as at FAIRFORD. The river here is the Ouse. DB *Fuleford*. SO ALSO: *Fulford*, Somerset, Staffs.

Fulham (district, Hammersmith & Ful): 'Fulla's land in a river bend'. OE *hamm*, 'enclosure', 'land in a river bend'. Fulham is in a bend of the Thames. *c.*705 *Fulanham*, DB *Fuleham*.

Fulking (village, W Sussex): '(settlement of) Folca's people'. OE *-ingas*, 'people of'. The DB form of the name below has omitted the *l*. DB *Fochinges*, *c.*1100 *Folkinges*.

Full Sutton (village, E Yorks): 'dirty southern farmstead'. OE *fūl*, 'foul', 'dirty', + *sūth*, 'southern', + *tūn*, 'farmstead'. DB *Sudtone*, 1234 *Fulesutton*.

Fulmer (village, Bucks): '(place by the) lake where birds are seen'. OE *fugol*, 'bird' (modern English *fowl*), + *mere*, 'pool'. Cp. FOWLMERE. The lake in question was partially drained in the 19C and converted into extensive watercress beds. 1198 *Fugelmere*.

Fulmodeston (hamlet, Norfolk): 'Fulcmod's farmstead'. OE *tūn*, 'farmstead'. The personal name is Old German. DB *Fulmotestuna*.

Fulney (district of Spalding, Lincs): '(place by the) dirty stream'. OE *fūl*, 'dirty' (modern English *foul*), + *ēa*, 'river', 'stream'. 1166 *Fuleneia*.

Fulstow (village, Lincs): 'Fugol's meeting place'. OE *stōw*, 'place of assembly'. The first part of the name could also represent OE *fugol*, 'bird' (modern English *fowl*), giving a sense 'place where birds abound'. DB *Fugelestou*.

Fulwell (district, Sunderland): '(place by the) muddy stream'. OE *fūl*, 'foul', 'dirty', + *wella*, 'spring', 'stream'. 12C *Fulewella*.

Fulwood (suburb of Preston, Lancs): '(place by the) dirty wood'. OE *fūl*, 'foul', 'dirty', + *wudu*, 'wood'. 1199 *Fulewde*. SO ALSO: *Fulwood*, Notts.

Funtington (village, W Sussex): 'farmstead at the place with a spring'. OE *funta*, 'spring', + *-ing*, 'place characterized by', + *tūn*, 'farmstead'. There are many springs here. 12C *Fundintune*.

Furness. See BARROW-IN-FURNESS.

Furneux Pelham. See BRENT PELHAM.

Fyfield (village, Essex): '(estate of) five hides'. OE *fīf*, 'five', + *hīd*, 'hide'. Cp. FIFIELD. DB *Fifhidam*. SO ALSO: *Fyfield*, Glos, Hants, Oxon, Wilts.

Fylde, The. See POULTON-LE-FYLDE.

Fylingdales (village, N Yorks): 'valleys (by the settlement of) Fygla's people'. OE *-ingas*, 'people of', + *dæl*, 'valley'. The district included by the settlement was probably the series of valleys that meet near the sea at Robin Hood's Bay here. DB *Figelinge*.

G

Gabrosentum. See MORESBY.

Gaddesby (village, Leics): 'Gaddr's farmstead'. OS *bý*, 'farmstead', 'village'. The personal name is Scandinavian. The first part of the name could also represent OS *gaddr*, 'spur of land'. DB *Gadesbi*.

Gailey (hamlet, Staffs): 'woodland clearing where bog myrtle grows'. OE *gagel*, 'gale', 'bog myrtle', + *lēah*, 'wood', 'clearing'. The DB form of the name below has an extraneous *r*. *c*.1002 *Gageleag*, DB *Gragelie*.

Gainford (village, Durham): '(place by the) direct ford'. OE *gegn*, 'direct' (related modern English *against*), + *ford*, 'ford'. The reference is to a ford on a direct route. The river here is the Tees. *c*.1040 *Gegnforda*.

Gainsborough (town, Lincs): 'Gegn's stronghold'. OE *burh*, 'fortified place'. The town, an inland port on the river Trent, long occupied a strategic defensive position. DB *Gainesburg*.

Gairloch (village, Highland): '(place on) Gair Loch'. The loch has a Gaelic name meaning 'short lake' (Gaelic *geàrr*, 'short', + *loch*, 'lake'). 1275 *Gerloth*, 1366 *Gerloch*.

Galashiels (town, Borders): 'huts by Gala Water'. ME *schele*, 'hut' (modern English *shieling*). The river name is of uncertain origin. The 'huts' would have been used by shepherds in summer pastures. 1237 *Galuschel*.

Galgate (village, Lancs): '(place by the) Galloway road'. OS *gata*, 'road'. Galgate is on a main road (now the A6) to and from southwest Scotland, and the name seems to imply that the route was used by cattle drovers from GALLOWAY. *c*.1190 *Galwaithegate*.

Galhampton (village, Somerset): 'farmstead of the rent-paying peasants'. OE *gafol-mann* (from *gafol*, 'rent', + *mann*, 'man'), + *tūn*, 'farmstead'. DB *Galmeton*.

Galloway (region, Dumfries & Gall): '(territory among the) stranger Gaels'. Gaelic *gall*, 'stranger', 'foreigner', + *Ghaidel*, 'Gael'. The reference is to the people of mixed Irish and Scandinavian descent who settled here in southwest Scotland in the 9C. Cp. GALSTON. *c*.970 *Galweya*.

Gallt Melyd. See MELIDEN.

Galmpton (village, Devon): 'farmstead of the rent-paying peasants'. OE *gafol-mann* (from *gafol*, 'rent', + *mann*, 'man'), + *tūn*, 'farmstead'. DB *Walementone*. SO ALSO: Galmpton, Torbay.

Galphay (village, N Yorks): 'enclosure with a gallows'. OE *galga*, 'gallows', + *haga*, 'enclosure' (related modern English *hedge*). 12C *Galghagh*.

Galston (town, E Ayrs): 'village of the strangers'. Gaelic *gall*, 'stranger', + OE *tūn*, 'farmstead', 'village'. The reference would be to 'immigrants' of a different race or background to the native Scots (Gaelic) dwellers here. 1260 *Gauston*.

Gamblesby (village, Cumbria): 'Gamall's farmstead'. OS *bý*, 'farmstead', 'village'. The personal name is Scandinavian. 1177 *Gamelesbi*.

Gamlingay (village, Cambs): 'enclosure associated with Gamela'. OE *-ing-*, 'associated with', + *hæg*, 'enclosure' (related modern English *hedge*). The name could also mean 'enclosure associated with Gamela's people' (OE *-inga-*, 'of the people of') and the last part of the name could represent OE *ēg*, 'island', here meaning well-watered land. DB *Gamelingei*.

Gamston (village, Notts): 'Gamall's farmstead'. OE *tūn*, 'farmstead'. The personal name is Scandinavian. The form of the name below relates to Gamston near East Retford, but Gamston near Nottingham has a name of identical origin. DB *Gamelestune*.

Ganarew (village, Herefords): '(place by the) pass of the hill'. Welsh *genau*, 'mouth', 'opening', + *rhiw*, 'hill'. This interpretation is rejected by some Celticists in favour of an origin in the Welsh personal name Gwynwarwy, otherwise St Gunguarui, who gave his name to

Wonastow (Welsh *Llanwarw*) near Monmouth. *c*.1150 *Genoreu*.

Ganstead (hamlet, E Yorks): 'Gagni's or Gagne's homestead'. OS *stathr*, 'homestead'. The personal names are Scandinavian. DB *Gagenestad*.

Ganthorpe (hamlet, N Yorks): 'Galmr's outlying farmstead'. OS *thorp*, 'outlying farmstead'. The personal name is Scandinavian (and corrupt in the DB form below). DB *Gameltorp*, 1169 *Galmestorp*.

Ganton (village, N Yorks): 'Galmr's farmstead'. OE *tūn*, 'farmstead'. The personal name is Scandinavian. DB *Galmeton*.

Gants Hill (district, Redbridge): 'le Gant's hill'. The le Gant family held land here in the 13C. The first form of the name below means 'Gant's grove', the second 'Gant's heath'. 1291 *Gantesgrave*, 1545 *Gauntes Hethe*.

Garboldisham (village, Norfolk): 'Gǣrbald's homestead'. OE *hām*, 'homestead', 'village'. DB *Gerboldesham*.

Garford (village, Oxon): '(place by) Gāra's ford'. OE *ford*, 'ford'. The first part of the name could also represent OE *gāra*, 'triangular plot of land'. The ford in question was where a Roman road crosses the river Ock here. The DB form of the name below is corrupt. 940 *Garanforda*, DB *Wareford*.

Garforth (town, Leeds): '(place by) Gǣra's ford'. OE *ford*, 'ford'. The name could also mean 'ford by the triangular piece of land' (OE *gāra*, 'point of land', modern English *gore*). The ford would have been over the stream known as The Beck at Garforth Bridge, and the land between the two main roads that intersect at this point. DB *Gereford*.

Gargrave (village, N Yorks): '(place by the) triangular wood'. OE *gāra*, 'triangular piece of land', + *grāf*, 'grove'. OE *gāra* has been replaced in the name by equivalent OS *geiri*. DB *Geregraue*.

Gariannum. See BURGH CASTLE.

Garras (hamlet, Cornwall): '(place in) rough moorland'. Cornish *garow*, 'rough', + *ros*, 'moorland'. The name is relatively modern. *c*.1696 *Garrows Common*.

Garrigill (village, Cumbria): 'Gerard's deep valley'. OS *gil*, 'deep valley'. The personal name is Old German. 1232 *Gerardgile*.

Garsdale (valley, Cumbria): 'Garthr's valley'. OS *dalr*, 'valley'. The personal name is Scandinavian. The name could also mean 'grass valley' (OE *gærs*, 'grass', + *dæl*, 'valley'). The valley in question is that of the river Clough. *c*.1240 *Garcedale*.

Garsdon (village, Wilts): '(place by the) grass hill'. OE *gærs*, 'grass', + *dūn*, 'hill'. 701 *Gersdune*, DB *Gardone*.

Garshall Green (hamlet, Staffs): 'Garnon's corner of land'. OE *halh*, 'nook', 'corner of land'. The Garnon family owned land here. Garshall later became associated with its green. 1310 *Garnonshale*.

Garsington (village, Oxon): '(place by the) grassy hill'. OE *gærsen*, 'growing with grass', + *dūn*, 'hill'. DB *Gersedun*.

Garstang (town, Lancs): '(place by the) spear post'. OS *geirr*, 'spear', + *stǫng*, 'post'. The allusion is to a boundary pole or post that marked a meeting place. The DB form of the name below is corrupt. DB *Cherestanc*, *c*.1195 *Gairstang*.

Garston (district, Liverpool): '(place by the) great stone'. OE *grēat*, 'great', + *stān*, 'stone'. The name may refer to a boundary marker or to some natural feature on the Mersey coast here. 1094 *Gerstan*.

Garswood (suburb of Ashton-in-Makerfield, St Helens): '(place by the) wood'. OE *wudu*, 'wood'. The first part of the name is of uncertain origin. It may represent a personal name. 1367 *Grateswode*.

Garthorpe (village, Leics): 'outlying farmstead in the triangle of land'. OE *gāra*, 'triangular piece of land', + OS *thorp*, 'outlying farmstead'. 12C *Garthorp*.

Garton-on-the-Wolds (village, E Yorks): 'farmstead on the triangular piece of ground in the Wolds'. OE *gāra*, 'triangular piece of land', + *tūn*, 'farmstead'. The second part of the name locates this Garton in the WOLDS, as distinct from the smaller Garton in Holderness. DB *Gartune*, 1347 *Garton in Wald*.

Garvestone (village, Norfolk): 'Geirulfr's or Gairulf's farmstead', + *tūn*, 'farmstead', 'village'. The personal names are respectively Scandinavian and Old German. DB *Gerolfestuna*.

Garway (village, Herefords): 'Guoruoe's church'. The 'church' element is absent in the first form of the name below (and in the current form), but present as Welsh *llan* in the second form. 1137 *Garou*, 1189 *Langarewi*.

Gasthorpe (hamlet, Norfolk): 'Gaddr's outlying farmstead'. OS *thorp*, 'outlying farmstead'. The personal name is Scandinavian. DB *Gadesthorp*.

Gatcombe (village, IoW): '(place in the) valley where goats are kept'. OE *gāt*, 'goat', + *cumb*, 'valley'. DB *Gatecome*.

Gateforth (village, N Yorks): '(place by the) ford used by goats'. OS *geit*, 'goat', + OE *ford*, 'ford'. The name implies that the ford was regularly used for herding goats from one pasture to another. *c*.1030 *Gæiteford*.

Gate Helmsley (village, N Yorks): 'Hemele's island on the (Roman) road'. OE *ēg*, 'island'. The 'island' is dry ground in marshland here. The first word of the name (OS *gata*, 'road'), referring to the Roman road from York to Malton on which the village lies, distinguishes this Helmsley from nearby *Upper Helmsley*, on higher ground. DB *Hamelsec*, 1438 *Gatehemelsay*.

Gateholm (island, Pemb): 'island of goats'. OS *geit*, 'goat', + *holmr*, 'island'. 1480 *Gateholme*.

Gatehouse of Fleet (town, Dumfries & Gall): 'gatehouse by the (river) Fleet'. The 'gatehouse' has 'gate' in the northern sense 'road', 'way' (OS *gata*). Cp. HARROGATE. A map of 1759 shows a single house by a road here. The river name means simply 'stream' (OS *fljót* or OE *flēot*).

Gateley (hamlet, Norfolk): 'clearing where goats are kept'. OE *gāt*, 'goat', + *lēah*, 'clearing'. DB *Gatelea*.

Gatenby (hamlet, N Yorks): 'Gaithan's farmstead'. OS *bȳ*, 'farmstead', 'village'. The personal name is Old Irish. DB *Ghetenesbi*.

Gateshead (town, Gateshead): 'goat's headland'. OE *gāt*, 'goat', + *hēafod*, 'headland'. Goats were probably kept on the headland here, or there may have been a site where a goat's head was displayed for cult reasons. The former interpretation is now generally favoured over the latter. 1196 *Gatesheued*.

Gathurst (district, Wigan): 'wooded hill where goats are kept'. OE *gāt*, 'goat', + *hyrst*, 'wooded hill'. 1547 *Gatehurst*.

Gatley (town, Stockport): 'bank where goats are kept'. OE *gāt*, 'goat', + *clif*, 'cliff', 'bank'. 1290 *Gateclyve*.

Gatwick (airport, W Sussex): 'farm where goats are kept'. OE *gāt*, 'goat', + *wīc*, 'specialized farm'. 19C Ordnance Survey maps show a farm here called *Gatwick Farm*. The airport dates from the 1930s. 1241 *Gatwik*.

Gawsworth (village, Cheshire): 'enclosure of the smith'. Welsh *gof*, 'smith', + OE *worth*, 'enclosure'. DB *Govesurde*.

Gaydon (village, Warwicks): '(place by) Gǣga's hill'. OE *dūn*, 'hill'. 1194 *Gaidone*.

Gayhurst (village, Milton K): 'wooded hill where goats are kept'. OE *gāt*, 'goat', + *hyrst*, 'wooded hill'. DB *Gateherst*.

Gayles (village, N Yorks): '(place by the) ravines'. OS *geil*, 'ravine'. 1534 *Gales*.

Gayton (village, Norfolk): 'farmstead where goats are kept'. OE *gāt*, 'goat', + *tūn*, 'farmstead'. DB *Gaituna*. SO ALSO: *Gayton*, Wirral.

Gayton (village, Northants): 'Gǣga's farmstead'. OE *tūn*, 'farmstead'. 1162 *Gaiton*. SO ALSO: *Gayton*, Staffs.

Gaywood (district of King's Lynn, Norfolk): 'Gǣga's wood'. OE *wudu*, 'wood'. DB *Gaiuude*.

Gazeley (village, Suffolk): 'Gǣgi's woodland clearing'. OE *lēah*, 'wood', 'clearing'. 1219 *Gaysle*.

Gedding (village, Suffolk): '(settlement of) Gydda's people'. OE *-ingas*, 'people of'. DB *Gedinga*.

Geddington (village, Northants): 'estate associated with Gǣte or Geiti'. OE *-ing-*, 'associated with', + *tūn*, 'farmstead', 'estate'. The personal names are respectively OE and Scandinavian. DB *Geitentone*.

Gedling (district of Nottingham, Notts): '(settlement of) Gēdel's people'. OE *-ingas*, 'people of'. The DB form of the name below is corrupt. DB *Ghellinge*, 1187 *Gedlinges*.

Gedney (village, Lincs): 'Gǣda's or Gydda's island'. OE *ēg*, 'island'. The 'island' is well-watered land here. DB *Gadenai*.

Geldeston (village, Norfolk): 'Gyldi's farmstead'. OE *tūn*, 'farmstead', 'village'. 1242 *Geldestun*.

Gelli Gandryll, Y. See HAY-ON-WYE.

Georgeham (village, Devon): '(place in) well-watered land with St George's church'. OE *hamm*, 'enclosure', 'riverside land'. Georgeham was originally just *Ham*, then *Netherham*, for distinction from nearby *Higher Ham*. DB *Hama*, 1356 *Hamme Sancti Georgii*, 1365 *Netherhamme*, 1535 *Georgeham*.

George Nympton. See KING'S NYMPTON.

Germansweek (village, Devon): 'dairy farm with St Germanus's church'. OE *wīc*, 'dwelling', 'specialized farm'. The place was originally *Wick*, but was then distinguished by the dedication of its church, perhaps to the same saint as at ST GERMANS. DB *Wica*, 1458 *Wyke Germyn*.

Germoe (village, Cornwall): '(chapel of) St Germoe'. The church here is dedicated to Germoe, a saint not known anywhere else. *c*.1176 *Sanctus Germoch*.

Gerrans (village, Cornwall): '(church of) St Guron'. The church here, now dedicated to St Saviour, was formerly dedicated to Guron, who may be the same as Gerennius or Geraint, a historical Cornish king of the early 8C. 1201 *Seint Geren*.

Gerrards Cross (town, Bucks): 'Gerrard's cross'. The town takes its name from a family called Gerrard or Garrard, here in the 14C or 15C. The 'cross' was probably a market by a boundary or crossroads. The present town grew from the 19C village. 1692 *Gerards Cross*.

Gestingthorpe (village, Essex): 'outlying farmstead of Gyrstel's people'. OE *-inga-*, 'of the people of', + *throp*, 'outlying farmstead'. Late 10C *Gyrstlingathorpe*, DB *Ghestingetorp*.

Gidea Park (district, Havering): 'park by Gidea Hall'. A medieval house here had a name meaning 'giddy hall' (ME *gidi*, 'giddy', + *hall*, 'hall'), presumably referring to its unusual design or construction. A park or garden was then added. 1258 *La Gidiehall*, 1668 *Guydie hall parke*.

Gidleigh (hamlet, Devon): 'Gydda's woodland clearing'. OE *lēah*, 'wood', 'clearing'. 1156 *Gideleia*.

Giggleswick (village, N Yorks): 'Gikel's or Gichel's dairy farm'. OE *wīc*, 'dwelling', 'specialized farm'. The personal names are respectively OE and ME. DB *Ghigeleswic*.

Gilberdyke (village, E Yorks): 'Gilbert's (estate by the) ditch or dyke'. OE *dīc*, 'ditch', 'dyke'. A person or family named Gilbert held land here. 1234 *Dyc*, 1376 *Gilbertdike*.

Gilcrux (village, Cumbria): 'retreat by a hill'. The name is Celtic in origin, from words related to modern Welsh *cil*, 'retreat', and *crug*, 'hillock'. The first part of the name was influenced by OS *gil*, 'ravine', 'gill', while the second has been assimilated to Latin *crux*, 'cross'. *c.*1175 *Killecruce*.

Gildersome (village, Leeds): '(place at the) guildhouses'. OS *gildi-hús*, 'guildhouse'. The name represents OS *gildi-húsum*, the dative plural form of *gildi-hús*. 1181 *Gildehusum*.

Gildingwells (village, Rotherham): '(place by the) gushing spring'. OE *gyldande*, 'gushing', + *wella*, 'spring', 'stream'. The spring in question is probably one of those to the south of the village. The name may have been influenced by that of nearby *Wallingwells* ('bubbling spring'), Notts. 13C *Gildanwell*.

Gillamoor (village, N Yorks): 'moorland of Gȳthla's or Gētla's people'. OE *-inga-*, 'of the people of', + *mōr*, 'moor'. The DB form of the name below has garbled the personal name. DB *Gedlingesmore*, late 12C *Gillingamor*.

Gilling East (village, N Yorks): 'eastern (settlement of) Gȳthla's or Gētla's people'. OE *-ingas*, 'people of'. The second word of the name distinguishes the village from *Gilling West* (or simply *Gilling*), some 34 miles to the northwest. (The two villages have also been respectively distinguished as *Gilling-near-Helmsley* and *Gilling-near-Richmond*.) DB *Ghellinge*.

Gillingham (town, Dorset): 'homestead of Gylla's people'. OE *-inga-*, 'of the people of', + *hām*, 'homestead'. The name is identical to those of GILLINGHAM, Medway, and GILLINGHAM, Norfolk, but it is unlikely the same man Gylla was involved. This Gillingham is pronounced with an initial hard G- (as in 'gig'). DB *Gelingeham*.

Gillingham (town, Medway): 'homestead of Gylla's people'. OE *-inga-*, 'of the people of', + *hām*, 'homestead'. Cp. GILLINGHAM, Dorset. This Gillingham is pronounced with an initial soft G- (as in 'gin'). 10C *Gyllingeham*, DB *Gelingeham*.

Gillingham (village, Norfolk): 'homestead of Gylla's people'. OE *-inga-*, 'of the people of', + *hām*, 'homestead'. Cp. GILLINGHAM, Dorset. This Gillingham is pronounced with an initial hard G- (as in 'gig'). The DB form of the name below has garbled the personal name. DB *Kildincham*, 12C *Gelingeham*.

Gilling West. See GILLING EAST.

Gilmorton (village, Leics): 'fertile farmstead in marshland'. OE *gylden*, 'golden', 'wealthy', + *mōr*, 'moor', 'marsh', + *tūn*, 'farmstead'. Cp. GUILDEN MORDEN. DB *Mortone*, 1327 *Gilden Morton*.

Gilsland (village, Cumbria): 'Gille's or Gilli's estate'. OE *land*, 'tract of land', 'estate'. The personal names are respectively Old Irish and Scandinavian. 12C *Gillesland*.

Gilston (hamlet, Herts): 'Gēdel's or Gydel's farmstead'. OE *tūn*, 'farmstead', 'village'. 1197 *Gedeleston*.

Gimingham (village, Norfolk): 'homestead of Gymi's or Gymma's people'. OE *-inga-*, 'of the people of', + *hām*, 'homestead'. DB *Gimingeham*.

Gipping. See IPSWICH.

Girsby (hamlet, N Yorks): 'Gríss's farmstead'. OS *bý*, 'farmstead'. The personal name is Scandinavian. The name could also mean 'farmstead where young pigs are reared' (OS *gríss*, 'young pig', + *bý*). DB *Grisebi*.

Girton (district of Cambridge, Cambs): 'farmstead on gravelly ground'. OE *grēot*, 'gravel' (modern English *grit*), + *tūn*, 'farmstead', 'village'. *c.*1060 *Grittune*, DB *Gretone*. SO ALSO: *Girton*, Notts.

Girvan (resort town and port, S Ayrs): '(place of the) thicket'. Gaelic *gar*, 'thicket'. The name has also been derived from the Water of Girvan here, its own name perhaps meaning 'short river' (Gaelic *gearr abhainn*), by contrast with the Stinchar, the next river south. 1275 *Girven*.

Gisburn (village, Lancs): '(place by the) gushing stream'. OE *gysel*, 'gushing', + *burna*, 'stream'. The first part of the name may originally have been the personal name Gysla. The stream in question originates just above the village. The DB form of the name below has omitted *l*. DB *Ghiseburna*, 12C *Giselburn*.

Gisleham (hamlet, Suffolk): 'Gysla's homestead'. OE *hām*, 'homestead', 'village'. DB *Gisleham*.

Gislingham (village, Suffolk): 'homestead of Gysla's people'. OE *-inga-*, 'of the people of', + *hām*, 'homestead'. c.1060 *Gyselingham*, DB *Gislingaham*.

Gissing (village, Norfolk): '(settlement of) Gyssa's or Gyssi's people'. OE *-ingas*, 'people of'. DB *Gessinga*.

Gittisham (village, Devon): 'Gyddi's homestead or enclosure'. OE *hām*, 'homestead', or *hamm*, 'enclosure'. DB *Gidesham*.

Glaisdale (village, N Yorks): '(place in the) valley of the (river) Glas'. OS *dalr*, 'valley'. The stream here was known by a Celtic name meaning 'grey-green' (modern Welsh *glas*). 12C *Glasedale*.

Glamis (village, Angus): 'open country'. Gaelic *glamhus*, 'wide gap'. The name would refer to the topography here, at the foot of the Sidlaw Hills. 1187 *Glames*.

Glamorgan (historic county, S Wales): 'Morgan's shore'. Welsh *glan*, 'bank', 'shore'. Morgan was a 7C prince of Gwent. The county name survives for the unitary authority *Vale of Glamorgan*, as the name of the fertile lowland region from the mouth of the river Ogmore in the west to Penarth Head in the east. The Welsh name of Glamorgan is *Morgannwg*, 'Morgan's territory', while that of the Vale of Glamorgan is *Bro Morgannwg*, from Welsh *bro*, 'lowlands', 'vale', a word implicitly contrasting with *blaenau*, 'uplands', as for Blaenau Ffestiniog.

Glanaman (town, Carm): '(place on the) bank of the (river) Aman'. Welsh *glan*, 'bank', 'shore'. For the river name, see AMMANFORD.

Glandford (village, Norfolk): '(place by the) ford where games are held'. OE *glēam*, 'revelry', + *ford*, 'ford'. The river *Glaven* here takes its name from that of the village. DB *Glamforda*.

Glanford. See BRIGG.

Glannoventa. See RAVENGLASS.

Glanton (village, Northd): '(place by the) hill with a lookout post'. OE *glente*, 'lookout place', + *dūn*, 'hill'. 1186 *Glentendon*.

Glanvilles Wootton (village, Dorset): 'Glanvilles's farmstead by a wood'. OE *wudu*, 'wood', + *tūn*, 'farmstead'. The Glanville family held the manor here in the 13C. The village is also sometimes known as *Wootton Glanville*. DB *Widetone*, 1288 *Wotton Glaunuill*, 1868 *Wootton-Glanville*.

Glapthorn (village, Northants): '(place by) Glappa's thorn bush'. OE *thorn*, 'thorn bush'. 12C *Glapethorn*.

Glapwell (village, Derbys): '(place by) Glappa's stream'. OE *wella*, 'spring', 'stream'. The name could also mean 'stream where the buckbean plant grows' (OE *glæppe*, 'buckbean', + *wella*). DB *Glappewelle*.

Glasbury (village, Powys): 'town of the monastic community'. Welsh *clas*, 'cloister', 'monastic community', + OE *burh*, 'fortified place', 'market town'. The village is near the English border. Hence the hybrid name. The Welsh name of the village is *Clas-ar-Wy*, 'monastic community on the (river) Wye'. (For the river name, see ROSS-ON-WYE.) 1056 *Clastbyrig*, 1191 *Glesburia*, 1322 *Classebury*.

Glascote (district of Tamworth, Staffs): 'hut where glass is made'. OE *glæs*, 'glass', + *cot*, 'cottage', 'hut'. 12C *Glascote*.

Glasgow (city, Glasgow): '(place in the) green hollow'. The name is of Celtic origin with words corresponding to modern Welsh *glas*, 'green', and *cau*, 'hollow'. The reference is to a natural feature here by the Clyde. 1136 *Glasgu*.

Glass Houghton (suburb of Castleford, Wakefield): 'farmstead on a hill spur where glass is made'. OE *hōh*, 'hill spur', + *tūn*, 'farmstead'. The first word of the name refers to the glassworks here. 'At the Glasshouse at Houghton near Pontefract is made ... all sorts of Window Glass' (*Extracts from the Leeds Mercury*, 1740); 'Sand largely used in iron foundries and by glass manufacturers is obtained here' (*Cassell's Gazetteer of Great Britain and Ireland*, 1896). DB *Hoctun*, 1793 *Glass Houton*.

Glasson (village, Cumbria): '(place by the river) Glasson'. The name seems to have been that of a stream or river here, from a Celtic word meaning 'green' (modern Welsh *glas*). 1259 *Glassan*.

Glasson (village, Lancs): '(place by the river) Glasson'. The name is apparently that of a former stream here, deriving from OE *glæsne*, 'clear one', 'bright one' (related modern English *glass*). *c.*1265 *Glassene*.

Glassonby (village, Cumbria): 'Glassán's farmstead'. OS *bý*, 'farmstead', 'village'. The personal name is Old Irish. 1177 *Glassanebi*.

Glaston (village, Rutland): 'Glathr's farmstead'. OE *tūn*, 'farmstead'. The personal name is Scandinavian. DB *Gladestone*.

Glastonbury (town, Somerset): 'stronghold of the dwellers at Glaston'. OE -*inga*-, 'of the dwellers at', + *burh*, 'fortified place'. *Glaston* is a Celtic name perhaps meaning 'place of woad' (modern Welsh *glaslys*, 'woad', from *glas*, 'blue'). This would refer to the original settlement here, where the Ancient Britons would have used the blue dye of the plant woad to decorate their bodies. The first form of the name below gave the modern Welsh name of Glastonbury, *Ynys Gwydrin*, explained as meaning 'island of glass' (Welsh *ynys*, 'island', + *gwydrin*, 'made of glass'), but this is probably a mistranslation of an earlier English name. It may be no coincidence, even so, that Latin *vitrum* meant both 'woad' and 'glass', and the suggestion of 'glass' in 'Glas-' could be more than folk etymology. The nature of a 'glass island' is hard to envisage, however, although the island referred to is certainly the marshy terrain on which the town lies. 601 *Ineswytrin*, 7C *Glastonia*, *c.*740 *Glestingaburg*.

Glatton (village, Cambs): 'pleasant farmstead'. OE *glæd*, 'bright', 'pleasant' (modern English *glad*), + *tūn*, 'farmstead'. DB *Glatune*.

Glazebury (village, Warrington): The name is recent, and based on that of *Glazebrook* here, itself named from *Glaze Brook*, from a Celtic word related to modern Welsh *glas*, 'greygreen', and OE *brōc*, 'brook'. 1896 *Glazebury*.

Glazeley (village, Shropshire): '(place by the) wood or clearing'. OE *lēah*, 'wood', 'clearing'. The first part of the name is of uncertain origin. It may represent OE *glæs*, 'glass', from the name of a stream here. DB *Gleslei*, 1255 *Glasele*.

Gleadless (district, Sheffield): 'woodland clearings where kites are seen'. OE *gleoda*, 'kite', + *lēah*, 'wood', 'clearing'. 13C *Gledeleys*.

Gleaston (village, Cumbria): 'bright farmstead'. OE *glǣs*, 'bright', + *tūn*, 'farmstead', 'village'. The first part of the name could also represent the name of the stream on which the village stands, meaning 'bright one'. The DB form of the name below is corrupt. DB *Glassertun*, 1269 *Gleseton*.

Glemsford (village, Suffolk): '(place by the) ford where games are held'. OE *glēam*, 'merri-

ment', + *ford*, 'ford'. The river here is the Stour. The DB form of the name below has C- for G-. *c.*1050 *Glemesford*, DB *Clamesforda*.

Glen Affric (tourist region, Highland): 'valley of the (river) Affric'. Gaelic *gleann*, 'valley'. The river name means 'dappled' (Gaelic *ath*, 'again', + *breac*, 'speckled').

Glencoe (valley, Highland): 'valley of the (river) Coe'. Gaelic *gleann*, 'valley'. The river name is of unknown meaning. The name as a whole has also been interpreted as 'narrow valley' (Gaelic *gleann comhann*). 1343 *Glenchomure*, 1491 *Glencole*.

Gleneagles (estate, Perth & Kin). *Glen Eagles*, the valley of the upper reaches of Ruthven Water, has a name meaning 'valley of the church' (Gaelic *gleann*, 'valley', + *eaglais*, 'church'). St Kentigern is said to have founded a religious establishment here in the 7C. *c.*1165 *Gleninglese*, 1508 *Glenegas*.

Glenelg (village, Highland): 'valley of Ireland'. Gaelic *gleann*, 'valley'. The name was given by Irish settlers who came to live here in early times, *Ealg* being one of their names for their mother country. Cp. ELGIN. 1292 *Glenelg*.

Glenfield (suburb of Leicester, Leics): 'clean open land'. OE *clǣne*, 'clean', + *feld*, 'open land' (modern English *field*). Cp. CLANFIELD. DB *Clanefelde*.

Glen Parva. See GREAT GLEN.

Glenrothes (town, Fife): 'valley of Rothes'. Gaelic *gleann*, 'valley'. Glenrothes was designated a New Town in 1948 and named after the earls of ROTHES, who have long had local connections. There is hardly a 'glen' here in the accepted sense, although the river Leven runs through the town.

Glentham (village, Lincs): 'homestead by a lookout place'. OE *glente*, 'lookout place' (related modern English *glance*, *glint*), + *hām*, 'homestead'. Glentham is situated on a hill. DB *Glentham*.

Glentworth (village, Lincs): 'enclosure by a lookout place'. OE *glente*, 'lookout place', + *worth*, 'enclosure'. Glentworth is barely 4 miles from GLENTHAM, and the names are probably related, although there is less of an obvious 'lookout place' at Glentworth. DB *Glentewrde*.

Glevum. See GLOUCESTER.

Glinton (village, Peterborough): 'fenced farmstead'. OE *glind*, 'fence', 'enclosure', + *tūn*, 'farmstead'. 1060 *Clinton*, DB *Glintone*.

Glooston (village, Leics): 'Glōr's farmstead'. OE *tūn*, 'farmstead'. DB *Glorstone*.

Glossop (town, Derbys): 'Glott's valley'. OE *hop*, 'small enclosed valley'. Glossop is in a narrow valley on the edge of the Peak District. DB *Glosop*, 1219 *Glotsop*.

Gloucester (city, Glos): 'Roman town of Glevum'. OE *ceaster*, 'Roman town'. The Roman name of Gloucester is of Celtic origin and means 'bright place' (related modern Welsh *gloyw*, 'bright', 'clear'), perhaps with reference to the river Severn here. DB *Glowecestre*.

Gloucestershire (county, W England): 'district based on Gloucester'. OE *scīr*, 'shire', 'district'. See GLOUCESTER. 11C *Gleaweceastrescire*.

Glusburn (village, N Yorks): '(place by the) shining stream'. OS *gluss*, 'bright', 'shining' (related modern English *gloss*), + *brunnr*, 'stream'. The stream in question is Glusburn Beck. DB *Glusebrun*.

Glympton (village, Oxon): 'farmstead on the (river) Glyme'. OE *tūn*, 'farmstead'. The river has a Celtic name meaning 'bright one'. *c.*1050 *Glimtuna*, DB *Glintone*.

Glyndebourne (country house, E Sussex): 'stream near Glynde'. OE *burna*, 'stream'. The nearby village of *Glynde* has a name meaning '(place at the) fence' (OE *glind*, 'fence', 'enclosure'). The form of the name below relates to the river, now called the Glynde Reach. 1288 *Burne juxta Glynde*.

Glynebwy. See EBBW VALE.

Glyn-neath (village, Neath PT): 'valley of the (river) Neath'. Welsh *glyn*, 'valley'. The Welsh form of the name is *Glyn-nedd*. For the river name, see NEATH. 1281 *Glynneth*, 15C *Glyn Nedd*.

Gnosall (village, Staffs): 'Gnēath's corner of land'. OE *halh*, 'nook', 'corner of land'. This interpretation is tentative, and Celticists see the first part of the name not as a personal name but as meaning 'mouth' (modern Welsh *genau*), referring to the wide stream valley that opens out to the south of the village. The DB clerk had problems over the name. DB *Geneshale*, 1140 *Gnowesala*.

Goadby (village, Leics): 'Gauti's farmstead'. OS *bý*, 'farmstead', 'village'. The personal name is Scandinavian. DB *Goutebi*.

Goadby Marwood (village, Leics): 'Maureward's (estate at) Gauti's farmstead'. OS *bý*, 'farmstead', 'village'. Gauti is a Scandinavian name. The Maureward family held the manor here in the 14C, their name distinguishing this Goadby from GOADBY, 17 miles to the south. DB *Goutebi*.

Goathill (hamlet, Dorset): '(place by the) hill where goats are pastured'. OE *gāt*, 'goat', + *hyll*, 'hill'. The DB form of the name below is garbled. DB *Gatelme*, 1176 *Gathulla*.

Goathland (village, N Yorks): 'Gōda's cultivated land'. OE *land*, 'tract of land'. The first part of the name could also represent OE *gōd*, 'good', giving a sense '(place by the) good cultivated land'. *c.*1110 *Godelandia*.

Goathurst (village, Somerset): 'wooded hill where goats are kept'. OE *gāt*, 'goat', + *hyrst*, 'wooded hill'. The DB form of the name below is corrupt. DB *Gahers*, 1292 *Gothurste*.

Gobanum. See ABERYSTWYTH.

Godalming (town, Surrey): '(settlement of) Godhelm's people'. OE *-ingas*, 'people of'. *c.*880 *Godelmingum*, DB *Godelminge*.

Goddington (district, Bromley): 'estate associated with Gōda'. OE *-ing-*, 'associated with', + *tūn*, 'farmstead', 'estate'. 1240 *Godinton*.

Godmanchester (town, Cambs): 'Roman station associated with Godmund'. OE *ceaster*, 'Roman camp'. The Roman station here was called *Durovigutum*, from a Celtic word meaning 'fort' and a second element of unknown meaning. DB *Godmundcestre*.

Godmanstone (village, Dorset): 'Godmann's farmstead'. OE *tūn*, 'farmstead'. 1166 *Godemanestone*.

Godney (hamlet, Somerset): 'Gōda's island'. OE *ēg*, 'island'. The 'island' is well-watered land here, by the river Brue. 10C *Godeneia*.

Godolphin Cross (hamlet, Cornwall): meaning uncertain. The second word refers to the crossroads where the village arose in the 19C. The first word gave the modern surname Godolphin, borne by various notables in the 17C.

Godshill (village, IoW): 'hill associated with a god'. OE *god*, 'god', + *hyll*, 'hill'. The god in question could be the Christian God, and the hill on which the village stands may have been a pagan site that was reconsecrated for Christian worship. 12C *Godeshella*. SO ALSO: *Godshill*, Hants.

Godstone (village, Surrey): 'Cōd's farmstead'. OE *tūn*, 'farmstead'. 1248 *Godeston*, 1279 *Codeston*.

Godstow (suburb of Oxford, Oxon): 'God's place'. OE *stōw*, 'holy place'. The name refers to the Benedictine nunnery founded here in the 12C. *c.*1150 *Godestowe*.

Golant (village, Cornwall): 'fair in a valley'. Cornish *goel*, 'fair', 'festival', + *nans* (earlier *nant*), 'valley'. This seems to be the meaning of the name, although no fair or festival has been recorded here. 1299 *Gulnant*.

Golberdon (village, Cornwall): '(place on the) hill'. OE *dūn*, 'hill'. The first part of the name is of uncertain origin. The village arose in the 18C, and the form of the name below refers to pastureland. 1620 *Golberton*.

Golborne (town, Wigan): 'stream where marsh marigolds grow'. OE *golde*, 'marigold', + *burna*, 'stream'. The stream is probably Millingford Brook, which flows through the town. 1187 *Goldeburn*.

Golcar (village, Kirklees): 'Guthleikr's or Guthlaugr's hill pasture'. OS *erg*, 'shieling', 'hill pasture'. The personal names are Scandinavian. DB *Gudlagesarc*.

Golders Green (district, Barnet): 'Golder's green'. A family called Golder (modern Goodyear) lived by the green here some time before the 17C. 1612 *Golders Greene*.

Goldhanger (village, Essex): '(place by the) wooded slope where marigolds grow'. OE *golde*, 'marigold', + *hangra*, 'wooded slope'. The village is on low-lying ground, suitable for marigolds or other yellow-flowering marsh plants. DB *Goldhangra*.

Goldsborough (village, N Yorks): 'Godel's stronghold'. OE *burh*, 'fortified place'. The personal name is either OE or Old German. The forms of the name below are for Goldsborough near Knaresborough, the DB form having *n* for *l*. DB *Godenesburg*, 1170 *Godelesburc*.

Goldsithney (village, Cornwall): 'fair of St Sithny'. Cornish *goel*, 'fair', 'festival'. The fair formerly held here was originally at SITHNEY, 6 miles to the east. 1403 *Golysithney*.

Goldthorpe (town, Barnsley): 'Golda's outlying farmstead'. OS *thorp*, 'secondary settlement', 'outlying farmstead'. DB *Goldetorp*.

Golspie (resort town, Highland): 'Gold's farm'. OS *bý*, 'farm'. The personal name is Scandinavian. 1330 *Goldespy*.

Gomeldon (village, Wilts): 'Gumela's hill'. OE *dūn*, 'hill'. 1189 *Gomeledona*.

Gomersal (district, Kirklees): 'Gūthmǣr's corner of land'. OE *halh*, 'nook', 'corner of land'. DB *Gomershale*.

Gomshall (village, Surrey): 'Guma's shelf of land'. OE *scelf*, 'shelf', 'area of flat ground'. The DB form of the name below has corrupted the OE word. DB *Gomeselle*, 1168 *Gumeselva*.

Gonalston (village, Notts): 'Gunnulf's farmstead'. OE *tūn*, 'farmstead'. The personal name is Scandinavian. DB *Gunnulvestune*.

Good Easter (village, Essex): 'Gōdgȳth's or Gōdgifu's sheepfold'. OE *eowestre*, 'sheepfold'. The personal names are those of women, and one or the other distinguishes this village from HIGH EASTER. 11C *Estre*, 1200 *Godithestre*.

Gooderstone (village, Norfolk): 'Gūthhere's farmstead'. OE *tūn*, 'farmstead'. The DB form of the name below has garbled the personal name. DB *Godestuna*, 1254 *Gutherestone*.

Goodleigh (village, Devon): 'Gōda's woodland clearing'. OE *lēah*, 'wood', 'clearing'. DB *Godelege*.

Goodmanham (village, E Yorks): 'homestead of Gōdmund's people'. OE *-inga-*, 'of the people of', + *hām*, 'homestead'. 731 *Godmunddingaham*, DB *Gudmundham*.

Goodnestone (village, Kent): 'Gōdwine's farmstead'. OE *tūn*, 'farmstead'. The form of the name below relates to Goodnestone near Aylesham, but Goodnestone near Faversham has a name of identical origin. 1196 *Godwineston*.

Goodrich (village, Herefords): 'Gōdrīc's castle'. Latin *castellum*, 'castle'. The Latin word has disappeared from the name to leave the personal name alone. Gōdrīc was a landholder here in 1086. 1102 *Castellum Godric*, 1868 *Goodrich, or Goderich*.

Goodrington (coastal district, Torbay): 'estate associated with Gōdhere'. OE *-ing-*, 'associated with', + *tūn*, 'farmstead', 'estate'. DB *Godrintone*.

Goodwin Sands (sandbanks, Kent): 'Godwin's sandbanks'. The sandbanks in the Strait of Dover are said to be the remains of an island owned by Earl Godwin in the 11C. But the meaning could be 'good friend' (OE *gōd*, 'good', + *wine*, 'friend'), a name given to 'placate' any evil spirits in the waters here. 1371 *Godewynesonde*.

Goodwood (country house, W Sussex): 'Gōdgifu's wood'. OE *wudu*, 'wood'. The personal name is that of a woman. (In its Latinized form it is more familiar as Godiva.) *c*.1200 *Godiuawuda*.

Goole (town and inland port, E Yorks): '(place by the) stream'. ME *goule*, 'ditch', 'channel' (related modern English *gully*). The name relates to the town's location on the river Ouse. The original 'stream' may be represented by the present canal called Dutch River. 1362 *Gulle*.

Goonhavern (village, Cornwall): '(place by the) downland ploughed in summer'. Cornish *goen*, 'downs', + *havar*, 'summer-ploughed land'. 1300 *Goenhavar*, 1748 *Goonhavern*.

Goosey (village, Oxon): 'island where geese are seen'. OE *gōs*, 'goose', + *ēg*, 'island'. The 'island' is land between Stutfield Brook and Land Brook here. 9C *Goseie*, DB *Gosei*.

Goosnargh (village, Lancs): 'Gussān's hill pasture'. OE *erg*, 'shieling', 'hill pasture'. The personal name is Old Irish. DB *Gusansarghe*.

Gordonstoun (estate, Moray): 'Gordon's estate'. ME *toun*, 'estate', 'village'. The estate here, formerly known as the Bog of Plewlands, was acquired in 1638 by Sir Robert Gordon.

Gorebridge (town, Midlothian): 'bridge by the triangular plot of land'. OE *gāra*, 'point of land', + *brycg*, 'bridge'. The river here, Water of Gore, took its name from the place.

Goring (town, Oxon): '(settlement of) Gāra's people'. OE -*ingas*, 'people of'. DB *Garinges*.

Goring-by-Sea (district of Worthing, W Sussex): '(settlement of) Gāra's people'. OE -*ingas*, 'people of'. The second part of the name is a recent touristic addition. DB *Garinges*.

Gorleston-on-Sea (district of Great Yarmouth, Norfolk): 'Gurl's farmstead by the sea'. OE *tūn*, 'farmstead'. The second part of the name is a recent commercial addition. DB *Gorlestuna*.

Gorran Haven (coastal village, Cornwall): 'harbour (in the parish of) Goran'. The parish is named from the dedication of its church to St Goran, who came here from Bodmin. Until the 18C Gorran Haven was known as *Porthjust*, 'St Just's harbour' (Cornish *porth*, 'harbour'). Cp. ST JUST. 1699 *Gurran hone*, 1748 *Gorranhaven*.

Gorseinon (town, Swansea): 'Einion's marsh'. Welsh *cors*, 'marsh'. The identity of the named man is unknown.

Gorton (district, Manchester): 'dirty farmstead'. OE *gor*, 'dung', 'dirt' (modern English *gore*), + *tūn*, 'farmstead'. 1282 *Gorton*.

Gosbeck (village, Suffolk): '(place by the) stream where geese are seen'. OE *gōs*, 'goose', + OS *bekkr*, 'stream'. 1179 *Gosebech*.

Gosberton (village, Lincs): 'Gosbert's church'. OE *cirice*, 'church'. The personal name is Old German, and OE *cirice* has been replaced in the name by OE *tūn*, 'farmstead', 'village'. DB *Gosbertechirche*, 1487 *Gosburton*.

Gosfield (village, Essex): 'open land where geese are seen'. OE *gōs*, 'goose', + *feld*, 'open land' (modern English *field*). The geese are more likely to have been wild than domestic. 1198 *Gosfeld*.

Gosforth (town, Newcastle): '(place at the) ford where geese are seen'. OE *gōs*, 'goose', + *ford*, 'ford'. Either of the two small streams here could have had the ford where wild geese were

seen or domestic ones driven across. 1166 *Goseford*. SO ALSO: *Gosforth*, Cumbria.

Gospel Oak (district, Camden): 'oak of the gospel'. The name alludes to the annual Rogationtide ceremony of 'beating the bounds', when the procession would have halted by an oak tree for the gospel to be read. Gospel Oak is on the parish boundary between Hampstead and St Pancras. The oak in question was cut down in the 19C.

Gosport (town and port, Hants): 'town where geese are sold'. OE *gōs*, 'goose', + *port*, 'town', 'market town'. The name could also mean 'port where geese are loaded'. Local lore explains it as 'God's port', referring to King Stephen's safe landing here after a storm. 1250 *Goseport*.

Goswick (hamlet, Northd): 'farm where geese are kept'. OE *gōs*, 'goose', + *wīc*, 'specialized farm'. 1202 *Gossewic*.

Gotham (village, Notts): 'homestead or enclosure where goats are kept'. OE *gāt*, 'goat', + *hām*, 'homestead', or *hamm*, 'enclosure'. DB *Gatham*.

Gotherington (village, Glos): 'estate associated with Gūthhere'. OE -*ing*-, 'associated with', + *tūn*, 'farmstead', 'estate'. DB *Godrinton*.

Goudhurst (village, Kent): 'Gūtha's wooded hill'. OE *hyrst*, 'wooded hill'. 11C *Guithyrste*.

Gourock (resort town, Inverclyde): '(place by the) hillock'. Gaelic *guireag*, 'pimple'. The 'hillock' in question may be Kempock Point here. 1661 *Ouir et Nether Gowrockis*.

Govan (district, Glasgow): 'dear rock'. OW *cu*, 'dear', + *faen*, 'rock'. The identity of the favoured rock is unknown. *c*.1150 *Gvuan*.

Gowdall (village, E Yorks): 'corner of land where marigolds grow'. OE *golde*, 'marigold', + *halh*, 'nook', 'corner of land'. The area of land in question would have been in one of the loops of the river Aire here. 12C *Goldale*.

Gower (peninsula, Swansea): 'curved (promontory)'. Welsh *gŵyr*, 'curved'. The name refers to the distinctive hook-like shape of the peninsula, whose Welsh name is simply *Gŵyr*.

Gowerton (town, Swansea): 'town of the Gower (peninsula)'. The original name of the location here was *Gower Road Station* (1860), from its position on a main rail route to the GOWER peninsula. The growing settlement received its present name in 1886. Its Welsh name is *Tre-Gŵyr* (Welsh *tre*, 'town').

Goxhill (village, N Lincs): '(place by the) gushing spring'. OS *gausli*, 'gushing spring'. The DB form of the name below has inverted *sl* as *ls*. DB *Golse*, 12C *Gousle*. SO ALSO: *Goxhill*, E Yorks.

Graffham (village, W Sussex): 'homestead or enclosure by a grove'. OE *grāf*, 'grove', + *hām*, 'homestead', or *hamm*, 'enclosure'. DB *Grafham*.

Grafton (hamlet, Oxon): 'farmstead by a grove'. OE *grāf*, 'grove', + *tūn*, 'farmstead'. The DB form of the name below has *p* for *f*. DB *Graptone*, 1130 *Graftona*. SO ALSO: *Grafton*, Herefords, N Yorks.

Grafton Flyford (village, Worcs): 'farmstead by a grove near Flyford'. OE *grāf*, 'grove', + *tūn*, 'farmstead'. *Flyford* is nearby FLYFORD FLAVELL. The first part of the DB form of the name below is garbled. 9C *Graftun*, DB *Garstune*.

Grafton Regis (village, Northants): 'farmstead by the grove of the king'. OE *grāf*, 'grove', + *tūn*, 'farmstead', + Latin *regis*, 'of the king'. Grafton was a royal manor. The DB form of the name below has *s* for *f*. DB *Grastone*, 12C *Graftone*.

Grafton Underwood (village, Northants): 'farmstead by the grove near the wood'. OE *grāf*, 'grove', + *tūn*, 'farmstead', + *under*, 'under', 'near', + *wudu*, 'wood'. The wood in question is Rockingham Forest. The DB form of the name below has *f* miscopied as *s*. DB *Grastone*, 1367 *Grafton Underwode*.

Grain, Isle of (peninsula, Medway): 'gravelly island'. OE *grēon*, 'gravel'. The name alludes to the gravelly or gritty shore of the peninsula, which was formerly an actual island, separated from the mainland by the Thames and the Medway. *c.*1100 *Grean*, 1610 *Ile of Greane*.

Grainsby (village, Lincs): 'Grein's farmstead'. OS *bý*, 'farmstead', 'village'. The personal name is Scandinavian. DB *Grenesbi*.

Grainthorpe (village, Lincs): 'Geirmundr's or Germund's outlying farmstead'. OS *thorp*, 'outlying farmstead'. The personal names are respectively Scandinavian and Old German. DB *Germundstorp*.

Grampians (mountain system, Scotland): meaning uncertain. The name was formerly thought to derive from *Mons Graupius*, but this was the Roman name, of unknown meaning, for the upland area of Bennachie, Aberdeens, which is not even in the Grampians. The earlier name of the region was *The Mounth* (Gaelic *monadh*, 'hilly district').

Grampound (village, Cornwall): '(place at the) great bridge'. OF *grant*, 'great', + *pont*, 'bridge'. The name refers to the crossing of the river Fal at the foot of the village. 1302 *Grauntpount*.

Granborough (village, Bucks): '(place on a) green hill'. OE *grēne*, 'green', + *beorg*, 'hill'. The DB form of the name below has an extraneous *s*. *c.*1060 *Grenebeorge*, DB *Grenesberga*, 1766 *Granborough*, 1868 *Grandborough*.

Granby (village, Notts): 'Grani's farmstead'. OS *bý*, 'farmstead', 'village'. The personal name is Scandinavian. DB *Granebi*.

Grandborough (village, Warwicks): '(place on a) green hill'. OE *grēne*, 'green', + *beorg*, 'hill'. DB *Greneberge*.

Grange (village, Cumbria): 'outlying farmstead belonging to a religious house'. ME *grange*, 'grange'. The Borrowdale village originally belonged to the monks of Furness Abbey. 1576 *The Grange*.

Grangemouth (town and port, Falkirk): 'mouth of the Grange Burn'. OE *mūtha*, 'mouth'. The river takes its name from the grange of Newbattle Abbey nearby. The town itself dates from 1777.

Grange-over-Sands (resort town, Cumbria): 'grange across the sands'. The 'grange' was an outlying farmstead owned by Cartmel Priory. The town is across the sands of Morecambe Bay. 1491 *Grange*.

Grangetown (town, Redcar & Clev): 'town by the grange'. The iron and steel town arose in the 19C and takes its name from nearby Eston Grange, a former possession of Fountains Abbey.

Gransmoor (hamlet, E Yorks): 'Grante's or Grentir's marshland'. OE *mor* or OS *mór*, 'moor', 'marsh'. The personal names are respectively OE and Scandinavian. DB *Grentesmor*.

Granston (hamlet, Pemb): 'Grand's farm'. OE *tūn*, 'farmstead'. The personal name is Old French. The Welsh name of Grandston is *Treopert*, 'Robert's farm' (Welsh *tre*, 'farm'), suggesting that the founder of the settlement may have been a Robert le Grand. 1291 *Villa Grandi*, 1535 *Grandiston*.

Grantchester (village, Cambs): '(place of the) settlers on the (river) Granta'. OE *sǣte*, 'settlers'. The '-chester' of the name is misleading, and does not denote a Roman station. The river has a Celtic name of unknown origin that also gave the name of CAMBRIDGE. *c.*730 *Grantacaestir*, DB *Granteseta*.

Grantham (town, Lincs): 'village built on gravel'. OE *grand*, 'gravel', + *hām*, 'homestead', 'village'. A meaning 'Granta's homestead' has also been proposed, but the lack of forms in *Grante-* does not support this. DB *Grantham*.

Granton (district, Edinburgh): 'farm built on gravel'. OE *grand*, 'gravel', + *tūn*, 'farmstead'. *c*.1200 *Grendun*.

Grantown-on-Spey (resort town, Highland): 'Grant's town on the (river) Spey'. The town arose as a model village planned by James Grant in 1765. The river has a pre-Celtic name of unknown meaning.

Grappenhall (district, Warrington): 'corner of land by a ditch'. OE *grōpe*, 'ditch', 'drain', + *halh*, 'nook', 'corner of land'. DB *Gropenhale*.

Grasby (village, Lincs): 'farmstead on gravelly ground'. OS *grjót*, 'gravel', + *bý*, 'farmstead', 'village'. DB *Grosebi*.

Grasmere (lake, Cumbria): 'grassy lake'. OE *gres*, 'grass', + *sǣ*, 'lake', + *mere*, 'lake'. A 'grassy lake' is one with either grassy shores or grass-like vegetation in its waters. The name was originally the equivalent of 'grass sea', to which 'mere' was added, giving a second 'lake'. 1245 *Gressemere*, 1375 *Grissemere*.

Grassendale (district, Liverpool): 'grassy valley'. OE *gærsen*, 'growing with grass', + *dæl*, 'valley'. The name could also mean 'valley used for grazing' (OE *gærsing*, 'grazing', + *dæl*). 13C *Gresyndale*.

Grassholm (island, Pemb): 'grassy island'. OS *gras*, 'grass', + *holmr*, 'island'. Latin *insula*, 'island', is redundant in the form of the name below, as '-holm' already has this meaning. 15C *Insula Grasholm*.

Grassington (village, N Yorks): 'farm with grazing'. OE *gærsing*, 'grazing' (from *gærs*, 'grass'), + *tūn*, 'farmstead'. DB *Ghersintone*.

Grassthorpe (village, Notts): 'grass farmstead'. OS *gres*, 'grass', + *thorp*, 'farmstead', 'hamlet'. A 'grass farmstead' is one given over to pasture. DB *Grestorp*.

Gratwich (hamlet, Staffs): 'dairy farm by the gravelly place'. OE *grēote*, 'gravelly place', + *wīc*, 'specialized farm'. The DB form of the name below has C- for G-. DB *Crotewiche*, 1176 *Grotewic*.

Graveley (village, Cambs): 'woodland clearing by the pit'. OE *græf*, 'pit', 'trench' (modern English *grave*), + *lēah*, 'wood', 'clearing'. The first part of the name could also represent OE *grǣfe* or *grāfa*, 'grove', 'copse'. 10C *Greflea*, DB *Gravelei*.

Graveley (village, Herts): 'clearing by a grove'. OE *grǣfe* or *grāf*, 'grove', + *lēah*, 'wood', 'clearing'. DB *Gravelai*.

Graveney (village, Kent): '(place by the) ditch stream'. OE *grafa*, 'ditch', + *ēa*, 'river', 'stream'.

The name was originally that of the stream here, which ran through a broad ditch. 9C *Grafonaea*.

Gravesend (town, Kent): '(place at the) end of the grove'. OE *grāf*, 'grove', 'copse', + *ende*, 'end'. The original 'grove' was probably to the east of the town centre where the old Fort Gardens (now the Riverside Leisure Area) are today. The DB form of the name below, with its garbled second element, gave the name of the local council district. DB *Gravesham*.

Gravesham. See GRAVESEND.

Grayrigg (village, Cumbria): '(place by the) grey ridge'. OS *grár*, 'grey', + *hryggr*, 'ridge'. The village lies in a small area of grey limestone. 12C *Grarigg*.

Grays (town, Thurrock): 'de Grai's (estate)'. The original (and present formal) name of the town is *Grays Thurrock*, with *Grays* from the de Grai family, here in the 12C, and *Thurrock* meaning 'place where foul water collects' (OE *thurruc*, 'bilge'). The latter name relates to Thurrock Marshes here. DB *Turruc*, 1248 *Turrokgreys*, 1399 *Grayes*, 1552 *Grace Thurrock*.

Grazeley (hamlet, Wokingham): 'place where wolves wallow'. OE *grǣg*, 'grey (one)', + *sol*, 'muddy place', 'place where animals wallow' (related modern English *slough*). The animal involved was formerly said to be the badger (at one time known as a 'grey'), but the wolf is now preferred, partly on linguistic grounds. *c*.950 *Grægsole*.

Greasbrough (district, Rotherham): '(place by the) grassy brook'. OE *gærs*, 'grass', + *brōc*, 'brook'. DB *Gersebroc*.

Greasby (suburb of Birkenhead, Wirral): 'stronghold by a wood'. OE *grǣfe*, 'grove', 'wood', + *burh*, 'fortified place'. OE *burh* was later replaced by equivalent OS *bý*. DB *Gravesberie*, *c*.1100 *Grauisby*.

Greasley (hamlet, Notts): '(place by the) wood or clearing'. OE *lēah*, 'wood', 'clearing'. The first part of the name is of uncertain origin. It may represent OE *grēosn*, 'gravel'. DB *Griseleia*.

Great Abington (village, Cambs): 'greater estate associated with Abba'. OE *-ing-*, 'associated with', + *tūn*, 'farmstead', 'estate'. The first word of the name distinguishes the village from nearby *Little Abington* and also from *Abington Pigotts*, 15 miles to the west, where the manor was held in the 15C by the Pykot family. DB *Abintone*.

Great Addington (village, Northants): 'greater estate associated with Eadda or Æddi'.

OE -*ing*-, 'associated with', + *tūn*, 'farmstead', 'estate'. The first word of the name distinguishes the village from nearby *Little Addington*. DB *Edintone*.

Great Alne (village, Warwicks): 'greater (place on the river) Alne'. For the river name, see ALCESTER. The first word of the name distinguishes the village from *Little Alne*, 2 miles to the northeast. DB *Alne*.

Great Altcar (village, Lancs): 'greater (place by the) marsh on the (river) Alt'. OS *kjarr*, 'marsh'. The river has a Celtic name meaning 'muddy one'. The first word of the name distinguishes the place from *Little Altcar*, a district of Formby, Sefton. The DB form of the name below is garbled. DB *Acrer*, 1251 *Altekar*.

Great Amwell (village, Herts): 'greater (place called) Æmma's spring'. OE *wella*, 'spring', 'stream'. The first word of the name distinguishes the village from nearby *Little Amwell*. DB *Emmewelle*.

Great Asby (village, Cumbria): 'greater farmstead where ash trees grow'. OS *askr*, 'ash', + *bý*, 'farmstead', 'village'. The first word of the name distinguishes the village from the hamlet of *Little Asby*, 2 miles to the southeast. *c*.1160 *Aschaby*.

Great Ashfield (village, Suffolk): 'greater (place on) open land where ash trees grow'. OE *æsc*, 'ash', + *feld*, 'open land' (modern English *field*). DB *Eascefelda*.

Great Ayton (village, N Yorks): 'greater farmstead or estate on a river'. OE *ēa*, 'river', + *tūn*, 'farmstead', 'estate'. OE *ēa* has been modified in the name by the OS equivalent, *á*, while the name itself is the equivalent of southern ETON. The river here is the Leven. The first word of the name distinguishes this Ayton from nearby *Little Ayton*. DB *Atun*.

Great Baddow (district of Chelmsford, Essex): 'greater (place on the river) Baddow'. The river name, of Celtic origin and uncertain meaning, is a former name for the Chelmer (see CHELMSFORD). The first word of the name distinguishes this village from *Little Baddow*, east of Chelmsford. *c*.975 *Beadewan*, DB *Baduuen*.

Great Badminton. See BADMINTON.

Great Bardfield (village, Essex): 'greater (place on) open land by a bank'. OE *byrde*, 'bank', 'border', + *feld*, 'open land' (modern English *field*). The first word of the name distinguishes this place from both *Little Bardfield*, to the northwest, and *Bardfield Saling*, to the south, the latter taking its name from GREAT SALING. DB *Byrdefelda*.

Great Barford (village, Beds): 'greater (place by the) barley ford'. OE *bere*, 'barley', + *ford*, 'ford'. A 'barley ford' is one used for barley at harvest time. The river here is the Ouse. The first word of the name distinguishes the village from *Little Barford*, 4 miles to the northeast on the same river, although its name means '(place by the) ford where birch trees grow' (OE *beorc*, 'birch', + *ford*). DB *Bereforde*.

Great Barr (district of West Bromwich, Sandwell): 'great hilltop'. The name is of Celtic origin, from a word related to modern Welsh *bar*, 'top'. The 'great hilltop' itself is Barr Beacon. Great Barr is 3 miles northwest of PERRY BARR. 957 *Bearre*, DB *Barre*.

Great Barrington (village, Glos): 'greater estate associated with Beorn'. OE -*ing*-, 'associated with', + *tūn*, 'farmstead', 'estate'. The first word of the name distinguishes the village from nearby *Little Barrington*. DB *Bernitone*.

Great Barrow (village, Cheshire): 'greater (place by the) wood'. OE *bearu*, 'wood', 'grove'. The first word of the name distinguishes the village from nearby *Little Barrow*. 958 *Barue*, DB *Bero*.

Great Barton (village, Suffolk): 'greater barley farm'. OE *bere-tūn* (from *bere*, 'barley', + *tūn*, 'farmstead'.) The first word of the name distinguishes the village from nearby *East Barton*. The first word of the second form of the name below is Latin *magna*, 'great'. 945 *Bertuna*, 1254 *Magna Bertone*.

Great Barugh (village, N Yorks): 'greater (place by the) hill'. OE *beorg*, 'hill'. The first word of the name distinguishes the village from nearby *Little Barugh*. DB *Berg*.

Great Bavington (hamlet, Northd): 'greater estate associated with Babba'. OE -*ing*-, 'associated with', + *tūn*, 'farmstead', 'estate'. The first word of the name distinguishes this Bavington from nearby *Little Bavington*. 1242 *Babington*.

Great Bealings (village, Suffolk): 'greater (settlement of the) dwellers in the glade'. OE *bel*, 'glade' (literally 'interval'), + -*ingas*, 'dwellers at'. The name could also mean '(settlement of the) dwellers by the funeral pyre' (OE *bēl*, 'fire', + -*ingas*). The first word of the name distinguishes the village from nearby *Little Bealings*. DB *Belinges*.

Great Bedwyn. See BEDWYN.

Great Bentley (village, Essex): 'greater woodland clearing where bents grow'. OE *beonet*, 'bent grass', + *lēah*, 'wood', 'clearing'. The first word of the name distinguishes this Bentley from *Little Bentley*, 2 miles to the north. *c.*1040 *Benetleye*, DB *Benetlea*.

Great Berkhamsted. See BERKHAMSTED.

Great Billing (suburb of Northampton, Northants): 'greater (settlement of) Bill's or Billa's people'. OE *-ingas*, 'people of'. The first word of the name distinguishes the place from nearby *Little Billing*. Northampton was designated a New Town in 1968 and the DB name *Bellinge* was adopted for the extended eastern district embracing the former villages of Great and Little Billing. DB *Bellinge*.

Great Bircham (village, Norfolk): 'greater homestead by newly cultivated land'. OE *brēc*, 'newly cultivated land' (related modern English *break*), + *hām*, 'homestead'. The first word of the name distinguishes the village from nearby *Bircham Newton* (OE *nīwe*, 'new', + *tūn*, 'farmstead') and *Bircham Tofts* (OS *toft*, 'homestead'). DB *Brecham*.

Great Blakenham (village, Suffolk): 'greater (place called) Blaca's homestead or enclosure'. OE *hām*, 'homestead', or *hamm*, 'enclosure'. The first word of the name distinguishes the village from nearby *Little Blakenham*. DB *Blacheham*.

Great Bolas (village, Wrekin): 'greater (place by) alluvial land'. OE *wæsse*, 'alluvial land' (related modern English *wash*). The name refers to a river that floods and drains quickly. Great Bolas lies near the junction of the rivers Meese and Tern. The first part of the name is of uncertain origin. It may represent OE *bogel*, 'small river bend', in a genitive plural form. The first word of the name distinguishes the village from *Little Bolas*, across the Tern. 1198 *Belewas*, 1199 *Boulewas*.

Great Bookham (suburban district, Surrey): 'greater homestead where birch trees grow'. OE *bōc*, 'birch', + *hām*, 'homestead'. The first word of the name distinguishes the village from nearby *Little Bookham*. DB *Bocheham*.

Great Bowden (village, Leics): 'greater (place by) Bucge's or Bugga's hill'. OE *dūn*, 'hill'. The first personal name is that of a woman. The first word of the name distinguishes the village from *Little Bowden*, 2 miles to the south, now a suburb of Market Harborough. DB *Bugedone*.

Great Braxted (hamlet, Essex): 'greater place where bracken grows'. OE *bracu*, 'bracken', + *stede*, 'place'. The first word of the name distinguishes the place from *Little Braxted*, 2 miles to the northwest. DB *Brachestedam*.

Great Bricett (village, Suffolk): 'greater (place by the) fold plagued with gadflies'. OE *brīosa*, 'gadfly', + *set*, 'fold' (for animals). The first word

of the name distinguishes the village from nearby *Little Bricett*. DB *Brieseta*.

Great Brickhill (village, Bucks): 'greater (place by) hill'. The first part of the main name represents a Celtic word meaning 'hilltop' related to modern Welsh *brig*, 'top', 'summit'. The second part represents OE *hyll*, 'hill', added when the meaning of the original was lost. The first word of the name distinguishes the village from nearby *Little Brickhill* and *Bow Brickhill* (both Milton K), the latter named after one Bolla, who must have held the manor here. The first word of the second form of the name below is Latin *magna*, 'great'. DB *Brichelle*, 1198 *Magna Brikehille*.

Great Brington (village, Northants): 'greater estate associated with Brȳni'. OE *-ing-*, 'associated with', + *tūn*, 'farmstead', 'estate'. The first word of the name distinguishes the village from nearby *Little Brington*. DB *Brinintone*.

Great Bromley (village, Essex): 'greater woodland clearing where broom grows'. OE *brōm*, 'broom', + *lēah*, 'wood', 'clearing'. The first word of the name distinguishes the village from *Little Bromley*, 2 miles to the north. DB *Brumleiam*.

Great Broughton (village, Cumbria): 'greater farmstead by a brook'. OE *brōc*, 'brook', + *tūn*, 'farmstead'. The first word of the name distinguishes this Broughton from nearby *Little Broughton*. 12C *Broctuna*.

Great Budworth (village, Cheshire): 'greater (place called) Budda's enclosure'. OE *worth*, 'enclosure'. The first word of the name distinguishes this Budworth from *Little Budworth*, 9 miles to the southwest. DB *Budewrde*.

Great Burstead (suburb of Billericay, Essex): 'greater (place on the) site of a stronghold'. OE *burh-stede* (from *burh*, 'fortified place', + *stede*, 'place'). The first word of the name distinguishes this Burstead from nearby *Little Burstead*. *c.*1000 *Burgestede*, DB *Burghesteda*.

Great Busby (village, N Yorks): 'greater (place called) Buski's farmstead'. OS *bý*, 'farmstead', 'village'. The personal name is Scandinavian. The name could also mean 'farmstead among the bushes or shrubs' (OS *buskr*, 'bush', or *buski*, 'shrub', + *bý*). There is no longer an adjoining *Little Busby*. DB *Buschebi*.

Great Canfield (hamlet, Essex): 'greater (place called) Cana's open land'. OE *feld*, 'open land' (modern English *field*). The first word of the name distinguishes this Canfield from nearby *Little Canfield*. DB *Canefelda*.

Great Casterton (village, Rutland): 'greater farmstead by the Roman fort'. OE *cæster*, 'Roman fort', + *tūn*, 'farmstead'. There are remains of a Romano-British settlement here, and Ermine Street crosses the river Gwash at this point. The first word distinguishes this village from nearby *Little Casterton*. DB *Castretone*.

Great Chart (village, Kent): 'greater (place on) rough ground'. OE *cert*, 'rough ground'. The first word of the name distinguishes the village from *Little Chart*, 3 miles to the northwest. The third form of the name below has Latin *magna*, 'great'. 762 *Cert*, DB *Certh*, 13C *Magna Chert*.

Great Chatwell (hamlet, Staffs): 'greater (place called) Ceatta's spring'. OE *wella*, 'spring', 'stream'. There is a spring here called St Chad's well, presumably based on the place name. The first word of the name distinguishes this Chatwell from nearby *Little Chatwell*. 1203 *Chattewell*.

Great Chell. See CHELL HEATH.

Great Chesterford (village, Essex): 'greater (place at the) ford by a Roman fort'. OE *ceaster*, 'Roman fort', + *ford*, 'ford'. The village, on the river Cam, stands on the site of a Roman town. The first word of the name distinguishes it from nearby *Little Chesterford*. 1004 *Ceasterford*, DB *Cestreforda*.

Great Cheverell (village, Wilts): 'greater small piece of common ploughed land'. The basic name is probably of Celtic origin from a word related to modern Welsh *cyfair*, 'acre', the '-ell' representing a diminutive suffix. The present name contrasts with that of nearby *Little Cheverell*. DB *Chevrel*.

Great Chishill (village, Cambs): 'greater (place by the) gravel hill'. OE *cis*, 'gravel', + *hyll*, 'hill'. The first word of the name distinguishes the village from nearby *Little Chishill*. DB *Cishella*.

Great Clacton. See CLACTON-ON-SEA.

Great Coates (village, NE Lincs): 'greater (place with) cottages'. OE *cot*, 'cottage'. The first word of the name distinguishes the village from nearby *Little Coates*, now a district of Grimsby. DB *Cotes*.

Great Comberton (village, Worcs): 'greater estate associated with Cumbra'. OE *-ing-*, 'associated with', + *tūn*, 'farmstead', 'estate'. The first word of the name distinguishes the village from nearby *Little Comberton*. 972 *Cumbrincgtun*, DB *Cumbrintune*.

Great Corby (village, Cumbria): 'greater (place called) Corc's farmstead'. OS *bý*, 'farmstead', 'village'. The personal name is Old Irish. The first word distinguishes this Corby from *Little Corby*, 2 miles to the north. c.1115 *Chorkeby*.

Great Cornard (suburb of Sudbury, Suffolk): 'greater (place on) cultivated land used for corn'. OE *corn*, 'corn', + *erth*, 'cultivated land' (modern English *earth*). The first word of the name distinguishes the place from nearby *Little Cornard*. DB *Cornerda*.

Great Cowden (hamlet, E Yorks): 'greater (place by the) hill where charcoal is made'. OE *col*, 'charcoal', + *dūn*, 'hill'. Woodland was formerly extensive here. The first word of the name distinguishes the place from nearby *Little Cowden*. DB *Coledun*.

Great Coxwell (village, Oxon): 'greater (place called) Cocc's spring'. OE *wella*, 'spring', 'stream'. The first word distinguishes this village from nearby *Little Coxwell*, and there are several springs at both Coxwells. DB *Cocheswelle*.

Great Crakehall (village, N Yorks): 'greater corner of land where crows are seen'. OS *kráka*, 'crow', + OE *halh*, 'nook', 'corner of land'. The first word of the name distinguishes the village from nearby *Little Crakehall*. DB *Crachele*.

Great Cransley (village, Northants): 'greater woodland clearing where cranes are seen'. OE *cran*, 'crane', + *lēah*, 'wood', 'clearing'. The first word of the name distinguishes the village from nearby *Little Cransley*. 956 *Cranslea*, DB *Cranesleia*.

Great Cressingham (village, Norfolk): 'greater homestead of Cressa's people'. OE *-inga-*, 'of the people of', + *hām*, 'homestead'. The main name could also mean 'homestead with cress beds' (OE *cærsing*, 'cress bed'). The first word of the name distinguishes the village from nearby *Little Cressingham*. DB *Cressingaham*.

Great Cumbrae. See CUMBRAE.

Great Dalby (village, Leics): 'greater village in a valley'. OS *dalr*, 'valley', + *bý*, 'farmstead', 'village'. The first word of the name contrasts the village with *Little Dalby*, 2 miles away. DB *Dalbi*.

Great Doddington (village, Northants): 'greater estate associated with Dodda'. OE *-ing-*, 'associated with', + *tūn*, 'farmstead', 'estate'. The first word of the name contrasts this Doddington with *Little Doddington*, now called DENTON, 5 miles to the southwest. DB *Dodintone*, 1290 *Great Dodington*.

Great Driffield. See DRIFFIELD.

Great Dunham (village, Norfolk): 'greater homestead by a hill'. OE *dūn*, 'hill', + *hām*, 'homestead', 'village'. The first word of the name distinguishes this Dunham from nearby *Little Dunham*. DB *Dunham*.

Great Dunmow. See DUNMOW.

Great Durnford (village, Wilts): 'greater (place with a) hidden ford'. OE *dierne*, 'hidden', + *ford*, 'ford'. A 'hidden' ford is one difficult to find, as when overgrown with vegetation. The village is on the river Avon, as is nearby *Little Durnford*. DB *Diarneford*.

Great Easton (village, Essex): 'greater (place with) stones by the island'. OE *ēg*, 'island', + *stān*, 'stone'. The 'island' is well-watered land here by the river Chelmer. The first word of the name distinguishes the village from nearby *Little Easton*. DB *Eistanes*.

Great Edstone (village, N Yorks): 'greater (place called) Ēadin's farmstead'. OE *tūn*, 'farmstead'. The first word of the name distinguishes this Edstone from nearby *Little Edstone*. The DB form of the name below has added OE *micel*, 'great'. DB *Micheledestun*.

Great Ellingham (village, Norfolk): 'greater homestead of Ella's people'. OE *-inga-*, 'of the people of', + *hām*, 'homestead'. The main name could also mean 'homestead at Ella's place' (OE *-ing*, 'place belonging to', + *hām*). The first word of the name distinguishes the village from nearby *Little Ellingham*. The first word of the second form of the name below is Latin *magna*, 'great'. DB *Elingham*, 1242 *Magna Elingham*.

Great Elm (village, Somerset): 'greater (place by the) elm tree'. OE *elm*, 'elm'. The first word of the name distinguishes the village from nearby *Little Elm*. The *T*- in the form of the name below comes from preceding OE *æt*, 'at'. DB *Telma*.

Greater London. See LONDON.

Great Everdon (village, Northants): 'greater (place by the) hill where wild boars are seen'. OE *eofor*, 'boar', + *dūn*, 'hill'. The first word of the name contrasts the village (also known simply as *Everdon*) with nearby *Little Everdon*. 944 *Eferdun*, DB *Everdone*.

Great Eversden (village, Cambs): 'greater (place by the) hill where wild boars are seen'. OE *eofor*, 'boar', + *dūn*, 'hill'. The name could also mean 'Eofor's hill'. The first word of the name distinguishes the village from nearby *Little Eversden*. DB *Euresdone*, 1240 *Everesdon Magna*.

Great Finborough (village, Suffolk): 'greater (place by the) hill where woodpeckers are seen'. OE *fina*, 'woodpecker', + *beorg*, 'mound', 'hill'. The first word of the name distinguishes the village from *Little Finborough*, 2 miles to the south. DB *Fineberga*.

Greatford (village, Lincs): '(place by the) gravelly ford'. OE *grēot*, 'gravel' (modern English *grit*), + *ford*, 'ford'. The gravel is still clearly visible in the river Glen here. DB *Greteford*.

Great Fransham (village, Norfolk): 'greater (place by the) homestead or enclosure'. OE *hām*, 'homestead', or *hamm*, 'enclosure'. The first part of the main name represents a personal name of uncertain form. The first word distinguishes the village from nearby *Little Fransham*. DB *Frandesham*.

Great Gable (mountain, Cumbria): 'great gable'. The earlier name of the mountain was *Mykelgavel* (OS *mikill*, 'great', + *gafl*, 'gable'), and this was subsequently replaced by the English equivalent. The reference is to the mountain's sharp triangular appearance. 1338 *Mykelgavel*, 1783 *Great Gavel*.

Great Gaddesden (village, Herts): 'greater (place called) Gǣte's valley'. OE *denu*, 'valley'. The first word of the name distinguishes this village from nearby *Little Gaddesden*. The common name gave that of the river Gade here. 10C *Gætesdene*, DB *Gatesdene*.

Great Gidding (village, Cambs): 'greater (settlement of) Gydda's people'. OE *-ingas*, 'people of'. The first word of the name distinguishes the village from nearby *Little Gidding* and *Steeple Gidding* (OE *stēpel*, 'steeple', 'tower'). The second form of the name below has Latin *magna*, 'great'. DB *Geddinge*, 1220 *Magna Giddinge*.

Great Givendale (hamlet, E Yorks): 'greater (place in the) valley of the (river) Gevel'. OS *dalr*, 'valley'. The stream here had a name of OS origin meaning 'giver of fish' (i.e. rich in them). The first word of the name distinguishes this place from what is now *Little Givendale Farm* on the opposite side of the valley of Whitekeld Dale. DB *Ghiuedale*.

Great Glemham (village, Suffolk): 'greater homestead where games are held'. OE *glēam*, 'merriment', + *hām*, 'homestead', 'village'. The first word of the name distinguishes the village from *Little Glemham*, 2 miles to the south. DB *Glaimham*.

Great Glen (village, Leics): 'greater (place in the) valley'. OE *glenn*, 'valley'. The first word of the name (Latin *magna*, 'great' in two of the forms below) distinguishes the village from *Glen Parva* (Latin *parva*, 'small'), now a suburb of Leicester. 849 *Glenne*, DB *Glen*, 1247 *Magna Glen*, 1868 *Glenn-Magna*.

Great Gonerby (village, Lincs): 'greater (place called) Gunnfrøthr's farmstead'. OS *bý*, 'farmstead', 'village'. The personal name is Scandinavian. The first word of the name contrasts the village with *Little Gonerby*, today represented by *Little Gonerby Farm*. DB *Gunfordebi*, 1868 *Gonerby Magna*.

Great Gransden (village, Cambs): 'greater (place in) Granta's or Grante's valley'. OE *denu*, 'valley'. The first word of the name distinguishes the village from nearby *Little Gransden*. 973 *Grantandene*, DB *Grantesdene*.

Great Grimsby. See GRIMSBY.

Great Habton (village, N Yorks): 'greater (place called) Habba's farmstead'. OE *tūn*, 'farmstead'. The first word of the name distinguishes the village from nearby *Little Habton*. DB *Habetun*.

Great Hallingbury (village, Essex): 'greater stronghold of Heall's people'. OE *-inga-*, 'of the people of', + *burh*, 'fortified place'. The 'stronghold' would have been the Iron Age hill fort here known as Wallbury Camp. The first word of the name distinguishes the village from nearby *Little Hallingbury*. DB *Hallingeberiam*.

Greatham (village, Hartlepool): 'gravelly homestead or enclosure'. OE *grēot*, 'gravel', + *hām*, 'homestead', or *hamm*, 'enclosure'. 1196 *Gretham*. SO ALSO: *Greatham*, Hants.

Great Hampden (hamlet, Bucks): 'greater (place in a) valley with an enclosure'. OE *hamm*, 'enclosure', + *denu*, 'valley'. The first word of the name contrasts the place with nearby *Little Hampden*. The main name gave that of *Hampden House* here. DB *Hamdena*.

Great Hanwood. See HANWOOD.

Great Harrowden (village, Northants): 'greater (place by the) hill of the heathen temple'. OE *hearg*, 'heathen temple', + *dūn*, 'hill'. The first word of the name distinguishes the village from nearby *Little Harrowden*. DB *Hargedone*.

Great Harwood (town, Lancs): 'greater (place by the) grey wood'. OE *hār*, 'grey', + *wudu*, 'wood'. The main name could also mean 'wood by the rocks' (OE *hær*, 'rock') or 'wood where hares are seen' (OE *hara*, 'hare'). In the form of the name below, the first word, distinguishing the town from nearby *Little Harwood*, derives from Latin *maior*, 'greater'. 1123 *Majori Harewuda*.

Great Haseley (village, Oxon): 'greater (place by the) hazel wood'. OE *hæsel*, 'hazel', + *lēah*, 'wood', 'clearing'. The first word distinguishes the village from nearby *Little Haseley*. 1002 *Hæseleia*, DB *Haselie*.

Great Hatfield (village, E Yorks): 'greater (place on) heathy open land'. OE *hǣth*, 'heath',

+ *feld*, 'open land' (modern English *field*). The first word of the name distinguishes the village from nearby *Little Hatfield*. DB *Haifeld*.

Great Haywood (village, Staffs): 'greater (place by the) enclosed wood'. OE *hæg*, 'enclosure', + *wudu*, 'wood'. The first word of the name distinguishes the village from nearby *Little Haywood*. DB *Haiwode*.

Great Heck (village, N Yorks): 'greater (place with a) gate'. OE *hæcc*, 'hatch', 'gate'. The gate in question was probably on some road here. The first word of the name distinguishes the village from nearby *Little Heck*. 1153 *Hech*.

Great Henny (hamlet, Essex): 'greater (place on a) high island'. OE *hēah*, 'high', + *ēg*, 'island'. Great Henny stands on a hill that slopes down to streams, and this is the 'high island'. The first word of the name distinguishes this hamlet from nearby *Little Henny*. DB *Heni*.

Great Hinton (village, Wilts): 'greater high farmstead'. OE *hēah*, 'high', + *tūn*, 'farmstead'. The first word of the name presumably distinguishes this Hinton from *Hinton Parva* or *Little Hinton*, 27 miles to the northeast, where the name has a different origin (see BROAD HINTON). 1216 *Henton*.

Great Hockham (village, Norfolk): 'greater (place called) Hocca's homestead'. OE *hām*, 'homestead'. The first part of the main name could also represent OE *hocc*, 'hock' (mallow), giving a sense 'homestead where hocks grow'. The first word of the name distinguishes the village from nearby *Little Hockham*. DB *Hocham*.

Great Holland. See HOLLAND-ON-SEA.

Great Horkesley (village, Essex): 'greater (place in a) woodland clearing with a shelter'. OE *horc*, 'shelter', + *lēah*, 'wood', 'clearing'. The first part of the main name could also represent OE *horsc*, 'dirty', 'muddy'. The first word of the name distinguishes the village from nearby *Little Horkesley*. c.1130 *Horchesleia*.

Great Hormead (village, Herts): 'greater (place in the) muddy meadow'. OE *horu*, 'filth', 'mud', + *mǣd*, 'meadow'. The first word of the name distinguishes the village from nearby *Little Hormead*. DB *Horemede*.

Great Horwood (village, Bucks): 'greater (place by the) dirty wood'. OE *horu*, 'filth', 'mud', + *wudu*, 'wood'. The first word of the name distinguishes the village from nearby *Little Horwood*. The DB form of the name below is corrupt. 792 *Horwudu*, DB *Herewode*.

Great Houghton (village, Barnsley): 'greater farmstead in a corner of land'. OE *halh*, 'nook', 'corner of land', + *tūn*, 'farmstead'. The first word of the name distinguishes this Houghton from nearby *Little Houghton*. The second form of the name below has Latin *magna*, 'great'. DB *Haltun*, 1303 *Magna Halghton*.

Great Houghton (suburb of Northampton, Northants): 'greater farmstead by a hill spur'. OE *hōh*, 'hill spur', + *tūn*, 'farmstead'. The first word of the name distinguishes this Houghton from nearby *Little Houghton*. The second form of the name below has Latin *magna*, 'great'. DB *Hohtone*, 1199 *Magna Houtona*.

Great Hucklow (village, Derbys): 'greater (place called) Hucca's hill'. OE *hlāw*, 'mound', 'hill'. The first word of the name contrasts the village with nearby *Little Hucklow*. The second form of the name below has Latin *magna*, 'great'. DB *Hochelai*, 1251 *Magna Hockelawe*.

Great Kelk (hamlet, E Yorks): 'greater (place on) chalky ground'. OE *celce*, 'chalky place'. The 'K-' of the name is due to Scandinavian influence. The first word of the name distinguishes the place from nearby *Little Kelk*. DB *Chelche*.

Great Kimble (village, Bucks): 'greater (place at the) royal bell-shaped hill'. OE *cyne-*, 'royal', + *belle*, 'bell'. The first word of the name contrasts the village with nearby *Little Kimble*. DB *Chenebelle*.

Great Langton (village, N Yorks): 'greater long farmstead'. OE *lang*, 'long', + *tūn*, 'farmstead', 'village'. The first word distinguishes the village from nearby *Little Langton*. DB *Langeton*, 1223 *Great Langeton*.

Great Leighs (village, Essex): 'greater (place in the) woodland clearing'. OE *lēah*, 'wood', 'clearing'. The first word distinguishes the village from nearby *Little Leighs*. DB *Lega*.

Great Limber (village, Lincs): 'greater (place by the) hill where lime trees grow'. OE *lind*, 'lime', + *beorg*, 'hill'. The first word of the name distinguishes the village from nearby *Little Limber*. *c.*1067 *Lindbeorhge*, DB *Lindberge*.

Great Livermere (village, Suffolk): 'greater (place by the) liver-shaped pool'. OE *lifer*, 'liver', + *mere*, 'pool'. The same source could give a meaning 'pool with muddy water' (cp. LIVERPOOL). The first word of the name contrasts the village with nearby *Little Livermere*. *c.*1050 *Leuuremer*, DB *Liuurmera*.

Great Longstone (village, Derbys): 'greater (place by the) hill (called) Lang'. OE *dūn*, 'hill'. *Lang* (OE *lang*, 'long') would have been the name of the ridge here. The first word of the name distinguishes the village from nearby *Little Longstone*. DB *Langesduna*.

Great Lumley (village, Durham): 'greater (place at the) woodland clearing by the pools'. OE *lumm*, 'pool', + *lēah*, 'wood', 'clearing'. The first word of the name distinguishes this Lumley from nearby *Little Lumley*. *c.*1050 *Lummalea*.

Great Malvern. See MALVERN HILLS.

Great Maplestead (village, Essex): 'greater place where maple trees grow'. OE *mapuldor*, 'maple tree', + *stede*, 'place'. The first word of the name distinguishes the village from nearby *Little Maplestead*. 1042 *Mapulderstede*, DB *Mapledestedam*.

Great Massingham (village, Norfolk): 'homestead of Mæssa's people'. OE *-inga-*, 'of the people of', + *hām*, 'homestead'. The first word of the name distinguishes the village from nearby *Little Massingham*. DB *Masingeham*.

Great Melton. See MELTON CONSTABLE.

Great Meols (coastal district of Hoylake, Wirral): 'greater (place with) sandhills'. OS *melr*, 'sandhill'. The first word of the name distinguishes the place from nearby *Little Meols*. Great Meols is now usually known as simply *Meols*, while Little Meols is a northern extension of West Kirby. DB *Melas*.

Great Milton (village, Oxon): 'greater middle farmstead'. OE *middel*, 'middle', + *tūn*, 'farmstead'. The first word of the name distinguishes this Milton from nearby *Little Milton*. DB *Mideltone*.

Great Missenden (town, Bucks): 'greater (place in the) valley where water plants grow'. OE *mysse*, 'water plant' (related modern English *moss*), + *denu*, 'valley'. The name refers to the river *Misbourne*, which rises near here, its own name meaning 'stream where water plants grow' (OE *burna*, 'stream'). The first word of the name distinguishes the town from nearby *Little Missenden*. DB *Missedene*.

Great Mitton (village, Lancs): 'greater farmstead at the confluence'. OE *mȳthe*, 'confluence' (related modern English *mouth*), + *tūn*, 'farmstead'. The confluence referred to is that of the rivers Hodder and Ribble. The first word of the name distinguishes the village from *Little Mitton* to the south, where the confluence is that of the Calder and Ribble. DB *Mitune*.

Great Musgrave (village, Cumbria): 'greater (place by the) grove running with mice'. OE *mūs*, 'mouse', + *grāf*, 'grove', 'copse'. The first word of the name distinguishes the village from nearby *Little Musgrave*. 12C *Musegrave*.

Great Ness. See NESSCLIFF.

Great Oakley (village, Essex): 'greater (place by the) oak wood'. OE *āc*, 'oak', + *lēah*, 'wood', 'clearing'. The first word of the name distinguishes the village from *Little Oakley*, 2 miles away. DB *Accleia*.

Great Offley (village, Herts): 'greater (place called) Offa's woodland clearing'. OE *lēah*, 'wood', 'clearing'. Offa, king of Mercia (d.796), who built OFFA'S DYKE, is said to be buried here. The first word of the name distinguishes the village from nearby *Little Offley*. 944 *Offanlege*, DB *Offelei*.

Great Ormes Head (peninsula, Conwy): 'snake headland'. OS *ormr*, 'snake' (English *worm*), + *hǫfuth*, 'headland'. The 'snake's head' would have been a landmark here for approaching ships. *Great Ormes Head* and *Little Ormes Head* are respectively the larger and smaller headlands west and east of Llandudno. Cp. WORMS HEAD. 15C *Ormeshede insula*.

Great Ormside (hamlet, Cumbria): 'greater (place called) Ormr's headland'. OE *hēafod*, 'headland'. The personal name is Scandinavian. The first word of the name distinguishes the place from nearby *Little Ormside*. *c.*1140 *Ormesheued*.

Great Orton (village, Cumbria): 'greater (place called) Orri's farmstead'. OE *tūn*, 'farmstead'. The personal name is Scandinavian. The first word distinguishes this Orton from nearby *Little Orton*. 1210 *Orreton*.

Great Ouseburn (village, N Yorks): 'greater (place by the) stream that flows into the Ouse'. OE *burna*, 'stream'. Great Ouseburn and *Little Ouseburn* are either side of a stream now called Ouse Gill Beck, but earlier probably *Ouseburn*, which flows into the *Ouse* (see OUSEFLEET). DB *Useburne*.

Great Oxendon (village, Northants): 'greater (place by the) hill where oxen are pastured'. OE *oxa*, 'ox', + *dūn*, 'hill'. The first word distinguishes the village from nearby *Little Oxendon*. 'Oxen-' represents OE *oxna*, the genitive plural form of *oxa*. DB *Oxendone*.

Great Palgrave (hamlet, Norfolk): 'greater (place called) Paga's grove'. OE *grāf*, 'grove'. The corrresponding *Little Palgrave* is now represented by *Little Palgrave Hall* nearby. DB *Pagraua*.

Great Parndon (district of Harlow, Essex): 'greater (place by the) hill where pears grow'. OE *peren*, 'growing with pears', + *dūn*, 'hill'. The first word of the name distinguishes the place from nearby *Little Parndon*. DB *Perenduna*.

Great Paxton (village, Cambs): 'greater (place called) Pæcc's farmstead'. OE *tūn*, 'farmstead'. The first word of the name distinguishes the village from *Little Paxton*, 2 miles to the southwest. DB *Pachstone*.

Great Ponton (village, Lincs): 'greater farmstead by a hill'. OE *pamp*, 'hill', 'mound' (related modern English *pamper*, originally 'to cram with food'). The first word of the name distinguishes the village from *Little Ponton*, 1 mile to the north. DB *Pamptune*.

Great Rissington (village, Glos): 'greater (place by the) hill where brushwood grows'. OE *hrīsen*, 'growing with brushwood', + *dūn*, 'hill'. The first word of the name contrasts the village with *Little Rissington*, 2 miles to the north, and with *Wick Rissington* or *Wyck Rissington* (OE *wīc*, 'building', 'specialized farm'), 7 miles to the north. DB *Risendune*.

Great Rollright. See ROLLRIGHT STONES.

Great Ryburgh (village, Norfolk): 'greater (place at the) old fortification where rye is grown'. OE *ryge*, 'rye', + *burh*, 'fortified place'. The first word of the name distinguishes the village from nearby *Little Ryburgh*. DB *Reieburh*.

Great Ryle (hamlet, Northd): 'greater (place by the) hill where rye is grown'. OE *ryge*, 'rye', + *hyll*, 'hill'. The first word of the name distinguishes the place from nearby *Little Ryle*. 1212 *Rihull*.

Great Saling (village, Essex): 'greater (settlement of the) dwellers among the willow trees'. OE *salh*, 'sallow', 'willow', + *-ingas*, 'dwellers at'. The first word of the name distinguishes the village from nearby *Bardfield Saling* (see GREAT BARDFIELD), which was formerly known as *Little Saling*. DB *Salinges*.

Great Salkeld (village, Cumbria): 'greater (place on the) slope where willows grow'. OE *salh*, 'sallow', 'willow', + *hilde*, 'slope'. The first word of the name distinguishes the village from nearby *Little Salkeld*, across the river Eden. *c.*1110 *Salchild*.

Great Sampford (village, Essex): 'greater (place by the) sandy ford'. OE *sand*, 'sand', + *ford*, 'ford'. The first word of the name distinguishes the village from *Little Sampford*, 2 miles to the southwest. Both are on the river Pant. DB *Sanfort*.

Great Sankey (district, Warrington): 'greater (place on the river) Sankey'. The river name is pre-English and of uncertain meaning. The first word of the name distinguishes the place from nearby *Little Sankey*. *c.*1180 *Sonchi*.

Great Saughall (village, Cheshire): 'greater (place in the) corner of land where willow trees grow'. OE *salh*, 'sallow', 'willow', + *halh*, 'nook', 'corner of land'. The first word of the name distinguishes the village from the hamlet of *Little Saughall* to the southeast. DB *Salhale*.

Great Saxham. See LITTLE SAXHAM.

Great Shefford (village, W Berks): 'greater (place by the) ford used for sheep'. OE *scīep*, 'sheep', + *ford*, 'ford'. The ford was probably near the point where the road from Wantage to Hungerford (the present A338) crosses the river Lambourn here. The first word of the name distinguishes the village, formerly also known as *West Shefford*, from the hamlet of *East Shefford*, further down the river. The first part of the DB form of the name below is corrupt. DB *Siford*, 1167 *Schipforda*.

Great Shelford (suburb of Cambridge, Cambs): 'greater (place by the) ford at a shallow place'. OE *sceldu*, 'shallow place', + *ford*, 'ford'. The river here is the Granta. The first word of the name distinguishes the village from *Little Shelford*, across the river. c.1050 *Scelford*, DB *Escelforde*.

Great Smeaton (village, N Yorks): 'greater farmstead of the smiths'. OE *smith*, 'smith', + *tūn*, 'farmstead'. The first word of the name distinguishes the village from nearby *Little Smeaton*. 966 *Smithatune*, DB *Smidetune*.

Great Snoring (village, Norfolk): 'greater (place of) Snear's people'. OE *-ingas*, 'people of'. The first word of the name distinguishes the village from nearby *Little Snoring*. DB *Snaringes*.

Great Somerford (village, Wilts): 'greater (place by the) ford usable in summer'. OE *sumor*, 'summer', + *ford*, 'ford'. The name implies that the ford over the river Avon here would be unusable in winter as the water would be too deep or the current too rapid. The first word of the name distinguishes the village from nearby *Little Somerford*. 937 *Sumerford*, DB *Sumreford*.

Great Stambridge (village, Essex): 'greater (place with a) stone bridge'. OE *stān*, 'stone', + *brycg*, 'bridge'. The first word of the name distinguishes the village from nearby *Little Stambridge*. DB *Stanbruge*.

Great Staughton (village, Cambs): 'greater farmstead by an outlying hamlet'. OE *stoc*, 'outlying hamlet', + *tūn*, 'farmstead'. The first word of the name distinguishes the village from *Little Staughton*, Beds, 2 miles to the southwest. The DB form of the name below is corrupt. c.1000 *Stoctun*, DB *Tochestone*.

Greatstone-on-Sea (resort town, Kent): '(place of the) big rock by the sea'. The resort takes its name from a former rocky headland here called *Great Stone*. *Littlestone-on-Sea*, to the north, took

its name similarly. (It was laid out as a 'marine town' in 1886 but did not properly develop until the 20C.) Both resorts are recent developments, as is the maritime addition for each.

Great Strickland (village, Cumbria): 'greater (place by) cultivated land where bullocks are kept'. OE *stirc*, 'bullock', + *land*, 'cultivated land'. The first word of the name distinguishes the village from *Little Strickland*, 2 miles to the south. Late 12C *Stircland*.

Great Tew (village, Oxon): 'greater (place by the) ridge'. OE *tīewe*, 'row', 'ridge'. The first word of the name distinguishes the village from nearby *Little Tew* and from *Duns Tew*, 4 miles to the east. All three places lie by a ridge. Duns Tew takes its name from one Dunn, who held the manor early here. 1004 *Tiwan*.

Great Tey. See MARKS TEY.

Great Thurlow (village, Suffolk): 'greater burial mound of the warriors'. OE *thrȳth*, 'troop', 'host', + *hlāw*, 'hill', 'mound'. The first word of the name distinguishes the village from nearby *Little Thurlow*. DB *Tridlauua*.

Great Torrington. See TORRINGTON.

Great Tosson (hamlet, Northd): 'greater (place by the) lookout stone'. OE *tōt*, 'lookout', + *stān*, 'stone'. The stone in question would have been on Tosson Hill here. The first word of the name distinguishes this Tosson from nearby *Little Tosson*. 1205 *Tossan*.

Great Totham (village, Essex): 'greater homestead by the lookout place'. OE *tōt*, 'lookout place', + *hām*, 'homestead'. The lookout place in question was probably nearby Beacon Hill, one of the highest points in the county. The first word of the name distinguishes the village from *Little Totham*, 2 miles to the east. c.950 *Totham*, DB *Totham*.

Great Urswick (village, Cumbria): 'greater dairy farm by the lake where wild cattle graze'. OE *ūr*, 'bison', + *wīc*, 'dwelling', 'specialized farm'. The lake in question is Urswick Tarn here. The first word of the name distinguishes the village from nearby *Little Urswick*. c.1150 *Ursewica*.

Great Wakering (village, Essex): 'greater (settlement of) Wacer's people'. OE *-ingas*, 'people of'. The first word of the name distinguishes the village from nearby *Little Wakering*. DB *Wacheringa*.

Great Waldingfield (village, Suffolk): 'greater (place on) open land of the forest dwellers'. OE *weald*, 'forest' (cp. WEALD), + *-inga-*, 'of the dwellers at', + *feld*, 'open land' (modern English *field*). The first word of the name distinguishes the village from nearby *Little Waldingfield*. *c.*995 *Wealdingafeld*, DB *Waldingefelda*.

Great Walsingham. See WALSINGHAM.

Great Waltham (village, Essex): 'greater homestead in a forest'. OE *weald*, 'forest', + *hām*, 'homestead', 'village'. The first word of the name distinguishes this Waltham from nearby *Little Waltham*. DB *Waltham*.

Great Warley (village, Essex): 'greater wood or clearing by a weir'. OE *wer*, 'weir', + *lēah*, 'wood', 'clearing'. The first part of the name could also represent OE *wǣr*, 'covenant', 'pledge', meaning that the place was subject to such. The first word of the name distinguishes the village from nearby *Little Warley*. *c.*1045 *Werle*, DB *Wareleia*.

Great Washbourne (hamlet, Glos): 'greater (place by the) stream with alluvial land'. OE *wæsce*, 'alluvial land' (related modern English *wash*), + *burna*, 'stream'. The hamlet lies by a meandering stream that joins the Carrant Brook near Beckford. The first word of the name distinguishes this Washbourne from nearby *Little Washbourne*. 780 *Uassanburnan*, DB *Waseborne*.

Great Weldon. See WELDON.

Great Welnetham (hamlet, Suffolk): 'greater enclosure where swans are seen by a circular feature'. OE *hwēol*, 'wheel', + *elfitu*, 'swan', + *hamm*, 'enclosure'. The 'circular feature' is perhaps a waterwheel, and this part of the name distinguishes Welnetham from THELNETHAM, 15 miles to the northeast. The '-n-' of the name arose through a misreading of *u* in the second form of the name below. The first word of the name distinguishes the place from nearby *Little Welnetham*. The DB form of the name below is corrupt. DB *Hvelfiham*, 1170 *Weluetham*.

Great Wenham (village, Suffolk): 'greater homestead or enclosure with pasture'. OE *wynn*, 'pasture', + *hām*, 'homestead', or *hamm*, 'enclosure'. The first word of the name distinguishes the village from nearby *Little Wenham*. DB *Wenham*.

Great Wigborough (village, Essex): 'greater (place by) Wicga's hill'. OE *beorg*, 'hill'. The first word of the name distinguishes the village from nearby *Little Wigborough*. DB *Wicgheberga*.

Great Wilbraham (village, Cambs): 'greater (place called) Wilburh's homestead'. OE *hām*, 'homestead', 'village'. The personal name is that of a woman. The first word of the name distinguishes the village from nearby *Little Wilbraham*. *c.*975 *Wilburgeham*, DB *Wiborgham*.

Great Wishford (village, Wilts): 'greater (place by the) ford where wych elms grow'. OE *wice*, 'wych elm', + *ford*, 'ford'. The river here is the Wylye. The first word of the name distinguishes the village from nearby *Little Wishford*. DB *Wicheford*.

Great Witchingham (hamlet, Norfolk): 'greater homestead of Wic's people'. OE *-inga-*, 'of the people of', + *hām*, 'homestead'. The first word of the name distinguishes the place from nearby *Little Witchingham*. DB *Wicinghaham*.

Great Witcombe (village, Glos): 'greater (place in the) wide valley'. OE *wīd*, 'wide', + *cumb*, 'valley'. The first word of the name distinguishes the village from nearby *Little Witcombe*. 1220 *Wydecomb*.

Great Witley (village, Worcs): 'greater woodland clearing in a bend'. OE *wīht*, 'bend', + *lēah*, 'wood', 'clearing'. The bend would have been in Shrawley Brook here. The first word of the name distinguishes the village from *Little Witley*, 2½ miles downstream. 964 *Wittlæg*, DB *Witlege*.

Great Wolford (village, Warwicks): 'greater place protected against wolves'. OE *wulf*, 'wolf', + *weard*, 'watch', 'protection' (modern English *ward*). The first word of the name distinguishes the village from *Little Wolford*. DB *Wolwarde*.

Greatworth (village, Northants): 'gravelly enclosure'. OE *grēot*, 'gravel' (modern English *grit*), + *worth*, 'enclosure'. The DB form of the name below has *n* for *u*. DB *Grentevorde*, 12C *Gretteworth*.

Great Wratting (village, Suffolk): 'greater place where crosswort grows'. OE *wrætt*, 'crosswort' (a type of bedstraw), + *-ing*, 'place characterized by'. The first word of the name distinguishes the village from *Little Wratting*, to the south, and *West Wratting*, Cambs, 6 miles to the northwest. DB *Wratinga*.

Great Wymondley (village, Herts): 'greater (place called) Wilmund's woodland clearing'. OE *lēah*, 'wood', 'clearing'. The first word of the name distinguishes the village from nearby *Little Wymondley*. 11C *Wilmundeslea*, DB *Wimundeslai*.

Great Wyrley (suburb of Cannock, Staffs): 'greater woodland clearing where bog myrtle grows'. OE *wīr*, 'bog myrtle', + *lēah*, 'wood', 'clearing'. The first word of the name distinguishes this Wyrley from nearby *Little Wyrley*. DB *Wereleia*.

Great Wytheford (hamlet, Shropshire): 'greater (place by the) ford where willow trees grow'. OE *wīthig*, 'willow' (modern English *withy*), + *ford*, 'ford'. The first word of the name distinguishes this place from nearby *Little Wytheford*, across the river Roden. The DB form of the name below is corrupt. DB *Wicford*, 1195 *Widiford*.

Great Yarmouth. See YARMOUTH (Norfolk).

Great Yeldham (village, Essex): 'greater taxable homestead'. OE *gield*, 'tax' (modern English *yield*), + *hām*, 'homestead'. The name implies a homestead liable to pay a certain tax. The first word of the name distinguishes the village from nearby *Little Yeldham*. DB *Geldeham*.

Greenacres (district, Oldham). The suburb developed when an Act of 1870 allowed the enclosure of the common land known as Greenacres Moor here.

Greenford (district, Ealing): '(place at the) green ford'. OE *grēne*, 'green', + *ford*, 'ford'. A 'green ford' is a grassy one, and probably so because less often used than a major crossing. The river here is the Brent. 845 *Grenan forda*, DB *Greneforde*.

Greenham (district of Newbury, W Berks): 'green river meadow'. OE *grēne*, 'green', + *hamm*, 'enclosure', 'river meadow'. Greenham is close to the river Kennet. DB *Greneham*.

Green Hammerton (village, N Yorks): 'farmstead with a smithy and a green'. OE *grēne*, 'village green', + *hamor*, 'hammer smithy', + *tūn*, 'farmstead'. (OE *hamor* also occurred in plant names, such as *hamor-secg*, 'hammer sedge', and this could equally be the sense here.) The first word of the name distinguishes this Hammerton from nearby *Kirk Hammerton* (OS *kirkja*, 'church'). DB *Hambretone*, 1176 *Grenhamerton*.

Greenhaugh (hamlet, Northd): '(place in the) green corner of land'. OE *grēne*, 'green', + *halh*, 'nook', 'corner of land'. 1326 *Le Grenehalgh*.

Greenhead (village, Northd): '(place by the) green hill'. OE *grēne*, 'green', + *hēafod*, 'head', 'hill'. 1290 *Le Greneheued*.

Greenhithe (suburb of Dartford, Kent): 'green landing place'. OE *grēne*, 'green', + *hȳth*, 'landing place'. Greenhithe is on the south bank of the Thames. 1264 *Grenethe*.

Greenhow Hill (village, N Yorks): '(place by the) green hill'. OE *grēne*, 'green', + OS *haugr*, 'hill'. Modern English *hill* is a late addition to the first word, presumably when its sense of 'hill' was lost. 1540 *Grenehoo*, 1701 *Greenhowhill*.

Greenock (town and port, Inverclyde): '(place on the) sunny hillock'. Gaelic *grianag* (from

grian, 'sun'). The town is on hilly ground to the south of the Firth of Clyde. *c*.1395 *Grenok*.

Greenodd (village, Cumbria): '(place on the) green promontory'. OS *grœnn*, 'green', + *oddi*, 'promontory'. The promontory in question is the tongue of land here at the confluence of the rivers Leven and Crake. 1774 *Green Odd*.

Greens Norton (village, Northants): 'Grene's northern farmstead'. OE *north*, 'northern', + *tūn*, 'farmstead', 'village'. The village lies northwest of Towcester. The Grene family held the manor here in the 14C. DB *Nortone*, 1465 *Grenesnorton*.

Greenstead (district of Colchester, Essex): 'green place'. OE *grēne*, 'green', + *stede*, 'place'. A 'green place' is a pasture used for grazing. 10C *Grenstede*, DB *Grensteda*.

Greenwich (borough, Greater London): 'green harbour'. OE *grēne*, 'green', + *wīc*, 'trading settlement', 'harbour'. A 'green harbour' is a grassy one, here by the Thames. 964 *Grenewic*, DB *Grenviz*.

Greete (village, Shropshire): 'gravelly place'. OE *grēote*, 'gravelly place' (from *grēot*, 'gravel', modern English *grit*). 'Soil mostly stiff gravel and strong loam, overlying clay' (*Cassell's Gazetteer of Great Britain and Ireland*, 1896). 1183 *Grete*.

Greetham (village, Lincs): 'homestead on gravelly soil'. OE *grēot*, 'gravel' (modern English *grit*), + *hām*, 'homestead'. DB *Gretham*. SO ALSO: *Greetham*, Rutland.

Greetland (village, Calderdale): '(place on) rocky cultivated land'. OS *grjót*, 'rock', 'boulder', + *land*, 'cultivated land'. The name refers to the steep rocky hillside here above the river Calder. The DB form of the name below has omitted the *t*. DB *Greland*, 13C *Greteland*.

Greinton (village, Somerset): 'Græga's farmstead'. OE *tūn*, 'farmstead'. DB *Graintone*.

Grendon (village, Northants): '(place by the) green hill'. OE *grēne*, 'green', + *dūn*, 'hill'. DB *Grendone*. SO ALSO: *Grendon*, Warwicks.

Grendon Green (hamlet, Herefords): '(place in the) green valley'. OE *grēne*, 'green', + *denu*, 'valley'. Grendon later became associated with its village green. DB *Grenedene*.

Grendon Underwood (village, Bucks): '(place by the) green hill near the wood'. OE *grēne*, 'green', + *dūn*, 'hill'. According to George Lipscomb's *History and Antiquities of the County of Buckingham* (1847), Grendon Underwood 'is supposed [i.e. believed] to derive its name from the verdure of a little hill near the village: and its vicinity to the forest of Bernwood ... and in ancient evidences it is sometimes called "under Bernwood"'. DB *Grennedone*.

Gresffordd. See GRESFORD.

Gresford (town, Wrexham): '(place by the) grassy ford'. OE *græs*, 'grass', + *ford*, 'ford'. A 'grassy ford', here over the river Alun, is one less frequently used than a major crossing. Cp. GREENFORD. The Welsh name of Gresford is *Gresffordd*, a version of the English original. The DB form of the name below has *s* miscopied as *t*. DB *Gretford*, 1273 *Gresford*.

Gresham (village, Norfolk): 'grassy homestead or enclosure'. OE *gærs*, 'grass', + *hām*, 'homestead', or *hamm*, 'enclosure'. DB *Gressam*.

Gressenhall (village, Norfolk): '(place in a) grassy corner of land'. OE *gærsen*, 'growing with grass', + *halh*, 'nook', 'corner of land'. The name could also mean '(place in a) gravelly corner of land' (OE *grēosn*, 'gravel', + *halh*). DB *Gressenhala*.

Gressingham (village, Lancs): 'homestead or enclosure with grazing'. OE *gærsing*, 'grazing', + *hām*, 'homestead', or *hamm*, 'enclosure'. The DB form of the name below has *tūn*, 'farmstead', for *hām* or *hamm*. DB *Ghersinctune*, 1183 *Gersingeham*.

Greta Bridge (village, Durham): '(place by the) bridge over the (river) Greta'. The river's name means 'stony stream' (OS *grjót*, 'gravel', 'stones', + *á*, 'river', 'stream').

Gretna Green (village, Dumfries & Gall): 'green by Gretna'. The nearby village of *Gretna* has a name meaning '(place by the) gravel hill' (OE *grēot*, 'gravel', + *hōh*, 'height', 'hill'). (The '-n-' of the name represents the ending of *grēotan*, the dative form of *grēot*.) 1223 *Gretenho*, *c*.1240 *Gretenhou*, 1576 *Gratnay*.

Gretton (village, Northants): 'gravel farmstead'. OE *grēot*, 'gravel' (modern English *grit*), + *tūn*, 'farmstead'. DB *Gretone*.

Gretton (hamlet, Shropshire): 'farmstead on gravelly ground'. OE *grēoten*, 'gravelly', + *tūn*, 'farmstead'. DB *Grotintune*.

Grewelthorpe (village, N Yorks): 'Gruel's outlying farmstead'. OS *thorp*, 'outlying farmstead'. The Gruel family held the manor early here. DB *Torp*, 1281 *Gruelthorp*.

Greysouthen (village, Cumbria): '(place by) Suthán's rock'. The first part of the name is Celtic in origin, from a word related to modern Welsh *craig*, 'rock', 'crag'. The rest is an Old Irish personal name. *c*.1187 *Craykesuthen*.

Greystoke (village, Cumbria): 'outlying farmstead by the (river) Cray'. OE *stoc*, 'outlying farmstead'. The former river name is of Celtic origin and means 'fresh', 'clean' (modern Welsh *crai*). Alternatively, the first part of the name may mean 'rock' (modern Welsh *craig*). 1167 *Creistoc*.

Griffithstown (district of Pontypool, Torfaen). The name is that of Henry Griffiths, the first stationmaster of Pontypool Road, who founded a new settlement here in *c*.1856 and named it after himself.

Grimley (village, Worcs): 'wood or clearing haunted by a goblin'. OE *grīma*, 'spectre', 'goblin', + *lēah*, 'wood', 'clearing'. 9C *Grimanleage*, DB *Grimanleh*.

Grimoldby (village, Lincs): 'Grimald's farmstead'. OS *bý*, 'farmstead', 'village'. The personal name is Old German. DB *Grimoldbi*.

Grimsargh (village, Lancs): 'Grímr's hill pasture'. OS *erg*, 'shieling', 'hill pasture'. The personal name is Scandinavian. DB *Grimesarge*.

Grimsby (town and port, NE Lincs): 'Grímr's farmstead'. OS *bý*, 'farmstead', 'village'. The OS personal name was popular as *Grim* in Anglo-Scandinavian regions and was a byname of the god Odin (Woden) meaning 'masked person', related to modern English *grimace* and *grim*. The Danes who occupied this part of Britain must have been aware of the association, and the following lines in *The Lay of Havelok the Dane*, the 13C romance from Lincolnshire, make it clear that Grim was popularly seen as the founder of Grimsby: 'And for that Grim that place aute / The stede of Grim the name laute, / So that Grimesbi it calle / That per-offe speken alle; / And so schulen men calle it ay / Bituene this and Domesday.' ('And as Grim had that place, the name "place of Grim" caught on, so that everyone called it Grimsby, and so shall it always be called from now till Doomsday'.) The town is formally *Great Grimsby* for distinction from the hamlet of *Little Grimsby*, 12 miles to the south, and this name was adopted for the local administrative district of the former county of Humberside. DB *Grimesbi*.

Grimscott (hamlet, Cornwall): 'Grim's cottage'. OE *cot*, 'cottage'. The personal name is an English variant of OS Grímr (as for GRIMSBY). 1284 *Grymescote*.

Grimsthorpe (village, Lincs): 'Grímr's outlying farmstead'. OS *thorp*, 'outlying farmstead', 'secondary settlement'. The Scandinavian personal name is as for GRIMSBY. Grimsthorpe was 'outlying' with regard to Edenham. 1212 *Grimestorp*.

Grimston (village, Leics): 'Grímr's farmstead'. OE *tūn*, 'farmstead'. The Scandinavian personal name is as for GRIMSBY. DB *Grimestone*. SO ALSO: *Grimston*, Norfolk.

Grindale (village, E Yorks): '(place in the) green valley'. OE *grēne*, 'green', + *dæl*, 'valley'. DB *Grendele*.

Grindleton (village, Lancs): 'farmstead by the gravelly stream'. OE *grendel*, 'gravelly stream', + *-ing*, 'place associated with', + *tūn*, 'farmstead'. The stream in question would be the one now known as Grindleton Brook. DB *Gretlintone*, 1251 *Grenlington*.

Grindley (hamlet, Staffs): 'green woodland clearing'. OE *grēne*, 'green', + *lēah*, 'wood', 'clearing'. 1251 *Grenleg*.

Grindlow (hamlet, Derbys): '(place on the) green hill'. OE *grēne*, 'green', + *hlāw*, 'hill', 'mound'. 1199 *Grenlawe*.

Grindon (village, Staffs): '(place on the) green hill'. OE *grēne*, 'green', + *dūn*, 'hill'. DB *Grendone*.

Gringley on the Hill (village, Notts): 'woodland clearing of the people living at the green place on the hill'. OE *grēne*, 'green', + *-inga-*, 'of the dwellers at', + *lēah*, 'wood', 'clearing'. The second part of the name distinguishes the village from *Little Gringley*, 7 miles to the south, where the name means 'green woodland clearing' (OE *grēne* + *lēah*). DB *Gringeleia*, 1535 *Grenly of the Hill*.

Grinsdale (village, Cumbria): 'valley by the green promontory'. OE *grēne*, 'green', + *næss*, 'promontory', + OS *dalr*, 'valley'. *c.*1180 *Grennesdale*.

Grinshill (village, Shropshire): '(place by the) hill'. OE *hyll*, 'hill'. The first part of the name is of uncertain origin. It may represent an OE word *grynel*, a derivative of *gryn*, 'noose', 'snare', as a device for trapping animals. The hill in question is probably the one now called Grinshill Hill. The DB form of the name below has *v* for *n*. DB *Grivelesul*, 1242 *Grineleshul*.

Grinton (village, N Yorks): 'green farmstead'. OE *grēne*, 'green', + *tūn*, 'farmstead'. DB *Grinton*.

Gristhorpe (village, N Yorks): 'Gríss's outlying farmstead'. OS *thorp*, 'outlying farmstead'. The personal name is Scandinavian. The name could also mean 'outlying farmstead where young pigs are reared' (OS *gríss*, 'young pig', + *thorp*). DB *Grisetorp*.

Griston (village, Norfolk): 'Gríss's farmstead'. OE *tūn*, 'farmstead'. The personal name is Scandinavian. The first part of the name could also represent OS *gríss*, 'young pig', or OE *gres*, 'grass'. DB *Gristuna*.

Grittenham (hamlet, Wilts): 'gravelly homestead or enclosure'. OE *grīeten*, 'gravelly' (related modern English *grit*), + *hām*, 'homestead', or *hamm*, 'enclosure'. 850 *Gruteham*.

Grittleton (village, Wilts): 'estate associated with Grytel'. OE *-ing-*, 'associated with', + *tūn*, 'farmstead', 'estate'. 940 *Grutelington*, DB *Gretelintone*.

Grizebeck (hamlet, Cumbria): '(place by the) brook where young pigs are kept'. OS *gríss*, 'young pig', + *bekkr*, 'brook'. The hamlet stands on a small stream. 13C *Grisebek*.

Grizedale (hamlet, Cumbria): '(place in the) valley where young pigs are kept'. OS *gríss*, 'young pig', + *dalr*, 'valley'. 1336 *Grysdale*.

Groby (village, Leics): 'farmstead by a hollow'. OS *gróf*, 'pit', 'hollow' (related modern English *grave*), + *bý*, 'farmstead'. The name probably alludes to the small lake here known as Groby Pool. DB *Grobi*.

Gronant (village, Flints): 'gravel brook'. Welsh *gro*, 'gravel', 'shingle', + *nant*, 'stream', 'valley'. DB *Gronant*.

Groombridge (village, E Sussex): 'bridge where young men meet'. ME *grome*, 'young man', 'servant' (modern English *groom*). The bridge over the Medway was probably one where servants met or regularly crossed. 1239 *Gromenebregge*.

Grosmont (village, Mon): '(place by the) big hill'. OF *gros*, 'big', + *mont*, 'hill'. The name refers to nearby Graig Hill, below which lie the ruins of the Norman castle first built by Henry II and rebuilt by Henry III. The Welsh form of the name is *Y Grysmwnt*. 1187 *Grosse Monte*, 1232 *Grosmont*.

Grosmont (village, N Yorks): '(place of the) big hill'. OF *gros*, 'big', + *mont*, 'hill'. The name was originally that of the priory founded here in 1200. It was itself named after its mother priory of Grandmont near Limoges in France. 1228 *Grosmunt*, 1301 *Grauntmount*.

Groton (village, Suffolk): '(place by the) gravelly stream'. OE *groten*, 'gravelly', + *ēa*, 'river', 'stream'. DB *Grotena*.

Grove (village, Oxon): '(place by the) grove'. OE *grāf*, 'grove', 'copse'. 1188 *la Graue*. SO ALSO: *Grove*, Notts.

Grundisburgh (village, Suffolk): 'stronghold by the foundation'. OE *grund*, 'foundation' (modern English *ground*), + *burh*, 'fortified place'. The 'foundation' would have been that of former buildings here. DB *Grundesburch*.

Grysmwnt, Y. See GROSMONT (Mon).

Guestling Green (village, E Sussex): '(settlement of) Gyrstel's people'. OE -*ingas*, 'people of'. The second word of the name, referring to the village green, is a recent addition distinguishing this Guestling from nearby *Guestling Thorn*, so called from a prominent thorn bush. DB *Gestelinges*.

Guestwick (village, Norfolk): 'clearing belonging to Guist'. OS *thveit*, 'clearing'. Guestwick is 4 miles east of GUIST. DB *Geghestueit*.

Guilden Morden (village, Cambs): 'rich (place by the) hill in marshland'. OE *gylden*, 'golden', 'rich', + *mōr*, 'moor', 'marshland', + *dūn*, 'hill'. A 'rich' place is a productive one. Cp. GILMORTON. The first word distinguishes this village from nearby *Steeple Morden*, which was originally called *South Morden* but is now named for its steeple (which fell in a storm of 1703). 1015 *Mordune*, 1204 *Gildene Mordon*.

Guilden Sutton (village, Cheshire): 'rich southern farmstead'. OE *gylden*, 'golden', 'rich', + *sūth*, 'southern', + *tūn*, 'farmstead'. A 'rich' place is a productive one. DB *Sudtone, c.*1200 *Guldenesutton*.

Guildford (city, Surrey): 'ford by the golden one'. OE *gylde*, 'golden one', + *ford*, 'ford'. The 'golden one' would have been the sandy soil to the south of the town, and the ford would have been over the river Wey there, probably at the point where Pilgrims Way joins Shalford Road, and not where Bridge Street crosses the river in central Guildford, where the current would have been too strong. See also HOG'S BACK. *c.*880 *Gyldeforda*, DB *Gildeford*.

Guilsborough (village, Northants): 'Gyldi's stronghold'. OE *burh*, 'fortified place'. The DB form of the name below has garbled the personal name. *c.*1070 *Gildesburh*, DB *Gisleburh*.

Guisborough (town, Redcar & Clev): 'Gígr's stronghold'. OE *burh*, 'fortified place'. The personal name is Scandinavian. DB *Ghigesburg*.

Guiseley (town, Leeds): 'Gīslic's woodland clearing'. OE *lēah*, 'wood', 'clearing'. *c.*972 *Gislicleh*, DB *Gisele*.

Guist (village, Norfolk): 'Gǣga's or Gǣgi's dwelling'. OE *sǣte*, 'house', 'dwelling'. *c.*1035 *Gǣssǣte*, DB *Gegeseta*.

Guiting Power (village, Glos): 'le Poer's (estate by the river) Guiting'. The river here now is the Windrush, but formerly it must have been the *Guiting*, 'running stream' (OE *gyte*, 'flood', + -*ing*, 'stream characterized by'). The manor was held early here by the le Poer family, their name distinguishing the village from *Temple Guiting*,

2 miles to the north, held by the Knights Templars. Cp. TEMPLE BALSALL. 814 *Gythinge*, DB *Getinge*, 1220 *Gettinges Poer*.

Gulval (village, Cornwall): '(church of) St Gulval'. The church here is dedicated to Gulval (probably originally Gwelvel), a saint who is generally believed to be female but about whom nothing is known. 1328 *Sancta Welvela*.

Gumfreston (hamlet, Pemb): 'Gunfrid's farm'. OE *tūn*, 'farmstead'. 1291 *Villa Gunfrid*, 1364 *Gonnfreiston*.

Gumley (village, Leics): 'Godmund's woodland clearing'. OE *lēah*, 'wood', 'clearing'. The personal name has been reduced to a single syllable. 8C *Godmundesleah*, DB *Godmundelai*.

Gunby (hamlet, E Yorks): 'Gunnhildr's farmstead'. OS *bȳ*, 'farmstead', 'village'. The Scandinavian personal name is that of a woman. 1066 *Gunelby*.

Gunnersbury (district, Hounslow): 'Gunnhildr's manor'. ME *bury*, 'manor' (from OE *byrig*, dative of *burh*, 'fortified place'). The Scandinavian personal name is that of a woman. (Local lore identifies her as Gunhilda, niece of King Canute.) 1334 *Gounyldebury*.

Gunnerton (village, Northd): 'Gunnvǫr's farmstead'. OE *tūn*, 'farmstead'. The Scandinavian personal name is that of a woman. 1170 *Gunwarton*.

Gunness (village, N Lincs): 'Gunni's headland'. OS *nes*, 'headland'. The personal name is Scandinavian. The headland in question is a promontory here into the river Trent. 1199 *Gunnesse*.

Gunnislake (village, Cornwall): '(place by) Gunni's stream'. OE *lacu*, 'stream' (related modern English *lake*). The personal name is Scandinavian. 1485 *Gonellake*.

Gunthorpe (village, Notts): 'Gunnhildr's outlying farmstead'. OS *thorp*, 'outlying farmstead'. The Scandinavian personal name is that of a woman. DB *Gulnetorp*.

Gunthorpe (district, Peterborough): 'Gunni's outlying farmstead'. OS *thorp*, 'outlying farmstead'. The personal name is Scandinavian. 1130 *Gunetorp*. SO ALSO: *Gunthorpe*, Norfolk.

Gunwalloe (coastal hamlet, Cornwall): '(church of) St Winwaloe'. The church here is dedicated to Winwaloe, said to have been born in Brittany. 1332 *Sanctus Wynwolaus*.

Gurnard (coastal village, IoW): '(place by the) muddy shore'. OE *gyre*, 'marsh', 'mud', + *ōra*, 'shore'. OE *ōra* can also mean 'flat-topped hill', and the reference could thus be to the hill behind the village. 280 *Gornore*.

Gurnard's Head (headland, Cornwall): 'gurnard's head'. The headland was thought to resemble the head of a gurnard fish. 1748 *Gurnards Head*.

Gussage All Saints (village, Dorset): '(place by the) gushing stream with All Saints church'. OE *gyse*, 'gush of water', + *sīc*, 'stream'. The church dedication distinguishes the village from nearby *Gussage St Andrew* and *Gussage St Michael*. The 'gushing stream' is a tributary of the river Allen. 10C *Gyssic*, DB *Gessic*, 1245 *Gussich All Saints*.

Guston (village, Kent): 'Gūthsige's farmstead'. OE *tūn*, 'farmstead'. DB *Gocistone*.

Guyhirn (village, Cambs): 'guide by the corner of land'. OF *guie*, 'guide', + OE *hyrne*, 'angle'. The reference is to some sort of guiding device to control the flow of the tide from the Wash up the river Wisbech at a critical corner here in the drainage of this part of the fens. 1275 *La Gyerne*.

Guyzance (hamlet, Northd): 'Guines' (estate)'. The Guines family held the manor here in the 13C. 1242 *Gynis*, 1868 *Guyson, or Guyzance*.

Gwalchmai (village, Anglesey): '(place of) Gwalchmai'. The name is that of the Welsh court poet Gwalchmai (*fl.*1130–80), whose own name is said to mean 'May hawk' (Welsh *gwalch*, 'hawk', + *Mai*, 'May'). The first two forms of the name below are prefixed with Welsh *tref*, 'town-ship'. 1291 *Trefwalkemyth*, 1350 *Trefwalghmey*, 1352 *Gwalghmey*.

Gweek (village, Cornwall): 'village'. Cornish *gwig*, 'village'. The name may have evolved as a Cornish form of OE *wīc*, 'hamlet'. 1201 *Wika*.

Gwenfo. See WENVOE.

Gwennap (village, Cornwall): '(place with the church of) St Wynup'. Nothing is known about the female saint to whom the church here is dedicated. 1269 *Sancta Weneppa*.

Gwent (historic county, SE Wales): 'special place'. Celtic *venta*, 'favoured place', 'market'. The name of the ancient kingdom, corresponding approximately in area to modern Monmouthshire (pre-1974), is based on a Celtic word found also for *Blaenau Gwent* (see BLAENAU FFESTINIOG), CAERWENT and WINCHESTER, and for the Welsh name of CHEPSTOW.

Gwinear (village, Cornwall): '(church of) St Winnear'. The church here is dedicated to Winnear, said to have come to Cornwall as the son of a pagan Irish king. 1258 *Sanctus Wynerus*.

Gwithian (village, Cornwall): '(church of) St Gothian'. Nothing is known of the saint to whom the church here is dedicated. 1334 *Sanctus Goythianus*.

Gwynedd (unitary authority, NW Wales): 'territory of Cunedda'. The former ancient kingdom and modern county (pre-1996) derives its name from Cunedda, a 5C ruler in this part of northwest Wales. One of his sons gave the name of Ceredigion.

H

Habberley (village, Shropshire): 'Hēathuburh's or Hēahburh's woodland clearing'. OE *lēah*, 'wood', 'clearing'. The personal names are those of women. 1242 *Habberleg*.

Habrough (village, NE Lincs): 'high stronghold'. OE *hēah*, 'high', 'chief', + *burh*, 'fortified place'. Original OE *hēah* was subsequently replaced by *hár*, the OS equivalent. The village stands on an 'island' of fairly high ground. The DB form of the name below is corrupt. DB *Haburne*, 1202 *Haburg*.

Haccombe (hamlet, Devon): '(place in the) valley with a hatch'. OE *hæcc*, 'hatch', 'fence', + *cumb*, 'valley'. DB *Hacome*, c.1200 *Hakcumbe*.

Hacheston (village, Suffolk): 'Hæcci's farmstead'. OE *tūn*, 'farmstead'. DB *Hacestuna*.

Hackforth (village, N Yorks): '(place at the) ford by a bend'. OE *haca*, 'hook', 'bend', + *ford*, 'ford'. The reference is probably to a bend in the road here. The name could also mean '(place by the) ford with a hatch' (OE *hæcc*, 'hatch', + *ford*), meaning a floodgate or sluice. DB *Acheford*.

Hackleton (village, Northants): 'estate associated with Hæccel'. OE *-ing-*, 'associated with', + *tūn*, 'farmstead', 'estate'. DB *Hachelintone*.

Hackness (village, N Yorks): '(place at the) hook-shaped headland'. OE *haca*, 'hook', + *nose*, 'headland', 'promontory'. The promontory in question is the distinctively shaped ridge that runs northwest from the village. 731 *Hacanos*, DB *Hagenesse*.

Hackney (borough, Greater London): 'Haca's island'. OE *ēg*, 'island'. The 'island' here is dry land among marshes. Hackney Marsh remains as an area of flat meadowland alongside the river Lea to the northeast of Hackney. 1198 *Hackeneia*.

Hackthorn (village, Lincs): '(place by the) hawthorn'. OE *hagu-thorn*, 'hawthorn'. DB *Hagetorne*.

Hackthorpe (village, Cumbria): 'Haki's outlying farmstead'. OS *thorp*, 'outlying farmstead'.

The personal name is Scandinavian. The first part of the name could also represent OS *haki* or OE *haca*, 'hook-shaped promontory'. c.1150 *Hakatorp*.

Haddenham (village, Bucks): 'Hæda's homestead'. OE *hām*, 'homestead', 'village'. The DB form of the name below may have arisen through a mishearing, although the Normans often substituted *r* for an original *n*. Cp. DURHAM. DB *Hedreham*, 1142 *Hedenham*. SO ALSO: *Haddenham*, Cambs.

Haddington (town, E Lothian): 'farmstead associated with Hada'. OE *-ing-*, 'associated with', + *tūn*, 'farmstead'. 1098 *Hadynton*.

Haddiscoe (village, Norfolk): 'Haddr's or Haddi's wood'. OS *skógr*, 'wood'. The personal names are Scandinavian. DB *Hadescou*.

Haddon Hall. See OVER HADDON.

Hadleigh (town, Essex): '(place in the) clearing where heather grows'. OE *hæth*, 'heath', 'heather', + *lēah*, 'wood', 'clearing'. The DB form of the name below is curiously corrupt. c.1000 *Hæthelege*, DB *Leam*.

Hadleigh (town, Suffolk): '(place in the) clearing where heather grows'. OE *hæth*, 'heath', 'heather', + *lēah*, 'wood', 'clearing'. The name has an identical origin to that of HADLEIGH, Essex. c.995 *Hædleage*, DB *Hetlega*.

Hadley (hamlet, Shropshire): '(place in the) clearing where heather grows'. OE *hæth*, 'heather', + *lēah*, 'wood', 'clearing'. DB *Hatlege*.

Hadley Wood (district, Enfield): 'wood by Hadley'. OE *wudu*, 'wood'. *Hadley* is nearby MONKEN HADLEY. 1248 *Hadlegh*.

Hadlow (village, Kent): '(place by the) mound where heather grows'. OE *hæth*, 'heather', + *hlāw*, 'mound', 'hill'. The DB form of the name below has *d* miscopied as *s*. DB *Haslow*, 1235 *Hadlou*.

Hadlow Down (village, E Sussex): 'woodland clearing where heather grows by the hill'. OE *hǣth*, 'heather', + *lēah*, 'wood', 'clearing', + *dūn*, 'hill'. 1254 *Hadleg*, 1333 *Hadledowne*.

Hadnall (village, Shropshire): 'Headda's corner of land'. OE *halh*, 'nook', 'corner of land'. The reference is to the slight valley here. The DB form of the name below has omitted the *n*. DB *Hadehelle*, 1242 *Hadenhale*.

Hadrian's Wall (Roman fortification, Cumbria/Northd). Construction of the wall across northern England was begun in AD 122 during the visit to Britain of the Roman emperor Hadrian (Publius Aelius Hadrianus) as a defence against the unconquered tribes of Caledonia (Scotland). The bridge at the eastern end of the wall also bore his name (see NEWCASTLE UPON TYNE).

Hadstock (village, Essex): 'Hada's outlying farmstead'. OE *stoc*, 'outlying farmstead'. 11C *Hadestoc*.

Hadzor (village, Worcs): 'Headd's ridge'. OE *ofer*, 'ridge'. DB *Hadesore*.

Hafren Forest (forest, Powys): 'forest of the (river) Severn'. The forest is traversed by the infant river SEVERN, whose Welsh name is *Hafren*. (The initial *H*- in this represents an early *S*.)

Haggerston (district, Hackney): 'Hærgod's stone'. OE *stān*, 'stone'. The reference is to a boundary stone. DB *Hergotestone*.

Haggerston (hamlet, Northd): 'Hagard's estate'. OE *tūn*, 'farmstead', 'estate'. The Hagard family held the manor here in the 12C. 1196 *Agardeston*.

Hagley (village, Worcs): 'woodland clearing where hawthorn grows'. OE *hagga*, 'hawthorn', + *lēah*, 'wood', 'clearing'. DB *Hageleia*.

Hagworthingham (village, Lincs): 'homestead of the dwellers at the hawthorn enclosure'. OE *hagga*, 'hawthorn', + *worth*, 'enclosure', + -*inga*-, 'of the dwellers at', + *hām*, 'homestead'. The DB form of the name below is corrupt, probably through a mishearing. DB *Hacberdingeham*, 1198 *Hagwrthingham*.

Haigh (district, Wigan): 'enclosure'. OS *hagi* or OE *haga*, 'enclosure' (related modern English *hedge*). 1194 *Hage*. SO ALSO: *Haigh*, Barnsley.

Haighton Green (hamlet, Lancs): 'farmstead in a corner of land'. OE *halh*, 'nook', 'corner of land', + *tūn*, 'farmstead'. Haighton came to be associated with its village green. DB *Halctun*.

Hailes (hamlet, Glos): '(place on the river) Hailes'. The name may have originally been that of the stream here. It is of Celtic origin and means 'dirty stream'. DB *Heile*, 1114 *Heilis*.

Hailey (village, Oxon): 'clearing where hay is made'. OE *hēg*, 'hay', + *lēah*, 'wood', 'clearing'. 1241 *Haylegh*. SO ALSO: *Hailey*, Herts.

Hailsham (town, E Sussex): 'Hægel's homestead or enclosure'. OE *hām*, 'homestead', or *hamm*, 'enclosure'. The DB form of the name below has corrupted the personal name. DB *Hamelesham*, 1189 *Helesham*.

Hail Weston (village, Cambs): 'western farmstead on the (river) Hail'. OE *west*, 'western', + *tūn*, 'farmstead', 'village'. The first word of the name, a former name of the river Kym here, is of Celtic origin and means 'dirty stream' (modern Welsh *halog*, 'polluted'). 1199 *Heilweston*.

Hainault (district, Redbridge): '(place by the) wood belonging to a religious community'. OE *hīwan*, 'household (of monks)', 'religious community', + *holt*, 'wood'. The first part of the name represents OE *hīgna*, the genitive form of the plural noun *hīwan*. The community in question is that of Barking Abbey, while the woodland is Hainault Forest. The present form of the name arose through a supposed connection with Philippa of Hainault (*c*.1314–69), wife of Edward III, whose father was count of Hainaut (in modern Belgium). 1221 *Hennehout*, 1323 *Hineholt*, 1654 *West Hainault*.

Hainford (village, Norfolk): '(place at the) ford by an enclosure'. OE *hægen*, 'enclosure', + *ford*, 'ford'. The river here is the Bure. DB *Hanforda*, 12C *Heinford*.

Hainton (village, Lincs): 'farmstead in an enclosure'. OE *hægen*, 'enclosure', + *tūn*, 'farmstead'. DB *Haintone*.

Haisthorpe (village, E Yorks): 'Họskuldr's outlying farmstead'. OS *thorp*, 'outlying farmstead'. The personal name is Scandinavian. DB *Ascheltorp*.

Halam (village, Notts): '(place by the) corners of land'. OE *halh*, 'nook', 'corner of land'. The name represents OE *halum*, the dative plural form of *halh*. 958 *Healum*.

Halberton (village, Devon): 'farmstead by a hazel wood'. OE *hæsel*, 'hazel', + *bearu*, 'wood', + *tūn*, 'farmstead'. DB *Halsbretone*.

Hale (village, Halton): '(place in the) corner of land'. OE *halh*, 'nook', 'corner of land'. The particular sense of OE *halh* here is 'raised ground in marshland'. Hale stands on a low ridge by the river Mersey. The form of the name below has *halh* in a plural form. 1094 *Halas*. SO ALSO: *Hale*, Hants.

Hale (town, Trafford): '(place in the) corner of land'. OE *halh*, 'nook', 'corner of land'. The 'corner of land' here is low-lying terrain in a bend of the river Bollin. Cp. HALESOWEN. DB *Hale*.

Hales (village, Norfolk): '(place by the) corners of land'. OE *halh*, 'nook', 'corner of land'. DB *Hals*. SO ALSO: *Hales*, Staffs.

Halesowen (town, Dudley): 'Owen's corners of land'. OE *halh*, 'nook', 'corner of land'. The 'nooks' here are hollows or shallow valleys. A Welsh prince Owen held the manor here in the early 13C. DB *Hala*, 1276 *Hales Ouweyn*.

Halesworth (town, Suffolk): 'Hæle's enclosure'. OE *worth*, 'enclosure'. DB *Healesuurda*.

Halewood (district, Knowsley): '(place by the) wood near Hale'. OE *wudu*, 'wood'. Halewood is near HALE, Halton. *c.*1200 *Halewode*.

Halford (hamlet, Shropshire): '(place by the) ford'. OE *ford*, 'ford'. The first part of the name is of uncertain meaning. It may represent OE *halh*, 'nook', 'corner of land'. The ford in question would have been over the river Onny here. 1155 *Hauerford*, 1221 *Haleford*.

Halford (village, Warwicks): 'ford by a corner of land'. OE *halh*, 'nook', 'corner of land', + *ford*, 'ford'. The ford in question would have been over the river Stour here, perhaps at the point where the ancient bridge crosses the river. 12C *Halchford*, 1868 *Halford, or Halford-Bridge*.

Halifax (town, Calderdale): '(place of) rough grass in a corner of land'. OE *halh*, 'nook', 'corner of land', + *gefeaxe*, 'coarse grass' (from OE *feax*, 'hair', 'tresses'). Two versions of local lore interpret the name as 'holy hair' (OE *hālig*, 'holy'), the first referring to the relic of hair from a murdered virgin, the second to the head of St John the Baptist, said to rest in or beneath the parish church dedicated to him. (The corporate seal of the borough of Halifax perpetuates the latter.) *c.*1095 *Halyfax*.

Hallamshire (historic district, Sheffield): 'district of Hallam'. OE *scīr*, 'district'. The name *Hallam*, surviving in street and school names in Fulwood, west Sheffield, means either '(place at the) corners of land' (OE *halum*, dative plural of *halh*, 'nook', 'corner of land') or '(place at the) rocks' (OE *hallum*, dative plural of *hall*, 'rock'). Cp. KIRK HALLAM. 1161 *Halumsira*.

Hallaton (village, Leics): 'farmstead in a corner of land'. OE *halh*, 'corner of land', 'nook', + *tūn*, 'farmstead'. DB *Alctone*.

Hallatrow (village, Bath & NE Somerset): '(place by the) holy tree'. OE *hālig*, 'holy', + *trēow*, 'tree'. DB *Helgetrev*.

Hall Dunnerdale (hamlet, Cumbria): '(place in the) valley of the (river) Duddon with a manor house'. OS *dalr*, 'valley'. The river name is of uncertain origin. OE *hall*, 'hall', 'manor house', was added to the original valley name. 1293 *Dunerdale*.

Halling (village, Medway): '(settlement of) Heall's people'. OE *-ingas*, 'people of'. 8C *Hallingas*, DB *Hallinges*.

Hallington (hamlet, Northd): '(place in the) holy valley'. OE *hālig*, 'holy', + *denu*, 'valley'. 1247 *Halidene*.

Halloughton (hamlet, Notts): 'farmstead in a corner of land'. OE *halh*, 'nook', 'corner of land', + *tūn*, 'farmstead'. 958 *Healhtune*.

Hallow (village, Worcs): 'enclosures in a corner of land'. OE *halh*, 'nook', 'corner of land', + *haga*, 'enclosure' (related modern English *hedge*). 9C *Halhagan*, DB *Halhegan*.

Hallworthy (hamlet, Cornwall): 'Gorgi's marsh'. Cornish *hal*, 'marsh'. The name has been influenced by English names ending in '-worthy'. 1439 *Halworgy*.

Halnaker (village, W Sussex): 'half an acre'. OE *healf*, 'half', + *æcer*, 'plot of land' (modern English *acre*). This interpretation has met with objections, partly because early forms of the name do not support it, partly because 'half an acre' seems inappropriate for such an important feudal centre. DB *Helnache*, 1105 *Hannac*.

Halsall (village, Lancs): 'Hæle's corner of land'. OE *halh*, 'nook', 'corner of land'. DB *Heleshale*.

Halse (hamlet, Northants): '(place at the) neck of land in the form of a ridge'. OE *hals*, 'neck', + *hōh*, 'hill spur'. The DB form of the name below has omitted the *l*. DB *Hasou*, *c.*1160 *Halsou*.

Halse (village, Somerset): '(place at the) neck of land'. OE *hals*, 'neck'. DB *Halse*.

Halsetown (village, Cornwall). The village was founded in the early 19C by James Halse (1769–1838), MP for St Ives, to provide homes for the local tin-miners. The second form of the name below has probably been influenced by HAYLE, 3 miles to the east. 1839 *Halse Town*, 1868 *Halestown, or Halsetown*.

Halsham (village, E Yorks): 'homestead on the neck of land'. OE *hals*, 'neck', + *hām*, 'homestead'. The 'neck of land' would be the higher ground here on which the church stands between two streams. 1033 *Halsaham*, DB *Halsam*.

Halstead (town, Essex): 'place of shelter'. OE *hald*, 'protection' (related modern English *hold*), + *stede*, 'place'. The name suits the location of Halstead, sheltered by the river Colne on one side and a hill on the other. DB *Haltesteda*. SO ALSO: *Halstead*, Kent, Leics.

Halstock (village, Dorset): 'outlying farmstead belonging to a religious house'. OE *hālig*, 'holy', + *stoc*, 'outlying farmstead'. 998 *Halganstoke*.

Haltemprice (district of Hull, E Yorks): '(place of the) high enterprise'. OF *haut*, 'high', 'noble', + *emprise*, 'enterprise'. The 'high enterprise' or great undertaking was the founding of an Augustinian priory at Cottingham in 1322. A few months later it moved to the present site, then called *Newton*, and took its present name. 1324 *Hautenprise*.

Halton (district of Runcorn, Halton): 'farmstead by a heathery place'. OE *hāthel*, 'heathery place', + *tūn*, 'farmstead'. Halton gave the name of the local unitary authority. DB *Heletune*, 1174 *Hethelton*.

Halton (village, Lancs): 'farmstead in a corner of land'. OE *halh*, 'nook', 'corner of land', + *tūn*, 'farmstead'. DB *Haltune*. SO ALSO: *Halton*, Bucks, Leeds.

Halton (hamlet, Northd): 'farmstead at the lookout hill'. OE *hāw*, 'lookout', + *hyll*, 'hill', + *tūn*, 'farmstead'. Halton lies on the slope of a hill whose top is known as Halton Shields. 1161 *Haulton*.

Halton East (village, N Yorks): 'eastern farmstead in a corner of land'. OE *halh*, 'nook', 'corner of land', + *tūn*, 'farmstead'. The second word of the name distinguishes this Halton from *Halton West*, 13 miles to the west. DB *Haltone*.

Haltwhistle (town, Northd): '(place at the) junction of two streams by a height'. OF *haut*, 'high', + OE *twisla*, 'confluence' (from *twi-*, 'two', the source of modern *twin*). The 'height' is Castle Hill here. Cp. OSWALDTWISTLE. 1240 *Hautwisel*.

Halvergate (village, Norfolk): '(land rated at) half a heriot'. OE *half*, 'half', + *here-geatu*, 'heriot' (from *here*, 'army', + *geatwa*, 'arms', 'trappings'). A heriot was a tribute paid to a lord out of the belongings of a tenant who had died, originally as military equipment that he had been lent in his lifetime. DB *Halfriate*.

Halwell (village, Devon): '(place by the) holy spring'. OE *hālig*, 'holy', + *wella*, 'spring'. The spring in question is just east of the church. 10C *Halganwylle*.

Halwill (village, Devon): '(place by the) holy spring'. OE *hālig*, 'holy', + *wella*, 'spring'. The spring still exists and has a ruined chapel by it. DB *Halgewilla*.

Ham (district, Richmond): 'land in a river bend'. OE *hamm*, 'enclosure', 'land in a river bend'. Ham lies in a great loop of the Thames. *c.*1150 *Hama*.

Ham (village, Wilts): 'enclosure'. OE *hamm*, 'enclosure'. Ham lies under a range of chalk hills, so that the specific application of OE *hamm* here is probably to wet land hemmed in by higher ground. 931 *Hamme*, DB *Hame*.

Hamble (village, Hants): '(place on the river) Hamble'. The river name means 'crooked river' (OE *hamel*, 'broken', 'crooked', + *ēa*, 'river'), perhaps alluding to the big bend at Bursledon. 1165 *Hamele*.

Hambleden (village, Bucks): '(place in the) crooked valley'. OE *hamel*, 'broken', 'crooked', + *denu*, 'valley'. There is a sharp bend in the valley at Fingest. 1015 *Hamelan dene*, DB *Hanbledene*.

Hambledon (village, Hants): '(place by the) crooked hill'. OE *hamel*, 'broken', 'crooked', + *dūn*, 'hill'. The reference may be to nearby Windmill Hill. 956 *Hamelandunæ*, DB *Hamledune*. SO ALSO: *Hambledon*, Surrey.

Hambleton (village, N Yorks): 'farmstead by the crooked hill'. OE *hamel*, 'broken', 'crooked', + *tūn*, 'farmstead'. The 'crooked hill' in question is nearby Hambleton Hough. DB *Hameltun*. SO ALSO: *Hambleton*, Lancs.

Hambleton Hills (hill range, N Yorks): 'hills by Hambleton Hill'. The hills are named from the single *Hambleton Hill*, 'broken hill' (OE *hamel*, 'broken', 'crooked', + *dūn*, 'hill'). *Hambleton* is the name of the local council district.

Hambrook (suburb of Bristol, S Glos): '(place at the) brook by the stone'. OE *hān*, 'stone', + *brōc*, 'brook'. DB *Hanbroc*.

Hamilton (town, S Lanarks): 'farmstead in broken country'. OE *hamel*, 'broken' (cp. HEMEL HEMPSTEAD), + *tūn*, 'farmstead'. The name is sometimes said to have been 'imported' here in the 13C by Sir Walter de Hameldone, from *Hamilton*, Leicester. 1291 *Hamelton*.

Hammersmith (district, Hammersmith & Ful): '(place with a) hammer smithy'. OE *hamor*, 'hammer', + *smiththe*, 'smithy'. A 'hammer smithy' was one with a forge, which would have been welcomed by travellers by horse on this main route out of London. Hammersmith and FULHAM form a single Greater London borough. 1294 *Hamersmythe*.

Hammerwich (village, Staffs): 'building with a smithy'. OE *hamor*, 'hammer', 'smithy', + *wīc*, 'specialized building'. The DB form of the name below has *u* for *a*. DB *Humeruuich*, 1191 *Hamerwich*.

Hammoon (village, Dorset): 'Moion's (estate in a) river bend'. OE *hamm*, 'enclosure', 'river bend'. The village is surrounded on three sides by the river Stour. The Moion family held the manor here in 1086. DB *Hame*, 1280 *Hamme Moun*.

Hampden. See GREAT HAMPDEN.

Hampden Park (district of Eastbourne, E Sussex): 'Hampden's park'. The name is that of Viscount Hampden, Sir Henry Brand (1814–92), Lord Lieutenant of Sussex, whose family owned land here.

Hampnett (village, Glos): 'little high farmstead'. OE *hēah*, 'high', + *tūn*, 'farmstead', + OF diminutive suffix *-ette*. Cp. WESTHAMPNETT. DB *Hantone*, 1213 *Hamtonett*.

Hampole (village, Doncaster): '(place by) Hana's pool'. OE *pōl*, 'pool'. The name could also mean 'pool where cockbirds are seen' (OE *hana*, 'cockbird', + *pōl*). DB *Hanepole*.

Hampreston (village, Dorset): 'riverside land by the priests' farmstead'. OE *hamm*, 'enclosure', 'riverside land', + *prēost*, 'priest', + *tūn*, 'farmstead'. Hampreston is on the river Stour, where lands belonged to the College of Wimborne Minster. DB *Hame*, 1244 *Hamme Preston*.

Hampshire (county, S England): 'district based on Hampton'. OE *scīr*, 'shire', 'district'. *Hampton* was the original name of SOUTHAMPTON. The present name is a contracted form of the equivalent of *Hamptonshire*, while the regular abbreviated form *Hants* comes from the DB form of the name below. Late 9C *Hamtunscir*, DB *Hantescire*.

Hampstead (district, Camden): 'homestead'. OE *hām-stede* (from *hām*, 'homestead', + *stede*, 'place'). A 'homestead' would have been a very small settlement, perhaps even a single farm. 959 *Hemstede*, DB *Hamestede*.

Hampstead Norreys (village, W Berks): 'Norreys' homestead'. OE *hām-stede* (see HAMPSTEAD). The Norreys family bought the manor here in 1448. The earlier form of the name was recently revived. DB *Hanstede*, 1517 *Hampstede Norreys*, 1868 *Hampstead Norris*.

Hampsthwaite (village, N Yorks): 'Hamr's or Hamall's clearing'. OS *thveit*, 'clearing'. The personal names are Scandinavian. *c.*1180 *Hamethwayt*.

Hampton (district, Richmond): 'farmstead in a river bend'. OE *hamm*, 'enclosure', 'land in a river bend', + *tūn*, 'farmstead'. Hampton lies to the west of a great bend in the Thames that encloses Hampton Court Park. DB *Hamntone*.

Hampton (district of Evesham, Worcs): 'high farmstead'. OE *hēah*, 'high', + *tūn*, 'farmstead'. 780 *Heantune*, DB *Hantun*. SO ALSO: *Hampton*, Shropshire.

Hampton Bishop (village, Herefords): 'bishop's farmstead in a river bend'. OE *hamm*, 'enclosure', 'river bend', + *tūn*, 'farmstead'. The village lies between the rivers Wye and Lugg. The manor here was held early by the Bishop of Hereford. DB *Hantune*, 1240 *Homptone*.

Hampton Gay. See HAMPTON POYLE.

Hampton in Arden (village, Solihull): 'high farmstead in Arden'. OE *hēah*, 'high', + *tūn*, 'farmstead'. For the district name, see HENLEY-IN-ARDEN. DB *Hantone*.

Hampton Lovett (village, Worcs): 'Luvet's home farm'. OE *hām-tūn* (from *hām*, 'homestead', + *tūn*, 'farmstead'). The Luvet family held the manor here in the 13C. 716 *Hamtona*, DB *Hamtune*.

Hampton Lucy (village, Warwicks): 'Lucy's farmstead in a river bend'. OE *hamm*, 'enclosure', 'land in a river bend', + *tūn*, 'farmstead'. The village lies in a large bend of the river Avon. The bishops of Worcester held the manor until 1556, when it passed to the Lucy family. 781 *Homtune*, DB *Hantone*, 1270 *Hampton Episcopi*, 1606 *Hampton Lucy*, 1868 *Hampton Lucy, or Bishop's Hampton*.

Hampton Poyle (village, Oxon): 'de la Puile's home farm'. OE *hām-tūn* (from *hām*, 'homestead', + *tūn*, 'farmstead'). The de la Puile family held the manor here in the 13C, their name distinguishing this Hampton from nearby *Hampton Gay*, held by the de Gay family. DB *Hantone*, 1428 *Hampton Poile*.

Hamsey (hamlet, E Sussex): 'de Say's (estate in the) river bend'. OE *hamm*, 'enclosure'. Hamsey is in a wide bend of the river Ouse. The de Say family held land here in the 13C. 961 *Hamme*, DB *Hame*, 1306 *Hammes Say*.

Hamstall Ridware (village, Staffs): '(settlement of the) dwellers at the ford by a homestead'. The second word of the name derives from a Celtic word meaning 'ford' related to modern Welsh *rhyd* followed by OE *-ware*, 'dwellers'. The ford would have been over the river Blyth here. The first word, representing OE *hām-stall*, 'homestead', distinguishes the village from nearby *Pipe Ridware*, where the Pipe family held the manor in the 13C. DB *Rideware*, 1242 *Hamstal Ridewar*.

Hamstead (district of West Bromwich, Sandwell): 'homestead'. OE *hām-stede* (see HAMPSTEAD). 1227 *Hamsted*. SO ALSO: *Hamstead*, IoW.

Hamstead Marshall (village, W Berks): 'Marshal's homestead'. OE *hām-stede* (see HAMP-STEAD). The Marshal family held the manor here in the 13C. DB *Hamestede*, 1284 *Hamsted Marchal*.

Hamsterley (village, Durham): '(place in the) clearing full of corn weevils'. OE *hamstra*, 'corn weevil' (related modern English *hamster*), + *lēah*, 'wood', 'clearing'. *c*.1190 *Hamsteleie*.

Hamstreet (village, Kent): 'enclosure on the street'. OE *hamm*, 'enclosure', + *strǣt*, 'street'. The 'street' is the main road from Canterbury and Ashford to the coast (now the A2070). DB *Hame*, 1254 *Hamme*, 1868 *Ham Street*.

Hamworthy (district, Poole): 'enclosure'. OE *hamm*, 'enclosure', + *worthig*, 'enclosure'. The first 'enclosure' (*hamm*) is probably the peninsula on which Hamworthy lies between Lytchett Bay and Holes Bay, a location 'enclosed' by water. The second 'enclosure' (*worthig*) was added later. 1236 *Hamme*, 1463 *Hamworthy*.

Hanbury (village, Worcs): 'high fortified place'. OE *hēah*, 'high', + *burh*, 'fortified place'. *c*.765 *Heanburh*, DB *Hambyrie*. SO ALSO: *Hanbury*, Staffs.

Hanchurch (hamlet, Staffs): 'high church'. OE *hēah*, 'high', + *cirice*, 'church'. The first part of the name represents OE *hēan*, the dative form of *hēah*. The DB form of the name below is corrupt. DB *Hancese*, 1212 *Hanchurche*.

Handcross (village, W Sussex): '(place by the) hand-like cross'. The name is modern, and may relate either to a cross used as a signpost, showing five routes in the forest radiating like the five fingers on a hand, or to the crossroads itself, where the five routes met. 1617 *Handcrosse*.

Handforth (suburb of Bramhall, Cheshire): '(place by the) ford where cockbirds are seen'. OE *hana*, 'cockbird' (related modern English *hen*), + *ford*, 'ford'. The first part of the name could also represent OE *hān*, 'stone', giving a sense '(place by the) ford with stones', meaning stones acting as markers. 12C *Haneford*.

Handley (village, Cheshire): 'high woodland clearing'. OE *hēah*, 'high', + *lēah*, 'wood', 'clearing'. DB *Hanlei*.

Handsacre (village, Staffs): 'Hand's arable piece of land'. OE *æcer*, 'plot of arable land' (modern English *acre*). The DB form of the name below has omitted the *n* of the personal name. DB *Hadesacre*, 1196 *Handesacra*.

Handsworth (district, Birmingham): 'Hūn's enclosure'. OE *worth*, 'enclosure'. DB *Honesworde*.

Handsworth (district, Sheffield): 'Hand's enclosure'. OE *worth*, 'enclosure'. DB *Handesuuord*.

Hanford (district of Stoke-on-Trent, Stoke): '(place by the) ford where cockbirds are seen'. OE *hana*, 'cockbird' (related modern English *hen*), + *ford*, 'ford'. The name could also mean 'ford by the stones' (OE *hān*, 'stone', + *ford*). Cp. HANFORTH. The river here is the Trent. The DB form of the name below has *e* for *a*. DB *Heneford*, 1212 *Honeford*.

Hanging Heaton. See KIRKHEATON (Kirklees).

Hanging Langford. See STEEPLE LANGFORD.

Hanham (district of Kingswood, S Glos): '(place by the) rocks'. OE *hān*, 'stone', 'rock'. The name represents OE *hānum*, the dative plural form of *hān*. The reference is to the many rocks and old quarries along the rocky gorge of the river Avon nearby. *Hanham Abbots* here is so called as a possession of Keynsham Abbey. DB *Hanun*.

Hankelow (village, Cheshire): 'Haneca's mound'. OE *hlāw*, 'mound', 'tumulus'. The personal name may be that of the man who is buried in the tumulus. 12C *Honcolawe*.

Hankerton (village, Wilts): 'estate associated with Haneca'. OE *-ing-*, 'associated with', + *tūn*, 'farmstead', 'estate'. 680 *Hanekyntone*.

Hanley (town, Stoke): '(place at the) high wood or clearing'. OE *hēah*, 'high', + *lēah*, 'wood', 'clearing'. Hanley is situated on a hill. 1212 *Henle*.

Hanley Castle (village, Worcs): '(place at the) high wood or clearing with a castle'. OE *hēah*, 'high', + *lēah*, 'wood', 'clearing'. The second word of the name refers to the early 13C castle here. DB *Hanlege*.

Hanley Child (hamlet, Worcs): '(estate of the) young monk in the high wood or clearing'. OE *hēah*, 'high', + *lēah*, 'wood', 'clearing', + *cild*, 'child', 'young monk'. The second word of the name distinguishes this Hanley from *Hanley William*, 2 miles to the northeast, where William de la Mare held the manor in 1242. DB *Hanlege*, 1255 *Cheldreshanle*.

Hanley William. See HANLEY CHILD.

Hanlith (hamlet, N Yorks): 'Hagni's or Hogni's hillside'. OS *hlíth*, 'slope', 'hillside'. The personal names are Scandinavian. The hillside in question lies to the east of the river Aire here. The DB form of the name below is garbled. DB *Hangelif*, 12C *Hahgenlid*.

Hannington (village, Northants): 'estate associated with Hana'. OE *-ing-*, 'associated with', + *tūn*, 'farmstead', 'estate'. DB *Hanintone*.

Hannington (village, Swindon): '(place by the) hill where cockbirds are seen'. OE *hana*, 'cockbird' (related modern English *hen*), + *dūn*, 'hill'. The name could also mean '(place by) Hana's hill'. DB *Hanindone*.

Hanslope (village, Milton K): 'Hamma's slippery place'. OE *slæp*, 'slippery place', 'muddy slope'. DB *Hamslape*.

Hanwell (district, Ealing): 'springs where cockbirds are seen'. OE *hana*, 'cockbird' (related modern English *hen*), + *wella*, 'spring', 'stream'. The original springs were probably not far from the river Brent here. 959 *Hanewelle*, DB *Hanewelle*.

Hanwell (village, Oxon): 'Hana's way'. OE *weg*, 'way'. OE *weg* was subsequently replaced by OE *wella*, 'stream', to give the present form of the name. DB *Hanewege*, 1236 *Haneuell*.

Hanwood (village, Shropshire): 'wood where cockbirds are seen'. OE *hana*, 'cockbird' (related modern English *hen*). The first part of the name could also represent OE *hān*, 'rock', 'stone', or the personal name Hana. The village is formally *Great Hanwood*, but is now usually regarded as a single entity with adjoining *Little Hanwood*. DB *Hanewde*.

Hanworth (district, Hounslow): 'Hana's enclosure'. OE *worth*, 'enclosure'. DB *Haneworde*.

Hanworth (village, Norfolk): 'Hagena's enclosure'. OE *worth*, 'enclosure'. DB *Haganaworda*.

Happisburgh (resort village, Norfolk): 'Hæp's stronghold'. OE *burh*, 'fortified place'. The 'fortified place' is said to have been a Roman fort here, but firm archaeological evidence is lacking for this. DB *Hapesburc*.

Hapsford (hamlet, Cheshire): '(place by) Hæp's ford'. OE *ford*, 'ford'. 13C *Happesford*.

Hapton (village, Lancs): 'farmstead by a hill'. OE *hēap*, 'hill' (modern English *heap*), + *tūn*, 'farmstead'. Hapton lies in a valley at the foot of a high hill. 1242 *Apton*.

Hapton (village, Norfolk): 'Habba's farmstead'. OE *tūn*, 'farmstead'. DB *Habetuna*.

Harberton (village, Devon): 'farmstead on the (river) Harbourne'. OE *tūn*, 'farmstead'. The river name means 'pleasant stream' (OE *hēore*, 'gentle', 'pleasant', + *burna*, 'stream'). 1108 *Herburnaton*.

Harbledown (district of Canterbury, Kent): 'Herebeald's hill'. OE *dūn*, 'hill'. 1175 *Herebolddune*.

Harborne (district, Birmingham): '(place by the) muddy stream'. OE *horu*, 'dirt', 'filth', + *burna*, 'stream'. The stream in question is Stonehouse Brook. DB *Horeborne*.

Harborough. See MARKET HARBOROUGH.

Harborough Magna (village, Warwicks): 'greater (place by the) hill of the herds'. OE *heord*, 'herd', 'flock', + *beorg*, 'hill', + Latin *magna*, 'great'. As explained by William Dugdale, in *The Antiquities of Warwickshire* (1656): 'The name at first arose, partly from the situation, and partly from the herds of cattell there kept'. The second word distinguishes the village from nearby *Harborough Parva* (Latin *parva*, 'small'). DB *Herdeberge*, 1498 *Hardeburgh Magna*.

Harbottle (village, Northd): 'dwelling of the hireling'. OE *hўra*, 'hireling', + *bōthl*, 'special building', 'dwelling'. c.1220 *Hirbotle*.

Harbury (village, Warwicks): 'Hereburh's stronghold'. OE *burh*, 'fortified place', 'manor house'. The personal name is that of a woman. There is no trace of any stronghold here now. 1002 *Hereburgebyrig*, DB *Erburgeberie*.

Harby (village, Leics): 'farmstead with a herd'. OS *hjorth*, 'herd', 'flock', + *bý*, 'farmstead'. DB *Herdebi*. SO ALSO: *Harby*, Notts.

Harden (village, Bradford): '(place in the) valley of rocks'. OE *hær*, 'rock', 'heap of stones', + *denu*, 'valley'. The name could also mean '(place in the) valley where hares are seen' (OE *hara*, 'hare', + *denu*). late 12C *Hareden*.

Hardham (hamlet, W Sussex): 'Heregyth's homestead or river meadow'. OE *hām*, 'homestead', or *hamm*, 'river meadow'. Hardham is situated at the junction of the rivers Rother and Arun. The personal name is that of a woman. DB *Heriedeham*.

Hardingham (village, Norfolk): 'homestead of Hearda's people'. OE *-inga-*, 'of the people of', + *hām*, 'homestead'. 1161 *Hardingeham*.

Hardingstone (district of Northampton, Northants): '(place by) Hearding's thorn bush'. OE *thorn*, 'thorn bush'. DB *Hardingestone*, 12C *Hardingesthorn*.

Hardington (village, Somerset): 'estate associated with Hearda'. OE *-ing-*, 'associated with', + *tūn*, 'farmstead', 'estate'. DB *Hardintone*.

Hardington Mandeville (village, Somerset): 'de Mandeville's (estate at the) estate associated with Hearda'. OE *-ing-*, 'associated with', + *tūn*, 'farmstead', 'estate'. The de Mandeville family held the manor here from the 12C. DB *Hardintone*.

Hardley Street (hamlet, Norfolk): 'hard clearing'. OE *heard*, 'hard', + *lēah*, 'wood', 'clearing'. The second word of the name amounts to 'hamlet' (on a road here). DB *Hardale*.

Hardwick (village, Northants): 'herd farm'. OE *heorde-wīc* (from *heord*, 'herd', + *wīc*, 'specialized farm'). A 'herd farm' was one devoted to livestock, as distinct from a 'barley farm' (see BERWICK-UPON-TWEED), devoted to arable farming. *c.*1067 *Heordewican*, DB *Herdewiche*. SO ALSO: *Hardwick*, Bucks, Cambs, Norfolk, Oxon (near Bicester, near Witney).

Hardwicke (village, Glos): 'herd farm'. OE *heorde-wīc* (see HARDWICK). The form of the name below relates to Hardwicke near Gloucester, but Hardwicke near Cheltenham has a name of identical origin. 12C *Herdewike*.

Harefield (district, Hillingdon): 'open land used by an army'. OE *here*, 'army', + *feld*, 'open land' (modern English *field*). The reference would be to a Viking army, although the role of their 'open land' here is uncertain. The DB form of the name below has *l* for *d*. DB *Herefelle*, 1206 *Herefeld*.

Haresfield (village, Glos): 'Hersa's open land'. OE *feld*, 'open land' (modern English *field*). DB *Hersefel*, 1213 *Hersefeld*.

Harewood (village, Leeds): 'wood where hares are seen'. OE *hara*, 'hare', + *wudu*, 'wood'. The name could also mean 'grey wood' (OE *hār*, 'grey') or 'wood by the rocks' (OE *hær*, 'rock', 'heap of stones'). 10C *Harawuda*, DB *Hareuuode*.

Harford (village, Devon): '(place by the) army ford'. OE *here-ford* (see HEREFORD). The river here is the Erme. DB *Hereford*.

Hargrave (village, Cheshire): '(place by the) boundary wood'. OE *hār*, 'boundary', + *grǣfe*, 'grove', 'wood'. The boundary was that between the hundreds of Broxton and Eddisbury. 1285 *Haregreve*.

Hargrave (village, Northants): '(place by the) boundary wood'. OE *hār*, 'boundary', + *grǣfe*, 'grove', 'wood'. The village is in the east of the county close to the boundary between Bedfordshire and (formerly) Huntingdonshire. DB *Haregrave*.

Hargrave (hamlet, Wirral): '(place by the) boundary wood'. OE *hār*, 'boundary', + *grǣfe*, 'grove', 'wood'. The wood probably marked the border of English territory here on the Wirral peninsula, as distinct from nearby RABY, at the limit of Scandinavian settlement. Hargrave is now represented on the map by *Hargrave Hall Farm* and *Hargrave House Farm*. DB *Haregrave*.

Haringey. See HORNSEY.

Harkstead (village, Suffolk): 'Hereca's pasture'. OE *stede*, 'pasture', 'place'. DB *Herchesteda*.

Harlaston (village, Staffs): 'Heorulwulf's farmstead'. OE *tūn*, 'farmstead'. 1002 *Heorelfestun*, DB *Horulvestone*.

Harlaxton (village, Lincs): 'Herelāf's or Heorulāf's farmstead'. OE *tūn*, 'farmstead'. The personal name may have originally been Scandinavian Hiǫrleifr. DB *Herlavestune*.

Harlech (coastal town, Gwynedd): '(place at the) fine rock'. Welsh *hardd*, 'fine', 'fair', + *llech*, 'rock', 'slab'. The name refers to the site of Harlech Castle, built in the 13C on the prominent crag here. The form of the name below is an anglicized approximation of the Welsh words. *c.*1290 *Hardelagh*.

Harlesden (district, Brent): 'Heoruwulf's or Herewulf's farmstead'. OE *tūn*, 'farmstead'. The original '-ton' of the name became '-den' under the influence of nearby NEASDEN and WILLESDEN. DB *Herulvestune*, 1195 *Herleston*, 1291 *Herlesdon*.

Harleston (town, Norfolk): 'Heoruwulf's or Herewulf's farmstead'. OE *tūn*, 'farmstead'. DB *Heroluestuna*. SO ALSO: *Harleston*, Devon, Suffolk.

Harley (village, Shropshire): 'rock wood or clearing'. OE *hær*, 'rock', + *lēah*, 'wood', 'clearing'. DB *Harlege*, *c.*1090 *Herleia*.

Harlington (district, Hillingdon): 'estate associated with Hygerēd'. OE *-ing-*, 'associated with', + *tūn*, 'farmstead', 'estate'. The original *d* of the personal name has been replaced by *l*. 831 *Hygereding tun*, DB *Herdintone*.

Harlow (town, Essex): 'mound associated with an army'. OE *here*, 'army', + *hlāw*, 'mound', 'hill'. The mound, serving both as an administrative centre and as a meeting place, was that of a Roman temple, now in Old Harlow just west of Harlow Mill railway station. The army was probably a Viking one. 1045 *Herlawe*, DB *Herlaua*.

Harlow Hill (hamlet, Northd): 'mound associated with an army'. OE *here*, 'army', + *hlāw*, 'mount', 'hill'. Cp. HARLOW. 1242 *Hirlawe*.

Harlthorpe (hamlet, E Yorks): 'Herleifr's or Herlaugr's outlying farmstead'. OS *thorp*, 'outlying farmstead'. The personal names are Scandinavian. 1150 *Herlesthorpia*.

Harlton (village, Cambs): 'Herela's farmstead'. OE *tūn*, 'farmstead'. DB *Herletone*.

Harmby (village, N Yorks): 'Hjarni's farmstead'. OS *bý*, 'farmstead', 'village'. The personal name is Scandinavian. DB *Hernebi*.

Harmondsworth (district, Hillingdon): 'Heremund's or Heremōd's enclosure'. OE *worth*, 'enclosure'. The name was formerly pronounced 'Harmsworth' and gave the present surname so spelt. DB *Hermodeswode*.

Harnhill (hamlet, Glos): '(place on the) grey hill'. OE *hār*, 'grey', + *hyll*, 'hill'. The name could also mean '(place on the) hill where hares are seen' (OE *hara*, 'hare', + *hyll*). The first part of the name would thus represent either OE *hāran*, the dative form of *hār*, or *harena*, the genitive plural form of *hara*. DB *Harehille*.

Harold Hill (district, Havering): '(place at the) hill by Harold Wood'. The district lies on rising ground immediately north of HAROLD WOOD. 1883 *Haroldshill Farm*.

Haroldston West (hamlet, Pemb): 'western (place called) Harold's farm'. OE *tūn*, 'farmstead'. The Harold family were here in the 13C, their name distinguishing this place from nearby *Haroldston St Issells*, with a church dedicated to the 6C Welsh bishop Ismael, also commemorated at ST ISHMAEL'S. 1307 *Harauldyston*.

Harold Wood (district, Havering): 'Harold's wood'. The name is that of King Harold, killed in the Battle of Hastings (1066), who held the nearby manor of Havering. *c.*1237 *Horalds Wood*.

Harome (village, N Yorks): '(place by the) rocks'. OE *hær*, 'stone', 'rock'. The name represents OE *harum*, the dative plural form of *hær*. DB *Harum*.

Harpenden (town, Herts): 'valley of the military road'. OE *here-pæth* (from *here*, 'army', + *pæth*, 'path'), + *denu*, 'valley'. Watling Street runs south of here to St Albans, and could have been used by both Anglo-Saxon and Danish armies following its exploitation by the Romans. The town's name was formerly explained as 'valley of the harp' (OE *hearpe*, 'harp'), but it is hard to rationalize such a sense. *c.*1060 *Herpedene*.

Harpford (village, Devon): '(place by the) ford on a main road'. OE *here-pæth* (see HARPENDEN), + *ford*, 'ford'. The reference is probably to the old road that crossed the river Otter just north of the Exeter to Lyme Regis road (the present A3052). 1167 *Harpeford*.

Harpham (village, E Yorks): 'homestead where the harp is played'. OE *hearpe*, 'harp', + *hām*, 'homestead'. The same OE words could also give a meaning 'homestead with a salt sieve' referring to a harp-like sieve for making salt, although modern *harp* in this sense is recorded by the *Oxford English Dictionary* only from the 18C. The DB form of the name below is corrupt. DB *Arpen*, 1100 *Harpam*.

Harpley (village, Norfolk): '(place by the) harp-shaped clearing'. OE *hearpe*, 'harp', + *lēah*, 'wood', 'clearing'. DB *Herpelai*. SO ALSO: *Harpley*, Worcs.

Harpole (village, Northants): '(place by the) muddy pool'. OE *horu*, 'dirt', 'filth', + *pōl*, 'pool'.

The pool in question may have been the one converted into an ornamental pond at Harpole Hall here. DB *Horpol*.

Harpsden (hamlet, Oxon): '(place in the) harp-shaped valley'. OE *hearpe*, 'harp', + *denu*, 'valley'. The valley here is hardly harp-shaped, and the first part of the name may instead represent a shortened form of OE *here-pæth*, 'highway' (literally 'army road', as for HARPENDEN). DB *Harpendene*.

Harpswell (village, Lincs): '(place by the) spring of the harper'. OE *hearpere*, 'harper', + *wella*, 'spring', 'stream'. The first part of the name could also represent a contracted form of OE *here-pæth*, 'highway' (literally 'army road', as for HARPENDEN), giving a sense 'spring of the highway'. DB *Herpeswelle*.

Harpurhey (district, Manchester): 'Harpour's enclosure'. OE *hæg*, 'enclosure' (related modern English *hedge*). Harpour is the surname of the 14C landowner here. 1320 *Harpourhey*.

Harrietsham (village, Kent): 'Heregeard's river meadow'. OE *hamm*, 'enclosure', 'river meadow'. Harrietsham is on the river Len. The first part of the name could also represent OE *here-geard*, 'army quarters' (*here*, 'army', + *geard*, 'enclosure', 'quarters'). 10C *Herigeardes hamm*, DB *Hariardesham*.

Harringay. See HORNSEY.

Harrington (coastal district of Workington, Cumbria): 'estate associated with Hæfer'. OE *-ing-*, 'associated with', + *tūn*, 'farmstead', 'estate'. *c.*1160 *Haueringtona*.

Harrington (village, Lincs): 'Hæring's farmstead'. OE *tūn*, 'farmstead'. The first part of the name could also represent OE *hæring*, 'stony place', or OE *hāring*, 'grey wood'. 12C *Haringtona*.

Harrington (village, Northants): 'estate associated with Heathuhere'. OE *-ing-*, 'associated with', + *tūn*, 'farmstead', 'estate'. The DB form of the name below has garbled the personal name. DB *Arintone*, 1184 *Hederingeton*.

Harringworth (village, Northants): 'enclosure of the dwellers at a stony place'. OE *hær*, 'rock', 'heap of stones', + *-inga-*, 'of the dwellers at', + *worth*, 'enclosure'. *c.*1060 *Haringwrth*, DB *Haringeworde*.

Harris (island region, W Isles): 'higher (island)'. Gaelic *na-h-earaidh*, 'that which is higher'. Harris is more mountainous than neighbouring Lewis. *c.*1500 *Heradh*, 1542 *Harrige*, 1588 *Harreis*.

Harrogate (town, N Yorks): '(place at the) road to the cairn'. OS *hǫrgr*, 'cairn', 'heap of stones', + *gata*, 'road', 'way'. OS *gata* also meant 'right of pasturage', and the name might more precisely thus mean 'pastureland by the cairn'. The whereabouts of the cairn in question is not known. The present town arose following William Slingsby's discovery of medicinal springs here in c.1571, and in consequence Harrogate was frequently called *Spaws*, from *Spa*, the Belgian resort with similar springs. 1332 *Harwegate*.

Harrold (village, Beds): 'high forestland by the boundary'. OE *hār*, 'boundary', + *weald*, 'high forestland' (cp. WEALD). The 'high forestland' is the high ground that rises up from the Ouse valley here, while the boundary is the point where Bedfordshire, Northamptonshire and Buckinghamshire meet, just southwest of Harrold. The second part of the DB form of the name below is corrupt. DB *Hareuuelle*, 1163 *Harewolda*.

Harrow (borough, Greater London): 'heathen shrine'. OE *hearg*. The implication is that there was a heathen shrine on the site of the present St Mary's Church, on the summit of Harrow-on-the-Hill, as Harrow is also known. 825 *Hearge*, DB *Herges*.

Harrowbarrow (village, Cornwall): (place by the) boundary wood'. OE *hār*, 'boundary', + *bearu*, 'grove', 'wood'. The name could also mean '(place by the) grey wood', from identical OE words, but the village is on the parish boundary, so the first meaning is more likely. c.1286 *Harebere*.

Harrow Weald (district, Harrow): 'woodland at Harrow'. OE *weald*, 'woodland' (cp. WEALD). See HARROW. 1282 *Wealde*, 1388 *Harewewelde*.

Harston (village, Cambs): 'Herel's farmstead'. OE *tūn*, 'farmstead'. DB *Herlestone*.

Harston (village, Leics): '(place by the) boundary stone'. OE *hār*, 'boundary', + *stān*, 'stone'. The village lies near the border with Lincolnshire. DB *Herstan*.

Hart (council district, Hants): '(district of the river) Hart'. The river takes its name either from HARTLEY WINTNEY or from the nearby hamlet of *Hartfordbridge*, 'bridge at the ford where stags are seen' (OE *heorot*, 'hart', 'stag', + *ford*, 'ford', + *brycg*, 'bridge').

Hart (village, Hartlepool): 'island where stags are seen'. OE *heorot*, 'hart', 'stag', + *ēg*, 'island'. The 'island' is the peninsula to the southeast on which HARTLEPOOL stands. 8C *Heruteu*.

Hartburn (district of Stockton-on-Tees, Stockton): '(place by the) stream where stags are seen'. OE *heorot*, 'hart', 'stag', + *burna*, 'stream'. The stream in question is Hartburn Beck. Hartburn is also known as *East Hartburn*. c.1190 *Herteburna*.

Hartest (village, Suffolk): '(place by the) wooded hill where stags are seen'. OE *heorot*, 'hart', 'stag', + *hyrst*, 'wooded hill'. c.1050 *Hertest*, DB *Herterst*.

Hartfield (village, E Sussex): 'open land where stags are seen'. OE *heorot*, 'hart', 'stag', + *feld*, 'open land' (modern English *field*). The DB form of the name below has omitted the final *d*. DB *Hertevel*, 12C *Hertefeld*.

Hartford (suburb of Northwich, Cheshire): '(place by the) ford where stags are seen'. OE *heorot*, 'hart', 'stag', + *ford*, 'ford'. Cp. HERTFORD. The river here is the Weaver. The DB form of the name below has omitted the *t* of *heorot*. DB *Herford*, late 12C *Hartford*.

Hartfordbridge. See HART (Hants).

Harthill (village, Cheshire): 'hill where stags are seen'. OE *heorot*, 'hart', 'stag', + *hyll*, 'hill'. 1259 *Herthil*. SO ALSO: *Harthill*, Rotherham.

Harting. See SOUTH HARTING.

Hartington (village, Derbys): '(place by the) hill where stags are seen'. OE *heorot*, 'hart', 'stag', + *dūn*, 'hill'. DB *Hortedun*.

Hartland Point (headland, Devon): 'farmstead on the headland where stags are seen'. OE *heorot*, 'hart', 'stag', + *īeg*, 'island', 'headland', + *tūn*, 'farmstead'. The second word of the name was added when the 'headland' part of the original had disappeared, while OE *tūn* was early replaced by *land*. c.880 *Heortigtun*, DB *Heritona*, 1130 *Hertilanda*.

Hartlebury (village, Worcs): 'Heortla's stronghold'. OE *burh*, 'fortified place'. 817 *Heortlabyrig*, DB *Huerteberie*.

Hartlepool (town and port, Hartlepool): 'pool by the peninsula where stags are seen'. OE *heorot*, 'hart', 'stag', + *ēg*, 'island', 'peninsula', + *pōl*, 'pool'. The peninsula in question is the low, rocky one on which the old town now stands, as distinct from the more modern West Hartlepool. The '-le-' of the name may have evolved by association with the OF *le* of such names as CHESTER-LE-STREET or HETTON-LE-HOLE, so that Hartlepool was understood as 'Hart-le-Pool'. c.1170 *Herterpol*.

Hartley (village, Cumbria): '(place by the) hard ridge'. OE *heard*, 'hard', + *clā*, 'claw'. The name implies a ridge of land that is hard to till, here the curving ridge between the river Eden and Hartley Beck. 1176 *Harteclo*.

Hartley (village, Kent): '(place by the) wood where stags are seen'. OE *heorot*, 'hart', 'stag', + *lēah*, 'wood', 'clearing'. The form of the name below applies to Hartley near Cranbrook, but

Hartley near Longfield has a name of identical origin. 843 *Heoratleag*.

Hartley (coastal village, Northd): '(place by the) hill where stags are seen'. OE *heorot*, 'hart', 'stag', + *hlāw*, 'mound', 'hill'. 1167 *Hertelawa*.

Hartley Wespall (village, Hants): 'Waspail's (estate) by the wood where stags are seen'. OE *heorot*, 'hart', 'stag', + *lēah*, 'wood', 'clearing'. The Waspail family held the manor here in the 13C, their name distinguishing this Hartley from HARTLEY WINTNEY, 4 miles to the east. DB *Harlei*, *c.*1270 *Hertlegh Waspayl*.

Hartley Wintney (village, Hants): 'wood where stags are seen belonging to Wintney'. OE *heorot*, 'stag', 'hart', + *lēah*, 'wood', 'clearing'. The manor here was held by the Prioress of Wintney ('Winta's island', from OE *ēg*, 'island', 'raised land in marsh') in the 13C, its name distinguishing this Hartley from HARTLEY WESPALL, 4 miles to the west. 1218 *Hertlega*, 13C *Hertleye Wynteneye*.

Hartlip (village, Kent): 'leaping place for harts'. OE *heorot*, 'hart', + *hlīep*, 'leap'. The name implies the presence of a gate or fence that harts could leap here. 11C *Heordlyp*.

Harton (village, N Yorks): 'farmstead by the rocks'. OE *hær*, 'rock', 'stone', + *tūn*, 'farmstead'. DB *Heretune*.

Harton (district of South Shields, S Tyneside): '(place by the) hill where stags are seen'. OE *heorot*, 'hart', 'stag', + *dūn*, 'hill'. 1104 *Heortedun*.

Hartpury (village, Glos): '(place by the) pear tree with hard fruit'. OE *heard*, 'hard', + *pirige*, 'pear tree'. 12C *Hardepiry*.

Hartshill (suburb of Nuneaton, Warwicks): '(place by) Heardrēd's hill'. OE *hyll*, 'hill'. The DB form of the name below has garbled the personal name. DB *Ardreshille*, 1151 *Hardredeshella*.

Hartshorne (village, Derbys): '(place by the) hart's horn'. OE *heorot*, 'hart', 'stag', + *horn*, 'horn'. The reference is to nearby Horn Hill, said to resemble a hart's horn. DB *Heorteshorne*.

Hartwell (village, Northants): '(place by the) stream where harts are seen'. OE *heorot*, 'hart', 'stag', + *wella*, 'spring', 'stream'. DB *Hertewelle*.

Harty, Isle of (district of Isle of Sheppey, Kent): 'stag island'. OE *heorot*, 'hart', 'stag', + *ēg*, 'island'. The Isle of Harty is separated from the Isle of Sheppey by the Capel Fleet, but was formerly part of it. DB *Hertei*, *c.*1100 *Heortege*.

Harvington (village, Worcs): 'farmstead by the army ford'. OE *here-ford*, 'army ford' (see HEREFORD), + *tūn*, 'farmstead'. The ford in question would have been over the Avon, to the east of the village. 709 *Herverton*, DB *Herferthun*.

Harwell (village, Oxon): '(place by the) stream by Hara'. OE *wella*, 'spring', 'stream'. *Hara* is the name of a hill meaning 'grey one' (OE *hār*, 'grey', modern English *hoar*). 956 *Haranwylle*, DB *Harvvelle*.

Harwich (town and port, Essex): '(place of the) army camp'. OE *here-wīc* (from *here*, 'army', + *wīc*, 'settlement'). There was a Danish military camp here in the 9C. 1248 *Herewic*.

Harwood Dale (village, N Yorks): '(place by the) grey wood in the valley'. OE *hār*, 'grey' (modern English *hoar*), + *wudu*, 'wood', + OS *dalr*, 'valley'. 1301 *Harewode*, 1577 *Harwoddale*.

Harworth (village, Notts): 'enclosure on the boundary'. OE *hār*, 'boundary', + *worth*, 'enclosure'. Harworth is near the historic county boundary with Yorkshire (now here the unitary authority of Doncaster). DB *Hareworde*.

Hascombe (village, Surrey): '(place by the) witch's valley'. OE *hætse*, 'witch' (related modern English *hex*), + *cumb*, 'valley'. 1232 *Hescumb*.

Haselbech (village, Northants): '(place by the) stream where hazels grow'. OE *hæsel*, 'hazel', + *bece*, 'stream'. The DB form of the name below is corrupt. DB *Esbece*, 12C *Haselbech*.

Haselbury Plucknett (village, Somerset): 'de Plugenet's (estate by the) hazel wood'. OE *hæsel*, 'hazel', + *bearu*, 'wood', 'grove'. The de Plugenet family held the manor here in the 13C, their name distinguishing the village from HAZELBURY BRYAN, Dorset, 16 miles to the east. The DB form of the name below is corrupt. DB *Halberge*, 1431 *Haselbare Ploukenet*.

Haselor (hamlet, Warwicks): 'hill where hazels grow'. OE *hæsel*, 'hazel', + *ofer*, 'hill'. The site of the hamlet is a good example of OE *ofer* in its particular application to a flat-topped ridge with a convex shoulder. DB *Haseloue*.

Hasfield (village, Glos): 'open land where hazels grow'. OE *hæsel*, 'hazel', + *feld*, 'open land' (modern English *field*). DB *Hasfelde*.

Hasguard (hamlet, Pemb): 'house cleft'. OS *hús*, 'house', + *skarth*, 'notch', 'cleft'. The name apparently refers to the small valley that cuts into the rising ground here. *c.*1200 *Huscart*.

Hasketon (village, Suffolk): 'Haseca's farmstead'. OE *tūn*, 'farmstead'. DB *Haschetuna*.

Hasland (district of Chesterfield, Derbys): '(place by the) hazel grove'. OS *hasl*, 'hazel', + *lundr*, 'grove'. 1129 *Haselont*.

Haslemere (town, Surrey): '(place by the) pool where hazels grow'. OE *hæsel*, 'hazel', +

mere, 'pool', 'lake'. There is no lake here now, but the original may have been on a site between the High Street and Derby Road. 1221 *Heselmere*.

Haslingden (town, Lancs): '(place in the) valley where hazels grow'. OE *hæsel*, 'hazel', + *denu*, 'valley'. The town is in a valley surrounded by high moorland. 1241 *Heselingedon*.

Haslingfield (village, Cambs): 'open land of Hæsel's people'. OE *-inga-*, 'of the people of', + *feld*, 'open land' (modern English *field*). The first part of the name could also represent OE *hæsling*, 'place growing with hazels'. DB *Haslingefeld*.

Haslington (village, Cheshire): 'farmstead where hazels grow'. OE *hæslen*, 'growing with hazels', + *tūn*, 'farmstead'. early 13C *Hasillinton*.

Hassall (hamlet, Cheshire): 'witch's corner of land'. OE *hægtesse*, 'witch' (related modern English *hag*), + *halh*, 'nook', 'corner of land'. The DB form of the name below is garbled. DB *Eteshale*, 13C *Hatishale*.

Hassingham (hamlet, Norfolk): 'homestead of Hasu's people'. OE *-inga-*, 'of the people of', + *hām*, 'homestead'. DB *Hasingeham*.

Hassocks (village, W Sussex): '(place by) Hassocks'. OE *hassuc*, 'clump of coarse grass' (modern English *hassock*). The village arose near a field called *Hassocks* following the opening of the London to Brighton railway in 1841.

Hassop (hamlet, Derbys): 'witch's valley'. OE *hægtesse*, 'witch' (related modern English *hag*), + *hop*, 'valley'. DB *Hetesope*.

Hastingleigh (village, Kent): 'woodland clearing of Hæsta's people'. OE *-inga-*, 'of the people of', + *lēah*, 'wood', 'clearing'. 993 *Hæstingalege*, DB *Hastingelai*.

Hastings (resort town, E Sussex): '(settlement of) Hæsta's people'. OE *-ingas*, 'people of'. The first form of the name below means 'Roman town of Hæsta's people' (OE *ceaster*, 'Roman camp'). The name of any Roman station here is unknown. *c*.915 *Hæstingaceaster*, DB *Hastinges*.

Haswell (village, Durham): '(place by the) stream where hazels grow'. OE *hæsel*, 'hazel', + *wella*, 'spring', 'stream'. 1131 *Hessewella*.

Hatch Beauchamp (village, Somerset): 'Beauchamp's (estate by the) gate'. OE *hæcc*, 'hatchgate'. A hatchgate leads to a forest. The manor here was held by the Beauchamp family in the 13C. DB *Hache*, 1243 *Hache Beauchampe*.

Hatch End (district, Harrow): 'district by the gate'. ME *hache*, 'hatch', + *ende*, 'end', 'district of an estate'. The district here was by a hatchgate

giving access to what is now Pinner Park. 1448 *Le Hacchehend*.

Hatcliffe (village, NE Lincs): 'Hadda's cliff'. OE *clif*, 'cliff', 'bank'. The 'cliff' is the steeply rising ground on each side of the village. DB *Hadecliue*.

Hatfield (town, Doncaster): 'open land where heather grows'. OE *hǣth*, 'heath', 'heather', + *feld*, 'open land' (modern English *field*). 731 *Haethfelth*, DB *Hedfeld*. SO ALSO: *Hatfield*, Herefords, Worcs.

Hatfield (town, Herts): 'open land where heather grows'. OE *hǣth*, 'heath', 'heather', + *feld*, 'open land' (modern English *field*). Hatfield was formerly known as *Bishops Hatfield*, as the Bishop of Ely held the manor here in 1086. 731 *Haethfelth*, DB *Hetfelle*, 1868 *Hatfield*, or *Bishop's Hatfield*.

Hatfield Broad Oak (village, Essex): 'open land where heather grows by the big oak tree'. OE *hǣth*, 'heath', 'heather', + *feld*, 'open land' (modern English *field*), + *brād*, 'broad', 'big', + *āc*, 'oak'. Philip Morant's *History of Essex* (1768) mentions the oak in question as 'a tree of extraordinary bigness'. Its addition to the name distinguishes this Hatfield from HATFIELD PEVEREL, 17 miles to the east. DB *Hadfelda*, *c*.1130 *Hatfeld Brodehoke*.

Hatfield Peverel (village, Essex): 'Peverel's (estate on the) open land where heather grows'. OE *hǣth*, 'heath', 'heather', + *feld*, 'open land' (modern English *field*). Ralph Peverel held the manor here in 1086, his name distinguishing this Hatfield from HATFIELD BROAD OAK, 17 miles to the west. DB *Hadfelda*, 1166 *Hadfeld Peurell*.

Hatherleigh (village, Devon): '(place by the) clearing where hawthorn grows'. OE *hagu-thorn*, 'hawthorn', + *lēah*, 'wood', 'clearing'. DB *Hadreleia*.

Hatherop. See SOUTHROP.

Hathersage (village, Derbys): 'ridge of the he-goat'. OE *hæfer*, 'he-goat', + *ecg*, 'edge', 'ridge'. The reference is to nearby Millstone Edge, a dramatically rocky escarpment, where a rock formation may have resembled the outline of a he-goat, or where goats actually lived. The first part of the name could also represent the personal name Hæfer, naming the man associated with the ridge. The DB form of the name below has corrupted the first part of the name. DB *Hereseige*, *c*.1220 *Hauersegge*.

Hatherton (hamlet, Staffs): '(place by the) hill where hawthorn grows'. OE *hagu-thorn*, 'hawthorn', + *dūn*, 'hill'. 996 *Hagenthorndun*, DB *Hargedone*.

Hatley St George (village, Cambs): 'de Sancto Giorgio's (estate at the) woodland clearing on the hill'. OE *hætt*, 'hill' (literally 'hat'), + *lēah*, 'wood', 'clearing'. The manor here was held in the 13C by the de Sancto Giorgio family, whose name distinguishes this Hatley from nearby *East Hatley*. DB *Hatelai*, 1279 *Hattele de Sancto Giorgio*.

Hatton (village, Derbys): 'farmstead on a heath'. OE *hǣth*, 'heath', + *tūn*, 'farmstead'. DB *Hatune*. SO ALSO: *Hatton*, Hounslow, Lincs, Shropshire, Warrington.

Haughley (village, Suffolk): '(place by the) wood with a hedge'. OE *haga*, 'hedge', + *lēah*, 'wood', 'clearing'. The name could also mean 'clearing where haws grow' (OE *haga*, 'haw'). *c.*1040 *Hagele*, DB *Hagala*.

Haughton (hamlet, Notts): 'farmstead on a spur of land'. OE *hōh*, 'spur of land', + *tūn*, 'farmstead'. There is a slight spur of land here. DB *Hoctun*.

Haughton (village, Staffs): 'farmstead by a corner of land'. OE *halh*, 'nook', 'corner of land', + *tūn*, 'farmstead'. DB *Haltone*. SO ALSO: *Haughton*, Shropshire (near Oswestry, near Shifnal, near Shrewsbury).

Haughton le Skerne (district, Darlington): 'farmstead by a corner of land on the (river) Skerne'. OE *halh*, 'nook', 'corner of land', + *tūn*, 'farmstead'. The river name means 'clear stream' (OE *scīr*, 'bright', 'clear', + *ēa*, 'river', 'stream'), with 'Sk-' from Scandinavian influence. *c.*1050 *Halhtun*.

Haunton (village, Staffs): 'Hagena's farmstead'. OE *tūn*, 'farmstead'. 942 *Hagnatun*.

Hauxley (village, Northd): 'mound where hawks are seen'. OE *hafoc*, 'hawk', + *hlāw*, 'mound', 'hill'. The name could also mean 'Hafoc's mound'. 1204 *Hauekeslaw*.

Hauxton (village, Cambs): 'Hafoc's farmstead'. OE *tūn*, 'farmstead'. *c.*975 *Hafucestune*, DB *Hauochestun*.

Havant (town, Hants): '(place by) Hāma's spring'. OE *funta*, 'spring'. Artesian wells ('springs') can occur when the local gravel is bored through here. The *m* of the personal name blended with the *f* of *funta* to give the present name. 935 *Hamanfuntan*, DB *Havehunte*.

Havenstreet (village, IoW): 'le Hethene's street'. OE *strǣt*, 'street'. The 'street' would have been a row of houses or a hamlet. The name has also been explained as 'street running through heathland' (OE *hǣthen*, 'heathy', + *strǣt*) and as 'heathen street' (OE *hǣthen*, 'heathen', + *strǣt*),

meaning a street built or used by pagans. But the first origin is the most likely. 1255 *Hethenestrete*.

Haverfordwest (town, Pemb): 'western (place by the) ford used by goats'. OE *hæfer*, 'goat', 'buck', + *ford*, 'ford', + *west*, 'western'. The ford would have been over the (Western) Cleddau here. The town's name was originally *Haverford*, but early forms of this suggested *Hereford* and *west* was added for distinction from the English town. The Welsh name of Haverfordwest is *Hwlffordd*, a corruption of the early English name. 1191 *Haverfordia*, 1283 *Hareford*, 1448 *Heverford West*, 1471 *Herefordwest*.

Haverhill (town, Suffolk): 'hill where oats are grown'. OS *hafri*, 'oats', + OE *hyll*, 'hill'. DB *Hauerhella*.

Havering-atte-Bower (village, Havering): '(settlement of) Hæfer's people by the residence'. OE *-ingas*, 'people of', + ME *atte*, 'at the', + OE *būr*, 'dwelling' (modern English *bower*). The 'residence' was the palace here owned by English kings from before the Norman Conquest until 1620. DB *Haueringas*, 1272 *Hauering atte Bower*.

Haversham (village, Milton K): 'Hæfer's homestead or river meadow'. OE *hām*, 'homestead', or *hamm*, 'river meadow'. 10C *Hæfæresham*, DB *Havresham*.

Haverthwaite (village, Cumbria): 'clearing where oats are grown'. OS *hafri*, 'oats', + *thveit*, 'clearing'. 1336 *Haverthwayt*.

Hawarden (town, Flints): 'high enclosure'. OE *hēah*, 'high', + *worthign*, 'enclosure'. Hawarden is on rising ground above the river Dee. The town's Welsh name is *Penarlâg*, from *pennardd*, 'high ground', and *alafog*, 'rich in cattle' (from *alaf*, 'cattle'). (The latter part of this could also be the personal name Alaog, from the same source.) DB *Haordine*, 1275 *Haworthyn*.

Hawes (town, N Yorks): '(place by the) neck'. OE *hals*, 'neck'. Hawes lies on the river Ure by a pass between the hills. 1614 *Hawes*.

Haweswater (lake, Cumbria): 'Hafr's lake'. OE *wæter*, 'water', 'lake'. The personal name is Scandinavian. 1199 *Havereswater*.

Hawick (town, Borders): 'high outlying farm'. OE *hēah*, 'high', + *wīc*, 'dwelling', 'outlying farm'. *c.*1167 *Hawic*.

Hawkchurch (village, Devon): 'Hafoc's church'. OE *cirice*, 'church'. 1196 *Hauekechierch*.

Hawkedon (village, Suffolk): '(place by the) hill where hawks are seen'. OE *hafoc*, 'hawk', + *dūn*, 'hill'. DB *Hauokeduna*.

Hawkesbury (village, S Glos): 'Hafoc's stronghold'. OE *burh*, 'fortified place'. The name could also mean 'stronghold where hawks are seen' (OE *hafoc*, 'hawk', + *burh*). DB *Havochesberie*.

Hawkhill (hamlet, Northd): '(place by the) hill where hawks are seen'. OE *hafoc*, 'hawk', + *hyll*, 'hill'. 1178 *Hauechil*.

Hawkhurst (village, Kent): '(place by the) wooded hill where hawks are seen'. OE *hafoc*, 'hawk', + *hyrst*, 'wooded hill'. 1254 *Hauekehurst*.

Hawkinge (village, Kent): 'place where hawks are seen'. OE *hafoc*, 'hawk', + *-ing*, 'place characterized by'. The name could also mean 'Hafoc's place' (OE *-ing*, 'place belonging to'). 1204 *Hauekinge*.

Hawkridge (village, Somerset): '(place by the) ridge where hawks are seen'. OE *hafoc*, 'hawk', + *hrycg*, 'ridge'. 1194 *Hauekerega*.

Hawkshead (village, Cumbria): 'Haukr's mountain pasture'. OS *sǽtr*, 'hill pasture'. The personal name is Scandinavian. *c.*1200 *Hovkesete*.

Hawkswick (hamlet, N Yorks): 'Haukr's dairy farm'. OE *wīc*, 'dwelling', 'specialized farm'. The personal name is Scandinavian (and corrupted in the DB form below). DB *Hochesuuic*, 1176 *Haukeswic*.

Hawksworth (village, Leeds): 'Hafoc's enclosure'. OE *worth*, 'enclosure'. *c.*1030 *Hafecesweorthe*, DB *Hauocesorde*.

Hawksworth (village, Notts): 'Hōc's enclosure'. OE *worth*, 'enclosure'. DB *Hochesuorde*.

Hawkwell (village, Essex): '(place by the) winding stream'. OE *haca*, 'hook', + *wella*, 'spring', 'stream'. There is a bend in a small stream here, a tributary of the river Roach. DB *Hacuuella*.

Hawling (village, Glos): '(settlement of the) people from Hallow'. OE *-ingas*, 'people of'. The village may have originally been settled by people from HALLOW, Worcs, 28 miles to the northwest. Alternatively, the name could mean '(settlement of the) people by the corner of land' (OE *halh*, 'nook', 'corner of land'). A third possibilty is that the name has the same origin as HALLING, Medway. DB *Hallinge*.

Hawnby (village, N Yorks): 'Halmi's farmstead'. OS *bȳ*, 'farmstead', 'village'. The personal name is Scandinavian. The first part of the name could also represent OS *halmr*, 'straw'. DB *Halmebi*.

Haworth (town, Bradford): 'enclosure with a hedge'. OE *haga*, 'hedge', + *worth*, 'enclosure'. OE *haga* also meant 'haw', so that the enclosure may have been one of hawthorn. 1209 *Hauewrth*.

Hawstead (village, Suffolk): 'place of shelter'. OE *hald*, 'protection', + *stede*, 'place'. DB *Haldsteda*.

Hawthorn (village, Durham): '(place by the) hawthorn'. OE *hagu-thorn*, 'hawthorn'. 1155 *Hagethorn*.

Hawton (hamlet, Notts): 'farmstead in a hollow'. OE *hol*, 'hole', 'hollow', + *tūn*, 'farmstead'. DB *Holtone*.

Haxby (village, York): 'Hákr's farmstead'. OS *bȳ*, 'farmstead', 'village'. The personal name is Scandinavian. DB *Haxebi*.

Haxey. See AXHOLME.

Haydock (town, St Helens): 'barley place'. Welsh *heiddiog* (modern Welsh *haidd*, 'barley'). The name essentially corresponds to English *Barton* (see BARTON-UPON-HUMBER). 1169 *Hedoc*.

Haydon (village, Dorset): '(place on the) hill where hay is made'. OE *hēg*, 'hay', + *dūn*, 'hill'. 1163 *Heydone*.

Haydon Bridge (town, Northd): '(place by a) bridge in the valley where hay is made'. OE *hēg*, 'hay', + *denu*, 'valley'. The town bridges the South Tyne. 1236 *Hayden*.

Hayes (district, Hillingdon): 'land overgrown with brushwood'. OE *hǽs*, 'brushwood'. The original site here would have been overgrown with rough bushes. 1177 *Hesa*. SO ALSO: *Hayes*, Bromley.

Hayfield (town, Derbys): 'open land where hay is obtained'. OE *hēg*, 'hay', + *feld*, 'open land' (modern English *field*). The DB form of the name below has *g* (or *y*) as *d*. DB *Hedfelt*, 1285 *Heyfeld*.

Hayle (town and port, Cornwall): '(place on the river) Hayle'. The river has a Celtic name meaning 'estuary' (Cornish *heyl*). The word for the river mouth thus became the name of the whole river and in turn gave that of the town. The first form of the name below is that of the river. The second is that of the town, a 19C industrial development. 1265 *Heyl*, 1816 *Hayle*.

Hayling Island (island, Hants): 'island of Hægel's people'. OE *-inga-*, 'of the people of', + *ēg*, 'island'. 956 *Heglingaegæ*, DB *Halingei*, *c.*1140 *Hailinges island*.

Hay-on-Wye (town, Powys): 'enclosure on the (river) Wye'. OE *hæg*, 'enclosure'. The name probably refers to an area of forest that was fenced off as a hunting ground. The town's Welsh name is *Y Gelli Gandryll*, 'the woodland of a hundred plots' (Welsh *y*, 'the', + *celli*, 'woodland', + *candryll*, from *cant*, 'hundred', + *dryll*, 'piece'). The former woodland here had apparently been divided into many plots. For the river name, see ROSS-ON-WYE. 958 *Hagan*, 1144 *Haya*.

Hayscastle (hamlet, Pemb): 'Hay's castle'. ME *castel*, 'castle', 'fort'. The Welsh name of Hayscastle is *Caslai* or *Castellhaidd*. Both these translate the English (*cas* is a short form of *castell*, 'castle'), with the second form influenced by Welsh *haidd*, 'barley'. 1293 *Castrum Hey*, 1326 *Heyscastel*.

Hayton (village, Cumbria): 'farmstead where hay is made or stored'. OE *hēg*, 'hay', + *tūn*, 'farmstead'. The form of the name below relates to Hayton near Brampton, but Hayton near Aspatria has a name of identical origin. *c*.1170 *Hayton*. SO ALSO: *Hayton*, E Yorks, Notts.

Haywards Heath (town, W Sussex): 'heath by an enclosure surrounded by a hedge'. OE *hege*, 'hedge', + *worth*, 'enclosure', + *hǣth*, 'heath'. The site here was simply heathland until the town developed following the opening of the London to Brighton railway in 1841. Local lore attributes the name to a highwayman called Hayward who carried out robberies on the heath. 1261 *Heyworth*, 1544 *Haywards Hoth*, 1868 *Hayward's Heath*.

Haywood Oaks (hamlet, Notts): 'enclosed wood'. OE *hæg* or *hege*, 'enclosure' (related modern English *hedge*), + *wudu*, 'wood'. The second word of the name presumably refers to some noted oak trees here. 1232 *Heywode*.

Hazelbury Bryan (village, Dorset): 'Bryene's (estate by the) hazel wood'. OE *hæsel*, 'hazel', + *bearu*, 'wood', 'grove'. The Bryene family held the manor here in the 14C, their name distinguishing the village from HASELBURY PLUCKNETT, Somerset, 16 miles to the west. 1201 *Hasebere*, 1547 *Hasilbere Bryan*.

Hazel Grove (town, Stockport): '(place by the) hazel copse'. OE *hæsel*, 'hazel', + *grāf*, 'grove', 'copse'. 1690 *Hesselgrove*.

Hazelwood (village, Derbys): '(place by the) hazel wood'. OE *hæsel*, 'hazel', + *wudu*, 'wood'. 1306 *Haselwode*.

Hazlemere (suburb of High Wycombe, Bucks): '(place by the) pool where hazels grow'. OE *hæsel*, 'hazel', + *mere*, 'pool'. Cp. HASLEMERE. 13C *Heselmere*.

Hazleton (village, Glos): 'farmstead where hazels grow'. OE *hæsel*, 'hazel', + *tūn*, 'farmstead'. The DB form of the name below is corrupt. DB *Hasedene*, 12C *Haselton*.

Heacham (village, Norfolk): 'homestead with a hedge'. OE *hecg*, 'hedge', + *hām*, 'homestead'.

The first part of the name could also represent OE *hecc*, 'hatchgate' (leading to a forest). DB *Hecham*.

Headbourne Worthy (village, Hants): 'enclosure by the Headbourne'. OE *worthig*, 'enclosure'. *Headbourne* is the former name of a stream here meaning 'stream by the hides' (OE *hīd*, 'hide', + *burna*, 'stream'), added to distinguish the village from nearby *Kings Worthy*, where the manor was held by the king, and *Martyr Worthy*, where it was held by the le Martre family. A hide was a unit of land supporting one family and household. 825 *Worthige*, DB *Ordie*, *c*.1270 *Hydeburne Worthy*.

Headcorn (village, Kent): 'Hydeca's tree trunk'. OE *hruna*, 'tree trunk'. The name perhaps implies that the tree trunk or fallen tree was used as a footbridge over a stream here. *c*.1100 *Hedekaruna*.

Headingley (district, Leeds): 'woodland clearing of Heada's people'. OE *-inga-*, 'of the people of', + *lēah*, 'wood', 'grove'. DB *Hedingeleia*.

Headington (district of Oxford, Oxon): 'Hedena's hill'. OE *dūn*, 'hill'. Headington is on rising ground northeast of Oxford city centre. 1004 *Hedenandun*, DB *Hedintone*.

Headley (village, Hants): 'woodland clearing where heather grows'. OE *hǣth*, 'heather', + *lēah*, 'wood', 'clearing'. Heather still grows on the sandy soil here in the east of the county. DB *Hallege*, *c*.1190 *Hetliga*.

Headon (village, Notts): '(place by the) high hill'. OE *hēah*, 'high', + *dūn*, 'hill'. DB *Hedune*.

Heage (village, Derbys): '(place by the) high edge'. OE *hēah*, 'high', + *ecg*, 'edge'. 1251 *Heyheg*, 1896 *Heage*, or *High Edge*.

Healaugh (village, N Yorks): '(place by the) high clearing or wood'. OE *hēah*, 'high', + *lēah*, 'clearing', 'wood'. The forms of the name below relate to Healaugh in Swaledale, but Healaugh near Tadcaster has a name of identical origin. The DB form is corrupt. DB *Hale*, 1200 *Helagh*.

Healey (village, N Yorks): '(place by the) high wood or clearing'. OE *hēah*, 'high', + *lēah*, 'wood', 'clearing'. *c*.1280 *Helagh*. SO ALSO: *Healey*, Northd (near Riding Mill).

Healing (village, NE Lincs): '(settlement of) Hǣgel's people'. OE *-ingas*, 'people of'. DB *Hegelinge*.

Heanor (town, Derbys): '(place at the) high ridge'. OE *hēah*, 'high', + *ofer*, 'ridge'. The fuller OE version of the name is *æt thǣm hēan ofre*, 'at the high ridge', with *hēah* in the dative. The town is on a hill. DB *Hainoure*.

Heanton Punchardon (village, Devon): 'Punchardon's (estate at the) high farm'. OE *hēah*, 'high', + *tūn*, 'farmstead'. The manor here was held in the 11C by the Punchardon family. DB *Hantone*, 1297 *Heantun Punchardun*.

Heath (village, Derbys): '(place by the) heath'. OE *hǣth*, 'heath'. The village was originally called *Lunt* (OS *lundr*, 'grove'). DB *Lunt*, 1257 *Heth*.

Heath and Reach (suburb of Leighton Buzzard, Beds): '(place by the) heath and the raised strip of land'. OE *hǣth*, 'heath', + *rǣc*, 'raised straight strip' (modern English *reach*). c.1220 *Reche*, 1276 *la Hethe*, c.1750 *Hetheredge*, 1785 *Heathanreach*, 1868 *Heath and Reach*.

Heather (village, Leics): 'place where heather grows'. OE *hǣddre*, 'heather'. DB *Hadre*.

Heathfield (town, E Sussex): 'open land where heather grows'. OE *hǣth*, 'heath', + *feld*, 'open land' (modern English *field*). 12C *Hadfeld*. SO ALSO: *Heathfield*, Somerset.

Heathrow (airport, Hillingdon): 'row by a heath'. ME *hethe*, 'heath', + *rewe*, 'row'. The 'row' would have been a line of cottages here by Hounslow Heath. The place was a hamlet until the airport was developed in the 1940s. c.1410 *La Hetherewe*, c.1530 *Hetherowfeyld*, 1822 *Heath Row*.

Heaton (district, Bradford): 'high farmstead'. OE *hēah*, 'high', + *tūn*, 'farmstead'. 1160 *Hetun*.

Heaton (district, Newcastle): 'high farmstead'. OE *hēah*, 'high', + *tūn*, 'farmstead'. 1256 *Heton*.

Hebburn (town, S Tyneside): 'high burial place'. OE *hēah*, 'high', + *byrgen*, 'burial place'. The location of the original burial place or tumulus is unknown. 1104 *Heabyrm*.

Hebden (village, N Yorks): '(place in the) valley where rose hips grow'. OE *hēope*, 'hip', + *denu*, 'valley'. The first part of the name could also represent OE *hēopa*, 'bramble'. DB *Hebedene*.

Hebden Bridge (town, Calderdale): 'bridge by the valley where rose hips grow'. OE *hēope*, 'hip', + *denu*, 'valley', + *brycg*, 'bridge'. The first part of the name could also represent OE *hēopa*, 'bramble'. The bridge here is over Hebden Water. 1399 *Hepdenbryge*.

Hebrides (island group, W Scotland): meaning uncertain. The Roman name for the islands was *Ebudae* or *Ebudes*, and the present form of the name resulted from a misreading of the latter, with *ri* for *u*. The Scandinavian name of the Hebrides was *Suthreyar*, 'southern islands', as they were south of Orkney and Shetland. Hence *Sodor* in the title of the Bishop of Sodor and Man, whose diocese is the Isle of Man, at one time grouped with the Hebrides. Cp. SUTHERLAND.

Hebron (hamlet, Northd): 'high burial place'. OE *hēah*, 'high', + *byrgen*, 'burial place'. Cp. HEBBURN. 1242 *Heburn*.

Heckfield (village, Hants): 'open land by a hedge'. OE *hecg*, 'hedge', + *feld*, 'open land' (modern English *field*). The first part of the name could also represent OE *hecc*, 'hatchgate' (leading to a forest). 1207 *Hechfeld*.

Heckingham (hamlet, Norfolk): 'homestead of Heca's people'. OE *-inga-*, 'of the people of', + *hām*, 'homestead'. DB *Hechingheam*, 1245 *Hekingeham*.

Heckington (village, Lincs): 'estate associated with Heca'. OE *-ing-*, 'associated with', + *tūn*, 'farmstead', 'estate'. DB *Hechintune*.

Heckmondwike (town, Kirklees): 'Hēahmund's dairy farm'. OE *wīc*, 'dwelling', 'specialized farm'. The DB form of the name below has *d* for *c*. DB *Hedmundewic*, 13C *Hecmundewik*.

Heddington (village, Wilts): 'estate associated with Hedde'. OE *-ing-*, 'associated with', + *tūn*, 'farmstead', 'estate'. DB *Edintone*.

Heddon-on-the-Wall (village, Northd): '(place by the) hill where heather grows on the wall'. OE *hǣth*, 'heather', + *dūn*, 'hill'. The second part of the name, referring to the location of the village on HADRIAN'S WALL, distinguishes this Heddon from *Black Heddon*, 7 miles to the northwest, so called for the dark colour of the heather or of the soil on which it grew. The second form of the name below has the Latin equivalent of the English. 1175 *Hedun*, 1242 *Hedon super murum*.

Hedenham (village, Norfolk): 'Hedena's homestead'. OE *hām*, 'homestead'. DB *Hedenaham*.

Hedge End (suburb of Botley, Hants): '(place at the) end of the hedge'. The hedge may originally have formed a boundary here. The first form of the name below has added *cut*, 'clipped'. 1759 *Cutt Hedge End*, 1826 *Hedge Ends*.

Hedgerley (village, Bucks): 'Hycga's woodland clearing'. OE *lēah*, 'wood', 'clearing'. 1195 *Huggeleg*.

Hednesford (town, Staffs): '(place by) Heddīn's ford'. OE *ford*, 'ford'. 13C *Hedenesford*.

Hedon (town, E Yorks): 'hill where heather grows'. OE *hǣth*, 'heather', + *dūn*, 'hill'. There is hardly a hill here in the normal sense. 12C *Hedon*.

Heeley (district, Sheffield): 'high wood or clearing'. OE *hēah*, 'high', + *lēah*, 'wood', 'clearing'. 1277 *Helegh*.

Heighington (village, Darlington): 'estate on the high ground'. OE *hēahing*, 'high ground' (from *hēah*, 'high', + *-ing*, 'place characterized by'), + *tūn*, 'farmstead', 'estate'. 1183 *Heghyngtona*.

Heighington (village, Lincs): 'estate associated with Hyht'. OE *-ing-*, 'associated with', + *tūn*, 'farmstead', 'estate'. 1242 *Hictinton*.

Helensburgh (coastal town, Argyll & Bute): 'Helen's town'. Modern Scottish English *burgh*, 'town' (related modern English *borough*). A new settlement was founded here in 1776 by Sir James Colquhoun of Luss, who named it after his wife, Lady Helen Sutherland, daughter of William, Lord Strathnaver.

Helford (village, Cornwall): '(place by the) estuary ford'. Cornish *heyl*, 'estuary', + OE *ford*, 'ford'. Helford lies on the estuary of the river of the same name. The 'ford' may have been a crossing at this point, with the village named after it and the river itself originally known as Heyl. The first form of the name below refers to the estuary, the second to the village. Cp. HAYLE. 1230 *Helleford*, 1564 *Haylford*.

Helhoughton (village, Norfolk): 'Helgi's farmstead'. OE *tūn*, 'farmstead'. The personal name is Scandinavian. Cp. HELLINGTON. DB *Helgatuna*.

Helions Bumpstead. See STEEPLE BUMPSTEAD.

Helland (village, Cornwall): 'old church site'. Cornish *hen*, 'old', + *lann*, 'church site'. 1284 *Hellaunde*.

Hellidon (village, Northants): '(place by the) holy valley'. OE *hǣlig*, 'holy', 'healthy', + *denu*, 'valley'. The village is on a hill overlooking a valley. 12C *Elliden*.

Hellifield (village, N Yorks): 'Helgi's open land'. OE *feld*, 'open land' (modern English *field*). The personal name is Scandinavian. DB *Helgefeld*.

Hellingly (village, E Sussex): 'woodland clearing of Hielle's people'. OE *-inga-*, 'of the people of', + *lēah*, 'wood', 'clearing'. The name could also mean 'woodland clearing of the people who live on the hill' (OE *hyll*, 'hill', + *-inga-*, 'of the dwellers at', + *lēah*). 13C *Hellingeleghe*.

Hellington (hamlet, Norfolk): 'Helgi's farmstead'. OE *tūn*, 'farmstead'. The personal name is Scandinavian. DB *Halgatune*.

Helmdon (village, Northants): 'Helma's valley'. OE *denu*, 'valley'. DB *Elmedene*.

Helmingham (village, Suffolk): 'homestead of Helm's people'. OE *-inga-*, 'of the people of', + *hām*, 'homestead'. DB *Helmingheham*.

Helmshore (district of Haslingden, Lancs): 'steep slope with a cattle shelter'. OE *helm*, 'shelter' (related modern English *helmet*), + *scora*, 'shore', 'steep slope'. Helmshore stands on a tongue of land between the rivers Irwell and Ogden. 1510 *Hellshour*.

Helmsley (town, N Yorks): 'Helm's woodland clearing'. OE *lēah*, 'wood', 'clearing'. The second part of the DB form of the name below is corrupt. DB *Elmeslac*, 12C *Helmesley*.

Helperby (village, N Yorks): 'Hjalp's farmstead'. OS *bý*, 'farmstead', 'village'. The first half of the name represents *Hjalpar*, the genitive form of the Scandinavian personal name, that of a woman. 972 *Helperby*, DB *Helprebi*.

Helperthorpe (village, N Yorks): 'Hjalp's outlying farmstead'. OS *thorp*, 'outlying farmstead'. The first half of the name represents *Hjalpar*, the genitive form of the Scandinavian personal name, that of a woman. DB *Elpetorp*.

Helpringham (village, Lincs): 'homestead of Helprīc's people'. OE *-inga-*, 'of the people of', + *hām*, 'homestead'. DB *Helperincham*.

Helpston (village, Peterborough): 'Help's farmstead'. OE *tūn*, 'farmstead'. 948 *Hylpestun*.

Helsby (village, Cheshire): 'farmstead on a ledge'. OS *hjallr*, 'hut', 'mountainside ledge', + *bý*, 'farmstead'. Helsby lies on a narrow shelf of land between the foot of Helsby Hill and the edge of Helsby Marsh. DB *Helesbe*, late 12C *Hellesbi*.

Helston (town, Cornwall): 'estate at an old court'. Cornish *hen-lys* (from *hen*, 'old', + *lys*, 'court'), + OE *tūn*, 'farmstead', 'estate'. DB *Henlistone*.

Helstone (village, Cornwall): 'estate at an old court'. Cornish *hen-lys* (from *hen*, 'old', + *lys*, 'court'), + OE *tūn*, 'farmstead', 'estate'. Cp. HELSTON. DB *Henliston*.

Helton (village, Cumbria): 'farmstead on a slope'. OE *helde*, 'slope', + *tūn*, 'farmstead'. c.1160 *Helton*.

Helvellyn (mountain, Cumbria): meaning uncertain. The name is probably Celtic, but early records of it are lacking. Even so, a meaning 'yellow (upland) moor' has been proposed, from words related to modern Welsh *hâl*, 'moor', and *melyn*, 'yellow'. The reference would be to the colour of the grass or bracken on the mountain slopes. 1577 *Helvillon*.

Hemblington (hamlet, Norfolk): 'estate associated with Hemele'. OE *-ing-*, 'associated with', + *tūn*, 'farmstead', 'estate'. DB *Hemelingetun*.

Hemel Hempstead (town, Herts): 'homestead in Hemel'. OE *hām-stede* (from *hām*, 'homestead', + *stede*, 'place'). Cp. HAMPSTEAD. *Hemel* is an old district name, meaning 'broken' (OE *hamel*, 'maimed', 'mutilated'). The countryside here is broken and uneven, with many steep hills and deep dells. The present form of the name has preserved the distinct parts of the original, which at one time was reduced to simply *Hempstead*. DB *Hamelamestede*.

Hemingbrough (village, N Yorks): 'Hemingr's stronghold'. OE *burh*, 'fortified place'. The personal name is Scandinavian. 1080 *Hemingburgh*, DB *Hamiburg*.

Hemingford Grey (village, Cambs): 'de Grey's (estate by the) ford of Hemma's or Hemmi's people'. OE *-inga-*, 'of the people of', + *ford*, 'ford'. The manor here was held early by the de Grey family, whose name distinguishes this village from nearby *Hemingford Abbots*, held by the Abbot of Ramsey. Both are on the river Ouse. 974 *Hemmingeford*, DB *Emingeford*, 1316 *Hemingford Grey*.

Hemingstone (village, Suffolk): 'Hemingr's farmstead'. OE *tūn*, 'farmstead'. The personal name is Scandinavian. DB *Hamingestuna*.

Hemington (village, Northants): 'estate associated with Hemma or Hemmi'. OE *-ing-*, 'associated with', + *tūn*, 'farmstead', 'estate'. 1077 *Hemmingtune*, DB *Hemintone*. SO ALSO: *Hemington*, Leics, Somerset.

Hemley (village, Suffolk): 'Helma's woodland clearing'. OE *lēah*, 'wood', 'clearing'. DB *Helmelea*.

Hempnall (village, Norfolk): 'Hemma's corner of land'. OE *halh*, 'nook', 'corner of land'. DB *Hemenhala*.

Hempstead (village, Essex): 'homestead'. OE *hām-stede* (from *hām*, 'homestead', + *stede*, 'place'). Cp. HAMPSTEAD. DB *Hamesteda*.

Hempstead (village, Norfolk): 'place where hemp is grown'. OE *hænep*, 'hemp', + *stede*, 'place'. This is Hempstead near Holt. Hempstead near Happisburgh has a name of identical origin to that of HEMPSTEAD, Essex. DB *Henepsteda*.

Hemsby (village, Norfolk): 'Hēmer's farmstead'. OS *bý*, 'farmstead', 'village'. The personal name is Scandinavian. DB *Heimesbei*.

Hemswell (village, Lincs): '(place by) Helm's spring'. OE *wella*, 'spring', 'stream'. There are a number of springs here. DB *Helmeswelle*.

Hemsworth (town, Wakefield): 'Hymel's enclosure'. OE *worth*, 'enclosure'. The DB form of the name below has corrupted the personal name. DB *Hamelesuurde*, 12C *Hymeleswrde*.

Hemyock (village, Devon): '(place by the river) Hemyock'. The river name is probably of Celtic origin based on a word related to modern Welsh *haf*, 'summer', meaning a stream that never dries up. Hemyock is actually on the river Culm. DB *Hamihoc*.

Henbury (district, Bristol): 'high fortified place'. OE *hēah*, 'high', + *burh*, 'fortified place'. The 'fortified place' is perhaps the encampment on Castle Hill nearby. 'High' may mean 'chief' rather than physically elevated. 692 *Heanburg*, DB *Henberie*.

Hendon (district, Barnet): '(place at the) high hill'. OE *hēah*, 'high', + *dūn*, 'hill'. Hendon grew up around St Mary's Church, which like many churches was built on a hill. The '-n-' of the name comes from the dative case of OE *hēah* in the phrase *æt thǣre hēan dūne*, 'at the high hill'. *c.*975 *Heandun*, DB *Handone*.

Hendy-gwyn. See WHITLAND.

Henfield (town, W Sussex): 'stony open land'. OE *hān*, 'stone' (related modern English *hone*), + *feld*, 'open land' (modern English *field*). 770 *Hanefeld*, DB *Hamfelde*.

Hengistbury Head (headland, Bournemouth): 'headland by Heddīn's fort'. OE *burh*, 'fortified place'. The name has been influenced by the OE personal name Hengest ('horse'). 877 *Heddinesburh*, 12C *Hedenesburia*, 1611 *Hengestbury heade*.

Hengrave (village, Suffolk): 'Hemma's grassy meadow'. OE *grēd*, 'grass'. The DB form of the name below has added OE *hām*, 'homestead'. DB *Hemegretham*, *c.*1095 *Hemegrede*.

Henham (village, Essex): 'high homestead or enclosure'. OE *hēah*, 'high', + *hām*, 'homestead', or *hamm*, 'enclosure'. The first part of the name represents OE *hēan*, the dative form of *hēah*. *c.*1045 *Henham*, DB *Henham*.

Henley (hamlet, Shropshire): 'wood or clearing where henbirds are seen'. OE *henn*, 'henbird' (modern English *hen*), + *lēah*, 'wood', 'clearing'. The name could also specifically mean 'clearing where hens are kept'. The second part of the DB form of the name below is corrupt. DB *Haneleu*, 1242 *Hennele*.

Henley (hamlet, Somerset): 'high wood or clearing'. OE *hēah*, 'high', + *lēah*, 'wood', 'clearing'. 973 *Henleighe*. SO ALSO: *Henley*, Suffolk.

Henley-in-Arden (village, Warwicks): 'high clearing in Arden'. OE *hēah*, 'high', + *lēah*, 'wood', 'clearing'. *Arden* is the Forest of Arden, its Celtic name meaning 'high district'. (The same base gave the name of the *Ardennes*, the forest upland in western Europe.) The second part of the name was added to distinguish this Henley from others, such as HENLEY-ON-THAMES. William Dugdale, in *The Antiquities of Warwickshire* (1656), comments: 'But in truth it ought to have been written *Heanley*, as the ordinary sort of people doe still pronounce it; for that was its original name, and occasioned from the ascending ground, whereunto it is so neerly situate, *hean* in our old English signifying *high*'. *c.*1180 *Henle*.

Henley-on-Thames (town, Oxon): 'high clearing by the (river) Thames'. OE *hēah*, 'high', + *lēah*, 'wood', 'clearing'. The town is not on elevated ground, so that 'high' here probably has the sense 'chief', 'important'. For the river name, see THAMES DITTON. *c.*1140 *Henleiam*.

Henlow (village, Beds): '(place by the) hill where henbirds are seen'. OE *henn*, 'henbird' (modern English *hen*), + *hlāw*, 'hill', 'mound'. DB *Haneslauue*.

Hennock (village, Devon): '(place by the) tall oak tree'. OE *hēah*, 'high', + *āc*, 'oak'. DB *Hainoc*.

Hensall (village, N Yorks): 'Hethīn's or Hethinn's corner of land'. OE *halh*, 'nook', 'corner of land'. The personal names are respectively OE and Scandinavian. The reference is to a piece of land partly surrounded by the river Aire here. The DB form of the name below has corrupted the personal name. DB *Edeshale*, 12C *Hethensale*.

Henshaw (village, Northd): 'Hethīn's or Hethinn's corner of land'. OE *halh*, 'nook', 'corner of land'. The personal names are respectively OE and Scandinavian. Cp. HENSALL. 12C *Hedeneshalch*.

Henstridge (village, Somerset): 'Hengest's ridge'. OE *hrycg*, 'ridge'. The first part of the name could also represent OE *hengest*, 'stallion', giving a sense 'ridge where stallions are kept'. 956 *Hengstesrig*, DB *Hengestrich*.

Henton (village, Oxon): 'high farmstead'. OE *hēah*, 'high', + *tūn*, 'farmstead'. 'High' could mean 'chief' here. DB *Hentone*.

Henton (village, Somerset): 'high farmstead'. OE *hēah*, 'high', + *tūn*, 'farmstead'. The name could also mean 'farmstead where hens are kept' (OE *henn*, 'hen', + *tūn*). 1065 *Hentun*.

Henwood (village, Cornwall): 'wood where henbirds are seen'. OE *henn*, 'henbird', + *wudu*, 'wood'. 1327 *Hennawode*.

Hepburn (hamlet, Northd): 'high burial place'. OE *hēah*, 'high', + *byrgen*, 'burial place'.

Cp. HEBBURN. The form of the name below has added OE *dūn*, 'hill'. *c.*1050 *Hybberndune*.

Hepple (village, Northd): 'corner of land where brambles grow'. OE *hēopa*, 'brambles', + *halh*, 'nook', 'corner of land'. The first part of the name could also represent OE *hēope*, 'rose hip'. 1205 *Hephal*.

Hepscott (village, Northd): 'Hebbi's cottage'. OE *cot*, 'cottage'. 1242 *Hebscot*.

Heptonstall (village, Calderdale): 'farmstead where brambles grow'. OE *hēopa*, 'brambles', + *tūn-stall*, 'farmstead' (see TUNSTALL). The first part of the name could also represent OE *hēope*, 'rose hip'. 1253 *Heptonstall*.

Hepworth (village, Kirklees): 'Heppa's enclosure'. OE *worth*, 'enclosure'. DB *Heppeuuord*. SO ALSO: *Hepworth*, Suffolk.

Herbrandston (village, Pemb): 'Herbrand's farm'. OE *tūn*, 'farm'. The name is said to allude to a Fleming who took refuge here in the early 12C. 13C *Villa Herbrandi*, 1307 *Herbraundistone*.

Hereford (city, Herefords): '(place by the) army ford'. OE *here*, 'army', + *ford*, 'ford'. An 'army ford' is one, here over the river Wye, where an army of men can cross in broad ranks without breaking formation. The ford itself would have been where the Roman road from Leintwardine to Monmouth crosses the river. 958 *Hereford*, DB *Hereford*.

Herefordshire (unitary authority, W central England): 'district based on Hereford'. OE *scīr*, 'shire', 'district'. See HEREFORD. 11C *Herefordscir*.

Hermitage (village, W Berks): '(place by the) hermitage'. ME *ermitage*, 'hermitage'. 1550 *Le Eremytage*.

Herne Bay (resort town, Kent): '(place at the) corner of land by the bay'. OE *hyrne*, 'angle', 'corner'. The original settlement here gave the name of the bay. *c.*1100 *Hyrnan*.

Hernhill (village, Kent): '(place by the) grey hill'. OE *hār*, 'grey' (modern English *hoar*), + *hyll*, 'hill'. *c.*1100 *Haranhylle*.

Herodsfoot (village, Cornwall): '(place at the) foot (of a stream) by Heriard'. Nearby *Heriard* has a name meaning 'long ridge' (Cornish *hir*, 'long', + *garth*, 'ridge'). 1613 *Herriott foote*.

Heronsgate (suburb of Chorleywood, Herts). The village arose in 1846 and was originally named *O'Connorville*, after the Irish Chartist leader Feargus O'Connor (1794–1855), who bought an estate here designed to be divided into smallholdings and let to subscribers to the National Land Company. The earlier name of the place, of obscure origin, was subsequently adopted. 1599 *Heryngarste*.

Herriard (village, Hants): 'army enclosure'. OE *here*, 'army', + *geard*, 'enclosure' (modern English *yard*). The reference is presumably to a Viking army camp. The DB form of the name below has *n* for *ri*. DB *Henerd*, c.1160 *Herierd*.

Herringfleet (village, Suffolk): '(place by the) stream of Herela's people'. OE *-inga-*, 'of the people of', + *flēot*, 'creek', 'stream'. DB *Herlingaflet*.

Herringswell (village, Suffolk): '(place by the) spring at the corner of land'. OE *hyrne*, 'corner', + *-ing*, 'place characterized by', + *wella*, 'spring', 'stream'. The 'corner of land' is probably the curving hill nearby. DB *Hyrningwella*.

Herrington. See EAST HERRINGTON.

Hersham (village, Surrey): 'Hæferic's river meadow'. OE *hamm*, 'enclosure', 'river meadow'. Hersham lies by a bend in the river Mole. 1175 *Hauerichesham*, 1868 *Hersham, or Heversham*.

Herstmonceux (village, E Sussex): 'Monceux's wooded hill'. OE *hyrst*, 'wooded hill'. The Monceux family held the manor here in the 12C. DB *Herst*, 1287 *Herstmonceux*.

Hertford (town, Herts): '(place by the) ford where stags are seen'. OE *heorot*, 'hart', 'stag', + *ford*, 'ford'. The ford over the river Lea here would have been one where stags gathered or regularly crossed. 731 *Herutford*, DB *Hertforde*.

Hertfordshire (county, S central England): 'district based on Hertford'. OE *scīr*, 'shire', 'district'. See HERTFORD. 11C *Heortfordscir*.

Hertingfordbury (district of Hertford, Herts): 'stronghold of the people of Hertford'. OE *-inga-*, 'of the people of', + *burh*, 'fortified place'. See HERTFORD. The name was originally *Hertfordingbury*, and the transposition of *-ford-* and *-ing-* was presumably made for ease of pronunciation. The DB form of the name below has *e* for *t*. DB *Herefordingberie*, 1220 *Hertfordingeberi*.

Hertsmere (council district, Herts). The name was created in 1974 for the new administrative district here as a combination of *Herts*, the abbreviated county name, and *mere* in the sense 'boundary' (OE *gemǣre*), referring to the county boundary with Greater London.

Hesketh Bank (hamlet, Lancs): 'course for horseracing'. OS *hestr*, 'horse', + *skeith*, 'course'. Horseracing was popular among the Vikings. The bank was formerly that of the river Ribble here. 1288 *Heschath*.

Hesket Newmarket (village, Cumbria): '(place by the) hill growing with ash trees with a new market'. OS *eski*, 'ash', + OE *hēafod*, 'headland', 'hill'. The main name was assimilated in form to that of HIGH HESKET. The second word is first recorded only in the 18C. 1227 *Eskeheued*, 1751 *Hesket New Market*.

Heskin Green (hamlet, Lancs): 'place where sedge grows'. The hamlet, on low land by a brook, has a Celtic name related to modern Welsh *hesg*, 'sedges'. It later became associated with its village green. 1257 *Heskyn*.

Heslington (village, York): 'farmstead by the hazel wood'. OE *hæsling*, 'place growing with hazels', + *tūn*, 'farmstead'. DB *Haslinton*.

Hessay (village, York): 'island where hazels grow'. OE *hæsel*, 'hazel', + *ēg*, 'island'. The 'island' here is dry ground in marshland. OE *hæsel* has been influenced by equivalent OS *hesli*. The DB form of the name below has *l* miscopied as *d*. DB *Hesdesai*, 12C *Heslesaia*.

Hessenford (village, Cornwall): '(place by the) ford of the witches'. OE *hægtesse*, 'witch' (related modern English *hag*), + *ford*, 'ford'. The first part of the name represents OE *hægtsena*, the genitive plural form of *hægtesse*. c.1286 *Heceneford*.

Hessett (village, Suffolk): 'fold with a hedge'. OE *hecg*, 'hedge', + *set*, 'dwelling', 'fold' (for animals). The DB form of the name below is garbled. DB *Heteseta*, 1225 *Heggeset*.

Hessle (town, E Yorks): '(place at the) hazel tree'. OE *hæsel*, 'hazel'. There must have been a grove of hazel trees here at one time. The OE word has been influenced by its OS equivalent, *hesli*. The DB form of the name below has omitted *l*. DB *Hase*, 12C *Hesel*.

Hest Bank (coastal village, Lancs): '(place in) undergrowth'. OE *hæst*, 'undergrowth', 'brushwood'. The village stands on marshes beside Morecambe Bay, hence 'Bank'. 1177 *Hest*.

Heston (district, Hounslow): 'farmstead in the brushwood'. OE *hǣs*, 'brushwood', + *tūn*, 'farmstead'. c.1125 *Hestone*.

Heswall (town, Wirral): '(place by the) spring where hazels grow'. OE *hæsel*, 'hazel', + *wella*, 'spring'. Local lore links the name with the Hessle Well, a roadside well in Heswall village. The first part of the DB form of the name below is corrupt. DB *Eswelle*, c.1200 *Haselwell*.

Hethe (village, Oxon): '(place on) uncultivated land'. OE *hēth*, 'heath', 'uncultivated land'. DB *Hedha*.

Hethersett (village, Norfolk): '(settlement of the) dwellers among the heather'. OE *hǣddre*, 'heather', + *sǣte*, 'dwellers'. DB *Hederseta*.

Hett (village, Durham): '(place by the) hat-shaped hill'. OE *hætt*, 'hat'. The name could also represent OS *hetti*, the dative form of *hǫttr*, 'hat'. There is a distinctive hill here. *c.*1168 *Het*.

Hetton (village, N Yorks): 'farmstead on a heath'. OE *hǣth*, 'heath', + *tūn*, 'farmstead'. DB *Hetune*.

Hetton-le-Hole (town, Sunderland): '(place by the) hill where rose hips grow in the hollow'. OE *hēope*, 'hip', + *dūn*, 'hill', + OF *le*, 'the', + OE *hol*, 'hole', 'hollow'. The second part of the name distinguishes this Hetton from others and emphasizes that it is not actually on the hill but in the valley below it. 1180 *Heppedun*.

Heveningham (village, Suffolk): 'homestead of Hefin's people'. OE *-inga-*, 'of the people of', + *hām*, 'homestead'. DB *Heueniggeham*.

Hever (village, Kent): '(place at the) high bank'. OE *hēah*, 'high', + *yfer*, 'bank'. Hever lies above Hever Castle, which is itself above the river Eden. The form of the name below preserves *hēan* as the dative of *hēah* in the original OE phrase *æt thǣm hēan yfre*, 'at the high bank'. 814 *Heanyfre*.

Heversham (village, Cumbria): 'Hēahfrith's homestead'. OE *hām*, 'homestead'. *c.*1050 *Hefresham*, DB *Eureshaim*.

Hevingham (village, Norfolk): 'homestead of Hefa's people'. OE *-inga-*, 'of the people of', + *hām*, 'homestead'. DB *Heuincham*.

Hewelsfield (village, Glos): 'Hygewald's open land'. OE *feld*, 'open land' (modern English *field*). The DB form of the name below has 'farmstead' (OE *tūn*), not 'open land'. DB *Hiwoldestone*, *c.*1145 *Hualdesfeld*.

Hewish (hamlet, Somerset): 'family holding'. OE *hīwisc*, 'household'. The OE word denoted a measure of land that would support a family. 1327 *Hywys*.

Hexham (town, Northd): 'bachelor's homestead'. OE *hagustald*, 'bachelor', + *hām*, 'homestead'. A *hagustald* (often translated 'bachelor', 'warrior', but literally meaning 'enclosure occupier') was a younger son of a family entitled to have his own holding outside the main village. 685 *Hagustaldes ham*, 1188 *Hexteldesham*.

Hexton (village, Herts): 'Hēahstān's farmstead'. OE *tūn*, 'farmstead'. DB *Hegestanestone*.

Heybridge (suburb of Maldon, Essex): '(place by the) high bridge'. OE *hēah*, 'high', + *brycg*, 'bridge'. 'High' probably means 'chief' here. Heybridge is on the river Blackwater. *c.*1200 *Heaghbregge*.

Heydon (village, Cambs): '(place in the) valley where hay is made'. OE *hēg*, 'hay', + *denu*, 'val-ley'. The first part of the name could also repre-sent OE *hæg*, 'enclosure' (related modern English *hedge*), giving a sense '(place in the) val-ley with an enclosure'. DB *Haidenam*.

Heydon (village, Norfolk): '(place by the) hill where hay is made'. OE *hēg*, 'hay', + *dūn*, 'hill'. 1196 *Heidon*.

Heysham (town, Lancs): 'homestead among the brushwood'. OE *hǣs*, 'brushwood', + *hām*, 'homestead', 'village'. DB *Hessam*.

Heyshott (village, W Sussex): 'corner of land where heather grows'. OE *hǣth*, 'heather', + *scēat*, 'corner of land'. *c.*1100 *Hethsete*.

Heytesbury (village, Wilts): 'Hēahthrȳth's stronghold'. OE *burh*, 'fortified place'. The per-sonal name is that of a woman. The DB form of the name below is corrupt. DB *Hestrebe*, *c.*1115 *Hehtredeberia*.

Heythrop (village, Oxon): 'high outlying farm-stead'. OE *hēah*, 'high', + *throp*, 'outlying farm-stead'. The DB form of the name below is corrupt. DB *Edrope*, 11C *Hethrop*.

Heywood (town, Rochdale): 'high wood'. OE *hēah*, 'high', + *wudu*, 'wood'. Heywood is not noticeably elevated but may have been regarded as 'high' by comparison with nearby Bury. 1246 *Heghwode*.

Heywood (village, Wilts): 'enclosed wood'. OE *hæg*, 'enclosure' (related modern English *hedge*), + *wudu*, 'wood'. 1225 *Heiwode*.

Hibaldstow (village, N Lincs): 'Hygebald's holy place'. OE *stōw*, 'holy place'. St Hygebald is said to be buried here and the church is dedi-cated to him. DB *Hiboldestou*.

Hickleton (village, Doncaster): 'farmstead where woodpeckers are seen'. OE *hicol*, 'wood-pecker', + *tūn*, 'farmstead'. DB *Icheltone*.

Hickling (village, Norfolk): '(settlement of) Hicel's people'. OE *-ingas*, 'people of'. DB *Hikelinga*. SO ALSO: *Hickling*, Notts.

Hidcote Bartrim (hamlet, Glos): 'Bertram's (estate by) Hydeca's or Huda's cottage'. OE *cot*, 'cottage'. The Bertram family held the manor here in the 13C, their name distinguishing this Hidcote from nearby *Hidcote Boyce*, where the manor was held by the de Bosco or Bois family in the 13C. DB *Hidicote*, 1274 *Hudcot Bertram*.

High Ackworth (village, Wakefield): 'higher Acca's enclosure'. OE *worth*, 'enclosure'. The first word of the name contrasts the village with nearby *Low Ackworth*. DB *Aceuurde*.

Higham (village, Suffolk): 'high enclosure'. OE *hēah*, 'high', + *hamm*, 'enclosure'. The village lies by a bend of the Stour, near the point where the Roman road from Colchester crosses the river. Hence the name of the Roman settlement here, *Ad Ansam*, '(place) at the bend'. *c.*1050 *Hecham*, DB *Heihham*. SO ALSO: *Higham*, Derbys, Kent, Lancs.

Higham (E Sussex). See NORTHIAM.

Higham Ferrers (town, Northants): 'Ferrers' high homestead'. OE *hēah*, 'high', + *hām*, 'homestead'. The town stands high above the Nene valley. The Ferrers family held the manor here in the 12C. DB *Hecham*, 1279 *Heccham Ferrar*.

Higham on the Hill (village, Leics): 'high homestead on the hill'. OE *hēah*, 'high', + *hām*, 'homestead'. The village stands on a hill near Watling Street, now represented by the A5 road. The second part of the name is first recorded only in the 16C. 1220 *Hecham*.

Highampton (village, Devon): 'high farmstead'. OE *hēah*, 'high', + *tūn*, 'farmstead'. The name was originally the equivalent of *Hampton*, from OE *hēan*, the dative form of *hēah*, 'high', + *tūn*, 'farmstead'. Another 'high' was then added to this when the original sense had been forgotten. DB *Hantone*, 1303 *Heghanton*.

High Barnet. See BARNET.

High Bentham (village, N Yorks): 'higher homestead or enclosure where bents grow'. OE *beonet*, 'bent grass', + *hām*, 'homestead', or *hamm*, 'enclosure'. The first word of the name distinguishes the village from nearby *Low Bentham*. The DB form of the name below has *m* miscopied as *in*. DB *Benetain*, 1214 *Benetham*.

High Bickington (village, Devon): 'high estate associated with Beocca'. OE *hēah*, 'high', + *-ing-*, 'associated with', + *tūn*, 'farmstead', 'estate'. The first word of the name distinguishes the village from the *Bickington* that is a suburb of Barnstaple, 8 miles to the northwest. DB *Bichentona*, 1423 *Heghebuginton*.

Highbridge (town, Somerset): '(place by the) high bridge'. OE *hēah*, 'high', + *brycg*, 'bridge'. 'High' may have had the sense 'important' for the bridge over the river Brue here. 1324 *Highbridge*.

Highbury (district, Islington): 'high manor'. OE *hēah*, 'high', + *burh*, 'fortified place', 'manor'. The manor here stood on higher ground than nearby Canonbury or Barnsbury. It was recorded in 1274 as *Neweton Barrewe*, after the de Barewe family, the first word indicating that it was at one time part of the parish of nearby STOKE NEWINGTON. *c.*1375 *Heybury*.

High Callerton. See BLACK CALLERTON.

High Catton (village, E Yorks): 'higher (place called) Catta's or Káti's farmstead'. OE *tūn*, 'farmstead'. The personal names are respectively OE and Scandinavian. The first word of the name distinguishes this Catton from nearby *Low Catton*. DB *Caton*.

Highclere. See KINGSCLERE.

Highcliffe (district of Christchurch, Dorset): '(place at the) high cliff'. The district is also known as *Highcliffe-on-Sea* and was earlier *Black Cliff*. 1610 *Black Cliffe*, 1759 *High Clift*.

High Coniscliffe (village, Darlington): 'high (place at the) king's cliff'. OE *cyning*, 'king', + *clif*, 'cliff', 'bank'. The first word of the name contrasts the village with the nearby smaller *Low Coniscliffe*. *c.*1050 *Cingcesclife*.

High Easter (village, Essex): 'high (place at the) sheepfold'. OE *hēah*, 'high', + *eowestre*, 'sheepfold'. The first word of the name distinguishes this village from GOOD EASTER. DB *Estra*, 1254 *Heyestre*.

High Eggborough. See LOW EGGBOROUGH.

High Ellington (village, N Yorks): 'high farmstead at the place where eels are found'. OE *ǣl* or *ēl*, 'eel', + *-ing*, 'place characterized by', + *tūn*, 'farmstead'. The basic name could also mean 'farmstead associated with Ella or Eli' (OE *-ing-*, 'associated with'). The first word of the name distinguishes the village from nearby *Low Ellington*. DB *Ellintone*.

High Ercall (village, Wrekin): 'higher (place in) Ercall'. The main name was originally a district name adopted from a hill now known as *The Ercall*, its own name probably originating as *Earcaluw*, 'muddy bare hill' (OE *ēar*, 'mud', 'gravel', + *caluw*, 'bare hill'). The first word (OE *hēah*, 'high') may indicate importance, rather than actual elevation, and distinguishes the village from *Child's Ercall*, 6 miles to the northeast, its own name prefixed with OE *cild*, 'nobleman's son' (modern English *child*). The second form of the name below has Latin *magna*, 'great'. DB *Archelou*, 1315 *Magna Ercaluwe*.

Higherford. See BARROWFORD.

Higher Kinnerton (village, Flints): 'higher (place called) Cyneheard's farmstead'. OE *tūn*, 'farmstead'. The first word of the name distinguishes the village from nearby *Lower Kinnerton*, across the border in Cheshire. 1240 *Kynarton*.

Higher Penwortham (suburb of Preston, Lancs): 'higher enclosed homestead by Penn'. OE *worth*, 'enclosure', + *hām*, 'homestead'. *Penn* is the Celtic name of the hill on which the former village stands, itself meaning simply 'hill' (modern Welsh *pen*, 'head', 'top'). The first word of the name contrasts the place with nearby *Lower Penwortham*. The DB form of the name below is the gallant effort of the Norman scribe. DB *Peneverdant*, 1149 *Penuertham*.

Higher Vexford. See LOWER VEXFORD.

Higher Whitley (village, Cheshire): 'higher (place by a) white wood'. OE *hwīt*, 'white', + *lēah*, 'wood'. A white wood is one in which trees have white bark or white blossom. The first word of the name distinguishes the village from nearby *Lower Whitley*. DB *Witelei*.

Higher Wych (hamlet, Cheshire): 'higher saltworks'. OE *wīc*, 'specialized farm', 'industrial settlement'. The first word of the name distinguishes this saltworks from nearby *Lower Wych*. 1208 *Upper Wych*.

Highgate (district, Camden): '(place by the) high gate'. OE *hēah*, 'high', + *geat*, 'gate'. The former tollgate here on the Great North Road was over 400 feet (122m) above sea level. 1354 *Le Heighgate*.

High Grantley (village, N Yorks): 'high (place called) Granta's or Grante's woodland clearing'. OE *lēah*, 'wood', 'clearing'. The first word of the name distinguishes the village from nearby *Low Grantley*. c.1030 *Grantelege*, DB *Grentelai*.

High Halden (village, Kent): 'high woodland pasture associated with Heathuwald'. OE *-ing-*, 'associated with', + *denn*, 'woodland pasture'. c.1100 *Hadingwoldungdenne*.

High Ham (village, Somerset): 'high enclosure'. OE *hamm*, 'enclosure'. High Ham (originally *Ham*) is on high ground overlooking Sedgemoor. The first word of the name distinguishes the village from nearby *Low Ham*. 873 *Hamme*, DB *Hame*, 1868 *Ham, or High Ham*.

High Hatton (hamlet, Shropshire): 'high farmstead by a heath'. OE *hæth*, 'heath', + *tūn*, 'farmstead'. The first word of the name (probably here meaning 'more important') distinguishes this Hatton from *Cold Hatton*, 'bleak farmstead by a heath', 2½ miles to the south. DB *Hetune*, 1327 *Heye Hatton*.

High Hawsker (village, N Yorks): 'higher (place called) Haukr's enclosure'. OS *garthr*, 'enclosure'. The personal name is Scandinavian. The first word of the name distinguishes the village from nearby *Low Hawsker*. c.1125 *Houkesgarth*.

High Hesket (village, Cumbria): 'high boundary land where horses graze'. OS *hestr*, 'horse', + *skeith*, 'course', 'track', 'boundary'. The same OS words could also mean 'racecourse for horses',

serving as a reminder of the Vikings' interest in horseracing. The first word of the name distinguishes the village from nearby *Low Hesket*. The second and third forms of the name below refer to Inglewood Forest. 1285 *Hescayth*, 1292 *Eskeyth in foresta*, 1896 *Hesket-in-the-Forest*.

High Hoyland. See HOYLAND NETHER.

High Hunsley (hamlet, E Yorks): 'higher (place called) Hund's woodland clearing'. OE *lēah*, 'wood', 'clearing'. The first word of the name distinguishes this Hunsley from what is now *Low Hunsley Farm* nearby. A former beacon at High Hunsley gave the name of the *Hunsley Beacon* division of Harthill wapentake. DB *Hundreslege*.

Highland (unitary authority, N Scotland): 'high land'. The mountainous region of northern Scotland is named the Highlands as distinct from the Lowlands to the south. There is no precise border between the two, but the Highlands as a natural region extend further south than the present unitary authority. 1529 *the heland*, c.1627 *the High-Lands of Scotland*.

High Laver (hamlet, Essex): 'high (place by the) water passage'. OE *lagu*, 'water' (related modern English *lake*), + *fær*, 'passage'. The first word of the name distinguishes the place from nearby *Little Laver* and *Magdalen Laver*, the latter named from the dedication of its church to St Mary Magdalen. All three hamlets are on the course of the Roman road from London to Great Dunmow, and this was presumably the 'passage' over marshland ('water') here. c.1010 *Lagefare*, DB *Lagafara*.

Highleadon. See UPLEADON.

High Legh (village, Cheshire): 'high (place at the) woodland clearing'. OE *hēah*, 'high', + *lēah*, 'wood', 'clearing'. The first word of the name distinguishes the village, on the crest of a broad ridge, from *Little Leigh*, 8 miles to the southwest. DB *Lege*.

Highley (village, Shropshire): 'Hugga's woodland clearing'. OE *lēah*, 'wood', 'clearing'. DB *Hugelei*.

High Littleton (village, Bath & NE Somerset): 'high little farmstead'. OE *hēah*, 'high', + *lȳtel*, 'little', + *tūn*, 'farmstead', 'estate'. DB *Liteltone*, 1324 *Heghelitleton*.

High Lorton (village, Cumbria): 'high farmstead on the (river) Lore'. OE *hēah*, 'high', + *tūn*, 'farmstead'. The river name, that of a stream here, represents OS *hlóra*, 'roaring one'. The first word of the name distinguishes the village from nearby *Low Lorton*. c.1150 *Loretona*.

High Marishes (hamlet, N Yorks): 'higher (place by the) marshes'. OE *mersc*, 'marsh'. High Marishes and nearby *Low Marishes* stand on a former extensive area of marshland. The DB names below are those of different manors distinguished by the names of their individual Scandinavian owners, respectively Ásketill, Ketilfrøthr and Authulfr. DB *Aschilesmares, Chiluesmares, Ouduluesmersc*.

High Marnham (village, Notts): 'high (place called) Mearna's homestead'. OE *hām*, 'homestead', 'village'. The first word of the name distinguishes the village from nearby *Low Marnham*. DB *Marneham*.

High Melton (village, Doncaster): 'high middle farmstead'. OE *middel*, 'middle', + *tūn*, 'farmstead'. The village is midway between Sprotborough and Barnburgh, and was earlier called *Melton on the Hill*. OE *middel* has been replaced by equivalent OS *methal*. DB *Middeltun*.

High Mickley (village, Northd): 'high large wood or clearing'. OE *hēah*, 'high', + *lēah*, 'wood', 'clearing'. The first word of the name distinguishes this Mickley from the nearby 19C mining village of *Mickley Square*, so named for its square. *c*.1190 *Michelleie*.

High Moorsley. See LOW MOORSLEY.

Highnam (village, Glos): '(place by the) river meadow belonging to a religious community'. OE *hīwan*, 'household (of monks)', + *hamm*, 'riverside meadow'. The first part of the name represents OE *hīgna*, the genitive form of the plural noun *hīwan*. The meadows in question lay between the rivers Severn and Leadon, while the religious community was that of the monks of St Peter's, Gloucester, to whom the estate here belonged. DB *Hamme*, 12C *Hinehamme*.

High Offley (village, Staffs): 'high (place called) Offa's woodland clearing'. OE *lēah*, 'wood', 'clearing'. The first word of the name distinguishes this Offley from *Bishop's Offley*, 2 miles to the north, where the manor was held early by the Bishop of Lichfield. DB *Offeleia*.

High Ongar. See CHIPPING ONGAR.

High Onn (hamlet, Staffs): 'high (place by the) ash trees'. Welsh *onn* (plural of *onnen*), 'ash trees'. The basic name may originally have been that of a stream here. The first word distinguishes this place from nearby *Little Onn*. The DB form of the name below is garbled. DB *Otne*, *c*.1130 *Onna*.

High Peak. See PEAK DISTRICT.

High Rochester. See ROCHESTER (Northd).

High Roding. See RODINGS.

High Salter (hamlet, Lancs): 'higher shieling where salt is kept'. OE *salt*, 'salt', + OS *erg*, 'shieling', 'hill pasture'. The first word of the name distinguishes the hamlet from nearby *Middle Salter* and *Lower Salter*. *c*.1150 *Salterge*.

High Stittenham (hamlet, N Yorks): 'higher (place at the) steep ascents'. OE *sticel*, 'steep place'. The name represents OE *sticelum*, the dative plural form of *sticel*. The DB form of the name below is corrupt. DB *Stidnun*, *c*.1260 *Stiklum*.

High Throston (district, Hartlepool): 'high (place called) Thórir's or Thórr's farmstead'. OE *tūn*, 'farmstead', 'village'. The personal names are Scandinavian. There is no corresponding *'Low Throston'*. *c*.1300 *Thoreston*.

Hightown (district of Congleton, Cheshire): 'high (part of the) town'. The name is modern.

High Trewhitt (hamlet, Northd): 'high (place by the) river bend where resinous wood is obtained'. OS *tyri*, 'dry resinous wood', + OE *wiht*, 'bend', 'curve'. High Trewhitt and nearby *Low Trewhitt* are on the Wreigh Burn, a tributary of the Coquet. 1150 *Tirwit*.

Highway (hamlet, Wilts): '(place by the) road where hay is carried'. OE *hēg*, 'hay', + *weg*, 'way'. DB *Hiwei*.

Highweek (suburb of Newton Abbot, Devon): 'high dairy farm'. OE *hēah*, 'high', + *wīc*, 'dwelling', 'specialized farm'. Highweek stands on a prominent hill by the river Teign. *c*.1270 *Hegewyk*.

High Worsall. See LOW WORSALL.

Highworth (town, Swindon): 'high enclosure'. OE *hēah*, 'high', + *worth*, 'enclosure', 'farmstead'. The settlement here was originally *Worth*. *High* was then added for distinctiveness. The town, as its name implies, is situated on high land, commanding extensive prospects' (*The National Gazetteer of Great Britain and Ireland*, 1868). DB *Wrde*, 1232 *Hegworth*.

High Wych (village, Herts): 'high dairy farm'. OE *wīc*, 'dwelling', 'specialized farm'. 1540 *Wyches*, 1676 *Highwick*.

High Wycombe (town, Bucks): 'high (place at the) dwellings'. OE *hēah*, 'high', + *wīc*, 'dwelling', 'outlying farm'. The basic name *Wycombe*, now in use for the local council district, represents OE *wīcum*, the dative plural of *wīc*. *High* was then added to distinguish this Wycombe from nearby *West Wycombe*. The sense of OE *hēah* here is probably 'important' rather than literally 'high'. *c*.970 *æt Wicumun*, DB *Wicumbe*.

Hilborough (village, Norfolk): 'Hildeburh's stream'. OE *wella*, 'spring', 'stream'. The personal name is that of a woman. The second part of the name could also represent OE *worth*, 'enclosure'. DB *Hildeburhwella*, 1242 *Hildeburwrthe*.

Hilbre Island (island, Wirral): 'Hildeburg's island'. OE *ēg*, 'island'. The personal name is that of a woman. There are two small islands here off the coast of West Kirby, the lesser being *Little Hilbre*. 12C *Hildeburgheye*.

Hildenborough (suburb of Tonbridge, Kent): 'manor at the woodland pasture by a hill'. OE *hyll*, 'hill', + *denn*, 'woodland pasture', + *burh*, 'manor', 'borough'. 1240 *Hyldenn*, 1389 *Hildenborough*.

Hildersham (village, Cambs): 'Hildrīc's homestead'. OE *hām*, 'homestead'. DB *Hildricesham*.

Hilderstone (village, Staffs): 'Hildulfr's or Hildwulf's farmstead'. OE *tūn*, 'farmstead'. The personal names are respectively Scandinavian and OE. DB *Hidulvestune*.

Hilderthorpe (district of Bridlington, E Yorks): 'Hildiger's or Hildigerthr's outlying farmstead'. OS *thorp*, 'outlying farmstead'. The Scandinavian personal names are respectively those of a man and a woman. DB *Hilgertorp*.

Hilfield (hamlet, Dorset): 'open land by a hill'. OE *hyll*, 'hill', + *feld*, 'open land' (modern English *field*). 934 *Hylfelde*.

Hilgay (village, Norfolk): 'island of Hȳthla's or Hydla's people'. OE *-inga-*, 'of the people of', + *ēg*, 'island'. The 'island' is dry ground in fenland beside the river Ouse. 974 *Hillingeiæ*, DB *Hidlingheia*.

Hill (village, S Glos): '(place on the) hill'. OE *hyll*, 'hill'. The church stands on a prominent hill here. DB *Hilla*.

Hillam (village, N Yorks): '(place by the) hills'. OE *hyll*, 'hill'. The name represents OE *hyllum*, the dative plural form of *hyll*. The terrain gradually rises in small hillocks here towards the hillier region in the west. 963 *Hillum*.

Hill Chorlton. See CHAPEL CHORLTON.

Hill Deverill. See KINGSTON DEVERILL.

Hillesden (village, Bucks): 'Hild's hill'. OE *dūn*, 'hill'. 949 *Hildesdun*, DB *Ilesdone*.

Hillfarance (village, Somerset): 'Furon's (estate by the) hill'. OE *hyll*, 'hill'. The Furon family held the manor here in the 12C. DB *Hilla*, 1253 *Hull Ferun*.

Hillingdon (borough, Greater London): 'Hilda's hill'. OE *dūn*, 'hill'. The '-ing-' of the name represents the genitive ending of the (male) personal name. c.1080 *Hildendune*, DB *Hillendone*.

Hillington (village, Norfolk): 'farmstead of Hȳthla's or Hydla's people'. OE *-inga-*, 'of the people of', + *tūn*, 'farmstead'. DB *Helingetuna*.

Hillmorton (district of Rugby, Warwicks). Originally two separate places: *Hill*, '(place at the) hill' (OE *hyll*, 'hill'), and *Morton*, 'farmstead in marshland' (OE *mōr*, 'moor', 'marshland', + *tūn*, 'farmstead'). As explained by William Dugdale in *The Antiquities of Warwickshire* (1656), the parish comprised '*Hill*, antiently written *Hull*, conteyning that part standing on the Bank, and *Moreton* where the Church is, that below in a moorish ground'. DB *Mortone*, 1247 *Hulle and Morton*.

Hillsborough (district, Sheffield). Hillsborough was originally represented by the hamlets *Hills*, *Hill Foot* and *Hill Top*, all referring to hills here. The second part of the name was added in modern times. 1817 *Hillsbro'*.

Hilmarton (village, Wilts): 'estate associated with Helmheard'. OE *-ing-*, 'associated with', + *tūn*, 'farmstead', 'estate'. 962 *Helmerdingtun*, DB *Helmerintone*.

Hilperton (village, Wilts): 'estate associated with Hylprīc'. OE *-ing-*, 'associated with', + *tūn*, 'farmstead', 'estate'. DB *Helperinton*.

Hilton (village, Cambs): 'farmstead by a hill'. OE *hyll*, 'hill', + *tūn*, 'farmstead'. 1196 *Hiltone*. SO ALSO: *Hilton*, Derbys, Stockton.

Hilton (village, Cumbria): 'farmstead on a slope'. OE *helde*, 'slope', + *tūn*, 'farmstead'. The village lies on the lower slope of Roman Fell. 1289 *Helton*.

Hilton (village, Dorset): 'farmstead on a slope'. OE *helde*, 'slope', + *tūn*, 'farmstead'. The name could also mean 'farmstead where tansy grows' (OE *helde*, 'tansy', + *tūn*). DB *Eltone*.

Himbleton (village, Worcs): 'farmstead where hops grow'. OE *hymele*, 'hop plant', + *tūn*, 'farmstead'. 816 *Hymeltun*, DB *Himeltun*.

Himley (village, Staffs): 'woodland clearing where hops grow'. OE *hymele*, 'hop plant', + *lēah*, 'wood', 'clearing'. DB *Himelei*.

Hincaster (hamlet, Cumbria): 'old fortification where henbirds are seen'. OE *henn*, 'henbird' (modern English *hen*), + *ceaster*, 'fortification'. OE *ceaster* usually denotes a Roman fortification, but none is known here. There may have been a Roman road nearby. DB *Hennecastre*.

Hinckley (town, Leics): 'Hȳnca's woodland clearing'. OE *lēah*, 'wood', 'clearing'. DB *Hinchelie*.

Hinderclay (village, Suffolk): 'tongue of land where elder trees grow'. OE *hyldre*, 'elder', + *clēa*, 'claw', 'tongue of land'. DB *Hilderclea*.

Hinderwell (village, N Yorks): 'spring associated with Hild'. OE *wella*, 'spring', 'well'. Hild is St Hilda (614–80), Abbess of Whitby, to whom the church here is dedicated. The '-er-' of the name represents -*ar*, a Scandinavian genitive ending. The spring is popularly (and perhaps actually) associated with St Hilda's Well in the churchyard. However, the name could also mean 'spring where elder trees grow' (OE *hyldre* or *hylder*, 'elder', + *wella*). DB *Hildrewell*.

Hindhead (town, Surrey): 'hill where does are seen'. OE *hind*, 'hind', 'doe', + *hēafod*, 'head', 'hill'. The name properly refers to *Hindhead Hill*, the high ground on the south side of the Devil's Punch Bowl, rising to Gibbet Hill. The present town developed only in the early 20C. 1571 *Hyndehed*.

Hindley (town, Wigan): 'wood or clearing where does are seen'. OE *hind*, 'hind', 'doe', + *lēah*, 'wood', 'clearing'. 1212 *Hindele*.

Hindlip (village, Worcs): '(place by the fence where) hinds leap over'. OE *hind*, 'hind', 'female deer', + *hlīep*, 'leap'. 966 *Hindehlep*, DB *Hindelep*.

Hindolveston (village, Norfolk): 'Hildwulf's farmstead'. OE *tūn*, 'farmstead'. DB *Hidolfestuna*.

Hindon (village, Wilts): 'hill belonging to a religious community'. OE *hīwan*, 'household (of monks)', 'religious community', + *dūn*, 'hill'. The first part of the name represents OE *hīgna*, the genitive form of the plural noun *hīwan*. 1268 *Hynedon*.

Hindringham (village, Norfolk): 'homestead of the people dwelling behind'. OE *hinder*, 'behind', + -*inga*-, 'of the dwellers at', + *hām*, 'homestead'. The reference is presumably to those dwelling behind the hills near which the place stands. DB *Hindringaham*.

Hingham (village, Norfolk): 'homestead of Hega's people'. OE -*inga*-, 'of the people of', + *hām*, 'homestead'. DB *Hincham*, 1173 *Heingeham*.

Hinstock (village, Shropshire): 'outlying farmstead of the household servants'. ME *hine*, 'household servants', + OE *stoc*, 'outlying farmstead'. DB *Stoche*, 1242 *Hinestok*.

Hintlesham (village, Suffolk): 'Hyntel's homestead or enclosure'. OE *hām*, 'homestead', or *hamm*, 'enclosure'. DB *Hintlesham*.

Hinton (village, Northants): 'farmstead belonging to a religious community'. OE *hīwan*, 'household (of monks)', 'religious community', + *tūn*, 'farmstead', 'estate'. The 'Hin-' of the name represents OE *hīgna*, the genitive form of the plural noun *hīwan*. DB *Hintone*. SO ALSO: *Hinton*, Herefords.

Hinton Admiral (hamlet, Hants): 'de Albemara's high farmstead'. OE *hēah*, 'high', + *tūn*, 'farmstead'. The de Albemara family held the manor here in the 13C, their name distinguishing this Hinton from HINTON AMPNER, 30 miles to the northeast. DB *Hentune*, 1379 *Henton Aumarle*.

Hinton Ampner (hamlet, Hants): 'high farmstead of the almoner'. OE *hēah*, 'high', + *tūn*, 'farmstead', + OF *aumoner*, 'almoner'. The manor here was held early by the almoner of St Swithin's Priory, Winchester, his title distinguishing this Hinton from HINTON ADMIRAL, 30 miles to the southwest. DB *Hentune*, 13C *Hinton Amner*.

Hinton Blewett (village, Bath & NE Somerset): 'Bluet's high farmstead'. OE *hēah*, 'high', + *tūn*, 'farmstead'. The Bluet family held the manor early here, the addition of their name distinguishing this Hinton from HINTON CHARTERHOUSE, 14 miles to the east. DB *Hantone*, 1246 *Hentun Bluet*.

Hinton Charterhouse (village, Bath & NE Somerset): 'high farmstead of the Carthusian monks'. OE *hēah*, 'high', + *tūn*, 'farmstead', + OF *chartrouse*, 'house of Carthusian monks'. The second word of the name, referring to a priory founded here in the early 13C, distinguishes this Hinton from HINTON BLEWETT, 14 miles to the west. DB *Hantone*, 1273 *Henton Charterus*.

Hinton-in-the-Hedges (village, Northants): 'farmstead belong to a religious community among the hedges'. OE *hīwan*, 'household (of monks)', 'religious community', + *tūn*, 'farmstead', 'estate'. The 'Hin-' of the name represents OE *hīgna*, the genitive form of the plural noun *hīwan*. DB *Hintone*, 1549 *Hynton in the edge*.

Hinton Martell (village, Dorset): 'Martell's (estate at the) farmstead belonging to a religious community'. OE *hīwan*, 'household (of monks)', 'religious community', + *tūn*, 'farmstead', 'estate'. The 'Hin-' of the name represents OE *hīgna*, the genitive form of the plural noun *hīwan*. The manor here was held in the 13C by the Martell family, whose name distinguishes this Hinton from *Hinton Parva* (Latin *parva*, 'little'), 1½ miles to the south. The religious community was the former monastery of Wimborne Minster. DB *Hinetone*, 1226 *Hineton Martel*.

Hinton on the Green (village, Worcs): 'farmstead belonging to a religious community'. OE *hīwan*, 'household (of monks)', 'religious community', + *tūn*, 'farmstead', 'estate'. The 'Hin-' of the name represents OE *hīgna*, the genitive form of the plural noun *hīwan*. Hinton belonged to St Peter's Abbey, Gloucester. The added words refer to the village green. DB *Hinetune*, 1537 *Hinton on the Green*.

Hinton Parva (Dorset). See HINTON MARTELL.

Hinton Parva (Swindon). See BROAD HINTON.

Hinton St George (village, Somerset): 'high farmstead with St George's church'. OE *hēah*, 'high', + *tūn*, 'farmstead'. The second part of the name, from the dedication of the church, distinguishes this Hinton from HINTON ST MARY, Dorset, 24 miles to the east. DB *Hantone*, 1246 *Hentun Sancti Georgii*.

Hinton St Mary (village, Dorset): 'high farmstead of St Mary's Abbey'. OE *hēah*, 'high', + *tūn*, 'farmstead'. The second part of the name, referring to the possession of the manor by the Abbey of St Mary, Shaftesbury, distinguishes this Hinton from HINTON ST GEORGE, Somerset, 24 miles to the west. 944 *Hamtune*, DB *Haintone*, 1626 *Hinton Marye*.

Hinton Waldrist (village, Oxon): '(de Sancto) Walerico's high farmstead'. OE *hēah*, 'high', + *tūn*, 'farmstead'. The de Sancto Walerico family held the manor here from the 12C. DB *Hentone*, 1676 *Hinton Walrush*, 1868 *Hinton-Waldridge, or Waldrist*.

Hints (village, Staffs): '(place on the) roads'. Welsh *hynt*, 'way', 'course'. Hints is on Watling Street. DB *Hintes*.

Hinxton (village, Cambs): 'estate associated with Hengest'. OE *-ing-*, 'associated with', + *tūn*, 'farmstead', 'estate'. The DB form of the name below has corrupted the personal name. DB *Hestitona*, 1202 *Hengstiton*.

Hinxworth (village, Herts): 'enclosure where stallions are kept'. OE *hengest*, 'stallion', + *worth*, 'enclosure'. DB *Haingesteuuorde*.

Hipperholme (village, Calderdale): '(place among the) osiers'. OE *hyper*, 'osier'. The name represents OE *hyperum*, the dative plural form of *hyper*. DB *Huperun*.

Hirst Courtney (village, N Yorks): 'Courtney's (estate at the) wooded hill'. OE *hyrst*, 'wooded hill'. The Courtney family held land here in the 13C, their name distinguishing the village from nearby *Temple Hirst*, held in the 12C by the Knights Templars. *c.*1030 *Hyrst*, 1303 *Hirst Courtenay*.

Hirwaun (village, Rhondda CT): 'long moor'. Welsh *hir*, 'long', + *gwaun*, 'moor'. The 'long moor' in question lies to the southwest of Hirwaun and the neighbouring village of *Penywaun*, 'head of the moor' (Welsh *pen*, 'head', + *y*, 'the', + *gwaun*, 'moor'). The forms of the name below include the name of Gwrgan, reputedly the last king of Glamorgan. 1203 *Hyrweunworgan*, 1536 *Hirwen Urgan*, 1638 *Hirwaun Wrgan*.

Histon (suburb of Cambridge, Cambs): 'farmstead of the young men'. OE *hyse*, 'son', 'young man', + *tūn*, 'farmstead'. DB *Histone*.

Hitcham (village, Suffolk): 'homestead with a hedge'. OE *hecg*, 'hedge', + *hām*, 'homestead'. The first part of the name could also represent OE *hecc*, 'hatchgate' (leading to a forest). DB *Hecham*.

Hitchin (town, Herts): '(place in the territory of the) Hicce'. Nothing is known about the people called Hicce who occupied this territory. Their name may derive from a Celtic river name meaning 'dry'. The river here now is called the Hiz, adopted from the DB form of the name below. The first name below represents the dative plural of the tribal name. *c.*945 *Hiccam*, DB *Hiz*.

Hither Green (district, Lewisham): 'nearer green'. The name apparently denotes a green near to Lewisham rather than a nearby green known as *Further Green*. English *hither* had the sense 'nearer', 'on this side', from the 14C. 18C *Hither Green*.

Hittisleigh (village, Devon): 'Hyttīn's woodland clearing'. OE *lēah*, 'wood', 'clearing'. DB *Hitenesleia*.

Hixon (village, Staffs): 'Hyht's hill'. OE *dūn*, 'hill'. The DB form of the name below has garbled the personal name. DB *Hustedone*, 1130 *Huchtesdona*.

Hoar Cross (hamlet, Staffs): '(place by the) grey cross'. OE *hār*, 'grey' (modern English *hoar*), + *cros*, 'cross'. OE *hār* also meant 'boundary', so the reference could equally be to a boundary cross here. 1230 *Horcros*.

Hoarwithy (village, Herefords): '(place by the) whitebeam'. OE *hār*, 'grey' (modern English *hoar*), + *wīthig*, 'withy', 'willow tree'. 13C *La Horewythy*.

Hôb, Yr. See HOPE (Flints).

Hoby (village, Leics): 'farmstead on a spur of land'. OE *hōh*, 'hill spur', + OS *bý*, 'farmstead', 'village'. DB *Hobie*.

Hockering (village, Norfolk): '(settlement of the) dwellers by the rounded hill'. OE *hocer*, 'hump', 'rounded hill', + *-ingas*, 'dwellers at'.

The DB form of the name below has *l* for *r*. DB *Hokelinka*, 12C *Hokeringhes*.

Hockerton (village, Notts): 'farmstead at the hump'. OE *hocer*, 'hump', + *tūn*, 'farmstead'. The 'hump' is a rounded hill here. DB *Hocretone*.

Hockley (suburb of Southend-on-Sea, Essex): 'Hocca's woodland clearing'. OE *lēah*, 'wood', 'clearing'. The name could also mean 'woodland clearing where hocks grow' (OE *hocc*, 'hock', 'mallow', + *lēah*). DB *Hocheleia*.

Hockley Heath (village, Solihull): '(place on the) heath by Hucca's hill'. OE *hlāw*, 'mound', 'hill', + *hǣth*, 'heath'. c.1280 *Huckeloweheth*.

Hockliffe (village, Beds): 'Hocga's bank'. OE *clif*, 'cliff', 'bank'. The DB form of the name below has garbled the second element (as if it were '-ley'). 1015 *Hocgan clif*, DB *Hocheleia*.

Hockwold cum Wilton. See METHWOLD.

Hockworthy (village, Devon): 'Hocca's enclosure'. OE *worth*, 'enclosure'. DB *Hocoorde*.

Hoddesdon (town, Herts): 'Hod's hill'. OE *dūn*, 'hill'. Hoddesdon lies to the east of the hill so named. DB *Hodesdone*.

Hoddlesdon (village, Blackburn with Dar): 'Hod's or Hodel's valley'. OE *denu*, 'valley'. 1296 *Hoddesdene*.

Hodgeston (village, Pemb): 'Hodge's farm'. OE *tūn*, 'farm'. Hodge is a form of the personal name Roger. 1291 *Villa Hogges*, 1376 *Hoggeston*.

Hodnet (village, Shropshire): '(place in the) pleasant valley'. The name is Celtic in origin, from words related to modern Welsh *hawdd*, 'easy', 'pleasant', and *nant*, 'valley'. The 'pleasant valley' is that of the river Tern, which Hodnet overlooks. DB *Odenet*, 1121 *Hodenet*.

Hoe (hamlet, Norfolk): '(place on the) spur of land'. OE *hōh*, 'hill spur'. The name represents OE *hōe*, the dative form of *hōh*. DB *Hou*.

Hoff (hamlet, Cumbria): 'heathen temple'. OS *hof*, 'temple', 'sanctuary'. There is no sign of a Viking temple here now. 1179 *Houf*.

Hoggeston (village, Bucks): 'Hogg's farmstead'. OE *tūn*, 'farmstead'. The DB form of the name below may have resulted from a mishearing. DB *Hocheston*, 1200 *Hoggeston*.

Hoghton (village, Lancs): 'farmstead by a hill spur'. OE *hōh*, 'hill spur', + *tūn*, 'farmstead'. The spur in question is the steep west bank of the river Darwen here. c.1160 *Hoctonam*.

Hognaston (village, Derbys): 'Hocca's grazing farm'. OE *æfēsn*, 'pasturage', + *tūn*, 'farmstead'. DB *Ochenavestun*.

Hog's Back (hill ridge, Surrey): 'hog's back'. The ridge is so called from its shape, resembling the broad back of a pig when seen from below. Its earlier name was *Guildown*, 'golden down' (OE *gylde*, 'golden one', + *dūn*, 'hill'), preserved in Guildown Road, GUILDFORD. 1195 *Geldedon*, 1495 *Gildowne*, 1744 *Gill Downe*, 1823 *Hogs Back*.

Hogsthorpe (village, Lincs): 'Hogg's secondary settlement'. OS *thorp*, 'outlying farmstead', 'secondary settlement'. The settlement probably depended on Mumby. 12C *Hocgestorp*.

Holbeach (town, Lincs): '(place by the) hollow stream'. OE *hol*, 'hollow', + *bece*, 'stream'. A 'hollow stream' is a deep one. The name could also mean 'hollow ridge' (OE *bæc*, modern English *back*), meaning slightly raised ground in a hollow place. This would better suit the topography of Holbeach. DB *Holebech*.

Holbeck (village, Notts): '(place by the) stream in a hollow'. OS *holr*, 'hollow', + *bekkr*, 'stream'. The stream in question runs between rocks called Cresswell Crags here. c.1180 *Holebek*.

Holbeton (village, Devon): 'farmstead in the hollow bend'. OE *hol*, 'hollow', + *boga*, 'bend', + *tūn*, 'farmstead'. 1229 *Holbouton*.

Holborn (district, Camden): '(place by the) hollow stream'. OE *hol*, 'hollow', + *burna*, 'stream'. A 'hollow stream' is one in a hollow, represented here by a dip in a section of Farringdon Road. DB *Holeburne*.

Holbrook (village, Suffolk): '(place by the) brook in a hollow'. OE *hol*, 'hollow', + *brōc*, 'brook'. DB *Holebroc*. SO ALSO: *Holbrook*, Derbys.

Holcombe (village, Somerset): '(place in the) deep valley'. OE *hol*, 'hollow', 'deep', + *cumb*, 'valley'. 1243 *Holecumbe*. SO ALSO: *Holcombe*, Bury, Devon (near Teignmouth).

Holcombe Rogus (village, Devon): 'Rogo's (estate in the) deep valley'. OE *hol*, 'hollow', 'deep', + *cumb*, 'valley'. One Rogo held the manor here in 1086, his name distinguishing this Holcombe from *Holcombe Burnell*, 20 miles to the southwest, where the manor was held in 1242 by the son of one Bernard. DB *Holecoma*, 1281 *Holecombe Roges*.

Holcot (village, Northants): 'cottage in the hollow'. OE *hol*, 'hole', 'hollow', + *cot*, 'cottage'. DB *Holecote*.

Holdenby (village, Northants): 'Halfdan's farmstead'. OS *bý*, 'farmstead', 'village'. The personal name is Scandinavian. DB *Aldenesbi*.

Holderness (peninsula, E Yorks): 'headland ruled by a hold'. OS *holdr*, 'hold', + *nes*, 'headland'. A 'hold' was a high-ranking officer in the

Danelaw, corresponding to the English high reeve. DB *Heldernesse*.

Holdgate (village, Shropshire): 'Helgot's castle'. The first two forms of the name below show that the name originally ended in 'castle' (Latin *castrum*, ME *castel*). This element eventually disappeared, leaving the OF personal name alone. 1109 *Castrum Helgoti*, 1199 *Hologodescastel*, 1294 *Holegot*.

Holford (village, Somerset): '(place by the) ford in a hollow'. OE *hol*, 'hollow', + *ford*, 'ford'. DB *Holeforde*.

Holkham (village, Norfolk): 'homestead by a hollow'. OE *holc*, 'hollow', + *hām*, 'homestead'. The 'hollow' may have been a lake in Holkham Park. DB *Holcham*.

Hollacombe (village, Devon): '(place by a) deep valley'. OE *hol*, 'hollow', + *cumb*, 'valley'. DB *Holecome*.

Holland (historic district, Lincs): 'land of hill spurs'. OE *hōh*, 'hill spur', + *land*, 'land'. This is the generally accepted origin of the name, although it seems unlikely for this fenland region. A Celtic source for the first part of the name has also been proposed, from a word related to modern Welsh *hoywal*, 'stream', 'current', referring to the many rivers here. The name is preserved in the council district of *South Holland*. DB *Hoiland*.

Holland-on-Sea (coastal district of Clacton-on-Sea, Essex): '(place on) cultivated land by a hill spur by the sea'. OE *hōh*, 'hill spur', + *land*, 'plot of cultivated land'. Holland-on-Sea was formerly *Little Holland*, as distinct from the village of *Great Holland*, 2 miles to the north and inland. *c*.1000 *Holande*, DB *Holanda*.

Hollesley (village, Suffolk): 'woodland clearing in a hollow'. OE *hol*, 'hollow', + *lēah*, 'wood', 'clearing'. The name could also mean 'Hōl's woodland clearing'. DB *Holeslea*.

Hollingbourne (village, Kent): '(place by the) stream of Hōla's people'. OE *-inga-*, 'of the people of', + *burna*, 'stream'. The name could also mean '(place by the) stream of the dwellers in the hollow' (OE *hol*, 'hollow', + *-inga-*, 'of the dwellers at'). The 'stream' is the river Len here. 10C *Holingeburna*, DB *Holingeborne*.

Hollington (village, Derbys): 'farmstead where holly grows'. OE *holegn*, 'holly', + *tūn*, 'farmstead'. DB *Holintune*. SO ALSO: *Hollington*, E Sussex, Staffs.

Hollingworth (village, Tameside): 'enclosure where holly grows'. OE *holegn*, 'holly', + *worth*, 'enclosure'. Holly bushes could have been used

to make the enclosure. The DB form of the name below is garbled. DB *Holisurde*, 13C *Holinewurth*.

Holloway (district, Islington): '(place by the) hollow road'. OE *hol*, 'hollow', + *weg*, 'way', 'road'. A 'hollow road' is one in a hollow, as represented by Holloway Road in the valley here between (significantly named) Highbury and Highgate. 1307 *Le Holeweye*.

Hollowell (village, Northants): '(place by the) spring in a hollow'. OE *hol*, 'hollow', + *wella*, 'spring', 'stream'. DB *Holewelle*.

Hollym (village, E Yorks): 'homestead or enclosure near the hollow'. OE *hol*, 'hollow', + *hām*, 'homestead', or *hamm* 'enclosure'. The name could also mean '(place at the) hollows', from OE or OS *holum*, the dative plural form of OE *hol* and OS *holr*. The village is in a slight hollow. DB *Holam*.

Holmbury St Mary (village, Surrey): '(place by a) fort with St Mary's church'. OE *burh*, 'fortified place'. The first part of the name is of uncertain origin. It may represent a personal name. The 'fort' is the ancient camp on nearby Holmbury Hill. early 15C *Homebery*, 1610 *Holmbury*.

Holme (village, Notts): '(place on an) island'. OS *holmr*, 'island'. The 'island' here is slightly raised ground in a wet area. Holme lies by the river Trent. 1203 *Holme*. SO ALSO: *Holme*, Cambs, Cumbria, N Yorks.

Holme (Kirklees). See HOLMFIRTH.

Holme Chapel (village, Lancs): '(place on an) island with a chapel'. OS *holmr*, 'island'. The 'island' is land by the river Calder here. The chapel was replaced by St John's church in 1788. 1305 *Holme*.

Holme Hale (village, Norfolk): '(place on an) island by a corner of land'. OS *holmr*, 'island', + OE *halh*, 'nook', 'corner of land'. The 'island' is raised ground by the river Wissey here. DB *Holm*, 1267 *Holmhel*.

Holme Lacy (village, Herefords): 'de Laci's (estate on) land in a river bend'. OE *hamm*, 'enclosure', 'land in a river bend'. The de Laci family held the manor here, in a loop of the river Wye, from 1086. DB *Hamme*, 1221 *Homme Lacy*.

Holme next the Sea (village, Norfolk): '(place at the) island by the sea'. OS *holmr*, 'island'. The 'island' is raised ground in marshland here, close to the sea. *c*.1035 *Holm*, DB *Holm*.

Holme on the Wolds. See HOLME UPON SPALDING MOOR.

Holme Pierrepont (village, Notts): 'de Perpount's (estate on the) island'. OS *holmr*, 'island'. The 'island' here is an area surrounded by watercourses and dykes by the river Trent. The de Perpount family held the manor here in the 14C. DB *Holmo*, 1571 *Holme Peyrpointe*.

Holmer (suburb of Hereford, Herefords): '(place at the) pool in a hollow'. OE *hol*, 'hollow', + *mere*, 'pool'. DB *Holemere*.

Holmes Chapel (village, Cheshire): 'chapel at Holme'. ME *chapel*, 'chapel'. The original name of the place here meant '(place at the) water meadow' (OS *holmr*). 12C *Hulm*, 1400 *Holme chapell*, 1868 *Church Hulme, or Holmes Chapel*.

Holmesfield (village, Derbys): 'open land near Holm'. OE *feld*, 'open land' (modern English *field*). *Holm* is the name of a now lost place meaning 'island' (OS *holmr*), referring to dry ground in marshland. DB *Holmesfelt*.

Holme upon Spalding Moor (village, E Yorks): '(place at the) island on Spalding Moor'. OS *holmr*, 'island'. The 'island' here is raised ground in a wet region. *Spalding Moor* is a district name from the people who gave the name of SPALD-ING, Lincs (+ OE *mōr*, 'moor'). The addition to the name distinguishes the village from *Holme on the Wolds*, 12 miles to the northwest (see WOLDS). DB *Holme*, 1293 *Holm in Spaldingmor*, 1868 *Holme-on-Spalding-Moor*.

Holmfirth (town, Kirklees): 'woodland by Holme'. OE *fyrhth*, 'sparse woodland'. The nearby village of *Holme* has a name meaning '(place at the) holly tree' (OE *holegn*, 'holly'). 1274 *Holnefrith*.

Holmpton (village, E Yorks): 'farmstead near the shore meadows'. OS *holmr*, 'meadow by the shore', + OE *tūn*, 'farmstead'. Holmpton is near the coast. DB *Holmetone*.

Holne (village, Devon): '(place by the) holly tree'. OE *holegn*, 'holly'. The DB form of the name below is corrupt. DB *Holle*, 1178 *Holna*.

Holnest (hamlet, Dorset): '(place by the) wooded hill where holly grows'. OE *holegn*, 'holly', + *hyrst*, 'wooded hill'. 1185 *Holeherst*.

Holsworthy (town, Devon): 'Heald's enclosure'. OE *worthig*, 'enclosure'. OE *worthig* is equivalent to *worth* in southwest England. DB *Haldeurdi*.

Holt (village, Dorset): '(place by the) wood'. OE *holt*, 'wood', 'thicket'. The first form of the name below has added the name of nearby WIMBORNE MINSTER. 1185 *Winburneholt*, 1372 *Holte*. SO ALSO: *Holt*, Wilts, Worcs.

Holt (town, Norfolk): '(place by the) wood'. OE *holt*, 'wood', 'thicket'. DB *Holt*.

Holtby (village, York): 'Holti's farmstead'. OS *bý*, 'farmstead', 'village'. The personal name is Scandinavian. DB *Holtebi*.

Holton (village, Lincs): 'farmstead on a spur of land'. OE *hōh*, 'hill spur', + *tūn*, 'farmstead'. The village is also known as *Holton cum Beckering*, after a nearby hamlet, for distinction from *Holton le Clay*, 18 miles to the northeast, on the clay, and *Holton le Moor*, 11 miles to the north, in fenland. DB *Houtone*.

Holton (village, Oxon): 'farmstead in a corner of land'. OE *healh*, 'nook', 'corner of land', + *tūn*, 'farmstead'. 956 *Healtun*, DB *Eltone*. SO ALSO: *Holton*, Somerset.

Holton Heath (hamlet, Dorset): 'farmstead by a hollow'. OE *hol*, 'hollow', + *tūn*, 'farmstead'. The name could also mean 'farmstead by a wood' (OE *holt*, 'wood', + *tūn*). The second word of the name refers to the area of heathland to the west. DB *Holtone*.

Holton le Clay. See HOLTON (Lincs).

Holton le Moor. See HOLTON (Lincs).

Holton St Mary (village, Suffolk): 'farmstead near a hollow with St Mary's church'. OE *hol*, 'hollow', + *tūn*, 'farmstead'. The main name could also mean 'Hōla's farmstead'. DB *Holetuna*.

Holwell (village, Dorset): '(place on a) ridge by a hollow'. OE *hol*, 'hollow', + *walu*, 'ridge', 'bank'. 1188 *Holewala*.

Holwell (village, Herts): '(place by the) spring in a hollow'. OE *hol*, 'hollow', + *wella*, 'spring', 'stream'. 969 *Holewelle*, DB *Holewelle*. SO ALSO: *Holwell*, Leics.

Holwell (village, Oxon): '(place by the) holy spring'. OE *hālig*, 'holy', + *wella*, 'spring', 'stream'. 1222 *Haliwell*.

Holwick (hamlet, Durham): 'farm in a hollow'. OE *hol*, 'hollow', + *wīc*, 'dwelling', 'specialized farm'. 1235 *Holewyk*.

Holworth (hamlet, Dorset): 'enclosure in a hollow'. OE *hol*, 'hollow', + *worth*, 'enclosure'. 934 *Holewertthe*, DB *Holverde*.

Holybourne (village, Hants): '(place by the) holy stream'. OE *hālig*, 'holy', + *burna*, 'stream'. The stream in question rises by the church here. DB *Haliburne*.

Holyhead (town and port, Anglesey): 'holy headland'. OE *hālig*, 'holy', + *hēafod*, 'headland'. Holyhead is a historic Christian centre. The 'headland' is Holyhead Mountain, to the west of the town. The Welsh name of Holyhead is *Caergybi*, 'Cybi's fort' (Welsh *caer*, 'fort'), for the 6C saint to whom the parish church here is dedicated. Cp. HOLY ISLAND (Anglesey). 1315 *Haliheved*, 1395 *Holyhede*.

Holy Island (island, Anglesey): 'holy island'. OE *hālig*, 'holy', + *ēg-land*, 'island'. The island, on which HOLYHEAD is situated, is associated with St Cybi, who founded a monastery here. Hence its Welsh name, *Ynys Gybi* (Welsh *ynys*, 'island').

Holy Island (island, Northd): 'holy island'. OE *hālig*, 'holy', + *ēg-land*, 'island' (from *ēg*, 'island', + *land*, 'land'). The island, also known as LINDISFARNE, has long associations with Christian missionaries. 1195 *Halieland*.

Holyport (village, Windsor & Maid): 'filthy market town'. OE *horig*, 'filthy' (from *horu*, 'filth', 'dirt'), + *port*, 'market town'. The undesirable first part of the original name was deliberately changed to *holy* by the late 14C. 1220 *Horipord*, 1395 *Holyport*.

Holystone (hamlet, Northd): '(place by a) holy stone'. OE *hālig*, 'holy', + *stān*, 'stone'. The reference is perhaps to a stone where the gospel was preached, not necessarily one of the so-called 'Five Kings' standing stones nearby. 1242 *Halistan*.

Holywell (town, Flints): '(place by the) holy well'. OE *hālig*, 'holy', + *wella*, 'spring', 'well'. The name refers to the sacred well of St Winifred, who founded a nunnery here in the 7C. The Welsh name of Holywell is *Treffynnon*, 'village of the well' (Welsh *tref*, 'village', + *ffynnon*, 'well', 'spring'). 1093 *Haliwel*.

Homersfield (village, Suffolk): 'Hūnbeorht's open land'. OE *feld*, 'open land' (modern English *field*). DB *Humbresfelda*.

Homerton (district, Hackney): 'Hūnburh's farmstead'. OE *tūn*, 'farmstead', 'estate'. The personal name is that of a woman. 1343 *Humburton*.

Homington (village, Wilts): 'estate associated with Humma'. OE *-ing-*, 'associated with', + *tūn*, 'farmstead', 'estate'. 956 *Hummingtun*, DB *Humitone*.

Honeyborough (hamlet, Pemb): 'manor where honey is produced'. OE *hunig*, 'honey', + *burh*, 'fortified place', 'manor'. The name implies that bees were kept at the manor. 1325 *Honyburgh*.

Honeybourne (village, Worcs): '(place by the) stream where honey is found'. OE *hunig*, 'honey', + *burna*, 'stream'. The village contains the parishes of *Church Honeybourne* and *Cow Honeybourne*, still identified individually on some maps. The former is distinguished from the latter by its church. The first word of the latter name represents OE *calu*, 'bare', meaning a place lacking vegetation. The second DB form of the name below (for Cow Honeybourne) is corrupt. 709 *Huniburna*, DB *Huniburne*, *Heniberge*, 1535 *Churchoniborne*; 1374 *Calewe Honiburn*.

Honeychurch (village, Devon): 'Hūna's church'. OE *cirice*, 'church'. In theory the name could also mean 'honey church', i.e. one where bees are kept, but this seems unlikely. DB *Honechercha*.

Honeystreet (hamlet, Wilts): '(place by the) muddy road'. The name applied to the Ridgeway as it crossed the Vale of Pewsey here, with mud of a honey-like consistency and colour. 1773 *Honey Street*.

Honiley (hamlet, Warwicks): 'woodland clearing where honey is found'. OE *hunig*, 'honey', + *lēah*, 'wood', 'clearing'. The name implies a place with many bees. 1208 *Hunilege*.

Honing (village, Norfolk): '(settlement of the) people by the stone'. OE *hān*, 'stone', 'rock', + *-ingas*, 'dwellers at'. The precise location of the stone or rock in question is uncertain. It may have been on the small hill here, or possibly the 'rock' was the hill itself. 1044 *Hanninge*, DB *Haninga*.

Honingham (village, Norfolk): 'homestead of Hūna's people'. OE *-inga-*, 'of the people of', + *hām*, 'homestead'. DB *Hunincham*.

Honington (village, Lincs): 'estate associated with Hund'. OE *-ing-*, 'associated with', + *tūn*, 'farmstead', 'estate'. DB *Hundintone*.

Honington (village, Suffolk): 'farmstead of Hūna's people'. OE *-inga-*, 'of the people of', + *tūn*, 'farmstead'. DB *Hunegetuna*.

Honington (village, Warwicks): 'farmstead where honey is made'. OE *hunig*, 'honey', + *tūn*, 'farmstead'. 1043 *Hunitona*, DB *Hunitone*.

Honiton (town, Devon): 'Hūna's farmstead'. OE *tūn*, 'farmstead'. DB *Honetone*.

Honley (town, Kirklees): 'woodland clearing where woodcock are seen'. OE *hana*, 'cockbird', 'woodcock', + *lēah*, 'wood', 'clearing'. The first part of the name could also mean 'rocks', 'stones' (OE *hān*, 'stone', modern English *hone*). DB *Haneleia*.

Honor Oak (district, Lewisham): '(place by the) oak of honour'. The oak in question, struck by lightning in the late 19C, probably served as a boundary marker between Camberwell (formerly in Surrey) and Lewisham (formerly in Kent). Local lore links the name with the honour of a visit here by Queen Elizabeth, who is said to have dined under the oak. The name preserves the old spelling of *honour*. 1609 *Oke of Honor*, 1763 *Oak of Honour Wood*.

Hooe (village, E Sussex): '(place on the) spur of land'. OE *hōh*, 'hill spur'. The village stands on a hill above marshland. DB *Hou*.

Hook (district, Kingston): '(place by the) hook of land'. OE *hōc*, 'hook'. The location of the hook-shaped hill or spur of land here is uncertain. 1227 *Hoke*. SO ALSO: *Hook*, Hants (near Basingstoke), Wilts.

Hook Norton (village, Oxon): 'farmstead of the dwellers by Hocca's hill slope'. The first word of the name and first part of the second word represent the tribal name *Hoccanere*, the latter part of which derives from OE *ōra*, 'hill slope'. This is followed by OE *tūn*, 'farmstead'. The name was humorously corrupted in the 16C or earlier to *Hogs Norton*, giving rise to a rhyme about 'Hogs Norton, where pigs play on the organ', and the 20C radio broadcaster Gillie Potter pursued the pleasantry in his invention of 'Lord Marshmallow of Hogsnorton'. Early 10C *Hocneratune*, c.1228 *Hogenartone*, 1381 *Hogesnorton*.

Hoole (district of Chester, Cheshire): '(place at the) hollow'. OE *hol*, 'hole', 'hollow'. A 12C manuscript refers to the place as *Vallis Demonum*, 'valley of devils', perhaps meaning a haunt of thieves. 1119 *Hole*.

Hooton Roberts (village, Rotherham): 'Robert's farmstead on a spur of land'. OE *hōh*, 'hill spur', + *tūn*, 'farmstead'. One Robert held the manor here in the 13C, his name distinguishing this Hooton from *Hooton Levitt*, to the south, where the Livet family owned the manor in the 13C, and *Hooton Pagnell*, Doncaster, 10 miles to the north, where the Painel family held the manor in the 11C. DB *Hotun*, 1285 *Hoton Robert*.

Hope (village, Derbys): 'enclosed land'. OE *hop*, 'remote valley'. The village is located below High Peak in Hope Valley at the entrance to the Vale of Edale. 926 *Hope*, DB *Hope*.

Hope (resort village, Devon): '(place by the) small bay'. OE *hōp*, 'hoop'. Hope has a small harbour sheltered by Bolt Head nearby. 1281 *La Hope*.

Hope (village, Flints): 'enclosed land'. OE *hop*, 'enclosure in marshland'. The village stands on fairly dry land beside the river Alun. The Welsh form of the English name is *Yr Hôb*. DB *Hope*.

Hope Bowdler (village, Shropshire): 'de Bulers' (estate in the) valley'. OE *hop*, 'enclosed valley'. The de Bulers family held the manor here in the 13C. The first part of the DB form of the name below represents the OE personal name Forthræd. DB *Fordritishope*, 1201 *Hop*, 1273 *Hopebulers*.

Hopeman (resort village, Moray): 'high hill'. French *haut*, 'high', + *mont*, 'hill'. The village was founded in 1805 by William Young of Inverugie and took its name from that of an estate here.

Hope Mansell (village, Herefords): 'Maloisel's (estate in the) valley'. OE *hop*, 'valley'. The Maloisel family held the manor early here, their name distinguishing this Hope from LONG-HOPE, Glos, 4 miles to the east. DB *Hope*, 12C *Hoppe Maloisel*.

Hopesay (village, Shropshire): 'de Say's (estate in the) valley'. OE *hop*, 'enclosed valley'. Picot de Say held the manor here in 1086. DB *Hope*, 1255 *Hope de Say*.

Hope under Dinmore (village, Herefords): '(place in the) valley below Dinmore'. OE *hop*, 'enclosed valley'. The added name is that of *Dinmore Hill*, perhaps representing Welsh *din mawr*, 'big fort', or else meaning 'Dynna's marsh' (OE *mōr*, 'moor', 'marshland'). DB *Hope*, 1291 *Hope sub' Dinnemor*.

Hopton (village, Suffolk): 'farmstead in an enclosed plot of land'. OE *hop*, 'valley', 'enclosed plot of land', + *tūn*, 'farmstead'. The 'enclosed plot of land' here by the north Suffolk border is probably the raised ground jutting into marshland on which Hopton lies. DB *Hopetuna*. SO ALSO: *Hopton*, Shropshire (near Hodnet), Staffs.

Hopton Wafers (village, Shropshire): 'Wafre's farmstead in a valley'. OE *hop*, 'enclosed valley', + *tūn*, 'farmstead'. The manor here was held early by the Wafre family, their name distinguishing this Hopton from *Hopton Cangeford*, 6 miles to the northwest, held by the Cangefot family, and *Hopton Castle*, 18 miles to the west, with a Norman castle. DB *Hopton*, 1236 *Hopton Wafre*.

Hopwas (village, Staffs): 'alluvial land by an enclosure'. OE *hop*, 'enclosure', + *wæsse*, 'alluvial land' (related modern English *wash*). 'Hopwas lies in the Tame valley, at the foot of a ridge, and much of it is liable to flood' (W. H. Duignan, *Notes on Staffordshire Place Names*, 1902). DB *Opewas*.

Hopwood (village, Worcs): '(place by the) wood near an enclosure'. OE *hop*, 'valley', 'enclosed plot of land', + *wudu*, 'wood'. 849 *Hopwuda*. SO ALSO: *Hopwood*, Rochdale.

Horbury (town, Wakefield): 'stronghold on muddy land'. OE *horu*, 'filth', 'dirt', + *burh*, 'fortified place'. Horbury stands on a hill overlooking the river Calder, but the original fortification may have been on the lower ground, nearer the river. DB *Horberie*.

Horden (district of Peterlee, Durham): '(place in a) muddy valley'. OE *horu*, 'filth', 'dirt', + *denu*, 'valley'. *c*.1050 *Horedene*.

Hordley (hamlet, Shropshire): 'woodland clearing where treasure was found'. OE *hord*, 'hoard', 'treasure', + *lēah*, 'wood', 'clearing'. A hoard of Roman coins was found here in recent times, and presumably similar discoveries were made in the Anglo-Saxon period. DB *Hordelei*.

Horfield (district, Bristol): 'muddy open land'. OE *horu*, 'dirt', 'filth', + *feld*, 'open land' (modern English *field*). DB *Horefelle*.

Horham (village, Suffolk): 'muddy homestead'. OE *horu*, 'dirt', 'filth', + *hām*, 'homestead'. *c*.950 *Horham*.

Horkstow (village, N Lincs): 'place of shelter'. OE *horc*, 'shelter', + *stōw*, 'place'. The name implies a place where animals or people could shelter. The DB form of the name below has omitted the *s* of *stōw*. DB *Horchetou*, 12C *Horkestowe*.

Horley (town, Surrey): 'woodland clearing in the horn-shaped area of land'. OE *horna*, 'horn', + *lēah*, 'wood', 'clearing'. 12C *Horle*. SO ALSO: *Horley*, Oxon.

Hornblotton (hamlet, Somerset): 'farmstead of the hornblowers'. OE *horn-blāwere* (from *horn*, 'horn', + *blāwere*, 'blower'), + *tūn*, 'farmstead'. 851 *Hornblawertone*, DB *Horblawetone*.

Hornby (village, Lancs): 'farmstead on a horn-shaped piece of land'. OS *horn*, 'horn', + *bý*, 'farmstead', 'village'. The village lies on a tongue of land formed by the confluence of the rivers Lune and Wenning. DB *Hornebi*. SO ALSO: *Hornby*, N Yorks (near Catterick, near Great Smeaton).

Horncastle (town, Lincs): 'Roman station on a horn-shaped area of land'. OE *horna*, 'horn', + *ceaster*, 'Roman camp'. (An expected '-caster' instead became '-castle'.) The 'horn of land' is that formed by the junction of the rivers Bain and Waring here. The Roman town here was *Bannovalium*, a Celtic name meaning 'strong horn of land', referring to the same feature. DB *Hornecastre*.

Hornchurch (town, Havering): 'church with horns'. OE *horn*, 'horn', + *cirice*, 'church'. The 'horns' would have been horn-shaped gables on the church. A representation of a bull's head with horns was fixed to the church roof in the 18C as a (misleading) 'visual aid' to the name. The first form of the name below is the Latin equivalent of the English. 1222 *Monasterium Cornutum*, 1233 *Hornechurch*.

Horncliffe (village, Northd): '(place on the) horn-shaped bank'. OE *horn*, 'horn-shaped piece of land', + *clif*, 'cliff', 'bank'. The reference is to the high bank of the river Tweed here. 1210 *Hornecliff*.

Horndean (town, Hants): 'valley where dormice are seen'. OE *hearma*, 'dormouse', + *denu*, 'valley'. The name could also mean 'Hearma's valley'. 1199 *Harmedene*.

Horndon on the Hill (village, Thurrock): '(place on the) horn-shaped hill'. OE *horning*, 'horn-shaped piece of land', + *dūn*, 'hill'. The tautological addition to the name distinguishes this Horndon from *East Horndon* and *West Horndon*, Essex, to the north. DB *Horninduna*.

Horne (hamlet, Surrey): '(place by the) horn-shaped piece of land'. OE *horn*, 'horn'. The name may refer to the projection of land by the church here. 1208 *Horne*.

Horning (village, Norfolk): '(settlement of the) dwellers on the horn-shaped piece of land'. OE *horn*, 'horn', + -*ingas*, 'dwellers at'. The 'horn-shaped piece of land' is a bend in the river Bure here. 1020 *Horningga*, DB *Horningam*.

Horninghold (village, Leics): 'woodland of the dwellers on the horn-shaped piece of land'. OE *horn*, 'horn', + -*inga*-, 'of the dwellers at', + *wald*, 'woodland'. The DB form of the name below is corrupt. DB *Horniwale*, 1163 *Horningewald*.

Horninglow (district of Burton upon Trent, Staffs): 'mound by the horn-shaped piece of land'. OE *horning*, 'horn-shaped piece of land', + *hlāw*, 'mound', 'hill'. 12C *Horninglow*.

Horningsea (village, Cambs): 'Horning's island'. OE *ēg*, 'island'. The 'island' is dry ground in marshland here. The first part of the name could also represent OE *horning*, 'horn-shaped piece of land'. *c*.975 *Horninges ige*, DB *Horningesie*.

Horningsham (village, Wilts): 'Horning's homestead'. OE *hām*, 'homestead'. The first part of the name could also represent OE *horning*, 'horn-shaped piece of land'. DB *Horningesham*.

Horningtoft (village, Norfolk): 'homestead of the dwellers on the horn-shaped piece of land'. OE *horn*, 'horn', + -*inga*-, 'of the dwellers at', + OS *toft*, 'homestead'. DB *Horninghetoft*.

Hornsea (resort town, E Yorks): '(place by the) lake with a horn-shaped peninsula'. OS *horn*, 'horn', + *nes*, 'headland', + *sǽr*, 'sea', 'inland lake'. The reference is to Hornsea Mere, a large lake to the west of the town, which has a 'horn' of land projecting into it. DB *Hornessei*.

Hornsey (district, Haringey): 'enclosure in the grey wood'. OE *hāring* (from *hār*, 'grey', modern

English *hoar*), + *hæg*, 'enclosure'. The name could also mean 'Hæring's enclosure'. Early forms of the name, as those below, gave that of the present unitary authority of *Haringey*, a 'restored' form of the formerly familiar alternative (but regularly evolved) name *Harringay*. 1201 *Haringeie*, 1243 *Haringesheye*, 1557 *Haringsaye alias Harnesey*, *c.*1580 *Haringay alias Hornesey*.

Hornton (village, Oxon): 'farmstead by the horn-shaped piece of land'. OE *horning*, 'horn-shaped piece of land', + *tūn*, 'farmstead'. The village stands on a tongue of land between two streams. 1194 *Hornigeton*.

Horrabridge (village, Devon): '(place by the) bridge on the boundary'. OE *hār*, 'boundary', + *brycg*, 'bridge'. The bridge over the river Walkham here is located at the boundary of three parishes. 1345 *Horebrigge*.

Horringer (village, Suffolk): '(place by the) ploughed land at the bend'. OE *horning*, 'bend', 'horn-shaped piece of land', + *erth*, 'ploughed land' (related modern English *earth*). The name could also mean 'Horning's ploughed land'. Until recently the village had the alternative name *Horningsheath*. DB *Horningeserda*, 1868 *Horningsheath, or Horringer*.

Horseheath (village, Cambs): 'heath where horses are kept'. OE *hors*, 'horse', + *hǣth*, 'heath'. The second part of the name is garbled in the DB form below. *c.*1080 *Horseda*, DB *Horsei*.

Horsell (suburb of Woking, Surrey): 'muddy shelter for animals'. OE *horu*, 'filth', 'dirt', + *sell*, 'shelter for animals'. 13C *Horisell*.

Horsey (village, Norfolk): 'island where horses are kept'. OE *hors*, 'horse', + *ēg*, 'island'. The 'island' is dry ground in marshes between Horsey Mere and the coast. DB *Horseia*, 1868 *Horsey-next-the-Sea*.

Horsford (village, Norfolk): '(place by the) ford where horses cross'. OE *hors*, 'horse', + *ford*, 'ford'. The ford in question would have been over the tributary of the river Bure on which the village lies. DB *Hosforda*.

Horsforth (district, Leeds): '(place by the) ford where horses cross'. OE *hors*, 'horse', + *ford*, 'ford'. The river here is the Aire. DB *Horseford*.

Horsham (town, W Sussex): 'homestead where horses are kept'. OE *hors*, 'horse', + *hām*, 'homestead', 'village'. The name implies that horses would have been bred here. A famous 17C folk etymology tells how the place had 'very very bad wayes, from whence it is sayd that towne had its name, the steps to it being up to the horses hams' (*Sussex Archaeological Collections*). 947 *Horsham*.

Horsham St Faith (village, Norfolk): 'homestead where horses are kept with St Faith's church'. OE *hors*, 'horse', + *hām*, 'homestead', 'village'. Horses would have been bred here. DB *Horsham*.

Horsington (village, Somerset): 'farmstead of the horsekeepers'. OE *hors-thegn* (from *hors*, 'horse', + *thegn*, 'servant'), + *tūn*, 'farmstead'. DB *Horstenetone*.

Horsley (village, Derbys): 'clearing where horses are kept'. OE *hors*, 'horse', + *lēah*, 'wood', 'clearing'. DB *Horselei*. SO ALSO: *Horsley*, Glos, Northd.

Horsmonden (village, Kent): 'woodland pasture by the stream where horses drink'. OE *hors*, 'horse', + *burna*, 'stream', + *denn*, 'woodland pasture'. *c.*1100 *Horsbundenne*.

Horspath (village, Oxon): '(place by the) horse path'. OE *hors*, 'horse', + *pæth*, 'path'. DB *Horspadan*.

Horstead (village, Norfolk): 'place where horses are kept'. OE *hors*, 'horse', + *stede*, 'place'. DB *Horsteda*.

Horsted Keynes (village, W Sussex): 'de Cahainges' (estate at the) place where horses are kept'. OE *hors*, 'horse', + *stede*, 'place'. William de Cahainges held the manor here in 1086, his name distinguishing this Horsted from *Little Horsted*, 9 miles to the southeast. DB *Horstede*, 1307 *Horsted Kaynes*.

Horton (village, Northants): 'muddy farmstead'. OE *horu*, 'filth', 'dirt', + *tūn*, 'farmstead'. DB *Hortone*. SO ALSO: *Horton*, Bucks (near Cheddington), Dorset, Oxon (now combined with STUDLEY as *Horton-cum-Studley*), Shropshire (near Wem), Staffs, Wilts.

Horton (village, S Glos): '(place by the) hill where stags are seen'. OE *heorot*, 'hart', 'stag', + *dūn*, 'hill'. DB *Horedone*.

Horton-cum-Studley. See HORTON (Northants).

Horton in Ribblesdale (village, N Yorks): 'muddy farmstead in the valley of the (river) Ribble'. OE *horu*, 'filth', 'dirt', + *tūn*, 'farmstead', + *dæl* or OS *dalr*, 'valley'. For the river name, see RIBCHESTER. The addition to the name distinguishes this Horton from the hamlet of *Horton*, Lancs, 15 miles to the south, with a name of the same origin. DB *Hortune*, 13C *Horton in Ribbelesdale*.

Horton Kirby (village, Kent): 'de Kirkeby's muddy farmstead'. OE *horu*, 'filth', 'dirt', + *tūn*, 'farmstead'. The de Kirkeby family held the manor here in the 13C. DB *Hortune*, 1346 *Horton Kyrkeby*.

Horwich (town, Bolton): '(place by the) grey wych elms'. OE *hār*, 'grey' (related modern English *hoary*), + *wice*, 'wych elm'. The '-wich' in the name does not represent the more common OE *wīc*, 'settlement'. 1221 *Horewic*, 1254 *Horewych*.

Horwood (village, Devon): '(place by the) grey wood'. OE *hār*, 'grey' (related modern English *hoary*), + *wudu*, 'wood'. The first part of the name could also represent OE *horu*, 'mud', giving a sense '(place by the) muddy wood'. DB *Horewoda*, *Hareoda*.

Hose (village, Leics): '(place by the) spurs of land'. OE *hōh*, 'hill spur'. The name represents the OE word in a plural form. There are a series of spurs to the south of the village. DB *Hoches*.

Hotham (village, E Yorks): '(place by the) shelters'. OE *hōd*, 'hood', 'shelter'. The name represents OE *hōdum*, the dative plural form of *hōd*. 963 *Hode*, DB *Hodhum*.

Hothfield (village, Kent): 'heathy open land'. OE *hǣth*, 'heath', + *feld*, 'open land' (modern English *field*). *c*.1100 *Hathfelde*.

Hoton (village, Leics): 'farmstead on a spur of land'. OE *hōh*, 'hill spur', + *tūn*, 'farmstead'. DB *Hohtone*.

Hough (village, Cheshire): '(place on a) hill spur'. OE *hōh*, 'hill spur', 'ridge'. The village lies on high ground south of Crewe. 1241 *Hohc*.

Hough-on-the-Hill (village, Lincs): 'enclosure on the hill'. OE *haga*, 'enclosure'. The village is on rising ground. DB *Hag*.

Houghton (village, Cambs): 'farmstead on a hill spur'. OE *hōh*, 'hill spur', + *tūn*, 'farmstead'. The 'hill spur' is the hill here known as Houghton Hill. DB *Hoctune*. SO ALSO: *Houghton*, Cumbria, Hants.

Houghton (village, W Sussex): 'farmstead on a hill spur'. OE *hōh*, 'hill spur', + *tūn*, 'farmstead'. The village stands on a spur of land projecting into the valley of the river Arun. 683 *Hohtun*.

Houghton Conquest (village, Beds): 'Conquest's farmstead on a hill spur'. OE *hōh*, 'hill spur', + *tūn*, 'farmstead'. The Conquest family held the manor here in the 13C. DB *Houstone*, 1316 *Houghton Conquest*.

Houghton-le-Side. See HOUGHTON-LE-SPRING.

Houghton-le-Spring (town, Sunderland): 'Spring's farmstead on a hill spur'. OE *hōh*, 'hill spur', + *tūn*, 'farmstead'. The Spring family held the manor here in the 13C, their name distinguishing this Houghton from *Houghton-le-Side*, Darlington, 'by the hill slope' (OE *sīde*, 'hillside'), 20 miles to the south. (Both Houghtons were originally in Co. Durham.) *c*.1220 *Hoctun*, *c*.1220 *Hoghton Springes*.

Houghton on the Hill (village, Leics): 'farmstead on a hill spur on a hill'. OE *hōh*, 'hill spur', + *tūn*, 'farmstead'. The essentially redundant second part of the name is first recorded only in the 17C. DB *Hohtone*.

Houghton Regis (suburb of Dunstable, Beds): 'farmstead on a hill spur of the king'. OE *hōh*, 'hill spur', + *tūn*, 'farmstead', + Latin *regis*, 'of the king'. The manor here was held early by the king. DB *Houstone*, 1287 *Kyngeshouton*.

Houghton St Giles (village, Norfolk): 'farmstead on a hill spur with St Giles' church'. OE *hōh*, 'hill spur', + *tūn*, 'farmstead'. DB *Hohttune*.

Hound (village, Hants): 'place where hoarhound grows'. OE *hūne*, 'hoarhound'. Cp. ARUNDEL. DB *Hune*.

Hounslow (borough, Greater London): '(place by the) mound where dogs are kept'. OE *hund*, 'dog' (modern English *hound*), + *hlāw*, 'mound'. The name could also mean 'Hund's mound', in which case the 'mound' could have been the burial place of the named man. The DB form of the name below has omitted the letter *d*. DB *Honeslaw*, 1217 *Hundeslawe*.

Housesteads (Roman camp site, Northd): 'sites of a house'. OE *hūs-stede* (from *hūs*, 'house', + *stede*, 'site', 'place'). The 'house' is the remains of the Roman fort of *Vercovicium* ('place of the Vercovices', i.e. 'effective fighters') on Hadrian's Wall. The original OE word has a later plural *-s*.

Houston (village, Renfrews): 'Hugo's village'. OE *tūn*, 'farmstead', 'village'. The name refers to Hugo de Paduinan, recorded here in the 12C. *c*.1200 *Villa Hugonis*, *c*.1230 *Huston*.

Hove (resort town, Brighton & Hove): '(place by the) hood-shaped hill'. OE *hūfe*, 'hood'. The 'hood' could also have been some natural feature that served as a shelter, but it is hard to say what this was. 1288 *La Houue*.

Hoveringham (village, Notts): 'homestead of the dwellers on the hump-shaped hill'. OE *hofer*, 'hump', + *-inga-*, 'of the dwellers at', + *hām*, 'homestead'. The DB form of the name below is corrupt. DB *Horingeham*, 1167 *Houeringeham*.

Hoveton (village, Norfolk): 'Hofa's farmstead'. OE *tūn*, 'farmstead'. The first part of the name could also represent OE *hōfe*, 'ale-hoof' (a type of ground ivy). The village is sometimes known as *Hoveton St John*, from its church dedication, for distinction from nearby *Hoveton St Peter*. 1044 *Houetonne*, DB *Houetuna*.

Hovingham (village, N Yorks): 'homestead of Hofa's people'. OE *-inga-*, 'of the people of', + *hām*, 'homestead'. DB *Hovingham*.

Howden (town, E Yorks): '(place in the) valley by the headland'. OE *hēafod*, 'headland', + *denu*, 'valley'. There is hardly a valley here in the normal sense, but the term may have been used of a particular defined area. The present form of the name evolved when OS *hǫfuth*, 'headland', replaced OE *hēafod*. 959 *Heafuddene*, DB *Hovedene*.

Howe (hamlet, Norfolk): '(place by the) hill'. OS *haugr*, 'hill', 'mound'. DB *Hou*.

Howick (hamlet, Northd): 'high dairy farm'. OE *hēah*, 'high', 'chief', + *wīc*, 'dairy farm'. *c*.1100 *Hewic*, 1230 *Hawic*.

Howle (hamlet, Wrekin): '(place by the) mound'. OE *hugol*, 'mound', 'hillock'. There is a small hill spur here. DB *Hugle*.

Howsham (village, N Lincs): '(place at the) houses'. OE *hūs* or OS *hús*, 'house'. The name represents *hūsum* or *húsum*, the dative plural form of the OE and OS words. DB *Usun*. SO ALSO: *Howsham*, N Yorks.

Howton (hamlet, Herefords): 'Hugh's estate'. OE *tūn*, 'farmstead', 'estate'. The personal name is Old French. *c*.1184 *Huetune*.

Hoxne (village, Suffolk): '(place on the) hock-shaped spur of land'. OE *hōhsinu*, 'sinew of the heel' (from *hōh*, 'hock', 'hill spur', + *sinu*, 'sinew'). *c*.950 *Hoxne*, DB *Hoxana*.

Hoxton (district, Hackney): 'Hōc's farmstead'. OE *tūn*, 'farmstead'. DB *Hochestone*.

Hoy (island, Orkney): 'lofty island'. OS *hár*, 'high', + *ey*, 'island'. Hoy is well known for the Old Man of Hoy, a massive column of rock 450 feet (137m) high. 1492 *Hoye*.

Hoylake (resort town, Wirral): '(place at the) lake by the hillock'. OE *hygel*, 'hillock', + *lacu*, 'lake'. The name refers to a former tidal lake, now silted up, that existed between the mainland and a sandbank known as the Hile or Hoyle, this being the 'hillock'. The present town grew up round a hotel built here for sea bathers in 1792. 1687 *Hyle Lake*.

Hoyland Nether (town, Barnsley): 'lower land by a hill spur'. OE *hōh*, 'hill spur', + *land*, 'cultivated land', + *neotherra*, 'nether'. The reversal of the two words of the name is quite recent, and today the town is often known as simply *Hoyland*, with *Upper Hoyland* adjoining to the north and *Hoyland Common* to the west. The second word distinguishes this Hoyland from *High Hoyland*, 9 miles to the northwest, high on the side of a ridge, and *Hoyland Swaine*, 8 miles to the northwest, where the manor was held in the 12C by a Scandinavian called Sveinn. Upper Hoyland, High Hoyland and Hoyland Swaine are all on or near the end of a ridge. DB *Hoiland*, 1390 *Nether Holand*, 1896 *Nether Hoyland*.

Hubberholme (hamlet, N Yorks): 'Hūnburh's homestead'. OE *hām*, 'homestead'. The personal name is that of a woman. The second part of the name has apparently been influenced by OS *holmr*, 'island'. DB *Huburgheham*, 1577 *Hubberham*, 1686 *Hubberholme*.

Hubberston (district of Milford Haven, Pemb): 'Hubert's farm'. OE *tūn*, 'farm'. 1291 *Villa Huberti*.

Huby (village, N Yorks): 'farmstead on the spur of land'. OE *hōh*, 'hill spur', + OS *bý*, 'farmstead'. This is Huby near Easingwold. Huby near Harrogate has a name meaning 'Hugh's farmstead', with an Old French personal name. DB *Hobi*.

Hucclecote (district of Gloucester, Glos): 'cottage associated with Hucel'. OE *-ing-*, 'associated with', + *cot*, 'cottage'. DB *Hochilicote*.

Hucking (hamlet, Kent): '(settlement of) Hucca's people'. OE *-ingas*, 'people of'. 1195 *Hugginges*.

Hucknall (town, Notts): 'Hucca's corner of land'. OE *halh*, 'corner of land'. The corner of land may have been a district by the river Leen here, close to the border with Derbyshire. Hucknall was formerly known as *Hucknall Torkard*, from the Torchard family who held the manor here in the 12C. DB *Hochenale*, 1287 *Hokenhale Torkard*.

Huddersfield (town, Kirklees): 'Hudrǣd's open land'. OE *feld*, 'open land' (modern English *field*). The first part of the name could also mean 'shelter' (OE *hūder*). DB *Odresfeld*.

Huddington (village, Worcs): 'estate associated with Hūda'. OE *-ing-*, 'associated with', + *tūn*, 'farmstead', 'estate'. DB *Hudintune*.

Hudswell (village, N Yorks): '(place by) Hūdel's spring'. OE *wella*, 'spring', 'stream'. The DB form of the name below has *r* for *l*. DB *Hudreswelle*, 12C *Hudeleswell*.

Huggate (village, E Yorks): '(place on the) road to the mounds'. OS *hugr*, 'mound', + *gata*, 'road'. A road from the village leads in the direction of tumuli on nearby Huggate Wold. DB *Hughete*.

Hughenden Valley (village, Bucks): 'Huhha's valley'. OE *denu*, 'valley'. The recent addition of the second word is etymologically tautological. DB *Huchedene*, 1868 *Hitchenden, or Hughendon*.

Hughley (village, Shropshire): 'Hugh's wood or clearing'. OE *lēah*, 'wood', 'clearing'. 1203 *Leg*, *c*.1291 *Huleye*.

Hugh Town (town and port, Scilly): 'town by the spur of land'. OE *hōh*, 'hill spur'. The St Mary's town takes its name from the nearby hill, recorded in 1593 as *the Hew Hill*, on which Star Castle stands. 1689 *Hugh Town*, 1868 *Heugh Town*.

Huish (village, Wilts): 'household'. OE *hīwisc*, 'household'. The OE word was a term for a measure of land that would support a family. DB *Iwis*.

Huish Champflower (village, Somerset): 'Champflur's household'. OE *hīwisc*, 'household'. Cp. HUISH. The manor here was held in the 13C by Thomas de Champflur, whose name distinguishes this village from the hamlet of *Beggearn Huish* ('of the beggars', i.e. friars), 5 miles to the north. DB *Hiwis*, 1274 *Hywys Champflur*.

Huish Episcopi (village, Somerset): 'household of the bishop'. OE *hīwisc*, 'household', + Latin *epsicopi*, 'of the bishop'. Cp. HUISH. The manor here was held early by the Bishop of Wells. 973 *Hiwissh*.

Hulcott (village, Bucks): 'hovel-like cottages'. OE *hulu*, 'hovel' (literally 'hull', 'husk'), + *cot*, 'cottage'. 1200 *Hoccote*, 1228 *Hulecote*.

Hull (city and port, Hull): '(place on the river) Hull'. The river has either an OS name, meaning 'deep one', or more likely a Celtic one, meaning 'muddy one'. Hull's official name is *Kingston upon Hull*, the first word of this meaning 'king's manor' (OE *cyning*, 'king', + *tūn*, 'enclosure', 'estate', 'manor'). The name came into use after 1292, when Edward I exchanged with the monks of Meaux lands he had in Wawne and Wilsby for the port here, then called *Wike* (OE *wīc*, 'harbour', or OS *vík*, 'creek'). 1299 *Kyngeston super Hul*.

Hulland (village, Derbys): 'cultivated land by a hill spur'. OE *hōh*, 'hill spur', + *land*, 'cultivated land'. DB *Hoilant*.

Hullavington (village, Wilts): 'estate associated with Hūnlāf'. OE *-ing-*, 'associated with', + *tūn*, 'farmstead', 'estate'. DB *Hunlavintone*.

Hullbridge (suburb of Rayleigh, Essex): '(place by the) bridge with arches'. OE *hwalf*, 'arch', 'vault', + *brycg*, 'bridge'. The river here is the Crouch. 1375 *Whouluebregg*.

Hullshire (historic county, E England): 'district based on Hull'. OE *scīr*, 'shire', 'district'. The former county was constituted by Henry VI and included the parishes of Kingston upon HULL, Hessle, Kirk Ella and North Ferriby. 1505 *Comitatus Hull*, 1546 *the Countie of Kyngeston upon Hulle*.

Hulme (district, Warrington): '(place on an) island'. OS *holmr*, 'island'. The 'island' is land between the rivers Irwell, Medlock and Cornbrook here. 1246 *Hulm*.

Humber (hamlet, Herefords): '(place on) Humber Brook'. The name of the stream has the same origin as that of the river *Humber* (see HUMBERSTON). DB *Humbre*.

Humber (river). See HUMBERSTON.

Humberston (district of Grimsby, NE Lincs): '(place at the) stone by the (river) Humber'. OE *stān*, 'stone'. The stone marked a boundary here. The river has a pre-English name of uncertain meaning. DB *Humbrestone*.

Humbleton (village, E Yorks): 'farmstead by a rounded hillock'. OE *humol*, 'rounded object', + *tūn*, 'farmstead'. The name could also mean 'farmstead where hops grow' (OE *humele*, 'hop', + *tūn*) or 'Humli's farmstead', with a Scandinavian personal name. DB *Humeltone*.

Humbleton (hamlet, Northd): '(place by the) crooked hill'. OE *hamel*, 'crooked', 'misshapen', + *dūn*, 'hill'. 1170 *Hameldun*.

Huncoat (suburb of Accrington, Lancs): 'Hūna's cottage'. OE *cot*, 'cottage'. The name could also mean 'shed where honey is stored' (OE *hunig*, 'honey', + *cot*). DB *Hunnicot*.

Huncote (village, Leics): 'Hūna's cottage'. OE *cot*, 'cottage'. DB *Hunecote*.

Hunderthwaite (hamlet, Durham): 'Húnrøthr's clearing'. OS *thveit*, 'clearing', 'meadow'. The personal name is Scandinavian. The first part of the name could also represent OE *hundred* or OS *hundrath*, 'hundred' (administrative district). DB *Hundredestoit*.

Hundleton (village, Pemb): 'farm where dogs are kept'. OE *hund*, 'hound', 'dog', + *tūn*, 'farm'. 1475 *Hundenton*.

Hundon (village, Suffolk): 'Hūna's valley'. OE *denu*, 'valley'. DB *Hunedana*.

Hungerford (town, W Berks): '(place by the) hunger ford'. OE *hungor*, 'hunger', + *ford*, 'ford'. A 'hunger ford' is one leading to barren land, that will leave one hungry. The name is popularly said to be an alteration of *Ingleford*, meaning 'ford of the Angles', on the basis that Ermine Street here marked the border between the Angles and Saxons. Another tradition derives the name from the Danish leader Hingwar, slayer of King Edmund (see BURY ST EDMUNDS), who was supposed to have drowned while crossing the river Kennet here. 1101 *Hungreford*.

Hunmanby (village, N Yorks): 'farmstead of the houndsmen'. OS *hunda-mathr* (from *hundr*, 'hound', + *mathr*, 'man', genitive plural *manna*), + *bȳ*, 'farmstead', 'village'. DB *Hundemanebi*.

Hunningham (village, Warwicks): 'homestead of Hūna's people'. OE -*inga*-, 'of the people of', + *hām*, 'homestead'. DB *Huningeham*.

Hunsdon (village, Herts): 'Hūn's hill'. OE *dūn*, 'hill'. DB *Honesdone*.

Hunsingore (village, N Yorks): '(place on the) promontory associated with Hūnsige'. OE -*ing*-, 'associated with', + *ofer*, 'promontory'. The promontory in question overlooks the river Nidd here. The DB form of the name below has *l* for *n*. DB *Hulsingoure*, 1194 *Hunsinghouere*.

Hunslet (district, Leeds): '(place by) Hūn's stream'. OE *flēot*, 'inlet', 'stream'. The stream in question may have been one flowing into the river Aire here. The DB form of the name below has omitted the *f*, which appeared in later forms of the name only to disappear again. DB *Hunslet*, 12C *Hunesflete*, 1868 *Hunslet, or Hunfleet*.

Hunsonby (hamlet, Cumbria): 'farmstead of the dogkeepers'. OS *hunda-sveinn* (from *hundr*, 'dog', + *sveinn*, 'servant'), + *bȳ*, 'farmstead', 'village'. 1292 *Hunswanby*.

Hunstanton (resort town, Norfolk): 'Hūn-stān's farmstead'. OE *tūn*, 'farmstead'. The name is locally shortened in speech to 'Hunston'. *c.*1035 *Hunstanestun*, DB *Hunestanestuna*.

Hunstanworth (hamlet, Durham): 'Hūnstān's enclosure'. OE *worth*, 'enclosure'. 1183 *Hunstan-wortha*.

Hunston (village, Suffolk): 'farmstead of the hunter'. OE *huntere*, 'hunter', + *tūn*, 'farmstead'. DB *Hunterstuna*.

Hunston (village, W Sussex): '(place by) Hūna's stone'. OE *stān*, 'stone'. The location of the stone in question is unknown. It probably marked a boundary. DB *Hunestan*.

Hunter's Quay (resort village, Argyll & Bute): 'Hunter's quay'. The name is that of the Hunter family of nearby Hafton House, who in 1872 gave the clubhouse here to the Royal Clyde Yacht Club, founded in 1856.

Huntingdon (town, Cambs): 'huntsman's hill'. OE *hunta*, 'huntsman', + *dūn*, 'hill'. The name could also mean 'Hunta's hill'. The hill in question would have been the low broad one on which the town lies, either favoured by huntsmen or owned by Hunta. It is sometimes stated that the Roman name of Huntingdon was *Venantodunum*, but this is simply a rendering of the English name (Latin *venatio*, 'hunting') coined by the 16C antiquary John Leland.

Huntingdon was not a Roman town. 973 *Huntandun*, DB *Huntedun*.

Huntingdonshire (historic county, E central England): 'district based on Huntingdon'. OE *scīr*, 'shire', 'district'. See HUNTINGDON. The county was abolished in 1974 but the name was revived for a council district of Cambridgeshire. 11C *Huntadunscir*.

Huntingfield (village, Suffolk): 'open land of Hunta's people'. OE -*inga*-, 'of the people of', + *feld*, 'open land' (modern English *field*). DB *Huntingafelde*.

Huntington (village, Staffs): 'huntsmen's hill'. OE *hunta*, 'huntsman', + *dūn*, 'hill'. The '-ing-' of the name comes from OE *huntena*, the genitive plural form of *hunta*. The DB form below represents an older name meaning 'hill to the east'. DB *Estendone*, 1167 *Huntendon*.

Huntington (village, York): 'hunting hill'. OE *hunting*, 'hunting', + *dūn*, 'hill'. The name implies a hill where hunting took place. DB *Huntindune*.

Huntley (village, Glos): 'huntsman's wood or clearing'. OE *hunta*, 'huntsman', + *lēah*, 'wood', 'clearing'. DB *Huntelei*.

Huntly (town, Aberdeens): 'Huntly's town'. The town was founded in 1769 by Alexander Gordon, 4th Duke of Gordon and Earl of Huntly, who took his title from the lost village of *Huntly* in southeast Scotland. Its own name means 'huntsman's wood' (OE *hunta*, 'huntsman', + *lēah*, 'wood').

Hunton (village, Kent): 'hill of the huntsmen'. OE *hunta*, 'huntsman', + *dūn*, 'hill'. The first part of the name represents OE *huntena*, the genitive plural form of *hunta*. 11C *Huntindone*.

Hunton (village, N Yorks): 'Hūna's farmstead'. OE *tūn*, 'farmstead'. DB *Huntone*.

Huntsham (village, Devon): 'Hūn's homestead or enclosure'. OE *hām*, 'homestead', or *hamm*, 'enclosure'. DB *Honesham*.

Huntspill (village, Somerset): 'Hūn's tidal creek'. OE *pyll*, 'tidal creek'. Huntspill is on an area of flat land known as Huntspill Level near the mouth of the river Parrett. DB *Honspil*.

Huntworth (village, Somerset): 'enclosure of the huntsman'. OE *hunta*, 'huntsman', + *worth*, 'enclosure'. The name could also mean 'Hunta's enclosure'. DB *Hunteworde*.

Hunwick (village, Durham): 'Hūna's dairy farm'. OE *wīc*, 'dwelling', 'dairy farm'. *c.*1050 *Hunewic*.

Hunworth (village, Norfolk): 'Hūna's enclosure'. OE *worth*, 'enclosure'. DB *Hunaworda*.

Hurdsfield (suburb of Macclesfield, Cheshire): 'open land by a hurdle'. OE *hyrdel*, 'hurdle', + *feld*, 'open land' (modern English *field*). The reference is probably to a hurdle fence. 13C *Hirdelesfeld*.

Hurley (village, Windsor & Maid): 'woodland clearing in a recess'. OE *hyrne*, 'corner', + *lēah*, 'wood', 'clearing'. The 'recess' is probably the curve in the high ground to the south of the village, which lies by the Thames. DB *Herlei*, 1106 *Hurnleia*. SO ALSO: *Hurley*, Warwicks.

Hurn (village, Dorset): '(place at the) corner of land'. OE *hyrne*, 'corner'. DB *Herne*.

Hursley (village, Hants): 'woodland clearing of the mare'. OE *hyrse*, 'mare', + *lēah*, 'wood', 'clearing'. 1171 *Hurselye*.

Hurstbourne Priors (village, Hants): 'prior's (estate by the) stream with trailing water plants'. OE *hysse*, 'tendril', + *burna*, 'stream'. The manor here was held early by Winchester Priory. The added word distinguishes this village from nearby *Hurstbourne Tarrant*, where the manor was held by Tarrant Abbey, Dorset, itself so named from the river Tarrant (see TARRANT HINTON). *c*.880 *Hysseburnan*, DB *Esseborne*, 1167 *Hesseburna Prioris*.

Hurstpierpoint (town, W Sussex): 'de Pierpoint's wooded hill'. OE *hyrst*, 'wooded hill'. Robert de Pierpoint held the manor here in 1086. DB *Herst*, 1279 *Herst Perepunt*.

Hurstwood (hamlet, Lancs): '(place by a) wood on a hill'. OE *hyrst*, 'wooded hill', + *wudu*, 'wood'. 1285 *Hurstwode*.

Hurworth (village, Darlington): 'enclosure of hurdles'. OE *hurth*, 'hurdle', + *worth*, 'enclosure'. The village is also known as *Hurworth-on-Tees* (for the river name, see TEESDALE). 1158 *Hurdewurda*.

Husbands Bosworth. See MARKET BOSWORTH.

Husborne Crawley (village, Beds). Originally two separate places: *Husborne*, '(place by the) stream with winding water plants' (OE *hysse*, 'tendril', + *burna*, 'stream'), and *Crawley*, 'wood or clearing where crows are seen' (OE *crāwe*, 'crow', + *lēah*, 'wood', 'clearing'). The two names subsequently combined. 969 *Hysseburnan*, DB *Crawelai*, 1276 *Husseburn Crouleye*.

Husthwaite (village, N Yorks): 'clearing with houses'. OS *hūs*, 'house', + *thveit*, 'clearing'. 1167 *Hustwait*.

Huttoft (village, Lincs): 'homestead on a spur of land'. OE *hōh*, 'hill spur', + OS *toft*, 'homestead'. DB *Hotoft*.

Hutton (district of Brentwood, Essex): 'farmstead by a hill spur'. OE *hōh*, 'hill spur', + *tūn*, 'farmstead'. The 'hill spur' in question is the one on which Hutton Hall stands, south of Hutton. The DB form of the name below represents the OE for '(place) at the hill spur'. DB *Atahou*, 1200 *Houton*. SO ALSO: *Hutton*, Cumbria, Lancs, N Somerset.

Hutton Buscel (village, N Yorks): 'Buscel's farmstead on a hill spur'. OE *hōh*, 'hill spur', + *tūn*, 'farmstead'. The Buscel family held the manor here in the 12C. DB *Hotun*, 1253 *Hoton Buscel*.

Hutton Conyers (hamlet, N Yorks): 'Conyers' farmstead on a hill spur'. OE *hōh*, 'hill spur', + *tūn*, 'farmstead'. The Conyers family held land here in the early 12C. DB *Hotone*, 1198 *Hotonconyers*.

Hutton Cranswick (village, E Yorks): 'farmstead on a hill spur by Cranswick'. OE *hōh*, 'hill spur', + *tūn*, 'farmstead'. *Cranswick* nearby has a name meaning 'Cranuc's dairy farm' (OE *wīc*, 'dairy farm'). DB *Hottune*.

Hutton Henry (village, Durham): 'Henry's farmstead on a hill spur'. OE *hōh*, 'hill spur', + *tūn*, 'farmstead'. Henry de Essh held the manor here in the 14C. 'The village ... is situated on an eminence commanding a view of the surrounding country' (*The National Gazetteer of Great Britain and Ireland*, 1868). *c*.1050 *Hoton*.

Hutton-le-Hole (village, N Yorks): 'farmstead on a hill spur in the hollow'. OE *hōh*, 'hill spur', + *tūn*, 'farmstead', + OF *le*, 'the', + OE *hol*, 'hollow'. DB *Hotun*.

Hutton Magna (village, Durham): 'greater farmstead on a hill spur'. OE *hōh*, 'hill spur', + *tūn*, 'farmstead'. The second word of the name (Latin *magna*, 'great') distinguishes the village from nearby *Little Hutton*. Hutton Magna was formerly also known as *Great Hutton*. The alternative third form of the name below refers to Johannes de Lungeviler, who held land here in the 13C. DB *Hotton*, 1157 *Magna Hoton*, 1868 *Hutton-Magna*, or *Hutton Long Villiers*.

Hutton Roof (hamlet, Cumbria): 'Rolf's estate on a hill spur'. OE *hōh*, 'hill spur', + *tūn*, 'farmstead', 'estate'. One Rolf held the manor here in or before the 13C. The form of the name below is for Hutton Roof near Hesket Newmarket. 1278 *Hotunerof*.

Hutton Rudby (village, N Yorks): 'farmstead on a hill spur by Rudby'. OE *hōh*, 'hill spur', + *tūn*, 'farmstead'. The second word of the name refers to RUDBY on the opposite bank of the river Leven. DB *Hotun*, 1310 *Hoton by Ruddeby*.

Hutton Sessay (village, N Yorks): 'farmstead on a hill spur by Sessay'. OE *hōh*, 'hill spur', + *tūn*, 'farmstead'. The second word of the name refers to nearby SESSAY. DB *Hottune*.

Hutton Wandesley (village, N Yorks): 'farmstead on a hill spur by Wandesley'. OE *hōh*, 'hill spur', + *tūn*, 'farmstead'. The second word of the name refers to former nearby *Wandesley*, 'Wand's or Wandel's woodland clearing' (OE *lēah*, 'wood', 'clearing'). c.1200 *Hoton*, 1253 *Hotun Wandelay*.

Huxley (village, Cheshire): 'Hucc's woodland clearing'. OE *lēah*, 'wood', 'clearing'. Early 13C *Huxelehe*.

Huyton (town, Knowsley): 'estate with a landing place'. OE *hȳth*, 'landing place', + *tūn*, 'farmstead', 'estate'. There could have been a landing stage on the river Alt or on Fitton Brook here. DB *Hitune*.

Hwlffordd. See HAVERFORDWEST.

Hyde (town, Tameside): '(estate assessed at one) hide'. OE *hīd*, 'hide'. A hide, as the standard unit for taxation purposes, was the amount of land that would support a single household. early 13C *Hyde*.

Hyndburn (council district, Lancs): '(district of the) Hyndburn Brook'. The name of the stream was selected for the new administrative district set up in 1974, when it was felt that none of the town names in the region (not even that of Accrington, which is on the Hyndburn) would serve as a district name.

Hythe (village, Hants): '(place by the) landing place'. OE *hȳth*, 'landing place'. Hythe is on Southampton Water. 1248 *La Huthe*.

Hythe (resort town, Kent): '(place by the) landing place'. OE *hȳth*, 'landing place'. The landing place in question would not have been on the sea coast here but on a river, a short distance inland. Coastal changes make it difficult to determine the original site. DB *Hede*.

Ibberton (village, Dorset): 'estate associated with Ēadbeorht'. OE -*ing*-, 'associated with', + *tūn*, 'farmstead', 'estate'. DB *Abristetone*.

Ible (hamlet, Derbys): '(place by) Ibba's hollow'. OE *hol*, 'hole', 'hollow'. DB *Ibeholon*.

Ibstock (village, Leics): 'Ibba's hamlet'. OE *stoc*, 'outlying farmstead', 'secondary settlement'. DB *Ibestoche*.

Ibstone (village, Bucks): '(place by) Ibba's stone'. OE *stān*, 'stone'. The stone marked the former county boundary with Oxfordshire here. (The actual boundary line passed through the parlour of the manor house.) DB *Ebestan*.

Ickburgh (village, Norfolk): 'Ica's stronghold'. OE *burh*, 'fortified place'. The stronghold of the name may relate to the Roman remains found here. DB *Iccheburc*, 1868 *Igborough, or Ickborough*.

Ickenham (district, Hillingdon): 'Ticca's homestead'. OE *hām*, 'homestead'. The initial *T*- of the personal name was lost when it was taken as the -*t* of OE *æt*, 'at', a word that often occurred as the first part of an OE place name. Cp. ILKESTON. DB *Ticheham*.

Ickford (village, Bucks): '(place by) Ica's ford'. OE *ford*, 'ford'. The river Ickford here takes its name from the village. The DB form of the name below has omitted the *c* of the personal name. DB *Iforde*, 1175 *Ycford*.

Ickham (village, Kent): 'homestead comprising a yoke of land'. OE *geoc*, 'yoke', + *hām*, 'homestead', 'village'. A yoke was an area of about 50 acres, so called as ploughed by yoked oxen. 785 *Ioccham*, DB *Gecham*.

Ickleford (village, Herts): '(place by the) ford associated with Icel'. OE -*ing*-, 'associated with', + *ford*, 'ford'. The river here is the Ivel. 12C *Ikelineford*.

Icklesham (village, E Sussex): 'Icel's promontory'. OE *hamm*, 'enclosure', 'promontory'. Icklesham lies on a promontory between marshes. 770 *Icoleshamme*.

Ickleton (village, Cambs): 'estate associated with Icel'. OE -*ing*-, 'associated with', + *tūn*, 'farmstead', 'estate'. *c*.975 *Icelingtune*, DB *Hichelintone*.

Icklingham (village, Suffolk): 'homestead of Ycel's people'. OE -*inga*-, 'of the people of', + *hām*, 'homestead'. DB *Ecclingaham*.

Icknield Way (trackway, England): meaning unknown. The name of the prehistoric trackway, running from Norfolk to Dorset, has been dubiously linked to that of the Iceni tribe. It was transferred in the 12C to the Roman road from Bourton-on-the-Water, Glos, to Templeborough, Sheffield, now known as *Icknield Street* or *Ryknild Street*. (The *R*- in the latter probably came about because ME *at there Ikenild stret*, 'at the Icknield Street', evolved to *at the Rikenild stret*.) 903 *Icenhylte*.

Ickwell Green (village, Beds): 'Gica's spring'. OE *wella*, 'spring', 'stream'. The name could also mean '(place by the) beneficial spring' (OE *gēoc*, 'help', + *wella*). The name passed to the (noted) village green here, then to the present village. *c*.1170 *Ikewelle*.

Icomb (village, Glos): '(place in) Icca's valley'. OE *cumb*, 'valley'. 781 *Iccacumb*, DB *Iccumbe*.

Idbury (village, Oxon): 'Ida's fortified place'. OE *burh*, 'fortified place'. DB *Ideberie*.

Iddesleigh (village, Devon): 'Ēadwīg's woodland clearing'. OE *lēah*, 'wood', 'clearing'. The DB form of the name below has garbled the personal name. DB *Edeslege*, 1107 *Edwislega*.

Ide (village, Devon): '(place on the river) Ide'. A stream here may have been known by this pre-English name, whose meaning is uncertain. DB *Ide*.

Ideford (village, Devon): '(place by) Giedda's ford'. OE *ford*, 'ford'. The first part of the name could also represent OE *giedd*, 'speech', 'song', giving a meaning '(place by the) ford where people gathered for speeches or songs'. DB *Yudaforda*.

Ide Hill (village, Kent): 'Ēadgȳth's hill'. OE *hyll*, 'hill'. The personal name is that of a woman. *c*.1250 *Edythehelle*.

Iden (village, E Sussex): 'woodland pasture where yew trees grow'. OE *īg*, 'yew', + *denn*, 'woodland pasture'. DB *Idene*.

Idle (district, Bradford): 'idle place'. OE *īdel*, 'idle', 'empty'. The reference is probably to unprofitable or uncultivated land here. *c*.1190 *Idla*, 13C *Idel*.

Idlicote (hamlet, Warwicks): 'cottage associated with Yttel'. OE -*ing*-, 'associated with', + *cot*, 'cottage'. DB *Etelincote*.

Idmiston (village, Wilts): 'Idmǣr's or Idhelm's farmstead'. OE *tūn*, 'farmstead'. 947 *Idemestone*.

Idridgehay (village, Derbys): 'Ēadrīc's enclosure'. OE *hæg*, 'enclosure' (related modern English *hedge*). 1230 *Edrichesei*.

Iffley (district of Oxford, Oxon): 'woodland clearing where plovers are seen'. OE *gīfete*, 'plover', 'lapwing', + *lēah*, 'wood', 'clearing'. 'The suggestion in Murray's *Handbook* to Oxfordshire that the name means "field of gifts" is absurd' (Henry Alexander, *The Place-Names of Oxfordshire*, 1912). 1004 *Gifetelea*, DB *Givetelei*.

Ifield (district of Crawley, W Sussex): 'open land where yew trees grow'. OE *īg*, 'yew', + *feld*, 'open land' (modern English *field*). DB *Ifelt*.

Iford (village, E Sussex): '(place by the) ford in the island'. OE *īeg*, 'island', + *ford*, 'ford'. The 'island' would be well-watered land here. Iford is not far from the river Ouse. The name could also mean '(place by the) ford where yew trees grow' (OE *īg*, 'yew', + *ford*). The DB form of the name below produced a legend that the place takes its name 'from the shrine or statue of a Saxon deity called Niorde' (*The National Gazetteer of Great Britain and Ireland*, 1868). DB *Niworde*, late 11C *Yford*.

Ightfield (village, Shropshire): 'open land by the river Ight'. OE *feld*, 'open land' (modern English *field*). The river, now called the Ray, had a pre-English name of uncertain meaning. DB *Istefelt*, 1210 *Ychtefeld*.

Ightham (village, Kent): 'Ehta's homestead'. OE *hām*, 'homestead', 'village'. *c*.1100 *Ehteham*.

Iken (village, Suffolk): '(place by the river) Iken'. The river here now is the Alde (see ALDEBURGH), but it originally seems to have been named identically to the *Itchen* (see ITCHEN ABBAS). 1212 *Ykene*.

Ilam (village, Staffs): '(place by the river) Ilam'. The river name, of Celtic origin and meaning 'trickling stream', was apparently an earlier name for the river Manifold here. The name could also represent OS *hylum*, the dative plural form of *hylr*, 'pool', meaning '(place) at the pools'. 1002 *Hilum*.

Ilchester (village, Somerset): 'Roman town on the (river) Gifl'. OE *ceaster*, 'Roman station'. The river is now known as the Yeo (see YEOVIL). The Roman town, on the Fosse Way, was *Lindinis*, '(place by the) pool', a Celtic name related to modern Welsh *llyn*, 'pond', 'lake'. DB *Givelcestre*.

Ilderton (hamlet, Northd): 'farmstead where elder trees grow'. OE *hyldre*, 'elder', + *tūn*, 'farmstead'. *c*.1125 *Ildretona*.

Ilford (town, Redbridge): '(place by the) ford over the (river) Hyle'. OE *ford*, 'ford'. The river has a Celtic name meaning 'trickling stream'. *Hyle* was a former name for the river Roding south of Ilford. See RODINGS. DB *Ilefort*.

Ilfracombe (resort town, Devon): 'valley associated with Ælfrēd'. OE -*ing*-, 'associated with', + *cumb*, 'valley'. The town's steep High Street runs up the valley in question. DB *Alfreincome*.

Ilkeston (town, Derbys): 'Ēalāc's hill'. OE *dūn*, 'hill'. In the DB form of the name below, the initial *T*- has been erroneously added from a preceding OE *æt*, 'at'. Cp. ICKENHAM. DB *Tilchestune*, early 12C *Elkesdone*.

Ilkley (town, Bradford): 'Yllica's or Illica's woodland clearing'. OE *lēah*, 'wood', 'clearing'. The Roman fort here is generally said to have been *Olicana*, but this identity has no etymological basis and recent scholarship names the fort as *Verbeia*, from the name of the river Wharfe here (see BURLEY IN WHARFEDALE). *c*.972 *Hillicleg*, DB *Illiclei*.

Illingworth (district of Halifax, Calderdale): 'enclosure associated with Illa or Ylla'. OE -*ing*-, 'associated with', + *worth*, 'enclosure'. 1276 *Illingworthe*.

Illogan (village, Cornwall): '(church of) St Illogan'. Nothing is known of the saint to whom the church here is dedicated. 1291 *Sanctus Illoganus*.

Ilmer (village, Bucks): '(place by the) pool where leeches are obtained'. OE *īl*, 'leech', + *mere*, 'pool'. The DB form of the name below has omitted the *l* of OE *īl*. DB *Imere*, 1161 *Ilmere*.

Ilmington (village, Warwicks): 'hill where elm trees grow'. OE *ylme*, 'elm wood', + *dūn*, 'hill'. The first part of the name represents OE *ylman*, the genitive form of *ylme*. 978 *Ylmandun*, DB *Ilmedone*.

Ilminster (town, Somerset): 'large church on the (river) Isle'. OE *mynster*, 'monastery', 'large church'. The river has a Celtic name of uncertain meaning ('swift one' has been suggested). 995 *Illemynister*, DB *Ileminstre*.

Ilsington (village, Devon): 'estate associated with Ielfstān'. OE *-ing-*, 'associated with', + *tūn*, 'farmstead', 'estate'. DB *Ilestintona*.

Ilton (village, N Yorks): 'Yllica's or Illica's farmstead'. OE *tūn*, 'farmstead'. DB *Ilcheton*.

Ilton (village, Somerset): 'farmstead on the (river) Isle'. OE *tūn*, 'farmstead'. For the river name, see ILMINSTER. The DB form of the name below is garbled. DB *Atiltone*, 1243 *Ilton*.

Imber (derelict village, Wilts): '(place by) Imma's pool'. OE *mere*, 'pool'. The DB form of the name below has garbled the second part. DB *Imemerie*, 1146 *Immemera*, 1291 *Imere*.

Immingham (town and port, NE Lincs): 'homestead of Imma's people'. OE *-inga-*, 'of the people of', + *hām*, 'homestead'. The DB form of the name below seems to have misread *u* for *mi*. DB *Imungeham*, c.1115 *Immingeham*.

Impington (village, Cambs): 'estate associated with Empa or Impa'. OE *-ing-*, 'associated with', + *tūn*, 'farmstead', 'estate'. c.1050 *Impintune*, DB *Epintone*.

Ince (village, Cheshire): '(place on an) island'. OW *inis*, 'island'. The 'island' here is the low ridge on which the village stands in marshland near the Mersey estuary. DB *Inise*.

Ince Blundell (village, Sefton): 'Blundell's (estate on the) island'. OW *inis*, 'island'. The 'island' is raised ground between the river Alt and the coast here. The manor was held in the early 13C by the Blundell family, whose name distinguishes the village from INCE-IN-MAKERFIELD. The DB form of the name below is corrupt. DB *Hinne*, 1332 *Ins Blundell*.

Ince-in-Makerfield (town, Wigan): '(place by the) island in Makerfield'. OW *inis*, 'island'. The exact nature or location of the 'island' here is uncertain. For the district name, see ASHTON-IN-MAKERFIELD. 1202 *Ines*.

Inchcolm (island, Fife): 'St Columba's island'. Gaelic *inis*, 'island'. Columba is said to have resided on this island, in the Firth of Forth, in the 6C and the ruins of a 12C abbey dedicated to him are here. c.1123 *Insula Sancti Columbae*, 1605 *St Colmes Ynch*.

Inchkeith (island, Fife): 'wooded island'. Gaelic *inis*, 'island'. The second part of the name is of Celtic origin and related to modern Welsh *coed*, 'wood'. Cp. KEITH. The island is in the Firth of Forth. c.1200 *Insula Ked*.

Indian Queens (village, Cornwall): '(village with the) Indian Queen inn'. The inn name has been popularly associated with Pocahontas, the famous 17C 'Red Indian queen'. 1802 *Indian Queens*.

Ingatestone (town, Essex): 'Ing at the stone'. OE *stān*, 'stone'. *Ing* was the name of a manor here, itself from a tribal name meaning 'people of the district' (OE *gē*, 'district', + *-ingas*, 'people of'). There are other places incorporating the name, among them FRYERNING, INGRAVE, MARGARETTING and MOUNTNESSING. Ingatestone was distinguished by its location near a particular stone, perhaps a Roman milestone (although there must have been many such). 1283 *Gynges Atteston*.

Ingbirchworth (village, Barnsley): 'enclosure where birch trees grow by a meadow'. OS *eng*, 'meadow', + OE *birce*, 'birch', + *worth*, 'enclosure'. The place was originally *Birchworth*. DB *Berceuuorde*, 1424 *Yngebyrcheworth*.

Ingham (village, Lincs): 'Inga's homestead'. OE *hām*, 'homestead'. The name has also been explained as meaning 'homestead of the Ingui-one', referring to a member of the Germanic tribe called the Inguiones. DB *Ingeham*. SO ALSO: *Ingham*, Norfolk, Suffolk.

Ingleby (hamlet, Derbys): 'farmstead of the Englishmen'. OS *Englar*, 'Englishmen', + *bý*, 'farmstead'. The name denotes an enclave of English inhabitants among a predominantly Scandinavian population. 1009 *Englaby*, DB *Englebi*. SO ALSO: *Ingleby*, Lincs.

Ingleby Greenhow (village, N Yorks): 'farmstead of the Englishmen by the green mound'. OS *Englar*, 'Englishmen', + *bý*, 'farmstead', 'village', + OE *grēne*, 'green', + OS *haugr*, 'mound'. Cp. INGLEBY. The second word of the name distinguishes this Ingleby from *Ingleby Arncliffe*, 10 miles to the southwest, near a steep wooded bank called *Arncliffe*, 'eagles' cliff' (cp. ARN-CLIFFE). The names denote a surviving 'pocket' of English inhabitants amid a predominantly Scandinavian population. DB *Englebi*.

Inglesham (hamlet, Swindon): 'Ingen's or Ingīn's enclosure'. OE *hamm*, 'enclosure', 'river meadow'. The 'enclosure' is land in a bend of the river Thames here. c.950 *Inggeneshamme*.

Ingleton (village, Durham): 'Ingeld's farmstead'. OE *tūn*, 'farmstead'. The personal name is Scandinavian. c.1050 *Ingeltun*.

Ingleton (village, N Yorks): 'farmstead near the peak'. OE *ingel*, 'peak', + *tūn*, 'farmstead'.

Ingleton lies at the foot of Ingleborough, one of the highest mountains in Yorkshire. DB *Inglestune*.

Inglewhite (hamlet, Lancs): '(place by the) river bend'. OE *wiht*, 'river bend'. The hamlet lies in the fork of two streams. The first part of the name is of uncertain origin. It may represent a personal name. 1662 *Inglewhite*.

Ingoe (hamlet, Northd): '(place by a) hill with a spur of land'. OE *ing*, 'hill', + *hōh*, 'spur of land'. Ingoe lies at the end of a ridge. 1229 *Hinghou*.

Ingoldisthorpe (village, Norfolk): 'Ingjaldr's outlying farmstead'. OS *thorp*, 'outlying farmstead'. The personal name is Scandinavian. DB *Torp*, 1203 *Ingaldestorp*.

Ingoldmells (resort village, Lincs): 'Ingólfr's sandbanks'. OS *melr*, 'sandbank'. The personal name is Scandinavian. The DB form of the name below has taken *in* as the Latin preposition and the final element as OE *mere*, 'lake'. DB *in Guldesmere*, 1180 *Ingoldesmeles*.

Ingram (village, Northd): 'homestead or enclosure with grassland'. OE *anger*, 'grassland', + *hām*, 'homestead', or *hamm*, 'enclosure'. 1242 *Angerham*.

Ingrave (suburb of Brentwood, Essex): 'Radulf's (manor called) Ing'. The manor (see INGATESTONE) was held here in 1086 by one Radulf. The personal name is Old German. DB *Ingam*, 1276 *Gingeraufe*.

Ingworth (village, Norfolk): 'Inga's enclosure'. OE *worth*, 'enclosure'. DB *Inghewurda*.

Inkberrow (village, Worcs): 'Inta's hills'. OE *beorg*, 'hill', 'mound'. The second half of the name represents OE *beorgas*, the plural form of *beorg*. 789 *Intanbeorgas*, DB *Inteberge*.

Inkpen (village, W Berks): 'enclosure by the hill'. OE *ing*, 'hill', 'peak', + *penn*, 'enclosure'. The 'hill' is the escarpment called Inkpen Hill, south of the village, while the 'enclosure' is the hill fort known as Walbury Camp, which surrounds the highest peak of the escarpment. *c.*935 *Ingepenne*, DB *Hingepene*.

Innerleithen (town, Borders): 'mouth of the Leithen Water'. Gaelic *inbhir*, 'river mouth'. The town stands at the confluence of the Leithen Water and the Tweed. The first part of the name corresponds to the more common 'Inver-', as in INVERNESS. *c.*1160 *Innerlethan*.

Innsworth (suburb of Gloucester, Glos): 'Ine's enclosure'. OE *worth*, 'enclosure'. 794 *Ineswurth*.

Inskip (village, Lancs): 'island by the osier basket'. The first part of the name derives from a Celtic word related to modern Welsh *ynys*, 'island', meaning raised ground in marshland. The second part is traditionally derived from OE *cȳpe*, 'osier basket (for catching fish)', but is more likely to be Celtic also, from a word related to modern Welsh *cib*, 'pod', 'husk', 'bowl', referring to the valley south of the village. The sense would then be 'raised ground by the bowl-shaped valley'. DB *Inscip*.

Instow (village, Devon): 'St John's holy place'. OE *stōw*, 'holy place'. The church here is dedicated to St John the Baptist. DB *Johannesto*.

Inveraray (town, Argyll & Bute): 'mouth of the (river) Aray'. Gaelic *inbhir*, 'river mouth'. The town stands where the Aray runs into Loch Fyne. The river's name may relate to that of the AYR and so mean simply 'river'.

Inverclyde (unitary authority, W central Scotland): 'mouth of the (river) Clyde'. Gaelic *inbhir*, 'mouth'. The name was earlier that of an administrative district in the region of Strathclyde.

Invergordon (town, Highland): 'Gordon's (place at the) river mouth'. Gaelic *inbhir*, 'river mouth'. The name is that of Alexander Gordon, landowner here in *c.*1760. Before that, the place was known as *Inverbreckie*, 'mouth of the Breckie', this stream name meaning 'speckled' (Gaelic *breac*).

Inverkeithing (town, Fife): 'mouth of the Keithing Burn'. Gaelic *inbhir*, 'river mouth'. The river's name means 'wooded stream'. Cp. KEITH. *c.*1057 *Hinhirkethy*, 1114 *Innerkethyin*.

Inverleith (district, Edinburgh): 'mouth of the Water of Leith'. Gaelic *inbhir*, 'river mouth'. Inverleith is not actually at the mouth of the Water of Leith, implying that the Firth of Forth, to the north of it, was originally much wider. The river itself gave the name of LEITH. *c.*1130 *Inerlet*.

Inverness (city, Highland): 'mouth of the (river) Ness'. Gaelic *inbhir*, 'river mouth'. The river has a pre-Celtic name perhaps meaning 'roaring', 'rushing'. 1300 *Invernis*.

Inverurie (town, Aberdeens): 'confluence of the (river) Urie'. Gaelic *inbhir*, 'river mouth', 'confluence'. The town stands at the confluence of the Urie and the Don. 1199 *Inverurie*, *c.*1300 *Innervwry*.

Inworth (hamlet, Essex): 'Ina's enclosure'. OE *worth*, 'enclosure'. 1206 *Inewrth*.

Iona (island, Argyll & Bute): '(place of) yew trees'. OI *eo*, 'yew'. At first the island was regularly called *I* or *Hi*. This was then incorporated into various forms of the name, and in *c.*700

appeared as *Ioua insula*, 'island of the yew tree place' (Latin *insula*, 'island'). The first word of this was misread as *Iona*, apparently by association with the biblical Jonah, and the form with *n* persisted. The second part of the second form of the name below means 'Columba's cell', referring to St Columba, who founded a monastery here in the 6C. 634 *Hiiensis*, *c.*1100 *Hiona-Columcille*.

Iping (village, W Sussex): '(settlement of) Ipa's people'. OE *-ingas*, 'people of'. DB *Epinges*.

Ipplepen (village, Devon): 'Ipela's enclosure'. OE *penn*, 'fold', 'enclosure' (modern English *pen*). 956 *Iplanpenne*, DB *Iplepene*.

Ipsden (village, Oxon): '(place in the) valley by the upland'. OE *yppe*, 'upland', + *denu*, 'valley'. The valley in question leads into the hills from the Icknield Way, which crosses the village near the church. DB *Yppesdene*.

Ipstones (village, Staffs): 'stone in the upland'. OE *yppe*, 'upland', + *stān*, 'stone'. Ipstones stands on high ground near the river Churnet. 1175 *Yppestan*.

Ipswich (town and port, Suffolk): 'Gip's harbour'. OE *wīc*, 'harbour', 'trading centre'. Ipswich lies at the confluence of the rivers Orwell and Gipping. The latter takes its name from the village of *Gipping*, 14 miles to the northwest. Its own name, meaning '(settlement of) Gip's people' (OE *-ingas*, 'people of'), relates to the same man. DB *Gipeswic*.

Irby (suburb of Heswall, Wirral): 'farmstead of the Irishmen'. OS *Íri*, 'Irishman', + *bý*, 'farmstead'. The 'Irishmen' were either Norwegian Vikings from Ireland or native Irishmen who came with the Vikings to England. *c.*1100 *Irreby*.

Irby upon Humber (village, NE Lincs): 'farmstead of the Irishmen on the (river) Humber'. OS *Íri*, 'Irishman', + *bý*, 'farmstead', 'village'. The river name (see HUMBERSTON) distinguishes this Irby from *Irby in the Marsh*, Lincs, 32 miles to the southeast. Irby upon Humber is actually 5 miles from the Humber estuary. DB *Iribi*.

Irchester (village, Northants): 'Roman station associated with Ira or Yra'. OE *ceaster*, 'Roman camp'. The name of the Roman town here is unknown. 973 *Yranceaster*, DB *Irencestre*.

Ireby (village, Cumbria): 'farmstead of the Irishmen'. OS *Íri*, 'Irishman', + *bý*, 'farmstead', 'village'. Cp. IRBY. *c.*1160 *Irebi*.

Ireleth (village, Cumbria): 'hill slope of the Irishmen'. OS *Íri*, 'Irishman', + *hlíth*, 'hill slope'. 1190 *Irlid*.

Irlam (town, Salford): 'homestead or enclosure on the (river) Irwell'. OE *hām*, 'homestead', or *hamm*, 'enclosure'. The river name means 'winding stream' (OE *irre*, 'winding', + *wella*, 'spring', 'stream'). *c.*1190 *Urwelham*.

Iron Acton (village, S Glos): 'farmstead by the oak tree where iron is found'. OE *īren*, 'iron', + *āc*, 'oak', + *tūn*, 'farmstead'. The first word of the name refers to old iron workings here. DB *Actune*, 1248 *Irenacton*.

Ironbridge (town, Wrekin): '(place by the) iron bridge'. The town takes its name from the iron bridge built across the river Severn here in 1779. 1868 *Iron-Bridge*.

Ironville (village, Derbys): 'town where iron is worked'. Modern English *iron* + French *ville*, 'town'. The village was built from *c.*1850 by the Butterley Iron Company here. 1837 *Ironville*.

Irthington (village, Cumbria): 'farmstead on the (river) Irthing'. OE *tūn*, 'farmstead'. The river has a name of Celtic origin and uncertain meaning. 1169 *Irthinton*.

Irthlingborough (town, Northants): 'fortified manor of the ploughmen'. OE *yrthling*, 'ploughman', + *burh*, 'fortified place', 'manor'. The DB form of the name below is corrupt. 780 *Yrtlingaburg*, DB *Erdinburne*.

Irton (village, N Yorks): 'farmstead of the Irishmen'. OS *Íri*, 'Irishman', + OE *tūn*, 'farmstead'. DB *Iretune*.

Irvine (town and port, N Ayrs): '(place on the river) Irvine'. The river name may mean 'green river', from Celtic words related to modern Welsh *ir*, 'fresh', 'green', and *afon*, 'river'. *c.*1190 *Hirun*, *c.*1200 *Irewin*, 1205 *Irving*.

Isca. See USK.

Isca Dumnoniorum. See EXETER.

Isca Legionis. See CAERLEON.

Isfield (village, E Sussex): 'Isa's open land'. OE *feld*, 'open land' (modern English *field*). 1214 *Isefeld*.

Isham (village, Northants): 'homestead or promontory by the (river) Ise'. OE *hām*, 'homestead', or *hamm*, 'enclosure', 'promontory'. The river name is of Celtic origin and means simply 'water'. 974 *Ysham*, DB *Isham*.

Isis (river). See THAMES DITTON.

Islay (island, Argyll & Bute): meaning uncertain. A Celtic sense 'swelling' is possible. The '-s-' is a recent insertion on an analogy with *island*,

and the final '-ay' was added as if from OS *ey*, 'island'. *c.*690 *Ilea*, 800 *Ile*.

Isle. For names beginning *Isle of* (apart from ISLE OF DOGS), see the next word, e.g. for *Isle of Wight*, see WIGHT.

Isle Abbotts (village, Somerset): 'abbot's (estate on the river) Isle'. Latin *abbatis*, 'of the abbot'. For the river name, see ILMINSTER. The manor here was held early by Muchelney Abbey, the abbot's title distinguishing the village from nearby *Isle Brewers*, where the manor was held by the Briwer family. 966 *Yli*, DB *Isle*, 1291 *Ile Abbatis*.

Isleham (village, Cambs): 'Gīsla's homestead'. OE *hām*, 'homestead'. 895 *Yselham*, DB *Gisleham*.

Isle of Dogs (district, Tower Hamlets): 'island where dogs are seen'. The dogs would probably have been wild or stray, rather than kept in kennels. The 'island' is actually a peninsula. A recent theory sees the name as a punning allusion to the Canary Islands (from Latin *canis*, 'dog'), the English island being a poor and puny counterpart to the rich and exotic Spanish Gran Canaria. 1520 *Isle of Dogs*.

Isleworth (district, Hounslow): 'Gīslhere's enclosure'. OE *worth* 'enclosure'. 'The name has somewhat puzzled enquirers ... Thistleworth appears to have been the local pronunciation down almost to our own day. It seems clear ... that the derivation from *isle* is inapplicable, and none quite satisfactory has been suggested. It is, probably, a patronymic combined with *worth*, an enclosure' (James Thorne, *Handbook to the Environs of London*, 1876). 677 *Gislheresuuyrth*, DB *Gistelesworde*, 1477 *Thystelworth*.

Islington (borough, Greater London): 'Gīsla's hill'. OE *dūn*, 'hill'. The '-ington' of the name is misleading, as the '-ing-' represents the ending of *Gīslan*, the genitive form of the personal name, while the '-ton' is really '-don'. *c.*1000 *Gislandune*, DB *Iseldone*.

Islip (village, Northants): 'slippery place by the (river) Ise'. OE *slæp*, 'slippery place'. The river has a pre-English name meaning simply 'water'. 10C *Isslepe*, DB *Islep*.

Islip (village, Oxon): 'slippery place by the (river) Ight'. OE *slæp*, 'slippery place'. The river name, pre-English and of uncertain meaning, is an old name for the river Ray here. The DB form of the name below is clearly corrupt. *c.*1050 *Githslepe*, DB *Letelape*.

Isurium Brigantum. See ALDBOROUGH.

Itchen Abbas (village, Hants): 'nuns' (estate by the river) Itchen'. The river has a pre-Celtic name of unknown meaning. The manor here was held in the 11C by St Mary's Abbey, Winchester. The second word of the name, a reduced form of Latin *abbatissa*, 'abbess', distinguishes the village from nearby *Itchen Stoke*, so named as a dependent settlement (OE *stoc*) of Itchen Abbas. DB *Icene*, 1167 *Ichene Monialum*, 1539 *Ichyn alias Abbesse Ichyn*.

Iver (village, Bucks): (place by the) brow of a hill'. OE *yfer*, 'hill brow'. The 'hill brow' is probably the low spur of land by which Iver lies. The *-am* of the DB form of the name below is a Latin ending. DB *Evreham*, *c.*1130 *Eura*.

Iveston (village, Durham): '(place by) Ifa's stone'. OE *stān*, 'stone'. The reference would be to a boundary stone here. 1183 *Ivestan*.

Ivinghoe (village, Bucks): 'hill spur of Ifa's people'. OE *-inga-*, 'of the people of', + *hōh*, 'hill spur'. The 'hill spur' in question is nearby Ivinghoe Beacon. Sir Walter Scott adopted an altered form of the name for his novel *Ivanhoe* (1820), exactly as the second form of the name below. But he could not have seen this record, which was published only in 1905. DB *Evinghehou*, 1665 *Ivanhoe*.

Ivington (hamlet, Herefords): 'estate associated with Ifa'. OE *-ing-*, 'associated with', + *tūn*, 'farmstead', 'estate'. DB *Ivintune*.

Ivybridge (town, Devon): '(place by the) ivy-covered bridge'. OE *īfig*, 'ivy', + *brycg*, 'bridge'. The river here is the Erme. 1292 *Ivebrugge*.

Ivychurch (village, Kent): '(place with an) ivy-covered church'. OE *īfig*, 'ivy', + *cirice*, 'church'. 11C *Iuecirce*.

Iwade (village, Kent): '(place by the) crossing place where yew trees grow'. OE *īw*, 'yew', + *wæd*, 'ford', 'crossing place' (related modern English *wade*). The crossing place would have been to the Isle of Sheppey here. 1179 *Ywada*.

Iwerne Minster (village, Dorset): '(place of the) monastery on the (river) Iwerne'. OE *mynster*, 'monastery', 'large church'. The river name is of Celtic origin and may mean either 'yew river' (modern Welsh *yw*, 'yew') or else represent the name of a goddess believed to dwell in its waters, itself meaning 'she who moves in a regular course'. The second word of the name, denoting the early possession of the manor by Shaftesbury Abbey, distinguishes the village from nearby *Iwerne Courtney* or *Shroton*, named either from the Courtenay family who held the manor in the 13C or as a 'sheriff's estate', as for SHREWTON, and, below it, *Steepleton Iwerne* or

Iwerne Stepleton, with its church steeple. 877 *Ywern*, DB *Evneministre*.

Ixworth (village, Suffolk): 'Gicsa's or Gycsa's enclosure'. OE *worth*, 'enclosure'. *c.*1025 *Gyxeweorde*, DB *Giswortha*.

Ixworth Thorpe (village, Suffolk): 'secondary settlement of Ixworth'. OS *thorp*, 'secondary settlement', 'dependent farmstead'. Ixworth Thorpe is 2 miles from IXWORTH. DB *Torp*, 1305 *Ixeworth thorp*.

J

Jacobstow (village, Cornwall): 'holy place of St James'. OE *stōw*, 'holy place'. The church here is dedicated to St James, whose Latin name is *Jacobus*. 1270 *Jacobestowe*.

Jacobstowe (village, Devon): 'holy place of St James'. OE *stōw*, 'holy place'. The church here is dedicated to St James, whose Latin name is *Jacobus*. 1331 *Jacopstoue*.

Jameston (hamlet, Pemb): 'St James's farm'. OE *tūn*, 'farm'. A fair was held here on St James's day. 1331 *Seint Jameston*.

Jarlshof (prehistoric site, Shetland): 'jarl's temple'. OS *jarl*, 'nobleman' (related modern English *earl*), + *hof*, 'temple'. The site was named by Sir Walter Scott, who was here in 1816 and who used the name for the medieval farmhouse that features in his novel *The Pirate* (1821).

Jarrow (town, S Tyneside): '(settlement of the) Gyrwe'. The tribal name means 'people of the fen', from OE *gyr*, 'mud', 'marsh'. The Gyrwe originated in the fenlands around Peterborough, but a group of them must have moved here, on the south bank of the river Tyne. *c*.730 *Gyruum*.

Jedburgh (town, Borders): 'enclosure by the (river) Jed'. OE *worth*, 'enclosure'. The river has a Celtic name meaning 'twisting one'. The '-burgh' of the name is misleading, and perhaps arose by association with *Roxburgh*, a few miles to the north. 800 *Gedwearde*, *c*.1100 *Geddewrde*, *c*.1160 *Jeddeburgh*.

Jeffreyston (village, Pemb): 'Geoffrey's farm'. OE *tūn*, 'farm'. The church here is dedicated to St Jeffry and St Oswald, but the first of these may in fact have been suggested by the place name. *c*.1214 *Villa Galfrid*, 1362 *Geffreiston*.

Jervaulx Abbey (monastic remains, N Yorks): 'abbey in the valley of the (river) Ure'. OF *val*, 'valley'. The river has a pre-English name of uncertain origin. *c*.1145 *Jorvalle*.

Jesmond (district, Newcastle): 'mouth of the (river) Ouseburn'. OE *mūtha*, 'mouth'. The name is a Norman adaptation of what might otherwise have been 'Ousemouth', with *J*-added to the river name and 'mouth' influenced by OF *mond*, 'mount'. For the river name, see OUSEFLEET. 1205 *Gesemue*.

Jevington (village, E Sussex): 'farmstead of Geofa's people'. OE *-inga-*, 'of the people of', + *tūn*, 'farmstead'. The DB form of the name below has *L*- for *G*-. DB *Lovingetone*, 1189 *Govingetona*.

Jodrell Bank (radio telescope site, Cheshire): 'Jodrell's hillside'. The Jodrell family were landowners here in the 19C. 1831 *Jodrell Bank*.

Johnby (hamlet, Cumbria): 'Johan's farmstead'. OS *bý*, 'farmstead', 'village'. The personal name is Old French. 1200 *Johannebi*.

John o'Groats (hamlet, Highland): 'John o'Groat's (place)'. John o'Groat (perhaps a Dutchman, Jan de Groot) was appointed bailee to the earls of Caithness here in the 15C.

Johnston (village, Pemb): 'John's farm'. OE *tūn*, 'farm'. 1296 *Villa Johannis*, 1393 *Johanneston*.

Johnstone (town, Renfrews): 'John's farm'. OE *tūn*, 'farmstead', 'village'. The identity of the original John is unknown. The town developed only from the 1780s. 1292 *Jonestone*.

Joppa (district, Edinburgh): '(place by) Joppa'. The name appears to have originated from that of a farm here in the 1780s, itself named after the biblical town by way of religious sentiment.

Jordanston (hamlet, Pemb): 'Jordan's farm'. OE *tūn*, 'farm'. The Welsh name of Jordanston is *Trefwrdan*, translating the English (Welsh *tref*, 'farm'). The first form of the name below has a miscopying of *n* as *h* in the personal name. 1291 *Villa Jordahi*, 1326 *Jordanyston*.

Juniper Green (district, Edinburgh): 'field of junipers'. The name is said to have been that of a farm here in the 18C. But the reference to junipers is suspect and the name may be a popular corruption.

Jura (island, Argyll & Bute): 'Doirad's island'. Gaelic *eilean*, 'island'. The name is a 'smoothed' form of the personal name, and the original 'island' element has been lost. 678 *Doirad Eilinn*.

K

Kaber (hamlet, Cumbria): '(place by the) hill where jackdaws are seen'. OE *cā* or OS *ká*, 'jackdaw', + OE *beorg* or OS *berg*, 'hill'. Late 12C *Kaberge*.

Katrine, Loch (loch, Stirling): 'loch of the wood of Eriu'. Gaelic *loch*, 'lake'. The first part of the name probably represents the Celtic word for 'forest', 'wood' (modern Welsh *coed*). The second is apparently the personal name Eriu. 1463 *Loch Ketyerne*.

Kea (village, Cornwall): '(church of) St Kea'. The name and church dedication were transferred here in the 19C from nearby *Old Kea*, where the church was dedicated to Kea, a saint said to have sailed to Cornwall from Ireland. The form of the name below relates to the original village. DB *Sanctus Che*.

Kearsley (town, Bolton): 'clearing where cress grows'. OE *cærse*, 'cress', + *lēah*, 'wood', 'clearing'. 'Clearing' here is perhaps better understood as 'meadow', given the watery context. Kearsley is on the river Croal. 1187 *Cherselawe*, *c*.1220 *Kersleie*.

Kearstwick (hamlet, Cumbria): '(place in the) valley clearing'. OS *kjóss*, 'valley', + *thveit*, 'clearing'. The hamlet lies in a small valley to the north of Kirkby Lonsdale. 1547 *Kesthwaite*.

Kearton (hamlet, N Yorks): 'Kærir's farmstead'. OE *tūn*, 'farmstead'. The personal name is Scandinavian. The first form of the name below is corrupt. 13C *Karretan*, 1298 *Kirton*.

Kedington (village, Suffolk): 'farmstead associated with Cydda'. OE *-ing-*, 'associated with', + *tūn*, 'farmstead'. 1043 *Kydington*, DB *Kidituna*.

Kedleston (hamlet, Derbys): 'Ketill's farmstead'. OE *tūn*, 'farmstead'. The personal name is Scandinavian. DB *Chetelestune*.

Keelby (village, Lincs): 'farmstead on a ridge'. OS *kjǫlr*, 'ridge' (modern English *keel*), + *bý*, 'farmstead', 'village'. DB *Chelebi*.

Keele (village, Staffs): 'hill where cows graze'. OE *cȳ*, 'cows', + *hyll*, 'hill'. The hill in question may be the one on which Keele Hall now stands as the nucleus of Keele University. 1169 *Kiel*.

Keeston (village, Pemb): 'Keting's farm'. OE *tūn*, 'farm'. The Welsh name of Keeston is *Tregetin*, translating the English (Welsh *tre*, 'farm'). 1289 *Villa Ketyng*, 1295 *Ketingeston*.

Keevil (village, Wilts): 'woodland clearing in a hollow'. OE *cȳf*, 'hollow' (literally 'vessel', 'tub'), + *lēah*, 'wood', 'clearing'. Celticists dispute this origin, preferring a source in a word related to modern Welsh *cyfyl*, 'neighbourhood' (earlier 'border'), or *cyfle*, 'place', 'district'. 964 *Kefle*, DB *Chivele*.

Kegworth (village, Leics): 'Cægga's enclosure'. OE *worth*, 'enclosure'. The DB form of the name below has garbled the personal name through a mishearing. DB *Cacheworde*, *c*.1125 *Caggworth*.

Keighley (town, Bradford): 'Cyhha's woodland clearing'. OE *lēah*, 'wood', 'clearing'. The modern pronunciation of the name as 'Keethly' arose in an attempt to preserve the original sound of OE *h* in the personal name. It is also represented by the middle *ch* in the DB form of the name below. DB *Chichelai*.

Keinton Mandeville (village, Somerset): 'Maundevill's royal manor'. OE *cyne-*, 'royal', + *tūn*, 'farmstead', 'manor'. The manor here was held in the 13C by the Maundevill family. DB *Chintune*, 1280 *Kyngton Maundevil*.

Keith (town, Moray): '(place by the) wood'. The name represents a Celtic word related to modern Welsh *coed*, 'wood'. 1187 *Geth*, *c*.1220 *Ket*.

Kelbrook (village, Lancs): '(place by the) brook flowing into a ravine'. OE *ceole*, 'throat', 'ravine', + *brōc*, 'brook'. The stream in question is Kelbrook Beck, which flows through a ravine that widens out at Kelbrook. The 'K-' of the name is due to Scandinavian influence. DB *Chelbroc*.

Keld (village, N Yorks): '(place by the) spring'. OS *kelda*, 'spring'. The first part of the first form of the name below means 'by the apple tree'. 1301 *Appeltrekelde*, 1538 *Kelde*.

Kelfield (village, N Yorks): 'open land where chalk is spread'. OE *celce*, 'chalky place', + *feld*, 'open land'. DB *Chelchefeld*. SO ALSO: *Kelfield*, N Lincs.

Kelham (village, Notts): '(place at the) ridges'. OS *kjǫlr*, 'ridge' (modern English *keel*). The name preserves the OS word in a dative plural form, the ridges themselves being the line of hills northwest of the village. The DB form of the name below is corrupt. DB *Calun*, 1156 *Kelum*.

Kelling (village, Norfolk): '(settlement of) Cylla's or Ceolla's people'. OE *-ingas*, 'people of'. *c.*970 *Chillinge*, DB *Kellinga*.

Kellington (village, N Yorks): 'estate associated with Ceolla'. OE *-ing-*, 'associated with', + *tūn*, 'farmstead', 'estate'. The 'K-' of the name is due to Scandinavian influence. DB *Chellinctone*.

Kelloe (village, Durham): '(place by the) hill where calves graze'. OE *celf*, 'calf', + *hlāw*, 'hill'. *c.*1170 *Kelflau*.

Kelly (hamlet, Devon): '(place by the) grove'. Cornish *kelli*, 'grove'. The DB form of the name below is corrupt. DB *Chenleie*, 1166 *Chelli*.

Kelly Bray (village, Cornwall): '(place by the) grove on a hill'. Cornish *kelli*, 'grove', + *bre*, 'hill'. The reference would be to nearby Kit Hill ('hill where kites are seen'). *c.*1286 *Kellibregh*.

Kelmarsh (village, Northants): '(place by the) marsh marked out with poles'. OE *cegel*, 'pole', 'post', + *mersc*, 'marsh'. The initial 'K-' of the name is due to Scandinavian influence. DB *Keilmerse*.

Kelmscot (village, Oxon): 'Cēnhelm's cottage'. OE *cot*, 'cottage'. 1234 *Kelmescote*.

Kelsale (village, Suffolk): 'Cēl's or Cēol's corner of land'. OE *halh*, 'nook', 'corner of land'. DB *Keleshala*.

Kelsall (village, Cheshire): 'Kell's corner of land'. OE *halh*, 'nook', 'corner of land'. The 'corner of land' is the valley here. 1257 *Kelsale*.

Kelshall (village, Herts): 'Cylli's hill'. OE *hyll*, 'hill'. *c.*1050 *Keleshelle*, DB *Cheleselle*.

Kelso (town, Borders): '(place on the) chalk hill spur'. OE *calc*, 'chalk', + *hōh*, 'hill spur'. The 'hill spur' in question is the low broad one to the north of the town. 1126 *Calkou*, *c.*1128 *Calcehou*.

Kelty (town, Fife): '(place by the) hard water'. The name is said to derive from Celtic words related to modern Welsh *caled*, 'hard', and *dwfr*, 'water'. It is not certain which particular watercourse is meant, and the second part of the

name may actually be of quite different origin. 1250 *Quilte*, 1329 *Quilt*.

Kelvedon (village, Essex): 'Cynelāf's valley'. OE *denu*, 'valley'. The Roman settlement here was *Canonium*, 'place on the reedy river', meaning the Blackwater. 998 *Cynlauedyne*, DB *Chelleuedana*.

Kelvedon Hatch (village, Essex): '(place at the) speckled hill with a gate'. OE *cylu*, 'spotted', 'speckled', + *dūn*, 'hill', + *hæcc*, 'hatchgate'. The first part of the main name represents OE *cylwan*, the dative form of *cylu*. The gate would have led to a forest. 1066 *Kylewendune*, DB *Keluenduna*, 1276 *Kelwedon Hacche*.

Kelvinside (district, Glasgow): '(place) beside the (river) Kelvin'. The river's name apparently derives from Gaelic *caol abhuinn*, 'narrow water'.

Kemberton (village, Shropshire): 'Cēnbeorht's farmstead'. OE *tūn*, 'farmstead'. DB *Chenbritone*.

Kemble (village, Glos): '(place at the) border'. The name is probably of Celtic origin from a word related to modern Welsh *cyfyl*, 'neighbourhood' (earlier 'border'). Cp. KEEVIL. The border was probably that of a tribal territory. 682 *Kemele*, DB *Chemele*.

Kemerton (village, Worcs): 'farmstead associated with Cyneburg'. OE *-ing-*, 'associated with', + *tūn*, 'farmstead'. The personal name is that of a woman. 840 *Cyneburgingctun*, DB *Chenemertune*.

Kempley (village, Glos): 'Cenep's woodland clearing'. OE *lēah*, 'wood', 'clearing'. DB *Chenepelei*.

Kempsey (village, Worcs): 'Cymi's island'. OE *ēg*, 'island'. The 'island' here is the higher ground on which the village stands by the river Severn. 799 *Kemesei*, DB *Chemesege*.

Kempsford (village, Glos): '(place at) Cynemǣr's ford'. OE *ford*, 'ford'. The ford in question was probably over a small stream that at one time flowed into the Thames here. 9C *Cynemæres forda*, DB *Chenemeresforde*.

Kempston (town, Beds): 'farmstead at the bend'. The first part of the name derives from a Celtic word related to modern Welsh *cam*, 'crooked'. The second part is OE *tūn*, 'farmstead'. Kempston lies by a large bend in the river Ouse. 1060 *Kemestan*, DB *Camestone*.

Kempton (hamlet, Shropshire): 'Cempa's farmstead'. OE *tūn*, 'farmstead'. The name could also mean 'farmstead of the warriors' (OE *cempa*, 'warrior', + *tūn*). DB *Chenpitune*.

Kempton Park (racecourse, Surrey): 'Cēna's farmstead'. OE *tūn*, 'farmstead'. The park here dates from at least the 13C. DB *Chenetone*, 1251 *Kenytun Park*.

Kemp Town (district of Brighton, Brighton & Hove): 'Kemp's town'. The district was laid out in the 1820s by Thomas Read Kemp (*c.*1781–1844), MP for Lewes.

Kemsing (village, Kent): 'Cymesa's place'. OE *-ing*, 'place belonging to'. 822 *Cymesing*.

Kenardington (village, Kent): 'estate associated with Cyneheard'. OE *-ing-*, 'associated with', + *tūn*, 'farmstead', 'estate'. 11C *Kynardingtune*.

Kenchester (hamlet, Herefords): 'Roman fort associated with Cēna'. OE *ceaster*, 'Roman fort'. Kenchester is the site of the Roman town of *Magnis* ('at the stones'), a name of Celtic origin related to modern Welsh *maen*, 'stone'. DB *Chenecestre*.

Kencot (village, Oxon): 'Cēna's cottage'. OE *cot*, 'cottage'. The second part of the DB form of the name below represents OE *tūn*, 'farmstead'. DB *Chenetone*, *c.*1130 *Chenicota*.

Kendal (town, Cumbria): 'village with a church in the valley of the (river) Kent'. The town was originally *Kirkby*, from OS *kirkju-bý* (*kirkja*, 'church', + *bý*, 'village'). It then added the district name *Kendal*, from the river Kent (a Celtic name of unknown meaning), and OS *dalr*, 'valley', to become *Kirkby Kendal*. The first word was then eventually dropped to leave the district name alone. DB *Cherchebi*, *c.*1095 *Kircabikendala*, 1452 *Kendale*, 1868 *Kendal*, or *Kirkby-in-Kendal*.

Kenilworth (town, Warwicks): 'Cynehild's enclosure'. OE *worth*, 'enclosure'. The DB form of the name below has omitted the second part of the personal name, that of a woman. DB *Chinewrde*, early 12C *Chenildeworda*.

Kenley (district, Croydon): 'Cēna's woodland clearing'. OE *lēah*, 'wood', 'clearing'. 1255 *Kenele*.

Kenn (village, Devon): '(place on the river) Kenn'. The name of the stream here is pre-English and of uncertain meaning. DB *Chent*. SO ALSO: *Kenn*, N Somerset.

Kennerleigh (village, Devon): 'Cyneweard's woodland clearing'. OE *lēah*, 'wood', 'clearing'. 1219 *Kenewarlegh*.

Kennet (river). See WEST KENNETT.

Kennett (hamlet, Cambs): '(place on the river) Kennett'. The river has a name of identical origin to that of the *Kennet* (see WEST KENNETT). DB *Chenet*.

Kennford (village, Devon): '(place by the) ford over the (river) Kenn'. OE *ford*, 'ford'. The river has a Celtic name of uncertain meaning. 1300 *Keneford*.

Kenninghall (village, Norfolk): 'corner of land of Cēna's people'. OE *-inga-*, 'of the people of', + *halh*, 'nook', 'corner of land'. DB *Keninchala*.

Kennington (district, Lambeth): 'farmstead associated with Cēna'. OE *-ing-*, 'associated with', + *tūn*, 'farmstead'. DB *Chenintune*.

Kennoway (town, Fife): meaning uncertain. The name has been popularly linked with that of St Caynicus. 1183 *Kennachin*, 1250 *Kennachyn*, *c.*1510 *Kennoquhy*.

Kennythorpe (hamlet, N Yorks): 'Cēnhere's outlying farmstead'. OS *thorp*, 'outlying farmstead'. The DB form of the name below is corrupt. DB *Cheretorp*, *c.*1180 *Kinnerthorp*.

Kensal Green (district, Brent): '(place by the) king's wood'. OE *cyning*, 'king', + *holt*, 'wood'. Kingsholt (as it originally was) was later associated with its village green. The '-al' of *Kensal* probably arose because OE *holt* was taken to be *halh*, 'corner of land'. 1253 *Kingisholte*, 1550 *Kynsale Green*.

Kensington (district, Kensington & Chel): 'estate associated with Cynesige'. OE *-ing-*, 'associated with', + *tūn*, 'farmstead', 'estate'. DB *Chenesitun*.

Kensworth (village, Beds): 'Cægīn's enclosure'. OE *worth*, 'enclosure'. 975 *Ceagnesworthe*, DB *Canesworde*.

Kent (county, SE England): 'coastal district'. The Celtic district name (modern Welsh *cant*, 'rim') is also explained as meaning 'land of the armies'. It in turn gave the name of CANTERBURY. 51 BC *Cantium*.

Kentchurch (hamlet, Herefords): 'St Keyn's church'. OE *cirice*, 'church'. The church here is now dedicated to St Mary, but the original dedication was to the female saint Keyn, patron of ST KEYNE, Cornwall. The first form of the name below has OW *lann* (modern Welsh *llan*) as the equivalent of OE *cirice*. *c.*1130 *Lan Cein*, 1341 *Keynchirche*.

Kentford (village, Suffolk): '(place at the) ford over the (river) Kennett'. OE *ford*, 'ford'. The river name has the same origin as that of the *Kennet* (see WEST KENNETT). 11C *Cheneteforde*.

Kentisbeare (village, Devon): 'Centel's wood'. OE *bearu*, 'wood', 'grove'. The DB form of the name below has omitted the *l* of the personal name. DB *Chentesbere*, 1242 *Kentelesbere*.

Kentisbury (hamlet, Devon): 'Centel's stronghold'. OE *burh*, 'fortified place'. The DB form of the name below has omitted the *l* of the personal name. DB *Chentesberie*, 1260 *Kentelesberi*.

Kentish Town (district, Camden): 'Kentish's estate'. OE *tūn*, 'farmstead', 'estate'. The ME surname Kentish means 'man from Kent'. 1208 *Kentisston*.

Kentmere (village, Cumbria): '(place at the) pool by the (river) Kent'. OE *mere*, 'pool'. The river has a Celtic name of uncertain meaning. 13C *Kentemere*.

Kenton (district, Brent): 'estate associated with Cēna'. OE *-ing-*, 'associated with', + *tūn*, 'farmstead', 'estate'. 1232 *Keninton*.

Kenton (village, Devon): 'farmstead on the (river) Kenn'. OE *tūn*, 'farmstead'. For the river name, see KENN. DB *Chentone*.

Kenton (village, Suffolk): 'royal manor'. OE *cyne-*, 'royal', + *tūn*, 'farmstead', 'manor'. The name could also mean 'Cēna's farmstead'. DB *Chenetuna*.

Kenwyn (village, Cornwall): '(place at the) white ridge'. Cornish *keyn*, 'ridge', + *gwynn*, 'white'. From the 14C the name was regarded as being that of a saint, and was subsequently equated with that of St Keyn, who gave the name of ST KEYNE. 1259 *Keynwen*.

Kenyon (district, Warrington). The name is said to be a shortened form of an OW name *Cruc Einion*, 'Einion's mound' (modern Welsh *crug*, 'hillock'). The mound in question could be a Bronze Age barrow known to have existed here. 1212 *Kenien*.

Kepwick (village, N Yorks): 'hamlet with a market'. OE *cēap*, 'market', + *wīc*, 'hamlet'. The initial 'K-' is due to Scandinavian influence. DB *Chipuic*.

Keresley (suburb of Coventry): 'Cēnhere's woodland clearing'. OE *lēah*, 'wood', 'clearing'. c.1144 *Keresleia*.

Kerne Bridge (hamlet, Herefords): 'bridge by a mill'. OE *cweorn*, 'mill' (modern English *quern*), + *brycg*, 'bridge'. Kerne Bridge is on the river Wye. 1272 *Kernebrigges*.

Kerrier (council district, Cornwall). The name is that of a former hundred here, perhaps meaning '(place of) rounds' (Cornish *ker*, 'fort', 'round'), a 'round' being a term for a special type of hill fort. 1201 *Kerier*.

Kersall (village, Notts): 'Cynehere's corner of land'. OE *halh*, 'nook', 'corner of land'. DB *Cherueshale*, 1196 *Kyrneshale*.

Kersey (village, Suffolk): 'island where cress grows'. OE *cærse*, 'cress', + *ēg*, 'island'. The 'island' is the higher ground on which the village stands northwest of Hadleigh. c.995 *Cæresige*, DB *Careseia*.

Kersoe (hamlet, Worcs): 'Criddi's hill spur'. OE *hōh*, 'hill spur'. Kersoe stands on a well-marked spur of land. 780 *Criddesho*.

Kesgrave (suburb of Ipswich, Suffolk): '(place by the) ditch where cress grows'. OE *cærse*, 'cress', + *græf*, 'trench', 'ditch' (modern English *grave*). The DB form of the name below has *G-* for *C-*. DB *Gressegraua*, 1231 *Kersigrave*.

Kessingland (village, Suffolk): 'cultivated land of Cyssi's people'. OE *-inga-*, 'of the people of', + *land*, 'tract of land', 'cultivated land'. DB *Kessingalanda*.

Kesteven (historic district, Lincs): 'meeting place in the wood'. The name combines the Celtic word for 'wood' (modern Welsh *coed*) with OS *stefna*, 'meeting'. The unusual mixture of languages implies that the same meeting place must have been used by both the Ancient Britons and, later, the Danes. The name survives today for the council districts of *North Kesteven* and *South Kesteven*. c.1000 *Ceostefne*, DB *Chetsteven*.

Keston (district, Bromley): '(place by) Cyssi's stone'. OE *stān*, 'stone'. The stone in question would have been a boundary marker here. 973 *Cysse stan*, DB *Chestān*.

Keswick (town, Cumbria): 'cheese farm'. OE *cēse*, 'cheese', + *wīc*, 'specialized farm'. The initial 'K-' is due to Scandinavian influence. Cp. CHISWICK. c.1240 *Kesewic*. SO ALSO: *Keswick*, Norfolk (near Bacton, near Norwich).

Kettering (town, Northants): '(settlement of) Cytra's people'. OE *-ingas*, 'people of'. 956 *Cytringan*, DB *Cateringe*.

Ketteringham (village, Norfolk): 'homestead of Cytra's people'. OE *-inga-*, 'of the people of', + *hām*, 'homestead'. c.1060 *Keteringham*, DB *Keterincham*.

Kettlebaston (village, Suffolk): 'Ketilbjǫrn's farmstead'. OE *tūn*, 'farmstead'. The personal name is Scandinavian. DB *Kitelbeornastuna*.

Kettleburgh (village, Suffolk): 'Ketil's hill'. OE *beorg* or OS *berg*, 'hill'. The personal name is Scandinavian. The name could also mean 'hill by a deep valley' (OE *cetel*, 'kettle', 'deep valley', + *beorg* or OS *berg*). DB *Ketelbiria*.

Kettleshulme (village, Cheshire): 'Ketil's island'. OS *holmr*, 'island', 'water meadow'. The personal name is Scandinavian. 1285 *Ketelisholm*.

Kettlestone (village, Norfolk): 'Ketil's farm-stead'. OE *tūn*, 'farmstead'. The personal name is Scandinavian. DB *Ketlestuna*.

Kettlewell (village, N Yorks): '(place by the) stream in a narrow valley'. OE *cetel*, 'narrow valley' (modern English *kettle*), + *wella*, 'spring', 'stream'. The 'K-' of the name is due to Scandinavian influence. DB *Cheteleuuelle*.

Ketton (village, Rutland): '(place on the river) Ketton'. The name is apparently an old name for the river Chater here, deriving from a Celtic word related to modern Welsh *coed*, 'wood'. This may itself have been a tribal name, meaning 'dwellers in the wood'. Early forms of the name ended in OE *ēa*, 'river', but this was later dropped. Some Celticists see the second part of the name as representing a word related to modern Welsh *hen*, 'old'. This would give a meaning 'old wood' and a name identical to that of *Hengoed* in Wales and Shropshire, but with the elements reversed. DB *Chetene*, 1175 *Ketene*.

Kew (district, Richmond): 'key-shaped spur of land'. OE *cǣg*, 'key', + *hōh*, 'hill spur'. An alternative meaning is 'spur of land by a landing place', with ME *key* (modern English *quay*) as the first element. The 'spur' is land in the bend of the Thames here, now half given over to the Royal Botanical Gardens. 1327 *Cayho*.

Kewstoke (village, N Somerset): 'Kew's secondary settlement'. OE *stoc*, 'outlying farmstead', 'secondary settlement'. Kew is a Celtic saint's name. DB *Chiwestoch*.

Kexbrough (hamlet, Barnsley): 'Keptr's stronghold'. OE *burh*, 'fortified place'. The personal name is Scandinavian. The DB form of the name below is corrupt. DB *Cezeburg*, *c*.1170 *Kesceburg*.

Kexby (village, York): 'Keikr's farmstead'. OS *bý*, 'farmstead', 'village'. The personal name is Scandinavian. 12C *Kexebi*.

Keyham (village, Leics): 'Cǣga's homestead'. OE *hām*, 'homestead', 'village'. The first part of the name could also represent OE *cǣg*, 'key', referring to a place that could be locked, or *cǣg*, 'stone'. DB *Caiham*.

Keyhaven (coastal village, Hants): 'harbour where cows are shipped'. OE *cū*, 'cow', + *hæfen*, 'harbour'. The first part of the name represents OE *cȳ*, the genitive form of *cū*. Presumably cows were shipped to and from the Isle of Wight here. *c*.1170 *Kihavene*.

Keyingham (village, E Yorks): 'homestead of Cǣga's people'. OE *-inga-*, 'of the people of', + *hām*, 'homestead'. DB *Caingeham*.

Keymer (town, W Sussex): '(place by the) cow pond'. OE *cū*, 'cow', + *mere*, 'pond'. The 'cow pond' was probably one of the streams of the river Adur here, where cows would have had a regular watering place. The name has OE *cū* in its genitive form *cȳ*. DB *Chemere*.

Keynsham (town, Bath & NE Somerset): 'Cǣgin's land in a river bend'. OE *hamm*, 'enclosure', 'land in a river bend'. Keynsham lies by a bend in the river Avon. *c*.1000 *Cægineshamme*, DB *Cainesham*.

Keysoe (village, Beds): '(place by the) key-shaped hill spur'. OE *cǣg*, 'key', + *hōh*, 'hillspur'. DB *Caissot*.

Keyston (village, Cambs): 'Ketil's boundary stone'. OE *stān*, 'stone'. Keyston was the westernmost village in Huntingdonshire, and the stone may have marked the county boundary here. The personal name is Scandinavian. DB *Chetelestan*.

Keyworth (village, Notts): '(place with an) enclosure'. OE *worth*, 'enclosure'. The origin of the first part of the name is uncertain. It probably represents a personal name. DB *Caworde*.

Kibblesworth (village, Gateshead): 'Cybbel's enclosure'. OE *worth*, 'enclosure'. 1185 *Kibleswrthe*.

Kibworth Beauchamp (village, Leics): 'de Beauchamp's (estate at) Cybba's enclosure'. OE *worth*, 'enclosure'. The de Beauchamp family held the manor early here, their name distinguishing this village from nearby *Kibworth Harcourt*, where the manor was held by the de Harewecurt family. DB *Chiburde*, 1315 *Kybeworth Beauchamp*.

Kidbrooke (district, Greenwich): '(place by the) brook where kites are seen'. OE *cȳta*, 'kite', + *brōc*, 'brook'. *c*.1100 *Chitebroc*.

Kidderminster (town, Worcs): 'Cydela's monastery'. OE *mynster*, 'monastery'. A monastery was founded here in the 8C on the site of the present All Saints church. The DB form of the name below has omitted the latter part of the personal name. DB *Chideminstre*, 1154 *Kedeleministre*.

Kiddington (hamlet, Oxon): 'estate associated with Cydda'. OE *-ing-*, 'associated with', + *tūn*, 'farmstead', 'estate'. DB *Chidintone*.

Kidlington (suburb of Oxford, Oxon): 'estate associated with Cydela'. OE *-ing-*, 'associated with', + *tūn*, 'farmstead', 'estate'. DB *Chedelintone*.

Kidsgrove (town, Staffs): 'Cyda's grove'. OE *grāf*, 'grove', 'copse'. This reading of the name is tentative. No early forms have been preserved, so an accurate interpretation is impossible.

Kidwelly (town, Carm): 'Cadwal's territory'. The identity of Cadwal is unknown. The Welsh form of the name is *Cydweli*, the final -*i* of which means 'territory'. The '-ll-' of the English spelling arose by association with Welsh names such as LLANELLI. IOC *Cetgueli*, *c*.1150 *Cedgueli*, 1191 *Kedwely*, 1458 *Kydwelly*.

Kielder Forest (forest region, Northd): 'forest by the Kielder Burn'. The river has a Celtic name meaning 'rapid stream' (modern Welsh *caled*, 'hard', and *dwfr*, 'water'). Kielder Forest and Kielder Water are modern creations in the Border Forest Park. 1326 *Keilder*.

Kilbirnie (town, N Ayrs): 'church of St Brendan'. Gaelic *cill*, 'church'. 1413 *Kilbyrny*.

Kilburn (district, Brent): '(place by the) cow stream'. OE *cū*, 'cow', + *burna*, 'stream'. The first part of the form of the name below represents OE *cūna*, the genitive plural of *cū*. There is no stream here now. *c*.1130 *Cuneburna*.

Kilburn (village, Derbys): '(place by) Cylla's stream'. OE *burna*, 'stream'. 1179 *Kileburn*.

Kilburn (village, N Yorks): '(place by) Cylla's stream'. OE *burna*, 'stream'. DB *Chilburne*.

Kilby (village, Leics): 'farmstead of the young men'. OE *cild*, 'child', 'young man', + OS *bý*, 'farmstead', 'village'. The 'K-' of the name is due to Scandinavian influence. DB *Cilebi*.

Kildale (village, N Yorks): '(place in the) narrow valley'. OS *kíll*, 'narrow bay', + *dalr*, 'valley'. DB *Childale*.

Kildwick (village, N Yorks): 'dairy farm of the young men'. OE *cild*, 'child', 'young man', + *wīc*, 'dairy farm'. The initial 'K-' of the name is due to Scandinavian influence. DB *Childeuuic*.

Kilgetty (village, Pemb): 'Ceti's corner of land'. Welsh *cil*, 'corner', 'nook'. The identity of Ceti is unknown. His name is also associated with *Sketty* (Welsh *Ynys Geti*, 'Ceti's island'), a district of Swansea. The Welsh form of the name is *Cilgeti*. 1330 *Kylketty*.

Kilham (village, E Yorks): '(place by the) kilns'. OE *cyln*, 'kiln'. The name represents OE *cylnum*, the dative plural form of *cyln*. DB *Chillun*.

Kilkhampton (village, Cornwall): 'farmstead by the circle'. Cornish *kylgh*, 'circle', + OE *tūn*, 'farmstead'. The 'circle' is probably a lost archaeological feature here. The '-ham-' probably appeared by association with names ending in '-hampton', such as *Littlehampton*. DB *Chilchetone*.

Killamarsh (village, Derbys): 'Cynewald's marsh'. OE *mersc*, 'marsh'. DB *Chinewoldemaresc*.

Killerby (village, Darlington): 'Ketilfrøthr's farmstead'. OS *bý*, 'farmstead', 'village'. The personal name is Scandinavian. 1091 *Culuerdebi*.

Killiecrankie (village, Perth & Kin): 'wood of aspens'. Gaelic *coille*, 'wood', + *critheann*, 'aspen'. There are still aspens here.

Killinghall (village, N Yorks): 'corner of land of Cylla's people'. OE *-inga-*, 'of the people of', + *halh*, 'nook', 'corner of land'. The land in question is a small valley in the hillside here. DB *Chilingale*.

Killington (hamlet, Cumbria): 'estate associated with Cylla'. OE *-ing-*, 'associated with', + *tūn*, 'farmstead', 'estate'. 1175 *Killintona*.

Killingworth (suburb of Newcastle upon Tyne, N Tyneside): 'enclosure associated with Cylla'. OE *-ing-*, 'associated with', + *worth*, 'enclosure'. 1242 *Killingwrth*.

Kilmacolm (town, Inverclyde): 'church of my Colm'. Gaelic *cill*, 'church', + *mo*, 'my'. Colm is St Columba, with 'my' added to his name to show a personal dedication to him. The name was regularly misspelt with a middle *l* in the 19C by wrong association with the name Malcolm. *c*.1205 *Kilmacolme*, 1868 *Kilmalcolm*.

Kilmarnock (town, E Ayrs): 'church of my little Ernan'. Gaelic *cill*, 'church', + *mo*, 'my'. Ernan is St Ernan, a disciple of St Columba, whose name here has the diminutive suffix -*oc*. The name as a whole indicates a personal dedication to him. Cp. KILMACOLM. 1299 *Kelmernoke*.

Kilmersdon (village, Somerset): 'Cynemær's hill'. OE *dūn*, 'hill'. 951 *Kunemersdon*, DB *Chenemeresdone*.

Kilmington (village, Devon): 'estate associated with Cynehelm'. OE *-ing-*, 'associated with', + *tūn*, 'farmstead', 'estate'. DB *Chenemetone*.

Kilnsea (coastal hamlet, E Yorks): '(place at the) pool near the kiln'. OE *cyln*, 'kiln', + *sæ*, 'pool'. There is no longer a pool here. DB *Chilnesse*.

Kilnsey (hamlet, N Yorks): '(place at the) marsh by the kiln'. OE *cyln*, 'kiln', + *sæge*, 'swamp', 'marsh'. The DB form of the name below has omitted the *n*. DB *Chileseie*, 1162 *Kilnesey*.

Kilnwick (village, E Yorks): 'farm associated with Cylla'. OE *-ing-*, 'associated with', + *wīc*, 'specialized farm'. The DB form of the name below is corrupt. DB *Chileuuit*, late 12C *Killingwic*.

Kilnwick Percy (hamlet, E Yorks): 'Percy's (estate at the) farm of Cylla's people'. OE *-inga-*, 'of the people of', + *wīc*, 'specialized farm'. Kiln-wick was associated with the Percy family from the 12C. DB *Chelingewic*.

Kilpeck (village, Herefords): '(place by the) corner'. The first part of the name represents Welsh *cil*, 'corner', 'nook'. The second part is of obscure origin. DB *Chipeete*.

Kilpin (village, E Yorks): 'enclosure for calves'. OE *celf*, 'calf', + *penn*, 'pen', 'enclosure'. The 'K-' of the name is due to Scandinavian influence. 959 *Celpene*, DB *Chelpin*.

Kilsby (village, Northants): 'Cild's farmstead'. OS *bȳ*, 'farmstead', 'village'. The first part of the name could also represent OE *cild*, 'child', 'young nobleman'. The 'K-' is due to Scandinavian influence. 1043 *Kildesbig*, DB *Chidesbi*.

Kilsyth (town, N Lanarks): meaning uncertain. The suggested interpretation 'church of St Syth' is quite untenable. 1210 *Kelvesyth*, 1217 *Kelnasydhe*, 1239 *Kilsyth*.

Kilton (village, Somerset): 'farmstead by the club-shaped hill'. OE *cylfe*, 'club', + *tūn*, 'farmstead'. *c.*880 *Cylfantun*, DB *Chilvetune*.

Kilve (village, Somerset): '(place by the) club-shaped hill'. OE *cylfe*, 'club'. 1243 *Kylve*.

Kilvington (village, Notts): 'estate associated with Cylfa or Cynelāf'. OE *-ing-*, 'associated with', + *tūn*, 'farmstead', 'estate'. DB *Chelvinctune*.

Kilwinning (town, N Ayrs): 'church of St Finnian'. Gaelic *cill*, 'church'. Finnian was a 6C Irish abbot of Clonard. *c.*1160 *Killvinin*, 1184 *Ecclesia Sti Vinini*, *c.*1300 *Kynwenyn*, 1357 *Kylvynnyne*.

Kimberley (hamlet, Norfolk): 'Cyneburg's woodland clearing'. OE *lēah*, 'wood', 'clearing'. The personal name is that of a woman. DB *Chineburlai*.

Kimberley (suburb of Nottingham, Notts): 'Cynemǣr's woodland clearing'. OE *lēah*, 'wood', 'clearing'. DB *Chinemarleie*.

Kimblesworth (village, Durham): 'Cynehelm's enclosure'. OE *worth*, 'enclosure'. 13C *Kymliswrth*.

Kimbolton (village, Cambs): 'Cynebald's village'. OE *tūn*, 'farmstead', 'village'. DB *Chenebaltone*. SO ALSO: *Kimbolton*, Herefords.

Kimcote (village, Leics): 'Cynemund's cottage'. OE *cot*, 'cottage'. DB *Chenemundescote*.

Kimmeridge (village, Dorset): 'Cȳma's strip of land'. OE *ric*, 'strip of land'. The first part of the name, garbled in the DB form below, could

also represent OE *cȳme*, 'convenient', describing a track that gives easy access to the sea. DB *Cameric*, 1212 *Kimerich*.

Kimmerston (hamlet, Northd): 'Cynemǣr's farmstead'. OE *tūn*, 'farmstead'. 1244 *Kynemereston*.

Kimpton (village, Herts): 'farmstead associated with Cȳma'. OE *-ing-*, 'associated with', + *tūn*, 'farmstead'. DB *Kamintone*. SO ALSO: *Kimpton*, Hants.

Kincardine (historic county, E Scotland): 'head of the copse'. Gaelic *cinn*, 'head'. The second part of the name comes from a Celtic word related to modern Welsh *cardden*, 'thicket' (cp. CARDENDEN). The county took its name from the now ruined Kincardine Castle, Aberdeens, north of Fettercairn. Other places of the name have the same sense, as the three Kincardines in Fife, Highland and Perth & Kin, and *Kincardine O'Neill*, Aberdeens, was owned by the O'Neill (Uí Néill) family of Northern Ireland. 1195 *Cincardin*.

Kinder Scout (mountain, Derbys): meaning uncertain. The second word of the name represents OS *skúti*, 'projecting cliff' (related modern English *shoot*). The first word is perhaps of Celtic origin meaning '(place) with wide views', from Celtic *com*, 'with' (related Latin *cum*), and a word related to Greek *derkomai*, 'to see'. DB *Chendre*, 1275 *Kinder*, 1767 *Kinder Scout*.

Kineton (village, Warwicks): 'king's manor'. OE *cyning*, 'king', + *tūn*, 'farmstead', 'manor'. 969 *Cyngtun*, DB *Quintone*.

Kingham (village, Oxon): 'homestead of Cǣga's people'. OE *-inga-*, 'of the people of', + *hām*, 'homestead'. The DB form of the name below has garbled the personal name. DB *Caningeham*, 11C *Keingaham*.

Kinghorn (resort town, Fife): 'head of the marsh'. Gaelic *cinn*, 'head', + *gorn*, 'marshland'. The town is built at a point where firmer ground rises above a marshy area. *c.*1136 *Chingor*, *c.*1140 *Kingornum*.

Kingsand (coastal village, Cornwall): 'King's sand'. The beach here must have been owned by a man or family called King. 1602 *Kings sand*.

Kingsbridge (town, Devon): 'king's bridge'. OE *cyning*, 'king', + *brycg*, 'bridge'. It is not known which Anglo-Saxon king gave his name to the bridge here at the head of Kingsbridge Estuary. 962 *Cinges bricge*.

Kings Bromley (village, Staffs): 'king's (estate at the) woodland clearing where broom grows'. OE *brōm*, 'broom', + *lēah*, 'wood', 'clearing'. The king held the manor here. The second form of the name below has Latin *regis*, 'of the king'. DB *Bromelei*, 1167 *Bramlea Regis*.

Kingsbury (district, Brent): 'king's manor'. OE *cyning*, 'king', + *burh*, 'fortified place', 'manor'. OE *byrig*, the dative form of *burh*, gave '-bury' in this and many other names. 1044 *Kynges Byrig*, DB *Chingesberie*.

Kingsbury (village, Warwicks): 'Cyne's stronghold'. OE *burh*, 'fortified place'. DB *Chinesberie*, 12C *Kinesburi*.

Kingsbury Episcopi (village, Somerset): 'bishop's (estate at the) king's manor'. OE *cyning*, 'king', + *burh*, 'fortified place', 'manor', + Latin *episcopi*, 'of the bishop'. The manor was held early by the Bishop of Bath. 1065 *Cyncgesbyrig*, DB *Chingesberie*.

Kingsclere (village, Hants): 'king's (manor at) Clere'. OE *cyning*, 'king'. The meaning of *Clere* is uncertain. It is also the base of the names of *Burghclere* (OE *burh*, 'fortified place', 'manor') and *Highclere* ('high'), to the west, and may be a Celtic river name meaning 'bright one' (modern Welsh *claer*, 'bright', 'shining'). early 12C *Kyngeclera*.

King's Cliffe (village, Northants): 'king's bank'. OE *cyning*, 'king', + *clif*, 'cliff', 'bank'. The place, on a hill slope above the Willow Brook, was often visited by Norman kings and was a royal manor in 1086. DB *Clive*, 1305 *Kyngesclive*, 1868 *Cliffe Regis*, or *King's-Cliffe*.

Kingscote (village, Glos): 'king's cottage'. OE *cyning*, 'king', + *cot*, 'cottage'. DB *Chingescote*.

King's Cross (district, Islington): 'king's cross'. 'Cross' means both 'stone monument in the form of a cross' and 'crossroads', and the name comes from the monument erected at the crossroads here in 1830 as a memorial to King George IV (1762–1830). It remained until 1845, when it was removed for King's Cross station to be built. The earlier name of the district was *Battlebridge*, preserved in Battlebridge Road here. This is a corruption of *Bradfordbridge*, 'bridge by the broad ford', referring to a ford and bridge over the Holborn. c.1378 *Bradefordebrigge*.

Kingsdon (village, Somerset): 'king's hill'. OE *cyning*, 'king', + *dūn*, 'hill'. 1194 *Kingesdon*.

Kingsdown (coastal village, Kent): 'king's hill'. OE *cyning*, 'king', + *dūn*, 'hill'. Kingsdown lies at the foot of cliffs. 1318 *Kyngesdoune*.

Kingsey (village, Bucks): 'king's island'. OE *cyning*, 'king', + *ēg*, 'island'. The 'island' is raised ground beside the river Thame here. 1174 *Eya*, 1197 *Kingesie*.

Kingsford (hamlet, Worcs): '(place by the) ford of Cēna's people'. OE *-inga-*, 'of the people of', + *ford*, 'ford'. 964 *Cenungaford*.

Kingsgate (resort suburb of Margate, Kent): 'king's gate'. The place is so called as it was at this gate (in the sense 'gap in the cliffs') that Charles II landed in 1683.

King's Heath (district, Birmingham): 'king's heath'. The former heathland here lay in the manor of KING'S NORTON. Hence the name. 1511 *Kyngesheth*.

Kingskerswell (suburb of Torquay, Devon): 'king's (estate at the) spring where watercress grows'. OE *cyning*, 'king', + *cærse*, 'cress', + *wella*, 'spring', 'stream'. The king held the manor here in 1086. DB *Carsewelle*, 1270 *Kyngescharsewell*, 1868 *Kinkerswell*, or *Kingskerswell*.

Kingsland (village, Herefords): 'king's (estate in) Leon'. OE *cyning*, 'king'. For the district name, see LEOMINSTER. DB *Lene*, 1213 *Kingeslan*.

Kings Langley (village, Herts): 'king's (estate in the) long wood or clearing'. OE *cyning*, 'king', + *lang*, 'long', + *lēah*, 'wood', 'clearing'. The king's manor was extracted in the early 12C from the manor granted to the Abbot of St Albans, leaving ABBOTS LANGLEY alone in monastic tenure. DB *Langelai*, 1436 *Kyngeslangeley*.

Kingsley (village, Staffs): 'king's wood'. OE *cyning*, 'king', + *lēah*, 'wood', 'clearing'. DB *Chingeslei*. SO ALSO: *Kingsley*, Cheshire, Hants.

King's Lynn (town and port, Norfolk): 'king's (estate in) Lynn'. The district name is of Celtic origin and means '(district by the) pool' (modern Welsh *llyn*, 'lake'), referring to the mouth of the river Ouse where the town now stands. The king in question is Henry VIII, who granted the town charters in 1525 and 1537. King's Lynn is generally known locally as *Lynn*. Also here are *North Lynn*, now an industrial estate adjoining the town to the north, and *West Lynn*, a district of King's Lynn on the west bank of the Ouse. DB *Lena*, c.1105 *Lynna*, 1868 *King's Lynn*, or *Lynn Regis*.

King's Meaburn (village, Cumbria): 'king's (estate by the) meadow stream'. OE *mæd*, 'meadow', + *burna*, 'stream'. The 'meadow stream' is the river Lyvennet here, where the manor was held in the 13C by the king. His title distinguishes the place from *Maulds Meaburn*, 3 miles upstream to the south, where the manor was held by Maud, wife of William de Vateriponte, who granted the estate to her in the late 12C. 12C *Maiburne*, 1279 *Meburne Regis*.

King's Newnham (village, Warwicks): 'king's new homestead or enclosure'. OE *nīwe*, 'new', + *hām*, 'homestead', or *hamm*, 'enclosure'. As William Dugdale explains in *The Antiquities of Warwickshire* (1656): 'This, for distinction from another *Newnham*, within the same Hundred, is called *Newnham-Regis*, in respect that the King was antiently possessed of it'. 1043 *Neowenham*, 1275 *Newham Kinges*.

King's Norton (district, Birmingham): 'king's northern farmstead'. OE *north*, 'northern', + *tūn*, 'farmstead', 'estate'. The farm was probably 'north' in relation to an early settlement at (or near) Bromsgrove. The king held the manor here in 1086. See also KING'S HEATH. DB *Nortune*, 1221 *Kinges Norton*.

King's Nympton (village, Devon): 'king's farmstead by the (river) Nymet'. OE *tūn*, 'farmstead'. The river here now is the Mole, but earlier it was the *Nymet*, from a Celtic word meaning 'holy place' (modern Welsh *nyfed*, 'sanctuary'). The king held the manor here in 1066, and the addition of his title distinguishes the village from *Bishop's Nympton*, 5 miles to the northeast, where the manor was held in 1086 by the Bishop of Exeter, and *George Nympton*, 2½ miles to the north, where the church is dedicated to St George. *Queen's Nympton*, a southern district of South Molton, was so named in 1900 in honour of Queen Victoria as a counterpart to King's Nympton. DB *Nimetone*, 1254 *Kingesnemeton*.

King's Pyon (village, Herefords): 'king's (estate at the) island plagued with insects'. OE *pīe*, 'parasite', 'insect', + *ēg*, 'island'. The 'island' is dry ground in a wet area. The second word of the name represents OE *pēona*, the genitive plural form of *pīe*. The manor here was held early by the king, whose title distinguishes the village from *Canon Pyon*, held by the canons of Hereford. DB *Pionie*, 1285 *Kings Pyon*.

King's Somborne (village, Hants): 'king's (estate on) stream where pigs come'. OE *swīn*, 'pig' (modern English *swine*), + *burna*, 'stream'. The stream in question is a tributary of the river Test. The king held the manor early here, his title distinguishing the village from nearby *Little Somborne* and *Upper Somborne*. 909 *Swinburnan*, DB *Sunburne*.

King's Stag (village, Dorset): '(place of the) king's stag'. The story goes that Thomas de la Lynde killed a stag of Henry III here in the 13C. The name has the alternative spelling *Kingstag*.

King's Stanley (village, Glos): 'king's (estate by the) stony woodland clearing'. OE *stān*, 'stone', + *lēah*, 'wood', 'clearing'. The manor

here belonged to the crown. The first word of the name distinguishes this Stanley from nearby *Leonard Stanley*, where the church was formerly dedicated to St Leonard. DB *Stanlege*, 1220 *Kingestanleg*.

Kings Sutton (village, Northants): 'king's southern farmstead'. OE *sūth*, 'southern', + *tūn*, 'farmstead'. King William held the manor here in 1086. DB *Sudtone*, 1294 *Kinges Sutton*.

Kingstanding (district, Birmingham): 'king's hunting station'. ME *standing*, 'hunter's post from which to shoot game'. Stebbing Shaw, in *History and Antiquities of Staffordshire* (1798–1801), describes Kingstanding as 'a little artificial mount where Charles I is said to have stood when he harangued the troops he brought out of Shropshire at the beginning of the civil war [in 1642]'.

Kingsteignton (town, Devon): 'king's estate on the (river) Teign'. OE *tūn*, 'farmstead', 'estate'. The king held the manor here in 1086. Cp. BISHOPSTEIGNTON. For the river name, see TEIGNMOUTH. DB *Teintona*, 1274 *Kingestentone*, 1868 *Kingsteignton, or Kingstanton*.

King Sterndale. See EARL STERNDALE.

Kingsthorpe (district of Northampton, Northants): 'outlying farmstead of the king'. OE *cyning*, 'king', + OS *thorp*, 'outlying farmstead'. The king held the manor here in 1086. DB *Torp*, 1190 *Kingestorp*.

Kingston Bagpuize (village, Oxon): 'de Bagpuize's royal manor'. OE *cyning*, 'king', + *tūn*, 'farmstead', 'manor'. Ralph de Bagpuize held the manor here in 1086. *c.*976 *Cyngestun*, DB *Chingestune*, 1284 *Kingeston Bagepuz*.

Kingston Blount (village, Oxon): 'le Blund's royal manor'. OE *cyning*, 'king', + *tūn*, 'farmstead', 'manor'. The le Blund family held the manor here in the 13C, their name distinguishing this Kingston from nearby *Kingston Stert* (OE *steort*, 'tongue of land'). DB *Chingestone*, 1379 *Kyngestone Blont*.

Kingston by Sea (district of Shoreham-by-Sea, W Sussex): 'de Busci's royal manor'. OE *cyning*, 'king', + *tūn*, 'farmstead', 'manor'. The manor was originally held by the king, but in the 12C passed to Robert de Busci, whose name was corrupted to 'by Sea' from the maritime location of the place. DB *Chingestune*, 1315 *Kyngeston Bouci*, 1730 *Kingston Bowsey al. Kingston by Sea*, 1868 *Kingston-by-Sea, or Kingston-Bowsey*.

Kingston Deverill (village, Wilts): 'king's manor on the (river) Deverill'. OE *cyning*, 'king', + *tūn*, 'farmstead', 'manor'. The river name, formerly that of the river Wylye here, is Celtic in origin and means 'watery one' (related modern Welsh *dwfr*, 'water'). The first (originally second) word of the name distinguishes this village from nearby *Brixton Deverill*, 'Beorhtrīc's estate', *Hill Deverill*, by a hill, *Monkton Deverill*, held by monks, and *Longbridge Deverill*, with a long bridge over the Wylye. Richard Colt Hoare writes of Kingston Deverill in his *History of Modern Wiltshire* (1822–44): 'Shortly after the Conquest it was in the Crown and was among the early grants to the Earl of Cornwall ... It followed the fate of the Earldom, which frequently reverted to the Crown and was finally entailed on the King's eldest son. This circumstance, perhaps, gave origin to the appellation of *Kingston*, by way of distinction from the other Deverills, none of which, since the Conquest, have been royal property'. The five villages are collectively known as *The Deverills*. DB *Devrel*, 1249 *Deverel Kyngeston*.

Kingstone (village, Herefords): 'king's manor'. OE *cyning*, 'king', + *tūn*, 'manor', 'estate'. DB *Chingestone*.

Kingstone (village, Somerset): '(place by the) king's stone'. OE *cyning*, 'king', + *stān*, 'stan'. The reference is probably to a boundary stone here. DB *Chingestana*.

Kingston Lacy (country house, Dorset): 'de Lacy's royal manor'. OE *cyning*, 'king', + *tūn*, 'farmstead', 'manor'. The de Lacy family held the manor here in the 13C. 1170 *Kingestune*, 1319 *Kyngesstone Lacy*.

Kingston Lisle (village, Oxon): 'del Isle's royal manor'. OE *cyning*, 'king', + *tūn*, 'farmstead', 'manor'. The del Isle family held the manor here in the 13C. 1220 *Kingeston*, 1322 *Kyngeston Lisle*.

Kingston near Lewes (village, E Sussex): 'king's manor near Lewes'. OE *cyning*, 'king', + *tūn*, 'farmstead', 'manor'. The second part of the name, locating this Kingston near LEWES, distinguishes it from KINGSTON BY SEA, W Sussex, 13 miles to the west. *c*.1100 *Kingestona*.

Kingston on Soar (village, Notts): '(place by the) royal stone on the (river) Soar'. OE *cyne-*, 'royal', + *stān*, 'stone'. The location of any such stone is unknown. For the river name, see BARROW UPON SOAR. DB *Chinestan*.

Kingston Stert. See KINGSTON BLOUNT.

Kingston upon Hull. See HULL.

Kingston upon Thames (borough, Greater London): 'king's manor by the (river) Thames'. OE *cyning*, 'king', + *tūn*, 'farmstead', 'estate', 'manor'. The town was a royal possession in Saxon times, and Edward the Elder was crowned here in 899, as were all his successors down to Ethelred II in 982. Hence the tradition that the name actually means 'king's stone', perpetuated by the so-called Coronation Stone: 'The name probably means that this was an estate belonging to the king, and not that Anglo-Saxon kings were crowned here on the stone that now stands on a site adjoining the modern Guildhall' (*The New Shell Guide to England*, 1981). The river name (see THAMES DITTON) was added subsequently to distinguish this Kingston from others. In 1927 Kingston was granted the title of Royal Borough by George V in recognition of its long-standing royal status. 838 *Cyninges tun*, DB *Chingestune*, 1321 *Kyngeston super Tamesiam*, 1589 *Kingestowne upon Thames*.

King's Walden. See ST PAUL'S WALDEN.

Kingswear (town, Devon): 'king's weir'. OE *cyning*, 'king', + *wer*, 'weir'. Kingswear is on the river Dart. 12C *Kingeswere*.

Kingswinford (district, Dudley): 'royal manor by the ford used by pigs'. OE *cyning*, 'king', + *swīn*, 'pig', + *ford*, 'ford'. The name is effectively 'King's Swinford'. Kingswinford was formerly sometimes known as *New Swinford*. Hence contrasting OLD SWINFORD. DB *Svinesford*, 1322 *Kyngesswynford*.

Kingswood (town, S Glos): 'king's wood'. OE *cyning*, 'king', + *wudu*, 'wood'. 1231 *Kingeswode*. SO ALSO: *Kingswood*, Glos, Surrey.

Kings Worthy. See HEADBOURNE WORTHY.

Kington (town, Herefords): 'royal manor', OE *cyne-*, 'royal' (later replaced by *cyning*, 'king'), + *tūn*, 'estate', 'manor'. DB *Chingtune*. SO ALSO: *Kington*, Worcs.

Kington Langley (village, Wilts): '(place at the) long wood or clearing near Kington'. OE *lang*, 'long', + *lēah*, 'wood', 'clearing'. The first word of the name was added in the 17C to distinguish this Langley from nearby LANGLEY BURRELL by locating it near KINGTON ST MICHAEL. DB *Langhelei*, 1699 *Kington Langley*.

Kington Magna (village, Dorset): 'greater royal manor'. OE *cyne-*, 'royal' (later replaced by *cyning*, 'king'), + *tūn*, 'estate', 'manor', + Latin *magna*, 'great'. The second word of the name distinguishes this Kington from what is now *Little Kington Farm*, West Stour. DB *Chintone*, 1243 *Magna Kington*.

Kington St Michael (village, Wilts): 'royal manor with St Michael's church'. OE *cyne-*, 'royal' (later replaced by *cyning*, 'king'), + *tūn*, 'farmstead', 'manor'. The addition of the church dedication distinguishes this village from nearby KINGTON LANGLEY. 934 *Kingtone*, DB *Chintone*, 1279 *Kyngton Michel*.

Kingussie (town, Highland): 'head of the pine-wood'. Gaelic *ceann*, 'head', + *giuthsach*, 'pine'. Pines are still numerous here. *c.*1210 *Kiguscy*.

Kinlet (hamlet, Shropshire): 'royal lot'. OE *cyning*, 'king', + *hlēt*, 'lot', 'share'. The manor here was held in 1066 by Queen Edith, widow of Edward the Confessor. DB *Chinlete*.

Kinlochleven (town, Highland): '(place at the) head of Loch Leven'. Gaelic *ceann*, 'head', + *loch*, 'lake'. The loch takes its name from the river that flows into it from the Blackwater Reservoir. Its own name means 'elm river' (Gaelic *leamhain*, 'elm'). There are other rivers and lochs of the name.

Kinnerley (village, Shropshire): 'Cyneheard's woodland clearing'. OE *lēah*, 'wood', 'clearing'. DB *Chenardelei*.

Kinnersley (village, Herefords): 'Cyneheard's woodland clearing'. OE *lēah*, 'wood', 'clearing'. 1123 *Chinardeslege*.

Kinnersley (Shropshire). See KYNNERSLEY.

Kinoulton (village, Notts): 'Cynehild's farmstead'. OE *tūn*, 'farmstead'. The personal name is that of a woman. *c.*1000 *Kinildetune*, DB *Chineltune*.

Kinross (town, Perth & Kin): 'end of the promontory'. Gaelic *ceann*, 'head', 'end', + *ros*, 'promontory'. Kinross is on a broad headland that projects into Loch Leven. *c.*1144 *Kynros*.

Kinsley (village, Wakefield): 'Cyne's woodland clearing'. OE *lēah*, 'wood', 'clearing'. DB *Chineslai*.

Kinson (district, Bournemouth): 'Cynestān's farmstead'. OE *tūn*, 'farmstead'. DB *Chinestanestone*, 1238 *Kinestaneston*, 1868 *Kingstone, or Kinson*.

Kintbury (village, W Berks): 'fortified place on the (river) Kennet'. OE *burh*, 'fortified place'. For the river name, see WEST KENNETT. *c.*935 *Cynetanbyrig*, DB *Cheneteberie*.

Kintyre (peninsula, Argyll & Bute): 'end of the land'. Gaelic *ceann*, 'head', 'end', + *tire*, 'land'. The peninsula runs south to the Mull of Kintyre, where *Mull* ('headland') is either from Gaelic *maol*, 'bald', or OS *múli*, 'snout'. Cp. LAND'S END. The Roman name for the Mull of Kintyre was *Epidium Promontorium*, 'headland of the Epidii' ('horse people'). 807 *Ciunntire*.

Kinver (town, Staffs): '(place by the) hill'. The name is Celtic, and originally applied to a forest here, now represented by Kinver Edge. The second part of the name is related to modern Welsh *bre*, 'hill'. The first part is of uncertain origin, but may have come to be associated with an OE personal name such as Cynehild. 736 *Cynibre*, DB *Chenevare*.

Kippax (village, Leeds): 'Cippa's or Cyppa's ash tree'. OE *æsc*, 'ash'. Scandinavian *K-* has replaced OE *C-* in the personal name and OS *askr*, 'ash', has replaced the original OE word. DB *Chipesch*.

Kirby Bedon (hamlet, Norfolk): 'de Bidun's village with a church'. OS *kirkju-bý* (from *kirkja*, 'church', + *bý*, 'village'). The de Bidun family held the manor here in the 12C. DB *Kerkebei*, 1291 *Kirkeby Bydon*.

Kirby Bellars (village, Leics): 'Beier's village with a church'. OS *kirkju-bý* (from *kirkja*, 'church', + *bý*, 'village'). The Beier family held the manor here from the 12C. DB *Chirchebi*, 1428 *Kirkeby Belers*.

Kirby Grindalythe (village, N Yorks): 'village with a church in Grindalythe'. OS *kirkju-bý* (from *kirkja*, 'church', + *bý*, 'village'). The district name means 'slope of the valley where cranes are seen' (OE *cran*, 'crane', + *dæl*, 'valley', + OS *hlíth*, 'slope'). DB *Chirchebi*, 1367 *Kirkby in Crendalith*.

Kirby Knowle (village, N Yorks): 'village with a church by Knowle'. OS *kirkju-bý* (from *kirkja*, 'church', + *bý*, 'village'). The second word of the name, referring to nearby *Knowle Hill* (OE *cnoll*, 'hilltop'), distinguishes this Kirby from COLD KIRBY, 4 miles to the southeast, where the main name has a different origin. DB *Chirchebi*.

Kirby-le-Soken. See THORPE-LE-SOKEN.

Kirby Misperton (village, N Yorks): 'village with a church by Misperton'. OS *kirkju-bý* (from *kirkja*, 'church', + *bý*, 'village'). The village takes its name from nearby *Misperton*, whose own name probably means 'farmstead with a dunghill' (OE *mist*, 'dung', + *beorg*, 'hill', + *tūn*, 'farm'). The two places are entered in the DB as two separate manors. The names were then combined. DB *Chirchebi*, *Mispeton*.

Kirby Muxloe (village, Leics): 'Muxloe's (estate at) Kærir's farmstead'. OS *bý*, 'farmstead', 'village'. The personal name is Scandinavian. The Muxloe family held lands here from at least the 17C. DB *Carbi*.

Kirdford (village, W Sussex): '(place at) Cynethrӯth's or Cynerēd's ford'. OE *ford*, 'ford'. The personal names are respectively those of a woman and a man. The ford in question was over the river Arun here, just south of the church. 1228 *Kinredeford*.

Kirkandrews upon Eden (village, Cumbria): 'St Andrew's church on the (river) Eden'.

OS *kirkja*, 'church'. The church here was dedicated to St Andrew. The river name (see EDEN-HALL) distinguishes the village from *Kirkandrews upon Esk* (see ESKDALE GREEN), 10 miles to the north. *c.*1200 *Kirkandres.*

Kirkbampton (village, Cumbria): 'farmstead made of beams by a church'. OS *kirkja*, 'church', + OE *bēam*, 'tree trunk', 'beam', + *tūn*, 'farmstead'. The original name could also mean 'farmstead by a tree'. *c.*1185 *Banton*, 1292 *Kyrkebampton.*

Kirk Bramwith (village, Doncaster): '(place by the) wood where broom grows with a church'. OS *kirkja*, 'church', + OE *brōm*, 'broom', + OS *vithr*, 'wood'. The first word of the name distinguishes the village from *South Bramwith*, on the opposite bank of the river Don. The DB form of the original name below is garbled. DB *Brannuet*, 1200 *Branwyth*, 1341 *Kyrkbramwith.*

Kirkbride (village, Cumbria): 'church of St Bride'. OS *kirkja*, 'church'. The church here is dedicated to the Irish saint Bride or Brigit (Bridget). 1163 *Chirchebrid*, 1868 *Bridekirk.*

Kirkburn (village, E Yorks): '(place on the) stream with a church'. OS *kirkja*, 'church', + OE *burna*, 'spring', 'stream'. The stream in question is Eastburn Beck. DB *Westburne*, 1272 *Kirkebrun.*

Kirkburton (town, Kirklees): 'farmstead by a fortified place with a church'. OS *kirkja*, 'church', + OE *byrh-tūn* (see BURTON UPON TRENT). The first part of the name was added only in the 16C. DB *Bertone.*

Kirkby (town, Knowsley): 'village with a church'. OS *kirkju-bý* (from *kirkja*, 'church', + *bý*, 'village'). The name is common in the Midlands and North of England and frequently adds a distinguishing element, as for the places below. See also KENDAL. DB *Cherchebi.*

Kirkby in Ashfield (town, Notts): 'village with a church in Ashfield'. OS *kirkju-bý* (from *kirkja*, 'church', + *bý*, 'village'). The district name means 'open land where ash trees grow' (OE *æsc*, 'ash', + *feld*, 'open land'). Cp. SUTTON IN ASHFIELD. DB *Chircebi*, 1216 *Kirkeby in Esfeld.*

Kirkby Lonsdale (town, Cumbria): 'village with a church in the valley of the (river) Lune'. OS *kirkju-bý* (from *kirkja*, 'church', + *bý*, 'village'). For the river name, here followed by OS *dalr*, 'valley', see LANCASTER. DB *Cherchebi*, 1090 *Kircabi Lauenesdale.*

Kirkby Malham (village, N Yorks): 'village with a church near Malham'. OS *kirkju-bý* (from *kirkja*, 'church', + *bý*, 'village'). The village is just over a mile south of MALHAM. DB *Chircebi.*

Kirkby Malzeard (village, N Yorks): 'village with a church in a bad clearing'. OS *kirkju-bý* (from *kirkja*, 'church', + *bý*, 'village'), + OF *mal*, 'bad', + *assart*, 'clearing'. A 'bad' clearing is an infertile one. DB *Chirchebi*, *c.*1105 *Kirkebi Malesard.*

Kirkbymoorside (town, N Yorks): 'village with a church at the head of the moor'. OS *kirkju-bý* (from *kirkja*, 'church', + *bý*, 'village'), + OE *mōr*, 'moor', + *hēafod*, 'head', 'top'. *Moorshead* later became *Moorside*, perhaps because the town, surrounded by hills, seems to occupy a lower rather than a higher site. DB *Chircebi*, *c.*1170 *Kirkeby Moresheved*, 1868 *Kirkby Moorside.*

Kirkby Overblow (village, N Yorks): 'village with a church of the smelters'. OS *kirkju-bý* (from *kirkja*, 'church', + *bý*, 'village'). The second word of the name represents OE *or-blāwere*, 'ore blower', referring to the smelters of iron ore formerly active here. DB *Cherchebi*, 1211 *Kirkeby Oreblowere.*

Kirkby Stephen (town, Cumbria): 'Stephen's village with a church'. OS *kirkju-bý* (from *kirkja*, 'church', + *bý*, 'village'). Stephen may have been an early owner of the manor here. More likely, the name is that of St Stephen, to whom the church is dedicated. *c.*1094 *Cherkaby Stephan.*

Kirkby Thore (village, Cumbria): 'Thórir's village with a church'. OS *kirkju-bý* (from *kirkja*, 'church', + *bý*, 'village'). The personal name is that of an early Scandinavian owner. 1179 *Kirkebythore.*

Kirkby Wharfe (village, N Yorks): 'village with a church on the (river) Wharfe'. OS *kirkju-bý* (from *kirkja*, 'church', + *bý*, 'village'). For the river name, see BURLEY IN WHARFEDALE. DB *Chircebi*, 1254 *Kirkeby super Werf.*

Kirkcaldy (town and port, Fife): 'fort at Caledin'. The name is Celtic, from a word meaning 'fort' (modern Welsh *caer*) added to *Caledin*, 'hard hill' (Welsh *caled*, 'hard', and *din*, 'hill'). The fort itself was probably on the site of the present 15C Ravenscraig Castle. 'Kirk-' was substituted for the 'fort' element when the latter was no longer understood. 12C *Kircalethyn.*

Kirkconnel (town, Dumfries & Gall): 'church of St Conall'. OS *kirkja*, 'church'. There are several Irish saints of the name. 1347 *Kyrkconwelle*, 1354 *Kirkconevel.*

Kirkcudbright (town, Dumfries & Gall): 'church of St Cuthbert'. OS *kirkja*, 'church'. The 'Kirk-' may have originally been 'Kil-' (Gaelic *cill*, 'church'), since the personal name follows the word, as is usual in Celtic names, such as KILMARNOCK, rather than preceding it, as in

ORMSKIRK. Cuthbert was a 7C Northumbrian monk who made many missionary journeys in Galloway. 1296 *Kircuthbright*.

Kirk Deighton (village, N Yorks): 'farmstead surrounded by a ditch with a church'. OE *dīc*, 'ditch', 'dyke', + *tūn*, 'farmstead'. The first word of the name (OS *kirkja*, 'church') distinguishes the village from nearby *North Deighton*. The DB form of the name below has *s* for *c*. DB *Distone*, 14C *Kirke Dighton*.

Kirk Ella (suburb of Hull, E Yorks): '(place at) Ælf's woodland clearing with a church'. OE *lēah*, 'wood', 'clearing'. The first word of the name (OS *kirkja*, 'church') distinguishes this Ella from nearby *West Ella*. The DB form of the name below suggests an original -*ing*-. DB *Aluengi*, 15C *Kirk Elley*.

Kirk Hallam (suburb of Ilkeston, Derbys): '(place at the) corners of land with a church'. OS *kirkja*, 'church', + OE *halh*, 'nook', 'corner of land'. The main name represents OE *halum*, the dative plural form of *halh*. The first word distinguishes this Hallam from nearby *West Hallam*. DB *Halun*, 12C *Kyrkehallam*.

Kirkham (town, Lancs): 'village with a church'. OE *cirice*, 'church', + *hām*, 'homestead', 'village'. OE *cirice* has been replaced in the name by equivalent OS *kirkja*. The DB form of the name below omits the *r*. DB *Chicheham*, 1094 *Kyrkham*.

Kirk Hammerton. See GREEN HAMMERTON.

Kirkharle (hamlet, Northd): 'Herela's woodland clearing'. OE *lēah*, 'wood', 'clearing'. 1177 *Herle*, 1242 *Kirkeherl*.

Kirkheaton (village, Kirklees): 'high farmstead with a church'. OS *kirkja*, 'church', + OE *hēah*, 'high', + *tūn*, 'farmstead'. The first part of the name distinguishes the village from nearby *Upper Heaton*, on higher ground, from *Earlsheaton*, 5 miles to the northeast, held by the earls of Warren, from *Hanging Heaton*, at the top of a steep hillside next to Earlsheaton, and from CLECKHEATON, 5 miles to the north. The DB form of the name below is corrupt. DB *Heptone*, 13C *Kirkheton*.

Kirkheaton (village, Northd): 'high farmstead with a church'. OS *kirkja*, 'church', + OE *hēah*, 'high', + *tūn*, 'farmstead'. The village was originally *Little Heaton*, its larger counterpart being the present *Capheaton*, 2 miles to the northeast, where *Cap*- represents Latin *caput*, 'head', 'chief'. 1242 *Heton*.

Kirkintilloch (town, E Dunbartons): 'fort at the head of the hillock'. As with KIRKCALDY, the first part of the name is a Celtic word meaning 'fort' (modern Welsh *caer*), not a Scandinavian

'Kirk-'. The rest of the name is made up of Gaelic *ceann*, 'head', and *tulach*, 'hillock'. The reference is to a Roman fort on the Antonine Wall here. *c*.1200 *Kirkintulach*.

Kirk Ireton (village, Derbys): 'farmstead of the Irishmen with a church'. OS *kirkja*, 'church', + *Íri*, 'Irishman', + OE *tūn*, 'farmstead'. DB *Hiretune*, 1370 *Kirkirton*.

Kirkland (hamlet, Cumbria): 'estate belonging to a church'. OS *kirkja*, 'church', + *land*, 'land', 'estate'. The form of the name below relates to Kirkland near Blencarn, but Kirkland near Ennerdale Bridge has a name of identical origin. *c*.1140 *Kyrkeland*.

Kirk Langley (village, Derbys): '(place by the) long wood or clearing with a church'. OS *kirkja*, 'church', + OE *lang*, 'long', + *lēah*, 'wood', 'clearing'. The first word of the name distinguishes this Langley from nearby *Meynell Langley*, where the Meynell family held the manor in the 13C. DB *Langelei*, 1269 *Kyrkelongeleye*.

Kirkleatham (village, Redcar & Clev): '(place by the) slopes with a church'. OS *kirkja*, 'church', + OE *hlith* or OS *hlíth*, 'slope'. The second part of the name (originally the sole name) represents a dative plural form of the OE or OS word for 'slope'. OS *kirkja*, 'church', subsequently replaced OE *west*, 'western', which distinguished the place from UPLEATHAM, 3 miles to the southeast. DB *Westlidum*, 1181 *Kyrkelidun*.

Kirklees (unitary authority, N England): '(district around) Kirklees'. The name is preserved in that of *Kirklees Hall*, north of Huddersfield, built on the site of a Cistercian nunnery. The name itself represents OE *cirice*, 'church' (or its OS equivalent, *kirkja*), and *lēah*, 'wood', giving an overall meaning 'wood belonging to a church' ('church' being the nunnery). 1246 *Kyrkelegh*.

Kirklevington (village, Stockton): 'farmstead on the (river) Leven with a church'. OE *tūn*, 'farmstead'. The river has a Celtic name perhaps meaning 'smooth one'. The first part of the name (OS *kirkja*, 'church') was added to distinguish the place from nearby *Castle Levington*, with its Norman castle. The church at Kirklevington is distinctive in its own right, and stands prominently in the highest part of the village. DB *Levetona*, 1230 *Kirkelevingtona*, 1868 *Linton-Kirk*, or *Kirk-Levington*.

Kirkley (district of Lowestoft, Suffolk): 'woodland clearing by the church'. OS *kirkja*, 'church', + OE *lēah*, 'wood', 'clearing'. DB *Kirkelea*.

Kirklington (village, Notts): 'estate associated with Cyrtla'. OE -*ing*-, 'associated with', + *tūn*, 'farmstead', 'estate'. 958 *Cyrlingtune*, DB *Cherlinton*. SO ALSO: *Kirklington*, N Yorks.

Kirklinton (hamlet, Cumbria): 'farmstead by the (river) Lyne'. OE *tūn*, 'farmstead'. The river has a Celtic name perhaps meaning 'smooth one'. OS *kirkja*, 'church', was added later to distinguish this Linton from *Westlinton*, 3 miles to the southwest. *c*.1170 *Leuenton*, 1278 *Kirkeleuinton*.

Kirk Merrington (village, Durham): 'estate associated with Mǣra with a church'. OE *-ing-*, 'associated with', + *tūn*, 'farmstead', 'estate'. OS *kirkja*, 'church', was added to the original name. *c*.1085 *Mǣrintun*, 1331 *Kyrke Merington*.

Kirknewton (village, Northd): 'new farmstead with a church'. OS *kirkja*, 'church', + OE *nīwe*, 'new', + *tūn*, 'farmstead'. 12C *Niwetona*.

Kirkoswald (village, Cumbria): 'church of St Oswald'. OS *kirkja*, 'church'. The church here is dedicated to Oswald, 7C king of Northumbria. 1167 *Karcoswald*.

Kirk Sandall (suburb of Doncaster): 'sandy corner of land with a church'. OS *kirkja*, 'church', + OE *sand*, 'sand', + *halh*, 'nook', 'corner of land'. The land is an area of flat ground in a bend of an old course of the river Don. The first word of the name distinguishes this Sandall from nearby straggling *Long Sandall*, formerly *Little Sandall*. Cp. SANDAL MAGNA. DB *Sandala*, 1261 *Kirke Sandale*.

Kirksanton (hamlet, Cumbria): 'church of St Sanctán'. OS *kirkja*, 'church'. The church here is dedicated to St Anne, as a corruption of the Irish saint's name. DB *Santacherche*, *c*.1150 *Kirkesantan*.

Kirk Smeaton (village, N Yorks): 'farmstead of the smiths with a church'. OS *kirkja*, 'church', + OE *smith*, 'smith', + *tūn*, 'farmstead'. The first word of the name distinguishes the village from *Little Smeaton*, on the opposite bank of the river Went. DB *Smedetone*.

Kirkstead (village, Lincs): 'church site'. OE *cirice*, 'church', + *stede*, 'place'. The reference is to the Cistercian abbey founded here in 1139. OE *cirice* was later replaced by equivalent OS *kirkja*. 1139 *Kirkestede*.

Kirkwall (town and port, Orkney): 'church by the bay'. OS *kirkja*, 'church', + *vágr*, 'bay'. The bay is the Bay of Kirkwall, to the north of the town, while the church is the 12C cathedral of St Magnus. The OS 'bay' word has given a misleading English *wall*. *c*.1225 *Kirkiuvagr*.

Kirkwhelpington (village, Northd): 'estate associated with Hwelp with a church'. OE *-ing-*, 'associated with', + *tūn*, 'farmstead', 'estate'. OS *kirkja*, 'church', was added to the original name. 1176 *Welpinton*.

Kirmington (village, N Lincs): 'estate associated with Cynehere'. OE *-ing-*, 'associated with', + *tūn*, 'farmstead', 'estate'. DB *Chernitone*.

Kirriemuir (town, Angus): 'big quarter'. Gaelic *ceathramh*, 'quarter', + *mór*, 'big'. A *ceathramh* (pronounced 'kerrow') was the fourth part of a *dabhach*, a variable area of land which, like the English hide, was considered large enough to support a single household. 1250 *Kerimor*.

Kirstead Green (village, Norfolk): 'site of a church'. OE *cirice*, 'church', + *stede*, 'site'. OE *cirice* was later replaced by equivalent OS *kirkja*, while Kirstead itself became associated with its village green. *c*.1095 *Kerkestede*.

Kirtling (village, Cambs): 'place associated with Cyrtla'. OE *-ing-*, 'place associated with'. DB *Chertelinge*.

Kirtlington (village, Oxon): 'estate associated with Cyrtla'. OE *-ing-*, 'associated with', + *tūn*, 'farmstead', 'estate'. *c*.1000 *Kyrtlingtune*, DB *Certelintone*.

Kirton (village, Lincs): 'village with a church'. OE *cirice*, 'church', + *tūn*, 'farmstead', 'village'. OE *cirice* was subsequently replaced by equivalent OS *kirkja*. DB *Chirchetune*. SO ALSO: *Kirton*, Notts, Suffolk.

Kirton in Lindsey (town, N Lincs): 'village with a church in Lindsey'. OE *cirice*, 'church', + *tūn*, 'farmstead', 'village'. OE *cirice* was subsequently replaced by equivalent OS *kirkja*. For the district name, added for distinction from KIRTON, Lincs, see LINDSEY. DB *Chirchetone*.

Kislingbury (village, Northants): 'stronghold of Cysel's people'. OE *-inga-*, 'of the people of', + *burh*, 'fortified place'. The name could also mean 'stronghold of the dwellers on the gravel' (OE *cisel*, 'gravel', + *-inga-*, 'of the dwellers at', + *burh*). DB *Ceselingeberie*.

Kiveton Park (village, Rotherham): 'farmstead with a tub-shaped feature'. OE *cȳf*, 'vessel', 'tub', + *tūn*, 'farmstead'. The park of the name is nearby Kiveton Park. DB *Ciuetone*, 1896 *Kiveton Park*.

Knaith (hamlet, Lincs): 'landing place by a river bend'. OE *cnēo*, 'knee', 'bend', + *hȳth*, 'landing place'. The river here is the Trent. DB *Cheneide*.

Knapton (village, Norfolk): 'servant's farmstead'. OE *cnapa*, 'boy', 'servant' (modern English *knave*), + *tūn*, 'farmstead'. The name could also mean 'Cnapa's farmstead'. The DB clerk has spaced the consonants out with vowels. Cp.

KNEBWORTH. DB *Kanapatone*. SO ALSO: *Knapton*, York.

Knapwell (village, Cambs): '(place by the) servant's spring'. OE *cnapa*, 'boy', 'servant' (modern English *knave*), + *wella*, 'spring', 'stream'. The name could also mean 'Cnapa's spring'. *c.*1045 *Cnapwelle*, DB *Chenepewelle*.

Knaresborough (town, N Yorks): 'Cēnheard's stronghold'. OE *burh*, 'fortified place'. The fortification in question was probably where Knaresborough Castle now stands. DB *Chenaresburg*.

Knarsdale (hamlet, Northd): '(place in the) valley of the rugged rock'. OE *cnearr*, 'rugged rock' (related modern English *gnarled*), + OS *dalr*, 'valley'. OE *Cnearr* was probably the name of this mountainous district. 1254 *Knaresdal*.

Knayton (village, N Yorks): 'Cēngifu's farmstead'. OE *tūn*, 'farmstead'. The personal name is that of a woman. DB *Cheniueton*.

Knebworth (town, Herts): 'Cnebba's enclosure'. OE *worth*, 'enclosure'. The DB clerk had problems with the many consonants and spaced them out with vowels. DB *Chenepeworde*, 1220 *Knebbewrth*.

Kneesall (village, Notts): 'Cynehēah's corner of land'. OE *halh*, 'nook', 'corner of land'. DB *Cheneshale*, 1175 *Cneshala*.

Kneesworth (village, Cambs): 'Cynehēah's enclosure'. OE *worth*, 'enclosure'. *c.*1218 *Cnesworth*.

Kneeton (village, Notts): 'Cēngifu's farmstead'. OE *tūn*, 'farmstead'. The personal name is that of a woman. DB *Cheniueton*.

Knightley (hamlet, Staffs): 'woodland clearing of the young men'. OE *cniht*, 'youth', 'servant' (modern English *knight*), + *lēah*, 'wood', 'clearing'. DB *Chenistelei*.

Knighton (town, Powys): 'farmstead of the young men'. OE *cniht*, 'youth', 'servant', + *tūn*, 'farmstead'. The 'young men' would have been the personal servants or followers of a baron or lord. The Welsh name of Knighton is *Trefyclo*, 'farm by the dyke' (Welsh *tref*, 'farm', + *y*, 'the', + *clawdd*, 'dyke'), referring to OFFA'S DYKE, to the west of the town. DB *Chenistetone*, 1193 *Cnicheton*. SO ALSO: *Knighton*, Leicester, Staffs.

Knightsbridge (district, Kensington & Chel): 'bridge of the young men'. OE *cniht*, 'youth', 'servant', + *brycg*, 'bridge'. As for KNIGHTON, the 'young men' would have been people of a baron or lord. The bridge where they congregated would have been where the present road of the name crosses the river Westbourne, near the present Albert Gate. *c.*1050 *Cnihtebricge*.

Knill (hamlet, Herefords): '(place on a) hillock'. OE *cnylle*, 'hillock' (related modern English *knoll*). Knill stands on a hillock overlooking a stream. DB *Chenille*.

Knipton (village, Leics): 'farmstead below a steep rock'. OS *gnipa*, 'steep rock', + OE *tūn*, 'farmstead'. The village lies in a valley with steep hills on either side. DB *Gniptone*.

Knitsley (hamlet, Durham): 'woodland clearing where knitches are obtained'. OE *cnycc*, 'knitch', 'faggot' (bundle of sticks bound together as fuel), + *lēah*, 'wood', 'clearing'. 1303 *Knyhtheley*.

Kniveton (village, Derbys): 'Cēngifu's farmstead'. OE *tūn*, 'farmstead'. The personal name is that of a woman. DB *Cheniuetun*.

Knock (hamlet, Cumbria): '(place by a) hillock'. OI *cnocc*, 'hillock'. The 'hillock' in question is the hill known as Knock Pike, to the north of the village. 12C *Chonoc*.

Knockholt (village, Kent): '(place at the) oak wood'. OE *āc*, 'oak', + *holt*, 'wood'. The *N-* of the second form of the name below (which gave the 'Kn-' of the present name) represents the final *-m* of the original preceding OE words *æt thǣm*, 'at the'. 1197 *Ocholt*, 1353 *Nocholt*.

Knockin (village, Shropshire): '(place by the) little hill'. The name is Celtic in origin, from a word related to modern Welsh *cnwc*, 'hillock'. Cp. KNOOK. 1165 *Cnochin*.

Knodishall (village, Suffolk): 'Cnott's corner of land'. OE *halh*, 'nook', 'corner of land'. DB *Cnotesheala*.

Knook (village, Wilts): '(place by the) hillock'. The name is of Celtic origin, from a word related to modern Welsh *cnwc*, 'hillock'. The reference may be to the tumulus to the south of the church. DB *Cunuche*.

Knossington (village, Leics): 'estate associated with Cnossa'. OE *-ing-*, 'associated with', + *tūn*, 'farmstead', 'village'. The DB form of the name below is corrupt. DB *Nossitone*, 12C *Cnossintona*.

Knott End-on-Sea (coastal village, Lancs): '(place at the) end of the hillock by the sea'. ME *knot*, 'hillock'. The village is at the northern point of the estuary of the river Wyre, and the 'end' is presumably that of the land here. 13C *Cnote*.

Knotting. See NOTTING HILL.

Knottingley (town, Wakefield): 'woodland clearing of Cnotta's people'. OE *-inga-*, 'of the people of', + *lēah*, 'wood', 'clearing'. DB *Notingeleia*.

Knotty Ash (district, Liverpool): '(place by the) gnarled ash tree'. A village arose around the ash tree in question in the late 17C or early 18C. The first word of the name, referring to the knots that made the tree gnarled, was added later. *c*.1700 *Ash*.

Knowle (district, Solihull): '(place at the) hill-top'. OE *cnoll*, 'hilltop', 'hillock' (modern English *knoll*). William Dugdale, in *The Antiquities of Warwickshire* (1656), writes of the former village 'having had its name originally from the situation: for in our old English, *cnolle* signifieth the knap of an Hill, or an ascending ground'. DB *La Cnolle*. SO ALSO: *Knowle*, Bristol.

Knowlton (hamlet, Kent): 'farmstead by a hill-ock'. OE *cnoll*, 'hillock' (modern English *knoll*), + *tūn*, 'farmstead'. DB *Chenoltone*.

Knowsley (village, Knowsley): 'Cēnwulf's or Cynewulf's woodland clearing'. OE *lēah*, 'wood', 'clearing'. The name gave that of the local unitary authority. DB *Chenulueslei*.

Knowstone (village, Devon): '(place by) Knútr's stone'. OE *stān*, 'stone'. The personal name is Scandinavian and as for KNUTSFORD. The stone in question was a boundary marker at the place called Rock just east of the village. DB *Chenutdestana*.

Knutsford (town, Cheshire): '(place by) Knútr's ford'. OE *ford*, 'ford'. The Scandinavian personal name has been popularly associated with that of King Canute (Cnut). Hence Canute Place as the name of the town's former Market Place. The location of the ford is uncertain, as Knutsford is on high ground away from any river. It may have taken the form of a causeway over the marshy ground south of Tatton Mere, a lake to the north of Knutsford. 'This place ... is situated on the banks of a small stream, over which Canute the Dane is said to have passed with his army for the conquest of the northern parts of the kingdom in the reign of Ethelred; hence its name of Canute's or Cnut's ford' (*The National Gazetteer of Great Britain and Ireland*, 1868). DB *Cunetesford*.

Kyleakin (village, Highland). The village on the island of Skye takes its name from *Kyle Akin*, the narrow strait between it and Kyle of Loch-alsh. The strait's name means 'Haakon's strait' (Gaelic *caol*, 'strait'). Haakon IV of Norway is said to have sailed through the strait in 1263 after his defeat at Largs.

Kyle of Lochalsh (village and port, High-land): '(place by the) Kyle of Lochalsh'. The village stands on the eastern side of the Kyle of Lochalsh, the narrow entrance (Gaelic *caol*, 'strait') to Loch Alsh. The name of the loch (lake) may mean 'foaming one' (Gaelic *aillseach*).

Kyles of Bute (sea channel, Argyll & Bute): 'straits of Bute'. The name is that of the narrow channel (Gaelic *caol*, 'strait') that surrounds the northern part of the island of BUTE, separating it from the mainland of ARGYLL. An English plural -*s* has been added to *kyle*, the English form of the Gaelic word.

Kynance Cove (cove, Cornwall): 'cove by the ravine'. Cornish *cow-nans*, 'ravine' (from *cow*, 'hollow', + *nans*, 'valley'). The 'ravine' is the narrow valley that leads down to the cove. The first form of the name below has added Cornish *penn*, 'head'. 1325 *Penkeunans*, 1613 *Kynans*, 1813 *Kinance Cove*.

Kynaston (hamlet, Shropshire): 'Cyneweard's farmstead'. OE *tūn*, 'farmstead'. The hamlet is close to the Welsh border and is also known by the Welsh translated name *Tregynferdd* (Welsh *tre*, 'farm', + *Cynferdd*, 'Cyneweard'). DB *Chimerestun*.

Kynnersley (village, Wrekin): 'Cyneheard's woodland clearing'. OE *lēah*, 'wood', 'clearing'. The DB form of the name below means 'Cyne-heard's island' (OE *ēg*, 'island'), referring to the large 'island' of land on which the village lies in the Weald Moors. The name is also spelt *Kinnersley* (thus in the Post Office's *Postal Addresses*, 1987) leading to confusion with KIN-NERSLEY. DB *Chinardeseie*, 1291 *Kynardesleye*.

Kyre (hamlet, Worcs): '(place by the river) Kyre'. The name, that of the stream here, is pre-English in origin and of uncertain meaning. DB *Cuer*.

L

Laceby (village, NE Lincs): 'Leifr's farmstead'. OS *bý*, 'farmstead', 'village'. The personal name is Scandinavian. DB *Levesbi*.

Lach Dennis (village, Cheshire): 'Danish (man's estate by the) boggy stream'. OE *lece*, 'stream', 'bog', + ME *danais*, 'Danish'. The manor here was held in 1086 by a Dane called Colben. DB *Lece*, 1260 *Lache Deneys*.

Lackford (village, Suffolk): '(place by the) ford where leeks grow'. OE *lēac*, 'leek', + *ford*, 'ford'. Lackford lies near the river *Lark*, which took its name from the village. DB *Lecforda*.

Lacock (village, Wilts): '(place by the) small stream'. OE *lacuc*, 'small stream' (related modern English *lake*). The 'small stream' is not the river Avon here but the minor tributary on which the village stands. 854 *Lacok*, DB *Lacoc*.

Lactodurum. See TOWCESTER.

Ladbroke (village, Warwicks): '(place by the) brook used for predicting the future'. OE *hlod*, 'lot', 'fate', + *brōc*, 'brook'. 998 *Hlodbroc*, DB *Lodbroc*.

Ladock (village, Cornwall): 'church of St Ladoc'. The church here is dedicated to Ladoc, a female saint about whom little is known. 1268 *Sancta Ladoca*, 1358 *Sent Ladek*.

Ladybank (town, Fife): 'damp slope'. Gaelic *leathad bog*, 'moist slope'. The name refers to the peat formerly dug here from the 13C. It appears to have been influenced by such names as *Ladykirk* ('Our Lady's Church'), Borders, or *Ladywell* ('Our Lady's Well'), Borders.

Lagentium. See CASTLEFORD.

Laindon (district of Basildon, Essex): '(place at the) hill by the (river) Lea'. OE *dūn*, 'hill'. The former river name, that of a lost stream here, is of Celtic origin and means 'light one'. *c.*1000 *Ligeandune*, DB *Leienduna*.

Lake (hamlet, Wilts): '(place by the) small stream'. OE *lacu*, 'stream', 'watercourse' (related modern English *lake*). The 'small stream' would

have been one of the many side channels of the river Avon here. 1289 *Lake*.

Lake District (national park, NW England). The region is characterized by its many lakes and tarns, of which 15 are of appreciable size. The name became prominent in the early 19C, as did the alternative *Lakeland*, which surprisingly did not prevail. 1829 *Lake-land*, 1835 *Lake District*.

Lakenham (district of Norwich, Norfolk): 'Lāca's homestead'. OE *hām*, 'homestead', 'village'. DB *Lakemham*.

Lakenheath. See FOREST HEATH.

Lake Vyrnwy (reservoir, Powys): 'lake of (the river) Vyrnwy'. The reservoir is named for the river that flows into it. The river's Welsh name is *Efyrnwy*, a form of *Hafren*, the Welsh name of the *Severn*, so has the same obscure origin as that name (see SEVERN STOKE). The Severn itself rises on Plynlimon, 23 miles to the southwest.

Laleham (suburb of Staines, Surrey): 'homestead or enclosure where brushwood is found'. OE *lǣl*, 'twig', 'switch', + *hām*, 'homestead', or *hamm*, 'enclosure'. 1042 *Lǣleham*, DB *Leleham*.

Laleston (village, Bridgend): 'Legeles' farm'. OE *tūn*, 'farmstead'. Thomas and Walter Legeles ('Lawless') are recorded in 13C documents as members of an Anglo-Scandinavian family that was probably already here in the 11C. The Welsh name of Laleston is *Trelales* (Welsh *tre*, 'farm'). *c.*1165 *Lagelestun*, 1268 *Laweleston*.

Lamarsh (village, Essex): '(place by the) marsh on loamy ground'. OE *lām*, 'loam', + *mersc*, 'marsh'. DB *Lamers*.

Lamas (hamlet, Norfolk): '(place by the) marsh on loamy ground'. OE *lām*, 'loam', + *mersc*, 'marsh'. Cp. LAMARSH. DB *Lamers*.

Lamberhurst (village, Kent): 'wooded hills where lambs graze'. OE *lamb*, 'lamb', + *hyrst*, 'wooded hill'. The first part of the name represents OE *lambra*, the genitive plural form of *lamb*. c.1100 *Lamburherste*.

Lambeth (borough, Greater London): 'landing place for lambs'. OE *lamb*, 'lamb', + *hȳth*, 'landing place'. Lambeth is on the south bank of the Thames. 1088 *Lamhytha*.

Lambley (village, Notts): 'clearing where lambs are pastured'. OE *lamb*, 'lamb', + *lēah*, 'wood', 'clearing'. DB *Lambeleia*.

Lambourn (town, W Berks): 'lambs' stream'. OE *lamb*, 'lamb', + *burna*, 'stream'. A 'lambs' stream' is probably one where they were washed. The name is that of the river here. c.880 *Lambburnan*, DB *Lamborne*.

Lambston (hamlet, Pemb): 'Lambert's farm'. OE *tūn*, 'farm'. The personal name is probably Flemish. 1291 *Villa Lamberti*, 1321 *Lamberteston*.

Lamerton (village, Devon): 'farmstead by the lambs' stream'. OE *lamb*, 'lamb', + *burna*, 'stream', + *tūn*, 'farmstead'. Cp. LAMBOURN. The name could also mean 'farmstead by the stream on loamy ground' (OE *lām*, 'loam', + *burna* + *tūn*). DB *Lambretona*.

Lamesley (village, Gateshead): 'pasture for lambs'. OE *lamb*, 'lamb', + *lēah*, 'clearing', 'pasture'. 1297 *Lamelay*.

Lammermuir (upland region, Borders): 'lambs' moor'. OE *lamb*, 'lamb', + *mōr*, 'moor'. The 'moor' would have been waste land on which lambs grazed. The first part of the name represents OE *lambra*, the genitive plural of *lamb*. 800 *Lambormore*.

Lamorna (village, Cornwall): 'valley of the (river) Mornow'. Cornish *nans*, 'valley'. The name of the stream that flows down to Lamorna Cove is conjectural, and of uncertain meaning. A word related to Welsh *mwrn*, 'close', 'sultry', has been suggested. 1302 *Nansmorno*, 1387 *Lamorna alias Nansmorna*.

Lamorran (hamlet, Cornwall): 'church site of Moran'. Cornish *lann*, 'church site'. Nothing is known of the female saint to whom the church here was dedicated. 969 *Lannmoren*.

Lampeter (town, Ceredigion): 'church of St Peter'. Welsh *llan*, 'church'. The Welsh name of Lampeter is *Llanbedr Pont Steffan*, 'church of St Peter by Stephen's bridge' (Welsh *llan*, 'church', + *Pedr*, 'Peter', + *pont*, 'bridge', + *Steffan*, 'Stephen'). The latter part of this name was added to distinguish this Llanbedr from others. Stephen was probably a Norman appointed to look after the bridge here over the river Teifi. 1284 *Lanpeder*, 1301 *Lampeter Pount Steune*.

Lamplugh (hamlet, Cumbria): '(place in the) bare valley'. The name is Celtic in origin, from words related to modern Welsh *nant*, 'valley', and Middle Welsh *blwch*, 'bare'. c.1150 *Lamplou*.

Lamport (village, Northants): 'long village'. OE *lang*, 'long', + *port*, 'village', 'market place'. DB *Langeport*.

Lamyatt (village, Somerset): '(place by a) gate for lambs'. OE *lamb*, 'lamb', + *geat*, 'gate'. Late 10C *Lambageate*, DB *Lamieta*.

Lanark (town, S Lanarks): '(place by the) glade'. OW *lannerch*, 'glade'. 1188 *Lannarc*.

Lancashire (county, NW England): 'district based on Lancaster'. OE *scīr*, 'shire', 'district'. See LANCASTER. 14C *Lancastreshire*.

Lancaster (city, Lancs): 'Roman fort on the (river) Lune'. OE *cæster*, 'Roman camp'. The river has a Celtic name probably meaning 'healthy', 'pure', perhaps referring to the god who lived in its waters, invoked to heal the sick. The name of the Roman station here is unknown, but it was probably based on the river name. (A Roman milestone found 4 miles from Lancaster ended its text with 'L MP IIII', interpreted as 'from L[ancaster] 4 miles'.) DB *Loncastre*.

Lanchester (town, Durham): 'long Roman fort'. OE *lang*, 'long', + *ceaster*, 'Roman camp'. This is the traditional origin of the name, but 'Lan-' may actually represent the first element of *Longovicium*, the name of the Roman fort, meaning 'place of the Longovices' (probably 'ship fighters', from a Celtic word related to modern Welsh *llong*, 'ship'). 1196 *Langecestr*.

Lancing (town, W Sussex): '(settlement of) Wlanc's people'. OE *-ingas*, 'people of'. There are many '-ing' names in W Sussex, suggesting that each of the named groups of people must have been quite small. Others nearby are ANGMERING and WORTHING. DB *Lancinges*.

Landbeach (village, Cambs): '(place on a) low ridge by dry land'. OE *land*, 'dry land', + *bæc*, 'ridge' (modern English *back*). The first part of the name was added to distinguish this place from nearby WATERBEACH, which is nearer the river Cam. DB *Bece*, 1218 *Landebeche*.

Landcross (hamlet, Devon): '(place by the) narrow buttock-shaped hill'. OE *hlanc*, 'long', 'narrow' (modern English *lank*), + *ears*, 'buttock' (modern English *arse*). The name could also mean 'church by the marsh', from Celtic words related to modern Welsh *llan*, 'church', and *cors*, 'marsh'. DB *Lanchers*.

Landford (village, Wilts): '(place by the) ford crossed by a lane'. OE *lanu*, 'lane', + *ford*, 'ford'. Early forms of the name suggest that the meaning may in fact be '(place by the) long ford' (OE *lang*, 'long', + *ford*). But the stream here is only a small one and the ford could not have been very long. DB *Langeford*, 1242 *Laneford*.

Landican (district of Birkenhead, Wirral): 'St Tegan's church'. OW *lann*, 'church'. The identity of the particular saint is uncertain. There is no known Welsh saint called Tegan and the reference may in fact be to the 7C Irish bishop Dagan. The church itself probably stood where the church of the Holy Cross, Woodchurch, stands now. DB *Landechene*.

Landkey (village, Devon): 'church site of St Ke'. Cornish *lann*, 'church site'. In the form of the name below, the *-de-* corresponds to OC *to-*, 'thy', used as a term of endearment. 1166 *Landechei*.

Landrake (village, Cornwall): '(place in a) clearing'. Cornish *lannergh*, 'clearing'. The form of the name below has added OE *tūn*, 'farmstead'. Late 11C *Landerhtun*.

Land's End (peninsula, Cornwall): 'end of the mainland'. OE *land*, 'land', + *ende*, 'end'. Land's End is the most westerly point of England. There are similar names in other countries, as *Finistère*, France, and Cape *Finisterre*, Spain, both from Latin *finis terrae*, 'end of the land'. Cp. KINTYRE, PEMBROKE. The Cornish name of Land's End is *Penwith*, 'end district' (Cornish *pennwedh*), now that of the local council district. 1337 *Londeseynde*.

Landulph (village, Cornwall): 'church site of Dilic'. Cornish *lann*, 'church site'. The name may be that of the saint to whom St Leonard's church here was formerly dedicated. The present dedication may have been suggested by the place name itself. DB *Landelech*.

Laneham (village, Notts): '(place at the) lanes'. OE *lanu*, 'lane'. The name represents OE *lanum*, the dative plural form of *lanu*. Various tracks and roads meet here. DB *Lanun*.

Lanercost (village, Cumbria): '(place by) Aust's glade'. The first part of the name is Celtic in origin, from a word related to modern Welsh *llanerch*, 'glade'. The second part is the personal name Aust, from Latin *Augustus*. The alternative second form of the name below refers to the 12C priory ruins here. 1169 *Lanrecost*, 1868 *Lanercost, or Abbey-Lanercost*.

Langar (village, Notts): '(place at the) long point of land'. OE *lang*, 'long', + *gāra*, 'point of land' (modern English *gore*). DB *Langare*.

Langbaurgh (hamlet, Redcar & Clev): '(place by the) long hill'. OE *lang*, 'long', + *berg*, 'hill'. The hill here, a long, high, narrow ridge, gave the name of the wapentake of Langbaurgh (for which its central position would have made it a good meeting place) and more recently the administrative district of Langbaurgh in the former county of Cleveland. 13C *Langberg*.

Langcliffe (village, N Yorks): '(place by the) long cliff'. OE *lang*, 'long', + *clif*, 'cliff', 'bank'. The name refers to the long steep bank above the river Ribble here, terminating in a great limestone cliff. DB *Lanclif*.

Langdale Pikes (mountain peaks, Cumbria): 'peaks of the long valley'. OE *lang*, 'long', + *denu*, 'valley'. 'Pikes' are 'peaks' (OE *pīc*, 'point'). OE *denu* was replaced by *dálr*, its OS equivalent. The peaks in question are at the summit of Langdale Fell. There are two 'long valleys': *Great Langdale* as the one to the north and *Little Langdale* as that of the river Brathay. The latter, also the name of a hamlet here, is recorded in *c*.1160 as *Langedenelittle*.

Langdon Hills (district of Basildon, Essex): '(place on the) long hill amid hills'. OE *lang*, 'long', + *dūn*, 'hill'. The 'long hill' is Langdon Hill itself, on which the village arose. DB *Langenduna*, 1485 *Langdon Hilles*.

Langenhoe (village, Essex): '(place by the) long hill spur'. OE *lang*, 'long', + *hōh*, 'hill spur'. DB *Langhou*.

Langford (village, Beds): '(place at the) long ford'. OE *lang*, 'long', + *ford*, 'ford'. The river here is the Ivel. 944 *Longaford*, DB *Langeford*.

Langford (village, Essex): '(place at the) long ford'. OE *lang*, 'long', + *ford*, 'ford'. The village is at the confluence of the rivers Blackwater and Chelmer. DB *Langheforda*.

Langford (village, Notts): '(place by) Landa's ford'. OE *ford*, 'ford'. The name could also mean '(place by the) ford on the (special tract of) land' (OE *land* + *ford*), referring to the county boundary with Lincolnshire nearby. DB *Landeforde*.

Langford (village, Oxon): '(place at the) long ford'. OE *lang*, 'long', + *ford*, 'ford'. The ford in question would have been over the stream here. DB *Langefort*.

Langford Budville (village, Somerset): 'de Buddevill's (estate by the) long ford'. OE *lang*, 'long', + *ford*, 'ford'. The de Buddevill family held the manor here in the 13C. 1212 *Langeford*, 1305 *Langeford Budevill*.

Langham (hamlet, Essex): 'homestead of Lahha's people'. OE *-inga-*, 'of the people of', + *hām*, 'homestead'. DB *Laingaham*.

Langham (village, Rutland): '(place by the) long water meadow'. OE *lang*, 'long', + *hamm*, 'enclosure', 'water meadow'. The village extends along both sides of a meandering stream. 1202 *Langham*.

Langham (village, Suffolk): 'long homestead or enclosure'. OE *lang*, 'long', + *hām*, 'homestead', or *hamm*, 'enclosure'. DB *Langham*. SO ALSO: *Langham*, Norfolk.

Langho (village, Lancs): '(place in the) long corner of land'. OE *lang*, 'long', + *halh*, 'nook', 'corner of land'. OE *halh* here probably has the particular sense 'land between rivers', referring to the location of Langho on an area of land between the rivers Ribble and Calder to the east and Park Brook and the Ribble to the west. 13C *Langale*.

Langholm (town, Dumfries & Gall): 'long island'. OE *lang*, 'long', + OS *holmr*, 'island'. The 'island' is the strip of land by the river Esk on which the town stands. 1376 *Langholm*.

Langley (district, Slough): 'long wood or clearing'. OE *lang*, 'long', + *lēah*, 'wood', 'clearing'. The place was until recently known as *Langley Marish*, from the Mareis family, who held the manor here in the 13C. 1208 *Langeley*, 1316 *Langele Marais*, 1868 *Langley-Marish*, 1965 *Langley Marish*. SO ALSO: *Langley*, Derbys, Kent.

Langley Burrell (village, Wilts): 'Burel's (estate by the) long wood or clearing'. OE *lang*, 'long', + *lēah*, 'wood', 'clearing'. The manor here was held by Peter Burel in the 13C. 940 *Langelegh*, DB *Lanhelei*, 1309 *Langele Burel*.

Langney (district of Eastbourne, E Sussex): 'long island'. OE *lang*, 'long', + *ēg*, 'island'. The 'long island' is a long stretch of dry ground in marshland here. The DB form of the name below has *l* for the final *n* of OE *langan*, the dative form of *lang*. DB *Langelie*, 1121 *Langania*.

Langold (village, Notts): 'long shelter'. OE *lang*, 'long', + *hald*, 'protection' (related modern English *hold*). 1246 *Langalde*.

Langport (town, Somerset): 'long market place'. OE *lang*, 'long', + *port*, 'town', 'market'. The 'long market place' would have originally been Bow Street, the long straight street that ascends through the town from the river Parrett. 10C *Longport*, DB *Lanport*.

Langridge (hamlet, Bath & NE Somerset): '(place by the) long ridge'. OE *lang*, 'long', +

hrycg, 'ridge'. The DB form of the name below has *s* for *g*. DB *Lancheris*, 1225 *Langerig*.

Langrigg (village, Cumbria): '(place by the) long ridge'. OS *langr*, 'long', + *hryggr*, 'ridge'. 1189 *Langrug*.

Langrish (village, Hants): '(place by the) long rush bed'. OE *lang*, 'long', + *rysce*, 'rush bed'. The rushes would have grown in a stream flowing into the river Rother here. 1236 *Langerishe*.

Langsett (hamlet, Barnsley): '(place by the) long hill slope'. OE *lang*, 'long', + *sīde*, 'hill slope' (modern English *side*). The slope in question is the long steep one on the north side of the valley of the Little Don here. 12C *Langeside*.

Langstone (coastal village, Hants): '(place by the) long stone'. OE *lang*, 'long', + *stān*, 'stone'. The reason for the name is unknown, unless some sort of marker is involved. A 'long' stone is a tall one. 1289 *Langeston*.

Langthorne (village, N Yorks): '(place by the) tall thorn bush'. OE *lang*, 'long', + *thorn*, 'thorn bush'. The DB form of the name below has taken OE *thorn* as OS *thorp*, 'outlying farmstead'. (The same slip occurs for SPENNITHORNE.) DB *Langetorp*, *c*.1100 *Langethorn*.

Langthorpe (village, N Yorks): 'Langlíf's outlying farmstead'. OS *thorp*, 'outlying farmstead'. The Scandinavian personal name is that of a woman. DB *Torp*, 12C *Langliuetorp*.

Langthwaite (hamlet, N Yorks): '(place in the) long clearing'. OS *langr*, 'long', + *thveit*, 'clearing'. 1167 *Langethwait*.

Langtoft (village, Lincs): 'long curtilage'. OS *langr*, 'long', + *toft*, 'curtilage', 'homestead'. A curtilage is an area of land attached to a house and forming a single enclosure with it, in this case as the nucleus of a straggling village. Langtoft may lie on the course of a Roman road. DB *Langetof*.

Langton (village, Durham): '(place on the) long hill'. OE *lang*, 'long', + *dūn*, 'hill'. *c*.1050 *Langadun*.

Langton Herring (village, Dorset): 'Harang's long farmstead'. OE *lang*, 'long', + *tūn*, 'farmstead', 'estate'. The Harang family held the manor here in the 13C. The same family gave the name of CHALDON HERRING, 12 miles to the east. DB *Langetone*, 1336 *Langeton Heryng*.

Langton Long Blandford (hamlet, Dorset): 'long farmstead near Blandford'. OE *lang*, 'long', + *tūn*, 'farmstead', 'estate'. The place was originally *Long Blandford*, to be distinguished from nearby BLANDFORD. The separate name *Langton* was then added to this. 1179 *Longa*

Bladeneford, 1273 *Langeton*, 1598 *Langton Long Blandford*.

Langton Matravers (village, Dorset): 'Mautravers' long farmstead'. OE *lang*, 'long', + *tūn*, 'farmstead', 'estate'. The Mautravers family held the manor here in the 13C. They also gave their name to nearby *Worth Matravers* (OE *worth*, 'enclosure') and *Lytchett Matravers*, 11 miles to the north across Poole Harbour (see LYTCHETT MINSTER). 1165 *Langeton*, 1428 *Langeton Mawtravers*.

Langtree (village, Devon): '(place by the) tall tree'. OE *lang*, 'long', + *trēow*, 'tree'. DB *Langtrewa*.

Langwathby (village, Cumbria): 'farmstead by the long ford'. OS *langr*, 'long', + *vath*, 'ford', + *bý*, 'farmstead', 'village'. The river here is the Eden. 1159 *Langwadebi*.

Langworth (village, Lincs): '(place by the) long ford'. OS *langr*, 'long', + *vath*, 'ford'. The second part of the name has been influenced by OE *worth*, 'enclosure'. *c*.1055 *Longwathe*.

Lanhydrock (country house, Cornwall): 'church site of St Hydrek'. Cornish *lann*, 'church site'. Nothing is known about Hydrek, whose name is unique to this place. 1201 *Lanhideroc*, 1327 *Lanhidrek*.

Lanivet (village, Cornwall): 'church site at the pagan sanctuary'. Cornish *lann*, 'church site', + *neved*, 'pagan sanctuary'. Cornish *neved* is related to the Celtic word that gave the names of KING'S NYMPTON and NYMET ROWLAND. 1268 *Lannived*.

Lanlivery (village, Cornwall): 'church site of Livri'. Cornish *lann*, 'church site'. The church here is actually dedicated to St Brevita (Bryvyth), about whom nothing is known. *c*.1170 *Lanliveri*.

Lanner (village, Cornwall): '(place in the) clearing'. Cornish *lannergh*, 'clearing'. 1327 *Lannergh*.

Lanreath (village, Cornwall): 'church site of Reydhogh'. Cornish *lann*, 'church site'. Nothing is known about the named person. DB *Lanredoch*, 1591 *Lanretha*.

Lansallos (village, Cornwall): 'church site of Salwys'. Cornish *lann*, 'church site'. Nothing is known about the named person. DB *Lansaluus*.

Lanteglos (church and farm, Cornwall): 'valley of the church'. Cornish *nans*, 'valley', + *eglos*, 'church'. The first part of the name has been influenced by Cornish *lann*, 'church site'. The hamlet of *Lanteglos Highway* lies nearby on the river Fowey. 1249 *Lanteglos*.

Lapford (village, Devon): '(place at) Hlappa's ford'. OE *ford*, 'ford'. The first part of the name

could also represent OE *læppa*, 'skirt of a garment' (modern English *lap*), in either a topographical or an administrative sense. The river here is the Taw. The DB form of the name below may have resulted from a mishearing. DB *Slapeforda*, 1107 *Lapeford*.

Lapley (village, Staffs): 'woodland clearing at the end (of the estate or parish)'. OE *læppa*, 'tag', 'end' (modern English *lap*), + *lēah*, 'wood', 'clearing'. Lapley lies at the eastern end of the parish. 1061 *Lappeley*, DB *Lepelie*.

Lapworth (village, Warwicks): 'Hlappa's enclosure'. OE *worth*, 'enclosure'. The second part of the name was originally OE *worthign*, in the same sense. The DB form of the name below has taken the second element to be OE *ford*, 'ford'. 816 *Hlappawurthin*, DB *Lapeforde*.

Larbert (town, Falkirk): 'farm by a thicket'. Gaelic *làrach*, 'farm', + Celtic *pert*, 'wood', 'thicket'. Early forms of the name apparently have Gaelic *leth*, 'portion', as the first element. 1195 *Lethberth*.

Largo (town, Fife): 'steep (place)'. Gaelic *leargach*, 'steep'. The ground rises steeply from Largo Bay to Largo Law, a hill north of Upper Largo. 1250 *Largauch*.

Largs (resort town, N Ayrs): '(places by) slopes'. Gaelic *learg*, 'slope'. The town is sheltered by lofty hills. An English plural -*s* has been added to the Gaelic word. 1140 *Larghes*.

Larkfield (urban development, Kent): 'open land where larks are seen'. OE *lāwerce*, 'lark', + *feld*, 'open land' (modern English *field*). DB *Lavrochesfel*.

Larkhall (town, S Lanarks): meaning uncertain. *Laverock* in the form of the name below represents a Scottish equivalent of English *lark*, but there is no evidence that the bird actually gave the name. 1620 *Laverockhall*.

Larling (hamlet, Norfolk): '(settlement of) Lyrel's people'. OE -*ingas*, 'people of'. DB *Lurlinga*.

Larnog. See LAVERNOCK.

Lartington (village, Durham): 'estate associated with Lyrti'. OE -*ing*-, 'associated with', + *tūn*, 'farmstead', 'estate'. *c*.1050 *Lyrtingtun*, DB *Lertinton*.

Larton (suburb of West Kirby, Wirral): 'farmstead on clay soil'. OS *leirr*, 'mud', 'clay', + OE *tūn*, 'farmstead'. Claypits near here were exploited commercially in the 14C. 1291 *Layrton*.

Lasham (village, Hants): 'smaller homestead'. OE *læssa*, 'smaller' (modern English *less*), + *hām*, 'homestead', 'estate'. The comparison would be with nearby Odiham. A sense 'Leassa's homestead' is also theoretically possible. The DB form of the name below is garbled. DB *Esseham*, 1175 *Lasham*.

Lasswade. See BONNYRIGG.

Lastingham (village, N Yorks): 'homestead of Læsta's people'. OE *-inga-*, 'of the people of', + *hām*, 'homestead'. DB *Lestingeham*.

Latchford (district, Warrington): '(place by a) ford at a boggy place'. OE *læcc*, 'bog', + *ford*, 'ford'. The ford in question took the Roman road from Warrington to Northwich over the river Mersey here. 12C *Lachford*.

Latchingdon (village, Essex): 'hill by the well-watered ground'. OE *læcen*, 'well watered' (related modern English *lake*), + *dūn*, 'hill'. *c.*1050 *Læcendune*, DB *Lacenduna*.

Latchley (village, Cornwall): 'wood by the marsh'. OE *læc*, 'marsh', 'wetland', + *lēah*, 'wood', 'clearing'. Mid-13C *Lachesleigh*.

Lathbury (village, Milton K): 'fortified place built with laths'. OE *lætt*, 'lath', + *burh*, 'fortified place'. DB *Lateberie*.

Latimer (village, Bucks): 'Latymer's (estate)'. The Latymer family held the manor here in the 14C. Their name was added to an earlier name, now disappeared, that meant 'Isa's homestead' (OE *hām-stede*). Cp. CHENIES, a neighbouring village with an identical original name. 1220 *Yselhamstede*, 1389 *Isenhampstede Latymer*.

Latteridge (village, S Glos): '(place at the) ridge by a watercourse'. OE *lād*, 'watercourse', + *hrycg*, 'ridge'. 1176 *Laderugga*.

Lattiford (hamlet, Somerset): '(place by the) ford where beggars gather'. OE *loddere*, 'beggar', 'vagabond', + *ford*, 'ford'. The ford would have been over Bow Brook here. DB *Lodereforda*.

Latton (village, Wilts): 'enclosure where leeks are grown'. OE *lēac-tūn* (from *lēac*, 'leek', + *tūn*, 'enclosure', 'farmstead'). DB *Latone*.

Lauder (town, Borders): '(place on the) Leader Water'. The river's name appears to derive from a Celtic word meaning 'wash', as perhaps for the LOWTHER HILLS, referring to a river that 'washes' the soil or land through which it flows. 1208 *Louueder*.

Laugharne (village, Carm): 'end (of the place)'. Welsh *tâl*, 'end'. The Welsh name of the village is *Talacharn*, and the English form of this has dropped the initial *Ta-*. The second part of the name is obscure in origin, although some associate it with the name of the brook Coran. The second form of the name below has this name prefixed by OW *aber*, 'river mouth'. 1191

Talacharn, 1191 *Abercoran*, 1868 *Laugharne*, or *Tal-Talcharn*.

Laughton (village, E Sussex): 'enclosure where leeks are grown'. OE *lēac-tūn*, 'herb garden' (from *lēac*, 'leek', + *tūn*, 'farmstead', 'enclosure'). DB *Lestone*. SO ALSO: *Laughton*, Leics.

Laughton en le Morthen (village, Rotherham): 'enclosure where leeks are grown in Morthen'. OE *lēac-tūn*, 'herb garden' (from *lēac*, 'leek', + *tūn*, 'farmstead', 'enclosure'). The district name means 'moorland district where an assembly is held' (OE *mōr* or OS *mór*, 'moorland', + *thing*, 'assembly'). The full name has been popularly perverted to *Lightning in the Morning*. DB *Lastone*, 1230 *Latton in Morthing*.

Launcells (hamlet, Cornwall): '(place on a) church site'. Cornish *lann*, 'church site'. The second part of the name is of uncertain origin, and is corrupt in the DB form below. DB *Landseu*, 1204 *Lanceles*.

Launceston (town, Cornwall): 'estate by the church site of St Stephen'. Cornish *lann*, 'church site', + *Stefan*, 'Stephen', + OE *tūn*, 'farmstead', 'estate'. The original name was *Lann-Stefan*, referring not to the present town but to the former village of *St Stephens* that is now a northern district of Launceston. The present town was originally *Dounhed*, 'end of the hill' (OE *dūn*, 'hill', + *hēafod*, 'head'), a name now revived in the archaic form *Dunheved* for the town's official name: 'Dunheved otherwise Launceston'. In 1155 the canons of St Stephens moved across the valley to what is now Launceston, and the name went with them. In the DB form of the name below, *t* has been miscopied as *c*. DB *Lanscavetone*, *c.*1125 *Lanstavaton*, 1303 *Lanceton*, 1868 *Launceston, or Launston*.

Launton (village, Oxon): 'long farmstead'. OE *lang*, 'long', + *tūn*, 'farmstead', 'estate'. *c.*1050 *Langtune*, DB *Lantone*.

Laurencekirk (town, Aberdeens): 'St Laurence's church'. The town was founded in *c.*1770 and was originally known as *Kirkton of St Laurence*, the first word of this meaning 'village with a church' (OE *cirice*, 'church', + *tūn*, 'village'). It later adopted its present name, after St Laurence of Canterbury.

Lavatris. See BOWES.

Lavendon (village, Milton K): 'Lāfa's valley'. OE *denu*, 'valley'. DB *Lavendene*.

Lavenham (town, Suffolk): 'Lāfa's homestead'. OE *hām*, 'homestead'. The first part of the name represents *Lāfan*, the genitive form of the personal name. *c.*995 *Lauanham*, DB *Lauenham*.

Lavernock (coastal village, Vale of Glam): 'lark hill'. OE *lāwerce*, 'lark', + *cnocc*, 'hill'. The Welsh form of the name is *Larnog*, from the English. 13C *Lawernach*.

Laversdale (hamlet, Cumbria): 'Lēofhere's valley'. OE *dæl*, 'valley'. *c.*1170 *Levirsdale*.

Laverstock (village, Wilts): 'outlying farmstead where larks are seen'. OE *lāwerce*, 'lark', + *stoc*, 'outlying farmstead', 'dependent settlement'. DB *Lavvrecestoches*.

Laverstoke (village, Hants): 'outlying farmstead where larks are seen'. OE *lāwerce*, 'lark', + *stoc*, 'outlying farmstead', 'dependent settlement'. DB *Lavrochestoche*.

Laverton (village, N Yorks): 'farmstead on the (river) Laver'. OE *tūn*, 'farmstead'. The river has a Celtic name meaning 'babbling brook'. DB *Lavretone*.

Laverton (hamlet, Somerset): 'farmstead where larks are seen'. OE *lāwerce*, 'lark', + *tūn*, 'farmstead'. DB *Lavretone*. SO ALSO: *Laverton*, Glos.

Lawford (village, Essex): '(place by) Lealla's ford'. OE *ford*, 'ford'. The ford here would have been over the river Stour. 1045 *Lalleford*, DB *Laleforde*.

Lawhitton (village, Cornwall): 'estate at the church site of Gwethen'. Cornish *lann*, 'church site'. The first part of the name could also represent Cornish *nans*, 'valley'. OE *tūn*, 'farmstead', 'estate', was added subsequently. 10C *Landuuithan*, DB *Languitetone*.

Lawkland (hamlet, N Yorks): 'arable land where leeks are grown'. OS *laukr*, 'leek', + *land*, 'cultivated land'. 12C *Laukeland*.

Lawley (district of Telford, Wrekin): 'Lāfa's woodland clearing'. OE *lēah*, 'wood', 'clearing'. DB *Lauelei*.

Lawrenny (village, Pemb): '(place on) low ground'. Welsh *llawr*, 'floor', 'bottom'. The second part of the name is of uncertain origin. The first part refers to the low-lying land by the estuary of the river Cresswell here. *c.*1200 *Leurenni*.

Lawshall (village, Suffolk): 'dwelling by a hill'. OE *hlāw*, 'hill', 'mound', + *sele*, 'dwelling', 'hall'. The name could also mean 'shelter by a hill' (*hlāw* + OE *sell*, 'shelter'). DB *Lawessela*.

Laxfield (village, Suffolk): 'Leaxa's open land'. OE *feld*, 'open land' (modern English *field*). DB *Laxefelda*.

Laxton (village, Northants): 'Leaxa's estate'. OE *tūn*, 'farmstead', 'estate'. DB *Lastone*.

Laxton (village, Notts): 'estate associated with Leaxa'. OE *-ing-*, 'associated with', + *tūn*, 'farm-stead', 'estate'. It was this Laxton that in 1713 gave the name of the US town of *Lexington*, Massachusetts. DB *Laxintune*, 1868 *Laxton, or Lexington*. SO ALSO: *Laxton*, E Yorks.

Layer Breton (village, Essex): 'Breton's (place on the) Layer Brook'. The river name is of Celtic origin but uncertain meaning. It could be related to that of the *Legra*, which may ultimately have given the name of LEICESTER. The manor here was held early by the Breton family, whose name distinguishes the village from nearby *Layer de la Haye* and *Layer Marney*, where the manors were held respectively by the de Haia and de Marinni families. DB *Legra*, 1254 *Leyre Bretoun*.

Layham (village, Suffolk): 'homestead with a shelter'. OE *hlīg*, 'shelter', + *hām*, 'homestead'. *c.*995 *Hligham*, DB *Leiham*.

Laytham (village, E Yorks): '(place by the) barns'. OS *hlatha*, 'barn'. The name represents OS *hlathum*, the dative plural form of *hlatha*. DB *Ladon*.

Lazenby (hamlet, Redcar & Clev): 'Leysingr's farmstead'. OS *bý*, 'farmstead', 'village'. The personal name is Scandinavian. The first part of the name could also represent OS *leysingi*, 'freedman', giving a sense 'farmstead of the freedmen'. DB *Lesingebi*.

Lazonby (village, Cumbria): 'Leysingr's farmstead'. OS *bý*, 'farmstead', 'village'. The personal name is Scandinavian. The name could also mean 'farmstead of the freedmen' (OS *leysingi*, 'freedman', + *bý*). 1165 *Leisingebi*.

Lea (village, Herefords): '(place by the) wood or clearing'. OE *lēah*, 'wood', 'clearing'. The DB form of the name below is corrupt. DB *Lecce*, 1219 *La Lee*. SO ALSO: *Lea*, Derbys, Lincs, Wilts.

Leadenham (village, Lincs): 'Lēoda's homestead'. OE *hām*, 'homestead', 'village'. DB *Ledeneham*.

Leaden Roding. See RODINGS.

Leadgate (suburb of Consett, Durham): '(place by the) swing gate'. OE *hlid-geat*, 'swing gate' (from *hlid*, 'door', 'gate', + *geat*, 'gate'). The gate would have been used to stop cattle straying across a road or on to arable land. Cp. LIDGATE, LYDIATE. 1590 *Lidgate*.

Leadhills (town, S Lanarks): '(place by the) lead hills'. OE *lēad*, 'lead', + *hyll*, 'hill'. Lead was long mined from the hills here but the mines were finally closed in 1928.

Leafield (village, Oxon): '(place by) the open land'. OF *la*, 'the', + OE *feld*, 'open land' (modern English *field*). The open land in question was probably an area in Wychwood Forest. 1213 *La Felde*.

Leake (hamlet, N Yorks): '(place by the) brook'. OS *lœkr*, 'brook'. DB *Lece*.

Lealholm (village, N Yorks): '(place among the) brushwood'. OE *lǣl*, 'twig'. Although influenced by OS *holmr*, 'island', the name really represents OE *lǣlum*, the dative plural form of *lǣl*. DB *Lelun*.

Lea Marston (village, Warwicks). Originally two separate names: *Lea*, '(place by the) woodland clearing' (OE *lēah*, 'wood', 'clearing'), and *Marston*, 'farmstead in the marsh' (OE *mersc*, 'marsh', + *tūn*, 'farmstead'). DB *Leth*, DB *Merstone*, 1306 *La Lee in Merston*, 1535 *Leemerston*.

Leamington (town, Warwicks): 'farmstead on the (river) Leam'. The river has a Celtic name meaning 'elm river'. The town's full official name is *Royal Leamington Spa*, granted by Queen Victoria in 1838 in token of her visit and in recognition of Leamington's medicinal springs. The manor here was held in 1160 by Kenilworthy Priory. Hence the second form of the name below, the second word distinguishing this Leamington from *Leamington Hastings*, 8 miles to the east, where the Hastings family held the manor in the 13C. DB *Lamintone*, 1868 *Leamington Priors, or Royal Leamington Spa*.

Leatherhead (town, Surrey): '(place by the) grey ford'. The name comes from Celtic words related to modern Welsh *llwyd*, 'grey', 'pale', 'brown', and *rhyd*, 'ford'. The ford in question would have been over the river Mole here. The name was long held to mean 'public ford', as if from OE *lēode*, 'people', + *ride*, 'ford that can be ridden across'. The Celtic origin was educed relatively recently (Richard Coates, 'Methodological Reflexions on Leatherhead', *Journal 12*, EPNS, 1980). The DB form of the name below is corrupt. *c.*880 *Leodridan*, DB *Leret*, 1868 *Leatherhead, or Letherhed*.

Leathley (village, N Yorks): 'woodland clearing on the slopes'. OE *hlith*, 'slope', + *lēah*, 'wood', 'clearing'. The first part of the name represents OE *hleotha*, the genitive plural of *hlith*. DB *Ledelai*.

Leaton (village, Shropshire): meaning uncertain. The second part of the name is OE *tūn*, 'farmstead'. The first part appears to be OE *lēah*, 'wood', 'clearing', but it would be unusual to find this as the first half of a compound name. DB *Letone*.

Leaveland (village, Kent): 'Lēofa's cultivated land'. OE *land*, 'cultivated land'. DB *Levelant*.

Leavening (village, N Yorks): '(settlement of) Lēofhēah's people'. OE *-ingas*, 'people of'. The DB form of the name below is corrupt. DB *Ledlinghe*, 1242 *Leyingges*.

Lebberston (village, N Yorks): 'Lēodbriht's farmstead'. OE *tūn*, 'farmstead'. DB *Ledbeztun*.

Lechlade (village, Glos): 'river crossing near the (river) Leach'. OE *gelād*, 'river crossing'. The river name means 'marshy stream', from OE *lœcc*, 'stream', 'bog'. The crossing in question would have been over the Thames here, which is joined by the Leach about ½ mile to the southeast. DB *Lecelade*.

Leckford (village, Hants): '(place at the) ford by a channel'. OE *leaht*, 'channel' (modern English *leat*), + *ford*, 'ford'. The channel in question would have been used to prevent the river Test from flooding here. 947 *Leahtforda*, DB *Lechtford*.

Leckhampstead (village, Bucks): 'homestead where leeks are grown'. OE *lēac*, 'leek', + *hāmstede* (see HAMPSTEAD). 956 *Lechamstede*. SO ALSO: *Leckhampstead*, W Berks.

Leckhampton (suburb of Cheltenham, Glos): 'home farm where leeks are grown'. OE *lēac*, 'leek', + *hām-tūn*, 'home farm' (from *hām*, 'homestead', + *tūn*, 'farmstead'). DB *Lechametone*.

Leconfield (village, E Yorks): '(place by) open land'. OE *feld*, 'open land' (modern English *field*). The first part of the name is of uncertain origin. It may represent a form of OE *lœc*, 'swampy stream'. DB *Lachinfeld*.

Ledbury (town, Herefords): 'fortified place on the (river) Leadon'. OE *burh*, 'fortified place'. The river has a Celtic name meaning 'broad stream'. DB *Liedeberge*.

Ledsham (hamlet, Cheshire): 'Lēofede's homestead'. OE *hām*, 'homestead'. DB *Levetesham*.

Ledsham (village, Leeds): 'homestead within the district of Leeds'. OE *hām*, 'homestead'. Ledsham is 10 miles east of LEEDS city centre. Cp. LEDSTON. *c.*1030 *Ledesham*.

Ledston (village, Leeds): 'farmstead within the district of Leeds'. OE *tūn*, 'farmstead'. Ledston is 9 miles east of LEEDS city centre. Cp. LEDSHAM. DB *Ledestune*.

Leebotwood (village, Shropshire): 'clearing in Botta's wood'. OE *lēah*, 'clearing', + *wudu*, 'wood'. The evolution of the name is *Botwood*, then *Lee in Botwood*, then *Leebotwood*. DB *Botewde*, *c.*1170 *Lega in Bottewode*, 1577 *Lebotwood*.

Lee Brockhurst (village, Shropshire): 'woodland clearing near Brockhurst'. OE *lēah*, 'wood', 'clearing'. The place was originally *Lee*. This Lee was subsequently distinguished from others by its proximity to the wood called *Brockhurst*, 'wooded hill where badgers are seen' (OE *brocc*, 'badger', + *hyrst*, 'wooded hill'). DB *Lege*, 1285 *Leye under Brochurst*.

Leece (village, Cumbria). The name is probably of Celtic origin from a word related to modern Welsh *llys*, 'court'. Cp. LISS. DB *Lies*.

Leeds (village, Kent): '(place by the river) Leeds'. The name of the stream here derives from OE *hlȳde*, 'loud one' (related modern English *loud*). DB *Esledes*, *c*.1100 *Hledes*.

Leeds (city, Leeds): '(place of the) people who live by the (river) Lat'. The name is Celtic, and originally that of a district here. Its inhabitants were known as the *Ladenses*, taking their name from the river, itself meaning 'strongly flowing'. The river name fell out of use, and Leeds is now on the Aire (see AIRMYN). The district name survives in the names of the villages of LEDSHAM and LEDSTON, some 10 miles east of the city centre. 731 *Loidis*, DB *Ledes*.

Leedstown (village, Cornwall). The village was created in the 19C by the Duke of Leeds, a major landowner here. 1867 *Leedstown*.

Leek (town, Staffs): '(place at the) brook'. OS *lœkr*, 'brook'. The 'brook' is the stream that flows through Leek as a tributary of the nearby river Churnet. DB *Lec*.

Leek Wootton (village, Warwicks): 'farmstead by a wood where leeks are grown'. OE *lēac*, 'leek', + *wudu*, 'wood', + *tūn*, 'farmstead'. The first word of the name presumably distinguishes this Wootton from WOOTTON WAWEN, 10 miles to the southwest. 1122 *Wottona*, 1285 *Lecwotton*.

Leeming (village, N Yorks): '(place on the) Leeming Beck'. The river name perhaps means 'bright stream', from a derivative of OE *lēoma*, 'ray', 'radiance'. 12C *Leming*.

Lee-on-the-Solent (resort village, Hants): '(place in the) clearing by the Solent'. OE *lēah*, 'wood', 'clearing'. The second part of the name was added only in the 19C. See also SOLENT. 1212 *Lie*, 1896 *Lee-on-the-Solent*.

Legborne (village, Lincs): '(place by the) swampy stream'. OE *lœc*, 'bog', + *burna*, 'stream'. DB *Lecheburne*.

Leicester (city, Leicester): 'Roman town of the Ligore'. OE *ceaster*, 'Roman camp'. The meaning of the tribal name is unknown. It may have derived from *Legra*, a former name of the river Soar here, itself of pre-English origin and probably related to that of the river Loire in France. (Cp. LEIRE.) The Roman name of Leicester was *Ratae Coritanorum*, 'fortifications of the Coritani'. Again, the meaning of the tribal name is unknown. (According to archaeological research carried out in the early 1980s, the tribal name is properly Corieltauvi.) The former theory that the river name gave *Lloegr* as the Welsh name for England is now rejected. Early 10C *Ligera ceaster*, DB *Ledecestre*.

Leicestershire (county, central England): 'district based on Leicester'. OE *scīr*, 'shire', 'district'. See LEICESTER. 11C *Lægreceastrescir*.

Leigh (town, Wigan): '(place at the) wood or clearing'. OE *lēah*, 'wood', 'clearing'. The 'woodland clearing' here was probably a meadow, as Leigh lies on an area of low marshland. 1276 *Legh*. SO ALSO: *Leigh*, Kent, Surrey.

Leigh (village, Worcs): '(place at the) wood or clearing'. OE *lēah*, 'wood', 'clearing'. The first form of the name below means 'Beornnōth's wood or clearing'. 972 *Beornothesleah*, DB *Lege*.

Leigh Delamare (village, Wilts): 'de la Mare's (estate by the) wood or clearing'. OE *lēah*, 'wood', 'clearing'. The manor here was held in the 13C by Adam de la Mare. 1236 *Leye*, 1637 *Lydallimore*.

Leigh-on-Sea (district, Southend): '(place in the) woodland clearing by the sea'. OE *lēah*, 'wood', 'clearing'. The second part of the name was added in the late 19C, presumably to match nearby SOUTHEND-ON-SEA. The DB clerk appears to have confused the name with that of Layer (see LAYER BRETON). DB *Legra*, 1226 *Legha*, 1896 *Leigh, or Leigh-on-Sea*.

Leigh Sinton (village, Worcs): '(place to the) south in the village of Leigh'. OE *sūth*, 'south', + *in*, 'in', + *tūn*, 'farmstead', 'village'. Leigh Sinton lies to the south of LEIGH in the same county. 13C *Sothyntone in Lega*.

Leighton (village, Shropshire): '(place by the) leek farm'. OE *lēac-tūn*, 'herb garden' (from *lēac*, 'leek', 'garlic', + *tūn*, 'enclosure', 'farmstead'). DB *Lestone*.

Leighton Bromswold (village, Cambs): OE *lēac-tūn*, 'herb garden by Bromswold' (from *lēac*, 'leek', 'garlic', + *tūn*, 'enclosure', 'farmstead'). *Bromswold*, a nearby place, has a name meaning 'Brūn's high forest land' (OE *weald*, 'woodland', 'high forest'). DB *Lectone*, 1254 *Letton super Bruneswald*.

Leighton Buzzard (town, Beds): 'Busard's leek farm'. OE *lēac-tūn*, 'herb garden' (from *lēac*, 'leek', 'garlic', + *tūn*, 'enclosure', 'farmstead'). The name implies that Leighton Buzzard was a medieval market-garden centre. The Busard family, landowners here in the 13C, had a name popularly derived from OF *beau desert* (as for BEAUDESERT), an interpretation sometimes offered for the town's name. 'The Buzzards are all gentlemen. We came in with the Conqueror. Our name (as the French has it) is Beau-desert; which signifies – Friends, what does it signify?' (Richard Brome, *The English Moor*, 1659). DB *Lestone*, 1254 *Letton Busard*.

Leigh upon Mendip (village, Somerset): '(place by the) wood or clearing in the Mendips'. OE *lēah*, 'wood', 'clearing'. This Leigh is distinguished from others by its location in the MENDIP HILLS. *c*.1000 *Leage*.

Leinthall Earls (village, Herefords): 'earl's (estate at the) corner of land by the (river) Lent'. OE *halh*, 'nook', 'corner of land'. For the river name, see LEINTWARDINE. The manor here was held early by an earl, whose title distinguishes the village from nearby *Leinthall Starkes*, where the manor was held by one Starker. The second word of the second form of the name below represents Latin *comitis*, 'of the earl'. DB *Lentehale*, 1275 *Leintall Comites*.

Leintwardine (village, Herefords): 'enclosure on the (river) Lent'. OE *worth*, 'enclosure'. The river name, of Celtic origin and meaning 'torrent', may at one time have been that of the Clun, which enters the Teme here. OE *worth* has been replaced by the equivalent *worthign* to give the present name. The Roman settlement here was *Branogenium*, 'Branogenos's place', the Celtic personal name meaning literally 'born of a raven'. DB *Lenteurde*.

Leire (village, Leics): '(place on the river) Leire'. The river, a tributary of the Soar, has a name of pre-English origin that may have given the name of LEICESTER. DB *Legre*.

Leiston (town, Suffolk): 'farmstead by a fire'. OE *lēg*, 'fire', + *tūn*, 'farmstead'. The name implies that the site here, near the coast, would have been suitable for lighting a beacon. DB *Leistuna*.

Leith (district, Edinburgh): 'damp (place)'. The name may represent a Celtic word related to modern Welsh *llaith*, 'moist'. Leith lies at the mouth of the Water of Leith, where it enters the Firth of Forth, and the name presumably relates to the location of the place rather than to the river itself. The forms of the name below have Gaelic *inbhir*, 'river mouth'. *c*.1130 *Inverlet*, *c*.1315 *Inverlethe*.

Lelant (hamlet, Cornwall): 'church site of Anta'. Cornish *lann*, 'church site'. Anta is a female saint who had a chapel nearby at the entrance to the river Hayle. *c*.1170 *Lananta*.

Lelley (hamlet, E Yorks): 'wood or clearing where brushwood is found'. OE *lǣl*, 'twig', 'brushwood', + *lēah*, 'wood', 'clearing'. 1246 *Lelle*.

Lenchwick. See ROUS LENCH.

Lenham (village, Kent): 'Lēana's homestead'. OE *hām*, 'homestead', 'village'. The village is on the river Len, named after it. The DB form of the name below has *r* for *n*, perhaps as a simple miscopying, although the Normans tended to make such substitution. Cp. DURHAM. 858 *Leanaham*, DB *Lerham*.

Lennoxtown (town, E Dunbartons): 'Lennox's town'. The town arose in the 1780s and took its name from the family of the earls and dukes of Lennox, whose title comes from the ancient territory of *Lennox*, from Gaelic *leamhanach*, 'abounding in elms' (*leamh*, 'elm').

Lenton (hamlet, Lincs): 'estate associated with Lēofa'. OE *-ing-*, 'associated with', + *tūn*, 'farmstead', 'estate'. *c*.1067 *Lofintun*, DB *Lavintone*.

Lenwade (village, Norfolk): '(place by the) ford crossed by a lane'. OE *lanu*, 'lane', + *gewæd*, 'ford'. 1199 *Langewade*.

Leominster (town, Herefords): 'church in Leon'. OE *mynster*, 'monastery', 'church'. The district name is Celtic in origin and means '(land) at the streams', referring to the triangle of land with Leominster at its point, the rivers Arrow and Lugg as its borders, and the streams enclosed within it. Cp. EARDISLAND. 10C *Leomynster*, DB *Leominstre*.

Leonard Stanley. See KING'S STANLEY.

Leppington (village, N Yorks): 'estate associated with Leppa'. OE *-ing-*, 'associated with', + *tūn*, 'farmstead', 'estate'. DB *Lepinton*.

Lepton (village, Kirklees): 'farmstead on a hill slope'. OE *hlēp*, 'slope', 'leaping place', + *tūn*, 'farmstead'. Lepton lies near the top of a hill. DB *Leptone*.

Lerryn (village, Cornwall): '(place on the river) Lerryn'. The river name may derive from the plural form of Cornish *lyr*, 'flood'. 1284 *Leryon*.

Lerwick (town, Shetland): '(place by) mud bay'. OS *leirr*, 'mud', + *vík*, 'bay', 'inlet'. The bay in question is Bressay Sound, on the east coast of Mainland. 1625 *Lerwick*.

Lesbury (village, Northd): 'fortified house of the physician'. OE *lǣce*, 'physician' (modern

English *leech*), + *burh*, 'fortified place'. *c*.1190 *Lechesbiri*.

Leslie (town, Fife): 'holly enclosure'. The town is said to have taken the name of the village of *Leslie* near Insch, Aberdeens, and the forms of the name below relate to that place. The name itself is Celtic, from words related to modern Welsh *llys*, 'court', and *celyn*, 'holly'. *c*.1180 *Lesslyn*, *c*.1232 *Lescelin*.

Lessingham (village, Norfolk): 'homestead of Lēofsige's people'. OE *-inga-*, 'of the people of', + *hām*, 'homestead'. DB *Losincham*.

Letchworth (town, Herts): 'enclosure that can be locked'. OE *lycce*, 'locked place' (related modern English *lock*), + *worth*, 'enclosure'. DB *Leceworde*.

Letheringham (hamlet, Suffolk): 'homestead of Lēodhere's people'. OE *-inga-*, 'of the people of', + *hām*, 'homestead'. DB *Letheringaham*.

Letheringsett (village, Norfolk): 'dwelling of Lēodhere's people'. OE *-inga-*, 'of the people of', + *set*, 'dwelling', 'fold'. DB *Leringaseta*.

Letocetum. See (1) LICHFIELD, (2) WALL (Staffs).

Letterston (village, Pemb): 'Letard's farm'. OE *tūn*, 'farm'. The Welsh name of Letterston is *Treletert*, translating the English (Welsh *tre*, 'farm'). 1230 *Villa Letardi*, 1332 *Lettardston*.

Letton (village, Herefords): 'enclosure where leeks are grown'. OE *lēac-tūn* (from *lēac*, 'leek', + *tūn*, 'enclosure'). The form of the name below is for Letton near Willersley, but Letton near Walford has a name of identical origin. DB *Letune*.

Letwell (village, Rotherham): '(place by the) spring with an obstruction'. ME *lette*, 'obstruction', 'stoppage' (modern English *let* in tennis), + *wella*, 'spring', 'stream'. There is no spring here now. *c*.1150 *Lettewelle*.

Leuchars (village, Fife): '(place of) rushes'. Gaelic *luachar*, 'rushes'. Leuchars is not far from the estuary of the river Eden. 1300 *Locres*.

Leven (village, E Yorks): '(place on the river) Leven'. The name must originally have been that of the stream here, from a Celtic word meaning 'smooth one'. DB *Leuene*.

Leven (resort town, Fife): '(place on the river) Leven'. The Leven enters the sea nearby and has a name meaning 'elm river' (Gaelic *leamhain*, 'elm'). Loch Leven takes its name from the same river. *c*.1535 *Levin*.

Levens (village, Cumbria): '(place at) Lēofa's promontory'. OE *næss*, 'headland', 'promontory'. The 'promontory' is probably the area of land between the rivers Kent and Gilpin, which join to the south of the village. DB *Lefuenes*.

Levenshulme (district, Manchester): 'Lēofwine's island'. OS *holmr*, 'island'. The 'island' here was raised ground in marshland. 1246 *Lewyneshulm*.

Leverington (village, Cambs): 'estate associated with Lēofhere'. OS *-ing-*, 'associated with', + *tūn*, 'farmstead', 'estate'. *c*.1130 *Leverington*.

Leverton (village, Lincs): 'farmstead where rushes grow'. OE *læfer*, 'rush', + *tūn*, 'farmstead'. DB *Leuretune*.

Levington (village, Suffolk): 'Lēofa's farmstead'. OE *tūn*, 'farmstead'. DB *Leuentona*.

Levisham (village, N Yorks): 'Lēofgēat's homestead'. OE *hām*, 'homestead', 'village'. The DB form of the name below is garbled. DB *Leuecen*, *c*.1230 *Leuezham*.

Lew (village, Oxon): '(place at the) mound'. OE *hlǣw*, 'mound', 'tumulus'. John Blair's *Anglo-Saxon Oxfordshire* (1994) describes the large tumulus here as 'one of the most conspicuous landmarks in west Oxfordshire'. 984 *Hlǣwe*, DB *Lewa*.

Lewannick (village, Cornwall): 'church site of Gwenek'. Cornish *lann*, 'church site'. The church here is actually dedicated to St Martin. *c*.1125 *Lanwenuc*.

Lewes (town, E Sussex): '(place by) burial mounds'. OE *hlǣw*, 'mound', 'hill'. The name, representing the OE word in a plural form, apparently alludes to the many tumuli in the area. But the OE word is rare in the south of England (cp. BASSETLAW, TOW LAW) and a Celtic meaning 'slope' (related modern Welsh *llechwedd*) was proposed in 1991 as a plausible alternative origin. The river Ouse here takes its name from that of the town. (It was recorded in *c*.1200 as *aqua de Lewes*. This was misdivided as *aqua del Ewes*, and *Ewes* was taken to be a form of the river name *Ouse*.) 961 *Læwes*, DB *Lewes*, 1868 *Lewes, or Lewis*.

Lewis (island, W Isles): 'marshy place'. Gaelic *leoghuis*, 'marshy' (*leoig*, 'marsh'). Much of Lewis is a huge tract of peat and moss, with many lochs and streams. The name is specifically applied to the northern part of the island, the southern part being HARRIS. *c*.1100 *Leodus*, 1449 *Leoghuis*.

Lewisham (borough, Greater London): 'Lēofsa's homestead'. OE *hām*, 'homestead', 'village'. The first form of the name below means 'boundary of the people of Lewisham' (OE *hǣme*, 'dwellers', + *mearc*, 'boundary'). 862 *Liofshema mearc*, DB *Levesham*.

Lewknor (village, Oxon): 'Lēofeca's hill slope'. OE *ōra*, 'hill slope'. The DB form of the name below has *l* for *r*. 990 *Leofecanoran*, DB *Levecanole*.

Lewtrenchard (village, Devon): 'Trenchard's (estate on the river) Lew'. For the river name, see NORTHLEW. The Trenchard family held the manor here in the 13C. DB *Lewe*, 1261 *Lyu Trencharde*.

Leybourne (village, Kent): '(place by) Lylla's stream'. OE *burna*, 'stream'. 10C *Lillanburna*, DB *Leleburne*.

Leyburn (town, N Yorks): '(place by the) stream with a shelter'. OE *hlēg*, 'shelter', + *burna*, 'stream'. The first part of the name is conjectural. The second part refers to the stream that enters the river Ure here. DB *Leborne*.

Leyland (town, Lancs): 'estate with untilled ground'. OE *lǣge*, 'fallow', 'unploughed' (related modern English *lie*), + *land*, 'land', 'estate'. Much of the land by the river Lostock here was probably used for grazing rather than for growing crops. DB *Lailand*.

Leysdown-on-Sea (resort village, Kent): '(place on a) hill with a beacon fire by the sea'. OE *lēg*, 'fire', + *dūn*, 'hill'. The rising ground here on the Isle of Sheppey on the Thames estuary would have been a suitable location for a beacon fire, and a coastguard station was later built on the site. The second part of the name is a commercial lure to the local holiday camps. *c*.1100 *Legesdun*.

Leyton (town, Waltham F): 'farmstead on the (river) Lea'. OE *tūn*, 'farmstead'. The river has a Celtic name probably meaning 'bright one'. It also gave the name of LUTON. Leyton was also known as *Low Leyton*, referring to its low-lying location by the Lea, but *Low* was dropped in 1867 following a petition to the Great Eastern Railway. *c*.1050 *Lugetune*, DB *Leintune*, 1594 *Leyton called Low Leyton*.

Leytonstone (district, Waltham F): 'Leyton at the stone'. ME *atte*, 'at the', + *stone*, 'stone'. The name is that of neighbouring LEYTON but with 'stone' added for differentiation. The stone in question is the so-called High Stone, said to stand on the site of a Roman milestone. 1370 *Leyton atte Stone*, 1426 *Leyton Stone*.

Lezant (village, Cornwall): 'church site of Sant'. Cornish *lann*, 'church site'. The name could also mean 'holy church site' (Cornish *lann* + *sans*, earlier *sant*, 'holy'). *c*.1125 *Lansant*.

Lichfield (city, Staffs): 'open land near Letocetum'. OE *feld*, 'open land' (modern English *field*). The first part of the name represents the Roman station *Letocetum* at what is now the village of WALL, 2 miles from Lichfield. Its name is of Celtic origin meaning 'grey wood' (related

modern Welsh *llwyd*, 'grey', 'pale', 'brown', + *coed*, 'wood'). Lichfield's name was long held to mean 'field of corpses' (OE *līc*, 'body', 'corpse', + *feld*), supposedly referring to an ancient battle here. As recounted by Robert Plot in *A Natural History of Staffordshire* (1686): 'A ground called Christianfield, near Stitchbrook, is said to be the place where St. Amphibalus taught the British Christians converted by the Martyrdom of St. Alban [in the 3C], who ... followed him hither, from the place of their conversion, where the Romans that were sent after them ... finding them in the exercise of their Religion, tooke them and carryed them to the place where Lichfield now is, and martyred 1,000 of them, leaving their bodies to be devoured by birds and beasts, whence the place yet retains the name of Lichfield, the field of dead bodies; to this day, the City bearing for their device, rather than Armes an Escocheon of Landskip [i.e. landscape] with many Martyrs in it, in severall manners massacred'. (The Corporation seal of Lichfield represents three slain kings lying on a field.) *c*.710 *Licitfelda*.

Liddington (village, Swindon): 'farmstead on the noisy stream'. OE *hlȳde*, 'noisy stream' (literally 'loud one'), + *tūn*, 'farmstead'. 940 *Lidentune*, DB *Ledentone*.

Lidgate (village, Suffolk): '(place at the) swing gate'. OE *hlid-geat*, 'swing gate' (from *hlid*, 'door', 'gate', + *geat*, 'gap', 'gate'). Cp. LEADGATE. DB *Litgata*.

Lifton (village, Devon): 'farmstead on the (river) Lew'. OE *tūn*, 'farmstead'. For the river name, see NORTHLEW. The DB form of the name below has *s* for *f*. *c*.880 *Liwtune*, DB *Listone*.

Lighthorne (village, Warwicks): '(place by the) light-coloured thorn bush'. OE *lēoht*, 'light', + *thyrne*, 'thorn bush'. The DB form of the name below is corrupt. DB *Listecorne*, 1235 *Litthethurne*.

Lilbourne (village, Northants): '(place by) Lilla's stream'. OE *burna*, 'stream'. DB *Lilleburne*.

Lilburn (hamlet, Northd): '(place by) Lilla's stream'. OE *burna*, 'stream'. 1170 *Lilleburn*.

Lilleshall (village, Wrekin): 'Lill's hill'. OE *hyll*, 'hill'. The DB form of the name below has an extraneous *n*. DB *Linleshelle*, 1162 *Lilleshull*.

Lilley (village, Herts): 'woodland clearing where flax is grown'. OE *līn*, 'flax' (related modern English *linen*), + *lēah*, 'wood', 'clearing'. DB *Linleia*.

Lillingstone Dayrell (village, Bucks): 'Dayrell's (estate by the) stone of Lȳtel's people'. OE *-inga-*, 'of the people of', + *stān*, 'stone'. The stone in question would have marked the county boundary with Northamptonshire here, where the manor was held early by the Dayrell family. Their name distinguishes this village from nearby *Lillingstone Lovell*, where it was held by the Lovell family. DB *Lillingestan*, 1166 *Litlingestan Daireli*.

Lillington (village, Dorset): 'estate associated with Lylla'. OE *-ing-*, 'associated with', + *tūn*, 'farmstead', 'estate'. 1166 *Lilletone*, 1200 *Lullinton*.

Lillington (district of Leamington, Warwicks): 'estate associated with Lilla'. OE *-ing-*, 'associated with', + *tūn*, 'farmstead', 'estate'. DB *Lillintone*.

Lilstock (hamlet, Somerset): 'Lylla's outlying farmstead'. OE *stoc*, 'outlying farmstead'. DB *Lulestoch*.

Limehouse (district, Tower Hamlets): 'lime kilns'. OE *līm*, 'lime', + *āst*, 'oast', 'kiln'. Limestone from Kent was brought here by the Thames for limeburning in medieval times. (The '-house' of the name was originally '-oast'.) 1367 *le Lymhostes*, 1496 *Lymost*, 1547 *Lymehouse*.

Limpley Stoke (village, Bath & NE Somerset): 'outlying farmstead associated with Limpley'. OE *stoc*, 'outlying farmstead'. The first word of the name refers to a former chapel here known in 1578 as *Our Lady of Limpley's Chapel*. The origin of *Limpley* is uncertain. The first form of the name below has OE *hangende*, 'hanging', referring to the location of the village below a steep hillside. 1263 *Hangyndestok*, 1333 *Stoke*, 1585 *Lymply Stoke*.

Limpsfield (village, Surrey): 'open land at Limen'. OE *feld*, 'open land' (modern English *field*). The first part of the name represents a Celtic name meaning 'elm wood'. DB *Limenesfelde*.

Linby (village, Notts): 'farmstead where lime trees grow'. OS *lind*, 'lime', + *bý*, 'farmstead'. The DB form of the name below has omitted the *n* of *lind*. DB *Lidebi*, 1163 *Lindebi*.

Linchmere (village, W Sussex): '(place by) Wlenca's pool'. OE *mere*, 'pool'. The pool in question is probably represented by the present Linchmere Marsh, south of the church. 1186 *Wlenchemere*.

Lincoln (city, Lincs): 'Roman colony by the pool'. Latin *colonia*, 'colony'. The first part of the name is Celtic, meaning 'pool' (related modern Welsh *llyn*, 'lake') and referring to the marshland and pools of the river Witham here. (The original pool is partly preserved in Brayford Pool.) A *colonia* was a Roman station for retired legionaries. The Roman town itself was called *Lindum*, from the same Celtic source. The

DB form of the name below has omitted the *n* of *colonia*, presumably because the Norman scribe found it difficult to pronounce after *l*. c.150-Lindon, late 7C *Lindum colonia*, DB *Lincolia*.

Lincolnshire (county, E England): 'district based on Lincoln'. OE *scīr*, 'shire', 'district'. See LINCOLN. 11C *Lindcolnescire*.

Lindale (village, Cumbria): 'valley where lime trees grow'. OS *lind*, 'lime', + *dalr*, 'valley'. 1246 *Lindale*.

Lindal in Furness (village, Cumbria): 'valley where lime trees grow in Furness'. OS *lind*, 'lime', + *dalr*, 'valley'. For the district name, see BARROW-IN-FURNESS. c.1220 *Lindale*.

Lindfield (district of Haywards Heath, W Sussex): 'open land where lime trees grow'. OE *lind*, 'lime', + *feld*, 'open land' (modern English *field*). c.765 *Lindefeldia*.

Lindinis. See ILCHESTER.

Lindisfarne (island, Northd): 'island of the travellers from Lindsey'. OE *fara*, 'traveller' (related modern English *farer*), + *ēg*, 'island'. This traditional interpretation of the name implies that people from LINDSEY, Lincs, made regular journeys to the island, probably as a religious pilgrimage. (Lindisfarne is also known as HOLY ISLAND.) Celticists point out that the name first appeared in 635, when the Irish monk St Aidan established a Christian missionary centre on Lindisfarne, and thus prefer an OI origin giving a meaning 'domain of Lindis', from *Lindis*, the name (meaning 'pool') of a river estuary on the island itself, and a word that gave modern Irish *fearann*, 'domain'. c.700 *Lindisfarnae*.

Lindridge (village, Worcs): '(place by the) ridge where lime trees grow'. OE *lind*, 'lime', + *hrycg*, 'ridge'. 11C *Lynderycge*.

Lindsell (village, Essex): 'dwelling among lime trees'. OE *lind*, 'lime', + *sele*, 'dwelling', 'hall'. DB *Lindesela*.

Lindsey (historic district, Lincs): 'island of the Lindes'. OE *ēg*, 'island'. The *Lindes* were the 'people of LINCOLN' or 'people of the pool'. *Lindsey* was an Anglo-Saxon kingdom in the north of what was later Lincolnshire, its name preserved in the council districts of *East Lindsey* and *West Lindsey*. The region was something like a real 'island' until the fens beside the river Witham here were drained. See also LINDISFARNE. c.704 (*prouincia*) *Lindissi*, DB *Lindesi*.

Lindsey (hamlet, Suffolk): 'Lelli's island'. OE *ēg*, 'island'. The 'island' here is dry ground in marshland. c.1095 *Lealeseia*.

Lindsey Tye (hamlet, Suffolk): 'common pasture by Lindsey'. Modern English dialect *tye*, 'area of common pasture'. Lindsey Tye is near LINDSEY (Suffolk).

Lindum. See LINCOLN.

Lingen (village, Herefords): '(place on the river) Lingen'. The name was probably that of a tributary of the river Lugg here. It is Celtic in origin and means 'clear stream'. 704 *Lingen*, DB *Lingham*.

Lingfield (village, Surrey): 'open land of the dwellers in the wood or clearing'. OE *lēah*, 'wood', 'clearing', + *-inga-*, 'of the dwellers at', + *feld*, 'open land' (modern English *field*). The initial 'L-' of the name is all that remains of OE *lēah*. 9C *Leangafelda*.

Linkinhorne (village, Cornwall): 'church site of Kenhoarn'. Cornish *lann*, 'church site'. The church here is actually dedicated to St Mylor. *c*.1175 *Lankinhorn*.

Linley (hamlet, Shropshire): 'wood or clearing where lime trees grow'. OE *lind*, 'lime', + *lēah*, 'wood', 'clearing'. The form of the name below is for Linley near Bridgnorth, but Linley near Bishop's Castle has a name of identical origin. *c*.1135 *Linlega*, 1204 *Lindleg*.

Linlithgow (town, W Lothian): '(place by) Linlithgow Loch'. The name of the loch means 'lake in the damp hollow', from Celtic words related to modern Welsh *llyn*, 'lake', *llaith*, 'damp', 'moist', and *cau*, 'field', 'hollow'. *c*.1138 *Linlidcu*.

Linshiels (hamlet, Northd): 'shieling where lime trees grow'. OE *lind*, 'lime', + *scēla*, 'shieling', 'temporary shelter'. 1292 *Lynsheles*.

Linslade (town, Beds): 'river crossing by a bank'. OE *hlinc*, 'bank', + *gelād*, 'river crossing'. Linslade is on the river Ouzel below a hill. 966 *Hlincgelad*, DB *Lincelada*.

Linstead Magna (hamlet, Suffolk): 'greater place where flax is grown'. OE *līn*, 'flax' (related modern English *linen*), + *stede*, 'place'. The main name could also mean 'place where maple trees grow' (OE *hlyn*, 'maple', + *stede*). The second word of the name (Latin *magna*, 'great') distinguishes this Linstead from nearby *Linstead Parva* (Latin *parva*, 'little'). DB *Linestede*.

Linstock (hamlet, Cumbria): 'outlying farmstead where flax is grown'. OE *līn*, 'flax' (related modern English *linen*), + *stoc*, 'outlying farmstead'. 1212 *Linstoc*.

Linthwaite (village, Kirklees): 'clearing where flax is grown'. OS *lín*, 'flax' (related modern English *linen*), + *thveit*, 'clearing'. The name could also mean 'clearing where lime trees grow' (OS *lind*, 'lime', + *thveit*). Late 12C *Lindthait*.

Linton (village, Cambs): 'farmstead where flax is grown'. OE *līn*, 'flax' (related modern English *linen*), + *tūn*, 'farmstead'. 1008 *Lintune*, DB *Lintone*. SO ALSO: *Linton*, Derbys, Herefords, Leeds.

Linton (village, Kent): 'estate associated with Lill or Lilla'. OE *-ing-*, 'associated with', + *tūn*, 'farmstead', 'estate'. *c*.1100 *Lilintuna*.

Linton (village, N Yorks): 'farmstead where flax is grown'. OE *līn*, 'flax' (related modern English *linen*), + *tūn*, 'farmstead'. The first part of the name could also represent OE *hlynn*, 'rushing stream', especially as Linton stands on the fast-flowing Linton Beck. The DB form of the name below has *p* for *n*. DB *Lipton*, 12C *Linton*.

Linton-on-Ouse (village, N Yorks): 'farmstead where flax is grown on the (river) Ouse'. OE *līn*, 'flax' (related modern English *linen*), + *tūn*, 'farmstead'. For the river name, see OUSEFLEET. The DB form of the name below contains a scribal error. DB *Luctone*, 1176 *Linton*.

Linwood (village, Lincs): '(place by the) wood where lime trees grow'. OE *lind*, 'lime', + *wudu*, 'wood'. DB *Lindude*.

Liphook (village, Hants): 'angle of land by the leap'. OE *hlīep*, 'leap', 'leaping place', + *hōc*, 'angle of land' (modern English *hook*). The 'leap' was probably the place where deer crossed the river Wey nearby, perhaps at the point where the present A3 runs over it. 1364 *Leophok*.

Liscard (district of Wallasey, Wirral): 'court at the rock'. The name derives from Celtic words related to modern Welsh *llys*, 'court', and *carreg*, 'rock'. The rock in question may have have been one of the reefs at Black Rock or Red Noses, or else the rocky hill on which Liscard itself lies. The second syllable of the form of the name below represents Celtic *en*, 'the'. *c*.1260 *Lisnecarke*.

Liskeard (town, Cornwall): 'Kerwyd's court'. Cornish *lys*, 'court'. *c*.1010 *Lys Cerruyt*, DB *Liscarret*.

Liss (village, Hants): '(place with a) court'. The name is Celtic, related to modern Welsh *llys*, 'court', and perhaps implies that a dwelling here was the chief one in its area. DB *Lis*, 1175 *Lisse*.

Lissett (village, E Yorks): 'dwelling by the pasture'. OE *lǣs*, 'pasture', + *geset*, 'seat', 'dwelling'. DB *Lessete*.

Litcham (village, Norfolk): 'homestead with an enclosure'. OE *lycce*, 'enclosure', + *hām*, 'homestead', 'village'. DB *Licham*.

Litchborough (village, Northants): 'hill with an enclosure'. OE *lycce*, 'enclosure', + *beorg*, 'hill'. The name could theoretically mean 'hill of the bodies' (OE *līc*, 'corpse'), but the origin above is generally preferred. DB *Liceberge*.

Litherland (town, Sefton): 'cultivated land on a slope'. OS *hlíth* (genitive *hlíthar*), 'slope', + *land*, 'cultivated land'. Litherland lies on rising ground by the mouth of the river Mersey. DB *Liderlant*.

Litlington (village, Cambs): 'farmstead of Lȳtel's people'. OE *-inga-*, 'of the people of', + *tūn*, 'farmstead'. DB *Lidlingtone*, 1183 *Litlingeton*.

Litlington (village, E Sussex): 'little farmstead'. OE *lȳtel*, 'little', + *tūn*, 'farmstead'. The first part of the name represents OE *lȳtlan*, the dative form of *lȳtel*. The name could also mean 'farmstead associated with Lȳtel' (OE *-ing-*, 'associated with', + *tūn*). 1191 *Litlinton*.

Little Abington. See GREAT ABINGTON.

Little Addington. See GREAT ADDINGTON.

Little Alne. See GREAT ALNE.

Little Altcar. See GREAT ALTCAR.

Little Amwell. See GREAT AMWELL.

Little Asby. See GREAT ASBY.

Little Ayton. See GREAT AYTON.

Little Baddow. See GREAT BADDOW.

Little Bardfield. See GREAT BARDFIELD.

Little Barford. See GREAT BARFORD.

Little Barrington. See GREAT BARRINGTON.

Little Barrow. See GREAT BARROW.

Little Barugh. See GREAT BARUGH.

Little Bavington. See GREAT BAVINGTON.

Little Bealings. See GREAT BEALINGS.

Little Bentley. See GREAT BENTLEY.

Little Benton. See LONGBENTON.

Little Berkhamsted (village, Herts): 'lesser homestead where birch trees grow'. OE *beorc*, 'birch', + *hām-stede*, 'homestead'. The first word of the name distinguishes the village from the town of BERKHAMSTED or *Great Berkhamsted*, 19 miles to the west, with a name formerly thought to be of identical origin. DB *Berchehamstede*, 1253 *Little Berchamstede*.

Little Billing. See GREAT BILLING.

Little Birch. See MUCH BIRCH.

Little Blakenham. See GREAT BLAKENHAM.

Little Bolas. See GREAT BOLAS.

Little Bookham. See GREAT BOOKHAM.

Littleborough (hamlet, Notts): 'little fort'. OE *lȳtel*, 'little', + *burh*, 'fortified place'. The fort in question was the Roman settlement of *Segelocum*, a name of Celtic origin perhaps meaning '(place by the) violent pool', referring to a pool in the river Trent here with a rapid current. DB *Litelburg*.

Littleborough (town, Rochdale): 'little fort'. OE *lȳtel*, 'little', + *burh*, 'fortified place'. No early forms of the name for this particular Littleborough have been found, and the nature of the fortification is uncertain. 1577 *Littlebrough*.

Littlebourne (village, Kent): 'little (estate on the river) Bourne'. OE *lȳtel*, 'little'. The river formerly called *Bourne* (OE *burna*, 'stream') is now the Little Stour. 696 *Littelburne*, DB *Liteburne*.

Little Bowden. See GREAT BOWDEN.

Little Braxted. See GREAT BRAXTED.

Littlebredy. See LONG BREDY.

Little Bricett. See GREAT BRICETT.

Little Brickhill. See GREAT BRICKHILL.

Little Brington. See GREAT BRINGTON.

Little Bromley. See GREAT BROMLEY.

Little Budworth. See GREAT BUDWORTH.

Little Burstead. See GREAT BURSTEAD.

Littlebury (village, Essex): 'little fort'. OE *lȳtel*, 'little', + *burh*, 'fortified place'. The fort in question is the prehistoric Ring Hill Camp here. c.1000 *Lytlanbyrig*, DB *Lytelbyria*.

Little Bytham. See CASTLE BYTHAM.

Little Canfield. See GREAT CANFIELD.

Little Casterton. See GREAT CASTERTON.

Little Chart. See GREAT CHART.

Little Chell. See CHELL HEATH.

Little Chesterford. See GREAT CHESTERFORD.

Little Cheverell. See GREAT CHEVERELL.

Little Chishill. See GREAT CHISHILL.

Little Clacton. See CLACTON-ON-SEA.

Little Coates. See GREAT COATES.

Little Comberton. See GREAT COMBERTON.

Little Cornard. See GREAT CORNARD.

Little Cowarne. See MUCH COWARNE.

Little Coxwell. See GREAT COXWELL.

Little Crakehall. See GREAT CRAKEHALL.

Little Cransley. See GREAT CRANSLEY.

Little Cressingham. See GREAT CRESSINGHAM.

Little Crosby. See CROSBY (Sefton).

Little Dalby. See GREAT DALBY.

Littledean. See MITCHELDEAN.

Little Dewchurch. See MUCH DEWCHURCH.

Little Dunham. See GREAT DUNHAM.

Little Dunmow. See DUNMOW.

Little Durnford. See GREAT DURNFORD.

Little Easton. See GREAT EASTON.

Little Eaton. See LONG EATON.

Little Edstone. See GREAT EDSTONE.

Little Ellingham. See GREAT ELLINGHAM.

Little Elm. See GREAT ELM.

Little England Beyond Wales (region, Pemb). The name or nickname is applied to the southern part of Pembrokeshire, which has been chiefly English-speaking since the Viking invasion of the 9C. 1519 *Ynglond beyond Walys*, 1594 *Little England beyond Wales*.

Little Everdon. See GREAT EVERDON.

Little Eversden. See GREAT EVERSDEN.

Little Faringdon (village, Oxon): 'lesser (place near a) fern-covered hill'. OE *fearn*, 'fern', + *dūn*, 'hill'. The name was transferred to the village from FARINGDON, formerly known as *Great Faringdon*, 6 miles to the southeast, and Little Faringdon has no 'fern-covered hill' of its own. DB *Ferendone*.

Little Fenton. See CHURCH FENTON.

Little Finborough. See GREAT FINBOROUGH.

Little Fransham. See GREAT FRANSHAM.

Little Gaddesden. See GREAT GADDESDEN.

Little Gidding. See GREAT GIDDING.

Little Glemham. See GREAT GLEMHAM.

Little Gonerby. See GREAT GONERBY.

Little Gransden. See GREAT GRANSDEN.

Little Grimsby. See GRIMSBY.

Little Gringley. See GRINGLEY ON THE HILL.

Little Habton. See GREAT HABTON.

Little Hadham. See MUCH HADHAM.

Little Hallingbury. See GREAT HALLINGBURY.

Littleham (village, Devon): '(place by a) little river meadow'. OE *lȳtel*, 'little', + *hamm*, 'enclosure', 'river meadow'. The forms of the name below are for Littleham near Exmouth. 1042 *Lytlanhamme*, DB *Liteham*.

Little Hampden. See GREAT HAMPDEN.

Littlehampton (resort town, W Sussex): 'little home farm'. OE *hām-tūn*, 'home farm' (from *hām*, 'homestead', + *tūn*, 'farmstead'). The name was originally *Hampton*, but *Little* was added later to distinguish this Hampton from the one that became SOUTHAMPTON, 40 miles

west along the coast. DB *Hantone*, 1482 *Lyttelhampton*.

Little Harrowden. See GREAT HARROWDEN.

Little Harwood. See GREAT HARWOOD.

Little Haseley. See GREAT HASELEY.

Little Hatfield. See GREAT HATFIELD.

Little Hautbois (hamlet, Norfolk): 'lesser (place by a) marshy meadow with tussocks'. OE *hobb*, 'tussock', + *wisse*, 'marshy meadow'. Corresponding *Great Hautbois*, 'vulgarly called "Hobbies"' (*The National Gazetteer of Great Britain and Ireland*, 1868), has now effectively merged with Coltishall, 2 miles to the southeast. The present form of the name has evolved by false association with French *haut bois*, 'high wood'. 1044 *Hobbesse*, DB *Hobuisse*, 1868 *Hautbois Parva*.

Little Haven (coastal village, Pemb): '(place with a) little harbour'. OE *hæfen*, 'haven', 'harbour'. The first word of the name distinguishes the village from nearby BROAD HAVEN. 1578 *the Lytel hauen*.

Little Haywood. See GREAT HAYWOOD.

Littlehempston. See BROADHEMPSTON.

Little Hereford (village, Herefords): 'lesser (place by the) army ford'. OE *lȳtel*, 'little', + *hereford*, 'army ford'. The first word of the name distinguishes the village from HEREFORD, 19 miles to the south. The river here is the Teme. The first part of the form of the name below represents OE *lȳtlan*, the dative form of *lȳtel*. DB *Lutelonhereford*.

Little Hinton. See BROAD HINTON.

Little Hockham. See GREAT HOCKHAM.

Little Horkesley. See GREAT HORKESLEY.

Little Hormead. See GREAT HORMEAD.

Little Horsted. See HORSTED KEYNES.

Little Horwood. See GREAT HORWOOD.

Littlehoughton. See LONGHOUGHTON.

Little Houghton (Barnsley). See GREAT HOUGHTON (Barnsley).

Little Houghton (Northants). See GREAT HOUGHTON (Northants).

Little Hucklow. See GREAT HUCKLOW.

Little Hutton. See HUTTON MAGNA.

Little Kelk. See GREAT KELK.

Little Kimble. See GREAT KIMBLE.

Little Langton. See GREAT LANGTON.

Little Laver. See HIGH LAVER.

Little Lawford. See CHURCH LAWFORD.

Little Leigh. See HIGH LEGH.

Little Leighs. See GREAT LEIGHS.

Little Lever (town, Bolton): 'lesser place where rushes grow'. OE *lǣfer*, 'rush', 'reed'. The first word of the name, though no longer appropriate, distinguishes this place from *Darcy Lever*, where the d'Arcy family held land in the 14C, and from *Great Lever*, now both districts of Bolton. The first word of the form of the name below represents Latin *parva*, 'little'. 1212 *Parua Lefre*.

Little Limber. See GREAT LIMBER.

Little Livermere. See GREAT LIVERMERE.

Little Longstone. See GREAT LONGSTONE.

Little Malvern. See MALVERN HILLS.

Little Maplestead. See GREAT MAPLESTEAD.

Little Marcle. See MUCH MARCLE.

Little Massingham. See GREAT MASSINGHAM.

Little Meols. See GREAT MEOLS.

Little Milton. See GREAT MILTON.

Little Missenden. See GREAT MISSENDEN.

Little Mitton. See GREAT MITTON.

Littlemore (suburb of Oxford, Oxon): '(place by the) little marsh'. OE *lȳtel*, 'little', + *mōr*, 'moor', 'marshy ground'. *c.*1130 *Luthlemoria*.

Little Musgrave. See GREAT MUSGRAVE.

Little Ness. See NESSCLIFF.

Little Oakley. See GREAT OAKLEY.

Little Offley. See GREAT OFFLEY.

Little Onn. See HIGH ONN.

Little Ormes Head. See GREAT ORMES HEAD.

Little Ormside. See GREAT ORMSIDE.

Little Orton. See GREAT ORTON.

Little Ouseburn. See GREAT OUSEBURN.

Littleover (district, Derby): 'lesser (place at the) ridge'. OE *ofer*, 'ridge'. The DB form of the name below has Latin *parva* ('Little-' in the present name) to distinguish this place from nearby MICKLEOVER. DB *Parva Ufre*.

Little Oxendon. See GREAT OXENDON.

Little Parndon. See GREAT PARNDON.

Little Paxton. See GREAT PAXTON.

Little Ponton. See GREAT PONTON.

Littleport (village, Cambs): 'little market town'. OE *lȳtel*, 'little', + *port*, 'town', 'market town'. DB *Litelport*.

Littler. See OVER (Cheshire).

Little Ribston (village, N Yorks): 'lesser (place by the) rock where ribwort grows'. OE *ribbe*, 'ribwort', + *stān*, 'stone', 'rock'. There is no longer a contrasting 'Great Ribston', but its site is represented by nearby *Ribston Park*. DB *Ripestan*.

Little Rissington. See GREAT RISSINGTON.

Little Ryburgh. See GREAT RYBURGH.

Little Ryle. See GREAT RYLE.

Little Salkeld. See GREAT SALKELD.

Little Sampford. See GREAT SAMPFORD.

Little Saughall. See GREAT SAUGHALL.

Little Saxham (village, Suffolk): 'lesser homestead of the Saxons'. OE *Seaxe*, 'Saxons', + *hām*, 'homestead'. Little Saxham is now actually bigger than nearby *Great Saxham*. DB *Saxham*.

Little Shefford. See GREAT SHEFFORD.

Little Shelford. See GREAT SHELFORD.

Little Smeaton (N Yorks, near Northallerton). See GREAT SMEATON.

Little Smeaton (N Yorks, near Pontefact). See KIRK SMEATON.

Little Snoring. See GREAT SNORING.

Little Sodbury. See CHIPPING SODBURY.

Little Somborne. See KING'S SOMBORNE.

Little Somerford. See GREAT SOMERFORD.

Little Stanney (village, Cheshire): 'lesser (place by a) rock island'. OE *stān*, 'stone', 'rock', + *ēg*, 'island'. The 'rock island' is Stanlow Point (see STANLOW) to the north. The first word of the name distinguished the village from *Great Stanney*, now part of Ellesmere Port. DB *Stanei*.

Little Staughton. See GREAT STAUGHTON.

Littlestone-on-Sea. See GREATSTONE-ON-SEA.

Little Stonham. See EARL STONHAM.

Little Stretton. See CHURCH STRETTON.

Little Strickland. See GREAT STRICKLAND.

Little Tew. See GREAT TEW.

Little Thetford (village, Cambs): 'lesser (place at the) people's ford'. OE *lȳtel*, 'little', + *thēod*, 'people', 'tribe', + *ford*, 'ford'. The river here is the Cam. The first word of the name distinguishes the village from THETFORD, Norfolk, 23 miles to the east. *c.*972 *Thiutforda*, DB *Liteltedford*.

Little Thurlow. See GREAT THURLOW.

Littleton (village, Surrey): 'little farmstead'. OE *lȳtel*, 'little', + *tūn*, 'farmstead', 'estate'. DB *Liteltone*. SO ALSO: *Littleton*, Cheshire, Hants, Somerset.

Littleton Drew (village, Wilts): 'Driwe's little farmstead'. OE *lȳtel*, 'little', + *tūn*, 'farmstead', 'estate'. The Driwe family held the manor here in the 13C. DB *Liteltone*, 1311 *Littleton Dru*.

Littleton Panell (village, Wilts): 'Paynel's little farmstead'. OE *lȳtel*, 'little', + *tūn*, 'farmstead', 'estate'. The Paynel family held the manor here in the 13C. DB *Liteltone*, 1317 *Lutleton Paynel*.

Littleton-upon-Severn (village, S Glos): 'little farmstead on the (river) Severn'. OE *lȳtel*, 'little', + *tūn*, 'farmstead', 'estate'. For the river name, see SEVERN STOKE. 986 *Lytletun*, DB *Liteltone*.

Little Torrington. See TORRINGTON.

Little Tosson. See GREAT TOSSON.

Little Totham. See GREAT TOTHAM.

Little Urswick. See GREAT URSWICK.

Little Wakering. See GREAT WAKERING.

Little Waldingfield. See GREAT WALDINGFIELD.

Little Walsingham. See WALSINGHAM.

Little Waltham. See GREAT WALTHAM.

Little Washbourne. See GREAT WASHBOURNE.

Little Weighton. See MARKET WEIGHTON.

Little Welnetham. See GREAT WELNETHAM.

Little Wenham. See GREAT WENHAM.

Little Wenlock. See MUCH WENLOCK.

Little Wilbraham. See GREAT WILBRAHAM.

Little Wishford. See GREAT WISHFORD.

Little Witchingham. See GREAT WITCHINGHAM.

Little Witcombe. See GREAT WITCOMBE.

Little Witley. See GREAT WITLEY.

Little Wittenham. See LONG WITTENHAM.

Little Wolford. See GREAT WOLFORD.

Littleworth (hamlet, Doncaster). The place was originally named *Shuttleworth*, 'locked enclosure' (OE *scytels*, 'bolt', 'bar', + *worth*, 'enclosure'), but this was subsequently changed to *Littleworth*, presumably for reasons of delicacy. Cp. MIDDLESTOWN. DB *Scitelesuuorde*, 1724 *Littleworth*.

Littleworth (village, Oxon): 'little enclosure'. OE *lȳtel*, 'little', + *worth*, 'enclosure'. The first part of the name distinguishes the village from LONGWORTH, 5 miles to the east. The DB form of the name below, representing a form of *worth*, is corrupt. *c.*971 *Wyrthæ*, DB *Ordia*, 1284 *Lytleworth*.

Little Wratting. See GREAT WRATTING.

Little Wymondley. See GREAT WYMONDLEY.

Little Wytheford. See GREAT WYTHEFORD.

Little Yeldham. See GREAT YELDHAM.

Litton (village, Derbys): 'farmstead on a slope'. OE *hlith*, 'hill slope', + *tūn*, 'farmstead'. DB *Litun*. SO ALSO: *Litton*, N Yorks.

Litton (village, Somerset): 'farmstead by a gate'. OE *hlid*, 'gate' (modern English *lid*), + *tūn*, 'farmstead'. The name could also mean 'farmstead by a slope' (OE *hlid*, 'hill slope', + *tūn*). *c.*1060 *Hlytton*, DB *Litune*.

Litton Cheney (village, Dorset): 'Cheyne's farmstead by a noisy stream'. OE *hlȳde*, 'loud one', + *tūn*, 'farmstead'. The Cheyne family held the manor here in the 14C. 1204 *Lideton*.

Liverpool (city and port, Liverpool): '(place by the) pool with muddy water'. OE *lifer*, 'liver', + *pōl*, 'pool'. The town arose by a 'livered pool', i.e. one that was clotted or coagulated with mud and weeds. The pool in question was *The Pool*, a former creek of the Mersey here that has now been filled in. The first part of the name gave birth to the liver, the fanciful bird that was said to be seen on The Pool and that supposedly appears on the city arms. 'It was intended for the eagle of St John the Evangelist, the patron saint of the corporation, but owing to the unskilful delineation there have been many guesses as to the identity of the bird represented' (*Oxford English Dictionary*). *c.*1190 *Liuerpul*.

Liversedge (town, Kirklees): 'Lēofhere's ridge'. OE *ecg*, 'edge', 'ridge'. Liversedge lies on a long low ridge above the river Calder. DB *Livresec*.

Liverton (village, Redcar & Clev): 'Lēofhere's farmstead'. OE *tūn*, 'farmstead'. The name could also mean 'farmstead on a stream with muddy water' (OE *lifer*, 'liver', + *tūn*), referring to Liverton Beck here. Cp. LIVERPOOL. DB *Liuretun*.

Livingston (town, W Lothian): 'Leving's farmstead'. OE *tūn*, 'farmstead'. *c.*1128 *Villa Leuing*, *c.*1150 *Leuinestun*.

Lizard (peninsula, Cornwall): 'court on a height'. Cornish *lys*, 'court', + *ardh*, 'height'. The original 'court' or dwelling was probably at or near the present village of *Lizard*. The Romans knew the Lizard as both *Dumnonium Promontorium*, 'headland of the Dumnonii' (see DEVON), and *Ocrinum Promontorium*, the latter name perhaps based on a word related to Greek *okris*, 'jagged point', referring not to the peninsula itself but to the group of rocks nearby called The MANACLES. DB *Lisart*.

Llanandras. See PRESTEIGNE.

Llanbadarn Fawr (district of Aberystwyth, Ceredigion): 'great church of St Padarn'. Welsh *llan*, 'church', + *mawr*, 'big', 'great'. St Padarn was a 5C or 6C abbot and bishop here, and the church dedicated to him was the principal one in the region. 1181 *Lampadervaur*, 1557 *Llanbadarn Vawr*.

Llanbedr Pont Steffan. See LAMPETER.

Llanberis (town, Gwynedd): 'church of St Peris'. Welsh *llan*, 'church'. Peris is said to have lived some time in the 11C or 12C. 1283 *Lanperis*.

Llanbethery (village, Vale of Glam): 'church of the deaf ones'. Welsh *llan*, 'church', + *byddair*, 'deaf ones' (plural of *byddar*, 'deaf'). The name appears to have the same origin as LLANYBY-DDER. The Welsh form of the name is *Llan-bydderi*. 13C *Landebither*.

Llanbydderi. See LLANBETHERY.

Llandaff (district, Cardiff): 'church on the (river) Taf'. Welsh *llan*, 'church'. The church in question is the cathedral church of St Teilo, whose name lies behind that of LLANDEILO. Cp. CARDIFF. *c.*1150 *Lanntaf*, 1191 *Landaph*.

Llanddewi Brefi (village, Ceredigion): 'church of St David on the (river) Brefi'. Welsh *llan*, 'church', + *Dewi*, 'David'. The river's name means 'noisy one' (Welsh *bref*, 'bleat', 'bray'). 13C *Landewi Brevi*.

Llanddewi Nant Hoddni. See LLANTHONY.

Llanddewi Velfrey (village, Pemb): 'church of St David in Efelffre'. Welsh *llan*, 'church', + *Dewi*, 'David'. The name of the commote (sub-division of a cantred, or hundred) is of uncertain origin, although the '-frey' may represent Welsh *bre*, 'hill'. 1488 *Landewi in Wilfrey*.

Llanddulas (coastal village, Conwy): 'church on the (river) Dulas'. Welsh *llan*, 'church'. The river name may mean 'black stream' (Welsh *du*, 'black', + *glais*, 'stream', 'river'). *c.*1700 *Llan Dhylas*.

Llandeilo (town, Carm): 'church of St Teilo'. Welsh *llan*, 'church'. Teilo, also known as Elid-ius, was a 6C saint and bishop whose work and cult was centred in South Wales. The second word of the forms of the name below means 'Great'. 1130 *Lanteliau Maur*, 1656 *Llandilo Vawr*.

Llandeloy (village, Pemb): 'Tylwyf's church'. Welsh *llan*, 'church'. The personal name, that of the owner of the site, is not recorded elsewhere and is conjectural. The church is now dedicated to St Teilo, the saint's name having been mistakenly associated with the original. 1291 *Landalee*.

Llandinabo (hamlet, Herefords): 'church of St Dinebo'. Welsh *llan*, 'church'. The saint's name seems to represent that of one Iunapui who owned the site here, with *ow di* (modern Welsh

dy), 'thy', prefixed to his name as a form of affectionate diminutive. *c.*1130 *Lann Hunapui*.

Llandovery (town, Carm): 'church near the waters'. Welsh *llan*, 'church', + *am*, 'near', + *dyfri*, 'waters' (plural of *dwfr*, 'water'). The town is near the point where the rivers Brân and Gwydderig join the Towy (see TYWI VALLEY). The Welsh form of the name is *Llanymddyfri*, but the *-ym-* of this has been lost in the English form. 12C *Llanamdewri*, 1194 *Lanandeveri*, 1383 *Lanymdevery*.

Llandrillo-yn-Rhos. See RHOS-ON-SEA.

Llandrindod Wells (town, Powys): 'church of the Trinity with wells'. Welsh *llan*, 'church', + *trindod*, 'trinity'. The original name of the church was *Llanddwy*, 'church of God' (Welsh *Dwy*, 'God'). The second (English) word of the name was added to draw attention to the local chalybeate springs, first exploited in the 18C. 1291 *Lando*, 1554 *Llandrindod*.

Llandudno (resort town, Conwy): 'church of St Tudno'. Welsh *llan*, 'church'. This is the only Welsh church dedicated to this saint, about whom little is known. 1291 *Llandudno*, 1376 *Lantudenou*.

Llandudoch. See ST DOGMAELS.

Llandysul (town, Ceredigion): 'church of St Tysul'. Welsh *llan*, 'church'. Little is known about the named saint. 1291 *Landessel*, 1299 *Lantissill*.

Llanelli (town, Carm): 'church of St Elli'. Welsh *llan*, 'church'. Elli is said to have been one of the daughters of the legendary prince Brychan, who gave the name of BRECON. 'The two *lls* in Llanelli are a little hard to pronounce, but practice makes it easier, so long as the abomination of "Lan-elthy" is avoided' (*The Shell Guide to Wales*, 1969). *c.*1173 *Lann elli*.

Llanelwy. See ST ASAPH.

Llanfair Caereinion (town, Powys): 'church of St Mary in Caereinion'. Welsh *llan*, 'church', + *Mair*, 'Mary'. *Caereinion*, the name of the cantref (hundred), means 'fort on the (river) Ein-ion' (Welsh *caer*, 'fort'). The addition distinguishes this *Llanfair* from the many others. 1279 *Llanveyr*, 1579 *Llanvair in Krynion*.

Llanfairfechan (resort town, Conwy): 'little church of St Mary'. Welsh *llan*, 'church', + *Mair*, 'Mary', + *bechan*, 'little'. The church here is 'little' compared to the 'big' church of St Mary at Conwy, 7 miles to the northeast. 1284 *Lanueyr*, 1291 *Llanbayar*, 1475 *Llanvair Vechan*.

Llanfair Pwllgwyngyll (village, Anglesey): 'church of St Mary in Pwllgwyngyll'. Welsh *llan*, 'church', + *Mair*, 'Mary'. The second word, added for purposes of distinction, is that of the township here, meaning 'pool of the white hazels' (Welsh *pwll*, 'pool', + *gwyn*, 'white', + *cyll*, 'hazels'). A further lengthy addition was notoriously made in the mid-19C (supposedly by a playful tailor) to give a fuller name *Llanfairpwllgwyngyllgogerychwyrndrobwllllantysiliogogogoch*. This incorporates Welsh *go*, 'rather', *ger*, 'near', *y*, 'the', *chwyrn*, 'rapid', *trobwyll*, 'whirlpool', *llantysilio*, 'church of St Tysilio', and *coch*, 'red', based on names or features in the local landscape. 1536 *Llan Vair y pwyll Gwinghill*, 1566 *ll.fair ymhwll gwingill*.

Llanfair Waterdine (village, Shropshire): 'church of St Mary in the wet valley'. Welsh *llan*, 'church', + *Mair*, 'Mary', + OE *wæter*, 'water', 'river', + *denu*, 'valley'. The village is on the river Teme, which here marks the border with Wales. Early forms of the name, as below, show that the second word is not a distinguishing addition, but the original. The second form of the name below has the *thl* still sometimes used by non-Welsh speakers in an attempt to pronounce the notorious *ll*. See LLANELLI. DB *Watredene*, 1284 *Thlanveyr*, 1376 *Lanweyrwaterden*.

Llanfair-ym-Muallt. See BUILTH WELLS.

Llanfihangel-ar-arth (village, Carm): 'St Michael's church on the high hill'. Welsh *llan*, 'church', + *Mihangel*, 'Michael the Archangel' (from Latin *Michangelus*, from *Michael*, 'Michael', + *angelus*, 'angel'), + *ar*, 'on', + *garth*, 'hill'. The second word of the form of the name below represents Welsh *gor-*, 'very', 'super-', + *garth*, 'hill', referring to the height of the hill. 1291 *Llanfihangel Orarth*.

Llanfihangel Dyffryn Arwy. See MICHAELCHURCH ESCLEY.

Llanfihangel-y-pwll. See MICHAELSTON-LE-PIT.

Llanfyllin (town, Powys): 'church of St Myllin'. Welsh *llan*, 'church'. Myllin (or Moling, or Mulling) was a 7C Irish saint, not known to have actually visited Wales. 1254 *Llanvelig*, 1291 *Lanvyllyn*, 1309 *Lanvethlyng*.

Llanfyrnach (village, Pemb): 'church of St Brynach'. Welsh *llan*, 'church'. 1291 *Ecclesia Sancti Bernaci*.

Llangadog (village, Carm): 'church of St Cadog'. Welsh *llan*, 'church'. Several other churches in Wales are dedicated to the 6C saint Cadog. 1281 *Lancadauc*, 1284 *Lankadoc*.

Llangarron (village, Herefords): 'church on the (river) Garron'. Welsh *llan*, 'church'. The river has a Celtic name meaning 'stream where

cranes are seen' (modern Welsh *garan*, 'crane'). c.1130 *Lann Garan*.

Llangefni (town, Anglesey): 'church on the (river) Cefni'. Welsh *llan*, 'church'. The church here is actually dedicated to St Cyngar. 1254 *Llangevni*.

Llangollen (town, Denb): 'church of St Collen'. Welsh *llan*, 'church'. Little is known of this 7C saint. 1234 *Lancollien*.

Llangolman (village, Pemb): 'church of St Colman'. Welsh *llan*, 'church'. The church here is dedicated to the 7C Irish bishop Colman. 1394 *Llangolman*.

Llangrove (village, Herefords): '(place by the) long grove'. OE *lang*, 'long', + *gräf*, 'grove', 'copse'. Llangrove is near the Welsh border, and the first part of its name has been influenced by the omnipresent Welsh *llan*, 'church'. 1372 *Longe grove*.

Llangwm (village, Pemb): 'church in the valley'. Welsh *llan*, 'church', + *cwm*, 'valley'. 1301 *Landegumme*.

Llanidloes (town, Powys): 'church of St Idloes'. Welsh *llan*, 'church'. This is the only church in Wales dedicated to the named saint, about whom almost nothing is known. 1254 *Lanidloes*.

Llanilltud Fawr. See LLANTWIT MAJOR.

Llanllyfni (village, Gwynedd): 'church on the (river) Llyfni'. Welsh *llan*, 'church'. The river name means 'smooth-flowing one' (Welsh *llyfn*, 'smooth'). The twice-occurring *thl* in the first form of the name below (with *n* miscopied as *u*) represents the famous Welsh *ll*. See LLANELLI. 1352 *Thlauthleueny*, 1432 *Llanllyfne*.

Llanrothal (hamlet, Herefords): '(place with a) church'. Welsh *llan*, 'church'. The second part of the name probably represents a saint's name. c.1130 *Lann Ridol*.

Llanrug (village, Gwynedd): 'church in Rug'. Welsh *llan*, 'church'. *Rug* is the name of the township (Welsh *grug*, 'heather'). The full name of the village was *Llanfihangel-yn-Rug*, 'church of St Michael the Archangel in Rug'. (Cp. LLANFIHANGEL-AR-ARTH.) 1566 *ll.v'el yn Ruc*, 1614 *Llanvihengle in Rug*.

Llanrwst (town, Conwy): 'church of St Gwrwst'. Welsh *llan*, 'church'. This is the only church in Wales dedicated to the named saint, about whom little is known. 1254 *lhannruste*, 1291 *Lannwrvst*.

Llansanffraid Glan Conwy (village, Conwy): 'church of St Ffraid on the bank of the (river) Conwy'. Welsh *llan*, 'church', + *sant*, 'saint', +

glan, 'bank', 'shore'. Ffraid is a Welsh form of the name of St Brigid (Bridget). For the river name, see CONWY. The lengthy village name is now often shortened to *Glan Conwy*. 1535 *Llansan-fraid*, *c*.1700 *Lhan St Ffraid*, 1713 *Llan Sanfraed Glan Conwy*.

Llansawel. See BRITON FERRY.

Llanstadwell (village, Pemb): 'church of St Tudwal'. Welsh *llan*, 'church'. The church here is dedicated to the 6C bishop Tudwal, suggesting that the original full form of the name may have been *Llan sant Tudwal*, with *llan* followed by Welsh *sant*, 'saint'. 12C *Lanstadhewal*.

Llanthony (village, Mon): 'church on the (river) Honddi'. Welsh *llan*, 'church'. The name is usually said to be an abbreviated form of the full Welsh name *Llanddewi Nant Hoddni*, 'church of St David on the river Hoddni' (Welsh *llan*, 'church', + *Dewi*, 'David', + *nant*, 'river'). More plausibly, *Llanthony* is simply a form of the river name, *Nant Hoddni*, with *llan* replacing *nant*. The river name itself means 'pleasant', 'quiet' (Welsh *hawdd*). 1160 *Lantony*.

Llantrisant (village, Mon): 'church of three saints'. Welsh *llan*, 'church', + *tri*, 'three', + *sant*, 'saint'. The three saints of Llantrisant are Dyfodwg, Gwynno and Illtud. 1246 *Landtrissen*.

Llantrithyd (village, Vale of Glam): 'Rhirid's valley'. Welsh *nant*, 'valley'. Although early forms of this name have *Llan-* (Welsh *llan*, 'church'), it seems likely that this replaced an original *nant*, as for LLANTHONY. The identity of Rhirid is unknown. A spelling *Llantriddyd* was recently also common. *c*.1126 *Landrirede*, 1545 *Nantririd*.

Llantwit Major (town, Vale of Glam): 'main church of St Illtud'. Welsh *llan*, 'church'. The name is a part translation, part contraction of the Welsh name *Llanilltud Fawr*, with Welsh *mawr*, 'great', represented by Latin *major*. Illtud established a monastery here in the 6C, and the place is 'great' in relation to Llantwit Fardre (Welsh *Llanilltud Faerdre*), Rhondda CT, and *Llantwit-juxta-Neath* (Welsh *Llanilltud Nedd*), Neath PT. 1106 *Landiltuit*, 1291 *Lannyltwyt*, 1480 *Lantwyt*.

Llantydewi. See ST DOGWELLS.

Llanwarne (village, Herefords): 'church by the alder grove'. Welsh *llan*, 'church', + *gwern*, 'swamp', 'alder grove'. The DB form of the name below is corrupt. DB *Ladgvern*, *c*.1130 *Lann Guern*.

Llanwnda (hamlet, Pemb): 'church of St Gwyndaf'. Welsh *llan*, 'church'. The church

here is dedicated to Gwyndaf, a saint about whom nothing is known. 1202 *Lanwndaph*.

Llanwrda (village, Carm): 'church of St Gwrdaf'. Welsh *llan*, 'church'. The dedication to the saint, about whom nothing is known, is unique in Wales. 1302 *Llanwrdaf*.

Llanwrtyd Wells (town, Powys): 'church of St Gwrtud with wells'. Welsh *llan*, 'church'. Nothing is known about the named saint, and the church here is actually dedicated to St David. The town developed as a spa in the 19C. Hence the second word of the name. 1553 *Llanwrtid*, 1566 *Ll. Wrtyd*.

Llanyblodwel (village, Shropshire): 'church of Blodwell'. Welsh *llan*, 'church'. *Blodwell* means 'blood spring' (OE *blōd*, 'blood', + *wella*, 'spring'), apparently referring to the colour of the water here or alluding to some local legend. The village is close to the Welsh border. 1535 *Llanblodwell*.

Llanybydder (village, Carm): 'church of the deaf ones'. Welsh *llan*, 'church', + *byddair*, 'deaf ones' (plural of *byddar*, 'deaf'). The name may allude to a congregation who were deaf to the call preached to them, or on the contrary whose hitherto deaf ears were opened by it. 1319 *Lannabedeir*, 1401 *Llanybyddeyr*.

Llanycefn (hamlet, Pemb): 'church on the ridge'. Welsh *llan*, 'church', + *y*, 'the', + *cefn*, 'ridge'. The ridge on which the church stands is a prominent local feature. 1499 *Llanekevyn*.

Llanychaer (hamlet, Pemb): meaning uncertain. Early forms of the name suggest that the first part may represent Welsh *llanerch*, 'glade'. The rest of the name is obscure. 1291 *Launerwayth*, 1408 *Llanerchaeth*.

Llanymddyfri. See LLANDOVERY.

Llanymynech (village, Shropshire): 'church of the monks'. Welsh *llan*, 'church', + *mynach*, 'monk'. The village is on the Welsh border. The reference to monks is unexplained. 1254 *Llanemeneych*.

Lleyn Peninsula (peninsula, Gwynedd): meaning uncertain. The name may have originally been that of a Celtic people here, with their own name perhaps coming from *Leinster*, Ireland, whence they may have emigrated to Wales. The peninsula is also known by the short English name of (the) *Lleyn* or the Welsh name of (the) *Llŷn*.

Llŷn. See LLEYN PENINSULA.

Llyn Tegid. See BALA.

Llys-y-fran (village, Pemb): 'Brân's court'. Welsh *llys*, 'court'. The 'court' is probably represented by the earthwork immediately north of the church here. 1326 *Lysurane*, 1402 *Lysfrane*.

Loanhead (town, Midlothian): '(place at the) end of a lane'. OE *lane*, 'lane', + *hēafod*, 'head'. *Loan* is a Scots form of standard English *lane*. The place name is common in Scotland. 1618 *Loneheid*.

Loch. For names beginning with this word, see the next word, e.g. for *Loch Lomond*, see LOMOND.

Lochaber (upland region, Highland): 'lake at the confluence'. Gaelic *loch*, 'lake', + Celtic *aber*, 'river mouth', 'confluence'. There are many lochs here and it is uncertain which particular one is meant. The second part of the name may actually be Gaelic *abar*, 'marsh', giving a general sense 'marshy lake'.

Lochgelly (town, Fife): '(place by) Loch Gelly'. Gaelic *loch*, 'lake'. The loch has a name meaning 'shining' (Gaelic *geal*). 1606 *Lochgellie*.

Lochgilphead (town, Argyll & Bute): '(place at the) head of Loch Gilp'. Gaelic *loch*, 'lake'. The name of the loch means 'chisel-shaped lake' (Gaelic *gilb*, 'chisel'). 1650 *Lochgilpshead*.

Lochinvar (loch, Dumfries & Gall): 'loch on the height'. Gaelic *loch an barrha*, from *loch*, 'lake', + *an*, 'on the', + *barr*, 'top', 'summit'. The loch is located among hills. 1540 *Lochinvar*.

Lochinver (town and port, Highland): '(place by) Loch Inver'. Gaelic *loch*, 'lake'. The town lies at the head of Loch Inver, a sea inlet at the mouth (Gaelic *inbhir*) of the river Inver, which in turn takes its name from the loch.

Lochmaben (town, Dumfries & Gall): meaning uncertain. Gaelic *loch*, 'lake'. The town lies among several small lochs, but none is named 'Maben'. It has been suggested the name may be that of some legendary youthful hero (related modern Welsh *mab*, 'boy', 'son', 'man'). 1166 *Locmaban*, c.1320 *Lochmalban*, 1502 *Lochmabane*.

Lochnagar (mountain ridge, Aberdeens): '(mountain by) Lochnagar'. The loch that gave the mountain its name is traditionally explained as 'loch of laughter' (Gaelic *loch an gàire*, from *loch*, 'lake', + *an*, 'of the', + *gàire*, 'laughter'), but it is not easy to rationalize this. 1640 *Loch Garr*, 1807 *Loch na Garr*.

Lochy, Loch (loch, Highland): 'loch of (the river) Lochy'. Gaelic *loch*, 'lake'. The loch takes its name from the river that flows from it to Loch Linnhe. Its own name means 'dark one' (Gaelic *lochaidh*).

Lockengate (hamlet, Cornwall): '(place by the) lockable gate'. The name refers to the former turnpike toll here, on the road (now the A391) from Bodmin to St Austell. 1748 *Locken Gate*.

Lockerbie (town, Dumfries & Gall): 'Locard's farm'. OS *bý*, 'farm'. The personal name is Scandinavian. 1306 *Lockardebie*.

Locking (village, N Somerset): 'place associated with Locc'. OE *-ing*, 'place associated with'. The name could also mean '(place by a) fold' (OE *locing*, 'fold', 'enclosure'). 1212 *Lockin*.

Lockington (village, E Yorks): 'estate associated with Loca'. OE *-ing-*, 'associated with', + *tūn*, 'farmstead', 'estate'. The first part of the name could also represent OE *locing*, 'enclosure' (related modern English *lock*). DB *Locheton*.

Lockton (village, N Yorks): 'Loca's farmstead'. OE *tūn*, 'farmstead'. The first part of the name could also represent OE *loca*, 'enclosure' (related modern English *lock*). DB *Lochetun*.

Loddington (village, Leics): 'estate associated with Luda'. OE *-ing-*, 'associated with', + *tūn*, 'farmstead', 'estate'. DB *Ludintone*.

Loddington (village, Northants): 'estate associated with Lodda'. OE *-ing-*, 'associated with', + *tūn*, 'farmstead', 'estate'. DB *Lodintone*.

Loddiswell (village, Devon): '(place by) Lod's spring'. OE *wella*, 'spring', 'stream'. DB *Lodeswille*.

Loddon (town, Norfolk): '(place by the river) Loddon'. The river here, now the Chet (from the nearby village of CHEDGRAVE), originally had a Celtic name meaning 'muddy stream'. 1043 *Lodne*, DB *Lotna*.

Lode (village, Cambs): '(place by the) watercourse'. OE *lād*, 'watercourse'. The reference is to the drainage channel known as Bottisham Lode here. 12C *Lada*.

Loders (village, Dorset): '(place on the river) Loder'. The old name of the river Asker here is of Celtic origin and means 'pool stream' (related modern Welsh *llwch*, 'lake', and *dwfr*, 'water'). DB *Lodre*.

Lodsworth (village, W Sussex): 'Lod's enclosure'. OE *worth*, 'enclosure'. DB *Lodesorde*.

Lofthouse (village, Leeds): 'house with an upper storey'. OS *lopt-hús* (from *lopt*, 'upper floor', modern English *loft*, + *hús*, 'house'). DB *Loftose*.

Loftus (town, Redcar & Clev): 'house with an upper storey'. OS *lopt-hús* (from *lopt*, 'upper floor', modern English *loft*, + *hús*, 'house'). The

DB form of the name below has the OS word with a dative plural ending. DB *Loctehusum*.

Lolworth (village, Cambs): 'Loll's or Lull's enclosure'. OE *worth*, 'enclosure'. 1034 *Lollesworthe*, DB *Lolesuuorde*.

Lomond, Loch (loch, Argyll & Bute): '(loch by) Ben Lomond'. Gaelic *loch*, 'lake'. The loch takes its name from nearby *Ben Lomond*, whose own name means 'beacon hill', from Gaelic *beinn*, 'mountain' and a Celtic word related to modern Welsh *llumon*, 'beacon', 'chimney'. Cp. PLYNLIMON. *c.*1340 *Lochlomond*.

Londesborough (village, E Yorks): 'Lothinn's stronghold'. OE *burh*, 'fortified place'. The personal name is Scandinavian. DB *Lodenesburg*.

Londinium. See LONDON.

London (city, London): meaning uncertain. The name has long been said to mean 'Londinos' place', from a Celtic personal name with an adjectival suffix, but modern scholarship disputes this, since the *u* of the OE forms of the name below shows that the Celtic original had a long *o*, whereas the vowel in *Londinos* is short. The *o* was later reinstated to avoid confusion between *u* and *n* in medieval texts. A recent theory derives the name from two Indo-European roots that combine to mean 'boat river', referring to the Thames as a river that needed a boat to be crossed (as distinct from one that could be forded). The name originally applied to the City of London, and spread to the surrounding area relatively recently, some years before the formation of the county of London in 1888, when the London County Council (LCC) inherited the administrative powers possessed from 1855 by the Metropolitan Board of Works. *Greater London*, a name already in use in the late 19C for the Metropolitan and City Police districts, became the official name for the entire administrative area in 1963, when the Greater London Council (GLC) superseded the LCC to embrace 32 London boroughs. (For further developments, see the Introduction, p. xxiv). The first form of the name below is the Roman name of London, found in Tacitus' *Annals*. *c.*115 *Londinium*, 731 *Lundonia*, *c.*890 *Lundeneceaster*, *c.*900 *Lundenburg*.

London Apprentice (village, Cornwall). The name is that of a former inn here, which took it from a contemporary ballad: 'The Honour of an Apprentice of London Wherein He Declared His Matchless Manhood and Brave Adventures Done by Him in Turkey and by What Means He Married the King's Daughter of that same Country'. The name is first recorded in 1747.

London Colney (district of St Albans, Herts): 'island by the (river) Colne on the road to London'. OE *ēg*, 'island'. 'Island' here means riverside land. The river name is pre-English and of uncertain meaning. The first word of the name distinguishes this place from nearby *Broad Colney* by locating it on the main road from St Albans to London, now represented by the A1081 bypass. 1209 *Colnea*, 1555 *London Colney*.

Long, Loch (loch, Argyll & Bute): 'ship loch'. Gaelic *loch*, 'lake', + *long*, 'ship'. The loch would have provided a safe anchorage for ships that had sailed up the Clyde.

Long Ashton (village, N Somerset): 'long farmstead where ash trees grow'. OE *æsc*, 'ash', + *tūn*, 'farmstead'. The first word refers to the length of the village. DB *Estune*, 1467 *Longe Asshton*.

Long Bennington (village, Lincs): 'long farmstead associated with Beonna'. OE *-ing-*, 'associated with', + *tūn*, 'farmstead'. The first word of the name denotes a long straggling village. DB *Beningtun*.

Longbenton (town, N Tyneside): 'long farmstead where bents grows'. OE *beonet*, 'bent grass', + *tūn*, 'farmstead'. The name could also mean 'farmstead where beans grow', from OE *bēan*, 'bean'. *Long* was added later for distinction from nearby *Little Benton*. The second form of the name below has Latin *magna*, 'great', while the third has northern modern English *mickle* in the same sense. *c.*1190 *Bentune*, 1256 *Magna Beneton*, 1868 *Long Benton*, or *Mickle Benton*.

Longborough (village, Glos): '(place by the) long hill'. OE *lang*, 'long', + *beorg*, 'hill', 'barrow'. The name probably refers to the long barrow about ½ mile above the village. DB *Langeberge*.

Long Bredy (village, Dorset): 'long (village by the river) Bride'. For the river name, see BRIDPORT. The first word of the name distinguishes the village from *Littlebredy*, 1½ miles to the southeast. 987 *Bridian*, DB *Langebride*.

Longbridge (district, Birmingham): '(place by the) long bridge'. The name is recent, referring to a long road bridge over the river Rea here. 1831 *Long Bridge*.

Longbridge Deverill. See KINGSTON DEVERILL.

Long Buckby (village, Northants): 'long (village called) Bukki's or Bucca's farmstead'. OS *bý*, 'farmstead', 'village'. The personal names are respectively Scandinavian and OE. The village is so called because of its length. DB *Buchebi*, 1565 *Longe Bugby*.

Longburton (village, Dorset): 'long fortified farm'. OE *lang*, 'long', + *burh-tūn*, 'fortified farm' (from *burh*, 'fortified place', + *tūn*, 'farmstead'). The first part of the name refers to the length of the village. 1244 *Burton*, 1460 *Langebourton*.

Long Clawson (village, Leics): 'long farmstead on a hill'. OE *lang*, 'long', + *clacc*, 'hill', + *tūn*, 'farmstead'. The main name could also mean 'Klakkr's farmstead', with a Scandinavian personal name. DB *Clachestone*.

Long Compton (village, Warwicks): 'long farmstead in a valley'. OE *lang*, 'long', + *cumb*, 'valley', + *tūn*, 'farmstead'. The first word refers to the length of the village and distinguishes it from nearby *Little Compton*. DB *Cuntone*, 1299 *Long Compton*.

Long Crendon (village, Bucks): 'long (place by) Creoda's hill'. OE *dūn*, 'hill'. The first word of the name, referring to the length of the village, has been present only since the 17C. DB *Credendone*.

Long Crichel. See MOOR CRICHEL.

Longden (village, Shropshire): '(place by the) long hill'. OE *lang*, 'long', + *dūn*, 'hill'. The hill in question is a distinctively shaped ridge here. DB *Langedune*.

Longdendale. See MOTTRAM IN LONGDENDALE.

Long Ditton. See THAMES DITTON.

Longdon (village, Worcs): '(place by the) long hill'. OE *lang*, 'long', + *dūn*, 'hill'. 969 *Langandune*, DB *Longedun*. SO ALSO: *Longdon*, Staffs.

Longdon upon Tern (village, Wrekin): '(place by the) long hill on the (river) Tern'. OE *lang*, 'long', + *dūn*, 'hill'. The 'long hill' is the ridge on which the village stands above the Weald Moors. The river has a Celtic name meaning 'strong one'. DB *Languedune*, 1491 *Longedon supra Tyren*.

Longdowns (village, Cornwall): '(place on the) long downs'. The village arose as a 19C settlement on former downland. 1841 *Long Downs*.

Long Drax (hamlet, N Yorks): '(place by the) long stretch of river'. OE *lang*, 'long', + *racu*, 'stream'. The river here is the Ouse. The name influenced that of neighbouring DRAX and was in turn subsequently influenced by that name. 1208 *Langrak*.

Long Duckmanton (village, Derbys): 'Ducemann's farmstead'. OE *tūn*, 'farmstead'. The two adjacent villages of *Duckmanton* and *Long Duckmanton*, the latter named for its length, combined in recent times under the latter name. c.1002 *Ducemannestune*, DB *Dochemanestun*.

Long Eaton (town, Derbys): 'long island farm'. OE *lang*, 'long', + *ēg*, 'island', + *tūn*, 'farm-stead'. An 'island farm' is one on well-watered land, as here, where the town is almost surrounded on three sides by the rivers Erewash and Trent. The farm was called 'long' partly for distinction from other Eatons, but also specifically because it extended further than the farm at *Little Eaton*, a village north of Derby. DB *Aitune*, 1288 *Long Eyton*.

Longfield (suburban development, Kent): 'long (stretch of) open land'. OE *lang*, 'long', + *feld*, 'open land' (modern English *field*). 10C *Langafelda*, DB *Langafel*.

Longfleet (district, Poole): '(place by the) long inlet'. OE *lang*, 'long', + *flēot*, 'creek', 'inlet'. The 'long inlet' in question is Holes Bay here. 1230 *Langeflete*.

Longford (village, Derbys): '(place at the) long ford'. OE *lang*, 'long', + *ford*, 'ford'. The village stands on a tributary of the river Dove. 1197 *Langeford*, DB *Langeford*. SO ALSO: *Longford*, Shropshire, Wrekin.

Longford (village, Glos): '(place at the) long ford'. OE *lang*, 'long', + *ford*, 'ford'. The Roman road from Gloucester to Worcester crossed Horsbere Brook here. 1107 *Langeford*.

Longframlington (village, Northd): 'long estate associated with Framela'. OE *lang*, 'long', + *-ing-*, 'associated with', + *tūn*, 'farmstead', 'estate'. The first part of the name refers to the length of the village. 1166 *Framelintun*, 1868 *Long Framlington*.

Longham (village, Norfolk): 'homestead of Lāwa's people'. OE *-inga-*, 'of the people of', + *hām*, 'homestead'. DB *Lawingham*.

Long Hanborough. See CHURCH HANBOROUGH.

Longhirst (village, Northd): '(place by the) long wooded hill'. OE *lang*, 'long', + *hyrst*, 'wooded hill'. 1200 *Langherst*.

Longhope (village, Glos): '(place in the) long valley'. OE *lang*, 'long', + *hop*, 'valley'. The first part of the name was added to distinguish this Hope from HOPE MANSELL, Herefords, 4 miles to the west. DB *Hope*, 1248 *Langehope*.

Longhorsley (village, Northd): 'long (place in the) woodland clearing where horses are kept'. OE *lang*, 'long', + *hors*, 'horse', + *lēah*, 'wood', 'clearing'. 1196 *Horsleg*.

Longhoughton (village, Northd): 'long farmstead by a hill spur'. OE *lang*, 'long', + *hōh*, 'hill spur', + *tūn*, 'farmstead'. The first part of the name distinguishes the village from nearby *Littlehoughton*, as does Latin *magna*, 'great', in the first form of the name below. 1242 *Houcton Magna*, 1868 *Long Houghton*.

Long Itchington (village, Warwicks): 'long farmstead on the (river) Itchen'. OE *lang*, 'long', + *tūn*, 'farmstead'. The river has a pre-Celtic name of unknown meaning. The first word of the name distinguishes the straggling village from *Bishops Itchington*, 5 miles to the south, held by the Bishop of Coventry and Lichfield. 1001 *Yceantune*, DB *Icentone*, c.1185 *Longa Hichenton*.

Long Lawford. See CHURCH LAWFORD.

Longleat (country house, Wilts): '(place by the) long stream'. OE *lang*, 'long', + *gelǣt*, 'stream', 'channel' (modern English *leat*). Longleat takes its name from the long water channel formerly here that was flooded to form ornamental lakes when the house was built in the 16C. 1235 *Langelete*.

Long Marston (village, N Yorks): 'long farmstead by a marsh'. OE *lang*, 'long', + *mersc*, 'marsh', + *tūn*, 'farmstead'. The first word of the name refers to the length of the village. DB *Mersetone*.

Long Marston (village, Warwicks): 'long farmstead by a marsh'. OE *lang*, 'long', + *mersc*, 'marsh', + *tūn*, 'farmstead'. The first word of the name refers to the length of the village and distinguishes it from nearby *Broad Marston*, so called from its broad shape. The fourth form of the name below has Latin *sicca*, 'dry', as the village stands above the surrounding marshland. Hence the former alternative name *Dry Marston*. 1043 *Merstuna*, DB *Merestone*, 1285 *Longa Merston*, 1535 *Marston Sicca*.

Long Marton (village, Cumbria): 'long (place with a) farmstead by a pool'. OE *mere*, 'pool', + *tūn*, 'farmstead'. The first word applies to the length of the parish, not of the village. c.1170 *Meretun*.

Long Melford (town, Suffolk): 'long (place with a) ford by a mill'. OE *lang*, 'long', + *myln*, 'mill', + *ford*, 'ford'. The town, on a tributary of the river Stour, where the ford would have been, has one of the longest main streets in the country. Hence the first word of the name. DB *Melaforda*.

Long Mynd, The (hill range, Shropshire): 'the long hill'. OE *lang*, 'long', + Welsh *mynydd*, 'hill'. The name refers to the central ridge of hills here, close to the Welsh border. Hence the mixed English and Welsh name. 12C *Longameneda*.

Longney (village, Glos): 'long island'. OE *lang*, 'long', + *ēg*, 'island'. The 'long island' here is probably the area of land enclosed on three sides by the river Severn. 972 *Longanege*, DB *Langenei*.

Longnor (village, Shropshire): '(place by the) long alder (copse)'. OE *lang*, 'long', + *alor*, 'alder'. The village is more likely to be named from a long alder copse rather than a single tall tree. 1155 *Longenalra*.

Longnor (village, Staffs): '(place by the) long ridge'. OE *lang*, 'long', + *ofer*, 'ridge'. 1227 *Langenoure*.

Longovicium. See LANCHESTER.

Longparish (village, Hants): 'long parish'. The earlier name of the place was *Middleton*, 'middle farmstead' (OE *middel*, 'middle', + *tūn*, 'farmstead'), so called as between *Easton*, 'eastern farm', and *Forton*, 'farm at the ford'. DB *Meddeltune*, 1389 *Langeparisshe*.

Long Preston (village, N Yorks): 'long farmstead of the priests'. OE *lang*, 'long', + *prēost*, 'priest', + *tūn*, 'farmstead'. The name refers to the length of the village. DB *Prestune*.

Longridge (town, Lancs): '(place by the) long ridge'. OE *lang*, 'long', + *hrycg*, 'ridge'. The name refers to Longridge Fell, the ridge to the northeast of the town. 1246 *Langrig*.

Long Riston (village, E Yorks): 'long farmstead by the brushwood'. OE *hrīs*, 'brushwood', + *tūn*, 'farmstead'. The first word of the name, denoting a straggling village, distinguishes this place from RUSTON PARVA, 14 miles to the northwest. DB *Ristune*.

Long Sandall. See KIRK SANDALL.

Longsdon (village, Staffs): '(place by the) hill (called) Lang'. OE *dūn*, 'hill'. *Lang* (OE *lang*, 'long') would have been the name of a ridge here. 1242 *Longesdon*.

Longships (island group, Cornwall). The cluster of islands with a lighthouse to the west of Land's End must have been named from their supposed resemblance to a long ship or ships. 1347 *Langeshipes*.

Longstanton. See FENSTANTON.

Long Stratton (village, Norfolk): 'long village by a Roman road'. OE *lang*, 'long', + *strǣt*, 'Roman road' (modern English *street*), + *tūn*, 'farmstead', 'village'. The first word of the name refers to the length of the village and distinguishes it from nearby *Stratton St Michael*, so called from the dedication of its church. Long Stratton is on (and Stratton St Michael is near) the Roman road (now followed by the A140) that led from Colchester to Caistor St Edmund, near Norwich. DB *Stretuna*.

Long Sutton (town, Lincs): 'long southern village'. OE *lang*, 'long', + *sūth*, 'southern', + *tūn*, 'farmstead', 'village'. The town is in the south of the county near the border with Cambridgeshire. The first word of the name, denoting a straggling village, distinguishes this Sutton from nearby *Sutton St Edmund* and *Sutton St James*, so called from the dedications of their churches. See also SUTTON BRIDGE. DB *Sudtone*, 1385 *Langsutton*.

Longton (town, Stoke): 'long estate'. OE *lang*, 'long', + *tūn*, 'farmstead', 'estate'. A 'long' estate is a straggling one. 1212 *Longeton*. SO ALSO: *Longton*, Lancs.

Longtown (town, Cumbria): 'long estate'. OE *lang*, 'long', + *tūn*, 'farmstead', 'estate'. The town is located beside the river Esk. 1267 *Longeton*.

Longtown (Herefords). See EWYAS HAROLD.

Longville in the Dale (village, Shropshire): 'long stretch of open land in the valley'. OE *lang*, 'long', + *feld*, 'open land' (modern English *field*), + *dæl*, 'valley'. The village lies below Wenlock Edge, while the 'dale' is Ape Dale, the valley of Eaton Brook and Byne Brook. 1255 *Longefewd*.

Long Whatton (village, Leics): 'long farmstead where wheat is grown'. OE *hwǣte*, 'wheat', + *tūn*, 'farmstead'. The first word of the name, recorded from the 14C, refers to the straggling village that evolved. 1190 *Watton*.

Long Wittenham (village, Oxon): 'long (place by) Witta's river bend'. OE *hamm*, 'enclosure', 'river bend'. The village lies at the base of a loop in the Thames. The first word, added in the 16C, indicates its size by comparison with nearby *Little Wittenham*. c.865 *Wittanham*, DB *Witeham*.

Longwitton (hamlet, Northd): 'long farmstead by a wood'. OE *lang*, 'long', + *wudu*, 'wood', + *tūn*, 'farmstead'. 1236 *Wttun*, 1340 *Langwotton*.

Longworth (village, Oxon): 'long enclosure'. OE *lang*, 'long', + *worth*, 'enclosure'. The first part of the name distinguishes the village from LITTLEWORTH, 5 miles to the west. 958 *Wurthe*, 1284 *Langewrth*.

Looe (resort town, Cornwall): '(place by the) pool'. Cornish *logh*, 'pool', 'inlet'. The name is properly that of the river here, which divides the town into *East Looe* and *West Looe*. c.1220 *Loo*.

Loose (village, Kent): '(place by the) pigsty'. OE *hlōse*, 'pigsty'. 11C *Hlose*.

Lopen (village, Somerset): '(place by the) hill'. The second part of the name represents either a

Celtic word related to modern Welsh *pen*, 'head', 'end', or else possibly OE *penn*, 'pen', 'enclosure'. The first part is of uncertain origin. DB *Lopene*.

Loppington (village, Shropshire): 'estate associated with Loppa'. OE *-ing-*, 'associated with', + *tūn*, 'farmstead', 'estate'. DB *Lopitone*.

Lossiemouth (resort town and port, Moray): 'mouth of the (river) Lossie'. The river has a Celtic name meaning 'water of herbs'. The town arose relatively recently. Hence English *mouth*.

Lostock Gralam (village, Cheshire): 'Gralam's outlying farmstead with a pigsty'. OE *hlōse*, 'pigsty', + *stoc*, 'outlying farmstead'. The manor here was held in the 12C by one Gralam. c.1100 *Lostoch*, 1288 *le Lostoke Graliam*.

Lostwithiel (town, Cornwall): '(place at the) tail end of the woodland'. Cornish *lost*, 'tail', + *gwydhyel*, 'wooded district' (from *gwydh*, 'trees', + adjectival ending *-yel*). Cp. WITHIEL. The surrounding country is still well wooded. 1194 *Lostwetell*.

Lothian. See MIDLOTHIAN.

Loughborough (town, Leics): 'Luhhede's fortified house'. OE *burh*, 'fortified place'. The second part of the DB form of the name below is corrupt. DB *Lucteburne*, 12C *Lucteburga*.

Loughor (town, Swansea): '(place by the river) Loughor'. The river name, of Celtic origin, means 'shining one' (modern Welsh *llychwr*, 'daylight', 'brightness'). The Welsh name of Loughor is *Casllwchwr*, with the river name prefixed by Welsh *cas*, a variant of *castell*, 'castle', referring to the former Norman castle here overlooking the estuary. 1691 *Caslougher*.

Loughton (town, Essex): 'estate associated with Luca'. OE *-ing-*, 'associated with', + *tūn*, 'farmstead', 'estate'. The original *-ing-* of the name has disappeared. 1062 *Lukintone*, DB *Lochetuna*.

Loughton (district of Milton Keynes, Milton K): 'estate associated with Luhha'. OE *-ing-*, 'associated with', + *tūn*, 'farmstead', 'estate'. The original *-ing-* of the name has been lost. DB *Lochintone*.

Loughton (hamlet, Shropshire): 'farmstead by a pool'. OE *luh*, 'pool', + *tūn*, 'farmstead'. There is no pool here now, but the hamlet stands on a hill spur between two streams. 1138 *Lochetona*.

Lound (village, Notts): '(place by the) grove'. OS *lundr*, 'grove'. DB *Lund*. SO ALSO: *Lound*, Lincs, Suffolk.

Louth (town, Lincs): '(place by the river) Lud'. The river name means 'loud one' (OE *hlūde*), as one with a noisy current. DB *Lude*.

Loversall (village, Doncaster): 'Lēofhere's corner of land'. OE *halh*, 'nook', 'corner of land'. DB *Loureshale*.

Loveston (hamlet, Pemb): 'Lovell's farm'. OE *tūn*, 'farm'. The personal name is Norman French in origin. 1362 *Lovelleston*.

Lovington (village, Somerset): 'estate associated with Lufa'. OE *-ing-*, 'associated with', + *tūn*, 'farmstead', 'estate'. DB *Lovintune*.

Low Ackworth. See HIGH ACKWORTH.

Low Bentham. See HIGH BENTHAM.

Low Catton. See HIGH CATTON.

Lowdham (village, Notts): 'Hlūda's homestead'. OE *hām*, 'homestead', 'village'. DB *Ludham*.

Low Dinsdale (hamlet, Darlington): 'lower corner of land belonging to Deighton'. OE *halh*, 'nook', 'corner of land'. The first part of the main name represents *Deighton*, N Yorks, 6 miles to the southeast, its own name having the same origin as DEIGHTON, York. The first word of the name distinguishes this Dinsdale from *Over Dinsdale*, N Yorks, on higher ground across the river Tees. c.1185 *Ditneshall*.

Low Eggborough (village, N Yorks): 'lower (place called) Ecga's stronghold'. OE *burh*, 'fortified place'. The first word of the name distinguishes the village from nearby *High Eggborough*. DB *Egeburg*.

Low Ellington. See HIGH ELLINGTON.

Lower Arncott. See UPPER ARNCOTT.

Lower Beeding. See UPPER BEEDING.

Lower Benefield. See UPPER BENEFIELD.

Lower Boddington. See UPPER BODDINGTON.

Lower Brailes. See UPPER BRAILES.

Lower Broadheath. See UPPER BROADHEATH.

Lower Bullingham (suburb of Hereford, Herefords): 'lower marsh enclosure associated with Bulla'. OE *-ing-*, 'associated with', + *hop*, 'marsh enclosure'. The name could also mean 'lower marsh enclosure at Bulla's place' (OE *-ing*, 'place belonging to', + *hop*). OE *hop* was later replaced by OE *hamm*, 'enclosure'. The first word of the name distinguished this Bullingham from nearby *Upper Bullingham*, now known by its earlier name as simply *Bullinghope*. The DB form of the name below is corrupt. DB *Boninhope*, 1242 *Bullingehope*.

Lower Cumberworth (village, Kirklees): 'lower (place called) Cumbra's enclosure'. OE *worth*, 'enclosure'. The main name could also mean 'enclosure of the Britons' (OE *Cumbre*, '(Ancient) Britons', + *worth*). The first word of the name distinguishes the village from nearby *Upper Cumberworth*. DB *Cumbreuurde*.

Lower Dicker (hamlet, E Sussex): 'lower (place of) ten'. ME *dyker*, 'ten' (related Latin *decem*, 'ten'). The name alludes to a plot of land for which ten iron rods were paid by way of rent, each rod being sufficient to make two horseshoes. The first word of the name distinguishes the hamlet from nearby *Upper Dicker*, while to the west of the latter and the river Cuckmere lies the area known as *The Dicker*. 1229 *Diker*.

Lower Dunsforth (village, N Yorks): 'lower (place called) Dunn's ford'. OE *ford*, 'ford'. The ford was probably over one of the streams that enter the river Ure nearby. The first word of the name distinguishes the village from nearby *Upper Dunsforth*. DB *Doneforde*.

Lower Farringdon. See UPPER FARRINGDON.

Lowerford. See BARROWFORD.

Lower Heyford. See UPPER HEYFORD (Oxon).

Lower Kinnerton. See HIGHER KINNERTON.

Lower Lemington (hamlet, Glos): 'lower farmstead by the (river) Limen'. OE *tūn*, 'farmstead'. *Limen*, the former name of the stream here, is of Celtic origin and means 'elm river'. The name of the former contrasting *Over Lemington* survives in that of *Lemington Manor*. DB *Limentone*.

Lower Lye. See UPPER LYE.

Lower Penn. See PENN (Wolverhampton).

Lower Penwortham. See HIGHER PENWORTHAM.

Lower Peover (village, Cheshire): 'lower (part of) Peover'. Lower Peover was the principal hamlet in the township of Peover, the others being *Nether Peover*, *Peover Superior* and *Peover Inferior*. *Peover* is the Celtic name of the river here, meaning 'bright one' (modern Welsh *pefr*, 'radiant', 'beautiful'). DB *Pevre*.

Lower Quinton (village, Warwicks): 'lower farmstead of the queen'. OE *cwēn*, 'queen', + *tūn*, 'farmstead', 'estate'. The first word of the name distinguishes the village from the nearby hamlet of *Upper Quinton*. 848 *Quentone*, DB *Quenintune*.

Lower Rochford. See UPPER ROCHFORD.

Lower Salter. See HIGH SALTER.

Lower Seagry. See UPPER SEAGRY.

Lower Shuckburgh (village, Warwicks): 'lower (place by the) hill haunted by an evil spirit'. OE *scucca*, 'goblin', 'evil spirit', + *beorg*, 'hill'. The first word of the name distinguishes the village from nearby *Upper Shuckburgh*. DB *Socheberge*.

Lower Slaughter. See UPPER SLAUGHTER.

Lower Swell. See UPPER SWELL.

Lower Tean. See UPPER TEAN.

Lower Thurnham. See UPPER THURNHAM.

Lower Tysoe. See UPPER TYSOE.

Lower Vexford (hamlet, Somerset): 'lower (place by the) fresh-water ford'. OE *fersc*, 'fresh', + *ford*, 'ford'. OE *fersc* is here used as a noun. The first word of the name distinguishes this Vexford from nearby *Higher Vexford*. DB *Fescheforde*.

Lower Whitley. See HIGHER WHITLEY.

Lower Winchendon. See UPPER WINCHEN-DON.

Lowesby (hamlet, Leics): 'Lauss's or Lausi's farmstead'. OS *bý*, 'farmstead', 'village'. The personal names are Scandinavian. The DB form of the name below must have resulted from a mishearing. DB *Glowesbi*, *c*.1125 *Lousebia*.

Lowestoft (town and port, Suffolk): 'Hlothvér's homestead'. OS *toft*, 'homestead'. The DB form of the name below misdivides the Scandinavian personal name. DB *Lothu Wistoft*.

Loweswater (lake, Cumbria): 'leafy lake'. OS *lauf*, 'leaf', + *sǽr*, 'lake', + OE *wæter*, 'water'. The lake gave the name of the hamlet of *Loweswater* between Loweswater and Crummock Water. *c*.1160 *Lousewater*.

Low Grantley. See HIGH GRANTLEY.

Low Ham. See HIGH HAM.

Low Hawsker. See HIGH HAWSKER.

Low Hesket. See HIGH HESKET.

Lowick (hamlet, Cumbria): '(place by a) leafy creek'. OS *lauf*, 'leaf', + *vík*, 'bay', 'creek'. Lowick stands on the river Crake, with *Lowick Bridge* to the north and *Lowick Green* to the south. 1202 *Lofwik*.

Lowick (village, Northants): 'Luhha's or Luffa's dairy farm'. OE *wīc*, 'dwelling', 'dairy farm'. DB *Luhwic*.

Lowick (village, Northd): 'dairy farm on the (river) Low'. OE *wīc*, 'dwelling', 'dairy farm'. The river name represents OE *luh*, 'pool' (related Scottish *loch*). 1181 *Lowich*.

Low Marishes. See HIGH MARISHES.

Low Marnham. See HIGH MARNHAM.

Low Moorsley (village, Sunderland): 'lower (place by the) hill of the moor'. OE *mōr*, 'moor', + *hlāw*, 'hill'. The first word of the name distinguishes the village from nearby *High Moorsley*. 12C *Moreslau*.

Lowther (hamlet, Cumbria): '(place on the river) Lowther'. The river name may mean 'foaming river' (OS *lauthr*, 'froth', 'foam', + *á*, 'river'), but could equally be of Celtic origin and uncertain meaning. *c*.1175 *Lauder*.

Lowther Hills (hill range, Dumfries & Gall): meaning uncertain. The name may be related to LAUDER.

Lowthorpe (village, E Yorks): 'Lági's or Logi's outlying farmstead'. OS *thorp*, 'outlying farmstead'. The personal names are Scandinavian. DB *Logetorp*.

Lowton (village, Wigan): 'farmstead on a hill'. OE *hlāw*, 'mound', 'hill', + *tūn*, 'farmstead'. Lowton stands on slightly elevated ground in marshland. 1202 *Lauton*.

Low Worsall (hamlet, N Yorks): 'lower (place called) Weorc's corner of land'. OE *halh*, 'nook', 'corner of land'. The first word of the name distinguishes the place from nearby *High Worsall*. DB *Wercheshale*.

Loxbeare (hamlet, Devon): 'Locc's grove'. OE *bearu*, 'wood', 'grove'. DB *Lochesbere*.

Loxford (district, Redbridge): '(place by) Locc's ford'. OE *ford*, 'ford'. The original ford would probably have been over the Loxford Water here. 1319 *Loxford*.

Loxhore (hamlet, Devon): 'Locc's hill slope'. OE *ōra*, 'hill slope'. DB *Lochesore*.

Loxley (village, Warwicks): 'Locc's woodland clearing'. OE *lēah*, 'wood', 'clearing'. DB *Locheslei*.

Loxton (village, N Somerset): 'farmstead on the (river) Lox Yeo'. OE *tūn*, 'farmstead'. The first word of the river name is of Celtic origin and uncertain meaning. The second represents OE *ēa*, 'river'. DB *Lochestone*.

Lubenham (village, Leics): 'Lubba's hill spurs'. OE *hōh*, 'hill spur'. The second part of the name represents OE *hōum*, the dative plural form of *hōh*. DB *Lubanham*.

Luccombe (village, Somerset): 'Lufa's valley'. OE *cumb*, 'valley'. DB *Locumbe*, 1896 *Luccombe, or Luckham*.

Luccombe Village (village, IoW): 'Lufa's valley'. OE *cumb*, 'valley'. DB *Lovecumbe*.

Lucker (village, Northd): '(place by the) marsh with a pool'. OE *luh*, 'pool' (related Scottish *loch*), + OS *kjarr*, 'marsh'. 1170 *Lucre*.

Luckett (village, Cornwall): 'Leofa's cottage'. OE *cot*, 'cottage'. 1557 *Lovecott*.

Luckington (village, Wilts): 'estate associated with Luca'. OE *-ing-*, 'associated with', + *tūn*, 'farmstead', 'estate'. DB *Lochintone*.

Lucton (village, Herefords): 'farmstead on the (river) Lugg'. OE *tūn*, 'farmstead'. For the river name, see LUGWARDINE. 1185 *Lugton*.

Ludborough (village, Lincs): 'fortified place associated with Louth'. OE *burh*, 'fortified place'. Ludborough is 6 miles north of LOUTH. Alternatively, the name could mean 'Luda's fortified place'. DB *Ludeburg*.

Ludchurch (village, Pemb): 'the grey church'. The Welsh name of Ludchurch is *Yr Eglwys Lwyd*, 'the grey church' (*yr*, 'the', + *eglwys*, 'church', + *llwyd*, 'grey') and the English name appears to be a part-translation of this, with 'Lud-' representing *llwyd*. 1324 *Ecclesia de Loudes*, 1353 *Loudeschirch*.

Luddenden (village, Calderdale): '(place in the) valley of Luddenden Brook'. OE *denu*, 'valley'. The stream name derives from that of the village, which in turn comes from the original name of the stream, *Hluding*, 'loud one' (OE *hlūd*, 'loud'). The nearby village of *Luddenden Foot*, at the bottom of the valley on the river Calder, derives the second word of its name from OE *ford*, 'ford'. (Its present form arose because the village is at the foot of Luddenden Dean.) 1284 *Luddingdene*.

Luddesdown (hamlet, Kent): '(place by) Hlūd's hill'. OE *dūn*, 'hill'. 10C *Hludesduna*, DB *Ledesdune*.

Luddington in the Brook (village, Northants): 'farmstead of Lulla's people in the brook'. OE *-inga-*, 'of the people of', + *tūn*, 'farmstead'. The name was originally *Lullington* but was influenced by nearby LUTTON. The brook of the name is Alconbury Brook, whose muddy water overflowed into the village. DB *Lullintone*, 1424 *Lodyngton in the Brooke*.

Ludford (village, Lincs): '(place by) Luda's ford'. OE *ford*, 'ford'. The location of the ford is unknown, but it probably carried a Roman road here. The village is properly divided into *Ludford Magna* (Latin *magna*, 'great') and *Ludford Parva* (Latin *parva*, 'little'). DB *Ludesforde*.

Ludford (village, Shropshire): '(place by the) ford on the noisy stream'. OE *hlūde*, 'loud one', + *ford*, 'ford'. Ludford lies on the south bank of

the river Teme at the point where the road crosses it to enter LUDLOW. DB *Ludeford*.

Ludgershall (town, Wilts): 'corner of land with a trapping spear'. OE *lūte-gār*, 'trapping spear' (from a word related to *lūtian*, 'to hide', 'to lurk', + *gār*, 'spear'), + *halh*, 'nook', 'corner of land'. A 'trapping spear' is a device set up to impale wild animals. The 'corner of land' may have been one of the valleys that run into the flat-topped hill on which the town now stands. The DB form of the name below is corrupt. 1015 *Lutegaresheale*, DB *Litlegarsele*. SO ALSO: *Ludgershall*, Bucks.

Ludgvan (village, Cornwall): 'place of ashes'. Cornish *lusow*, 'ashes', + suffix *-an*, 'place of'. The reason for the name is uncertain. The reference may be to a former burial site. DB *Luduhan*.

Ludham (village, Norfolk): 'Luda's homestead'. OE *hām*, 'homestead', 'village'. DB *Ludham*.

Ludlow (town, Shropshire): '(place on the) mound by the noisy one'. OE *hlūde*, 'noisy one', + *hlāw*, 'mound', 'hill'. The 'noisy one' is the rapid current of a crossing over the river Teme here. Cp. LUDFORD. The 'mound' is a former large tumulus that was demolished in 1199 when the parish church was enlarged. 1138 *Ludelawe*.

Ludworth (village, Durham): 'Luda's enclosure'. OE *worth*, 'enclosure'. 12C *Ludeuurthe*.

Luffincott (hamlet, Devon): 'cottages of Luhha's people'. OE *-inga-*, 'of the people of', + *cot*, 'cottage'. 1242 *Lughyngecot*.

Luguvalium. See CARLISLE.

Lugwardine (village, Herefords): 'enclosure on the (river) Lugg'. OE *worthign*, 'enclosure'. The river has a Celtic name meaning 'bright stream'. DB *Lucvordine*.

Lullingstone (castle, Kent): 'Lulling's farmstead'. OE *tūn*, 'farmstead'. DB *Lolingestone*.

Lullington (village, Derbys): 'estate associated with Lulla'. OE *-ing-*, 'associated with', + *tūn*, 'farmstead', 'estate'. DB *Lullitune*. SO ALSO: *Lullington*, Somerset.

Lulsley (village, Worcs): 'Lull's island'. OE *ēg*, 'island'. The 'island' is low-lying land by the river Teme here. The *l* after *s* in the name is a relatively modern development. 12C *Lulleseia*, 1649 *Lullesey*.

Lulworth Cove. See EAST LULWORTH.

Lumby (hamlet, N Yorks): 'farmstead by a grove'. OS *lundr*, 'grove', + *bȳ*, 'farmstead'. 963 *Lundby*.

Lund (village, E Yorks): '(place by the) grove'. OS *lundr*, 'grove'. DB *Lont*. SO ALSO: *Lund*, E Yorks.

Lundy (island, Devon): 'puffin island'. OS *lundi*, 'puffin', + *ey*, 'island'. Lundy is still noted for its puffins, which are rare on the mainland. Cp. PUFFIN ISLAND. 1189 *Lundeia*.

Lune (river). See LANCASTER.

Luppitt (village, Devon): 'Lufa's pit'. OE *pytt*, 'pit', 'hollow'. DB *Lovapit*.

Lupton (hamlet, Cumbria): 'Hluppa's farmstead'. OE *tūn*, 'farmstead'. DB *Lupetun*.

Lurgashall (village, W Sussex): 'corner of land with a trapping spear'. OE *lūte-gār*, 'trapping spear' (from a word related to *lūtian*, 'to hide', 'to lurk', + *gār*, 'spear'), + *halh*, 'nook', 'corner of land'. Cp. LUDGERSHALL. 12C *Lutegareshale*.

Lustleigh (village, Devon): 'Lēofgiest's woodland clearing'. OE *lēah*, 'wood', 'clearing'. 1242 *Leuestelegh*.

Luston (village, Herefords): 'farmstead full of lice'. OE *lūs*, 'louse', + *tūn*, 'farmstead'. DB *Lustone*.

Luton (town, Luton): 'farmstead on the (river) Lea'. OE *tūn*, 'farmstead'. The named river rises north of the town and flows through it. The name itself is exactly the same in meaning as that of LEYTON, but the reason for the different forms is uncertain. 792 *Lygetun*, DB *Loitone*.

Luton Hoo (country house, Beds): 'spur of land near Luton'. OE *hōh*, 'spur of land'. The house is 2 miles southeast of LUTON and takes its name from it.

Lutterworth (town, Leics): 'enclosure on the (river) Lutter'. OE *worth*, 'enclosure'. The river here now is the Swift, but it seems to have been earlier known as the *Hlūtre*, 'clear one' (OE *hlūttor*, 'clear', 'bright'). DB *Lutresurde*.

Lutton (village, Northants): 'estate associated with Luda'. OE *tūn*, 'farmstead', 'estate'. The first form of the name below has an extraneous *n* in the personal name. c.970 *Lundingtun*, DB *Luditone*.

Luxborough (village, Somerset): 'Lulluc's stronghold'. OE *burh*, 'fortified place'. The second part of the name could also represent OE *beorg*, 'mound', 'hill'. DB *Lolochesberie*.

Luxulyan (village, Cornwall): 'chapel of St Sulyen'. Cornish *log*, 'chapel'. Sulyen was probably a Breton saint, and Cornish *log* has its counterpart in Brittany in the names of places such as *Locmaria*, 'St Mary's chapel', *Locronan*, 'St Ronan's chapel'. 1282 *Luxulian*.

Lydbury North (village, Shropshire): 'northern manor by the (river) Lyd'. OE *burh*, 'fortified place', 'manor'. The river here now is the Kemp, but it appears to have been originally known as the *Hlȳde*, 'loud one' (OE *hlūd*, 'loud'). The second word of the name distinguishes the village from LEDBURY, Herefords, some 40 miles to the southeast, but with a name of different origin. DB *Lideberie*, 1221 *Ledebir North*.

Lydd (town, Kent): '(place at the) gates'. OE *hlid*, 'covering', 'door', 'gate' (modern English *lid*). The 'gates' may have been ways of access to common pastureland here. The form of the name below represents the OE word in a dative plural form. 774 *Hlidum*.

Lydden (village, Kent): '(place in the) sheltered valley'. OE *hlēo*, 'shelter' (modern English *lee*), + *denu*, 'valley'. The village lies in a valley surrounded by hills northwest of Dover. c.1100 *Hleodaena*.

Lyddington (village, Rutland): 'farmstead associated with Hlȳda'. OE *-ing-*, 'associated with', + *tūn*, 'farmstead', 'estate'. The name could also mean 'farmstead on the loud stream' (OE *hlȳde*, 'loud one', + *tūn*). Lyddington lies on a tributary of the river Welland. DB *Lidentone*.

Lydeard St Lawrence. See BISHOP'S LYDEARD.

Lydford (village, Devon): '(place at the) ford over the (river) Lyd'. OE *ford*, 'ford'. The river name means 'loud one' (OE *hlȳde*). c.1000 *Hlydanforda*, DB *Lideforda*.

Lydham (village, Shropshire): '(place at the) slopes'. OE *hlid*, 'slope'. The name represents OE *hlidum*, the dative plural form of *hlid*. It is uncertain which slopes are meant. DB *Lidum*.

Lydiard Millicent (village, Wilts): 'Millisent's (place by the) grey ridge'. The first word of the name is of Celtic origin, from words related to modern Welsh *llwyd*, 'grey', and *garth*, 'hill'. One Millisent held the manor here in the late 12C, her name distinguishing the village from nearby *Lydiard Tregoze*, Swindon, held by the Tresgoz family. 901 *Lidgeard*, DB *Lidiarde*, 1275 *Lidiard Milisent*.

Lydiate (district, Sefton): '(place by the) swing gate'. OE *hlid-geat*, 'swing gate' (from *hlid*, 'door', 'gate', + *geat*, 'gap', 'gate'). The gate would have been used to prevent cattle straying from pasture on to arable land. The DB form of the name below is corrupt. DB *Leiate*, 1202 *Liddigate*.

Lydlinch (village, Dorset): '(place on a) ridge by the (river) Lydden'. OE *hlinc*, 'ridge', 'bank'. The name could also mean '(place on the) bank of the Lydden'. The river has a Celtic name meaning 'broad one' (modern Welsh *llydan*, 'broad'). 1182 *Lidelinz*.

Lydney (town, Glos): 'Lida's island'. OE *ēg*, 'island'. The 'island' is the area of land on which the town lies between two streams that enter the Severn to the south. The personal name means 'sailor', and the town's name itself could even mean 'sailor's island'. c.853 *Lideneg*, DB *Ledenei*.

Lyford (village, Oxon): '(place by the) ford where flax grows'. OE *līn*, 'flax' (related modern English *linen*), + *ford*, 'ford'. The ford in question was probably where Lyford Bridge crosses the river Ock here. 944 *Linforda*, DB *Linford*.

Lyme Regis (resort town, Dorset): 'king's (place on the river) Lim'. Latin *regis*, 'of the king'. The river has a Celtic name meaning simply 'river'. The town acquired its royal suffix at the end of the 13C, when Edward I declared it a free borough. 774 *Lim*, DB *Lime*, 1285 *Lyme Regis*.

Lyminge (village, Kent): 'district around the (river) Limen'. OE *gē*, 'district'. For the river name, see LYMPNE. 689 *Liminge*, DB *Leminges*.

Lymington (town, Hants): 'farmstead on the (river) Limen'. OE *tūn*, 'farmstead'. The river here now is the Lymington, but originally it must have been something like *Limen*, a Celtic name meaning 'elm river'. Cp. LEAMINGTON. The DB form of the name below is corrupt. DB *Lentune*, 1185 *Limington*.

Lyminster (village, W Sussex): 'monastery associated with Lulla'. OE *-ing-*, 'associated with', + *mynster*, 'monastery', 'large church'. c.880 *Lullyngmynster*, DB *Lolinminstre*.

Lymm (town, Warrington): '(place on the river) Lymm'. The river in question is Slitten Brook, running down a ravine in the middle of the town, which formerly had a name meaning 'noisy stream' (OE *hlimme*, 'torrent'). DB *Lime*.

Lympne (village, Kent): '(place on the river) Limen'. The river here now is the Rother, but at one time it was the *Limen*, a Celtic name meaning either 'elm river' or 'marshy river'. 4C *Lemanis*.

Lympsham (village, Somerset): '(place with a) homestead or enclosure'. OE *hām*, 'homestead', or *hamm*, 'enclosure'. The first part of the name is of uncertain origin, but may represent a personal name. 1189 *Limpelesham*.

Lympstone (village, Devon): 'Lēofwine's farmstead'. OE *tūn*, 'farmstead'. The DB form of the name below has omitted the *n* of the personal name. DB *Levestone*, 1238 *Leveneston*.

Lyndhurst (town, Hants): 'wooded hill with lime trees'. OE *lind*, 'lime', + *hyrst*, 'wooded hill'. The town has been nicknamed 'capital of the New Forest', although the trees there are not predominantly limes. DB *Linhest*.

Lyndon (village, Rutland): '(place by the) hill where lime trees grow'. OE *lind*, 'lime', + *dūn*, 'hill'. 1167 *Lindon*.

Lyneham (village, Wilts): 'homestead or enclosure where flax is grown'. OE *līn*, 'flax' (related modern English *linen*), + *hām*, 'homestead', or *hamm*, 'enclosure'. 1224 *Linham*. SO ALSO: *Lyneham*, Oxon.

Lynemouth (village, Northd): 'mouth of the (river) Lyne'. OE *mūtha*, 'mouth'. The river has a Celtic name meaning simply 'river'. 1342 *Lynmuth*.

Lyng (village, Norfolk): '(place by the) bank'. OE *hlinc*, 'bank', 'ridge'. The bank or ridge in question runs beside the river Wensum here. DB *Ling*.

Lyng (village, Somerset): 'long place'. OE *lengen*, 'length'. The name refers to a long, narrow settlement. The DB form of the name below has omitted the *n*. Early 10C *Lengen*, DB *Lege*.

Lynmouth (resort town, Devon): 'mouth of the (river) Lym'. OE *mūtha*, 'mouth'. The river name means 'torrent' (OE *hlynn*). 1330 *Lymmouth*.

Lynsted (village, Kent): 'place where lime trees grow'. OE *lind*, 'lime', + *stede*, 'place'. 1212 *Lindestede*.

Lynton (resort town, Devon): 'farmstead on the (river) Lyn'. OE *tūn*, 'farmstead'. The river name means 'torrent'. Cp. LYNMOUTH. DB *Lintone*.

Lyonshall (village, Herefords): 'corner of land in Leon'. OE *halh*, 'nook', 'corner of land'. For the district name, see LEOMINSTER. DB *Lenehalle*.

Lytchett Matravers. See LANGTON MATRAVERS.

Lytchett Minster (village, Dorset): '(place by the) grey wood with a large church'. OE *mynster*, 'monastery', 'large church'. The first word of the name is Celtic in origin, from words related to modern Welsh *llwyd*, 'grey', and *coed*, 'wood'. The second word distinguishes the village from nearby *Lytchett Matravers* (see LANGTON MATRAVERS). DB *Lichet*, 1244 *Licheminster*.

Lytham St Anne's (resort town, Lancs): '(place at the) slopes with St Anne's (church)'. OE *hlith*, 'slope'. The first (and original) word of the name represents OE *hlithum*, the dative plural form of *hlith*. The 'slopes' are probably those of the sandhills along the coast here. In 1922 Lytham amalgamated with nearby *St Anne's*, named after its parish church, built in 1873 as the first building to be constructed in a new planned town. *St Annes* (officially *St Annes-on-the-Sea*) is now a district of Lytham St Anne's. The site where St Annes arose was known as *Kilgrimol*, 'Kelgrímr's hollow' (OS *hol*, 'hollow', with a Scandinavian personal name), a name preserved in Kilgrimol Gardens here. DB *Lidun*.

Lythe (village, N Yorks): '(place on the) slope'. OS *hlíth*, 'hillside'. The slope in question borders on the coast to the north of Whitby. DB *Lid*.

M

Mabe Burnthouse (village, Cornwall): 'Mab's church site with the burnt house'. Cornish *lann*, 'church site'. The 'church site' element later disappeared from the name. The second word of the name is first recorded only in the 19C, and presumably alludes to a fire here. 1524 *Lavabe*, 1549 *Mape*.

Mablethorpe (resort town, Lincs): 'Malbert's outlying farmstead'. OS *thorp*, 'outlying farmstead'. The personal name is Old German. DB *Malbertorp*.

Macclesfield (town, Cheshire): 'Maccel's open country'. OE *feld*, 'open land' (modern English *field*). The 'open country' was probably part of the former forest in the Peak District here. DB *Maclesfeld*.

Macduff (town and port, Aberdeens): '(place of) Macduff'. The town owes its name to James Duff, 2nd Earl of Fife, who rebuilt the settlement here at the end of the 18C. He claimed to be descended from the semi-mythical Macduff in Shakespeare's *Macbeth*, but he actually named the town after his father, William Duff, 1st Earl of Fife, who had acquired land here earlier in the 18C. As Scottish 'Mac' means 'son of', the name can thus be seen as a tribute from a son to his father.

Machen (town, Caerphilly): 'Cein's plain'. Welsh *ma*, 'plain', 'low-lying ground'. The identity of Cein is unknown. 1102 *Mahhayn*.

Machynlleth (town, Powys): 'Cynllaith's plain'. Welsh *ma*, 'plain', 'low-lying ground'. The 'plain' was probably the low-lying ground on the left bank of the river Dyfi (Dovey) here. The 17C antiquarian William Camden claimed that the name derived from the former Roman station of *Maglona*, but this was actually the old fort at Carlisle. The identity of Cynllaith is unknown. 1254 *Machenleyd*.

Mackworth (village, Derby): 'Macca's enclosure'. OE *worth*, 'enclosure'. DB *Macheuorde*.

Maddington (hamlet, Wilts): 'estate of the maidens'. OE *mægden*, 'maiden', + *tūn*, 'farmstead', 'estate'. The 'maidens' are the nuns of Amesbury, who had a holding here in the 12C. Cp. MAIDEN BRADLEY. The place was originally *Winterbourne* (see WINTERBOURNE), from the earlier name of the infant river Till here. DB *Wintreburne*, 1178 *Maydenewynterburna*, 1198 *Medinton*.

Madehurst (hamlet, W Sussex): 'wooded hill by meadowland'. OE *mǣd*, 'meadow', + *hyrst*, 'wooded hill'. 1255 *Medhurst*.

Madeley (village, Staffs): 'Māda's woodland clearing'. OE *lēah*, 'wood', 'clearing'. 975 *Madanlieg*, DB *Madelie*. SO ALSO: *Madeley*, Wrekin.

Madingley (village, Cambs): 'woodland clearing of Māda's people'. OE *-inga-*, 'of the people of', + *lēah*, 'wood', 'clearing'. DB *Madingelei*.

Madley (village, Herefords): 'Māda's woodland clearing'. OE *lēah*, 'wood', 'clearing'. There is some uncertainty about the first part of the name, which may not be a personal name. DB *Medelagie*.

Madresfield (village, Worcs): 'open land of the mower'. OE *mǣthere*, 'mower', + *feld*, 'open land' (modern English *field*). The name could also mean 'Mǣthhere's open land'. *c.*1086 *Madresfeld*, 1192 *Metheresfeld*.

Madron (village, Cornwall): '(church of) St Madern'. The church here is dedicated to Madern, a saint about whom nothing is known. 1203 *Sanctus Madernus*, 1310 *Madern*.

Maenclochog (village, Pemb): '(place by the) stone sounding like a bell'. Welsh *maen*, 'stone', + *clochog*, 'sounding like a bell' (from *cloch*, 'bell', related English *clock*). According to Richard Fenton's *A Historical Tour through Pembrokeshire* (1811), there were two large stones near the church which had a ringing property. The first part of the name might thus perhaps represent Welsh plural *main*, 'stones'. 1257 *Maenclochawc*.

Maenorbŷr. See MANORBIER.

Maentwrog (village, Gwynedd): 'rock of St Twrog'. Welsh *maen*, 'rock', 'stone'. The stone in question is a plain round block, about 4 feet (1.2m) high, at the southwest corner of St Twrog's church, where it is traditionally said to mark the saint's grave. 1292 *Mayntwroc*.

Maer (village, Staffs): '(place by the) pool'. OE *mere*, 'pool'. There is a lake of about 25 acres in extent, the source of the river Tern, a tributary of the Severn' (*The National Gazetteer of Great Britain and Ireland*, 1868). DB *Mere*.

Maesbrook (hamlet, Shropshire): '(place by the) brook of the boundary'. OE *mǽre*, 'boundary', + *brōc*, 'brook'. The first part of the name could also represent Welsh *maes*, 'open field', 'plain', implying an erroneous DB form below. DB *Meresbroc*, 1272 *Maysbrok*.

Maesbury (hamlet, Shropshire): 'manor house of the boundary'. OE *mǽre*, 'boundary', + *burh*, 'fortified place', 'manor'. DB *Meresberie*.

Maesteg (town, Bridgend): '(place in the) fair field'. Welsh *maes*, 'field', + *teg*, 'fair'. The name was originally that of a farm here. When an ironworks was opened in 1826 on the site of the farm, the name was adopted for the industrial town that grew up round it.

Maesyfed. See NEW RADNOR.

Magdalen Laver. See HIGH LAVER.

Maghull (town, Sefton): 'corner of land where mayweed grows'. OE *mǽgthe*, 'mayweed', + *halh*, 'nook', 'corner of land'. There is no obvious 'corner of land' here, and it is possible the latter part of the name actually represents OE *hyll*, 'hill', which suits the topography better. The DB form of the name below is seemingly corrupt. DB *Magele*, 1219 *Maghal*.

Magnis. See KENCHESTER.

Maida Vale (district, Westminster): 'vale (of) Maida'. The district evolved in the mid-19C and was named for Sir John Stuart's victory over the French at the Battle of Maida (1806) in Calabria, Italy. 'Vale' refers to the fact that the new houses were built at the foot of a hill, which was called *Maida Hill*. *Maida*, 1822.

Maiden Bradley (village, Wilts): 'broad wood of the maidens'. OE *mǽgden*, 'maiden', + *brād*, 'broad', + *lēah*, 'wood', 'clearing'. The first word of the name, which also distinguishes the village from *North Bradley*, 13 miles to the north, refers to the nuns of Amesbury who had a cell here. DB *Bradelie*, early 13C *Maydene Bradelega*.

Maidenhead (town, Windsor & Maid): 'landing place of the maidens'. OE *mǽgden*, 'maiden', + *hŷth*, 'landing place'. Maidenhead is on the Thames, and the landing place may have been a place where young women regularly gathered rather than one where they actually landed. Any landing place is always a centre of activity, with much coming and going. 1202 *Maidenhee*, 1262 *Maydenhith*.

Maiden Newton (village, Dorset): 'new estate of the maidens'. OE *mǽgden*, 'maiden', + *nīwe*, 'new', + *tūn*, 'farmstead', 'estate'. The first word of the name may allude to the early possession of the manor by nuns here. DB *Newetone*, 1288 *Maydene Neweton*.

Maiden Wells (hamlet, Pemb): '(place by the) spring of the maidens'. OE *mǽgden*, 'maiden', + *wielle*, 'spring'. The name may refer to a spring here visited by girls and young women in connection with fertility rites. 1336 *Mayden Welle*.

Maidford (village, Northants): '(place by the) ford of the maidens'. OE *mǽgden*, 'maiden', + *ford*, 'ford'. The ford over a tributary of the river Tove here would have been a regular meeting place for young women and girls. The DB form of the name below is corrupt. DB *Merdeford*, 1166 *Maideneford*.

Maids' Moreton (village, Bucks): 'farmstead in moorland of the maidens'. OE *mōr*, 'moor', 'marshy ground', + *tūn*, 'farmstead', 'estate'. According to George Lipscomb's *History and Antiquities of the County of Buckingham* (1847), the first word of the name refers to a tradition that the church here was built in the 15C by two maiden ladies of the Peyvre family. DB *Mortone*, c.1488 *Maidenes Morton*.

Maidstone (town, Kent): 'stone of the maidens'. OE *mǽgden*, 'maiden', + *stān*, 'stone'. As for MAIDENHEAD, the name describes a regular meeting place for young women and girls. The stone in question would probably have been a focal point for traditional ceremonies. Late 10C *Mægthan stan*, DB *Meddestane*.

Maidwell (village, Northants): '(place by the) spring of the maidens'. OE *mǽgden*, 'maiden', + *wella*, 'spring', 'stream'. The reference is to a spring or stream where young women and girls gathered. Cp. CHILWELL. DB *Medewelle*.

Mainland (island, Orkney): 'chief district'. OS *megin*, 'main', + *land*, 'land'. Mainland, Orkney, and Mainland, Shetland, are not only the largest islands in their respective groups but the most important administratively. OS *megin* is a noun, as in English 'might and main'. c.1150 *Meginland*.

Mainstone (village, Shropshire): '(place by the) stone of strength'. OE *mægen*, 'might', 'strength', + *stān*, 'stone'. The stone in question is a small boulder here used by local young men as a test of muscular strength in which it was raised to the height of the face, then thrown over the left shoulder. The stone formerly lay outside the church but is now installed inside it. 1284 *Meyneston*.

Maisemore (village, Glos): '(place in the) great field'. Welsh *maes*, 'field', + *mawr*, 'big'. 1138 *Mayesmora*.

Malborough (village, Devon): 'Mærla's hill'. OE *beorg*, 'hill', 'mound'. The name could also mean 'hill where gentian grows' (OE *meargealla*, 'gentian', + *beorg*). Cp. MARLBOROUGH. 1249 *Malleberge*.

Maldon (town, Essex): 'hill with a crucifix'. OE *mæl*, 'cross', 'crucifix', + *dūn*, 'hill'. Maldon stands in a commanding position over the river Blackwater, and the Anglo-Saxons probably erected a crucifix here as a focus for religious services. The actual site may have been the one on which All Saints church now stands. Early 10C *Mældune*, DB *Malduna*.

Malham (village, N Yorks): '(settlement by the) gravelly places'. OS *malgr*, 'gravelly place'. The second part of the name represents a dative plural ending. The 'gravelly places' could be scattered boulders or the like. DB *Malgun*.

Mallaig (town and port, Highland): 'bay of gulls'. OS *mar*, 'gull', + *vágr*, 'bay'. There are gulls in most sea bays, so their presence here must have been in some way remarkable.

Malmesbury (town, Wilts): 'Maeldub's stronghold'. OE *burh*, 'fortified place'. The Old Irish personal name, meaning 'black chief', has been influenced by that of Bishop Aldhelm, who built a chapel here in the 7C. 685 *Maldumesburg*, DB *Malmesberie*.

Malpas (town, Cheshire): '(place at the) difficult passage'. OF *mal*, 'bad', + *pas*, 'pass'. The reference is to the Roman road from Chester to Wroxeter, which must have become a miry track here in the valley of Bradley Brook. The earlier DB name below means '(place at the) deep valley with a stream in it' (OE *dēop*, 'deep', + *bece*, 'stream'). DB *Depenbach*, *c*.1125 *Malpas*.

Malpas (village, Cornwall): '(place at the) difficult passage'. OF *mal*, 'bad', + *pas*, 'pass'. There must have been an unpleasant river crossing here, at the confluence of the Tresillian and Truro. There is now a ferry. Late 12C *Le Mal Pas*.

Maltby (town, Rotherham): 'Malti's farm'. OS *bý*, 'farm'. Instead of the Scandinavian personal name, the first part of the name could be OS

malt, 'malt', giving a meaning 'farm where malt is made'. DB *Maltebi*. SO ALSO: *Maltby*, Stockton.

Maltby le Marsh (village, Lincs): 'Malti's farm by the marsh'. OS *bý*, 'farm'. The personal name is Scandinavian. The village is on low-lying ground near the coast. DB *Maltebi*.

Malton (town, N Yorks): 'farmstead where an assembly is held'. OE *mæthel*, 'assembly', + *tūn*, 'farmstead'. The first part of the name could equally be OS *methal*, 'middle', giving a meaning 'middle farm'. The Roman fort here was *Derventio*, named after the river Derwent (see DERWENT WATER). The town was long alternatively known as *New Malton* for distinction from the adjoining village of *Old Malton*, and these are still separate parish names. DB *Maltune*.

Malvern Hills (hill range, Worcs): 'bare hill'. The name is Celtic, from words related to modern Welsh *moel*, 'bare', and *bryn*, 'hill'. The Malvern Hills have given the names of many local places, including the town of *Great Malvern*, villages of *Little Malvern* and *West Malvern*, hamlet of *Malvern Wells*, and district of Great Malvern, *Malvern Link*, whose second word represents OE *hlinc*, 'ledge', 'terrace' (modern English *link* in 'golf links'). *c*.1030 *Mælfern*, DB *Malferna*.

Mamble (village, Worcs): '(place by the) breast-shaped hill'. The name is Celtic in origin. Cp. MAM TOR. DB *Mamele*.

Mam Tor (hill, Derbys): 'breast-shaped hill'. The first word of the name is Celtic, related to modern Welsh *mam*, 'mother' (and indirectly English *mammary*). The second word is OE *torr*, 'rocky hill'. 1577 *Manhill*, 1630 *Mantaur*.

Mamucium. See MANCHESTER.

Manaccan (village, Cornwall): '(church of) St Manacca'. The church here now is dedicated to St Dunstan, but was earlier dedicated to the 5C or 6C Irish abbess Manacca. 1309 *Sancta Manaca*, 1395 *Managhan*, 1868 *Manaccan, or Monathon*.

Manacles, The (group of rocks, Cornwall): 'church rocks'. Cornish *men*, 'stone', + *eglos*, 'church' (cp. ECCLES). The name refers either to the sharpness of the rocks, like church spires, or possibly to the actual spire of the church at St Keverne, serving as a landmark from the sea here, northeast of Lizard Point. *c*.1605 *Manacles*, 1619 *Mannahackles alias Manacles*.

Manaton (village, Devon): 'communal farmstead'. OE *mǣne*, 'communal', 'held in common' (related modern English *man*), + *tūn*, 'farmstead'. The name could also mean 'Manna's farmstead'. DB *Manitone*.

Mancetter (village, Warwicks): 'Roman station at Manduessedum'. OE *ceaster*, 'Roman camp'. The name of the Roman station is of Celtic origin and means 'horse chariot' (Gaulish *essedum* is related to modern Welsh *sedd*, 'seat'), perhaps referring to some local topographical feature. 1195 *Manacestre*.

Manchester (city, Manchester): 'Roman station of Mamucium'. OE *ceaster*, 'Roman fort'. The name of the Roman station here (not *Mancunium*, as often stated) probably derives from a local hill name of Celtic origin meaning 'breast-shaped', as for MAM TOR. The fort itself was probably at the confluence of the rivers Irwell and Medlock. DB *Mamecestre*.

Manduessedum. See MANCETTER.

Manea (village, Cambs): '(place on an) island'. OE *ēg*, 'island'. The first part of the name is of uncertain origin. The 'island' is well-watered land here in the fens. 1177 *Moneia*.

Manfield (village, N Yorks): 'Manna's open land'. OE *feld*, 'open land' (modern English *field*). The name could also mean 'open land held communally' (OE *mǣne*, 'communal', + *feld*). DB *Mannefelt*.

Mangotsfield (town, S Glos): 'Mangod's open land'. OE *feld*, 'open land' (modern English *field*). The personal name is Old German. DB *Manegodesfelle*.

Manley (village, Cheshire): '(place in a) common wood or clearing'. OE *mǣne*, 'communal' (related modern English *man*), + *lēah*, 'wood', 'clearing'. DB *Menlie*.

Manningford Bruce (village, Wilts): 'Breuse's (estate by the) ford of Manna's people'. OE *-inga-*, 'of the people of', + *ford*, 'ford'. The ford was by the mill over the river Avon here. The Breuse family held the manor here in the 13C, their name distinguishing this village from nearby *Manningford Abbots*, where it was held by the Abbot of Hyde, Winchester, and *Manningford Bohune*, where it was held by the de Boun family. 987 *Maningaford*, DB *Maniford*, 1279 *Manyngeford Breuse*.

Mannington (hamlet, Dorset): 'estate associated with Manna'. OE *-ing-*, 'associated with', + *tūn*, 'farmstead', 'estate'. DB *Manitone*.

Manningtree (town, Essex): 'Manna's tree'. OE *trēow*, 'tree'. The name could equally mean '(place of) many trees', with the first part representing OE *manig*, 'many'. 1248 *Manitre*.

Manorbier (village, Pemb): 'Pŷr's manor'. Welsh *maenor*, 'manor'. It is not certain who Pŷr was, or whether he was the same person who gave the name of *Ynys Bŷr*, the Welsh name of CALDY ISLAND. The Welsh name of Manorbier is *Maenorbŷr*. 1136 *Mainour pir*, 1331 *Manerbire*.

Manordeifi (hamlet, Pemb): 'estate on the (river) Teifi'. Welsh *maenor*, 'manor', 'estate'. The river name is of Celtic origin and means simply 'stream'. In the first form of the name below, *Main-* has been miscopied as *Mam-*. 1219 *Mamardeyvi*, 1291 *Menordaun*.

Manorowen (hamlet, Pemb): 'Gnawan's manor'. Welsh *maenor*, 'manor'. 1326 *Maynornawan*.

Mansell Lacy (village, Herefords): 'de Lacy's (estate by the) hill of the gravel ridge'. OE *malu*, 'sand', 'gravel', + *hyll*, 'hill'. The de Lacy family held the manor here in 1086. Their name distinguishes this village from nearby *Mansell Gamage*, where the manor was held in the 12C by the de Gamagis family. c.1045 *Mǣlueshylle*, DB *Malveselle*, 1242 *Maumeshull Lacy*.

Mansfield (town, Notts): 'open land by the (river) Maun'. OE *feld*, 'open land' (modern English *field*). The river derives its name from that of a hill about 4 miles away formerly known as *Mammeshead*. This means 'headland of Mam', the latter being the Celtic name of the hill itself, in turn meaning 'breast-shaped'. Cp. MAM TOR. DB *Mamesfelde*.

Mansfield Woodhouse (town, Notts): 'woodland hamlet near Mansfield'. OE *wudu*, 'wood', + *hūs*, 'house', 'hamlet'. The town lies immediately north of MANSFIELD and has taken its name. The name overall thus implies that a separate settlement was established here by people from Mansfield. 1230 *Wodehuse*, 1280 *Mamesfeud Wodehus*.

Manston (suburb of Ramsgate, Kent): 'Mann's farmstead'. OE *tūn*, 'farmstead'. 1254 *Manneston*. SO ALSO: *Manston*, Dorset.

Manthorpe (village, Lincs): 'Manni's outlying farmstead'. OS *thorp*, 'outlying farmstead', 'secondary settlement'. The personal name is Scandinavian. The form of the name below relates to Manthorpe near Grantham, although Manthorpe near Thurlby has a name of identical origin. 1185 *Mannetorp*.

Manton (hamlet, N Lincs): 'farmstead on sandy soil'. OE *malm*, 'sand', + *tūn*, 'farmstead'. 'Soil light, sandy, and black peat, overlying ironstone' (*Cassell's Gazetteer of Great Britain and Ireland*, 1896). 1060 *Malmetun*, DB *Mameltune*.

Manton (village, Rutland): 'Manna's farmstead'. OE *tūn*, 'farmstead', 'estate'. 1120 *Mannatonam*, c.1130 *Manatona*.

Manuden (village, Essex): 'valley of Manna's people'. OE -*inga*-, 'of the people of', + *denu*, 'valley'. The DB form of the name below has garbled the personal name. DB *Magghedana*, *c*.1130 *Manegedan*.

Maplebeck (village, Notts): '(place by the) stream where maple trees grow'. OE *mapel*, 'maple', + OS *bekkr*, 'stream'. DB *Mapelbec*.

Mapledurham (village, Oxon): 'homestead where maple trees grow'. OE *mapuldor*, 'maple tree', + *hām*, 'homestead'. DB *Mapeldreham*.

Mapleton (village, Derbys): 'farmstead where maple trees grow'. OE *mapel*, 'maple', + *tūn*, 'farmstead'. The name is also spelt *Mappleton*. DB *Mapletune*.

Mapperley (village, Derbys): 'wood or clearing where maple trees grow'. OE *mapuldor*, 'maple tree', + *lēah*, 'wood', 'clearing'. DB *Maperlie*.

Mapperton (hamlet, Dorset): 'farmstead where maple trees grow'. OE *mapuldor*, 'maple tree', + *tūn*, 'farmstead'. The form of the name below is for Mapperton near Beaminster. DB *Malperetone*.

Mappleton (village, E Yorks): 'farmstead where maple trees grow'. OE *mapel*, 'maple', + *tūn*, 'farmstead'. DB *Mapletone*.

Mappowder (village, Dorset): '(place by the) maple tree'. OE *mapuldor*, 'maple tree'. DB *Mapledre*.

Marazion (coastal town, Cornwall): '(place with a) little market'. Cornish *marghas*, 'market', + *byghan*, 'little'. The market here would have been 'little' by comparison with that at Penzance, 3 miles away. The alternative name of Marazion is *Market Jew*, 'Thursday market' (Cornish *marghas*, 'market', + *yow*, 'Thursday'). Hence Market Jew Street, Penzance, leading east towards Marazion. This name gave rise to a story that Jews were banished by Roman emperors to Cornwall to work in the tin mines. 'Then a town among us, too, which we call Market Jew, but the old name was Marazion, that means the Bitterness of Zion, they tell me; and bitter work it was for them, no doubt, poor souls!' (Charles Kingsley, *Yeast*, 1851). *c*.1265 *Marghasbigan*, 1868 *Marazion, or Market-Jew*.

March (town, Cambs): '(place at the) boundary'. OE *mearc*, 'boundary' (modern English *mark*). March is not on a county boundary, but it may have been at the western limit of the district of ELY. The name was originally that of a settlement some 2 miles south of the present town, near the old church of St Wendreda. The

OE word gave the name in an old locative form. DB *Merche*.

Marcham (village, Oxon): '(place by the) river meadow where smallage grows'. OE *merece*, 'smallage' (wild celery), + *hamm*, 'river meadow'. The river here is the Ock. 900 *Merchamme*, DB *Merceham*.

Marchamley (village, Shropshire): 'Merchelm's woodland clearing'. OE *lēah*, 'wood', 'clearing'. The name could also mean 'woodland clearing in the (territory of the) Mercians', the first part of the name representing OE *Mierce*, 'Mercians', in the dative plural form *Miercum*. Marchamley is in the northeast of the county, within the territory of the Anglo-Saxon kingdom of Mercia. DB *Marcemeslei*, 1227 *Marchemeleg*.

Marchington (village, Staffs): 'farmstead of the dwellers at a homestead where smallage grows'. OE *merece*, 'smallage' (wild celery), + *hǣme*, 'dwellers' (related modern English *home*), + *tūn*, 'farmstead'. 1002 *Mæchamtun*, DB *Merchametone*.

Marchwood (village, Hants): '(place by the) wood where smallage grows'. OE *merece*, 'smallage' (wild celery), + *wudu*, 'wood'. DB *Merceode*.

Marden (village, Herefords): 'enclosed settlement in Maund'. OE *worthign*, 'enclosure'. The district name may mean 'place at the hollows' (OE *maga*, 'stomach', in a transferred sense) or else represent a Celtic name *Magnis*, meaning '(place) at the rocks', as for the Roman name of KENCHESTER. Marden is barely 4 miles from MAUND BRYAN, with a similar name. The DB form of the name below is corrupt. DB *Maurdine*, 1177 *Magewurdin*.

Marden (village, Kent): 'woodland pasture where mares are kept'. OE *mere*, 'mare', + *denn*, 'woodland pasture'. The first part of the name could also represent OE *mǣre*, 'boundary'. *c*.1100 *Maeredaen*.

Marden (village, Wilts): '(place in the) boundary valley'. OE *mearc*, 'boundary' (modern English *mark*), + *denu*, 'valley'. The river Avon here forms the boundary between the parishes of Marden and Beechingstoke. 941 *Mercdene*, DB *Meresdene*, 1868 *Marden, or Merton*.

Marefield (hamlet, Leics): 'open land where martens are seen'. OE *mearth*, 'marten', 'weasel', + *feld*, 'open land' (modern English *field*). DB *Merdefelde*.

Mareham le Fen (village, Lincs): '(place by the) pools in the marshland'. OE *mere*, 'pool'. The main name represents OE *merum*, the dative plural form of *mere*. The second part of the name distinguishes the village from *Mareham*

on the Hill, 4 miles to the north. DB *Marun*, *c.*1200 *Marum*.

Maresfield (village, E Sussex): 'open land by a pool'. OE *mere*, 'pool', + *feld*, 'open land' (modern English *field*). There are still pools nearby, including one formerly used to provide water power for the iron mill here. 1234 *Mersfeld*.

Marfleet (district, Hull): '(place by the) pool stream'. OE *mere*, 'pool', + *flēot*, 'stream'. A small stream here flows from a pool, now a swamp, into the river Hull. DB *Mereflet*.

Margaret Marsh (village, Dorset): 'Margaret's (land on the) marsh with a church'. OE *mersc*, 'marsh', + *cirice*, 'church'. The 'church' part of the name later disappeared. The village church is dedicated to St Margaret, but the name was originally that of an early owner of the site here (perhaps an abbess of Shaftesbury Abbey). 1395 *Maragaretysmerschchurche*, 1575 *Margaret Marsh*.

Margaret Roding. See RODINGS.

Margaretting (village, Essex): '(manor called) Ing of St Margaret'. For the manor name, see INGATESTONE. The church here is dedicated to St Margaret. DB *Ginga*, 1291 *Gynge Margarete*.

Margate (resort town, Kent): 'gate to the sea'. OE *mere*, 'pool', 'sea', + *geat*, 'gate'. The 'gate' would have been a gap in the cliffs here which either led to the sea or passed by a particular pool. (The town's Latin motto is *Porta maris, portus salutis*, 'Gate to the sea, haven of health'.) 1254 *Meregate*.

Margidunum. See WEST BRIDGFORD.

Marham (village, Norfolk): 'homestead by a pond'. OE *mere*, 'pond', + *hām*, 'homestead'. There is no pond here now. *c.*1050 *Merham*, DB *Marham*.

Marhamchurch (village, Cornwall): 'church of St Marwen'. OE *cirice*, 'church'. The church here is dedicated to Marwen, according to Cornish tradition one of the daughters of Brychan (see BRECON), although she could also be Merewenna, 10C Abbess of Romsey, Hants. DB *Maronecirce*.

Marholm (village, Peterborough): 'homestead by a pond'. OE *mere*, 'pool', 'pond', + *hām*, 'homestead'. There are ponds by the manor here. *c.*1060 *Marham*.

Mariansleigh (village, Devon): '(place by the) wood or clearing with St Marina's church'. OE *lēah*, 'wood', 'clearing'. The church here now is dedicated to St Mary, but earlier it was presumably dedicated to Marina (or perhaps Marian, as a diminutive of Mary). DB *Lege*, 1238 *Marinelegh*.

Mark (village, Somerset): 'building by a boundary'. OE *mearc*, 'boundary', + *ærn*, 'building'. The second part of the original name has disappeared. 1065 *Mercern*.

Markby (village, Lincs): 'Marke's farmstead'. OS *bȳ*, 'farmstead', 'village'. The personal name is Scandinavian. DB *Marchebi*.

Markeaton (district, Derby): 'Mearca's farmstead'. OE *tūn*, 'farmstead'. DB *Marchetone*.

Market Bosworth (town, Leics): 'Bōsa's enclosure with a market'. OE *worth*, 'enclosure'. The addition of the first word (ME *merket*, 'market') emphasizes the importance of the market here and also distinguishes this Bosworth from *Husbands Bosworth*, 'Bār's enclosure of the farmers' (late OE *hūsbonda*, 'husbandman'), 20 miles to the southeast. DB *Boseworde*.

Market Deeping (town, Lincs): 'deep place with a market'. ME *merket*, 'market', + OE *dēoping*, 'deep place'. The name alludes to the location of the town in the fens and applies equally to neighbouring *Deeping St James* and *Deeping St Nicholas*, named for their church dedications, and *West Deeping*, to the west, collectively known as *The Deepings*. DB *Depinge*, 1412 *Markyddepyng*.

Market Drayton (town, Shropshire): 'farmstead by a portage with a market'. ME *merket*, 'market', + OE *dræg*, 'portage' (modern English *drag*, *draw*), + *tūn*, 'farmstead'. Market Drayton is on the river Tern, and there must have been a place where boats were dragged from the water or loads hauled to or from it. The first word indicates the important commercial activity here. DB *Draitune*.

Market Harborough (town, Leics): '(place by a) hill where oats are grown with a market'. ME *merket*, 'market', + OS *hafri* or OE *hæfera*, 'oats', + OS *berg* or OE *beorg*, 'hill'. The first part of the second word could also represent OE *hæfer* or OS *hafr*, 'he-goat', giving a meaning 'hill where goats are kept'. The first word indicates the importance of the market. The second alone is now the name of the local council district of *Harborough*. 1153 *Haverbergam*, 1312 *Mercat Heburgh*.

Market Jew. See MARAZION.

Market Lavington (village, Wilts): 'estate associated with Lāfa with a market'. OE *-ing-*, 'associated with', + *tūn*, 'farmstead', 'estate'. The first word of the name was added in the 17C to distinguish this Lavington from nearby *West Lavington*. DB *Laventone*, 1681 *Steeple Lavington al. Markett Lavington*, 1868 *East, or Market Lavington*.

Market Overton (village, Rutland): 'farmstead on a ridge with a market'. ME *merket* + OE *ofer*, 'ridge', + *tūn*, 'farmstead'. The first part of the main name could also represent OE *ōfer*, 'bank', giving a sense 'farmstead by a bank'. DB *Overtune*, 1200 *Marketesoverton*.

Market Rasen (town, Lincs): '(place at the) planks with a market'. ME *merket*, 'market', + *ræsn*, 'plank'. The 'planks' would either have been laid over marshy ground or formed a plank bridge over the river Rase (named after the town). The second word of the name represents the OE word in a dative plural form. The first word emphasizes the importance of the market and also distinguishes this Rasen from nearby *Middle Rasen* and *West Rasen*, respectively 2 and 3 miles away. The first form of the name below means simply 'at the planks'. 973 *æt ræsnan*, DB *Resne*, 1358 *Marketrasyn*.

Market Weighton (town, E Yorks): 'farmstead by a settlement with a market'. OE *wīc*, 'settlement', + *tūn*, 'farmstead'. Market Weighton lies on a Roman road, and the 'settlement' would have been a Romano-British *vicus* or village. The first word of the name was added in the 19C to denote the importance of the market and to distinguish this Weighton from *Little Weighton*, 9 miles to the southeast, although its name means 'farmstead where willow trees grow' (OE *withig*, 'willow', + *tūn*). DB *Wicstun*.

Markfield (village, Leics): 'open land of the Mercians'. OE *Merce*, 'Mercians', + *feld*, 'open land' (modern English *field*). Mercia was the kingdom in central England established by the Angles in the 6C. The first part of the name represents OE *Mercna*, the genitive plural form of *Merce*. DB *Merchenefeld*.

Markinch (town, Fife): 'meadow where horses are kept'. Gaelic *marc*, 'horse', + *innis*, 'island', 'riverside meadow'. Markinch is on the river Leven. 1055 *Marchinke*, c.1290 *Markynchs*.

Markington (village, N Yorks): 'farmstead of the Mercians'. OE *Merce*, 'Mercians', + *tūn*, 'farmstead'. Cp. MARKFIELD. The name could also mean 'farmstead of the boundary dwellers' or 'farmstead by a boundary' (OE *merce*, 'boundary', + *-inga-*, 'of the dwellers at', or *-ing*, 'place characterized by', + *tūn*). c.1030 *Mercingtune*, DB *Merchinton*.

Marksbury (village, Bath & NE Somerset): 'Mæerc's or Mearc's stronghold'. OE *burh*, 'fortified place'. The stronghold in question presumably have been on Stantonbury Hill here. The name could also mean 'stronghold by the boundary' (OE *mearc*, 'boundary', + *burh*),

with a presumed reference to Wansdyke nearby. 936 *Merkesburi*, DB *Mercesberie*.

Marks Tey (village, Essex): 'de Merck's enclosure'. OE *tīege*, 'enclosure' (modern English dialect *tye*). The de Merck family held the manor here, their name distinguishing this village from *Great Tey*, 2 miles to the northwest, and *Little Tey*, 3 miles to the west. c.950 *Tygan*, DB *Teia*, 1475 *Merkys Teye*.

Markyate (village, Herts): 'gate at the boundary'. OE *mearc*, 'boundary' (modern English *mark*), + *geat*, 'gate'. Markyate is close to the county border with Bedfordshire, and the 'gate' would have led into the former forest here. 12C *Markyate*.

Marlborough (town, Wilts): 'Mæerla's hill'. OE *beorg*, 'hill', 'mound'. The name could also mean '(place by the) hill where gentian grows' (OE *meargealla*, 'gentian', + *beorg*). The plant would have been used for its medicinal properties. The name is popularly said to mean 'Merlin's hill', on the basis that the magician of Arthurian legend is supposedly buried in the Castle Mound here. DB *Merleberge*.

Marlcliff (village, Warwicks): 'Mearna's cliff'. OE *clif*, 'cliff', 'bank'. 872 *Mearnanclyfe*.

Marldon (village, Devon): '(place by the) hill where gentian grows'. OE *meargealla*, 'gentian', + *dūn*, 'hill'. 1307 *Mergheldone*.

Marlesford (village, Suffolk): 'Mæerel's ford'. OE *ford*, 'ford'. The river here is the Alde. DB *Merlesforda*.

Marlingford (village, Norfolk): '(place by the) ford of Mearthel's people'. OE *-inga-*, 'of the people of', + *ford*, 'ford'. The ford in question would have been over the stream here, a tributary of the river Yare. c.1000 *Marthingforth*, DB *Marthingeforda*.

Marlow (town, Bucks): '(place by the) lake leavings'. OE *mere*, 'pool', 'lake', + *lāf*, 'thing left'. The name implies a place that arose by the remains of a lake, which would itself have been linked to the river Thames here. 1015 *Merelafan*, DB *Merlaue*.

Marnhull (village, Dorset): 'Mearna's hill'. OE *hyll*, 'hill'. 1267 *Marnhulle*.

Marple (town, Stockport): 'pool by the boundary'. OE *mære*, 'boundary', 'border', + *pyll*, 'pool'. The pool is one in the river Goyt here, while the boundary is the historic one between the counties of Cheshire and Derbyshire. Early 13C *Merpille*.

Marr (village, Doncaster): '(place by the) marsh'. OS *marr*, 'marsh'. Marr stands on a hillside, so that the name presumably refers to a former marshy site below it. DB *Marra*.

Marrick (village, N Yorks): '(place by the) boundary ridge'. OE *mǣre*, 'boundary', + *hrycg*, 'ridge'. The nature of the boundary is uncertain. DB *Marige*.

Marsden (town, Kirklees): 'boundary valley'. OE *mearc*, 'boundary', + *denu*, 'valley'. Marsden lies on the river Colne in a deep valley. The boundary is the historic one, 2 miles to the southwest of the town, between the counties of Yorkshire and Lancashire. 12C *Marchesden*.

Marsham (village, Norfolk): 'homestead by a marsh'. OE *mersc*, 'marsh', + *hām*, 'homestead', 'village'. DB *Marsam*.

Marsh Baldon (village, Oxon): 'Bealda's hill by a marsh'. OE *mersc*, 'marsh', + *dūn*, 'hill'. The first word of the name distinguishes this village from nearby *Toot Baldon* (OE *tōt*, 'lookout hill'). DB *Baldedone*, 1241 *Mersse Baldindon*.

Marsh Chapel (village, Lincs): '(place in the) marsh with a chapel'. OE *mersc*, 'marsh'. The place was long known as either *Fulstow Marsh* (referring to nearby FULSTOW) or *Marsh Chapel*. The latter name, referring to the chapel there, eventually prevailed. 1277 *Fulestowmersk*, 1347 *Mersch Chapel*.

Marshfield (village, S Glos): 'open land by the boundary'. OE *mǣre*, 'boundary', + *feld*, 'open land' (modern English *field*). Marshfield is close to the county boundaries with both Wiltshire and Somerset. A meaning 'open land by a marsh' (OE *mersc*, 'marsh', + *feld*) has also been proposed, but this cannot be justified topographically. DB *Meresfelde*.

Marsh Gibbon (village, Bucks): 'Gibwen's (estate by the) marsh'. OE *mersc*, 'marsh'. The Gibwen family held the manor here in the 12C. DB *Merse*, 1292 *Mersh Gibwyne*.

Marshwood (village, Dorset): '(place at the) wood by a marsh'. OE *mersc*, 'marsh', + *wudu*, 'wood'. 1188 *Merswude*.

Marske (village, N Yorks): '(place by the) marsh'. OE *mersc*, 'marsh'. DB *Mersche*.

Marske-by-the-Sea (resort town, Redcar & Clev): '(place at the) marsh by the sea'. OE *mersc*, 'marsh'. Marske lies on marshy terrain by the North Sea. The '-sk-' of the name is due to Scandinavian influence. The latter part of the name distinguishes the town from MARSKE, N Yorks, 37 miles to the southwest. DB *Mersc*.

Marston (suburb of Oxford, Oxon): 'farmstead by a marsh'. OE *mersc*, 'marsh', + *tūn*, 'farmstead'. c.1069 *Mersttune*.

Marston Magna (village, Somerset): 'greater farmstead by a marsh'. OE *mersc*, 'marsh', + *tūn*, 'farmstead', + Latin *magna*, 'great'. The second word of the name distinguishes this Marston from *Marston Bigot*, 17 miles to the north, where the manor was held by the le Bigod family. DB *Merstone*, 1248 *Great Merston*.

Marston Meysey. See MEYSEY HAMPTON.

Marston Montgomery (village, Derbys): 'de Mungumeri's farmstead by a marsh'. OE *mersc*, 'marsh', + *tūn*, 'farmstead'. The manor here was held in the 13C by the de Mungumeri family, their name distinguishing this Marston from *Marston on Dove*, 9 miles to the southeast, on the river Dove (see DOVE DALE). 1243 *Merstone*, c.1350 *Marston Mountegomery*.

Marston Moor (upland region, N Yorks): 'moor by a farmstead in a marsh'. OE *mersc*, 'marsh', + *tūn*, 'farmstead', + *mōr*, 'moor'. The moor takes its name from the village of *Long Marston*, near York. 1281 *mora de Marston*, 1499 *Marston More*.

Marston Moretaine (village, Beds): 'Morteyn's farmstead by a marsh'. OE *mersc*, 'marsh', + *tūn*, 'farmstead'. The manor here was held early by the Morteyn family. DB *Merestone*, 1383 *Merston Morteyn*.

Marston on Dove. See MARSTON MONTGOMERY.

Marston Trussell (village, Northants): 'Trussel's farmstead by a marsh'. OE *mersc*, 'marsh', + *tūn*, 'farmstead'. The Trussel family held the manor here in the 13C. DB *Mersitone*, 1235 *Merston Trussel*.

Marstow (hamlet, Herefords): 'St Martin's church'. OE *stōw*, 'holy place'. The name comes from the dedication of the church (now to St Matthew). In the first form of the name below, OW *lann* (modern Welsh *llan*) is the equivalent of OE *stōw*. c.1130 *Lann Martin*, 1291 *Martinestowe*.

Marsworth (village, Bucks): 'Mæssa's enclosure'. OE *worth*, 'enclosure'. The DB form of the name below is garbled. 10C *Mæssanwyrth*, DB *Missevorde*.

Marthall (hamlet, Cheshire): 'corner of land where martens are seen'. OE *mearth*, 'marten', 'weasel', + *halh*, 'nook', 'corner of land'. Late 13C *Marthale*.

Martham (village, Norfolk): 'homestead or enclosure where martens are seen'. OE *mearth*, 'marten', 'weasel', + *hām*, 'homestead', or *hamm*, 'enclosure'. DB *Martham*.

Martin (village, Hants): 'farmstead by the boundary'. OE *mǣre*, 'boundary', + *tūn*, 'farmstead'. The village was formerly in Wiltshire near the border with Hampshire and Dorset. The name could also mean 'farmstead by a pool', as for MARTIN, Lincs. 946 *Mertone*.

Martin (village, Lincs): 'farmstead by a pool'. OE *mere*, 'pool', + *tūn*, 'farmstead'. The form of the name below applies to Martin near Woodhall Spa, although Martin near Horncastle has a name of identical origin. 12C *Martona*.

Martindale (hamlet, Cumbria): 'St Martin's valley'. OS *dalr*, 'valley'. The reference is to the old St Martin's church, in the valley of the Howe Grain. It is possible that the valley was owned by a man called Martin, and that this gave the church dedication, as for PATTERDALE. 1256 *Martindale*.

Martinhoe (coastal village, Devon): 'hill spur of Matta's people'. OE *-inga-*, 'of the people of', + *hōh*, 'hill spur'. DB *Matingeho*.

Martin Hussingtree (village, Worcs). Originally two separate places: *Martin*, 'farmstead by a pool' (OE *mere*, 'pool', + *tūn*, 'farmstead') or 'farmstead by a boundary' (OE *mǣre*, 'boundary', + *tūn*), and *Hussingtree*, '(place by) Hūsa's tree' (OE *trēow*, 'tree'). The second meaning of *Martin* would refer to the boundary between the hundreds of Oswaldslow and Pershore. 972 *Meretun, Husantreo*, DB *Husentre*, 1535 *Marten Hosentre*.

Martinscroft (district, Warrington): 'Martin's enclosure'. OE *croft*, 'enclosure'. 1332 *Martinescroft*.

Martinstown (village, Dorset): 'Martin's town'. The church here is dedicated to St Martin. The original name of the village was *Winterborne*, as for nearby WINTERBOURNE ABBAS. DB *Wintreburne*, 1280 *Wynterburn Seynt Martyn*, 1494 *Martyn towne*.

Martlesham (village, Suffolk): 'homestead by a woodland clearing where martens are seen'. OE *mearth*, 'marten', 'weasel', + *lēah*, 'wood', 'clearing', + *hām*, 'homestead'. The name could also mean 'Mertel's homestead'. The DB form of the name below has omitted the *t*. DB *Merlesham*, 1254 *Martlesham*.

Martletwy (village, Pemb): '(place with the) grave of a saint'. Welsh *merthyr*, 'martyr', 'grave of a saint', + 'shrine'. If the first part of the name represents Welsh *merthyr*, the second part would be the name of the (unidentified) saint. c.1230 *Martletwye*.

Martley (village, Worcs): 'woodland clearing where martens are seen'. OE *mearth*, 'marten', 'weasel', + *lēah*, 'wood', 'clearing'. c.1030 *Mærtleag*, DB *Mertelai*.

Martock (town, Somerset): 'outlying farmstead by a pool'. OE *mere*, 'pool', + *stoc*, 'outlying farmstead', 'dependent settlement'. The name lacks the *s* of OE *stoc* through Norman influence. DB *Mertoch*.

Marton (village, Lincs): 'farmstead by a pool'. OE *mere*, 'pool', + *tūn*, 'farmstead'. DB *Martone*. SO ALSO: *Marton*, Shropshire (near Baschurch, near Worthen), Warwicks.

Marton-in-the-Forest (hamlet, N Yorks): 'farmstead by a pool in the forest'. OE *mere*, 'pool', + *tūn*, 'farmstead'. The second part of the name, referring to the ancient forest of Galtres, distinguishes this Marton from MARTON-LE-MOOR, 15 miles to the west. DB *Martun*.

Marton-le-Moor (village, N Yorks): 'farmstead by a pool on the moor'. OE *mere*, 'pool', + *tūn*, 'farmstead'. The second part of the name (OE *mōr*, 'moor', 'marsh') distinguishes this Marton from MARTON-IN-THE-FOREST, 15 miles to the east. 1198 *Marton*, 1292 *Marton on the Moor*.

Martyr Worthy. See HEADBOURNE WORTHY.

Marwood (village, Devon): '(place by a) wood at the boundary'. OE *mǣre*, 'boundary', + *wudu*, 'wood'. The village lies on the boundary between the hundreds of Braunton and Shirwell. DB *Mereuda*.

Marylebone (district, Westminster): '(place by) St Mary's stream'. OE *burna*, 'stream'. 'St Mary's stream', named after St Mary's church, built in the 15C, was originally the *Tyburn*, 'boundary stream' (OE *tēo*, 'boundary', + *burna*), as it formed the boundary between the manors of Ebury and Westminster, but this name was changed because of its undesirable association with Tyburn gallows. The middle *-le-* was added in the 17C, possibly by association with St Maryle-Bow. The name is still popularly explained as 'St Mary the Good', as if from French, and has prompted spurious pedantry to the effect that the *-le-* should 'really' be feminine *-la-*. The old name still exists for Tyburn Way, Marble Arch, the site of Tyburn Tree, the original place of execution. DB *Tiburne*, 1453 *Maryburne*, 1490 *Tyborne otherwise called Maryborne*, 1626 *Marylebone*.

Maryport (town and port, Cumbria): 'Mary's port'. The harbour here was built in the mid-18C by Humphrey Senhouse, who named it after his wife, Mary, daughter of Sir George Fleming, Bishop of Carlisle. A local legend takes the name from Mary, Queen of Scots, who is said to have landed here when fleeing from Scotland in 1568. The original settlement was called *Elnefoot*, from its location at the mouth of the river Ellen, which also gave *Alauna* as the name of the Roman fort here. Cp. ALCESTER. 1762 *Mary-port*.

Marystow (hamlet, Devon): 'St Mary's holy place'. OE *stōw*, 'holy place'. The church here is dedicated to St Mary. 1266 *Sancte Marie Stou*.

Mary Tavy. See TAVISTOCK.

Masham (town, N Yorks): 'Mæssa's homestead'. OE *hām*, 'homestead', 'village'. The DB form of the name below has garbled the second part. DB *Massan*, 1153 *Masham*.

Mashbury (hamlet, Essex): 'Mæssa's or Mæcca's stronghold'. OE *burh*, 'fortified place'. 1068 *Maisseberia*, DB *Masseberig*.

Matching (hamlet, Essex): '(settlement of) Mæcca's people'. OE *-ingas*, 'people of'. The name could also mean simply 'Mæcca's place' (OE *-ing*, 'place belonging to'). DB *Matcinga*.

Matfen (village, Northd): 'Matta's fen'. OE *fenn*, 'fen'. Matfen lies near the river Pont. 1159 *Matefen*.

Mathon (village, Herefords): 'treasure'. OE *māthm*, 'treasure', 'gift'. The reason for the name is unknown. It may have originally applied to a gift of a piece of land. 1014 *Matham*, DB *Matma*.

Mathry (village, Pemb): '(place with the) grave of a saint'. Welsh *merthyr*, 'martyr', 'grave of a saint'. This meaning is conjectural, but early records of the name have the middle *r* of *merthyr* (or a related word) that was apparently later dropped. The final '-y' is unexplained. *c*.1150 *Marthru*.

Matlaske (village, Norfolk): '(place by the) ash tree where assemblies are held'. OE *mæthel*, 'assembly', + *æsc* or OS *askr*, 'ash'. Cp. MATLOCK. DB *Matelasc*.

Matlock (town, Derbys): '(place by the) oak tree where assemblies are held'. OE *mæthel*, 'assembly', + *āc*, 'oak'. The reference is to a particular oak where meetings were held to discuss legal and administrative matters. The DB form of the name below has *t* miscopied as *s*. DB *Meslach*, 1196 *Matlac*.

Matson (district of Gloucester, Glos): 'Mæthhere's or Mattere's hill'. OE *dūn*, 'hill'. 1121 *Mattresdone*.

Matterdale (hamlet, Cumbria): '(place in the) valley where madder grows'. OS *mathra*, 'madder', + *dalr*, 'valley'. The first form of the name below has *y* for *th*. *c*.1250 *Mayerdale*, 1323 *Matherdal*.

Mattersey (village, Notts): 'Mæthhere's island'. OE *ēg*, 'island'. The 'island' is well-watered land by the river Idle here. DB *Madressei*.

Mattingley (village, Hants): 'woodland clearing of Matta's people'. OE *-inga-*, 'of the people of', + *lēah*, 'wood', 'clearing'. DB *Matingelege*.

Mattishall (village, Norfolk): 'Matt's corner of land'. OE *halh*, 'nook', 'corner of land'. DB *Mateshala*.

Mauchline (town, E Ayrs): 'plain by the pool'. Gaelic *magh*, 'plain', + *linn*, 'pool'. *c*.1130 *Machline*, *c*.1177 *Mauhhelin*, *c*.1200 *Mauchlyn*.

Maugersbury (hamlet, Glos): 'Mæthelgār's stronghold'. OE *burh*, 'fortified place'. 714 *Meilgaresbyri*, DB *Malgeresberie*.

Maulden (village, Beds): '(place by the) hill with a crucifix'. OE *mǣl*, 'cross', 'crucifix', + *dūn*, 'hill'. Cp. MALDON. DB *Meldone*.

Maulds Meaburn. See KING'S MEABURN.

Maunby (village, N Yorks): 'Magni's farmstead'. OS *bȳ*, 'farmstead', 'village'. The personal name is Scandinavian. DB *Mannebi*.

Maund Bryan (hamlet, Herefords): 'Brian's (estate at the) hollows'. OE *maga*, 'stomach' (used in a topographical sense). The main name could also represent Celtic *Magnis*, '(place) at the rocks', as for the Roman name of KENCHESTER. One Brian held the manor here in the 12C. DB *Magene*, 1242 *Magene Brian*.

Mautby (hamlet, Norfolk): 'Malti's farmstead'. OS *bȳ*, 'farmstead', 'village'. The personal name is Scandinavian. The name could also mean 'farm where malt is made' (OS *malt*, 'malt', + *bȳ*). DB *Malteby*.

Mavis Enderby (village, Lincs): 'Malebisse's (estate at) Eindrithi's farmstead'. OS *bȳ*, 'farmstead'. The personal name is Scandinavian. The Malebisse family held the manor here in the 13C, their name distinguishing this Enderby from *Bag Enderby*, 4 miles to the north, where the village encloses the church as if in a bag, and *Wood Enderby*, 6 miles to the west, by former woodland. DB *Endrebi*, 1229 *Malebisse Enderby*.

Mawdesley (village, Lancs): 'Maud's woodland clearing'. OE *lēah*, 'wood', 'clearing'. The OF (from Old German) personal name is that of a woman. 1219 *Madesle*.

Mawgan (village, Cornwall): '(church of) St Mawgan'. Cp. ST MAWGAN. DB *Scantus Mawan*.

Mawnan (village, Cornwall): '(church of) St Mawnan'. Nothing is known about the saint to whom the church is dedicated here. 1281 *Sanctus Maunanus*.

Maxey (village, Peterborough): 'Maccus's island'. OE *ēg*, 'island'. The 'island' is dry ground in marshland here by the river Welland. The personal name is Scandinavian. *c*.963 *Macuseige*.

Maxstoke (village, Warwicks): 'Macca's outlying farmstead'. OE *stoc*, 'outlying farmstead'. 1169 *Makestoka*.

May, Isle of (island, Fife): 'seagull island'. OS *már*, 'seagull', + *ey*, 'island'. 1143 *Mai*, 1250 *Maeyar*.

Maybole (town, S Ayrs): 'plain of danger'. Gaelic *magh*, 'plain', + *baoghail*, 'danger'. At one time the open land here must have afforded little protection. 1275 *Mayboill*.

Mayfair (district, Westminster): '(place of the) May fair'. An annual May fair was held here on Brook Field near Hyde Park Corner from the 17C to the late 18C. 1701 *May-fair*.

Mayfield (village, E Sussex): 'open land where mayweed grows'. OE *mægthe*, 'mayweed', + *feld*, 'open land' (modern English *field*). 12C *Magavelda*.

Mayfield (village, Staffs): 'open land where madder grows'. OE *mæddre*, 'madder', + *feld*, 'open land' (modern English *field*). The DB form of the name below lacks an *r*. DB *Medevelde*, *c*.1180 *Matherfeld*.

Mayford (district of Woking, Surrey): '(place by the) ford where mayweed grows'. OE *mægthe*, 'mayweed', + *ford*, 'ford'. The name could also mean 'maidens' ford' (OE *mægth*, 'maiden'), meaning a ford (here over the Hoe Stream) where young women and girls gathered. 1212 *Maiford*.

Mayland (hamlet, Essex): 'estate where mayweed grows'. OE *mægthe*, 'mayweed', + *land*, 'land', 'estate'. Another possible meaning is '(place at the) island' (OE *ēg-land*, from *ēg*, 'island', + *land*, 'land'), with initial 'M-' from the OE phrase *æt thǣm ēg-lande*, 'at the island'. Mayland is on low-lying land west of Dengie Marshes. 1188 *La Mailanda*.

Meare (village, Somerset): '(place by the) pool'. OE *mere*, 'pool', 'lake'. DB *Mere*.

Mears Ashby (village, Northants): 'de Mares' farmstead where ash trees grow'. OS *askr*, 'ash', + *bý*, 'farmstead', 'village'. The de Mares family held the manor here in the 13C, their name distinguishing this Ashby from CASTLE ASHBY, 5 miles to the south. DB *Asbi*, 1281 *Esseby Mares*.

Measham (village, Leics): 'homestead on the (river) Mease'. OE *hām*, 'homestead'. The river name means 'mossy one' (OE *mēos*, 'moss'). DB *Messeham*.

Meathop (hamlet, Cumbria): 'middle enclosure in marshland'. OE *midd*, 'middle', + *hop*, 'enclosure in marshland'. OE *midd* was subsequently replaced by the equivalent OS *mithr*. *c*.1185 *Midhop*.

Meaux (hamlet, E Yorks): '(place by the) sandbank pool'. OS *melr*, 'sandbank', + *sǣr*, 'pool'. The pool no longer exists. There was an important monastery here and the name is thus popularly said to derive from the famous French abbey of *Meaux*, as in the following (translated) account of the name in the medieval *Chronica monasterii de Melsa*: 'This monastery, *Melsa* in Latin, *Meaux* in French or English, was named by our priors. The place itself was allotted a name by the first occupants, who in the Norman Conquest came from a certain town in France called *Meldis* in Latin, *Meaux* in French and inhabiting this place gave it the name of *Meaux* in memory of their former city'. The chronicler then gives various etymologies for the name, such as Latin *sapor mellis*, 'flavour of honey', *rixa*, 'strife', and so on, all of which are supposedly appropriate, *sapor mellis* because of 'the amenities of the place, the sweetness of religion', *rixa* because of 'the strife over the site at the foundation of the monastery or because of the continual strife against the triple enemy, the world, the flesh and the devil'. DB *Melse*.

Meavy (village, Devon): '(place on the river) Meavy'. The river has a name of Celtic origin meaning 'lively one'. 1031 *Mǣwi*, DB *Mewi*.

Medbourne (village, Leics): '(place by the) meadow stream'. OE *mǣd*, 'meadow', + *burna*, 'stream'. DB *Medburne*.

Medina (historic district, IoW): '(district of the river) Medina'. The river *Medina* that gave the name of the former administrative district has a name meaning 'middle (one)' (OE *medume*, 'middle') because it rises near the south coast and flows north, dividing the island into two almost equal halves. 1196 *Medine*.

Mediolanum. See WHITCHURCH (Shropshire).

Medmenham (village, Bucks): 'middle enclosure'. OE *medume*, 'middle', 'medium-sized', + *hamm*, 'enclosure'. Medmenham lies in a bend of the Thames, and can be regarded as a 'middle enclosure' between REMENHAM to the west and BISHAM to the east. DB *Medmeham*.

Medway (unitary authority, SE England): '(region of the river) Medway'. The first part of the river's name may mean 'mead' (OE *medu*), referring to the colour or sweetness of the water. The second part is identical to the name of the river *Wey* at WEYBRIDGE. Local lore prefers an 'obvious' origin in *midway*, as the river bisects the county, those born west of it being Kentishmen, and those born east, Men of Kent. 8C *Medeuuæge*.

Meesden (village, Herts): '(place on the) boggy hill'. OE *mēos*, 'moss', 'bog', + *dūn*, 'hill'. DB *Mesdone*.

Meeth (village, Devon): '(place at the) confluence of rivers'. OE *mȳthe*, 'confluence' (related modern English *mouth*). The name would presumably refer to the meeting of streams here. On the other hand, the meaning could be 'place where grass is cut' (OE *mǣth*, 'mowing'). DB *Meda*.

Meirionnydd. See MERIONETH.

Melbourn (village, Cambs): 'stream where orach grows'. OE *melde*, 'orach', + *burna*, 'stream'. Orach is a plant of the goosefoot family with edible leaves. Local evidence suggests, however, that this particular plant is not likely to have grown here, so the name may refer to some similar plant. 970 *Meldeburne*, DB *Melleburna*.

Melbourne (town, Derbys): '(place by the) millstream'. OE *myln*, 'mill', + *burna*, 'stream'. The 'millstream' here would have been the Carr Brook, which flows through Melbourne to the Trent. DB *Mileburne*.

Melbourne (village, E Yorks): '(place by the) middle stream'. OE *middel*, 'middle', + *burna*, 'stream'. Original OE *middel* in the name was replaced by equivalent OS *methal*. DB *Middelburne*, 1285 *Medelbornn*.

Melbury Abbas (village, Dorset): 'multicoloured fortified place of the abbess'. OE *mǣle*, 'multicoloured', + *burh*, 'fortified place', + Latin *abbatissa*, 'abbess'. The fortified place referred to is the earthwork on nearby Melbury Hill. The manor here was held early by Shaftesbury Abbey. 956 *Meleburge*, DB *Meleberie*, 1291 *Melbury Abbatisse*.

Melcombe Regis (district of Weymouth, Dorset): 'royal (estate in the) valley where milk is produced'. OE *meoluc*, 'milk', + *cumb*, 'valley', + Latin *regis*, 'of the king'. The valley is that of the river Wey. 1223 *Melecumb*.

Meldreth (village, Cambs): '(place by the) millstream'. OE *myln*, 'mill', + *rīth*, 'stream'. The form of the name, with inserted *d*, may have been influenced by early forms of the name of nearby MELBOURN. DB *Melrede*.

Meliden (village, Denb): '(hill of) St Melydn'. The word for 'hill' is missing in the English form of the name, but present in the Welsh *Allt Melyd* (Welsh *allt*, 'hill'). The saint in question has not

been identified. An alternative Welsh form of the name is *Gallt Melyd*, *gallt* being modern Welsh for 'hill'. 1291 *Altmelyden*.

Melkinthorpe (hamlet, Cumbria): 'Maelchon's outlying farmstead'. OS *thorp*, 'outlying farmstead'. The personal name is Old Irish. *c.*1150 *Melcanetorp*.

Melkridge (village, Northd): '(place on the) ridge where milk is produced'. OE *meoluc*, 'milk', + *hrycg*, 'ridge'. 1279 *Melkrige*.

Melksham (town, Wilts): 'homestead or riverside pasture where milk is produced'. OE *meoluc*, 'milk', + *hām*, 'homestead', or *hamm*, 'enclosure'. Melksham lies by the river Avon. DB *Melchesham*.

Melling (village, Lancs): '(settlement of) Mealla's people'. OE *-ingas*, 'people of'. The name could also mean simply 'Mealla's place' (OE *-ing*, 'place belonging to'). DB *Mellinge*. SO ALSO: *Melling*, Sefton.

Mellis (village, Suffolk): '(place with) mills'. OE *myln*, 'mill'. Cp. MELLS. DB *Melles*.

Mellor (village, Lancs): '(place by the) bare hill'. The name is Celtic in origin, from words related to modern Welsh *moel*, 'bald', and *bre*, 'hill'. Cp. MOELFRE. *c.*1130 *Malver*.

Mells (village, Somerset): '(place with) mills'. OE *myln*, 'mill'. 942 *Milne*, DB *Mulle*.

Melmerby (village, Cumbria): 'Maelmuire's farmstead'. OS *bý*, 'farmstead', 'village'. The personal name is Old Irish. 1201 *Malmerbi*.

Melmerby (village, N Yorks): 'Maelmuire's farmstead'. OS *bý*, 'farmstead', 'village'. The personal name is Old Irish. The first part of the name could also represent OS *malmr*, 'sandy field'. The form of the name below relates to Melmerby near Ripon, but Melmerby near Middleham has a name of identical origin. DB *Malmerbi*.

Melplash (village, Dorset): '(place by the) multicoloured pool'. OE *mǣle*, 'multicoloured', + *plæsc*, 'pool' (modern English *plash*). 1155 *Melpleys*.

Melrose (town, Borders): '(place by the) bare moor'. The name derives from Celtic words related to modern Welsh *moel*, 'bald', 'bare', and *rhos*, 'moor', 'heath'. The name originally applied to what is now *Old Melrose*, 3 miles to the east by the river Tweed, where a monastery was founded in the 7C. The name of that place became that of the present town after David I founded a new monastery here in 1136 for Cistercian monks from Rievaulx. *c.*700 *Mailros*.

Melsonby (village, N Yorks): 'Maelsuithan's farmstead'. OS *bý*, 'farmstead', 'village'. The personal name is Old Irish. DB *Malsenebi*.

Meltham (town, Kirklees): 'village where smelting is carried out'. OE *melt*, 'melting', 'smelting', + *hām*, 'homestead', 'village'. Smelting is the extraction of metal from ore by a process involving heating and melting. 'The village is situated in a valley adjoining a mountainous moorland ridge ... and abounds with mineral wealth. ... There is an extensive iron foundry. In this township are quarries of good flagstone, also coal' (*The National Gazetteer of Great Britain and Ireland*, 1868). DB *Meltham*.

Melton (village, Suffolk): 'farmstead with a crucifix'. OE *mǣl*, 'cross', 'crucifix', + *tūn*, 'farmstead'. *c.*1050 *Meltune*, DB *Meltuna*.

Melton (Leics). See MELTON MOWBRAY.

Melton Constable (village, Norfolk): 'constable's farmstead with a crucifix'. OE *mǣl*, 'cross', 'crucifix', + *tūn*, 'farmstead'. The manor here was held in the 12C by the constable of the Bishop of Norwich. His title distinguishes this Melton from *Great Melton*, 17 miles to the south, and nearby *Little Melton*. DB *Maeltuna*, 1320 *Melton Constable*.

Melton Mowbray (town, Leics): 'de Moubray's middle farmstead'. OE *middel*, 'middle', + *tūn*, 'farmstead'. OS *methal*, 'middle', has replaced the OE word to give the present form of the name. The 'middle farmstead' must have been so called for distinction from two (or more) others, but their location is unknown. Roger de Moubray held the manor here in the 12C. The local council district of *Melton* is named after the town. DB *Medeltone*, 1284 *Melton Moubray*.

Melton Ross (village, N Lincs): 'de Ros's middle farmstead'. OE *middel*, 'middle', + *tūn*, 'farmstead'. OS *methal*, 'middle', has replaced the OE word to give the present form of the name. The de Ros family held the manor here in the 14C. DB *Medeltone*, 1375 *Melton Roos*.

Melverley (hamlet, Shropshire): 'woodland clearing by the mill ford'. OE *myln*, 'mill', + *ford*, 'ford', + *lēah*, 'wood', 'clearing'. The ford would have been over the river Severn here. The DB form of the name below is somewhat garbled. DB *Meleurlei*, 1311 *Milverlegh*.

Membury (village, Devon): 'fortified place'. OE *burh*, 'fortified place'. The first part of the name is of uncertain origin. It may derive from a Celtic word meaning 'stone' (modern Welsh *maen*) or from OE *mǣne*, 'communal', as for MANATON. The 'fortified place' is the ancient entrenchment known as Membury Castle here. DB *Manberia*.

Menai Bridge (town, Anglesey): '(town by the) bridge over the Menai Strait'. A bridge was built across the Menai Strait by Thomas Telford in 1826 and the town developed soon after. The name of the strait itself is of uncertain origin but may mean 'carrying one', referring to the swift current. The Welsh name of the town is *Porthaethwy*, 'ferry of Daethwy' (Welsh *porth*, 'ferry'), from a tribal name.

Mendham (village, Suffolk): 'Mynda's homestead'. OE *hām*, 'homestead', 'village'. *c.*950 *Myndham*, DB *Mendham*.

Mendip Hills (hill range, Somerset): 'hills with a plateau'. The first part of the name is probably of Celtic origin, related to modern Welsh *mynydd*, 'hill'. The second part may be OE *yppe*, 'upland', 'plateau'. The western Mendips form a plateau almost 6 miles wide. *Mendip* is the name of the local council district. 1185 *Menedepe*.

Mendlesham (village, Suffolk): 'Myndel's homestead'. OE *hām*, 'homestead', 'village'. DB *Mundlesham*.

Menheniot (village, Cornwall): 'Hynyed's plain'. Cornish *ma*, 'plain'. 1260 *Mahiniet*, 1868 *Menheniot*, or *Menhynnet*.

Menston (village, Bradford): 'estate associated with Mensa'. OE *-ing-*, 'associated with', + *tūn*, 'farmstead', 'estate'. The original *-ing-* has disappeared from the name. *c.*972 *Mensinctun*, DB *Mersintone*.

Menstrie (town, Clack): 'farmstead in the meadow'. The town has a Celtic name from words related to modern Welsh *maes*, 'field', and *tref*, 'farmstead', 'village'. 1261 *Mestryn*, 1315 *Mestry*.

Mentmore (village, Bucks): 'Menta's moor'. OE *mōr*, 'moor'. DB *Mentemore*.

Meole Brace (district of Shrewsbury, Shropshire): 'de Braci's (estate by) Meole Brook'. The former name of Rea Brook here may represent OE *melu*, 'meal', describing a stream with cloudy water. The de Braci family held the manor here in the 13C. DB *Mela*, 1273 *Melesbracy*.

Meols. See GREAT MEOLS.

Meonstoke (village, Hants): 'dependent settlement on the (river) Meon'. OE *stoc*, 'outlying farmstead', 'dependent settlement'. Meonstoke was dependent on *Meon*, i.e. on WEST MEON (see for the river name) and *East Meon*. DB *Menestoche*.

Meopham (village, Kent): 'Mēapa's homestead'. OE *hām*, 'homestead', 'village'. 788 *Meapaham*, DB *Mepeham*.

Mepal (village, Cambs): 'Mēapa's corner of land'. OE *halh*, 'nook', 'corner of land'. 12C *Mepahala*.

Merchiston (district, Edinburgh): 'Merchiaun's farm'. OE *tūn*, 'farmstead'. The personal name is an OW form of Latin *Marcianus*. 1266 *Merchinstoun*, 1278 *Merchammeston*, 1371 *Merchenstoun*.

Mere (village, Cheshire): '(place by the) lake': OE *mere*, 'pool', 'lake'. The village takes its name from the nearby lake known as *The Mere*. DB *Mera*.

Mere (village, Wilts): '(place by the) pool'. OE *mere*, 'pool', 'lake'. There is a small lake near the village. DB *Mere*.

Mereworth (village, Kent): 'Mǣra's enclosure'. OE *worth*, 'enclosure'. 843 *Meranworth*, DB *Marovrde*.

Meriden (village, Solihull): 'pleasant valley'. OE *myrge*, 'pleasing' (modern English *merry*), + *denu*, 'valley'. The name may imply that merrymaking took place here. The place appears to have lost its good reputation by the time of William Dugdale's *The Antiquities of Warwickshire* (1656), where he interprets the name as *Miredene*, 'for the foulness thereof'. 1230 *Mereden*.

Merioneth (historic county, NW Wales): 'seat of Meirion'. Meirion (Meriaun) is said to be the grandson of Cunedda, who gave the name to GWYNEDD. The Welsh form of the name, *Meirionnydd*, was adopted for the administrative district formed in the new county of Gwynedd in 1974.

Merrington (hamlet, Shropshire): '(place by the) pleasant hill'. OE *myrig*, 'merry', 'pleasant', + *dūn*, 'hill'. The name could imply a hill where merrymaking took place. 1254 *Muridon*.

Merriott (village, Somerset): '(place by the) boundary gate'. OE *mǣre*, 'boundary', + *geat*, 'gate'. DB *Meriet*.

Merrow (district of Guildford, Surrey): origin uncertain. Attempts to derive the name from OE *mearg*, 'marrow', as if denoting fertile ground, are unsatisfactory. An origin in a Celtic word meaning 'marl' (from Latin *marga*, itself said to come from Gaulish) seems more plausible. 1185 *Marewe*.

Merrymeet (hamlet, Cornwall): 'pleasant meeting place'. English *merry* meant 'pleasant' (as in *Merry England*) before it gained its present sense of 'cheerful'. The name is quite common

for a place where several roads meet, as here on the road (now the A390) from Liskeard to Callington. 1699 *Merrymeet*.

Mersea Island (island, Essex): 'island of the pool'. OE *mere*, 'pool', + *ēg*, 'island'. The 'pool' may be the wetland here rather than an actual area of water, although Mersea Island lies between the mouths of the rivers Blackwater and Colne. The second word of the name was added when the sense of 'island' was lost in the original. Early 10C *Meresig*.

Mersey (river, NW England): 'boundary river'. OE *mǣre*, 'boundary', + *ēa*, 'river'. The Mersey originally formed the boundary between the Anglo-Saxon kingdoms of Mercia and Northumbria. It then served as the border between the counties of Cheshire and Lancashire. This long historic link was broken overnight in 1974 when the 'new' county of Merseyside was created. 1002 *Mærse*.

Mersham (village, Kent): 'Mǣrsa's homestead'. OE *hām*, 'homestead', 'village'. 858 *Mersaham*, DB *Merseham*.

Merstham (suburb of Reigate, Surrey): 'homestead by a trap for martens'. OE *mearth*, 'marten', 'weasel', + *sǣt*, 'ambush', + *hām*, 'homestead'. 947 *Mearsætham*, DB *Merstan*.

Merston (village, W Sussex): 'farmstead on marshy ground'. OE *mersc*, 'marsh', + *tūn*, 'farmstead'. Merston lies on well-watered land southeast of Chichester. DB *Mersitone*.

Merthyr Tydfil (town, M Tydfil): 'Tudful's grave'. Welsh *merthyr*, 'martyr', 'grave of a saint'. Tudful is said to have been one of the daughters of Brychan, who gave the name of BRECON. According to tradition she was murdered by pagans in the 5C at the site of the present town and buried here. 1254 *Merthir*, 13C *Merthyr Tutuil*.

Merton (borough, Greater London): 'farmstead by the pool'. OE *mere*, 'pool', + *tūn*, 'farmstead'. The 'pool' was probably in the river Wandle here. 967 *Mertone*, DB *Meretone*. SO ALSO: *Merton*, Devon, Norfolk, Oxon.

Meshaw (village, Devon): '(place by the) bad clearing'. OF *mal*, 'bad', + *assart*, 'clearing'. A 'bad' clearing is an infertile one. The second part of the name was later wrongly associated with OE *sceaga*, 'wood', as for SHAW. DB *Mauessart*.

Messing (hamlet, Essex): '(settlement of) Mæcca's people'. OE *-ingas*, 'people of'. DB *Metcinges*.

Messingham (village, N Lincs): 'homestead of Mæssa's people'. OE *-inga-*, 'of the people of', +

hām, 'homestead'. *c*.1067 *Mæssingaham*, DB *Messingeham*.

Metfield (village, Suffolk): 'open land with a meadow'. OE *mǣd*, 'meadow', + *feld*, 'open land' (modern English *field*). 1214 *Medefeld*.

Metheringham (village, Lincs): 'Mæthelrīc's homestead'. OE *hām*, 'homestead'. The name could also mean 'homestead of Mæthelrīc's people' (OE *-inga-*, 'of the people of', + *hām*). DB *Medricesham*, 1193 *Mederingeham*.

Methley (village, Leeds): '(place at the) clearing where grass is mown'. OE *mǣth*, 'mowing', + *lēah*, 'wood', 'clearing'. The name could also mean 'middle island' (OS *methal*, 'middle', + OE *ēg*, 'island'), referring to land between the rivers Calder and Aire here. DB *Medelai*.

Methwold (village, Norfolk): 'middle forest'. OE *middel*, 'middle', + *wald*, 'woodland', 'forest'. OE *middel* was later replaced by equivalent OS *methal*. Methwold occupies a central position in relation to *Hockwold cum Wilton* ('woodland where hocks grow', + Latin *cum*, 'with', + 'farmstead where willows grow') and *Northwold* ('northern forest'). *c*.1050 *Medelwolde*, DB *Methelwalde*.

Mettingham (village, Suffolk): 'homestead of Metti's people'. OE *-inga-*, 'of the people of', + *hām*, 'homestead'. DB *Metingaham*.

Mevagissey (coastal town, Cornwall): '(church of) St Meva and St Issey'. The '-ag-' of the name represents Cornish *hag*, 'and'. Nothing is known of Meva, while Issey, according to Cornish legend, is said to be one of the sons of the Welsh king Brychan, who gave the name of BRECON. *c*.1400 *Meffagesy*, 1637 *Meva and Issey alias Mevagissey*.

Mexborough (town, Doncaster): 'Mēoc's or Mjúkr's stronghold'. OE *burh*, 'stronghold'. The personal names are respectively OE and Scandinavian. DB *Mechesburg*.

Meynell Langley. See KIRK LANGLEY.

Meysey Hampton (village, Glos): 'de Meisi's home farm'. OE *hām-tūn*, 'home farm' (from *hām*, 'homestead', + *tūn*, 'farmstead'). The de Meisi family held the manor here from the 12C. Their name also belongs to *Marston Meysey*, Wilts, 2 miles to the south, where it distinguishes that village from *South Marston*, 7 miles to the southeast. (*Marston* is as for MARSTON MAGNA.) DB *Hantone*, 1287 *Meseishampton*.

Michaelchurch (hamlet, Herefords): 'St Michael's church'. OE *cirice*, 'church'. The form of the name below is the Welsh equivalent. Cp. LLANFIHANGEL-AR-ARTH. *c*.1150 *Lann mihacgel*.

Michaelchurch Escley (village, Herefords): 'St Michael's church by Escley Brook'. OE *cirice*, 'church'. The church here is dedicated to St Michael. The river name represents a Celtic word for 'water' (as for the *Esk* at ESKDALE GREEN), + OE *hlynn*, 'torrent'. Its addition distinguishes the village from *Michaelchurch-on-Arrow*, Powys, 12 miles to the northwest, itself particularized by its location on the river Arrow (with a name of identical origin to that of ARROW). The latter Michaelchurch has the Welsh name *Llanfihangel Dyffryn Arwy*, 'St Michael's church (in the) valley (of the river) Arrow'. *c*.1257 *Michaeleschirche*.

Michaelston-le-Pit (village, Vale of Glam): 'St Michael's holy place in the pit'. OE *stōw*, 'holy place', + OF *le*, 'the', + OE *pytt*, 'pit'. The church here is dedicated to St Michael, and the 'pit' is the wide, basin-like depression in which the village lies. The addition to the basic name distinguishes this Michaelston from nearby *Michaelston-super-Ely*, 'Michaelston on the (river) Ely'. The Welsh name of the village is *Llanfihangel-y-pwll*, 'St Michael's church in the pit', with the addition as Welsh *y*, 'the', + *pwll*, 'pool', 'pit'. The '-ton' in the English name was originally '-stow', as can be seen from the forms below. *c*.1291 *Michelstowe*, 1483 *Mighelstowe*, 1535 *Michaelstown*, 1567 *Mighelston in le Pitt*.

Michaelstow (village, Cornwall): 'holy place of St Michael'. OE *stōw*, 'holy place'. The church here is dedicated to St Michael. 1279 *Sanctus Michael*, 1311 *Mihelstou*.

Micheldever (village, Hants): '(place on the) boggy waters'. The name is of Celtic origin and refers to a stream here, from words related to modern Welsh *mign*, 'bog', and *dwfr*, 'water'. The first part of the name became associated with OE *micel*, 'great'. 862 *Mycendefr*, DB *Miceldevere*.

Mickfield (village, Suffolk): 'large expanse of open land'. OE *micel*, 'large', + *feld*, 'open land' (modern English *field*). DB *Mucelfelda*.

Mickleby (village, N Yorks): 'large farmstead'. OS *mikill*, 'large', + *bý*, 'farmstead'. DB *Michelbi*.

Mickleham (village, Surrey): 'large enclosure'. OE *micel*, 'large', + *hamm*, 'enclosure'. Mickleham is by the river Mole, so a more precise sense of *hamm* is 'river meadow'. The name is popularly associated with the dedication of the church to St Michael. DB *Micleham*.

Mickleover (district, Derby): 'large (place at the) ridge'. OE *micel*, 'large', + *ofer*, 'ridge'. The third form of the name below has Latin *magna* ('great') to distinguish the place from nearby

LITTLEOVER. 1011 *Vfre*, DB *Ufre*, *c*.1100 *Magna Oufra*.

Mickleton (village, Glos): 'large farmstead'. OE *micel*, 'large', + *tūn*, 'farmstead'. 1005 *Micclantun*, DB *Muceltvne*. SO ALSO: *Mickleton*, Durham.

Mickle Trafford (village, Cheshire): 'great (place by the) trough ford'. OS *mikill*, 'great', + OE *trog*, 'trough', + *ford*, 'ford'. A 'trough ford' is either a deeply worn ford or one with a trough by it. The river here is the Gowy. The first word of the name distinguishes this Trafford from nearby *Bridge Trafford*, with a bridge over the Gowy, and *Wimbolds Trafford*, with the personal name Winebald. DB *Traford*, 1379 *Mekeltrogh-ford*.

Mickley Square. See HIGH MICKLEY.

Middle Aston (village, Oxon): 'middle eastern farmstead'. OE *ēast*, 'eastern', + *tūn*, 'farmstead'. The first word of the name locates this Aston between NORTH ASTON and STEEPLE ASTON. DB *Estone*.

Middle Claydon. See STEEPLE CLAYDON.

Middleham (village, N Yorks): 'middle homestead'. OE *middel*, 'middle', + *hām*, 'homestead'. The sense of 'middle' here is obscure. The DB form of the name below is garbled. DB *Medelai*, 12C *Midelham*.

Middle Harling. See EAST HARLING.

Middle Herrington. See EAST HERRINGTON.

Middle Littleton. See NORTH LITTLETON.

Middle Rainton. See EAST RAINTON.

Middle Rasen. See MARKET RASEN.

Middle Salter. See HIGH SALTER.

Middlesbrough (town and port, Middlesbrough): 'middlemost stronghold'. OE *midlest*, 'middlemost', + *burh*, 'fortified place', 'stronghold'. It is uncertain of which two (or more) strongholds this was the 'middlemost'. It is possible that 'Middle' was simply the name of a district here, with the Tees, on which Middlesbrough stands, as its northern boundary. *c*.1165 *Midelesburc*.

Middlesex (historic county, SE England): '(territory of the) Middle Saxons'. The 'Middle Saxons' (OE *middel*, 'middle', + *Seaxe*, 'Saxons') inhabited a region between the East Saxons of ESSEX and the West Saxons of WESSEX. See also SUSSEX. The original territory was much larger than the former county (whose name is still active for postal purposes). 704 *Middelseaxan*, DB *Midelsexe*.

Middlestown (village, Wakefield). The name is a contracted form of *Middle Shitlington*, where the main name means 'estate associated with Scyttel' (OE *-ing-*, 'associated with', + *tūn*, 'farmstead', 'estate'). Middlestown lies between *Netherton* (formerly *Nether Shitlington*) and *Overton* (formerly *Over Shitlington*). 1325 *Midle Shitlington*, 1551 *Myddleston*, 1817 *Middles Town*.

Middleton (hamlet, Cumbria): 'middle farmstead'. OE *middel*, 'middle', + *tūn*, 'farmstead', 'village'. Middleton is perhaps so called as it is roughly midway between Castleton and Killington. DB *Middeltun*.

Middleton (town, Rochdale): 'middle farmstead'. OE *middel*, 'middle', + *tūn*, 'farmstead', 'village'. Middleton may have been so called because it lies midway between Manchester and Rochdale. 1194 *Middelton*.

Middleton (village, Warwicks): 'middle farmstead'. OE *middel*, 'middle', + *tūn*, 'farmstead'. Middleton lies halfway between Tamworth and Coleshill. DB *Mideltone*.

Middleton Cheney (village, Northants): 'de Chendut's middle farmstead'. OE *middel*, 'middle', + *tūn*, 'farmstead'. The de Chendut family held the manor here in the 12C. The farm may have been so called as lying midway between Wardington, Oxon, to the north, and Great Purston, Northants, to the south. DB *Mideltone*, 1342 *Middleton Cheyndut*.

Middleton in Teesdale (town, Durham): 'middle farmstead in Teesdale'. OE *middel*, 'middle', + *tūn*, 'farmstead'. The addition to the name distinguishes this Middleton from others by locating it in TEESDALE. *c*.1164 *Middeltun*.

Middleton-on-Sea (resort town, W Sussex): 'middle farmstead by the sea'. OE *middel*, 'middle', + *tūn*, 'farmstead'. Middleton may have been regarded as midway between Felpham to the south and Flansham to the north. The second part of the name is chiefly a touristic enticement. DB *Middeltone*.

Middleton on the Hill (village, Herefords): 'large farmstead on the hill'. OE *micel*, 'large', + *tūn*, 'farmstead'. The second part of the name distinguishes this Middleton from *Middleton*, Shropshire, 8 miles to the north (although its name means 'middle farmstead'). DB *Miceltune*.

Middleton-on-the-Wolds (village, E Yorks): 'middle farmstead in the Wolds'. OE *middel*, 'middle', + *tūn*, 'farmstead'. This Middleton is distinguished from others by its location in the (Yorkshire) WOLDS. DB *Middeltun*.

Middleton Priors. See MIDDLETON SCRIVEN.

Middleton Scriven (village, Shropshire): 'Scriven's (estate at the) middle farmstead'. OE *middel*, 'middle', + *tūn*, 'farmstead'. The family name, first recorded in the 16C, distinguishes this Middleton from *Middleton Priors*, 4 miles to the northwest, which was held by Wenlock Priory. DB *Middeltone*, 1577 *Skrevensmyddleton*.

Middleton Stoney (village, Oxon): 'middle farmstead on stony soil'. OE *middel*, 'middle', + *tūn*, 'farmstead'. The second word of the name, first recorded in 1552, perhaps distinguishes this Middleton from MIDDLETON CHENEY, Northants, 13 miles to the north. DB *Mideltone*, 1552 *Myddylton Stony*.

Middleton Tyas (village, N Yorks): 'le Tyeis's middle estate'. OE *middel*, 'middle', + *tūn*, 'farmstead', 'estate'. The le Tyeis family may have held lands early here. DB *Middeltun*, 14C *Midilton Tyas*.

Middle Tysoe. See UPPER TYSOE.

Middle Wallop. See NETHER WALLOP.

Middlewich (town, Cheshire): 'middlemost saltworks'. OE *midlest*, 'middlemost', + *wīc*, 'specialized farm', 'trading settlement'. Middlewich is roughly halfway between NORTHWICH and NANTWICH (the three collectively known as *The Wiches*), and all three names have OE *wīc* in the same sense, with salt production an important commercial activity at all three. The Roman settlement at Middlewich was *Salinae*, 'saltworks' (Latin *sal*, 'salt'), as at DROITWICH. DB *Wich*, *Mildestuich*.

Middlezoy (village, Somerset): 'middle island on the (river) Sow'. OE *ēg*, 'island'. The 'island' here is raised ground in a damp area. The river here now is the Parrett, but its former name is of pre-English origin and uncertain meaning. See also OTHERY. 725 *Soweie*, DB *Sowi*, 1227 *Middlesowy*.

Midge Hall (suburb of Leyland, Lancs): 'corner of land full of midges'. OE *mycg*, 'midge', + *halh*, 'nook', 'corner of land'. Midge Hall is on low-lying ground near the river Lostock. 1390 *Miggehalgh*.

Midgham (village, W Berks): 'homestead or enclosure plagued with midges'. OE *mycg*, 'midge', + *hām*, 'homestead', or *hamm*, 'enclosure'. Midgham lies by the river Kennet. DB *Migeham*.

Midgley (village, Calderdale): 'wood or clearing full of midges'. OE *mycg*, 'midge', + *lēah*, 'wood', 'clearing'. DB *Micleie*. SO ALSO: *Midgley*, Wakefield.

Midhurst (town, W Sussex): 'middle wooded hill'. OE *midd*, 'middle', + *hyrst*, 'wooded hill'. This is the traditional interpretation of the name, but the topography favours 'place amid wooded hills', from OE *mid*, 'amid'. Midhurst lies between high woodland to the north and the woods of the South Downs to the south. 1186 *Middeherst*.

Mid Lambrook. See EAST LAMBROOK.

Midlands (central region, England): '(region in the) middle of the country'. Modern English *mid* + *lands*. The name for the central counties of England has been current since the 16C and in 1974 gave *West Midlands* as a metropolitan county (to 1986). 1610 *Mid-lands*.

Mid Lavant. See EAST LAVANT.

Midlothian (unitary authority, S Scotland): 'middle Lothian'. The name is that of the historic county in which Edinburgh was located (and also known by the name), between *East Lothian* and *West Lothian*. The name is ultimately that of the region of *Lothian*, named after Leudonus, a man whose identity and ethnic origin are uncertain. *c.*970 *Loonia*, 1098 *Lodoneó*, *c.*1200 *Louthion*.

Midsomer Norton (town, Bath & NE Somerset): 'northern settlement of the midsummer'. OE *north*, 'northern', + *tūn*, 'farmstead', 'settlement'. The first word of the name, perhaps added to distinguish this Norton from NORTON ST PHILIP, refers to the Midsummer Day festival of St John the Baptist, to whom the parish church is dedicated. 1248 *Midsomeres Norton*.

Milborne Port (town, Somerset): '(place by the) millstream (with the status of a) market town'. OE *myln*, 'mill', + *burna*, 'stream', + *port*, 'market town'. The second word of the name was added when Milborne was declared a borough in 1225. *c.*880 *Mylenburnan*, DB *Meleburne*, 1249 *Milleburnport*.

Milborne St Andrew (village, Dorset): '(place by the) millstream with St Andrew's church'. OE *myln*, 'mill', + *burna*, 'stream'. The church here is dedicated to St Andrew. 934 *Muleburne*, DB *Meleburne*, 1294 *Muleburne St Andrew*.

Milbourne (village, Northd): '(place by the) millstream'. OE *myln*, 'mill', + *burna*, 'stream'. 1158 *Meleburna*.

Milburn (village, Cumbria): '(place by the) millstream'. OE *myln*, 'mill', + *burna*, 'stream'. 1178 *Milleburn*.

Milcombe (village, Oxon): '(place in the) middle valley'. OE *middel*, 'middle', + *cumb*, 'valley'. DB *Midelcumbe*.

Milden (hamlet, Suffolk): '(settlement of) Melda's people'. OE -*ingas*, 'people of'. The name could also mean 'place where orach grows' (OE *melde*, 'orach', + -*ing*, 'place characterized by'). Orach is an edible plant of the goosefoot family. The DB form of the name below has *l* for *d*. DB *Mellinga*, *c*.1130 *Meldinges*.

Mildenhall (village, Suffolk): 'middle corner of land'. OE *middel*, 'middle', + *halh*, 'nook', 'corner of land'. The name could also be identical with that of MILDENHALL, Wilts. The DB form of the name below has *l* miscopied as *t*. *c*.1050 *Mildenhale*, DB *Mitdenehalla*.

Mildenhall (village, Wilts): 'Milda's corner of land'. OE *halh*, 'nook', 'corner of land'. The 'corner of land' is an indentation in nearby Mildenhall Hill. The Roman town here was *Cunetio*, a name of Celtic origin but uncertain meaning that gave that of the river Kennet (see WEST KENNETT). 803 *Mildanhald*, DB *Mildenhalle*, 1868 *Mildenhall, or Minal*.

Mile End (district, Tower Hamlets): '(place at the) end of a mile'. ME *mile*, 'mile', + *ende*, 'end'. Mile End is situated a mile from Aldgate. 1288 *La Mile ende*.

Mileham (village, Norfolk): 'homestead with a mill'. OE *myln*, 'mill', + *hām*, 'homestead'. DB *Meleham*.

Milford (village, Surrey): '(place by a) ford with a mill'. OE *myln*, 'mill', + *ford*, 'ford'. 1235 *Muleford*. SO ALSO: *Milford*, Derbys.

Milford Haven (town and port, Pemb): 'harbour at Milford'. The original site here was *Milford*, 'sandy inlet' (OS *melr*, 'sandy bank', + *fjorthr*, 'fjord', 'inlet'). English *haven* was then added when the meaning of the OS original was forgotten. The Welsh name of Milford Haven is *Aberdaugleddau*, 'mouth of the two (rivers) Cleddau' (Welsh *aber*, 'river mouth', + *dau*, 'two'). The river Cleddau, divided into the Eastern Cleddau and Western Cleddau here, has a Celtic name meaning 'sword', referring either to its straight course or to its shining waters. *c*.1191 *de Milverdico portu*, 1207 *Mellferth*, 1219 *Milford*, 15C *Aber Dav Gleddyf*.

Milford on Sea (resort town, Hants): 'ford by a mill by the sea'. OE *myln*, 'mill', + *ford*, 'ford'. The ford would have been over Danes Stream here. The second part of the name was added both to distinguish this Milford from others and to serve as a touristic label. DB *Melleford*.

Millbrook (village, Beds): '(place at the) brook by a mill'. OE *myln*, 'mill', + *brōc*, 'brook'. DB *Melebroc*. SO ALSO: *Millbrook*, Southampton.

Miller's Dale (village, Derbys): '(place in the) valley with a millhouse'. OE *myln*, 'mill', + *hūs*, 'house', + *dæl*, 'valley', 'dale'. The name has been influenced by modern English *miller*. 1633 *Milhousdale*, 1767 *Millers-dale*.

Mill Hill (district, Barnet): 'hill with a mill'. ME *mille*, 'mill', + *hill*, 'hill'. The name refers to a windmill formerly on a hill here. The hill in question may have been the one now known as Highwood Hill. 1547 *Myllehill*.

Millington (village, E Yorks): 'farmstead with a mill'. OE *myln*, 'mill', + *tūn*, 'farmstead'. DB *Milleton*.

Millom (town, Cumbria): '(place at the) mills'. OE *myln*, 'mill'. The name represents OE *mylnum*, the dative plural form of *myln*. The mills may have been on the hill where Millom Castle now stands. *c*.1180 *Millum*.

Millport (resort and port, N Ayrs): 'port with a mill'. The town on the island of Great Cumbrae arose in the early 19C and took its name from the grain mill that stood over the harbour.

Millwall (district, Tower Hamlets): 'wall with a mill'. The 'wall' here, formerly called *Marsh Wall*, was an embankment by the Thames on which mills stood in the 18C.

Milngavie (town, E Dunbartons): '(place by the) windmill'. Gaelic *muileann gaoithe* (from *muileann*, 'mill', + *gaoth*, 'wind'). The site of the windwill here is uncertain.

Milnrow (town, Rochdale): 'row (of houses) by a mill'. OE *myln*, 'mill', + *rāw*, 'row'. 1554 *Mylnerowe*.

Milnthorpe (village, Cumbria): 'outlying farmstead with a mill'. OE *myln*, 'mill', + OS *thorp*, 'outlying farmstead'. 1272 *Milntorp*.

Milson (village, Shropshire): 'Myndel's farmstead'. OE *tūn*, 'farmstead'. The name could also represent OE *myln-stān*, 'millstone', referring to a distinctive one here by Mill Brook. DB *Mulstone*.

Milstead (village, Kent): 'middle place'. OE *middel*, 'middle', + *stede*, 'place'. late 11C *Milstede*.

Milston (village, Wilts): 'middlemost farmstead'. OE *midlest*, 'middlemost', + *tūn*, 'farmstead'. This is probably the meaning of the name, although it is hard to identify the places of which Milston is the 'middlemost'. DB *Mildestone*.

Milton (village, Cambs): 'middle farmstead'. OE *middel*, 'middle', + *tūn*, 'farmstead'. The farm was perhaps so called as lying between Impington and Fen Ditton. *c*.975 *Middeltune*, DB *Middeltone*. SO ALSO: *Milton*, Oxon (near Didcot).

Milton (hamlet, Cumbria): 'farmstead with a mill'. OE *myln*, 'mill', + *tūn*, 'farmstead', 'village'. 1285 *Milneton*. SO ALSO: *Milton*, Staffs.

Milton (district, Portsmouth): 'middle farmstead'. OE *middel*, 'middle', + *tūn*, 'farmstead'. The farm was perhaps so called as lying between Eastney and Fratton. 1186 *Middelton*.

Milton Abbas (village, Dorset): 'middle farmstead of the abbot'. OE *middel*, 'middle', + *tūn*, 'farmstead', + Latin *abbas*, 'abbot'. The farm was seen as lying in the middle of the county. The second word of the name refers to the former 10C abbey here, today represented by the (unfinished) church that is the chapel of Milton Abbey School. 934 *Middeltone*, DB *Mideltune*, 1268 *Middelton Abbatis*.

Milton Abbot (village, Devon): 'abbot's middle farmstead'. OE *middel*, 'middle', + *tūn*, 'farmstead'. The manor here was held early by Tavistock Abbey. The farm was perhaps 'middle' with regard to Dunterton and Lamerton. DB *Middeltone*, 1297 *Middelton Abbots*.

Milton Bryan (village, Beds): 'Brian's middle farmstead'. OE *middel*, 'middle', + *tūn*, 'farmstead'. The manor here was held in the 12C by one Brian. DB *Middelton*, 1303 *Mideltone Brian*, 1868 *Milton-Bryant*.

Milton Clevedon (village, Somerset): 'de Clyvedon's middle farmstead'. OE *middel*, 'middle', + *tūn*, 'farmstead'. The de Clyvedon family held the manor here in the early 13C. DB *Mideltune*, 1408 *Milton Clyvedon*.

Milton Damerel (village, Devon): 'de Albemarle's middle farmstead'. OE *middel*, 'middle', + *tūn*, 'farmstead'. Robert de Albemarle held the manor here in 1086. DB *Mideltone*, 1301 *Middelton Aubemarle*.

Milton Ernest (village, Beds): 'Erneis' middle farmstead'. OE *middel*, 'middle', + *tūn*, 'farmstead'. The manor here was held early by one Erneis. DB *Middeltone*, 1330 *Midelton Orneys*.

Milton Keynes (town, Milton K): 'de Cahaignes' middle farmstead'. OE *middel*, 'middle', + *tūn*, 'farmstead'. The second word of the name, added to distinguish this Milton from others, refers to Lucas de Cahaignes, lord of the manor here in the 12C. The place was probably seen as 'middle' with regard to Broughton and Walton. The forms of the name below relate to the present Milton Keynes Village, in the eastern part of the New Town of Milton Keynes, designated in 1967. DB *Middeltone*, 1227 *Middeltone Kaynes*, 1868 *Milton-Keynes, or Middelton Keynes*.

Milton Lilbourne (village, Wilts): 'de Lilebone's middle farmstead'. OE *middel*, 'middle', +

tūn, 'farmstead'. The de Lilebone family held the manor here in the 13C, midway between Pewsey and Easton. DB *Mideltone*, 1249 *Mydilton Lillebon*.

Milton Malsor (village, Northants): 'Malsor's middle farmstead'. OE *middel*, 'middle', + *tūn*, 'farmstead'. The Malsor family held the manor here in the 12C. DB *Mideltone*, 1781 *Milton alias Middleton Malsor*, 1868 *Milton-Mazor, or Middleton Malsor*.

Milton under Wychwood (village, Oxon): 'middle farmstead near (the forest of) Wychwood'. OE *middel*, 'middle', + *tūn*, 'farmstead'. For the forest name, see SHIPTON UNDER WYCHWOOD. DB *Mideltone*.

Milverton (town, Somerset): 'farmstead by the mill ford'. OE *myln*, 'mill', + *ford*, 'ford', + *tūn*, 'farmstead', 'estate'. Milverton is on a tributary of the river Tone. 11C *Milferton*, DB *Milvertone*. SO ALSO: *Milverton*, Warwicks.

Milwich (village, Staffs): 'farmstead with a mill'. OE *myln*, 'mill', + *wīc*, 'farmstead'. DB *Mulewiche*.

Minch (sea strait, W Isles/Highland): '(sea of the) great headlands'. OS *megin*, 'great', + *nes*, 'headland'. The headlands in question are those on the northwest coast of mainland Scotland. The strait is traditionally divided into *North Minch* and the more southerly *Little Minch*.

Minchinhampton (village, Glos): 'high farmstead of the nuns'. OE *myncen*, 'nun', + *hēah*, 'high', + *tūn*, 'farmstead'. The '-hamp-' of the name represents OE *hēan*, the dative of *hēah*. The nuns, from Caen, Normandy, were given the manor here in the 11C. DB *Hantone*, 1221 *Minchenhamtone*.

Mindrum (hamlet, Northd): '(place by the) mountain ridge'. The name is Celtic, from words related to modern Welsh *mynydd*, 'mountain', and *trum*, 'ridge'. Mindrum lies near the Cheviot Hills. *c*.1050 *Minethrum*.

Minehead (resort town, Somerset): 'headland by the hill'. The first part of the name is Celtic and means 'hill', from a word related to modern Welsh *mynydd*, 'mountain'. The second part is OE *hēafod*, 'headland'. Minehead is below and on the face of a hill that may have been called *The Myne*. The first form of the name below seems to have added OE *dūn*, 'hill'. 1046 *Mynheafdon*, DB *Maneheve*.

Minety (village, Wilts): 'island where mint grows'. OE *minte*, 'mint', + *ēg*, 'island'. The 'island' would be dry ground in marshland here. Celticists, however, prefer a meaning 'house of young goats' or 'house on the edge', from words related to modern Welsh *myn*, 'kid', or *min*, 'edge', 'brink', and *tŷ*, 'house'. 844 *Mintig*, 1868 *Minty, or Minety*.

Minginish (region, Highland): 'great headland'. OS *megin*, 'great', + *nes*, 'headland'. Cp. MINCH. The central region of the island of Skye has the Gaelic equivalent name *Rubha Mór*.

Mingulay (island, W Isles): 'great island'. OS *mikill*, 'great', + *ey*, 'island'. The island is 'great' in its gaunt appearance, with high cliffs, rather than its actual area. 1580 *Megala*.

Minions (village, Cornwall). Minions arose in the 19C as a mining village and took its name from a nearby tumulus now known as Minions Mound. Its own name is of uncertain origin, but the first part may represent Cornish *men*, 'stone'. The first form of the name below, with *m* for *nn*, refers to the tumulus (the second word is 'barrow'), the second to the village. 1613 *Mimiens borroughe*, 1897 *Minions*.

Minskip (village, N Yorks): 'communal holding'. OE *mænscipe*, 'community'. DB *Minescip*.

Minstead (village, Hants): 'place where mint grows'. OE *minte*, 'mint', + *stede*, 'place'. It is not clear whether mint was cultivated here or whether it grew naturally. DB *Mintestede*.

Minster (village, Kent): '(place by the) monastery'. OE *mynster*, 'monastery', 'large church'. The original 'monastery' here was a 7C nunnery, which was destroyed by the Danes. The forms of the name below relate to Minster near Ramsgate. 694 *Menstre*, 1868 *Minster-in-Thanet*.

Minster (village, Kent): '(place by the) monastery'. OE *mynster*, 'monastery', 'large church'. The original 'monastery' here was a 7C nunnery, which was destroyed by the Danes but rebuilt for Benedictine nuns in the 12C. The forms of the name below relate to Minster near Sheerness. 1203 *Menstre*, 1868 *Minster-in-Sheppey*.

Minsterley (village, Shropshire): 'woodland clearing by a church'. OE *mynster*, 'monastery', 'large church', + *lēah*, 'wood', 'clearing'. Minsterley was in the ancient parish of Westbury, and the church referred to is probably the one there, 3 miles to the northwest. DB *Menistrelie*.

Minster Lovell (village, Oxon): 'Luvel's (estate by the) monastery'. OE *mynster*, 'monastery', 'large church'. The monastery in question is the former Benedictine priory here, where the Luvel family held the manor in the 13C. DB *Minstre*, 1279 *Ministre Lovel*.

Minsterworth (village, Glos): 'enclosure of the monastery'. OE *mynster*, 'monastery', + *worth*, 'enclosure'. The monastery in question

was that of St Peter's, Gloucester. *c.*1030 *Mynsterworthig*.

Minterne Magna (village, Dorset): 'greater building near the place where mint grows'. OE *minte*, 'mint', + *ærn*, 'house', 'building', + Latin *magna*, 'great'. The second word of the name distinguishes the village from nearby *Minterne Parva* (Latin *parva*, 'small'). 987 *Minterne*.

Minto (village, Borders): '(place by the) mountain'. The village takes its name from the nearby Minto Hills, the name itself deriving from a Celtic word related to modern Welsh *mynydd*, 'mountain', + OE *hōh*, 'hill spur'. The latter was added when the Celtic word was no longer understood. 1296 *Myntowe*.

Minton (village, Shropshire): 'farmstead by the mountain'. Welsh *mynydd*, 'mountain', + OE *tūn*, 'farmstead'. The mountain referred to is the Long Mynd nearby. DB *Munetune*.

Mirfield (town, Kirklees): 'pleasant open land'. OE *myrge*, 'pleasing' (modern English *merry*), + *feld*, 'open land' (modern English *field*). If the first part of the name is from OE *myrgen*, 'pleasure', the sense could be 'open land where festivities are held'. Mirfield lies by the river Calder, not far from WAKEFIELD on the same river, with a name of similar meaning. DB *Mirefeld*.

Miserden (village, Glos): 'Musard's (manor)'. The earlier name of the place was *Greenhamstead*, 'green homestead' (OE *grēne*, 'green', + *hām-stede*, 'homestead'), and the Musard family already held the manor in 1086. The '-den' of Miserden is not from OE *denu*, 'valley', although this suits the situation of the village, but an altered form of *-dere*, from the final letter of the French personal name and the OF place-name suffix *-ere*, from Latin *-aria*. DB *Grenhamstede*, 1186 *Musardera*.

Misson (village, Notts): 'marshy place'. OE *mos*, 'moss', 'marsh'. DB *Misne*.

Misterton (village, Notts): 'estate with a church'. OE *mynster*, 'monastery', 'large church', + *tūn*, 'farmstead'. The name could also mean 'estate belonging to a monastery', but there is no record of any monastery here. DB *Ministretone*. SO ALSO: *Misterton*, Leics, Somerset.

Mistley (village, Essex): 'wood or clearing where mistletoe grows'. OE *mistel*, 'mistletoe', + *lēah*, 'wood', 'clearing'. The DB form of the name below is corrupt. DB *Mitteslea*, 1225 *Misteleg*.

Mitcham (district, Merton): 'large homestead'. OE *micel*, 'great', + *hām*, 'homestead'. Mitcham may have been regarded as 'large' by comparison with nearby Streatham. DB *Michelham*.

Mitcheldean (village, Glos): 'great (place in the) valley'. OE *micel*, 'great', + *denu*, 'valley'. The first part of the name distinguishes the village from *Littledean*, 4 miles to the south. The 'valley' is that of the FOREST OF DEAN. 1220 *Dena*, 1224 *Muckeldine*, 1868 *Mitchelldean, or Micheldean*.

Mitchell (village, Cornwall): 'maiden's hollow'. OE *mægd*, 'maiden', + *hol*, 'hollow'. The 'hollow' is the dip in the main road here (now the A30) where the village lies. The sense of 'maiden' is obscure. 1239 *Meideshol*.

Mitford (village, Northd): '(place by the) ford at a confluence'. OE *mȳthe*, 'confluence' (related modern English *mouth*), + *ford*, 'ford'. The reference is to the junction of the rivers Wansbeck and Font here. 1196 *Midford*.

Mitton (hamlet, Staffs): 'farmstead at the confluence'. OE *gemȳthe*, 'confluence' (related modern English *mouth*), + *tūn*, 'farmstead'. Two streams, Church Eaton Brook and Whiston Brook, meet nearby. DB *Mutone*.

Mixbury (village, Oxon): 'fortified place by a dunghill'. OE *mixen*, 'dunghill', + *burh*, 'fortified place'. DB *Misseberie*.

Mobberley (village, Cheshire): 'clearing at the fortified place where assemblies are held'. OE *mōt*, 'meeting', 'assembly', + *burh*, 'fortified place', + *lēah*, 'wood', 'clearing'. DB *Motburlege*.

Moccas (hamlet, Herefords): '(place on the) moor where pigs are kept'. Welsh *moch*, 'pigs', + *rhos*, 'moor'. *c*.1130 *Mochros*, DB *Moches*.

Modbury (village, Devon): 'fortified place where assemblies are held'. OE *mōd*, 'meeting', 'assembly', + *burh*, 'fortified place'. DB *Motberia*.

Moddershall (hamlet, Staffs): 'Mōdrēd's corner of land'. OE *halh*, 'nook', 'corner of land'. DB *Modredeshale*.

Moelfre (coastal village, Anglesey): '(place by the) bare hill'. Welsh *moel*, 'bare', + *bre*, 'hill'. There are many hills in Wales named *Moel*, such as *Moel Hebog* ('bare hill of the hawk') and *Moel Tryfan* (see RHOSTRYFAN), Gwynedd, and *Moel Sych* ('dry bare hill'), Powys. Cp. MALVERN HILLS. 1399 *Moylvry*, 1528 *Moelvre*.

Moffat (town, Dumfries & Gall): '(place in the) long plain'. Gaelic *magh*, 'plain', + *fada*, 'long'. The first part of the name represents Gaelic *mo*, the locative form of *magh*. The 'long plain' here is the valley of the river Annan. 1179 *Moffet*, 1296 *Moffete*.

Mogerhanger (village, Beds): '(place by the) wooded slope'. OE *hangra*, 'wooded slope'. The first part of the name is of uncertain origin. 1216 *Mogarhangre*.

Moira (village, Leics). Moira is in the parish of Ashby-de-la-Zouch, which was the property of Francis Rawdon-Hastings, 2nd Earl of Moira (1754–1826), when fireclay and coal were discovered here in the late 18C. The earl's own title comes from Moira, Co Down, Northern Ireland.

Mold (town, Flints): '(place by the) high hill'. OF *mont*, 'hill', + *hault*, 'high'. The 'high hill' is Bailey Hill, where there was an (Ancient) British fort and possibly a Roman one. The Welsh name of Mold is *Yr Wyddgrug*, 'the burial mound' (Welsh *yr*, 'the', + *gwydd*, 'tomb', 'cairn', + *crug*, 'mound'), referring to the same hill, which may have had a tumulus or cairn of stones on it. The present name arose from a 'fusing' of the two OF words. 1267 *de Monte alto*, 1278 *Montem Altum*, 1284 *Moald*.

Mole (river). See EAST MOLESEY.

Molescroft (suburb of Beverley, E Yorks): 'Mūl's enclosure'. OE *croft*, 'enclosure'. DB *Molescroft*.

Mole Valley. See EAST MOLESEY.

Molland (village, Devon): '(place with) cultivated land'. OE *land*, 'cultivated land', 'estate'. The first part of the name is of uncertain origin. It may represent the pre-English name of a hill. See also SOUTH MOLTON. DB *Mollande*.

Mollington (village, Cheshire): 'estate associated with Moll'. OE *-ing-*, 'associated with', + *tūn*, 'farmstead', 'estate'. The village was earlier known as *Great Mollington* or *Mollington Tarrant* (from the Torold family who owned land here in the 13C), distinguishing it from nearby *Little Mollington*, or *Mollington Banastre* (from the Banastre family, who held the manor here in the 13C). DB *Molintone*. SO ALSO: *Mollington*, Oxon.

Môn. See ANGLESEY.

Mona. See ANGLESEY.

Monewden (village, Suffolk): 'valley of Munda's people'. OE *-inga-*, 'of the people of', + *denu*, 'valley'. DB *Munegadena*.

Monk Bretton (district, Barnsley): 'monks' (estate at the) farmstead of the Britons'. OE *munuc*, 'monk', + *Brettas*, '(Ancient) Britons', + *tūn*, 'farmstead'. The first word of the name, distinguishing this Bretton from *West Bretton*, Wakefield, 8 miles to the northwest, refers to the monks of Bretton Priory. DB *Brettone*, 1225 *Munkebretton*.

Monken Hadley (district, Barnet): 'monks' (estate by the) clearing where heather grows'. ME *monken*, 'of the monks', + OE *hǣth*, 'heather', + *lēah*, 'wood', 'clearing'. The manor here was held early by the monks of Walden Abbey, Essex. 1248 *Hadlegh*, 1489 *Monken Hadley*.

Monk Fryston (village, N Yorks): 'monks' (estate at the) farmstead of the Frisians'. OE *munuc*, 'monk', + *Frīsa*, 'Frisian', + *tūn*, 'farmstead'. The monks of Selby Abbey held the manor here in the 11C, their title distinguishing this Fryston from *Ferry Fryston*, 5 miles to the southwest, near FERRYBRIDGE, its site now occupied by a power station, and from *Water Fryston*, northwest of Ferrybridge on the river Aire. *New Fryston* has in turn recently arisen northwest of Water Fryston. *c.*1030 *Fristun*, 1166 *Munechesfryston*.

Monkhopton (village, Shropshire): 'monks' farmstead in a valley'. OE *hop*, 'enclosed valley', + *tūn*, 'farmstead'. The first part of the name refers to the possession of the place by Wenlock Priory. 1255 *Hopton*, 1577 *Munkehopton*.

Monkland (village, Herefords): 'monks' (estate in) Leon'. OE *munuc*, 'monk'. For the district name, see LEOMINSTER. Before 1086 the manor here was held by Conches Abbey, Normandy. DB *Leine*, *c.*1180 *Munkelen*.

Monkleigh (village, Devon): 'monks' (estate) at the wood or clearing'. OE *munuc*, 'monk', + *lēah*, 'wood', 'clearing'. The manor here was held by the monks of Montacute Priory from the 12C. DB *Lega*, 1244 *Munckenelegh*.

Monkokehampton (village, Devon): 'monks' estate on the (river) Okement'. OE *munuc*, 'monk', + *tūn*, 'farmstead', 'estate'. For the river name, see OKEHAMPTON. The manor here was at one time held by the monks of Glastonbury Abbey. DB *Monacochamentona*, 1868 *Monk Okehampton*.

Monkseaton (district of Whitley Bay, N Tyneside): 'monks' (estate at the) farmstead by the sea'. OE *sǣ*, 'sea', + *tūn*, 'farmstead'. The manor here was held early by the monks of Tynemouth. The form of the name below has Latin *monachorum*, 'of the monks'. 1380 *Seton Monachorum*.

Monks Eleigh. See BRENT ELEIGH.

Monk Sherborne. See SHERBORNE ST JOHN.

Monksilver (village, Somerset): 'monks' (estate by the river) Silver'. OE *munuc*, 'monk'. *Silver* is an old river name meaning something like 'bright stream' (OE *seolfor*, 'silver'). The manor here was held early by the monks of Goldcliff Priory. DB *Selvere*, 1249 *Monkesilver*.

Monks Kirby (village, Warwicks): 'village with a church of the monks'. OS *kirkju-bý* (from *kirkja*, 'church', + *bý*, 'village'). Land here was given to St Nicholas Priory, Angers, France, in the 11C. 1077 *Kirkeberia*, DB *Chircheberie*, 1416 *Monkenkirkeby*.

Monk Soham. See EARL SOHAM.

Monks Risborough. See PRINCES RISBOROUGH.

Monkton (village, Devon): 'farmstead of the monks'. OE *munuc*, 'monk', + *tūn*, 'farmstead'. 1244 *Muneketon*. SO ALSO: *Monkton*, Kent.

Monkton Combe (village, Bath & NE Somerset): 'estate of the monks in the valley'. OE *munuc*, 'monk', + *tūn*, 'farmstead', 'estate', + *cumb*, 'valley'. DB *Cume*.

Monkton Deverill. See KINGSTON DEVERILL.

Monkton Farleigh (village, Wilts): 'monks' woodland clearing where ferns grow'. OE *munuc*, 'monk', + *tūn*, 'estate', + *fearn*, 'fern', + *lēah*, 'wood', 'clearing'. The first word of the name refers to the priory that was founded here in 1125. 1001 *Farnleghe*, DB *Farleghe*, 1321 *Monekenefarlegh*.

Monkton Up Wimborne. See WIMBORNE MINSTER.

Monkwearmouth (district, Sunderland): '(place at the) mouth of the (river) Wear of the monks'. OE *mūtha*, 'mouth'. Monkwearmouth was originally *Wearmouth*, from its location at the mouth of the river Wear, whose name is probably of Celtic origin and perhaps related to obsolete Welsh *gweir*, 'bend', 'circle', referring to its winding course. (The Wear describes a great loop at DURHAM, whose name in a Welsh 10C text is *Caer Weir*, 'fortress of the Wear'. In modern times the river gave the name of *Wear Valley*, the Durham council district that includes the region of Weardale, between Wearhead and Crook.) The Benedictine abbey founded at Wearmouth in 674 came early into the possession of the monks of Durham. Hence the first part of the name, represented in the second form of the name below by Latin *monachorum*, 'of the monks'. *c.*730 *Uuiremutha*, 1291 *Wermuth Monachorum*.

Monmouth (town, Mon): 'mouth of the (river) Monnow'. OE *mūtha*, 'mouth'. The river's name may mean 'fast-flowing' (cp. MENAI BRIDGE). The Welsh name of Monmouth is *Trefynwy*, 'homestead on the (river) Mynwy' (Welsh *tref*, 'homestead', 'town'). 11C *Munwi Mutha*, 1190 *Munemuda*, 1267 *Monmouth*.

Monnington on Wye (village, Herefords): 'Manna's estate on the (river) Wye'. OE *tūn*, 'farmstead', 'estate'. The basic name could also mean 'communal estate' (OE *mǣne*, 'communal', 'held in common'). For the river name, see ROSS-ON-WYE. DB *Manitune*.

Mons Graupius. See GRAMPIANS.

Montacute (village, Somerset): '(place by the) pointed hill'. OF *mont*, 'hill', + *aigu*, 'sharp', 'pointed'. The name, probably transferred from France, refers to nearby Flamdon Hill. DB *Montagud*.

Montford (village, Shropshire): '(place by the) ford where people gather'. OE *gemāna*, 'fellowship', 'association', + *ford*, 'ford'. The name probably refers to the crossing of the river Severn here, near the Welsh border, as the place where important negotiations between the English and the Welsh were held. The '-t-' in the name probably arose by association with French *mont*, 'hill'. DB *Maneford*, 1204 *Moneford*.

Montgomery (town, Powys): '(place of) Montgomery'. The Norman lord Roger de Montgomery built a castle here (on what is now Castle Hill) and named it after his other castle at Montgommery in Calvados, Normandy. In 1102 this castle passed into the hands of another Norman, Baldwin de Bollers, who gave the Welsh name of the present town, *Trefaldwyn*, 'Baldwin's town' (Welsh *tref*, 'town'). DB *Montgomeri*.

Montrose (town and port, Angus): 'moor on the promontory'. Gaelic *moine*, 'moor', + *ros*, 'promontory'. Montrose lies on a low peninsula at the entrance to the large tidal lagoon known as Montrose Basin. *c*.1178, *Munros*.

Monyash (village, Derbys): '(place with) many ash trees'. OE *manig*, 'many', + *æsc*, 'ash'. DB *Maneis*.

Moor Allerton. See CHAPEL ALLERTON (Leeds).

Moor Crichel (village, Dorset): '(place on) marshy ground by Crich'. OE *mōr*, 'moor', 'marshy ground'. *Crich* is a Celtic hill name meaning simply 'hill' (modern Welsh *crug*). The first word of the name distinguishes this village from *Long Crichel*, 1½ miles to the northwest, so named for its length. The name is also spelt *More Crichel*. DB *Circel*, 1212 *Mor Kerchel*.

Moorlinch (village, Somerset): '(place by a) pleasant ledge'. OE *myrge*, 'pleasant' (modern English *merry*), + *hlinc*, 'ledge', 'terrace'. A terrace road winds up from the village to the Polden Hills. 971 *Mirieling*.

Moor Monkton. See NUN MONKTON.

Moorsholm (village, Redcar & Clev): '(place by the) houses on the moor'. OE *mōr* or OS *mōr*, 'moor', + OE *hūs* or OS *hús*, 'house'. The name represents the OE or OS words in a dative plural form ending in *-um*. DB *Morehusum*.

Moortown. See CHAPEL ALLERTON (Leeds).

Morar (coastal region, Highland): 'great water'. Gaelic *mór*, 'big', 'great', + *dobhar*, 'water'. The name ultimately refers to the river Morar that flows into Loch Morar here. 1292 *Morderer*, 14C *Mordhowar*.

Moray (unitary authority, NE Scotland): 'sea settlement'. The name comes from Celtic words related to modern Welsh *môr*, 'sea', and *tref*, 'home', 'town'. The ancient province here gave the name of the Moray Firth, the great arm of the North Sea that extends inland to Inverness. *c*.970 *Moreb*, 1124 *Morauia*, *c*.1185 *Murewe*.

Morchard Bishop (village, Devon): 'bishop's (estate by the) great wood'. The main name is of Celtic origin, from words related to modern Welsh *mawr*, 'big', and *coed*, 'wood'. The manor here was held by the Bishop of Exeter in 1086. Hence the second word of the name, distinguishing the village from *Cruwys Morchard*, where the manor was held by the de Crues family in the 13C. DB *Morchet*, 1311 *Bisschoppes-morchard*, 1868 *Bishop Morchard*.

Morcombelake (village, Dorset): '(place by the) stream in the marshy valley'. OE *mōr*, 'moor', 'marsh', + *cumb*, 'valley', + *lacu*, 'stream' (related modern English *lake*). The first part of the name could also represent OE *mort*, 'young salmon', as perhaps for MORTLAKE. 1240 *Mortecumbe*, 1558 *Morecomblake*.

Morcott (village, Rutland): 'cottage in the marshland'. OE *mōr*, 'moor', 'marshland', + *cot*, 'cottage'. DB *Morcote*.

Morden (district, Merton): 'hill in marshland'. OE *mōr*, 'moor', 'marshland', + *dūn*, 'hill'. There is no hill here in the accepted sense, but the ground rises between Beverley Brook and the river Wandle. 969 *Mordune*, DB *Mordone*. SO ALSO: *Morden*, Dorset.

Mordiford (village, Herefords): '(place with a) ford'. OE *ford*, 'ford'. The meaning of the first part of the name is uncertain. The river here is the Lugg. 12C *Mordeford*.

Mordon (hamlet, Durham): '(place by the) hill in marshland'. OE *mōr*, 'moor', 'marsh', + *dūn*, 'hill'. *c*.1050 *Mordun*.

More (village, Shropshire): '(place by the) marsh'. OE *mōr*, 'moor', 'marsh'. The village lies by the river West Onny. 1181 *La Mora*.

Morebath (village, Devon): 'bathing place in marshy ground'. OE *mōr*, 'moor', 'marshland', + *bæth*, 'bath'. There are natural springs here near the river Exe and marshy land nearby. DB *Morbatha*.

Morecambe (resort town, Lancs): '(place by) Morecambe Bay'. The old Celtic name for the estuary of the river Lune to the south of modern Morecambe was *Morikambe*, 'curved inlet', from words related to modern Welsh *môr*, 'sea', and *cam*, 'crooked', and this was recorded by Ptolemy in the 2C AD. The name was revived in the 18C for what is now Morecambe Bay, and in 1870 was adopted for the growing resort formerly known as *Poulton-le-Sands* (see POULTON-LE-FYLDE). (The suggestion of 'more come' in the name is said to have influenced the adoption.) The name was by then already in use for certain coastal buildings: 'Overlooking the bay is Morecambe Lodge, a modern edifice' (*The National Gazetteer of Great Britain and Ireland*, 1868).

More Crichel. See MOOR CRICHEL.

Moreleigh (village, Devon): 'woodland clearing by a moor'. OE *mōr*, 'moor', + *lēah*, 'wood', 'clearing'. DB *Morlei*.

Moresby (hamlet, Cumbria): 'Maurice's farmstead'. OS *bȳ*, 'farmstead', 'village'. The personal name is Old French. The Roman fort here was *Gabrosentum*, a Celtic name meaning literally 'goat path', probably referring to a steep path up the sea cliffs nearby. *c*.1160 *Moresceby*.

Moreton (village, Dorset): 'farmstead in marshland'. OE *mōr*, 'moor', 'marshland', + *tūn*, 'farmstead'. DB *Mortune*.

Moreton (district of Wallasey, Wirral): 'farmstead in marshland'. OE *mōr*, 'moor', 'marshland', + *tūn*, 'farmstead'. 1278 *Moreton*.

Moreton Corbet (village, Shropshire): 'Corbet's farmstead in marshland'. OE *mōr*, 'moor', 'marshland', + *tūn*, 'farmstead'. The manor here was held in the 13C by the Corbet family, whose name distinguishes this Moreton from *Moreton Say*, 9 miles to the northeast, held by the de Say family. DB *Mortone*, 1255 *Morton Corbet*.

Moretonhampstead (town, Devon): 'farmstead on a moor with a homestead'. OE *mōr*, 'moor', + *tūn*, 'farmstead', + *hām-stede* (see HAMPSTEAD). The reason for the 'homestead' addition is uncertain, as *Hampstead* occurs nowhere else in Devon. It may be a reference to a nearby place originally known by a different name. DB *Mortone*, 1493 *Morton Hampsted*, 1868 *Moreton-Hampstead*.

Moreton-in-Marsh (town, Glos): 'farmstead on a moor in marshland'. OE *mōr*, 'moor', + *tūn*, 'farmstead'. The name was originally *Moreton*. As shown by the third form of the name below, the district name *Henmarsh* was then added, meaning 'marshland where henbirds are seen' (OE *henn*, 'hen', + *mersc*, 'marsh'). 'Henmarsh' then became 'in-Marsh' and even sometimes 'in-the-Marsh'. 714 *Mortun*, DB *Mortune*, 1253 *Morton in Hennemersh*, 1868 *Moreton-in-the-Marsh*.

Moreton Morrell (village, Warwicks). Originally two places: *Moreton*, 'farmstead by marshland' (OE *mōr*, 'moor', 'marsh', + *tūn*, 'farmstead'), and *Morrell*, 'boundary hill' (OE *mǣre*, 'boundary', + *hyll*, 'hill'). William Dugdale, in *The Antiquities of Warwickshire* (1656), describes the village: '*Moreton-Morell*, for so it is vulgarly called, but more truly *Morton-Merhull*, in regard that [i.e. because] the town is divided into two parts, whereof the one … is called Morton from the low moorish ground adjoining thereto, and the other … *Merehill*'. DB *Mortone*, 1279 *Merehull*, 1285 *Morton Merehill*.

Moreton Pinkney (village, Northants): 'de Pinkney's farmstead in marshland'. OE *mōr*, 'moor', 'marshland', + *tūn*, 'farmstead'. The de Pinkney family held the manor here in the 13C. DB *Mortone*.

Moreton Say. See MORETON CORBET.

Moreton Valence (village, Glos): 'de Valence's farmstead in marshland'. OE *mōr*, 'moor', 'marshland'. The de Valence family held the manor here in the 13C. DB *Mortune*, 1276 *Mortun Valence*.

Morgannwg. See GLAMORGAN.

Moridunum. See CARMARTHEN.

Morland (village, Cumbria): '(place by the) grove on the moor'. OS *mór*, 'moor', + *lundr*, 'grove'. *c*.1140 *Morlund*.

Morley (town, Leeds): 'woodland clearing by a moor'. OE *mōr*, 'moor', + *lēah*, 'wood', 'clearing'. The many '-ley' names here are evidence that the region must at one time have been heavily wooded. DB *Moreleia*. SO ALSO: *Morley*, Derbys, Durham.

Morningside (district, Edinburgh): 'morning hillside'. The name is first recorded for an estate formed here in 1657 on the amalgamation of two adjoining properties. It is probably a fanciful creation, with a generally agreeable meaning.

Morningthorpe (village, Norfolk): 'outlying farmstead of the dwellers by the lake'. OE *mere*, 'lake', + -*inga*-, 'of the dwellers at', + OS *thorp*, 'outlying farmstead'. The first part of the name could also represent OE *mǣre*, 'boundary'. DB *Maringatorp*.

Morpeth (town, Northd): 'murder path'. OE *morth*, 'murder', + *pæth*, 'path', 'way'. The name must refer to a road or track where a notorious murder took place and that was thus regarded as dangerous. The potentially unfavourable name has probably been accepted through its popular interpretation as 'moor path', a meaning in fact apt for a town that is the 'gateway to the moors'. *c.*1200 *Morthpath*.

Morriston (district, Swansea). The settlement was built in *c.*1768 by Sir John Morris to provide housing for local colliery and copper workers. The Welsh name of Morriston is *Treforys* (Welsh *tre*, 'town', + *Morys*, 'Morris').

Morston (village, Norfolk): 'farmstead by a marsh'. OE *mersc*, 'marsh', + *tūn*, 'farmstead'. DB *Merstona*.

Mortehoe (coastal village, Devon): 'hill spur by Morte'. OE *hōh*, 'hill spur'. The name refers to the distinctive headland here called *Morte Point*. Its own name means 'stump' (OE *mort*). DB *Morteho*.

Mortlake (district, Richmond): 'Morta's stream'. OE *lacu*, 'stream', 'body of water' (related modern English *lake*). The first part of the name could also represent OE *mort*, 'young salmon', referring to the presence of this or some similar fish, perhaps in nearby Beverley Brook, which enters the Thames here. DB *Mortelage*.

Morton (village, Derbys): 'farmstead in moorland'. OE *mōr*, 'moor', + *tūn*, 'farmstead'. 956 *Mortun*, DB *Mortune*. SO ALSO: *Morton*, Lincs (near Bourne, near Gainsborough).

Morton Bagot (village, Warwicks): 'Bagod's farmstead in moorland'. OE *mōr*, 'moor', 'marsh', + *tūn*, 'farmstead'. The Bagod family held the manor here in the 12C. DB *Mortone*, 1262 *Morton Bagod*.

Morvah (coastal village, Cornwall): 'grave by the sea'. Cornish *mor*, 'sea', + *bedh*, 'grave'. A saint's grave was revered here at one time, but the saint's name is unknown. 1327 *Morveth*.

Morval (hamlet, Cornwall): '(place by the) sea'. Cornish *mor*, 'sea'. The second part of the name is of obscure origin. Morval is 2 miles from the sea but close to the head of a tidal creek. 1238 *Morval*.

Morville (village, Shropshire): '(place by) open land'. OE *feld*, 'open land' (modern English *field*). The meaning of the first part of the name is uncertain. It may represent a Celtic word meaning 'breast-shaped hill', as for MAM TOR. The reference would be to nearby Aston Hill. DB *Membrefelde*, *c.*1138 *Mamerfeld*.

Morwenstow (coastal village, Cornwall): 'St Morwenna's holy place'. OE *stōw*, 'holy place'. According to Cornish legend, Morwenna was a daughter of Brychan of BRECON. 1201 *Morwestewe*.

Mosborough (district, Sheffield): 'fortified place in the moor'. OE *mōr*, 'moor', + *burh*, 'fortified place'. The *r* of OE *mōr* has dropped from the name. *c.*1002 *Moresburh*, DB *Moresburg*.

Mosedale (hamlet, Cumbria): '(place in the) valley with a bog'. OS *mosi*, 'moss', 'bog', + *dalr*, 'valley'. 1285 *Mosedale*.

Moseley (district, Birmingham): 'woodland clearing where mice are seen'. OE *mūs*, 'mouse', + *lēah*, 'wood', 'clearing'. The name refers to a place overrun by field mice. DB *Museleie*.

Moseley (district, Wolverhampton): 'Moll's woodland clearing'. OE *lēah*, 'wood', 'clearing'. DB *Moleslei*.

Moseley (hamlet, Worcs): 'woodland clearing by a swamp'. OE *mos*, 'swamp' (modern English *moss*), + *lēah*, 'wood', 'clearing'. Cp. MOSSLEY. 816 *Mosleage*.

Moss (village, Doncaster): '(place by the) swamp'. OE *mos* or OS *mosi*, 'swamp' (modern English *moss*). The reference is to marshland between the rivers Aire and Don here. 1416 *Mose*.

Mossley (town, Tameside): 'woodland clearing by a swamp'. OE *mos* or OS *mosi*, 'swamp' (modern English *moss*), + *lēah*, 'wood', 'clearing'. Mossley lies by the river Tame. 1319 *Moselegh*.

Moss Side (district, Manchester): 'edge of the mossy land'. OE *mos*, 'moss', + *sīde*, 'hillside'. The name is common locally. 1530 *Mossyde*.

Mosterton (village, Dorset): 'Mort's thorn bush'. OE *thorn*, 'thorn bush'. DB *Mortestorne*.

Moston (district, Manchester): 'farmstead by marshy land'. OE *mos*, 'moss', 'marsh', + *tūn*, 'farmstead'. 1195 *Moston*.

Motcombe (village, Dorset): '(place in the) valley where meetings are held'. OE *mōt*, 'meeting', + *cumb*, 'valley'. Motcombe was probably the meeting place of a local hundred. 1244 *Motcumbe*.

Motherby (hamlet, Cumbria): 'Mothir's farmstead'. OS *bý*, 'farmstead', 'village'. The personal name is Scandinavian. 1279 *Motherby*.

Motherwell (town, N Lanarks): 'Our Lady's well'. OE *mōdor*, 'mother', + *wella*, 'well'. The site of the original well dedicated to the Virgin Mary (Mother of God) is marked by a plaque in Ladywell Road. *c.*1250 *Matervelle*, 1265 *Moydirwal*.

Mottingham (district, Lewisham): 'homestead or enclosure of Mōda's people'. OE *-inga-*, 'of the people of', + *hām*, 'homestead', or *hamm*, 'enclosure'. 1044 *Modingeham*.

Mottisfont (village, Hants): '(place by the) spring near the confluence'. OE *mōt*, 'meeting', + *funta*, 'spring'. The spring in question is probably the one on the lawn of Mottisfont Priory, while the confluence is that of the rivers Test and Dunn. The DB form of the name below is corrupt. DB *Mortesfunde*, 1167 *Motesfont*.

Mottistone (village, IoW): '(place by the) stone of the speaker at an assembly'. OE *mōtere*, 'speaker at an assembly', + *stān*, 'stone'. The stone in question, the menhir now called The Longstone that stands on a hill overlooking the village, would have served as a site for important meetings during the Anglo-Saxon period. The name would have been transferred to the settlement here some time before the DB recorded its name. DB *Modrestan*.

Mottram in Longdendale (village, Tameside): 'place where assemblies are held in Longdendale'. OE *mōt*, 'meeting', 'assembly', or *mōtere*, 'speaker at an assembly', + *rūm*, 'space'. The district name, meaning 'dale of the long valley' (OE *lang*, 'long', + *denu*, 'valley', + OS *dalr*, 'dale'), distinguishes this Mottram from *Mottram St Andrew*, Cheshire, 15 miles to the southwest, named after its church dedication. *c.*1220 *Mottrum*, 1308 *Mottram in Longedenedale*.

Mouldsworth (village, Cheshire): 'enclosure by a hill'. OE *molda*, 'crown of the head', + *worth*, 'enclosure'. The village lies at the foot of a considerable hill. 12C *Moldeworthe*.

Moulsecoomb (district of Brighton, Brighton & Hove): 'Mūl's valley'. OE *cumb*, 'valley'. *c.*1100 *Mulescumba*.

Moulsford (village, Oxon): '(place by) Mūl's ford'. OE *ford*, 'ford'. Moulsford is on the Thames. *c.*1110 *Muleforda*.

Moulsoe (village, Milton K): 'Mūl's hill spur'. OE *hōh*, 'hill spur'. The name could also mean 'hill spur where mules are kept' (OE *mūl*, 'mule', + *hōh*). DB *Moleshou*.

Moulton (village, Lincs): 'Mūla's farmstead'. OE *tūn*, 'farmstead', 'village'. The name could also mean 'farmstead where mules are kept' (OE *mūl*, 'mule', + *tūn*). DB *Multune*. SO ALSO: *Moulton*, Cheshire, Northants, N Yorks, Suffolk.

Mountain Ash (town, Rhondda CT): '(place by the) mountain ash'. The town arose as an industrial development in the 19C and took its name from an inn here, itself named (perhaps punningly, given its location) after a nearby mountain ash or rowan. The Welsh name of Mountain Ash is *Aberpennar*, 'confluence of the (river) Pennar' (Welsh *aber*, 'river mouth', 'confluence'). The stream Pennar flows into the river Cynon here. The stream takes its name from a nearby mountain, *Cefn Pennar*, 'ridge of the height' (Welsh *cefn*, 'ridge', + *pennardd*, 'height').

Mount Bures (hamlet, Essex): '(place by the) hill near Bures'. ME *munt*, 'hill'. The hamlet, near BURES, 'takes its distinguishing name from an artificial mount near the church, one acre in extent at the base, and upwards of 100 feet high, the top of which is crowned with large oak and other trees' (Samuel Lewis, *A Topographical Dictionary of England*, 1840). 1328 *Bures atte Munte*.

Mount Edgcumbe (mansion, Cornwall). The house was built on a prominent site facing Plymouth Sound in *c.*1547 by Sir Richard Edgcumbe, who gave it the family name. 1579 *Monte Edgecomb*.

Mountfield (village, E Sussex): 'Munda's open land'. OE *feld*, 'open land' (modern English *field*). The DB form of the name below is corrupt. DB *Montifelle*, 12C *Mundifeld*.

Mountjoy (hamlet, Cornwall): 'stone house'. Cornish *meyn-ji* (from *meyn*, plural of *men*, 'stone', + *chi*, 'house'). The name has been assimilated to an English equivalent of *Mount Pleasant*. 1277 *Meyndi*.

Mountnessing (village, Essex): 'de Mounteney's (manor called) Ing'. The de Mounteney family held the manor here. For its name, see INGATESTONE. DB *Ginga*, 1237 *Gynges Munteny*.

Mount's Bay (bay, Cornwall): 'bay of (St Michael's) Mount'. The extensive bay, stretching from Gwennap Head near Land's End in the west to Lizard Point in the east, takes its name from its most distinctive feature, ST MICHAEL'S MOUNT. 1354 *Le Mountesbaye*.

Mountsorrel (village, Leics): '(place by the) sorrel-coloured hill'. OF *mont*, 'hill', + *sorel*, 'sorrel'. The name refers to the local pinkish-brown stone. 1152 *Munt Sorel*.

Mousehold Heath (district of Norwich, Norfolk): 'mousehold heath'. The elevated open space 'derives its name from the numerous caves made by digging for chalk clunch used by builders' (*The National Gazetteer of Great Britain* *and Ireland*, 1868). 1868 *Mousehold, or Mousewold Heath*.

Mousehole (coastal village, Cornwall): '(place by a) mousehole'. OE *mūs*, 'mouse', + *hol*, 'hole'. The original 'mousehole' was a large cave nearby in the cliffs. The first form of the name below is the Latin equivalent. 1242 *Pertusum muris*, 1284 *Musehole*, 1302 *Mousehole*.

Mow Cop (hill, Cheshire/Staffs): 'heap hill'. OE *mūga*, 'heap', + *hyll*, 'hill', + *copp*, 'hilltop'. The 'heap' would probably have been a cairn here, marking the county boundary. The second word of the name was added when the sense of 'hill' in the original was lost. *c.*1270 *Mowel*, 1621 *Mowle-coppe*.

Mowsley (village, Leics): 'woodland clearing overrun with mice'. OE *mūs*, 'mouse', + *lēah*, 'wood', 'clearing'. DB *Muselai*.

Moylgrove (village, Pemb): 'Matilda's grove'. OE *grāfa*, 'grove'. The Welsh name of Moylgrove is *Trewyddel*, 'grove farm' (Welsh *tre*, 'farm', + *gwyddel*, 'grove'). 1291 *Ecclesia de grava Matild'*.

Much Birch (village, Herefords): 'greater (place by the) birch tree'. OE *micel*, 'great', + *birce*, 'birch'. The first word of the name distinguishes the village from nearby *Little Birch*. 1252 *Birches*.

Much Cowarne (village, Herefords): 'greater (place with a) cowhouse'. OE *cū*, 'cow', + *ærn*, 'house', 'building'. The first word of the name (OE *mycel*, 'great') distinguishes the village from *Little Cowarne*, 3 miles to the northwest. The DB form of the name below has omitted *n*. DB *Cuure*, 1255 *Couern*.

Much Dewchurch (village, Herefords): 'greater (place with) St Dewi's church'. OE *cirice*, 'church'. The first word of the name (OE *mycel*, 'great') distinguishes this Dewchurch from *Little Dewchurch*, 4 miles to the east. The churches at both places are dedicated to St David, whose Welsh name is Dewi. The first form of the name below has OW *lann* (modern Welsh *llan*) as the equivalent of OE *cirice*. 7C *Lann Deui*, *c.*1150 *Dewischirche*.

Muchelney (village, Somerset): 'large island'. OE *micel*, 'great', + *ēg*, 'island'. The 'island' is the raised ground liable to flood on which Muchelney stands by the rivers Yeo and Parrett. *c.*900 *Miclanige*, DB *Micelenye*.

Much Hadham (village, Herts): 'greater homestead on the heath'. OE *mycel*, 'great', + *hæth*, 'heath', + *hām*, 'homestead'. The first word of the name distinguishes this Hadham from *Little Hadham*, 2 miles to the north. An old joke runs that Much Hadham is so called from the many lawyers living there ('much had 'em'). 957 *Hædham*, DB *Hadham*, 1373 *Muchel Hadham*.

Much Hoole (village, Lancs): 'greater (place with a) shed'. OE *mycel*, 'great', + *hulu*, 'shed', 'hovel'. The first word of the name distinguishes the village from nearby *Little Hoole*. The second form of the name below has Latin *magna*, 'great'. 1204 *Hulle*, *c.*1235 *Magna Hole*.

Muchlarnick (hamlet, Cornwall): 'greater (place in the) clearing'. The place was originally *Larnick* (Cornish *lannergh*, 'clearing'). It was then divided in two and the parts were distinguished as 'Much' (ME *muchel*, 'great') and 'Little' (ME *lutel*, 'little'). DB *Lanher*, 1307 *Muchele Lanrak*.

Much Marcle (village, Herefords): 'greater (place by the) wood or clearing on a boundary'. OE *mycel*, 'great', + *mearc*, 'boundary', + *lēah*, 'wood', 'clearing'. Much Marcle is close to the county boundary with Gloucestershire. The first word of the name distinguishes the village from *Little Marcle*, 3 miles to the north. DB *Merchelai*.

Much Wenlock (town, Shropshire): 'greater enclosure by the white place'. The main word of the name represents OE *loca*, 'enclosed place' (perhaps in the sense 'monastery') preceded by a Celtic word related to modern Welsh *gwyn*, 'white', referring to the nearby limestone hill ridge of Wenlock Edge. The first word (OE *mycel*, 'great') distinguishes the town from the village of *Little Wenlock*, 5 miles to the north. DB *Wenloch*.

Muck (island, Highland): '(island of) pigs'. Gaelic *muc*, 'pig'. Pigs must have been pastured here at some time. The first part of the form of the name below represents Gaelic *eilean*, 'island'. 1370 *Helantmok*.

Mucking (hamlet, Thurrock): '(settlement of) Mucca's people'. OE *-ingas*, 'people of'. The name could also mean simply 'Mucca's place' (OE *-ing*, 'place belonging to'). DB *Muchinga*.

Muckle Flugga (island, Shetland): '(island of) great cliffs'. OS *mikill*, 'great', + *flugga*, 'cliffs', 'precipices'. The island is the highest of three rocks here.

Mucklestone (village, Staffs): 'Mucel's farmstead'. OE *tūn*, 'farmstead'. DB *Moclestone*.

Muddiford (village, Devon): 'Mōda's enclosure'. OE *worthig*, 'enclosure'. The OE word was later replaced by *ford*, 'ford'. 1303 *Modeworthi*.

Mudeford (coastal district of Christchurch, Dorset): '(place by the) muddy ford'. OE *muddig*, 'muddy', + *ford*, 'ford'. The ford would have been over one of the streams here. 13C *Modeford*, 1868 *Muddiford*.

Mudford (village, Somerset): '(place by the) muddy ford'. OE *muddig*, 'muddy', + *ford*, 'ford'. The river here is the Yeo. DB *Mudiford*.

Mudgley (hamlet, Somerset): '(place by the) wood or clearing'. OE *lēah*, 'wood', 'clearing'. The first part of the name is of uncertain origin. It may represent a personal name. 1157 *Mudesle*.

Mugginton (village, Derbys): 'estate associated with Mogga or Mugga'. OE *-ing-*, 'associated with', + *tūn*, 'farmstead', 'estate'. DB *Mogintun*.

Muggleswick (hamlet, Durham): 'Mucel's farmstead'. OE *wīc*, 'specialized farm'. The form of the name below has OE *-ing-*, 'associated with'. *c.*1170 *Muclingwic*.

Muirkirk (town, E Ayrs): 'moorland church'. OS *mōr*, 'moor', + *kirkja*, 'church'. Muirkirk is near the barren tract of moorland known as Airds Moss.

Muker (village, N Yorks): '(place with a) narrow plot of land'. OS *mjór*, 'narrow', + *akr*, 'plot of land' (related modern English *acre*). The Muker Beck here takes its name from that of the village. 1274 *Meuhaker*.

Mulbarton (village, Norfolk): 'outlying farm where milk is produced'. OE *meoluc*, 'milk', + *bere-tūn*, 'outlying farm' (see BARTON). DB *Molkebertuna*.

Mull (island, Argyll & Bute): '(island of the) headland'. OS *múli*, 'snout', 'headland'. The name suits the topography, although an alternative derivation in Gaelic *muileach*, 'dear', 'beloved', has also been proposed, alluding to a place that was specially favoured in some way. *c.*150 *Malaios*.

Mullion (village, Cornwall): '(church of) St Melaine'. The church here is dedicated to Melaine, a 6C Breton or Frankish bishop of Rennes. *c.*1225 *Sanctus Melanus*, 1284 *Seynt Melan*, 1569 *Moullian*.

Mull of Kintyre. See KINTYRE.

Mumbles (district, Swansea): '(place by) Mumbles Head'. The second part of the name of the headland probably comes from OS *múli*, 'snout', as possibly for MULL. The first part is obscure. 1549 *Mommulls*.

Mumby (village, Lincs): 'Mundi's farmstead'. OS *bý*, 'farmstead', 'village'. The personal name is Scandinavian. DB *Mundebi*.

Mundesley (resort village, Norfolk): 'Mūl's or Mundel's woodland clearing'. OE *lēah*, 'wood', 'clearing'. DB *Muleslai*.

Mundford (village, Norfolk): '(place by) Munda's ford'. OE *ford*, 'ford'. The village is near the river Wissey. DB *Mundeforda*.

Mundham (village, Norfolk): 'Munda's homestead or enclosure'. OE *hām*, 'homestead', or *hamm*, 'enclosure'. DB *Mundaham*.

Mundon (village, Essex): '(place by the) hill offering protection'. OE *mund*, 'protection', + *dūn*, 'hill'. The low hill here by the marshes of the Blackwater estuary would have afforded protection from floods. DB *Munduna*.

Mungrisdale (hamlet, Cumbria): '(place in the) valley where young pigs are kept'. OS *gríss*, 'pig', + *dalr*, 'valley'. The church here is dedicated to St Kentigern, otherwise known as St Mungo, whose name was subsequently added to the original. 1285 *Grisedale*, 1600 *Mounge Grieesdell*.

Munsley (hamlet, Herefords): 'Mūl's or Mundel's woodland clearing'. OE *lēah*, 'wood', 'clearing'. DB *Muleslage*, *Muneslai*.

Munslow (village, Shropshire): '(place with a) mound'. OE *hlāw*, 'mound', 'tumulus'. The first part of the name is of unknown meaning. The mound in question, of which there is now no trace, may have marked the meeeting place of the Munslow hundred. 1167 *Mosselawa*, 1252 *Munselowe*.

Murcott (hamlet, Oxon): 'cottage in marshy ground'. OE *mōr*, 'moor', 'marshy ground', + *cot*, 'cottage'. *c.*1191 *Morcot*.

Murrayfield (district, Edinburgh): 'Murray's field'. The name is that of Archibald Murray, later Lord Henderland, who bought the estate known as Nisbet's Parks here in 1733 and named it after himself.

Mursley (village, Bucks): 'Myrsa's woodland clearing'. OE *lēah*, 'wood', 'clearing'. The DB form of the name below has omitted the *r* of the personal name. DB *Muselai*, 12C *Murselai*.

Murton (town, Durham): 'farmstead in moorland'. OE *mōr*, 'moor', + *tūn*, 'farmstead'. 1155 *Mortun*. SO ALSO: *Murton*, Cumbria, York.

Musbury (village, Devon): 'fort full of mice '. OE *mūs*, 'mouse', + *burh*, 'fortified place'. The name denotes the old fort known as Musbury Castle, which must have been overrun by mice. DB *Musberia*.

Muscoates (hamlet, N Yorks): 'cottages overrun with mice'. OE *mūs*, 'mouse', + *cot*, 'cottage'. *c.*1160 *Musecote*.

Musselburgh (coastal town, E Lothian): 'mussel town'. OE *musele*, 'mussel', + *burh*, 'town'. The town has been famous for its seafood since the 11C. *c.*1100 *Muselburge*.

Muston (village, Leics): 'farmstead full of mice'. OE *mūs*, 'mouse', + *tūn*, 'farmstead'. 12C *Mustun*.

Muston (village, N Yorks): 'farmstead running with mice'. OE *mūs*, 'mouse', + *tūn*, 'farmstead'. The name could also mean 'Músi's farmstead', with a Scandinavian personal name. DB *Mustone*.

Muswell Hill (district, Haringey): 'hill by the mossy spring'. OE *mēos*, 'moss', + *wella*, 'spring', + modern English *hill*. A plaque in Muswell Road locates the original site of the spring, dedicated to St Mary and said to have curative properties. The hill is the one on which St James's church stands. *c.*1155 *Mosewella*.

Myddle (village, Shropshire): '(place at the) confluence of streams'. OE *mȳthe*, 'junction of streams' (related modern English *mouth*). The DB form of the name below is corrupt. DB *Mulleht*, 1121 *Muthla*, 1868 *Middle*.

Mylor Bridge (village, Cornwall): 'bridge in (the parish of) Mylor'. The main name means '(church of) St Melorus', from the saint, said to be a Cornish prince, to whom Mylor parish church is dedicated. The bridge is over the head of Mylor Creek. The first form of the name below means 'new bridge' (Cornish *pons*, 'bridge', + *nowydh*, 'new'). 1562 *Ponsnowythe*, 1697 *New bridge*, 1745 *Mylor Bridge*.

Myndtown (hamlet, Shropshire): 'place by the mountain'. Welsh *mynydd*, 'mountain', + modern English *town*. The mountain is the Long Mynd nearby. DB *Munete*, 1577 *Myntowne*.

Mynyddoedd Duon, Y. See BLACK MOUNTAINS.

Mytholmroyd (town, Calderdale): 'clearing at the river mouths'. OE *mȳthe*, 'confluence of rivers' (related modern English *mouth*), + *rodu*, 'clearing'. The river mouths in question are those of Cragg Brook and the river Calder. The first part of the name represents OE *mȳthum*, the dative plural form of *mȳthe*. For the second part, see also BLACKROD. late 13C *Mithomrode*.

Myton-on-Swale (village, N Yorks): 'farmstead at the river junction on the (river) Swale'. OE *mȳthe*, 'river junction' (related modern English *mouth*), + *tūn*, 'farmstead'. The village is near the confluence of the Swale and the Ure. For the river name, see BROMPTON-ON-SWALE. 972 *Mytun*, DB *Mitune*.

Mytton (hamlet, Shropshire): 'farmstead at the river junction'. OE *mȳthe*, 'river junction' (related modern English *mouth*), + *tūn*, 'farmstead'. The river Perry joins the river Severn here. DB *Mutone*.

Naburn (village, York): '(place by the) narrow stream'. OE *naru*, 'narrow', + *burna*, 'stream'. The first part of the name is speculative. The stream in question enters the river Ouse here. DB *Naborne*.

Nackington (hamlet, Kent): 'hill by the wet place'. OE *næting*, 'wet place' (from *næt*, 'wet', + *-ing*, 'place characterized by'), + *dūn*, 'hill'. The DB form of the name below has *L-* for *N-*. late 10C *Natyngdun*, DB *Latintone*.

Nacton (village, Suffolk): 'Hnaki's farmstead'. OE *tūn*, 'farmstead'. The personal name is Scandinavian. DB *Nachetuna*.

Nafferton (village, E Yorks): 'Náttfari's farmstead'. OE *tūn*, 'farmstead'. The personal name is Scandinavian. DB *Nadfartone*.

Nailsea (town, N Somerset): 'Nægl's island'. OE *ēg*, 'island'. The 'island' is the raised ground on which Nailsea stands, to the east of Nailsea Moor. 1196 *Nailsi*.

Nailstone (village, Leics): 'Nægl's farmstead'. OE *tūn*, 'farmstead'. 1225 *Naylestone*.

Nailsworth (town, Glos): 'Nægl's enclosure'. OE *worth*, 'enclosure'. The named Anglo-Saxon is not necessarily the same as the man who gave the name to NAILSEA, although the two towns are only some 30 miles apart. 1196 *Nailleswurd*.

Nairn (resort town, Highland): '(place at the mouth of the river) Nairn'. The river has a Celtic name meaning something like 'penetrating one'. The town's location is indicated by the first form of the name below, which has Gaelic *inbhir*, 'river mouth'. c.1195 *Inuernaren*, 1382 *Narne*.

Nanstallon (village, Cornwall): '(place in the) valley of the (river) Alan'. Cornish *nans* (earlier *nant*), 'valley'. The river here now is the Camel (see CAMELFORD), but formerly it was the *Alan*, a Celtic name of uncertain meaning. 1201 *Lantalan*.

Nantwich (town, Cheshire): 'famous salt-works'. ME *named*, 'famous' (modern English *named*), + *wīc*, 'specialized farm', 'industrial settlement'. Nantwich was noted for the excellence and whiteness of its salt. See also MIDDLEWICH, NORTHWICH. DB *Wich*, 1194 *Nametwihc*.

Nantyglo (village, Blaenau Gwent): 'valley of coal'. Welsh *nant*, 'valley', + *y*, 'the', + *glo*, 'charcoal', 'coal'. The name indicates a valley where coal was extracted, or where a stream was associated with charcoal-burning. The village of *Coalbrookvale*, a little further down the valley of the river Ebbw Fach, translates the Welsh name. (Welsh *nant* means both 'valley' and 'stream'.) 1752 *Nantygloe*.

Nappa (hamlet, N Yorks): 'enclosure in a bowl-shaped hollow'. OE *hnæpp*, 'bowl', + *hæg*, 'enclosure' (related modern English *hedge*). The DB form of the name below is corrupt. DB *Napars*, 1182 *Nappai*.

Napton on the Hill (village, Warwicks): 'farmstead on the bowl-shaped hill'. OE *hnæpp*, 'bowl', + *tūn*, 'farmstead'. The hill on which the village stands must have suggested the shape of an inverted bowl. The second part of the name is strictly speaking tautologous. DB *Neptone*.

Narberth (town, Pemb): '(place) near the hedge'. Welsh *yn*, 'at', + *ar*, 'near', + *perth*, 'hedge'. The original name of Narberth was *Arberth*, its Welsh name today. The 'N-' of the English name comes from the first word of the phrase *yn Arberth*, 'in Arberth'. 1291 *Nerberth*, 1331 *la Nerbert*.

Narborough (village, Norfolk): 'stronghold by a narrow pass'. OE *neru*, 'narrow place', + *burh*, 'fortified place'. The river Nar here took its name from that of the village. DB *Nereburh*.

Naseby (village, Northants): 'Hnæf's stronghold'. OE *burh*, 'fortified place'. The name was originally *Navesbury*. When the Danes arrived, they substituted OS *bȳ*, 'village', for OE *burh*. DB *Navesberie*.

Nash (village, Bucks): '(place) at the ash tree'. OE *æsc*, 'ash'. The 'N-' of the name comes from preceding ME *atten*, 'at the'. 1231 *Esse*, 1520 *Nassche*. SO ALSO: *Nash*, Herefords, Shropshire.

Nassington (village, Northants): 'farmstead on the promontory'. OE *næss*, 'promontory', + *-ing*, 'place characterized by', + *tūn*, 'farmstead'. The promontory in question is the broad headland on which the village stands above the river Nene. 1017 *Nassingtona*, DB *Nassintone*.

Nateby (village, Cumbria): 'farmstead where nettles grow'. OS *nata*, 'nettle', + *bȳ*, 'farmstead', 'village'. The name could also mean 'Nati's farmstead', with a Scandinavian personal name. 1242 *Nateby*.

Nately Scures. See UP NATELY.

Natland (village, Cumbria): 'grove where nettles grow'. OS *nata*, 'nettle', + *lundr*, 'grove'. The name could also mean 'Nati's grove', with a Scandinavian personal name. c.1175 *Natalund*.

Naughton (hamlet, Suffolk): 'Nagli's farmstead'. OE *tūn*, 'farmstead'. The personal name is Scandinavian. c.1150 *Nawelton*.

Naunton (village, Glos): 'new farmstead'. OE *nīwe*, 'new', + *tūn*, 'farmstead', 'estate'. The first part of the name represents OE *nīwan*, the dative form of *nīwe*. DB *Niwetone*.

Naunton Beauchamp (village, Worcs): 'Beauchamp's new estate'. OE *nīwe*, 'new', + *tūn*, 'farmstead', 'estate'. The first word of the name is a local variant of NEWINGTON. The Beauchamp family held the manor here in the 11C. 972 *Niwantune*, DB *Newentune*, 1370 *Newenton Beauchamp*.

Navenby (village, Lincs): 'Nafni's farmstead'. OS *bȳ*, 'farmstead', 'village'. The personal name is Scandinavian. DB *Navenebi*.

Navestock (hamlet, Essex): 'outlying farmstead on the promontory'. OE *næss*, 'promontory', + *-ing*, 'place characterized by', + *stoc*, 'outlying farmstead'. The name could also mean 'outlying farmstead of the dwellers on the promontory', referring to the inhabitants of NAZEING, 10 miles to the northwest. 867 *Nasingestok*, DB *Nassestoca*.

Navio. See BROUGH (Derbys).

Nawton (village, N Yorks): 'Nagli's farmstead'. OE *tūn*, 'farmstead'. The personal name is Scandinavian. DB *Nagletune*.

Nayland (town, Suffolk): '(place) at the island'. OE *ēg-land*, 'island'. The 'island' is the land that lies in a bend of the river Stour here.

The initial 'N-' of the name comes from preceding ME *atten*, 'at the'. DB *Eilanda*.

Naze (headland, Essex): 'promontory'. OE *næss*, 'promontory'. The form of the name below means 'Eadwulf's promontory'. 1052 *Eadulfes næsse*.

Nazeing (village, Essex): '(settlement of the) dwellers on the promontory'. OE *næss*, 'promontory', + *-ingas*, 'dwellers at'. The promontory in question is the spur of land on which Nazeing lies, overlooking the Lea valley. 1062 *Nassingan*, DB *Nasinga*.

Near Sawrey. See FAR SAWREY.

Neasden (district, Brent): '(place by the) nose-shaped hill'. OE *neosu*, 'nose', + *dūn*, 'hill'. It is not clear which hill gave the name, but it may have been in the region of the present Gladstone Park, towards Dollis Hill. c.1000 *Neosdune*, 1876 *Neasdon*.

Neasham (village, Darlington): 'homestead or enclosure by the nose-shaped piece of land'. OE *nes*, 'nose-shaped piece of land', + *hām*, 'homestead', or *hamm*, 'enclosure'. Neasham lies in a nose-shaped bend of the river Tees. 1158 *Nesham*.

Neath (town, Neath PT): '(place on the river) Neath'. The river, known in Welsh as *Nedd*, has a Celtic name perhaps meaning 'shining one'. The Welsh name of Neath is *Castell-Nedd*, 'castle on the Nedd' (Welsh *castell*, 'castle'), referring to the Roman fort here, known as *Nidum*. 1191 *Neth*, 1306 *Neeth*.

Neatishead (village, Norfolk): 'household of the vassal'. OE *genēat*, 'vassal', 'retainer', + *hīred*, 'household'. The DB form of the name below is corrupt. 1020 *Netheshird*, DB *Snateshirda*.

Necton (village, Norfolk): 'farmstead by a neck of land'. OE *hnecca*, 'neck', + *tūn*, 'farmstead'. DB *Nechetuna*, 1868 *Necton, or Neighton*.

Nedging (hamlet, Suffolk): 'place associated with Hnydda'. OE *-ing*, 'place associated with'. c.995 *Hnyddinge*, DB *Niedinga*.

Nedging Tye (hamlet, Suffolk): 'common pasture near Nedging'. Modern English dialect *tye*, 'area of common pasture'. Nedging Tye is 2 miles northeast of NEDGING.

Needham Market (town, Suffolk): 'poor homestead with a market'. OE *nēd*, 'need', + *hām*, 'homestead', + ME *merket*, 'market'. The name implies that the people of Needham were poor and often went hungry. But things must have improved, for by the 16C they had a market. 13C *Nedham*, 1511 *Nedeham Markett*.

Needham Street (hamlet, Suffolk): 'poor homestead'. OE *nēd*, 'need', + *hām*, 'homestead'. The second word of the name amounts to 'hamlet'. *c*.1185 *Nedham*.

Needingworth (village, Cambs): 'enclosure of Hnydda's people'. OE *-inga-*, 'of the people of', + *worth*, 'enclosure'. 1161 *Neddingewurda*.

Needles, The (group of rocks, IoW): 'the needles'. OE *nǣdl*, 'needle'. The name refers to the pointed shape of the three chalk stacks off the western end of the island. The first form of the name below represents a dialect plural form. 1333 *Nedlen*, 1409 *Les nedeles*, 1583 *The Nedells*.

Needwood (hamlet, Staffs): '(place by the) wood of need'. OE *nēd*, 'need', + *wudu*, 'wood'. The reference is to Needwood Forest here, so named as a wood where timber could be obtained in time of need or where refuge could be found when necessary. 1248 *Nedwode*.

Neen Savage (village, Shropshire): 'le Savage's (estate on the river) Neen'. The former name of the river Rea is of identical origin to that of the *Nene* (see NENE VALLEY). The le Savage family held the manor here in the 13C, their name distinguishing this village from *Neen Sollers*, 4 miles to the south, where the manor was held by the de Solers family in the late 12C. DB *Nene*, 13C *Nenesauvage*, 1868 *Neen-Savage*, or *Upper Neen*.

Neenton (village, Shropshire): 'farmstead on the (river) Neen'. OE *tūn*, 'farmstead', 'estate'. For the river name, see NEEN SAVAGE. The DB form of the name below appears to have been influenced by OE *nīwe*, 'new'. DB *Newentone*, 1242 *Nenton*.

Nelson (town, Lancs). The town arose in the early 19C and took its name from the Lord Nelson inn here, itself so called to commemorate Nelson's victory at Trafalgar (1805).

Nempnet Thrubwell (village, Bath & NE Somerset). Originally two places: *Nempnet*, '(place on) level ground' (OE *emnet*, 'plain'), with the initial 'N-' from preceding ME *atten*, 'at the', and *Thrubwell*, '(place by the) stream' (OE *wella*, 'spring', 'stream'), with the first part of the name of uncertain origin. (It may be related to modern English *throb*, giving a sense of 'gushing stream'). *c*.1200 *Emnet*, 1201 *Trubewel*.

Nene Valley (valley, Peterborough): 'valley of the (river) Nene'. The name of the river is of Celtic or pre-Celtic origin and uncertain meaning. 948 *Nyn*.

Nenthead (village, Cumbria): '(place at the) source of the (river) Nent'. OE *hēafod*, 'head'.

The river has a Celtic name meaning 'valley' (modern Welsh *nant*). 1631 *Nentheade*.

Ness, Loch (loch, Highland): 'loch of (the river) Ness'. The river Ness flows from the northern end of Loch Ness to INVERNESS (which see for its name).

Nesscliff (village, Shropshire): '(place by) Nesscliff Hill'. The hill here (OE *ness*, 'promontory', 'headland', + *clif*, 'cliff') is perhaps so called as it was seen as a rocky headland jutting into marshland. It also gave the name of the nearby villages of *Great Ness* and *Little Ness*. DB *Nesse*.

Neston (town, Cheshire): 'farmstead by the promontory'. OE *nǣss*, 'promontory', + *tūn*, 'farmstead'. Neston is on the Wirral peninsula, which may itself have been known as *Ness* at one time. If so, the name would mean 'farmstead in Ness'. The reference could also be to the promontory at Burton Point. DB *Nestone*.

Nether Alderley (village, Cheshire): 'lower (place called) Althrȳth's clearing'. OE *lēah*, 'wood', 'clearing'. The personal name is that of a woman. The first word of the name contrasts the village with nearby *Over Alderley*, and their basic name gave that of ALDERLEY EDGE, 2 miles to the north. DB *Aldredelie*.

Netheravon. See UPAVON.

Netherbury (village, Dorset): 'lower fortified place'. OE *neotherra*, 'lower', 'nether', + *burh*, 'fortified place'. DB *Niderberie*.

Netherby (hamlet, Cumbria): 'lower farmstead'. OS *nethri*, 'lower', + *bý*, 'farmstead'. The Roman fort here was *Castra Exploratorum*, 'camp of the scouts'. 1279 *Netherby*.

Nether Cerne. See UP CERNE.

Nether Compton. See OVER COMPTON.

Nether Exe. See UP EXE.

Netherfield (village, E Sussex): 'open land crawling with adders'. OE *nǣddre*, 'adder', + *feld*, 'open land' (modern English *field*). DB *Nedrefelle*.

Netherhampton (village, Wilts): 'lower homestead'. OE *neotherra*, 'lower', + *hām-tūn*, 'homestead' (from *hām*, 'homestead', + *tūn*, 'farmstead'). The village is probably 'lower' as lying south of the river Nadder with regard to Wilton. 1242 *Notherhampton*.

Nether Heyford. See UPPER HEYFORD (Northants).

Nether Langwith (village, Notts): 'lower (place by the) long ford'. OS *langr*, 'long', + *vath*, 'ford'. The village is lower down the river

Poulter than *Upper Langwith*, Derbys, nearer its source. *c.*1179 *Languath*, 1252 *Netherlangwat*.

Nether Padley (village, Derbys): 'lower (place called) Padda's woodland clearing'. OE *lēah*, 'wood', 'clearing'. The main name could also mean 'woodland clearing where toads are seen' (OE *padde*, 'toad', + *lēah*). The first word of the name distinguishes this Padley from nearby smaller *Upper Padley*. *c.*1230 *Paddeley*.

Nether Poppleton (village, York): 'lower farmstead on pebbly soil'. OE *popel*, 'pebble', + *tūn*, 'farmstead'. The first word of the name distinguishes the village, lying low beside the river Ouse, from nearby *Upper Poppleton*, away from the river. *c.*972 *Popeltune*, DB *Popletone*.

Netherseal. See OVERSEAL.

Nether Silton (village, N Yorks): 'lower farmstead by a ledge'. OE *scylfe*, 'shelf', 'edge', + *tūn*, 'farmstead'. The name could also mean 'Sylfa's farmstead', with a Scandinavian personal name. The first word of the name distinguishes the village from nearby *Over Silton*. DB *Silftune*.

Nether Stowey (village, Somerset): 'lower (place by the) stone way'. OE *stān*, 'stone', + *weg*, 'way'. The first word of the name distinguishes the village from *Over Stowey*, to the south, on the lower slopes of the Quantock Hills. A stony track leads from both villages up to a saddle on the Quantocks. DB *Stawei*.

Netherthong (village, Kirklees): 'lower (place at the) narrow strip of land'. OE *neotherra*, 'nether', 'lower', + *thwang*, 'thong', 'narrow strip of land'. The first part of the name distinguishes the village from nearby *Upperthong*. 13C *Thoying*, 1448 *Nethyrthonge*.

Netherton (hamlet, Northd): 'lower farmstead'. OE *neotherra*, 'nether', 'lower', + *tūn*, 'farmstead', 'estate'. *c.*1050 *Nedertun*. SO ALSO: *Netherton*, Herefords (near Evesham).

Netherton (Wakefield). See MIDDLESTOWN.

Nether Wallop (village, Hants): 'lower (place in a) valley with a spring'. OE *wella*, 'spring', 'stream', + *hop*, 'remote valley'. OE *hop* is mostly found in northern names, and this is the only known example of it south of the Thames. The village is downstream on the Wallop Brook in relation to *Over Wallop*, with *Middle Wallop* between them. The three are sometimes known collectively as *The Wallops*. DB *Wallope*, 1271 *Netherwellop*.

Nether Whitacre (village, Warwicks): 'lower (place by the) white arable land'. OE *hwīt*, 'white', + *æcer*, 'cultivated land' (modern English *acre*). The first word of the name distin-

guishes the village from *Over Whitacre*, 2 miles to the southeast. DB *Witacre*.

Nether Winchendon. See UPPER WINCHEN-DON.

Nether Worton. See OVER WORTON.

Netley (village, Hants): 'wood where laths are obtained'. OE *lætt*, 'lath', + *lēah*, 'wood', 'clearing'. The name originally began with *L-*, not *N-*, as shown by the forms below. 955 *Lætanlia*, DB *Latelei*, 1239 *Lettelege*.

Nettlebed (village, Oxon): '(place by the) plot of land overgrown with nettles'. OE *netele*, 'nettle', + *bedd*, 'bed'. 1246 *Nettlebed*.

Nettlecombe (hamlet, Dorset): '(place in the) valley where nettles grow'. OE *netele*, 'nettle', + *cumb*, 'valley'. DB *Netelcome*.

Nettleden (village, Herts): 'valley of the woodland clearing where nettles grow'. OE *netele*, 'nettle', + *lēah*, 'wood', 'clearing', + *denu*, 'valley'. Nettleden lies in a narrow valley. *c.*1200 *Neteleydene*.

Nettlestead (village, Kent): 'homestead where nettles grow'. OE *netele*, 'nettle', + *hām-stede*, 'homestead' (see HAMPSTEAD). The DB form of the name below is corrupt. 9C *Netelamstyde*, DB *Nedestede*.

Nettlestone (village, IoW): 'farmstead by the nut pasture or nut wood'. OE *hnutu*, 'nut', + *lǣs*, 'pasture', or *lēah*, 'wood', + *tūn*, 'farmstead'. The DB form of the name below has a mistranscription of *N-* as *H-*. DB *Hoteleston*, 1248 *Nutelastone*.

Nettleton (village, Lincs): 'farmstead where nettles grow'. OE *netele*, 'nettle', + *tūn*, 'farmstead'. DB *Neteltone*.

Nettleton (village, Wilts): 'farmstead (at the) place overgrown with nettles'. OE *netele*, 'nettle', + *-ing*, 'place characterized by', + *tūn*, 'farmstead'. 940 *Netelingtone*, DB *Niteletone*.

Nevendon (hamlet, Essex): '(place by the) level valley'. OE *efen*, 'even', 'level', + *denu*, 'valley'. The initial 'N-' of the name comes from the last letter of preceding ME *atten*, 'at the'. The DB form of the name below has *z* for *v*. DB *Nezendena*, 1218 *Neuendene*.

New Alresford. See ALRESFORD (Hants).

Newark-on-Trent (town, Notts): 'new building on the (river) Trent'. OE *nīwe*, 'new', + *weorc*, 'building', 'fortification' (modern English *work*). The 'new building' here would have been contrasted with the Roman fort of *Margidunum* ('marly fort'), at what is now Castle Hill, East Bridgford. The addition of the river name (see STOKE-ON-TRENT) is recent. *c.*1080 *Niweweorce*, DB *Neuuerche*.

New Barnet. See BARNET.

Newbiggin (village, Cumbria): 'new building'. OE *nīwe*, 'new', + ME *bigging*, 'building'. The name implies that new buildings were erected on or near the site of old buildings. Newbiggin is a common North of England name, and there are eight in Cumbria alone. The form of the name below relates to the one near Appleby. 1179 *Neebigging*. SO ALSO: *Newbiggin*, Durham.

Newbiggin-by-the-Sea (resort town and port, Northd): 'new building by the sea'. OE *nīwe*, 'new', + ME *bigging*, 'building'. See NEWBIGGIN. The latter part of the name differentiates this Newbiggin from others. 1187 *Niwebiginga*.

Newbold (district of Chesterfield, Derbys): 'new building'. OE *nīwe*, 'new', + *bold*, 'building'. DB *Newebold*. SO ALSO: *Newbold*, Leics.

Newbold on Avon (district of Rugby, Warwicks): 'new building on the (river) Avon'. OE *nīwe*, 'new', + *bold*, 'building'. The Avon here has a name of the same origin as that at AVON-MOUTH. 1077 *Neobaldo*, DB *Newebold*.

Newbold-on-Stour (village, Warwicks): 'new building on the (river) Stour'. OE *nīwe*, 'new', + *bold*, 'building'. For the river name, see STOURBRIDGE. 991 *Nioweboldan*.

Newbold Pacey (village, Warwicks): 'de Pasci's new building'. OE *nīwe*, 'new', + *bold*, 'building'. The de Pasci family held the manor here in the 13C. DB *Niwebold*, 1235 *Neubold Pacy*.

New Bolingbroke. See OLD BOLINGBROKE.

Newborough (village, Anglesey): 'new borough'. OE *nīwe*, 'new', + *burh*, 'borough'. The 'new borough' was established here in the late 13C by Edward I. The Welsh name of Newborough is *Niwbwrch*, a phonetic version of the English. 1305 *Novus Burgus*, 1324 *Neuburgh*, 1379 *Newborough*.

Newborough (village, Peterborough): 'new borough'. The parish of Newborough here was formed in 1822 from *Borough Fen*, an extraparochial district comprising the area of fenland to the north of PETERBOROUGH. On the formation of the parish, the rest of the area accordingly became *Oldborough*. 1823 *Newborough*.

Newborough (village, Staffs): 'new fortification'. OE *nīwe*, 'new', + *burh*, 'fortified place'. 1280 *Neuboreg*.

Newbottle (hamlet, Northants): 'new building'. OE *nīwe*, 'new', + *bōthl*, 'building'. DB *Niwebotle*. SO ALSO: *Newbottle*, Sunderland.

Newbourne (village, Suffolk): '(place by the) new stream'. OE *nīwe*, 'new', + *burna*, 'stream'. A 'new' stream is one that has changed its course. DB *Neubrunna*.

New Bradwell (town, Milton K): 'new Bradwell'. The town evolved in the 19C from a settlement for railway workers near the village of *Bradwell*, '(place by the) broad spring' (OE *brād*, 'broad', + *wella*, 'spring', 'stream').

Newbridge (hamlet, Oxon): '(place by the) new bridge'. Newbridge stands by what is in fact an ancient bridge over the Thames at the confluence of that river and the Windrush. 1822 *Newbridge*.

New Brighton (district of Emsworth, Hants): 'new Brighton'. The name was adopted from the famous resort of BRIGHTON, 35 miles to the east. The place came to be so called following the visit to take the waters in 1805 of Princess Amelia (1783–1810), the delicate 15th and last child of George III. The royal link lay in the association of her brother, the Prince Regent, with Brighton, where his Royal Pavilion was built in the 1780s.

New Brighton (district of Wallasey, Wirral): 'new Brighton'. The resort arose in the first half of the 19C and took its name from the noted south-coast resort of BRIGHTON. 'This place ... has, from its local advantages, attracted the attention of the public; and a plan of a new town, adapted to the purposes of a bathing-place, has been approved, and numerous houses have been erected' (Samuel Lewis, *A Topographical Dictionary of England*, 1840).

Newbrough (village, Northd): 'new fortification'. OE *nīwe*, 'new', + *burh*, 'fortified place'. 1203 *Nieweburc*.

New Buckenham (village, Norfolk): 'new (place called) Bucca's homestead'. OE *hām*, 'homestead'. The first word of the name contrasts the village with nearby smaller *Old Buckenham*. DB *Bucheham*.

Newburgh (coastal town, Fife): 'new borough'. OE *nīwe*, 'new', + *burh*, 'borough'. The town is not new but an ancient royal burgh dating from at least the 12C. *c*.1130 *Niwanbyrig*, 1266 *Novus burgus*.

Newburn (district, Newcastle): '(place by the) new stream'. OE *nīwe*, 'new', + *burna*, 'stream'. A 'new' stream is one that has changed its course. 1121 *Neuburna*.

Newbury (town, W Berks): 'new borough'. OE *nīwe*, 'new', + *burh*, 'borough'. The town arose as a trading centre after the Norman Conquest, so the name could equally be rendered 'new market town'. *c*.1080 *Neuberie*.

Newby (village, Cumbria): 'new farmstead'. OE *nīwe*, 'new', + OS *bȳ*, 'farmstead', 'village'. 12C *Neubi*.

Newby Bridge (village, Cumbria): '(place by the) new bridge'. *Newby* usually means 'new farmstead' (see NEWBY), but here the '-by' was apparently not part of the original name. The river here is the Leven. No early forms of the name are known. 1577 *New bridge*, 1659 *Newbybridge*.

Newby Wiske (village, N Yorks): 'new farmstead on the (river) Wiske'. OE *nīwe*, 'new', + OS *bȳ*, 'farmstead'. For the river name, see APPLETON WISKE. 1157 *Neuby*.

Newcastle (village, Shropshire): 'new castle'. OE *nīwe*, 'new', + *castel*, 'castle'. The form of the name below is the Latin equivalent of the English. 1284 *Novum castrum*.

Newcastle Emlyn (town, Carm): 'new castle in Emlyn'. OE *nīwe*, 'new', + *castel*, 'castle'. The 13C castle here was 'new' by comparison with the one at Cilgerran, 8 miles away. This Newcastle was distinguished from others by being located in the cantref (hundred) of *Emlyn*, 'around the valley' (Welsh *am*, 'around', + *glyn*, 'valley'). The Welsh name of the town is *Castell-newydd Emlyn*. c.1240 *Novum castrum de Emlyn*, 1257 *Emlyn with New Castle*, 1295 *Newcastle Emlyn*.

Newcastle-under-Lyme (town, Staffs): 'new castle by Lyme'. OE *nīwe*, 'new', + *castel*, 'castle'. A 'new castle' was built here in the 12C near the ancient Lyme Forest, whose Celtic name means 'place of elms'. Cp. ASHTON-UNDER-LYNE. The castle was 'new' by comparison with the one at Chesterton, 2 miles to the northwest. The form of the name below is the Latin equivalent. 1173 *Novum castellum subtus Lymam*.

Newcastle upon Tyne (city and port, Newcastle): 'new castle on the (river) Tyne'. OE *nīwe*, 'new', + *castel*, 'castle'. A 'new castle' was built here in the 11C on the site of the old Roman fort known as *Pons Aelii* ('Hadrian's Bridge'). (The original name of the Roman emperor Hadrian was Publius Aelius Hadrianus, and the bridge here was designed as the original starting point of HADRIAN'S WALL, named after him, which in the event began at WALLSEND, now an eastern extension of Newcastle.) For the river name, see TYNEMOUTH. 1130 *Novem Castellum*.

Newchapel (suburb of Kidsgrove, Staffs): '(place with a) new chapel'. The earlier name of the place was *Thursfield*, 'Thorvaldr's open land' (OE *feld*, 'open land'), with a Scandinavian personal name, and this is preserved in Thurs-

field Lodge here. St James' church stands on the site of the 'old chapel', built in the 16C as a chapel of ease to Wolstanton. DB *Turvoldesfeld*, 1868 *Thursfield, or Newchapel*.

Newchurch (village, Kent): '(place with a) new church'. OE *nīwe*, 'new', + *cirice*, 'church'. The original 'new church' probably stood on the site of the present St Peter and St Paul's church. DB *Nevcerce*. SO ALSO: *Newchurch*, IoW.

New Cross (district, Lewisham): '(place by the) new cross'. The name was probably that of an inn here, perhaps replacing an earlier 'Golden Cross'.

New Delph (district, Oldham): 'new Delph'. The original village takes its name from OE *delf*, 'quarry' (modern English *delve*). 1544 *Delfe*, 1817 *New Delph*.

Newdigate (village, Surrey): '(place at the) gate by the new wood'. OE *nīwe*, 'new', + *wudu*, 'wood', + *geat*, 'gate'. c.1167 *Niudegate*.

New Edlington (suburb of Doncaster): 'new estate associated with Ēdla'. OE *-ing-*, 'associated with', + *tūn*, 'farmstead', 'estate'. New Edlington arose in recent times to the north of the original village of Edlington, now called *Old Edlington*. The DB form of the name below has *l* for *d*. DB *Ellintone*, 1194 *Edelington*.

Newenden (village, Kent): 'new woodland pasture'. OE *nīwe*, 'new', + *denn*, 'woodland pasture'. The first part of the name represents OE *nīwan*, the dative form of *nīwe*. DB *Newedene*.

Newent (town, Glos): 'new place'. The name is believed to be Celtic in origin, and related to the French town name *Nogent*, from the Roman name *Novientum*, from Gaulish *novio*, 'new'. DB *Noent*.

New Forest (woodland region, Hants): 'new forest'. A 'new forest' was created here as a hunting preserve by William the Conqueror in the 11C. DB *Nova Foresta*.

New Fryston. See MONK FRYSTON.

New Galloway (town, Dumfries & Gall): 'new Galloway'. The town dates from 1629, when a royal charter was granted by Charles I to Sir John Gordon, who chose a name to mark his family ties with Lochinvar in what was then the county of GALLOWAY.

Newhall (village, Cheshire): 'new hall'. OE *nīwe*, 'new', + *hall*, 'hall'. The hall in question was a new house built in c.1227 by the lords Audley. It was fortified and had a tower. 1252 *La Nouehall*. SO ALSO: *Newhall*, Derbys.

Newham (borough, Greater London): 'new (borough of East and West) Ham'. The name dates from 1965, when the borough of Newham was created as an amalgamation of the towns of *East Ham* and WEST HAM, the name uniting the two as a 'new Ham'. The name was originally pronounced as two distinct words, unlike Newham, Northd, pronounced 'Newam'.

Newham (hamlet, Northd): 'new homestead or enclosure'. OE *nīwe*, 'new', + *hām*, 'homestead', or *hamm*, 'enclosure'. 1242 *Neuham*.

Newhaven (town and port, E Sussex): '(place with a) new harbour'. OE *nīwe*, 'new', + *hæfen*, 'harbour' (modern English *haven*). A 'new harbour' was created here in the 1580s when the lower section of the river Ouse was canalized so that it entered the sea at this point instead of at Seaford. The earlier name of the place was *Meeching*, '(settlement of) Mēce's people' (OE *-ingas*, 'people of'), preserved in Meeching Road here. 1121 *Mechingas*, 1204 *Mecinges*, 1587 *Newehaven al. Michinge*, 1685 *Meetching al. Newhaven*, 1868 *Newhaven, or Meeching*.

New Herrington. See EAST HERRINGTON.

New Holland (village, N Lincs): 'new (place named after) Holland'. The village arose in the early 19C on the south side of the Humber estuary. White's *Directory of Lincolnshire* (1828) describes it as 'the modern hamlet of the New Holland, where a large Inn was built on the Humber bank about ten years ago'. The name does not apparently relate to the district of HOLLAND, and according to a report in the *Hull Advertiser* of 8 December 1848: 'On the 4th instant, in Caister [died], Mr. Thomas Linley ... from whom New Holland first received its name, he having landed there a cargo of smuggled goods.'

Newick (village, E Sussex): 'new farm'. OE *nīwe*, 'new', + *wīc*, 'dwelling', 'specialized farm'. 1121 *Niwicha*.

Newington (district, Southwark): 'new farmstead'. OE *nīwe*, 'new', + *tūn*, 'farmstead', 'estate'. The '-ing-' of the name represents the ending of OE *nīwan*, the dative form of *nīwe* in the phrase *æt thǣm nīwan tūne*, 'at the new farmstead'. Cp. STOKE NEWINGTON. *c*.1200 *Neuton*, 13C *Niwentone*, 1325 *Neuwyngton juxta Suthwerk*. SO ALSO: *Newington*, Kent (near Folkestone, near Sittingbourne), Oxon.

New Invention (district, Walsall). The name of the original settlement here is first recorded in the 17C and has attracted a number of local legends to account for it. It may have originally been an inn name, punning on the long-established *New Inn* name. 1663 *New Invention*.

Newland (village, Glos): '(place by) new arable land'. OE *nīwe*, 'new', + *land*, 'cultivated land'. At the time the name was given, land here had been newly acquired by the Priory of Malvern. 1221 *Nova terra*, 1248 *Neweland*. SO ALSO: *Newland*, N Yorks, Worcs.

Newlyn (village and port, Cornwall): 'pool for a fleet of boats'. Cornish *lu*, 'army', 'fleet of boats', + *lynn*, 'pool'. The name originally began with *L*- but this changed to *N*- under the influence of names beginning New-. 1290 *Lulyn*, 1337 *Nywelyn*.

Newlyn East (village, Cornwall): 'eastern (place with the) church of St Newlyn'. The church here is dedicated to Newlyn (Newelina), a female saint said to have been martyred nearby by her father, a king. The village was originally known as *St Newlyn*, but the prefix was subsequently dropped. *East* was then added in the 19C to distinguish this Newlyn from NEWLYN, almost 30 miles to the southwest. 1259 *Sancta Niwelina*, 1543 *Nulyn*, 1884 *Newlyn East*.

New Malden (district, Kingston): 'new Malden'. The district of this name arose in the early 19C as an extension of *Malden*, 'hill with a crucifix' (cp. MALDON). It is uncertain which hill is meant, but it may have been the small rise on which the church of St John the Baptist stands in what is now *Old Malden*. DB *Meldone*.

Newmarket (town, Suffolk): 'new market town'. OE *nīwe*, 'new', + ME *merket*, 'market'. The name implies a new settlement that has been granted the right to hold a market. The first form of the name below is the Latin equivalent. 1200 *Novum Forum*, 1418 *la Newmarket*.

New Mills (town, Derbys): 'new mill'. The town grew up around a mill known as New Mill, operating in the late 16C. A second mill was built in the 18C, and the present plural form of the name may date from then. 1625 *New Miln*.

Newnham (village, Kent): 'new homestead or enclosure'. OE *nīwe*, 'new', + *hām*, 'homestead', or *hamm*, 'enclosure'. 1177 *Newenham*. SO ALSO: *Newnham*, Glos, Herts, Northants.

Newport (village, E Yorks): 'new town'. OE *nīwe*, 'new', + *port*, 'town'. The village arose on reclaimed fenland. A former alternative name *River Bridge* referred to the bridge that crossed the Market Weighton Canal here. 1368 *Newport*. SO ALSO: *Newport*, Devon, Essex.

Newport (town and port, IoW): 'new town'. OE *nīwe*, 'new', + *port*, 'market town'. The name could also mean 'new harbour'. The town, at the head of the Medina estuary, is the island's commercial capital. 1202 *Neweport*.

Newport (city and port, Newport): 'new town'. OE *nīwe*, 'new', + *port*, 'market town'. The 12C castle here was regarded as 'new' by comparison with the Roman fort at Caerleon. The Welsh name of Newport is thus *Casnewydd-ar-Wysg*, 'new castle on the (river) Usk' (Welsh *cas*, 'castle', + *newydd*, 'new', + *ar* 'on'). For the river name, see USK. 1138 *Novus Burgus*, 1290 *Nova Villa*, 1291 *Neuborh*.

Newport (coastal town, Pemb): 'new town'. OE *nīwe*, 'new', + *port*, 'market town'. The original town with market rights here may have been regarded as 'new' by comparison with Fishguard, 6 miles away. The Welsh name of Newport is *Trefdraeth*, 'town by the shore' (Welsh *tref*, 'town', + *traeth*, 'shore'). 1282 *Nuport*, 1296 *Newburgh*, 1316 *Novus Burgus*.

Newport (town, Wrekin): 'new town'. OE *nīwe*, 'new', + *port*, 'market town'. The 'new market town' is believed to have been founded by Henry I. 12C *Novus Burgus*, 1237 *Newport*.

Newport-on-Tay (coastal town, Fife): 'new port on the (river) Tay'. OE *nīwe*, 'new', + *port*, 'port'. The town was a ferry port across the Firth of Tay to Dundee for some 800 years. For the river name, see TAYPORT.

Newport Pagnell (town, Milton K): 'Paynel's new town'. OE *nīwe*, 'new', + *port*, 'market town'. The town arose as a 'new town' with market rights. The Paynel family held the manor here in the 12C. (*Pagnell* is from *Paganellus*, the Latinized form of their name.) DB *Neuport*, 1220 *Neuport Paynelle*.

New Quay (resort town, Ceredigion): '(place with a) new quay'. A new quay was built here in 1835 to replace an older and smaller harbour. The Welsh name of New Quay is *Ceinewydd* (Welsh *cei*, 'quay', + *newydd*, 'new').

Newquay (resort town, Cornwall): '(place with a) new quay'. OE *nīwe*, 'new', + ME *key*, 'quay'. A 'new quay' was built here in the 15C to provide shelter for ships. The Cornish name of Newquay is *Towan Blistra*, from *tewynn*, 'sand dunes', and a word of uncertain meaning. 1602 *Newe Kaye*.

New Radnor (village, Powys): 'new Radnor'. The original *Radnor*, '(place at the) red bank' (OE *rēad*, 'red', + *ōra*, 'bank') was the present *Old Radnor*, known in Welsh as *Pencraig*, 'head of the rock' (Welsh *pen*, 'top', 'head', + *craig*, 'rock'). In 1064 the present Radnor was granted rights as the new administrative centre of the region, and became the county town of Radnorshire. Its Welsh name is *Maesyfed*, 'Hyfaidd's field'

(Welsh *maes*, 'field'). DB *Raddrenoue*, 1191 *Radenoura*, 1201 *Radnore*, 1298 *New Radenore*.

New Romney (town, Kent): 'new Romney'. The town is 'new' by comparison with the village of *Old Romney*, which took its name from what is now Romney Marsh and was originally simply *Romney*, '(district of the) broad river' (OE *rūm*, 'broad', + *ēa*, 'river'). There must have been several streams here, giving the overall effect of a 'broad river'. 895 *Rumenea*, DB *Romenel*.

Newsham (village, N Yorks): '(place at the) new houses'. OE *nīwe*, 'new', + *hūs*, 'house'. The name represents OE *nīwum hūsum*, the dative plural form of *nīwe hūs*. The form of the name below is for Newsham near Richmond. DB *Neuhuson*. SO ALSO: *Newsham*, Northd.

Newsholme (hamlet, Lancs): '(place at the) new houses'. OE *nīwe*, 'new', + *hūs*, 'house'. The origin of the name is as for NEWSHAM. DB *Neuhuse*. SO ALSO: *Newsholme*, E Yorks.

New Silksworth. See SILKSWORTH.

Newstead (village, Borders): 'new place'. OE *nīwe*, 'new', + *stede*, 'place'. The Roman fort here was *Trimontium*, '(place by the) three hills', referring to the three Eildon Hills nearby. 1189 *Novo Loco*.

Newstead (village, Notts): 'new place'. OE *nīwe*, 'new', + *stede*, 'place'. The 'new place' here was the site of the 12C abbey. The first form of the name below is the Latin equivalent of the English. 12C *Novus Locus*, 1302 *Newstede*.

Newton (village, Lincs): 'new farmstead'. OE *nīwe*, 'new', + *tūn*, 'farmstead', 'village'. This is the most common English place name, found in all parts of the British Isles. DB *Neutone*.

Newton Abbot (town, Devon): 'new estate of the abbot'. OE *nīwe*, 'new', + *tūn*, 'farmstead', 'estate', + Latin *abbatis*, 'of the abbot'. The estate was given to Torre Abbey (see TORQUAY) in 1196. Hence the second word of the name, which also serves to distinguish this Newton from others. *c.*1200 *Nyweton*, 1270 *Nyweton Abbatis*.

Newton Arlosh (village, Cumbria): 'new farmstead in Arlosh'. OE *nīwe*, 'new', + *tūn*, 'farmstead', 'estate'. The district name, originally the sole name, means 'burnt place', from Celtic words related to modern Welsh *ār*, 'ground', and *llosg*, 'burning'. 1185 *Arlosk*, 1345 *Neutonarlosk*.

Newton Aycliffe (town, Durham): 'new town of Aycliffe'. The first word of the name is an adoption of OE *Newton* for the New Town designated here in 1947. The second word names the nearby village of *Aycliffe*, 'oak tree wood or clearing' (OE *āc*, 'oak', + *lēah*, 'wood', 'clearing'). *c.*1085 *Ayclea*.

Newton Blossomville (village, Milton K): 'de Blosseville's new estate'. OE *nīwe*, 'new', + *tūn*, 'farmstead', 'estate'. The de Blosseville family held the manor here in the 13C. 1175 *Niwetone*, 1254 *Newenton Blosmevill*.

Newton Burgoland (village, Leics): 'Burgilon's new estate'. OE *nīwe*, 'new', + *tūn*, 'farmstead', 'estate'. Lands here were held early by the Burgilon family. DB *Neutone*, 1390 *Neuton Burgilon*.

Newton by Toft. See TOFT NEXT NEWTON.

Newton Ferrers (town, Devon): 'de Ferers' new estate'. OE *nīwe*, 'new', + *tūn*, 'farmstead', 'estate'. William de Ferers held the manor here in the 13C. DB *Niwetone*, 1303 *Neweton Ferers*.

Newtongrange (town, Midlothian): 'grange of the new estate'. OE *nīwe*, 'new', + *tūn*, 'farmstead', 'estate', + OF *grange*, 'grange'. A grange was not simply a granary but a place where an abbey's tithes were paid. This grange was so named for distinction from the one at *Prestongrange*, near Prestonpans. Both were owned by the abbots of Newbattle Abbey.

Newton-le-Willows (town, St Helens): 'new farmstead by the willow trees'. OE *nīwe*, 'new', + *tūn*, 'farmstead'. As recently as the 19C the place was known as *Newton-in-Makerfield* (see ASHTON-IN-MAKERFIELD), and it seems odd that the present distinguishing addition should have been adopted, leading to confusion with the identically named *Newton-le-Willows*, N Yorks. DB *Neweton*, 1257 *Neuton Macreffeld*, 1868 *Newton-in-Mackerfield*, 1897 *Newton-in-Makerfield* (*otherwise Newton-le-Willows*).

Newton Longville (village, Bucks): '(estate at the) new farmstead belonging to Longueville'. OE *nīwe*, 'new', + *tūn*, 'farmstead'. The second word of the name relates to the church of St Faith of Longueville, France, to which the manor here was granted in the mid-12C. DB *Nevtone*, 1254 *Newenton Longevile*.

Newton Mearns (district of Glasgow, E Renfrews): 'new town in Mearns'. The parish name means 'land of the steward', from Gaelic *maor*, 'steward' (from Latin *maior*, 'greater'). 1609 *Newtoun de Mernis*.

Newton Morrell. See NEWTON PURCELL.

Newton on Trent (village, Lincs): 'new farmstead on the (river) Trent'. OE *nīwe*, 'new', + *tūn*, 'farmstead'. For the river name, see STOKE-ON-TRENT. DB *Neutone*.

Newton Poppleford (village, Devon): 'new farmstead by the (place at the) pebble ford'. OE *nīwe*, 'new', + *tūn*, 'farmstead', + *popel*, 'pebble', + *ford*, 'ford'. The ford would have been over the river Otter here, and the pebbles are the round stones known locally as 'Budleigh pobbles'. 1226 *Poplesford*, 1305 *Neweton Popilford*.

Newton Purcell (hamlet, Oxon): 'Purcel's new farmstead'. OE *nīwe*, 'new', + *tūn*, 'farmstead'. The manor here was held in the 12C by the Purcel family, their name distinguishing this Newton from nearby *Newton Morrell*, held by the Morell family. 1198 *Niweton*, 1285 *Newentone Purcel*.

Newton Regis (village, Warwicks): 'royal new farmstead'. OE *nīwe*, 'new', + *tūn*, 'farmstead', + Latin *regis*, 'of the king'. The manor here was held by the king in the 13C. 1155 *Newintone*, 1259 *Kingesneuton*.

Newton Reigny (village, Cumbria): 'de Reigni's new farmstead'. OE *nīwe*, 'new', + *tūn*, 'farmstead'. The de Reigni family held the manor here in the 12C. 1185 *Niweton*, 1275 *Neutonreygnye*.

Newton Solney (village, Derbys): 'de Solenneio's new farmstead'. OE *nīwe*, 'new', + *tūn*, 'farmstead', 'estate'. The de Solenneio family held the manor here in the 13C. DB *Newetun*, 1321 *Newton Solney*.

Newton St Cyres (village, Devon): 'new farmstead with (the church of) St Cyres'. OE *nīwe*, 'new', + *tūn*, 'farmstead'. The church here is dedicated to St Ciricius. *c.*1070 *Niwantune*, 1330 *Nywetone Sancti Ciricii*.

Newton Stewart (town, Dumfries & Gall): 'new village of Stewart'. OE *nīwe*, 'new', + *tūn*, 'farmstead', 'village'. The village was laid out in 1677 by William Stewart, son of the 2nd Earl of Galloway.

Newton Tony (village, Wilts): 'de Toenye's new farmstead'. OE *nīwe*, 'new', + *tūn*, 'farmstead'. The de Toenye family held the manor here in the 13C. DB *Newentone*, 1338 *Newenton Tony*.

Newton with Scales. See SCALES.

Newtown (village, IoW): 'new town'. OE *nīwe*, 'new', + *tūn*, 'village', 'borough'. Newtown was originally the borough of *Francheville*, 'free town' (OF *franche*, 'free', + *ville*, 'town'), a name used as an alternative down to the 16C. *c.*1200 *Niwetune*, 1254 *nouum burgum de Francheuile*.

Newtown (town, Powys): 'new village'. OE *nīwe*, 'new', + *tūn*, 'farmstead', 'village'. The original 'new town' was designated a modern New Town in 1967. The Welsh name of Newtown is *Y Drenewydd*, 'the new town' (Welsh *y*, 'the', + *tref*, 'town', + *newydd*, 'new'). 1250 *Newentone*, 1360 *the Newtown*.

New Tredegar (town, Caerphilly): 'new Tredegar'. The town arose in the 19C around a colliery which was regarded as 'new' by comparison with the ironworks at TREDEGAR, 5 miles to the north.

New Village (suburb of Newport, E Yorks): 'new village'. The village is a recent development, its name first recorded in 1828.

New York (hamlet, Lincs): '(place named after) New York'. The name is essentially a nickname for a remote place, as the hamlet is near the parish boundary. The choice of this particular name may have been influenced by the proximity of the place to Boston, 9 miles to the southeast. 1824 *New York*.

Neyland (town, Pemb): '(place at the) island'. OE *ēg-land*, 'island'. The 'island' is the virtual peninsula on which the town stands. The 'N-' of the name came from preceding ME *atten*, 'at the'. Until recently Neyland was also known as *New Milford*, by contrast with MILFORD HAVEN. 1596 *Nailand*, 1896 *New Milford, or Neyland*.

Nidd (village, N Yorks): '(place by the river) Nidd'. The village stands about a mile north of the Nidd, whose name is of Celtic or pre-Celtic origin and uncertain meaning. DB *Nith*.

Nidum. See NEATH.

Ninfield (village, E Sussex): '(place by) newly reclaimed open land'. OE *nīwe*, 'new', + *numen*, 'taken', 'reclaimed', + *feld*, 'open land' (modern English *field*). The DB form of the name below is garbled. DB *Nerewelle*, 1255 *Nimenefeld*.

Nithsdale (valley, Dumfries & Gall): 'valley of the (river) Nith'. OS *dalr*, 'valley'. The river has a Celtic name meaning 'new one', perhaps referring to its constantly changing course. The first two forms of the name below have Gaelic *srath*, 'valley'. *c.*1124 *Stranit*, 1181 *Stranud*, 1256 *Niddesdale*.

Niton (village, IoW): 'new farmstead'. OE *nīwe*, 'new', + *tūn*, 'farmstead'. The form of more usual NEWTON has been influenced by local dialect. DB *Neeton*, 1868 *Niton, or Neighton*.

Niwbwrch. See NEWBOROUGH.

Nocton (village, Lincs): 'farmstead where wethers are kept'. OE *hnoc*, 'wether' (castrated ram), + *tūn*, 'farmstead'. DB *Nochetune*.

Noctorum (district of Birkenhead, Wirral): '(place on a) dry hill'. OI *cnocc*, 'hill', + *tírim*, 'dry'. This is a purely Irish name, from words corresponding to modern Irish *cnoc* and *tirim*. Noctorum is on raised ground above marshland. The name has now assumed the form of a bogus genitive plural of Latin *nox, noctis*, 'night', 'darkness'. DB *Chenoterie*, 1553 *Knocktoram*.

Noke (village, Oxon): '(place at the) oak tree'. OE *āc*, 'oak'. The 'N-' comes from the ME phrase *atten oke*, 'at the oak'. DB *Acam*, 1382 *Noke*.

Nolton (village, Pemb): 'old farm'. OE *ald*, 'old', + *tūn*, 'farm'. The initial 'N-' of the name has been added as for NEYLAND. The original 'old farm' here may have been taken over from the native Welsh by English settlers. 1317 *Noldeton*, 1403 *Nolton*.

Nomansland (village, Wilts): 'no man's land'. The village evolved as an extraparochial district on the county border with Hampshire. 1817 *Nomans Land*.

Nonington (village, Kent): 'estate associated with Nunna'. OE *-ing-*, 'associated with', + *tūn*, 'farmstead', 'estate'. *c.*1100 *Nunningitun*.

Nonsuch Park (park, Ewell, Surrey). The park is the site of Nonsuch Palace, built in 1538 by Henry VIII and so named as it was intended to be without equal (there would be 'none such' elsewhere). It was never finished and the original had been almost entirely demolished by the end of the 17C.

Norbiton (district, Kingston): 'northern outlying grange'. OE *north*, 'northern', + *bere-tūn*, 'outlying grange' (from *bere*, 'barley', + *tūn*, 'farmstead'). The name contrasts with that of SURBITON, and both granges originally belonged to the royal manor of Kingston. 1205 *Norberton*.

Norbury (hamlet, Cheshire): 'northern manor'. OE *north*, 'northern', + *burh*, 'fortified place', 'manor'. Norbury was in the most northerly part of the parish of Whitchurch, Shropshire. DB *Norberie*.

Norbury (district, Croydon): 'northern manor'. ME *north*, 'northern', + *bury*, 'manor'. The manor was in the north of the parish of Croydon. 1359 *Northbury*, 1422 *Norbury*.

Norbury (village, Derbys): 'northern stronghold'. OE *north*, 'northern', + *burh*, 'fortified place'. The place was presumably regarded as 'north' with regard to Rocester, Staffs. DB *Nortberie*.

Norbury (village, Shropshire): 'northern manor house'. OE *north*, 'northern', + *burh*, 'fortified place', 'manor'. Norbury was probably regarded as 'north' in relation to Lydbury North, 5 miles to the south. 1237 *Norbir*.

Norbury (village, Staffs): 'northern stronghold'. OE *north*, 'northern', + *burh*, 'fortified place'. Norbury was probably seen as 'north' in relation to Stafford Castle, although this is more east than south. DB *Nortberie*.

Norbury (Derbys). See SUDBURY (Derbys).

Norfolk (county, E England): '(territory of the) northern people'. OE *north*, 'northern', + *folc*, 'folk', 'people'. The name refers to the 'northern people' of the East Angles who inhabited this part of East Anglia, as distinct from the 'southern people' of SUFFOLK. DB *Nordfolc*.

Norfolk Broads. See BROADS.

Norham (village, Northd): 'northern homestead or enclosure'. OE *north*, 'northern', + *hām*, 'homestead', or *hamm*, 'enclosure'. The village is on the county's northern border, on the river Tweed. *c*.1050 *Northham*.

Normanby (village, Lincs): 'farmstead of the Northmen'. OE *Northman*, 'Northman', + OS *bý*, 'farmstead'. The Northmen were the Norwegian Vikings. OS *bý* shows that the name was given by other Scandinavians, in this case Danes. The village is also known as *Normanby by Spital*, after SPITAL IN THE STREET, 2½ miles to the northwest, for distinction from NORMANBY LE WOLD, 10 miles to the northeast, and from *Normanby by Stow*, 9 miles to the southwest, near STOW. There is also NORMANBY, N Lincs, 20 miles to the northwest. DB *Normanebi*, 1545 *Normanby next Spittal*, 1868 *Normanby-by-Spittal*. SO ALSO: *Normanby*, N Yorks, Redcar & Clev.

Normanby (village, N Lincs): 'farmstead of the Northmen'. OE *Northman*, 'Northman', + OS *bý*, 'farmstead'. The Northmen were the Norwegian Vikings. Cp. NORMANBY (Lincs). DB *Normanebi*.

Normanby by Spital. See NORMANBY (Lincs).

Normanby by Stow. See NORMANBY (Lincs).

Normanby le Wold (village, Lincs): 'farmstead of the Northmen in the Wolds'. OE *Northman*, 'Northman', + OS *bý*, 'farmstead'. The Northmen were the Norwegian Vikings. The second part of the name denotes the location of this Normanby in the Lincolnshire WOLDS, as distinct from NORMANBY (or *Normanby by Spital*), 10 miles to the southwest. DB *Normanesbi*, 1294 *Normanby super Waldam*, 1868 *Normanby-on-the-Wolds*.

Normandy (village, Surrey). The village takes its name from a former inn here, the Duke of Normandy. 1656 *Normandie*.

Normanton (town, Wakefield): 'farmstead of the Northmen'. OE *Northman*, 'Northman', + *tūn*, 'farmstead'. The Northmen were the Norwegian Vikings. DB *Normantone*.

Normanton on Soar (village, Notts): 'farmstead of the Northmen on the (river) Soar'. OE *Northman*, 'Northman', + *tūn*, 'farmstead'. Cp. NORMANTON. The river name (see BARROW UPON SOAR) distinguishes this Normanton from NORMANTON-ON-THE-WOLDS, 9 miles to the northeast. DB *Normanton*.

Normanton-on-the-Wolds (village, Notts): 'farmstead of the Northmen on the Wolds'. OE *Northman*, 'Northman', + *tūn*, 'farmstead'. Cp. NORMANTON. The second part of the name (see WOLDS) distinguishes this Normanton from NORMANTON ON SOAR, 9 miles to the southwest. DB *Normantone*.

Normanton on Trent (village, Notts): 'farmstead of the Northmen on the (river) Trent'. OE *Northman*, 'Northman', + *tūn*, 'farmstead'. Cp. NORMANTON. The river name (see STOKE-ON-TRENT) distinguishes this Normanton from its namesake 11 miles to the southwest. DB *Normentone*.

Northallerton (town, N Yorks): 'northern Allerton'. OE *north*, 'northern'. The name contrasts with other places called ALLERTON. Unlike them, however, this one is 'Ælfhere's farmstead' (OE *tūn*, 'farmstead'). DB *Aluretune*, 1293 *North Alverton*.

Northam (town, Devon): 'northern enclosure'. OE *north*, 'northern', + *hamm*, 'enclosure'. It is not clear where the corresponding 'southern enclosure' was. DB *Northam*. SO ALSO: *Northam*, Southampton.

Northampton (town, Northants): 'northern home farm'. OE *north*, 'northern', + *hām-tūn*, 'home farm' (from *hām*, 'homestead', + *tūn*, 'farmstead'). The town came to be called 'northern' by contrast with SOUTHAMPTON (although there *Hampton* has a different origin). The need to distinguish the two arose when the towns became the centres of their respective counties. early 10C *Hamtun*, DB *Northantone*.

Northamptonshire (county, central England): 'district based on Northampton'. OE *scīr*, 'shire', 'district'. See NORTHAMPTON. 11C *Hamtunscir*, DB *Northantonescir*.

North Anston (village, Rotherham): 'northern (place by the) solitary stone'. OE *āna*, 'solitary', + *stān*, 'stone'. The first word of the name distinguishes the village from nearby *South Anston*. DB *Anestan*, 1297 *Northanstan*.

North Aston (village, Oxon): 'northern eastern farmstead'. OE *ēast*, 'eastern', + *tūn*, 'farmstead'. The first word of the name locates this Aston to the north of MIDDLE ASTON and STEEPLE ASTON. DB *Estone*.

Northaw (village, Herts): 'northern enclosure'. OE *north*, 'northern', + *haga*, 'enclosure' (related modern English *hedge*). A contrary 'southern enclosure' in East Barnet (1432 *South-awe*) is now lost. 11C *North Haga*.

North Baddesley (village, Hants): 'northern (place called) Bæddi's clearing'. OE *lēah*, 'wood', 'clearing'. The village is 17 miles north of *South Baddesley*, south of Southampton Water. DB *Bedeslei*.

North Barrow (village, Somerset): 'northern (place by the) wood'. OE *bearu*, 'grove', 'wood'. The first word of the name distinguishes the village from nearby *South Barrow*. DB *Berue*.

North Benfleet. See SOUTH BENFLEET.

North Berwick (resort town, E Lothian): 'northern barley farm'. OE *bere-wīc* (from *bere*, 'barley', + *wīc*, 'farm'). The town is 'north' in relation to BERWICK-UPON-TWEED. *c.*1225 *Beruvik*, 1250 *Northberwyk*.

Northborough (village, Peterborough): 'northern fortification'. OE *north*, 'northern', + *burh*, 'fortified place'. The village arose near the northern boundary of Northamptonshire. It may also have been regarded as a 'northern borough' in relation to PETERBOROUGH. 12C *North-burh*, 1868 *Northborough, or Northburgh*.

Northbourne (village, Kent): '(place by the) northern stream'. OE *north*, 'northern', + *burna*, 'stream'. The stream in question may have been the one that flows to the north of Deal. 618 *Northburne*, DB *Norborne*.

North Bovey. See BOVEY TRACEY.

North Bradley. See MAIDEN BRADLEY.

North Brentor (village, Devon): 'northern (place by) Brent Tor'. OE *torr*, 'rocky hill'. The nearby hill has a name of Celtic origin meaning simply 'high place' (modern Welsh *bre*, 'hill', 'highland'). The first word of the name distinguishes the village from nearby *South Brentor*. 1232 *Brentetor*.

North Brewham (village, Somerset): 'northern homestead or enclosure on the (river) Brue'. OE *hām*, 'homestead', or *hamm*, 'enclosure'. For the river name, see BRUTON. Both North Brewham and nearby *South Brewham* are on the Brue. DB *Briweham*.

North Burlingham (village, Norfolk): 'northern homestead of Bærla's or Byrla's people'. OE *-inga-*, 'of the people of', + *hām*, 'homestead'. The first word of the name distinguishes the village from *South Burlingham*, 2 miles to the south. DB *Berlingeham*.

North Burton. See BURTON AGNES.

North Cadbury (village, Somerset): 'northern (place by) Cadbury Castle. The village is 1 mile north of *South Cadbury*, both places taking their name from *Cadbury Castle* (see CADBURY) to the southwest. *c.*1000 *Cadanbyrig*, DB *Cadeberie*.

North Cave. See SOUTH CAVE.

North Cerney (village, Glos): 'northern (place on the) river Churn'. OE *ēa*, 'stream', 'river'. The river has a Celtic name from the same source as the first part of the name of CIRENCESTER. The first word of the name distinguishes the village from *South Cerney*, 5 miles to the south. 852 *Cyrnea*, DB *Cernei*, 1291 *Northcerneye*.

Northchapel (village, W Sussex): 'northern chapel'. ME *north*, 'northern', + *chapele*, 'chapel'. The place was formerly a chapelry of Petworth and lies to the north of that town. 1514 *North-Chapell*.

North Charlton (hamlet, Northd): 'northern farmstead of the freemen'. OE *ceorl*, 'freeman', 'peasant' (modern English *churl*), + *tūn*, 'farmstead'. The first word of the name distinguishes this Charlton from nearby *South Charlton*. 1242 *Charleton del North*.

North Cheriton (village, Somerset): 'northern village with a church'. OE *cirice*, 'church', + *tūn*, 'farmstead', 'village'. The first word of the name distinguishes the village from nearby *South Cheriton*. DB *Ciretona*.

Northchurch (district of Berkhamsted, Herts): '(place by the) northern church'. OE *north*, 'northern', + *cirice*, 'church'. The place arose by the northern church of Berkhamsted. 1254 *Ecclesia de North Berchamstede*, 1347 *le North-cherche*.

North Clifton (village, Notts): 'northern farmstead by a bank'. OE *clif*, 'cliff', 'bank', + *tūn*, 'farmstead'. The village lies on the slope of a low hill, and this could be the 'bank'. The first word of the name distinguishes it from nearby *South Clifton*. DB *Cliftone*, *c.*1160 *Nort Clifton*.

North Coker. See EAST COKER.

North Collingham. See COLLINGHAM.

North Cotes (village, Lincs): 'northern cottages'. OE *north*, 'northern', + *cot*, 'cottage'. There is no corresponding 'South Cotes', and the village was probably regarded as 'north' in relation to Fulstow, 2 miles to the southwest. *c.*1115 *Nordcotis*.

North Cove (village, Suffolk): 'northern (place by the) cove'. OE *cofa*, 'cove'. North Cove is 6 miles north of *South Cove*, which is near the coast (with its coves), and is probably named after it. Also near the coast here is *Covehithe*, 'harbour (near the) cove' (OE *hȳth*, 'harbour'), which must have also taken its name from South Cove. 1204 *Cove*.

North Cowton. See EAST COWTON.

North Crawley (village, Milton K): 'northern (place by the) wood or clearing where crows are seen'. OE *crāwe*, 'crow', + *lēah*, 'wood', 'clearing'. The village was also known as *Great Crawley*, in relation to nearby *Little Crawley*. DB *Crauelai*.

North Cray. See ST MARY CRAY.

North Creake (village, Norfolk): 'northern (place by the) cliff'. The basic name is Celtic in origin, from a word related to modern Welsh *craig*, 'rock' (modern English *crag*). The first word of the name distinguishes the village from nearby *South Creake*. DB *Creic*, 1211 *Northcrec*.

North Curry. See CURRY RIVEL.

North Dalton (village, E Yorks): 'northern farmstead in a valley'. OE *dæl*, 'valley', + *tūn*, 'farmstead'. The first word of the name distinguishes the village from *South Dalton*, 5 miles to the south. DB *Dalton*, c.1155 *Northdaltona*.

North Deighton. See KIRK DEIGHTON.

North Elmham (village, Norfolk): 'northern homestead where elm trees grow'. OE *elm*, 'elm', + *hām*, 'homestead'. The first word of the name distinguishes North Elmham from the group of villages and hamlets known collectively as the *South Elmhams*, Suffolk. Most of these are named from the dedications of their churches: *All Saints South Elmham, St James South Elmham, St Margaret South Elmham, St Michael South Elmham, St Nicholas South Elmham* and *St Peter South Elmham*. However, the first part of the name of *St Cross South Elmham* is really *Sandcroft*, 'sandy enclosure' (OE *sand*, 'sand', + *croft*, 'enclosure'). c.1035 *Ælmham*, DB *Elmenham*.

North Elmsall. See SOUTH ELMSALL.

Northenden (district, Manchester): 'northern enclosure'. OE *north*, 'northern', + *worthign*, 'enclosure'. DB *Norwordine*.

North Fambridge (village, Essex): 'northern bridge by a fen'. OE *fenn*, 'fen', 'marsh', + *brycg*, 'bridge'. The village lies on the northern side of the river Crouch estuary, the first word of the name distinguishing it from *South Fambridge*, on the southern side. DB *Fanbruge*, 1291 *North Fambregg*.

North Ferriby. See SOUTH FERRIBY.

Northfield (district, Birmingham): '(place by) the northern open land'. OE *north*, 'northern', + *feld*, 'open land' (modern English *field*). Northfield lies to the north of King's Norton. DB *Nordfeld*.

Northfleet (town, Kent): 'northern (place by the) stream'. OE *north*, 'northern', + *flēot*, 'stream'. The place was regarded as 'north' in relation to what is now the village of *Southfleet*. The stream in question is a creek of the Thames. 10C *Flyote*, DB *Norfluet*.

North Frodingham (village, E Yorks): 'northern homestead of Frōda's people'. OE *-inga-*, 'of the people of', + *hām*, 'homestead'. The first word of the name distinguished the village from the former *South Frodingham*, now represented by *Frodingham Grange*, 24 miles to the southeast. DB *Frotingham*, 1297 *North Frothyngham*.

North Grimston (village, N Yorks): 'northern (place called) Grímr's farmstead'. OE *tūn*, 'farmstead'. The personal name is Scandinavian. The village is presumably 'north' in relation to *Grimston*, York, 17 miles to the southwest, with a name of the same origin. DB *Grimeston*.

North Hayling. See SOUTH HAYLING.

North Hill (village, Cornwall): 'northern (place by the) wood or clearing where hinds are seen'. OE *hind*, 'hind', 'doe', + *lēah*, 'wood', 'clearing'. The second word of the name was later replaced by OE *hyll*, 'hill'. The first word distinguishes the village from *South Hill*, 5 miles to the southeast. 1238 *Henle*, 1260 *Northindle*.

North Hinksey (suburb of Oxford, Oxon): 'northern island where stallions are kept'. OE *hengest*, 'stallion', + *ēg*, 'island'. The name could also mean 'Hengest's island'. The 'island' is land by the Thames here. The first word of the name distinguishes this Hinksey from nearby *South Hinksey*. 10C *Hengestesige*.

North Holme. See SOUTH HOLME.

North Huish (hamlet, Devon): 'northern household property'. OE *hīwisc*, 'household'. The OE word was the term for a measure of land that would support a family. The first word of the name distinguishes this Huish from *South Huish*, 10 miles to the south. DB *Hewis*.

Northiam (village, E Sussex): 'northern hay meadow'. OE *north*, 'northern', + *hīg*, 'hay', + *hamm*, 'enclosure', 'meadow'. It is possible the 'hay' element is actually 'high' (OE *hēah*). Northiam would then be 'north' by comparison with what is now the hamlet of *Higham* ('high meadow'), recorded in 1339 as *Suthyhomme*, 'southern high meadow'. DB *Hiham*, c.1200 *Nordhyam*, 1868 *Northiam, or Nordiham*.

Northill. See SOUTHILL.

North Kelsey (village, Lincs): 'northern (place called) Cēol's island'. OE *ēg*, 'island'. The 'island' here is dry ground in marshland. The first word of the name distinguishes the village from *South Kelsey*, 2 miles to the south. DB *Chelsi*, DB *Nortchelesei*.

North Killingholme (village, N Lincs): 'northern homestead of Cēolwulf's people'. OE *-inga-*, 'of the people of', + *hām*, 'homestead'. (Original OE *hām* has been replaced by OS *holmr*, 'island'.) The first word of the name distinguishes the village from nearby *South Killingholme*. DB *Chelvingeholm*.

North Kilvington. See SOUTH KILVINGTON.

North Kilworth (village, Leics): 'northern enclosure associated with Cyfel'. OE *-ing-*, 'associated with', + *worth*, 'enclosure'. The first word of the name distinguishes the village from *South Kilworth*, to the southwest. DB *Chivelesworde*, 1191 *Kiuelingwurda*.

North Kyme (village, Lincs): 'northern (place by the) hollow'. OE *cymbe*, 'hollow'. The first word of the name distinguishes the village from *South Kyme*, and the places lie respectively north and south of a shallow depression here. DB *Chime*.

Northleach (village, Glos): 'northern (place) on the (river) Leach'. OE *lǣcc*, 'stream', 'bog'. The river name derives from OE *lǣcc*, 'stream', 'bog'. The first part of the name distinguishes this place from EASTLEACH, to the southeast. DB *Lecce*, 1200 *Northlecche*.

Northleigh (village, Devon): 'northern (place by the) wood or clearing'. OE *north*, 'northern', + *lēah*, 'wood', 'clearing'. The first part of the name distinguishes the village from *Southleigh*, 1½ miles to the south. DB *Lege*, 1291 *Northleghe*.

North Leigh (village, Oxon): 'northern (place by the) wood or clearing'. OE *lēah*, 'wood', 'clearing'. The first word of the name distinguishes the village from *South Leigh*, 3 miles to the south. DB *Lege*, 1225 *Northleg*.

North Leverton (village, Notts): 'northern farmstead on the (river) Legre'. OE *tūn*, 'farmstead'. The former name of a stream here is of Celtic origin and uncertain meaning. The first word of the name distinguishes the village from nearby *South Leverton*. The village is also known as *North Leverton with Habblesthorpe*, the latter name meaning 'Hæppel's outlying farmstead' (OS *thorp*, 'outlying farmstead'). DB *Legretone*.

Northlew (village, Devon): 'northern (place by the river) Lew'. The river name is Celtic in origin and means 'bright stream'. The village is 'north' with regard to LEWTRENCHARD, 9 miles to the south. DB *Leuia*, 1282 *Northlyu*.

North Littleton (village, Worcs): 'northern little farmstead'. OE *lȳtel*, 'little', + *tūn*, 'farmstead'. The first word of the name distinguishes the village from nearby *Middle Littleton* and *South Littleton*. A text of c.860 refers to the group as *thry litlen tunes*, 'three little farms'. 709 *Litletona*, DB *Liteltune*.

North Lopham (village, Norfolk): 'northern (place called) Loppa's homestead'. OE *hām*, 'homestead'. The first word of the name distinguishes the village from nearby *South Lopham*. DB *Lopham*.

North Luffenham (village, Rutland): 'northern (place called) Luffa's homestead'. OE *hām*, 'homestead'. The first word of the name distinguishes the village from nearby *South Luffenham*. DB *Luffenham*.

North Marden. See EAST MARDEN.

North Milford. See SOUTH MILFORD.

North Mimms. See SOUTH MIMMS.

North Molton. See SOUTH MOLTON.

Northmoor (village, Oxon): 'northern (place by the) marsh'. OE *north*, 'northern', + *mōr*, 'moor', 'marshland'. 1059 *More*, 1367 *Northmore*.

North Mundham (village, W Sussex): 'northern (place called) Munda's homestead or enclosure'. OE *hām*, 'homestead', or *hamm*, 'enclosure'. The first word of the name distinguishes the village from nearby *South Mundham*. c.692 *Mundhame*, DB *Mundreham*.

North Muskham (village, Notts): 'northern (place called) Musca's homestead'. OE *hām*, 'homestead', 'village'. The first word of the name distinguishes the village from nearby *South Muskham*. DB *Muscham*.

North Newbald (village, E Yorks): 'northern new building'. OE *nīwe*, 'new', + *bold*, 'building'. The first word of the name distinguishes the village from the smaller *South Newbald*, to the south. 972 *Neoweboldan*, DB *Niuuebold*.

North Newington (village, Oxon): 'northern new farmstead'. OE *nīwe*, 'new', + *tūn*, 'farmstead'. The '-ing-' of the name represents the ending of OE *nīwan*, the dative form of *nīwe*. The first word distinguishes the village from *South Newington*, 5 miles to the south. 1200 *Newinton*.

North Newton (village, Wilts): 'northern new farmstead'. OE *nīwe*, 'new', + *tūn*, 'farmstead'. The first word of the name distinguishes the village from *South Newton*, 15 miles to the south. 892 *Northniwetune*, DB *Newetone*.

North Newton (village, Somerset): 'northern new farmstead'. OE *nīwe*, 'new', + *tūn*, 'farmstead'. DB *Newetune*.

North Nibley (village, Glos): 'northern (place by a) woodland clearing with a peak'. OE *hnybba*, 'peak' (related modern English *nib*), + *lēah*, 'wood', 'clearing'. The 'peak' is the nearby lofty hill known as Nibley Knoll. The first word of the name distinguishes the village from the much smaller *Nibley*, S Glos, 10 miles to the south. 940 *Hnibbanlege*.

North Ockendon. See SOUTH OCKENDON.

Northolt (district, Ealing): '(place by the) northern corners of land'. OE *north*, 'northern', + *halh*, 'nook', 'corner of land'. The corresponding 'southern corners of land' were at SOUTHALL. The *-um* of the first form of the name below represents the dative plural ending of *halh*. The modern form of the name has been influenced by OE *holt*, 'wood'. 960 *Northhealum*, DB *Northala*, 1631 *Northall alias Northolt*, 1868 *Northolt, or Northalt*.

North Ormsby (village, Lincs): 'northern (place called) Ormr's farmstead'. OS *bý*, 'farmstead', 'village'. The personal name is Scandinavian. The first word of the name distinguishes the village from SOUTH ORMSBY, 13 miles to the south, with a name of different origin. 1066 *Vrmesbyg*, DB *Ormesbi*.

North Otterington. See SOUTH OTTERINGTON.

North Owersby (village, Lincs): 'northern (place called) Ávarr's farmstead'. OS *bý*, 'farmstead', 'village'. The personal name is Scandinavian. The first word of the name distinguishes the village from nearby *South Owersby*. DB *Aresbi*.

Northowram. See SOUTHOWRAM.

North Perrott (village, Somerset): 'northern (place by the river) Parrett'. The river name is pre-English and of obscure origin. The first word of the name distinguishes the village from *South Perrott*, Dorset, 2 miles to the south. *c.*1050 *Peddredan*, DB *Peret*.

North Petherton. See SOUTH PETHERTON.

North Petherwin (village, Cornwall): 'northern (church of) Padern the Blessed'. Cornish *gwynn*, 'white', 'blessed'. The churches here and at *South Petherwin*, 5 miles to the south, are dedicated to Padern, a saint of uncertain identity. 1259 *North Piderwine*.

North Pickenham (village, Norfolk): 'northern (place called) Pīca's homestead'. OE *hām*, 'homestead'. The first word of the name distinguishes the village from *South Pickenham*, 2 miles to the south. DB *Pichenham*.

North Piddle. See WYRE PIDDLE.

North Poorton (village, Dorset): 'northern (place with a) farmstead'. OE *tūn*, 'farmstead'. The first part of the main name is of uncertain origin. It may represent a former name of the stream here. The first word of the name distinguishes the village from nearby *South Poorton*. DB *Pourtone*.

Northrepps (village, Norfolk): 'northern strips of land'. OE *north*, 'northern', + *reopul*, 'strip of land' (related modern English *rip*). The first part of the name distinguishes the village from *Southrepps*, 2 miles to the south. DB *Norrepes*, 1185 *Nordrepples*.

North Riding. See EAST RIDING.

North Ronaldsay (island, Orkney): 'northern Ringan's island'. OS *ey*, 'island'. 'Ringan' is said to be a form of the name of St Ninian, while 'North' distinguishes this island, the northernmost of the Orkneys, from SOUTH RONALDSAY, where the personal name is different. *c.*1150 *Rinarsey*.

North Runcton (village, Norfolk): 'northern farmstead enclosed by poles'. OE *hrung*, 'pole' (modern English *rung*), + *tūn*, 'farmstead'. The poles could also have been used to make a causeway here. The first word of the name distinguishes the village from the hamlet of *South Runcton*, 5 miles to the south. To the west of South Runcton is *Runcton Holme*, the latter word representing OS *holmr*, 'island', meaning raised ground in marsh. DB *Runghetuna*.

North Scarle (village, Lincs): 'northern (place by a) dirty clearing'. OE *scearn*, 'dung', 'muck', + *lēah*, 'wood', 'clearing'. The first word of the name distinguishes the village from *South Scarle*, Notts, 2 miles to the south. DB *Scornelei*.

North Shields (town, N Tyneside): 'northern sheds'. ME *north*, 'northern', + *schele*, 'shed', 'shieling'. The 'sheds' would have been temporary huts used by fishermen on the north bank of the Tyne here, opposite SOUTH SHIELDS. 1268 *Chelis*, 1275 *Nortscheles*.

North Somercotes (village, Lincs): 'northern huts or cottages used in summer'. OE *sumor*, 'summer', + *cot*, 'cottage'. The hamlet of *South Somercotes* lies 2 miles to the south. DB *Summercotes*.

North Stainley. See SOUTH STAINLEY.

North Stainmore (hamlet, Cumbria): 'northern (place by the) rocky moor'. OE *stān*, 'stone', + *mōr*, 'moor'. OE *stān* was later replaced by equivalent OS *steinn*. The first word of the name distinguishes this Stainmore from nearby *South Stainmore*. Stainmore Moor here is strewn with boulders. *c.*990 *Stanmoir*.

North Stifford (village, Thurrock): 'northern (place by the) ford where lamb's cress grows'. OE *stīthe*, 'lamb's cress', + *ford*, 'ford'. Lamb's cress (*Cardamine hirsuta*) is a type of bitter cress. The ford would have been over the Mar Dyke here, perhaps where Stifford Bridge now crosses it. The first word distinguishes the village from *South Stifford*, immediately to the south. *c.*1090 *Stithforde*, DB *Stiforda*.

North Sunderland (village, Northd): 'northern (place on the) southern cultivated land'. OE *sūtherra*, 'southern', + *land*, 'cultivated land'. The place was originally *Southland* or *Sutherland*, presumably so called as south of NORHAM, 23 miles to the northwest. It then became *Sutherlandland* or *Sunderland*, apparently under the influence of SUNDERLAND, and finally added *North* to be distinguished from that town, 50 miles to the south. 1177 *Suthlanda*, 12C *Sutherlannland*.

North Tawton. See BISHOP'S TAWTON.

North Thoresby (village, Lincs): 'northern (place called) Thórir's farmstead'. OS *bý*, 'farmstead', 'village'. The personal name is Scandinavian. The first word of the name distinguishes this Thoresby from *South Thoresby*, 16 miles to the south. DB *Toresbi*.

North Tidworth. See TIDWORTH.

Northumberland (county, NE England): 'land of the north Humber people'. OE *land*, 'land', 'estate'. The name alludes to the territory of the people who lived north of the *Humber* (see HUMBERSTON), which was originally more extensive than the present county (whose southern border is some way north of the Humber). As *Northumbria* the name became familiar for the Anglo-Saxon kingdom in this region, and this is still sometimes misused as the county name, doubtless under the influence of the revived historic name of CUMBRIA ('A parachutist plunged to his death during a jump near Chathill, Northumbria', *Sunday Times*, 26 November 2000). The name is still in official use for the Northumbria Police, however, based at Ponteland. 1130 *Norhumberland*.

North Walsham (town, Norfolk): 'northern (place called) Walh's homestead' (OE *hām*, 'homestead', 'village'). The first word of the name distinguishes the town from the village of *South Walsham*, 12 miles to the south. 1044 *Northwalsham*, DB *Walsam*.

North Warnborough (village, Hants): 'northern (place by the) stream where criminals were drowned'. OE *wearg*, 'felon', 'criminal' (related modern English *wary*), + *burna*, 'stream'. The first word of the name contrasts the village with *South Warnborough*, 2½ miles to the south. 973 *Weargeburnan*, DB *Wergeborne*.

North Weald Bassett (village, Essex): 'Basset's (estate by the) northern woodland'. OE *weald*, 'woodland', 'forest'. Cp. WEALD. The Basset family held the manor here in the 13C. The first word of the name distinguishes the village from *South Weald*, 8 miles to the southeast. DB *Walda*, 1291 *Welde Basset*.

North Wheatley (village, Notts): 'northern clearing where wheat is grown'. OE *hwǣte*, 'wheat', + *lēah*, 'clearing'. The first word of the name distinguishes the village from *South Wheatley*, immediately to the southeast. DB *Wateleie*.

Northwich (town, Cheshire): 'northern saltworks'. OE *north*, 'northern', + *wīc*, 'special farm', 'trading settlement'. Northwich is the northernmost of the three salt towns or 'saltwiches', the others being MIDDLEWICH and NANTWICH. See also DROITWICH. The salt industry at Northwich is still active. The Roman settlement here was *Condate*, a Celtic name meaning '(place at the) confluence', referring to the rivers Dane and Weaver. DB *Norwich*.

Northwick (hamlet, S Glos): 'northern dairy farm'. OE *north*, 'northern', + *wīc*, 'dairy farm'. The place is 'north' with regard to nearby REDWICK. 955 *Northwican*.

North Widcombe. See SOUTH WIDCOMBE.

North Willingham (village, Lincs): 'northern homestead of Wifel's people'. OE *-inga-*, 'of the people of', + *hām*, 'homestead'. The first word of the name distinguishes the village from SOUTH WILLINGHAM, 4 miles to the southeast, and also from CHERRY WILLINGHAM, 14 miles to the southwest, each with a basic name of different origin. DB *Wiuilingeham*.

North Wingfield (village, Derbys): 'northern open land used for pasture'. OE *winn*, 'pasture', + *feld*, 'open land' (modern English *field*). The first word of the name distinguishes the village from *South Wingfield*, 8 miles to the south. 1002 *Wynnefeld*, DB *Winnefelt*.

North Witham (village, Lincs): 'northern (place by the river) Witham'. The river's name is Celtic or pre-Celtic and of uncertain meaning. The first word of the name contrasts this village with *South Witham*. DB *Widme*, *c.*1160 *Nort Widham*.

Northwold. See METHWOLD.

Northwood (district, Hillingdon): '(place by the) northern wood'. OE *north*, 'northern', +

wudu, 'wood'. The wood here was north of Ruislip. The present district developed from the late 19C. Cp. NORWOOD. 1435 *Northwode*.

Northwood (village, IoW): '(place by the) northern wood'. OE *north*, 'northern', + *wudu*, 'wood'. The wood here was north of the forest of Parkhurst. 1181 *Nortwuda*, early 13C *Northwwde*.

North Wootton (village, Dorset): 'northern farmstead by a wood'. OE *wudu*, 'wood', + *tūn*, 'farmstead'. This Wootton is 'north' with regard to GLANVILLES WOOTTON, 4 miles to the south. *c.*1180 *Wotton*.

North Wootton (village, Norfolk): 'northern farmstead by a wood'. OE *wudu*, 'wood', + *tūn*, 'farmstead'. The first word of the name distinguishes the village from *South Wootton*, 2 miles to the south, now a suburb of King's Lynn. DB *Wdetuna*, 1166 *Nordwitton*.

North Wraxall (village, Wilts): 'northern corner of land where buzzards are seen'. OE *wrocc*, 'buzzard', + *halh*, 'nook', 'corner of land'. (OE *wrocc* could also apply to some other bird of prey.) The first word of the name distinguishes the village from *South Wraxall*, 7 miles to the south. DB *Werocheshalle*.

Norton (village, Doncaster): 'northern farmstead'. OE *north*, 'northern', + *tūn*, 'farmstead'. Norton was a township in the north of the parish of Campsall, as distinct from *Sutton*, 2 miles to the south, in the south of the parish. DB *Nortone*. SO ALSO: *Norton*, Suffolk, Worcs.

Norton (town, N Yorks): 'northern farmstead'. OE *north*, 'northern', + *tūn*, 'farmstead'. The town, also known as *Norton-on-Derwent* (see DERWENT WATER), is 'north' in relation to the former hamlet of *Sutton* to the south (cp. SUTTON), now part of Norton itself. DB *Nortone*.

Norton (district, Sheffield): 'northern farmstead'. OE *north*, 'northern', + *tūn*, 'farmstead'. The original settlement was presumably 'north' in relation to Dronfield. DB *Nortune*.

Norton Bavant (village, Wilts): 'de Bavent's northern farmstead'. OE *north*, 'northern', + *tūn*, 'farmstead'. The de Bavent family held the manor here in the 14C. The village is north with regard to nearby SUTTON VENY. DB *Nortone*, 1381 *Nortonbavent*.

Norton Canon (village, Herefords): 'northern farmstead of the canons'. OE *north*, 'northern', + *tūn*, 'farmstead'. The manor here was held early by the canons of Hereford Cathedral. DB *Nortune*, 1327 *Norton Canons*.

Norton Disney (village, Lincs): 'de Isney's northern farmstead'. OE *north*, 'northern', +

tūn, 'farmstead'. The de Isney family held the manor here in the 12C. The village was probably regarded as 'north' in relation to nearby Stapleford. DB *Nortune*, 1299 *Norton de Iseny*.

Norton Fitzwarren (suburb of Taunton, Somerset): 'Fitzwarren's northern farmstead'. OE *north*, 'northern', + *tūn*, 'farmstead'. The Fitzwarren family held land here. DB *Nortone*.

Norton in Hales (village, Shropshire): 'northern farmstead in Hales'. OE *north*, 'northern', + *tūn*, 'farmstead'. The village had a northern location in the district, whose name has the same origin as that of HALES, Norfolk. DB *Nortune*, 1291 *Norton in Hales*.

Norton juxta Twycross (village, Leics): 'northern farmstead near Twycross'. OE *north*, 'northern', + *tūn*, 'farmstead', + Latin *juxta*, 'near'. This Norton is distinguished from others by its proximity to TWYCROSS, 1½ miles to the southeast. DB *Nortone*.

Norton-on-Derwent. See NORTON (N Yorks).

Norton St Philip (village, Somerset): 'northern farmstead with St Philip's church'. OE *north*, 'northern', + *tūn*, 'farmstead'. The dedication of the church was probably added to distinguish this Norton from MIDSOMER NORTON, 7 miles to the west. DB *Nortune*, 1315 *Norton Sancti Phillipi*.

Norton sub Hamdon (village, Somerset): 'northern farmstead under Hamdon'. OE *north*, 'northern', + *tūn*, 'farmstead'. The second part of the name refers to nearby *Hamdon Hill* (see STOKE SUB HAMDON). DB *Nortune*, 1246 *Norton under Hamedon*.

Norwell. See SOUTHWELL.

Norwich (city, Norfolk): 'northern trading centre'. OE *north*, 'northern', + *wīc*, 'specialized farm', 'trading centre'. There were originally four separate settlements here on the river Wensum, three of them south of the river and one, *Norwich*, to the north of it. The latter was more important than the others and gave its name to the subsequent merger of the four. 10C *Northwic*, DB *Norwic*.

Norwood (district, Lambeth): 'northern wood'. OE *north*, 'northern', + *wudu*, 'wood'. The 'northern wood' here, to the north of Croydon, was not entirely cut down until the 19C. 1176 *Norwude*.

Noss Mayo (village, Devon): 'Matheu's (estate on the) headland'. OE *næss*, 'headland', 'promontory'. The 'headland' is land between two streams here, where the manor was held by one Matheu in the 13C. (*Mayo* represents the OF form of English *Matthew*.) 1286 *Nesse Matheu*.

Nosterfield (hamlet, N Yorks): 'open land with a sheepfold'. OE *eowestre*, 'sheepfold', +

feld, 'open land' (modern English *field*). The first part of the name could also represent OE *ōster*, 'hillock'. The 'N-' of the name is said to come from the final letter of ME *atten*, 'at the'. But the first part of the name could in fact represent some unexplained word beginning with this letter. 1204 *Nostrefeld*.

Notgrove (village, Glos): '(place by the) wet grove'. OE *næt*, 'wet', + *grāf*, 'grove', 'copse'. 716 *Natangrafum*, DB *Nategraua*.

Nottingham (city, Notts): 'homestead of Snot's people'. OE *-inga-*, 'of the people of', + *hām*, 'homestead'. The initial *S-* has been lost from Snot's name, but survives in the name of *Sneinton*, 'farmstead of Snot's people' (OE *tūn*, 'farmstead'), now a district of Nottingham itself. Late 9C *Snotengaham*, DB *Snotingeham*.

Nottinghamshire (county, central England): 'district based on Nottingham'. OE *scīr*, 'shire', 'district'. See NOTTINGHAM. 11C *Snotingaham-scir*.

Notting Hill (district, Kensington & Chel): 'hill (at the place) associated with Cnotta'. OE *-ing*, 'place belonging to', + *hyll*, 'hill'. Alternatively, *Notting* may have been the name of a family who held land here and who came from *Knotting* '(settlement of) Cnotta's people' (OE *-ingas*, 'people of'), Beds. 1356 *Knottynghull*.

Nottington (hamlet, Dorset): 'estate associated with Hnotta'. OE *-ing-*, 'associated with', + *tūn*, 'farmstead', 'estate'. 1212 *Notinton*.

Notton (village, Wakefield): 'farmstead where wethers are kept'. OE *hnoc*, 'wether' (castrated ram), + *tūn*, 'farmstead'. DB *Notone*.

Noviomagus. See (1) CHICHESTER, (2) CRAYFORD.

Nuffield (village, Oxon): '(place on the) tough open land'. OE *tōh*, 'tough', + *feld*, 'open land' (modern English *field*). The name was originally *Tuffield*, with initial *T-* becoming *N-* in the 14C. c.1181 *Tofeld*.

Nun Appleton (hamlet, N Yorks): 'nuns' farmstead where apples grow'. OE *æppel*, 'apple', + *tūn*, 'farmstead'. A priory of Cistercian nuns was founded here in the 12C, their title distinguishing this Appleton from APPLETON ROEBUCK, 2 miles to the north. c.1140 *Appelton*.

Nunburnholme (village, E Yorks): 'nuns' (place by the) springs'. OS *brunnr*, 'spring', 'stream'. There are many springs and small streams here. The second part of the name represents OS *brunnum*, the dative plural form of *brunnr*. The first part refers to the Benedictine

nunnery here. DB *Brunha'*, 1530 *Nonnebrynholme*.

Nuneaton (town, Warwicks): 'river farmstead of the nuns'. OE *nunne*, 'nun', + *ēa*, 'river', + *tūn*, 'farmstead'. The original farmstead by the river Anker here passed to the Benedictine nunnery founded in the 12C. DB *Etone*, 1247 *Nonne Eton*.

Nuneham Courtenay (village, Oxon): 'Curtenay's new homestead'. OE *nīwe*, 'new', + *hām*, 'homestead'. The Curtenay family held the manor here in the 13C. Their name also gave that of *Sutton Courtenay* ('southern farmstead'), 5 miles to the south, so called as lying south of Abingdon. DB *Neuham*, 1320 *Newenham Courteneye*.

Nun Monkton (village, N Yorks): 'nuns' (estate at the) farmstead of the monks'. OE *nunne*, 'nun', + *munuc*, 'monk', + *tūn*, 'farmstead'. The first word of the name, referring to the nunnery founded here in the 12C, distinguishes the village from *Moor Monkton* (OE *mōr*, 'moor', 'marsh'), to the south across the river Nidd, and *Bishop Monkton*, 13 miles to the northwest, which was in the Ripon estates of the archbishops of York. DB *Monechetone*, 1402 *Moremonketon*.

Nunney (village, Somerset): 'Nunna's island'. OE *ēg*, 'island'. The first part of the name could also represent OE *nunne*, 'nun'. The 'island' is land beside a tributary of the river Frome here. 954 *Nuni*, DB *Nonin*.

Nunnington (village, N Yorks): 'estate associated with Nunna'. OE *-ing-*, 'associated with', + *tūn*, 'farmstead', 'estate'. DB *Noningtune*.

Nunthorpe (suburb of Middlesbrough): 'outlying farmstead of the nuns'. OS *thorp*, 'outlying farmstead'. 'This place takes the prefix to its name from a Cistercian nunnery, which was removed here from Hutton in 1160' (*The National Gazetteer of Great Britain and Ireland*, 1868). DB *Torp*, 1240 *Nunnethorp*.

Nursling (village, Hants): 'nutshell place'. OE *hnutu*, 'nut', + *scell*, 'shell', + *-ing*, 'place characterized by'. The place was perhaps (unusually) so called for its small size, as if 'in a nutshell'. c.800 *Hnutscelle*, DB *Notesselinge*, 1868 *Nursling*, *or Nutshalling*.

Nutbourne (village, W Sussex): '(place by the) northern stream'. OE *north*, 'northern', + *burna*, 'stream'. The stream is probably 'north' with respect to the rivers Chilt and Stor, to the south. The present form of the name came about by popular association. The form of the name below relates to Nutbourne near Pulborough. DB *Nordborne*.

Nutfield (village, Surrey): 'open land where nut trees grow'. OE *hnutu*, 'nut', + *feld*, 'open land' (modern English *field*). DB *Notfelle*.

Nuthall (suburb of Nottingham, Notts): 'corner of land where nut trees grow'. OE *hnutu*, 'nut', + *halh*, 'nook', 'corner of land'. DB *Nutehale*.

Nuthampstead (village, Herts): 'homestead where nut trees grow'. OE *hnutu*, 'nut', + *hām-stede*, 'homestead' (see HAMPSTEAD). *c.*1150 *Nuthamstede*.

Nuthurst (hamlet, W Sussex): 'wooded hill where nut trees grow'. OE *hnutu*, 'nut', + *hyrst*, 'wooded hill'. 1228 *Nothurst*.

Nutley (village, E Sussex): 'wood or clearing where nut trees grow'. OE *hnutu*, 'nut', + *lēah*, 'wood', 'clearing'. 1249 *Nutleg*.

Nyetimber (village, W Sussex): 'new timbered building'. OE *nīwe*, 'new', + *timbre*, 'timber'. 12C *Neuetunbra*.

Nymet Rowland (village, Devon): 'Roland's holy place'. The first word of the name represents a Celtic word related to modern Welsh *nyfed*, 'sanctuary', perhaps as an old name for the river Taw here. The manor was held by one Roland in the 12C, and his name distinguishes the village from *Nymet Tracey* to the south, held by the de Trascy family in the 13C. The DB form of the name below may have resulted from a mishearing rather than a miscopying. See also BOW (Devon). 974 *Nymed*, DB *Limet*, 1242 *Nimet Rollandi*.

Nympsfield (village, Glos): 'open land by the holy place'. The first part of the name represents a Celtic word related to modern Welsh *nyfed*, 'sanctuary'. The second part is OE *feld*, 'open land' (modern English *field*). 862 *Nymdesfelda*, DB *Nimdesfelde*, 1868 *Nymphsfield*.

Nynehead (hamlet, Somerset): '(estate of) nine hides'. OE *nigon*, 'nine', + *hīd*, 'hide'. A hide was an area of land, usually about 120 acres, that would support a family and its dependants. 11C *Nigon Hidon*, DB *Nichehede*.

Nyton (village, W Sussex): 'new farmstead'. OE *nīwe*, 'new', + *tūn*, 'farmstead'. The name could also mean 'farmstead on an island' (OE *īeg*, 'island', + *tūn*), referring to the well-watered land here. In the latter case, the initial 'N-' would come from the last letter of preceding ME *atten*, 'at the'. 1327 *Nyton*.

O

Oadby (town, Leics): 'Authi's farmstead'. OS *bȳ*, 'farmstead', 'village'. The personal name is Scandinavian. The DB form of the name below has an erroneous *l*. DB *Oldebi*, 1199 *Outheby*.

Oake (village, Somerset): '(place by the) oak trees'. OE *āc*, 'oak'. The name represents OE *ācum*, the dative plural form of *āc*. 11C *Acon*, DB *Acha*.

Oaken (village, Staffs): '(place by the) oak trees'. OE *āc*, 'oak'. The name represents OE *ācum*, the dative plural form of *āc*. DB *Ache*.

Oakengates (district of Telford, Wrekin): '(place in the) gap where oak trees grow'. OE *ācen*, 'growing with oaks', + *geat*, 'gate', 'gap'. 1414 *Okenyate*.

Oakenshaw (village, Kirklees): 'copse where oak trees grow'. OE *ācen*, 'growing with oaks', + *sceaga*, 'wood', 'copse'. 1246 *Acescahe*.

Oakford (village, Devon): '(place at the) ford by the oak tree'. OE *āc*, 'oak', + *ford*, 'ford'. The DB form of the name below has *l* for *c*. DB *Alforda*, 1166 *Acford*.

Oakham (town, Rutland): 'Occa's homestead or enclosure'. OE *hām*, 'homestead', or *hamm*, 'enclosure'. If 'enclosure', the reference could be to the tongue of land between two streams on which Oakham is situated. 1067 *Ocham*, DB *Ocheham*, 1868 *Oakham, or Okeham*.

Oakington (village, Cambs): 'estate associated with Hocca'. OE *-ing-*, 'associated with', + *tūn*, 'farmstead', 'estate'. The name has its lore. 'Near Cambridge is a village, called phonetically by its inhabitants "Hokinton." This the railway company imagined to be a local mispronunciation for "Oakington," which name they have painted up on the spot and stereotyped by their timetables. Archæological researches, however, proved that the real name is Hockynton, and that it is derived from an ancient family once resident there – the Hockings' (A. Smythe Palmer, *Folk-Etymology*, 1882). DB *Hochinton*.

Oakley (village, Beds): 'wood or clearing where oak trees grow'. OE *āc*, 'oak', + *lēah*, 'wood', 'clearing'. DB *Achelai*. SO ALSO: *Oakley*, Poole.

Oaksey (village, Wilts): 'Wocc's island'. OE *ēg*, 'island'. The 'island' is well-watered land here. DB *Wochesie*.

Oakthorpe (village, Leics): 'Áki's outlying farmstead'. OS *thorp*, 'outlying farmstead'. The personal name is Scandinavian. DB *Achetorp*.

Oakworth (village, Bradford): 'enclosure where oak trees grow'. OE *āc*, 'oak', + *worth*, 'enclosure'. DB *Acurde*.

Oare (hamlet, Somerset): '(place on the) Oare Water'. The stream here has a Celtic name of the same origin as that of the AYR in Scotland. DB *Are*.

Oare (village, Wilts): '(place by the) hill slope'. OE *ōra*, 'hill slope'. The village lies below a hill with a level top and a convex slope, a distinctive feature to which the OE word often applies. 934 *Oran*.

Oban (resort town and port, Argyll & Bute): '(place by the) little bay'. Gaelic *òban*, 'little bay'. The Gaelic word, a diminutive of *òb*, 'bay', refers to the virtually landlocked bay on which Oban stands.

Oborne (village, Dorset): '(place by the) winding stream'. OE *wōh*, 'crooked', + *burna*, 'stream'. The 'winding stream' is the river Yeo here. Cp. WOBURN. 975 *Womburnan*, DB *Wocburne*.

Occold (village, Suffolk): '(place by the) oak-tree wood'. OE *āc*, 'oak', + *holt*, 'wood'. Cp. ACOL. *c*.1050 *Acholt*, DB *Acolt*.

Ochil Hills (hill range, Perth & Kin): 'high ones'. The name is Celtic, from a word related to modern Welsh *uchel*, 'high'. The Ochils have their summit in Ben Cleugh at 2363 feet (720m). 1461 *Oychellis*, 1580 *Ocelli montes*.

Ockbrook (village, Derbys): '(place by) Occa's brook'. OE *brōc*, 'brook'. The nearby stream here is still called Ock Brook. DB *Ochebroc*.

Ockham (village, Surrey): 'Occa's homestead or enclosure'. The DB form of the name below has added an initial *B-*, perhaps through confusion with nearby Bookham. DB *Bocheham*, 1170 *Hocham*.

Ockley (village, Surrey): 'Occa's woodland clearing'. OE *lēah*, 'wood', 'clearing'. DB *Hoclei*.

Ocle Pychard (village, Herefords): 'Pichard's (estate by the) oak wood'. OE *āc*, 'oak', + *lēah*, 'wood', 'clearing'. Cp. ACLE. The Pichard family held the manor here in the 13C. *c*.1030 *Aclea*, DB *Acle*, 1242 *Acle Pichard*.

Ocrinum Promontorium. See LIZARD.

Octapitarum Promontorium. See ST DAVID'S.

Odcombe (village, Somerset): '(place in) Uda's valley'. OE *cumb*, 'valley'. DB *Udecome*.

Oddingley (village, Worcs): 'woodland clearing of Odda's people'. OE *-inga-*, 'of the people of', + *lēah*, 'wood', 'clearing'. 816 *Oddingalea*, DB *Oddunclei*.

Oddington (village, Oxon): '(place by) Otta's hill'. OE *dūn*, 'hill'. The '-ing-' represents the ending of *Ottan*, the genitive form of the personal name. DB *Otendone*.

Odell (village, Beds): '(place by the) hill where woad is grown'. OE *wād*, 'woad', + *hyll*, 'hill'. DB *Wadehelle*.

Odiham (village, Hants): 'wooded homestead or enclosure'. OE *wudig*, 'wooded', + *hām*, 'homestead', or *hamm*, 'enclosure'. The *w-* of OE *wudig* has been lost, probably through Norman influence. DB *Odiham*.

Odstock (village, Wilts): 'Odda's outlying farmstead'. OE *stoc*, 'outlying farmstead'. DB *Odestoche*.

Odstone (hamlet, Leics): 'Oddr's farmstead'. OE *tūn*, 'farmstead'. The personal name is Scandinavian. DB *Odestone*.

Offa's Dyke (earthwork, Wales/England): 'Offa's earthwork'. OE *dīc*, 'ditch', 'dyke', 'embankment'. The lengthy earthwork was built in the 8C by Offa, king of Mercia, to mark the boundary between Anglo-Saxon and Welsh territory. The Welsh name of Offa's Dyke is *Clawdd Offa*. Hence *Trefyclo* as the Welsh name of KNIGHTON. 854 *Offan dic*.

Offchurch (village, Warwicks): 'Offa's church'. OE *cirice*, 'church'. The name is popularly associated with King Offa of OFFA'S DYKE: 'This hath been a town of no small note in the Saxons time, if we may believe Tradition; for in one part of the Lordship is a place called the *Berye*, which signifies no less than *burgus* or *curia*; and accordingly 'tis said that Offa, K. of Mercia had here a Palace;

as also, the Church first, and so consequently the Village, had this name' (William Dugdale, *The Antiquities of Warwickshire*, 1656). ('The *Berye*' is Offchurch Bury, a country house.) 1139 *Offechirch*.

Offenham (village, Worcs): 'Offa's or Uffa's homestead'. OE *hām*, 'homestead'. 709 *Offeham*, DB *Offenham*.

Offham (village, Kent): 'Offa's homestead'. OE *hām*, 'homestead'. 10C *Offaham*.

Offton (village, Suffolk): 'Offa's farmstead'. OE *tūn*, 'farmstead'. DB *Offetuna*.

Offwell (village, Devon): '(place by) Uffa's spring'. OE *wella*, 'spring', 'stream'. DB *Offewille*.

Ogbourne St George (village, Wilts): '(place by) Occa's stream with St George's church'. OE *burna*, 'stream'. The church dedication distinguishes this village from nearby *Ogbourne St Andrew*. The river Og here takes its name from one or other of these. 10C *Oceburnan*, DB *Ocheburne*, 1332 *Okeburne Sancti Georgii*.

Ogle (hamlet, Northd): '(place by) Ocga's hill'. OE *hyll*, 'hill'. 1170 *Hoggel*.

Ogmore (village, Vale of Glam): '(place on the river) Ogmore'. The river, in Welsh *Ogwr*, has a name basically meaning 'sharp', 'rapid' (Welsh *og*). The name is also found in the region for the coastal village of *Ogmore-by-Sea*, the village of *Ogmore Vale* north of Bridgend, and as part of the Welsh name of BRIDGEND itself, *Pen-y-Bont ar Ogwr*.

Okeford Fitzpaine. See CHILD OKEFORD.

Okehampton (town, Devon): 'farmstead on the (river) Okement'. OE *tūn*, 'farmstead'. The river has a Celtic name meaning 'swift stream', from a root source that gave modern Welsh *og* (see OGMORE). The '-hampton' of the town's name is thus misleading. *c*.970 *Ocmundtun*, DB *Ochenemitona*.

Old (village, Northants): '(place by the) woodland'. OE *wald*, 'woodland', 'forest'. DB *Walda*, 1868 *Old, or Wold*.

Old Basing. See BASINGSTOKE.

Oldberrow (hamlet, Warwicks): '(place by) Ulla's hill'. OE *beorg*, 'hill', 'mound'. 709 *Ulenbeorge*, DB *Oleberge*.

Old Bolingbroke (village, Lincs). The main name means '(place by the) brook at Bula's or Bola's place' (OE *-ing*, 'place belonging to', + *brōc*, 'brook'). The first word of the name was added when the village of *New Bolingbroke* arose, 5 miles to the southwest. According to White's *Directory of Lincolnshire* (1842), the latter was founded in *c*.1817 by John Parkinson, lessee of crown lands here, 'upon that part of West Fen which was allotted at the enclosure to Bolingbroke parish'. DB *Bolinbroc*, 1202 *Bulingbroc*.

Old Buckenham. See NEW BUCKENHAM.

Oldbury (hamlet, Kent): 'old fort'. OE *eald*, 'old', + *burh*, 'fortified place'. The name refers to the early Roman fort on Oldbury Hill at nearby Ightham Common. 1302 *Ealdebery*. SO ALSO: *Oldbury*, Shropshire.

Oldbury (district, Sandwell): 'old fort'. OE *eald*, 'old', + *burh*, 'fortified place'. The name usually indicates a pre-Anglo-Saxon fortification, although the location of such a fort here is unknown. 1174 *Aldeberia*.

Oldbury (hamlet, Warwicks): 'old fort'. OE *eald*, 'old', + *burh*, 'fortified place'. The name refers to the Iron Age fort nearby, as noted by William Dugdale in *The Antiquities of Warwickshire* (1656): 'A place of great antiquitie, as may appear by that quadrangular Fort, whence at first it has this name'. 12C *Aldburia*.

Oldbury-on-Severn (village, S Glos): 'old fort on the (river) Severn'. OE *ald*, 'old', + *burh*, 'fortified place'. The name probably refers to the ancient circular encampment just north of the village, rather than the Roman camp a mile to the south. For the river name, see SEVERN STOKE. 1185 *Aldeburhe*.

Oldcastle Heath (hamlet, Cheshire): 'old castle'. OE *ald*, 'old', + *castel*, 'castle'. The name refers to the former castle on nearby Castle Hill. The place was later associated with its heath. 13C *Oldcastil*.

Old Cleeve (village, Somerset): 'old (place by the) cliff'. OE *clif*, 'cliff', 'bank'. The village is near the Bristol Channel coast. The first word of the name distinguishes it from nearby *Chapel Cleeve*, with a chapel. DB *Clive*.

Old Fletton (district, Peterborough): 'old farmstead on a stream'. OE *flēot*, 'stream', + *tūn*, 'farmstead'. The 'stream' here is the river Nene. The addition of the first word is recent, and contrasts the place with *New Fletton*, within the borough of Peterborough itself. DB *Fletun*.

Oldham (town, Oldham): '(place on the) old island'. OE *ald* + OS *holmr*, 'island'. The 'island' is the ridge on which Oldham lies at the western end of Saddleworth Moor. It is said to be 'old' because it has long been inhabited. The interpretation is not convincing, however, and early forms of the name have led Celticists to take the first part (*Ald-*) from a word related to modern Welsh *allt*, 'hill', giving a meaning 'island at *Alt*', this being the actual name of the ridge.

Other names in the region seem to confirm this origin, such as *Alt* and *Alt Hill* southeast of Oldham. 1212 *Aldhulme*, 1226 *Aldholm*.

Old Kea. See KEA.

Oldland (suburb of Bristol, S Glos): 'old land'. OE *ald*, 'old', + *land*, 'land'. 'Old' land is agricultural land that has long been in use. DB *Aldelande*.

Old Leake (village, Lincs): 'old (place by the) brook'. OS *lœkr*, 'brook'. DB *Leche*.

Old Radnor. See NEW RADNOR.

Old Romney. See NEW ROMNEY.

Old Sarum. See SALISBURY.

Old Sodbury. See CHIPPING SODBURY.

Old Swan (district, Liverpool). The name was originally that of an inn here. Until 1824 the inn was called *The Three Swans*, but that same year was renamed for distinction from a newly opened rival called *The Swan*.

Old Swinford (district of Stourbridge, Dudley): 'old (place by the) ford used by pigs'. OE *swīn*, 'pig', + *ford*, 'ford'. The first word of the name distinguishes the place from KINGSWINFORD, 5 miles to the north, which was sometimes formerly known as *New Swinford*. c.950 *Swinford*, DB *Suineford*.

Old Trafford (district, Salford): 'old Trafford'. The name distinguishes the original manor here from *Trafford Park*, now a district of Stretford. *Trafford*, now the name of the local unitary authority, means 'ford on a Roman road' (OE *strǣt*, 'Roman road + *ford*, 'ford'), but without the initial *s-* of *strǣt* and with its final *-t* blended with the *f-* of *ford* to give the '-ff-'. Cp. STRATFORD, STRETFORD. 1206 *Stratford*.

Old Windsor. See WINDSOR.

Olicana. See ILKLEY.

Ollerton (town, Notts): 'farmstead where alder trees grow'. OE *alor*, 'alder', + *tūn*, 'farmstead'. The name is shared by *New Ollerton*, a recent residential development to the north. DB *Alretun*. SO ALSO: *Ollerton*, Cheshire.

Olney (town, Milton K): 'Olla's island'. OE *ēg*, 'island'. Olney lies in a bend of the river Ouse and this is the 'island'. The '-n-' of the name represents the genitive ending of the personal name. 979 *Ollanege*, DB *Olnei*.

Olveston (village, S Glos): 'Ælf's farmstead'. OE *tūn*, 'farmstead'. 955 *Ælvestune*, DB *Alvestone*.

Ombersley (village, Worcs): 'Ambre's woodland clearing'. OE *lēah*, 'wood', 'clearing'. The name could also mean 'woodland clearing where buntings are seen' (OE *amer*, 'bunting', + *lēah*). 706 *Ambreslege*.

Ompton (village, Notts): 'Alhmund's farmstead'. OE *tūn*, 'farmstead'. DB *Almuntone*.

Onecote (village, Staffs): 'lonely cottage'. OE *āna*, 'lonely', + *cot*, 'cottage'. 1199 *Anecote*.

Onibury (village, Shropshire): 'manor (on the river) Onny'. OE *burh*, 'fortified place', 'manor'. The river name means 'single river' (OE *āna*, 'lonely', + *ēa*, 'river'), i.e. one that is formed by the uniting of two streams. DB *Aneberie*, 1247 *Onebur*.

Onneley (village, Staffs): 'Onna's woodland clearing'. OE *lēah*, 'wood', 'clearing'. The name could also mean 'isolated clearing' (OE *āna*, 'lonely', + *lēah*). DB *Anelege*.

Openshaw (district, Manchester): '(place by the) open wood'. OE *open*, 'open', + *sceaga*, 'wood', 'copse'. An 'open' wood is one that is not enclosed. 1282 *Opinschawe*.

Orcades. See ORKNEY.

Orchard Portman (village, Somerset): 'Portman's (estate at the) orchard'. OE *orceard*, 'garden', 'orchard'. The Portman family held the manor here in the 15C. 854 *Orceard*.

Orcheston (village, Wilts): 'Ordrīc's farmstead'. OE *tūn*, 'farmstead'. The village properly comprises neighbouring *Orcheston St George* and *Orcheston St Mary*, named after their respective churches. DB *Orchestone*.

Orcop (village, Herefords): '(place by the) top of the ridge'. OE *ōra*, 'slope', 'ridge', + *copp*, 'top'. Orcop lies below a steep-sided hill with a rounded summit. 1138 *Orcop*.

Ordsall (district, Salford): 'Ord's corner of land'. OE *halh*, 'nook', 'corner of land'. The original 'corner of land' could have been any of the small local valleys. 1177 *Ordeshala*.

Orford (village, Suffolk): '(place by the) ford near the shore'. OE *ōra*, 'shore', + *ford*, 'ford'. Orford is on the river Ore (named after it) close to the coast. 1164 *Oreford*.

Orgreave (hamlet, Staffs): '(place by the) pointed grove'. OE *ord*, 'point', + *grǣfe*, 'grove'. The allusion is probably to the shape of the grove. 1195 *Ordgraue*.

Orkney (island group, N Scotland): 'islands of (the) Orcos'. OS *ey*, 'island'. The islands may have originally had a Celtic tribal name meaning 'boar', a popular Celtic totemic animal. This was then apparently taken by the Vikings to mean 'seal' (OS *orkn*). The Romans knew the Orkneys as *Orcades*. 970 *Orkaneya*.

Orleton (village, Herefords): 'farmstead where alder trees grow'. OE *alor*, 'alder', + *tūn*, 'farmstead'. DB *Alretune*.

Orlingbury (village, Northants): '(place by the) hill associated with Ordla'. OE *-ing-*, 'associated with', + *beorg*, 'hill'. The DB form of the name below is corrupt. DB *Ordinbaro*, 1202 *Ordelinberg*.

Ormesby (suburb of Middlesbrough, Redcar & Clev): 'Ormr's farmstead'. OS *bý*, 'farmstead'. The personal name is Scandinavian. DB *Ormesbi*.

Ormesby St Margaret (village, Norfolk): 'Ormr's farmstead with St Margaret's church'. OS *bý*, 'farmstead'. The personal name is Scandinavian. The church dedication distinguishes the village from nearby *Ormesby St Michael*. c.1020 *Ormesby*, DB *Ormesbei*.

Ormskirk (town, Lancs): 'Ormr's church'. OS *kirkja*, 'church'. The personal name is Scandinavian, and OS *kirkja* may have been substituted for an original equivalent OE *cirice*. c.1190 *Ormeshirche*.

Oronsay (island, Argyll & Bute): 'St Oran's island'. OS *ey*, 'island'. Oran, a disciple of St Columba, founded a monastery here in the 6C. 1549 *Orvansay*.

Orphir (village, Orkney): 'tidal island'. The name relates to the coastline here, regarded as an island that appears above the waterline only at low tide. The derivation is thus in OS *ór*, 'out of', + *fjara*, 'low water', 'foreshore', + *ey*, 'island'. c.1225 *Orfura*, c.1500 *Orfiara*.

Orpington (town, Bromley): 'estate associated with Orped'. OE *-ing-*, 'associated with', + *tūn*, 'farmstead', 'estate'. 1032 *Orpedingtun*, DB *Orpinton*.

Orrell (town, Wigan): '(place by the) hill where iron ore is found'. OE *ōra*, 'ore', + *hyll*, 'hill'. 1202 *Horhill*. SO ALSO: *Orrell*, Sefton.

Orsedd, Yr. See ROSSETT.

Orsett (village, Thurrock): '(place at the) pits where ore is dug'. OE *ōra*, '(iron) ore', + *sēath*, 'pit', 'hole'. 957 *Orseathan*, DB *Orseda*.

Orston (village, Notts): 'estate associated with Ōsica'. OE *-ing-*, 'associated with', + *tūn*, 'farmstead', 'estate'. Cp. OSSINGTON. DB *Oschintone*.

Orton (village, Cumbria): 'farmstead by a hill'. OE *ofer*, 'ridge', 'hill', + *tūn*, 'farmstead'. The hill in question is nearby Orton Scar. 1239 *Overton*.

Orton (village, Northants): 'farmstead on a hill'. OE *ofer*, 'hill', + *tūn*, 'farmstead'. Orton is on a fairly steep hillside. DB *Overtone*.

Orton on the Hill (village, Leics): 'higher farmstead on the hill'. OE *uferra*, 'higher', + *tūn*, 'farmstead'. The DB form of the name below is corrupt. DB *Wortone*, *c*.1215 *Overton*.

Ortons, The. See ORTON WATERVILLE.

Orton Waterville (district, Peterborough): 'de Waltervilla's farmstead by the bank'. OE *ōfer*, 'bank', + *tūn*, 'farmstead'. The bank in question is that of the river Nene. The de Waltervilla family held the manor here in the 12C, their name distinguishing this Orton from nearby *Orton Longueville*, held by the de Longauilla family. Other members of *The Ortons*, as this southern district of Peterborough is known, are *Orton Brimbles*, *Orton Goldhay*, *Orton Malborne*, *Orton Southgate* and *Orton Wistow*. Orton Waterville was also known as *Cherry Orton* from its cherry trees (cp. CHERRY HINTON), and the name survives in Cherry Orton Road. 958 *Ofertune*, DB *Ovretune*, 1248 *Ouertone Wateruile*, 1573 *Overton Watervile al. Cherihorton*, 1868 *Orton Waterville, or Cherry Orton*.

Orwell (village, Cambs): '(place at the) spring by a pointed hill'. OE *ord*, 'point', + *wella*, 'spring'. The hill in question is the one that projects into the valley here. DB *Ordeuuelle*.

Orwell (river, Suffolk): 'stream of the (river) Or'. OE *wella*, 'stream', 'spring'. The river here, a tidal part of the river Gipping, has a pre-Celtic name of uncertain meaning. 11C *Arewan*, 1341 *Orewell*.

Osbaldeston (village, Lancs): 'Ōsbald's farmstead'. OE *tūn*, 'farmstead'. *c*.1200 *Ossebaldiston*.

Osbaston (hamlet, Leics): 'Ásbjǫrn's farmstead'. OE *tūn*, 'farmstead'. The OS personal name has lost its initial vowel in the DB form of the name below. DB *Sbernestun*, 1200 *Osberneston*.

Osborne (mansion, IoW): '(place by the) stream at the sheepfold'. OE *eowestre*, 'sheepfold', + *burna*, 'stream'. 1316 *Austeburn*.

Osbournby (village, Lincs): 'Ásbjǫrn's farmstead'. OS *bȳ*, 'farmstead'. The personal name is Scandinavian. DB *Osbernebi*.

Oscroft (village, Cheshire): 'enclosure for sheep'. OE *eowe*, 'sheep' (related modern English *ewe*), + *croft*, 'croft', 'enclosure'. 1288 *Ouescroft*.

Osgathorpe (village, Leics): 'Ásgautr's outlying farmstead'. OS *thorp*, 'outlying farmstead'. The personal name is Scandinavian. DB *Osgodtorp*.

Osgodby (village, Lincs): 'Ásgautr's farmstead'. OS *bȳ*, 'farmstead', 'village'. The personal name is Scandinavian. DB *Osgotebi*. SO ALSO: *Osgodby*, N Yorks.

Osmaston (district, Derby): 'Ōsmund's farmstead'. OE *tūn*, 'farmstead'. This Osmaston is sometimes distinguished as *Osmaston by Derby* from the village of *Osmaston*, Derbys, which is correspondingly distinguished as *Osmaston by Ashbourne*. Both names are of identical origin. DB *Osmundestune*.

Osmington (village, Dorset): 'estate associated with Ōsmund'. OE *-ing-*, 'associated with', + *tūn*, 'farmstead', 'estate'. The church dedication to the Norman St Osmond here was probably suggested by the OE personal name. 934 *Osmingtone*, DB *Osmentone*.

Osmotherley (village, N Yorks): 'Ásmundr's woodland clearing'. OE *lēah*, 'wood', 'clearing'. The personal name is Scandinavian. The DB form of the name below has garbled the latter part. DB *Asmundrelac*, 1088 *Osmunderle*.

Osney (district of Oxford, Oxon): 'Ōsa's island'. OE *ēg*, 'island'. The 'island' is raised ground by the river Thames here. 1004 *Osanig*.

Ospringe (hamlet, Kent): '(place at the) spring'. OE *or-spring*, 'spring'. (OE *or-* is an intensive prefix corresponding to modern German *ur-*, as in *alt*, 'old', *uralt*, 'ancient'.) DB *Ospringes*.

Ossett (town, Wakefield): 'Ōsla's fold'. OE *set*, 'dwelling', 'stable', 'fold'. The first part of the name could also be OE *ōsle*, 'blackbird' (modern English *ouzel*), giving a meaning 'fold where blackbirds are seen'. DB *Osleset*.

Ossington (village, Notts): 'estate associated with Ōsica'. OE *-ing-*, 'associated with', + *tūn*, 'farmstead', 'estate'. Cp. ORSTON. DB *Oschintone*.

Osterley (district, Hounslow): 'woodland clearing with a sheepfold'. OE *eowestre*, 'sheepfold', + *lēah*, 'wood', 'clearing'. 1274 *Osterle*.

Oswaldkirk (village, N Yorks): 'St Oswald's church'. OE *cirice*, 'church'. OE *cirice* has been replaced in the name by equivalent OS *kirkja*. Oswald (d.992) was first Bishop of Worcester, then Archbishop of York. DB *Oswaldescherca*.

Oswaldtwistle (town, Lancs): 'Ōswald's river junction'. OE *twisla*, 'fork of a river', 'junction of streams'. Two streams meet at Oswaldtwistle. The identity of Oswald is uncertain, despite attempts to name him as St Oswald, 7C king of Northumbria. Cp. OSWESTRY. 1246 *Oswaldestwisel*.

Oswestry (town, Shropshire): 'Ōswald's tree'. OE *trēow*, 'tree'. The name is traditionally associated with St Oswald: 'The field where the

Roman Catholic church now stands is believed to be the site of the Battle of Maserfield in AD 642, when the pagan King Penda of Mercia defeated and killed Oswald, the Christian king of Northumbria: this was the origin of the name Oswestry' (*The New Shell Guide to England*, 1981). The historical connection is doubtful, however, and the dedication of St Oswald's church here was probably suggested by the place name. 1191 *Oswaldestroe*.

Otford (village, Kent): '(place by) Otta's ford'. OE *ford*, 'ford'. The river here is the Darent. 832 *Otteford*, DB *Otefort*.

Otham (village, Kent): 'Otta's homestead'. OE *hām*, 'homestead', 'village'. DB *Oteham*.

Otherton (hamlet, Staffs): 'the other farmstead'. OE *ōther*, 'second', 'other', + *tūn*, 'farmstead'. The name denotes a second farmstead in relation to some previous one. DB *Orretone*.

Othery (village, Somerset): 'the other island'. OE *ōther*, 'second', 'other', + *ēg*, 'island'. Othery is 'the other island' with regard to nearby MIDDLEZOY, the 'island' being raised ground by the river Parrett. 1225 *Othri*.

Othona. See BRADWELL-ON-SEA.

Otley (town, Leeds): 'Otta's woodland clearing'. OE *lēah*, 'wood', 'clearing'. The many names ending '-ley' in the region testify to the former extensive woodland here. *c.*972 *Ottanlege*, DB *Otelai*.

Ot Moor. See CHARLTON-ON-OTMOOR.

Otterbourne (village, Hants): '(place by the) stream where otters are seen'. OE *oter*, 'otter', + *burna*, 'stream'. The stream in question is a tributary of the Itchen. *c.*970 *Oterburna*, DB *Otreburne*.

Otterburn (village, Northd): '(place by the) stream where otters are seen'. OE *oter*, 'otter', + *burna*, 'stream'. The river here is the Rede. 1217 *Oterburn*. SO ALSO: *Otterburn*, N Yorks.

Otterden Place (hamlet, Kent): 'woodland pasture of Oter's people'. OE *-inga-*, 'of the people of', + *denn*, 'woodland pasture'. The second word of the name refers to the Tudor mansion *Otterden Place* here. DB *Otringedene*.

Otterham (village, Cornwall): 'river meadow by the (river) Ottery'. OE *hamm*, 'enclosure', 'river meadow'. The river is named for its otters (OE *oter*, 'otter', + *ēa*, 'river'). Cp. OTTERY ST MARY. DB *Otrham*.

Ottershaw (village, Surrey): '(place by the) wood where otters are seen'. OE *oter*, 'otter', + *sceaga*, 'wood'. *c.*980 *Otershaghe*.

Otterton (village, Devon): 'farmstead by the (river) Otter'. OE *tūn*, 'farmstead'. For the river name, see OTTERY ST MARY. DB *Otritone*.

Ottery St Mary (town, Devon): '(place by the river) Otter with St Mary's church'. The river is named for its otters, and OE *oter* + *ēa* ('river') gave the name of the town, which is distinguished by its church dedication from the villages of *Upottery* ('up the Otter'), 10 miles to the northeast, and *Venn Ottery* ('fenny place on the Otter'), 3 miles to the southwest. DB *Otri*, 1242 *Otery Sancte Marie*.

Ottringham (village, E Yorks): 'homestead of Oter's people'. OE *-inga-*, 'of the people of', + *hām*, 'homestead'. DB *Otringeham*.

Oughtibridge (village, Sheffield): 'Ūhtgifu's bridge'. OE *brycg*, 'bridge'. The personal name is that of a woman. 1161 *Uhtiuabrigga*.

Oulston (village, N Yorks): 'Wulf's or Ulfr's farmstead'. OE *tūn*, 'farmstead'. The personal names are respectively OE and Scandinavian. DB *Uluestun*.

Oulton (village, Cumbria): 'Wulfa's farmstead'. OE *tūn*, 'farmstead'. *c.*1200 *Ulveton*.

Oulton (district of Rothwell, Leeds): 'Áli's farmstead'. OE *tūn*, 'farmstead'. The personal name is Scandinavian. The first part of the name could also represent OE *ald*, 'old'. 1180 *Aleton*.

Oulton (hamlet, Norfolk): 'Authulfr's farmstead'. OE *tūn*, 'farmstead'. The personal name is Scandinavian. DB *Oulstuna*.

Oulton Broad (lake, Suffolk): 'stretch of water by Oulton'. *Oulton*, now a suburb of Lowestoft, has a name meaning either 'Áli's farmstead' (OE *tūn*, 'farmstead'), with a Scandinavian personal name, or 'old farmstead' (OE *ald*, 'old'). Oulton Broad is one of The BROADS, also known as the *Norfolk Broads*, although this one is south of the county boundary. 1203 *Aleton*.

Oundle (town, Northants): '(settlement of the) Undalas'. The OE tribal name means 'those without a share', from OE *un-*, 'not' (modern English *un-*), and *dāl*, 'share' (modern English *dole*). The name implies that the territory here was given to the people who remained after the rest of the land had been apportioned elsewhere. The name was long popularly explained as 'Avon dale', from a supposed earlier name of the river Nene here. *c.*710 *Undolum*, DB *Undele*.

Ousby (village, Cumbria): 'Ulfr's farmstead'. OS *bý*, 'farmstead', 'village'. The personal name is Scandinavian. 1195 *Uluesbi*.

Ousden (village, Suffolk): '(place in the) valley where owls are heard'. OE *ūf*, 'owl', + *denu*, 'valley'. DB *Uuesdana*.

Ouse (river). See OUSEFLEET.

Ousefleet (village, E Yorks): '(place by the) channel of the (river) Ouse'. OE *flēot*, 'inlet', 'stream'. There is no channel here now, on the southern bank of the Ouse, but there must have been once, presumably one through which the river flowed between the mainland and a sandbank. The Ouse has a name of Celtic or pre-Celtic origin meaning simply 'water'. Other rivers of this name have the same meaning with the exception of the Ouse in W Sussex, which takes its name from LEWES. 1100 *Useflete*.

Ouston (village, Durham): 'Ulfkell's stone'. OE *stān*, 'stone'. The personal name is Scandinavian. The reference would be to a boundary stone here. 1244 *Vlkilstan*.

Outwell (village, Norfolk): '(place) further down the stream'. OE *ūte*, 'outer', 'further down', + *wella*, 'spring', 'stream'. The first part of the name distinguishes the village from UPWELL, immediately to the southwest, which is further up the (original course of the) river Nene. 963 *Wellan*, DB *Utuuella*.

Outwood (village, Surrey): '(place by the) outlying wood'. OE *ūt*, 'outside', + *wudu*, 'wood'. An 'outlying' wood is one on the outskirts of a manor or parish. 1640 *Outwood*. SO ALSO: *Outwood*, Wakefield.

Ovenden (district of Halifax, Calderdale): '(place in) Ōfa's valley'. OE *denu*, 'valley'. 1219 *Ovenden*.

Over (village, Cambs): '(place by a) ridge'. OE *ofer*, 'ridge'. The ridge or slope in question is by the river Ouse. 1060 *Ouer*, DB *Ovre*. SO ALSO: *Over*, S Glos.

Over (hamlet, Cheshire): '(place on a) ridge'. OE *ofer*, 'ridge'. The hamlet lies on a ridge by the river Weaver. It is formally *Great Over*, as distinct from nearby *Littler* (i.e. Little Over), names that parallel Derby's MICKLEOVER and LITTLEOVER. DB *Ovre*.

Over Alderley. See NETHER ALDERLEY.

Overbury (village, Worcs): 'higher fortification'. OE *uferra*, 'higher', + *burh*, 'fortified place'. The 'higher fortification' is probably the old earthwork at North Conderton, which is higher than nearby Bredon. 975 *Uferebiri*, DB *Ovrebeberie*.

Over Compton (village, Dorset): 'higher farmstead in a valley'. OE *cumb*, 'valley', + *tūn*, 'farmstead'. The first word of the name (OE *uferra*, 'higher') contrasts this Compton with nearby *Nether Compton* (OE *neotherra*, 'lower'). DB *Contone*, 1268 *Ouerecumton*.

Over Haddon (village, Derbys): 'higher (place by the) hill where heather grows'. OE *uferra*, 'higher', + *hǣth*, 'heather', + *dūn*, 'hill'. The first word of the name contrasts the village with *Nether Haddon* (OE *neotherra*, 'lower'). DB *Hadun*, 1206 *Uverehaddon*.

Over Norton. See CHIPPING NORTON.

Overseal (village, Derbys): 'higher (place by the) wood'. OE *uferra*, 'higher', + *scegel*, 'wood', 'copse'. The first part of the name distinguishes the village from *Netherseal*, 'lower (place by the) wood' (OE *neotherra*, 'lower', + *scegel*), to the south. DB *Scela*, 13C *Overe Scheyle*.

Over Silton. See NETHER SILTON.

Overstone (village, Northants): 'Ufic's farmstead'. OE *tūn*, 'farmstead'. 12C *Oveston*.

Over Stowey. See NETHER STOWEY.

Overstrand (resort village, Norfolk): 'land along the shore'. OE *ōfer*, 'edge', 'margin', + *strand*, 'shore'. The first part of the DB form of the name below is corrupt. DB *Othestranda*, 1231 *Overstrand*.

Overton (village, Hants): 'higher farmstead'. OE *uferra*, 'higher', + *tūn*, 'farmstead'. The sense 'higher' here is probably 'further upstream', comparing the location of Overton further up the river Test than Laverstoke or some other place below it. 909 *Uferantun*, DB *Ovretune*.

Overton (village, Wrexham): 'farmstead by a bank'. OE *ōfer*, 'bank', + *tūn*, 'farmstead'. The village overlooks the river Dee. The Welsh form of the name is *Owrtyn*. 1201 *Overtone*. SO ALSO: *Overton*, Lancs, N Yorks.

Overton (Wakefield). See MIDDLESTOWN.

Over Wallop. See NETHER WALLOP.

Over Whitacre. See NETHER WHITACRE.

Over Worton (hamlet, Oxon): 'higher farmstead by a bank'. OE *ōra*, 'bank', 'slope', + *tūn*, 'farmstead'. The first word of the name distinguishes this Worton from nearby *Nether Worton*. 1050 *Ortune*, DB *Hortone*.

Oving (village, Bucks): '(settlement of) Ūfa's people'. OE *-ingas*, 'people of'. The DB form of the name below is corrupt. DB *Olvonge*, 12C *Vuinges*. SO ALSO: *Oving*, W Sussex.

Ovingdean (district, Brighton & Hove): 'valley of Ūfa's people'. OE *-inga-*, 'of the people of', + *denu*, 'valley'. DB *Hovingedene*.

Ovingham (village, Northd): 'homestead of Ōfa's people'. OE *-inga-*, 'of the people of', +

hām, 'homestead'. The name could also mean 'homestead at Ōfa's place' (OE *-ing*, 'place belonging to', + *hām*). 1238 *Ovingeham*.

Ovington (village, Durham): 'estate associated with Wulfa'. OE *-ing-*, 'associated with', + *tūn*, 'farmstead', 'estate'. DB *Ulfeton*.

Ovington (hamlet, Essex): 'estate associated with Ūfa'. OE *-ing-*, 'associated with', + *tūn*, 'farmstead', 'estate'. DB *Ouituna*. SO ALSO: *Ovington*, Hants, Norfolk.

Ovington (village, Northd): '(place by the) hill of Ōfa's people'. OE *-inga-*, 'of the people of', + *dūn*, 'hill'. 699 *Ofingadun*.

Ower (village, Hants): '(place by the) bank'. OE *ōra*, 'bank', 'slope'. The village overlooks a tributary of the river Blackwater. DB *Hore*.

Owermoigne (village, Dorset): 'Moigne's (estate by the) windy gap'. The first part of the name is Celtic in origin from a word related to modern Welsh *oerddrws*, 'wind gap', referring to the gaps in the chalk hills nearby that channel the wind off the sea. The Moigne family held the manor here in the 13C. DB *Ogre*, 1314 *Oure Moyngne*.

Owlerton (district, Sheffield): 'farmstead by the alders'. OE *alor*, 'alder', + *tūn*, 'farmstead'. 1310 *Olerton*.

Owmby (village, Lincs): 'Authunn's farmstead'. OS *bý*, 'farmstead', 'village'. The personal name is Scandinavian. The first part of the name could also represent OS *authn*, 'uncultivated land', implying a deserted farm. DB *Odenebi*.

Owrtyn. See OVERTON (Wrexham).

Owston (hamlet, Doncaster): 'eastern farmstead'. OS *austr*, 'eastern', + OE *tūn*, 'farmstead'. DB *Austun*.

Owston (village, Leics): 'Ōswulf's farmstead'. OE *tūn*, 'farmstead'. DB *Osulvestone*.

Owstwick (hamlet, E Yorks): 'eastern dairy farm'. OS *austr*, 'eastern', + OE *wīc*, 'dairy farm'. OS *austr* may have replaced an original equivalent OE *ēast*. DB *Osteuuic*.

Owthorpe (village, Notts): 'Ūfi's or Ōfa's outlying farmstead'. OS *thorp*, 'outlying farmstead'. The personal names are respectively Scandinavian and OE. DB *Ovetorp*.

Oxborough (village, Norfolk): 'fortification where oxen are kept'. OE *oxa*, 'ox', + *burh*, 'fortified place'. The 'fortification' would be the old earthwork at nearby Warren Hill. DB *Oxenburch*, 1868 *Oxborough, or Oxburgh*.

Oxenhope (village, Bradford): '(place in the) valley where oxen are kept'. OE *oxna*, 'valley'. The first part of the name represents OE *oxna*, the genitive plural form of *oxa*. The valley in question is probably the deep one that runs off the main valley of the river Worth here. 12C *Hoxnehop*.

Oxenton (village, Glos): '(place on the) hill where oxen are pastured'. OE *oxa*, 'ox', + *dūn*, 'hill'. The first part of the name represents OE *oxna*, the genitive plural form of *oxa*. DB *Oxendone*.

Oxford (city, Oxon): '(place by the) ford where oxen cross'. OE *oxa*, 'ox', + *ford*, 'ford'. A ford over the river Thames here, perhaps just south of Folly Bridge, was at one time used regularly by oxen. The forms of the name below have OE *oxna* as the genitive plural of *oxa*. This simple 'rustic' origin of the name for the scholarly city has led some to propose a worthier etymology. One favourite, quoted by Henry Alexander in *The Place-Names of Oxfordshire* (1912), is to see the name as a 'corruption' of *Ousenford*, '(place by the) ford over the (river) Ouse', the latter being the supposed original name of the Isis here. Alexander's verdict: 'This is a good example of what can be produced by the application of a healthy imagination to the science of place-names'. 10C *Oxnaforda*, DB *Oxeneford*.

Oxfordshire (county, S central England): 'district based on Oxford'. OE *scīr*, 'shire', 'district'. See OXFORD. 11C *Oxnafordscire*.

Oxhill (village, Warwicks): 'Ohta's shelf of land'. OE *scelf*, 'shelf', 'ledge'. The reference is to the long tongue of land to the northwest of the village. DB *Octeselve*.

Oxley (district, Wolverhampton): 'woodland clearing where oxen are pastured'. OE *oxa*, 'ox', + *lēah*, 'wood', 'clearing'. DB *Oxelie*.

Oxshott (village, Surrey): 'Ocga's projecting piece of land'. OE *scēat*, 'angle of land'. Oxshott is in the northeast corner of the parish of Stoke d'Abernon. 1179 *Okesseta*.

Oxspring (village, Barnsley): '(place by the) spring where oxen drink'. OE *oxa*, 'ox', + *spring*, 'spring'. The DB form of the name below has *s* for *x*. DB *Ospring*, 1154 *Oxspring*.

Oxted (town, Surrey): 'place where oak trees grow'. OE *āc*, 'oak', + *stede*, 'place'. DB *Acstede*.

Oxton (village, Notts): 'farmstead where oxen are kept'. OE *oxa*, 'ox', + *tūn*, 'farmstead'. DB *Oxetune*.

Oystermouth (district, Swansea): '(place at the river) mouth with oysters'. The name relates to the oyster beds formerly here off Mumbles Head. The Welsh name of Oystermouth is *Ystumllwynarth*, an impressive phonetic rendering of the English.

Ozleworth (hamlet, Glos): 'Ōsla's enclosure'. OE *worth*, 'enclosure'. The name could also mean 'enclosure where blackbirds are seen' (OE *ōsle*, 'blackbird', modern English *ouzel*). 940 *Oslan wyrth*, DB *Osleuuorde*.

P

Packington (village, Leics): 'estate associated with Pacca'. OE *-ing-*, 'associated with', + *tūn*, 'farmstead', 'estate'. 1043 *Pakinton*, DB *Pachintone*.

Padbury (village, Bucks): 'Padda's fortified place'. OE *burh*, 'fortified place'. DB *Pateberie*.

Paddington (district, Warrington). The name was created by Robert Halton, who established a soapworks here in 1820. Although influenced by London's PADDINGTON, it is said to be a blend of the names of nearby *Padgate* and WARRINGTON.

Paddington (district, Westminster): 'estate associated with Padda'. OE *-ing-*, 'associated with', + *tūn*, 'farmstead', 'estate'. *c.*1050 *Padington*.

Paddlesworth (village, Kent): 'Pæddel's enclosure'. OE *worth*, 'enclosure'. 11C *Peadleswurthe*.

Paddock Wood (town, Kent): 'wood by the small enclosure'. OE *pearroc*, 'small enclosure' (related modern English *paddock*). The town grew up around the railway junction here in the 19C. 1279 *Parrok*.

Padiham (town, Lancs): 'homestead or enclosure associated with Padda'. OE *-ing-*, 'associated with', + *hām*, 'homestead', or *hamm*, 'enclosure'. 1251 *Padiham*.

Padstow (resort town, Cornwall): 'St Petroc's holy place'. OE *stōw*, 'assembly place', 'holy place'. St Petroc, who lived in the 6C, is Cornwall's most famous saint, and the church here is dedicated to him. The *a* in *Padstow* probably arose by association with the name of St Patrick. 981 *Sancte Petroces stow*, 1318 *Patristowe*, 1525 *Padstowe*.

Padworth (village, W Berks): 'Peada's enclosure'. OE *worth*, 'enclosure'. 956 *Peadanwurthe*, DB *Peteorde*.

Pagham (district of Bognor Regis, W Sussex): 'Pæcga's homestead'. OE *hām*, 'homestead'. 680 *Pecganham*, DB *Pageham*.

Paglesham (village, Essex): 'Pæccel's homestead'. OE *hām*, 'homestead', 'village'. The DB form of the name below has *ch* for *cl*. 1066 *Paclesham*, DB *Pachesham*.

Paignton (resort town, Devon): 'estate associated with Pæga'. OE *-ing-*, 'associated with', + *tūn*, 'farmstead', 'estate'. As shown by the forms of the name below, the spelling *Paington* gradually evolved. The present spelling was introduced by the railway company in the 19C, perhaps suggested by TEIGNMOUTH further up the coast. DB *Peintone*, 1259 *Peynctone*, 1267 *Peington*, 1837 *Paington*, 1868 *Paignton*.

Pailton (village, Warwicks): 'estate associated with Pægel'. OE *-ing-*, 'associated with', + *tūn*, 'farmstead', 'estate'. 1077 *Pallentuna*.

Painswick (town, Glos): 'Pain's dwelling'. OE *wīc*, 'dwelling', 'specialized farm'. The personal name is that of Pain Fitzjohn, who held the manor here in the early 12C. DB *Wiche*, 1237 *Painswike*.

Paisley (town, Renfrews): '(place with a) church'. The name represents a Celtic word for 'church', ultimately deriving from Latin *basilica*. It was given by the 'Scots' from Ireland who came to settle in eastern Scotland from the late 6C. 1161 *Passeleth*, 1298 *Passelek*.

Pakefield (district of Lowestoft, Suffolk): 'Pacca's open land'. OE *feld*, 'open land' (modern English *field*). DB *Paggefella*.

Pakenham (village, Suffolk): 'Pacca's homestead'. OE *hām*, 'homestead', 'village'. *c.*950 *Pakenham*, DB *Pachenham*.

Palgrave (village, Suffolk): '(place by the) grove where poles are obtained'. OE *pāl*, 'pole', + *grāf*, 'grove'. 962 *Palegrave*, DB *Palegraua*.

Palmers Green (district, Enfield): 'Palmer's green'. The village green here was named after a family called Palmer, known locally from the 14C. 1608 *Palmers grene*.

Pamber Green (village, Hants): '(place by a) hill with an enclosure'. OE *penn*, 'enclosure', 'fold', + *beorg*, 'hill'. The village later became associated with its green. The basic name also gave that of *Pamber End*, *Pamber Forest* and *Pamber Heath* here. 1165 *Penberga*.

Pamphill (village, Dorset): 'Pampa's or Pempa's hill'. OE *hyll*, 'hill'. The first part of the name could also represent OE *pamp*, 'hill' (related modern English *pamper*, originally 'to cram with food'), to which OE *hyll* was added when it was no longer understood. 1168 *Pamphilla*.

Pampisford (village, Cambs): 'Pamp's enclosure'. OE *worth*, 'enclosure'. DB *Pampesuuorde*.

Pancrasweek (hamlet, Devon): 'hamlet with St Pancras' church'. OE *wīc*, 'dwelling', 'hamlet'. The church here is dedicated to St Pancras. 1197 *Pancradeswike*.

Panfield (village, Essex): 'open land by the (river) Pant'. OE *feld*, 'open land' (modern English *field*). The river has a Celtic name meaning 'valley' (related modern Welsh *pant*). DB *Penfelda*.

Pangbourne (town, W Berks): 'stream of Pæga's people'. OE *-inga-*, 'of the people of', + *burna*, 'stream'. The stream gave the name of the town, which in turn gave the name of the river Pang on which it lies. 844 *Pegingaburnan*, DB *Pangeborne*.

Pannal (suburb of Harrogate, N Yorks): 'pan-shaped corner of land'. OE *panne*, 'pan', + *halh*, 'nook', 'corner of land'. The reference is perhaps to a hollow near the confluence of Crimple Beck and Clark Beck. 1170 *Panhal*.

Papcastle (village, Cumbria): 'Roman fort where a hermit lives'. OS *papi*, 'hermit' (related Latin *papa*, 'pope', 'priest'), + OE *cæster*, 'Roman fort'. The fort in question was *Derventio*, named after the river Derwent here (see DERWENT WATER). 1260 *Pabecastr*.

Papplewick (village, Notts): 'dairy farm in the pebbly place'. OE *papol*, 'pebble', + *wīc*, 'special place', 'dairy farm'. DB *Papleuuic*.

Papworth Everard (village, Cambs): 'Evrard's (estate at) Pappa's enclosure'. OE *worth*, 'enclosure'. One Evrard held the manor in the 12C here, his name distinguishing this Papworth from nearby *Papworth St Agnes*, so called not from the dedication of its church but from a lady named Agnes who held the manor similarly. 1012 *Pappawyrthe*, DB *Papeuuorde*, 1254 *Pappewrth Everard*.

Par (resort town and port, Cornwall): '(place with a) harbour'. Cornish *porth*, 'cove', 'harbour'. 1573 *Le Pare*, 1665 *the Parre*, 1748 *Par*.

Paradise (hamlet, Glos): '(place resembling) paradise'. ME *paradis*, 'paradise'. The name was given to places regarded as particularly pleasant. 1327 *Paradys*.

Parbold (village, Lancs): 'dwelling where pears grow'. OE *peru*, 'pear', + *bold*, 'building', 'dwelling'. 1200 *Perebold*.

Pardshaw (hamlet, Cumbria): 'Perdi's hill'. OS *haugr*, 'hill'. The personal name is Scandinavian. *c.*1205 *Perdishaw*.

Parham (village, Suffolk): 'homestead or enclosure where pears grow'. OE *peru*, 'pear', + *hām*, 'homestead', or *hamm*, 'enclosure'. DB *Perreham*.

Parkeston (district of Harwich, Essex): 'Parkes's town'. The Great Eastern Railway transferred their continental service from Harwich to a new quay here in 1883 and named it *Parkeston Quay* after their chairman, Charles Henry Parkes. The port here is now known as Harwich International Port.

Parkgate (suburb of Neston, Cheshire): '(place by the) park gate'. The former port for passengers to Ireland took its name from the gate of the former Neston Park. 1610 *the Parkgate*.

Parkham (village, Devon): 'enclosure with paddocks'. OE *pearroc*, 'paddock', + *hamm*, 'enclosure'. DB *Percheham*.

Parkhurst (village, IoW): '(place by the) wooded hill in the park'. ME *park*, 'park', + OE *hyrst*, 'wooded hill'. The 'park' was a royal chase (area of land for hunting) or forest from the time of DB. *c.*1200 *Perkehurst*.

Park Royal (district, Brent). The name relates to an area of land where the Royal Agricultural Society attempted to establish a permanent base for their annual show. The venture came to nothing, however, and in 1905 the enterprise was abandoned.

Parkstone (district, Poole): 'park stone'. ME *park*, 'park', + OE *stān*, 'stone'. The 'park' was probably a medieval hunting park in Canford, the stone marking its boundary. 1326 *Parkeston*.

Parracombe (village, Devon): '(place in the) valley of the pedlars'. OE *peddere*, 'pedlar', + *cumb*, 'valley'. The DB form of the name below may be corrupt, in which case the first part could represent OE *pearroc*, 'enclosure'. DB *Pedrecumbe*, 1238 *Parrecumbe*, 1297 *Pearecumbe*.

Parrett (river). See NORTH PERROTT.

Parson Drove (village, Cambs): 'parson's drove'. ME *persone*, 'parson', + *drove*, 'drove'. The name implies a cattle road used or owned by a parson. 1324 *Personesdroue*.

Parsons Green (district, Hammersmith & Ful): 'parson's green'. ME *persone*, 'parson', + *grene*, 'green'. The district arose round the parsonage of Fulham which stood to the west of the former village green. 1391 *Personesgrene*.

Partick (district, Glasgow): 'bushy place'. ow *perthog*. The Celtic word that gave the name is represented by modern Welsh *perth*, 'wood', 'bush'. Cp. PERTH. *c.*1136 *Perdeyc*.

Partington (town, Trafford): 'estate associated with Pearta'. OE *-ing-*, 'associated with', + *tūn*, 'farmstead', 'estate'. 1260 *Partinton*.

Partney (village, Lincs): 'Pearta's island'. OE *ēg*, 'island'. The 'island' is dry ground surrounded by marsh here. 731 *Peartaneu*, DB *Partenay*.

Parwich (village, Derbys): 'dairy farm on the (river) Pever'. OE *wīc*, 'dwelling', 'specialized farm'. The former name for the stream that flows through the village is Celtic in origin and means 'bright one' (modern Welsh *pefr*, 'radiant', 'beautiful'). 963 *Piowerwic*, DB *Pevrewic*.

Passenham (village, Northants): 'Passa's river meadow'. OE *hamm*, 'river meadow'. The river here is the Ouse. Early 10C *Passanhamme*, DB *Passeham*, 1868 *Passenham, or Pasham*.

Paston (hamlet, Norfolk): 'Pæcci's farmstead'. OE *tūn*, 'farmstead'. The first part of the name could also represent OE *pæsc*, 'pool', 'muddy place'. DB *Pastuna*.

Patcham (district of Brighton, Brighton & Hove): 'Pæcca's homestead'. OE *hām*, 'homestead'. The DB form of the name below is corrupt. DB *Piceham*, *c.*1090 *Peccham*.

Patching (village, W Sussex): '(settlement of) Pæcci's people'. OE *-ingas*, 'people of'. 960 *Pæccingas*, DB *Petchinges*.

Pateley Bridge (town, N Yorks): '(place by the) woodland clearing near the paths with a bridge'. OE *pæth*, 'path', + *lēah*, 'wood', 'clearing'. The 'paths' are probably now represented by the roads from Knaresborough (the present B6165) and Ripon (B6265) that join here near this important crossing of the river Nidd, where there was probably a ford before there was a bridge, first mentioned in the 14C. 1202 *Pathlay*, 1320 *Patheleybrigg*.

Patney (village, Wilts): 'Peatta's island'. OE *ēg*, 'island'. The 'island' is well-watered land by the river Avon here. 963 *Peattanige*.

Patrick Brompton (village, N Yorks): 'Patric's farmstead where broom grows'. OE *brōm*, 'broom', + *tūn*, 'farmstead'. The manor here was held early by one Patric (an Old Irish name). DB *Brunton*, 1157 *Patricbrunton*.

Patrington (village, E Yorks): '(place with a) farmstead'. OE *tūn*, 'farmstead'. The first part of the name is of uncertain origin. It may represent a personal or tribal name. The dedication of the church here to St Patrick was almost certainly suggested by the place name. 1033 *Patringtona*, DB *Patrictone*.

Patrixbourne (village, Kent): 'Patricius' (estate on the river) Bourne'. The river here now is the Little Stour, but it was originally the *Bourne* (OE *burna*, 'stream'). The manor here was held in the 12C by William Patricius. DB *Borne*, 1215 *Patricburn*.

Patterdale (village, Cumbria): '(place in) Patric's valley'. OS *dalr*, 'valley'. The personal name is Old Irish. The valley is that of Goldrill Beck, at the head of Ullswater. The dedication of the church here to St Patrick was probably suggested by the name of the valley. *c.*1180 *Patrichesdale*.

Pattingham (village, Staffs): 'homestead of Patta's people'. OE *-inga-*, 'of the people of', + *hām*, 'homestead'. The name could also mean 'homestead at Patta's place' (OE *-ing*, 'place belonging to', + *hām*). DB *Patingham*.

Pattishall (village, Northants): 'Pætti's hill'. OE *hyll*, 'hill'. The DB form of the name below is corrupt. DB *Pascelle*, 12C *Patesshille*.

Paul (village, Cornwall): '(church of) St Paul'. The church here is dedicated to the 6C bishop Paul (Paulinus), said to have been born in Wales and to have founded monasteries in Brittany, notably at Saint-Pol-de-Léon (which also bears his name). 1259 *Beatus Paulus, Sanctus Paulinus*, 1437 *Pawle*.

Paulerspury (village, Northants): 'de Pavelli's (estate by the) pear tree'. OE *pirige*, 'pear tree'. The di Pavelli family held the manor here from 1085, their name distinguishing it from POTTERSPURY, 3 miles to the southeast. DB *Pirie*, *c.*1280 *Pirye Pavely*.

Paull (village, E Yorks): '(place at the) stake'. OE *pagol*, 'stake' (related modern English *pawl*). The stake would have been a landmark or guidemark here on the banks of the Humber. DB *Pagele*, 1868 *Paul, or Paghill*.

Payhembury. See BROADHEMBURY.

Paythorne (hamlet, Lancs): 'Pái's thorn bush'. OE *thorn*, 'thorn bush'. The personal name is Scandinavian. DB *Pathorme*.

Peacehaven (coastal town, E Sussex). The town arose as a 'plotland' during the First World

War and was given a name that denoted not only a 'peaceful haven' for its residents but also a desire for peace to end the war. The settlement was originally named *New Anzac-on-Sea* to honour the Australian and New Zealand Army Corps, but after the butchery at Gallipoli (1915–16) the present name was adopted.

Peak District (upland region, Derbys): 'district of peaks'. OE *pēac*, 'peak'. The Peak proper is the region known as *High Peak*, a name contrasting with *Low Peak* and now that of the local council district. Neither of these relates to a particular individual peak. The first form of the name below means 'land of the peak dwellers' (OE *sǣte*, 'dwellers', + *land*, 'land'). 7C *Pecsǣtna lond*, DB *Pec*.

Peakirk (village, Peterborough): 'St Pega's church'. OE *cirice*, 'church'. The church at Peakirk is dedicated to the 8C St Pega, an anchoress here not far from her brother Guthlac's hermitage at Crowland. OE *cirice* was subsequently replaced by equivalent OS *kirkja*. 1016 *Pegecyrcan*.

Peasenhall (village, Suffolk): 'corner of land where peas grow'. OE *pisen*, 'growing with peas', + *halh*, 'nook', 'corner of land'. DB *Pesehala*.

Pease Pottage (hamlet, W Sussex): '(place by) muddy ground'. The name probably refers to soft muddy ground, the consistency of pease pottage (thick pea soup). Local lore relates it to the meal provided here for prisoners on their way to Horsham jail, or specifically to that eaten by the guards who preceded George IV here on his way to Brighton. But the name is recorded several years before the king was even born (in 1762). 1724 *Peaspottage Gate*.

Peaslake (village, Surrey): '(place on a) stream by which peas grow'. OE *pise*, 'pea', + *lacu*, 'stream' (related modern English *lake*). 15C *Pysshelake*, 1662 *Pislake*.

Peasmarsh (village, E Sussex): '(place by) marshy ground where peas grow'. OE *pise*, 'pea', + *mersc*, 'marsh'. 12C *Pisemerse*.

Peatling Magna (village, Leics): 'greater (settlement of) Pēotla's people'. OE *-ingas*, 'people of'. The second word of the name (Latin *magna*, 'great') distinguishes the village from *Peatling Parva* (Latin *parva*, 'little'), 2 miles to the south. DB *Petlinge*.

Pebmarsh (village, Essex): 'Pybba's ploughed field'. OE *ersc*, 'ploughed land'. DB *Pebeners*.

Pebworth (village, Worcs): 'Peobba's enclosure'. OE *worth*, 'enclosure'. 848 *Pebewrthe*, DB *Pebeworde*.

Peckforton (hamlet, Cheshire): 'farmstead at the ford by a peak'. OE *pēac*, 'peak', 'hill', + *ford*, 'ford', + *tūn*, 'farmstead'. The 'peak' is nearby Peckforton Hill. DB *Pevreton*.

Peckham (district, Southwark): 'homestead by a peak'. OE *pēac*, 'peak', + *hām*, 'homestead'. There is hardly a 'peak' at Peckham, but the old village is on higher ground west of the area known as Telegraph Hill (its name implying an ascent), and this could be the site in question. DB *Pecheham*.

Peckham Rye (district, Southwark): '(place at the) stream by Peckham'. OE *rīth*, 'stream'. Peckham Rye is south of PECKHAM proper and takes its name from a stream formerly here, now covered over. 1520 *Peckham Rithe*.

Peckleton (village, Leics): 'estate associated with Peohtel'. OE *-ing-*, 'associated with', + *tūn*, 'farmstead', 'estate'. The DB form of the name below has garbled the personal name. DB *Pechintone*, 1180 *Petlington*.

Pedmore (district of Stourbridge, Dudley): 'Pybba's marsh'. OE *mōr*, 'moor', 'marsh'. The DB form of the name below has *v* for *b*. DB *Pevemore*, 1176 *Pubemora*.

Peebles (resort town, Borders): '(place with) shelters'. The name comes from a Celtic word related to modern Welsh *pabell*, 'tent' (plural *pebyll*), referring to shepherds' temporary huts (shielings) used in summer on the pastures here. Cp. GALASHIELS. *c.*1125 *Pebles*.

Pegswood (village, Northd): 'Pecg's enclosure'. OE *worth*, 'enclosure'. 1242 *Peggiswrth*, 1868 *Pegswood, or Pegswsrth*.

Pegwell (district of Ramsgate, Kent): '(place by the) pig well'. The name is modern, and may refer to a spring where pigs drank regularly. 1799 *Pegwell*.

Pelaw (district of Felling, Gateshead): '(place on a) hill spur with a palisade'. ME *pel*, 'palisade', + *hough*, 'hill spur' (from OE *hōh*). Pelaw stands on raised ground by the river Trent. 1242 *Pellowe*.

Peldon (village, Essex): '(place on) Pylta's hill'. OE *dūn*, 'hill'. The village lies on rising ground. *c.*950 *Piltendone*, DB *Peltenduna*.

Pelsall (suburb of Walsall): 'Pēol's corner of land'. OE *halh*, 'nook', 'corner of land'. 996 *Peoleshale*, DB *Peleshale*.

Pelton (village, Durham): 'Pēola's farmstead'. OE *tūn*, 'farmstead'. 1312 *Pelton*.

Pelynt (village, Cornwall): 'Nennyd's parish'. Cornish *plu*, 'parish'. Nennyd is said to be St Nonn, the mother of St David, to whom the church here is dedicated. DB *Plunent*, 1868 *Pelynt, or Plynt*.

Pemberton (district, Wigan): 'barley farm on the hill'. Celtic *penn*, 'head', 'top', + OE *bere-tūn* (from *bere*, 'barley', + *tūn*, 'farm'). Celticists prefer an interpretation 'farmstead on the small hill', with the second element from a word related to modern Welsh *byr*, 'short'. 1201 *Penberton*, 1212 *Pemberton*.

Pembridge (village, Herefords): 'Pena's or Pægna's bridge'. OE *brycg*, 'bridge'. The bridge in question would have been over the river Arrow here. Celticists see the first half of the name as Welsh, as if *Pen-y-bridge*, 'end of the bridge' (cp. BRIDGEND), especially as the existence of an OE personal name Pena is uncertain. DB *Penebruge*.

Pembroke (town, Pemb): 'land at the end'. Pembroke is on the southwestern tip of Wales and its name comes from Celtic words related to modern Welsh *pen*, 'end', 'head', and *bro*, 'region', 'land'. An exact English equivalent is LAND'S END. Cp. KINTYRE. The Welsh name of Pembroke is thus *Penfro*. c.1150 *Pennbro*, 1191 *Pembroch*.

Pembroke Dock (town and port, Pemb): 'Pembroke dock'. The port was established by the government in 1814 near the head of Milford Haven estuary and took the name of nearby PEMBROKE. The original settlement here was *Paterchurch*, 'St Patrick's church', and the dockyard is still known locally as *Pater Dock*. 1817 *Pembroke Dockyard*.

Pembury (village, Kent): 'fortified place of Pepa's people'. OE *-inga-*, 'of the people of', + *burh*, 'fortified place'. There is some doubt about the personal name, which may not even be OE. c.1100 *Peppingeberia*.

Penally (village, Pemb): 'Alun's headland'. Welsh *pen*, 'head', 'promontory'. 9C *Pennalun*, 1136 *Penn Alun*.

Penarlâg. See HAWARDEN.

Penarth (resort town and port, Vale of Glam): 'top of the headland'. Welsh *pen*, 'end', 'head', + *garth*, 'hill', 'promontory'. The town takes its name from the high promontory on which it lies, overlooking the Bristol Channel. 1254 *Penarth*.

Pencombe (village, Herefords): '(place in the) valley with an enclosure'. OE *penn*, 'enclosure', + *cumb*, 'valley'. The name could also mean '(place at the) end of the valley', from Celtic words related to modern Welsh *pen*, 'head', 'end', and *cwm*, 'valley'. 12C *Pencumbe*.

Pencoyd (hamlet, Herefords): '(place at the) end of the wood'. The name is Celtic in origin, from words related to modern Welsh *pen*, 'head', 'end', and *coed*, 'wood'. 1291 *Pencoyt*.

Pencraig. See NEW RADNOR.

Pendeen (village, Cornwall): '(place on the) headland with a fort'. Cornish *penn*, 'headland', + *din*, 'fort'. The name was transferred from the headland here to the mining village that arose in the 19C. 1284 *Pendyn*, 1588 *Pendeen*.

Pendennis Point (headland, Cornwall): 'headland with a fort'. Cornish *penn*, 'headland', + *dinas*, 'fort'. The name implies an early fortified place of some kind, but none is known here. c.1540 *Pendinas*.

Pendle. See PENDLE HILL.

Pendlebury (town, Salford): 'manor by Pendle'. OE *burh*, 'fortified place', 'manor'. There must have been a hill called *Pendle* here at one time, its name, now that of the local council district, having the same origin as that of PENDLE HILL. 1202 *Penelbiri*.

Pendle Hill (hill, Lancs): 'hill of Pendle'. The name of the prominent hill here is based on a Celtic word meaning 'hill' related to modern Welsh *pen*, 'hill'. OE *hyll*, 'hill', was then added to this when it was no longer understood. Modern English *hill* was further added when *Pendle* in turn ceased to be meaningful. The name thus has 'hill' three times. Cp. BREEDON ON THE HILL. 1296 *Pennehille*.

Pendleton (village, Lancs): 'farmstead by Pendle'. OE *tūn*, 'farmstead'. *Pendle* is PENDLE HILL, to the northeast of the village. DB *Peniltune*.

Pendleton (district, Salford): 'manor by Pendle'. OE *tūn*, 'farmstead', 'manor'. *Pendle* is the hill that gave the name of PENDLEBURY. 1200 *Penelton*.

Pendock (village, Worcs): 'hill where barley is grown'. The name is Celtic in origin, from words related to modern Welsh *pen*, 'head', 'top', and *heiddiog*, 'of barley'. Cp. HAYDOCK. 875 *Penedoc*.

Pendoggett (village, Cornwall): '(place at the) head of two woods'. Cornish *penn*, 'head', 'top', + *dew*, 'two', + *coes* (earlier *cuit*), 'wood'. The village stands at the head of two wooded valleys. 1289 *Pendeugod*.

Pendragon Castle (ruined castle, Cumbria). The 12C castle, near Kirkby Stephen, was named after Uther Pendragon, father of King Arthur in the Arthurian romances. Local lore tells how Pendragon tried to fortify the castle by diverting the river Eden round it but failed to do so. Hence the local rhyme: 'Let Uther Pendragon do what he can, Eden will run where Eden ran'. The name itself means 'chief war leader' (Welsh *pen*, 'head', + *dragon*, 'leader'.) 1309 *Pendragon*.

Penfro. See PEMBROKE.

Penge (district, Bromley): '(place at the) top of the wood'. The name comes from two Celtic words related to modern Welsh *pen*, 'head', 'top', and *coed*, 'wood'. Cp. PENCOYD, PENKETH. Penge was at one time an important woodland pasture. 1067 *Penceat*.

Penhurst (hamlet, E Sussex): 'Pena's wooded hill'. OE *hyrst*, 'wooded hill'. The DB form of the name below has omitted the *r* of *hyrst*. DB *Penehest*.

Penicuik (town, Midlothian): '(place by the) hill where cuckoos are heard'. OW *penn y cog* (from *penn*, 'hill', + *y*, 'the', + *cog*, 'cuckoo'). 1250 *Penikok*.

Penistone (town, Barnsley): 'farmstead by Penning'. *tūn*, 'farmstead'. *Penning*, 'place on the hill' (Celtic *penn*, 'hill', + OE -*ing*, 'place characterized by'), was presumably the name of the great ridge between the rivers Don and Little Don, with Penistone at the foot of its northern side. DB *Pengestone*, 1199 *Peningeston*.

Penketh (district, Warrington): '(place at the) end of the wood'. The name consists of two Celtic words related to modern Welsh *pen*, 'head', 'end', and *coed*, 'wood'. 1242 *Penket*.

Penkridge (village, Staffs): '(place by the) chief mound'. The name originally applied to the nearby Roman settlement of *Pennocrucium*, from Celtic words related to modern Welsh *pen*, 'head', 'chief', and *crug*, 'hillock', 'tumulus'. The reference is presumably to a burial mound, although none is evident here. The river Penk takes its name from that of the village, misdivided as 'Penk/ridge'. DB *Pancriz*.

Penmaenmawr (resort town, Conwy): '(place by) Penmaen Mawr'. The town takes its name from a nearby mountain. Its own name means 'great stone headland' (Welsh *pen*, 'head', 'top', + *maen*, 'stone', 'rock', + *mawr*, 'great'). 1473 *Penmayne mawre*, 1795 *Penmaen mawr*.

Penmark (village, Vale of Glam): 'height of the horse'. Welsh *pen*, 'head', 'height', + *march*, 'horse'. Horses were presumably kept or pastured here at some time. The village church is dedicated to St Mark, from the notion that the name means 'Mark's head'. 1153 *Penmarc*, 13C *Penmarch*.

Penn (village, Bucks): '(place on the) hill'. The name is Celtic, from a word related to modern Welsh *pen*, 'head', 'top'. The village stands on a prominent rise. 1188 *Penna*.

Penn (district, Wolverhampton): '(place on the) hill'. The origin of the name is as for PENN, Bucks. Penn now includes the former village of *Upper Penn*, whose name contrasts with that of nearby *Lower Penn*, Staffs. DB *Penne*.

Pennines (mountain range, England): '(range of) hills'. The name is not recorded before the 18C. It could either derive from Celtic *penn*, 'hill', or have been based on the name of the *Apennines* in Italy, as a range that similarly runs the length of the country.

Pennington (village, Cumbria): 'farmstead paying a penny rent'. OE *pening*, 'penny', + *tūn*, 'farmstead'. DB *Pennigetun*.

Pennocrucium. See PENKRIDGE.

Penny Bridge (village, Cumbria): 'Penny's bridge'. The bridge over the river Crake here takes its name from the Penny family of Crake Side who settled nearby in the late 16C.

Pennycomequick (district of Plymouth, Devon). The name means what it says, as if 'get rich quick', referring to a prosperous farm or a growing settlement. It was also an early name of Falmouth, Cornwall, where it has been said to derive from Cornish to mean 'head of the valley creek', 'but there are several reasons why that derivation cannot possibly be right, and anyway the phrase does not mean that, nor anything else, in Cornish' (O.J. Padel, *A Popular Dictionary of Cornish Place-Names*, 1988). 1643 *Penicomequick*.

Penrhyndeudraeth (coastal village, Gwynedd): 'promontory between two beaches'. Welsh *penrhyn*, 'promontory', + *dau*, 'two', + *traeth*, 'beach'. The 'promontory' is the ridge of land on which the village stands, while the two beaches are *Traeth Mawr* ('big beach') and *Traeth Bach* ('little beach'), where two rivers flow on either side of Penrhyndeudraeth. 1292 *Penrindeudrait*.

Penrith (town, Cumbria): '(place at the) ford by a hill'. The name derives from two Celtic words represented by modern Welsh *pen*, 'hill', and *rhyd*, 'ford'. The hill is Penrith Beacon, to the east of the town, while the ford was probably over the river Eamont, to the southeast. *c*.1100 *Penrith*.

Penruddock (village, Cumbria): '(place by a) hill'. The first part of the name represents a Celtic word related to modern Welsh *pen*, 'head', 'end'. The second part is of obscure origin. (A word related to Welsh *rhyd*, 'ford', has been suggested.) 1278 *Penreddok*.

Penryn (town, Cornwall): '(place on the) promontory'. Cornish *penn rynn*, 'promontory' (from *penn*, 'head', 'end', + *rynn*, 'point of land'). Penryn lies on a ridge between two valleys. 1236 *Penryn*.

Pensax (village, Worcs): '(place by the) hill of the Saxons'. The first part of the name is Celtic, and related to modern Welsh *pen*, 'head', 'top'. The second part is OE *Sachson*, 'Saxon'. The name would apply to a pocket of English speakers among Welsh speakers here. 11C *Pensaxan*.

Pensby (district of Heswall, Wirral): 'farmstead by Penn'. OS *bý*, 'farmstead', 'village'. *Penn* is a Celtic hill name meaning simply 'hill' (modern Welsh *pen*, 'head', 'top'). The hill in question is probably nearby Heswall Hill. *c*.1229 *Penisby*.

Penselwood (village, Somerset): '(place by the) hill in Selwood'. The first part of the name is Celtic and related to modern Welsh *pen*, 'head', 'top'. The second part names Selwood Forest (see ZEALS). DB *Penne*, 1345 *Penne in Selewode*.

Pensford (village, Bath & NE Somerset): '(place with a) ford'. OE *ford*, 'ford'. The first part of the name is of uncertain origin but may represent a personal name. The river here is the Chew. 1400 *Pensford*.

Penshurst (village, Kent): 'Pefen's wooded hill'. OE *hyrst*, 'wooded hill'. 1072 *Pensherst*.

Pensilva (village, Cornwall). The village arose as a miners' settlement in the 19C and was given a name that combined common Cornish *Pen-* ('head', 'top') with an existing local name. 1868 *Pensilva*.

Pentewan (village, Cornwall): '(place at the) foot of the sand dunes'. Cornish *ben*, 'foot', + *tewynn*, 'sand dunes'. The second part of the name is inappropriate for the location of the place and may in fact represent a former river name. DB *Bentewoin*, 1297 *Bentewyn*.

Pentland Firth (sea strait, N Scotland): 'sea inlet in the land of the Picts'. OS *Pett*, 'Pict', + *land*, 'land', + *fjǫrthr*, 'inlet', 'fjord'. 'Pictland' was the name used by the Vikings for the north of Scotland generally. *c*.1085 *Pettaland fjorthr*.

Pentland Hills (hill range, S Lanarks/W Lothian): 'land of hills'. Celtic *penn*, 'hill', 'head', + OE *land*, 'land'. 1250 *Pentland*.

Pentlow (hamlet, Essex): '(place by) Penta's hill'. OE *hlāw*, 'hill', 'tumulus'. *c*.1045 *Pentelawe*, DB *Pentelauua*.

Pentney (village, Norfolk): 'Penta's island'. OE *ēg*, 'island'. The 'island' is dry ground by the river Nene here. The DB form of the name below is garbled. DB *Penteleiet*, 1200 *Pentenay*.

Pentonville (district, Islington): 'Penton's town'. French *ville*, 'town'. The name is that of Henry Penton (d.1812), MP for Winchester, who owned land here which he began to develop for building in the 1770s. 1822 *Pentonville*.

Pentraeth (village, Anglesey): '(place at the) end of the beach'. Welsh *pen*, 'head', 'end', + *traeth*, 'beach'. The village is at the head of the valley through which the river Nodwydd flows into Red Wharf Bay. 1254 *Pentrayth*.

Pentrich (village, Derbys): 'hill where wild boars are seen'. The name is Celtic in origin, from words related to modern Welsh *pen*, 'head', 'top', and *twrch*, 'boar'. Cp. PENTRIDGE. DB *Pentric*.

Pentridge (village, Dorset): 'boar hill'. The name is Celtic in origin, from words related to modern Welsh *pen*, 'head', 'top', and *twrch*, 'boar'. The reference is to Pentridge Hill, where a promontory was apparently thought to be shaped like a boar's head. DB *Pentric*.

Penwith. See LAND'S END.

Penwithick (village, Cornwall): '(place at the) top of the group of trees'. Cornish *penn*, 'head', 'top', + *gwydhek* (from *gwydh*, 'trees', + adjectival ending *-ek*). 1357 *Penwythyk*.

Pen-y-bont ar Ogwr. See BRIDGEND.

Penygroes (village, Gwynedd): '(place at the) top of the crossroads'. Welsh *pen*, 'end', 'top', + *y*, 'the', + *croes*, 'cross', 'crossroads'. Penygroes is on the main road (now the A487) from Caernarfon to Porthmadog at the point where it is joined by roads from Carmel and Pontllyfni. 1838 *Pen-y-groes*.

Penywaun. See HIRWAUN.

Penzance (resort town and port, Cornwall): '(place by the) holy headland'. Cornish *penn*, 'headland', + *sans*, 'holy'. The name refers to the old chapel of St Mary, which stood on the headland at what is now the bottom end of Chapel Street. HOLYHEAD has an exactly equivalent name. 1284 *Pensans*, 1582 *Penzaunce*.

Peopleton (village, Worcs): 'estate associated with Pyppel'. OE *-ing-*, 'associated with', + *tūn*, 'farmstead', 'estate'. 972 *Piplincgtun*, DB *Piplintune*.

Peper Harow (hamlet, Surrey): 'heathen temple of the pipers'. OE *pīpere*, 'piper', + *hearg*, 'heathen temple'. The name implies that musical instruments were used in pagan worship here. DB *Pipereherge*.

Perivale (district, Ealing): 'pear tree valley'. ME *perie*, 'pear tree', + *vale*, 'valley'. The earlier name of Perivale was *Little Greenford*, for distinction from *Great Greenford*, now GREENFORD. 'This place was formerly known as "Greenford Parva" … and has only borne its present name, which [Daniel] Lysons regards as a corruption of Parva, since the 16th cent.' (*Cassell's Gazetteer of Great Britain and Ireland*, 1897). 1508 *Pyryvale*, 1868 *Perrivale, or Greenford-Parva*.

Perranarworthal (village, Cornwall): '(church of) St Piran in Arwothel'. The manor name *Arwothel* means '(estate) beside the marsh' (Cornish *ar*, 'beside', + *goethel*, 'marsh'), and distinguishes this parish from St Piran's two other parishes, PERRANUTHNOE and PERRANZABULOE. Piran was a 5C monk who came from Ireland (or Wales) to settle in Cornwall. 1181 *Arewethel*.

Perranporth (resort village, Cornwall): '(place by the) cove of St Piran's (parish)'. Modern English dialect *porth*, 'cove', 'harbour' (modern English *port*). The parish in question is PERRANZABULOE. Perranporth arose as a 19C mining village. 1577 *St Perins creeke*, 1810 *Perran Porth*.

Perranuthnoe (village, Cornwall): '(church of) St Piran in Uthno'. The meaning of the manor name *Uthno* is obscure. It was added to distinguish this parish from St Piran's two other parishes, PERRANARWORTHAL and PERRANZABULOE. DB *Odenol*.

Perranzabuloe (hamlet, Cornwall): '(church of) St Piran in the sand'. Latin *in sabulo*, 'in the sand'. The second part of the name distinguishes this parish from St Piran's two other parishes, PERRANARWORTHAL and PERRANUTHNOE. The DB form of the name below has Cornish *lann*, 'church site'. DB *Lanpiran*, 1535 *Peran in Zabulo*, 1868 *Perran-Zabuloe, or Perran-in-the-Sands*.

Perry Barr (district, Birmingham): '(place at the) pear tree by Barr'. OE *pirige*, 'pear tree'. There must have been a hill here named *Barr*, its own name simply meaning 'hill' (Celtic *barr*). Perry Barr is 3 miles southeast of GREAT BARR. DB *Pirio*.

Pershore (town, Worcs): '(place by the) osier bed below a bank'. OE *persc*, 'twig', 'osier', + *ōra*, 'bank', 'slope'. Pershore, by the river Avon, is overlooked by a bank or ridge to the west of the town. 972 *Perscoran*, DB *Persore*.

Pertenhall (village, Beds): 'Pearta's corner of land'. OE *halh*, 'nook', 'corner of land'. DB *Partenhale*.

Perth (town, Perth & Kin): '(place by a) thicket'. The name is Celtic in origin, from a word related to modern Welsh *perth*, 'bush', 'thicket'. *c*.1128 *Pert*.

Perton (village, Staffs): 'farmstead where pears grow'. OE *peru*, 'pear', + *tūn*, 'farmstead'. 1167 *Pertona*.

Peterborough (city, Peterborough): 'St Peter's town'. OE *burh*, 'fortified place', 'borough', 'town'. The name comes from the dedication of the abbey (now the cathedral). The original name of the site of the monastery here, founded in the 7C, was *Medeshamstede*, 'Mēde's homestead' (OE *hām-stede*, 'homestead'). DB *Burg*, 1333 *Petreburgh*.

Peterchurch (village, Herefords): 'St Peter's church'. OE *cirice*, 'church'. The church here is dedicated to St Peter. 1302 *Peterescherche*.

Peterhead (town and port, Aberdeens): 'St Peter's headland'. OE *hēafod*, 'head', 'headland'. The town takes its name from the headland here, itself named after the former St Peter's Kirk. An earlier name was *Inverugie*, 'mouth of the (river) Ugie' (Gaelic *inbhir*, 'river mouth'). 1544 *Petyrheid*.

Peterlee (town, Durham). A New Town was designated here in 1948 and named after the popular local miner and trade union leader Peter Lee (1864–1935). The name itself was proposed by C. W. Clark, surveyor to Easington Rural District Council, who wrote in his report *Farewell Squalor* (1947): 'At the moment, the naming of the new town has not been considered. Many names have come to my mind; some having their derivatives from local history, some coined from the names of our present villages and others from the names of members of the Government. I have reviewed each one of them from all angles and have come to the conclusion that this new town should bear the name of some local man who, during his life time, went fearlessly and courageously forward for the good and uplift of the people of the district … Having all these virtues in one single frame seems well nigh impossible. I am convinced, however, that there was one person whose life was moulded on these virtues and whose memory could be appropriately perpetuated by the naming of the New Town – PETERLEE.'

Petersfield (town, Hants): '(settlement on the) open land with St Peter's church'. OE *feld*, 'open land' (modern English *field*). The town arose as a Norman 'new town' in the 12C, and apparently took its name from the church already here. But the church dedication may itself have been suggested by the OE personal name in an unrecorded earlier place name meaning 'Peohthere's open land'. 1182 *Peteresfeld*.

Petersham (district, Richmond): 'Peohtrīc's land in the bend of a river'. OE *hamm*, 'enclosure', 'land in a river bend'. Petersham lies in the same loop of the Thames as HAM. The church here is dedicated to St Peter, this particular saint being suggested by the personal name. DB *Patricesham*.

Peters Marland (hamlet, Devon): 'St Peter's (place on) cultivated land by a pool'. OE *mere*, 'pool', + *land*, 'cultivated land'. The church here is dedicated to St Peter. DB *Mirlanda*, 1244 *Merlond Sancti Petri*.

Peterstow (village, Herefords): 'holy place of St Peter'. OE *stōw*, 'holy place'. The church here is dedicated to St Peter. 1207 *Peterestow*.

Peter Tavy. See TAVISTOCK.

Petham (village, Kent): 'homestead or enclosure in a hollow'. OE *pytt*, 'pit', 'hollow', + *hām*, 'homestead', or *hamm*, 'enclosure'. DB *Piteham*.

Petrockstow (village, Devon): 'holy place of St Petroc'. OE *stōw*, 'holy place'. The church here is dedicated to the Cornish saint Petroc (who gave the name of PADSTOW). DB *Petrochestou*.

Pett (village, E Sussex): '(place by the) pit'. OE *pytt*, 'pitt'. The nature or location of the pit in question is unknown. 1195 *Pette*.

Pettaugh (village, Suffolk): 'Pēota's enclosure'. OE *haga*, 'hedged enclosure'. DB *Petehaga*.

Pettistree (village, Suffolk): 'Peohtrēd's tree'. OE *trēow*, 'tree'. 1253 *Petrestre*.

Petton (hamlet, Shropshire): 'farmstead by a pointed hill'. OE *pēac*, 'peak', + *tūn*, 'farmstead'. The church here stands on a conical hill. DB *Pectone*.

Petts Wood (district, Bromley): 'Pett's wood'. The district is said to take its name from William Pett, a master shipwright, who leased an oak wood here in the 16C.

Petuaria. See BROUGH (E Yorks).

Petworth (town, W Sussex): 'Pēota's enclosure'. OE *worth*, 'enclosure'. DB *Peteorde*.

Pevensey (village, E Sussex): '(place by) Pefen's river'. OE *ēa*, 'river'. The river is the small stream on which Pevensey stands. The Roman fort here was *Anderitum*, '(place at the) great ford', alluding to the crossing of some former coastal inlet here. 947 *Pevenesea*, DB *Pevenesel*.

Pewsey (town, Wilts): 'Pefe's island'. OE *ēg*, 'island'. The 'island' is the land beside a branch of the river Avon on which the town stands. *c*.880 *Pefesigge*, DB *Pevesie*.

Phillack (hamlet, Cornwall): '(church of) St Felek'. The church here is dedicated to Felek, about whom nothing is known. The first form of the name below shows an attempt to equate the saint with one of the several called Felicity. The 'Ph-' of the name emerged only in the 17C. 1259 *Sancta Felicitas*, 1388 *Felok*, 1613 *Phillacke*.

Philleigh (village, Cornwall): '(church of) St Fily'. The church here is dedicated to Fily, about whom nothing is known. The name was originally spelt with *F*-. 1312 *Sanctus Filius*, 1450 *Fili*, 1613 *Phillie*.

Pickering (town, N Yorks): '(settlement of) Pīcer's people'. OE *-ingas*, 'people of'. The name could also perhaps be tribal in origin, meaning '(place of the) hill dwellers', from a derivative of OE *pīc*, 'point', + *-ingas*, 'dwellers at'. DB *Picheringa*.

Pickhill (village, N Yorks): 'corner of land by the pointed hills'. OE *pīc*, 'point', + *halh*, 'nook', 'corner of land'. The name could also mean 'Pīca's corner of land'. DB *Picala*.

Pickmere (village, Cheshire): '(place by the) lake where pike are found'. OE *pīc*, 'pike', + *mere*, 'lake'. The lake in question is nearby Pick Mere. 12C *Pichemere*.

Pickwell (village, Leics): '(place at the) stream by the pointed hill'. OE *pīc*, 'point', + *wella* 'spring', 'stream'. There are conical hills to the south and east of the village. DB *Pichewelle*.

Pickwick (village, Wilts): 'dairy farm by a pointed hill'. OE *pīc*, 'point', + *wīc*, 'dairy farm'. 1268 *Pykewyke*.

Pickworth (village, Lincs): 'Pīca's enclosure'. OE *worth*, 'enclosure'. DB *Picheuuorde*. SO ALSO: Pickworth, Rutland.

Picton (village, Cheshire): 'Pīca's farmstead'. OE *tūn*, 'farmstead'. DB *Picheton*. SO ALSO: *Picton*, N Yorks.

Piddinghoe (village, E Sussex): 'hill spur of Pyda's people'. OE *-inga-*, 'of the people of', + *hōh*, 'hill spur'. 12C *Pidingeho*.

Piddington (village, Northants): 'estate associated with Pyda'. OE *-ing-*, 'associated with', + *tūn*, 'farmstead', 'estate'. DB *Pidentone*. SO ALSO: *Piddington*, Oxon.

Piddlehinton (village, Dorset): 'estate on the (river) Piddle belonging to a religious community'. OE *hīwan*, 'household (of monks)', 'religious communtiy', + *tūn*, 'farmstead', 'estate'. The '-hin-' of the name represents OE *hīgna*, the genitive form of the plural noun *hīwan*. The religious community was the Abbey of Marmoutier, France. For the river name, see PUDDLETOWN. DB *Pidele*, 1244 *Pidel Hineton*.

Piddletrenthide (village, Dorset): '(estate on the river) Piddle (assessed at) thirty hides'. OF *trente*, 'thirty', + OE *hīd*, 'hide'. For the river name, see PUDDLETOWN. 966 *Uppidelen*, DB *Pidrie*, 1212 *Pidele Trentehydes*.

Pidley (village, Cambs): 'Pyda's woodland clearing'. OE *lēah*, 'wood', 'clearing'. 1228 *Pydele*.

Piercebridge (village, Darlington): '(place by the) bridge where osiers grow'. OE *persc*, 'osier', + *brycg*, 'bridge'. The bridge in question would have been over the river Tees. Local lore claims it was built by two priests. Hence the second alternative for the second form of the name below. *c.*1050 *Persebrigc*, 1868 *Pierse-Bridge*, *Piercebridge*, or *Priest-Bridge*.

Pigdon (hamlet, Northd): 'Pīca's valley'. OE *denu*, 'valley'. The name could also mean '(place in the) valley by the pointed hills' (OE *pīc*, 'point', + *denu*). 1205 *Pikedenn*.

Pilgrims Hatch (suburb of Brentwood, Essex): '(place by the) pilgrims' hatchgate'. ME *pilegrim*, 'pilgrim', + OE *hæcc*, 'hatch'. Pilgrims passed through a gate here to visit the chapel of St Thomas. 1483 *Pylgremeshacch*.

Pilgrims' Way (trackway, SE England). The ancient trackway along the southern slope of the South Downs was used by pilgrims making their way to the shrine of St Thomas Becket at Canterbury, Kent. Hence the name, which dates only from the 18C.

Pillerton Priors (village, Warwicks): 'prior's estate associated with Pīlheard'. OE *-ing-*, 'associated with', + *tūn*, 'farmstead', 'estate'. The manor here was held in the 13C by the Prior of Sheen, whose title distinguishes the village from nearby *Pillerton Hersey*, where it was held by the de Hersy family. DB *Pilardintone*, 1247 *Pilardinton Prior*.

Pilling (village, Lancs): '(place on the) Pilling Water'. The river name probably represents OE *pyll*, 'creek', + *-ing*, 'stream characterized by'. Pilling is on a tidal creek. *c.*1195 *Pylin*.

Pilning (village, S Glos): 'district by the stream'. OE *pyll*, 'pool', 'stream', + *ende*, 'district' (modern English *end*). 1529 *Pyllyn*.

Pilsdon (hamlet, Dorset): '(place by the) hill with a peak'. OE *pīl*, 'pointed stake' (modern English *pile*), + *dūn*, 'hill'. DB *Pilesdone*.

Pilsley (village, Derbys): 'Pinnel's woodland clearing'. OE *lēah*, 'wood', 'clearing'. The forms of the name below are for Pilsley near Clay Cross. *c.*1002 *Pilleslege*, DB *Pinneslei*.

Pilton (village, Northants): 'Pīleca's farmstead'. OE *tūn*, 'farmstead'. DB *Pilchetone*.

Pilton (village, Rutland): 'farmstead by a stream'. OE *pyll*, 'pool', 'stream', + *tūn*, 'farmstead'. The 'stream' in question is the upper reaches of the river Chater here. 1202 *Pilton*. SO ALSO: *Pilton*, Somerset.

Pimlico (district, Westminster). The name was long thought to be that of a local innkeeper, Ben Pimlico, but a theory proposed in 1995 saw the name as a borrowing of *Pamlico*, a place in America mentioned in connection with Walter Raleigh's abortive settlements of the 1580s. 1626 *Pimlico*.

Pimperne (village, Dorset): '(place among) five trees'. The name is apparently Celtic in origin, from words related to modern Welsh *pum*, 'five', and *pren*, 'tree'. Another possibility is 'place among the hills', from an OE word ultimately related to modern English *pimple*. 935 *Pimpern*, DB *Pinpre*.

Pinchbeck (village, Lincs): '(place by the) stream of minnows'. OE *pinc*, 'minnow', + *bece*, 'stream'. The name could also mean 'ridge where finches are seen' (OE *pinca*, 'finch', + *bæc*, 'ridge'). In the former case the spelling has been influenced by OS *bekkr*, 'stream'. DB *Pincebec*.

Pinhoe (district of Exeter, Devon): '(place by the) hill spur Pen'. OE *hōh*, 'hill spur'. The hill spur was known by a Celtic name related to modern Welsh *pen*, 'head', 'top'. *c.*1050 *Peonho*, DB *Pinnoc*.

Pinner (district, Harrow): '(place by the) pointed bank'. OE *pinn*, 'point', 'peg' (modern English *pin*), + *ōra*, 'bank'. The reference is to the elongated ridge that crosses Pinner Park. 1232 *Pinnora*.

Pinvin (village, Worcs): '(place by) Penda's fen'. OE *fenn*, 'fen'. 1187 *Pendefen*.

Pinxton (village, Derbys): 'Penec's farmstead'. OE *tūn*, 'farmstead'. 1208 *Penkeston*.

Pipe and Lyde (village, Herefords). Originally two separate places: *Pipe*, '(place by the) pipe' (OE *pīpe*, 'pipe', 'conduit'), referring to the stream here, and *Lyde*, 'loud one' (OE *hlūd*, 'loud'), naming it. DB *Pipe*, *Lude*, 1868 *Pipe-cum-Lyde*.

Pipe Ridware. See HAMSTALL RIDWARE.

Pirbright (village, Surrey): 'sparse woodland where pear trees grow'. OE *pirige*, 'pear tree', + *fyrhth*, 'sparse woodland', 'scrubland on the edge of a forest'. 1166 *Perifrith*.

Pirton (village, Worcs): 'farmstead where pear trees grow'. OE *pirige*, 'pear tree', + *tūn*, 'farmstead'. 972 *Pyritune*, DB *Peritune*. SO ALSO: *Pirton*, Herts.

Pishill (hamlet, Oxon): '(place by the) hill where peas grow'. OE *pise*, 'pea', + *hyll*, 'hill'. 1195 *Pesehull*.

Pitchcott (village, Bucks): 'cottage where pitch is made or kept'. OE *pīc*, 'pitch', + *cot*, 'cottage'. 1176 *Pichecote*.

Pitchford (village, Shropshire): '(place by a) ford where pitch is found'. OE *pīc*, 'pitch', + *ford*, 'ford'. Pitch still oozes from a well near the former stream crossing here. 'On the surface of a well near the village petroleum is obtained, from which circumstance the village takes its name, the oil having a strong pitchy smell' (*The National Gazetteer of Great Britain and Ireland*, 1868). DB *Piceforde*.

Pitcombe (village, Somerset): '(place in the) marshy valley'. OE *pide*, 'marsh', + *cumb*, 'valley'. DB *Pidecombe*.

Pitlochry (town, Perth & Kin): 'portion of the stones'. Celtic *pett*, 'portion', + Gaelic *cloichreach*, 'stony'. The reference is probably to stepping stones over the river Tummel here. 'Pit-' in this and other names in eastern Scotland is of Pictish origin, with *pett* ultimately related to English *piece*.

Pitminster (village, Somerset): 'church associated with Pippa'. OE *-ing-*, 'associated with', + *mynster*, 'monastery', 'large church'. 938 *Pipingmynstre*, DB *Pipeminstre*.

Pitney (village, Somerset): 'Pytta's or Pēota's island'. OE *ēg*, 'island'. The 'island' is dry ground in marshland here. DB *Petenie*.

Pitsea (district of Basildon, Essex): 'Pīc's island'. OE *ēg*, 'island'. The 'island' here is dry ground in marshland by a creek of the Thames. DB *Piceseia*.

Pitsford (village, Northants): '(place by) Peoht's ford'. OE *ford*, 'ford'. DB *Pitesford*.

Pittenweem (town and port, Fife): 'portion of the cave'. Celtic *pett*, 'portion' (cp. PITLOCHRY), + Gaelic *na h-uama*, 'of the cave'. *c*.1150 *Petnaweme*.

Pittington (village, Durham): '(place by the) hill associated with Pytta'. OE *-ing-*, 'associated with', + *dūn*, 'hill'. *c*.1085 *Pittindun*.

Pitton (village, Wilts): 'Putta's farmstead'. OE *tūn*, 'farmstead'. The name could also mean 'farmstead where hawks are seen or kept' (OE *putta*, 'hawk', + *tūn*, 'farmstead'). 1165 *Putenton*.

Pity Me (village, Durham). The name probably arose as a semi-humorous term for a barren or desolate piece of land. It is popularly said to be a corruption of OF *petit mer*, 'little pool', given by Norman monks to a small lake here, while the following has also found favour at a local level: 'Mr. W. A. Ingledew, of Henshaw Hall, Bardon Mill, has received a letter from the assistant private secretary to the Prince of Wales thanking him "for the interesting explanation of the name of the village of Pity Me," which he sent to His Royal Highness. Mr. Ingledew's explanation ... stated that the monks sang the 51st Psalm at that place during their flight with St. Cuthbert's remains during a Danish invasion, the Latin words of the Psalm, "Miserere mei, Deus," meaning in English, "Pity me, O God"' (*Durham Evening Chronicle*, 14 December 1934).

Plaish (hamlet, Shropshire): '(place by the) shallow pool'. OE *plæsc*, 'shallow pool' (modern English *plash*). 963 *Plesc*, DB *Plesham*.

Plaistow (district, Bromley): 'place for play'. OE *pleg-stōw* (from *plega*, 'play', 'sport', + *stōw*, 'place'). The name implies an open place, something like a modern village green, where people gathered for sport and meetings. 1278 *Pleystowe*. SO ALSO: *Plaistow*, Newham, W Sussex.

Plaitford (village, Hants): '(place by the) ford where sports are held'. OE *pleget*, 'playing', + *ford*, 'ford'. The ford may have been over the stream that formed the county boundary with Wiltshire here. Such a site would have been appropriate for games or contests. DB *Pleiteford*.

Plawsworth (village, Durham): 'enclosure for games'. OE *plaga*, 'play', + *worth*, 'enclosure'. The first part of the name could also represent a personal name. 1297 *Plauworth*.

Plaxtol (village, Kent): 'place for play'. OE *pleg-stōw* (from *plega*, 'play', 'sport', + *stōw*, 'place'). Cp. PLAISTOW. 1386 *Plextole*.

Playden (village, E Sussex): 'woodland pasture where sports are held'. OE *plega*, 'play', 'sport', + *denn*, 'woodland pasture'. DB *Pleidena*.

Playford (village, Suffolk): '(place by the) ford where sports are held'. OE *plega*, 'play', 'sport', + *ford*, 'ford'. The village is on a tributary of the river Deben. DB *Plegeforda*.

Playing Place (village, Cornwall). The village arose in the 20C near a circular area that at one time must have been used for games. 1813 *Kea Playing Place*, 1884 *Playing Place*.

Pleasington (village, Blackburn with Dar): 'estate associated with Plēsa'. OE -*ing*-, 'associated with', + *tūn*, 'farmstead', 'estate'. 1196 *Plesigtuna*.

Pleasley (village, Derbys): 'Plēsa's woodland clearing'. OE *lēah*, 'wood', 'clearing'. 1166 *Pleseleia*.

Plenmeller (hamlet, Northd): '(place at the) top of the bare hill'. The name is Celtic, from words related to modern Welsh *blain*, 'top', 'summit', *moel*, 'bare', 'bald', and *bre*, 'hill'. 1279 *Playnmelor*.

Pleshey (village, Essex): 'enclosure made with interlaced fencing'. OF *plaisseis*, 'enclosure formed by a plashed hedge'. *c.*1150 *Plaseiz*.

Pluckley (village, Kent): 'Plucca's woodland clearing'. OE *lēah*, 'wood', 'clearing'. DB *Pluchelei*.

Plumbland (village, Cumbria): 'grove where plum trees grow'. OE *plūme*, 'plum tree', + OS *lundr*, 'grove'. *c.*1150 *Plumbelund*.

Plumley (village, Cheshire): 'wood or clearing where plum trees grow'. OE *plūme*, 'plum tree', + *lēah*, 'wood', 'clearing'. 1119 *Plumleia*.

Plumpton (village, E Sussex): 'farmstead where plum trees grow'. OE *plūme*, 'plum tree', + *tūn*, 'farmstead'. DB *Pluntune*.

Plumpton Wall (village, Cumbria): 'farmstead where plum trees grow by the wall'. OE *plūme*, 'plum tree', + *tūn*, 'farmstead'. The wall in question would have been that of the Roman fort here. 1212 *Plumton*, 1597 *Le Plumpton Wall*.

Plumstead (district, Greenwich): 'place where plum trees grow'. OE *plūme*, 'plum tree', + *stede*, 'place'. 961 *Plumstede*. SO ALSO: *Plumstead*, Norfolk.

Plumtree (village, Notts): '(place by the) plum tree'. OE *plȳm-trēow* (from *plūme*, 'plum', + *trēow*, 'tree'). DB *Pluntre*.

Plungar (village, Leics): 'triangular plot of land where plum trees grow'. OE *plūme*, 'plum tree', + *gāra*, 'triangular plot'. *c.*1125 *Plungar*.

Plush (village, Dorset): '(place by the) shallow pool'. OE *plysc*, 'shallow pool' (related modern English *plash*). There is still a pool here south of the village. 891 *Plyssch*.

Plymouth (city and port, Plymouth): 'mouth of the (river) Plym'. OE *mūtha*, 'mouth'. The river took its name from *Plympton*, now a district of Plymouth, whose own name means 'farmstead of the plum tree' (OE *plūme*, 'plum tree', + *tūn*, 'farmstead'). The earlier name of Plymouth was *Sutton*, 'southern village' (OE *sūth*, 'southern', + *tūn*, 'village'), preserved in *Sutton Har-*

bour, one of Plymouth's three harbours. Sutton may have been seen as 'south' with respect to Stoke, now part of Plymouth itself. 1230 *Plymmue*, 1234 *Plimmuth*.

Plympton. See PLYMOUTH.

Plymstock (district, Plymouth): 'outlying farmstead associated with Plympton'. OE *stoc*, 'outlying farmstead', 'secondary settlement'. The settlement depended on *Plympton* (see PLYMOUTH), to the north of it. DB *Plemestocha*.

Plymtree (village, Devon): '(place by the) plum tree'. OE *plȳm-trēow* (from *plūme*, 'plum', + *trēow*, 'tree'). DB *Plumtrei*.

Plynlimon (mountain, Ceredigion): 'five beacons'. Welsh *pum*, 'five', + *llumon*, 'chimney'. The mountain has five distinct summits, on one or more of which beacons could have been lit in medieval times. The Welsh form of the name is *Pumlumon*.

Pockley (village, N Yorks): 'Poca's woodland clearing'. OE *lēah*, 'wood', 'clearing'. The second part of the DB form of the name below is corrupt. DB *Pochelac*, *c.*1190 *Pokelai*.

Pocklington (town, E Yorks): 'estate associated with Pocela'. OE -*ing*-, 'associated with', + *tūn*, 'farmstead', 'estate'. DB *Poclinton*.

Podimore (village, Somerset): '(place by the) marsh where frogs abound'. ME *pode*, 'frog', 'toad', + OE *mōr*, 'moor', 'marsh'. The original name of the village was *Milton*, 'middle farmstead' (OE *middel*, 'middle', + *tūn*, 'farmstead'), with *Podimore* a place nearby. DB *Mideltone*, 1868 *Milton-Podimore*, 1897 *Podymore Milton*.

Podmore (hamlet, Staffs): '(place by the) marsh full of frogs'. ME *pode*, 'frog', 'toad', + OE *mōr*, 'moor', 'marsh'. Cp. PODIMORE. DB *Podemore*.

Polbathick (village, Cornwall): '(place by the) pool'. Cornish *poll*, 'pool'. The second part of the name is of obscure origin. It may be a river name. The village is at the head of a tidal creek, and this is probably the 'pool'. 1365 *Polbarthek*.

Polden Hills. See CHILTON POLDEN.

Poldhu Cove (bay, Cornwall): 'dark cove'. Cornish *poll*, 'pool', 'cove', + *du*, 'black', 'dark'. 1533 *Polsewe*, 1699 *Poll jew*.

Polebrook (village, Northants): '(place by the) brook with a pouch-shaped feature'. OE *pohha*, 'pouch', + *brōc*, 'brook'. The name could also mean '(place by the) brook where frogs are found' (OE *pocce*, 'frog', + *brōc*). DB *Pochebroc*.

Polegate (district of Eastbourne, E Sussex): 'gate by the pool'. OE *pōl*, 'pool', + *geat*, 'gate'. The name has no early records, and it is hard to say which gate was by which pool. 1563 *Powle-gate Corner*.

Polesden Lacey (country house, Surrey): 'Lacey's (estate in) Pāl's valley'. OE *denu*, 'valley'. The second word of the name may not be genuinely manorial. 12C *Polesdene*, 1538 *Polesdon Lacy*.

Polesworth (village, Warwicks): 'Poll's enclosure'. OE *worth*, 'enclosure'. *c*.1000 *Polleswyrth*.

Poling (village, W Sussex): '(settlement of) Pāl's people'. OE *-ingas*, 'people of'. 1199 *Palinges*.

Polkerris (coastal village, Cornwall): '(place by a) cove'. Cornish *poll*, 'pool', 'cove'. The second part of the name is of uncertain origin. *c*.1605 *Polkeryes*.

Pollington (village, E Yorks): 'farmstead associated with Pofel'. OE *-ing-*, 'associated with', + *hām*, 'homestead'. *Pofel* was the name, of unknown meaning, of a piece of ground here. *c*.1185 *Pouelington*.

Pollokshaws (district, Glasgow): '(place by the) little pool in the woods'. Celtic *poll*, 'pool', + OE *sceaga*, 'wood', 'copse'. The place was originally *Pollok*. The second part of the name was then added to distinguish it from nearby *Pollokshields*, '(place by the) little pool with sheds' (ME *schele*, 'shed'). 1158 *Pullock*.

Pollokshields. See POLLOKSHAWS.

Polmassick (village, Cornwall): 'Madek's bridge'. Cornish *pons*, 'bridge'. 1301 *Ponsmadek*.

Polperro (resort village, Cornwall): 'Pyra's harbour'. Cornish *porth*, 'cove', 'harbour'. 1303 *Portpira*, 1355 *Porthpera*, 1748 *Polparrow*.

Polruan (coastal village, Cornwall): 'Ruveun's harbour'. Cornish *porth*, 'cove', 'harbour'. Early 13C *Porruwan*, 1284 *Porthruan*, 1292 *Polruan*.

Polstead (village, Suffolk): 'place by a pool'. OE *pōl*, 'pool', + *stede*, 'place'. There is a large pool in the river Box here. *c*.975 *Polstede*, DB *Polesteda*.

Poltimore (village, Devon): 'Pulta's marshy ground'. OE *mōr*, 'moor', 'marshland'. DB *Pultimore*.

Polyphant (village, Cornwall): '(place by the) pool where toads are seen'. Cornish *poll*, 'pool', + *lefant*, 'toad'. DB *Polefand*.

Polzeath (coastal village, Cornwall): '(place by the) dry cove'. Cornish *poll*, 'pool', 'cove', + *sygh*, 'dry'. A 'dry' cove is presumably one that dries out at low tide. *c*.1605 *Pulsath baye*, 1748 *Polzeath*.

Ponders End (district, Enfield): 'Ponder's district'. ME *ende*, 'end', 'district of an estate'. A

family named Ponder were here in the 14C. 1593 *Ponders ende*.

Pons Aelii. See NEWCASTLE UPON TYNE.

Ponsanooth (village, Cornwall): 'bridge of the watercourse'. Cornish *pons*, 'bridge', + *an*, 'the', + *goeth*, 'watercourse'. 1521 *Pons an Oeth*.

Pontardawe (town, Neath PT): 'bridge over the (river) Tawe'. Welsh *pont*, 'bridge', + *ar*, 'over', 'on'. For the river name, see SWANSEA. The forms of the name below relate to a house (Welsh *tŷ*), giving a meaning 'house at the end of the bridge over the Tawe'. Cp. *Pen-y-bont ar Ogwr* as the Welsh name of BRIDGEND. 1583 *Tir penybont ardawe*, 1675 *Ty pen y bont ar y Tawe*, 1706 *Ty pen y bont ar tawey*.

Pontarddulais (town, Swansea): 'bridge over the (river) Dulais'. Welsh *pont*, 'bridge', + *ar*, 'over', 'on'. The river's name means 'dark water' (Welsh *du*, 'black', + *glais*, 'stream'). 1557 *Ponte ar theleys*.

Pontefract (town, Wakefield): 'broken bridge'. Latin *pons*, 'bridge', + *fractus*, 'broken'. The bridge in question was probably where Bubwith Bridge is now, over the small stream called Wash Dike, to the east of the town. This would have given key access to the Great North Road. It is not known how or why the bridge came to be broken. One implausible account runs: 'Seven hundred years ago, an Archbishop of York was passing with his train over the bridge at this spot when the structure gave way. Lives were lost, and maimed survivors as well as bereaved relatives had ample reason to remember the "broken bridge"' (Flavell Edmunds, *Traces of History in the Names of Places*, 1872). The present name preserves the Latin ablative singular (*ponte fracto*), while an OF form *Pomfret* also evolved. 1090 *Pontefracto*, 1868 *Pontefract, or Pomfret*.

Ponteland (town, Northd): 'cultivated land by the (river) Pont'. OE *ēa-land*, 'river land' (from *ēa*, 'river', + *land*, 'land'). The river has a Celtic name meaning 'valley' (modern Welsh *pant*). The name is pronounced 'Pont-eeland', as if two words. 1203 *Punteland*.

Pontesbury (village, Shropshire): 'Pant's fortified place'. OE *burh*, 'fortified place'. DB *Pantesberie*.

Pontesford (hamlet, Shropshire): '(place by) Pant's ford'. OE *ford*, 'ford'. The personal name is the same as for nearby PONTESBURY. The road crosses a tributary of Rea Brook here. 1255 *Pontesford*.

Pontfaen (hamlet, Pemb): '(place by the) stone bridge'. Welsh *pont*, 'bridge', + *maen*, 'stone'. The river here is the Gwaun. The first form of the name below is the Latin equivalent. 13C *Pons Lapideus*, 13C *Pontvaen*.

Pontibus. See STAINES.

Pontllanfraith (village, Caerphilly): 'bridge by the speckled pool'. Welsh *pont*, 'bridge', + *llyn*, 'lake', 'pool', + *braith*, 'speckled'. The pool may have seemed 'speckled' when the sun shone on its waters. The bridge in question was over a pool in the river Sirhywi. The first two words of the first form of the name below mean 'farm at the end of the bridge'. 1492 *tre penybont llynvraith*, 1713 *Pontllynfraith*.

Pontycymer (town, Bridgend): 'bridge at the confluence'. Welsh *pont*, 'bridge', + *y*, 'the', + *cymer*, 'confluence'. The town stands at a point where two streams meet.

Pontypool (town, Torfaen): 'bridge by the pool'. Welsh *pont*, 'bridge', + *y*, 'the', + modern English *pool*. The bridge here crosses a pool in the river Llwyd (Welsh *llwyd*, 'grey', 'dark'). The Welsh name of Pontypool is *Pont-y-pŵl*, with *pŵl* a Welsh form of English *pool*, rather than Welsh *pwll*. 1614 *Pont y poole*.

Pontypridd (town, Rhondda CT): 'bridge by the earthen house'. Welsh *pont*, 'bridge', + *y*, 'the', + *tŷ*, 'house', + *pridd*, 'earth'. The house in question would have had earthen walls. Pontypridd stands at the junction of the rivers Rhondda and Taff. Welsh *tŷ* was later dropped from the original name, as it was already represented by the -*t* of *pont* and the word *y*. c.1700 *Pont y Tŷ Pridd*.

Pont-y-pŵl. See PONTYPOOL.

Pool (village, Leeds). The name derives from OE *pofel*, a word of uncertain meaning but perhaps related to modern English *pebble*. c.1030 *Pofle*, DB *Pouele*.

Poole (town and port, Poole): '(place at the) pool'. OE *pōl*, 'pool'. The 'pool' is Poole Harbour. 1183 *Pole*.

Poole Keynes. See SOMERFORD KEYNES.

Pooley Bridge (village, Cumbria): 'mound by the pool with a bridge'. OE *pol*, 'pool', + OS *haugr*, 'mound', + modern English *bridge*. The 'pool' is probably one at the lower end of Ullswater, while the 'mound' is the ancient camp site on the hill known as Bowerbank to the west of the village. The bridge is over the river Eamont. 1252 *Pulhoue*, 1549 *Pulley*, 1671 *Powley-Bridge*.

Poplar (district, Tower Hamlets): '(place at the) poplar tree'. ME *popler*, 'poplar'. One or more prominent poplars here would have given the original name. All three forms of the name below predate the *Oxford English Dictionary*'s earliest record of the tree name in 1356. 1327 *Popler*, 1340 *Popeler*, 1351 *Le Popler*.

Poringland (village, Norfolk): 'cultivated land of the Porringas'. OE *land*, 'arable land'. The Porringas were the people of (OE -*inga*-) a man whose personal name is uncertain. The village is properly *East Poringland*, as distinct from the smaller nearby *West Poringland*. DB *Porringalanda*.

Porkellis (village, Cornwall): '(place by a) hidden entrance'. Cornish *porth*, 'harbour', 'entrance', + *kellys*, 'lost'. The reference may be to a former hidden pass over a ridge here. 1286 *Porthkelles*.

Porlock (resort village, Somerset): 'enclosure by the harbour'. OE *port*, 'harbour', + *loca*, 'enclosure' (related modern English *lock*). 10C *Portloca*, DB *Portloc*.

Portbury (village, N Somerset): 'fortified place near the harbour'. OE *port*, 'harbour', + *burh*, 'fortified place'. Roman remains have been found here, near the Severn estuary. DB *Porberie*.

Portchester (town, Hants): 'Roman fort by the harbour'. OE *port*, 'harbour', + *ceaster*, 'Roman station'. Portchester is on the north shore of Portsmouth Harbour. The Roman fort there was called *Portus Adurni* (see SHOREHAM-BY-SEA) or *Portus Ardaoni*, the latter word coming from a Celtic source meaning 'height', referring to the hill known as PORTSDOWN, below which Portchester lies. c.690 *Porteceaster*, DB *Portcestre*, 1868 *Porchester, or Portchester*.

Port Dinorwic (town, Gwynedd): 'port of Dinorwic'. Modern English *port*. The town arose as a port for the export of slate from the quarries at *Dinorwic*, whose name means 'fort of the Ordovices', referring to an ancient tribe. The Welsh name of Port Dinorwic, now preferred since the demise of the slate industry, is *Y Felinheli*, 'the sea mill' (Welsh *y*, 'the', + *melin*, 'mill', + *heli*, 'brine', 'sea water'). 1851 *the port of Dinorwic*, 1868 *Port-Dinorwig*.

Port Ellen (town and port, Argyll & Bute): 'Ellen's port'. The town takes its name from Lady Ellenor Campbell of Islay, widow of the Gaelic scholar W. F. Campbell, who planned the settlement in 1821.

Portesham (village, Dorset): 'enclosure belonging to the town'. OE *port*, 'town', + *hamm*, 'enclosure'. The town in question was probably nearby Abbotsbury. 1024 *Porteshamme*.

Port Gate (hamlet, Northd): '(place by the) gate'. OE *port*, 'gate', + *geat*, 'gate'. The second word of the name was added when the first was no longer understood. Port Gate stands at the gap ('gate') in Hadrian's Wall where Watling Street runs through it. 1269 *Portyate*.

Portgaverne (coastal hamlet, Cornwall): '(place with a) harbour'. Cornish *porth*, 'cove', 'harbour'. The second part of the name is of unknown meaning. 1337 *Porcaveran*.

Port Glasgow (town, Inverclyde): 'port for Glasgow'. The town arose on the Firth of Clyde in the 1660s with the aim of becoming a port for GLASGOW. The deepening of the Clyde prevented this, however, and instead the town concentrated on shipbuilding, with Glasgow being its own port.

Porth (town, Rhondda CT): 'gateway'. Welsh *porth*, 'gateway'. Porth stands at the confluence of the rivers Rhondda and Little Rhondda, and this serves as a 'gateway' to places further south in the valley.

Porthaethwy. See MENAI BRIDGE.

Porthallow (coastal village, Cornwall): '(place by the) cove of the (river) Alaw'. Cornish *porth*, 'cove'. The stream here has a name of uncertain origin. The first form of the name below has *W*-for *P*-. 967 *Worthalaw*, 1333 *Porthaleu*.

Porthcawl (resort town, Bridgend): 'harbour where seakale grows'. Welsh *porth*, 'harbour', + *cawl*, 'seakale' (related modern English *cole*). Seakale, cultivated for its edible roots, must have grown here at some time. 1632 *Portcall*, 1825 *Porth Cawl*.

Porthcurno (village, Cornwall): '(place by the) cove of horns'. Cornish *porth*, 'cove', + *corn*, 'horn'. The 'horns' are the two prominent headlands to the east and west of Porth Curno, the bay that lies to the south of the village. The village itself arose only in the 20C. 1580 *Porthe Cornowe*.

Porthleven (town and port, Cornwall): '(place by the) smooth harbour'. Cornish *porth*, 'harbour', + *leven*, 'smooth'. *Leven* may originally have been the name of the stream here, referring to its smooth waters, in which case the name means 'harbour of the Leven'. c.1605 *Port-levan*.

Porthmadog (resort town, Gwynedd): 'port of Madocks'. The town takes its name from William Alexander Madocks (1772–1828), MP for Boston, Lincolnshire, who developed the nearby village of *Tremadoc* (see TREMADOC BAY) and built a harbour here for the region's slate industry. The spelling of the name may have been influenced by the Welsh first name Madog. The form of the name below was in regular use to the 20C. 1838 *Portmadoc*.

Portholland (coastal hamlet, Cornwall): '(place on the) cove'. Cornish *porth*, 'cove'. The second part of the name is of uncertain meaning. It may have originally been that of a stream here. 1288 *Portalan*.

Porthoustock (coastal village, Cornwall): '(place with a) cove'. Cornish *porth*, 'cove'. The second part of the name is of unknown origin. It may represent a personal name. c.1255 *Portheustech*.

Porthpean (coastal village, Cornwall): '(place by a) little harbour'. Cornish *porth*, 'harbour', + *byghan*, 'little'. The harbour here was 'little' by contrast with the one at nearby *Polmear*, 'great harbour', the Cornish name of CHARLESTOWN. 1297 *Porthbyhan*.

Porthtowan (coastal village, Cornwall): '(place by the) cove of sand dunes'. Cornish *porth*, 'cove', + *tewan*, 'sand dunes'. 1628 *Porthtowan*.

Portington (hamlet, E Yorks): 'farmstead belonging to a market town'. OE *port*, 'market town', + *-ing-*, 'associated with', + *tūn*, 'farmstead'. The town in question was probably Howden. DB *Portinton*.

Portinscale (village, Cumbria): 'sheds of the townswomen'. OE *port-cwēn* (from *port*, 'town', + *cwēn*, 'woman', modern English *queen*), + OS *skáli*, 'shed', 'temporary shelter'. 'Townswomen' is a euphemism for prostitutes, the town in question being nearby Keswick. c.1160 *Porqeneschal*.

Port Isaac (coastal village, Cornwall): '(place by the) harbour of chaff'. Cornish *porth*, 'harbour'. The origin of the second word of the name is uncertain. It may be Cornish *usek*, the adjective of *usyon*, 'chaff', perhaps referring to tidal debris. 1337 *Portusek*, c.1540 *Porthissek*.

Portishead (resort town and port, N Somerset): 'headland by the harbour'. OE *port*, 'harbour', + *hēafod*, 'headland'. The headland is Portishead Point, just to the north of the town. The DB form of the name below omits the final *-d*. DB *Portesheve*, 1200 *Portesheved*.

Portland, Isle of (peninsula, Dorset): 'estate by the harbour'. OE *port*, 'harbour', + *land*, 'estate'. The 'harbour' is Portland Harbour, between the Isle of Portland (in fact a peninsula) and Weymouth. 9C *Port*, 862 *Portlande*, DB *Porland*.

Portloe (coastal village, Cornwall): '(place by the) harbour of an inlet'. Cornish *porth*, 'harbour', + *logh*, 'pool', 'inlet'. c.1653 *Portlowe*.

Portmadoc. See PORTHMADOG.

Portmahomack (village, Highland): 'harbour of Machalmac'. Gaelic *port*, 'harbour'. *Machalmac* literally means 'my little Colman', from Gaelic *ma*, 'my', the saint's name *Colman*, and the Gaelic diminutive suffix *-oc*. The whole is a 'reverential' or affectionate form of address. Cp. KILMARNOCK. 1678 *Portmachalmok*.

Portmeirion (resort village, Gwynedd): 'port of Meirion'. The name was devised in the 1920s by the architect Clough William-Ellis (1883–1978) for his Italianate creation here. Meirion was the grandson of Cunedda, who gave the name of GWYNEDD. His name is also present in *Meirionnydd*, the Welsh name of the old county of MERIONETH in which Portmeirion originated. 'I should perhaps explain why I dropped its old Welsh place name of Aber Ia ... First I disliked its chilly sound; and I was aiming even then at a world public and I thought my new name for a new thing both euphonious and indicative of its whereabouts, "Meirion" giving its county and "Port" placing it on the coast. Also it was a little in affectionate memory of [the Italian fishing port of] Portofino ... to which I had immediately and hopelessly lost my heart' (Clough William-Ellis, *Portmeirion: The Place and its Meaning*, 1963).

Portobello (district, Edinburgh): '(place named after) Portobello'. The district derives its name from the Portobello Hut, a house built here in the mid-18C. This was itself named commemoratively for the capture of Portobello, Panama, by Admiral Vernon in 1739. The literal meaning of the name, 'fine port', happened to be appropriate for the district, with its extensive sands and coastal attractions. 1753 *Porto-Bello*, 1779 *Portobello*.

Porton (village, Wilts): '(place with a) farmstead'. OE *tūn*, 'farmstead'. The first part of the name is of uncertain origin. It may represent a former name of the river Bourne here. DB *Portone*.

Portpatrick (resort town and port, Dumfries & Gall): 'harbour of St Patrick'. The saint's name comes from the dedication of the chapel here, and was appropriate for the former main crossing point to Ireland. 1630 *Portpatrick*.

Portquin (coastal hamlet, Cornwall): '(place by the) white harbour'. Cornish *porth*, 'harbour', + *gwynn*, 'white'. The reference may be to the colour of the sand here. 1201 *Porquin*.

Portreath (coastal village, Cornwall): '(place by the) beach cove'. Cornish *porth*, 'cove', + *treth*, 'beach'. 1495 *Porthtreath*.

Portree (town and port, Highland): 'harbour of the slope'. Gaelic *port*, 'harbour', + *righe*, 'slope'. The name implies a summer pasture on the rising ground near Portree, the chief town on the island of Skye. A formerly favoured meaning was 'royal harbour' (Gaelic *port righe*), commemorating a visit of James V to Skye in 1540. But local pronunciation of the name supports the first origin. 1549 *Portri*, 1868 *Portree, or Port a Roi*.

Portscatho (coastal village, Cornwall): '(place by the) harbour of boats'. Cornish *porth*, 'harbour', + *scath*, 'boat'. Cornish *scath* is believed to be the term for a large type of rowing boat, so the harbour here would have been for such boats. 1592 *Porthskathowe*.

Portsdown (chalk ridge, Portsmouth): 'hill by the harbour'. OE *port*, 'harbour', + *dūn*, 'hill', 'down'. The harbour in question is the present Portsmouth Harbour, which Portsdown overlooks. See PORTSMOUTH. DB *Portesdone*.

Portsea Island (island, Portsmouth): 'island by the harbour'. OE *port*, 'harbour', + *ēg*, 'island'. The harbour is the present Portsmouth Harbour. See PORTSMOUTH. The second word of the name was added when the sense of 'island' in the original was no longer understood. 982 *Portesig*.

Portslade-by-Sea (coastal town, W Sussex): 'river crossing by a harbour by the sea'. OE *port*, 'harbour', + *gelād*, 'river crossing'. The name implies a former inlet here which had to be crossed by a special causeway. The second part of the name properly relates to the resort that developed here in the 20C, while Portslade Village, an inland district of the town, represents the original settlement. The DB form of the name below has *g* for *d*. DB *Porteslage*, *c*.1095 *Portes Ladda*.

Portsmouth (city and port, Portsmouth): '(place at the) mouth of the harbour'. OE *port*, 'harbour', + *mūtha*, 'mouth'. The harbour in question is the present Portsmouth Harbour, the town arising at its mouth. The Roman name of the harbour was *Portus* accordingly. Cp. PORTCHESTER, PORTSDOWN. Late 9C *Portesmuthan*.

Port Sunlight (model village, Wirral): 'port of sunlight'. The village on the Mersey estuary arose as a residential estate laid out in 1888 by William Hesketh Lever (later Lord Leverhulme) for workers at his soap factory. The name is properly that of Sunlight soap, the factory's leading brand, but it also evokes the village's garden suburb planning, with green areas open to sun and air, unlike the nearby smoking factories and railways. 'The first sod of the new factory was cut by the late Lady Lever on 3rd March, 1888, when the land acquired for Port Sunlight was allocated in certain proportions to works and village' (William Henry Beable, *Romance of Great Businesses*, 1926).

Port Talbot (town and port, Neath PT): 'Talbot's port'. The town dates from 1836, when docks were built on Swansea Bay on land owned by the Talbot family of nearby Margam Abbey, which they had inherited in the 18C.

Portus. See PORTSMOUTH.

Portus Adurni. See (1) PORTCHESTER, (2) SHOREHAM-BY-SEA.

Portway (Roman road, Hants/Wilts): 'town way'. OE *port*, 'town', + *weg*, 'way', 'road'. The Roman road from Silchester to Old Sarum came to be seen in medieval times as the 'town way' leading to Salisbury. 1298 *Portweye*.

Port William (resort village, Dumfries & Gall): 'William's port'. A settlement was founded here on Luce Bay in 1770 by Sir William Maxwell of Monreith.

Portwrinkle (coastal village, Cornwall): '(place on the) cove'. Cornish *porth*, 'cove'. The second part of the name is of uncertain origin. 1605 *Port Wrickel*.

Poslingford (village, Suffolk): 'enclosure of Possel's people'. OE *-inga-*, 'of the people of', + *worth*, 'enclosure'. DB *Poslingeorda*.

Postbridge (hamlet, Devon): '(place by the) post bridge'. The hamlet has a medieval clapper bridge that predates a later 'post bridge' which took the post road from Exeter to Plymouth (the present B3212) over the East Dart river nearby. 1675 *a stone bridge of three arches called Post Bridg*.

Postwick (village, Norfolk): 'Possa's dairy farm'. OE *wīc*, 'dwelling', 'dairy farm'. DB *Possuic*.

Potter Brompton (hamlet, N Yorks): 'potmaker's farmstead where broom grows'. OE *brōm*, 'broom', + *tūn*, 'farmstead'. The first word of the name presumably refers to early potmaking here. DB *Brunetona*, 1285 *Potter Brumton*.

Potter Heigham (village, Norfolk): 'potmaker's homestead with a hedge'. OE *pottere*, 'potmaker', + *hecg*, 'hedge', + *hām*, 'homestead'. The name was originally *Heigham*, the first part of which could also represent OE *hecc*, 'hatchgate', and the second OE *hamm*, 'enclosure'. The first word was added when pot-making became established here. DB *Echam*, 1182 *Hegham Pottere*.

Potteries, The (region, N Staffs). The name arose in the early 19C for the home of the china

and earthenware industry in England, the chief centres being Stoke-on-Trent, Burslem, Hanley, Longton, Fenton and Tunstall. 'The district abounds with coal, potters' clay, and iron ore, and is one vast factory, being covered with the furnaces, ovens, and chimneys of the banks or pottery works, which were originated by Mr. Wedgwood, whose seat was at Etruria' (*The National Gazetteer of Great Britain and Ireland*, 1868).

Potterne (village, Wilts): 'building where pots are made'. OE *pott*, 'pot', + *ærn*, 'house', 'building'. The local clayey soil would have been suitable for making pottery here. Cp. POTTON. DB *Poterne*.

Potters Bar (town, Herts): 'Potter's gate'. ME *barre*, 'gate'. A gate or 'bar' leading into Enfield Chase here was owned in the 16C by a man named Potter. 1509 *Potterys Barre*, 1868 *Potter's-Bar*.

Potterspury (village, Northants): 'potters' (place by the) pear tree'. OE *pottere*, 'potter', + *pirie*, 'pear tree'. The first part of the name, referring to the former pottery here, distinguishes this village from PAULERSPURY, 3 miles to the northwest. DB *Perie*, 1287 *Potterispirye*.

Potter Street (district of Harlow, Essex): 'Potter's (place on the) street'. A family named le Pottere ('potmaker') were here in the 13C, with Kiln Lane a reminder of the surname's origin. 1594 *Potters streete*, 1868 *Potter's-street*.

Potto (village, N Yorks): '(place by the) hill where pots were found'. OE *pott*, 'pot', + OS *haugr*, 'mound', 'hill'. 1202 *Pothow*.

Potton (town, Beds): 'farmstead where pots are made'. OE *pott*, 'pott', + *tūn*, 'farmstead'. *c.*960 *Pottun*, DB *Potone*.

Poughill (village, Cornwall): '(place by the) pouch-shaped hill'. OE *pohha*, 'pouch', + *hyll*, 'hill'. The name could also mean '(place by) Pohha's spring' (OE *wella*, 'spring', 'stream'). The DB form of the name below has *h* for *w*. DB *Pochehelle*, 1227 *Pochewell*.

Poughill (village, Devon): '(place by the) pouch-shaped hill'. OE *pohha*, 'pouch', + *hyll*, 'hill'. The name could also mean '(place by) Pohha's hill'. DB *Pochehille*.

Poulshot (village, Wilts): 'Paul's wood'. OE *holt*, 'wood'. The DB form of the name below is corrupt. DB *Paveshou*, 1187 *Paulesholt*.

Poulton (hamlet, Cheshire): 'farmstead by a creek'. OE *pull*, 'pool', 'stream', + *tūn*, 'farmstead'. The stream in question is Pulford Brook, a tributary of the river Dee. 1260 *Pulton*.

Poulton (village, Glos): 'farmstead by a pool'. OE *pōl*, 'pool', + *tūn*, 'farmstead'. 855 *Pultune*.

Poulton-le-Fylde (town, Lancs): 'farmstead by a pool in The Fylde'. OE *pōl*, 'pool', + *tūn*, 'farmstead'. *The Fylde* is a former open area here with a name meaning 'plain' (OE *filde*, related to *feld*, 'open land', modern English *field*). The addition was made to distinguish this Poulton from *Poulton-le-Sands*, the original name of MORECAMBE, 17 miles to the north. DB *Poltun*.

Poundon (village, Bucks): '(place by the) hill'. OE *dūn*, 'hill'. The first part of the name is of uncertain origin. It may be a personal name. 1255 *Paundon*.

Poundstock (village, Cornwall): 'outlying farmstead with a pound'. OE *pund*, 'pound' (for animals), + *stoc*, 'outlying farmstead'. DB *Pondestoch*.

Powderham (hamlet, Devon): 'promontory in reclaimed marshland'. OE *polra* (low-lying land reclaimed from the sea), + *hamm*, 'promontory'. Powderham lies low by the estuary of the river Exe. DB *Poldreham*.

Powerstock (village, Dorset): '(place by an) outlying farmstead'. OE *stoc*, 'outlying farmstead'. The first part of the name, identical to that of nearby NORTH POORTON, is of uncertain origin. DB *Povrestoch*.

Powick (village, Worcs): 'farm associated with Pohha'. OE *-ing-*, 'associated with', + *wīc*, 'specialized farm'. 972 *Poincguuic*, DB *Poiwic*.

Powys (unitary authority, central Wales): 'provincial (place)'. Low Latin *pagensis*, 'provincial', from classical Latin *pagus*, 'district', 'region', 'province' (related French *pays*, Italian *paese*, 'country'). The name of the historic kingdom implies that those who lived here were 'country folk', inhabiting an open upland tract that was not protected in the same way as the regions to the north and south, with their hills and valleys.

Poxwell (manor house, Dorset): '(place by) Poca's rising ground'. OE *swelle*, 'rising ground' (modern English *swell*). Poxwell lies in a gap by a long ridge. The name could also mean 'Poc's spring' (OE *wella*, 'spring', 'stream'). 987 *Poceswylle*, DB *Pocheswelle*.

Poynings (village, W Sussex): '(settlement of) Pūn's people'. OE *-ingas*, 'people of'. 960 *Puningas*, DB *Poninges*.

Poyntington (village, Dorset): 'estate associated with Punt'. OE *-ing-*, 'associated with', + *tūn*, 'farmstead', 'estate'. DB *Ponditone*.

Poynton (town, Cheshire): 'estate associated with Pofa'. OE *-ing-*, 'associated with', + *tūn*, 'farmstead', 'estate'. 1249 *Povinton*.

Poynton (hamlet, Wrekin): 'estate associated with Pēofa'. OE *-ing-*, 'associated with', + *tūn*, 'farmstead', 'estate'. DB *Peventone*.

Praa Sands (resort village, Cornwall). The name, properly that of the beach here, is of obscure origin. It may have originally meant 'hag's cove' (Cornish *porth*, 'cove', + *gwragh*, 'hag') or 'hag's pool' (Cornish *poll*, 'pool', + *gwragh*), but the forms are too late to be certain. 1714 *Prah*, 1813 *Pra Sand*, 1888 *Prah Sands*.

Pratt's Bottom (district, Bromley): 'Pratt's valley'. OE *botm*, 'valley bottom'. A family named Pratt are known to have been here from the 14C. 1791 *Sprats Bottom*, 1799 *Pratts Bottom*.

Praze-an-Beeble (village, Cornwall): 'meadow of the conduit'. Cornish *pras*, 'meadow', + *an*, 'the', + *pibell*, 'pipe', 'conduit'. 1697 *Praze-an-beble*.

Prees (village, Shropshire): '(place by the) thicket'. OW *pres*, 'brushwood'. DB *Pres*.

Preesall (village, Lancs): '(place on the) headland covered in brushwood'. OW *pres*, 'brushwood', + OS *hofuth* or OE *hēafod*, 'headland'. The village stands on a headland near the mouth of the river Wyre. DB *Pressouede*.

Prendwick (hamlet, Northd): 'Prend's dairy farm'. OE *wīc*, 'dwelling', 'dairy farm'. 1242 *Prendewic*.

Prenton (district of Birkenhead, Wirral): 'Præn's farmstead'. OE *tūn*, 'farmstead'. The name is mistranscribed as if PRESTON in the DB form below. DB *Prestune*, 1260 *Prenton*.

Prescelly Hills. See PRESELI HILLS.

Prescot (town, Knowsley): 'priests' cottage'. OE *prēost*, 'priest', + *cot*, 'cottage'. The name probably denotes an endowment for the church at nearby Eccleston. 1178 *Prestecota*.

Preseli Hills (hill range, Pemb). The name is an English rendering of Welsh *Mynydd Preseli* (Welsh *mynydd*, 'mountain'), probably from Welsh *prys*, 'wood', 'grove'. The English spelling *Prescelly* was formerly common. 1868 *Precelly, or Percelly*.

Prestatyn (resort town, Denb): 'priests' farmstead'. OE *prēost*, 'priest', + *tūn*, 'farmstead'. The farm would probably have been an endowment for priests who worked elsewhere. The name is a Welsh-style form of English PRESTON, but with the middle syllable of OE *prēosta-tūn* stressed in the regular Welsh manner and the English *-ton* becoming *-tyn* (as in Welsh names such as *Mostyn*). DB *Prestetone*, 1301 *Prestatton*.

Prestbury (village, Cheshire): 'priests' manor'. OE *prēost*, 'priest', + *tūn*, 'farmstead', 'manor'. The pretentious style of many of Prestbury's homes and buildings have earned it the nickname *Mansionville* from neighbouring Bollington residents. 1181 *Presteberi*.

Prestbury (suburb of Cheltenham, Glos): 'priests' manor'. OE *prēost*, 'priest', + *tūn*, 'farmstead', 'manor'. The priests were probably those of Cheltenham Minster. *c.*900 *Preosdabyrig*, DB *Presteberie*.

Presteigne (town, Powys): 'priests' household'. OE *prēost*, 'priest', + *hǣmed*, 'household'. The name probably denotes a religious community here. The Welsh name of Presteigne is *Llanandras*, 'church of St Andrew' (Welsh *llan*, 'church', + *Andras*, 'Andrew'). 1137 *Prestehemed*, 1548 *Prestene*, 1868 *Presteign, or Llan-Andras of the Welsh*.

Preston (city, Lancs): 'farmstead of the priests'. OE *prēost*, 'priest', + *tūn*, 'farmstead'. The name does not necessarily imply that priests worked on the farm but that it was probably an endowment for priests who served a church elsewhere. DB *Prestune*. SO ALSO: *Preston*, Brighton & Hove, Dorset, E Yorks, Northd.

Preston Brockhurst (village, Shropshire): 'priests' estate by Brockhurst'. OE *prēost*, 'priest', + *tūn*, 'farmstead', 'estate'. The wood name *Brockhurst* (see LEE BROCKHURST) distinguishes this Preston from others, such as *Preston Gubbals*, 5 miles to the southwest, where the manor was held in 1086 by a priest called Godebold. DB *Prestone*, 1385 *Preston Brokhurst*.

Preston Candover (village, Hants): 'priests' Candover'. The original name of the place was *Candover*, from the stream here, whose own name is of Celtic origin and means 'pleasant waters' (related modern Welsh *cain*, 'pleasant', + *dwfr*, 'water'). It then passed into the possession of priests (ME *prestene*, the genitive plural form of *prest*) and their title was added to distinguish this Candover from nearby *Brown Candover*, where the manor was held by the Brun family, and *Chilton Candover*, with a basic name as for CHILTON, Bucks. *c.*880 *Cendefer*, DB *Candovre*, 1262 *Prestecandevere*.

Preston Capes (village, Northants): 'de Capes' (estate at the) farmstead of the priests'. OE *prēost*, 'priest', + *tūn*, 'farmstead'. The de Capes family held the manor here in the 13C. DB *Prestetone*, 1300 *Preston Capes*.

Preston Gubbals. See PRESTON BROCKHURST.

Prestonpans (coastal town, E Lothian): '(salt) pans by Preston'. OE *panne*, 'pan'. The monks of Newbattle Abbey laid out salt pans here by the Firth of Forth in the early 13C. *Preston*, with a name as PRESTON, is now a district of Prestonpans itself. 1587 *Saltprestoun*, 1654 *Prestonpans*.

Preston-under-Scar (village, N Yorks): 'priests' farm under the rocky hill'. OE *prēost*, 'priest', + *tūn*, 'farmstead'. The village lies below a high range of crags at the western end of Leyburn Shawl. *Scar* is OS *sker*, 'rock'. DB *Prestun*, 1568 *Preston undescar*.

Preston upon the Weald Moors (village, Wrekin): 'priests' estate on the Weald Moors'. OE *prēost*, 'priest', + *tūn*, 'farmstead', 'estate'. The *Weald Moors* ('wild moors') is an extensive area of low-lying wetland here. DB *Prestune*, 1392 *Preston upon Wyldemore*.

Prestwich (town, Bury): 'priests' farm'. OE *prēost*, 'priest', + *wīc*, 'specialized farm'. The farm was probably an endowment, with the priests themselves working elsewhere. 1194 *Prestwich*.

Prestwick (hamlet, Northd): 'priests' farm'. OE *prēost*, 'priest', + *wīc*, 'specialized farm'. Cp. PRESTWICH. 1242 *Prestwic*.

Prestwick (resort town, S Ayrs): 'priests' farm'. OE *prēost*, 'priest', + *wīc*, 'specialized farm'. Cp. PRESTWICH. *c.*1170 *Prestwic*.

Prickwillow (village, Cambs): '(place by the) willow used for making skewers'. OE *pricca*, 'prick', 'skewer', + *wilig*, 'willow'. 1251 *Prickewylev*.

Priddy (village, Somerset): 'earthen house'. The name is Celtic in origin, from words related to modern Welsh *pridd*, 'earth', and *tŷ*, 'house'. Cp. PONTYPRIDD. 1182 *Pridia*.

Priestholm. See PUFFIN ISLAND.

Primethorpe (hamlet, Leics): 'Prim's outlying farmstead'. OS *thorp*, 'farmstead'. DB *Torp*, 1316 *Prymesthorp*.

Primrose Hill (district, Camden): 'hill where primroses grow'. ME *primerose*, 'primrose', + OE *hyll*, 'hill'. The name is first recorded in a song title of 1586, *A Sweete and Courtly Songe of the Flowers that grow on Prymrose Hill*.

Princes Risborough (town, Bucks): 'prince's (estate on the) hill where brushwood grows'. OE *hrīsen*, 'growing with brushwood' (from *hrīs*, 'brushwood'), + *beorg*, 'hill'. The 'prince' is the Black Prince, no less, otherwise Edward, Prince of Wales (1330–76), eldest son of Edward III, who held the manor of Risborough. The royal title was added to distinguish this Risborough from adjoining *Monks Risborough*, held by the monks of Christ Church, Canterbury. 1004 *Risenbeorgas*, DB *Riseberge*, 1433 *Pryns Risburgh*.

Princethorpe (village, Warwicks): 'Præn's or Pren's outlying farmstead'. OS *thorp*, 'outlying farmstead'. William Dugdale, in *The Antiquities of Warwickshire* (1656), comments: 'As for the name it proceeds, doubtless, from some antient possessor thereof, the latter sillable, viz. *thorpe*, signifying a Village or Hamlet, for so in the Saxon time they were called: the Dutch to this day (whose language hath a great affinity with our old English) calling such Villages *Dropes*, pronouncing *d* instead of *th*'. 1221 *Prandestorpe*.

Princetown (town, Devon): 'prince's town'. The town arose on Dartmoor in the early 19C around a prison built in 1806 to house French and American prisoners taken in the Napoleonic Wars. It was named in honour of the Prince Regent, the future George IV (1762–1830), who owned Dartmoor as part of his Duchy of Cornwall.

Prinknash (abbey, Glos): 'Princa's ash tree'. OE *æsc*, 'ash'. 1121 *Prinkenesse*.

Prior's Frome. See BISHOP'S FROME.

Priors Hardwick (village, Warwicks): 'prior's farmstead for livestock'. OE *heorde-wīc* (see HARDWICK). The manor here was granted to Coventry Priory in 1043. 1043 *Herdewyk*, DB *Herdewiche*, 1310 *Herdewyk Priour*.

Priors Marston (village, Warwicks): 'prior's farmstead by a marsh'. OE *mersc*, 'marsh', + *tūn*, 'farmstead'. There are many streams to the southeast of the village, where the manor was held by the Prior of Coventry in 1242. 1236 *Merston*, 1316 *Prioris Merston*.

Priston (village, Bath & NE Somerset): 'farmstead near the brushwood'. The first part of the name is Celtic, from a word related to modern Welsh *prysg*, 'copse'. The second part is OE *tūn*, 'farmstead'. 931 *Prisctun*, DB *Priscone*.

Prittlewell (district of Southend-on-Sea, Southend): '(place by the) babbling spring'. OE *pritol*, 'babbling', + *wella*, 'spring', 'stream'. 'The actual Prittle*well* appears to be the spring which feeds the smaller and most easterly of the two fishponds of Priory Park' (*Our Town: An Encyclopaedia of Southend-on-Sea & District*, 1947). See also SOUTHEND-ON-SEA. DB *Pritteuuella*.

Probus (village, Cornwall): '(church of) St Probus'. The church here is dedicated to Probus, a saint about whom nothing is known. DB *Sanctus Probus*.

Prudhoe (town, Northd): 'Prūda's hill spur'. OE *hōh*, 'heel of land', 'hill spur'. The 'hill spur'

in question is the one on which Prudhoe Castle stands, above the river Tyne. 1173 *Prudho*.

Puckeridge (village, Herts): '(place by the) ridge haunted by a goblin'. OE *pūca*, 'goblin' (modern English *Puck*), + *hrycg*, 'ridge'. 1294 *Pucherugge*.

Puckington (village, Somerset): 'estate associated with Pūca'. OE *-ing-*, 'associated with', + *tūn*, 'farmstead', 'estate'. DB *Pokintuna*.

Pucklechurch (village, S Glos): 'Pūcela's church'. OE *cirice*, 'church'. Pūcela was the owner of the church, not the person to whom it was dedicated. 950 *Pucelancyrcan*, DB *Pulcrecerce*.

Puddington (village, Cheshire): 'estate associated with Putta'. OE *-ing-*, 'associated with', + *tūn*, 'farmstead', 'estate'. DB *Potitone*. SO ALSO: *Puddington*, Devon.

Puddletown (village, Dorset): 'farmstead on the (river) Piddle'. OE *tūn*, 'farmstead'. The river's name means 'marsh', 'fen' (OE *pidele*). In 1956 Dorset County Council wanted to change the name to 'Piddletown' to make it conform to places such as PIDDLEHINTON and PIDDLETRENTHIDE, but this was opposed, mainly on the grounds of expense but also because *Puddletown* sounded 'nicer'. The first part of the DB form of the name below is garbled. DB *Pitretone*, 1212 *Pideleton*.

Pudleston (village, Herefords): 'Pyttel's hill'. OE *dūn*, 'hill'. The name could also mean 'hill where mousehawks are seen' (OE *pyttel*, 'mousehawk', + *dūn*). A mousehawk is a type of hawk that catches mice. The first part of the DB form of the name below is garbled. DB *Pillesdune*, 1212 *Putlesdone*.

Pudsey (town, Leeds): 'Pudoc's enclosure'. OE *hæg*, 'enclosure' (related modern English *hedge*). The first part of the name could also represent OE *puduc*, 'wart', as the name of a local hill, giving a sense 'enclosure by The Wart'. DB *Podechesaie*.

Puffin Island (island, Anglesey): 'island where puffins are seen'. Puffins still nest on the island, which is also known as *Priestholm*, 'priests' island' (OS *holmr*, 'island'), referring to the monastery founded here in the 6C by St Seriol, who gave the island's Welsh name, *Ynys Seiriol*, 'Seriol's island' (Welsh *ynys*, 'island'). Cp. LUNDY.

Pulborough (town, W Sussex): 'hill by the pools'. OE *pōl*, 'pool', + *beorg*, 'hill', 'mound'. The 'pools' would have been in the bend of the river Arun here, while the hill is the one on which the older part of the town stands, including its parish church. DB *Poleberge*.

Pulford (village, Cheshire): '(place by a) ford over a stream'. OE *pull*, 'pool', 'stream', + *ford*, 'ford'. The ford here would have been over Pulford Brook, a tributary of the Dee. DB *Pulford*.

Pulham (village, Dorset): 'homestead or enclosure by the pools'. OE *pōl*, 'pool', + *hām*, 'homestead', or *hamm*, 'enclosure'. The river Lydden flows nearby. DB *Poleham*.

Pulham Market (village, Norfolk): 'homestead or enclosure by the pools or streams with a market'. OE *pōl* or *pull*, 'pool', 'stream', + *hām*, 'homestead', or *hamm*, 'enclosure'. The second word of the name, referring to the important market here, distinguishes the village from nearby *Pulham St Mary*, named from the dedication of its church. The latter is formally *Pulham St Mary the Virgin*, as against *Pulham St Mary Magdalene*, the alternative name of Pulham Market. *c.*1050 *Polleham*, DB *Pullaham*.

Pumlumon. See PLYNLIMON.

Puncheston (village, Pemb): '(place by the) bridge where thistles grow'. OF *pont*, 'bridge', + *chardon*, 'thistle'. The name is said to have been transferred from *Pontchardon*, Normandy, by a Norman settler. An alternative meaning may be 'Ponchard's hill' (OE *dūn*, 'hill'), with an Old French personal name. The Welsh name of Puncheston is *Casmael*, 'Mael's fort' (Welsh *cas*, short for *castell*, 'castle', 'fort'). 1291 *Pounchardon*.

Puncknowle (village, Dorset): '(place by) Puma's hillock'. OE *cnoll*, 'hillock' (modern English *knoll*). DB *Pomacanole*.

Purbeck Hills (hill range, Dorset): 'beak-shaped ridge where bittern are seen'. OE *pūr*, 'bittern', 'snipe', + *bic*, 'pointed ridge' (related modern English *beak*). The hills form a conspicuous 'pointed' range, suggesting the outline of a bittern's long bill, and their name gave that of the *Isle of Purbeck* and so the local council district of *Purbeck*. The first form of the name below means 'dwellers in Purbeck' (OE -*ingas*, 'dwellers in'). 948 *Purbicinga*, DB *Porbi*.

Purbrook (village, Hants): '(place by the) brook haunted by a goblin'. OE *pūca*, 'goblin' (modern English *Puck*), + *brōc*, 'brook'. 1248 *Pukebrok*.

Purfleet (district, Thurrock): 'Purta's creek'. OE *flēot*, 'creek', 'stream'. The 'creek' would have been the Mar Dyke, which enters the Thames just west of Purfleet. 1285 *Purteflyete*.

Puriton (village, Somerset): 'farmstead where pear trees grow'. OE *pirige*, 'pear tree', + *tūn*, 'farmstead'. DB *Peritone*.

Purleigh (village, Essex): 'wood or clearing where bittern are seen'. OE *pūr*, 'bittern', 'snipe', + *lēah*, 'wood', 'clearing'. The bird would have been common in the former marshland here, south of Maldon. 998 *Purlea*, DB *Purlai*.

Purley (town, Croydon): 'wood where pear trees grow'. OE *pirige*, 'pear tree', + *lēah*, 'wood', 'clearing'. This is still a well-wooded district, especially to the south and east. 1200 *Pirlee*.

Purse Caundle. See BISHOP'S CAUNDLE.

Purslow (hamlet, Shropshire): 'Pussa's tumulus'. OE *hlāw*, 'mound', 'tumulus'. The burial mound in question no longer exists. DB *Possalau*.

Purston Jaglin (hamlet, Wakefield): 'Jakelyn's (estate at the) priests' farmstead'. OE *prēost*, 'priest', + *tūn*, 'farmstead'. The manor here was held early by one Jakelyn, his name a diminutive of OF Jacques. DB *Preston*, 1269 *Preston Jakelin*.

Purton (village, Wilts): 'farmstead where pear trees grow'. OE *pirige*, 'pear tree', + *tūn*, 'farmstead'. 796 *Puritone*, DB *Piritone*. SO ALSO: *Purton*, Glos (near Berkeley, near Blakeney).

Pusey (village, Oxon): 'island where peas grow'. OE *pise*, 'pea', + *ēg*, 'island'. The 'island' here is raised ground between two streams. DB *Pesei*.

Putley (village, Herefords): 'Putta's woodland clearing'. OE *lēah*, 'wood', 'clearing'. The name could also mean 'woodland clearing where hawks are seen' (OE *putta*, 'hawk', + *lēah*). The DB form of the name below is corrupt. DB *Poteslepe*, *c.*1180 *Putelega*.

Putney (district, Wandsworth): 'Putta's landing place'. OE *hȳth*, 'landing place'. Putney is on the Thames. The name could also mean 'landing place where hawks are seen' (OE *putta*, 'hawk', + *hȳth*). The DB form of the name below has *l* for *n*. DB *Putelei*, 1279 *Puttenhuthe*, 1474 *Putneth*.

Puttenham (village, Surrey): 'Putta's homestead or enclosure'. OE *hām*, 'homestead', or *hamm*, 'enclosure'. The name could also mean 'homestead or enclosure where hawks are seen' (OE *putta*, 'hawk', + *hām* or *hamm*). 1199 *Puteham*. SO ALSO: *Puttenham*, Herts.

Puxton (village, N Somerset): 'Pukerel's estate'. OE *tūn*, 'farmstead', 'estate'. The surname is Old French in origin. 1212 *Pukereleston*.

Pwllheli (town and port, Gwynedd): '(place by the) brine pool'. Welsh *pwll*, 'pool', + *heli*, 'brine', 'salt water'. A 'brine pool' is one near the sea, as here, as distinct from an inland pool. The pool in question may have been the enclosed inlet that forms the harbour. 1292 *Pwllhely*.

Pyecombe (village, W Sussex): '(place in the) valley by the pointed hill'. OE *pīc*, 'point', + *cumb*, 'valley'. The hill in question may be the southern end of Wolstonbury Hill, which projects into the valley here. late 11C *Picumba*.

Pylle (village, Somerset): '(place by the) stream'. OE *pyll*, 'pool', 'stream'. Pylle is near *Pilton*, with a name as for PILTON, Rutland. 705 *Pil*, DB *Pille*.

Pyrford (village, Surrey): '(place at the) ford by a pear tree'. OE *pirige*, 'pear tree', + *ford*, 'ford'. The name relates to the present Pyrford Village,

where the ford would have been over the river Wey, and not nearby Pyrford that is a suburb of Woking. The DB form of the name below has *l* for *r*. 956 *Pyrianforda*, DB *Peliforde*.

Pyrton (village, Oxon): 'farmstead where pear trees grow'. OE *pirige*, 'pear tree', + *tūn*, 'farmstead'. 987 *Pirigtune*, DB *Peritone*.

Pytchley (village, Northants): 'Peoht's woodland clearing'. OE *lēah*, 'wood', 'clearing'. 956 *Pihteslea*, DB *Pihteslea*.

Pyworthy (village, Devon): 'enclosure plagued with gnats'. OE *pīe*, 'gnat', 'insect', + *worthig*, 'enclosure'. The DB form of the name below is corrupt. DB *Paorda*, 1239 *Peworthy*.

Quadring (village, Lincs): 'muddy place of Hæfer's people'. OE *cwēad*, 'mud', 'dirt', + *-ingas*, 'people of'. The 'muddy place' is the fen here. The '-r-' is all that remains of the personal name. DB *Quedhaveringe*.

Quainton (village, Bucks): 'queen's farmstead'. OE *cwēn*, 'queen', + *tūn*, 'farmstead'. The first part of the DB form of the name below is corrupt. DB *Chentone*, 1167 *Quentona*.

Quantock Hills (hill range, Somerset): 'border hills'. The name is of Celtic origin, related to a word meaning 'border' (modern Welsh *cant*, 'ring', 'rim') also found behind the name of KENT. A section of the hill chain would probably have been seen as forming a border or 'edge'. The second part of the form of the name below represents OE *wudu*, 'wood'. 682 *Cantucuudu*.

Quarley (village, Hants): 'woodland clearing where millstones are obtained'. OE *cweorn*, 'millstone' (modern English *quern*), + *lēah*, 'wood', 'clearing'. The name could also mean 'woodland clearing with a mill'. 1167 *Cornelea*.

Quarndon (village, Derbys): '(place by the) hill where millstones are obtained'. OE *cweorn*, 'millstone' (modern English *quern*), + *dūn*, 'hill'. The DB form of the name below is corrupt. DB *Cornun*, *c.*1200 *Querendon*.

Quarrendon (suburb of Aylesbury, Bucks): '(place by the) hill where millstones are obtained'. OE *cweorn*, 'millstone' (modern English *quern*), + *dūn*, 'hill'. Cp. QUARNDON. DB *Querendone*.

Quarrington Hill (village, Durham): '(place by the) hill where millstones are obtained'. OE *cweorn*, 'millstone' (modern English *quern*), + *dūn*, 'hill'. Cp. QUARNDON. The second word of the name was added when the sense of 'hill' in the basic name was forgotten. *c.*1190 *Querendune*.

Quatford (village, Shropshire): '(place by the) ford in Cwatt'. OE *ford*, 'ford'. The district name is of obscure origin and meaning. Quatford is on

the river Severn, and 2 miles south is the village of *Quatt*, with a name of the same unexplained origin. DB *Quatford*.

Quatt. See QUATFORD.

Quedgeley (village, Glos): 'Cwēod's woodland clearing'. OE *lēah*, 'wood', 'clearing'. *c.*1140 *Quedesleya*.

Queenborough (town, Kent): 'borough of the queen'. OE *cwēn*, 'queen', + *burh*, 'borough'. The borough received its charter in 1367 and was named after Queen Philippa of Hainault (*c.*1314–69), wife of Edward III. 1376 *Queneburgh*.

Queen Camel (village, Somerset): 'queen's (estate in) Camel'. The district name is perhaps of Celtic origin from words related to modern Welsh *cant*, 'rim', and *moel*, 'bare hill'. The first word of the name refers to Queen Eleanor, who held the manor here in the 13C. Her title distinguishes the village from *West Camel*, immediately to the west. 995 *Cantmæl*, DB *Camelle*.

Queen Charlton (hamlet, Bath & NE Somerset): 'queen's (estate at the) farmstead of the freemen'. OE *ceorl*, 'freeman', 'peasant' (modern English *churl*), + *tūn*, 'farmstead'. The queen in question is Catherine Parr (1512–48), who was given the manor here by Henry VIII. 1291 *Cherleton*.

Queensbury (town, Bradford): 'town of the queen'. The town was originally a village called *Queen's Head*, named after an inn. In 1863 the present name was adopted as a compliment to Queen Victoria.

Queensbury (district, Harrow). The district takes its name from the local Underground station, opened in 1934 and named as a counterpart to KINGSBURY, Brent, the next station south.

Queensferry (town, Flints): '(town with a) ferry of the queen'. There were originally several ferries across the river Dee here before it was canalized. One was the *Lower Ferry*, renamed

King's Ferry in 1828 in honour of George IV and *Queensferry* in 1837 to mark the coronation of Queen Victoria.

Queen's Nympton. See KING'S NYMPTON.

Quemerford (village, Wilts): '(place by a) ford at the confluence'. The first part of the name represents a Celtic word related to modern Welsh *cymer*, 'confluence'. The second is OE *ford*, 'ford'. Quemerford is not far from the point where two streams meet. 1199 *Quemerford*, 1476 *Comerford*.

Quendon (village, Essex): '(place in the) valley of the women'. OE *cwene*, 'woman' (related modern English *queen*), + *denu*, 'valley'. DB *Kuenadana*.

Queniborough (village, Leics): 'fortified manor of the queen'. OE *cwēn*, 'queen', + *burh*, 'fortified place', 'manor'. DB *Cuinburg*, 12C *Queniburg*.

Quenington (village, Glos): 'farmstead of the women'. OE *cwene* 'woman' (related modern English *queen*), + *tūn*, 'farmstead'. The first part of the name represents OE *cwenene*, the genitive plural form of *cwene*. Alternatively, the name could mean 'farmstead associated with Cwēn' (OE *-ing-*, 'associated with'), the latter being a woman's name. DB *Quenintone*.

Quernmore (hamlet, Lancs): '(place on the) moor where millstones are obtained'. OE *cweorn*, 'millstone' (modern English *quern*), + *mōr*, 'moor'. 1228 *Quernemor*.

Quethiock (village, Cornwall): 'wooded place'. OC *cuidoc* (Middle Cornish *coes*, 'wood', + adjectival ending *-ek*). 1201 *Quedoc*.

Quidenham (hamlet, Norfolk): 'Cwida's homestead'. OE *hām*, 'homestead', 'village'. DB *Cuidenham*.

Quidhampton (village, Wilts): 'muddy home farm'. OE *cwēad*, 'dirt', 'mud', + *hām-tūn*, 'home farm' (from *hām*, 'homestead', + *tūn*, 'farmstead'). OE *cwēad* also meant 'dung', so that another possible sense is 'home farm with good manure'. 1249 *Quedhampton*. SO ALSO: *Quidhampton*, Hants.

Quies (island group, Cornwall): '(islands of the) sow'. Cornish *gwis*, 'sow'. The rocks here, south of Trevose Head, were presumably thought to resemble a sow. 1813 *Quies*.

Quorndon (village, Leics): 'hill where millstones are obtained'. OE *cweorn*, 'millstone' (modern English *quern*), + *dūn*, 'hill'. The village is also known as simply *Quorn*. c.1220 *Querendon*.

R

Raasay (island, Highland): 'island with a ridge where deer are seen'. OS *rár*, 'roe deer', + *áss*, 'ridge', + *ey*, 'island'. The 'ridge' is the mountain chain in the southern part of the island. Red deer are still found on this island off Skye. 1263 *Raasa*.

Raby (village, Wirral): 'farmstead at the boundary'. OS *rá*, 'boundary', + *bý*, 'farmstead'. Raby was probably at the limit of Scandinavian territory here on the Wirral peninsula. Cp. HARGRAVE (Wirral). DB *Rabie*.

Rackenford (village, Devon): '(place by the) ford near gullies'. OE *hraca*, 'throat', 'gully', + *ford*, 'ford'. The precise meaning of the name is uncertain. It has also been derived from OE *racu*, 'bed of a stream', and *ærne-ford*, 'ford that can be ridden over (on horseback)'. The river here is the Little Dart. DB *Racheneforda*.

Rackham (hamlet, W Sussex): 'homestead or enclosure with ricks'. OE *hrēac*, 'rick', + *hām*, 'homestead', or *hamm*, 'enclosure'. 1166 *Recham*.

Rackheath (hamlet, Norfolk): 'landing place by a gully'. OE *hraca*, 'throat', 'gully', + *hýth*, 'landing place'. The name could also mean 'landing place by a watercourse' (OE *racu*, 'watercourse', + *hýth*). Rackheath is near the source of a tributary of the river Bure that enters the river through a wide but deep valley ('gully'), and there may have originally been enough water to allow transport from the Bure. DB *Racheitha*.

Radcliffe (town, Bury): '(place at the) red cliff'. OE *rēad*, 'red', + *clif*, 'cliff', 'bank'. The name refers to the red sandstone cliff beside the river Irwell here. DB *Radecliue*.

Radcliffe on Trent (town, Notts): '(place at the) red bank by the (river) Trent'. OE *rēad*, 'red', + *clif*, 'cliff', 'bank'. The name alludes to the red loamy clay that slopes down to the Trent here. The river name (see STOKE-ON-TRENT) distinguishes this Radcliffe from RATCLIFFE ON SOAR, 12 miles to the southwest. DB *Radeclive*.

Radclive (village, Bucks): '(place at the) red bank'. OE *rēad*, 'red', + *clif*, 'cliff', 'bank'. The village stands on soil of a reddish hue above the river Ouse. DB *Radeclive*.

Radcot (hamlet, Oxon): 'red cottage'. OE *rēad*, 'red', + *cot*, 'cottage'. The name could also mean 'reed cottage', i.e. one thatched with reeds (OE *hrēod*, 'reed', + *cot*). 1163 *Rathcota*.

Radford (district, Nottingham): '(place by the) red ford'. OE *rēad*, 'red', + *ford*, 'ford'. The name alludes to the red sandstone here by the river Leen. DB *Redeford*.

Radford Semele (village, Warwicks): 'Simely's (estate by the) red ford'. OE *rēad*, 'red', + *ford*, 'ford'. The soil is red here, where the manor was held by the Simely family in the 12C. DB *Redeford*, 1314 *Radeford Symely*.

Radipole (district of Weymouth, Dorset): '(place by the) reedy pool'. OE *hrēod*, 'reed', + *pōl*, 'pool'. The pool in question is Radipole Lake, which opens into the sea to the south. DB *Retpole*.

Radlett (town, Herts): '(place at the) road junction'. OE *rād*, 'road', + *gelǣt*, 'junction'. Radlett is on Watling Street (the modern A5183), and the 'junction' was an important medieval crossroads here. 1453 *Radelett*.

Radley (village, Oxon): 'red wood or clearing'. OE *rēad*, 'red', + *lēah*, 'wood', 'clearing'. The colour probably refers to bark or foliage rather than to the soil, which is anyway not noticeably red at Radley. *c*.1180 *Radelege*.

Radnage (hamlet, Bucks): '(place by the) red oak tree'. OE *rēad*, 'red', + *āc*, 'oak'. The present form of the name represents OE *rēadan ǣc*, the dative form of the two words. 1162 *Radenhech*.

Radnor Forest (woodland region, Powys): 'forest with a red bank'. OE *rēad*, 'red', + *ōra*, 'bank'. The 'red bank' is the red loamy soil on the hill slopes here. The name gave that of the historic county of *Radnorshire* and is also found for NEW RADNOR. DB *Raddrenoue*.

Radstock (town, Bath & NE Somerset): 'outlying farmstead by the road'. OE *rād*, 'road', + *stoc*, 'outlying farmstead'. The 'road' is the Fosse Way here, today represented by the A367. The place was originally known simply as *Stoke*, and the first part of the name must have been added to distinguish this Stoke from some other, such as *Stoke St Michael*, Somerset, 5 miles to the south, or *Southstoke*, Bath & NE Somerset, 5 miles to the northeast. DB *Stoche*, 1221 *Radestok*.

Radstone (village, Northants): '(place at the) rood stone'. OE *rōd-stān* (from *rōd*, 'rood', 'cross', 'crucifix', + *stān*, 'stone'). The reference may be to a stone serving as the socket of a cross. DB *Rodestone*.

Radur. See RADYR.

Radway · (village, Warwicks): '(place by the) red way'. OE *rēad*, 'red', + *weg*, 'way'. The name refers to the colour of the soil here. 'The place being situat on the skirt, and neer the passage up *Edg-hill*, had its name originally, as I guesse, from the red colour of the earth, which sheweth it self at a good distance upon that road by reason of the ascending ground' (William Dugdale, *The Antiquities of Warwickshire*, 1656). A meaning 'way for riding on' (OE *rād-weg*) is also theoretically possible. DB *Radwei*, 1198 *Radewey*.

Radwell (village, Herts): '(place by the) red spring'. OE *rēad*, 'red', + *wella*, 'spring', 'stream'. DB *Radeuuelle*.

Radwinter (village, Essex): 'Rædwynn's tree'. OE *trēow*. The personal name is that of a woman. The name could also mean 'red vineyard', from OE *rēad*, 'red', + *winter*, 'vineyard' (from Latin *vinitorium*). There were several vineyards in medieval Essex. DB *Redeuuintra*.

Radyr (village, Cardiff): '(place by the) oratory'. Latin *oratorium*, 'oratory'. The name refers to a small chapel for private worship here. The Welsh form of the name is *Radur*. 1254 *Radur*, 1291 *Rador*.

Rafborough (district of Farnborough, Hants). Rafborough lies by the airfield of the former Royal Aircraft Establishment (now the UK Defence Evaluation and Research Agency). Hence the 20C name, from the initials of the RAF (which happen to invert the 'Far-' of 'Farnborough') and the latter part of the town's name.

Ragdale (village, Leics): '(place by the) narrow valley'. OE *hraca*, 'throat', 'gully', + *dæl*, 'valley'. Ragdale lies in the Leicestershire Wolds. The DB form of the name below has an extraneous *n*. DB *Ragendele*, *c*.1125 *Rachedal*, 1868 *Ragdale*, *Rakedale*, or *Wreakdale*.

Raglan (village, Mon): '(place) before the bank'. Welsh *rhag*, 'before', 'against', + *glan*, 'bank'. The name refers to the former castle here, on the site of the remains of the 15C castle to the north of the village. The Welsh spelling of the name is *Rhaglan*. 1254 *Raghelan*.

Ragnall (village, Notts): 'Ragni's hill'. OE *hyll*, 'hill'. The personal name is Scandinavian. DB *Ragenehil*.

Rainford (town, St Helens): '(place by) Regna's ford'. OE *ford*, 'ford'. The first part of the name could also represent OS *rein*, 'boundary', perhaps referring to the point where the road through the former morass here crossed the Sankey Brook. Cp. RAINHILL. 1198 *Raineford*.

Rainham (town, Havering): 'homestead of the Roegingas'. OE *hām*, 'homestead'. The tribal name is of uncertain origin. The name could also mean 'Regna's homestead'. DB *Renaham*.

Rainham (district of Gillingham, Medway): 'homestead of the Roegingas'. OE *hām*, 'homestead'. The tribal name is of uncertain meaning. 811 *Roegingaham*.

Rainhill (town, St Helens): 'Regna's hill'. OE *hyll*, 'hill'. The first part of the name could also represent OS *rein*, 'boundary'. Rainhill lies on the northern side of a sandstone ridge, and this could be the 'boundary hill'. Cp. RAINFORD. *c*.1190 *Raynhull*.

Rainow (village, Cheshire): '(place on the) hill spur where ravens are seen'. OE *hræfn*, 'raven', + *hōh*, 'hill spur'. The village lies on the shoulder of a hill. 1285 *Rauenouh*.

Rainton (village, N Yorks): 'estate associated with Rægen or Regna'. OE -*ing*-, 'associated with', + *tūn*, 'farmstead', 'estate'. DB *Rainincton*.

Rainworth (village, Notts): '(place by the) clean ford'. OS *hreinn*, 'clean', + *vath*, 'ford'. The name could also mean '(place by the) boundary ford' (OS *rein*, 'boundary'), in which case the reference would be to the boundary between Broxtow and Bassetlaw wapentakes. The river here is Rainworth Water. 1268 *Reynwath*.

Rake (village, Hants): '(place at the) pass'. OE *hraca*, 'throat'. The reference is to a gap in the hills here. 1296 *Rake*.

Rame (village, Cornwall): origin uncertain. A meaning 'barrier' has been proposed, from an unrecorded OE word related to modern German *Rahmen*, 'frame'. The reference could be to the ancient fort on nearby Rame Head. DB *Rame*.

Rampisham (village, Dorset): 'enclosure where wild garlic grows'. OE *hramsa*, 'wild garlic', + *hamm*, 'enclosure'. The name could also mean 'enclosure where rams are kept' (OE *ramm*, 'ram', + *hamm*) or 'Ramm's enclosure'. DB *Ramesham*.

Rampside (coastal village, Cumbria): 'headland where rams are kept'. OE *ramm*, 'ram', + *hēafod*, 'headland'. The second part of the name has been confused with OE *sīde*, 'hillside'. 1292 *Rameshede*.

Rampton (village, Cambs): 'farmstead where rams are kept'. OE *ramm*, 'ram', + *tūn*, 'farmstead'. DB *Rantone*. SO ALSO: *Rampton*, Notts.

Ramsbottom (town, Bury): 'valley where rams are pastured'. OE *ramm*, 'ram', + *bothm*, 'valley bottom'. The name could also refer to a rock formation resembling a ram's head. The first part of the name could also represent OE *hramsa*, 'wild garlic', giving a meaning 'valley where wild garlic grows'. The valley is that of the river Irwell. 1324 *Romesbothum*.

Ramsbury (village, Wilts): 'fortification where ravens are seen'. OE *hræfn*, 'raven', + *burh*, 'fortified place'. The name may be figurative rather than literal, as the raven was associated with battlefields in OE literature and was symbolic of Woden, the Teutonic god of victory and the dead. 947 *Rammesburi*, DB *Ramesberie*.

Ramsden (village, Oxon): '(place in the) valley where wild garlic grows'. OE *hramsa*, 'wild garlic', + *denu*, 'valley'. 1246 *Rammesden*.

Ramsden Bellhouse (village, Essex): 'de Belhus' (estate in the) valley where wild garlic grows'. OE *hramsa*, 'wild garlic', + *denu*, 'valley'. The de Belhus family held the manor here in the 13C. DB *Ramesdana*, 1254 *Ramesden Belhous*.

Ramsey (town, Cambs): 'island where wild garlic grows'. OE *hramsa*, 'wild garlic', + *ēg*, 'island'. Ramsey is a fenland town, and the 'island' is an area of dry ground in marshland. *c*.1000 *Hramesege*. SO ALSO: *Ramsey*, Essex.

Ramsey Island (island, Pemb): 'island where wild garlic grows'. OS *hramsa*, 'wild garlic', + *ey*, 'island'. The Welsh name of the island is *Ynys Dewi*, 'St David's island' (Welsh *ynys*, 'island', + *Dewi*, 'David'). 1326 *Ramesey*.

Ramsgate (resort town, Kent): 'Hræfn's gap'. OE *geat*, 'gap'. The 'gap' is a way through the cliffs here. The name could also mean 'gap by The Raven' (OE *hræfn*, 'raven'), referring to a rock here, so named from its resemblance to the bird. It could even mean 'gap of the ravens', if the birds were frequently seen here. 1275 *Remmesgate*.

Ramsgill (village, N Yorks): '(place by the) ravine where rams graze'. OE *ramm*, 'ram', + OS *gil*, 'ravine'. The first part of the name could also represent OE *hramsa*, 'wild garlic'. 1198 *Ramesgile*.

Randwick (village, Glos): 'dwelling on the border'. OE *rend*, 'edge', 'border', + *wīc*, 'dwelling', 'specialized farm'. The border in question may have been that of a hundred here. 1121 *Rendewiche*.

Rangeworthy (village, S Glos): 'Hrencga's enclosure'. OE *worthig*, 'enclosure'. The name could also mean 'enclosure made of stakes' (OE *hrynge*, 'stake'). 1167 *Rengeswurda*.

Rannoch Moor (upland region, Highland): '(place of) bracken'. Gaelic *raineach*, 'fern', 'bracken'. The name also applies to *Rannoch Forest* and *Loch Rannoch*, Perth & Kin. 1505 *Rannach*.

Ranskill (village, Notts): '(place on a) shelf where ravens are seen'. OS *hrafn*, 'raven', + *skjalf*, 'shelf'. The name could also mean 'Hrafn's shelf (of land)', with a Scandinavian personal name. The village is on a slight slope above level ground beside the river Idle. The DB form of the name below is corrupt. DB *Raveschel*, 1275 *Ravenskelf*.

Ranton (village, Staffs): 'farmstead where rams are kept'. OE *ramm*, 'ram', + *tūn*, 'farmstead'. DB *Rantone*.

Ranworth (village, Norfolk): 'enclosure by a border'. OE *rand*, 'edge', 'border', + *worth*, 'enclosure'. The name could also mean 'Randi's enclosure', with a Scandinavian personal name. *c*.1045 *Randwrthe*.

Raskelf (village, N Yorks): '(place by the) ridge where roe deer are seen'. OS *rá*, 'roe deer', + *skjalf*, 'shelf', 'ridge'. Raskelf is on a ridge of land overlooking the river Kyle. DB *Raschel*.

Rastrick (district of Brighouse, Calderdale): '(place on the) ridge with a resting place'. OS *rost*, 'resting place', + OE *ric*, 'ridge'. Rastrick lies on the side of a long narrow ridge above the river Calder. DB *Rastric*.

Ratae Coritanorum. See LEICESTER.

Ratby (village, Leics): 'Rōta's farmstead'. OS *bý*, 'farmstead'. The personal name is the same as that behind RUTLAND, and it is possible the same Anglo-Saxon was involved. DB *Rotebie*.

Ratcliffe Culey (village, Leics): 'de Culy's (estate by the) red bank'. OE *rēad*, 'red', + *clif*, 'cliff', 'bank'. The de Culy family held the manor here in the 13C. DB *Redeclive*.

Ratcliffe on Soar (village, Notts): '(place by the) red bank on the (river) Soar'. OE *rēad*, 'red', + *clif*, 'cliff', 'bank'. The reference is to the colour of the clay hills here along the river Soar (see BARROW UPON SOAR). The river name distinguishes this Ratcliffe from both RADCLIFFE ON TRENT, 12 miles to the northeast, and RATCLIFFE ON THE WREAKE, Leics, 12 miles to the southeast. DB *Radeclive*.

Ratcliffe on the Wreake (village, Leics): '(place by the) red bank on the (river) Wreake'. OE *rēad*, 'red', + *clif*, 'cliff', 'bank'. The river name (see FRISBY ON THE WREAKE) distinguishes this Ratcliffe from RATCLIFFE ON SOAR, Notts, 12 miles to the northwest. DB *Radeclive*.

Rathmell (village, N Yorks): '(place by the) red sandbank'. OS *rauthr*, 'red', + *melr*, 'sandbank'. DB *Rodemele*.

Ratley (village, Warwicks): '(place in the) clearing with (tree) roots'. OE *rōt*, 'root', + *lēah*, 'wood', 'clearing'. The name could also mean 'Rōta's clearing'. DB *Rotelei*.

Ratlinghope (village, Shropshire): '(place in the) valley associated with Rōtel'. OE *-ing-*, 'associated with', + *hop*, 'enclosed valley'. DB *Rotelingehope*.

Rattery (village, Devon): '(place by the) red tree'. OE *rēad*, 'red', + *trēow*, 'tree'. DB *Ratreu*.

Rattlesden (village, Suffolk): '(place in the) valley'. OE *denu*, 'valley'. The first part of the name is of uncertain origin. It may represent a personal name. DB *Ratlesdena*.

Rattray (town, Perth & Kin): 'farm by the fort'. The first part of the name is Gaelic *ràth*, 'fort', while the second is a Celtic word related to modern Welsh *tref*, 'farm'. The name makes no mention of the town's location by the river Ericht. 1291 *Rotrefe*.

Raughton Head (hamlet, Cumbria): 'farmstead where moss grows'. OE *ragu*, 'moss', 'lichen', + *tūn*, 'farmstead'. The second word (OE *hēafod*, 'headland') was added later. 1182 *Ragton*, 1367 *Raughtonheved*.

Raunds (town, Northants): '(place at the) borders'. OE *rand*, 'border', 'edge', 'boundary'. Raunds is not far from the point where three counties meet: Northamptonshire, Cambridgeshire (formerly Huntingdonshire) and Bedfordshire. Hence the name. *c*.980 *Randan*, DB *Rande*.

Ravenfield (village, Rotherham): 'Hræfn's open land'. OE *feld*, 'open land' (modern English *field*). The name could also mean 'open land where ravens are seen' (OE *hræfn*, 'raven', + *feld*). DB *Rauenesfeld*.

Ravenglass (village, Cumbria): 'Glas's share'. The name is Celtic, with the first part related to modern Gaelic *rann* and modern Welsh *rhan*,

'part', 'portion'. The second part is either an OI personal name or a word meaning 'blue-green' (modern Welsh *glas*), giving a sense 'green portion'. The Roman fort here was *Glannoventa*, a name of Celtic origin meaning literally 'shore field'. *c*.1180 *Rengles*.

Raveningham (village, Norfolk): 'homestead of Hræfn's people'. OE *-inga-*, 'of the people of', + *hām*, 'homestead'. DB *Rauenicham*.

Ravenscar (hamlet, N Yorks): '(place by the) rock where ravens are seen'. OS *hrafn*, 'raven', + *sker*, 'rock'. Ravenscar lies on lofty cliffs by the coast. 1312 *Rauenesere*.

Ravenshead (village, Notts): 'hill where ravens are seen'. OE *hræfn*, 'raven', + *hēafod*, 'head', 'hill'. The name, which could also mean 'Hræfn's hill', was originally that of a hill, then that of a wood on it. 1205 *Ravenesheved*.

Ravensthorpe (village, Northants): 'Hrafn's outlying farmstead'. OS *thorp*, 'outlying farmstead'. The personal name is Scandinavian. DB *Ravenestorp*. SO ALSO: *Ravensthorpe*, Kirklees.

Ravenstone (village, Milton K): 'Hræfn's or Hrafn's farmstead'. OE *tūn*, 'farmstead'. The personal names are respectively OE and Scandinavian. DB *Raveneston*. SO ALSO: *Ravenstone*, Leics.

Ravenstonedale (village, Cumbria): '(place in the) valley of the raven stone'. OE *hræfn*, 'raven', + *stān*, 'stone', + OS *dalr*, 'valley'. The 'raven stone' is a distinctive rock here. 12C *Rauenstandale*.

Ravensworth (village, N Yorks): '(place by) Hrafn's ford'. OS *vath*, 'ford'. The personal name is Scandinavian. The river here is the Holme Beck. The second part of the DB form of the name below is corrupt. DB *Raveneswet*, 1157 *Raveneswad*.

Rawcliffe (village, E Yorks): '(place by the) red bank'. OS *rauthr*, 'red', + *klif*, 'cliff', 'bank'. The bank in question would have been that of the river Aire here. DB *Routheclif*. SO ALSO: *Rawcliffe*, York.

Rawdon (district, Leeds): '(place by the) red hill'. OS *rauthr*, 'red', + OE *dūn*, 'hill'. DB *Roudun*.

Rawmarsh (town, Rotherham): '(place by the) red marsh'. OS *rauthr*, 'red', + OE *mersc*, 'marsh'. A 'red' marsh is one with red earth. Cp. REDCAR. Rawmarsh is on the river Don. The DB form of the name below has omitted the *r* of the OE word. DB *Rodemesc*, *c*.1200 *Rowmareis*.

Rawreth (village, Essex): '(place by the) stream where herons are seen'. OE *hrāgra*, 'heron', + *rīth*, 'stream'. 1177 *Raggerea*.

Rawtenstall (town, Lancs): 'rough cow pasture'. OE *rūh*, 'rough', + *tūn-stall*, 'cow pasture' (from *tūn*, 'farmstead' + *stall*, 'stall', 'site'). Rawtenstall is on the edge of high moorland, and this would have been the original 'rough cow pasture'. 1324 *Routonstall*.

Raydon (village, Suffolk): '(place by the) hill where rye is grown'. OE *rygen*, 'growing with rye', + *dūn*, 'hill'. DB *Reindune*.

Rayleigh (town, Essex): 'woodland clearing where deer are seen'. OE *rǣge*, 'roe deer', + *lēah*, 'wood', 'clearing'. DB *Ragheleia*.

Rayne (village, Essex): '(place by the) shelter'. OE *hrægene*, 'shelter', 'hut'. *c*.1000 *Hrǣgenan*, DB *Raines*.

Reach (village, Cambs): '(place on a) raised strip of land'. OE *rǣc*, 'raised straight strip' (modern English *reach*). The village stands on the northern tip of the post-Roman earthwork known as the Devil's Dyke, and this is the 'raised strip of land'. Cp. HEATH AND REACH. DB *Reche*.

Read (village, Lancs): 'headland where female roe deer are seen'. OE *rǣge*, 'female roe deer', + *hēafod*, 'headland'. The headland in question is the rising ground between Sabden Brook and the river Calder. 1202 *Revet*.

Reading (town, Reading): '(settlement of) Rēad's people'. OE *-ingas*, 'people of'. *c*.900 *Readingum*, DB *Reddinges*.

Reagill (hamlet, Cumbria): '(place by the) ravine where foxes are seen'. OS *refr*, 'fox', + *gil*, 'ravine'. 1176 *Reuegile*.

Rearsby (village, Leics): 'Hreitharr's farmstead'. OS *bý*, 'farmstead', 'village'. The personal name is Scandinavian. DB *Redresbi*.

Reculver (coastal village, Kent): '(place by the) great headland'. The name is Celtic, from a prefix *ro-*, 'great', and a word related to modern Welsh *gylfin*, 'beak', understood metaphorically as 'headland'. There is no actual 'great headland' at Reculver itself, and the reference is probably to the Isle of Thanet to the east. The name of the Roman fort here, *Regulbium*, has the same origin. DB *Roculf*.

Redberth (village, Pemb): '(place by the) ford with bushes'. Welsh *rhyd*, 'ford', + *perth*, 'wood', 'bush'. The ford would have been over the river Carew here. 1361 *Ridebard*.

Redbourn (village, Herts): '(place by the) reedy stream'. OE *hrēod*, 'reed', + *burna*, 'stream'. *c*.1060 *Reodburne*, DB *Redborne*.

Redbourne (village, N Lincs): '(place by the) reedy stream'. OE *hrēod*, 'reed', + *burna*, 'stream'. DB *Radburne*.

Redbridge (borough, Greater London): '(place by the) red bridge'. The bridge in question is one formerly across the river Roding, which here forms the boundary between Wanstead and Ilford. It was made of red brick and was designed to carry wheeled transport, unlike the nearby *White Bridge*, for foot passengers only. The bridge itself, demolished in 1922, was located at the point where modern Eastern Avenue (the A12) now crosses the Roding at Wanstead. 1746 *Red Bridge*.

Redcar (resort town, Redcar & Clev): '(place by the) red marsh'. OE *rēad*, 'red', + OS *kjarr*, 'marsh'. The reference is to the red-coloured rocks here. However, the first part of the name could also represent OE *hrēod*, 'reed', giving a sense 'reedy marshland', referring to the low-lying land by the sea on which Redcar lies. *c*.1170 *Redker*.

Reddish (district, Stockport): '(place by the) reedy ditch'. OE *hrēod*, 'reed', + *dīc*, 'ditch'. 1212 *Rediche*.

Redditch (town, Worcs): '(place by the) red ditch'. OE *rēad*, 'red', + *dīc*, 'ditch'. The reference would be to a ditch with red soil rather than one with red-coloured water. However, the first part of the name could equally represent OE *hrēod*, 'reed', giving a sense 'reedy ditch'. Either way, the ditch itself would probably have linked with the river Arrow, on which Redditch stands. 1247 *La Rededich*.

Rede (village, Suffolk): '(place by the) reed bed'. OE *hrēod*, 'reed'. DB *Reoda*.

Redenhall (village, Norfolk): 'corner of land where reeds grow'. OE *hrēoden*, 'growing with reeds', + *halh*, 'nook', 'corner of land'. Redenhall is on the river Waveney. DB *Redanahalla*.

Redgrave (village, Suffolk): '(place by the) reedy pit'. OE *hrēod*, 'reed', + *grǽf*, 'pit' (modern English *grave*). The name could also mean '(place by the) red grove' (OE *rēad*, 'red', + *grāf*, 'grove'). 11C *Redgrafe*.

Redhill (town, Surrey): '(place by the) red slope'. OE *rēad*, 'red', + *helde*, 'slope'. The form of the name below shows that the second part is not OE *hyll*, 'hill', as it appears. The 'red slope' was probably the one with red soil now known as Redstone Hill, to the southeast. The town itself did not develop until the mid-19C. 1301 *Redehelde*.

Redisham (village, Suffolk): 'Rēad's homestead'. OE *hām*, 'homestead', 'village'. DB *Redesham*.

Redland (district, Bristol): 'third part of an estate'. OE *thridda*, 'third', + *land*, 'land', 'estate'.

'The particular circumstances in which the name Redland arose are not known' (A. H. Smith, *The Place-Names of Gloucestershire*, 1964). 1209 *Thriddeland*.

Redlingfield (village, Suffolk): 'open land of Rædel's or Rædla's people'. OE *-inga-*, 'of the people of', + *feld*, 'open land' (modern English *field*). The DB form of the name below has omitted *l* from the personal name. DB *Radinghefelda*, 1166 *Radlingefeld*.

Redlynch (hamlet, Somerset): '(place by the) reedy marsh'. OE *hrēod*, 'reed', + *lisc*, 'marsh'. DB *Redlisc*.

Redmarley D'Abitot (village, Glos): 'd'Abitot's (estate in the) woodland clearing with a reedy pond'. OE *hrēod*, 'reed', + *mere*, 'pond', + *lēah*, 'wood', 'clearing'. The d'Abitot family held the manor here in 1086, their name distinguishing this village from the smaller *Redmarley*, Worcs, 22 miles to the north. 963 *Reodemæreleage*, DB *Ridmerlege*, 1324 *Rudmarleye Dabetot*.

Redmarshall (village, Stockton): '(place on the) hill by a reedy pond'. OE *hrēod*, 'reed', + *mere*, 'pond', + *hyll*, 'hill'. 1208 *Rodmerehil*.

Redmile (village, Leics): '(place with) red earth'. OE *rēad*, 'red', + *mylde*, 'earth'. DB *Redmelde*.

Redmire (village, N Yorks): '(place by the) reedy pool'. OE *hrēod*, 'reed', + *mere*, 'pool'. DB *Ridemare*.

Redruth (town, Cornwall): '(place by the) red ford'. Cornish *rys* (earlier *rid*), 'ford', + *rudh*, 'red'. Despite appearances, it is the second part of the name that means 'red', not the first, as in Celtic languages the adjective usually follows the noun. The 'red ford' was probably over the small stream on which St Euny's church stands, to the west of the town. 1259 *Ridruth*.

Redwick (hamlet, S Glos): 'dairy farm among the reeds'. OE *hrēod*, 'reed', + *wīc*, 'dairy farm'. 955 *Hreodwican*, DB *Redeuuiche*.

Redworth (hamlet, Darlington): 'enclosure where reeds grow'. OE *hrēod*, 'reed', + *worth*, 'enclosure'. 1183 *Redwortha*.

Reed (village, Herts): 'rough area of ground'. OE *rȳhth*, 'rough land' (related modern English *rough*). DB *Retth*.

Reedham (village, Norfolk): 'homestead or enclosure where reeds grow'. OE *hrēod*, 'reed', + *hām*, 'homestead', or *hamm*, 'enclosure'. Reedham is on the river Yare. 1044 *Redham*, DB *Redeham*.

Reedness (village, E Yorks): '(place on the) reedy headland'. OE *hrēod*, 'reed', + *næss*, 'head-

land'. The village lies on a curving piece of land on the southern bank of the river Ouse. *c*.1170 *Rednesse*.

Reepham (village, Norfolk): 'manor run by a reeve'. OE *rēfa*, 'reeve', + *hām*, 'homestead', 'manor'. A reeve arranged the day-to-day business of a manor in Anglo-Saxon times. DB *Refham*. SO ALSO: *Reepham*, Lincs.

Reeth (village, N Yorks): '(place by the) stream'. OE *rīth*, 'stream'. DB *Rie*, 1184 *Rithe*.

Regulbium. See RECULVER.

Reigate (town, Surrey): '(place by the) gate for roe deer'. OE *rǣge*, 'roe deer', + *geat*, 'gate'. The reference is to an entrance to a deer park, perhaps where Reigate Park is today, or else to a gap in a boundary fence where a doe could pass with her young. Cp. ROGATE. *c*.1170 *Reigata*.

Reighton (village, N Yorks): 'farmstead by the ridge'. OE *ric*, 'ridge', + *tūn*, 'farmstead'. The 'ridge' is the line formed by Speeton Hills and Speeton Cliffs to the east of Reighton. DB *Rictone*.

Remenham (village, Wokingham): 'homestead or enclosure by the river bank'. OE *reoma*, 'border', 'edge' (modern English *rim*), + *hām*, 'homestead', or *hamm*, 'enclosure'. The river here is the Thames. DB *Rameham*.

Rempstone (village, Notts): 'Hrempi's farmstead'. OE *tūn*, 'farmstead'. DB *Rampestune*.

Rendcomb (village, Glos): '(place in the) valley of the Rend Brook'. OE *cumb*, 'valley'. The stream that flows past Rendcomb originally had the OE name *Hrinde*, meaning 'pusher', 'thruster', referring to a fast-flowing stream. DB *Rindecumbe*.

Rendham (village, Suffolk): 'cleared homestead'. OE *rȳmed*, 'cleared', + *hām*, 'homestead'. The name could also mean 'homestead by a hill' (OE *rind*, 'hill', + *hām*). DB *Rindham*.

Rendlesham (village, Suffolk): 'Rendel's homestead'. OE *hām*, 'homestead'. *c*.730 *Rendlæsham*, DB *Rendlesham*.

Renfrew (town, Renfrews): '(place at the) point of the current'. The name derives from two Celtic words represented by modern Welsh *rhyn*, 'point', and *ffrwyd*, 'current'. The 'point of the current' is the one where the river Gryfe enters the Clyde here. *c*.1128 *Reinfry*, *c*.1150 *Renfriu*.

Rennington (village, Northd): 'estate associated with Regna'. OE *-ing-*, 'associated with', + *tūn*, 'farmstead', 'estate'. 12C *Reiningtun*.

Renton (town, W Dunbartons). The town was founded in 1782 by the family of the novelist

Tobias Smollett (1721–71), who was born near here, and named by Jean Telfer, Smollett's sister, after her daughter-in-law, Cecilia Renton.

Renwick (village, Cumbria): 'Hrafn's or Hræfn's dwelling'. OE *wīc*, 'dwelling', 'specialized farm'. The personal names are respectively Scandinavian and OE. 1178 *Rauenwich*.

Repps (hamlet, Norfolk): '(place by the) strips of land'. OE *reopul*, 'strip of land' (related modern English *rip*). The name probably refers to arable strips of land in marshland. Cp. NORTH-REPPS. DB *Repes*, 1191 *Repples*.

Repton (town, Derbys): 'hill of the Hrype'. OE *dūn*, 'hill'. The Hrype, a people about whom nothing is known except their name, also gave the name of RIPON. There is hardly a hill at Repton in the accepted sense, but the ground does rise gradually from the river Trent, near which the town stands. 730 *Hrypadun*, DB *Rapendune*.

Restormel (castle ruins, Cornwall): 'moor by the bare hill'. Cornish *ros*, 'moor', + *tor*, 'hill', + *moyl*, 'bald', 'bare'. The location of the hill in question is uncertain, but it may have been on the headland on which the remains of Restormel Castle stand. The name is now also that of the local council district. 1310 *Rostormel*.

Retford (town, Notts): '(place by the) red ford'. OE *rēad*, 'red', + *ford*, 'ford'. The ford in question would have been one with red soil over the river Idle, on which Retford stands. The town is also known as *East Retford*, for distinction from *West Retford* across the river. DB *Redforde*.

Rettendon (village, Essex): '(place by the) hill running with rats'. OE *rætten*, 'running with rats', + *dūn*, 'hill'. *c.*1000 *Rettendun*, DB *Ratenduna*.

Revesby (village, Lincs): 'Refr's farmstead'. OS *bý*, 'farmstead', 'village'. The personal name is Scandinavian. DB *Resuesbi*.

Rewe (village, Devon): 'row of houses'. OE *rǣw*, 'row (of houses)'. DB *Rewe*.

Reydon (suburb of Southwold, Suffolk): 'hill where rye is grown'. OE *rygen*, 'growing with rye', + *dūn*, 'hill'. DB *Rienduna*.

Reymerston (village, Norfolk): 'Raimar's farmstead'. OE *tūn*, 'farmstead'. The personal name is Old German. DB *Raimerestuna*.

Reynalton (village, Pemb): 'Reynald's farm'. OE *tūn*, 'farm'. The Norman personal name, itself of Germanic origin, corresponds to English Reginald. 1394 *Reynaldeston*.

Rhaeadr. See RHAYADER.

Rhaglan. See RAGLAN.

Rhayader (town, Powys): '(place by the) waterfall'. Welsh *rhaeadr*, 'waterfall'. The spectacular waterfall here is on the river Wye (Gwy). The Welsh name of the town is *Rhaeadr*, or *Rhaeadr Gwy*, with the river name added (as in the forms below) to distinguish this waterfall from the many others. 1191 *Raidergoe*, 14C *Rayadyr Gwy*, 1543 *Raiadergwy*.

Rhisga. See RISCA.

Rhiwabon. See RUABON.

Rhondda (town, Rhondda CT): '(place on the river) Rhondda'. The river name means 'noisy one', from Welsh *rhoddni*, 'noisy', 'babbling'. (The *dd* and *n* have changed places in the modern name.) Rhondda stands on the *Rhondda Fawr* ('Great Rhondda'), which gave the name of the *Rhondda Valley* here and hence the name of the whole district as *The Rhondda*. The town arose only in the mid-19C. 12C *Rotheni*.

Rhosllanerchrugog (district, Wrexham): 'moor of the heather glade'. Welsh *rhos*, 'moor', + *llanerch*, 'clearing', 'glade', + *grugog*, 'of heather' (*grug*, 'heather'). The form of the name below was probably recorded by an English writer who did not understand the meaning of the Welsh words. The length of the name means that it is now often abbreviated to *Rhos* (cp. RHOS-ON-SEA). 1544 *Rose lane aghregog*.

Rhos-on-Sea (resort town, Conwy): 'headland by the sea'. Welsh *rhos*, 'headland'. The name refers to the small promontory here. The second part of the name distinguishes this Rhos from the many others, especially in North Wales, and also serves to attract visitors. The resort developed in the 19C from the village of *Llandrillo-yn-Rhos*, 'St Trillo's church in Rhos' (Welsh *llan*, 'church', + *yn*, 'in', 'on'), and this now serves as the Welsh name. *Rhos* was itself the name of a cantref (hundred) here.

Rhostryfan (village, Gwynedd): 'moor by (Moel) Tryfan'. Welsh *rhos*, 'moor'. The hill near Rhostryfan is *Moel Tryfan*, 'bare hill with a distinctive summit' (Welsh *moel*, 'bare hill', + *tryfan*, 'sharp peak', from *try*, 'exceptional', + *ban*, 'summit'). 1827 *Rhos Tryfan*.

Rhostyllen (village, Wrexham): 'moor on a shelf'. Welsh *rhos*, 'moor', + *astell*, 'shelf', 'ledge'. The name refers to the ledge of rock here, above the river Clywedog. 1546 *Rhos Stellan*.

Rhuddlan (village, Denb): 'red bank'. Welsh *rhudd*, 'red', + *glan*, 'bank'. The banks of the river Clwyd are noticeably red here. DB *Roelend*, 1191 *Ruthelan*.

Rhum. See RUM.

Rhuthun. See RUTHIN.

Rhydaman. See AMMANFORD.

Rhyl (resort town, Denb): '(place by) the hill'. Welsh *yr*, 'the', + ME *hull*, 'hill'. There is no obvious hill here, but the ground rises slightly to the south of the town and in such a flat region any elevation could perhaps be reckoned a 'hill'. 1301 *Ryhull*, 1578 *Yrhill*, 1660 *Rhyll*.

Rhymney (town, Caerphilly): '(place on the river) Rhymney'. The river name means 'auger', 'borer' (Welsh *rhwmp* + adjectival ending *-ni*), describing its boring or cutting action. The Welsh spelling of the name is *Rhymni*, for both river and town. 1101 *Remni*, 1296 *Rempny*, 1541 *Rymney*.

Ribbesford (village, Worcs): '(place at a) ford by a bed of ribwort'. OE *ribbe*, 'ribwort', + *bedd*, 'bed', + *ford*, 'ford'. The river here is the Severn. 1023 *Ribbedford*, DB *Ribeford*.

Ribble (river). See RIBCHESTER.

Ribbleton (district of Preston, Lancs): 'farmstead on the (river) Ribble'. OE *tūn*, 'farmstead'. For the river name, see RIBCHESTER. 1201 *Ribleton*.

Ribchester (village, Lancs): 'Roman fort on the (river) Ribble'. OE *ceaster*, 'Roman fort'. The river has a name meaning 'tearing one' (OE *ripel*, 'tearing'), alluding to its scouring action. The Roman fort was *Bremetenacum Veteranorum*, '(place of the) roaring one of the veterans', the 'roaring one' being the Ribble. This name for the river is Celtic, from a word related to modern Welsh *brefu*, 'to roar' (cp. ROCHESTER, Northd). *Ribble Valley* is now the name of the local council district. DB *Ribelcastre*.

Riby (hamlet, Lincs): 'farmstead where rye is grown'. OE *ryge*, 'rye', + OS *bȳ*, 'farmstead'. DB *Ribi*.

Riccall (village, N Yorks): 'Rīca's corner of land'. OE *halh*, 'nook', 'corner of land'. DB *Richale*.

Richards Castle (village, Herefords): 'Richard's castle'. OF *castel*, 'castle'. The name is that of the Frenchman Richard Scrope, whose son Osbern held the (now ruined) castle here in 1086. *c.*1180 *Castellum Ricardi*, 1346 *Richardescastel*.

Richborough (Roman fort remains, Kent): 'stronghold (called) Repta'. OE *burh*, 'fortified place'. The first part of the name is Celtic in origin and gave the Roman name of the fort, *Rutupiae*, meaning 'muddy waters' (related modern Welsh *rhwd*, 'dirt'), referring to the streams of Richborough Creek. 1197 *Ratteburg*.

Richmond (town, N Yorks): '(place by the) strong hill'. OF *riche*, 'strong', + *mont*, 'hill'. The name was given by Earl Alan Rufus ('the Red'), kinsman of William the Conqueror, to the new castle he built here after the Norman Conquest. The name referred to the site, on a lofty precipice overlooking the river Swale, but was also probably adopted from one of the places called *Richemont* in France. The name was later transferred to RICHMOND UPON THAMES. See also RICHMONDSHIRE. *c.*1110 *Richemund*.

Richmondshire (council district, N Yorks): 'district based on Richmond'. OE *scīr*, 'shire', 'district'. At the time of the DB survey (1086), the wapentakes of Hang and Gilling, corresponding to the lordships of Catterick and Gilling, formed an 'honour' belonging to Edwin, earl of Mercia. They then passed to Earl Alan Rufus ('the Red'), a kinsman of William the Conqueror, and were known as *terra Alani Comitis*, 'land of Earl Alan'. The lands later became known as *Richmondshire* from the new castle at RICHMOND built and named by Earl Alan himself. 1174 *shira de Richmond*, 1198 *Richemundesir*.

Richmond upon Thames (borough, Greater London): '(town of) Richmond on the (river) Thames'. The settlement here by the Thames was originally called *Sheen*, 'shelters' (OE *shēo*, 'shelter'), or *West Sheen*, referring to shepherds' shelters in summer pastures. This name survives for the adjacent district of *East Sheen*. Edward I built a palace here in the 13C and it was enlarged by Henry VII in the late 15C. After its destruction by fire in 1499, however, Henry renamed the rebuilt (and even grander) palace *Richmond*, after his earlier title of Earl of Richmond, from RICHMOND, N Yorks. The borough's full name is shortened to *Richmond* for the town alone. 1502 *Richemount*.

Rickerscote (district of Stafford, Staffs): 'Ricard's cottage'. OE *cot*, 'cottage'. The personal name is Old French. DB *Ricardescote*.

Rickinghall Inferior (village, Suffolk): 'lower (place at the) corner of land of Rīca's people'. OE *-inga-*, 'of the people of', + *halh*, 'nook', 'corner of land', + Latin *inferior*, 'lower'. Immediately to the west is the village of *Rickinghall Superior* (Latin *superior*, 'higher'). 10C *Rikinghale*, DB *Rikingahala*.

Rickling (village, Essex): '(settlement of) Rīcela's or Rīcola's people'. OE *-ingas*, 'people of'. The first personal name is that of a man, the second that of a woman. DB *Richelinga*.

Rickmansworth (town, Herts): 'Rīcmǣr's enclosure'. OE *worth*, 'enclosure'. The final 'r' of the personal name became 'n', probably by association with obsolete English *richman*, 'rich man'. The DB form of the name below has a prefixed *P-*, perhaps because the Norman scribe misheard a rolled *r* as *pr*. DB *Prichemareworde*, c.1180 *Richemaresworthe*, 1248 *Rikemanneswrthe*.

Riddlesden (district, Bradford): 'Rēdel's or Hrēthel's valley'. OE *denu*, 'valley'. DB *Redelesden*.

Ridge (village, Herts): '(place on a) ridge'. OE *hrycg*, 'ridge'. The village lies on a narrow ridge of land. 1248 *La Rigge*.

Ridgewell (village, Essex): '(place by the) stream where reeds grow'. OE *hrēod*, 'reed', + *wella*, 'spring', 'stream'. DB *Rideuuella*.

Ridgmont (village, Beds): '(place by the) red hill'. OF *rouge*, 'red', + *mont*, 'hill'. 1227 *Rugemund*.

Riding. See EAST RIDING.

Riding Mill (village, Northd): '(place by the) clearing'. OE *ryding*, 'clearing'. The second word of the name is a recent addition. 1262 *Ryding*, 1897 *Riding, or Riding Mill*.

Ridlington (village, Norfolk): 'estate associated with Rēdel or Hrēthel'. OE *-ing-*, 'associated with', + *tūn*, 'farmstead', 'estate'. DB *Ridlinketuna*. SO ALSO: *Ridlington*, Rutland.

Rievaulx (village, N Yorks): '(place in the) valley of the (river) Rye'. OF *val*, 'valley'. The river has a Celtic name probably meaning simply 'stream'. The name originally applied to the 12C monastery here. 1157 *Rievalle*.

Rillington (village, N Yorks): 'estate associated with Rēdel or Hrēthel'. OE *-ing-*, 'associated with', + *tūn*, 'farmstead', 'estate'. DB *Redlintone*.

Rimington (village, Lancs): 'farmstead on the boundary stream'. OE *rima*, 'rim', 'boundary', + *-ing*, 'stream characterized by', + *tūn*, 'farmstead'. The boundary in question is the historic one between Lancashire and the West Riding of Yorkshire, formed here by the stream now known as Ings Beck. The DB form of the name below is corrupt. DB *Renitone*, 1182 *Rimingtona*.

Rimpton (village, Somerset): 'farmstead on the boundary'. OE *rima*, 'rim', 'boundary', + *tūn*, 'farmstead'. Rimpton is (still) near the county border with Dorset. 938 *Rimtune*, DB *Rintone*.

Ringland (village, Norfolk): 'cultivated land of Rӯmi's people'. OE 'of the people of', + *land*, 'cultivated land'. DB *Remingaland*.

Ringmer (village, E Sussex): '(place by the) circular pool'. OE *hring*, 'ring', + *mere*, 'pool'. The name could also be understood as '(place by the) pool with a circular feature'. The where-abouts of any such pool is not known. 1276 *Ryngemere*.

Ringmore (village, Devon): '(place by the) reedy moor'. OE *hrēod*, 'reed', + *mōr*, 'moor'. The DB form of the name below is corrupt. DB *Reimore*, 1242 *Redmore*.

Ringsfield (village, Suffolk): 'Hring's open land'. OE *feld*, 'open land' (modern English *field*). The name could also mean 'open land by a circular feature' (OE *hring*, 'ring', + *feld*). DB *Ringesfelda*.

Ringshall (hamlet, Suffolk): 'Hring's corner of land'. OE *halh*, 'nook', 'corner of land'. The name could also mean 'corner of land by a circular feature' (OE *hring*, 'ring', + *halh*). DB *Ringeshala*.

Ringstead (village, Northants): 'circular enclosure'. OE *hring*, 'ring', + *stede*, 'enclosed pasture', 'place'. The name could also be understood as 'place by a circular feature'. 12C *Ringstede*. SO ALSO: *Ringstead*, Norfolk.

Ringway (village, Trafford): 'enclosure with a circular hedge'. OE *hring*, 'ring', + *hæg*, 'enclosure'. 1260 *Ringheye*.

Ringwood (town, Hants): 'wood on a boundary'. OE *rimuc*, 'boundary' (related modern English *rim*), + *wudu*, 'wood'. The 'boundary' was probably the fringe of the New Forest here, or possibly the nearby county boundary with Dorset. 955 *Rimucwuda*, DB *Rincvede*.

Ringwould (village, Kent): 'woodland of Rēdel's or Hrēthel's people'. OE *-inga-*, 'of the people of', + *weald*, 'woodland' (cp. WEALD). 861 *Roedligwealda*.

Rinns of Galloway (peninsula, Dumfries & Gall): 'headlands of Galloway'. Gaelic *rinn*, 'point', 'headland'. See GALLOWAY. An English plural *-s* has been added to the Gaelic word. 1460 *Le Rynnys*.

Rinns of Islay (peninsula, Argyll & Bute): 'divisions of Islay'. Gaelic *rann*, 'division'. The name refers to the three districts into which the island of ISLAY was formerly divided.

Ripe (village, E Sussex): '(place by the) strip of land'. OE *rip*, 'strip'. DB *Ripe*.

Ripley (town, Derbys): 'woodland clearing in the form of a strip'. OE *ripel*, 'strip', + *lēah*, 'wood', 'clearing'. DB *Ripelei*. SO ALSO: *Ripley*, Hants, Surrey.

Ripley (village, N Yorks): 'woodland clearing of the Hrype'. OE *lēah*, 'wood', 'clearing'. The tribal name also gave the name of RIPON. DB *Ripeleia*.

Riplingham (hamlet, E Yorks): 'homestead associated with Rippel'. OE *-ing-*, 'associated with', + *hām*, 'homestead'. The name could also mean 'homestead by the strip of land' (OE *ripel*, 'strip', + *-ing-* + *hām*). The DB form of the name below has omitted the *l*. DB *Ripingham*, 1180 *Ripplingeham*.

Ripon (city, N Yorks): '(place in the territory of the) Hrype'. The tribal name, of obscure origin and meaning, is that of a people here who also gave their name to REPTON and RIPLEY (N Yorks). The town name represents *Hrypum*, the dative plural form of *Hrype*. *c*.715 *Hripis*, DB *Ripum*.

Ripple (village, Worcs): '(place by the) strip of land'. OE *ripel*, 'strip of land'. The village lies on a tongue of land. 708 *Rippell*, DB *Rippel*. SO ALSO: *Ripple*, Kent.

Ripponden (town, Calderdale): '(place in the) valley of the (river) Ryburn'. OE *denu*, 'valley'. The river name means either 'fierce stream' (OE *hrīfe*, 'fierce', + *burna*, 'stream') or 'reedy stream' (OE *hrēod*, 'reed', + *burna*). 1307 *Ryburnedene*.

Risbury (hamlet, Herefords): 'fortress among the brushwood'. OE *hrīs*, 'brushwood', + *burh*, 'fortified place'. The fortress in question is the prehistoric fort here known as Risbury Camp. DB *Riseberia*.

Risby (hamlet, N Lincs): 'farmstead among brushwood'. OS *hrís*, 'brushwood', + *bý*, 'farmstead', 'village'. DB *Risebi*. SO ALSO: *Risby*, Suffolk.

Risca (town, Caerphilly): '(place of) bark'. Welsh *rhisg*, 'bark'. The name may allude to a house built of bark-covered logs, or else to bark used as shingles on walls. The Welsh form of the name is *Rhisga*. 1330 *Risca*.

Rise (hamlet, E Yorks): '(place among) brushwood'. OE *hrīs*, 'brushwood'. The name represents OE *hrīsum*, the dative plural form of *hrīs*. DB *Risun*.

Riseley (village, Wokingham): '(place in the) clearing where brushwood grows'. OE *hrīs*, 'brushwood', + *lēah*, 'wood', 'clearing'. Cp. RISLEY. 1300 *Rysle*. SO ALSO: *Riseley*, Beds.

Rishangles (village, Suffolk): '(place on the) wooded slope where brushwood grows'. OE *hrīs*, 'brushwood', + *hangra*, 'wooded slope'. DB *Risangra*.

Rishton (town, Lancs): 'farmstead where rushes grow'. OE *risc*, 'rush', + *tūn*, 'farmstead'. Rushes would have been widespread in the region, which has many streams and rivers. *c*.1205 *Riston*.

Rishworth (village, Calderdale): 'enclosure where rushes grow'. OE *risc*, 'rush', + *worth*, 'enclosure'. Rushes still grow in parts of the river valley here. 12C *Risseworde*.

Risley (village, Derbys): '(place in the) clearing where brushwood grows'. OE *hrīs*, 'brushwood', + *lēah*, 'wood', 'clearing'. Cp. RISELEY. DB *Riselei*. SO ALSO: *Risley*, Warrington.

Rivenhall (hamlet, Essex): '(place by the) rough corner of land'. OE *hrēof*, 'rough', 'rugged', + *halh*, 'nook', 'corner of land'. The first part of the name represents OE *hrēofan*, the dative form of *hrēof*. 1068 *Reuenhala*, DB *Ruenhale*.

Riverhead (district of Sevenoaks, Kent): 'landing place for cattle'. OE *hrīther*, 'cattle', + *hȳth*, 'landing place'. Riverhead is near the source of the river Darent, which may account for the present form of the name. 1278 *Reddride*.

Rivington (village, Lancs): 'farmstead by the rough hill'. OE *hrēof*, 'rough', 'rugged', + *-ing-*, 'associated with', + *tūn*, 'farmstead'. The village lies below the high hill known as Rivington Pike. 1202 *Revington*.

Roade (village, Northants): '(place in the) clearing'. OE *rod*, 'clearing'. DB *Rode*.

Robertsbridge (village, E Sussex): '(place by) Robert's bridge'. The name is that of Robert de St Martin, founder of the 12C abbey here. The bridge in question was over the river Rother. Hence the somewhat similar-sounding alternative for the third form of the name below. The first form has Latin *pons*, 'bridge'. 1176 *Pons Roberti*, 1445 *Robartesbregge*, 1868 *Robertsbridge*, or *Rotherbridge*.

Robeston Wathen (village, Pemb): 'Robert's farm by Llangwathen'. OE *tūn*, 'farm'. The second word of the name comes from neighbouring *Llangwathen*, 'Gwaiddan's grove' (Welsh *llwyn*, 'grove', replaced by *llan*, 'church'), and distinguishes the village from nearby *Robeston West*. 1282 *Villa Roberti*, 1357 *Roberdeston*, 1545 *Robertson Wathen*.

Robin Hood's Bay (resort village, N Yorks): 'Robin Hood's bay'. The bay, named for the famous folk hero, gave the name of the village. Robin Hood was especially associated with Nottinghamshire and Yorkshire and there are many places with local legends about him. 1532 *Robin Hoode Baye*.

Roborough (village, Devon): '(place by the) rough hill'. OE *rūh*, 'rough', + *beorg*, 'hill'. DB *Raweberge*.

Roby (town, Knowsley): 'farmstead by a boundary'. OS *rá*, 'landmark', 'boundary mark', + *bý*, 'farmstead', 'village'. The boundary was probably that of a hundred here. The DB form of the name below has an extraneous *l*. DB *Rabil*, 1185 *Rabi*.

Rocester (village, Staffs): '(place by a) Roman fort'. OE *ceaster*, 'Roman fort'. The first part of the name is of uncertain origin. It may represent OE *rūh*, 'rough (place)', or a personal name. Rocester is on the Roman road from Little Chester, Derby, to Chesterton, Staffs. DB *Rowcestre*.

Rochdale (town, Rochdale): '(place in the) valley of the (river) Roch'. OS *dalr*, 'valley'. The river derives its name from the first part of the former name of the settlement here, *Recedham*, 'homestead with a hall' (OE *reced*, 'building', 'hall', + *hām*, 'homestead'). DB *Recedham*, c.1195 *Rachedal*.

Roche (village, Cornwall): '(place by the) rock'. OF *roche*, 'rock'. The 'rock' is the prominent granite tor here, now known tautologically as Roche Rock. 1233 *La Roche*.

Roche Abbey (ruined abbey, Rotherham): 'abbey by a rock'. OF *roche*, 'rock'. The 12C Cistercian abbey was built near a rocky bank, now called Table Rock. The first form of the name below derives from Latin *rupes*, 'rock'. 1147 *Rupe*, 1253 *Roche*.

Rochester (town, Medway): '(place by the) Roman fort Durobrivae'. OE *ceaster*, 'Roman station'. The initial 'Ro-' is all that remains of *Durobrivae* (stressed on -*ro*-), the Roman name of the fort here, itself of Celtic origin and meaning 'walled town with bridges'. The river here is the Medway. 731 *Hrofaescaestir*, DB *Rovecestre*.

Rochester (hamlet, Northd): '(place by the) rough fort'. OE *rūh*, 'rough', + *ceaster*, 'Roman fort'. The Roman fort of *Bremenium* was located nearby, its name based on a Celtic word meaning 'roaring one' (modern Welsh *brefu*, 'to roar'), referring to the Sills Burn here. Cp. RIBCHESTER. The village is also known as *High Rochester*. 1242 *Rucestr*.

Rochford (town, Essex): '(place by the) ford of the hunting dog'. OE *ræcc*, 'hunting dog', + *ford*, 'ford'. There must have been a regular crossing point for hunting dogs over the river Roach here, its own name coming from that of the town. The DB form of the name below was probably influenced by the French place of that name. DB *Rochefort*. SO ALSO: *Rochford*, Worcs.

Rock (village, Cornwall): '(place by the) rock'. The original name of the settlement here on the estuary of the river Camel meant 'black crag' (OE *blæc*, 'black', + *torr*, 'crag', 'tor'). The second part of this was then replaced by ME *roke*, 'rock',

and the first part subsequently dropped altogether. The forms of the name below show the evolution. 1337 *Blaketore*, 1748 *Black Rock*, 1813 *Rock House*.

Rock (village, Northd): '(place by the) rock'. ME *rokke*, 'rock', 'peak'. 1242 *Rok*.

Rock (village, Worcs): '(place by the) oak tree'. OE *āc*, 'oak'. The initial 'R-' of the name comes from preceding ME *atter*, 'at the'. 1224 *Ak*, 1259 *Roke*.

Rockbeare (village, Devon): '(place by the) grove where rooks are seen'. OE *hrōc*, 'rook', + *bearu*, 'grove'. DB *Rochebere*.

Rockbourne (village, Hants): '(place by the) stream where rooks are seen'. OE *hrōc*, 'rook', + *burna*, 'stream'. The stream in question is a tributary of the Avon. DB *Rocheborne*.

Rockcliffe (village, Cumbria): '(place by the) red cliff'. OS *rauthr*, 'red', + OE *clif*, 'cliff', 'bank'. The OS word has become assimilated to modern English *rock*. 1185 *Rodcliua*.

Rockhampton (village, S Glos): 'homestead by the rock'. OE *rocc*, 'rock', + *hām*, 'homestead'. The name could also mean 'homestead where rooks are seen' (OE *hrōc*, 'rook', + *hām*). DB *Rochemtune*.

Rockingham (village, Northants): 'homestead of Hrōc's people'. OE *-inga-*, 'of the people of', + *hām*, 'homestead'. The name passed to the former royal hunting preserve of *Rockingham Forest*. DB *Rochingeham*.

Rockland All Saints (village, Norfolk): '(place at the) grove where rooks are seen with All Saints church'. OS *hrókr*, 'rook', + *lundr*, 'grove'. The church dedication distinguishes the village from *Rockland St Peter*, immediately to the north, and *Rockland St Mary*, 22 miles to the east. DB *Rokelund*.

Rodbourne (district, Swindon): '(place by the) reedy stream'. OE *hrēod*, 'reed', + *burna*, 'stream'. The place is properly *Rodbourne Cheney*, after Ralph le Chanu, who held the manor here in 1242. His name distinguished this Rodbourne from *Rodbourne*, Wilts, 15 miles to the west. DB *Redborne*, 1304 *Rodburne Chanu*.

Rodd (hamlet, Herefords): '(place at the) clearing'. OE *rod*, 'clearing'. 1220 *La Rode*.

Roddam (hamlet, Northd): '(place at the) clearings'. OE *rod*, 'clearing'. The name represents OE *rodum*, the dative plural form of *rod*. 1201 *Rodun*.

Rodings, The (village group, Essex): '(settlement of) Hrōth's people'. OE *-ingas*, 'people of'. *The Rodings* encompasses eight different places:

Abbess Roding (held by the Abbess of Barking), *Aythorpe Roding* (manor held by Aitrop), *Beauchamp Roding* (manor held by de Beauchamp family), *Berners Roding* (manor held by Hugh de Berners), *High Roding* (in a higher location), *Leaden Roding* (with a leaden-roofed church), *Margaret Roding* (with St Margaret's church) and *White Roding* (with a white-walled church). All these are near the river *Roding*, named after them. (It was originally the *Hyle*, giving the name of ILFORD.) DB *Rodinges*.

Rodington (village, Wrekin): 'farmstead on the (river) Roden'. OE *tūn*, 'farmstead'. The river has a Celtic name meaning 'swift one' (modern Welsh *rhuthro*, 'to rush'). DB *Rodintone*.

Rodmarton (village, Glos): 'farmstead by a reedy pool'. OE *hrēod*, 'reed', + *mere*, 'pool', + *tūn*, 'farmstead'. The pool in question is still here. See also TORMARTON. DB *Redmertone*.

Rodmell (village, E Sussex): '(place with) red soil'. OE *rēad*, 'red', + *mylde*, 'soil', 'earth' (related modern English *mould*, 'soft loose earth'). The DB form of the name below has *ll* for *ld*. DB *Redmelle*, 1202 *Radmelde*.

Rodmersham (village, Kent): 'Hrōthmǣr's homestead'. OE *hām*, 'homestead', 'village'. *c*.1100 *Rodmaeresham*.

Rodney Stoke (village, Somerset): 'de Rodeney's outlying farmstead'. OE *stoc*, 'outlying farmstead', 'secondary settlement'. The de Rodeney family held the manor here in the 14C. DB *Stoches*.

Rodsley (village, Derbys): origin uncertain. The second part of the name is almost certainly OE *lēah*, 'woodland clearing'. The first part may be OE *hrēod*, 'reed bed'. DB *Redeslei*.

Roedean (suburb of Brighton, Brighton & Hove): '(place in the) rough valley'. OE *rūh*, 'rough', + *denu*, 'valley'. There is a break in the South Downs near the coast at this point. 1724 *Rowdean Gap*.

Roehampton (district, Wandsworth): 'home farm where rooks are seen'. OE *hrōc*, 'rook', + *hām-tūn* (from *hām*, 'homestead', + *tūn*, 'farmstead'). The name was originally *Hampton*, and 'rook' was probably added for distinction from HAMPTON, not too far away across the Thames from Kingston. 1332 *Hampton*, 1350 *Rokehampton*.

Roffey (district of Horsham, W Sussex): 'enclosure for roe deer'. OE *rāh-hege* (from *rāh*, 'roe deer', + *hege*, 'hedge', 'fence'). The first part of the name could also represent OE *rūh*, 'rough', giving a sense 'rough enclosure'. 1281 *La Rogheye*.

Rogate (village, W Sussex): '(place by the) gate for roe deer'. OE *rā*, 'roe deer', + *geat*, 'gate'. The roe deer referred to here are bucks (male), unlike the does (female) at REIGATE. 12C *Ragata*.

Rollesby (village, Norfolk): 'Hrólfr's farmstead'. OS *bý*, 'farmstead', 'village'. The personal name is Scandinavian. 1044 *Rollesby*, DB *Rotholfuesby*.

Rolleston (village, Leics): 'Hrōthwulf's or Hrólfr's farmstead'. OE *tūn*, 'farmstead'. The personal names are respectively OE and Scandinavian. DB *Rovestone*.

Rolleston (village, Notts): 'Hróaldr's farmstead'. OE *tūn*, 'farmstead'. The personal name is Scandinavian. DB *Roldestun*.

Rolleston (village, Staffs): 'Hrōthwulf's or Hrólfr's farmstead'. OE *tūn*, 'farmstead'. The personal names are respectively OE and Scandinavian. 941 *Rothulfeston*, DB *Rolvestune*.

Rollright Stones (ancient stone circle, Oxon): 'stones by Rollright'. The Bronze Age stone circle takes its name from the nearby villages of *Great Rollright* and *Little Rollright*, whose basic name may mean 'Hrolla's property' (OE *land-riht*, 'land rights'). Celticists reject this in favour of a sense 'groove by Rodland', where the 'Roll-' of the present name represents a reconstructed form *Rodland*, meaning 'wheel precinct' (related modern Welsh *rhod*, 'wheel', and *llan*, 'church'), referring to the stone circle, and the '-right' represents a word related to modern Welsh *rhych*, 'groove', referring to a little gorge nearby now known as Danes Bottom. DB *Rollandri*, 1091 *Rollendricht*, 1607 *Rolle-rich stones*.

Rolvenden (village, Kent): 'woodland pasture associated with Hrōthwulf'. OE *-ing-*, 'associated with', + *denn*, 'woodland pasture'. The DB form of the name below has corrupted the personal name. DB *Rovindene*, 1185 *Ruluinden*.

Romaldkirk (village, Durham): 'St Rūmwald's church'. OS *kirkja*, 'church'. The church here is dedicated to Rumwald, supposedly a grandson of Penda, king of Mercia (d.654). DB *Rumoldescerche*.

Romanby (suburb of Northallerton, N Yorks): 'Róthmundr's farmstead'. OS *bý*, 'farmstead', 'village'. The personal name is Scandinavian. DB *Romundrebi*.

Romansleigh (village, Devon): 'Rumon's woodland clearing'. OE *lēah*, 'wood', 'clearing'. The personal name is that of St Rumon, the Celtic saint to whom the church here is dedicated. DB *Liega*, 1228 *Reymundesle*.

Romford (town, Havering): '(place by the) wide ford'. OE *rūm*, 'roomy', 'wide', + *ford*, 'ford'. The ford in question would have been where the old Roman road to Colchester crossed the river Rom here, its own name coming from that of the town. (This historical association has prompted the popular interpretation of the name as 'Roman ford'.) 1177 *Romfort*.

Romiley (town, Stockport): '(place in a) spacious woodland clearing'. OE *rūm*, 'wide', 'spacious', + *lēah*, 'wood', 'clearing'. DB *Rumelie*.

Romney Marsh. See NEW ROMNEY.

Romsey (town, Hants): 'Rūm's island'. OE *ēg*, 'island'. The 'island' here is the somewhat higher land away from the river Test around Romsey Abbey, where the town arose in the 10C. *c*.970 *Rummæsig*, DB *Romesy*.

Romsley (village, Worcs): '(place by the) wood or clearing where ravens are seen'. OE *hræfn* or *hremn*, 'raven', + *lēah*, 'wood', 'clearing'. 1270 *Romesle*. SO ALSO: *Romsley*, Shropshire.

Rona (island, W Isles): 'rough island'. OS *hraun*, 'rough', 'rocky', + *á*, 'island'.

Rood Ashton. See STEEPLE ASHTON.

Rookhope (village, Durham): '(place in the) valley where rooks are seen'. OE *hrōc*, 'rook', + *hop*, 'valley'. 1242 *Rochop*.

Rookley (village, IoW): '(place by the) wood or clearing where rooks are seen'. OE *hrōc*, 'rook', + *lēah*, 'wood', 'clearing'. 1202 *Roclee*.

Roos (village, E Yorks): '(place by the) moor'. The name is Celtic in origin, from a word related to modern Welsh *rhos*, 'moor'. Roos is not far from the coast on the Holderness peninsula. DB *Rosse*.

Roose (district of Barrow-in-Furness, Cumbria): '(place by the) moor'. The name is identical in origin to ROOS. Roose lies in a valley. DB *Rosse*.

Rorrington (hamlet, Shropshire): 'estate associated with Hrōr'. OE -*ing*-, 'associated with', + *tūn*, 'farmstead', 'estate'. DB *Roritune*.

Roseacre (hamlet, Lancs): 'cultivated land with a cairn'. OS *hreysi*, 'cairn', 'heap of stones', + *akr*, 'cultivated land' (related modern English *acre*). The stones in question also gave the name of nearby WHARLES. 1283 *Raysacre*.

Rose Ash (village, Devon): 'Ralph's (estate by the) ash tree'. OE *æsc*, 'ash'. One Ralph held the manor here in the late 12C. DB *Aissa*, 1281 *Assherowes*, 1400 *Rowesassche*.

Roseberry Topping (hill, Redcar & Clev): 'Othin's hill'. OS *berg*, 'hill'. The name was orig-

inally *Othenesberg*, after Othin (Odin), the Scandinavian god who was the equivalent of Woden. His name with its possessive -*s* gave the 'Rose-' of the present name, while OS *berg* gave '-berry'. *Topping* (from OE *top*, 'hill') was subsequently added to this as a word for a large conical hill. The initial 'R-' of *Roseberry* appears to have come from the final -*r* of *under* in the name of the nearby hamlet *Newton under Roseberry*, earlier *Newton under Ouesbergh* (the second form of the name below). 1119 *Othenesberg*, 1404 *Ouesbergh*, 1610 *Ounsbery or Rosebery Topping*.

Rosedale Abbey (village, N Yorks): '(place in the) valley of the horses'. OS *hross*, 'horse', + *dalr*, 'valley'. The abbey referred to is the (now ruined) 12C priory here. *c*.1140 *Russedal*.

Roseden (hamlet, Northd): '(place in the) valley where rushes grow'. OE *rysc*, 'rush', + *denu*, 'valley'. 1242 *Russeden*.

Rosemarket (village, Pemb): 'Roose market'. The medieval market here took its name from the cantref (hundred) of *Roose* (Welsh *rhos*, 'moor', 'peninsula'). *c*.1230 *Rosmarche*.

Rosenannon (hamlet, Cornwall): 'moorland of the ash tree'. Cornish *ros*, 'moorland', + *an*, 'the', + *onnenn*, 'ash'. 1326 *Rosnonnen*.

Rosherville (district of Gravesend, Kent): 'Rosher's town'. French *ville*, 'town'. The riverside resort, on the Thames estuary, was founded in *c*.1853. 'The place owes its name to its founder, Jeremiah Rosher, formerly largely engaged in chalk and lime-works here, who created on the cliffs overlooking the abandoned pits a village of smart villas and "cottages of gentility"' (James Thorne, *Handbook to the Environs of London*, 1876).

Rosliston (village, Derbys): 'Hrōthlāf's farmstead'. OE *tūn*, 'farmstead'. The DB form of the name below has *e* for *o*. DB *Redlauestun*, *c*.1232 *Rosliston*.

Ross (historic county, Scotland): 'moorland'. Gaelic *ros*, 'moorland', 'headland'. The former county, extending west from the Moray Firth to the Atlantic, derives its name as much from the headlands and promontories of its eastern and western seaboards as from its inland moors and forests. The old county of *Ross and Cromarty* (see CROMARTY) owed its origin to Sir George Mackenzie of Tarbat (1630–1714), created Earl of Cromarty in 1703, who was granted the privilege of having his various estates throughout Ross erected into a separate county of Cromarty, its geographical formation being a number of 'islands' surrounded by the 'sea' of Ross. The awkward arrangement lasted almost 200 years, but was ended by the Local Government (Scotland) Act of 1889, when the areas were united as the county of Ross and Cromarty.

Rossendale (valley, Lancs): 'valley in the moors'. Celtic *ros*, 'moor', + OE *del*, 'valley'. The name is that of the valley of the river Irwell, and may relate to the surrounding moorland, especially that of the Forest of Rossendale to the north. Doubts have been raised, however, about the validity of a Celtic source for the first part of the name. 1242 *Rocendal*, 1292 *Rossendale*.

Rossett (village, Wrexham): '(place by) the hill'. Welsh *yr*, 'the', + *gorsedd*, 'throne', 'hill'. The hill in question is probably nearby Marford Hill, or specifically that part of it on which Roft Castle was built inside an Iron Age fort. The Welsh form of the name is *Yr Orsedd*. *c*.1700 *Rhossedh*.

Rossington (village, Doncaster): 'farmstead on the moor'. Celtic *ros*, 'moor', + OE *-ing-*, 'associated with', + *tūn*, 'farmstead'. *c*.1190 *Rosington*.

Ross-on-Wye (town, Herefords): 'hill spur by the (river) Wye'. Celtic *ros*, 'hill spur', 'moor'. The town is on a steep hill overlooking the Wye, whose own name is of uncertain origin. It is pre-English and may mean 'conveyor', 'mover', referring to its current. DB *Rosse*.

Rostherne (village, Cheshire): '(place by) Rauthr's thorn bush'. OE *thorn*, 'thorn bush'. The personal name is Scandinavian. DB *Rodestorne*.

Rosyth (town, Fife): meaning uncertain. The first part of the name may represent Gaelic *ros*, 'headland', perhaps referring to the rock by the river Forth on which the ruins of the town's castle stand. The latter part of the name has been derived from either OE *hȳth*, 'landing place', or Gaelic *suidhe*, 'seat', meaning a level place on a hillside. But support for these is lacking. *c*.1170 *Rossyth*, 1363 *Westir Rossith*.

Rothbury (town, Northd): 'Hrōtha's stronghold'. OE *burh*, 'fortified place'. The first part of the name could also represent OS *rauthr*, 'red', referring to the colour of the local bedrock. *c*.1125 *Routhebiria*.

Rother (council district, E Sussex): '(district of the river) Rother'. The river, now sometimes known as the *Western Rother*, takes its name from the historic hundred of *Rotherbridge*, 'cattle bridge' (OE *hrȳther*, 'cattle', + *brycg*, 'bridge'), referring to the bridge where cattle crossed what was originally the river *Shire*, 'bright one' (OE *scīr*, 'bright', 'clear'). The *Eastern Rother* rises near ROTHERFIELD, and similarly takes its name

from it. It was earlier known as the *Limen*, from a Celtic word meaning 'elm'. DB *Redrebrige*.

Rotherby (village, Leics): 'Hreitharr's or Hreithi's farmstead'. OS *bȳ*, 'farmstead', 'village'. The personal names are Scandinavian. DB *Redebi*.

Rotherfield (village, E Sussex): 'open land where cattle graze'. OE *hrȳther*, 'cattle', + *feld*, 'open land' (modern English *field*). The DB form of the name below is corrupt. See also ROTHER. *c*.880 *Hrytheranfeld*, DB *Reredfelle*.

Rotherfield Greys (village, Oxon): 'de Gray's (estate on) open land where cattle graze'. OE *hrȳther*, 'cattle', + *feld*, 'open land' (modern English *field*). The manor here was held early by the de Gray family, their name distinguishing this village from nearby *Rotherfield Peppard*, where it was held by the Pipard family. DB *Redrefeld*, 1313 *Retherfeld Grey*.

Rotherham (town, Rotherham): 'homestead on the (river) Rother'. OE *hām*, 'homestead'. The river has a Celtic name meaning 'chief river'. DB *Rodreham*.

Rotherhithe (district, Southwark): 'landing place for cattle'. OE *hrȳther*, 'cattle', + *hȳth*, 'landing place'. Rotherhithe lies by the Thames. The alternative form *Redriff* was at one time current and is preserved in Redriff Road here. *c*.1105 *Rederheia*, 1127 *Retherhith*, 1868 *Rotherhithe, or Redriff*.

Rothersthorpe (village, Northants): 'outlying farmstead of the counsellor'. OE *rædere*, 'counsellor', 'advocate', + OS *thorp*, 'outlying farmstead'. DB *Torp*, 1231 *Retherestorp*.

Rothes (town, Moray): '(place by the) fort'. Gaelic *ràth*, 'circular fort'. The fort referred to probably stood where the old castle ruins now lie, in a loop of the river Spey. See also GLENROTHES. 1238 *Rothes*.

Rothesay (town and port, Argyll & Bute): 'Rother's island'. OS *ey*, 'island'. The personal name is that of Roderick, the son of Reginald, to whom Bute was granted in the 13C. 1321 *Rothersay*.

Rothley (village, Leics): '(place by the) wood with clearings'. OE *roth*, 'clearing', + *lēah*, 'wood'. DB *Rodolei*.

Rothwell (town, Northants): 'spring by the clearing'. OE *roth*, 'clearing', + *wella*, 'spring', 'stream'. DB *Rodewelle*. SO ALSO: *Rothwell*, Leeds, Lincs.

Rotsea (hamlet, E Yorks): '(place by the) scummy pool'. OE *hrot*, 'scum', + *sǣ*, 'pool'. The name could also mean '(place by) Rōta's pool'. There is no pool here now. DB *Rotesse*.

Rottingdean (coastal village, Brighton & Hove): 'valley of Rōta's people'. OE *-inga-*, 'of the people of', + *denu*, 'valley'. DB *Rotingedene*.

Rottington (hamlet, Cumbria): 'estate associated with Rōta'. OE *-ing-*, 'associated with', + *tūn*, 'farmstead', 'estate'. *c.*1125 *Rotingtona*.

Rougham (village, Norfolk): 'homestead on rough ground'. OE *rūh*, 'rough', + *hām*, 'homestead', 'village'. DB *Ruhham*.

Roughton (village, Norfolk): 'farmstead on rough ground'. OE *rūh*, 'rough', + *tūn*, 'farmstead'. The first part of the name could also represent OS *rugr*, 'rye' (replacing earlier OE *ryge*), giving a sense 'farm where rye is grown'. DB *Rugutune*. SO ALSO: *Roughton*, Lincs.

Rough Tor (rocky hill, Cornwall): 'rough crag'. OE *rūh*, 'rough', + *torr*, 'crag', 'tor'. The name is pronounced 'Rowter' (rhyming with 'outer'). 1284 *Roghetorr*, 1478 *Rowtor*.

Roundhay (district, Leeds): 'round enclosure'. OF *rond*, 'round', + OE *hæg*, 'enclosure' (related modern English *hedge*). *c.*1180 *La Rundehaia*.

Roundway (village, Wilts): '(place by the) cleared way'. OE *rȳmed*, 'cleared' (related modern English *room*), + *weg*, 'way'. 1149 *Rindweiam*.

Rousdon (hamlet, Devon): 'Ralph's (estate by the) hill'. OE *dūn*, 'hill'. The manor here was held in the 12C by the Ralph family. DB *Done*, 1285 *Rawesdon*.

Rousham (hamlet, Oxon): 'Hrōthwulf's homestead'. OE *hām*, 'homestead', 'village'. DB *Rowesham*.

Rous Lench (village, Worcs): 'Rous's (estate in) Lench'. OE *hlenc*, 'extensive hill slope'. *Lench* was the district extending north from Evesham, and the OE word appears in the names of a line of villages: *Lenchwick*, with a dairy farm (OE *wīc*), *Sheriff's Lench*, held by the sheriff, *Atch Lench*, held by Æcci, *Church Lench*, with a church, *Abbots Lench*, held by Abba, and *Rous Lench*, where the manor was held in the 14C by the Rous family (but in 1086 by the Bishop of Worcester). 983 *Lenc*, DB *Biscopesleng*, 1445 *Rous Lench*.

Routh (village, E Yorks): '(place in a) clearing'. OS *ruth*, 'clearing'. DB *Rutha*.

Rowde (village, Wilts): '(place at the) reed bed'. OE *hrēod*, 'reed'. The name is appropriate for the village's low-lying location. DB *Rode*.

Rowland (hamlet, Derbys): 'boundary grove'. OS *rá*, 'boundary', + *lundr*, 'grove'. OS *rá* could also mean 'roe deer', giving an alternative sense 'grove where roe deer are seen'. DB *Ralunt*.

Rowland's Castle (village, Hants): 'Rolok's castle'. ME *castel*, 'castle'. The castle here was originally named after one Rolok, but his name, apparently of Frankish origin, was later associated with that of the heroic knight Roland of medieval legend. *c.*1315 *Rolokescastel*, 1369 *Roulandes Castell*.

Rowley (hamlet, E Yorks): '(place in the) rough wood or clearing'. OE *rūh*, 'rough', + *lēah*, 'wood', 'clearing'. The former village here was depopulated in 1638 when the inhabitants left for America and founded Rowley, Massachusetts. 1150 *Rowlee*.

Rowley Regis (district of Warley, Sandwell): 'king's (estate in the) rough wood or clearing'. OE *rūh*, 'rough', + *lēah*, 'wood', 'clearing', + Latin *regis*, 'of the king'. The king held the manor early here. Hence the second word of the name. 1173 *Roelea*.

Rowsley (village, Derbys): 'Hrōthwulf's or Hrólfr's woodland clearing'. OE *lēah*, 'wood', 'clearing'. The personal name, respectively OE or OS, is corrupt in the DB form of the name below. DB *Reuslege*, 1204 *Rolvesle*.

Rowton (village, Cheshire): 'rough part of Christleton'. OE *rūh*, 'rough'. The first part of the name of CHRISTLETON disappeared early from the name. 12C *Rowa Christletona*, 13C *Roweton*.

Rowton (hamlet, Wrekin): 'farmstead by a rough hill'. OE *rūh*, 'rough', + *hyll*, 'hill', + *tūn*, 'farmstead'. The first part of the name could also represent OE *rūhel*, 'small rough place'. The forms of the name below relate to Rowton northwest of Wellington, the DB form lacking any trace of OE *hyll*. DB *Routone*, 1195 *Rowelton*.

Roxburgh (village, Borders): 'Hrōc's fortress'. OE *burh*, 'fortified place'. The name gave that of the historic county of *Roxburghshire*. 1127 *Rocisburc*.

Roxby (village, N Lincs): 'Hrókr's farmstead'. OS *bȳ*, 'farmstead', 'village'. The personal name is Scandinavian. DB *Roxebi*.

Roxby (village, N Yorks): 'Rauthr's farmstead'. OS *bȳ*, 'farmstead', 'village'. The personal name is Scandinavian. DB *Roscebi*.

Roxwell (village, Essex): '(place by) Hrōc's spring'. OE *wella*, 'spring', 'stream'. 1291 *Rokeswelle*.

Royal British Legion Village (village, Kent). The village was set up near Maidstone as a residential and rehabilitation centre for ex-servicemen soon after the founding of the British Legion in 1921, and was originally known as *British Legion Village*. When the name of the organization was prefixed with *Royal* in 1971, the name of the village was similarly adjusted.

Royal Leamington Spa. See LEAMINGTON.

Royal Tunbridge Wells. See TUNBRIDGE WELLS.

Roydon (village, Essex): '(place by the) hill where rye is grown'. OE *rygen*, 'growing with rye', + *dūn*, 'hill'. DB *Ruindune*.

Royston (town, Barnsley): 'Hrōr's or Róarr's farmstead'. OE *tūn*, 'farmstead'. The personal names are respectively OE and Scandinavian. DB *Rorestone*.

Royston (town, Herts): 'village by Rohesia's cross'. OE *tūn*, 'farmstead', 'village'. The first form of the name below shows the original meaning as 'Rohesia's cross' (Latin *crux*, 'cross'), referring to a stone cross erected here at the junction of Icknield Way and Ermine Street by a lady called Rohesia. The name was then condensed to *Cruceroys* and finally shortened to *Roys*, with OE *tūn* added in the 13C. The identity of Rohesia is disputed, but she is traditionally said to be the daughter of Aubrey de Vere (d.1141), Great Chamberlain under Henry I, who married Geoffrey Mandeville, Earl of Essex (d.1144), then after his early death Payne de Beauchamp of Bedford. 1184 *Crux Roaisie*, 1286 *Roiston*.

Royton (town, Oldham): 'farmstead where rye is grown'. OE *ryge*, 'rye', + *tūn*, 'farmstead'. 1226 *Ritton*.

Ruabon (town, Wrexham): 'Mabon's hill'. Welsh *rhiw*, 'hill'. The identity of Mabon is uncertain, despite attempts to identify him with the legendary Mabon, son of Modron, in Welsh mythology. The Welsh form of the name, *Rhiwabon*, is now often preferred. 1291 *Rywuabon*, 1394 *Rhiwvabon*.

Ruan Lanihorne (village, Cornwall): '(parish of) St Ruan by Lanihorne'. The village, with a church dedicated to St Ruan, is distinguished from RUAN MINOR and *Ruan Major*, some 20 miles to the southwest, by the name of the manor here, *Lanihorne*, meaning 'church site of Rihoarn' (Cornish *lann*, 'church site'). 1270 *Lanryhorn*.

Ruan Minor (village, Cornwall): 'lesser (church of) St Ruan'. The church here is dedicated to Ruan (Rumon), a saint about whom nothing is known. The second word of the name (Latin *minor*, 'lesser') distinguishes the village from nearby *Ruan Major* (Latin *major*, 'greater'), which although larger in area is

smaller in population. The form of the name below has Latin *parvus*, 'small'. 1277 *Sanctus Rumonus Parvus*.

Ruardean (village, Glos): 'enclosure where rye is grown'. OE *ryge*, 'rye', + *worthign*, 'enclosure'. The first part of the name could also be of Celtic origin and mean 'hill' (modern Welsh *rhiw*). DB *Rwirdin*.

Rubery (suburb of Birmingham): '(place by the) rough hill'. OE *rūh*, 'rough', + *beorg*, 'hill'. 1650 *Robery Hills*.

Ruckcroft (hamlet, Cumbria): 'enclosure where rye is grown'. OS *rugr*, 'rye', + OE *croft*, 'enclosure', 'croft'. 1211 *Rucroft*.

Ruckinge (village, Kent): 'place where rooks are seen'. OE *hrōc*, 'rook', + *-ing*, 'place characterized by'. The name could also mean 'place associated with Hrōc' (OE *-ing*, 'place belonging to'). 786 *Hroching*, DB *Rochinges*.

Rudby (village, N Yorks): 'Ruthi's farmstead'. OS *bȳ*, 'farmstead', 'village'. The personal name is Scandinavian. The village gave the distinguishing word of the name of HUTTON RUDBY, on the opposite bank of the river Leven. DB *Rodebi*.

Ruddington (village, Notts): 'estate associated with Rudda'. OE *-ing-*, 'associated with', + *tūn*, 'farmstead', 'estate'. DB *Roddintone*.

Rudford (village, Glos): '(place by the) ford among the reeds'. OE *hrēod*, 'reed', + *ford*, 'ford'. The ford would have been over the river Leadon here. DB *Rudeford*.

Rudge (hamlet, Shropshire): '(place by the) ridge'. OE *hrycg*, 'ridge'. DB *Rigge*.

Rudgwick (village, W Sussex): 'dwelling or farm on a ridge'. OE *hrycg*, 'ridge', + *wīc*, 'dwelling', 'specialized farm'. 1210 *Regwic*.

Rudston (village, E Yorks): '(place by the) rood stone'. OE *rōd-stān* (from *rōd*, 'rood', 'cross', 'crucifix', + *stān*, 'stone'). '[Rudston] is supposed [i.e. believed] to derive its name from a gritstone pillar in the churchyard, which resembles both in shape and substance the well-known stones called Devil's Arrows, near Boroughbridge' (*The National Gazetteer of Great Britain and Ireland*, 1868). DB *Rodestan*.

Rudyard (village, Staffs): 'enclosure where rue is grown'. OE *rūde*, 'rue', + *geard*, 'yard', 'enclosure'. 1002 *Rudegeard*, DB *Rudierd*.

Rufford (village, Lancs): '(place by the) rough ford'. OE *rūh*, 'rough', + *ford*, 'ford'. The ford would have been over the river Douglas here. 1212 *Ruchford*.

Rufforth (village, York): '(place by the) rough ford'. OE *rūh*, 'rough', + *ford*, 'ford'. The ford in question probably crossed Moor Drain near Rufforth Hall here. DB *Ruford*.

Rugby (town, Warwicks): 'Hrōca's fortified place'. OE *burh*, 'fortified place'. Another interpretation of the name could be 'fort where rooks are seen', with the first element as OE *hrōc*, 'rook'. Either way, the original OE *burh* has been replaced by OS *bȳ*, 'village'. DB *Rocheberie*.

Rugeley (town, Staffs): 'woodland clearing by a ridge'. OE *hrycg*, 'ridge', + *lēah*, 'wood', 'clearing'. There is no obvious ridge at Rugeley, but the town is near the northeastern edge of Cannock Chase. 'The natives keep up the old pronunciation "Ridgeley"' (W. H. Duignan, *Notes on Staffordshire Place Names*, 1902). DB *Rugelie*.

Ruishton (village, Somerset): 'farmstead where rushes grow'. OE *rysc*, 'rush', + *tūn*, 'farmstead'. 9C *Risctun*.

Ruislip (district, Hillingdon): 'leaping place where rushes grow'. OE *rysc*, 'rush', + *hlȳp*, 'leaping place'. The reference is to a point on the river Pinn where it was possible to jump across. DB *Rislepe*.

Rum (island, Highland): 'spacious place'. Gaelic *rùim*, 'room', 'space'. The name compares the island with smaller neighbouring Eigg and Muck. The spelling *Rhum* still appears in many maps and guides. The bogus *h* was inserted in the early 20C by the island's English owner, Sir George Bullough, perhaps suggested by the alternative spelling of *rinn* (as in RINNS OF GALLOWAY) as *rhinn*. 677 *Ruim*.

Rumburgh (village, Suffolk): 'wide stronghold'. OE *rūm*, 'wide', + *burh*, 'fortified place'. The name could also mean 'fortification built of tree trunks' (OE *hruna*, 'log', + *burh*). The DB form of the name below is corrupt. *c.*1050 *Romburch*, DB *Ramburc*.

Rumford (village, Cornwall): '(place by the) wide ford'. OE *rūm*, 'roomy', 'wide', + *ford*, 'ford'. The ford in question would have been over the stream here. Cp. ROMFORD. 1699 *Rumford*.

Runcorn (town, Halton): '(place by the) wide bay'. OE *rūm*, 'wide', 'spacious', + *cofa*, 'bay', 'cove'. There was formerly a broad bay ('roomy cove') here between Widnes and Castle Rock on the southern bank of the Mersey. *c.*1000 *Rumcofan*.

Runcton (village, W Sussex): 'estate associated with Hrōc'. OE *-ing-*, 'associated with', + *tūn*, 'farmstead', 'estate'. DB *Rochintone*.

Runcton Holme. See NORTH RUNCTON.

Runfold (hamlet, Surrey): 'place where trees have been felled'. OE *hrune*, 'tree trunk', 'log', + *feall*, 'felling (of trees)'. 974 *Hrunigfeall*.

Runhall (village, Norfolk): 'corner of land with tree trunks'. OE *hruna*, 'tree trunk', + *halh*, 'nook', 'corner of land'. The reference is probably to fallen trees here. DB *Runhal*.

Runham (village, Norfolk): 'Rūna's homestead or enclosure'. OE *hām*, 'homestead', or *hamm*, 'enclosure'. The first part of the name could also represent OE *hruna*, 'tree trunk', referring to its use as a footbridge over marshland here in the Norfolk Broads. DB *Ronham*.

Runnington (hamlet, Somerset): 'Rūna's farmstead'. OE *tūn*, 'farmstead'. The first part of the name represents *Rūnan*, the genitive form of the personal name. DB *Runetone*.

Runnymede (historic meadows, Egham, Surrey): 'meadow at the island where councils are held'. OE *rūn*, 'secret', 'council' (modern English *rune*), + *ēg*, 'island', + *mǣd*, 'meadow'. The 'island', or land by the Thames, was already a meeting place for assemblies before King John negotiated with the barons here in 1215 as a prelude to drawing up the Magna Carta. Egham's association with racing led to a popular interpretation of the name as 'running meadow', but the true origin was already known to several writers from the 13C, such as John Leland in his 16C *Collectanea*: '*Runnimede, id est, Pratum Consilii ... eo quod antiquis temporibus ibi de pace regni sæpius consilia tractabant*' ('Runnymede, i.e. Field of Council ... because in ancient times councils concerning the peace of the realm usually assembled here'). The name is now (appropriately) that of the local council district. 1215 *Ronimede*.

Runswick (resort village, N Yorks): '(place by) Reinn's creek'. OS *vík*, 'creek'. The personal name is Scandinavian. 1273 *Reneswike*.

Runwell (village, Essex): '(place at the) well of secrets'. OE *rūn*, 'secret', 'council' (modern English *rune*), + *wella*, 'spring', 'well'. A 'well of secrets' is a wishing well. *c.*940 *Runewelle*, DB *Runewella*.

Ruscombe (village, Wokingham): 'Rōt's enclosed land'. OE *camp*, 'enclosed piece of land' (modern English *camp*). 1091 *Rothescamp*.

Rushall (village, Norfolk): '(place in a) corner of land'. OE *halh*, 'nook', 'corner of land'. The first part of the name is of uncertain origin. It may represent a personal name. DB *Riuessala*.

Rushall (village, Wilts): 'Rust's corner of land'. OE *halh*, 'nook', 'corner of land'. The second part of the DB form of the name below is corrupt. DB *Rusteselve*, 1160 *Rusteshala*.

Rushbrooke (village, Suffolk): '(place by the) brook where rushes grow'. OE *rysc*, 'rush', + *brōc*, 'brook'. *c*.950 *Ryssebroc*, DB *Ryscebroc*.

Rushbury (village, Shropshire): 'fortified manor among the rushes'. OE *rysc*, 'rush', + *burh*, 'fortified place'. There is no sign of any kind of fortification here now. DB *Riseberie*.

Rushcliffe (council district, Notts): 'slope where brushwood grows'. OE *hrīs*, 'brushwood', 'shrubs', + *clif*, 'cliff', 'slope'. The name is that of a former wapentake here, with a meeting place at Rushcliffe Moat in the parish of Gotham. The 'slope' was probably that of nearby Court Hill. DB *Riseclive*.

Rushden (town, Northants): 'valley where rushes grow'. OE *ryscen*, 'growing with rushes', + *denu*, 'valley'. The land is mostly low-lying here, and Rushden is not far from the river Nene. DB *Risedene*. SO ALSO: *Rushden*, Herts.

Rushford (hamlet, Norfolk): 'enclosure where rushes grow'. OE *rysc*, 'rush', + *worth*, 'enclosure'. *c*.1060 *Rissewrth*, DB *Rusceuuorda*.

Rushmere (hamlet, Suffolk): '(place by the) pool where rushes grow'. OE *rysc*, 'rush', + *mere*, 'pool'. DB *Ryscemara*.

Rushmoor (council district, Hants). The administrative district formed in 1974 was named after the little valley called *Rushmoor Bottom*, itself so called from the rushes that grew there. 1567 *Rushe more*.

Rushock (village, Worcs): '(place by the) rush bed'. OE *ryscuc*, 'rushy place'. The DB form of the name below appears to have a duplicated syllable. DB *Russococ*, 1166 *Rossoc*.

Rusholme (district, Manchester): '(place by) rushes'. OE *rysc*, 'rush'. The name represents OE *ryscum*, the dative plural form of *rysc*. 1235 *Russum*.

Rushton (village, Northants): 'farmstead where rushes grow'. OE *rysc*, 'rush', + *tūn*, 'farmstead'. DB *Risetone*. SO ALSO: *Rushton*, Cheshire.

Rushton Spencer (village, Staffs): 'Spencer's farmstead where rushes grow'. OE *rysc*, 'rush', + *tūn*, 'farmstead'. The Spencer family held the manor early here. DB *Risetone*.

Rushwick (village, Worcs): 'dairy farm among the rushes'. OE *rysc*, 'rush', + *wīc*, 'dairy farm'. 1275 *Russewyk*.

Ruskington (village, Lincs): 'farmstead where rushes grow'. OE *ryscen*, 'growing with rushes', + *tūn*, 'farmstead'. The '-k-' in the name is due to Scandinavian influence. DB *Rischintone*.

Rusland (hamlet, Cumbria): 'Hrólfr's or Hróaldr's cultivated land'. OS *land*, 'cultivated land'. The personal names are Scandinavian. 1336 *Rolesland*.

Rusper (village, W Sussex): '(place by the) rough beam of wood'. OE *rūh*, 'rough', + *spearr*, 'beam of wood' (related modern English *spar*). 1219 *Rusparre*.

Rustington (coastal town, W Sussex): 'estate associated with Rust'. OE *-ing-*, 'associated with', + *tūn*, 'farmstead', 'estate'. 1180 *Rustinton*.

Ruston (village, N Yorks): 'farmstead with special roof beams or rafters'. OE *hrōst*, 'roof beam' (modern English *roost*, 'perch for fowls'), + *tūn*, 'farmstead'. DB *Rostune*.

Ruston Parva (village, E Yorks): 'lesser (place called) Hrōr's or Róarr's farmstead'. OE *tūn*, 'farmstead'. The personal names are respectively OE and Scandinavian. The second word of the name (Latin *parva*, 'little') distinguishes the village from LONG RISTON, 14 miles to the southeast. DB *Roreston*.

Ruswarp (village, N Yorks): 'silted land overgrown with brushwood'. OE *hrīs*, 'brushwood', + *wearp*, 'silted land' (modern English *warp*). Ruswarp lies by the river Esk. *c*.1146 *Risewarp*.

Rutherglen (town, Glasgow): '(place in the) red valley'. Gaelic *ruadh*, 'red', + *gleann*, 'valley'. The reference would be to the red-coloured soil here, in the valley of the river Clyde. *c*.1160 *Ruthirglen*.

Ruthin (town, Denb): 'red fort'. Welsh *rhudd*, 'red', + *din*, 'fort'. Fragments of the original red sandstone can still be made out in the ruins of the 13C castle here, which in 1545 was referred to as *Y Castell Coch yng gwernfor*, 'the red castle in the great marsh' (Welsh *castell*, 'castle', + *coch*, 'red', + *yn*, 'in', + *gwern*, 'marsh', + *mawr*, 'great'). The Welsh form of the name is *Rhuthun*. 1253 *Ruthin*.

Ruthvoes (village, Cornwall): '(place by the) red bank'. Cornish *rudh*, 'red', + *fos*, 'bank'. 1298 *Ruthfos*.

Rutland (unitary authority, central England): 'Rōta's estate'. OE *land*, 'tract of land', 'estate'. OE *land* in the historic county name here denotes a relatively small estate, unlike the same word in such county names as *Cumberland* (see CUMBRIA) or NORTHUMBERLAND. *c*.1060 *Roteland*.

Rutupiae. See RICHBOROUGH.

Ruyton-XI-Towns (village, Shropshire): 'farmstead where rye is grown'. OE *ryge*, 'rye', + *tūn*, 'farmstead'. The second part of the name refers to the 11 townships that originally formed the parish. DB *Ruitone*, 1758 *Royton of the Eleven Towns*.

Ryal (hamlet, Northd): 'hill where rye is grown'. OE *ryge*, 'rye', + *hyll*, 'hill'. 1242 *Ryhill*.

Rydal Water (lake, Cumbria): 'lake by Rydal'. The lake takes its name from the village of *Rydal*, '(village in the) valley where rye is grown' (OE *ryge*, 'rye', + OS *dalr*, 'valley', 'dale'). The name is quite recent, and the lake's earlier name was *Routhmere*, 'lake of the (river) Rothay' (OE *mere*, 'lake'). Its own name means 'trout stream' (OS *rauthi*, 'red one', 'trout'). 13C *Routhemere*, 1576 *Rydal Water*.

Ryde (resort town, IoW): '(place by the) small stream'. OE *rīth*, 'stream'. The stream in question is Monktonmead Brook, which enters the sea here. 1257 *La Ride*.

Rye (town, E Sussex): '(place at the) island'. OE *īeg*, 'island'. The original OE phrase to describe this location was *æt thǣre īege*, 'at the island'. This was then 'smoothed' to ME *atter ie*, later misdivided as *atte Rie* on the basis that *atte* is found in other names (as HAVERING-ATTE-BOWER). Rye was actually built on an island in the flooded marshes here, and was long an important port. It is now 2 miles from the sea. 1130 *Ria*.

Ryedale (council district, N Yorks): 'valley of the (river) Rye'. OS *dalr*, 'valley'. The name, that of a former wapentake here, is an exact equivalent of that of RIEVAULX, located in the modern district. *c.*1160 *Rydal*.

Rye Foreign (village, E Sussex): '(place) outside Rye'. The village is 2 miles northwest of RYE and geographically outside its authority. It is thus 'foreign' (Latin *forinseca*, 'outside the bounds').

Ryhall (village, Rutland): 'land in a river bend where rye is grown'. OE *ryge*, 'rye', + *halh*, 'corner of land'. Ryhall lies in a loop of the river Gwash. *c.*1050 *Righale*, DB *Riehale*.

Ryhill (hamlet, Wakefield): 'hill where rye is grown'. OE *ryge*, 'rye', + *hyll*, 'hill'. DB *Rihella*.

Ryhope (district, Sunderland): 'rough valleys'. OE *hrēof*, 'rough', + *hop*, 'valley', 'enclosure'. The first part of the name could also represent OE *rēfa*, 'reeve', 'bailiff'. *c.*1050 *Reofhoppas*.

Ryknild Street. See ICKNIELD WAY.

Rylstone (village, N Yorks): '(particular) farmstead'. OE *tūn*, 'farmstead'. The first part of the name is of uncertain origin. It may represent OE *rynel*, 'small stream' (modern English *runnel*). DB *Rilestun*.

Ryme Intrinseca (village, Dorset): 'inner (place at the) edge'. OE *rima*, 'edge', 'border' (modern English *rim*), + Latin *intrinsecus*, 'inner' (modern English *intrinsic*). The 'edge' is the nearby county boundary with Somerset. The second word of the name distinguishes this place from the former manor of *Ryme Extrinseca* (Latin *extrinsecus*, 'outer'). 1160 *Rima*.

Ryther (village, N Yorks): '(place at the) clearing'. OE *ryther*, 'clearing'. DB *Ridre*.

Ryton (town, Gateshead): 'farm where rye is grown'. OE *ryge*, 'rye', + *tūn*, 'farmstead'. 1183 *Ritona*. SO ALSO: *Ryton*, Shropshire.

Ryton (hamlet, N Yorks): 'farmstead on the (river) Rye'. OE *tūn*, 'farmstead'. For the river name, see RIEVAULX. DB *Ritun*.

Ryton-on-Dunsmore (village, Warwicks): 'farm where rye is grown on Dunsmore'. OE *ryge*, 'rye', + *tūn*, 'farmstead'. 'The soyl here is of a light sandy disposition, and beareth Rye best of any Grain' (William Dugdale, *The Antiquities of Warwickshire*, 1656). For the district name, see CLIFTON UPON DUNSMORE. *c.*1045 *Ruyton*, DB *Rietone*.

S

Sabden (village, Lancs): '(place in the) valley where fir trees grow'. OE *sæppe*, 'fir', + *denu*, 'valley'. The valley in question is the one through which Sabden Brook flows. *c*.1140 *Sapeden*.

Sabrina. See SEVERN STOKE.

Sacombe (village, Herts): 'Swæfa's enclosed land'. OE *camp*, 'enclosed piece of land' (modern English *camp*). DB *Sueuecampe*.

Sacriston (village, Durham): 'hill spur of the sacristan'. ME *secrestein*, 'sacristan', + OE *hōh*, 'hill spur'. The name refers to the sacristan of Durham. Until recently the full name was *Sacriston Heugh*, but the second word of this has been dropped. 1312 *Segrysteynhogh*.

Sadberge (village, Darlington): '(place on a) flat-topped hill'. OS *set-berg* (from *set*, 'seat', + *berg*, 'hill'). 1169 *Sadberge*.

Saddington (village, Leics): '(particular) farmstead'. OE *tūn*, 'farmstead', 'estate'. The first part of the name is obscure. It could represent a reduced form of a personal name such as Sǣgēat or Sǣhæth with OE *-ing-*, 'associated with', or else OE *sēath*, 'pit', with *-ing*, 'place characterized by'. DB *Sadintone*.

Saddle Bow (hamlet, Norfolk): '(place by the) saddle bow'. OE *sadol*, 'saddle', + *boga*, 'bow'. The name refers to some arched or curved feature here. 1198 *Sadelboge*.

Saddleworth (district, Oldham): 'enclosure on a saddle-shaped ridge'. OE *sadol*, 'saddle', + *worth*, 'enclosure'. Late 12C *Sadelwrth*.

Saffron Walden (town, Essex): 'valley of the Britons where saffron is grown'. ME *safron* + OE *walh*, '(Ancient) Briton', 'Welshman', + *denu*, 'valley'. The first word of this name, added to distinguish this Walden from others (such as ST PAUL'S WALDEN, Herts, 25 miles to the southwest), refers to the fields of saffron (*Crocus sativus*) grown here from the early 15C for use in cloth-dyeing and medicine. In 1545 the town made a gift of saffron to 'my ladye Pagett', wife of a secretary of state. *c*.1000 *Wealadene*, DB *Waledana*, 1582 *Safornewalden*.

Sageston (hamlet, Pemb): 'Sager's farm'. OE *tūn*, 'farm'. 1362 *Sagerston*.

Saham Toney (village, Norfolk): 'de Toni's homestead by the pool'. OE *sǣ*, 'pool', + *hām*, 'homestead'. The manor here was held by the de Toni family in the late 12C. DB *Saham*, 1498 *Saham Toney*.

Saighton (village, Cheshire): 'farmstead where willow trees grow'. OE *salh*, 'sallow', 'willow', + *tūn*, 'farmstead'. DB *Saltone*.

St Agnes (resort village, Cornwall): '(parish of) St Agnes'. The church here is dedicated to the 4C martyr Agnes. (Here and in most similar entries below, the Latin form of the saint's name, when cited on its own, is given in the nominative case, although in the original text it may well occur in some other case following a word meaning 'church', 'castle', or the like, as in the DB form for ST ALBANS.) 1327 *Sancta Agnes*.

St Agnes (island, Scilly): 'pasture headland'. OS *hagi*, 'pasture', + *nes*, 'headland'. The name of one of the headlands here was extended to the whole island. 'St' was then added on an analogy with the names of other Scilly islands, such as ST MARY'S and ST MARTIN'S. Local people usually refer to the island as simply 'Agnes'. 1193 *Aganas*, 1244 *Agnas*, *c*.1540 *St Agnes*.

St Albans (city, Herts): 'holy place of St Alban'. OE *stōw*, 'holy place'. St Alban was martyred in the Roman amphitheatre outside the town in the early 3C and the abbey is dedicated to him. See also WATLING STREET. The Roman city nearby was *Verulamium*, a name of uncertain origin that gave that of the river Ver here. The DB form of the name below has Latin *villa*, 'town'. 1007 *Sancte Albanes stow*, DB *Villa Sancti Albani*.

St Andrews (coastal town, Fife): '(place with the shrine of) St Andrew'. The relics of St

Andrew are said to have been brought here in the 8C. The final '-s' of the name is the last letter of *Androis*, the Scottish form of 'Andrew'. *c.*1158 *Sancti Andree.*

St Annes. See LYTHAM ST ANNES.

St Anthony in Meneage (village, Cornwall): '(church of) St Entenin in Meneage'. The name of the Cornish saint has been altered to English 'Anthony'. The district name, meaning '(region) of monks' (Cornish *managh*, 'monk', + adjectival suffix *-ek*), was added for distinction from *St Anthony in Roseland*, 6 miles to the northeast across Falmouth Bay, where the district name means 'land by the headland' (Cornish *ros*, 'headland', + OE *land*, 'land'). The second form of the name below has Cornish *lann*, 'church site'. 1269 *Sanctus Antoninus*, 1344 *Lanyntenin*, 1522 *St Antony.*

St Asaph (village, Denb): '(church of) St Asaph'. The cathedral here is dedicated to the 6C bishop and saint Asaph. The Welsh name of St Asaph is *Llanelwy*, 'church by the (river) Elwy' (Welsh *llan*, 'church'). The river's own name means 'driving one'. 1291 *Sanctus Asaph.*

St Austell (town, Cornwall): '(church of) St Austol'. The church here is dedicated to the 6C monk and saint Austol. *c.*1150 *Austol*, 1169 *Sanctus Austolus.*

St Bees (village, Cumbria): '(church of) St Bega' The church here is dedicated to the 7C Irish (female) saint Bega. The village gave the name of the nearby headland *St Bees Head*. *c.*1135 *Sancta Bega.*

St Blazey (town, Cornwall): '(church of) St Blaise'. The church here is dedicated to the 4C Armenian martyr Blaise. 1440 *Sanctus Blasius*, 1525 *Seynt Blazy.*

St Boniface Down. See BONCHURCH.

St Breock (village, Cornwall): '(church of) St Brioc'. The church here is dedicated to the 6C saint, who is said to have been born in Cardiganshire. He lived and worked mainly in Brittany, where he gave the name of the town of *Saint-Brieuc*. 1259 *Sanctus Briocus.*

St Briavels (village, Glos): '(castle of) St Briavel'. The name is that of the Welsh saint Briavel, about whom little is known. 1130 *Sanctus Briauel.*

St Brides (village, Pemb): '(church of) St Bridget'. The church here is dedicated to the 6C Irish abbess Bridget (Brigid). The village gave the name of *St Brides Bay*. 1242 *Sancta Brigida.*

St Budeaux (district, Plymouth): '(church of) St Budoc'. The church here is dedicated to the 6C Celtic saint Budoc. The place is or was locally called 'Buddocks'. The DB form of the name below means 'Budoc's hide (of land)' (OE *hīd*, 'hide'). DB *Bucheside*, 1520 *Seynt Bodokkys.*

Saintbury (village, Glos): 'Sǽwine's fortified place'. OE *burh*, 'fortified place'. The 'fortified place' in question may be the remains of ancient entrenchments just south of the village. The DB form of the name below has garbled the personal name. DB *Svineberie*, 1186 *Seinesberia.*

St Buryan (village, Cornwall): '(church of) St Buryan'. The church here is dedicated to the female saint Beryan, said to have been of Irish origin. *c.*939 *Sancta Beriana*, DB *Sancta Berriona.*

St Clears (village, Carm): '(church of) St Clear'. The 9C saint, to whom the church here is dedicated, is also commemorated in ST CLEER. The Welsh form of the name is *Sanclêr*. 1291 *Sanctus Clarus*, 1331 *Seint Cler.*

St Cleer (village, Cornwall): '(church of) St Cleer'. The church here is dedicated to the 9C saint Cleer, who is also commemorated in ST CLEARS. His main cult is in *Saint-Clair-sur-Epte*, Normandy. 1212 *Sanctus Clarus.*

St Clether (village, Cornwall): '(church of) St Cleder'. The church here is dedicated to the saint, who according to Cornish legend is said to have been a son of Brychan of BRECON. 1249 *Sanctus Clederus.*

St Columb (village, Cornwall): '(church of) St Columba'. The churches at both *St Columb Major* and *St Columb Minor* are dedicated to the obscure female saint Columba (not the famous male Columba). *c.*1240 *Sancta Columba.*

St Cross South Elmham. See NORTH ELMHAM.

St David's (city, Pemb): '(church of) St David'. The 12C cathedral here, built on the site of an earlier church, is dedicated to the 6C monk and bishop David, patron saint of Wales. The Welsh name of St David's is *Tyddewi*, 'house of Dewi' (Welsh *tŷ*, 'house', + *Dewi*, 'David'), with 'house' in the biblical sense 'house of the Lord'. (St David is known in Welsh as *Dewi Sant*.) The nearby headland *St David's Head* was known to the Romans as *Octapitarum Promontorium*, a name of uncertain origin but with a first element perhaps meaning 'eight' and referring to the group of islets here known as Bishops and Clerks. 12C *Sancti Deuui*, *c.*1480 *Dyddewi.*

St Devereux (hamlet, Herefords): '(church of) St Dyfrig'. The church here is dedicated to Dyfrig, a 6C Welsh monk and bishop said by

Geoffrey of Monmouth to have crowned Arthur 'King of Britain'. 1291 *Sanctus Dubricius*.

St Dogmaels (village, Pemb): '(church of) St Dogmael'. The church here is dedicated to the 6C Welsh bishop Dogmael. The Welsh name of St Dogmaels is *Llandudoch*, apparently meaning 'St Tydoch's church' (Welsh *llan*, 'church'), although no such saint is known. (It is possible *Tydoch* is a pet form of *Dogmael*, based on Welsh *ty*, 'thy', and the first part of his name.) *c.*1208 *Sanctis Dogmaelis*.

St Dogwells (hamlet, Pemb): '(church of) St Dogmael'. The church here is dedicated to the same saint as at ST DOGMAELS. The Welsh name of St Dogwells is *Llantydewi*, a name apparently meaning 'church of the house of St David' (Welsh *llan*, 'church', + *tŷ*, 'house', + *Dewi*, 'David'), perhaps linking it specifically with ST DAVID'S, 15 miles to the west. 1215 *Ecclesia St. Dogmaelis*.

St Edmundsbury. See BURY ST EDMUNDS.

St Endellion (hamlet, Cornwall): '(church of) St Endilient'. The church here is dedicated to Endilient, according to Cornish lore a daughter of the Welsh king Brychan, who gave the name of BRECON. 1260 *Sancta Endelienta*.

St Florence (village, Pemb): '(church of) St Florence'. The church here is dedicated to Florence, otherwise Florent of Anjou. 1248 *Sanctus Florencius*.

St Germans (village, Cornwall): '(church of) St Germanus'. It is unclear whether the church here is dedicated to the 5C Germanus of Auxerre or to a local saint of the same name. Cp. GERMANSWEEK. Mid-10C *Sanctus Germanus*.

St Giles in the Wood (village, Devon): 'holy place of St Giles in the wood'. OE *stōw*, 'holy place'. The church here is dedicated to St Giles. The OE word was subsequently dropped from the name, which later added the last three words for distinction from *St Giles on the Heath*, 22 miles to the southwest. 1330 *Stow St Giles*.

St Helen Auckland. See BISHOP AUCKLAND.

St Helens (village, IoW): '(church of) St Helena'. The church here is dedicated to the 4C empress Helen, mother of Constantine the Great. 12C *Sancta Elena*.

St Helens (town, St Helens): '(chapel of) St Helen'. The town arose in the 17C and takes its name from a medieval chapel of ease here, first mentioned in 1552, that was dedicated to the 4C empress Helen, mother of Constantine the Great. Four different buildings have occupied the site, the third (1816–1916) being dedicated to St Mary.

St Hilary (hamlet, Cornwall): '(church of) St Hilary'. The church here is dedicated to Hilary, 4C Bishop of Poitiers. 1178 *Sanctus Hilarius*.

St Ippollitts (village, Herts): '(church of) St Hippolytus'. The church here is dedicated to the 3C Roman priest and martyr Hippolytus. 1283 *S. Ypollitus*.

St Ishmael's (village, Pemb): '(church of) St Ishmael'. The church here is dedicated to Ishmael, otherwise the 6C Welsh bishop Ismael. 1291 *Ecclesia Sancti Ismael*.

St Issey (village, Cornwall): '(church of) St Idi'. The church here is dedicated to Idi, according to Cornish legend a son of Brychan, the Welsh king who gave the name of BRECON. 1195 *Sanctus Ydi*.

St Ive (village, Cornwall): '(church of) St Ive'. The church here is dedicated to a Persian bishop named Ive, whose relics are said to have been found in ST IVES, Cambs, in 1001. 1201 *Sanctus Yvo*.

St Ives (town, Cambs): '(place of) St Ive'. The relics of St Ive, who gave the name of ST IVE, are said to have been found here in 1001. The form of the name below includes the earlier name of St Ives as *Slepe*, from OE *slǣp*, 'slippery place', referring to its location by the river Ouse. 1110 *Sancto Ivo de Slepe*.

St Ives (resort town, Cornwall): '(church of) St Ya'. The church here is dedicated to the Irish (female) saint Ya. The Cornish name of the town was *Porthia*, 'harbour of Ya' (Cornish *porth*, 'harbour'). 1284 *Sancta Ya*.

St Ives (hamlet, Dorset): '(place overgrown with) ivy'. OE *īfet*, 'clump of ivy'. *St* was added in recent times on an analogy with the names above. 1167 *Iuez*.

St James South Elmham. See NORTH ELMHAM.

St John's Wood (district, Westminster): 'wood of St John'. The name refers to the Knights Hospitallers of St John, to whom land here was transferred from the Knights Templars on the suppression of the latter in the early 14C. The first form of the name below is Latin for 'wood of the priory of St John'. 1294 *Boscum Prioris Sancti Johannis*, 1524 *Seynt Johns Woode*.

St Just (town, Cornwall): '(church of) St Just'. The church here is dedicated to the obscure saint Just. The town is sometimes called *St Just in Penwith*, from the Cornish name of LAND'S

END, for distinction from *St Just in Roseland* (see ST ANTHONY IN MENEAGE). 1291 *Sanctus Justus*.

St Keverne (village, Cornwall): '(church of) St Aghevran'. The church here is dedicated to Aghevran, a saint about whom nothing is known. DB *Sanctus Achebrannus*.

St Kew (village, Cornwall): '(church of) St Kew'. The church here is dedicated to Kew, a female saint said to have come to Cornwall from Wales. The first form of the name below has *p* in error for *w*. c.962 *Sancta Cypa*, DB *Sanctus Cheus*.

St Keyne (village, Cornwall): '(church of) St Keyn'. The church here is dedicated to Keyn, according to Welsh (but not Cornish) legend a daughter of the Welsh king Brychan, who gave the name of BRECON. 1291 *Sancta Keyna*.

St Kilda (island, W Isles): '(place of) shields'. OS *skildar*, 'shields' (related modern English *shield*). The name may have originally applied not to St Kilda itself but to a group of neighbouring islands, whose outline resembled shields lying on the surface of the sea. The name created a bogus saint (included in the 1978 edition of the *Oxford Book of Saints* but subsequently disavowed).

St Lawrence (hamlet, IoW): '(church of) St Lawrence'. The church here is dedicated to the 3C deacon and martyr Lawrence. The place was also formerly known as *Wathe*, '(place at the) ford' (OE *wæd*, 'ford', related modern English *wade*). There is no longer a ford here, or even a stream. 1255 *Sanctus Laurencius*.

St Leonards (resort town, E Sussex): '(church of) St Leonard'. The original parish church here, washed away by the sea in the 15C, was dedicated to the 6C hermit Leonard. As for the resort: 'It is entirely of recent origin, having been begun in 1828 by James Burton, Esq., who purchased this valley from the Eversfield estate. In 1832, having laid out the general plan of the town, Mr. Burton obtained an Act of Parliament "for the better lighting, watching, paving, &c., the town of St. Leonard's-on-Sea"' (*The National Gazetteer of Great Britain and Ireland*, 1868). The medieval name below means 'manor of St Leonard near Hastings'. 1288 *Villa de Sancto Leonardo juxta Hasting*.

St Levan (hamlet, Cornwall): '(parish of) St Selevan'. The church here is dedicated to Selevan, a local Cornish saint. (The 'Se-' of his name in its spoken form was taken to be 'St'. Hence the form 'Levan'.) His name is from *Solomon*, but was early turned into *Silvanus* in official records, as below. 1327 *Sanctus Silvanus*.

St Margarets (district, Richmond): 'St Margaret's (House)'. The name was originally given by the 1st Marquess of Ailsa to his mansion here in c.1820, no doubt in honour of St Margaret of Scotland (1046–93). It subsequently transferred to the surrounding district.

St Margarets (Herts). See STANSTED.

St Margaret's at Cliffe (resort village, Kent): '(church of) St Margaret at Cliffe'. The church here is dedicated to St Margaret of Antioch. The second part of the name, from OE *clif*, 'cliff', refers to the location of the resort on high cliffs above St Margaret's Bay. DB *Sancta Margarita*.

St Margaret's Island (island, Pemb): 'St Margaret's island'. The island, between Caldy and the mainland, takes its name from a former chapel dedicated to St Margaret here. It was originally known as *Little Caldy*. 1718 *Little Caldey alias St Margaretts Island*.

St Margaret South Elmham. See NORTH ELMHAM.

St Martin's (island, Scilly): '(church of) St Martin'. The church here is dedicated to Martin of Tours (d.397), whose name is traditionally given to churches away from urban areas. The name then passed to the whole island. c.1540 *Seynt Martyns*, c.1540 *St Martines Isle*.

St Martin's (village, Shropshire): '(church of) St Martin'. The church here is dedicated to Martin of Tours (d.397). The village is near the Welsh border and is also known by the Welsh name *Llanfarthin* (Welsh *llan*, 'church', + *Martin*). c.1222 *Sanctus Martinus*.

St Mary Bourne (village, Hants): '(chapel of) St Mary by the stream'. OE *burna*, 'spring', 'stream'. The former chapel here was dedicated to St Mary. The stream is the Bourne Rivulet. 1185 *Borne*, 1476 *Maryborne*.

St Mary Cray (district, Bromley): '(church of) St Mary on the (river) Cray'. For the river name, see CRAYFORD. The church dedication distinguishes this Cray from nearby *St Paul's Cray*, where the church is dedicated to St Paulinus, first bishop of York. Further north on the same river are *Foots Cray*, Bexley, where the manor was held in 1086 by one Fot, and *North Cray*, Bexley, the northernmost of the four, which are locally known collectively as *The Crays*. 1257 *Creye Sancte Marie*.

St Mary's (island, Scilly): '(church of) St Mary'. The parish church at Hugh Town, the island's 'capital', is dedicated to St Mary, and the name passed to the whole island. c.1175 *Sancta Maria*, 1478 *Seynt Mary island*.

St Mawes (coastal town, Cornwall): '(town of) St Maudyth'. The chapel here is dedicated to the 5C Breton bishop Maudyth (Maudez). 1284 *Sanctus Maudetus*, 1342 *Saint Mauduyt*.

St Mawgan (village, Cornwall): '(church of) St Mawgan'. The church here is dedicated to the obscure saint Mawgan, venerated in Wales as St Meugan. 1257 *Sanctus Mauchanus*.

St Mellion (village, Cornwall): '(church of) St Melaine'. The church here is dedicated to Melaine, 6C Bishop of Rennes, France. 1259 *Sanctus Melanus*.

St Merryn (village, Cornwall): '(church of) St Marina'. The church here is dedicated to Marina, an early (female) saint of Asia Minor. The original dedication may actually have been to the Celtic (male) saint Merin. 1259 *Sancta Marina*.

St Michael's Mount (island, Cornwall): '(chapel of) St Michael on the mount'. St Michael the Archangel is said to have appeared here in 710, and in the 11C The Mount (a small rocky island) and its priory were given to *Mont-Saint-Michel* in France, presumably because of the similarity of the two sites. Mid-11C *Sanctus Michael*, 1478 *Mount Mychell*, 1479 *Seynt Mychell Mount*.

St Michael's on Wyre (village, Lancs): '(church of) St Michael on the (river) Wyre'. The church here is dedicated to St Michael. The river has a Celtic name meaning 'winding one'. DB *Michelescherche*.

St Michael South Elmham. See NORTH ELMHAM.

St Monance (town and port, Fife): '(church of) St Monans'. The church here is dedicated to the 6C Irish Bishop of Clonfert, Monans. 1565 *Sanct Monanis*.

St Neot (village, Cornwall): '(church of) St Neot'. The church here is dedicated to Neot, said to have been a relative of Alfred the Great. His relics were later removed to ST NEOTS. DB *Sanctus Neotus*.

St Neots (town, Cambs): '(town of) St Neot'. The relics of St Neot, a 9C monk of Glastonbury, were brought here in the 10C from the Cornish village of ST NEOT, where he had died. 12C *S' Neod*.

St Nicholas (village, Pemb): '(church of) St Nicholas'. The church here is dedicated to St Nicholas. The Welsh name of the village is either *Sain Nicolas* or *Tremarchog*, 'knight's farm' (Welsh *tre*, 'farm', + *marchog*, 'knight'), a 'knight' being an official of the episcopal estates here. The first form of the name below has the

Latin equivalent, 'manor of the chamberlain'. 1287 *Villa Camerarii*, 1551 *Tremarchoc*, 1554 *Saynt Nycolas*.

St Nicholas at Wade (village, Kent): '(church of) St Nicholas at Wade'. The church here is dedicated to St Nicholas. *Wade*, from OE *wæd*, 'ford' (related modern English *wade*), is the name of a former crossing place over some stream here leading to the Isle of Thanet. 1254 *Villa Sancti Nicholai*, 1458 *St Nicholas at Wade*.

St Nicholas South Elmham. See NORTH ELMHAM.

St Osyth (village, Essex): '(priory of) St Ōsgyth'. Ōsgyth (d.*c.*700) was a granddaughter of Penda, king of Mercia, and was betrothed to Sighere, king of the East Saxons, but because of her vow of perpetual virginity the marriage was not consummated. She retired to this place, then called *Chich*, '(place at the) bend' (OE *cicc*), referring to the stream here, and founded a nunnery of which she became abbess. 1046 *Seynte Osithe*.

St Pancras (district, Camden): '(church of) St Pancras'. The church here is dedicated to the 4C boy martyr Pancras. DB *Sanctum Pancratium*.

St Paul's Cray. See ST MARY CRAY.

St Paul's Walden (village, Herts): 'St Paul's (estate in) Walden'. The Dean and Chapter of St Paul's, London, became patrons of the living here in 1544, their name distinguishing this village from *King's Walden*, 2 miles to the northwest, where the manor was held by the king in 1086. For the main name, see SAFFRON WALDEN. 888 *Waledene*, DB *Waldene*.

St Peter's (district of Broadstairs, Kent): '(church of) St Peter'. The church here is dedicated to St Peter. The form of the name below means 'borough of St Peter'. 1254 *Borgha sancti Petri*.

St Peter South Elmham. See NORTH ELMHAM.

St Petrox (hamlet, Pemb): '(church of) St Petroc'. The church here was dedicated to the 6C abbot Petroc, Cornwall's most famous saint. 1291 *Ecclesia de Sancto Petroco*, 1603 *St Petrocks*.

St Stephen (village, Cornwall): '(church of) St Stephen'. The church here is dedicated to St Stephen, the first martyr. *c.*1166 *Sanctis Stephanus*.

St Stephens. See LAUNCESTON.

St Tudy (village, Cornwall): '(church of) St Tudy'. The church here is dedicated to Tudy, a 6C monk and bishop. The first part of the form of the name below represents Cornish *eglos*, 'church'. DB *Hecglostudic*.

St Weonards (village, Herefords): '(church of) St Gwennarth'. The church here is dedicated to Gwennarth, a Celtic monastic saint. The first word of the form of the name below represents OW *lann*, 'church'. *c.*1130 *Lann Sant Guainerth*.

St Winnow (hamlet, Cornwall): '(church of) St Winnoc'. The church here is dedicated to the 8C Welsh monk Winnoc, although his name may have evolved as a pet form of Winwaloe, the Cornish saint to whom the church at GUNWALLOE is dedicated. DB *San Winnuc*, 1166 *Sanctus Winnocus*.

Salcey Forest (wooded region, Northants): 'willow wood'. OF *salceie* (from Latin *salix*, 'willow'). 1206 *bosco de Sasceya*.

Salcombe (resort town, Devon): '(place in the) salt valley'. OE *sealt*, 'salt', + *cumb*, 'valley'. The reference is to the production of salt here, rather than simply the presence of salt water in the Kingsbridge Estuary. 1244 *Saltecumbe*.

Salcombe Regis (village, Devon): 'king's (place in the) salt valley'. OE *sealt*, 'salt', + *cumb*, 'valley'. The manor here was held early by the Dean and Chapter of Exeter, and the late (18C) appearance of the second word (Latin *regis*, 'of the king') is unexplained. It may represent a local field name such as *Kingsdown* and have been added to distinguish this Salcombe from the town of SALCOMBE, although that is over 40 miles away. *c.*1060 *Sealtcumbe*, DB *Selcome*.

Salcott (village, Essex): 'building where salt is made or stored'. OE *sealt*, 'salt', + *cot*, 'cottage', 'building'. Cp. SALTCOATS. Saltpans were formerly common in the Essex marshes. *c.*1200 *Saltcot*.

Sale (town, Trafford): '(place at the) willow tree'. OE *salh*, 'willow' (modern English *sallow*). The original site here would have been among willows by the river Mersey. *c.*1205 *Sale*.

Salehurst (village, E Sussex): 'wooded hill where willow trees grow'. OE *salh*, 'sallow', 'willow', + *hyrst*, 'wooded hill'. The DB form of the name below has omitted an *s*. DB *Salhert*, *c.*1210 *Salhirst*.

Salesbury (village, Lancs): 'fortified place where willow trees grow'. OE *salh*, 'sallow', 'willow', + *burh*, 'fortified place', 'manor'. 1246 *Salesbyry*.

Salford (village, Oxon): '(place by the) ford over which salt is carried'. OE *salt*, 'salt', + *ford*, 'ford'. Salford was probably on a saltway that led from the Four Shire Stone, near Moreton-in-Marsh, Glos, to Chipping Norton, Oxon. 777 *Saltford*, DB *Salford*.

Salford (city, Salford): '(place by the) ford where willows grow'. OE *salh*, 'sallow', 'willow', + *ford*, 'ford'. The ford would have been over the river Irwell here. DB *Salford*. SO ALSO: *Salford*, Beds.

Salford Priors (village, Warwicks): 'prior's (estate by the) ford over which salt is carried'. OE *salt*, 'salt', + *ford*, 'ford'. The river here is the Arrow. The manor was held early by Kenilworth Priory, and the second word of the name distinguishes the village from nearby *Abbots Salford*, where it was held by Evesham Abbey. 714 *Saltford*, DB *Salford*.

Salfords (suburb of Redhill, Surrey): '(place by the) ford where willows grow'. OE *salh*, 'sallow', 'willow', + *ford*, 'ford'. The ford would have been over Salfords Stream here. 1279 *Salford*.

Salhouse (village, Norfolk): '(place by the) willow trees'. OE *salh*, 'sallow', 'willow'. The name represents the OE word in a plural form. 1291 *Salhus*.

Salinae. See (1) DROITWICH, (2) MIDDLEWICH.

Salisbury (city, Wilts): 'stronghold (called) Sorvio'. OE *burh*, 'fortified place'. The first part of the name represents a reduced and altered form of *Sorviodunum*, the Roman name of Salisbury. The last part of this is of Celtic origin and means 'fort' (modern Welsh *dinas*). The first part is also probably Celtic and may represent a personal name Sorwjos, giving an overall sense 'fort of Sorwjos' (just as *Camulodunum*, the Roman name of COLCHESTER, means 'fort of Camulos'). Salisbury originated on the ancient hill fort to the north of the present city called *Old Sarum*, with *Sarum* arising as an abbreviated form of *Sarisberie*, the DB form of the name, which was conventionally contracted in medieval manuscripts by writing *Sa*- followed by a symbol resembling the figure 4. This same sign was used for the common ending *-rum*, hence *Sarum*. Modern Salisbury is now officially known as *New Sarum*. The first *r* in *Sarisberie* became *l* under Norman influence. *c.*900 *Searobyrg*, DB *Sarisberie*.

Salle (hamlet, Norfolk): '(place by the) wood or clearing where willow trees grow'. OE *salh*, 'sallow', 'willow', + *lēah*, 'wood', 'clearing'. Until recently the name was spelt *Sall*. DB *Salla*.

Salop. See SHROPSHIRE.

Salperton (hamlet, Glos): 'farmstead by a saltway'. OE *salt*, 'salt', + *here-pæth*, 'through road' (from *here*, 'army', + *pæth*, 'path'), + *tūn*, 'farmstead'. Salperton lies near the Saltway, a route for conveying salt from Droitwich, Worcs, some 30 miles to the north. DB *Salpretune*.

Salt (hamlet, Staffs): 'place where salt is made'. OE *selte*, 'saltpit', 'saltworks'. DB *Selte*.

Saltaire (district of Shipley, Bradford). In 1850 Sir Titus Salt (1803–76), whose family originated in SALT, founded a model village here on the river Aire for workers at his worsted mills. The streets retain the names of Salt's family, which numbered 11 children. For the river name, see AIRMYN.

Saltash (town, Cornwall): '(place by the) ash tree where salt is produced'. OE *sealt*, 'salt', + *æsc*, 'ash'. The first form of the name below relates simply to the ash tree. The reference to salt appeared later. 1201 *Esse*, 1302 *Saltehasche*.

Saltburn-by-the-Sea (resort town, Redcar & Clev): '(place by the) salt stream by the sea'. OE *salt*, 'salt', + *burna*, 'stream'. The reference is probably not to a saltwater stream here but to the nearby brine wells. Brine baths were opened in Saltburn in the 1890s. The second part of the name is a commercial lure. *c.*1185 *Salteburnam*.

Saltby (village, Leics): 'Salti's or Salt's farmstead'. OS *bý*, 'farmstead', 'village'. The personal names are Scandinavian. The name could also mean 'farmstead where salt is found or kept' (OS *salt*, 'salt', + *bý*). DB *Saltebi*.

Saltcoats (resort town, N Ayrs): 'buildings where salt is made or stored'. OE *sealt*, 'salt', + *cot*, 'cottage', 'shed'. The saltworks here were established by James V in the 16C. 1548 *Saltcoates*.

Saltdean (district, Brighton & Hove): '(place in the) salt valley'. OE *sealt*, 'salt', + *denu*, 'valley'. The name refers to a gap in the cliffs by the sea here. Such 'deans' are a feature of this coastal region between Brighton and Newhaven. Cp. OVINGDEAN, ROEDEAN, ROTTINGDEAN. 1740 *Saltdean Gap*.

Salterforth (village, Lancs): '(place by the) ford used by salt merchants'. OE *saltere*, 'salt dealer', + *ford*, 'ford'. The ford in question would have crossed Salterforth Beck here. 13C *Salterford*.

Saltfleet (coastal village, Lincs): '(place by the) salt stream'. OE *salt*, 'salt', + *flēot*, 'stream'. DB *Salfluet*.

Saltfleetby All Saints (hamlet, Lincs): 'farmstead by the salt streams with All Saints church'. OE *salt*, 'salt', + *flēot*, 'stream', + OS *bý*, 'farmstead', 'village'. The church dedication distinguishes this Saltfleetby from nearby *Saltfleetby St Clement* and *Saltfleetby St Peter*. DB *Salflatebi*.

Saltford (village, Bath & NE Somerset): '(place by the) ford over which salt is carried'. OE *salt*, 'salt', + *ford*, 'ford'. The name could also mean

'salt-water ford', as the river Avon here was formerly tidal. Cp. FRESHFORD. Alternatively, the first part of the name (corrupted in the DB form below) may have originally represented OE *salh*, 'willow tree', giving a sense '(place by the) ford where willows grow'. DB *Sanford*, 1229 *Salford*, 1291 *Saltford*.

Salthouse (village, Norfolk): 'building where salt is stored'. OE *salt*, 'salt', + *hūs*, 'house', 'building'. DB *Salthus*.

Saltmarshe (village, E Yorks): '(place by the) salty marsh'. OE *salt*, 'salt', + *mersc*, 'marsh'. There would have been a brackish marsh by the river Ouse here. DB *Saltemersc*.

Salton (village, N Yorks): 'farmstead where willow trees grow'. OE *salh*, 'sallow', 'willow', + *tūn*, 'farmstead'. DB *Saletun*.

Saltwood (suburb of Hythe, Kent): '(place by the) wood where salt is stored'. OE *sealt*, 'salt', + *wudu*, 'wood'. *c.*1000 *Sealtwuda*, DB *Salteode*.

Salvington (district of Worthing, W Sussex): 'estate associated with Sǣlāf or Sǣwulf'. OE *-ing-*, 'associated with', + *tūn*, 'farmstead', 'estate'. 1249 *Saluinton*.

Salwarpe (village, Worcs): '(place on) dark-coloured silted land'. OE *salu*, 'sallow', 'dark-coloured', + *wearp*, 'silt'. 817 *Salouuarpe*, DB *Salewarpe*.

Sambourne (village, Warwicks): '(place by the) sandy stream'. OE *sand*, 'sand', + *burna*, 'stream'. William Dugdale, in *The Antiquities of Warwickshire* (1656), describes the place as 'having its originall denomination from that little Sandy brook nigh unto which it stands'. 714 *Samburne*, DB *Sandburne*.

Sambrook (village, Wrekin): '(place by the) sandy brook'. OE *sand*, 'sand', + *brōc*, 'brook'. The DB form of the name below is corrupt. DB *Semebre*, 1256 *Sambroc*.

Samlesbury (village, Lancs): 'stronghold by a ledge of land'. OE *scamol*, 'shelf', 'ledge', + *burh*, 'fortified place'. 1188 *Samelesbure*.

Sampford Arundel (village, Somerset): 'Arundel's (estate by the) sandy ford'. OE *sand*, 'sand', + *ford*, 'ford'. Roger Arundel held the manor here in 1086, his name distinguishing this Sampford from *Sampford Brett*, 15 miles to the north, where the Bret family held the manor in the 12C. DB *Sanford*, 1240 *Samford Arundel*.

Sampford Brett. See SAMPFORD ARUNDEL.

Sampford Courtenay (village, Devon): 'Curtenay's (estate by the) sandy ford'. OE *sand*, 'sand', + *ford*, 'ford'. The ford would have been over the river Taw. The Curtenay family held the manor here in the 13C. DB *Sanfort*, 1262 *Saunforde Curtenay*.

Sampford Peverell (village, Devon): 'Peverel's (estate by the) sandy ford'. OE *sand*, 'sand', + *ford*, 'ford'. The ford would have been over the river Lynor. The Peverel family held the manor here in the 12C. DB *Sanforda*, 1275 *Saunford Peverel*.

Sampford Spiney (hamlet, Devon): 'Spiney's (estate by the) sandy ford'. OE *sand*, 'sand', + *ford*, 'ford'. The ford would have been over the river Walkham. The Spiney family held the manor here in the 13C. DB *Sanforda*, 1304 *Saundford Spyneye*.

Samson (island, Scilly): '(chapel of) St Samson'. There is no record of a chapel on this island, now uninhabited, but there was presumably one dedicated to Samson, 6C Bishop of Dol. *c.*1160 *Sanctus Sampson*.

Sanclêr. See ST CLEARS.

Sancreed (village, Cornwall): '(church of) St Sancred'. The church here is dedicated to Sancred, who is said to have lived his life in contrition as a swineherd after accidentally killing his father. The first part of the first form of the name below represents Cornish *eglos*, 'church', while the second part implies an alternative form Sant for the saint's name. *c.*1176 *Eglossant*, 1235 *Sanctus Sancretus*.

Sancton (village, E Yorks): 'farmstead with sandy soil'. OE *sand*, 'sand', + *tūn*, 'farmstead'. 'Soil loam, overlying chalk and sand' (*Cassell's Gazetteer of Great Britain and Ireland*, 1897). DB *Santun*.

Sandal Magna (district, Wakefield): 'greater sandy corner of land'. OE *sand*, 'sand', + *halh*, 'nook', 'corner of land'. The second word of the name (Latin *magna*, 'great'), referring to the important castle here, distinguishes this Sandal from KIRK SANDALL, Doncaster, 28 miles to the southeast. DB *Sandal*.

Sanday (island, Orkney): 'sandy island'. OS *sand*, 'sand', + *ey*, 'island'. *Sanday* in the Inner Hebrides, Highland, has a name of identical origin.

Sandbach (town, Cheshire): '(place by the) sandy valley stream'. OE *sand*, 'sandy', + *bæce*, 'valley stream'. Sandbach is on a small tributary of the river Wheelock. DB *Sanbec*.

Sandbanks (coastal district, Poole): '(place by) sandbanks'. Sandbanks, with its modern name, lies on a spit of land at the entrance to Poole Harbour. *c.*1800 *Sandbanks*.

Sanderstead (district, Croydon): 'sandy homestead'. OE *sand*, 'sand', + *hām-stede*, 'homestead' (from *hām*, 'homestead', + *stede*, 'place'). The soil is noticeably sandy here. *c.*880 *Sondenstede*, DB *Sandestede*.

Sandford (village, Devon): '(place by the) sandy ford'. OE *sand*, 'sand', + *ford*, 'ford'. The ford in question would have been over the small tributary here of the river Creedy. 930 *Sandforda*. SO ALSO: *Sandford*, Cumbria, Shropshire.

Sandford-on-Thames (village, Oxon): '(place by the) sandy ford on the (river) Thames'. OE *sand*, 'sand', + *ford*, 'ford'. The river name (see THAMES DITTON) distinguishes this Sandford from SANDFORD ST MARTIN, 19 miles to the southeast. 1050 *Sandforda*, DB *Sanford*.

Sandford Orcas (village, Dorset): 'Orescuils' (estate by the) sandy ford'. OE *sand*, 'sand', + *ford*, 'ford'. The ford would have been over the stream here now called Mill Stream. The Orescuils family held the manor here from the 12C. DB *Sanford*, 1372 *Sandford Horscoys*.

Sandford St Martin (village, Oxon): '(place by the) sandy ford with St Martin's church'. OE *sand*, 'sand', + *ford*, 'ford'. The river here is the Dorn. DB *Sanford*.

Sandgate (district of Folkestone, Kent): '(place by the) gap leading to the sandy shore'. OE *sand*, 'sand', + *geat*, 'gate', 'gap'. 1256 *Sandgate*.

Sandhoe (village, Northd): '(place by the) sandy hill spur'. OE *sand*, 'sand', + *hōh*, 'hill spur'. 1225 *Sandho*.

Sandhurst (town, Bracknell F): '(place by the) sandy wooded hill'. OE *sand*, 'sand', + *hyrst*, 'wooded hill'. The sandy hill in question is the low promontory on which the town lies, overlooking the river Blackwater. 1175 *Sandherst*. SO ALSO: *Sandhurst*, Glos, Kent.

Sandhutton (village, N Yorks): 'farmstead on a sandy hill spur'. OE *sand*, 'sand', + *hōh*, 'hill spur', + *tūn*, 'farmstead'. DB *Hotune*, 12C *Sandhoton*.

Sand Hutton (village, N Yorks): 'farmstead on a sandy hill spur'. OE *sand*, 'sand', + *hōh*, 'hill spur', + *tūn*, 'farmstead'. DB *Hotone*, 1219 *Sandhouton*.

Sandiacre (district of Stapleford, Derbys): 'sandy plot of cultivated land'. OE *sandig*, 'sandy', + *æcer*, 'plot of cultivated land' (modern English *acre*). DB *Sandiacre*.

Sandon (village, Essex): '(place on the) sandy hill'. OE *sand*, 'sand', + *dūn*, 'hill'. As described by White's *Gazetteer and Directory of Essex* (1848): 'The soil is various, mostly a wet loam, resting on clay; but the elevated ground occupied by the village is rather light and sandy.' 1199 *Sandun*. SO ALSO: *Sandon*, Herts, Staffs.

Sandown (resort town, IoW): 'sandy riverside land'. OE *sand*, 'sand', + *hamm*, 'enclosure', 'riverside land'. The 'riverside land' is probably the flat ground between the upper reaches of the river Yar and the sea. The name does not thus refer to the town's sandy beaches, or to the downs behind it: 'Sandown, as the name suggests, has the best beaches and is backed by downs' (*The Shell Book of the Islands of Britain*, 1981). The DB form of the name below is corrupt. DB *Sande*, 1271 *Sandham*.

Sandown Park (park and racecourse, Surrey): 'park by the sandy hill'. OE *sand*, 'sand', + *dūn*, 'hill'. The park and racecourse were opened in 1875. 1235 *Sandone*.

Sandplace (hamlet, Cornwall): 'sand place'. It has been suggested that boats would have brought sand from the coast up the East Looe River to be unloaded here and spread on the fields. The first form of the name below is Latin for 'sanding places'. 1326 *Placeae sabulonis*, 1667 *Sandplace*.

Sandridge (village, Herts): '(place by the) sandy ridge'. OE *sand*, 'sand', + *hrycg*, 'ridge'. DB *Sandrige*.

Sandringham (village, Norfolk): 'sandy part of Dersingham'. OE *sand*, 'sand'. Sandringham is immediately south of *Dersingham*, 'homestead of Dēorsige's people' (OE *-inga-*, 'of the people of', + *hām*, 'homestead'). 'The name [of Sandringham] is derived from its deep sandy soil, of which more than 200 acres are on the extensive heath stretching hence to Wolferton' (*Cassell's Gazetteer of Great Britain and Ireland*, 1897). DB *Santdersincham*.

Sandwell (district of West Bromwich, Sandwell): '(place by the) sandy spring'. OE *sand*, 'sand', + *wella*, 'spring'. 'The spring which gave rise to this name still flows in the grounds [of Sandwell Park] at Sandwell' (W. H. Duignan, *Notes on Staffordshire Place Names*, 1902). The name is now that of the local unitary authority. 13C *Saundwell*.

Sandwich (town and former port, Kent): '(place with a) sandy harbour'. OE *sand*, 'sand', + *wīc*, 'specialized farm', 'trading settlement', 'harbour'. The former cinque port is now 2 miles inland. *c*.710 *Sandwīcæ*, DB *Sandwice*.

Sandy (town, Beds): 'sandy island'. OE *sand*, 'sand', + *ēg*, 'island'. The 'island' here is the slightly higher ground, to the east of the river Ivel, on which the town stands. DB *Sandeie*.

Sandy Lane (village, Wilts). Sandy Lane arose as a model village around an 18C inn on the same Lower Greensand ridge as SEEND, 5 miles to the south. Hence the modern name of obvious origin. The Roman settlement nearby was *Verlucio*, a Celtic name meaning 'very bright place'.

Sanquhar (town, Dumfries & Gall): '(place by the) old fort'. Gaelic *sean*, 'old', + *cathair*, 'fort'. The 'old fort' is the ancient earthwork to the west of the town known as Devil's Dyke. 1150 *Sanchar*.

Sapcote (village, Leics): 'shed for sheep'. OE *scēap*, 'sheep', + *cot*, 'shed', 'shelter'. DB *Scepecote*.

Sapiston (village, Suffolk): '(particular) farmstead'. OE *tūn*, 'farmstead'. The first part of the name is of uncertain origin. It may represent a personal name. DB *Sapestuna*.

Sapperton (village, Glos): 'farmstead of the soapmakers'. OE *sāpere*, 'soapmaker', + *tūn*, 'farmstead'. The DB form of the name below is corrupt. *c*.1075 *Sapertun*, DB *Sapletorne*. SO ALSO: *Sapperton*, Lincs.

Sarisbury (village, Hants): origin uncertain. The name is popularly said to have been adopted from SALISBURY, almost 30 miles away. 13C *Sarebury*, 1538 *Sarisbury*.

Sarnesfield (village, Herefords): 'open land by a road'. The first part of the name is an early form of modern Welsh *sarn*, 'causeway'. The second part is OE *feld*, 'open land' (modern English *field*). DB *Sarnesfelde*.

Sarratt (village, Herts): 'dry place'. OE *sīeret*, from *sēar*, 'dry', 'barren' (modern English *sere*). Sarratt is situated high on the chalk not far from SEER GREEN, Bucks, with a name of identical origin. *c*.1085 *Syreth*.

Sarre (village, Kent): origin uncertain. The name may derive from a pre-English name for the river Wantsum here. 761 *Serræ*.

Sarsden (hamlet, Oxon): '(place in the) valley of the church'. OE *cirice*, 'church', + *denu*, 'valley'. The DB form of the name below is corrupt. DB *Secendene*, *c*.1180 *Cherchesdena*.

Satley (village, Durham): 'woodland clearing with a fold'. OE *set*, 'fold' (for animals), + *lēah*, 'wood', 'clearing'. 1228 *Sateley*.

Satterleigh (hamlet, Devon): 'woodland clearing of the robbers'. OE *sætere*, 'robber', + *lēah*, 'wood', 'clearing'. DB *Saterlei*.

Satterthwaite (village, Cumbria): 'clearing by a shieling'. OS *sǽtr*, 'shieling', 'hill pasture', + *thveit*, 'clearing'. 1336 *Saterthwayt*.

Saughall Massie (district of Wallasey, Wirral): 'de Mascy's (estate at the) corner of land where willows grow'. OE *salh*, 'sallow', 'willow', + *halh*, 'nook', 'corner of land'. The manor here was held in the 14C by the de Mascy family, their name distinguishing this Saughall from GREAT SAUGHALL, Cheshire, 14 miles to the southeast. 1202 *Saham*, 1322 *Salghalle Mascy*.

Saul (village, Glos): 'wood or clearing where willows grow'. OE *salh*, 'sallow', 'willow', + *lēah*, 'wood', 'clearing'. 12C *Salle*.

Saundby (village, Notts): 'Sandi's farmstead'. OS *bý*, 'farmstead'. The personal name is Scandinavian. The first part of the name could also represent OS *sandr*, 'sand', giving a meaning 'farmstead on sandy ground'. DB *Sandebi*.

Saundersfoot (resort town, Pemb): 'Saunders' foot'. The 'foot' is probably that of a hill or cliff here owned by one Saunders, a local family name. 1602 *Saunders foot*.

Saunderton (village, Bucks): '(place by the) hill'. OE *dūn*, 'hill'. The first part of the name is of uncertain meaning. It may represent a personal name. DB *Santesdune*, 1196 *Santredon*.

Savernake Forest (wooded region, Wilts): 'district of (the river) Severn'. The river name, now familiar from the Severn (see SEVERN STOKE), was perhaps originally that of the river Bedwyn here (see BEDWYN). The '-ake' of the name represents a Celtic element meaning 'district', seen also as the *-acum* of *Eboracum*, the Roman name of YORK. 934 *Safernoc*.

Sawbridgeworth (town, Herts): 'Sæbeorht's enclosure'. OE *worth*, 'enclosure'. The second part of the personal name has been rationalized into a coincidentally appropriate *bridge*. (Sawbridgeworth is on the river Stort.) DB *Sabrixteworde*, 1868 *Sawbridgeworth, or Sabsworth*.

Sawdon (hamlet, N Yorks): 'valley where willow trees grow'. OE *salh*, 'sallow', 'willow', + *denu*, 'valley'. early 13C *Saldene*.

Sawley (district of Long Eaton, Derbys): 'hill where willow trees grow'. OE *salh*, 'sallow', 'willow', + *hlāw*, 'mound', 'hill'. The 'hill' is the slight rise on which the church stands by the river Trent. The DB form of the name below is corrupt, with *e* for *o*. DB *Salle*, 1166 *Sallawa*.

Sawley (village, Lancs): 'woodland clearing where willow trees grow'. OE *salh*, 'sallow', 'willow', + *lēah*, 'wood', 'clearing'. The DB form of the name below is corrupt. DB *Sotleie*, 1147 *Sallaia*.

Sawley (village, N Yorks): 'woodland clearing where willow trees grow'. OE *salh*, 'sallow', 'willow', + *lēah*, 'wood', 'clearing'. c.1030 *Sallege*.

Sawston (village, Cambs): 'farmstead of Salse's people'. OE *-inga-*, 'of the people of', + *tūn*, 'farmstead'. The original *-inga-* has disappeared from the name. 970 *Salsingetune*, DB *Salsiton*.

Sawtry (village, Cambs): '(place by the) salty stream'. OE *salt*, 'salt', + *rīth*, 'stream'. The reference is to the brackish taste of the water in the stream here, which flows to the fens. 974 *Saltreiam*, DB *Saltrede*.

Saxby (village, Leics): 'farmstead of the Saxons'. OE *Seaxe*, 'Saxons', + OS *bý*, 'farmstead'. The name could also mean 'Saksi's farmstead', with a Scandinavian personal name. DB *Saxebi*. SO ALSO: *Saxby*, Lincs.

Saxby All Saints (village, N Lincs): 'Saksi's farmstead with All Saints church'. The personal name is Scandinavian. The first part of the first word of the name could also represent OS *Saksar*, 'Saxons'. The second part of the name refers to the dedication of the church, which distinguishes this Saxby from *Saxby*, Lincs, 20 miles to the south. DB *Saxebi*.

Saxelbye (hamlet, Leics): 'Saksulfr's farmstead'. OS *bý*, 'farmstead', 'village'. The personal name is Scandinavian. The name was formerly regularly spelt *Saxelby*. The present final *e*, as in the DB form below, was presumably added to avoid confusion with SAXBY, 8 miles to the east. DB *Saxelbie*.

Saxilby (village, Lincs): 'Saksulfr's farmstead'. OS *bý*, 'farmstead', 'village'. The personal name (garbled in the DB form below) is Scandinavian. DB *Saxebi*, c.1115 *Saxlabi*.

Saxlingham (village, Norfolk): 'homestead of Seaxel's or Seaxhelm's people'. OE *-inga-*, 'of the people of', + *hām*, 'homestead'. DB *Saxelingaham*.

Saxlingham Nethergate (village, Norfolk): 'homestead of Seaxel's or Seaxhelm's people with a lower street'. OE *-inga-*, 'of the people of', + *hām*, 'homestead'. The second word of the name, perhaps relating to the road running beside the river Tas to Norwich, 7 miles to the north, distinguishes the village from nearby *Saxlingham Thorpe* (OS *thorp*, 'outlying farmstead') and *Saxlingham Green*, with a village green. All three are 30 miles south of SAXLINGHAM. 1046 *Seaxlingaham*, DB *Saiselingaham*.

Saxmundham (town, Suffolk): 'Seaxmund's homestead'. OE *hām*, 'homestead'. The personal name is unique to this town. DB *Sasmundeham*.

Saxondale (hamlet, Notts): '(place in the) valley of the Saxons'. OE *Seaxe*, 'Saxons', + *dæl*, 'valley'. The second part of the name was originally OE *denu*, 'valley'. DB *Saxeden*, c.1130 *Saxendala*.

Saxtead (village, Suffolk): 'Seaxa's place'. OE *stede*, 'place'. The name also gave those of the nearby villages of *Saxtead Green* and *Saxtead Little Green*. DB *Saxteda*.

Saxthorpe (village, Norfolk): 'Saksi's outlying farmstead'. OS *thorp*, 'outlying farmstead'. The personal name is Scandinavian. DB *Saxthorp*.

Saxton (village, N Yorks): 'farmstead of the Saxons'. OE *Seaxe*, 'Saxons', + *tūn*, 'farmstead'. The name could also mean 'Saksi's farmstead', with a Scandinavian personal name. DB *Saxtun*.

Scackleton (village, N Yorks): '(place in the) valley by a point of land'. OE *scacol*, 'point of land' (related modern English *shackle*), + *denu*, 'valley'. The 'point of land' is presumably the small steep hill on which the village lies. Scandinavian influence has given 'Sca-' instead of expected 'Sha-'. DB *Scacheldene*.

Scafell Pike (mountain, Cumbria): 'hill with a summer pasture'. OS *skáli*, 'temporary hut', 'shieling', + *fjall*, 'rough hill'. 'Pike' means 'peak'. 1578 *Scallfeild*.

Scaftworth (village, Notts): 'Sceafta's or Skapti's enclosure'. OE *worth*, 'enclosure'. The personal names are respectively OE and Scandinavian. The name could also mean 'enclosure made with poles' (OE *sceaft*, 'shaft', 'pole', + *worth*), with 'Sc-' (rather than expected 'Sh-') as a result of Scandinavian influence. DB *Scafteorde*.

Scagglethorpe (village, N Yorks): 'Skakull's or Skakli's outlying farmstead'. OS *thorp*, 'outlying farmstead'. The personal names are Scandinavian. DB *Scachetorp*.

Scalby (town, N Yorks): 'Skalli's farmstead'. OS *bý*, 'farmstead'. The personal name is Scandinavian. DB *Scallebi*. SO ALSO: *Scalby*, E Yorks.

Scaldwell (village, Northants): '(place by the) shallow spring'. OE *scald*, 'shallow', + *wella*, 'spring', 'stream'. The 'Sc-' of the name (instead of the expected 'Sh-') is due to Scandinavian influence. DB *Scaldewelle*.

Scaleby (village, Cumbria): 'farmstead by the huts'. OS *skáli*, 'shed', 'shieling', + *bý*, 'farmstead', 'village'. c.1235 *Schaleby*.

Scales (village, Cumbria): 'huts'. OS *skáli*, '(temporary) hut', 'shed'. The form of the name below relates to Scales near Dalton-in-Furness, but Scales near Keswick has a name of identical origin. 1269 *Scales*. SO ALSO: *Scales*, Lancs (now often *Newton with Scales*).

Scalford (village, Leics): '(place by the) shallow ford'. OE *scald*, 'shallow', + *ford*, 'ford'. Scandinavian influence has given this form of the name (with 'Sca-') rather than as for SHALFORD. DB *Scaldeford*.

Scalloway (coastal town, Shetland): 'bay by the summer pastures'. OS *skáli*, 'shed', 'shieling', + *vágr*, 'bay', 'creek'. The shielings would have been set up by shepherds in the summer months.

Scamblesby (village, Lincs): 'Skammel's farmstead'. OS *bý*, 'farmstead', 'village'. The personal name is Scandinavian. DB *Scamelesbi*.

Scampston (village, N Yorks): 'Skammr's or Skammel's farmstead'. OE *tūn*, 'farmstead'. The personal names are Scandinavian. DB *Scameston*.

Scampton (village, Lincs): 'Skammi's farmstead'. OE *tūn*, 'farmstead'. The personal name is Scandinavian. The name could also mean 'short farmstead' (OS *skammr*, 'short', + OE *tūn*). DB *Scantone*.

Scapa Flow (sea area, Orkney): 'sea bay of the boat isthmus'. OS *skalpr*, 'boat', + *eith*, 'isthmus', + *flóa*, 'flood' (related modern English *flow*). The 'isthmus' is the stretch of land south of Kirkwall on the eastern side of Scapa Bay. 1579 *Scalpay*.

Scarborough (resort town and port, N Yorks): 'Skarthi's stronghold'. OE *burh*, 'fortified place'. Scarborough is said to have been founded in c.996 by a Norseman called Thorgils Skarthi. (The second word is a nickname, 'Harelip'.) The account of this must have been widely known, as it is quoted (in the summary of a story by 'Mayster Edmund') in Robert Mannyng of Brunne's *The Story of Inglande* (completed 1338): 'When Engle had the londe al thorow, / He gaf to Scardyng Scardeburghe – / Toward the northe, by the see side, / An hauene hit is, schipes to ryde.' ('When the Angle had all the land, he gave Skarthi Scarborough, towards the north, by the seaside. It is a harbour where ships can ride at anchor'.) The name of Scarborough appears in Scandinavian sagas as *Skarthaborg* and *Skarthabork*. The first part of the name could also represent OS *skarth*, 'gap', and the second part *berg*, 'hill', giving a sense 'hill by a gap'. This suits the topography, with the 'gap' being the valley through which the present A64 road approaches the town from the south. c.1160 *Escardeburg*.

Scarcliffe (village, Derbys): '(place by the) cliff with a gap'. OE *sceard*, 'gap' (modern English *shard*), + *clif*, 'cliff'. The 'gap' is a valley that cuts into the limestone escarpment ('cliff') here. The spelling with 'Sc-' (instead of the expected 'Sh-') is due to Scandinavian influence. DB *Scardeclif*.

Scarcroft (district, Leeds): 'enclosure in a gap'. OE *sceard*, 'cleft', 'gap' (modern English *shard*), + *croft*, 'enclosure'. The precise nature of the gap is uncertain. OE *sceard* has been influenced by OS *sk-*. 1166 *Scardecroft*.

Scargill (hamlet, Durham): '(place by the) ravine where mergansers are seen'. OS *skraki*, 'merganser', + *gil*, 'ravine'. OS *skraki* could also refer to some other seabird. DB *Scracreghil*.

Scarisbrick (village, Lancs): '(place on the) hillside by a ditch'. OS *skor*, 'ditch', 'ravine', + *brekka*, 'slope' (related modern English *brink*). The name may relate to the slight rise between two streams near which Scarisbrick Hall stands. *c.*1200 *Scharisbrec*.

Scarning (village, Norfolk): 'dirty place'. OE *scearn*, 'dung', 'muck', + *-ing*, 'place characterized by'. Scandinavian influence has given the 'Sc-' of the name, instead of the expected 'Sh-'. DB *Scerninga*.

Scarrington (village, Notts): 'dirty farmstead'. OE *scearnig*, 'mucky', + *tūn*, 'farmstead'. The first part of the name could also represent OE *scearning*, 'dirty place' (cp. SCARNING). Either way, the 'Sc-', rather than 'Sh-', has resulted from Scandinavian influence. DB *Scarintone*.

Scartho (district of Grimsby, NE Lincs): '(place on the) mound by a gap'. OS *skarth*, 'gap', + *haugr*, 'mound'. The name could also mean '(place by the) mound where cormorants are seen' (OS *skarfr*, 'cormorant', + *haugr*). Scartho is near the North Sea coast. DB *Scarhou*.

Scawby (village, N Lincs): 'Skalli's farmstead'. OS *bý*, 'farmstead', 'village'. The personal name is Scandinavian. DB *Scallebi*.

Scawton (hamlet, N Yorks): 'farmstead in a hollow'. OS *skál*, 'hollow' (modern English *scale*, 'pan of a balance'), + OE *tūn*, 'farmstead'. The village lies in a steep-sided valley. DB *Scaltun*.

Scholar Green (hamlet, Cheshire): 'corner of land with a hut'. OS *skáli*, 'hut', 'shieling', + OE *halh*, 'nook', 'corner of land'. The place was later associated with its green. Late 13C *Scholehalc*, 1668 *Schollers Greene*.

Scholes (village, Kirklees): 'huts'. OS *skáli*, '(temporary) hut', 'shed'. This is Scholes near Holmfirth, but Scholes near Cleckheaton has a name of identical origin. 1284 *Scholes*.

Scilly Isles (island group, Scilly): meaning uncertain. The name is pre-English and first recorded as *Silumnus* in the 1C AD. It has been suggested that an earlier Roman name may have been *Silina*, going back to the Celtic pagan goddess Sulis, who gave *Aquae Sulis* as the Roman name of BATH, and that some Romano-British remains on the islands may have been a shrine to her. The *c* of the name was added in the 16C or 17C, either to avoid an undesirable association with modern English *silly* or, according to another theory, on an analogy with *Sicily*, an island that lies off the 'toe' of Italy just as Scilly lies off the 'toe' of England (Penwith, Cornwall). 1176 *Sully*, 1460 *Sylly*.

Scole (village, Norfolk): 'temporary sheds'. OS *skáli*, 'temporary shed', 'hut' (related modern English *shieling*). The sheds would have been used by shepherds here in the summer months. 1191 *Escales*.

Scone Palace (mansion, Perth & Kin): 'mass of rock'. Gaelic *sgonn*, 'lump', 'mass'. The 'mass of rock' is the Moot Hill here, the traditional ritual site of Scottish kings and at one time the site of the coronation Stone of Scone. 1020 *Sgoinde*.

Scopwick (village, Lincs): 'sheep farm'. OE *scēap*, 'sheep', + *wīc*, 'special farm'. The 'Sc-' of the name is due to Scandinavian influence. Cp. SHAPWICK. DB *Scapeuic*.

Scorborough (village, E Yorks): 'booth in a wood'. OS *skógr*, 'wood', + *búth*, 'booth', 'shelter'. The second part of the name was replaced by OE *burh*, 'fortified place', when a castle was built here. DB *Scogerbud*, 13C *Scorburgh*.

Scorrier (village, Cornwall): '(place with) mining waste'. Latin *scoria*, 'dross'. 1330 *Scoria*.

Scorton (village, N Yorks): 'farmstead by a ditch'. OS *skor*, 'ditch', 'ravine', + OE *tūn*, 'farmstead'. The 'ditch' is presumably Scorton Beck here. DB *Scortone*. SO ALSO: *Scorton*, Lancs.

Sco Ruston. See EAST RUSTON.

Scotby (suburb of Carlisle, Cumbria): 'farmstead of the Scots'. OS *Skoti*, 'Scot', + *bý*, 'farmstead', 'village'. 1130 *Scoteby*.

Scotch Corner (road junction, N Yorks). The junction on the Great North Road (now the A1) is so called because the main road (now the A66) to southwest Scotland via Carlisle branches off here. 1860 *Scotch Corner*.

Scotforth (district of Lancaster, Lancs): '(place at the) ford used by the Scots'. OE *Scot*, 'Scot', + *ford*, 'ford'. The place is probably so called as it stood on the route used by cattle drovers from

Galloway. Cp. GALGATE. The 'Sc-' of the name is due to Scandinavian influence. DB *Scozforde*.

Scotland (country, N Britain): 'land of the Scots'. The original 'Scots' were the Celtic raiders from northern Ireland who came to settle in *Caledonia* (see CALEDONIAN CANAL) in the 5C and 6C. *Scotia* became the name of the whole country in the 9C. The meaning of the people's name is uncertain.

Scotter (village, Lincs): '(place by the) tree of the Scots'. OE *Scot*, 'Scot', + *trēow*, 'tree'. The 'Sc-' of the name is the result of Scandinavian influence. DB *Scotere*.

Scotton (village, N Yorks): 'farmstead of the Scots'. OE *Scot*, 'Scot', + *tūn*, 'farmstead'. This is Scotton near Catterick, but Scotton near Knaresborough has a name of identical origin. DB *Scottune*. SO ALSO: *Scotton*, Lincs.

Scottow (hamlet, Norfolk): '(place by the) hill spur of the Scots'. OE *Scot*, 'Scot', + *hōh*, 'hill spur'. The 'Sc-' of the name is due to Scandinavian influence. 1044 *Scoteho*, DB *Scotohou*.

Scott Willoughby. See SILK WILLOUGHBY.

Scoulton (village, Norfolk): 'Skúli's farmstead'. OE *tūn*, 'farmstead'. The personal name is Scandinavian. DB *Sculetuna*.

Scrabster (village and port, Highland): 'rocky homestead'. OS *skjære*, 'rocky', + *bólstathr*, 'homestead'. 1201 *Skarabolstad*.

Scrainwood (hamlet, Northd): 'wood where shrewmice are seen'. OE *scrēawa*, 'shrewmouse', + *wudu*, 'wood'. The same OE words could also mean 'wood associated with villains'. The first half of the name represents OE *scrēawena*, the genitive plural form of *scrēawa*. 'Scr-' rather than expected 'Shr-' is due to Scandinavian influence. 1242 *Scravenwod*.

Scraptoft (village, Leicester): 'Skrápi's homestead'. OS *toft*, 'homestead'. The personal name is Scandinavian. The DB form of the name below is corrupt. 1043 *Scraptoft*, DB *Scrapentot*.

Scratby (resort village, Norfolk): 'Skrauti's farmstead'. OS *bý*, 'farmstead', 'village'. The personal name is Scandinavian. *c.*1020 *Scroutebi*, DB *Scroteby*.

Scrayingham (village, N Yorks): 'homestead of Scīrhēah's people'. OE *-inga-*, 'of the people of', + *hām*, 'homestead'. The name could also mean 'homestead with a structure of poles' (OE *scræging*, 'structure made of poles', 'slanting', + *hām*). DB *Escraingham*.

Scremerston (village, Northd): 'Skermer's estate'. OE *tūn*, 'farmstead', 'estate'. The Skermer family held the manor here in the 12C. 1196 *Schermereton*.

Scriven (village, N Yorks): 'hollow place with pits'. OE *screfen* (from *scræf*, 'hole', 'pit'). There are old quarries and gravel pits near the village. DB *Scrauinge*.

Scrooby (village, Notts): 'Skropi's farmstead'. OS *bý*, 'farmstead', 'village'. The personal name is Scandinavian. DB *Scrobi*.

Scruton (village, N Yorks): 'Skurfa's farmstead'. OE *tūn*, 'farmstead'. The personal name is Scandinavian. DB *Scurvetone*.

Sculthorpe (village, Norfolk): 'Skúli's outlying farmstead'. OS *thorp*, 'outlying farmstead'. The personal name is Scandinavian. DB *Sculatorpa*.

Scunthorpe (town, N Lincs): 'Skúma's outlying farmstead'. OS *thorp*, 'outlying farmstead', 'secondary settlement'. The personal name is Scandinavian. Scunthorpe was probably secondary with regard to Frodingham, in whose parish it was originally located. The town is recent, and developed following the discovery of iron ore locally in 1859. The DB form of the name below was the Norman scribe's way of making the name pronounceable. DB *Escumetorp*.

Seaborough (hamlet, Dorset): 'seven hills'. OE *seofon*, 'seven', + *beorg*, 'hill', 'barrow'. DB *Seveberge*.

Seacombe (district of Wallasey, Wirral): '(place in the) valley by the sea'. OE *sǣ*, 'sea', + *cumb*, 'valley'. The valley in question was probably the 'dale' at nearby Oakdale. *c.*1277 *Secumbe*.

Seacroft (district, Leeds): 'enclosure by a pool'. OE *sǣ*, 'sea', 'pool', + *croft*, 'enclosure'. There is no pool here now. DB *Sacroft*.

Seaford (resort town, E Sussex): '(place at the) ford by the sea'. OE *sǣ*, 'sea', + *ford*, 'ford'. The ford in question would have been near the mouth of the Ouse here before its course was diverted by great storms in the 16C to enter the sea at NEWHAVEN, 3 miles to the northwest. 12C *Saforde*.

Seaforth (district of Crosby, Sefton). The name came from *Seaforth House*, the Litherland home of the Scottish merchant Sir John Gladstone (1764–1851), father of prime minister W. E. Gladstone, who so named it on moving there in 1813 with his second wife, Anne Robertson, a member of the Mackenzie clan whose chief was Francis Mackenzie Humberston, Baron Seaforth and Mackenzie (1754–1815).

Seagrave (village, Leics): '(place by the) grove near a pit'. OE *sēath*, 'pit', 'pool', + *grāf*, 'grove'. The first part of the name could also represent OE *set*, 'fold' (for animals). DB *Setgraue*.

Seaham (town and port, Durham): 'homestead by the sea'. OE *sǣ*, 'sea', + *hām*, 'homestead', 'village'. *c*.1050 *Sǣham*.

Seahouses (village resort and port, Northd): 'houses by the sea'. The village is a 19C development with a harbour opened in 1889. 1897 *Sea Houses*.

Seal (village, Kent): 'dwelling'. OE *sele*, 'dwelling', 'house', 'hall'. The name could also mean 'willow-tree copse' (OE *sele*, 'willow copse', related modern English *sallow*). DB *La Sela*.

Seale (village, Surrey): 'dwelling'. OE *sele*, 'dwelling', 'house', 'hall'. The name could also mean 'willow-tree copse' (OE *sele*, 'willow copse', related modern English *sallow*). 1210 *Sela*.

Seamer (village, N Yorks): '(place by the) pool'. OE *sǣ*, 'lake', + *mere*, 'pool'. The pool in question was probably located on the piece of land to the southwest of the village called *The Mere*, where a number of drains run in different directions. The second part of the name was added when the meaning of the first was forgotten. The form of the name below relates to Seamer near Scarborough, but Seamer near Stokesley has a name of identical origin. DB *Semœr*.

Sea Palling (resort village, Norfolk): '(settlement of) Pælli's people by the sea'. OE *-ingas*, 'people of'. The first word of the name, added relatively recently, refers to the coastal location of the village. DB *Pallinga*, 1868 *Palling-near-the-Sea*, 1897 *Palling-next-the-Sea*.

Searby (village, Lincs): 'Sæfari's farmstead'. OS *bý*, 'farmstead', 'village'. The personal name is Scandinavian. DB *Seurebi*.

Seasalter (suburb of Whitstable, Kent): '(place with) saltworks by the sea'. OE *sǣ*, 'sea', + *sealt-ærn*, 'saltworks' (from OE *sealt*, 'salt', + *ærn*, 'building'). DB *Seseltre*.

Seascale (resort town, Cumbria): 'sheds by the sea'. OS *sǽr*, 'sea', + *skáli*, 'hut', 'shieling'. The reference is to shepherds' temporary shelters used in the summer months here. *c*.1165 *Sescales*.

Seathwaite (hamlet, Cumbria): '(place in the) clearing where sedge grows'. OS *sef*, 'sedge', + *thveit*, 'clearing'. The name relates to Seathwaite near Borrowdale. 1292 *Seuethwayt*.

Seathwaite (hamlet, Cumbria): '(place in the) clearing by the lake'. OS *sǽr*, 'lake', + *thveit*, 'clearing'. The name relates to Seathwaite near Coniston, the lake in question being Seathwaite Tarn. 1592 *Seathwhot*.

Seatoller (hamlet, Cumbria): 'summer pasture by the alder tree'. OS *sǽtr*, 'summer pasture', + OE *alor*, 'alder'. No early forms of the name are known, but this is the apparent meaning. 1563 *Settaller*.

Seaton (coastal village, Cornwall): '(place on the river) Seaton'. The river name is of Cornish origin but uncertain meaning. It has evolved to resemble an English name, partly because the coastal village is in fact a 'sea town'. 1601 *Seythen*.

Seaton (resort town, Devon): 'village by the sea'. OE *sǣ*, 'sea', + *tūn*, 'farmstead', 'village'. 1238 *Seton*. SO ALSO: *Seaton*, Cumbria.

Seaton (village, Rutland): 'Sǣga's farmstead'. OE *tūn*, 'farmstead'. DB *Segentone*.

Seaton Carew (suburb of Hartlepool): 'Carou's estate by the sea'. OE *sǣ*, 'sea', + *tūn*, 'farmstead', 'village'. The Carou family held the manor here in the 12C. late 12C *Setona*, 1345 *Seton Carrowe*.

Seaton Delaval (town, Northd): 'de la Val's estate by the sea'. OE *sǣ*, 'sea', + *tūn*, 'farmstead', 'village'. The de la Val family held the manor here, near the sea, in the 13C. 1270 *Seton de la Val*.

Seaton Ross (village, E Yorks): 'Ross's estate by the pool'. OE *sǣ*, 'pool', + *tūn*, 'farmstead', 'village'. The Ross family held the manor here from the 12C. There is no pool here now. DB *Seton*, 1618 *Seaton Rosse*.

Seaton Sluice (coastal village, Northd). A huge sluice was built here in the 18C across the mouth of the Seaton Burn by the Delaval family, of neighbouring SEATON DELAVAL. The aim was to dam the waters of the river before releasing them to flush out the silt of the harbour. The plan did not work, however, and instead in the 1760s a great cut was made through solid rock to reach the sea. This became the harbour, now abandoned, with large boulders blocking the entrance.

Seaview (resort village, IoW): '(resort with a) sea view'. The name originated with a 19C lodging house here that commanded wide views over the Solent. 1839 *Sea View*.

Seavington St Mary (village, Somerset): 'village of seven homesteads with St Mary's church'. OE *seofon*, 'seven', + *hām-tūn*, 'homestead' (from *hām*, 'homestead', + *tūn*, 'farmstead'). The church dedication distinguishes the village from nearby *Seavington St Michael*. *c*.1025 *Seofenempton*, DB *Sevenehantune*.

Sebergham (village, Cumbria): 'Sæburh's homestead'. OE *hām*, 'homestead'. The personal name is that of a woman. 1223 *Saburgham*.

Seckington (village, Warwicks): 'Secca's hill'. OE *dūn*, 'hill'. late 9C *Seccandun*, DB *Sechintone*.

Sedbergh (town, Cumbria): '(place on a) flat-topped hill'. OS *set-berg* (from *set*, 'seat', + *berg*, 'hill'). The hill in question is the one on which Sedbergh stands in the valley of the river Raw-ther. DB *Sedberge*.

Sedgeberrow (village, Worcs): 'Secg's grove'. OE *bearu*, 'grove'. 777 *Segcgesbearuue*, DB *Segges-barue*.

Sedgefield (village, Durham): 'Cedd's or Secg's open land'. OE *feld*, 'open land' (modern English *field*). The name is now also that of the local council district. *c*.1050 *Ceddesfeld*.

Sedgeford (village, Norfolk): '(place by) Secci's ford'. OE *ford*, 'ford'. The ford would have been over the small stream here. DB *Secesforda*.

Sedgehill (village, Wilts): 'Secga's hill'. OE *hyll*, 'hill'. The name could also mean 'hill where sedge grows' (OE *secg*, 'sedge', + *hyll*). early 12C *Seghulle*.

Sedgemoor (marshland region, Somerset): 'tract of land where sedge grows'. OE *secg*, 'sedge', + *mōr*, 'moor'. The name, now also that of the local council district, is descriptive of the region between Bridgwater and Street. 1263 *Seggemore*.

Sedgley (district, Dudley): 'Secg's woodland clearing'. OE *lēah*, 'wood', 'clearing'. The DB form of the name below has garbled the personal name. 985 *Secgesleage*, DB *Segleslei*.

Sedgwick (village, Cumbria): 'Sicg's dairy farm'. OE *wīc*, 'dwelling', 'specialized farm'. *c*.1185 *Sigghiswic*.

Sedlescombe (village, E Sussex): 'valley with a dwelling'. OE *sedl*, 'dwelling', 'house', + *cumb*, 'valley'. The DB form of the name below is corrupt. DB *Selescome*, *c*.1210 *Sedelescumbe*.

Seend (village, Wilts): 'sandy place'. OE *sende*, 'sandy place'. The village lies on a Lower Green-sand ridge. Cp. SANDY LANE. 1190 *Sinda*.

Seer Green (village, Bucks): 'dry place'. OE *sēar*, 'dry', 'barren' (modern English *sere*). Although originally dry, the settlement was fertile enough to have a village green. Cp. SARRATT. 1223 *La Sere*.

Seething (village, Norfolk): '(settlement of) Sīth's people'. OE *-ingas*, 'people of'. DB *Sithinges*.

Sefton (village, Sefton): 'farmstead where rushes grow'. OS *sef*, 'sedge', 'rush', + OE *tūn*, 'farmstead'. The village gave the name of the unitary authority. In the DB form of the name below, the scribe has copied *f* as *x*. DB *Sextone*, *c*.1220 *Sefftun*.

Segedunum. See WALLSEND.

Segelocum. See LITTLEBOROUGH (Notts).

Seghill (village, Northd): 'corner of land by the (river) Sege'. OE *halh*, 'nook', 'corner of land'. The stream here now called the Seaton Burn was earlier called *Sege*, an OE name meaning 'slow-moving'. 1198 *Syghall*.

Segontium. See CAERNARFON.

Seighford (village, Staffs): '(place at the) ford by an old fortification'. OE *ceaster*, 'Roman fort', + *ford*, 'ford'. The ford in question would have been over the river Sow here. DB *Cesteforde*.

Selattyn (village, Shropshire): 'settlement of the gullies'. OE *sulh*, 'plough', + *tūn*, 'farmstead', 'settlement'. OE *sulh* meant 'ploughland' as well as 'plough', and so in a transferred sense 'gully', referring to broken land. The first part of the name represents OE *sula*, the genitive plural of *sulh*. The formation of the name is similar to that of PRESTATYN, although the '-tt-' is peculiar to Selattyn. 1254 *Sulatun*.

Selborne (village, Hants): 'stream by (a copse of) willow trees'. OE *sealh*, 'willow', + *burna*, 'stream'. The name was originally that of Oakhanger Stream here, so that one tree name was replaced by another. 903 *Seleborne*, DB *Selesburne*.

Selby (town, N Yorks): 'village by (a copse of) willow trees'. OE *sele*, 'willow copse', or OS *selja*, 'sallow', 'willow', + OS *bý*, 'farmstead', 'village'. It seems likely that OS *bý* replaced earlier OE *tūn* in the same sense. Selby stands on the bank of the river Ouse, a favourable place for willows to grow. *c*.1030 *Seleby*, DB *Salebi*.

Selham (village, W Sussex): 'homestead by a willow copse'. OE *sele*, 'willow copse', + *hām*, 'homestead'. DB *Seleham*.

Selhurst (district, Croydon): 'willow tree wood'. OE *sealh*, 'willow', + *hyrst*, 'wooded hill'. There was a willow wood here to the 18C but little sign remains of it now. 1229 *Selherst*.

Selkirk (town, Borders): 'church by a hall'. OE *sele*, 'hall', + *cirice*, 'church'. Despite the '-kirk', early forms of the name show an entirely OE origin. *c.*1120 *Selechirche, c.*1190 *Seleschirche,* 1306 *Selkirk.*

Sellack (village, Herefords): '(church of) St Suluc'. The church here is dedicated to the 7C Welsh saint Tysilio. (*Suluc* is a pet form of *Suliau,* as is *Tysilio,* prefixed by the affectionate Welsh *ty,* 'thy'.) The form of the name below has OW *lann,* 'church'. *c.*1130 *Lann Suluc.*

Sellafield (hamlet, Cumbria): 'open land by the mound where willows grow'. OS *selja,* 'willow', + *haugr,* 'mound', + OE *feld,* 'open land' (modern English *field*). 1576 *Sellofeld.*

Sellindge (village, Kent): '(settlement of) those sharing a house'. OE *sedl,* 'house', 'building', + -*ingas,* 'dwellers at'. The name could also mean 'place by a house' (OE *sedl* + -*ing,* 'place characterized by'). DB *Sedlinges.*

Selly Oak (district, Birmingham): 'woodland clearing on a ledge with an oak'. OE *scelf,* 'shelf', 'ledge', + *lēah,* 'wood', 'clearing', + modern English *oak.* The former village is said to have had a prominent oak tree. DB *Escelie,* 1204 *Selvele.*

Selmeston (village, E Sussex): 'Sigehelm's farmstead'. OE *tūn,* 'farmstead'. DB *Sielmestone.*

Selsdon (district, Croydon): 'Sele's or Seli's hill'. OE *dūn,* 'hill'. *c.*880 *Selesdune.*

Selsey (resort town, W Sussex): 'seal island'. OE *seolh,* 'seal', + *ēg,* 'island'. The reference is to the peninsula here with beaches where seals were seen or stranded. The name was correctly interpreted by Bede in his *Ecclesiastical History of the English People* (completed 731): '*quod dicitur Latine insula vituli marini*' ('which is called in Latin the island of the sea calf', i.e. 'the seal'). Selsey was an island until as recently as the early 19C. The name gave that of the nearby headland *Selsey Bill,* the latter word meaning 'promontory' (OE *bile,* 'bill', 'beak'). *c.*715 *Seolesiae,* DB *Seleisie.*

Selston (village, Notts): 'Sele's or Seli's farmstead'. OE *tūn,* 'farmstead'. DB *Salestune.*

Selwood Forest. See ZEALS.

Selworthy (village, Somerset): 'enclosure by a willow copse'. OE *sele,* 'willow copse' (related modern English *sallow*), + *worthig,* 'enclosure'. DB *Seleuurde.*

Semington (village, Wilts): 'farmstead on the (river) Semnet'. OE *tūn,* 'farmstead'. The river name, formerly that of Semington Brook, is of pre-English origin and uncertain meaning. 13C *Semneton.*

Semley (village, Wilts): 'woodland clearing on the (river) Sem'. OE *lēah,* 'wood', 'clearing'. The river has a pre-English name of uncertain meaning. 955 *Semeleage.*

Sempringham (hamlet, Lincs): 'homestead of Sempa's people'. OE -*inga-,* 'of the people of', + *hām,* 'homestead'. All the early forms of the name lack the middle *r,* while the DB form below omits the *m* of the personal name. 852 *Sempingaham,* DB *Sepingeham,* 1150 *Sempringham.*

Send (village, Surrey): 'sandy place'. OE *sende,* 'sandy place'. Cp. SEEND. 960 *Sendan,* DB *Sande.*

Sennen (village, Cornwall): '(parish of) St Sennen'. The church here is dedicated to the female saint Sennen, about whom little is known. 1327 *Sancta Senana.*

Sessay (village, N Yorks): 'island where sedge grows'. OE *secg,* 'sedge', + *ēg,* 'island'. The 'island' is well-watered land here. DB *Sezai.*

Setchey (hamlet, Norfolk): 'Secci's landing place'. OE *hȳth,* 'landing place'. Setchey is on the river Nar. DB *Seche,* 13C *Sechithe,* 1868 *Setchey, or Setch.*

Settle (town, N Yorks): '(place by the) house'. OE *setl,* 'house', 'dwelling place' (related modern English *seat*). DB *Setel.*

Settrington (village, N Yorks): 'estate associated with Sætere'. OE -*ing-,* 'associated with', + *tūn,* 'farmstead', 'estate'. The first part of the name could also represent OE *sætere,* 'robber', giving a sense 'estate associated with a robber'. The DB form of the name below is corrupt. DB *Sendriton, c.*1090 *Seteringetune.*

Sevenhampton (village, Glos): '(village of) seven homesteads'. OE *seofon,* 'seven', + *hāmtūn,* 'homestead' (from *hām,* 'homestead', + *tūn,* 'farmstead'). A village of this size would bear a special tax burden. DB *Sevenhamtone.* SO ALSO: *Sevenhampton,* Swindon.

Seven Kings (district, Redbridge): '(settlement of) Seofeca's people'. OE -*ingas,* 'people of'. The original name was gradually corrupted, giving rise to a legend that seven Saxon kings met here. 1285 *Sevekynnges.*

Sevenoaks (town, Kent): '(place by) seven oak trees'. OE *seofon,* 'seven', + *āc,* 'oak'. There may be a local legend behind the name, with seven more a 'mystic' number than a precise enumeration. Seven oaks from nearby Knole Park were actually planted in the east of the town in 1955. *c.*1100 *Seouenaca.*

Seven Sisters (cliff group, E Sussex): 'seven cliffs'. The name is that of a stretch of seven chalk cliffs, individually named, to the west of Beachy Head. The name is an old phrase for seven linked females or objects, as in classical mythology for the seven daughters of Atlas and Pleione. 1588 *the Seven Cliffes*.

Seven Sisters (village, Neath PT). The name was originally that of a colliery here, begun in 1872 and named after the seven daughters of the pit owner, David Bevan: Nancy Isabella (then 23), Mary Diana (21), Sarah Jane (20), Margreta (17), Frances Matilda (14), Maria Louisa (10) and Sophia Annie (10).

Severn Stoke (village, Worcs): 'outlying farmstead on the (river) Severn'. OE *stoc*, 'outlying farmstead', 'secondary settlement'. The river name, distinguishing this Stoke from others, is of uncertain meaning. It is pre-English and possibly even pre-Celtic. The Severn was known to the Romans as *Sabrina*. Its Welsh name is *Hafren* (cp. LAKE VYRNWY), which is essentially the same name. 972 *Stoc*, DB *Stoche*, 1212 *Savernestok*.

Sewerby (village, E Yorks): 'Sigvarthr's farmstead'. OS *bý*, 'farmstead', 'village'. The personal name is Scandinavian. DB *Siuuardbi*.

Seworgan (hamlet, Cornwall): 'Goedhgen's ford'. Cornish *rys*, 'ford'. 1302 *Reswoethgen*.

Sewstern (village, Leics): 'Sǣwīg's thorn bush'. OE *thyrne*, 'thorn bush'. DB *Sewesten*.

Sezincote (hamlet, Glos): 'gravelly cottages'. OE *cisen*, 'gravelly', + *cot*, 'cottage'. DB *Chiesnecote*.

Shabbington (village, Bucks): 'estate associated with Scobba'. OE *-ing-*, 'associated with', + *tūn*, 'farmstead', 'estate'. DB *Sobintone*.

Shackerstone (village, Leics): 'farmstead of the robber'. OE *scēacere*, 'robber', + *tūn*, 'farmstead'. DB *Sacrestone*.

Shadforth (village, Durham): '(place by the) shallow ford'. OE *sceald*, 'shallow', + *ford*, 'ford'. The ford would have been over the Shadforth Beck here, a tributary of the Wear. 1183 *Shaldeford*.

Shadingfield (village, Suffolk): 'open land by the boundary valley'. OE *scēad*, 'boundary', + *denu*, 'valley', + *feld*, 'open land' (modern English *field*). Shadingfield is near Hundred River, which marked the boundary of the hundred of Wangford. DB *Scadenafella*.

Shadoxhurst (village, Kent): '(place by the) wooded hill'. OE *hyrst*, 'wooded hill'. The first part of the name is of uncertain origin. It may represent a personal or family name. 1239 *Schettokesherst*.

Shadwell (district, Tower Hamlets): '(place by the) shallow spring'. OE *sceald*, 'shallow', + *wella*, 'spring', 'stream'. 1222 *Schadewelle*.

Shaftesbury (town, Dorset): 'Sceaft's fortified place'. OE *burh*, 'fortified place'. The first part of the name could also represent OE *sceaft*, 'shaft', referring to the steep (shaft-shaped) hill on which Shaftesbury stands. The alternative name *Shaston* below may have resulted from a shortening of the medieval Latin form *Shaftonia*, with *f* misread as *s*. 877 *Sceaftesburi*, DB *Sceftesberie*, 1868 *Shaftesbury, or Shaston*.

Shafton (village, Barnsley): 'farmstead made of poles'. OE *sceaft*, 'shaft', 'pole', + *tūn*, 'farmstead'. The name could also mean 'farmstead marked by a pole'. The DB form of the name below has *p* for *f*. DB *Sceptun*, c.1160 *Scaftona*.

Shalbourne (village, Wilts): '(place by the) shallow stream'. OE *sceald*, 'shallow', + *burna*, 'stream'. 955 *Scealdeburnan*, DB *Scaldeburne*.

Shaldon (resort town, Devon): '(place in the) shallow valley'. OE *sceald*, 'shallow', + *denu*, 'valley'. The meaning of the name is uncertain as early forms are lacking. 17C *Shaldon*.

Shalfleet (village, IoW): '(place by the) shallow creek'. OE *sceald*, 'shallow', + *flēot*, 'creek'. The name refers to the narrow creek, just north of the village, that flows into the stream called Caul Bourne. 838 *Scealdan fleote*, DB *Seldeflet*.

Shalford (village, Essex): '(place by the) shallow ford'. OE *sceald*, 'shallow', + *ford*, 'ford'. The river here is the Pant. DB *Scaldefort*.

Shalford (village, Surrey): '(place by the) shallow ford'. OE *sceald*, 'shallow', + *ford*, 'ford'. The ford in question would have been over the Tilling Bourne, just to the north of the village. DB *Scaldefor*.

Shalstone (village, Bucks): 'farmstead at the shallow place'. OE *sceald*, 'shallow (place)', + *tūn*, 'farmstead'. The name presumably denotes a shallow crossing of a stream here. DB *Celdestone*, 1868 *Shalstone, or Shaldestone*.

Shamley Green (village, Surrey): '(place by the) woodland clearing with ridges'. OE *sceamel*, 'ledge', 'bench', + *lēah*, 'wood', 'clearing'. The village was later characterized by its green. 1544 *Shambles*, 1548 *Shameleigh*.

Shangton (village, Leics): 'farmstead by a hill spur'. OE *scanca*, 'shank', 'hill spur', + *tūn*, 'farmstead'. The name could also mean 'Scanca's farmstead'. DB *Sanctone*.

Shanklin (resort town, IoW): 'bank by the cup'. OE *scenc*, 'cup', + *hlinc*, 'bank', 'ridge'. The 'cup' is the waterfall at Shanklin Chine, where the water was seen to fall as from a drinking cup. The 'bank' was probably a feature of the waterfall itself. DB *Sencliz*.

Shap (village, Cumbria): '(place by the) heap of stones'. OE *hēap*, 'heap'. The name refers to the remains of an ancient stone circle by the main road (now the A6) south of the town. *c.*1190 *Hep*.

Shapwick (village, Dorset): 'sheep farm'. OE *scēap*, 'sheep', + *wīc*, 'farm'. DB *Scapeuuic*. SO ALSO: *Shapwick*, Somerset.

Shardlow (village, Derbys): 'mound with a notch'. OE *sceard*, 'gap', 'notch' (modern English *shard*), + *hlāw*, 'mound'. Shardlow arose on a low gravel mound by the river Trent. DB *Serdelau*.

Shareshill (village, Staffs): 'Scearf's hill'. OE *hyll*, 'hill'. Early forms of the name have OE *scylf*, 'shelf' (i.e. shelving terrain) alternating with *hyll*, while the DB form below is corrupt. DB *Servesed*, 1213 *Sarueshull*, 1298 *Sarushulf*.

Sharlston (village, Wakefield): 'Scearf's farmstead'. OE *tūn*, 'farmstead'. *c.*1180 *Scharueston*.

Sharnford (village, Leics): '(place by the) dirty ford'. OE *scearn*, 'dung', 'muck', + *ford*, 'ford'. The river here is the Soar. 1002 *Scearnford*, DB *Scerneforde*.

Sharow (village, N Yorks): '(place by the) boundary hill spur'. OE *scearu*, 'boundary', + *hōh*, 'hill spur'. The hill in question is probably the one known as The Mount, by the main road to Thirsk (now the A61), which is near the historic border between the North Riding and West Riding of Yorkshire. *c.*1130 *Sharou*.

Sharperton (hamlet, Northd): 'farmstead by the steep hill'. OE *scearp*, 'sharp', 'steep', + *beorg*, 'hill', + *tūn*, 'farmstead'. The hill in question is Sharperton Edge here. 1242 *Scharberton*.

Sharpness (location of docks, Glos): 'Scobba's headland'. OE *næss*, 'headland'. Sharpness is on the Severn estuary. DB *Nesse*, 1368 *Schobbenasse*.

Sharrington (village, Norfolk): 'dirty farmstead'. OE *scearn*, 'dung', 'filth', 'mud', + *tūn*, 'farmstead'. The first part of the name represents OE *scearnan*, the dative form of *scearn*. DB *Scarnetuna*.

Shaugh Prior (village, Devon): 'prior's (estate by the) copse'. OE *sceaga*, 'wood', 'copse'. The manor here was held early by Plympton Priory. DB *Scage*.

Shavington (village, Cheshire): 'estate associated with Scēafa'. OE *-ing-*, 'associated with', + *tūn*, 'farmstead', 'estate'. The DB form of the name below is garbled. DB *Santune*, 1260 *Shawynton*.

Shaw (town, Oldham): '(place by the) small wood'. OE *sceaga*, 'copse'. 1555 *Shaghe*. SO ALSO: *Shaw*, Swindon, W Berks, Wilts.

Shawbury (village, Shropshire): 'manor house by a copse'. OE *sceaga*, 'wood', 'copse', + *burh*, 'fortified place', 'manor'. DB *Sawesberie*, *c.*1165 *Shawberia*.

Shawell (village, Leics): '(place by the) boundary spring'. OE *scēath*, 'boundary' (modern English *sheath*), + *wella*, 'spring', 'stream'. Shawell lies near Watling Street, which here forms the county boundary between Leicestershire and Warwickshire. DB *Sawelle*, 1224 *Schadewelle*.

Shearsby (village, Leics): 'Swæf's or Skeifr's farmstead'. OS *bý*, 'farmstead', 'village'. The personal names are respectively OE and Scandinavian. DB *Svevesbi*.

Shebbear (village, Devon): '(place by the) grove where poles are obtained'. OE *sceaft*, 'shaft', 'pole', + *bearu*, 'grove'. 1050 *Sceftbeara*, DB *Sepesberie*.

Sheen (village, Staffs): 'shelters'. OE *scēo*, 'shed', 'shelter' (related modern English *shieling*). The name represents OE *scēon*, the plural form of *scēo*. Sheen or *West Sheen* was the earlier name for RICHMOND UPON THAMES. 1002 *Sceon*, DB *Sceon*.

Sheepstor (village, Devon): 'craggy hill resembling a bolt'. OE *scytels*, 'bolt', 'bar', + *torr*, 'craggy hill', 'tor'. The first part of the name could equally represent OE *scitels*, 'dung'. 1168 *Sitelestorra*.

Sheepwash (village, Devon): 'place where sheep are dipped'. OE *scēap-wæsce* (from *scēap*, 'sheep', + *wæsc*, 'washing'). The river here is the Torridge. 1166 *Schepewast*.

Sheepy Magna (village, Leics): 'greater island where sheep graze'. OE *scēap*, 'sheep', + *ēg*, 'island', + Latin *magna*, 'great'. The 'island' is dry ground in marshland here by the river Sence. The second word of the name distinguishes the village from *Sheepy Parva* (Latin *parva*, 'small') across the river. DB *Scepehe*.

Sheering (village, Essex): '(settlement of) Scear's people'. OE *-ingas*, 'people of'. DB *Sceringa*.

Sheerness (resort town and port, Kent): '(place on the) bright headland'. OE *scīr*, 'bright', 'clear', + *næss*, 'headland'. A 'bright headland' is probably an open one, as here, overlooking the estuaries of both the Thames and Medway. The first part of the name could also represent OE *scear*, 'ploughshare', referring to the shape of the headland. 1203 *Scerhnesse*.

Sheet (village, Hants): '(place by the) corner of land'. OE *scīete*, 'angle of land'. The village lies in the angle of two streams. c.1210 *Syeta*.

Sheffield (city, Sheffield): 'open land by the (river) Sheaf'. OE *feld*, 'open land' (modern English *field*). The name of the river, which enters the Don here, means 'dividing one', 'boundary' (OE *scēath*, modern English *sheath*), as it marked the boundary between Derbyshire and the West Riding of Yorkshire. DB *Scafeld*.

Sheffield Green (hamlet, E Sussex): 'open land where sheep graze'. OE *scēap*, 'sheep', + *feld*, 'open land' (modern English *field*). Sheffield later became associated with its green. The DB form of the name below may have resulted from a mishearing. DB *Sifelle*, 1272 *Shipfeud*.

Shefford (town, Beds): '(place by the) ford for sheep'. OE *scēap*, 'sheep', + *ford*, 'ford'. A ford over the river Ivel here, where the Roman road crossed it (now the A600), would have been regularly used by sheep. 1220 *Sepford*.

Sheinton (village, Shropshire): 'estate associated with Scēna'. OE *-ing-*, 'associated with', + *tūn*, 'farmstead', 'estate'. DB *Schentune*, 1222 *Sheinton*.

Sheldon (district, Birmingham): '(place by the) hill with a ledge'. OE *scelf*, 'shelf', 'ledge', + *dūn*, 'hill'. There is a slight slope here. 1189 *Scheldon*.

Sheldon (village, Derbys): 'heathy hill with a ledge'. OE *scelf*, 'shelf', 'ledge', + *hǣth*, 'heath', + *dūn*, 'hill'. The village lies on the edge of a flat hill above a valley. DB *Scelhadun*.

Sheldon (village, Devon): '(place in the) valley with a shelf'. OE *scelf*, 'shelf', 'ledge', + *denu*, 'valley'. The name is descriptive of the steeply shelving hillside here. DB *Sildene*.

Sheldwich (village, Kent): 'farm with a shelter'. OE *sceld*, 'shelter', + *wīc*, 'dwelling', 'special farm'. 784 *Scilduuic*.

Shelf (hamlet, Calderdale): '(place on) level terrain'. OE *scelf*, 'shelf'. Shelf is located on an area of level ground in hilly country southwest of Bradford. DB *Scelf*.

Shelfanger (village, Norfolk): '(place by the) wood on sloping ground'. OE *scelf*, 'shelf', + *hangra*, 'wood on a slope'. DB *Sceluangra*.

Shelfield (district, Walsall): '(place on the) hill with a plateau'. OE *scelf*, 'shelf', + *hyll*, 'hill'. The second part of the DB form of the name below wrongly implies OE *feld*, 'open land' (modern English *field*), as does the present form. DB *Scelfeld*, 1271 *Schelfhul*. SO ALSO: *Shelfield*, Warwicks.

Shelford (village, Notts): '(place by the) ford at a shallow place'. OE *sceldu*, 'shallow place', + *ford*, 'ford'. The village is near the river Trent. DB *Scelforde*.

Shelley (hamlet, Essex): 'woodland clearing on shelving terrain'. OE *scelf*, 'shelf', + *lēah*, 'wood', 'clearing'. The DB form of the name below has an extraneous *n*. DB *Senleiam*, 1197 *Sellege*.

Shellingford (village, Oxon): '(place by the) ford of Scear's people'. OE *-inga-*, 'of the people of', + *ford*, 'ford'. The ford in question was probably over a tributary of the river Ock here. The *r* of the personal name has become *l* as for SALISBURY. 931 *Scaringaford*, DB *Serengeford*.

Shellow Bowells (village, Essex): 'de Bueles' (estate on the) winding river'. OE *sceolh*, 'twisted'. The river referred to is the Roding. The du Bueles family held the manor here in the 13C. DB *Scelga*, 1303 *Schuele Boueles*.

Shelsley Walsh (village, Worcs): 'le Waleys' (estate at) Sceld's woodland clearing'. OE *lēah*, 'wood', 'clearing'. The le Waleys family held the manor here in the early 13C, their name distinguishing the village from *Shelsley Beauchamp*, across the river Severn, where the manor was held by the Beauchamp family in the 12C. DB *Caldeslei*, 1275 *Seldesle Waleys*.

Shelton (village, Beds): 'farmstead on a shelf of ground'. OE *scelf*, 'shelf', + *tūn*, 'farmstead'. DB *Eseltone*. SO ALSO: *Shelton*, Norfolk, Notts, Shropshire.

Shelve (village, Shropshire): '(place on the) shelf'. OE *scelf*, 'shelf'. The village stands on a small area of level ground among hills. 1180 *Schelfe*.

Shelwick (hamlet, Herefords): 'dwelling with a shelter'. OE *sceld*, 'shelter', + *wīc*, 'dwelling', 'dairy farm'. DB *Scelwiche*.

Shenfield (district of Brentwood, Essex): '(place on) beautiful open land'. OE *scēne*, 'bright', 'beautiful' (modern English *sheen*), + *feld*, 'open land' (modern English *field*). DB *Scenefelda*.

Shenington (village, Oxon): (place by the) beautiful hill'. OE *scēne*, 'beautiful', + *dūn*, 'hill'. The '-ing-' of the name represents the ending of OE *scēnan*, the dative form of *scēne*. DB *Senendone*.

Shenley (village, Herts): '(place by the) bright glade'. OE *scēne*, 'bright', 'beautiful' (modern English *sheen*), + *lēah*, 'wood', 'clearing'. DB *Scenlai*.

Shenstone (village, Staffs): '(place by the) beautiful stone'. OE *scēne*, 'bright', 'beautiful' (modern English *sheen*), + *stān*, 'stone'. The DB form of the name below is corrupt. DB *Seneste*, 11C *Scenstan*.

Shenton (village, Leics): 'farmstead on the (river) Sence'. OE *tūn*, 'farmstead'. The river name represents OE *scenc*, 'drink', 'drinking cup', perhaps implying a good supply of drinking water. 1002 *Scenctun*, DB *Scentone*.

Shepherds Bush (district, Hammersmith & Ful): 'Shepherd's bush'. The name probably refers to an area of bushy land owned by a family named Shepherd, rather than a bush where shepherds sheltered. 1635 *Sheppards Bush Green*.

Shepherdswell (village, Kent): 'Swīthbeorht's woodland'. OE *wald*, 'woodland'. The present name was introduced in the 19C by the local railway company as a 'popular' form of modern *Sibertswold*, a name still found as an alternative in modern gazetteers and preserved in that of Sibertswold primary school. 940 *Swythbrihteswealde*, DB *Sibertswald*, 1610 *Sibertwood*, 1868 *Sibertswold, or Shepherdswell*, 2001 *Shepherdswell or Sibertswold*.

Shepley (village, Kirklees): '(place by the) clearing where sheep graze'. OE *scēap*, 'sheep', + *lēah*, 'wood', 'clearing'. DB *Scipelei*.

Shepperton (suburban district, Surrey): 'farmstead of the shepherds'. OE *scēap-hirde*, 'shepherd' (from *scēap*, 'sheep', + *hierde*, 'herdsman'), + *tūn*, 'farmstead'. Shepherds would have gathered or pastured their flocks at this location by the Thames. 959 *Scepertune*, DB *Scepertone*.

Sheppey (island, Kent): 'sheep island'. OE *scēap*, 'sheep', + *ēg*, 'island'. An island is a good place for pasturing sheep, with its natural boundaries. Sheppey is now often referred to as *Isle of Sheppey*, although the word for 'island' is already present in the original name. 696 *Scepeig*, DB *Scape*.

Shepreth (village, Cambs): '(place by the) sheep stream'. OE *scēap*, 'sheep', + *rīth*, 'stream'. A 'sheep stream' is one where sheep come to drink or where they are washed. DB *Esceprid*.

Shepshed (town, Leics): 'sheep headland'. OE *scēap*, 'sheep', + *hēafod*, 'headland'. The 'headland' must be the high ground on which Shepshed is located. A meaning 'sheep's head' is also possible, referring to a place where sheep were sacrificed and their heads impaled, although this sense is now generally disavowed. Cp. GATESHEAD. DB *Scepeshefde*.

Shepton Mallet (town, Somerset): 'Malet's sheep farm'. OE *scēap*, 'sheep', + *tūn*, 'farmstead'.

The Malet family held the manor here in the 12C, their name distinguishing this Shepton from *Shepton Beauchamp*, 22 miles to the southwest, where the manor was held in the 13C by the de Beauchamp family, and *Shepton Montague*, 9 miles to the southeast, where the tenant in 1086 was Drogo de Montacute. DB *Sepetone*, 1228 *Scheopton Malet*.

Shepway (council district, Kent): 'sheep way'. OE *scēap*, 'sheep', + *weg*, 'way', 'track'. The name is that of a former lathe (administrative division) here. A 'sheep way' is a track regularly followed by sheep. One such may have been the route now followed by the Roman road known as Stone Street, leading across the North Downs towards Canterbury.

Sheraton (hamlet, Durham): 'Skurfa's farmstead'. OE *tūn*, 'farmstead'. The personal name is Scandinavian. *c*.1040 *Scurufatun*.

Sherborne (town, Dorset): '(place by the) bright stream'. OE *scīr*, 'bright', 'clear', + *burna*, 'stream'. The name was probably that of the river here, now the Yeo. 864 *Scireburnan*, DB *Scireburne*. SO ALSO: *Sherborne*, Glos.

Sherborne St John (village, Hants): 'de Sancto Johanne's (estate by the) bright stream'. OE *scīr*, 'bright', + *burna*, 'stream'. The manor here was held in the 13C by Robert de Sancto Johanne, whose name distinguishes the village from *Monk Sherborne*, immediately to the west, where it was held by the priory. Sherborne St John has also been known as *East Sherborne*, and Monk Sherborne as *West Sherborne*. DB *Sireburne*, 1167 *Shireburna Johannis*.

Sherbourne (village, Warwicks): '(place by the) bright stream'. OE *scīr*, 'bright', 'clear', + *burna*, 'stream'. William Dugdale, in *The Antiquities of Warwickshire* (1656), describes Sherbourne as a place 'which had its name originally from the said brook *Scireburne*, in our old English signifying a clear running stream, for so is this'. DB *Scireburne*.

Sherburn (village, N Yorks): '(place by the) bright stream'. OE *scīr*, 'bright', 'clear', + *burna*, 'stream'. DB *Scireburne*. SO ALSO: *Sherburn*, Durham.

Sherburn in Elmet (village, N Yorks): '(place by the) bright stream in Elmet'. OE *scīr*, 'bright', 'clear', + *burna*, 'stream'. For the district name, see BARWICK IN ELMET. *c*.900 *Scirburnan*, DB *Scireburne*.

Shere (village, Surrey): '(place by the) bright (stream)'. OE *scīr*, 'bright', 'clear'. The 'bright stream' here is the Tilling Bourne, a tributary of the Wey. DB *Essira*.

Shereford (hamlet, Norfolk): '(place by the) bright ford'. OE *scīr*, 'clear', 'bright', + *ford*, 'ford'. Shereford is on the river Wensum. DB *Sciraford*, 1868 *Shereford, or Sheringford*.

Sherfield on Loddon (village, Hants): '(place by the) bright open land on the (river) Loddon'. OE *scīr*, 'bright', 'clear', + *feld*, 'open land' (modern English *field*). 'Bright open land' was probably land that was sparsely wooded. The addition of the river name, of Celtic origin and perhaps meaning 'muddy one', distinguishes this village from *Sherfield English*, 35 miles to the south-west, where the manor was held in 1325 by Richard le Engleys. 1167 *Sirefelda*, 1868 *Sherfield-upon-Loddon*.

Sherford (village, Devon): '(place by the) bright ford'. OE *scīr*, 'bright', 'clear', + *ford*, 'ford'. *c*.1050 *Scireford*, DB *Sirefort*.

Sheriffhales (village, Shropshire): 'sheriff's corners of land'. OE *scīr-rēfa*, 'sheriff' (from *scīr*, 'shire', + *rēfa*, 'reeve'), + *halh*, 'nook', 'corner of land'. In 1086 the manor here was held by Reginald of Balliol, Sheriff of Shropshire. DB *Halas*, 1301 *Shiruehales*.

Sheriff Hutton (village, N Yorks): 'sheriff's farmstead by a hill spur'. OE *hōh*, 'hill spur', + *tūn*, 'farmstead'. The manor here was held from the mid-12C by the Sheriff of York. DB *Hotone*, *c*.1200 *Shirefhoton*.

Sheriff's Lench. See ROUS LENCH.

Sheringham (resort town, Norfolk): 'homestead of Scīra's people'. OE *-inga-*, 'of the people of', + *hām*, 'homestead'. The DB form of the name below has *l* for *r*, but the *r* prevailed, unlike with SALISBURY. DB *Silingeham*, 1242 *Scheringham*.

Sherington (village, Milton K): 'estate associated with Scīra'. OE *-ing-*, 'associated with', + *tūn*, 'farmstead', 'estate'. DB *Serintone*.

Shernborne (hamlet, Norfolk): '(place by the) muddy stream'. OE *scearn*, 'dung', 'muck', + *burna*, 'stream'. DB *Scernebrune*.

Sherrington (village, Wilts): 'mucky farmstead'. OE *scearn*, 'dung', + *tūn*, 'farmstead'. 968 *Scearntune*, DB *Scarentone*.

Sherston (village, Wilts): '(place by the) stone on a steep slope'. OE *scora*, 'steep slope' (modern English *shore*), + *stān*, 'stone'. Sherston is near the county border with Gloucestershire and the stone may thus have been a boundary marker. 896 *Scorranstan*, DB *Sorestone*.

Sherwood Forest (wooded region, Notts): 'wood of the shire'. OE *scīr*, 'shire', + *wudu*, 'wood'. The wood was owned by the shire (county), either as a hunting ground or as common pastureland. In the latter case, pigs would have fed on the acorns of the oak trees here. The addition of 'forest' is strictly speaking superfluous. 955 *Scirwuda*.

Shetland (island group, N Scotland): 'Hjalti's land'. OS *land*, 'land'. The *l* of the Scandinavian personal name has disappeared, as it has in the alternative name *Zetland*, where the *Z*- represents the medieval letter known as yogh (used where modern English has *gh* or *y*) as a way of expressing the sound of *hj*. *c*.1100 *Haltland*, 1289 *Shetland*.

Shevington (suburb of Wigan): 'farmstead near Shevin'. OE *tūn*, 'farmstead'. *Shevin* is a hill name of Celtic origin meaning 'ridge' (related modern Welsh *cefn*). *c*.1225 *Shefinton*.

Sheviock (village, Cornwall): 'strawberry place'. Cornish *sevi*, 'strawberries', + adjectival ending *-ek*. DB *Savioch*.

Shide (district of Newport, IoW): '(place by the) plank bridge'. OE *scīd*, 'plank', 'footbridge'. The reference would be to an early bridge over the river Medina here. DB *Sida*.

Shifnal (town, Shropshire): '(place by) Scuffa's corner of land'. OE *halh*, 'nook', 'corner of land'. The 'corner of land' is the large shallow depression in which the town lies. The personal name is not recorded elsewhere. Shifnal was also long known as *Idsall*, 'Idi's corner of land', and the two names may have originally applied respectively to the districts lying east and west of the stream that runs through the town. 12C *Scuffanhalch*, 1733 *Idsal alias Shiffnall*, 1868 *Shiffnal*.

Shilbottle (village, Northd): 'dwelling of the people of Shipley'. OE *-inga-*, 'of the people of', + *botl*, 'building', 'dwelling'. The first part of the name represents that of *Shipley*, 7 miles to the north, with a name of identical origin to that of SHIPLEY. 1242 *Schipplingbothill*.

Shildon (town, Durham): '(place by the) hill with shelves'. OE *scylfe*, 'shelf', + *dūn*, 'hill'. Shildon is surrounded by hills. 1214 *Sciluedon*.

Shillingford (village, Oxon): '(place by the) ford of Sciella's people'. OE *-inga-*, 'of the people of', + *ford*, 'ford'. The river here is the Thames. 1156 *Sillingeforda*. SO ALSO: *Shillingford*, Devon.

Shillingstone (village, Dorset): 'Schelin's estate'. OE *tūn*, 'farmstead', 'estate'. The manor here was held in 1086 by one Schelin. The village was earlier the equivalent of *Okeford Shilling* (see CHILD OKEFORD). 1220 *Akeford Skelling*, 1444 *Shillyngeston*, 1868 *Shilling-Okeford, or Shillingstone*.

Shillington (village, Beds): 'hill of Scyttel's people'. OE *-inga-*, 'of the people of', + *dūn*, 'hill'.

The dropping of *t* in the personal name is relatively recent and doubtless introduced for reasons of propriety. 1060 *Scytlingedune*, DB *Sethlindone*, 1780 *Shilindon*, 1868 *Shitlington, or Shillingdon*.

Shilton (village, Warwicks): 'farmstead on a ledge'. OE *scylfe*, 'shelf', 'ledge', + *tūn*, 'farmstead'. Shilton stands on a wide expanse of level ground. DB *Scelftone*. SO ALSO: *Shilton*, Oxon.

Shimpling (hamlet, Suffolk): '(settlement of) Scimpel's people'. OE *-ingas*, 'people of'. DB *Simplinga*. SO ALSO: *Shimpling*, Norfolk.

Shincliffe (village, Durham): '(place by the) cliff haunted by a phantom'. OE *scinna*, 'spectre', + *clif*, 'cliff', 'bank'. *c.*1085 *Scinneclif*.

Shinfield (village, Wokingham): 'open land of Scīene's people'. OE *-inga-*, 'of the people of', + *feld*, 'open land' (modern English *field*). The DB form of the name below has *l* for *n* in the personal name. DB *Selingefelle*, 1167 *Schiningefeld*.

Shipbourne (village, Kent): '(place by the) stream where sheep are washed'. OE *scēap*, 'sheep', + *burna*, 'stream'. The first form of the name below has omitted the *p*. *c.*1100 *Sciburna*, 1198 *Scipburn*.

Shipdham (village, Norfolk): 'homestead with a flock of sheep'. OE *scīpde*, 'flock of sheep', + *hām*, 'homestead'. DB *Scipdham*.

Shiplake (village, Oxon): '(place on the) stream where sheep are washed'. OE *scēap*, 'sheep', + *lacu*, 'stream' (related modern English *lake*). The stream would have flowed into the Thames here. 1163 *Siplac*.

Shipley (town, Bradford): 'woodland clearing where sheep graze'. OE *scēap*, 'sheep', + *lēah*, 'wood', 'clearing'. DB *Scipeleia*. SO ALSO: *Shipley*, Northd, Shropshire, W Sussex.

Shipmeadow (village, Suffolk): 'meadow for sheep'. OE *scēap*, 'sheep', + *mǣd*, 'meadow'. The second part of the name represents OE *mǣdwe*, the dative form of *mǣd*. DB *Scipmedu*.

Shipston on Stour (town, Warwicks): 'farmstead by the sheepwash on the (river) Stour'. OE *scēap-wǣsc*, 'sheepwash' (from *scēap*, 'sheep', + *wǣsc*, 'washing'), + *tūn*, 'farmstead'. There would have been a sheepdip on the Stour here. For the river name, see STOURBRIDGE. *c.*770 *Scepuuæisctune*, DB *Scepwestun*.

Shipton (village, N Yorks): 'farmstead where rose hips grow'. OE *hēope*, 'hip', + *tūn*, 'farmstead'. DB *Hipton*.

Shipton Gorge (village, Dorset): 'de Gorges' (estate at the) sheep farm'. OE *scēap*, 'sheep', + *tūn*, 'farmstead'. The de Gorges family held the manor here in the 13C. DB *Sepetone*, 1594 *Shipton Gorges*.

Shipton Moyne (village, Glos): 'Moygne's (estate at the) sheep farm'. OE *scēap*, 'sheep', + *tūn*, 'farmstead'. The Moygne family held the manor here in the 13C. DB *Sciptone*, 1287 *Schipton Moine*.

Shipton-on-Cherwell. See SHIPTON UNDER WYCHWOOD.

Shipton under Wychwood (village, Oxon): 'sheep farm near (the forest of) Wychwood'. OE *scēap*, 'sheep', + *tūn*, 'farmstead'. The name of *Wychwood* Forest, distinguishing this Shipton from *Shipton-on-Cherwell*, 13 miles to the east on the river Cherwell (see CHARWELTON), means 'wood of the Hwicce', referring to an Anglo-Saxon people who occupied a region approximating to present Gloucestershire, Worcestershire and western Warwickshire. Wychwood Forest would have been at the eastern edge of their territory. DB *Sciptone*.

Shirburn (village, Oxon): '(place by the) bright stream'. OE *scīr*, 'clear', 'bright', + *burna*, 'stream'. DB *Scireburne*.

Shirebrook (town, Derbys): '(place by the) boundary brook'. OE *scīr*, 'shire', + *brōc*, 'brook'. The stream marks the county boundary between Nottinghamshire and Derbyshire. The first part of the name could also represent OE *scīr*, 'bright', giving a sense 'bright brook', 'clear stream'. But the former meaning is more likely. 1202 *Scirebroc*.

Shirehampton (district, Bristol): 'dirty home farm'. OE *scearnig*, 'dirty', + *hām-tūn*, 'home farm' (from *hām*, 'homestead', + *tūn*, 'farmstead'). *c.*855 *Scearamtone*.

Shireoaks (village, Notts): '(place by the) oak trees on the county boundary'. OE *scīr*, 'county', 'shire', + *āc*, 'oak'. Shireoaks is close to the historic county boundary with Yorkshire. 12C *Shirakes*.

Shirland (village, Derbys): '(place by the) bright grove'. OE *scīr*, 'bright' (modern English *sheer*), + OS *lundr*, 'grove'. A 'bright' grove is a sparsely wooded one. DB *Sirelunt*.

Shirley (district, Croydon): 'bright woodland clearing'. OE *scīr*, 'bright', + *lēah*, 'wood', 'clearing'. The first part of the name could also represent OE *scīr*, 'shire', referring to the location of the place near the historic county boundary between Surrey and Kent. 1314 *Shirleye*. SO ALSO: *Shirley*, Derbys, Hants, Solihull.

Shirwell (village, Devon): '(place by the) bright spring'. OE *scīr*, 'bright', 'clear', + *wella*, 'spring', 'stream'. DB *Sirewelle*.

Shobdon (village, Herefords): 'Sceobba's hill'. OE *dūn*, 'hill'. The DB form of the name below has *p* for *b* in the personal name. DB *Scepedune*, 1242 *Scobbedun*.

Shobrooke (village, Devon): '(place by the) brook haunted by an evil spirit'. OE *sceocca*, 'evil spirit', 'demon', + *brōc*, 'brook'. 938 *Sceocabroc*, DB *Sotebroca*.

Shocklach (village, Cheshire): '(place by the) boggy stream haunted by an evil spirit'. OE *sceocca*, 'evil spirit', 'goblin', + *læcc*, 'stream', 'bog'. DB *Socheliche*.

Shoeburyness (district, Southend): 'promontory by the fortress providing shelter'. OE *scēo*, 'shelter', + *burh*, 'fortified place', + *næss*, 'promontory'. The promontory is at the mouth of the Thames estuary. The 'sheltering fortress' may be the ancient camp whose remains still exist here. Early 10C *Sceobyrig*, DB *Soberia*, 16C *Shoberynesse*.

Sholing (district, Southampton): 'sloping place'. OE *sceolh*, 'twisted', + *-ing*, 'place characterized by'. The original village lay on land between two streams, shelving gently to the point where they joined. The name could also represent OE *Scēolingas*, '(place of the) people of Scēolh' (OE *-ingas*, 'people of'). 1251 *Sholling*.

Shooters Hill (district, Greenwich): 'shooter's hill'. OE *scēotere*, 'shooter', 'archer', + *hyll*, 'hill'. The allusion may be to hunters on the formerly wooded hill here, or alternatively to highwaymen on the main road (following the course of Watling Street) which crosses the hill. The latter, more colourful origin has been preferred by many: 'Shooter's Hill, so called for the thievery there practised' (John Philipot, *Villare Cantianum*, 1659). 1226 *Shitereshell*.

Shop (village, Cornwall): '(place with a) workshop'. The form of the name below, with the workshop owner's surname, is for Shop near Padstow, although Shop near Bude has a name of identical origin. 1748 *Parkens Shop*.

Shoreditch (district, Hackney): 'ditch by a bank'. OE *scora*, 'bank', 'slope' (modern English *shore*), + *dīc*, 'ditch'. The exact location of the ditch in question is uncertain. It would not have been by the bank of the Thames, as Shoreditch is some distance north of the river. *c.*1148 *Soredich*.

Shoreham-by-Sea (town and port, W Sussex): 'homestead by a bank by the sea'. OE *scora*, 'bank' (modern English *shore*), + *hām*, 'homestead'. The bank in question is the steep slope of the downs here east of the river Adur, at whose mouth Shoreham is situated. The river takes its name (now that of the local council district) from *Portus Adurni*, 'harbour of Adurnos', the name of the Roman fort at PORTCHESTER, which the 17C antiquarian Michael Drayton wrongly located at Shoreham. The second part of the name distinguishes this Shoreham (earlier called *New Shoreham*) from *Old Shoreham* (the original place of the name) as well as indicating its maritime location. 1073 *Sorham*, DB *Soreham*.

Shorncote (hamlet, Glos): 'cottage in a mucky place'. OE *scearn*, 'dung', + *cot*, 'cottage'. DB *Schernecote*.

Shortlanesend (village, Cornwall): '(place at the) end of the short lane'. The first part of the name could also represent the surname Short. 1678 *Shortlane end*.

Shortstown (village, Beds). The garden village here was built from 1917 by the aircraft manufacturers Short Brothers. It later became RAF property.

Shorwell (village, IoW): 'spring by a steep slope'. OE *scora*, 'steep slope', + *wella*, 'spring', 'stream'. Shorwell is in a deep valley at the foot of the downs, and the stream that rises here flows into the sea at Brighstone. DB *Sorewelle*.

Shotesham (village, Norfolk): 'Scot's homestead'. OE *hām*, 'homestead'. 1044 *Shotesham*, DB *Scotesham*.

Shotley (hamlet, Suffolk): '(place by the) clearing where pigeons are seen'. OE *sceote*, 'pigeon', + *lēah*, 'wood', 'clearing'. DB *Scoteleia*.

Shotley Bridge (suburb of Consett, Durham): '(place by the) clearing where pigeons are seen'. OE *sceote*, 'pigeon', + *lēah*, 'wood', 'clearing'. The second word of the name denotes the important bridge over the river Derwent here connecting the counties of Durham and Northumberland. 1242 *Schotley*.

Shotover (hamlet, Oxon): '(place by the) ridge with a steep place'. OE *scēot*, 'steep place', + *ofer*, 'flat-topped ridge'. The reference is to nearby Shotover Hill. The name, formerly that of Shotover Forest here, has been popularly derived both from a legendary shot fired over the hill and from French *château vert*, 'green castle'. 'Yet old Sir Harry Bath was not forgot, / In the remembrance of whose wondrous shot / The forest by (believe it they that will) / Retains the surname of Shotover still' (George Wither, *Abuses Stript and Whipt*, 1613). DB *Scotorne*.

Shottermill (village, Surrey): 'Shotover's mill'. The first part of the name represents the

ME family name Shotover. 1537 *Shottover*, 1607 *Schotouermyll*, 1868 *Shotter Mills*.

Shottery (district of Stratford-upon-Avon, Warwicks): '(place by the) stream of the Scots'. OE *Scot*, 'Scot', + *rīth*, 'stream'. The first part of the name could also represent OE *sceota*, 'trout', giving a sense '(place by the) trout stream'. 699 *Scotta rith*.

Shottesbrooke (hamlet, Windsor & Maid): '(place by) Scot's brook'. OE *brōc*, 'brook'. DB *Sotesbroc*, 1187 *Schottesbroc*.

Shotteswell (village, Warwicks): '(place by) Scot's spring'. OE *wella*, 'spring', 'stream'. *c.*1140 *Soteswell*.

Shottisham (village, Suffolk): 'Scot's or Scēot's homestead'. OE *hām*, 'homestead'. DB *Scotesham*.

Shottle (hamlet, Derbys): 'hill with a steep slope'. OE *scēot*, 'steep slope', + *hyll*, 'hill'. The DB form of the name below is corrupt. DB *Sothelle*, 1191 *Schethell*.

Shotton (district of Peterlee, Durham): 'farmstead by a steep slope'. OE *scēot*, 'slope', 'steep hill', + *tūn*, 'farmstead'. *c.*1165 *Sotton*.

Shotton (town, Flints): 'farm on a hill'. OE *scēot*, 'hill', + *tūn*, 'farmstead'. The original farm of the name was where *Higher Shotton* now is, on the hill above *Lower Shotton* by the river Dee. 1283 *Schotton*.

Shotton (hamlet, Northd): '(place by the) hill of the Scots'. OE *Scot*, 'Scot', + *dūn*, 'hill'. The form of the name below relates to Shotton near Kirk Yetholm. *c.*1050 *Scotadun*.

Shotwick (village, Cheshire): 'dwelling by a steep promontory'. OE *scēot*, 'steep slope', + *hōh*, 'hill spur', + *wīc*, 'dwelling', 'farm'. DB *Sotowiche*.

Shouldham (village, Norfolk): 'homestead owing a debt'. OE *sculd*, 'debt', 'due', + *hām*, 'homestead'. DB *Sculdeham*.

Shoulton (hamlet, Worcs): 'farmstead by the (river) Shoul'. OE *tūn*, 'farmstead'. The river name, formerly that of a stream here, means 'winding one' (OE *sceolh*, 'twisted'). *c.*1220 *Scolegeton*.

Shrawardine (village, Shropshire): '(place in the) enclosure near a hollow'. OE *scræf*, 'cave', 'den', 'hollow', + *worthign*, 'enclosure'. The hollow in question was probably some feature now obscured by Shrawardine Pool. The DB form of the name below is corrupt. DB *Saleurdine*, 1166 *Scrawardin*.

Shrawley (village, Worcs): 'woodland clearing by a hollow'. OE *scræf*, 'hollow', 'hovel', + *lēah*, 'wood', 'clearing'. 804 *Scræfleh*.

Shrewsbury (town, Shropshire): 'fortified place of the scrubland'. OE *scrubb*, 'scrubland', + *burh*, 'fortified place'. The present spelling of the name evolved because words like *shrew* and *shrewd* were formerly pronounced to rhyme with *show* and *showed*. Hence the modern pronunciation 'Shrowsbury'. The Welsh name of Shrewsbury is *Amwythig*, a rendering of the English name, from *am*, 'about', + *gwydd*, 'trees', + the adjectival suffix -*ig*. See also SHROPSHIRE. 11C *Scrobbesbyrig*, DB *Sciropesberie*.

Shrewton (village, Wilts): 'sheriff's manor'. OE *scīr-rēfa*, 'sheriff' (literally 'shire reeve', from *scīr*, 'shire', + *rēfa*, 'reeve'), + *tūn*, 'farmstead', 'village', 'manor'. The original name of Shrewton was *Winterbourne*, after the stream here (see WINTERBOURNE), now called the Till (from TILSHEAD, the next village). DB *Wintreburne*, 1232 *Winterbourne Syreveton*, 1255 *Schyrreveton*.

Shrivenham (village, Oxon): 'riverside land allotted by decree'. OE *scrifen*, 'allotted' (modern English *shriven*), + *hamm*, 'enclosure', 'riverside land'. The name indicates that land by the river Cole here was allotted by decree to the church following a dispute about ownership. *c.*950 *Scrifenanhamme*, DB *Seriveham*.

Shropham (village, Norfolk): '(particular) homestead'. OE *hām*, 'homestead'. The first part of the name is of uncertain origin. It probably represents a personal name. DB *Screpham*.

Shropshire (county, W central England): 'district based on Shrewsbury'. OE *scīr*, 'district', 'shire'. The first part of the name is a shortening of the old form of SHREWSBURY. The first part of the last form of the name below, with its Norman substitution of *l* for *r*, gave *Salop* as an abbreviation for the county name (adopted officially from 1974 to 1980) and *Salopian* as a term for an inhabitant of Shrewsbury or Shropshire. 1006 *Scrobbesbyrigscir*, DB *Sciropescire*, 1094 *Salopescira*.

Shroton. See IWERNE MINSTER.

Shucknall (village, Herefords): '(place by the) hill with an evil spirit'. OE *scucca*, 'demon', 'goblin', + *hyll*, 'hill'. 1377 *Shokenhulle*.

Shudy Camps (village, Cambs): 'enclosures with a hovel'. OE *scydd*, 'shed', 'hovel', + *camp*, 'enclosed piece of land' (modern English *camp*). The first word of the name was added to distinguish this village from nearby *Castle Camps*, where there was a medieval castle. (The comparison may have been made in mockery, contrasting lowly 'hovel' with grand 'castle'.) DB *Campas*, 1219 *Sudekampes*.

Shurdington (village, Glos): 'estate associated with Scyrda'. OE -*ing*-, 'associated with', + *tūn*, 'farmstead', 'estate'. *c.*1150 *Surditona*.

Shurton (village, Somerset): 'sheriff's manor'. OE *scīr-rēfa*, 'sheriff' (from *scīr*, 'shire', + *rēfa*, 'reeve'), + *tūn*, 'manor'. 1219 *Shureveton*.

Shustoke (village, Warwicks): 'Scēot's outlying farmstead'. OE *stoc*, 'outlying farmstead'. If the DB form below is not a mistranscription, the second part of the name was originally OE *cot*, 'cottage'. DB *Scotescote*, 1247 *Schutestok*.

Shute (village, Devon): '(place by the) corner of land'. OE *scīete*, 'corner of land'. *c.*1200 *Schieta*.

Shutford (village, Oxon): '(place by) Scytta's ford'. OE *ford*, 'ford'. *c.*1160 *Schiteford*.

Shutlanger (village, Northants): '(place by the) wooded slope where shuttles are obtained'. OE *scytel*, 'shuttle', + *hangra*, 'wooded slope'. The 'shuttles' would probably have been wooden gate bars. 1162 *Shitelhanger*.

Shuttington (village, Warwicks): 'estate associated with Scytta'. OE -*ing*-, 'associated with', + *tūn*, 'farmstead', 'estate'. The DB form of the name below is corrupt. DB *Cetitone*, *c.*1160 *Schetintuna*.

Shuttleworth (village, Bury): '(place by the) barred enclosure'. OE *scytel*, 'bar', 'bolt' (modern English *shuttle*), + *worth*, 'enclosure'. 1227 *Suttelsworth*.

Sibbertoft (village, Northants): 'Sigebeorht's or Sigbjǫrn's homestead'. OS *toft*, 'homestead'. The personal names are respectively OE and Scandinavian. The DB form of the name below has miscopied OS *toft*. DB *Sibertod*, 1198 *Sibertoft*.

Sibdon Carwood (village, Shropshire): 'Sibba's farmstead near Carwood'. OE *tūn*, 'farmstead'. *Carwood*, the name of a former nearby wood, means 'rock wood' (OE *carr*, 'rock', + *wudu*, 'wood'). DB *Sibetune*, 1672 *Sipton Carswood*.

Sibford Ferris (village, Oxon): 'de Ferrers' (estate by) Sibba's ford'. OE *ford*, 'ford'. The manor here was held early by the de Ferrers family, whose name distinguishes the village from nearby *Sibford Gower*, held by the Guher family. DB *Sibeford*, early 18C *Sibbard Ferreys*.

Sible Hedingham (town, Essex): 'Sibil's (estate at the) homestead of Hyth's people'. OE -*inga*-, 'of the people of', + *hām*, 'homestead'. The first element of the main name could also be OE *hȳth*, 'landing place', referring to the nearby river Colne. The first word of the name comes from a lady called Sibil whose family held the manor here in the 13C. The addition distinguishes this place from nearby *Castle Hed-*

ingham, where there was a Norman castle. DB *Hedingham*, 1231 *Heyngham Sibille*.

Sibsey (village, Lincs): 'Sigebald's island'. OE *ēg*, 'island'. The 'island' here is raised ground in fenland. DB *Sibolci*.

Sibson (village, Leics): 'Sigebed's hill'. OE *dūn*, 'hill'. DB *Sibetesdone*.

Sibthorpe (village, Notts): 'Sibba's or Sibbi's outlying farm'. OS *thorp*, 'outlying farm'. The personal names are respectively OE and Scandinavian. DB *Sibetorp*.

Sibton (hamlet, Suffolk): 'Sibba's farmstead'. OE *tūn*, 'farmstead'. DB *Sibbetuna*.

Sicklinghall (village, N Yorks): 'corner of land of Sicel's people'. OE -*inga*-, 'of the people of', + *halh*, 'nook', 'corner of land'. The DB form of the name below has *cl* miscopied as *d*. DB *Sidingale*, *c.*1150 *Sicclinghala*.

Sidbury (village, Devon): 'fortified place by the (river) Sid'. OE *burh*, 'fortified place'. For the river name, see SIDMOUTH. DB *Sideberia*.

Sidbury (village, Shropshire): 'southern fortified place'. OE *sūth*, 'southern', + *burh*, 'fortified place'. The place lies south of Middleton Scriven. DB *Sudberie*.

Sidcup (district, Bexley): '(place on the) flat-topped hill'. OE *set-copp* (from *set*, 'seat', + *copp*, 'hill'). The name implies that Sidcup arose as a place 'seated' on a hilltop. It is hard to envisage a hill here now, but the ground does fall away to the north and south of the High Street. 1254 *Cetecopp*.

Siddington (hamlet, Cheshire): '(place to the) south of the hill'. OE *sūthan*, 'south', + *dūn*. 'hill'. It is not clear which hill is referred to. DB *Sudendune*.

Siddington (village, Glos): '(estate in the) south in the township'. OE *sūth*, 'south', + *in*, 'in', + *tūn*, 'farmstead', 'township'. Siddington is just south of Cirencester, the 'township' in question. DB *Sudintone*.

Sidestrand (village, Norfolk): '(place by the) broad shore'. OE *sīd*, 'large', 'broad', + *strand*, 'shore'. Sidestrand is near the coast. The DB form of the name below has omitted each *d*. DB *Sistran*, late 12C *Sidestrande*.

Sidford (suburb of Sidmouth, Devon): '(place by the) ford on the (river) Sid'. OE *ford*, 'ford'. For the river name, see SIDMOUTH. 1238 *Sideford*.

Sidlaw Hills (hill range, Angus): 'seat hills'. Gaelic *suidhe*, 'seat', + OE *hlāw*, 'hill'. The 'seat' would be the flat hilltops found at various points in the range. 1799 *Seedlaws*.

Sidlesham (village, W Sussex): 'Sidel's homestead'. OE *hām*, 'homestead'. 683 *Sidelesham*.

Sidmouth (resort town, Devon): 'mouth of the (river) Sid'. OE *mūtha*, 'mouth'. The river name means 'broad one' (OE *sīd*, 'spacious', 'extensive', related modern English *side*). DB *Sedemuda*.

Siefton (hamlet, Shropshire): 'Sigegifu's farmstead'. OE *tūn*, 'farmstead'. The personal name is that of a woman. The first part of the name could also represent the name, of unknown origin, of the stream on which Siefton stands. The DB form of the name below has r for v. DB *Sireton*, 1257 *Siveton*.

Sigglesthorne (village, E Yorks): 'Sigulfr's thorn bush'. OS *thorn*, 'thorn bush'. The personal name is Scandinavian. DB *Siglestorne*.

Silbury Hill (ancient earthwork, Wilts): 'hill by a hall'. OE *sele*, 'dwelling', 'hall', + *beorg*, 'hill'. The first part of the name is of uncertain origin. The second part could also represent OE *burh*, 'fortified place'. *c.*1235 *Selleboruwe*, 1281 *Seleburgh*.

Silchester (village, Hants): 'Roman station by a willow copse'. OE *siele*, 'willow copse', + *ceaster*, 'Roman station'. The Celtic-based name of the Roman camp here was *Calleva Atrebatum*, and it is possible the first word of this, meaning '(place in the) woods' (related modern Welsh *celli*, 'grove'), gave 'Sil-'. However, forms of the name with C- do not appear until the 13C. The second word is a tribal name, that of the Atrebates, who had their capital here. DB *Silcestre*, 1227 *Cilcestre*.

Sileby (village, Leics): 'Sigulfr's farmstead'. OS *bý*, 'farmstead', 'village'. The personal name is Scandinavian. DB *Siglebi*.

Silecroft (village, Cumbria): 'enclosure where willows grow'. OS *selja*, 'willow', + OE *croft*, 'enclosure'. 1211 *Selecroft*.

Sili. See SULLY.

Silina. See SCILLY ISLES.

Silkstone (village, Barnsley): 'Sigelāc's farmstead'. OE *tūn*, 'farmstead'. DB *Silchestone*.

Silksworth (district, Sunderland): 'Sigelāc's enclosure'. OE *worth*, 'enclosure'. The district is now more generally known as *New Silksworth*. *c.*1050 *Sylceswurthe*.

Silk Willoughby (village, Lincs): 'farmstead where willows grow by Silkby'. OE *wilig*, 'willow', + OS *bý*, 'farmstead'. (The OS word may have replaced earlier OE *tūn* in the same sense.) This Willoughby is distinguished from *Scott Willoughby*, 4 miles to the south, where the Scot family held the manor, and *West Willoughby*, 6

miles to the west, by adding the name of nearby *Silkby*, 'Silki's farmstead' (OS *bý*, 'farmstead', with a Scandinavian personal name). The latter name no longer exists, but the hamlet to which it applied survives to the west of the church. DB *Wilgebi*.

Silloth (town and port, Cumbria): 'barns by the sea'. OS *sǽr* or OE *sǽ*, 'sea', + OS *hlatha*, 'barn', 'storehouse'. 1292 *Selathe*.

Silpho (hamlet, N Yorks): '(place on the) flat-topped hill spur'. OE *scylfe*, 'shelf', + *hōh*, 'hill spur'. *c.*1160 *Silfhou*.

Silsden (town, Bradford): 'Sigulfr's valley'. OE *denu*, 'valley'. The personal name is Scandinavian. The valley in question is the one that runs north from the main valley of the river Aire to Silsden Moor. DB *Siglesdene*.

Silsoe (village, Beds): '(place by) Sifel's hill spur'. OE *hōh*, 'hill spur'. DB *Siuuilessou*.

Silverdale (village, Lancs): '(place in the) silver-coloured valley'. OE *seolfor*, 'silver', + *dæl*, 'valley'. The reference is to the grey limestone here. The DB form of the name below is corrupt. DB *Selredal*, 1292 *Celverdale*.

Silverstone (village, Northants): 'Sǽwulf's or Sigewulf's farmstead'. OE *tūn*, 'farmstead'. The '-r-' of the name entered by association with *silver*. 942 *Sulueston*, DB *Silvestone*.

Silverton (village, Devon): 'farmstead near the gully ford'. OE *sulh*, 'gully', + *ford*, 'ford', + *tūn*, 'farmstead'. The village lies between the rivers Exe and Culm. DB *Sulfretone*.

Silvertown (district, Newham). The firm of S. W. Silver & Co., rubber and telegraph manufacturers, were here by the Thames in the 19C. 1888 *Silvertown*.

Simonburn (village, Northd): '(place by) Sigemund's stream'. OE *burna*, 'stream'. 1229 *Simundeburn*.

Simonstone (village, Lancs): 'Sigemund's stone'. OE *stān*, 'stone'. The reference is probably to a boundary stone. 1278 *Simondestan*.

Simpson (village, Milton K): 'Sigewine's farmstead'. OE *tūn*, 'farmstead'. DB *Siwinestone*.

Sinderby (village, N Yorks): 'southern farmstead'. OS *syndri*, 'southern', + *bý*, 'farmstead', 'village'. The farmstead could have been 'southern' with regard to Pickhill. An alternative meaning is 'Sindri's farmstead', with a Scandinavian personal name. DB *Senerebi*.

Sinfin (district, Derby): '(place by the) wide fen'. OE *sīd*, 'wide' (related modern English *side*), + *fenn*, 'fen'. If this interpretation of the name is correct, the DB form below is corrupt. DB *Sedenefeld*, early 13C *Sidenfen*.

Singleton (village, Lancs): 'farmstead with shingled roof'. OE *scingol*, 'shingle', + *tūn*, 'farmstead'. DB *Singletun*.

Singleton (village, W Sussex): 'farmstead with tufts of grass'. OE *sengel*, 'bundle', 'tuft', + *tūn*, 'farmstead'. The first part of the DB form of the name below is corrupt. DB *Silletone*, 1185 *Sengelton*.

Sinnington (village, N Yorks): 'farmstead by the (river) Seven'. OE *-ing-*, 'associated with', + *tūn*, 'farmstead'. The river has a pre-English name of uncertain meaning. DB *Siuenintun*.

Sissinghurst (village, Kent): 'wooded hill of Seaxa's people'. OE *-inga-*, 'of the people of', + *hyrst*, 'wooded hill'. *c*.1180 *Saxingherste*.

Siston (village, S Glos): 'Sige's farmstead'. OE *tūn*, 'farmstead'. DB *Sistone*.

Sithney (village, Cornwall): '(church of) St Sithney'. The church here is dedicated to Sithney, a saint also venerated in Brittany, who is said to have been buried here. 1230 *St Sythninus*.

Sittingbourne (town, Kent): 'stream of the dwellers on the slope'. OE *sīde*, 'slope' (modern English *side*), + *-inga-*, 'of the dwellers at', + *burna*, 'stream'. Sittingbourne lies on the lower slope of a ridge by Milton Creek, the 'stream' of the name. 1200 *Sidingeburn*.

Six Mile Bottom (village, Cambs). The village lies in a hollow (OE *botm*, 'valley bottom') 6 miles from Newmarket. Hence the name. 1801 *Six Mile Bottom*.

Sixpenny Handley (village, Dorset): 'high wood or clearing by the hill of the Saxons'. OE *hēah*, 'high', + *lēah*, 'wood', 'clearing'. The first word of the name is that of a hundred here, from OE *Seaxe*, 'Saxons', and a Celtic word meaning 'hill' (modern Welsh *pen*, 'head', 'top'). A nearby signpost long bore the name as *6º HANDLEY* . 877 *Hanlee*, DB *Hanlege*, 1575 *Sexpennyhanley*.

Sizergh Castle (castle, Cumbria): 'Sigríthr's hill pasture'. OS *erg*, 'shieling', 'hill pasture'. The Scandinavian personal name is that of a woman. 1170 *Sigaritherge*.

Sizewell (coastal hamlet, Suffolk): '(place by) Sigehere's spring'. OE *wella*, 'spring', 'stream'. 1240 *Syreswell*.

Skara Brae (historic village, Orkney): 'steep bank by the shore'. OS *skari*, 'shore', + *brá*, 'brow' (modern Scottish *brae*).

Skeeby (village, N Yorks): 'Skíthi's farmstead'. OS *bý*, 'farmstead', 'village'. The personal name

is Scandinavian. The DB form of the name below has *r* for *t*. DB *Schireby*, 1187 *Schittebi*.

Skeffington (village, Leics): 'estate associated with Sceaft'. OE *-ing-*, 'associated with', + *tūn*, 'farmstead', 'estate'. The 'Sk-' of the name is the result of Scandinavian influence. DB *Sciftitone*.

Skeffling (village, E Yorks): '(settlement of) Sceaftel's people'. OE *-ingas*, 'people of'. The 'Sk-' of the name is due to Scandinavian influence. 12C *Sckeftling*.

Skegby (suburb of Sutton in Ashfield, Notts): 'Skeggi's farmstead'. OS *bý*, 'farmstead', 'village'. The personal name is Scandinavian. The name could also mean 'farmstead on a beard-shaped promontory' (OS *skegg*, 'beard', + *bý*). DB *Schegebi*.

Skegness (resort town, Lincs): 'Skeggi's promontory'. OS *nes*, 'promontory'. The personal name is Scandinavian. There is no promontory now at Skegness, following changes in the coastline, but there must have been once. Skegness has been identified with the DB name *Tric*, perhaps ultimately from Latin *traiectus*, 'crossing point', referring to a former ferry link here. A Roman road (the present A52) leads south from Skegness to Wainfleet. 12C *Sceggenesse*.

Skellow (village, Doncaster): 'corner of land with a shieling'. OE *scēla*, 'shieling', 'hut', + *halh*, 'nook', 'corner of land'. OE *scēla* has been influenced by equivalent OS *skáli*. The first part of the DB form of the name below is corrupt. DB *Scanhalle*, *c*.1190 *Scalehale*.

Skelmanthorpe (town, Kirklees): 'Skjaldmarr's outlying farmstead'. OS *thorp*, 'secondary settlement', 'dependent outlying farmstead'. The same Scandinavian personal name also lies behind SKELMERSDALE. DB *Scelmertorp*.

Skelmersdale (town, Lancs): 'Skjaldmarr's valley'. OS *dalr*, 'valley'. The personal name is Scandinavian. The valley in question is probably that of the river Tawd here. Cp. SKELMANTHORPE. DB *Schelmeresdele*.

Skelton (village, Cumbria): 'farmstead on a ledge'. OE *scelf*, 'shelf', 'ledge', + *tūn*, 'farmstead'. The name is the equivalent of SHELTON, but with OS influence giving the initial 'Sk-'. *c*.1160 *Sheltone*. SO ALSO: *Skelton*, E Yorks, N Yorks, Redcar & Clev, York.

Skelwith Bridge (hamlet, Cumbria): '(place at a) ford by a waterfall with a bridge'. OS *skjallr*, 'resounding (thing)', + *vath*, 'ford'. The waterfall in question is Skelwith Force. The second word of the name dates from the 17C. 1246 *Schelwath*.

Skendleby (village, Lincs): 'farmstead by a beautiful slope'. OE *scēne*, 'beautiful' (modern English *sheen*), + *helde*, 'slope', + OS *bý*, 'farmstead'. The 'Sk-' of the name is the result of Scandinavian influence. The DB form of the name below is garbled. DB *Scheueldebi*, *c.*1150 *Schendelebia*.

Skerne (village, E Yorks): '(place by) Skerne Beck'. The river name means 'clear stream', from OS *skirn*, 'cleansing', or OE *scīr*, 'bright', 'clear', + *ēa*, 'river'. DB *Schirne*.

Skerries, The (island group, Anglesey): 'the reefs'. OS *sker*, 'reef'. The Welsh name of The Skerries is *Ynysoedd y Moelrhoniaid*, 'islands of the seals' (Welsh *ynys*, 'island', plural *ynysoedd*, + *y*, 'the', + *moelrhon*, 'seal', plural *moelrhoniaid*).

Sketty. See KILGETTY.

Skewsby (hamlet, N Yorks): 'farmstead in the wood'. OS *skógr*, 'wood', + *bý*, 'farmstead', 'village'. DB *Scoxebi*.

Skeyton (hamlet, Norfolk): 'Skeggi's farmstead'. OE *tūn*, 'farmstead'. The personal name is Scandinavian. DB *Scegutuna*.

Skidby (village, E Yorks): 'Skyti's farmstead'. OS *bý*, 'farmstead'. The personal name is Scandinavian. The first part of the name could also represent OS *skítr*, 'dung', giving a sense 'mucky farmstead'. 972 *Scyteby*, DB *Schitebi*.

Skiddaw (mountain, Cumbria): 'snowshoe mound'. OS *skith*, 'snowshoe' (modern English *ski*), + *haugr*, 'mound'. The allusion is to the outline of the mountain, like that of a snowshoe. 1230 *Skithoc*.

Skilgate (village, Somerset): '(place by) shaly gap'. OE *scilig*, 'shaly', + *geat*, 'gate', 'gap'. DB *Schiligata*.

Skillington (village, Lincs): 'estate associated with Scilla'. OE *-ing-*, 'associated with', + *tūn*, 'farmstead', 'estate'. The first part of the name could also represent OE *scilling*, 'shilling', referring to a local rent. The 'Sk-' is due to Scandinavian influence. DB *Schillintune*.

Skinburness (coastal village, Cumbria): 'promontory by Skinburgh'. OS *nes*, 'promontory'. *Skinburgh* is the name of a now lost place meaning 'stronghold haunted by demons' (OE *scinna*, 'demon', + *burh*, 'fortified place'). The 'Sk-' is due to Scandinavian influence. 1175 *Skyneburg*, 1298 *Skynburneyse*.

Skinningrove (coastal hamlet, Redcar & Clev): 'pit used by skinners'. OS *skinnari*, 'skinner', 'tanner', + *gryfja*, 'pit'. *c.*1175 *Scineregrive*.

Skipsea (village, E Yorks): '(place by the) lake where ships can sail'. OS *skip*, 'ship', + *sǽr*, 'lake'. Skipsea is near the North Sea coast. 1160 *Skipse*.

Skipton (town, N Yorks): 'sheep farm'. OE *scīp*, 'sheep', + *tūn*, 'farmstead'. The spelling with 'Sk-' is due to Scandinavian influence. DB *Scipton*.

Skipton-on-Swale (village, N Yorks): 'sheep farm on the (river) Swale'. OE *scīp*, 'sheep', + *tūn*, 'farmstead'. The 'Sk-' is due to Scandinavian influence. For the river name, see BROMPTON-ON-SWALE. DB *Schipetune*.

Skipwith (village, N Yorks): 'sheep farm'. OE *scīp*, 'sheep', + *wīc*, 'special farm'. Original OE *wīc* has been replaced by OS *vithr*, 'wood', with the 'Sk-' due to Scandinavian influence. DB *Schipewic*.

Skirlaugh (village, E Yorks): 'bright woodland clearing'. OE *scīr*, 'bright', + *lēah*, 'wood', 'clearing'. The 'Sk-' is the result of Scandinavian influence. The village was originally *South Skirlaugh*, as distinct from the adjoining hamlet of *North Skirlaugh*, but the two have now combined. DB *Schirelai*.

Skirmett (village, Bucks): 'meeting place of the shire court'. OE *scīr*, 'shire', + *mōt*, 'assembly', 'meeting' (modern English *moot*). Cp. FINGEST. The 'Sk-' of the name is due to Scandinavian influence. *c.*1307 *La Skiremote*.

Skirpenbeck (village, E Yorks): '(place by the) dried-up stream'. OS *skarpr*, 'dried up', + *bekkr*, 'stream'). The name implies a stream that frequently dries up. DB *Scarpenbec*.

Skirwith (village, Cumbria): 'wood belonging to the shire'. OE *scīr*, 'shire', + OS *vithr*, 'wood'. The spelling with 'Sk-' resulted from Scandinavian influence. 1205 *Skirewit*.

Skokholm (island, Pemb): 'island in a channel'. OS *stokkr*, 'stock', 'trunk', 'channel', + *holmr*, 'island'. The 'channel' is Broad Sound, between Skokholm and the neighbouring island of SKOMER. The latter's name influenced the spelling of this one, with 'Sk-' instead of the expected 'St-'. 1219 *Scogholm*, 1275 *Stokholm*.

Skomer (island, Pemb): 'cloven island'. OS *skálm*, 'cleft', + *ey*, 'island'. Two bays on opposite sides of Skomer seem to cut into it to form the peninsula known as The Kneck. 1324 *Skalmey*.

Skye (island, Highland): 'winged (island)'. Gaelic *sgiath*, 'wing'. The name alludes to the island's great peninsulas, which thrust out north and south like wings. *c.*150 *Scitis*, *c.*700 *Scia*, *c.*1250 *Skith*, 1266 *Skye*.

Slad (village, Glos): '(place in the) valley'. OE *slæd*, 'valley'. This is the Slad Valley between

Stroud and Painswick, made famous by Laurie Lee's *Cider with Rosie*. No early forms of the name are known. 1779 *Slad*, 1868 *Slade*.

Slaggyford (hamlet, Northd): '(place by the) muddy ford'. ME *slaggi*, 'muddy', + *ford*, 'ford'. The ford here would have been over the South Tyne. 13C *Slaggiford*.

Slaidburn (village, Lancs): '(place on the) stream by the sheep pasture'. OE *slæget*, 'pasture', 'sheepwalk', + *burna*, 'stream'. The stream originally so called is now known as Croasdale Brook. DB *Slateborne*.

Slaithwaite (town, Kirklees): 'clearing where timber was felled'. OS *slag*, 'blow', 'stroke', + *thveit*, 'clearing'. 1178 *Sladweit*, 1277 *Sclagtwayt*.

Slapton (village, Devon): 'farmstead by a slippery place'. OE *slæp*, 'slippery place', + *tūn*, 'farmstead'. The road descends steeply from the village to the coast, and this was probably the 'slippery place'. A slightly different interpretation would be 'muddy farmstead' (OE *slæp*, 'muddy', 'slippery', + *tūn*). The DB form of the name below is corrupt (*pt* has become *d*). DB *Sladone*, 1244 *Slapton*. SO ALSO: *Slapton*, Bucks, Northants.

Slaugham (village, W Sussex): 'homestead or enclosure where sloes grow'. OE *slāh*, 'sloe', + *hām*, 'homestead', or *hamm*, 'enclosure'. *c*.1100 *Slacham*.

Slawston (village, Leics): 'Slagr's farmstead'. OE *tūn*, 'farmstead'. The personal name is Scandinavian. DB *Slagestone*.

Sleaford (town, Lincs): '(place by the) ford over the (river) Slea'. OE *ford*. The river has a name meaning 'muddy one', from a Germanic source ultimately related to modern English *slime*. 852 *Slioford*, DB *Eslaforde*.

Sleagill (hamlet, Cumbria): '(place by the) ravine of the trickling stream'. OS *slefa*, 'saliva', + *gil*, 'ravine'. The reference would be to Sleagill Beck here. The name could also mean '(place by) Slefa's ravine', with a Scandinavian personal name. *c*.1190 *Slegill*.

Sledmere (village, E Yorks): '(place by the) pool in the valley'. OE *slæd*, 'valley', + *mere*, 'pool'. The village is in a very wide valley and the pool in question may be the one on the hillside near the church. DB *Slidemare*.

Sleightholme (hamlet, Durham): '(place on) smooth raised ground'. OS *slēttr*, 'smooth', + *holmr*, 'island', 'raised ground'. 1234 *Slethholm*.

Sleights (village, N Yorks): '(place by) smooth fields'. OS *slétta*, 'smooth level field'. *c*.1223 *Sleghtes*.

Slimbridge (village, Glos): 'bridge over a muddy place'. OE *slim*, 'slime', 'mud', + *brycg*, 'bridge'. The 'bridge' was probably a causeway. The DB form of the name below shows the Norman clerk's way of dealing with the 'Sl-'. DB *Heslinbruge*, *c*.1153 *Slimbrugia*.

Slindon (village, W Sussex): '(place by the) sloping hill'. OE *slim*, 'slope', + *dūn*, 'hill'. DB *Eslindone*. SO ALSO: *Slindon*, Staffs.

Slinfold (village, W Sussex): 'fold on the sloping hill'. OE *slind*, 'slope', + *fald*, 'fold' (for animals). The village lies on the side of a hill. 1225 *Slindefold*.

Slingsby (village, N Yorks): 'Slengr's farmstead'. OS *bý*, 'farmstead'. The personal name is Scandinavian. DB *Selungesbi*.

Slipton (village, Northants): 'muddy farmstead'. OE *slipa*, 'slime', 'mud', + *tūn*, 'farmstead'. DB *Sliptone*.

Sloley (hamlet, Norfolk): 'woodland clearing where sloe grows'. OE *slāh*, 'sloe', 'blackthorn', + *lēah*, 'wood', 'clearing'. DB *Slaleia*.

Slough (town, Slough): 'miry place'. OE *slōh*, 'slough'. The name refers to the low-lying marshy terrain formerly here, to the north of the Thames. 1195 *Slo*.

Slyne (village, Lancs): '(place on the) slope'. OE *slinu*, 'slope'. The slope in question is the ridge on which the village stands. DB *Sline*.

Smallburgh (village, Norfolk): '(place by the) hill on the (river) Smale'. OE *beorg*, 'mound', 'hill'. The river here now is the Ant, but formerly it was the *Smale*, from OE *smæl*, 'narrow' (modern English *small*), + *ēa*, 'river'. DB *Smaleberga*.

Smalley (village, Derbys): '(place in the) narrow woodland clearing'. OE *smæl*, 'narrow' (modern English *small*), + *lēah*, 'wood', 'clearing'. 1009 *Smælleage*, DB *Smalei*.

Small Hythe (hamlet, Kent): 'narrow landing place'. OE *smæl*, 'narrow' (modern English *small*), + *hȳth*, 'landing place'. Small Hythe is now on the stream known as Reading Sewer, but in medieval times was a thriving port on the river Rother. 13C *Smalide*, 1289 *Smalhede*.

Smarden (village, Kent): 'woodland pasture where butter is made'. OE *smeoru*, 'grease', 'butter' (modern English *smear*), + *denn*, 'woodland pasture'. *c*.1100 *Smeredaenne*.

Smeeth (village, Kent): 'smithy'. OE *smiththe*, 'smithy'. 1018 *Smitha*.

Smethwick (town, Sandwell): 'building of the smiths'. OE *smith*, 'smith', 'metalworker', + *wīc*, 'special building'. DB *Smedeuuich*.

Smisby (village, Derbys): 'farmstead of the smith'. OS *smithr*, 'smith', + *bý*, 'farmstead'. DB *Smidesbi*.

Snailwell (village, Cambs): '(place by the) stream full of snails'. OE *snægl*, 'snail', + *wella*, 'spring', 'stream'. *c.*1050 *Sneillewelle*, DB *Snelleuuelle*.

Snainton (village, N Yorks): 'farmstead associated with Snoc'. OE *-ing-*, 'associated with', + *tūn*, 'farmstead'. DB *Snechintune*.

Snaith (village, E Yorks): 'detached piece of land'. OS *sneith*, 'slice'. The reference may have been to a piece of land cut off by the river Aire or some stream here. *c.*1080 *Snaith*, DB *Esneid*.

Snape (village, Suffolk): '(place in) marshland'. OE *snæp*, 'boggy piece of land'. Snape lies on low ground beside the river Alde. DB *Snapes*. SO ALSO: *Snape*, N Yorks.

Snaresbrook (district, Waltham F): '(place by the) brook'. OE *brōc*, 'brook'. The first part of the name is of uncertain origin. It may represent a surname or relate to animal snares. 1599 *Snaresbrook*.

Snarestone (village, Leics): 'Snarc's farmstead'. OE *tūn*, 'farmstead'. DB *Snarchetone*.

Snave (hamlet, Kent): '(place by) strips of land'. OE *snafa*, 'spit of land'. 1182 *Snaues*.

Sneaton (village, N Yorks): 'Snær's farmstead'. OE *tūn*, 'farmstead'. The personal name is Scandinavian. The name could also mean 'farmstead with a detached piece of land' (OE *snǣd*, 'thing cut off', + *tūn*). DB *Snetune*.

Sneinton. See NOTTINGHAM.

Snelston (village, Derbys): 'Snell's farmstead'. OE *tūn*, 'farmstead'. DB *Snellestune*.

Snettisham (village, Norfolk): 'Snæt's or Sneti's homestead'. OE *hām*, 'homestead'. DB *Snetesham*.

Snitterby (village, Lincs): 'Snytra's farmstead'. OS *bý*, 'farmstead', 'village'. DB *Snetrebi*.

Snitterfield (village, Warwicks): 'open land where snipe are seen'. OE *snīte*, 'snipe', + *feld*, 'open land' (modern English *field*). DB *Snitefeld*.

Snodhill (hamlet, Herefords): '(place by the) snowy hill'. OE *snāwede*, 'snowy', + *hyll*, 'hill'. 1195 *Snauthil*.

Snodland (village, Kent): 'land associated with Snodd'. OE *-ing-*, 'associated with', + *land*, 'land'. The land in question would have been newly worked agricultural land by the Medway here. The DB form of the name below is corrupt. 838 *Snoddingland*, DB *Esnoiland*.

Snowdon (mountain, Gwynedd): 'snow hill'. OE *snāw*, 'snow', + *dūn*, 'hill'. The heights of Snowdon are snow-clad for much of the year. The Welsh name of Snowdon is *Yr Wyddfa*, 'the mound' (Welsh *yr*, 'the', + *gwyddfa*, 'mound', 'tumulus'), referring to its use as a burial place. The region centring on Snowdon is known as *Snowdonia* in English, *Eryri* in Welsh. The latter name is said to derive from *eryr*, 'eagle', but more likely originated as a translation of the English, from *eira*, 'snow'. 1095 *Snawdune*.

Snowshill (village, Glos): '(place by the) hill where snow lies long'. OE *snāw*, 'snow', + *hyll*, 'hill'. DB *Snawesille*.

Soar (river). See BARROW UPON SOAR.

Soberton (village, Hants): 'southern grange'. OE *sūth*, 'southern', + *bere-tūn*, 'grange', 'outlying farm' (see BARTON). The grange was south with regard to the farm at Meonstoke. DB *Sudbertune*.

Sodor. See HEBRIDES.

Soham (village, Cambs): 'homestead by a swampy pool'. OE *sǣge*, 'swamp', 'lake', + *hām*, 'homestead'. The former lake here was drained in medieval times. *c.*1000 *Sægham*, DB *Saham*.

Soho (district, Westminster). The fields formerly here were associated with hunting, and 'Soho' was a cry similar to 'Tally ho' used by a huntsman to draw the attention of the rest of the field to a hare that had been sighted or started. The Duke of Monmouth lived in Soho Square, and the name has been popularly derived from his password during the 1685 Rising. However, the form of the name below shows that it dates from some time before this, although the duke's followers could have adopted the watchword with at least partial reference to their leader's place of residence. 1632 *So Ho*.

Solent, The (sea channel, Hants/IoW): meaning uncertain. The name is pre-English, with a sense on the lines of 'place of cliffs' postulated by some scholars. 731 *Soluente*.

Solfach. See SOLVA.

Solihull (town, Solihull): '(place by the) muddy hill'. OE *solig*, 'muddy' (related modern English *soil*), + *hyll*, 'hill'. The hill in question is probably the one south of St Alphege's church, where the road runs through red clayey soil. The first part of the name could also represent OE *sulig*, 'pigsty'. 12C *Solihull*.

Sollers Hope (village, Herefords): 'de Solariis' (estate in the) valley'. OE *hop*, 'valley'. The de Solariis family held the manor here in the 13C, their name distinguishing this Hope from nearby FOWNHOPE and WOOLHOPE. DB *Hope*, 1242 *Hope Solers*.

Sollom (hamlet, Lancs): 'muddy enclosure'. OS *sol*, 'muddy place' (related modern English *soil*), + *hegn*, 'enclosure' (related modern English *hedge*). The name could also mean 'sunny slope' (OS *sól*, 'sun', + *hlein*, 'slope'). *c*.1200 *Solayn*.

Solva (coastal village, Pemb): '(place on the river) Solfach'. The river name may mean 'poor one' (modern Welsh *salw*, 'ugly'). The Solfach enters the sea here and gives the Welsh name of the village. *c*.1200 *Saleuuach*.

Solway Firth (sea inlet, Dumfries & Gall/Cumbria): 'inlet of the pillar ford'. OS *súla*, 'pillar', + *vath*, 'ford', + *fjǫrthr*, 'inlet'. The name probably refers to the Lochmaben Stone, a granite boulder that marks the end of the ford across the Solway Firth on the Scottish side. 1229 *Sulewad*.

Somerby (village, Lincs): 'Sumarlithi's farmstead'. OS *bý*, 'farmstead', 'village'. The personal name is Scandinavian. Cp. SOMERLEYTON. DB *Sumertebi*. SO ALSO: *Somerby*, Leics.

Somerford Keynes (village, Glos): 'de Keynes' (estate by the) ford used in summer'. OE *sumor*, 'summer', + *ford*, 'ford'. The river here is the Thames. The de Keynes family held the manor here in the 13C and also at *Ashton Keynes* ('farmstead where ash trees grow'), Wilts, 2 miles to the southeast, and *Poole Keynes* ('(place by the) pool'), 1 mile to the southwest. 685 *Sumerford*, 1291 *Somerford Keynes*.

Somerleyton (village, Suffolk): 'Sumarlithi's farmstead'. OE *tūn*, 'farmstead'. The personal name is Scandinavian. DB *Sumerledetuna*.

Somersal Herbert (village, Derbys): 'Fitzherbert's (estate at) Sumor's corner of land'. OE *halh*, 'nook', 'corner of land'. The Fitzherbert family held the manor here in the 13C. DB *Summersale*, *c*.1300 *Somersale Herbert*.

Somersby (village, Lincs): 'Sumarlithi's farmstead'. OS *bý*, 'farmstead', 'village'. The personal name is Scandinavian. Cp. SOMERLEYTON. DB *Summerdebi*.

Somerset (county, SW England): '(district of the) settlers around Somerton'. OE *sǣte*, 'settlers'. The first part of the name is a shortened form of SOMERTON. 'Some will have it so called from the *summerliness*, or temperate pleasantness thereof: with whom we concur, whilst they confine their etymologies to the air; *dissent*, if they extend it to the earth, which in winter is as *winterly*, deep, and dirty, as any in England. The truth is, it is so named from *Somerton*, the most ancient town in the county' (Thomas Fuller, *The Worthies of England*, 1662). The alternative name *Somersetshire* has OE *scīr*, 'shire', 'district'. 12C *Sumersæton*, *Sumersetescir*.

Somersham (village, Cambs): 'Sumor's or Sunmær's homestead'. OE *hām*, 'homestead'. *c*.1000 *Summeresham*, DB *Sumersham*.

Somersham (village, Suffolk): 'Sumor's homestead'. OE *hām*, 'homestead'. DB *Sumersham*.

Somers Town (district, Camden). The district here grew up in the late 18C on the estate of Lord Somers, a descendant of the 1st Baron Somers of Evesham (1651–1716), Lord Chancellor. 1795 *Sommers Town*.

Somerton (town, Somerset): 'farmstead used in summer'. OE *sumor*, 'summer', + *tūn*, 'farmstead'. The name refers to a farm whose pastures were usable only in summer, since they were too wet or swampy for use in winter. The area around Somerton has now been drained, so there is no longer marshland. The favourable pasturing here no doubt attracted the settlers who gave the name of SOMERSET. 901 *Sumortun*, DB *Summertone*. SO ALSO: *Somerton*, Oxon.

Somerton (village, Suffolk): 'Sumarlithi's farmstead'. OE *tūn*, 'farmstead'. The personal name is Scandinavian. Cp. SOMERLEYTON. DB *Sumerledetuna*.

Sompting (district of Worthing, W Sussex): '(settlement of the) dwellers at the marsh'. OE *sumpt*, 'swamp', 'marsh' (related English *sump*), + *-ingas*, 'dwellers at'. The terrain is low-lying here, and not far from the sea. 956 *Suntinga*, DB *Sultinges*.

Sonning (village, Wokingham): '(settlement of) Sunna's people'. OE *-ingas*, 'people of'. DB *Soninges*.

Sopley (village, Hants): 'Soppa's woodland clearing'. OE *lēah*, 'wood', 'clearing'. The first part of the name could also represent OE *soppa*, 'marsh' (related modern English *sopping*), giving a sense 'marshy wood'. Sopley is in the valley of the river Avon. DB *Sopelie*.

Sopworth (village, Wilts): 'Soppa's enclosure'. OE *worth*, 'enclosure'. DB *Sopeworde*.

Sorviodunum. See SALISBURY.

Sotterley (hamlet, Suffolk): '(place by the) woodland clearing'. OE *lēah*, 'wood', 'clearing'. The first part of the name is of uncertain origin. It may represent a personal name. DB *Soterlega*.

Sotwell (village, Oxon): '(place by) Sutta's spring'. OE *wella*, 'spring', 'stream'. Sotwell is formally joined (via Latin *cum*, 'with') to nearby BRIGHTWELL, both places taking their name from a spring. DB *Sotwelle*.

Soulbury (village, Bucks): 'stronghold by a gully'. OE *sulh*, 'gully', + *burh*, 'fortified place'. DB *Soleberie*.

Soulby (village, Cumbria): 'Súla's farmstead'. OS *bý*, 'farmstead'. The personal name is Scandinavian. The name could also mean 'farmstead made of posts' (OS *súla*, 'post', + *bý*). The form of the name below applies to Soulby near Kirkby Stephen, but Soulby near Pooley Bridge has a name of identical origin. *c.*1160 *Sulebi*.

Souldern (village, Oxon): '(place by the) thorn bush in a gully'. OE *sulh*, 'gully', + *thorn*, 'thorn bush'. *c.*1160 *Sulethorne*.

Souldrop (village, Beds): 'outlying farmstead near a gully'. OE *sulh*, 'gully', + *throp*, 'outlying farmstead'. OE *sulh* properly means 'plough', hence 'furrow made by a plough', hence 'gully', which is here the valley through which a river and railway run. 1196 *Sultrop*.

Sourton (village, Devon): 'farmstead by a neck of land'. OE *swēora*, 'neck', 'col', + *tūn*, 'farmstead'. The 'neck of land' is the hill to the east of Sourton that separates two deep valleys. *c.*970 *Swurantune*, DB *Surintone*.

Southall (district, Ealing): 'southern corners of land'. OE *sūth*, 'southern', + *halh*, 'nook', 'corner of land'. The corresponding 'northern corners of land' were at NORTHOLT. 1198 *Suhaull*.

Southam (town, Warwicks): 'southern homestead'. OE *sūth*, 'southern', + *hām*, 'homestead'. The identity of the corresponding northern place is uncertain. The second part of the name could also represent OE *hamm*, 'land in a river bend'. Southam is on the river Stowe. The DB form of the name below has *c* for *t*. 998 *Suthham*, DB *Sucham*. SO ALSO: *Southam*, Glos.

South Ambersham (hamlet, W Sussex): 'southern (place called) Æmbre's homestead or riverside land'. OE *hām*, 'homestead', or *hamm*, 'riverside land'. The river here is the Rother. The first word of the name distinguishes this Ambersham from the former *North Ambersham*, 8 miles to the north. 963 *Æmbresham*.

Southampton (city, Southampton): 'southern estate on a promontory'. OE *sūth*, 'southern', + *hamm*, 'enclosure', 'promontory', + *tūn*, 'farmstead', 'estate'. The original name was *Hampton* (which gave the name of HAMPSHIRE). Hence Bevis of Hampton, hero of the medieval verse romance named after him. 'South' was subsequently added to distinguish this Hampton from NORTHAMPTON, although that *Hampton* has a different origin. The 'promontory' is the land between the Itchen and Test estuaries

where the modern city arose. 825 *Homtun*, 962 *Suthhamtunan*, DB *Hantone*.

South Anston. See NORTH ANSTON.

South Barrow. See NORTH BARROW.

South Barsham. See EAST BARSHAM.

South Benfleet (town, Essex): 'southern (place by the) tree-trunk creek'. OE *bēam*, 'beam', 'tree trunk', + *flēot*, 'creek'. A 'tree-trunk creek' is one with a rudimentary bridge, here Benfleet Creek, an inlet of the Thames. The first word of the name distinguishes the town from the nearby village of *North Benfleet*. 10C *Beamfleote*, DB *Benflet*.

South Bersted (district of Bognor Regis, W Sussex): 'southern homestead by a tumulus'. OE *beorg*, 'mound', 'tumulus', + *hām-stede*, 'homestead' (see HAMPSTEAD). The first word of the name distinguishes the place from the smaller *North Bersted*. 680 *Beorganstede*.

Southborough (town, Kent): 'southern borough'. OE *sūth*, 'southern', + *burh*, 'fortified place', 'borough'. The borough was 'south' by contrast with Tonbridge, to which it belonged. 1270 *bo. de Suth*, 1450 *la South Burgh*.

Southbourne (district, Bournemouth). The name dates only from the 19C. Geographically, 'Eastbourne' would have been more appropriate, but that name was already in use for EASTBOURNE. The name therefore remained, matching *Northbourne* and *Westbourne*. The second part of the name reflects both the river *Bourne* here and BOURNEMOUTH itself.

South Brent (village, Devon): 'southern high place'. The basic name is Celtic in origin, related to modern Welsh *bre*, 'hill', 'upland'. The 'high place' is nearby Brent Hill, and the village is 'south' in relation to a former *Over Brent*, further up the river Avon. DB *Brenta*.

South Brentor. See NORTH BRENTOR.

South Brewham. See NORTH BREWHAM.

Southburgh (village, Norfolk): '(place by the) southern hill'. OE *sūth*, 'southern', + *beorg*, 'hill'. The hill may be 'south' with regard to WHIN-BURGH, 2 miles to the north. The DB form of the name below has *c* for *g*. DB *Berc*, 1291 *Suthberg*.

South Burlingham. See NORTH BURLINGHAM.

South Cadbury. See NORTH CADBURY.

South Cave (village, E Yorks): 'southern (place by the) rapid stream'. OE *cāf*, 'swift', 'quick'. The stream in question is probably the one now known as Mire Beck, which flows from the Yorkshire Wolds through nearby *North Cave* to be joined by Cave Beck not far from South Cave. DB *Cave*.

South Cerney. See NORTH CERNEY.

South Charlton. See NORTH CHARLTON.

South Cheriton. See NORTH CHERITON.

Southchurch (district of Southend-on-Sea, Southend): 'southern church'. OE *sūth*, 'southern', + *cirice*, 'church'. The church was in the south of Rochford hundred here. 1042 *Suthcyrcan*, DB *Sudcerca*.

South Clifton. See NORTH CLIFTON.

South Collingham. See COLLINGHAM.

South Cove. See NORTH COVE.

South Cowton. See EAST COWTON.

South Creake. See NORTH CREAKE.

South Croxton (village, Leics): 'southern farmstead in a corner of land'. OE *crōc*, 'crook', 'corner of land', + *tūn*, 'farmstead'. The name could also mean 'Krókr's farmstead', with a Scandinavian personal name. South Croxton is 15 miles southwest of CROXTON KERRIAL. DB *Crochestone*, 1212 *Sudcroxton*.

South Dalton. See NORTH DALTON.

Southease (village, E Sussex): 'southern (land overgrown with) brushwood'. OE *sūth*, 'southern', + *hǣse*, 'brushwood'. The name contrasts with that of nearby *Northease Farm*. 966 *Sueise*, DB *Suesse*.

South Elmhams. See NORTH ELMHAM.

South Elmsall (town, Wakefield): 'southern corner of land by the elm tree'. OE *elm*, 'elm', + *halh*, 'nook', 'corner of land'. The first word of the name distinguishes the town from nearby *North Elmsall*. The DB form of the name below has *r* for *l*. DB *Ermeshale*, 1230 *Suthelmeshal*.

Southend-on-Sea (resort town, Southend): '(place at the) southern end'. ME *south*, 'southern', + *ende*, 'end'. The resort arose at the southern end of the parish of Prittlewell (and also on the south coast of Essex). The second part of the name was added as a holiday lure, especially originally to day visitors ('trippers') from London, some 35 miles to the west. 1481 *Sowthende*.

Southery (village, Norfolk): 'southerly island'. OE *sūtherra*, 'southerly', + *ēg*, 'island'. The village lies on the edge of extensive fenland. 942 *Suthereye*, DB *Sutreia*.

South Fambridge. See NORTH FAMBRIDGE.

South Ferriby (village, N Lincs): 'southern farmstead by the ferry'. OS *ferja*, 'ferry', + *bý*, 'farmstead', 'village'. The name refers to the early ferry crossing on the Humber here

between what are now the villages of South Ferriby and *North Ferriby*, E Yorks. DB *Ferebi*, *c*.1130 *Suthferebi*.

Southfields (district, Wandsworth): 'southern arable open land'. OE *sūth*, 'southern', + *feld*, 'open land' (modern English *field*). The name contrasts with a former *Northfields*, nearer the Thames, whose name is preserved in that of the street called Northfields, Wandsworth. 1247 *Suthfeld*.

Southfleet. See NORTHFLEET.

Southgate (district, Enfield): '(place by the) southern gate'. OE *sūth*, 'southern', + *geat*, 'gate'. The gate in question would have led into Enfield Chase. 1370 *Suthgate*.

South Hams (council district, Devon): 'southern enclosures'. OE *sūth*, 'southern', + *hamm*, 'enclosure'. *The South Hams* is the name of the fertile district between Plymouth and the estuary of the river Dart, with Dartmoor as its northern boundary. It is therefore south of the latter. OE *hamm* here has the particular sense 'cultivated area of land' rather than simply 'enclosure'. 1396 *Southammes*.

South Hanningfield. See EAST HANNINGFIELD.

South Harting (village, W Sussex): 'southern (settlement of) Heort's people'. OE *-ingas*, 'people of'. The parish of *Harting* contains the villages of *East Harting* and *South Harting* and the hamlet of *West Harting*. 970 *Hertingas*, DB *Hertinges*, 1248 *Suthhertlinges*.

South Hayling (town, Hants): 'southern (place in) Hayling'. The town is located at the southern end of HAYLING ISLAND, its name contrasting with that of the village of *North Hayling*, near the northern end. *c*.1140 *Hailinges*.

South Heighton (village, E Sussex): 'southern high farmstead'. OE *sūth*, 'southern', + *hēah*, 'high', + *tūn*, 'farmstead'. The village is 'south' in relation to nearby *Heighton Street*. DB *Hectone*, 1327 *Sutheghton*.

South Hiendley (village, Wakefield): 'southern wood or clearing where does are seen'. OE *hind*, 'hind', 'doe', + *lēah*, 'wood', 'clearing'. The first part of the name distinguishes this Hiendley from former adjacent *Upper Hiendley*, now represented by *Upper Hiendley Farm*, and from nearby *Cold Hiendley*, so called from its bleak, exposed position. DB *Hindeleia*.

South Hinksey. See NORTH HINKSEY.

South Holme (hamlet, N Yorks): 'southern island'. OS *holmr*, 'island'. The 'island' is well-watered land here between Hole Beck, the river Rye and Wath Beck. The first word of the name distinguishes the place from nearby *North Holme*. DB *Holme*, 1301 *Southolme*.

South Huish. See NORTH HUISH.

Southill (village, Beds): 'southern (settlement of the) Gifle'. OE *sūth*, 'southern'. The tribal name derives from the river Ivel here, whose own name is of Celtic origin and means 'forked stream'. Cp. YEOVIL. The village is 'south' with regard to *Northill*, 3 miles to the north near the same river. Its own name thus means 'northern (settlement of the) Gifle'. DB *Sudgiuele*.

South Kelsey. See NORTH KELSEY.

South Killingholme. See NORTH KILLING-HOLME.

South Kilvington. (village, N Yorks): 'southern estate associated with Cylfa or Cynelāf'. OE -*ing*-, 'associated with', + *tūn*, 'farmstead', 'estate'. The first word of the name distinguishes the village from the nearby much smaller *North Kilvington*. DB *Chelvinctune*.

South Kilworth. See NORTH KILWORTH.

South Kirkby (town, Wakefield): 'southern village with a church'. OE *sūth*, 'southern', + OS *kirkju-bý* (from *kirkja*, 'church', + *bý*, 'village'). This Kirkby was 'south' in relation to a former Kirkby in Pontefract, 6 miles to the north. DB *Cherchebi*, 1129 *Sudkirkebi*.

South Kyme. See NORTH KYME.

Southleigh. See NORTHLEIGH.

South Leigh. See NORTH LEIGH.

South Littleton. See NORTH LITTLETON.

South Lopham. See NORTH LOPHAM.

South Luffenham. See NORTH LUFFENHAM.

South Malling (district of Lewes, E Sussex): 'southern (settlement of) Mealla's people'. OE -*ingas*, 'people of'. There is no 'North Malling'. Cp. WEST MALLING. 838 *Mallingum*, DB *Mellinges*.

South Marston. See MEYSEY HAMPTON.

South Milford (village, N Yorks): 'southern (place by the) ford at a mill'. OE *myln*, 'mill', + *ford*, 'ford'. The ford here took the Roman road to Tadcaster over the stream now known as Mill Dyke. The first word of the name distinguishes the village from the smaller *North Milford*, 5 miles to the north. *c.*1030 *Myleford*.

South Mimms (village, Herts): 'southern (territory of the) Mimmas'. The tribal name is of uncertain origin. The first word of the name distinguishes the village from *North Mimms*, 2 miles to the north, now best known for *North Mymms Park*. DB *Mimes*.

Southminster (village, Essex): 'southern church'. OE *sūth*, 'southern', + *mynster*, 'monastery', 'church'. The corresponding 'northern church' may have been at STEEPLE, 2 miles to north. Despite the name, it is unlikely to have been UPMINSTER, 25 miles away. *c.*1000 *Suthmynster*, DB *Sudmunstra*.

South Molton (town, Devon): 'southern farmstead by Molland'. OE *sūth*, 'southern', + *tūn*, 'farmstead'. Both South Molton and the corresponding *North Molton*, 3 miles to the northeast, share the first part of their main name with that of MOLLAND, to the east of them. DB *Sudmoltone*.

South Mundham. See NORTH MUNDHAM.

South Muskham. See NORTH MUSKHAM.

South Newington. See NORTH NEWINGTON.

South Newton. See NORTH NEWNTON.

South Normanton. See TEMPLE NORMAN-TON.

South Ockendon (suburb of Grays, Thurrock): 'southern (place called) Wocca's hill'. OE *dūn*, 'hill'. The first word of the name distinguishes this place from nearby *North Ockendon*, Havering. DB *Wochenduna*.

Southolt (village, Suffolk): '(place by the) southern wood'. OE *sūth*, 'southern', + *holt*, 'wood'. DB *Sudholda*.

South Ormsby (village, Lincs): 'southern (place called) Ormarr's farmstead'. OS *bý*, 'farmstead', 'village'. The personal name is Scandinavian. The first word of the name distinguishes this Ormsby from NORTH ORMSBY, 13 miles to the north, but with a name of different origin. DB *Ormesbi*, early 12C *Ormeresbi*, 1323 *Suth Ormesby*.

Southorpe (village, Peterborough): 'southern outlying farmstead'. OE *sūthr*, 'southern', + *thorp*, 'outlying farmstead'. The farm was probably regarded as 'south' in relation to Barnack. DB *Sudtorp*.

South Otterington (village, N Yorks): 'southern estate associated with Oter'. OE -*ing*-, 'associated with', + *tūn*, 'farmstead', 'estate'. The first word of the name distinguishes the village from nearby *North Otterington*. DB *Otrinctun*.

South Owersby. See NORTH OWERSBY.

Southowram (village, Calderdale): 'southern (place by the) ridge'. OE *sūth*, 'southern', + *ufer*, 'ridge'. The second and original part of the name represents OE *uferum*, the dative plural form of *ufer*. The first part was added to distinguish this place from *Northowram*, 2 miles to the north. The names refer to two long ridges here, separated from each other by Shibden Brook. DB *Overe*, *c*.1275 *Sudhouerum*.

South Perrott. See NORTH PERROTT.

South Petherton (town, Somerset): 'southern farmstead on the (river) Parrett'. OE *sūth*, 'southern', + *tūn*, 'farmstead'. For the river name, see NORTH PERROTT. The first word of the name distinguishes the town from the village of *North Petherton*, 15 miles to the northwest. DB *Sudperetone*.

South Petherwin. See NORTH PETHERWIN.

South Pickenham. See NORTH PICKENHAM.

South Pool (village, Devon): 'southern (place by the) pool'. OE *pōl*, 'pool', 'creek'. The 'pool' is Southpool Creek, a tidal arm of the Kingsbridge estuary. The first word of the name distinguishes the village from nearby *North Pool*, a hamlet in the same parish. DB *Pole*.

South Poorton. See NORTH POORTON.

Southport (resort town, Sefton): 'southern port'. The name was given to a development here in 1798 in a location formerly known as *South Hawes*. It seems to have adopted the first word of this name, perhaps adding *port* for a generally more important maritime place. It may also have been seen as 'south' in relation to North Meols, 2 miles to the northeast, now absorbed into Southport itself.

South Raynham. See EAST RAYNHAM.

Southrepps. See NORTHREPPS.

South Ronaldsay (island, Orkney): 'southern Rögnvaldr's island'. OS *ey*, 'island'. Rögnvaldr was the brother of Sigurd, first Jarl of Orkney in the late 9C. The island, the southernmost of the Orkneys, is 'south' in relation to NORTH RONALDSAY, where the personal name is different. *c*.1150 *Rögnvalsey*.

Southrop (village, Glos): 'southern outlying farmstead'. OE *sūth*, 'southern', + *throp*, 'outlying farmstead'. Southrop is the most southerly of the *throps* in this part of the county. 6 miles to the northwest is *Hatherop*, 'high outlying farmstead' (OE *hēah*, 'high', + *throp*). *c*.1140 *Sudthropa*.

South Runcton. See NORTH RUNCTON.

South Scarle. See NORTH SCARLE.

Southsea (resort district, Portsmouth): '(place in the) south by the sea'. The name was originally that of the castle that Henry VIII built in 1538 at the entrance to Portsmouth Harbour. The second part of the name may have been influenced by that of nearby PORTSEA ISLAND. 1545 *le South castell of Portesmouth*, 1579 *Southsea ca*.

South Shields (town and port, S Tyneside): 'southern sheds'. ME *south*, 'southern', + *schele*, 'shed', 'shieling'. The 'sheds' would have been temporary huts used by fishermen on the south bank of the Tyne here, opposite NORTH SHIELDS. 1235 *Scheles*.

South Somercotes. See NORTH SOMERCOTES.

South Stainley (village, N Yorks): 'southern stony woodland clearing'. OE *stān*, 'stone', + *lēah*, 'wood', 'clearing'. OE *stān* has been replaced by equivalent OS *steinn*. The first word of the name distinguishes the village from *North Stainley*, 9 miles to the north. DB *Stanlai*, 1198 *Southstainlei*.

South Stifford. See NORTH STIFFORD.

South Tawton. See BISHOP'S TAWTON.

South Thoresby. See NORTH THORESBY.

South Walsham. See NORTH WALSHAM.

Southwark (borough, Greater London): 'southern fort'. OE *sūth*, 'southern', + *weorc*, 'building', 'fortification' (modern English *work*). The 'southern fort' was a defensive post here south of the Thames as an outpost of the City of London. (Cp. BOROUGH, THE.) Its name in the 10C was *Suthriganaweorc*, 'fort of the men of Surrey'. DB *Sudwerca*.

South Warnborough. See NORTH WARNBOROUGH.

South Weald. See NORTH WEALD BASSETT.

Southwell (town, Notts): '(place by the) southern spring'. OE *sūth*, 'southern', + *wella*, 'spring' (modern English *well*). The 'southern spring' is the Lady Well by the minster church here, while the corresponding 'northern spring' was at the village of *Norwell*, 7 miles to the northeast. 958 *Suthwellan*, DB *Sudwelle*.

South Weston (village, Oxon): 'southern western farmstead'. OE *west*, 'western', + *tūn*, 'farmstead'. The first word of the name distinguishes this Weston from the smaller *North Weston*, 4 miles to the north. DB *Westone*.

South Wheatley. See NORTH WHEATLEY.

Southwick (village, Hants): 'southern dairy farm'. OE *sūth*, 'southern', + *wīc*, 'specialized farm'. The identity of a corresponding 'northern dairy farm' is uncertain. *c*.1140 *Sudwic*. SO ALSO: *Southwick*, Sunderland.

Southwick (village, Northants): 'southern dairy farm'. OE *sūth*, 'southern', + *wīc*, 'specialized farm'. The farm may have been regarded as 'south' in relation to Apethorpe. *c*.980 *Suthwycan*.

Southwick (coastal town, W Sussex): 'southern dwelling'. OE *sūth*, 'southern', + *wīc*, 'dwelling', 'specialized farm'. The place was originally a 'southern dwelling' or farm of the manor of Kingston. 1073 *Sudewic*.

Southwick (village, Wilts): 'southern dairy farm'. OE *sūth*, 'southern', + *wīc*, 'specialized farm'. The farm was probably seen as south with regard to Trowbridge. 1196 *Sudwich*.

South Widcombe (hamlet, Bath & NE Somerset): 'southern (place in the) wide valley'. OE *wīd*, 'wide', + *cumb*, 'valley'. The main name could also mean '(place in the) valley where willows grow' (OE *wīthig*, 'willow', + *cumb*). The first word of the name distinguishes this Widcombe from nearby *North Widcombe*. 1303 *Widecomb*.

South Willingham (village, Lincs): 'southern homestead of Willa's people'. OE *-inga-*, 'of the people of', + *hām*, 'homestead'. The first word of the name contrasts this Willingham with NORTH WILLINGHAM, 4 miles to the northwest (with a name of different origin), and with CHERRY WILLINGHAM, 13 miles to the southwest (with a name of identical origin). DB *Ulingeham*.

South Wingfield. See NORTH WINGFIELD.

South Witham. See NORTH WITHAM.

Southwold (resort town, Suffolk): '(place by the) southern forest'. OE *sūth*, 'southern', + *wald*, 'woodland', 'forest'. The woodland here was probably regarded as being south of Lowestoft. See WOLDS. DB *Sudwolda*.

South Wootton. See NORTH WOOTTON.

South Wraxall. See NORTH WRAXALL.

South Zeal (village, Devon): 'southern hall'. OE *sele*, 'hall'. The name is perhaps more likely to represent OE *sealh*, 'sallow', 'willow'. The identity of the corresponding northern place is uncertain. 1168 *La Sele*.

Sowerby Bridge (town, Calderdale): 'bridge by Sowerby'. The name was originally that of the nearby village of *Sowerby*, 'farmstead on sour ground' (OS *saurr*, 'sour', + *bý*, 'farmstead'), meaning swampy terrain, as here, where the soil is liable to be waterlogged. The name then passed to the bridge over the Calder here and this was adopted for the modern industrial town, which evolved in the early 19C as a suburb of Halifax. A bridge is known to have existed in 1315, when the township of *Sourby* was fined 13s. 4d. for not repairing it. The first form of the name below is that of the village, the second that of the bridge. DB *Sorebi*, 15C *Sourebybrigge*.

Sowton (village, Devon): 'southern farmstead'. OE *sūth*, 'southern', + *tūn*, 'farmstead', 'village'. The place was probably south with

regard to Monkerton, to the north. Its earlier name was *Clis*, referring to its position by the river Clyst (see CLYST HONITON). DB *Clis*, 1420 *Southton*.

Spadeadam Forest (moorland region, Cumbria): origin uncertain. The name may be of Celtic origin, from a word related to modern Welsh *ysbyddaden*, 'hawthorn'. 1295 *Spathe Adam*, 1399 *Spadadam*.

Spalding (town, Lincs): '(settlement of the) people in Spald'. OE *-ingas*, 'dwellers in'. The old district name perhaps means '(region of the) ditch' (OE *spald*, 'ditch', 'trench'), referring to some natural feature. DB *Spallinge*, c.1115 *Spaldingis*.

Spaldington (village, E Yorks): 'farmstead of the Spaldingas'. OE *tūn*, 'farmstead'. The tribal name (OE *-inga-*, 'of the people of') is that of the people who gave the name of SPALDING. DB *Spellinton*.

Spaldwick (village, Cambs): 'farm by a ditch'. OE *spald*, 'ditch', 'trench', + *wīc*, 'dwelling', 'specialized farm'. DB *Spalduice*.

Spalford (village, Notts): '(place by the) ford over a trickling stream'. OE *spāld*, 'spittle', 'saliva', + *ford*, 'ford'. The first part of the name could also represent OE *spald*, 'ditch', 'trench', giving a meaning '(place by the) ford over a ditch'. DB *Spaldesforde*.

Sparham (village, Norfolk): 'homestead or enclosure made with spars'. OE *spearr*, 'spar', 'shaft', + *hām*, 'homestead', or *hamm*, 'enclosure'. DB *Sparham*.

Sparkbrook (district, Birmingham): '(place by) Spark's brook'. A family named Spark are recorded as living here in the 13C and gave their name to the stream nearby.

Sparkford (village, Somerset): '(place by the) ford among brushwood'. OE *spearca*, 'brushwood', + *ford*, 'ford'. DB *Sparkeforda*.

Sparkwell (village, Devon): '(place by the) stream where brushwood grows'. OE *spearca*, 'brushwood', + *wella*, 'spring', 'stream'. c.1070 *Spearcanwille*, DB *Sperchewelle*.

Sparsholt (village, Hants): '(place by the) wood of the spar'. OE *spearr*, 'spar', 'rafter'. The reference is to a wood where spars and rafters were obtained. 901 *Speoresholte*.

Sparsholt (village, Oxon): '(place by the) wood of the spear'. OE *spere*, 'spear', + *holt*, 'wood'. The name may refer to a wood where spear shafts were obtained or else to a 'spear trap' for wild animals. 963 *Speresholte*, DB *Spersolt*.

Spaunton (hamlet, N Yorks): 'farmstead with a shingled roof'. OS *spánn*, 'chip', 'shingle', + OE *tūn*, 'farmstead'. DB *Spantun*.

Spaxton (village, Somerset): 'Spakr's farmstead'. OE *tūn*, 'farmstead'. The personal name is Scandinavian. DB *Spachestone*.

Speen (district of Newbury, W Berks): 'place of woodchips'. OE *spēne*, 'woodchip'. The name, originally that of a wood here, was adapted (but not directly adopted) from the Roman name *Spinis*, '(place) at the thorn bushes', from Latin *spina*, 'thorn' (modern English *spine*). 821 *Spene*, DB *Spone*.

Speeton (village, N Yorks): 'enclosure where meetings are held'. OE *spēc*, 'speech', 'meeting', + *tūn*, 'enclosure'. The local hundred may have met here. DB *Specton*.

Speke (district, Liverpool): '(place of) brushwood'. OE *spēc*, 'branches', 'brushwood'. DB *Spec*.

Speldhurst (village, Kent): '(place by the) wooded hill where woodchips are found'. OE *speld*, 'splinter', + *hyrst*, 'wooded hill'. 8C *Speldhirst*.

Spelsbury (village, Oxon): 'Spēol's stronghold'. OE *burh*, 'fortified place'. early 11C *Speolesbyrig*, DB *Spelesberie*.

Spelthorne (council district, Surrey): 'thorn bush where speeches are made'. OE *spell*, 'speech' (modern English *spell*, 'words of magic charm'), + *thorn*, 'thorn bush'. The name is that of a former hundred of Middlesex, referring to its meeting place. The site of this is uncertain, but it may have been somewhere near Ashford, east of Staines, as in 1819 the road leading from Ashford to Kempton Park is known to have been called Spelthorne Lane. This name exists today for the road running along the eastern edge of Queen Mary Reservoir. DB *Spelethorne*.

Spenborough (district, Kirklees). The modern industrial borough was formed in 1915 as an urban district in the valley of the river Spen, which takes its name from *Spen* near Gomersal, from ME *spenne*, 'fence', 'enclosure'. 1308 *Spen*.

Spennithorne (village, N Yorks): '(place at the) thorn bush by the fence'. OE or OS *spenning*, 'hedge', 'fence' (related modern English *span*), + *thorn*, 'thorn bush'. The DB form of the name below has taken *thorn* as OS *thorp*, 'outlying farmstead'. DB *Speningetorp*, 1184 *Speningthorn*.

Spennymoor (town, Durham): '(place on the) moor with a fence'. OE or OS *spenning*, 'hedge', 'fence' (related modern English *span*), + *mōr*, 'moor'. c.1336 *Spendingmor*.

Spetchley (village, Worcs): 'woodland clearing where speeches are made'. OE *spēc*, 'speech',

+ *lēah*, 'wood', 'clearing'. The speeches would have been made at the meetings of Oswaldslow hundred, whose meeting place was at nearby Low Hill. 967 *Spæclea*, DB *Speclea*.

Spetisbury (village, Dorset): 'fortified place where woodpeckers are seen'. OE *speoht*, 'green woodpecker', + *burh*, 'fortified place'. The 'fortified place' is the nearby Iron Age hill fort of Spettisbury Rings, whose subsequent earthwork was doubtless regularly visited by green woodpeckers. DB *Spehtesberie*.

Spexhall (hamlet, Suffolk): 'corner of land where woodpeckers are seen'. OE *speoht*, 'woodpecker', + *halh*, 'nook', 'corner of land'. 1197 *Specteshale*.

Spey (river). See GRANTOWN-ON-SPEY.

Spilsby (town, Lincs): 'Spillir's farmstead'. OS *bý*, 'farmstead', 'village'. The personal name is Scandinavian. DB *Spilesbi*.

Spindlestone (hamlet, Northd): '(place by the) rock resembling a spindle'. OE *spinele*, 'spindle', + *stān*, 'stone', 'rock'. 1187 *Spindlestan*.

Spinis. See SPEEN.

Spital (district of Bebington, Wirral): 'hospital'. ME *spitel*, 'hospital', 'religious house'. The hospital here was for lepers, and associated with St Thomas the Martyr's chapel. 1385 *le Spitell*.

Spitalfields (district, Tower Hamlets): 'hospital fields'. ME *spitel*, 'hospital', 'religious house', + *feld*, 'field'. The land here belonged to the Priory of St Mary Spital, founded in 1197. 1394 *Seintmariespitel in Shordich*.

Spital in the Street (hamlet, Lincs): 'hospital on the Roman road'. ME *spitel*, 'hospital', 'religious house', + OE *strǣt*, 'Roman road' (modern English *street*). Little is known about the early history of the hospital here, but the chapel is dedicated to St Edmund, king and martyr. The Roman road is Ermine Street, between Lincoln and York. 1158 *Hospitali*, 1295 *Spytelothestrete*.

Spithead (sea strait, Hants): 'headland of the sandspit'. OE *spitu*, 'spit of land', + *hēafod*, 'headland'. The name, not recorded before the 17C, originally referred to the 'head' or end of the sandbank on the Hampshire coast called *Spit Sand*, now built over. It then passed to the whole strait. 1619 *Spithead*.

Spithurst (hamlet, E Sussex): 'wooded hill with a gap'. ME *split*, 'split', 'gap', + OE *hyrst*, 'wooded hill'. The name implies a wood divided in two by a path or track. 1296 *Splytherst*.

Spixworth (village, Norfolk): 'Spic's enclosure'. OE *worth*, 'enclosure'. DB *Spikesuurda*.

Spofforth (village, N Yorks): 'ford by a small plot of ground'. OE *spot*, 'small piece', 'bit' (modern English *spot*), + *ford*, 'ford'. The ford would have been over the Crimple Beck here, a tributary of the Nidd. DB *Spoford*, 1218 *Spotford*.

Spondon (district, Derby): '(place by the) hill where woodchips are obtained'. OE *spōn*, 'woodchip' (modern English *spoon*), + *dūn*, 'hill'. DB *Spondune*.

Sporle (village, Norfolk): '(place by the) wood or clearing where spars are obtained'. OE *spearr*, 'spar', 'shaft', + *lēah*, 'wood', 'clearing'. DB *Sparlea*.

Spratton (village, Northants): 'farmstead made of poles'. OE *sprēot*, 'pole', + *tūn*, 'farmstead'. DB *Spretone*.

Spreyton (village, Devon): 'farmstead among brushwood'. OE *sprǣg*, 'twigs', 'brushwood' (modern English *spray*), + *tūn*, 'farmstead'. DB *Spreitone*.

Spridlington (village, Lincs): 'estate associated with Sprytel'. OE *-ing-*, 'associated with', + *tūn*, 'farmstead', 'estate'. DB *Spredelintone*.

Springfield (suburb of Chelmsford, Essex): 'open land of the dwellers by the springs'. OE *spring*, 'spring', + *-inga-* 'of the dwellers at', + *feld*, 'open land' (modern English *field*). The whereabouts of any springs here is uncertain, and OE *spring* may have some other sense, such as 'young woodland'. This interpretation depends on the DB form below, which may be corrupt, with a reduplicated *-ing-*. DB *Springinghefelda*.

Sprinkling Tarn (lake, Cumbria): origin uncertain. The name probably comes from that of a stream here. Its own name is perhaps related to that of the river *Sprint* that rises by Haweswater and that itself may derive from OS *spretta* (earlier *sprenta*), 'to jump', 'to start'. 1774 *Sparkling Tarn*, *c.*1784 *Sprinkling Tarn*.

Sproatley (village, E Yorks): 'woodland clearing where young shoots grow'. OE *sprota*, 'shoot' (related modern English *sprout*), + *lēah*, 'wood', 'clearing'. DB *Sprotele*.

Sproston Green (hamlet, Cheshire): 'Sprow's farmstead'. OE *tūn*, 'farmstead'. The village was later associated with its green. DB *Sprostune*.

Sprotbrough (village, Doncaster): 'Sprota's stronghold'. OE *burh*, 'fortified place'. The name could also mean 'stronghold overgrown with young shoots' (OE *sprota*, 'shoot', + *burh*). DB *Sproteburg*.

Sproughton (village, Suffolk): 'Sprow's farmstead'. OE *tūn*, 'farmstead'. 1191 *Sproeston*.

Sprowston (suburb of Norwich, Norfolk): 'Sprow's farmstead'. OE *tūn*, 'farmstead'. DB *Sprowestuna*.

Sproxton (village, Leics): 'Sprok's farmstead'. OE *tūn*, 'farmstead'. The personal name is Scandinavian. The name could also mean 'farmstead amid brushwood' (OS *sprogh*, 'brushwood', + OE *tūn*). The DB form of the name below has omitted the *x*. DB *Sprotone*, *c.*1125 *Sproxcheston*. SO ALSO: *Sproxton*, N Yorks.

Spurn Head (headland, E Yorks): 'headland of the spur'. ME *spurn*, 'spur', 'projecting piece of land'. The name refers to the spur-like outline of the headland. The form of the name below refers to *Ravenser*, 'Hrafn's sandbank' (OS *eyrr*, 'gravel bank', with a Scandinavian personal name), the former settlement here, now long submerged by the sea. 1399 *Ravenserespourne*.

Spurstow (village, Cheshire): 'meeting place on a trackway'. OE *spor*, 'track', 'footprint' (related modern English *spoor*), + *stōw*, 'place'. Spurstow stands near the point where the Roman road from Tarporley to Whitchurch, Shropshire, crosses the old saltway from Nantwich to Farndon, and this could be the 'meeting point on a trackway'. But the first part of the name could also represent OE *spura*, 'spur (of land)', referring to the location of the village on a slight ridge. The DB form of the name below is corrupt. DB *Spuretone*, *c.*1200 *Sporstow*.

Stackpole Elidor. See CHERITON (Pemb).

Stadhampton (village, Oxon): 'riverside land where horses are kept'. OE *stōd*, 'stud', 'herd of horses', + *hamm*, 'enclosure', 'riverside land'. Stadhampton is by the Thames. The '-ton' of the name is a fairly recent addition, probably made under the influence of nearby Brookhampton and Chislehampton. *c.*1135 *Stodeham*.

Staffa (island, Argyll & Bute): 'pillar island'. OS *stafr*, 'pillar', 'rod' (related modern English *staff*), + *ey*, 'island'. The reference is to the columns of basaltic rock on the island.

Staffield (hamlet, Cumbria): 'round hill with a staff'. OS *stafr*, 'staff', 'post', + *hóll*, 'hill'. *c.*1225 *Stafhole*.

Stafford (town, Staffs): '(place at the) ford by a landing place'. OE *stæth*, 'landing place', + *ford*, 'ford'. Stafford is on the river Sow, and the ford in question was probably at the limit of navigation, where the landing place would have been, very likely where Bridge Street crosses the river today. The name has its own popular etymology: '[The English] made another settlement at Stafford, or the ford over the broadening stream, which could be crossed by the help of a staff' (Mandell Creighton, *The Story of Some English Shires*, 1897). Mid-11C *Stæfford*, DB *Stadford*.

Staffordshire (county, central England): 'district based on Stafford'. OE *scīr*, 'shire', 'district'. See STAFFORD. 11C *Stæffordscir*.

Stagsden (village, Beds): '(place in the) valley of stakes'. OE *staca*, 'stake', + *denu*, 'valley'. The 'stakes' may have been boundary markers. DB *Stachedene*.

Stainburn (village, N Yorks): '(place by the) stony stream'. OE *stān*, 'stone', + *burna*, 'stream'. OE *stān* has been replaced in the name by equivalent OS *steinn*. c.972 *Stanburne*, DB *Stainburne*.

Staincross (suburb of Barnsley): '(place by the) stone cross'. OE *steinn*, 'stone', + *kros*, 'cross'. The cross here marked the meeting place of the local wapentake. DB *Staincros*.

Staindrop (village, Durham): '(place in the) valley with stony ground'. OE *stǣner*, 'stony ground', + *hop*, 'valley'. Staindrop lies on a tributary of the river Tees, in a valley near Raby Park. c.1040 *Standropa*, 1868 *Staindrop, or Stainthorp*.

Staines (town, Surrey): '(place at the) stone'. OE *stān*, 'stone'. The stone in question was perhaps a Roman milestone on the road from London to Silchester, although popularly identified as a boundary stone here that marked the western limit of the jurisdiction of the City of London. The London Stone, as it is called, has an inscription 'God preserve the City of London. A.D. 1285', but the name predates this by many years. A plural -s was added by the time of the DB record of the name below. The Roman settlement at Staines was *Pontibus*, '(place at the) bridges', referring to the crossing of the Thames here. 11C *Stane*, DB *Stanes*.

Stainforth (town, Doncaster): '(place by the) stony ford'. OE *stān*, 'stone', + *ford*, 'ford'. The river here is the Don. Cp. STAMFORD. The original OE *stān* has been replaced in the name by the equivalent OS *steinn*. DB *Steinforde*. SO ALSO: *Stainforth*, N Yorks.

Staining (village, Lancs): '(settlement of) Stān's people'. OE *-ingas*, 'people of'. The name could also mean '(settlement of the) dwellers on stony ground' (OE *stān*, 'stone', influenced by equivalent OS *steinn* + *-ingas*, 'dwellers at') or simply 'stony place' (OE *stāning*). DB *Staininghe*.

Stainland (village, Calderdale): '(place on) stony cultivated land'. OE *stān*, 'stone', + *land*, 'cultivated land'. OS *stān* has been replaced in the name by equivalent OS *steinn*. DB *Stanland*.

Stainsacre (village, N Yorks): 'Steinn's plot of arable land'. OS *akr*, 'cultivated land' (related modern English *acre*). The personal name is Scandinavian. 1090 *Stainsaker*.

Stainton (village, Cumbria): 'farmstead on stony ground'. OE *stān*, 'stone', + *tūn*, 'farmstead'. OE *stān* has been replaced in the name by equivalent OS *steinn*. The form of the name below relates to Stainton near Penrith, but Stainton near Kendal has a name of identical origin. 1166 *Stainton*. SO ALSO: *Stainton*, Doncaster, Durham.

Staintondale (village, N Yorks): 'farmstead on stony ground in the valley'. OE *stān*, 'stone', + *tūn*, 'farmstead', + ME *dale*, 'valley'. OE *stān* was later replaced by equivalent OS *steinn*. DB *Steintun*, 1562 *Staynton Dale*.

Stainton le Vale (village, Lincs): 'farmstead on stony ground in the valley'. OE *stān*, 'stone', + *tūn*, 'farmstead', + ME *vale*, 'valley'. The village lies in a valley in the Lincolnshire Wolds. OE *stān* was later replaced by equivalent OS *steinn*. DB *Staintone*.

Staithes (coastal village, N Yorks): 'landing places'. OE *stæth*, 'landing place' (modern English *staithe*). The form of the name below is prefixed with the name of nearby *Seaton* ('farmstead by the sea'), which the landing places must have been designed to serve. 1415 *Setonstathes*.

Stalbridge (village, Dorset): '(place by the) bridge built on piles'. OE *stapol*, 'post', 'pile' (modern English *staple*), + *brycg*, 'bridge'. According to K. J. Penn's *Historic Towns in Dorset* (1980), the name 'may refer to a bridge over the Stour or Bibbern Brook (and thus presumably some way from the present settlement)'. 998 *Stapulbreicge*, DB *Staplebrige*.

Stalham (village, Norfolk): 'homestead or enclosure by the fishing pool'. OE *stall*, 'stall', 'fishing pool', + *hām*, 'homestead', or *hamm*, 'enclosure'. Stalham lies near Sutton Broad. 1044 *Stalham*, DB *Stalham*.

Stalisfield Green (village, Kent): 'open land with a stall'. OE *stall*, 'stall', 'stable', + *feld*, 'open land' (modern English *field*). The second word, alluding to the village green, was added later. The DB form of the name below is corrupt. DB *Stanefelle*, c.1100 *Stealesfelde*.

Stallingborough (village, NE Lincs): 'fortified place of Stalla's people'. OE *-inga-*, 'of the people of', + *burh*, 'fortified place'. DB *Stalingeburg*.

Stalling Busk (hamlet, N Yorks): '(place by the) stallion's bush'. ME *stalun*, 'stallion', + OS *buski*, 'bush'. 1218 *Stalunebusc*.

Stalmine (village, Lancs): '(place at the) mouth of the pool'. OE *stœll*, '(fishing) pool', + OS *mynni*, 'mouth'. DB *Stalmine*.

Stalybridge (town, Tameside): 'bridge by a wood where staves are cut'. OE *stæf*, 'staff', 'stave', + *lēah*, 'wood', 'clearing', + *brycg*, 'bridge'. The name was originally that of a hamlet in Lancashire across the river Tame from the Cheshire township of *Stayley*, its own name having the same meaning as the first part of the longer name. Cp. STAVELEY. The Lancashire name then superseded that of the Cheshire place (the present Tameside town). 13C *Stauelegh*, 1560 *Stayley*, 1687 *Stalybridge*.

Stambourne (village, Essex): '(place by the) stony stream'. OE *stān*, 'stone', + *burna*, 'stream'. DB *Stanburna*.

Stamford (town, Lincs): '(place by the) stony ford'. OE *stān*, 'stone', + *ford*, 'ford'. A 'stony ford' is either one with a gravelly bed or, as here, a ford where stones have been laid for ease of crossing. The site of the original ford across the river Welland is just below the Town Bridge. The alternative for the third form of the name below (now *Newstead*) means 'new place' (OE *nīwe*, 'new', + *stede*, 'place'), referring to the Augustinian priory founded here in the late 12C. 10C *Steanford*, DB *Stanford*, 1868 *Stamford, or Newstead*.

Stamford Bridge (village, E Yorks): 'bridge by the stony ford'. OE *stān*, 'stone', + *ford*, 'ford', + *brycg*, 'bridge'. The ford across the river Derwent here was replaced by a bridge at an early date. *c.*1075 *Stanford brycg*.

Stamfordham (village, Northd): 'homestead by the stony ford'. OE *stān*, 'stone', + *ford*, 'ford', + *hām*, 'homestead', 'village'. The ford would have been over the river Pont here. 1188 *Stanfordham*.

Standish (town, Wigan): 'stony enclosure'. OE *stān*, 'stone', + *edisc*, 'enclosure', 'enclosed park'. 1178 *Stanesdis*.

Standlake (village, Oxon): '(place by the) stony stream'. OE *stān*, 'stone', + *lacu*, 'stream', 'channel' (related modern English *lake*). The stream in question is a tributary of the river Windrush here. According to a piece of 18C popular etymology, the place is so called as it is 'situate upon a damn'd standing Puddle, long Deep and Dirty'. *c.*1155 *Stanlache*.

Standon (village, Herts): '(place by the) stony hill'. OE *stān*, 'stone', + *dūn*, 'hill'. 944 *Standune*, DB *Standone*.

Stanfield (village, Norfolk): '(place on) stony open land'. OE *stān*, 'stone', + *feld*, 'open land' (modern English *field*). DB *Stanfelda*.

Stanford on Avon. See STANFORD ON SOAR.

Stanford in the Vale (village, Oxon): '(place by the) stony ford in the valley'. OE *stān*, 'stone', + *ford*, 'ford'. The ford in question was probably over Frogmore Brook here. The village lies in the VALE OF WHITE HORSE. DB *Stanford*, 1496 *Stanford in le Vale*.

Stanford-le-Hope (town, Thurrock): '(place by the) stony ford in the Hope'. OE *stān*, 'stone', + *ford*, 'ford'. The stony ford across a stream by the Thames here was distinguished from STANFORD RIVERS, Essex, 15 miles to the northwest, by nearby *Broad Hope*, at a broad curve in the Thames. 'Hope' represents OE *hop*, which usually means 'valley', but which here is better rendered 'bay'. 1267 *Staunford*, 1361 *Stanford in the Hope*.

Stanford on Soar (village, Notts): '(place by the) stony ford on the (river) Soar'. OE *stān*, 'stone', + *ford*, 'ford'. The river name (see BARROW UPON SOAR) probably distinguishes the village from *Stanford on Avon* (see AVONMOUTH), Northants, 28 miles to the south. DB *Stanford*.

Stanford on Teme (village, Worcs): '(place by the) stony ford on the (river) Teme'. OE *stān*, 'stone', + *ford*, 'ford'. For the river name, see TENBURY WELLS. DB *Stanforde*.

Stanford Rivers (hamlet, Essex): 'Rivers' (estate by the) stony ford'. OE *stān*, 'stone', + *ford*, 'ford'. The ford would have been over the river Roding. The manor here was held in the 13C by the Rivers family. The second word of the name (popularly referred to the river) distinguishes the hamlet from STANFORD LE HOPE, Thurrock, 15 miles to the southeast. 1068 *Stanford*, DB *Stanfort*, 1289 *Stanford Ryueres*.

Stanhoe (village, Norfolk): '(place on a) stony hill spur'. OE *stān*, 'stone', + *hōh*, 'hill spur'. DB *Stanhou*.

Stanhope (town, Durham): '(place in a) stony valley'. OE *stān*, 'stone', + *hop*, 'valley'. The reference is to a valley full of stones, or one with stony soil. OE *hop* often specifically described an enclosed place, as here at Stanhope, which is sheltered by hills and moorland. 1183 *Stanhopa*.

Stanion (village, Northants): 'stone buildings'. OE *stān*, 'stone', + *œrn*, 'house', 'building'. The DB form of the name below has omitted the *n* of *œrn*. DB *Stanere*, 1162 *Stanerna*.

Stanley (town, Durham): 'stony woodland clearing'. OE *stān*, 'stone', + *lēah*, 'wood', 'clearing'. The name relates to a clearing with stony or rocky soil. 1297 *Stanley*. SO ALSO: *Stanley*, Derby, Staffs, Wakefield.

Stanlow (oil refinery, Cheshire): 'rock hill'. The present oil refinery and former abbey take their name from the rocky promontory on the Mersey estuary known as Stanlow Point (OE *stān*, 'stone', 'rock', + *hlaw*, 'hill'). The abbey, founded in 1172 with the name *Locus Benedictus*, 'Blessed Place', was evacuated to Whalley in 1296 following serious flooding. 1172 *Stanlawa*.

Stanmer (village, Brighton & Hove): '(place by the) stony pool'. OE *stān*, 'stone', + *mere*, 'pool'. The pool in question is now in the grounds of the University of Sussex. Just over the border in East Sussex is another pool at FALMER. 765 *Stanmere*, DB *Stanmere*.

Stanmore (district, Harrow): '(place by the) stony pool'. OE *stān*, 'stone', + *mere*, 'pool'. There was probably a gravelly pool here at one time. DB *Stanmere*.

Stanningfield (hamlet, Suffolk): '(place on) stony open land'. OE *stān*, 'stone', or *stānen*, 'stony', + *feld*, 'open land' (modern English *field*). DB *Stanfelda*, 1197 *Stanefeld*.

Stannington (village, Northd): 'farmstead at the stony place'. OE *stāning*, 'stony place', + *tūn*, 'farmstead'. 1242 *Stanigton*.

Stansfield (village, Suffolk): 'Stān's open land'. OE *feld*, 'open land' (modern English *field*). DB *Stanesfelda*.

Stanstead Abbots. See STANSTED.

Stansted (village, Essex): 'stony place'. OE *stān*, 'stone', + *stede*, 'place'. The reference is probably to a prominent stone building here, rather than to a place with stony soil. The village is properly *Stansted Mountfitchet*, after the Muntfichet family, who held the manor here in the 12C. Their name distinguishes this Stansted from *Stanstead Abbots*, Herts, 12 miles to the southwest, where the manor was held in the 13C by the Abbot of Waltham, and, across the river Lea from it, *Stanstead St Margarets*, Herts, now known as *St Margarets*, named after the dedication of its church. DB *Stanesteda*, c.1290 *Stansted Mounfichet*.

Stanton (village, Glos): 'farmstead on stony ground'. OE *stān*, 'stone', + *tūn*, 'farmstead'. DB *Stantone*. SO ALSO: *Stanton*, Suffolk.

Stanton by Dale (village, Derbys): 'farmstead on stony ground near Dale'. OE *stān*, 'stone', + *tūn*, 'farmstead'. The second part of the name relates to nearby DALE (Abbey). DB *Stantone*.

Stanton Drew (village, Bath & NE Somerset): 'Drogo's farmstead by the stones'. OE *stān*, 'stone', + *tūn*, 'farmstead'. The name alludes to the ancient stone circles here. The manor was held in 1225 by one Drogo or Drew. DB *Stantone*, 1253 *Stanton Drogonis*.

Stanton Fitzwarren (village, Swindon): 'fitz Waryn's farmstead by the stone'. OE *stān*, 'stone', + *tūn*, 'farmstead'. There is a large standing stone here. The manor was held in 1196 by Fulco filius Warini. DB *Stantone*, 1394 *Staunton Fitz Waryn*.

Stanton Harcourt (village, Oxon): 'de Harecurt's farmstead by the stones'. OE *stān*, 'stone', + *tūn*, 'farmstead'. The name refers to the ancient stones nearby known as the Devil's Coits. The de Harecurt family held the manor here in the 12C, their name distinguishing this Stanton from STANTON ST JOHN, 10 miles to the east. DB *Stantone*, c.1275 *Stantone Harecurt*.

Stanton Lacy (village, Shropshire): 'de Lacy's farmstead on stony ground'. OE *stān*, 'stone', + *tūn*, 'farmstead'. Roger de Lacy held the manor here in 1086, his name distinguishing this Stanton from *Stanton Long*, 9 miles to the northeast, where the village straggles along the road, by contrast with the compact Stanton Lacy at the southern end of Corve Dale. DB *Stantone*, 1255 *Stanton Lacy*.

Stanton Long. See STANTON LACY.

Stanton on the Wolds. See STAUNTON IN THE VALE.

Stanton St Bernard (village, Wilts): 'Bernard's farmstead on stony ground'. OE *stān*, 'stone', + *tūn*, 'farmstead'. 'Bernard' appears to go back ultimately to the name of Erebetus, known to have held the manor here in 1242. (The Fits Herbard in the second form of the name below was presumably a descendant.) The 'St' is unexplained, but may have been added on analogy with STANTON ST QUINTIN, 17 miles to the northwest. DB *Stantone*, 1402 *Staunton Fits Herbard*, 1553 *Staunton Barnarde*.

Stanton St John (village, Oxon): 'de Sancto Johanne's farmstead on stony ground'. OE *stān*, 'stone', + *tūn*, 'farmstead'. John de Sancto Johanne held land here in the 12C, his name distinguishing this Stanton from STANTON HARCOURT, 10 miles to the west. DB *Stantone*, 1155 *Stantona Johannis de Sancto Johanne*.

Stanton St Quintin (village, Wilts): 'de Sancto Quintino's farmstead on stony ground'. OE *stān*, 'stone', + *tūn*, 'farmstead'. The de Sancto Quintino family held the manor here in the 13C. DB *Stantone*, 1283 *Staunton St Quintin*.

Stanton upon Hine Heath (village, Shropshire): 'farmstead on stony ground on the heath of the domestic servants'. OE *stān*, 'stone', + *tūn*, 'farmstead', + ME *hine*, 'servant', + *hethe*, 'heath'. The significance of the second part of the name is uncertain. DB *Stantune*, 1327 *Staunton super Hyne Heth*.

Stanwardine in the Fields (hamlet, Shropshire): 'enclosure on stony ground in open country'. OE *stān*, 'stone', + *worthign*, 'enclosure', + *feld*, 'open land' (modern English *field*). The second part of the name distinguishes this Stanwardine from *Stanwardine in the Wood*, 2½ miles to the northeast. DB *Staurdine*, 1271 *Stanwarthin in Le Felde*.

Stanway (village, Essex): '(place by the) stony roads'. OE *stān*, 'stone', + *weg*, 'way', 'road'. Stanway lies between two parallel Roman roads to Colchester, and these would have been the 'stony roads'. *c*.1000 *Stanwǣgun*, DB *Stanwega*.

Stanway (village, Glos): '(place by the) stony road'. OE *stān*, 'stone', + *weg*, 'way', 'road'. The 'stony road' would have been the salt route from Droitwich, which passed through the settlement. 12C *Stanwege*.

Stanwell (district of Staines, Surrey): '(place by the) stony spring'. OE *stān*, 'stone', + *wella*, 'spring', 'stream'. The soil is gravelly here, on the course of the Roman road Stane Street ('stony street'). DB *Stanwelle*.

Stanwick (village, Northants): '(place by the) rocking stone'. OE *stān*, 'stone', + *wigga*, 'wiggler' (literally 'beetle'). The reference is to a local logan stone, which can be easily rocked. 10C *Stanwigga*, DB *Stanwige*.

Stanwix (district of Carlisle, Cumbria): '(place of) stone walls'. OS *steinn*, 'stone', + *veggr*, 'wall'. The walls are those of the Roman fort on Hadrian's Wall here known as *Uxelodunum*, 'high fort', a name of Celtic origin (related modern Welsh *uchel*, 'high', and *dinas*, 'fort'). *c*.1160 *Steynweuga*.

Stapenhill (district of Burton upon Trent, Staffs): '(place by the) steep hill'. OE *stēap*, 'steep', + *hyll*, 'hill'. The first part of the name represents OE *stēapan*, the dative form of *stēap*. DB *Stapenhille*.

Staple Fitzpaine (village, Somerset): 'Fitzpaine's (estate by the) post'. OE *stapol*, 'post', 'pillar'. The reference is to a wood or stone post here, presumably set up as a marker. The Fitzpaine family held the manor here in the 14C. DB *Staple*.

Stapleford (town, Notts): '(place by the) ford marked by a post'. OE *stapol*, 'post', 'pillar', + *ford*, 'ford'. The name implies that a ford across the river Erewash here needed special marking, presumably because it was dangerous. DB *Stapleford*. SO ALSO: *Stapleford*, Cambs.

Stapleford Abbots (village, Essex): 'abbot's (place by the) ford marked by a post'. OE *stapol*, 'post', 'pillar', + *ford*, 'ford'. The ford would have been over the river Roding, perhaps at Passingford Bridge. The manor here was held early by the Abbot of Bury St Edmunds, whose title distinguishes this Stapleford from nearby *Stapleford Tawney*, where it was held by the de Tany family. DB *Staplefort*, 1255 *Staplford Abbatis Sancti Edmundi*.

Staplegrove (suburb of Taunton, Somerset): '(place by the) grove where posts are obtained'. OE *stapol*, 'post', + *grāf*, 'grove'. 1327 *Stapilgrove*.

Staplehurst (village, Kent): '(place by the) wooded hill where posts are obtained'. OE *stapol*, 'post', + *hyrst*, 'wooded hill'. 1226 *Stapelherst*.

Stapleton (village, Leics): 'farmstead by a post'. OE *stapol*, 'post', 'pillar', + *tūn*, 'farmstead'. The name could also imply that the farm was actually built on posts. DB *Stapletone*. SO ALSO: *Stapleton*, Bristol.

Stapleton (village, Shropshire): 'farmstead by a steep place'. OE *stēpel*, 'steep place' (modern English *steeple*), + *tūn*, 'farmstead'. 12C *Stepleton*. SO ALSO: *Stapleton*, Herefords.

Starbeck (hamlet, N Yorks): '(place by the) brook where sedge grows'. OS *star*, 'sedge', + *bekkr*, 'brook'. The name is first recorded only in 1817 but seems to have this origin and meaning.

Starbotton (village, N Yorks): '(place in the) valley where stakes are obtained'. OE *stæfer*, 'stake' (related modern English *staff*, *stave*), + OS *botn*, 'valley'. OE *stæfer* has replaced OS equivalent *stafn* in the (garbled) DB form of the name below. DB *Stamphotne*, 12C *Stauerboten*.

Starcross (village, Devon): 'cross where starlings are seen'. Modern English dialect *stare*, 'starling', + modern English *cross*. The name could apply to a crossroads as well as a cross. 1689 *Star Crosse*.

Starston (village, Norfolk): 'Styrr's farmstead'. OE *tūn*, 'farmstead', 'village'. The personal name is Scandinavian. DB *Sterestuna*.

Startforth (village, Durham): '(place by the) ford on a Roman road'. OE *strǣt*, 'Roman road' (modern English *street*), + *ford*, 'ford'. Startforth stands at the point where Watling Street crosses the river Tees. The name is more common in the form STRATFORD. *c.*1050 *Stretford*, DB *Stradford*.

Start Point (headland, Devon): 'headland at the tongue of land'. OE *steort*, 'tail', 'tongue of land'. The name refers to the outline of the headland. 1310 *La Sterte*, 1586 *Start point*.

Stathe (village, Somerset): '(place by the) landing place'. OE *stæth*, 'landing place'. Stathe is on the river Parrett. 1233 *Stathe*.

Stathern (village, Leics): 'thorn bush serving as a stake'. OE *staca*, 'stake', + *thyrne*, 'thorn bush'. The name implies that the thorn bush marked a boundary. DB *Stachedirne*.

Staunton (village, Glos): 'farmstead on stony ground'. OE *stān*, 'stone', + *tūn*, 'farmstead'. The name could also mean 'farm by a standing stone', and Samuel Rudder, in *A New History of Gloucestershire* (1779), mentions such a stone here. This Staunton is the one near Coleford, not the one north of Gloucester, whose name has the first meaning above. 12C *Stantune*.

Staunton in the Vale (village, Notts): 'farmstead on stony ground in the valley'. OE *stān*, 'stone', + *tūn*, 'farmstead'. The second part of the name, referring to the Vale of Belvoir, distinguishes the village from *Stanton on the Wolds* (see WOLDS), 15 miles to the southwest. DB *Stantone*.

Staunton on Arrow (village, Herefords): 'farmstead on stony ground on the (river) Arrow'. OE *stān*, 'stone', + *tūn*, 'farmstead'. For the river name, see ARROW. 958 *Stantun*, DB *Stantune*, 1868 *Stanton-upon-Arrow*.

Staunton on Wye (village, Herefords): '(place by the) stony hill on the (river) Wye'. OE *stān*, 'stone', + *dūn*, 'hill'. For the river name, see ROSS-ON-WYE. DB *Standune*.

Staveley (town, Derbys): '(place by the) wood where staves are cut'. OE *stæf*, 'staff', 'stave', + *lēah*, 'wood', 'clearing'. Cp. STALYBRIDGE. DB *Stavelie*. SO ALSO: *Staveley*, Cumbria, N Yorks.

Staverton (village, Devon): 'farmstead by a stony ford'. OE *stān*, 'stone', + *ford*, 'ford', + *tūn*, 'farmstead'. The river here is the Dart. *c.*1070 *Stofordtune*, DB *Stovretona*.

Staverton (village, Glos): 'farmstead made of stakes'. OE *stæfer*, 'stake', + *tūn*, 'farmstead'. The name could also mean 'farmstead marked out by stakes'. DB *Staruenton*. SO ALSO: *Staverton*, Northants, Wilts.

Stawell (village, Somerset): '(place by the) stony stream'. OE *stān*, 'stone', + *wella*, 'spring', 'stream'. DB *Stawelle*.

Stearsby (hamlet, N Yorks): 'Styrr's farmstead'. OS *bý*, 'farmstead', 'village'. The personal name is Scandinavian. DB *Stirsbi*.

Stebbing (village, Essex): '(settlement of) Stybba's people'. OE *-ingas*, 'people of'. The first part of the name could also represent OE *stybb*, 'stump', giving a meaning '(settlement of the) dwellers among the tree stumps'. DB *Stibinga*.

Stechford (district, Birmingham): '(place by the) sticky ford'. OE *sticce*, 'sticky', + *ford*, 'ford'. A ford over the river Cole here must have been clayey or muddy. 1267 *Stichesford*.

Stedham (village, W Sussex): 'homestead or enclosure of the stallion'. OE *stēda*, 'stallion' (modern English *steed*), + *hām*, 'homestead', or *hamm*, 'enclosure'. The name could also mean 'Stedda's homestead or enclosure'. 960 *Steddanham*, DB *Stedeham*.

Steep (village, Hants): 'steep place'. OE *stīepe*, 'steep place'. There is quite a steep drop from the downs here. 12C *Stepe*.

Steeple (hamlet, Dorset): 'steep place'. OE *stēpel*, 'steeple' (from *stēap*, 'steep', 'high'). The hamlet stands below a steep hill. DB *Stiple*.

Steeple (village, Essex): 'steep place'. OE *stēpel*, 'steeple' (from *stēap*, 'steep', 'high'). The village could be regarded as 'steep' by comparison with the surrounding flat terrain. DB *Stepla*.

Steeple Ashton (village, Wilts): 'farmstead where ash trees grow with a steeple'. OE *stīepel*, 'steeple', + *æsc*, 'ash', + *tūn*, 'farmstead'. The first word of the name distinguishes the village from nearby *Rood Ashton*, where there was presumably a wayside cross (OE *rōd*), and *West Ashton*. 964 *Æystone*, DB *Aistone*, 1268 *Stepelaston*.

Steeple Aston (village, Oxon): 'eastern farmstead with a steeple'. OE *stīepel*, 'steeple', + *ēast*, 'eastern', + *tūn*, 'farmstead'. DB *Estone*, 1220 *Stipelestun*.

Steeple Bumpstead (village, Essex): 'place where rushes grow with a steeple'. OE *stēpel*, 'steeple', + *bune*, 'reeds', 'rushes', + *stede*, 'place'. The first word of the name distinguishes the village from nearby *Helions Bumpstead*, where Tihel de Helon held one of the manors in 1086. DB *Bumesteda*, 1261 *Stepilbumstede*.

Steeple Claydon (village, Bucks): '(place on the) clayey hill with a steeple'. OE *stēpel*, 'steeple', 'tower', + *clǣgig*, 'clayey', + *dūn*, 'hill'. East of Steeple Claydon is *East Claydon*, and between them *Middle Claydon*. South of East Claydon is *Botolph Claydon*, where the first word has been altered from OE *bōtl*, 'house', 'building', by popular association with the saint's name. All four places are collectively known as *The Claydons*. DB *Claindone*, 13C *Stepel Cleydon*.

Steeple Gidding. See GREAT GIDDING.

Steeple Langford (village, Wilts): '(place by the) long ford with a steeple'. OE *stēpel*, 'steeple', + *lang*, 'long', + *ford*, 'ford'. The ford would have been over the river Wylye here. The first word of the name distinguishes the village from *Hanging Langford*, across the river, so called from its position below a steep hillside, and from nearby *Little Langford*. 943 *Langanforda*, DB *Langeford*, 1294 *Stupellangeford*.

Steeple Morden. See GUILDEN MORDEN.

Steeton (village, Bradford): 'farmstead among tree stumps'. OE *styfic*, 'stump', + *tūn*, 'farmstead'. The name could also refer to a farmstead actually built of tree stumps. DB *Stiuetune*.

Stella (district, Gateshead): 'pasture with a shelter for cattle'. OE *stelling*, 'cattle fold' (related modern English *stall*), + *lēah*, 'wood', 'clearing'. 1183 *Stelyngleye*.

Stenalees (village, Cornwall): '(place of) tin'. Cornish *stenek* (from *sten*, 'tin', + adjectival ending *-ek*). The second part of the name is of uncertain origin. It may represent Cornish *lys*, 'court', although the place has no administrative importance. 1621 *Senaglease alias Stenylease*.

Stenhousemuir (town, Falkirk): 'moorland by the stone house'. OE *stān*, 'stone', + *hūs*, 'house', + *mōr*, 'moor'. *c*.1200 *Stan house*, 1601 *Stenhous*.

Stepaside (village, Pemb). The village would have arisen by a wayside cottage or modest alehouse inviting the traveller to 'step aside' for rest and refreshment. 1694 *Stepaside*.

Stepney (district, Tower Hamlets): 'Stybba's landing place'. OE *hȳth*, 'landing place'. Stepney is on the Thames. The '-n-' of the name comes from *Stybban*, the genitive form of the personal name. *c*.1000 *Stybbanhythe*, DB *Stibanhede*.

Sternfield (village, Suffolk): 'Sterne's open land'. OE *feld*, 'open land' (modern English *field*). DB *Sternesfelda*.

Stert (village, Wilts): '(place by the) projecting piece of land'. OE *steort*, 'tail', 'point of land'. DB *Sterte*.

Stetchworth (village, Cambs): 'enclosure among the tree stumps'. OE *styfic*, 'tree stump', + *worth*, 'enclosure'. The name could also mean 'Styfic's enclosure'. *c*.1050 *Steuicheswrthe*, DB *Stiuicesuuorde*.

Stevenage (town, Herts): '(place by the) strong oak tree'. OE *stīth*, 'strong', + *āc*, 'oak'. There must have been a particular sturdy oak

here at one time. The spelling of the name reflects the dative forms of the two OE words after OE *æt*, 'at'. *c*.1060 *Stithenæce*, DB *Stigenace*.

Stevenston (town, N Ayrs): 'Steven's farm'. OE *tūn*, 'farmstead'. The identity of Steven is unknown. 1246 *Stevenstoun*.

Steventon (village, Hants): 'estate associated with Stīfa'. OE *-ing-*, 'associated with', + *tūn*, 'farmstead', 'estate'. The name could also mean 'farmstead at the place where trees have been grubbed up', with 'Steven-' representing OE *styfing*, from *styfic*, 'stump'. DB *Stivetune*. SO ALSO: *Steventon*, Oxon.

Stevington (village, Beds): 'estate associated with Stīfa'. OE *-ing-*, 'associated with', + *tūn*, 'farmstead', 'estate'. The name could also mean 'farmstead at the place where trees have been grubbed up', with 'Steven-' representing OE *styfing*, from *styfic*, 'stump'. DB *Stiuentone*.

Stewartby (village, Beds). The model village was built in 1926 for employees at the brickworks here by Sir Malcolm Stewart (1872–1951), who named it after his father, Sir Halley Stewart (1838–1937), vice chairman of the London Brick Company. 'Stewart took great pride in converting the drab hamlet of Wootton Pillinge in Bedfordshire into a garden village which bore the new name of Stewartby' (*Dictionary of National Biography*).

Stewarton (town, E Ayrs): 'steward's estate'. OE *tūn*, 'farmstead', 'estate'. The reference is to Walter, Seneschal (High Steward) to King David I, who owned the estate here in the 12C. 1201 *Stewartoun*.

Stewkley (village, Bucks): 'woodland clearing with tree stumps'. OE *styfic*, 'tree stump', + *lēah*, 'wood', 'clearing'. The DB form of the name below has omitted the *c* of *styfic*. DB *Stiuelai*, 1182 *Stiuecelea*.

Steyning (town, W Sussex): '(settlement of) Stān's people'. OE *-ingas*, 'people of'. The name could also mean '(settlement of the) dwellers at the stony place' (OE *stǣne*, 'stony place', + *-ingas*, 'dwellers at') or simply 'stony places', from a plural form of OE *stāning* or *stǣning*. *c*.880 *Stæningum*, DB *Staninges*.

Steynton (village, Pemb): 'farm built of stone'. OS *steinn*, 'stone', + OE *tūn*, 'farmstead'. 1291 *Steinton*.

Stibb (hamlet, Cornwall): '(place by the) tree stump'. OE *stybb*, 'tree stump'. 1327 *Stybbe*.

Stibbard (village, Norfolk): '(place on a) bank beside a path'. OE *stīg*, 'path', + *byrde*, 'bank'. OE *byrde* could be a river bank or a roadside. Stibbard is not on a river so the latter may apply here. The DB form of the name below is corrupt. DB *Stabyrda*, 1202 *Stiberde*.

Stibbington (village, Cambs): 'estate associated with Stibba'. OE *-ing-*, 'associated with', + *tūn*, 'farmstead', 'estate'. The first part of the name could also represent OE *stybbing*, 'tree-stump clearing'. DB *Stebintune*.

Sticker (village, Cornwall): '(place by) tree stumps'. Cornish *stekyer* (from *stok*, 'tree stump', + plural ending *-yer*). 1319 *Stekyer*.

Sticklepath (village, Devon): '(place by a) steep path'. OE *sticol*, 'steep' (related modern English *stile*), + *pæth*, 'path'. There is a steep ascent here over a northern spur of Dartmoor. 1280 *Stikelepethe*.

Stickney (village, Lincs): '(place on a) stick-like island'. OE *sticca*, 'stick', + *ēg*, 'island'. The village is located on land that forms an elongated island ('stick') between two streams, now catchment drains. DB *Stichenai*.

Stiffkey (village, Norfolk): 'island with tree stumps'. OE *styfic*, 'tree stump', + *ēg*, 'island'. The 'island' is raised ground here beside the river Stiffkey, whose own name comes from that of the village. DB *Stiuekai*.

Stillingfleet (village, N Yorks): 'stream belonging to Stȳfel's people'. OE *-inga-*, 'of the people of', + *flēot*, 'stream'. The name implies that a stretch of the river Ouse here belonged to the named people. DB *Steflingefled*.

Stillington (village, N Yorks): 'estate associated with Stȳfel'. OE *-ing-*, 'associated with', + *tūn*, 'farmstead', 'estate'. DB *Stiuelinctun*. SO ALSO: *Stillington*, Stockton.

Stilton (village, Cambs): 'farmstead at a stile'. OE *stigel*, 'stile', + *tūn*, 'farmstead'. Stilton is on Ermine Street, and there was presumably a point where a fence had to be climbed to continue northwards to Peterborough, as Ermine Street itself (now followed by the A1) turns to the northwest here. DB *Stichiltone*.

Stinchcombe (village, Glos): 'valley where sandpipers are seen'. OE *stint*, 'dunlin', 'sandpiper', + *cumb*, 'valley'. *c*.1155 *Stintescombe*.

Stinsford (village, Dorset): '(place by the) ford where sandpipers are seen'. OE *stint*, 'dunlin', 'sandpiper', + *ford*, 'ford'. The ford would have been over the river Frome here, or some branch of it. DB *Stincteford*.

Stirchley (hamlet, Wrekin): 'clearing where young bullocks are pastured'. OE *styrc*, 'young bullock', + *lēah*, 'clearing'. 1002 *Styrcleage*.

Stirling (city, Aberdeens): meaning uncertain. The name may have originally been that of the river, now the Forth, on which Stirling stands. An alternative possibility is 'enclosure by a stream' (Gaelic *sruth*, 'stream', + *lann*, 'enclosure'). 1124 *Strevelin*, *c*.1470 *Sterling*.

Stisted (village, Essex): 'place where lamb's cress grows'. OE *stīthe*, 'lamb's cress', + *stede*, 'place'. Lamb's cress is the bitter cress *Cardamine hirsuta*, which must have been plentiful here. DB *Stistede*, 1198 *Stidsted*.

Stithians (village, Cornwall): '(church of) St Stithian'. The church here is dedicated to Stithian, a female saint about whom nothing is known. 1268 *Sancta Stethyana*.

Stivichall (district, Coventry): 'corner of land with tree stumps'. OE *styfic*, 'stump', + *halh*, 'nook', 'corner of land'. *c*.1144 *Stivichall*.

Stoborough (village, Dorset): '(place by the) stony hill'. OE *stān*, 'stone', + *beorg*, 'hill', 'barrow'. DB *Stanberge*.

Stock (village, Essex): 'Hereweard's outlying farmstead'. OE *stoc*, 'outlying farmstead', 'secondary settlement'. The personal name was eventually dropped from the original name. 1234 *Herewardestoc*, 1476 *Herford Stoke*, 1608 *Harward alias Harrard Stock*, 1627 *Stocke alias Haverstocke*.

Stockbridge (village, Hants): '(place by the) bridge made of logs'. OE *stocc*, 'stock', 'tree trunk', + *brycg*, 'bridge'. The river Test is narrow enough to have been bridged here in this way. 1221 *Stochbrugge*.

Stockerston (village, Leics): 'stronghold built of logs'. OE *stocc*, 'tree trunk', 'log', + *fæsten*, 'stronghold' (related modern English *fastness*). The name denotes a basic blockhouse. The DB form of the name below has taken it as for STOCKTON. DB *Stoctone*, *c*.1130 *Stocfaston*.

Stock Green (village, Worcs): '(place by the) tree stump'. OE *stocc*, 'tree stump'. The village later became associated with its green, distinguishing it from nearby *Stock Wood*. 1271 *La Stokke*.

Stockingford (district of Nuneaton, Warwicks): '(place at the) ford by the tree-stump clearing'. OE *stoccing*, 'tree-stump clearing', + *ford*, 'ford'. 1157 *Stoccingford*.

Stocking Pelham. See BRENT PELHAM.

Stockland (village, Devon): 'cultivated land of the outlying farmstead'. OE *stoc*, 'outlying farmstead', + *land*, 'cultivated land'. 998 *Stocland*.

Stockland Bristol (village, Somerset): '(cultivated land of the outlying farmstead belonging to Bristol'. OE *stoc*, 'outlying farmstead', + *land*, 'cultivated land'. The manor here was held by the chamber of Bristol. DB *Stocheland*.

Stockleigh English (village, Devon): 'Engles' (estate by the) woodland clearing with tree stumps'. OE *stocc*, 'tree stump', + *lēah*, 'wood', 'clearing'. The manor here was held early by the Engles family, their name distinguishing this Stockleigh from *Stockleigh Pomeroy*, 2½ miles to the southeast, where the manor was held by the de Pomerei family. DB *Stochelie*, 1268 *Stokeley Engles*.

Stockport (town, Stockport): 'market place at an outlying hamlet'. OE *stoc*, 'place', 'secondary settlement', + *port*, 'town', 'market place'. *c.*1170 *Stokeport*.

Stocksbridge (town, Sheffield): '(place by the) bridge made of logs'. OE *stocc*, 'stock', 'tree trunk', + *brycg*, 'bridge'. There are no early records of the name, but it probably has the same origin as STOCKBRIDGE. The bridge in this case would have been over the Little Don. The form of the name below is on an early Ordnance Survey map. 1841 *Stocks Br*.

Stocksfield (village, Northd): 'open land belonging to an outlying hamlet'. OE *stoc*, 'outlying hamlet', + *feld*, 'open land' (modern English *field*). 1242 *Stokesfeld*.

Stockton (village, Warwicks): 'farmstead built of logs'. OE *stocc*, 'tree stump', 'log', + *tūn*, 'farmstead'. 1249 *Stocton*.

Stockton Heath (district, Warrington): 'farmstead at an outlying hamlet with a heath'. OE *stoc*, 'outlying hamlet', + *tūn*, 'farmstead'. The former heath here has left its name in Heath Street. *c.*1200 *Stocton*, 1682 *Stoaken Heath*.

Stockton-on-Tees (town, Stockton): 'farmstead at an outlying hamlet on the (river) Tees'. OE *stoc*, 'outlying hamlet', + *tūn*, 'farmstead'. For the river name, see TEESDALE. 1196 *Stocton*.

Stockton on Teme (village, Worcs): 'farmstead built of logs on the (river) Teme'. OE *stocc*, 'tree trunk', 'log', + *tūn*, 'farmstead'. For the river name, see TENBURY WELLS. *c.*957 *Stoctun*, DB *Stotune*.

Stockton on the Forest (village, York): 'farmstead built of logs on the (edge of the) forest'. OE *stocc*, 'tree trunk', 'log', + *tūn*, 'farmstead'. The village stands on the eastern side of the ancient forest of Galtres. Cp. SUTTON-ON-THE-FOREST. DB *Stochetun*.

Stockwell (district, Lambeth): '(place at the) spring by a tree stump'. OE *stocc*, 'tree stump', + *wella*, 'spring', 'stream'. 1197 *Stokewell*.

Stodmarsh (village, Kent): '(place by the) marsh where a herd of horses is kept'. OE *stōd*, 'stud', + *mersc*, 'marsh'. Stodmarsh lies beside the marshes of the Great Stour. 675 *Stodmerch*.

Stoford (hamlet, Wilts): '(place by the) stony ford'. OE *stān*, 'stone', + *ford*, 'ford'. See STAMFORD. The river here is the Avon. 943 *Stanford*.

Stogumber (village, Somerset): 'Gumer's outlying farmstead'. OE *stoc*, 'outlying farmstead'. One Gumer held the manor early here. 1225 *Stoke Gunner*.

Stogursey (village, Somerset): 'de Curci's outlying farmstead'. OE *stoc*, 'outlying farmstead'. The de Curci family held the manor here in the 12C. DB *Stoche*, 1212 *Stok Curcy*, 1868 *Stogursey, or Stoke-Courcy*.

Stoke Bishop (district, Bristol): 'outlying farmstead of the bishop'. OE *stoc*, 'outlying farmstead'. Stoke Bishop was held by the Bishop of Worcester for many years from the 10C. Cp. STOKE PRIOR. 804 *Stoc*, DB *Stoche*, 1285 *Stoke Episcopi*.

Stoke Bruerne (village, Northants): 'Briwere's outlying farmstead'. OE *stoc*, 'outlying farmstead'. The Briwere family held the manor here in the 13C. DB *Stoche*, 1254 *Stokbruer*.

Stoke-by-Nayland (village, Suffolk): 'place near Nayland'. OE *stoc*, 'place', 'secondary settlement'. OE *stoc* could have the sense 'religious place', and this applies in the case of Stoke, which was known to have a monastery. The second part of the name, locating Stoke near NAYLAND, distinguishes the village from *Stoke by Clare*, 16 miles to the northwest, near CLARE. *c.*950 *Stoke*, 1272 *Stokeneylond*.

Stoke Charity (village, Hants): 'de la Charite's outlying farmstead'. OE *stoc*, 'outlying farmstead'. The farm was originally a secondary settlement dependent on Micheldever. The manor here was held in 1276 by Henry de la Charite. DB *Stoches*, *c.*1270 *Stokecharite*.

Stoke Climsland (village, Cornwall): 'outlying farmstead in (the manor of) Climsland'. OE *stoc*, 'outlying farmstead'. *Climsland* has OE *land*, 'estate', added to an original name *Climes* of uncertain meaning. The manor name distinguishes this *Stoke* from others across the border in Devon, such as *Stoke Damerel* (now part of Devonport), 13 miles to the southeast, held by the de Albamarla family. 1266 *Stoke*.

Stoke D'Abernon (village, Surrey): 'de Abernun's outlying farmstead'. OE *stoc*, 'outlying farmstead'. The de Abernun family held the manor here in the 12C. DB *Stoche*, 1253 *Stokes de Abernun*.

Stoke Dry (village, Rutland): 'outlying farmstead on dry land'. OE *stoc*, 'outlying farmstead'. The second word of the name, referring to the location of the village on a hill above former marshland, distinguishes it from some other *stoc*, perhaps the one represented by the field called *Big Stockwell* in nearby Caldecott. DB *Stoche*.

Stoke Ferry (village, Norfolk): 'outlying farmstead with a ferry'. OE *stoc*, 'outlying farmstead', + OS *ferja*, 'ferry'. The ferry would have been over the river Wissey here, now crossed by the A134. DB *Stoches*, 1248 *Stokeferie*.

Stoke Fleming. See STOKE GABRIEL.

Stoke Gabriel (village, Devon): 'outlying farmstead with (the church of) St Gabriel'. OE *stoc*, 'outlying farmstead', 'secondary settlement'. The church dedication distinguishes this Stoke from *Stoke Fleming*, 6 miles to the south, where the manor was held by the le Flemeng family in the 13C. 1307 *Stoke*, 1309 *Stokegabriel*.

Stoke Gifford (village, S Glos): 'Gifard's outlying farmstead'. OE *stoc*, 'outlying farmstead', 'secondary settlement'. The Gifard family held the manor here from the 11C to the 14C. DB *Stoche*, 1243 *Stokes Giffard*.

Stokeham (village, Notts): '(place by the) outlying farmsteads'. OE *stoc*, 'outlying farmstead'. The name represents OE *stocum*, the dative plural form of *stoc*. DB *Estoches*, 1242 *Stokum*.

Stokeinteignhead (village, Devon): 'outlying farmstead in Tenhide'. OE *stoc*, 'outlying farmstead', 'secondary settlement'. The district has a name meaning 'ten hides' (OE *tēn*, 'ten', + *hīd*, 'hide'), denoting its extent. Cp. COMBEINTEIGNHEAD. The spelling has been influenced by the name of the nearby river Teign (see TEIGNMOUTH). DB *Stoches*, 1279 *Stokes in Tynhide*.

Stoke Mandeville (village, Bucks): 'Mandeville's outlying farmstead'. OE *stoc*, 'outlying farmstead'. The Mandeville family held the manor here in the 13C. DB *Stoches*, 1284 *Stoke Mandeville*.

Stokenchurch (village, Bucks): '(place with a) church made of logs'. OE *stoccen*, 'of logs', + *cirice*, 'church'. *c*.1200 *Stockenechurch*.

Stoke Newington (district, Hackney): 'new farmstead by the tree stumps'. OE *stoccen*, 'tree stumps', + *nīwe*, 'new', + *tūn*, 'farmstead'. The name is misleading, as the 'Stoke' is not as in STOKE-ON-TRENT and the '-ing-' represents the ending of OE *nīwan*, the dative form of *nīwe* in the phrase *æt thām nīwan tūne*, 'at the new farm'. The first word of the name was added to distinguish this Newington (or *Newton*) from HIGHBURY, which was formerly the manor of *Neweton Barrewe*. DB *Neutone*, 1274 *Neweton Stoken*, 1294 *Stokene Neuton*, 1535 *Stokenewington*.

Stokenham (village, Devon): 'outlying farmstead in an area of cultivated land'. OE *stoc*, 'outlying farmstead', + *in*, 'in', + *hamm*, 'enclosure'. Stokenham is in the district of SOUTH HAMS, with *hamm* in its specialized sense in that name. 1242 *Stokes*, 1276 *Stok in Hamme*.

Stoke-on-Trent (city, Stoke): 'outlying farmstead on the (river) Trent'. OE *stoc*, 'outlying farmstead', 'secondary settlement'. This Stoke is distinguished from the others by the addition of the river name, which is of Celtic origin and means 'trespasser' (related modern Welsh *trwy*, 'through', and *hynt*, 'way'), denoting a river liable to flooding. DB *Stoche*, 1232 *Stoke*.

Stoke Orchard (village, Glos): 'archer's (land at the) outlying farmstead'. ME *archere*, 'archer', + OE *stoc*, 'outlying farmstead'. The second word of the name, assimilated to modern *orchard*, refers to land here being held by the service to the king of supplying an archer equipped with bows and arrows for 40 days a year. 967 *Stoce*, DB *Stoches*, 1269 *Stokes le Archer*.

Stoke Poges (village, Bucks): 'le Pugeis' outlying farmstead'. OE *stoc*, 'outlying farmstead', 'secondary settlement'. The le Pugeis family held the manor here in the 13C. DB *Stoches*, 1292 *Stokepogeis*.

Stoke Prior (village, Worcs): 'outlying farmstead of the prior'. OE *stoc*, 'outlying farmstead'. The manor here was held by the Prior of Worcester, whereas STOKE BISHOP was an episcopal possession. 770 *Stoke*, DB *Stoche*, 1275 *Stoke Prioris*.

Stokesay (village, Shropshire): 'de Say's outlying farmstead'. OE *stoc*, 'place', 'outlying farmstead'. The de Say family held the manor here in the 13C. DB *Stoches*, 1256 *Stok Say*.

Stokesby (village, Norfolk): 'village with an outlying farmstead'. OE *stoc*, 'outlying farmstead', + OS *bý*, 'village'. The name could also mean 'village with an outlying pasture', from another sense of OE *stoc*. DB *Stokesbei*.

Stokesley (town, N Yorks): 'woodland clearing belonging to an outlying farmstead'. OE *stoc*, 'outlying farmstead', + *lēah*, 'wood', 'clearing'. DB *Stocheslage*.

Stoke St Gregory (village, Somerset): 'outlying farmstead with St Gregory's church'. OE *stoc*, 'outlying farmstead'. The church dedication distinguishes this Stoke from *Stoke St Mary*, 7 miles to the southwest. 1225 *Stokes*.

Stoke St Mary. See STOKE ST GREGORY.

Stoke St Milborough (village, Shropshire): 'St Milborough's outlying farmstead'. OE *stoc*, 'outlying farmstead'. The settlement here belonged to the Priory of St Milborough, Much Wenlock, founded in *c*.670 by Milburga (d.715), daughter of Merewald, king of Mercia. The DB form of the name below, referring to the same nunnery, is the equivalent of 'God's Stoke'. DB *Godestoch*, 1271 *Stok Milburge*.

Stoke sub Hamdon (village, Somerset): 'outlying farmstead below Hamdon'. OE *stoc*, 'outlying farmstead'. The second part of the name refers to nearby *Hamdon Hill*, whose name appears to mean 'hill of the enclosures' (OE *hamm*, 'enclosure', + *dūn*, 'hill'). DB *Stoca*, 1248 *Stokes under Hamden*.

Stoke upon Tern (village, Shropshire): 'outlying farmstead on the (river) Tern'. OE *stoc*, 'outlying farmstead'. The river has a Celtic name meaning 'strong one' (modern Welsh *tren*, 'strong', 'fierce'). DB *Stoche*.

Stondon Massey (village, Essex): 'de Marci's (estate by the) stony hill'. OE *stān*, 'stone', + *dūn*, 'hill'. The de Marci family held the manor here in the 13C. 1062 *Staundune*, 1238 *Standon de Marcy*.

Stone (town, Staffs): '(place at the) stone or stones'. OE *stān*, 'stone'. The reference may have been to a prominent stone building here. 'What "stone" or "stones," Stone took its name from we do not and probably never shall know' (W. H. Duignan, *Notes on Staffordshire Place Names*, 1902). 1187 *Stanes*. SO ALSO: *Stone*, Bucks, Glos, Kent.

Stone Allerton. See CHAPEL ALLERTON (Somerset).

Ston Easton (village, Somerset): 'stony eastern farmstead'. OE *stānig*, 'stony', + *ēast*, 'eastern', + *tūn*, 'farmstead'. The reference is to stony ground. DB *Estone*, 1230 *Stonieston*.

Stonegrave (village, N Yorks): 'quarry of the people living by the rock'. OE *stān*, 'stone', 'rock', + *-inga-*, 'of the dwellers at', + *græf*, 'quarry' (modern English *grave*). The DB form of the name below has been influenced by OS

gryfja, the equivalent of OE *græf*. 757 *Staningagrave*, DB *Stainegrif*.

Stonehaven (town and port, Aberdeens): 'stone landing place'. OE *stān*, 'stone', + *hȳth*, 'landing place'. Early forms of the name show that the second part is the equivalent of obsolete English *hithe*, not modern English *haven*. 1587 *Stanehyve*, 1629 *Steanhyve*.

Stonehenge (ancient stone circle, Wilts): 'stone gallows'. OE *stān*, 'stone', + *hengen*, '(instrument for) hanging', 'gallows'. The name alludes to the gallows-like appearance of the trilithons, with two upright stones and a third across the top as a lintel. The second form of the name below comes from Geoffrey of Monmouth's *Historia Regum Britanniae* (*c*.1136): '*Intra lapidum structuram sepultus fuit, quae haud longe a Salesberia mira arte composita, Anglorum lingua Stanheng nuncupatur*' ('He [King Constantine] was buried within the structure of the stones, which was set up with wonderful art not far from Salisbury, and called in the English tongue Stonehenge'). *c*.1130 *Stanenges*, *c*.1136 *Stanheng*.

Stonehouse (town, Glos): '(place by the) stone-built house'. OE *stān*, 'stone', + *hūs*, 'house'. DB *Stanhus*.

Stoneleigh (village, Warwicks): '(place in the) stony woodland clearing'. OE *stān*, 'stone', + *lēah*, 'wood', 'clearing'. 'As for the name, there needs not much to be said, in regard [i.e. since] 'tis obvious enough, considering that the nature of the soil where the Town stands is rocky' (William Dugdale, *The Antiquities of Warwickshire*, 1656). DB *Stanlei*.

Stonesby (village, Leics): 'farmhouse by a tree stump'. OE or OS *stofn*, 'tree stump', + OS *bý*, 'farmstead', 'village'. DB *Stovenebi*.

Stonesfield (village, Oxon): 'Stunt's open land'. OE *feld*, 'open land' (modern English *field*). DB *Stuntesfeld*.

Stonham Aspal. See EARL STONHAM.

Stonnall (village, Staffs): '(place in the) stony corner of land'. OE *stān*, 'stone', + *halh*, 'nook', 'corner of land'. Stonnall was formerly *Upper Stonnall* or *Over Stonnall*, in contrast to nearby *Lower Stonnall*. 1143 *Stanahala*.

Stonor (village, Oxon): '(place by the) stony hill slope'. OE *stān*, 'stone', + *ōra*, 'hill slope'. The hill in question is the one to the north of Stonor House. late 10C *Stanora*.

Stonton Wyville (village, Leics): 'de Wivill's farmstead on stony ground'. OE *stān*, 'stone', + *tūn*, 'farmstead'. The de Wivill family held the manor here in the 13C. DB *Stantone*, 1265 *Staunton Wyvile*.

Stony Stratford (town, Milton K): 'stony (place by a) ford on a Roman road'. OE *stānig*, 'stony', + *strǣt*, 'Roman road' (modern English *street*), + *ford*, 'ford'. Stony Stratford lies on Watling Street, which must have crossed the river Ouse here over a stony or gravelly ford. The first word of the name distinguishes this Stratford from FENNY STRATFORD, 6 miles to the southeast. 1202 *Stani Stratford*.

Stoodleigh (hamlet, Devon): 'woodland clearing where a herd of horses is kept'. OE *stōd*, 'stud', 'herd of horses', + *lēah*, 'wood', 'clearing'. DB *Stodlei*.

Stopham (village, W Sussex): 'Stoppa's homestead or river meadow'. OE *hām*, 'homestead', or *hamm*, 'river meadow'. Stopham stands at the confluence of the river Arun and the western Rother. The name could also mean 'homestead or river meadow by a hollow' (OE *stoppa*, 'hollow', + *hām* or *hamm*). DB *Stopeham*.

Storeton (hamlet, Wirral): 'large farmstead'. OS *stórr*, 'big', + OE *tūn*, 'farmstead'. The first part of the name could also represent OS *storth*, 'young wood', 'plantation'. DB *Stortone*.

Stornoway (town and port, W Isles): 'steering bay'. OS *stjórn*, 'steering' (modern English *stern*), + *vágr*, 'bay'. Ships presumably had to make special manoeuvres when entering or leaving the original harbour here on the island of Lewis. The Gaelic form of the name is *Steornabhagh*. 1511 *Stornochway*.

Storridge (hamlet, Herefords): '(place by the) stony ridge'. OE *stān*, 'stone', + *hrycg*, 'ridge'. 13C *Storugge*.

Storrington (town, W Sussex): 'farmstead where storks are seen'. OE *storc*, 'stork', + *tūn*, 'farmstead'. The mention of storks in this name appears to be unique in Britain. DB *Storgetune*.

Stotfold (suburb of Baldock, Beds): 'enclosure for horses'. OE *stōd-fald* (from *stōd*, 'stud', + *fald*, 'fold'). 1007 *Stodfald*, DB *Stotfalt*.

Stottesdon (village, Shropshire): '(place by the) hill where a herd of horses is kept'. OE *stōd*, 'stud', 'herd of horses', + *dūn*, 'hill'. DB *Stodesdone*.

Stoughton (village, W Sussex): 'farmstead at an outlying hamlet'. OE *stoc*, 'outlying hamlet', + *tūn*, 'farmstead'. The DB form of the name below is corrupt. DB *Estone*, 1121 *Stoctona*. SO ALSO: *Stoughton*, Leics, Surrey.

Stoulton (village, Worcs): 'farmstead with a seat'. OE *stōl*, 'seat' (modern English *stool*), + *tūn*,

'farmstead', 'village'. The seat would have been used during meetings of the local hundred here. 840 *Stoltun*, DB *Stoltun*, 1868 *Stoulton, or Stoughton*.

Stourbridge (town, Dudley): 'bridge over the (river) Stour'. OE *brycg*, 'bridge'. The river has a Celtic or OE name probably meaning 'strong one'. There are no less than five major rivers in England called Stour, all with this meaning. 1255 *Sturbrug*.

Stourhead (country house, Wilts): '(place at the) head of the (river) Stour'. The Stour (see STOURBRIDGE) rises near the house, which was built in 1720.

Stourpaine (village, Dorset): 'Payn's (estate on the river) Stour'. The Payn family held the manor here in the 13C. For the river name, see STOURBRIDGE. DB *Sture*, 1243 *Stures Paen*.

Stourport-on-Severn (town and port, Worcs): 'port at (the confluence of the rivers) Stour and Severn'. The town arose only in the 18C, when the Staffordshire and Worcester canal linked the Trent and Mersey canal with the Severn here. For the river names, see STOURBRIDGE, SEVERN STOKE. *c.*1775 *Stourport*.

Stour Provost (village, Dorset): '(estate on the river) Stour belonging to Préaux'. For the river name, see STOURBRIDGE. The manor here was held in the 13C and 14C by the Abbey of St Leger, Préaux, France. The French place name was assimilated to *Provost* when the manor was given by Edward IV in the 15C to the Provost of King's College, Cambridge (who sold it in 1925). DB *Stur*, 1270 *Sture Preauus*, 1535 *Stoure Provys*.

Stourton (village, Wilts): 'farmstead on the (river) Stour'. OE *tūn*, 'farmstead'. For the river name, see STOURBRIDGE. DB *Stortone*. SO ALSO: *Stourton*, Staffs, Warwicks.

Stourton Caundle. See BISHOP'S CAUNDLE.

Stoven (village, Suffolk): '(place by the) tree stumps'. OE or OS *stofn*, 'stem', 'stump'. DB *Stouone*.

Stow (village, Lincs): 'holy place'. OE *stōw*, 'place of assembly', 'holy place'. The Saxon-to-Norman church of St Mary here stands on the site of an earlier monastery. 1053 *Stowe*, DB *Stou*.

Stow Bardolph (village, Norfolk): 'Bardulf's (estate at the) place of assembly'. OE *stōw*, 'place of assembly', 'holy place'. The Bardulf family held the manor here in the 13C. DB *Stou*.

Stow Bedon (village, Norfolk): 'de Bidun's (estate at the) place of assembly'. OE *stōw*, 'place of assembly', 'holy place'. The de Bidun family held the manor here in the 13C. DB *Stou*, 1287 *Stouwebidun*.

Stow cum Quy (village, Cambs): 'place with a cow island'. OE *stōw*, 'place of assembly', 'holy place', + Latin *cum*, 'with', + OE *cū*, 'cow', + *ēg*, 'island'. A 'cow island' is a raised area of pasture in fenland. DB *Stoua*, 1316 *Stowe cum Quey*.

Stowell (village, Somerset): '(place by the) stony stream'. OE *stān*, 'stone', + *wella*, 'spring', 'stream'. DB *Stanwelle*.

Stowford (village, Devon): '(place by the) stony ford'. OE *stān*, 'stone', + *ford*, 'ford'. See STAMFORD. The form of the name below is for Stowford near Launceston. DB *Staford*.

Stowlangtoft (village, Suffolk): 'de Langetot's (estate at the) place of assembly'. OE *stōw*, 'place of assembly', 'holy place'. The de Langetot family held the manor here in the 13C. DB *Stou*, 13C *Stowelangetot*.

Stow Maries (village, Essex): 'Mareys' (estate at the) place of assembly'. OE *stōw*, 'place of assembly', 'holy place'. The Mareys family held the manor here in the 13C. The dedication of the church to St Mary (and St Margaret) here is a coincidence. 1222 *Stowe*, 1420 *Stowe Mareys*.

Stowmarket (town, Suffolk): 'place with a market'. OE *stōw*, 'place', + ME *merket*, 'market'. OE *stōw* could mean either 'place of assembly' or 'holy place'. The latter sense is probably right here, as the full DB form of the name below is *ecclesia de Stou*. DB *Stou*, 1268 *Stowmarket*.

Stow-on-the-Wold (town, Glos): 'place by the upland wood'. OE *stōw*, 'place', + *wald*, 'upland wood'. OE *stōw* meant both 'assembly place' and 'holy place'. The latter is appropriate here, with the Norman parish church, on its hilltop site, probably representing an even earlier building. The DB form of the name below thus means 'St Edward's holy place'. The second part of the modern name distinguishes this Stow from others. See WOLDS. DB *Eduuardesstou*, 1213 *Stoua*, 1574 *Stowe on the Olde*.

Stowting (village, Kent): 'place with a lumpy hillock'. OE *stūt*, 'hill', + *-ing*, 'place characterized by'. The name could also mean 'place associated with Stūt' (OE *-ing*, 'place belonging to'). 1044 *Stuting*, DB *Stotinges*.

Stradbroke (village, Suffolk): 'brook by a paved road'. OE *strǣt*, 'paved road' (modern English *street*), + *brōc*, 'brook'. The suggestion is of a Roman road here, although none is known. The DB form of the name below is corrupt. DB *Statebroc*, 1168 *Stradebroc*.

Stradsett (hamlet, Norfolk): 'dwelling on a Roman road'. OE *strǣt*, 'Roman road' (modern English *street*), + *set*, 'dwelling'. The name of Stradsett is a corrupted form of Streat-sett, the place on the Street, and lends strong support to the inclusion of this part of the road [a continuation of Fen Road, from Castor to the east coast] as Roman' (Ivan D. Margary, *Roman Roads in Britain*, 1973). DB *Strateseta*.

Straiton (district of Edinburgh, Midlothian): 'village on a Roman road'. OE *strǣt*, 'Roman road' (modern English *street*), + *tūn*, 'farmstead', 'village'. The name is the equivalent of the common *Stratton*, as for STRATTON (Dorset), although the route of the particular Roman road here is uncertain. 1296 *Stratone*.

Stramshall (village, Staffs): 'Strangrīc's hill'. OE *hyll*, 'hill'. The DB form of the name below is corrupt. 'One can readily imagine the ... Norman scribe being "staggered" by the name, and pitying us poor savages' (W. H. Duignan, *Notes on Staffordshire Place Names*, 1902). DB *Stagrigesholle*, 1227 *Strangricheshull*.

Strangeways (district, Manchester): '(place by a) stream with a strong current'. OE *strang*, 'strong', + *gewæsc*, 'stream' (related modern English *wash*). Strangeways is on a tongue of land between two rivers and was formerly subject to flooding from their strong currents. 1322 *Strangwas*.

Stranraer (resort town and port, Dumfries & Gall): '(place by the) thick promontory'. Gaelic *sròn*, 'promontory', + *reamhar*, 'thick'. There is no promontory at Stranraer itself, at the head of Loch Ryan, so the name presumably refers to the Rinns of Galloway to the west. 1320 *Stranrever*.

Stratfield Mortimer (village, W Berks): 'de Mortemer's (estate on) open land by the Roman road'. OE *strǣt*, 'Roman road' (modern English *street*), + *feld*, 'open land' (modern English *field*). The de Mortemer family held the manor here from 1086. The village is on the Roman road from Silchester to London. DB *Stradfeld*, 1275 *Stratfeld Mortimer*.

Stratfield Saye (village, Hants): 'de Say's (estate on) open land by the Roman road'. OE *strǣt*, 'Roman road' (modern English *street*), + *feld*, 'open land' (modern English *field*). The de Say family held the manor here in the 13C. Their name distinguishes this Stratfield from nearby *Stratfield Turgis*, held by the Turgis family, with both villages on the same Roman road as STRATFIELD MORTIMER. *c*.1060 *Stratfeld*, DB *Stradfelle*, 1277 *Stratfeld Say*.

Stratford (town, Newham): '(place by the) ford on a Roman road'. OE *strǣt*, 'Roman road' (modern English *street*), + *ford*, 'ford'. Stratford stands by the Roman road that ran from London to Colchester and that crossed the river Lea here. 1177 *Stratford*.

Stratford St Andrew. See STRATFORD ST MARY.

Stratford St Mary (village, Suffolk): '(place by the) ford on a Roman with St Mary's church'. OE *strǣt*, 'Roman road' (modern English *street*), + *ford*, 'ford'. The village, on the river Stour, stands on the Roman road between Colchester and Caistor St Edmund, its church dedication distinguishing it from *Stratford St Andrew*, 27 miles to the northeast. c.995 *Stredford*, DB *Stratfort*.

Stratford sub Castle (suburb of Salisbury, Wilts): '(place by the) ford on a Roman road under the castle'. OE *strǣt*, 'Roman road' (modern English *street*), + *ford*, 'ford', + Latin *sub*, 'under'. Stratford, on the river Avon, stands on the stretch of Roman road between Old Sarum (the 'castle') and Badbury Rings. 1091 *Stratford*, 1651 *Stratford under the Castle*.

Stratford Tony (village, Wilts): 'de Touny's (estate at the place by the) ford on a Roman road'. OE *strǣt*, 'Roman road' (modern English *street*), + *ford*, 'ford'. The village stands on the same Roman road as STRATFORD SUB CASTLE, 5 miles to the northwest. Here the river is the Ebble. 672 *Stretford*, DB *Stradford*, 14C *Stratford Touny*, 1868 *Stratford Tony, or Stratford St Anthony*.

Stratford-upon-Avon (town, Warwicks): '(place by the) ford over the (river) Avon on a Roman road'. OE *strǣt*, 'Roman road' (modern English *street*), + *ford*, 'ford'. The Roman road from Eatington to Alcester and Droitwich joined the settlements at Alcester and Tiddington, east of the town, and probably crossed the Avon where Bridgefoot crosses it now. For the river name, see AVONMOUTH. c.700 *Stretfordæ*, DB *Stradforde*.

Strathaven (town, S Lanarks): 'valley of the Avon Water'. Gaelic *srath*, 'valley'. The river here has a name of the same origin as the English Avons (see AVONMOUTH). c.1190 *Strathouen*.

Strathclyde (region, W Scotland): 'valley of the (river) Clyde'. Gaelic *srath*, 'valley'. The name is that of a former administrative region enclosing the whole of the basin of the river Clyde (see CLYDEBANK).

Strathmiglo (town, Fife): 'valley of the (river) Miglo'. Gaelic *srath*, 'valley'. Strathmiglo is actually in the valley of the river Eden, whose former name must thus have been *Miglo*, referring to the marshy lake here, from Celtic words related to modern Welsh *mign*, 'bog', 'quagmire', and *llwch*, 'loch'. The change of name came about when the swampy lake became a proper river. c.1200 *Scradimigglock*, 1294 *Stramygloke*.

Strathmore (valley, Perth & Kin/Angus): 'great valley'. Gaelic *srath*, 'valley', + *mór*, 'great'. The long valley separates the Scottish Highlands, to the north, from the Central Lowlands, to the south.

Strathpeffer (village, Highland): 'valley of the (river) Peffery'. Gaelic *srath*, 'valley'. The village lies in the valley of the Peffery, whose own name is of Celtic origin and means 'radiant', from a word related to modern Welsh *pefr*, 'radiant', 'beautiful'. 1350 *Strathpefir*.

Stratton (town, Cornwall): 'village in the valley of the (river) Neet'. Cornish *stras*, 'valley', + OE *tūn*, 'village'. The name of the river, of uncertain meaning, has disappeared from that of the town. The river is now also known as the Strat, from the town's name. c.880 *Strætneat*, DB *Stratone*, 1187 *Stratton*.

Stratton (village, Dorset): 'farmstead on a Roman road'. OE *strǣt*, 'Roman road' (modern English *street*), + *tūn*, 'farmstead', 'village'. The village stands on the Roman road from Dorchester to Ilchester. 1212 *Stratton*.

Stratton Audley (village, Oxon): 'de Alditheleg's farmstead on a Roman road'. OE *strǣt*, 'Roman road' (modern English *street*), + *tūn*, 'farmstead', 'village'. The manor here was held in the 13C by the de Alditheleg family. The village stands by the Roman road from Dorchester to Towcester, Northants. DB *Stratone*, 1318 *Stratton Audeley*.

Stratton-on-the-Fosse (village, Somerset): 'farmstead on a Roman road on the Fosse Way'. OE *strǣt*, 'Roman road' (modern English *street*), + *tūn*, 'farmstead', 'village'. The village stands on the Roman road from Ilchester to Bath that followed the course of the FOSSE WAY. DB *Stratone*.

Stratton St Margaret (suburb of Swindon): 'farmstead on a Roman road with St Margaret's church'. OE *strǣt*, 'Roman road' (modern English *street*), + *tūn*, 'farmstead', 'village'. The former village stands on Ermine Street, adapted by the Romans for a road between Gloucester and Silchester. DB *Stratone*.

Stratton St Michael. See LONG STRATTON.

Stratton Strawless (village, Norfolk): 'strawless village on a Roman road'. OE *strǣt*, 'Roman road' (modern English *street*), + *tūn*, 'farmstead', 'village', + *strēaw*, 'straw', + *-lēas*, '-less'. A 'strawless' village is presumably an infertile one, while the Roman road would have been an east–west route. DB *Stratuna*, 1446 *Stratton Streles*.

Strawberry Hill (district, Richmond). The name was originally given by the writer Horace Walpole (1717–97) to the villa he bought here in 1748. It was earlier known as *Chopped Straw Hall*. Walpole based his name on a local field name, *Strawberry Hill Shot*, referring to the strawberries formerly cultivated here: 'I am now returning to my villa, where I have been making some alterations: you shall hear from me from STRAWBERRY HILL, which I have found out in my lease is the old name of my house; so pray, never call it Twickenham again' (letter to Sir Horace Mann, 7 June 1748).

Streat (village, E Sussex): '(place by a) Roman road'. OE *strǣt*, 'Roman road' (modern English *street*). Streat is on the 25-mile-long Roman road that branched off from the London to Lewes road to join Stane Street at Hardham, near Pulborough. DB *Estrat*.

Streatham (district, Lambeth): 'homestead on a Roman road'. OE *strǣt*, 'Roman road' (modern English *street*), + *hām*, 'homestead', 'village'. The Roman road here from London to the Brighton area of the South Downs lay on a course now followed by Streatham High Road (the A23). The DB form of the name below omits the second *t*. DB *Estreham*, 1247 *Streteham*.

Streatley (village, Beds): 'woodland clearing by a Roman road'. OE *strǣt*, 'Roman road' (modern English *street*), + *lēah*, 'wood', 'clearing'. The stretch of Roman road here is now represented by the A6 from Luton to Bedford. *c*.1053 *Strǣtlea*, DB *Stradlei*.

Streatley (village, W Berks): 'woodland clearing by a Roman road'. OE *strǣt*, 'Roman road', + *lēah*, 'wood', 'clearing'. Streatley, on the Thames, lies on the Icknield Way as it passes through Goring Gap. The DB form of the name below omits the second *t*. *c*.690 *Stretlea*, DB *Estralei*.

Street (town, Somerset): '(place by a) Roman road'. OE *strǣt*, 'Roman road' (modern English *street*). The Roman road here ran from Ilchester to the Bristol Channel coast. 725 *Stret*.

Strelley (village, Notts): 'woodland clearing by a Roman road'. OE *strǣt*, 'Roman road' (modern English *street*), + *lēah*, 'wood', 'clearing'. No Roman road has been discovered here. DB *Straleia*.

Strensall (village, York): 'corner of land given as a reward'. OE *strēon*, 'property', 'treasure', + *halh*, 'nook', 'corner of land'. OE *strēon* also meant 'procreation' (modern English *strain*, 'line of descent'), so that a sense amounting to 'lovers' nook' is also possible. DB *Strenshale*.

Strensham (village, Worcs): 'Strenge's homestead or enclosure'. OE *hām*, 'homestead', or *hamm*, 'enclosure'. The second part of the first form of the name below represents OE *hōh*, 'promontory'. 972 *Strengesho*, *c*.1086 *Strenchesham*.

Strete (coastal village, Devon): '(place on a) Roman road'. OE *strǣt*, 'Roman road' (modern English *street*). The main road here (now the A379) probably follows the course of an ancient trackway. 1194 *Streta*.

Stretford (town, Trafford): 'ford on a Roman road'. OE *strǣt*, 'Roman road' (modern English *street*), + *ford*, 'ford'. Stretford arose on the Roman road that ran from Chester to Manchester at the point where it crossed the Mersey. The site of the actual crossing is the present Crossford Bridge. 1212 *Stretford*.

Strethall (village, Essex): 'corner of land by a Roman road'. OE *strǣt*, 'Roman road' (modern English *street*), + *halh*, 'nook', 'corner of land'. Strethall lies on a section of the Roman road that ran from London to Great Chesterford. DB *Strathala*.

Stretham (village, Cambs): 'homestead on a Roman road'. OE *strǣt*, 'Roman road' (modern English *street*), + *hām*, 'homestead', 'village'. Stretham lies on Akeman Street between Cambridge and Ely. *c*.970 *Stratham*, DB *Stradham*.

Strettington (village, W Sussex): 'farmstead of the dwellers by the Roman road'. OE *strǣt*, 'Roman road' (modern English *street*), + *hǣme*, 'dwellers' (related modern English *home*), + *tūn*, 'farmstead'. The Roman road here is Stane Street. DB *Stratone*, 12C *Estretementona*.

Stretton (village, Cheshire): 'farmstead on a Roman road'. OE *strǣt*, 'Roman road' (modern English *street*), + *tūn*, 'farmstead', 'village'. Stretton, near Warrington, is on the Roman road from Warrington to Northwich. 12C *Stretton*.

Stretton (hamlet, Cheshire): 'farmstead on a Roman road'. OE *strǣt*, 'Roman road' (modern English *street*), + *tūn*, 'farmstead', 'village'. Stretton, near Holt, Wrexham, is on the Roman road from Chester to Wroxeter. 12C *Stretton*.

Stretton (village, Derbys): 'farmstead on a Roman road'. OE *strǣt*, 'Roman road' (modern English *street*), + *tūn*, 'farmstead', 'village'. Stretton is on Ryknild Street. *c*.1002 *Strǣttune*, DB *Stratune*.

Stretton (village, Rutland): 'farmstead on a Roman road'. OE *strǣt*, 'Roman road' (modern English *street*), + *tūn*, 'farmstead', 'village'. Stretton is on Ermine Street. DB *Stratune*.

Stretton (village, Staffs): 'farmstead on a Roman road'. OE *strǣt*, 'Roman road' (modern English *street*), + *tūn*, 'farmstead', 'village'. Stretton is on Watling Street. DB *Estretone*.

Stretton Baskerville Village (hamlet, Warwicks): 'de Baskervill's farmstead on a Roman road'. OE *strǣt*, 'Roman road' (modern English *street*), + *tūn*, 'farmstead', 'village'. The de Baskervill family held the manor here in the 12C. As noted by William Dugdale in *The Antiquities of Warwickshire* (1656): 'As all the other *Strettons* take their names from some great road near unto which they are situate, so doth this of that known Roman way, called *Watlingstreet* lying on the North side of it'. DB *Stratone*, 1247 *Stretton Baskeruill*.

Stretton Grandison (village, Herefords): 'Grandison's farmstead on a Roman road'. OE *strǣt*, 'Roman road' (modern English *street*), + *tūn*, 'farmstead', 'village'. The Grandison family held the manor here in the 14C. The village lies on a Roman road (now represented by the A417) running northwest from Gloucester, while another Roman road ran west from Stretton Grandison to Kenchester. DB *Stratune*, 1350 *Stretton Graundison*, 1868 *Stretton-Grandsome*.

Stretton-on-Dunsmore. See STRETTON UNDER FOSSE.

Stretton-on-Fosse. See STRETTON UNDER FOSSE.

Stretton Sugwas (village, Herefords): 'farmstead on a Roman road over alluvial land where sparrows are seen'. OE *strǣt*, 'Roman road' (modern English *street*), + *tūn*, 'farmstead', 'village', + *sugge*, 'sparrow', + *wæsse*, 'alluvial land'. Stretton Sugwas lies on a stretch of Roman road that runs west from a point north of Hereford to Kenchester. The terrain here is low-lying and liable to flood. Hence OE *wæsse*, as for BROADWAS and BUILDWAS. DB *Stratone*, 1334 *Strattone by Sugwas*.

Stretton under Fosse (village, Warwicks): 'farmstead on a Roman road by the Fosse Way'. OE *strǣt*, 'Roman road' (modern English *street*), + *tūn*, 'farmstead', 'village'. The village lies near the FOSSE WAY, its name contrasting with that of *Stretton-on-Dunsmore* (see CLIFTON UPON DUNSMORE), 6 miles further down Fosse Way, and more obviously with *Stretton-on-Fosse*, 30 miles down. 1303 *Stretton*.

Stringston (village, Somerset): 'Strenge's farmstead'. OE *tūn*, 'farmstead', 'village'. DB *Strengestune*.

Strixton (village, Northants): 'Stríkr's farmstead'. OE *tūn*, 'farmstead', 'village'. The personal name is Scandinavian. 12C *Strixton*.

Stroma (island, Highland): 'island in the stream'. OS *straumr*, 'stream', + *ey*, 'island'. Stroma lies in the Pentland Firth, whose current is said to flow like a river. Cp. STROMNESS. 1150 *Straumsey*.

Stromness (town and port, Orkney): 'headland of the stream'. OS *straumr*, 'stream', 'current', + *nes*, 'headland'. The name alludes to the strong current off the headland here. 1150 *Straumsness*.

Strood (district of Rochester, Medway): 'marshy land overgrown with brushwood'. OE *strōd*, 'marshy land with scrub'. Strood is on low-lying land by the Medway. Cp. STROUD. 889 *Strod*.

Stroud (town, Glos): 'marshy land overgrown with brushwood'. OE *strōd*, 'marshy land with scrub'. Although on a hill slope, Stroud lies behind the river Frome, and the name would have applied to this lower-lying area to the south of the town. 1200 *La Strode*. SO ALSO: *Stroud*, Hants.

Strubby (village, Lincs): 'Strútr's farmstead'. OS *bý*, 'farmstead', 'village'. The personal name is Scandinavian. DB *Strobi*.

Strumble Head (headland, Pemb): 'stormy headland'. *Strumble* perhaps originated as a sailors' nickname for this windswept point, based on *storm* and *bill*, the latter as for *Selsey Bill* (see SELSEY). The second word was then added when the sense of 'headland' in the original was forgotten. Locally the headland is known as simply *Strumble*. 1578 *Strumble head*.

Strumpshaw (village, Norfolk): '(place by the) wood full of trees stumps'. OE *strump*, 'stump', + *sceaga*, 'wood', 'copse'. DB *Stromessaga*.

Stubbington (suburb of Fareham, Hants): 'estate associated with Stubba'. OE *-ing-*, 'associated with', + *tūn*, 'farmstead', 'estate'. The name could also mean 'farmstead in a clearing of tree stumps' (OE *stubbing*, 'clearing of tree stumps', + *tūn*). DB *Stubitone*.

Stubbins (village, Lancs): 'place with tree stumps'. OE *stubbing*, 'clearing of tree stumps'. 1563 *Stubbyng*.

Studdal. See EAST STUDDAL.

Studland (village, Dorset): 'cultivated land where horses are kept'. OE *stōd*, 'herd of horses', 'stud', + *land*, 'tract of land'. The village gave the name of *Studland Bay* here. DB *Stollant*.

Studley (village, Oxon): 'woodland clearing where a herd of horses is kept'. OE *stōd*, 'stud', 'herd of horses', + *lēah*, 'wood', 'clearing'. Studley now forms a single village with Horton as *Horton-cum-Studley* (Latin *cum*, 'with'). See HORTON (Northants). *c.*1185 *Stodleya*. SO ALSO: *Studley*, Warwicks, Wilts.

Studley Roger (hamlet, N Yorks): 'Roger's (estate at the) woodland clearing where a herd of horses is kept'. OE *stōd*, 'stud', 'herd of horses', + *lēah*, 'wood', 'clearing'. The manor here was held early by Roger de Mowbray or Archbishop Roger of York, their name distinguishing it from nearby *Studley Royal*, with an uncertain royal connection. *c.*1030 *Stodlege*, DB *Stollai*, 1228 *Stodelay Roger*.

Sturmer (village, Essex): '(place by the) pool on the (river) Stour'. OE *mere*, 'pool'. For the river name, see STOURBRIDGE. *c.*1000 *Sturmere*, DB *Sturmere*.

Sturminster Newton (town, Dorset): 'church on the (river) Stour by Newton'. OE *mynster*, 'monastery', 'church'. *Newton*, meaning 'new farmstead' (OE *nīwe*, 'new', + *tūn*, 'farmstead'), and originally the name of a place across the river, was added to distinguish this Sturminster from *Sturminster Marshall*, 17 miles to the south-east, where the Mareschal family held the manor in the 13C. For the river name, see STOURBRIDGE. 968 *Nywetone*, DB *Newentone*, 1291 *Sturminstr Nyweton*.

Sturry (village, Kent): 'district by the (river) Stour'. OE *gē*, 'district'. For the river name, see STOURBRIDGE. 878 *Sturgeh*, DB *Esturai*.

Sturton (village, N Lincs): 'village by a Roman road'. OE *strǣt*, 'Roman road' (modern English *street*), + *tūn*, 'farmstead', 'village'. Sturton lies close to Ermine Street. DB *Straitone*.

Sturton le Steeple (village, Notts): 'village on a Roman road with a steeple'. OE *strǣt*, 'Roman road' (modern English *street*), + *tūn*, 'farmstead', 'village'. The village stands on the Roman road from Doncaster to Lincoln. The second part of the name, referring to the tower of the church, distinguishes this Sturton from *Sturton by Stow*, Lincs, 7 miles to the southeast on the same Roman road. DB *Estretone*, 1732 *Sturton le Steeple*.

Stuston (village, Suffolk): 'Stūt's farmstead'. OE *tūn*, 'farmstead', 'village'. DB *Stutestuna*.

Stutton (village, N Yorks): 'Stúfr's farmstead'. OE *tūn*, 'farmstead'. The personal name is Scandinavian. The name could also mean 'farmstead built among tree stumps' (OS *stúfr*, 'stump', + *tūn*). DB *Stouetun*.

Stutton (village, Suffolk): 'farmstead plagued with gnats'. OE *stūt*, 'gnat', + *tūn*, 'farmstead'. The name could also mean 'farmstead where bullocks are kept' (OS *stútr*, 'bullock', + OE *tūn*). DB *Stuttuna*.

Styal (village, Cheshire): '(place in the) corner of land by a path'. OE *stīg*, 'path', + *halh*, 'nook', 'corner of land'. *c.*1200 *Styhale*.

Styrrup (village, Notts): '(place by the) stirrup-shaped hill'. OE *stīg-rāp*, 'stirrup' (literally 'climbing rope', from *stīge*, 'climbing', + *rāp*, 'rope'). Presumably early settlers here regarded the hill to the east of the village as similar in some way to a stirrup. DB *Estirape*.

Suckley (village, Worcs): 'woodland clearing where sparrows are seen'. OE *succa*, 'sparrow', + *lēah*, 'wood', 'clearing'. DB *Suchelei*.

Sudborough (village, Northants): 'southern fortification'. OE *sūth*, 'southern', + *burh*, 'fortified place'. The fortification here may have been regarded as 'south' with regard to Brigstock, 2 miles to the north. DB *Sutburg*.

Sudbourne (village, Suffolk): '(place by the) southern stream'. OE *sūth*, 'southern', + *burna*, 'stream'. *c.*1050 *Sutborne*, DB *Sutburna*.

Sudbury (district, Brent): 'southern manor'. OE *sūth*, 'southern', + *burh*, 'fortified place', 'manor'. The corresponding 'northern manor' may have been Harrow. 1292 *Suthbery*, 1294 *Sudbery*.

Sudbury (village, Derbys): 'southern fortification'. OE *sūth*, 'southern', + *burh*, 'fortified place'. The contrary 'northern fortification' is *Norbury*, 7 miles to the north. DB *Sudberie*.

Sudbury (town, Suffolk): 'southern fortification'. OE *sūth*, 'southern', + *burh*, 'fortified place'. The corresponding 'northern fortification' was probably Bury St Edmunds. *c.*995 *Suthbyrig*, DB *Sutberia*.

Suffield (hamlet, Norfolk): 'southern open land'. OE *sūth*, 'southern', + *feld*, 'open land' (modern English *field*). DB *Sudfelda*.

Suffolk (county, E England): '(territory of the) southern people'. OE *sūth*, 'southern', + *folc*, 'people'. The name refers to the southern people of the East Angles who inhabited this part of East Anglia, as distinct from the 'northern people' of NORFOLK. 895 *Suthfolchi*, DB *Sudfulc*.

Sugnall (hamlet, Staffs): '(place on the) hill where sparrows are seen'. OE *sugge*, 'sparrow', +

hyll, 'hill'. The first part of the name represents OE *suggena*, the genitive plural form of *sugge*. The DB form of the name below is corrupt. DB *Sotehelle*, 1222 *Sugenhulle*.

Sulgrave (village, Northants): 'grove near a gully'. OE *sulh*, 'ploughland', + *grāf*, 'grove'. OE *sulh*, 'plough', could also mean 'furrow made by a plough', and hence by extension 'gully'. The 'gully' was probably that of the river Tove, which rises near here. DB *Sulgrave*.

Sulham (village, W Berks): 'homestead by a gully'. OE *sulh*, 'ploughland', 'gully', + *hām*, 'homestead'. The 'gully' is presumably that of the nearby stream. DB *Soleham*.

Sullington (hamlet, W Sussex): 'farmstead by a willow copse'. OE *sieling*, 'willow copse', + *tūn*, 'farmstead', 'village'. The first part of the name could also represent OE *sielling*, 'gift', referring to land given as a gift here. 959 *Sillinctune*, DB *Sillintone*.

Sullom Voe (sea inlet, Shetland): 'bay of gannets'. OS *súla*, 'gannet' (modern English *solan*), + *vágr*, 'bay'.

Sully (coastal village, Vale of Glam): origin uncertain. The name may derive from the Norman family de Sully, who held the manor here in the late 12C. The Welsh form of the name is *Sili*. 1193 *Sulie*, 1254 *Sulye*.

Sumburgh Head (headland, Shetland): 'headland of Sveinn's fort'. OS *borg*, 'fort', 'stronghold'. The personal name is Scandinavian. The headland, at the southern tip of Mainland, derives its name from *Sumburgh*, to the north of it. 1506 *Swynbrocht*.

Summercourt (village, Cornwall): 'summer court'. The meaning of the name is uncertain. The reference may be to a courtyard used only in summer. An important fair is held here every September, but 'court' is not recorded in this sense. 1711 *Somercourt*.

Summerseat (district, Bury): 'shieling used in summer'. OS *sumarr*, 'summer', + *sǽtr*, 'shieling', 'hill pasture'. 1556 *Sumersett*.

Summerstown (district, Wandsworth). The land here was probably owned by a family called Summer or Sumner, recorded locally from the 17C. The name itself is found no earlier than the 19C. 1823 *Summers Town*.

Summertown (district of Oxford, Oxon). The name is said to derive from a signboard displayed here in the late 18C or early 19C by the first settler, which read: 'James Lambourn horsedealer Somers Town'. Lambourn reportedly gave the name because the place seemed

pleasant to him. 1822 *Summerstown*, 1832 *Summer-Town*.

Sunbury (town, Surrey): 'Sunna's stronghold'. OE *burh*, 'fortified place'. The town is also known, mainly for postal purposes, as *Sunbury-on-Thames*. 960 *Sunnanbyrg*, DB *Sunneberie*.

Sunderland (city, Sunderland): 'detached estate'. OE *sundor-land*, 'private property'. The OE term denotes an estate set apart for a particular purpose, literally 'sundered land'. *c.*1168 *Sunderland*. SO ALSO: *Sunderland*, Cumbria.

Sundridge (village, Kent): 'detached ploughed field'. OE *sundor*, 'in separate ownership', + *ersc*, 'ploughed field'. DB *Sondresse*.

Sunk Island (hamlet, E Yorks): 'sunken island'. The land on which the hamlet stands arose from the water as an island off the northern coast of the Humber estuary in the 17C. 1678 *Sunk Island*.

Sunningdale (district, Windsor & Maid): 'valley by Sunninghill'. The name is that of a parish formed in 1841 from parts of Old Windsor and *Sunninghill*, 'hill of Sunna's people' (OE -*inga*-, 'of the people of', + *hyll*, 'hill'). The same people gave the names of SONNING and SUNNINGWELL. 1800 *Sunning Hill Dale*.

Sunningwell (village, Oxon): '(place at the) spring of Sunna's people'. OE -*inga*-, 'of the people of', + *wella*, 'spring', 'stream'. 9C *Sunningauuille*, DB *Soningeuuel*.

Surbiton (district, Kingston): 'southern outlying farm'. OE *sūth*, 'southern', + *bere-tūn*, 'grange' (from *bere*, 'barley', + *tūn*, 'farm'). The corresponding 'northern outlying farm' was at NORBITON, and both farms or granges were dependent on the royal manor of Kingston. 1179 *Suberton*.

Surfleet (village, Lincs): '(place by the) sour stream'. OE *sūr*, 'sour', + *flēot*, 'creek', 'stream'. The DB form of the name below is garbled. DB *Sverefelt*, 1167 *Surfliet*.

Surlingham (village, Norfolk): 'southern homestead of Herela's people'. OE -*inga*-, 'of the people of', + *hām*, 'homestead'. The first part of the name represents OE *sūth*, 'southern'. The name could be analysed as OE *sūther* + -*linga*- + *hām*, 'homestead of the dwellers to the south', meaning those living south of Norwich. DB *Sutherlingaham*.

Surrey (county, SE England): 'southern district'. OE *sūther*, 'southern', + *gē*, 'district'. Surrey was inhabited by the Saxons of the middle Thames valley and was so named by contrast with MIDDLESEX, to the north. South of them again were the South Saxons of SUSSEX. 722 *Suthrige*, DB *Sudrie*.

Surrey Heath (council district, Surrey). The district lies in the northwest part of SURREY, a region of former barren commons and moorland, especially at Bagshot, Bisley and Chobham.

Sussex (historic county, S England): '(territory of the) South Saxons'. OE *sūth*, 'southern', + *Seaxe*, 'Saxons'. The name contrasts geographically with ESSEX, MIDDLESEX and WESSEX. See also SURREY. The two divisions of *East Sussex* and *West Sussex* have long existed, and in 1974 each gained county status. late 9C *Suth Seaxe*, DB *Sudsexe*.

Sustead (village, Norfolk): 'southern place'. OE *sūth*, 'southern', + *stede*, 'place'. DB *Sutstede*.

Sutcombe (village, Devon): '(place in) Sutta's valley'. OE *cumb*, 'valley'. DB *Sutecome*.

Sutherland (historic county, N Scotland): 'southern territory'. OS *suthr*, 'southern', + *land*, 'land'. This region of northern Scotland was a 'southern territory' to the Vikings who settled in Orkney and Shetland. Hence the apparently anomalous name. See also HEBRIDES. *c.*1250 *Suthernelande*.

Sutterton (village, Lincs): 'farmstead of the shoemakers'. OE *sūtere*, 'shoemaker', + *tūn*, 'farmstead'. 1200 *Suterton*.

Sutton (village, Cambs): 'southern farmstead'. OE *sūth*, 'southern', + *tūn*, 'farmstead', 'village'. Sutton lies in the south of the Isle of Ely. DB *Sudtone*. SO ALSO: *Sutton*, Suffolk.

Sutton (borough, Greater London): 'southern farmstead'. OE *sūth*, 'southern', + *tūn*, 'farmstead', 'village'. The place may be 'south' in relation to Mitcham and Morden. DB *Sudtone*.

Sutton at Hone (village, Kent): 'southern farmstead at the stone'. OE *sūth*, 'southern', + *tūn*, 'farmstead', 'village', + *hān*, 'stone' (modern English *hone*). The reference is probably to a boundary stone here by the river Darent. DB *Sudtone*, 1240 *Sutton atte hone*.

Sutton Benger (village, Wilts): 'Berenger's southern farmstead': OE *sūth*, 'southern', + *tūn*, 'farmstead', 'village'. The corresponding 'northern farmstead' may have been Hullavington. The Berenger family held the manor here in the 11C. 854 *Suttune*, DB *Sudtone*.

Sutton Bonington (village, Notts). Originally two separate manors: *Sutton*, 'southern farmstead' (OE *sūth*, 'southern', + *tūn*, 'farmstead', 'village'), and *Bonington*, 'estate associated with Buna' (OE *-ing-*, 'associated with', +

tūn, 'farmstead', 'estate'). Sutton was 'south' with regard to Bonington. DB *Sudtone*, DB *Bonniton*, 1332 *Sutton cum Bonyngton*.

Sutton Bridge (town, Lincs): '(place by the) bridge near Sutton'. Sutton Bridge was formed in 1894 as a separate parish of LONG SUTTON. The bridge is over the river Nene.

Sutton Coldfield (town, Birmingham): 'southern farmstead in open land where charcoal is made'. OE *sūth*, 'southern', + *tūn*, 'farmstead', + *col*, 'charcoal' (modern English *coal*), + *feld*, 'open land' (modern English *field*). The second word distinguishes this Sutton from others. The farm may have been 'south' in relation to Shenstone, 6 miles to the north, although William Dugdale, in *The Antiquities of Warwickshire* (1656), suggests: 'This Sutton was originally so called from its situation, there is no doubt; and therefore as it stands South to Lichfield I am inclin'd to believe that the name at first arose'. DB *Sutone*, 1269 *Sutton in Colefeud*.

Sutton Courtenay. See NUNEHAM COURTENAY.

Sutton in Ashfield (town, Notts): 'southern farmstead in Ashfield'. OE *sūth*, 'southern', + *tūn*, 'farmstead'. The farm was probably 'south' in relation to Skegby, now a northern suburb of the town. For the district name, see KIRKBY IN ASHFIELD. DB *Sutone*, 1276 *Sutton in Essefeld*.

Sutton Maddock (village, Shropshire): 'Madoc's southern farmstead'. OE *sūth*, 'southern', + *tūn*, 'farmstead'. The Welsh family Madoc held the manor over three generations in the 12C and 13C. DB *Sudtone*, 1255 *Sutton Madok*.

Sutton Mandeville (village, Wilts): 'de Mandeville's southern farmstead'. OE *sūth*, 'southern', + *tūn*, 'farmstead'. The de Mandeville family held the manor here in the 13C, their name distinguishing this Sutton from SUTTON VENY, 11 miles to the northwest. DB *Sudtone*, 1276 *Sutton Maundeville*.

Sutton-on-Hull (district, Hull): 'southern farmstead on the (river) Hull'. OE *sūth*, 'southern', + *tūn*, 'farmstead'. The distinguishing part of the name refers to the river that gave HULL its own name. DB *Sudtone*, 1172 *Sutune iuxta Hul*.

Sutton on Sea (resort town, Lincs): 'southern farm by the sea'. OE *sūth*, 'southern', + *tūn*, 'farmstead'. The identity of the corresponding 'northern farm' is uncertain, especially as Sutton is surrounded by places with OS names. The second part of the name was added to help the resort compete with nearby Mablethorpe. DB *Sudtone*, 1898 *Sutton-in-the-Marsh*.

Sutton-on-the-Forest (village, N Yorks): 'southern farmstead on the (edge of the) forest'. OE *sūth*, 'southern', + *tūn*, 'farmstead'. The village once formed part of the ancient forest of Galtres. Cp. STOCKTON ON THE FOREST. DB *Sudtune*, 1242 *Sutton sub Galtris*.

Sutton on Trent (village, Notts): 'southern farmstead on the (river) Trent'. OE *sūth*, 'southern', + *tūn*, 'farmstead', 'village'. The farm may have been regarded as 'south' in relation to Normanton to the north or Weston to the northwest. For the river name, see STOKE-ON-TRENT. DB *Sudtone*.

Sutton Scotney (village, Hants): 'de Scotney's southern farmstead'. OE *sūth*, 'southern', + *tūn*, 'farmstead', 'village'. The farm was 'south' here with regard to *Norton* in the same parish. The de Scotney family held the manor here in the 13C. DB *Sudtune*.

Sutton St Edmund. See LONG SUTTON.

Sutton St James. See LONG SUTTON.

Sutton-under-Brailes (village, Warwicks): 'southern farmstead near Brailes'. OE *sūth*, 'southern', + *tūn*, 'farmstead'. The village is 2 miles from UPPER BRAILES. DB *Sudtune*.

Sutton-under-Whitestonecliffe (village, N Yorks): 'southern farmstead under Whitestone Cliff'. OE *sūth*, 'southern', + *tūn*, 'farmstead', 'village'. The village is in the south of the parish of Felixkirk at the foot of the named high hill ('cliff of white stone'). DB *Sudtone*, 13C *Sutton subtus Whitstanclif*.

Sutton upon Derwent (village, E Yorks): 'southern farmstead on the (river) Derwent'. OE *sūth*, 'southern', + *tūn*, 'farmstead'. This Derwent has a name of the same origin as that of DERWENT WATER. DB *Sudtone*.

Sutton Valence (village, Kent): 'Valence's southern farmstead'. OE *sūth*, 'southern', + *tūn*, 'farmstead'. The Valence family held the manor here in the 13C, their name distinguishing the village from nearby *East Sutton*. 814 *Suthtun*, DB *Sudtone*, 1316 *Sutton Valence*.

Sutton Veny (village, Wilts): 'marshy southern farmstead'. OE *sūth*, 'southern', + *tūn*, 'farmstead', + *fennig*, 'muddy', 'marshy'. The village is 'south' with regard to NORTON BAVANT. The second word of the name has Wiltshire *v* for *f* (as *vly* for *fly*). DB *Sudtone*, 1268 *Fennisutton*, 1535 *Veny Sutton*.

Sutton Waldron (village, Dorset): 'Waleran's southern farmstead'. OE *sūth*, 'southern', + *tūn*, 'farmstead', 'village'. The farmstead was probably 'south' with regard to Fontmell Magna. One

Waleran held the manor here in 1086. DB *Sudtone*, 1297 *Sutton Walerand*.

Swaby (village, Lincs): 'Sváfi's farmstead'. OS *bý*, 'farmstead', 'village'. The personal name is Scandinavian. DB *Suabi*.

Swadlincote (town, Derbys): 'Sweartling's or Svartlingr's cottage'. OE *cot*, 'cottage'. The personal names are respectively OE and Scandinavian. DB *Sivardingescotes*.

Swaffham (town, Norfolk): 'homestead of the Swabians'. OE *Swǣfe*, 'Swabians', + *hām*, 'homestead'. The named people came from Swabia, a former duchy of medieval Germany. DB *Suafham*.

Swaffham Prior (village, Cambs): 'prior's homestead of the Swabians'. OE *Swǣfe*, 'Swabians', + *hām*, 'homestead'. Cp. SWAFFHAM. The manor here was held by the Prior of Ely, whose title distinguishes the village from nearby *Swaffham Bulbeck*, where it was held by the Bolebech family. DB *Suafham*, 1261 *Swafham Prior*.

Swafield (village, Norfolk): 'open land with a track over it'. OE *swæth*, 'swathe', 'track', + *feld*, 'open land' (modern English *field*). The DB form of the name below has omitted *th*. DB *Suafelda*, c.1150 *Suathefeld*.

Swainby (village, N Yorks): 'farmstead of the young men'. OS *sveinn*, 'lad', 'young man' (modern English *swain*), + *bý*, 'farmstead', 'village'. 1314 *Swaneby*.

Swainsthorpe (village, Norfolk): 'Sveinn's outlying farmstead'. OS *thorp*, 'outlying farmstead'. The personal name is Scandinavian. DB *Sueinestorp*.

Swalcliffe (village, Oxon): '(place by the) cliff where swallows are seen'. OE *swealwe*, 'swallow', + *clif*, 'cliff', 'bank'. Cp. SWALLOWCLIFFE. c.1166 *Sualewclive*.

Swale (river). See (1) BROMPTON-ON-SWALE, (2) SWALECLIFFE.

Swalecliffe (district of Whitstable, Kent): 'bank by the (river) Swale'. OE *clif*, 'cliff', 'bank'. Swalecliffe lies on the estuary of the river Swale, whose name, meaning 'rushing water' (OE *swalwe*, 'whirlpool', related modern English *swallow*), was adopted for that of the local council district. The DB form of the name below has garbled the river name. 949 *Swalewanclife*, DB *Soaneclive*.

Swallow (village, Lincs): '(place on the) rushing stream'. OE *swalwe*, 'whirlpool'. The stream that rises here could also have a pre-Celtic name with a meaning something like 'shining one'. DB *Sualun*.

Swallowcliffe (village, Wilts): '(place by the) cliff where swallows are seen'. OE *swealwe*, 'swallow', + *clif*, 'cliff', 'bank'. The village stands at the head of a steep coomb below the scarp of Swallowcliffe Down. The first form of the name below translates from the Latin as 'cliff of the swallow, that is, Swallowcliffe'. 940 *rupis irundinis, id est Swealewanclif*, DB *Svaloclive*.

Swallowfield (village, Wokingham): 'open land by the (river) Swallow'. OE *feld*, 'open land' (modern English *field*). The former river name, meaning 'rushing water', is identical with that of the *Swale* at SWALECLIFFE. The river is now known as the Blackwater, as at BLACKWATER. DB *Sualefelle*.

Swanage (resort town, Dorset): 'farm of the herdsmen'. OE *swān*, 'herdsman' (modern English *swain*), + *wīc*, 'farm'. The name could also mean 'farm where swans are bred', with OE *swan*, 'swan', as the first element. The former seems more likely, as the pastures by the sea here were probably used by dairy farmers in the summer months. late 9C *Swanawic*, DB *Swanwic*.

Swanbourne (village, Bucks): '(place by the) stream where swans are seen'. OE *swan*, 'swan', + *burna*, 'stream'. There is not much of a stream here now. 792 *Suanaburna*, DB *Sueneborne*.

Swanland (village, E Yorks): 'Svanr's or Sveinn's grove'. OS *lundr*, 'grove'. The personal names are Scandinavian. 1189 *Suenelund*.

Swanley (town, Kent): 'woodland clearing of the herdsmen'. OE *swān*, 'herdsman' (modern English *swain*), + *lēah*, 'wood', 'clearing'. The name could also mean 'woodland clearing where swans are seen' (OE *swan*, 'swan', + *lēah*). 1203 *Swanleg*.

Swanmore (village, Hants): '(place by the) pool where swans are seen'. OE *swan*, 'swan', + *mere*, 'pool'. 1205 *Suanemere*.

Swannington (village, Leics): 'estate associated with Swan'. OE *-ing-*, 'associated with', + *tūn*, 'farmstead', 'estate'. Late 12C *Suaninton*. SO ALSO: *Swannington*, Norfolk.

Swanscombe (town, Kent): 'enclosed land of the herdsmen'. OE *swān*, 'herdsman' (modern English *swain*), + *camp*, 'enclosure' (modern English *camp*). The name is popularly interpreted as 'Sweyn's camp', after the 11C Danish king, who is said to have landed and set up his winter quarters here, but earlier forms of the name (as below) date from long before his time. 695 *Suanescamp*, DB *Svinescamp*.

Swansea (city and port, Swansea): 'Sveinn's island'. OS *ey*, 'island'. The identity of the named Viking is not known, but he was presumably associated with an island in the estuary of the river Tawe here. The Welsh name of Swansea is *Abertawe*, 'mouth of the Tawe' (OW *aber*, 'river mouth'). The name of the river itself is of Celtic origin and means either 'dark one' or simply 'water'. c.1165 *Sweynnesse*, 1190 *Sueinesea*, 1322 *Swanesey*.

Swanton Morley (village, Norfolk): 'de Morle's (estate at the) farmstead of the herdsmen'. OE *swān*, 'herdsman', + *tūn*, 'farmstead', 'village'. The manor here was held in the 14C by the de Morle family, their name distinguishing the village from *Swanton Novers*, 10 miles to the north, where the manor was held in the 13C by the de Nuiers family, and from *Swanton Abbot*, 17 miles to the east, held early by Holme Abbey. DB *Suanetuna*.

Swanwick (village, Derbys): 'dairy farm of the herdsmen'. OE *swān*, 'herdsman', + *wīc*, 'specialized farm'. Late 13C *Swanwyk*.

Swardeston (village, Norfolk): 'Sweord's farmstead'. OE *tūn*, 'farmstead', 'village'. DB *Suerdestuna*.

Swarkestone (village, Derbys): 'Swerkir's farmstead'. OE *tūn*, 'farmstead', 'village'. The personal name is Scandinavian. DB *Suerchestune*.

Swarland (hamlet, Northd): 'heavily cultivated land'. OE *swǣr*, 'heavy', + *land*, 'cultivated land'. 1242 *Swarland*.

Swaton (village, Lincs): 'Swafa's or Sváfi's farmstead'. OE *tūn*, 'farmstead', 'village'. The personal names are respectively OE and Scandinavian. DB *Svavetone*.

Swavesey (village, Cambs): 'Swǣf's landing place'. OE *hȳth*, 'landing place'. The village lies at a point where firm ground meets fenland. The personal name means 'Swabian' (see SWAFFHAM). DB *Suauesye*.

Sway (town, Hants): '(place by the river) Sway'. The former name of the river here, now the Little Avon, means 'noisy stream' (OE *swēge*, 'sounding'). The name could also mean 'swathe', 'track' (OE *swæth*), perhaps referring to a royal route here by the New Forest. DB *Sueia*, 1227 *Sweia*.

Swaythling (district, Southampton). The name is probably a former name of the stream here now known as Monk's Brook. It may represent OE *swætheling*, 'misty stream', from *swathul*, 'smoke'. 909 *Swæthelinge*.

Swefling (village, Suffolk): '(settlement of) Swiftel's people'. OE *-ingas*, 'people of'. DB *Sueflinga*, c.1150 *Sueftlinges*.

Swepstone (village, Leics): 'Sweppi's farmstead'. OE *tūn*, 'farmstead'. The DB form of the name below is corrupt. DB *Scopestone*, *c.*1125 *Swepeston*.

Swerford (village, Oxon): '(place at the) ford by a neck of land'. OE *swēora*, 'neck', + *ford*, 'ford'. The river Swere here takes its name from that of the village. DB *Surford*, 1194 *Swereford*.

Swettenham (village, Cheshire): 'Swēta's homestead or enclosure'. OE *hām*, 'homestead', or *hamm*, 'enclosure'. Late 12C *Suetenham*.

Swilland (village, Suffolk): 'tract of land where pigs are kept'. OE *swīn*, 'pig', 'swine', + *land*, 'tract of land'. DB *Suinlanda*.

Swillington (village, Leeds): 'farmstead by the hill where pigs are pastured'. OE *swīn*, 'swine', + *hyll*, 'hill', + *-ing-*, 'associated with', + *tūn*, 'farmstead'. The second element of the name could also represent OE *lēah*, 'clearing'. DB *Suillintune*.

Swimbridge (village, Devon): '(place by) Sæwine's bridge'. OE *brycg*, 'bridge'. The named man held the manor here in 1086. The bridge is over a tributary of the river Taw. DB *Birige*, 1225 *Svimbrige*, 1868 *Swinbridge*.

Swinbrook (village, Oxon): '(place by the) brook where pigs drink'. OE *swīn*, 'swine', + *brōc*, 'brook'. DB *Svinbroc*.

Swinderby (village, Lincs): 'southern farmstead'. OS *sundri*, 'southern', + *bý*, 'farmstead', 'village'. The place was probably regarded as lying to the south of Morton. DB *Sunderby*.

Swindon (town, Swindon): 'hill where pigs are kept'. OE *swīn*, 'swine', 'pig', + *dūn*, 'hill'. Old Swindon, the oldest part of the town, stands on a prominent hill. DB *Svindune*. SO ALSO: *Swindon*, Glos, Staffs.

Swine (village, E Yorks): '(place by the) creek'. OE *swīn*, 'creek', 'channel'. The original creek here is now represented by Swine Church Drain. DB *Suuine*.

Swinefleet (village, E Yorks): '(place on the) stretch of river where pigs are kept'. OE *swīn*, 'swine', 'pig', + *flēot*, 'creek', 'stream'. The river here is the Ouse. *c.*1195 *Swyneflet*.

Swineshead (village, Beds): '(place at the) pig's head'. OE *swīn*, 'pig', + *hēafod*, 'head'. The reference is probably to a headland that projects like a pig's snout, rather than to one where pigs were kept or to one where a pig's head was displayed following a ritual sacrifice. DB *Suineshefet*.

Swineshead (village, Lincs): '(place by the) source of the creek'. OE *swīn*, 'creek', + *hēafod*, 'head', 'source'. Swineshead is in fenland country. *c.*675 *Swineshæfed*, 786 *Suinesheabde*, 1163 *Suinesheued*.

Swinford (village, Leics): '(place by the) ford used by pigs'. OE *swīn*, 'swine', 'pig', + *ford*, 'ford'. The river here is the Avon. DB *Svineford*. SO ALSO: *Swinford*, Oxon.

Swingfield Minnis (village, Kent): 'open land where pigs are kept (held as) common land'. OE *swīn*, 'swine', 'pig', + *feld*, 'open land' (modern English *field*), + *mænnes*, 'common land'. *c.*1100 *Suinafeld*.

Swinhoe (hamlet, Northd): 'headland where pigs are kept'. OE *swīn*, 'swine', 'pig', + *hōh*, 'hill spur'. 1242 *Swinhou*.

Swinhope (hamlet, Lincs): '(place in the) valley where pigs are kept'. OE *swīn*, 'pig', + *hop*, 'valley'. There is no village here today, but the church remains in a very long curving valley, a typical OE *hop*. DB *Suinhope*.

Swinithwaite (hamlet, N Yorks): 'place cleared by burning'. OS *svithningr*, 'place cleared by burning', + *thveit*, 'clearing'. 1202 *Swiningethwait*.

Swinscoe (hamlet, Staffs): '(place by the) wood where pigs are kept'. OS *svín*, 'swine', 'pig', + *skógr*, 'wood'. 1248 *Swyneskow*.

Swinton (town, Rotherham): 'pig farm'. OE *swīn*, 'swine', 'pig', + *tūn*, 'farmstead'. DB *Suintone*. SO ALSO: *Swinton*, N Yorks.

Swinton (town, Salford): 'pig farm'. OE *swīn*, 'swine', 'pig', + *tūn*, 'farmstead'. 1258 *Suinton*.

Swithland (village, Leics): 'grove by the burnt clearing'. OS *svitha*, 'land cleared by burning', + *lundr*, 'wood', 'grove'. *c.*1215 *Swithellund*.

Swyncombe (estate, Oxon): '(place in the) valley where pigs are kept'. OE *swīn*, 'swine', 'pig', + *cumb*, 'valley'. DB *Svinecumbe*.

Swynnerton (village, Staffs): 'farmstead by the ford used by pigs'. OE *swīn*, 'swine', 'pig', + *ford*, 'ford', + *tūn*, 'farmstead'. The river here is the Sow. The DB form of the name below is corrupt. DB *Sulvertone*, 1242 *Suinuerton*.

Swyre (village, Dorset): '(place on a) neck of land'. OE *swēora*, 'col'. DB *Suere*.

Syde (village, Glos): '(place on the) long hill slope'. OE *sīde*, 'hillside', 'slope' (modern English *side*). DB *Side*.

Sydenham (district, Lewisham): 'Cippa's homestead'. OE *hām*, 'homestead'. One would have expected the name to evolve on the lines of CHIPPENHAM (Cambs), but a 17C copyist's error put *d* for *p*. 1206 *Chipeham*, 1315 *Shippenham*, 1690 *Sidenham*.

Sydenham (village, Oxon): '(place at the) broad enclosure'. OE *sīd*, 'broad' (related modern English *side*), + *hamm*, 'enclosure'. The DB form of the name below is corrupt. DB *Sidreham*, 1216 *Sidenham*.

Sydenham Damerel (village, Devon): 'de Albemarle's (estate at the) broad enclosure'. OE *sīd*, 'broad' (related modern English *side*), + *hamm*, 'enclosure'. The manor here was held in the 13C by the de Albemarle family. The DB form of the name below has *l* for *n*. DB *Sidelham*, 1297 *Sydenham Albemarlie*.

Syderstone (village, Norfolk): '(place by) Siduhere's pool'. OS *tjǫrn*, 'pool' (modern English *tarn*). The name could also mean 'extensive property' (OE *sīd*, 'broad', + *sterne*, 'property'). DB *Cidesterna*.

Sydling St Nicholas (village, Dorset): '(place on the) broad ridge with St Nicholas's church'. OE *sīd*, 'broad' (related modern English *side*), + *hlinc*, 'ridge'. 934 *Sidelyng*, DB *Sidelince*.

Syerston (village, Notts): 'Sigehere's farmstead'. OE *tūn*, 'farmstead', 'village'. DB *Sirestune*.

Sykehouse (village, Doncaster): 'house by the stream'. OS *sík*, 'stream', + *hús*, 'house'. 1404 *Sikehouse*.

Symondsbury (village, Dorset): 'Sigemund's hill'. OE *beorg*, 'hill', 'barrow'. DB *Simondesberge*.

Symonds Yat (hill pass, Herefords): 'Sigemund's gap'. OE *geat*, 'gate', 'gap'. The 'gap' is the narrow gorge through which the river Wye flows here. 1256 *Symundesyate*.

Syon House (mansion, Hounslow). The 18C house derives its name from a 15C monastery originally known as the Monastery of the Holy Saviour and St Brigid. The words *de Syon* ('of Zion'), perhaps referring to the biblical 'daughters of Zion' (Song of Solomon 3:11), were for some reason then added to this. 'Zion' was subsequently regarded as the 'official' name of the religious house and persisted after the monastery was suppressed in the 16C. The first word of the form of the name below refers to ISLEWORTH. 1564 *Istelworth Syon*.

Syresham (village, Northants): 'Sigehere's homestead or enclosure'. OE *hām*, 'homestead', or *hamm*, 'enclosure'. DB *Sigresham*.

Syston (suburb of Leicester, Leics): 'Sigehæth's farmstead'. OE *tūn*, 'farmstead', 'village'. DB *Sitestone*.

Syston (village, Lincs): '(place by the) broad stone'. OE *sīd*, 'broad' (related modern English *side*), + *stān*, 'stone'. DB *Sidestan*.

Sywell (village, Northants): '(place with) seven springs'. The number may have some 'mystic' significance. OE *seofon*, 'seven', + *wella*, 'spring'. DB *Siwella*.

T

Tackley (village, Oxon): 'Tæcca's woodland clearing'. OE *lēah*, 'wood', 'clearing'. The name could also mean 'woodland clearing where young sheep are kept', from OE *tacca* (related modern English *teg*). DB *Tachelie*.

Tacolneston (village, Norfolk): 'Tātwulf's farmstead'. OE *tūn*, 'farmstead', 'village'. The middle '-n-' of the name arose from a misreading of earlier *u* (the *w* of the personal name). DB *Tacoluestuna*.

Tadcaster (town, N Yorks): 'Tāta's or Tāda's Roman town'. OE *cæster*, 'Roman station'. The Roman settlement here was *Calcaria*, 'limeworks', as identified by the Venerable Bede in *The Ecclesiastical History of the English People* (completed 731): '*ciuitatem calcariam quae a gente anglorum kælcacaestir appellatur*' ('the town of Calcaria, which is called by the English people Kælcacaestir'). The latter name means 'Roman station in the chalky place' (OE *celce*, 'chalky place', + *cæster*), and refers to the magnesian limestone on which the town stands. DB *Tatecastre*.

Taddington (village, Derbys): 'estate associated with Tāda'. OE *-ing-*, 'associated with', + *tūn*, 'farmstead', 'estate'. DB *Tadintune*.

Tadley (village, Hants): 'Tāda's woodland clearing'. OE *lēah*, 'wood', 'clearing'. 909 *Tadanleage*.

Tadlow (village, Cambs): 'Tāda's tumulus'. OE *hlāw*, 'mound', 'tumulus'. *c.*1080 *Tadeslaue*, DB *Tadelai*.

Tadmarton (village, Oxon): 'farmstead by a pool where toads are seen'. OE *tāde*, 'toad', + *mere*, 'pool', + *tūn*, 'farmstead'. The village lies beside a stream in a damp valley, a favourable habitat for toads. 956 *Tademærtun*, DB *Tademertone*.

Tadworth (district of Banstead, Surrey): 'Thædda's enclosure'. OE *worth*, 'enclosure'. 1062 *Thæddeuurthe*, DB *Tadeorde*.

Taf (river). See CARDIFF.

Tain (town, Highland): '(place of the) river'. Gaelic *tain*, 'water', 'river'. The name may be pre-Celtic, but the sense seems likely for the stream here. 1226 *Tene*, 1257 *Thayn*.

Takeley (village, Essex): 'Tæcca's woodland clearing'. OE *lēah*, 'wood', 'clearing'. The name could also mean 'woodland clearing where young sheep are kept' (OE *tacca*, 'teg', 'young sheep', + *lēah*). DB *Tacheleia*.

Talacharn. See LAUGHARNE.

Talaton (village, Devon): 'farmstead on the (river) Tale'. OE *tūn*, 'farmstead', 'village'. The river has an OE name meaning 'swift one'. DB *Taletone*.

Talbenny (village, Pemb): '(place at the) end'. The first part of the name is Welsh *tâl*, 'end'. The second is of uncertain origin. It may represent a form of Welsh *ban*, 'mountain', 'peak', although this hardly suits the local topography. 1291 *Talbenny*.

Talbot Village (district, Bournemouth). The district arose as a model village built for impoverished local families in the 1860s by two wealthy sisters, Georgina Charlotte Talbot and Mary Anne Talbot, who are also commemorated in Georgina Close and Marianne Road here.

Talgarth (town, Powys): '(place at the) end of the ridge'. Welsh *tâl*, 'end', + *garth*, 'ridge', 'hillside'. Talgarth is at the edge of hill country northwest of the Black Mountains.

Talke (district of Kidsgrove, Staffs): origin uncertain. The name may be of Celtic origin, from a word related to modern Welsh *talcen*, 'forehead', referring to the prominent ridge here. The former village was also known as *Talko'-th'-Hill*, 'popularly supposed to have got its name from a conference or council of war held there either by Charles I, or according to others, by Charles Edward in 1745' (A. Smythe Palmer, *Folk-Etymology*, 1882). The second part of this name merely emphasizes the lofty situation of the place ('on the hill'). DB *Talc*.

Talkin (hamlet, Cumbria): '(place by the) white brow'. The name is Celtic in origin, from words related to modern Welsh *tâl*, 'forehead', and *can*, 'white'. The reference is to a hill. *c.*1195 *Talcan*.

Talland (hamlet, Cornwall): '(church of) Tallan'. The church here is dedicated to St Tallan, but his name probably evolved from a combination of Cornish *tal*, 'hill brow', and *lann*, 'church site', and the church was earlier dedicated to St Catherine. *c.*1205 *Tallan*, 1440 *Tallant*.

Tallentire (village, Cumbria): '(place at the) end of the land'. The name is Celtic, from words related to modern Welsh *tâl*, 'end', and *tir*, 'land'. *c.*1160 *Talentir*.

Tallington (village, Lincs): 'estate associated with Tæl or Talla'. OE *-ing-*, 'associated with', + *tūn*, 'farmstead', 'estate'. DB *Talintune*.

Tal-y-bont (village, Ceredigion): '(place at the) end of the bridge'. Welsh *tâl*, 'end', + *y*, 'the', + *pont*, 'bridge'. The village is at the northern end of the bridge over the river Leri. Cp. BRIDGEND.

Talysarn (village, Gwynedd): '(place at the) end of the causeway'. Welsh *tâl*, 'end', + *y*, 'the', + *sarn*, 'causeway'. The causeway in question carried the route from Rhyd-ddu and Llyn Nantlle to Talysarn across the marshland either side of the river Llydni. 1795 *Talysarn*.

Tamar (river). See TAMERTON FOLIOT.

Tame (river). See TAMWORTH.

Tamerton Foliot (district, Plymouth): 'Foliot's farmstead on the (river) Tamar'. OE *tūn*, 'farmstead', 'village'. The river name is Celtic in origin and means 'dark one' or, more likely, simply 'river'. The Foliot family held the manor here in the 13C. DB *Tambretone*, 1262 *Tamereton Foliot*.

Tameside (unitary authority, NW England): '(district) beside the (river) Tame'. There are at least three major rivers of the name in England. This one rises on the moors northeast of Oldham and flows south to join the Goyt and form the Mersey. For the name itself, see TAMWORTH.

Tamesis. See THAMES DITTON.

Tamworth (town, Staffs): 'enclosure on the (river) Tame'. OE *worthig*, 'enclosure'. The river has a Celtic name meaning either 'dark one' or, more likely, simply 'river'. For another river of the name, see TAMESIDE. 781 *Tamouuorthig*, DB *Tamuuorde*.

Tandridge (village, Surrey): 'ridge with a pasture for pigs'. OE *hrycg*, 'ridge', 'hill'. The origin of the first part of the name is uncertain. It may be *denn*, 'woodland pasture for pigs'. The 'ridge', or a section of it, is probably nearby Tandridge Hill. The name is now also that of the local council district. *c.*965 *Tenhric*, DB *Tenrige*.

Tanfield (village, Durham): 'open land on the (river) Team'. OE *feld*, 'open land' (modern English *field*). The river has a name of Celtic origin meaning 'dark one' or, more likely, simply 'river'. Cp. THAMES DITTON. 1179 *Tamefeld*.

Tangmere (village, W Sussex): '(place by the) tongs-shaped pool'. OE *tang*, 'tongs', + *mere*, 'pool'. There is no pool here now. 680 *Tangmere*, DB *Tangemere*.

Tankersley (village, Barnsley): 'Tancred's or Tancrad's woodland clearing'. OE *lēah*, 'wood', 'clearing'. The personal names are Old German. DB *Tancresleia*.

Tankerton (district of Whitstable, Kent): 'Tancred's or Tancrad's farmstead'. OE *tūn*, 'farmstead', 'estate'. The personal names are Old German. 1240 *Tangerton*.

Tannington (village, Suffolk): 'estate associated with Tāta'. OE *-ing-*, 'associated with', + *tūn*, 'farmstead', 'estate'. DB *Tatintuna*.

Tansley (village, Derbys): 'Tān's woodland clearing'. OE *lēah*, 'wood', 'clearing'. The first part of the name could also represent OE *tān*, 'branch', perhaps referring to a valley that branched off from the main valley. Alternatively it could refer to a site where shoots or branches were obtained. Cp. TANSOR. DB *Taneslege*.

Tansor (village, Northants): 'Tān's ridge'. OE *ofer*, 'flat-topped ridge'. The first part of the name could also be OE *tān*, 'branch', perhaps referring to a valley that branched off from a main valley, as for TANSLEY. Alternatively it could refer to a site where branches were obtained. DB *Tanesovre*.

Tanton (hamlet, N Yorks): 'farmstead on the (river) Tame'. OE *tūn*, 'farmstead', 'village'. The river name has the same origin as that of the Tame behind TAMWORTH. DB *Tametun*.

Tanworth-in-Arden (village, Warwicks): 'enclosure made with branches in Arden'. OE *tān*, 'branch', + *worth*, 'enclosure'. For the district name, see HENLEY-IN-ARDEN. 1201 *Tanewrthe*.

Taplow (village, Bucks): 'Tæppa's tumulus'. OE *hlāw*, 'mound', 'tumulus'. The tumulus in question is a barrow in the old churchyard (now in the grounds of Taplow Court) in which a hoard of Anglo-Saxon arms and ornaments was found in 1883 and presented to the British Museum. DB *Thapeslau.*

Tarbat Ness (headland, Highland): 'headland by a portage'. Gaelic *tairbeart*, 'isthmus', 'portage' (from *tar*, 'over', 'across', + *beir*, 'to bear'). A portage is a site on a narrow promontory, as here between Dornoch Firth and Moray Firth, where boats and their contents can be carried or dragged from one stretch of water to another. Cp. TARBERT, TARBET.

Tarbert (village, Argyll & Bute): '(place by a) portage'. Gaelic *tairbeart*, 'isthmus', 'portage'. The isthmus here, between Loch Tarbert and West Loch Tarbert, at the north end of Kintyre, is over 2 miles wide. Magnus Barfot ('Barefoot') of Norway is said to have been dragged across it in a galley in 1093. See TARBAT NESS.

Tarbet (village, Argyll & Bute): '(place by a) portage'. Gaelic *tairbeart*, 'isthmus', 'portage'. In 1263 Haakon IV Haakonsson of Norway dragged his ships from here, on the western shore of Loch Lomond, across the narrow strip of land to Arrochar, at the head of Loch Long. See TARBAT NESS.

Tarbock Green (hamlet, Knowsley): '(place by the) brook where thorn bushes grow'. OE *thorn*, 'thorn bush', + *broc*, 'brook'. Tarbock was later associated with its village green. DB *Torboc*, *c.*1240 *Thornebrooke.*

Tardebigge (village, Worcs): origin uncertain. Despite plentiful early forms of the name, its origin and meaning remain obscure. The DB form below appears to be garbled. *c.*1000 *Tærdebigcan*, DB *Terdeberie.*

Tarleton (village, Lancs): 'Tharaldr's farmstead'. OE *tūn*, 'farmstead'. The personal name is Scandinavian. *c.*1200 *Tarleton.*

Tarporley (town, Cheshire): 'woodland clearing of the peasants'. OE *thorpere*, 'peasant' (related OS *thorp*, 'outlying farmstead'), + *lēah*, 'wood', 'clearing'. DB *Torpelei*, 1281 *Thorperlegh.*

Tarrant Hinton (village, Dorset): 'estate of the religious community on the (river) Tarrant'. The river name is Celtic in origin and means 'trespasser', as for the *Trent* (see STOKE-ON-TRENT). The second word of the name derives from OE *hīgna*, the genitive form of the plural noun *hīwan*, 'household (of monks)', 'religious community', + *tūn*, 'estate', and refers to Shaftesbury Abbey. There are several villages here east of Blandford named after the same river. Others include *Tarrant Crawford*, at a ford where crows were seen, *Tarrant Gunville*, where the Gundeville family held the manor in the 12C,

Tarrant Keyneston, where the manor was held by the de Cahaignes family from the 12C, *Tarrant Launceston*, with an estate held by Lēofwine or a family called Lewin, *Tarrant Monkton*, owned by the monks of Tewkesbury Abbey, *Tarrant Rawston*, where one Ralph held the estate, and *Tarrant Rushton*, where the manor was held by the de Rusceaus family in the 13C. DB *Tarente*, 1280 *Tarente Hyneton.*

Tarring Neville (village, E Sussex): 'de Neville's (estate at the settlement of) Teorra's people'. OE *-ingas*, 'people of'. The de Neville family held the manor here in the 13C. The village is also known as *East Tarring*, for distinction from WEST TARRING. DB *Toringes*, 1339 *Thoring Nevell.*

Tarrington (village, Herefords): 'estate associated with Tāta'. OE *-ing-*, 'associated with', + *tūn*, 'farmstead', 'estate'. DB *Tatintune.*

Tarvedunum. See THURSO.

Tarvin (village, Cheshire): '(place by the river) Tarvin'. The river here now is the Gowy, but its former name was *Tarvin*, from a Celtic word meaning 'boundary' (modern Welsh *terfyn*). The boundary in question was probably that of a tribal territory. The DB form below lacks the final *n*. DB *Terve*, 1185 *Teruen.*

Tasburgh (village, Norfolk): 'Tæsa's stronghold'. OE *burh*, 'fortified place'. The river Tas here is named after the village. DB *Taseburc.*

Tasley (hamlet, Shropshire): '(place by the) wood or clearing'. OE *lēah*, 'wood', 'clearing'. The first part of the name is of uncertain meaning. *c.*1143 *Tasseleya.*

Tatenhill (village, Staffs): 'Tāta's hill'. OE *hyll*, 'hill'. 942 *Tatenhyll.*

Tatham (hamlet, Lancs); 'Tāta's homestead'. OE *hām*, 'homestead'. DB *Tathaim.*

Tatsfield (village, Surrey): 'Tātel's open land'. OE *feld*, 'open land' (modern English *field*). Tatsfield stands high on the bare chalk downs. DB *Tatelefelle.*

Tattenhall (village, Cheshire): 'Tāta's corner of land'. OE *halh*, 'nook', 'corner of land'. DB *Tatenale.*

Tatterford (hamlet, Norfolk): '(place by) Tāthere's ford'. OE *ford*, 'ford'. The river here is the Wensum. DB *Taterforda.*

Tattersett (village, Norfolk): 'Tāthere's fold'. OE *set*, 'dwelling', 'fold' (for animals). Tattersett is only 1½ miles from TATTERFORD, and Tāthere has given his name to both places. DB *Tatessete.*

Tattershall (village, Lincs): 'Tāthere's corner of land'. OE *halh*, 'nook', 'corner of land'. DB *Tateshale.*

Tattingstone (village, Suffolk): 'Tāting's farmstead'. OE *tūn*, 'farmstead'. The name could also mean 'farmstead at the place associated with Tāta' (OE *-ing*, 'place associated with', + *tūn*). The DB form of the name below has omitted the first *n*. DB *Tatistune*, 1219 *Tatingestone*.

Taunton (town, Somerset): 'farmstead on the (river) Tone'. OE *tūn*, 'farmstead', 'village'. The river has a Celtic name traditionally said to mean 'roaring one', although recent scholarship prefers a sense 'fire' (modern Welsh *tân*), referring to its bright and sparkling waters. 737 *Tantun*, DB *Tantone*.

Taunton Deane (council district, Somerset). The name is that of a former hundred, surviving today for the *Vale of Taunton Deane*, a fertile valley (OE *denu*, 'valley') centring on TAUNTON. (The modern name is tautologous, as the sense of *Vale* is already present in *Deane*.)

Taverham (suburb of Norwich, Norfolk): 'vermilion homestead or enclosure'. OE *tēafor*, 'red lead', 'vermilion', + *hām*, 'homestead' or *hamm*, 'enclosure'. If the second part of the name is OE *hām*, the reference might be to red-painted buildings, but if it is *hamm*, it could be to red soil. DB *Taverham*.

Tavistock (town, Devon): 'outlying farmstead by the (river) Tavy'. OE *stoc*, 'outlying farmstead', 'dependent settlement'. The river has a Celtic name perhaps meaning 'dark stream'. Tavistock may have been a dependent settlement of *Mary Tavy* and *Peter Tavy*, now two villages northeast of the town on either side of the river. The distinguishing first words of their names are from the respective dedications of their churches to St Mary and St Peter. 981 *Tauistoce*.

Tawstock (village, Devon): 'outlying farmstead on the (river) Taw'. OE *stoc*, 'outlying farmstead'. For the river name, see BISHOP'S TAWTON. DB *Tauestoca*.

Tawton. See BISHOP'S TAWTON.

Taxal (hamlet, Derbys): 'corner of land held on lease'. ME *tak*, 'lease', 'tenure' (related modern English *take*), + OE *halh*, 'nook', 'corner of land'. *c*.1251 *Tackeshale*.

Tay (river). See TAYPORT.

Taynton (village, Glos): 'estate associated with Tæta'. OE *-ing-*, 'associated with', + *tūn*, 'farmstead', 'estate'. DB *Tetinton*.

Tayport (town, Fife): 'port on the (river) Tay'. The town has had various names over the years, including *Scotscraig* (13C), *South Ferry of Portincraig* (17C) and *South Ferry* (19C). This last name distinguished the former port from *Broughty Ferry* on the northern side of the Tay. (The earlier names refer to the rock or crag on which the town lies.) The present name dates from 1888, when the Tay Bridge was built. The river has a Celtic name perhaps meaning 'silent one'.

Tealby (village, Lincs): 'farmstead of the Tāflas'. OS *bý*, 'farmstead', 'village'. The tribal name apparently represents the East Germanic *Taifali* people, who are recorded in Britain by the early 5C. DB *Tavelesbi*.

Tean (island, Scilly): '(island of) St Tean'. The former chapel on this uninhabited island was dedicated to the female saint Tean, about whom nothing is known. *c*.1160 *Sancta Teona*.

Tebay (village, Cumbria): 'Tiba's island'. OE *ēg*, 'island'. The 'island' would be raised ground in wet land here, near the river Lune. *c*.1160 *Tibeia*.

Tedburn St Mary (village, Devon): '(place by) Tette's or Tetta's stream with St Mary's church'. OE *burna*, 'stream'. The first personal name is that of a woman, the second that of a man. The river Ted here takes its name from that of the village. DB *Teteborne*.

Teddington (village, Glos): 'estate associated with Teotta'. OE *-ing-*, 'associated with', + *tūn*, 'farmstead', 'estate'. 780 *Teottingtun*, DB *Teotintune*.

Teddington (district, Richmond): 'estate associated with Tuda'. OE *-ing-*, 'associated with', + *tūn*, 'farmstead', 'estate'. 'It is a favourite legend at Teddington ... that the place owes its name to the tide being arrested here—*Tide-end-town*' (James Thorne, *Handbook to the Environs of London*, 1876). The fancy was popularized by Rudyard Kipling in his poem about the Thames, *The River's Tale* (1911): 'Up I go till I end my run / At Tide-end-town, which is Teddington.' 969 *Tudintun*.

Tedstone Wafer (village, Herefords): 'le Wafre's (estate by) Tēod's thorn bush'. OE *thorn*, 'thorn bush'. The le Wafre family held the manor early here, their name distinguishing the village from nearby *Tedstone Delamere*, held by the de la Mare family. DB *Tedesthorne*, 1249 *Teddesthorne Wafre*.

Tees (river). See TEESDALE.

Teesdale (district, Durham): 'valley of the (river) Tees'. The name is that of the district around the Tees in the southwest of the county, now also that of the local council district. The river has a Celtic or pre-Celtic name perhaps meaning 'surging one'. *c*.1130 *Tesedale*.

Teeton (hamlet, Northants): '(place on the hill with a) beacon'. OE *tǣcne*, 'beacon' (related modern English *token*). Teeton stands on an elevated site, with the ground descending on three sides. The DB form of the name below has omitted the *n*. DB *Teche*, 1195 *Teacne*.

Teffont Evias (village, Wilts): 'Ewyas' (estate by the) boundary spring'. OE *tēo*, 'boundary', + *funta*, 'spring'. The village is on the border of two hundreds, although the name dates earlier than the formation of OE hundreds in the 10C. The manor here was held by the barons of Ewyas in the 13C, their name distinguishing the village from nearby *Teffont Magna* (Latin *magna*, 'great'). 860 *Tefunte*, DB *Tefonte*, 1275 *Teffunt Ewyas*, 1868 *Teffont-Evias*, or *Teffont-Ewyas*.

Teigh (village, Rutland): 'small enclosure'. OE *tēag*, 'small enclosure'. DB *Tie*.

Teignbridge (council district, Devon): 'bridge over the (river) Teign'. OE *brycg*, 'bridge'. The name is that of a former hundred here, referring to a bridge over the Teign at KINGSTEIGNTON. For the river name, see TEIGNMOUTH. 1187 *Teingnebrige*, 1212 *Teinnebrig*.

Teigngrace (village, Devon): 'Gras' (estate by the river) Teign'. The Gras family held the manor here in the 14C. For the river name, see TEIGNMOUTH. DB *Taigne*, 1331 *Teyngegras*.

Teignmouth (resort town, Devon): 'mouth of the (river) Teign'. OE *mūtha*, 'mouth'. The river has a Celtic name perhaps related to modern Welsh *taenu*, 'to spread', 'to expand', referring to its liability to flood. 1044 *Tengemutha*.

Telford (town, Wrekin). Telford was designated a New Town in 1963 and named after the Scottish civil engineer Thomas Telford (1757–1834), appointed surveyor of Shropshire (the town's original county) in 1786.

Telscombe (village, E Sussex): 'Titel's valley'. OE *cumb*, 'valley'. 966 *Titelescumbe*.

Temple Balsall (district, Solihull): 'estate of the Knights Templars at Bǣll's corner of land'. ME *tempel*, 'temple', + OE *halh*, 'nook', 'corner of land'. The Knights Templars held many estates in England and *Temple* was often added to an existing name, as here, where they had taken possession by 1185. 1185 *Beleshale*.

Temple Cloud (village, Bath & NE Somerset): 'estate of the Knights Templars by the hill'. ME *tempel*, 'temple', + OE *clūd*, 'rocky hill' (modern English *cloud*). Cp. TEMPLE BALSALL. 1199 *La Clude*.

Templecombe (town, Somerset): 'estate of the Knights Templars in the valley'. ME *tempel*, 'temple', + OE *cumb*, 'narrow valley'. Cp. TEMPLE BALSALL. DB *Come*, 1291 *Cumbe Templer*.

Temple Cowley (district of Oxford, Oxon): 'estate of the Knights Templars at Cowley'. ME *tempel*, 'temple'. Cp. TEMPLE BALSALL. In 1139 Queen Matilda gave land at COWLEY to the Knights Templars, and Cowley itself was formerly distinguished accordingly as *Church Cowley*. c.1200 *Temple Couele*.

Temple Ewell (suburb of Dover, Kent): 'estate of the Knights) Templars at the river source'. ME *tempel*, 'temple', + OE *æwell*, 'river source'. Cp. TEMPLE BALSALL. The river here is the Dour (see DOVER). The first word of the name distinguishes the place from the nearby village of *Ewell Minnis*, where the second word represents OE *mǣnnes*, 'common land'. c.722 *Æwille*, DB *Ewelle*.

Temple Grafton (village, Warwicks): 'estate of the Knights Templars at the farmstead by the pit'. ME *tempel*, 'temple', + OE *græf*, 'pit', 'trench' (modern English *grave*), + *tūn*, 'farmstead'. Cp. TEMPLE BALSALL. The DB form of the name below has *f* miscopied as *s*. 10C *Greftone*, DB *Grastone*, 1363 *Temple Grafton*.

Temple Guiting. See GUITING POWER.

Temple Hirst. See HIRST COURTNEY.

Temple Normanton (village, Derbys): 'estate of the Knights Templars at the farmstead of the Northmen'. ME *tempel*, 'temple', + OE *Northman*, 'Northman', + *tūn*, 'farmstead'. Cp. TEMPLE BALSALL. The Northmen were the Norwegian Vikings. The first word of the name distinguishes this Normanton from *South Normanton*, 7 miles to the south. DB *Normantune*, 1330 *Normanton Templer*.

Temple Sowerby (village, Cumbria): 'estate of the Knights) Templars at the farmstead on sour ground'. ME *tempel*, 'temple', + OS *saurr*, 'sour', + *bȳ*, 'farmstead'. Cp. TEMPLE BALSALL. The first word of the name distinguishes the village from the hamlet of *Brough Sowerby*, 15 miles to the southeast, near BROUGH. 1179 *Sourebi*, 1292 *Templessoureby*.

Templeton (village, Devon): 'village of the (Knights) Templars'. ME *tempel*, 'temple', + OE *tūn*, 'farmstead', 'village'. Cp. TEMPLE BALSALL. 1206 *Templum*, 1334 *Templeton*.

Tempsford (village, Beds): '(place by the) ford over the (river) Thames'. OE *ford*, 'ford'. Tempsford is on the Great North Road (now the A1) on the Great Ouse, and it is thus not clear whether the name means 'ford on the road (south) to the Thames' or whether this stretch of the Ouse was at one time itself known as the Thames. For the river name, see THAMES DITTON. 921 *Tæmeseford*, DB *Tamiseforde*, 1526 *Tempisford*.

Tenbury Wells (town, Worcs): 'stronghold on the (river) Teme with wells'. OE *burh*, 'fortified place', + modern English *wells*. The river has a Celtic name perhaps meaning 'dark one', as the Tame at TAMWORTH or the Thame at THAME. Saline springs were discovered here in *c.*1840. DB *Tamedeberie*.

Tenby (resort town, Pemb): 'little fort'. Welsh *dinas*, 'fort', + *bych*, 'little'. The original 'little fort' was on Castle Hill, the site of the present ruins of 13C Tenby Castle. The Welsh name of Tenby is *Dinbych-y-pysgod*, the first word of which gave the English name. Cp. DENBIGH. The additions are Welsh *y*, 'the', and *pysgod*, 'fish', referring to the town's importance as a fishing port with a daily fish market. *c.*1275 *Dinbych*, 1369 *Tynby*.

Tendring (village, Essex): 'place where tinder is gathered'. OE *tynder*, 'tinder', + *-ing*, 'place characterized by'. The name was originally that of a hundred here and is now also that of the local council district. DB *Tendringa*.

Tenterden (town, Kent): 'woodland pasture of the dwellers in Thanet'. OE *denn*, 'woodland pasture'. An area of woodland here must have been granted to a group of people from the Isle of THANET. This gave the 'Tent-' of the name, while the '-er-' represents OE *-ware*, 'dwellers'. OE *denn* usually denoted a woodland pasture where pigs fed on acorns. 1179 *Tentwardene*.

Terling (village, Essex): '(settlement of) Tyrhtel's people'. OE *-ingas*, 'people of'. The river Ter here takes its name from that of the village. 1017 *Terlinges*, DB *Terlingas*.

Terrington (village, N Yorks): 'estate associated with Teofer'. OE *-ing-*, 'associated with', + *tūn*, 'farmstead', 'estate'. DB *Teurinctune*.

Terrington St Clement (village, Norfolk): 'farmstead of Tir's people with St Clement's church'. OE *-inga-*, 'of the people of', + *tūn*, 'farmstead'. The church dedication distinguishes this Terrington from *Terrington St John*, 3 miles to the south. DB *Tilinghetuna*, 1121 *Terintona*.

Test (river). See TESTWOOD.

Testwood (village, Hants): 'wood by the (river) Test'. OE *wudu*, 'wood'. The river has a Celtic or pre-Celtic name perhaps related to obsolete Welsh *tres*, 'toil', 'labour' (earlier 'tumult', 'agitation') or to modern Welsh *trais*, 'force', 'violence', referring to its strong current. *Test Valley* is now the name of the local council district. The DB form of the name below has *T-* miscopied as *L-*. DB *Lesteorde*, *c.*1185 *Terstewode*.

Tetbury (town, Glos): 'Tette's fortified place'. OE *burh*, 'fortified place'. The fortification in question is the encampment just south of the parish church. The personal name is that of an abbess of Wimborne who was the sister of King Ine of Wessex (reigned 688–726). *c.*900 *Tettanbyrg*, DB *Teteberie*.

Tetcott (village, Devon): 'Tette's or Tetta's cottage'. OE *cot*, 'cottage'. The first personal name is that of a woman, the second that of a man. DB *Tetecote*.

Tetney (village, Lincs): 'Tǣta's island'. OE *ēg*, 'island'. Tetney lies on an 'island' of raised ground in a low-lying marshy coastal area. DB *Tatenai*.

Tetsworth (village, Oxon): 'Tætel's enclosure'. OE *worth*, 'enclosure'. *c.*1150 *Tetleswrthe*.

Tettenhall (district, Wolverhampton): 'Teotta's corner of land'. OE *halh*, 'nook', 'corner of land'. Early 10C *Teotanheale*, DB *Totenhale*.

Teversal (village, Notts): 'shelter of the painter or sorcerer'. OE *tiefrere*, 'painter', + *hald*, 'shelter'. A 'painter' here may have been a man who marked sheep. OE *tiefrere* also meant 'sorcerer'. Alternatively, the name could mean 'Teofer's shelter'. DB *Tevreshalt*.

Teversham (village, Cambs): 'homestead of the painter or sorcerer'. OE *tiefrere*, 'painter', 'sorcerer', + *hām*, 'homestead'. Cp. TEVERSAL. The name could also mean 'Teofer's homestead'. DB *Teuersham*.

Tewin (village, Herts): '(settlement of) Tīwa's people'. OE *-ingas*, 'people of'. 944 *Tiwingum*, DB *Teuuinge*.

Tewkesbury (town, Glos): 'Tēodec's fortified place'. OE *burh*, 'fortified place'. The name is popularly derived from a 7C missionary monk called Theocus, said to have built the first church here. DB *Teodekesberie*.

Teynham (village, Kent): 'Tēna's homestead'. OE *hām*, 'homestead'. The DB form of the name below has garbled the personal name. 798 *Teneham*, DB *Therham*.

Thakeham (village, W Sussex): 'homestead with a thatched roof'. OE *thaca*, 'thatched roof', + *hām*, 'homestead'. DB *Taceham*.

Thame (town, Oxon): '(place on the river) Thame'. The river has a Celtic name perhaps meaning 'dark one' or, more likely, simply 'river'. *c.*1000 *Tame*, DB *Tame*.

Thames Ditton (town, Surrey): 'farmstead by a ditch on the (river) Thames'. OE *dīc*, 'ditch', 'dyke', + *tūn*, 'farmstead'. The ditch in question was excavated to drain the land and channel the standing water of the Thames. The first word of the name was added to distinguish this Ditton from nearby *Long Ditton*, so called from the length of the village. The Thames has a Celtic or pre-Celtic name perhaps meaning 'dark one' or, more likely, simply 'river'. The alternative name for the Thames at Oxford is *Isis*, a formation obtained by dividing *Tamesis*, an early name for the Thames, into *Thame* and *Isis*. For rivers with related names, see TAMERTON FOLIOT, TAMWORTH, TANFIELD, TENBURY WELLS, THAME. DB *Ditune*, 1235 *Temes Ditton*.

Thamesmead (town, Bexley): 'meadows by the (river) Thames'. The town is a modern development planned beside the Erith Marshes on the south bank of the Thames (see THAMES DITTON) in 1967. The second part of the name is generally evocative rather than precisely descriptive.

Thanet (district, Kent): 'bright island'. The name is of Celtic origin and perhaps alludes to a beacon formerly here (related modern Welsh *tân*, 'fire'). The name is familiar for the *Isle of Thanet*, which is now a peninsula, not an island. It is also that of the local council district. 3C *Tanatus*, DB *Tanet*.

Thanington (district of Canterbury, Kent): 'estate associated with Tān'. OE *-ing-*, 'associated with', + *tūn*, 'farmstead', 'estate'. 833 *Taningtune*.

Tharston (village, Norfolk): 'Therir's farmstead'. OE *tūn*, 'farmstead', 'village'. The personal name is Scandinavian. DB *Therstuna*.

Thatcham (village, W Berks): 'riverside meadow where thatching materials are obtained'. OE *thæc*, 'thatch', + *hamm*, 'enclosure', 'riverside meadow'. Thatcham is beside the river Kennet. The name could also mean 'thatched homestead' (OE *thæc* + *hām*, 'homestead'). c.954 *Thæcham*, DB *Taceham*.

Thatto Heath (district, St Helens): '(place by the) spring with a conduit'. OE *thēote*, 'torrent', 'conduit', 'waterpipe', + *wella*, 'spring', 'stream'. Thatto was later associated with its heath. 12C *Thetwall*.

Thaxted (town, Essex): 'place where thatching materials are obtained'. OE *thæc*, 'thatch', + *stede*, 'place'. Thaxted is on the river Chelmer. DB *Tachesteda*.

Theakston (hamlet, N Yorks): 'Thēodec's farmstead'. OE *tūn*, 'farmstead', 'village'. The DB form of the name below has garbled the personal name. DB *Eston*, 1157 *Thekeston*.

Thealby (village, N Lincs): 'Thjóthulfr's farmstead'. OS *bý*, 'farmstead', 'village'. The personal name is Scandinavian. DB *Tedulfbi*.

Theale (village, W Berks): '(place by the) planks'. OE *thel*, 'plank'. The reference is to some sort of wooden structure here, perhaps a plank bridge over the river Kennet, or a platform for the meetings of the local hundred. 1208 *Teile*. SO ALSO: *Theale*, Somerset.

Thearne (hamlet, E Yorks): '(place by the) thorn bush'. OE *thorn*, 'thorn bush'. 1297 *Thoren*.

Theberton (village, Suffolk): 'Thēodbeorht's farmstead'. OE *tūn*, 'farmstead', 'village'. The DB form of the name below has garbled the personal name. DB *Thewardetuna*, 1176 *Tiberton*.

Theddingworth (village, Leics): 'enclosure of Thēoda's people'. OE *-inga-*, 'of the people of', + *worth*, 'enclosure'. The DB form of the name below has an extraneous *s*. DB *Tedingesworde*, 1206 *Tedingewrth*.

Theddlethorpe All Saints (village, Lincs): 'Thēodlāc's outlying farmstead with All Saints church'. OS *thorp*, 'outlying farmstead'. The church dedication distinguishes the village from nearby *Theddlethorpe St Helen*, where the church is dedicated to St Helen. DB *Tedlagestorp*.

Thelbridge (hamlet, Devon): '(place by the) plank bridge'. OE *thel*, 'plank', + *brycg*, 'bridge'. The bridge in question was probably over the small stream to the north of the church. DB *Talebrige*.

Thelnetham (village, Suffolk): 'enclosure where swans are seen by a plank bridge'. OE *thel*, 'plank', + *elfitu*, 'swan', + *hamm*, 'enclosure'. Thelnetham is by the Little Ouse. DB *Thelueteham*.

Thelwall (suburb of Warrington): '(place by a) deep pool with a plank bridge'. OE *thel*, 'plank', + *wēl*, 'deep pool'. The 'deep pool' would have been in the Mersey here. 923 *Thelwæle*.

Themelthorpe (village, Norfolk): 'Thȳmel's or Thymill's outlying farmstead'. OS *thorp*, 'outlying farmstead'. The personal names are respectively OE and Scandinavian. The first part of the name could also represent OE *thȳmel*, 'thimble', denoting a small-size settlement. 1203 *Timeltorp*.

Thenford (village, Northants): '(place by the) ford of the thegns'. OE *thegn*, 'thegn', 'retainer', + *ford*, 'ford'. The village is on a tributary of the Cherwell. The reason for the name is unknown. DB *Taneford*.

Therfield (village, Herts): '(place on) dry open land'. OE *thyrre*, 'dry', + *feld*, 'open land' (modern English *field*). 1060 *Therefeld*, DB *Derevelde*.

Thetford (town, Norfolk): '(place at the) people's ford'. OE *thēod*, 'people', 'tribe', + *ford*, 'ford'. The reference is to a public ford across the Little Ouse here, rather than the river Thet (named after the town). Late 9C *Theodford*, DB *Tedfort*.

Theydon Bois (village, Essex): 'de Bosco's (estate in the) valley where thatching materials are obtained'. OE *thæc*, 'thatch', + *denu*, 'valley'. The de Bosco or de Bois family held the manor here in the 13C. The second word of the name is popularly associated with French *bois*, 'wood', as if referring to Epping Forest here. 1062 *Thecdene*, DB *Teidana*, 1257 *Teidon Boys*.

Thimbleby (hamlet, N Yorks): 'Thymill's or Thymli's farmstead'. OS *bý*, 'farmstead', 'village'. The personal names are Scandinavian. DB *Timbelbi*. SO ALSO: *Thimbleby*, Lincs.

Thingwall (district of Birkenhead, Wirral): 'field of the assembly'. OS *thing-vǫllr* (from *thing*, 'assembly', + *vǫllr*, 'field'. The name refers to the meeting place of the Scandinavian community in Wirral. Cp. DINGWALL. DB *Tinguelle*.

Thirkleby (village, N Yorks): 'Thorkell's farmstead'. OS *bý*, 'farmstead', 'village'. The personal name is Scandinavian. DB *Turchilebi*.

Thirlby (village, N Yorks): 'Thrylli's farmstead'. OS *bý*, 'farmstead', 'village'. The personal name is Scandinavian. The name could also mean 'farmstead of the thralls' (OS *thrǽll*, 'thrall', 'slave'). 1187 *Trillebia*.

Thirlmere (lake, Cumbria): 'hollow lake'. OE *thyrel*, 'hole', 'opening' (related modern English *thrill*), + *mere*, 'lake'. The 'hollow' may have been the narrow strip of water that originally formed the 'waist' of the lake before the water level rose when the lake was dammed to form a reservoir. Early forms of the name are lacking. 1574 *Thyrlemere*.

Thirn (hamlet, N Yorks): '(place by the) thorn bush'. OE *thyrne*, 'thorn bush'. DB *Thirne*.

Thirsk (town, N Yorks): '(place in a) marsh'. OS *thresk*, 'marsh'. The town is on low-lying land in the Vale of Mowbray on the Cod Beck, a tributary of the Swale. DB *Tresch*.

Thistleton (village, Rutland): 'farmstead where thistles grow'. OE *thistel*, 'thistle', + *tūn*, 'farmstead', 'village'. DB *Tisteltune*. SO ALSO: *Thistleton*, Lancs.

Thixendale (village, N Yorks): 'Sigsteinn's valley'. OS *dalr*, 'valley'. The personal name is Scandinavian. DB *Sixtendale*.

Tholthorpe (village, N Yorks): 'Thórulfr's outlying farmstead'. OS *thorp*, 'outlying farmstead'. The personal name is Scandinavian. DB *Turulfestorp*.

Thompson (village, Norfolk): 'Tumi's farmstead'. OE *tūn*, 'farmstead', 'village'. The personal name is Scandinavian. DB *Tomestuna*.

Thoralby (village, N Yorks): 'Thóraldr's farmstead'. OS *bý*, 'farmstead', 'village'. The personal name is Scandinavian. DB *Turoldesbi*.

Thoresway (village, Lincs): '(place by) Thórir's way'. OE *weg*, 'way', 'road'. The personal name is Scandinavian. The meaning could also be '(place at the) shrine dedicated to Thor', from the name of the pagan god Thor and OS *vé*, 'heathen shrine', the latter being subsequently taken as OE *weg*. DB *Toreswe*, 1187 *Thoresweie*.

Thorganby (village, Lincs): 'Thorgrímr's farmstead'. OS *bý*, 'farmstead', 'village'. The personal name is Scandinavian. DB *Turgrimbi*. SO ALSO: *Thorganby*, N Yorks.

Thorington (hamlet, Suffolk): 'farmstead where thorn bushes grow'. OE *thorn* or *thyrne*, 'thorn bush', + *tūn*, 'farmstead'. DB *Torentuna*.

Thorlby (hamlet, N Yorks): 'Thóraldr's or Thórhildr's farmstead'. OS *bý*, 'farmstead', 'village'. The OS personal names are respectively those of a man and a woman. DB *Toreilderebi*.

Thorley (village, Herts): 'wood or clearing with thorn bushes'. OE *thorn*, 'thorn bush', + *lēah*, 'wood', 'clearing'. DB *Torlei*. SO ALSO: *Thorley*, IoW.

Thormanby (village, N Yorks): 'Thormóthr's farmstead'. OS *bý*, 'farmstead', 'village'. The personal name is Scandinavian. DB *Tormozbi*.

Thornaby-on-Tees (town, Stockton): 'Thormóthr's farmstead on the (river) Tees'. OS *bý*, 'farmstead'. The personal name is Scandinavian. Before incorporation as a borough in 1892, Thornaby was known as *South Stockton*, from its location on the south side of the Tees opposite Stockton-on-Tees. For the river name, see TEESDALE. DB *Tormozbi*.

Thornage (village, Norfolk): 'enclosure with thorn bushes'. OE *thorn*, 'thorn bush', + *edisc*, 'enclosure', 'pasture'. DB *Tornedis*.

Thornborough (village, Bucks): '(place by the) hill where thorn bushes grow'. OE *thorn*, 'thorn bush', + *beorg*, 'hill'. The hill in question is probably the one to the southwest of the village. DB *Torneberge*. SO ALSO: *Thornborough*, N Yorks.

Thornbury (town, S Glos): 'fortified place where thorn bushes grow'. OE *thorn*, 'thorn bush', + *burh*, 'fortified place'. No fortified place is known here, although Thornbury Castle is ½ mile to the north. DB *Turneberie*. SO ALSO: *Thornbury*, Devon, Herefords.

Thornby (village, Northants): 'farmstead where thorn bushes grow'. OS *thyrnir*, 'thorn bush', + *bý*, 'farmstead', 'village'. The name was originally identical with that of THORNBURY, but when the Danes arrived they replaced OE *burh*, 'fortified place', with OS *bý*, as with NASEBY. DB *Torneberie*, c.1160 *Thirnebi*.

Thorncombe (village, Dorset): '(place in the) valley where thorn bushes grow'. OE *thorn*, 'thorn bush', + *cumb*, 'valley'. DB *Tornecoma*.

Thorndon (village, Suffolk): 'hill where thorn bushes grow'. OE *thorn*, 'thorn bush', + *dūn*, 'hill'. DB *Tornduna*.

Thorne (town, Doncaster): '(place at the) thorn bush'. OE *thorn*, 'thorn bush'. The name could denote a place by a single prominent thorn bush or one among many such bushes. DB *Torne*.

Thorner (village, Leeds): 'ridge where thorn bushes grow'. OE *thorn*, 'thorn bush', + *ofer*, 'ridge'. DB *Tornoure*.

Thorne St Margaret (hamlet, Somerset): '(place by the) thorn bush with St Margaret's church'. OE *thorn*, 'thorn bush'. The church dedication distinguishes the hamlet from *Thornfalcon*, 12 miles to the east, where the manor was held early by the Fagun family. DB *Torne*, 1251 *Thorn St Margaret*.

Thorney (village, Notts): 'enclosure of thorn bushes'. OE *thorn*, 'thorn bush', + *haga*, 'enclosure' (related modern English *hedge*). The reference is to an enclosure protected by a thorn hedge. DB *Torneshaie*.

Thorney (village, Peterborough): 'island where thorn bushes grow'. OE *thorn*, 'thorn bush', + *ēg*, 'island'. The 'island' would have been raised ground in waterland, in what is now the Bedford Level. c.960 *Thornige*, DB *Torny*.

Thorney Island (island, W Sussex): 'island where thorn bushes grow'. OE *thorn*, 'thorn bush', + *ēg*, 'island'. The name is properly that of the village now known as WEST THORNEY, from which it passed to the island. The second word of the name is properly redundant, as 'island' is present in the original. 11C *Thorneg*, DB *Tornei*.

Thornfalcon. See THORNE ST MARGARET.

Thornford (village, Dorset): '(place by the) ford where thorn bushes grow'. OE *thorn*, 'thorn bush', + *ford*, 'ford'. The ford would have been over the river Yeo here. 951 *Thornford*, DB *Torneford*.

Thorngumbald (village, E Yorks): 'Gumbald's (estate by the) thorn bush'. OE *thorn*, 'thorn bush'. The Gumbald family held the manor here in the 13C. DB *Torne*, 1297 *Thoren Gumbaud*.

Thornham (village, Norfolk): 'homestead where thorn bushes grow'. OE *thorn*, 'thorn bush', + *hām*, 'homestead', 'village'. DB *Tornham*.

Thornham Magna (village, Suffolk): 'greater homestead where thorn bushes grow'. OE *thorn*, 'thorn bush', + *hām*, 'homestead', 'village', + Latin *magna* ('great'). The second word of the name distinguishes the village from nearby *Thornham Parva* (Latin *parva*, 'small'). DB *Thornham*.

Thornhaugh (village, Peterborough): 'enclosure where thorn bushes grow'. OE *thorn*, 'thorn bush', + *haga*, 'enclosure' (related modern English *hedge*). The name implies an enclosure protected by a thorn hedge. 1189 *Thornhawe*.

Thornhill (village, Derbys): 'hill where thorn bushes grow'. OE *thorn*, 'thorn bush', + *hyll*, 'hill'. 1200 *Tornhull*. SO ALSO: *Thornhill*, Kirklees.

Thornley (village, Durham): 'hill where thorn bushes grow'. OE *thorn*, 'thorn bush', + *hlāw*, 'mound', 'hill'. This is Thornley near Peterlee. 1071 *Thornhlawa*.

Thornley (hamlet, Durham): 'wood or clearing where thorn bushes grow'. OE *thorn*, 'thorn bush', + *lēah*, 'wood', 'clearing'. This is Thornley near Tow Law. 1382 *Thornley*.

Thornthwaite (hamlet, Cumbria): 'clearing where thorn bushes grow'. OS *thorn*, 'thorn bush', + *thveit*, 'clearing'. 1254 *Thornthwayt*.

Thornton (town, Lancs): 'farmstead where thorn bushes grow'. OE *thorn*, 'thorn bush', + *tūn*, 'farmstead'. DB *Torentun*. SO ALSO: *Thornton*, Bradford.

Thornton Curtis (village, N Lincs): 'farmstead where thorn bushes grow'. OE *thorn*, 'thorn bush', + *tūn*, 'farmstead'. The second word of the name, of unknown origin, distinguishes this Thornton from low-lying *Thornton le Moor*, Lincs, 15 miles to the south. DB *Torentune*, 1430 *Thornton Curteys*.

Thornton Dale (village, N Yorks): 'farmstead where thorn bushes grow in the valley'. OE *thorn*, 'thorn bush', + *tūn*, 'farmstead', + OS *dalr*, 'valley'. DB *Torentune*.

Thornton Heath (district, Croydon): 'heath by Thornton'. OE *hǣth*, 'heath'. The first word of the name is as for THORNTON. Vestiges of the common land that was part of the original heath exist today in Grangewood Park. 1511 *Thorneton hethe*.

Thornton Hough (village, Wirral): 'del Hogh's (estate at the) farmstead where thorn bushes grow'. OE *thorn*, 'thorn bush', + *tūn*, 'farmstead'. The del Hogh family held the manor here in the 14C. DB *Torintone*, 1624 *Thorneton Hough*.

Thornton-le-Beans (village, N Yorks): 'farmstead where thorn bushes grow where beans are grown'. OE *thorn*, 'thorn bush', + *tūn*, 'farmstead'. The second part of the name distinguishes this Thornton from nearby THORNTON-LE-MOOR. The DB form of the name below is prefixed with the OS personal name Gríss. DB *Gristorentun*, 1534 *Thornton in le Beyns*.

Thornton le Moor. See THORNTON CURTIS.

Thornton-le-Moor (village, N Yorks): 'farmstead where thorn bushes grow in marshland'. OE *thorn*, 'thorn bush', + *tūn*, 'farmstead'. The second part of the name (OE *mōr*, 'moor', 'marsh') distinguishes this Thornton from nearby THORNTON-LE-BEANS. 1114 *Torentona*, 1327 *Thornton in the More*.

Thornton-le-Moors (village, Cheshire): 'farmstead where thorn bushes grow in marshland'. OE *thorn*, 'thorn bush', + *tūn*, 'farmstead', + OF *le*, 'the', + OE *mōr*, 'moor', 'marshland'. The second part of the name refers to the nearby marshes of the river Gowy. DB *Torentune*, 1299 *Thorneton in le Moore*.

Thornton-le-Street (hamlet, N Yorks): 'farmstead where thorn bushes grow by the Roman road'. OE *thorn*, 'thorn bush', + *tūn*, 'farmstead'. The hamlet stands on the Roman road from Stamford Bridge to Durham. DB *Torentun*.

Thoroton (village, Notts): 'Thorfrøthr's farmstead'. OE *tūn*, 'farmstead', 'estate'. The personal name is Scandinavian. DB *Toruertune*.

Thorp Arch (village, Leeds): 'de Arches' outlying farmstead'. OS *thorp*, 'outlying farmstead'. The three manors here were held by the de Arches family. DB *Torp*, 1272 *Thorp de Arches*.

Thorpe Bassett (village, N Yorks): 'Basset's outlying farmstead'. OS *thorp*, 'outlying village'. William Basset held land here in 1204. DB *Torp*, 1267 *Thorp Basset*.

Thorpe by Water (village, Rutland): 'outlying farmstead near water'. OS *thorp*, 'outlying farmstead'. The second part of the name refers to the proximity of the village to the river Welland. DB *Torp*.

Thorpe-le-Soken (village, Essex): 'outlying village in the soke'. OS *thorp*, 'outlying village', 'secondary settlement', + OE *sōcn*, 'soke'. A soke is a district with special jurisdiction, as formerly for the Soke of Peterborough. *Kirby-le-Soken* ('village with a church in the soke') is 3 miles to the east, with *Walton-le-Soken* (now WALTON ON THE NAZE) beyond it on the coast. 12C *Torp*, 1612 *Thorpe in ye Sooken*.

Thorpeness (resort village, Suffolk): '(place by) Thorpe Ness'. The village takes its name from the nearby headland of *Thorpe Ness*, itself so called from the settlement's original name of *Thorpe*, 'outlying village' (OS *thorp*). Construction of the holiday village began in 1910 with the making of an artificial lake called *The Meare* and continued, with interruptions, into the 1930s.

Thorpe Salvin (village, Rotherham): 'Salvain's outlying farmstead'. OS *thorp*, 'outlying farmstead'. The Salvain family held the manor here in the 13C. DB *Torp*, 1255 *Thorpe Saluayn*.

Thorpe St Andrew (suburb of Norwich, Norfolk): 'secondary settlement with St Andrew's church'. OS *thorp*, 'outlying farmstead', 'secondary settlement'. Thorpe St Andrew was formerly known as *Thorpe-next-Norwich*. DB *Torp*, 1302 *Thorp juxta Norwycum*.

Thorpe Willoughby (village, N Yorks): 'de Willeby's outlying farmstead'. OS *thorp*, 'outlying farmstead'. The de Willeby family held the manor here in the 13C. DB *Torp*, 1276 *Thorp Wyleby*.

Thorrington (village, Essex): 'enclosure made of thorn bushes'. OE *thorn*, 'thorn bush', + *tūn*, 'enclosure', 'farmstead'. The DB form of the name below is corrupt. DB *Torinduna*, 1202 *Torritona*.

Thorverton (village, Devon): 'farmstead by the ford where thorn bushes grow'. OE *thorn*, 'thorn bush', + *ford*, 'ford', + *tūn*, 'farmstead'. The village lies near the river Exe. 1182 *Toruerton*.

Thrandeston (village, Suffolk): 'Thrándr's farmstead'. OE *tūn*, 'farmstead', 'village'. The personal name is Scandinavian. *c*.1035 *Thrandeston*, DB *Thrandestuna*.

Thrapston (village, Northants): 'Thræpst's farmstead'. OE *tūn*, 'farmstead', 'village'. DB *Trapestone*.

Threapwood (village, Cheshire): '(place by the) disputed wood'. OE *thrēap*, 'dispute', 'quarrel', + *wudu*, 'wood'. The wood here is on a county boundary, partly in Cheshire and partly in Flintshire. It was at one time outside almost all jurisdiction, and no rates or taxes were payable on property in the region. 1548 *Threpewood*.

Three Bridges (district of Crawley, W Sussex): '(place by) three bridges'. The present district developed in the 19C with the coming of the railway, but the name is earlier. The bridges would have been over the river Mole. 1534 *two bridges called the Three bridges leading from Charlewood to Crawley*, 1598 *three bridges between Worth and Crawley*, 1613 *Le three bridges*.

Threekingham (village, Lincs): 'homestead of the Tricingas'. OE *hām*, 'homestead'. The tribal name is of obscure origin. DB *Trichingeham*, 1868 *Threckingham*.

Threemilestone (village, Cornwall). The village arose in the 19C at a location three miles from Truro. 1884 *Three Mile Stone*.

Three Rivers (council district, Herts). The district, in the southwest of the county, takes its name from the three rivers Chess (see CHESHAM), Gade (see GREAT GADDESDEN) and Colne (see LONDON COLNEY), the first two being tributaries of the third.

Threlkeld (village, Cumbria): '(place by the) spring of the serfs'. OS *thrǽll*, 'thrall', 'serf', + *kelda*, 'spring'. 1197 *Trellekeld*.

Threshfield (village, N Yorks): 'open land where corn is threshed'. OE *thresc*, 'threshing', + *feld*, 'open land' (modern English *field*). The DB form of the name below has F- for Th-, perhaps by confusion with *Freshfield*. DB *Freschefelt*, 12C *Threskefeld*.

Thrigby (hamlet, Norfolk): 'Thrykki's farmstead'. OS *bý*, 'farmstead', 'village'. The personal name is Scandinavian. DB *Trikebei*.

Thringstone (village, Leics): 'Thrǽingr's farmstead'. OE *tūn*, 'farmstead', 'village'. The personal name is Scandinavian. OE *tūn* replaced original OS *bý* in the same sense, as seen in the DB form of the name below. DB *Trangesbi*, *c*.1200 *Trengeston*.

Thrintoft (village, N Yorks): 'homestead by a thorn bush'. OS *thyrnir*, 'thorn bush', + *toft*, 'homestead'. The name could also mean 'Thyrnir's farmstead', with a Scandinavian personal name DB *Tirnetofte*.

Thriplow (village, Cambs): 'Tryppa's tumulus'. OE *hlāw*, 'hill', 'tumulus'. The first form of the name below is corrupt. *c*.1050 *Tripelan*, DB *Trepeslau*.

Throcking (village, Herts): 'place where beams are obtained'. OE *throc*, 'beam', + *-ing*, 'place characterized by'. DB *Trochinge*.

Throckley (suburb of Newcastle upon Tyne, Newcastle): '(place on the) hill where beams are obtained'. OE *throc*, 'beam', + *hlāw*, 'hill'. 1177 *Trokelawa*.

Throckmorton (village, Worcs): 'farmstead by a pool with a platform'. OE *throc*, 'support', 'post', + *mere*, 'pool', + *tūn*, 'farmstead'. The 'platform' may have been some kind of beam bridge here. 1176 *Trochemerton*.

Thropton (village, Northd): 'estate with an outlying farmstead'. OE *throp*, 'outlying farmstead', + *tūn*, 'farmstead', 'estate'. 1177 *Tropton*.

Throwleigh (village, Devon): 'woodland clearing with a conduit'. OE *thrūh*, 'water pipe', 'conduit' (related modern English *trough*), + *lēah*, 'wood', 'clearing'. DB *Trule*.

Throwley (hamlet, Kent): 'woodland clearing with a conduit'. OE *thrūh*, 'water pipe', 'conduit' (related modern English *trough*), + *lēah*, 'wood', 'clearing'. DB *Trevelai*.

Thrumpton (village, Notts): 'Thormóthr's farmstead'. OE *tūn*, 'farmstead', 'village'. The personal name is Scandinavian. The form of the name below relates to Thrumpton southwest of East Bridgford, but the Thrumpton that is a district of Retford has a name of identical origin. DB *Turmodestun*.

Thrupp (village, Glos): 'outlying farmstead'. OE *throp*, 'outlying farmstead'. 1261 *Trop*. SO ALSO: *Thrupp*, Oxon.

Thrushelton (hamlet, Devon): 'farmstead where thrushes are seen'. OE *thryscele*, 'thrush' (related modern English *throstle*), + *tūn*, 'farmstead', 'village'. DB *Tresetone*.

Thruxton (village, Hants): 'Thorkell's estate'. OE *tūn*, 'farmstead', 'estate'. The personal name is Scandinavian. 1167 *Turkilleston*. SO ALSO: *Thruxton*, Herefords.

Thrybergh (village, Rotherham): '(place between) three hills'. OE *thrī*, 'three', + *beorg*, 'hill'. Thrybergh lies near the river Don between three hills. DB *Triberge*, 1868 *Thribergh, or Thrybergh*.

Thundersley (town, Essex): 'Thunor's wood'. OE *lēah*, 'wood', 'clearing'. Thunor was a pagan god corresponding to the more familiar Thor, and the wood here would have been his sacred grove. DB *Thunreslea*.

Thundridge (village, Herts): 'Thunor's ridge'. OE *hrycg*, 'ridge'. Cp. THUNDERSLEY. DB *Tonrinch*.

Thurcaston (village, Leics): 'Thorketill's farmstead'. OE *tūn*, 'farmstead', 'village'. The personal name is Scandinavian. DB *Turchitelestone*.

Thurcroft (village, Rotherham): 'Thórir's enclosure'. OE *croft*, 'enclosure'. The personal name is Scandinavian. 1319 *Thurscroft*.

Thurgarton (village, Notts): 'Thorgeirr's farmstead'. OE *tūn*, 'farmstead', 'village'. The personal name is Scandinavian. DB *Turgarstune*. SO ALSO: *Thurgarton*, Norfolk.

Thurgoland (village, Barnsley): 'Thorgeirr's cultivated land'. OS *land*, 'cultivated land'. The personal name is Scandinavian. DB *Turgesland*.

Thurlaston (village, Warwicks): 'Thorleifr's farmstead'. OE *tūn*, 'farmstead', 'village'. The personal name is Scandinavian. DB *Torlauestone*. SO ALSO: *Thurlaston*, Leics.

Thurlby (village, Lincs): 'Thórulfr's farmstead'. OS *bý*, 'farmstead', 'village'. The personal name is Scandinavian. The DB form of the name below relates to Thurlby near Bourne, but Thurlby near Lincoln has a name of identical origin. DB *Turolvebi*.

Thurleigh (village, Beds): '(place) at the wood or clearing'. OE *lēah*, 'wood', 'clearing'. The first part of the name derives from the OE phrase *æt thǣre lēage*, 'at the wood'. DB *La Lega*, 1372 *Thyrleye*.

Thurlestone (village, Devon): '(place by the) rock with a hole in it'. OE *thyrel*, 'having a hole', + *stān*, 'stone', 'rock'. The name relates to Thurlestone Rock, a natural arch off the coast here in Bigbury Bay. 847 *Thyrelanstane*, DB *Torlestan*.

Thurloxton (village, Somerset): 'Thorlákr's farmstead'. OE *tūn*, 'farmstead'. The personal name is Scandinavian. 1195 *Turlakeston*.

Thurlstone (village, Barnsley): 'Thórulfr's farmstead'. OE *tūn*, 'farmstead', 'village'. The personal name is Scandinavian. DB *Turulfestune*.

Thurlton (village, Norfolk): 'Thorfrithr's farmstead'. OE *tūn*, 'farmstead', 'village'. The personal name is Scandinavian. DB *Thuruertuna*.

Thurmaston (district, Leicester): 'Thormóthr's farmstead'. OE *tūn*, 'farmstead', 'village'. The personal name is Scandinavian. DB *Turmodestone*.

Thurnby (village, Leics): 'Thyrnir's farmstead'. OS *bý*, 'farmstead', 'village'. The personal name is Scandinavian. The name could also mean 'farmstead where thorn bushes grow' (OS *thyrnir*, 'thorn bush', + *bý*). 1156 *Turneby*.

Thurne (village, Norfolk): '(place by the) thorn bush'. OE *thyrne* or OS *thyrnir*, 'thorn

bush'. The river Thurne here takes its name from that of the village. 1044 *Thirne*, DB *Thura*.

Thurning (village, Northants): 'place where thorn bushes grow'. OE *thyrne*, 'thorn bush', + -*ing*, 'place characterized by'. DB *Torninge*. SO ALSO: *Thurning*, Norfolk.

Thurnscoe (town, Barnsley): 'wood of thorn bushes'. OS *thyrnir*, 'thorn bush', + *skógr*, 'wood'. DB *Ternusche*, c.1090 *Thirnescoh*.

Thurrock. See GRAYS.

Thursby (village, Cumbria): 'Thórir's farmstead'. OS *bý*, 'farmstead', 'village'. The personal name is Scandinavian. c.1165 *Thoresby*.

Thursford (hamlet, Norfolk): '(place by the) ford associated with a giant'. OE *thyrs*, 'giant', 'demon', + *ford*, 'ford'. Some local legend must be involved here. Thursford is near the river Stiffkey. DB *Turesfort*.

Thursley (village, Surrey): 'Thunor's grove'. OE *lēah*, 'wood', 'clearing'. There must have been a sacred grove here dedicated to the pagan god Thunor, as at THUNDERSLEY. 1292 *Thoresle*.

Thurso (town and port, Highland): '(place on the river) Thurso'. Thurso stands at the mouth of the river. Hence its Gaelic name, *Inbhir Thorsa* (as if 'Inverthurso'). The river has a Celtic name meaning 'bull river', based on the old name of nearby Dunnet Head, known to the Romans as *Tarvedunum*, 'bull fort', presumably because of its outline, suggesting a bull's head. 1152 *Thorsa*.

Thurstaston (village, Wirral): 'Thorsteinn's farmstead'. OE *tūn*, 'farmstead', 'village'. The personal name is Scandinavian. A local outcrop of sandstone has given rise to the folk etymology 'Thor's-stone-town'. DB *Turstanetone*.

Thurston (village, Suffolk): 'Thóri's farmstead'. OE *tūn*, 'farmstead', 'village'. The personal name is Scandinavian. DB *Thurstuna*.

Thurstonfield (village, Cumbria): 'Thorsteinn's open land'. OE *feld*, 'open land' (modern English *field*). The personal name is Scandinavian. c.1210 *Turstanfeld*.

Thurton (village, Norfolk): 'enclosure where thorn bushes grow'. OE *thyrne*, 'thorn bush', + *tūn*, 'enclosure', 'farmstead'. DB *Tortuna*.

Thuxton (hamlet, Norfolk): 'Thorsteinn's farmstead'. OE *tūn*, 'farmstead', 'village'. The personal name is Scandinavian. DB *Turstanestuna*.

Thwaite (village, Suffolk): '(place in the) clearing'. OS *thveit*, 'clearing', 'meadow'. 1228 *Theyt*.

Thwaite St Mary (village, Norfolk): '(place in the) clearing with St Mary's church'. OS *thveit*, 'clearing', 'meadow'. The church dedication appears to distinguish this Thwaite from THWAITE, Suffolk, formerly *Thwaite St George*, 35 miles to the southwest. 1254 *Thweit*.

Thwing (village, E Yorks): '(place by on a) narrow strip of land'. OS *thvengr* or OE *thweng*, 'thong', 'strap'. DB *Tuuenc*.

Tibberton (village, Glos): 'Tīdbeorht's farmstead'. OE *tūn*, 'farmstead', 'village'. DB *Tebriston*. SO ALSO: *Tibberton*, Worcs, Wrekin.

Tibshelf (village, Derbys): 'Tibba's shelf'. OE *scelf*, 'shelf', 'ledge'. The name refers to the stretch of level ground here. DB *Tibecel*, 1179 *Tibbeshelf*.

Tibthorpe (village, E Yorks): 'Tibbi's or Tibba's outlying farmstead'. OS *thorp*, 'outlying farmstead'. The personal names are respectively Scandinavian and OE. DB *Tibetorp*.

Ticehurst (village, E Sussex): 'wooded hill where young goats are kept'. OE *ticce*, 'kid', 'young goat', + *hyrst*, 'wooded hill'. 1248 *Tycheherst*.

Tichborne (village, Hants): '(place by the) stream where young goats come'. OE *ticce*, 'kid', + *burna*, 'stream'. The stream in question is the upper course of what is now part of the river Itchen. *c.*909 *Ticceburna*.

Tickencote (village, Rutland): 'shelter for young goats'. OE *ticcen*, 'kid', + *cot*, 'cottage', 'shelter'. DB *Tichecote*.

Tickenham (village, N Somerset): 'Tica's homestead or enclosure'. OE *hām*, 'homestead', or *hamm*, 'enclosure'. The name could also mean 'homestead or enclosure where young goats are kept' (OE *ticcen*, 'young goat', + *hām* or *hamm*). DB *Ticaham*.

Tickhill (town, Doncaster): 'Tica's hill'. OE *hyll*, 'hill'. The name could also mean 'hill where young goats are kept' (OE *ticce*, 'kid', 'young goat', + *hyll*). 12C *Tikehill*.

Ticknall (village, Derbys): 'corner of land where young goats are kept'. OE *ticcen*, 'kid', 'young goat', + *halh*, 'nook', 'corner of land'. *c.*1002 *Ticenheale*.

Tickton (village, E Yorks): 'Tica's farmstead'. OE *tūn*, 'farnstead'. The name could also mean 'farmstead where young goats are kept' (OE *ticce*, 'kid', 'young goat', + *tūn*). DB *Tichetone*.

Tidcombe (hamlet, Wilts): 'Titta's valley'. OE *cumb*, 'valley'. DB *Titicome*.

Tiddington (village, Oxon): 'Tytta's hill'. OE *dūn*, 'hill'. The '-ing-' of the name represents the OE genitive ending of the personal name (as *Tyttan*). DB *Titendone*.

Tiddington (village, Warwicks): 'estate associated with Tīda'. OE *-ing-*, 'associated with', + *tūn*, 'farmstead', 'estate'. 969 *Tidinctune*.

Tideford (village, Cornwall): '(place by the) ford over the (river) Tiddy'. OE *ford*, 'ford'. The river name is of uncertain origin. (The village name is popularly explained as meaning 'tidal ford' as the tide comes up to the bridge here.) 1201 *Tutiford*, 1813 *Tidiford*.

Tidenham (village, Glos): 'Dydda's enclosure'. OE *hamm*, 'enclosure'. 956 *Dyddanhamme*, DB *Tedeneham*.

Tideswell (town, Derbys): 'Tīdi's spring'. OE *wella*, 'spring', 'stream'. DB *Tidesuuelle*.

Tidmarsh (village, W Berks): 'people's marsh'. OE *thēod*, 'people', + *mersc*, 'marsh'. The name denotes a marsh given over to communal use. 1196 *Tedmerse*.

Tidmington (village, Warwicks): 'estate associated with Tīdhelm'. OE *-ing-*, 'associated with', + *tūn*, 'farmstead', 'estate'. 977 *Tidelminctune*, DB *Tidelmintun*.

Tidworth (town, Wilts): 'Tuda's enclosure'. OE *worth*, 'enclosure'. The town is now properly *North Tidworth*, with *South Tidworth*, formerly in Hampshire, adjacent. *c.*990 *Tudanwyrthe*, DB *Todeorde*.

Tiffield (village, Northants): 'open land by a meeting place'. OE *tīg*, 'meeting place', + *feld*, 'open land' (modern English *field*). DB *Tifelde*.

Tilbrook (village, Cambs): 'Tila's brook'. OE *brōc*, 'brook'. The river here is the Til, which took its name from that of the village. DB *Tilebroc*.

Tilbury (town and port, Thurrock): 'Tila's stronghold'. OE *burh*, 'fortified place'. The first part of the name could represent the former name of a stream here, meaning 'useful one' (OE *til*, 'useful', 'good'). 731 *Tilaburg*, DB *Tiliberia*.

Tilehurst (district, Reading): 'wooded hill where tiles are made'. OE *tigel*, 'tile', + *hyrst*, 'wooded hill'. The name evokes the brickworks for which Reading itself was long noted. (Hence Thomas Hardy's fictional *Aldbrickham* for Reading.) 1167 *Tigelherst*.

Tilford (village, Surrey): '(place by the) convenient ford'. OE *til*, 'useful', 'good' (modern English *till*, 'cultivate land'), + *ford*, 'ford'. The name could also mean 'Tila's ford'. Either way the ford here would have been over the river Wey. *c.*1140 *Tileford*.

Tillicoultry (town, Clack): 'hill at the back of the land'. Gaelic *tulach*, 'small hill', + *cùl*, 'back', 'ridge', + *tīr*, 'land', 'country'. Tillicoultry is on the edge of the Ochill Hills. 1195 *Tulycultri*, c.1199 *Tullicultre*.

Tillingham (village, Essex): 'homestead of Tilli's people'. OE *-inga-*, 'of the people of', + *hām*, 'homestead'. c.1000 *Tillingaham*, DB *Tillingham*.

Tillington (village, Herefords): 'estate associated with Tulla or Tylla'. OE *-ing-*, 'associated with', + *tūn*, 'farmstead', 'estate'. c.1180 *Tullinton*.

Tillington (village, W Sussex): 'estate associated with Tulla'. OE *-ing-*, 'associated with', + *tūn*, 'farmstead', 'estate'. 960 *Tullingtun*.

Tilney All Saints (village, Norfolk): '(place at the) convenient island with All Saints church'. OE *til*, 'useful', 'good' (modern English *till*, 'cultivate land'), + *ēg*, 'island'. The name must refer to raised ground suitable for settlement in marshland. The church dedication distinguishes the village from *Tilney St Lawrence*, 7 miles to the southwest. 1170 *Tilnea*.

Tilshead (village, Wilts): 'Tīdwulf's hide'. OE *hīd*, 'hide'. A hide was an area of land big enough to support a free family and its dependants. The river Till here, earlier the Winterbourne (see SHREWTON), takes its name from the village. DB *Tidulfhide*.

Tilstock (village, Shropshire): 'Tīdhild's outlying farmstead'. OE *stoc*, 'outlying farmstead'. The personal name is that of a woman. 1211 *Tildestok*.

Tilston (village, Cheshire): 'Tilli's or Tilla's stone'. OE *stān*, 'stone'. The stone in question may have been a milestone on the Roman road here. DB *Tilleston*.

Tilstone Fearnall (hamlet, Cheshire): 'Tīdwulf's stone by Fearnall'. OE *stān*, 'stone'. *Fearnall* is the name of a former nearby place meaning 'corner of land where ferns grow' (OE *fearn*, 'fern', + *halh*, 'nook', 'corner of land'.) DB *Tidulstane*, 1427 *Tilston Farnhale*.

Tilton (village, Leics): 'Tila's farmstead'. OE *tūn*, 'farmstead', 'village'. The village, on high ground, is also known as *Tilton on the Hill*. DB *Tiletone*.

Timberland (village, Lincs): 'grove where timber is obtained'. OE *timber* or OS *timbœr*, 'timber', + *lundr*, 'grove'. DB *Timberlunt*.

Timberscombe (village, Somerset): '(place in the) valley where timber is obtained'. OE *timber*, 'timber', + *cumb*, 'valley'. DB *Timbrecumbe*.

Timble (village, N Yorks): '(place by a) fall'. OE *tymbel*, 'fall' (related modern English *tumble*).

The nature of the 'fall' is uncertain, and it could be a fall of earth or a tumbling stream. The village stands on a prominent hill overlooking the valley of the river Washburn. c.972 *Timmel*, DB *Timble*.

Timperley (district, Trafford): 'wood where timber is obtained'. OE *timber*, 'timber', + *lēah*, 'wood', 'clearing'. 1211 *Timperleie*.

Timsbury (village, Bath & NE Somerset): 'grove where timber is obtained'. OE *timber*, 'timber', + *bearu*, 'grove'. The DB form of the name below is corrupt. DB *Timesberua*, 1233 *Timberesberwe*.

Timworth (hamlet, Suffolk): 'Tima's enclosure'. OE *worth*, 'enclosure'. DB *Timeworda*.

Tincleton (village, Dorset): 'valley of the small farms'. OE *tўnincel*, 'small farm', + *denu*, 'valley'. The valley is that of the river Frome. DB *Tincladene*.

Tingewick (village, Bucks): 'dairy farm at the place associated with Tīda or Tēoda'. OE *-ing*, 'place associated with', + *wīc*, 'dwelling', 'specialized farm'. Local legend tells of a river called *Tinge* here, now covered over. DB *Tedinwiche*.

Tingrith (village, Beds): 'stream by which assemblies are held'. OE *thing*, 'assembly', + *rīth*, 'stream'. The meeting place of the local hundred was here. The DB form of the name below has omitted final *-th*. DB *Tingrei*, c.1215 *Tingrith*.

Tinsley (district, Sheffield): '(place by) Tynni's mound'. OE *hlāw*, 'mound'. DB *Tineslauue*.

Tintagel (village, Cornwall): 'fort by the neck of land'. Cornish *din*, 'fort', + *tagell*, 'constriction', 'narrow neck'. The 'fort' is represented by the castle ruins on the peninsula known as Tintagel Island, while the 'constriction' is the narrow neck that joins it to the mainland. Until the 20C the name referred to the castle, the manor and the church here, but not to the village, which was called *Trevena*, 'farm on a hill' (Cornish *tre*, 'farm', + *war*, 'upon', + *menydh*, 'hill'). c.1137 *Tintagol*.

Tintern Abbey (ruined abbey, Mon): 'abbey by Tintern'. The abbey takes its name from the village now known as *Tintern Parva*. Its own name is of Celtic origin and means 'king's fortress' (modern Welsh *dinas*, 'fort', + *teyrn*, 'monarch', 'sovereign'). The Welsh form of the name is *Tyndyrn*.

Tintinhull (village, Somerset): 'fort by the hill'. Celtic *din*, 'fort', + OE *hyll*, 'hill'. The middle part of the name (the second '-tin-') is of uncertain origin. 10C *Tintanhulle*, DB *Tintenella*.

Tintwistle (village, Derbys): '(place at the) river fork of the prince'. OE *thengel*, 'prince', + *twisla*, 'river fork'. DB *Tengestvisie*.

Tinwell (village, Rutland): '(place by the) spring of Tȳni's people'. OE *-inga-*, 'of the people of', + *wella*, 'spring', 'stream'. The DB form of the name below has *d* for *n* in the personal name. DB *Tedinwelle*, mid-13C *Tiningewelle*.

Tipton (district, Sandwell): 'estate associated with Tibba'. OE *-ing-*, 'associated with', + *tūn*, 'farmstead', 'estate'. The original *-ing-* has disappeared from the name. DB *Tibintone*, 1868 *Tipton, or Tibbington*.

Tiptree (town, Essex): 'Tippa's tree'. OE *trēow*, 'tree'. The 'tree' could have been an actual prominent tree or a manmade cross or crucifix. 12C *Tipentrie*.

Tiree (island, Argyll & Bute): 'Ith's land'. Gaelic *tīr*, 'land'. Ith has not been identified. *c*.850 *Tir Iath*, 1343 *Tiryad*.

Tirley (village, Glos): 'circular woodland clearing'. OE *trind*, 'circle', + *lēah*, 'wood', 'clearing'. DB *Trineleie*.

Tisbury (village, Wilts): 'Tyssi's stronghold'. OE *burh*, 'fortified place'. *c*.800 *Tyssesburg*, DB *Tisseberie*.

Tissington (village, Derbys): 'estate associated with Tīdsige'. OE *-ing-*, 'associated with', + *tūn*, 'farmstead', 'estate'. DB *Tizinctun*.

Titchfield (village, Hants): 'open land where young goats are kept'. OE *ticce*, 'kid', 'young goat', + *feld*, 'open land' (modern English *field*). DB *Ticefelle*.

Titchmarsh (village, Northants): 'Tyccea's marsh'. OE *mersc*, 'marsh'. 973 *Tuteanmersc*, DB *Ticemerse*.

Titchwell (village, Norfolk): '(place by the) spring where young goats drink'. OE *ticce*, 'kid', 'young goat', + *wella*, 'spring', 'stream'. *c*.1035 *Ticeswelle*, DB *Tigeuuella*.

Titley (village, Herefords): 'Titta's woodland clearing'. OE *lēah*, 'wood', 'clearing'. DB *Titelege*.

Titlington (hamlet, Northd): 'estate associated with Titel'. OE *-ing-*, 'associated with', + *tūn*, 'farmstead', 'estate'. 12C *Titlingtona*.

Titsey (hamlet, Surrey): 'Tydic's island'. OE *ēg*, 'island'. The 'island' is the well-watered land here. 10C *Tideces eg*, DB *Ticesel*.

Tittensor (village, Staffs): 'Titten's ridge'. OE *ofer*, 'ridge'. The DB form of the name below has omitted *n* from the personal name. DB *Titesovre*, 1236 *Titneshovere*.

Tittleshall (village, Norfolk): 'Tyttel's corner of land'. OE *halh*, 'nook', 'corner of land'. The DB form of the name below has omitted the *l* of the personal name. DB *Titeshala*, 1200 *Titleshal*.

Tiverton (village, Cheshire): 'red-lead farmstead'. OE *tēafor*, 'vermilion', 'red lead', + *tūn*, 'farmstead'. The name implies that the farm was painted red or that red lead was available there. DB *Tevreton*.

Tiverton (town, Devon): 'farmstead at the double ford'. OE *twī-fyrde*, 'double ford' (see TWYFORD, Bucks), + *tūn*, 'farmstead', 'village'. Tiverton is located at the confluence of the river Exe and its tributary, the Loman. 880 *Twyfyrde*, DB *Tovretona*.

Tivetshall St Margaret (village, Norfolk): '(place in the) corner of land where lapwings are seen with St Margaret's church'. The first word of the name derives from an old form of English dialect *tewit*, 'lapwing', so called from its cry (hence also its alternative name *peewit*), and OE *halh*, 'nook', 'corner of land'. The church dedication distinguishes the village from nearby *Tivetshall St Mary*. DB *Teueteshala*.

Tixall (village, Staffs): 'corner of land where young goats are kept'. OE *ticce*, 'kid', 'young goat', + *halh*, 'nook', 'corner of land'. DB *Ticheshale*.

Tixover (village, Rutland): 'ridge where young goats are kept'. OE *ticce*, 'kid', 'young goat', + *ofer*, 'ridge'. DB *Tichesovre*.

Tobermory (resort town, Argyll & Bute): '(place by) St Mary's well'. Gaelic *tiobar*, 'well', + *Moire*, 'Mary'. The well in question is by the ruins of the old chapel to the west of the present town, which arose here on the island of Mull in the 18C. 1540 *Tibbermore*.

Tockenham (village, Wilts): 'Toca's homestead or enclosure'. OE *hām*, 'homestead', or *hamm*, 'enclosure'. 854 *Tockenham*, DB *Tocheham*.

Tockholes (village, Blackburn with Dar): 'Toca's or Tóki's hollows'. OE or OS *hol*, 'hollow'. The personal names are respectively OE and Scandinavian. *c*.1200 *Tocholis*.

Tockwith (village, N Yorks): 'Tóki's wood'. OS *vithr*, 'wood'. The personal name is Scandinavian. DB *Tocvi*.

Todber (village, Dorset): 'Tota's hill'. OE *beorg*, 'hill'. The name could also mean 'Tota's grove' (OE *bearu*, 'grove'). DB *Todeberie*.

Toddington (village, Beds): 'hill of Tuda's people'. OE *-inga-*, 'of the people of', + *dūn*, 'hill'. DB *Totingedone*.

Toddington (village, Glos): 'estate associated with Tuda'. OE -*ing*-, 'associated with', + *tūn*, 'farmstead', 'estate'. DB *Todintun*.

Todenham (village, Glos): 'Tēoda's enclosure'. OE *hamm*, 'enclosure'. The 'enclosure' here is land by the river Stour that is hemmed in by higher ground. 804 *Todanhom*, DB *Teodeham*.

Todmorden (town, Calderdale): 'Totta's boundary valley'. OE *mǣre*, 'boundary', + *denu*, 'valley'. The 'boundary valley' is probably the one to the north-west of the town, the boundary itself being the historic one between the West Riding of Yorkshire and Lancashire. 1246 *Tottemerden*.

Todwick (village, Rotherham): 'Tāta's dairy farm'. OE *wīc*, 'dwelling', 'specialized farm'. DB *Tatewic*.

Toft (village, Cambs): 'homestead'. OS *toft*, 'homestead', 'curtilage'. DB *Tofth*.

Toft next Newton (village, Lincs): 'homestead near Newton'. OS *toft*, 'homestead', 'curtilage'. The village is near *Newton by Toft*, so that the two are mutually distinguished from other Tofts and Newtons. (*Newton* is 'new farmstead'.) DB *Tofte*.

Toftrees (hamlet, Norfolk): 'homestead'. OS *toft*, 'homestead', 'curtilage'. DB *Toftes*, 1868 *Toft-Trees, or Tofts*.

Togston (village, Northd): '(place in) Tocg's valley'. OE *denu*, 'valley'. 1130 *Toggesdena*.

Tolland (village, Somerset): 'cultivated land by the (river) Tone'. OE *land*, 'cultivated land'. For the river name, see TAUNTON. DB *Talanda*.

Tollard Royal (village, Wilts): 'royal (estate by the) hollow hill'. The basic name is of Celtic origin, from words related to modern Welsh *twll*, 'hole', and *ardd*, 'high', 'hill'. Lands here were held in *c*.1200 by King John. Hence the second word of the name, which distinguishes the village from nearby *Tollard Farnham*, Dorset, so named as close to *Farnham*, 'homestead or enclosure where ferns grow' (OE *fearn*, 'fern', + *hām*, 'homestead', or *hamm*, 'enclosure'). DB *Tollard*, 1535 *Tollard Ryall*.

Toller Porcorum (village, Dorset): '(estate on the river) Toller of the pigs'. Latin *porcorum*, 'of the pigs'. The river, now the Hooke, has a Celtic name meaning 'hollow stream'. The second word of the name, referring to the village's herds of swine, humorously distinguishes it from nearby *Toller Fratrum*, where Latin *fratrum*, 'of the brethren', refers to its early possession by the Knights Hospitallers. DB *Tolre*, 1340 *Tolre Porcorum*.

Tollerton (village, N Yorks): 'farmstead of the tax gatherers'. OE *tolnere*, 'tax gatherer' (related modern English *toll*), + *tūn*, 'farmstead'. 972 *Toletun*, DB *Tolentun*.

Tollerton (village, Notts): 'Thorleifr's farmstead'. OE *tūn*, 'farmstead', 'village'. The personal name is Scandinavian. DB *Troclauestune*.

Tollesbury (village, Essex): 'Toll's stronghold'. OE *burh*, 'fortified place'. DB *Tolesberia*.

Tolleshunt D'Arcy (village, Essex): 'Darcy's (estate at the place called) Toll's spring'. OE *funta*, 'spring'. The Darcy family held the manor here in the 15C, their name distinguishing the village from nearby *Tolleshunt Knights*, where the parish apparently comprised a knight's fee, and *Tolleshunt Major*, where the manor was held in 1086 by one Malger. *c*.1000 *Tollesfuntan*, DB *Toleshunta*.

Tolpuddle (village, Dorset): 'Tóla's estate on the (river) Piddle'. The Scandinavian personal name is that of the widow of Urc, the royal bodyguard of Edward the Confessor, who in *c*.1060 obtained Edward's permission to give her lands, including Tolpuddle, to Abbotsbury Abbey. For the river name, see PUDDLETOWN. DB *Pidele*, 1210 *Tollepidele*.

Tolworth (district, Kingston): 'Tala's enclosure'. OE *worth*, 'enclosure'. The personal name has not been recorded elsewhere. DB *Taleorde*, 1352 *Talworth*, 1601 *Tolworth*.

Tomintoul (village, Moray): 'knoll of the barn'. Gaelic *tom an t-sabhail* (from *tom*, 'little hill', 'knoll', + *an*, 'of', + *sabhal*, 'barn', 'granary'). The name is found elsewhere in Scotland.

Tonbridge (town, Kent): '(place by the) bridge belonging to the manor'. OE *tūn*, 'farmstead', 'manor', + *brycg*, 'bridge'. The bridge would have led over the Medway here from some part of the manor. See also TUNBRIDGE WELLS. DB *Tonebrige*.

Tone (river). See TAUNTON.

Tong (village, Bradford): '(place on the) tong-shaped feature'. OE *tang*, 'forceps' (modern English *tongs*). The feature in question is the ridge on which the village lies between Tyersal Beck and Cockers Dale. The DB form of the name below is corrupt. DB *Tuinc*, 1176 *Tange*.

Tong (village, Shropshire): '(place on the) tong-shaped feature'. OE *tang*, 'forceps' (modern English *tongs*). The reference is to the location of the village between the two headstreams of the river Worfe. *c*.975 *Tweongan*, DB *Tvange*.

Tonge (hamlet, Leics): '(place on a) tongue of land'. OS *tūnga*, 'tongue'. DB *Tunge*.

Tongham (village, Surrey): 'homestead or enclosure by the river fork'. OE *twang*, 'tongs', 'river fork', + *hām*, 'homestead' or *hamm*, 'enclosure'. The fork in question would be the junction of the river Wey with a smaller tributary here. 1189 *Tuangham*.

Tonypandy (town, Rhondda CT): 'grassland of the fulling mill'. Welsh *ton*, 'grassland', + *y*, 'the', + *pandy*, 'fulling mill'. The fulling mill beside the river Rhondda here was in existence from the 18C until the early 20C.

Toot Baldon. See MARSH BALDON.

Toothill (district of Brighouse, Calderdale): '(place on the) lookout hill'. OE *tōt-hyll* (from *tōt*, 'lookout place', + *hyll*, 'hill'). Toothill stands on a prominent round-topped hill overlooking the valley of the river Calder. 1309 *Tothil*.

Tooting (district, Wandsworth): '(settlement of) Tōta's people'. OE *-ingas*, 'people of'. There were two manors here: *Upper Tooting* or *Tooting Bec*, held by the Norman abbey of Bec-Hellouin, and *Lower Tooting* or *Tooting Graveney*, held by the de Gravenel family. 675 *Totinge*, DB *Totinges*.

Topcliffe (village, N Yorks): 'Toppa's cliff'. OE *clif*, 'cliff', 'bank'. The name could also mean '(place at the) top of a cliff' (OE *topp*, 'top', + *clif*). Topcliffe is on the upper edge of a steep bank overlooking the river Swale. DB *Topeclive*.

Topcroft (village, Norfolk): 'Tópi's enclosure'. OE *croft*, 'enclosure'. The personal name is Scandinavian. DB *Topecroft*.

Toppesfield (village, Essex): 'Topp's open land'. OE *feld*, 'open land' (modern English *field*). DB *Topesfelda*.

Topsham (district of Exeter, Devon): 'Topp's promontory'. OE *hamm*, 'promontory'. Topsham stands on a promontory in the estuary of the river Exe. The first part of the name could also represent OE *topp*, 'top', as a name for the highest point of the promontory. The second part of the DB form of the name below is garbled. 937 *Toppeshamme*, DB *Topeshant*.

Torbay (unitary authority, SW England): '(district by) Tor Bay'. The bay is so called from the hill called Torre that gave the name of TORQUAY. A document of 1412 tells how a French ship laden with wine was seized and brought into Devon '*a un lieu appelle le Getee de Torrebaie*' ('at a place called the Jetty of Tor Bay'), where the 'jetty' may be the original quay of Torquay. 1401 *Torrebay*.

Torbryan (hamlet, Devon): 'de Brione's (estate by the) rocky hill'. OE *torr*, 'rocky hill', 'tor'. The de Brione family held the manor here in the 13C. DB *Torre*, 1238 *Torre Briane*.

Torcross (coastal village, Devon): '(place by the) rocky hill with a cross'. The rocky hill or tor would have been the hill and promontory to the south of the present village, but there is no cross here now. 1714 *Tarcross*.

Torfaen (unitary authority, S Wales): 'stone gap'. Welsh *tor*, 'gap', 'break', + *maen*, 'stone'. The name is that of the valley of the river Lwyd, which flows south through the district to join the Usk.

Torksey (village, Lincs): 'Turec's island'. OE *ēg*, 'island'. The 'island' is raised ground here at the junction of the river Trent and the Roman canal known as the Fosse Dyke (now Fossdyke Navigation). 11C *Turecesieg*, DB *Torchesey*.

Tormarton (village, S Glos): 'boundary settlement where thorn bushes grow'. OE *thorn*, 'thorn tree', + *mǣre*, 'boundary', + *tūn*, 'farmstead', 'settlement'. Like DIDMARTON and ROD-MARTON, Tormarton is near the boundary with Wiltshire. But also like those villages, it is known to have had a pond, so that the name could equally mean 'farmstead by the pool where thorn bushes grow' (OE *mere*, 'pool'). The DB form of the name below has *n* for *r*. DB *Tormentone*, 1166 *Tormarton*.

Torpenhow (village, Cumbria): 'ridge of the hill with a rocky peak'. The second part of the name is Celtic, from a word related to modern Welsh *pen*, 'head', 'top'. The first part represents OE *torr*, 'rocky peak', and the last OE *hōh*, 'hill spur', 'ridge'. The village lies on the slope of a long hill. The name is popularly said to reveal the three successive races to occupy Britain: Celtic ('-pen-'), Anglo-Saxon ('Tor-') and Viking ('-how'). But this last is not OS *haugr*. 1163 *Torpennoc*.

Torpoint (town, Cornwall): '(place by the) rocky headland'. OE *torr*, 'rocky hill', 'tor', + ME *point*, 'point', 'headland'. Torpoint arose as a town in the 18C, taking its name from the headland here on the Hamoaze, the estuary of the river Tamar. 1746 *Tor-point*, 1748 *Torr Point*.

Torquay (resort town, Torbay): '(place with a) quay near Torre'. ME *key*, 'quay'. The quay here was built by monks from Torre Abbey, which took its name from the nearby hill called *Torre* (OE *torr*, 'rocky hill', 'tor'). The town is mainly of 19C origin. See also TORBAY. 1591 *Torrekay*.

Torridge (river). See TORRINGTON.

Torrington (town, Devon): 'farmstead by the (river) Torridge'. OE *tūn*, 'farmstead'. The river name, now also that of the local council district, is Celtic in origin with a meaning 'turbulent one'. The town is officially known as *Great Torrington*, for distinction from nearby *Little Torrington*. *Black Torrington*, so called from the dark colour of the river, is 9 miles to the south. DB *Torintona*.

Torrisholme (district of Morecambe, Lancs): 'Thóraldr's island'. OS *holmr*, 'island'. The personal name is Scandinavian. The 'island' is the end of the ridge on which the place stands, above low-lying country. DB *Toredholme*.

Tortington (hamlet, W Sussex): 'estate associated with Torhta'. OE *-ing-*, 'associated with', + *tūn*, 'farmstead', 'estate'. DB *Tortinton*.

Tortworth (village, S Glos): 'Torhta's enclosure'. OE *worth*, 'enclosure'. DB *Torteword*.

Torver (hamlet, Cumbria): 'turf-roofed shed'. OS *torf*, 'turf', + *erg*, 'shed', 'shelter'. The name could also mean 'Thorfi's shed', with a Scandinavian personal name. Either way, the shed would have been a temporary one used by shepherds here in the summer months. 1190 *Thoruergh*.

Torworth (village, Notts): 'Thórthr's enclosure'. OE *worth*, 'enclosure'. The personal name is Scandinavian. DB *Turdeworde*.

Tostock (village, Suffolk): 'outlying farmstead by the lookout place'. OE *tōt*, 'lookout place', + *stoc*, 'outlying farmstead'. DB *Totestoc*.

Totland (resort village, IoW): 'cultivated land by a lookout place'. OE *tōt*, 'lookout place', + *land*, 'cultivated land', 'estate'. The lookout place in question was probably Headon Hill here, where it is known a beacon was formerly lit. The resort is also known as *Totland Bay*, from the bay here named after the original settlement. *c.*1240 *Toteland*, 1608 *Totland*.

Totley (district, Sheffield): 'woodland clearing of Tota's people'. OE *-inga-*, 'of the people of', + *lēah*, 'wood', 'clearing'. The original *-inga-* has disappeared from the name. DB *Totingelei*.

Totnes (town, Devon): 'Totta's promontory'. OE *næss*, 'promontory'. The name refers to the promontory on which the ruins of the 12C castle stand. *c.*1000 *Totanæs*, DB *Toteneis*.

Tottenham (district, Haringey): 'Totta's homestead'. OE *hām*, 'homestead'. London's Tottenham Court Road is not named from this place but from *Tottenhale*, 'Totta's corner of land' (OE *halh*, 'nook', 'corner of land'), with the two Anglo-Saxons named Totta probably distinct. DB *Toteham*.

Tottenhill (village, Norfolk): 'Totta's hill'. OE *hyll*, 'hill'. DB *Tottenhella*.

Totteridge (district, Barnet): 'Tāta's ridge'. OE *hrycg*, 'ridge'. Totteridge stands on a ridge of high ground extending westward from Whetstone to Highwood Hill. *c.*1150 *Taderege*.

Totternhoe (village, Beds): 'hill spur with a lookout building'. OE *tōt*, 'lookout', + *ærn*, 'house', 'building', + *hōh*, 'hill spur'. The location of the 'lookout building' was probably the nearby promontory topped by the Bronze Age fort known as Totternhoe Castle. DB *Totenehou*.

Tottington (town, Bury): 'estate associated with Totta'. OE *-ing-*, 'associated with', + *tūn*, 'farmstead', 'estate'. The first part of the name could also represent OE *tōt*, 'lookout hill'. Tottington is on a hill. 1212 *Totinton*.

Totton (town, Hants): 'estate associated with Tota'. OE *-ing-*, 'associated with', + *tūn*, 'farmstead', 'estate'. The original *-ing-* of the name has disappeared. DB *Totintone*.

Towcester (town, Northants): 'Roman fort on the (river) Tove'. OE *ceaster*, 'Roman station'. The river has an OE name meaning 'slow one'. The Roman town here was *Lactodunum*, a name of Celtic origin apparently meaning 'milky fort' (modern Welsh *llaeth*, 'milk', and *dinas*, 'fort'). The reference was probably not to the fort itself but to the river and its 'milky' water. 10C *Tofeceaster*, DB *Tovecestre*.

Towednack (hamlet, Cornwall): '(parish of) St Winwaloe'. The church here is dedicated to Winwaloe (see GUNWALLOE), whose name in this case is prefixed by Cornish *to-*, 'thy', by way of a pet form. 1327 *Sanctus Tewennocus*.

Tower Hamlets (borough, Greater London): 'hamlets of the Tower (of London)'. The name dates from the 16C, when there were various hamlets here under the jurisdiction of the Tower of London, including Shadwell, Bethnal Green, Poplar, Mile End, Whitechapel and Ratcliff.

Towersey (village, Oxon): 'de Turs' (estate on the) island'. OE *ēg*, 'island'. The village has water on three sides. Hence 'island'. The de Turs family held the manor here in the 13C. DB *Eie*, 1240 *Turrisey*.

Tow Law (town, Durham): '(place by the) lookout hill'. OE *tōt*, 'lookout', + *hlāw*, 'hill', 'mound'. The town stands on rising ground east of Wolsingham Moor. 1423 *Tollawe*.

Townshend (village, Cornwall). The village was created in the 19C by the Townshend family (the dukes of Leeds), who had inherited lands here. Cp. LEEDSTOWN. 1867 *Townsend*.

Towthorpe (village, York): 'Tófi's outlying farmstead'. OS *thorp*, 'outlying farmstead'. The personal name is Scandinavian. DB *Touetorp*.

Towton (village, N Yorks): 'Tófi's farmstead'. OE *tūn*, 'farmstead', 'village'. The personal name is Scandinavian. DB *Touetun*.

Towy (river). See TYWI VALLEY.

Towyn. See TYWYN.

Toxteth (district, Liverpool): 'Tóki's landing place'. OS *stoth*, 'landing place'. The landing place itself was probably on the banks of the Mersey here. The DB form of the name below has added an initial *S-* to the OS personal name. DB *Stochestede*, 1212 *Tokestath*.

Trafford. See OLD TRAFFORD.

Trallwng, Y. See WELSHPOOL.

Tranent (town, E Lothian): 'farm on the stream'. The name comes from Celtic words related to modern Welsh *tref*, 'farm', and *nant*, 'stream'. Cp. TREFNANT. 1210 *Tranent*.

Tranmere (district of Birkenhead, Wirral): 'sandbank where cranes are seen'. OS *trani*, 'crane', + *melr*, 'sandbank'. Cranes must have frequented the former sands here by the Mersey. A bogus origin in (pseudo-)Welsh *Tre-yn-Moel*, 'village at the bare hill', is sometimes quoted, as is equally spurious Latin *trans*, 'across', + *mare*, 'sea' (as viewed from Liverpool). Late 12C *Tranemul*.

Trawden (village, Lancs): '(place in the) trough-shaped valley'. OE *trog*, 'trough', + *denu*, 'valley'. The reference is to the river valley in which the village stands. 1296 *Trochdene*.

Trawsfynydd (village, Gwynedd): '(place by a route) across the mountain'. Welsh *traws*, 'across', + *mynydd*, 'mountain'. The village is at the centre of several mountain routes, including those to Bala, Ffestiniog and Dolgellau. See also TROSSACHS. 1292 *Trausvenith*.

Treales (village, Lancs): 'farmstead of a court'. Welsh *tref*, 'farmstead', + *llys*, 'court'. The name implies a persistent Celtic presence in the region. DB *Treueles*.

Treamlod. See AMBLESTON.

Trearddur Bay (resort village, Anglesey): '(place by the) bay of Trearddur'. The resort took its name from the bay, whose own name comes from the village of *Trearddur*, 'Iarddur's farm' (Welsh *tre*, 'farm'). In medieval times, Iarddur owned one of the largest farms in northwest Anglesey. 1609 *Tre Iarthur*, 1691 *Treyarddur*.

Trebetherick (village, Cornwall): 'Pedrek's farm'. Cornish *tre*, 'farm'. The name is probably

connected with that of St Petroc at PADSTOW, just across Padstow Bay. 1284 *Trebederich*.

Treborough (hamlet, Somerset): '(place by the) hill growing with trees'. OE *trēow*, 'tree', + *beorg*, 'mound', 'hill'. DB *Traberge*.

Trebudannon (village, Cornwall): 'Pydannan's farm'. Cornish *tre*, 'farm'. 1279 *Trebedannan*.

Treburley (village, Cornwall): 'Borlay's farm'. Cornish *tre*, 'farm'. The Borlay family were here in the 14C. 1538 *Treburley*.

Tredegar (town, Blaenau Gwent). The town arose around ironworks in the 19C on land owned by Baron Tredegar, who took his title from the family home at *Tredegar*, near Newport, where the original name meant 'Tegyr's farm' (Welsh *tre*, 'farm'). Cp. NEW TREDEGAR.

Tredington (village, Warwicks): 'estate associated with Tyrdda'. OE *-ing-*, 'associated with', + *tūn*, 'farmstead', 'estate'. 757 *Tredingctun*, DB *Tredinctun*.

Treen (village, Cornwall): 'farm by a fort'. Cornish *tre*, 'farm', + *din*, 'fort'. The name refers to the nearby ancient fort called Treryn Dinas. 1284 *Trethyn*, 1699 *Treen*.

Treeton (village, Rotherham): 'farmstead built with posts'. OE *trēow*, 'tree', 'post', + *tūn*, 'farmstead'. DB *Tretone*.

Trefaldwyn. See MONTGOMERY.

Trefdraeth. See NEWPORT (Pemb).

Treffynnon. See HOLYWELL.

Trefgarn (village, Pemb): 'farm by the rock'. Welsh *tref*, 'farm', + *carn*, 'rock'. The reference may be to the nearby rocky mass known as Trefgarn Mountain, although early forms of the name throw doubt on this derivation. 1324 *Traueger*, 1368 *Trefgarn*.

Trefnant (village, Denb): 'farm on the stream'. Welsh *tref*, 'farm', + *nant*, 'stream'. In the form of the name below, the middle vowel probably represents Welsh *y*, 'the'. 1661 *Trevenant*.

Treforys. See MORRISTON.

Trefriw (village, Conwy): 'farm on the hill'. Welsh *tref*, 'farm', + *rhiw*, 'hill'. The original farm here was built by a steep hill that is now within the village. 1254 *Treffruu*.

Trefwrdan. See JORDANSTON.

Trefyclo. See KNIGHTON.

Trefynwy. See MONMOUTH.

Tregadillett (village, Cornwall): 'Cadyled's farm'. Cornish *tre*, 'farm'. 1076 *Tregadylet*.

Tregaron (town, Ceredigion): 'village on the (river) Caron'. Welsh *tre*, 'village'. The river here took the name of the saint to whom the church is dedicated. 1566 *tre garon*, 1763 *Caron alias Tre Garon*.

Tregatwg. See CADOXTON.

Tregetin. See KEESTON.

Treglemais (hamlet, Pemb): 'Clement's farm'. Welsh *tref*, 'farm'. 1326 *Trefclemens*.

Tregony (village, Cornwall): 'Rigni's farm'. Cornish *tre*, 'farm'. The DB form of the name below has *l* for *r*.1049 *Trefhrigoni*, DB *Treligani*.

Tre-Gŵyr. See GOWERTON.

Treknow (village, Cornwall): 'farm by a valley'. Cornish *tre*, 'farm', + *tnow*, 'valley'. The village lies at the head of a short side valley to the north of the main valley running down to the coast. DB *Tretdeno*.

Trelales. See LALESTON.

Treletert. See LETTERSTON.

Trelights (village, Cornwall): '(place with a) farm'. Cornish *tre*, 'farm'. The second part of the name is of obscure origin. It may represent a personal name. 1302 *Trefflectos*.

Tremadoc Bay (bay, Gwynedd): 'bay by Tremadog'. The bay takes its name from the village of *Tremadog*, 'village of Madocks' (Welsh *tre*, 'village'). Its own name comes from William Alexander Madocks, who gave the name of nearby PORTHMADOG.

Tremaine (village, Cornwall): 'farm by a stone'. Cornish *tre*, 'farm', + *men*, 'stone'. *c.*1230 *Tremen*.

Tremar (village, Cornwall): 'Margh's farm'. Cornish *tre*, 'farm'. 1284 *Tremargh*.

Tremarchog. See ST NICHOLAS.

Trematon (village, Cornwall): '(place with a) farm'. Cornish *tre*, 'farm'. The second part of the name is of uncertain origin. OE *tūn*, 'farmstead', 'estate', was subsequently added to the original. Mid-11C *Tref meu tun*, DB *Tremetone*.

Trenance (coastal village, Cornwall): 'farm in a valley'. Cornish *tre*, 'farm', + *nans*, 'valley'. The original village lay at the head of a short valley running down to the coast. 1327 *Trenans*.

Treneglos (village, Cornwall): 'farm by the church'. Cornish *tre*, 'farm', + *an*, 'the', + *eglos*, 'church'. 1269 *Treneglos*.

Trent (village, Dorset): '(place on the river) Trent'. The original name of the stream here is of the same origin as that of the river *Trent* (see STOKE-ON-TRENT). DB *Trente*.

Trent (river). See STOKE-ON-TRENT.

Trentham (district, Stoke): 'homestead or river meadow on the (river) Trent'. OE *hām*, 'homestead', or *hamm*, 'river meadow'. For the river name, see STOKE-ON-TRENT. DB *Trenham*.

Trentishoe (coastal hamlet, Devon): '(place by the) round hill spur'. OE *trendel*, 'circle', + *hōh*, 'hill spur'. The reference is to Trentishoe Down here, a circular hill with a projecting spur of land. The second part of the DB form of the name below is corrupt (as if OE *holt*, 'wood'). DB *Trendesholt*, 1203 *Trenlesho*.

Treopert. See GRANSTON.

Treorchy (town, Rhondda CT): 'village on the (river) Orci'. Welsh *tre*, 'village'. The town stands on the Orci, a tributary of the Rhondda. The meaning of the name is unknown. The Welsh form of the name is *Treorci*.

Tresco (island, Scilly): 'farm of elder trees'. Cornish *tre*, 'farm', + *scaw*, 'elder tree'. The name was originally that of a farm where Tresco Abbey stands now. It then spread to the whole island. For a time Tresco was known as *Iniscaw*, 'island of elders' (Cornish *ynys*, 'island'), but the name did not last. 1305 *Trescau*, *c.*1540 *Trescaw*.

Tresillian (village, Cornwall): 'Sulyen's farm'. Cornish *tre*, 'farm'. 1325 *Tresulyan*.

Tresimwn. See BONVILSTON.

Tresmeer (village, Cornwall): 'Gwasmeur's farm'. Cornish *tre*, 'farm'. 1076 *Treguasmer*.

Treswell (village, Notts): '(place by) Tīr's spring'. OE *wella*, 'spring', 'stream'. DB *Tireswelle*.

Trethurgy (village, Cornwall): 'Devergi's farm'. Cornish *tre*, 'farm'. *c.*1230 *Tretheverki*.

Tretire (hamlet, Herefords): '(place by the) long ford'. Welsh *rhyd*, 'ford', + *hir*, 'long'. The ford in question was presumably over the river Garren here, a tributary of the Wye. The first part of the name became associated with Welsh *tre*, 'farm'. 1212 *Rythir*.

Trevalga (village, Cornwall): '(place with a) farm'. Cornish *tre*, 'farm'. The second part of the name probably represents a personal name. 1238 *Trevalga*.

Trevellas (village, Cornwall): '(place with a) farm'. Cornish *tre*, 'farm'. The second part of the name is of uncertain origin. It may represent a personal name. 1306 *Trevelles*.

Treviscoe (village, Cornwall): 'Otker's farm'. Cornish *tre*, 'farm'. 1049 *Trefotcere*.

Trevone (coastal village, Cornwall): origin uncertain. A meaning 'farm on a river' has been proposed, from Cornish *tre*, 'farm', and *avon*, 'river', with *avon* perhaps referring to the sea. 1302 *Treavon*.

Trevose Head (headland, Cornwall): 'headland by Trevose'. *Trevose* is the name of a nearby farm, meaning 'farm by the bank' (Cornish *tre*, 'farm', + *an*, 'the', + *fos*, 'bank'). 1302 *Trenfos*.

Trewen (village, Cornwall): 'white farm'. Cornish *tre*, 'farm', + *gwenn* (feminine form of *gwynn*), 'white'. *c.*1293 *Trewen*.

Trewidland (village, Cornwall): 'Gwydhelan's farm'. Cornish *tre*, 'farm'. The name could also mean 'farm by a cemetery' (Cornish *tre*, + *gwydh-lann*, 'cemetery', from *gwydh*, 'trees', + *lann*, 'church site'), although there is no record of the latter here. 1297 *Trewithelon*.

Trewoon (village, Cornwall): 'farm on the downs'. Cornish *tre*, 'farm', + *goen*, 'downs'. DB *Tregoin*.

Trewyddel. See MOYLGROVE.

Treyford (hamlet, W Sussex): '(place at the) ford marked by a tree'. OE *trēow*, 'tree', + *ford*, 'ford'. The name could also mean '(place at the) ford with a tree-trunk bridge'. The stream here is a small one. DB *Treverde*.

Triangle (village, Calderdale). The name of the modern industrial village comes from the Triangle Inn here, so called because it stood on a triangular piece of ground southwest of Halifax between the turnpike to Lancashire and Oak Hill. The original name of the location was *Stansfield Pond*, preserved in Stansfield Mill Lane. 1777 *Triangle*.

Trimdon (village, Durham): 'hill with a wooden cross'. OE *trēow*, 'tree', + *mǣl*, 'cross', + *dūn*, 'hill'. There would have been a wooden preaching cross here before the church was built. 1196 *Tremeldon*.

Trimingham (village, Norfolk): 'homestead of Trymma's people'. OE *-inga-*, 'of the people of', + *hām*, 'homestead'. 1185 *Trimingeham*.

Trimley (village, Suffolk): 'Trymma's woodland clearing'. OE *lēah*, 'wood', 'clearing'. The village is properly *Trimley St Mary*, from the dedication of its church, as distinct from nearby *Trimley St Martin*. The churches are only 100 yards (91m) apart. DB *Tremelaia*, 1254 *Tremle Beate Marie*.

Trimontium. See NEWSTEAD (Borders).

Trimpley (hamlet, Worcs): 'Trympa's woodland clearing'. OE *lēah*, 'wood', 'clearing'. DB *Trinpelei*.

Tring (town, Herts): '(place by the) tree-covered hillside'. OE *trēow*, 'tree', + *hangra*, 'wooded hillside'. The DB form of the name below is corrupt. DB *Treunge*, 1199 *Trehangr*.

Trispen (village, Cornwall): '(place with a) farm'. Cornish *tre*, 'farm'. The second part of the name is of uncertain origin and meaning. 1324 *Tredespan*.

Tritlington (village, Northd): 'estate associated with Tyrhtel'. OE *-ing-*, 'asociated with', + *tūn*, 'farmstead', 'estate'. *c.*1170 *Turthlyngton*.

Troon (village, Cornwall): 'farm on the downs'. Cornish *tre*, 'farm', + *goen*, 'downs'. Cp. TREWOON. 1327 *Trewoen*.

Troon (resort town and port, S Ayrs): '(place by the) headland'. Troon, on a prominent headland, has a Celtic name from a word related to modern Welsh *trwyn*, 'nose', 'cape'. 1371 *Le Trone*, 1464 *Le Trune*.

Trossachs (hill country, Stirling): 'transverse hills'. The name is said to be a Gaelic adaptation (*Tròsaichean*) of Welsh TRAWSFYNYDD, referring specifically to the hills that divide Loch Katrine from Loch Achray.

Troston (village, Suffolk): 'estate associated with Trost'. OE *-ing-*, 'associated with', + *tūn*, 'farmstead', 'estate'. *c.*1000 *Trostingtun*, DB *Trostuna*.

Trottiscliffe (village, Kent): '(place by) Trott's cliff'. OE *clif*, 'cliff', 'hill slope'. The village lies at the foot of the North Downs. The DB form of the name below has omitted the *r* of the personal name. 788 *Trottes clyva*, DB *Totesclive*, 1868 *Trosley, or Trotterscliffe*.

Trotton (hamlet, W Sussex): 'estate associated with Trætt'. OE *-ing-*, 'associated with', + *tūn*, 'farmstead', 'estate'. The first part of the original form of the name could also represent OE *trǣding*, 'path', 'stepping stones' (related modern English *tread*), presumably referring to a way over the river Rother here. The DB form of the name below is corrupt. DB *Traitone*, 12C *Tratinton*.

Troutbeck (village, Cumbria): '(place on the) Trout Beck'. OE *truht*, 'trout', + OS *bekkr*, 'stream'. The form of the name below refers to the trout stream that flows south past the village into Lake Windermere, but Troutbeck near Penruddock has a name of identical origin. 1272 *Trutebek*.

Trowbridge (town, Wilts): '(place by the) bridge made of logs'. OE *trēow*, 'tree', 'beam', + *brycg*, 'bridge'. The bridge in question probably crossed the small river Biss to the west of the town centre. The seriously garbled DB form of the name below has OE *burh*, 'fortified place', for *brycg*, and an initial extraneous *S-*. DB *Straburg*, 1184 *Trobrigge*.

Trowell (village, Notts): '(place by the) tree stream'. OE *trēow*, 'tree', + *wella*, 'spring', 'stream'. The reference is perhaps to a tree trunk used as a bridge. DB *Trowalle*.

Trowse Newton (village, Norfolk). Originally two separate places: *Trowse*, 'wooden house' (OE *trēow*, 'tree', 'beam', + *hūs*, 'house'), and *Newton*, 'new farmstead' (OE *nīwe*, 'new', + *tūn*, 'farmstead'). DB *Treus*, *Newotona*.

Trull (village, Somerset): '(place by the) circular feature'. OE *trendel*, 'circle', 'ring'. The reference is to a feature such as a round hill or circular earthwork. 1225 *Trendle*.

Trumpington (village, Cambs): 'estate associated with Trump'. OE *-ing-*, 'associated with', + *tūn*, 'farmstead', 'estate'. *c.*1050 *Trumpintune*, DB *Trumpintone*.

Trunch (village, Norfolk): '(place in the) upland wood'. The name is probably Celtic in origin, from words related to modern Welsh *trum*, 'ridge', 'upland', and *coed*, 'wood'. Trunch lies on a plateau, with valleys to north and south and woods to the west. DB *Trunchet*, 1203 *Truch*, 1254 *Trunch*.

Truro (city, Cornwall): '(place of) turbulent water'. The first part of the name is Cornish *try-*, 'triple' (i.e. 'very'), while the second is probably *berow*, 'boiling'. Truro is liable to flooding in winter, as two rapid rivers, the Kenwyn and the Allen, meet the sea here at the head of Truro River. *c.*1173 *Triueru*, 1201 *Triwereu*, *c.*1280 *Truru*.

Trusham (village, Devon): '(place overgrown with) brushwood'. OE *trūs*, 'fallen leaves', 'brushwood'. This meaning of the name is disputed by Celticists, who prefer a sense 'place of thorns', from a word related to modern Welsh *drysi*, 'thorns', 'briars'. The final *-ma* in the DB form of the name below would thus mean 'place', as in *Caesaromagus*, 'Caesar's (market) place', the Romano-Celtic name of CHELMSFORD. The hills around Trusham are still heavily wooded, and there are farms called *Upper Bramble* and *Lower Bramble* not far from Trusham church. DB *Trisma*.

Trusley (village, Derbys): '(place by the) clearing where brushwood lies'. OE *trūs*, 'fallen leaves', 'brushwood', + *lēah*, 'wood', 'clearing'. 1166 *Trusselai*.

Trusthorpe (coastal village, Lincs): 'Drjúgr's or Dreus's outlying farmstead'. OS *thorp*, 'outlying farmstead'. The personal names are respectively Scandinavian and Old French. DB *Dreuistorp*.

Trysull (village, Staffs): '(place on the river) Trysull'. The river name is of Celtic origin and traditionally said to mean 'strongly flowing', from a word related to modern Welsh *tres*, 'toil', 'labour'. The Welsh word earlier meant 'uproar', 'tumult', however, giving a better sense 'tumultuous one', 'noisy one'. DB *Treslei*.

Tuddenham (village, Suffolk): 'Tūda's homestead'. OE *hām*, 'homestead', 'village'. DB *Todenham*.

Tudhoe (village, Durham): 'Tūda's hill spur'. OE *hōh*, 'hill spur'. 1279 *Tudhow*.

Tuesley (village, Surrey): 'Tīw's wood or clearing'. OE *lēah*, 'wood', 'clearing'. The name implies a dedication to the heathen god Tīw (who gave the name of Tuesday). Alternatively, the name may mean 'Tīwhere's wood'. DB *Tiwesle*.

Tufnell Park (district, Islington): 'Tufnell's park'. The district arose in the 19C and commemorates the name of William Tufnell, lord of the manor of Barnsbury in 1753.

Tugby (village, Leics): 'Tóki's farmstead'. OS *bý*, 'farmstead', 'village'. The personal name is Scandinavian. DB *Tochebi*.

Tugford (village, Shropshire): '(place by) Tucga's ford'. OE *ford*, 'ford'. Tugford is on a tributary of the river Corve. The DB form of the name below is corrupt. DB *Dodefort*, *c.*1138 *Tuggeford*.

Tullibody (town, Clack): 'hill of the hut'. Gaelic *tulach*, 'small hill', + *both*, 'hut', 'cottage' (modern English *bothy*). The name would have originally applied to a single hut or cottage here. 1195 *Tullibotheny*.

Tumby (hamlet, Lincs): 'Tumi's farmstead'. OS *bý*, 'farmstead', 'village'. The personal name is Scandinavian. The first part of the name could also represent OE *tūn* or OS *tún*, 'enclosure'. DB *Tunbi*.

Tunbridge Wells (town, Kent): 'wells near Tonbridge'. The town arose around the medicinal springs ('wells') discovered here by Lord North in 1606 and took its name from TONBRIDGE, 5 miles to the north. Tonbridge gradually adopted the spelling *Tunbridge* in medieval times but on the rise of Tunbridge Wells reverted to the DB spelling with *Ton-* for purposes of distinction. Tunbridge Wells was granted the prefix *Royal* by Edward VII in 1909. 1868 *Tonbridge Wells*.

Tunstall (town, Staffs): 'farm site'. OE *tūn-stall* (from *tūn*, 'farmstead', + *stall*, 'place', 'site'). 1212 *Tunstal*. SO ALSO: *Tunstall*, Kent, Suffolk.

Tunstead (hamlet, Norfolk): 'farmstead'. OE *tūn-stede* (from *tūn*, 'farmstead', + *stede*, 'place'). 1044 *Tunstede*, DB *Tunesteda*.

Tupsley (suburb of Hereford, Herefords): 'pasture for rams'. ME *tup*, 'ram', + OE *lēah*, 'clearing', 'pasture'. The first part of the name could also represent a personal name. DB *Topeslage*.

Turkdean (village, Glos): '(place in the) valley of the (river) Turk'. OE *denu*, 'valley'. The former river name *Turce* is of Celtic origin and probably means 'boar' (modern Welsh *twrch*), referring to a stream that 'roots' or digs out its course. 743 *Turcandene*, DB *Turchedene*.

Tur Langton (village, Leics): 'estate associated with Tyrhtel or Tyrli'. OE *-ing-*, 'associated with', + *tūn*, 'farmstead', 'estate'. The name was originally the equivalent of 'Turlington' but was refashioned under the influence of the nearby villages of CHURCH LANGTON and *East Langton*. DB *Terlintone*.

Turnastone (hamlet, Herefords): 'de Turnei's estate'. OE *tūn*, 'farmstead', 'estate'. The de Turnei family are recorded as living locally in the 12C. 1242 *Thurneistun*.

Turners Puddle (hamlet, Dorset): 'Toner's (estate on the river) Piddle'. For the river name, see PUDDLETOWN. The Toner family held the manor here in 1086. DB *Pidele*, 1268 *Tonerespydele*.

Turnhouse (district, Edinburgh): 'house by a turnpike'. This is just one possible interpretation of the name, which is of uncertain origin. It presumably indicates some kind of 'turning' process or action.

Turnworth (hamlet, Dorset): 'enclosure formed by thorn bushes'. OE *thyrne*, 'thorn bush', + *worth*, 'enclosure'. DB *Torneworde*.

Turriff (town, Aberdeens): 'place of the mound'. Gaelic *torr*, 'hill', 'mound'. The origin of the name is uncertain, despite attempts to derive it from an OS source meaning 'Thor's gift'. 1273 *Turrech*, *c.*1300 *Turreth*, *c.*1500 *Turreff*.

Turton Bottoms (village, Blackburn with Dar): 'Thóri's or Thórr's farmstead in the valley'. OE *tūn*, 'farmstead', + *botm*, 'valley bottom'. The personal names are Scandinavian. 1212 *Turton*.

Turvey (village, Beds): '(place on the) island with turf'. OE *turf*, 'turf', + *ēg*, 'island'. The name implies a place on raised riverside land where there is good turf or grass. Turvey is by the river Ouse. DB *Torueie*.

Turville (village, Bucks): 'dry open land'. OE *thyre*, 'dry', + *feld*, 'open land' (modern English *field*). The name probably refers to the upland now known as Turville Heath. In the DB form of the name below, the scribe seems to have misentered the name of nearby *Tilbury*. 796 *Thyrefeld*, DB *Tilleberie*.

Turweston (village, Bucks): 'Thorfrøthr's or Thorfastr's farmstead'. OE *tūn*, 'farmstead', 'village'. The personal names are Scandinavian. DB *Turvestone*.

Tutbury (village, Staffs): 'Tutta's stronghold'. OE *burh*, 'fortified place'. The second form of the name below suggests that the original personal name may have been Stūt, with loss of the initial *S*- as for the Snot who gave the name of NOTTINGHAM. DB *Toteberia*, *c.*1150 *Stutesberia*.

Tutnall (hamlet, Worcs): 'Totta's hill'. OE *hyll*, 'hill'. The DB form of the name below is garbled. DB *Tothehel*, 1262 *Tottenhull*.

Tuttington (village, Norfolk): 'estate associated with Tutta'. OE *-ing-*, 'associated with', + *tūn*, 'farmstead', 'estate'. DB *Tuttincghetuna*.

Tuxford (village, Notts): '(place by) Tuk's ford'. OE *ford*, 'ford'. The personal name is Scandinavian. The first part of the name could also represent an early form of *tusk*, 'tussock'. The second part of the DB form of the name below is corrupt. DB *Tuxfarne*, 12C *Tukesford*.

Tweed (river). See BERWICK-UPON-TWEED.

Tweedmouth (district of Berwick-upon-Tweed, Northd): 'mouth of the (river) Tweed'. OE *mūtha*, 'mouth'. For the river name, see BERWICK-UPON-TWEED. 1208 *Tuedemue*.

Twelveheads (village, Cornwall): '(place with) twelve heads'. The 'heads' in question are the hammers in a set of tinstamps (used for stamping tin). early 17C *the Twelfe Heades*.

Twemlow Green (hamlet, Cheshire): '(place by) two tumuli'. OE *twēgen*, 'two' (modern English *twain*), + *hlāw*, 'tumulus'. The '-m-' of the name comes from OE *twǣm*, the dative form of *twēgen*. The identity of the tumuli in question is uncertain, although five tumuli in a line were noted here in 1819. The village was later associated with its green. 12C *Twamlawe*.

Twerton (district of Bath, Bath & NE Som): 'farm at the double ford'. OE *twī-fyrde* (see TWYFORD, Bucks), + *tūn*, 'farmstead'. The river with the 'double ford' here is the Avon. DB *Twertone*.

Twickenham (district, Richmond): 'Twicca's land in a river bend'. OE *hamm*, 'enclosure', 'land in a river bend'. The name could also mean 'river fork at the river bend', with the first element OE *twicce*, 'confluence' (from *twi-*, 'two'), referring to the point where the river Crane joins the Thames. Either way, Twickenham lies by a great bend in the Thames. The name, popularly rendered *Twittenham* by writers such as Alexander Pope and Horace Walpole, has been the subject of various absurd etymologies, as the following: 'The word *ken* signifies to look; so that *Twy-ken-ham* may signify a village with two views, as it hath a view of Kingston one way, and Isleworth, as also Richmond, the other way' (Edward Ironside, *The History and Antiquities of Twickenham*, 1797). 704 *Tuicanhom*.

Twigworth (village, Glos): 'Twicga's enclosure'. OE *worth*, 'enclosure'. The name could also mean 'enclosure made with twigs' (OE *twigge*, 'twig', + *worth*). 1216 *Tuiggewrthe*.

Twineham (hamlet, W Sussex): '(place) between the streams'. OE *betwēonan*, 'between', + *ēa*, 'river', 'stream'. The second half of the name represents OE *ēam*, the dative plural form of *ēa*. As the name indicates, Twineham lies between two streams. CHRISTCHURCH, Dorset, had an identical earlier name. Late 11C *Tuineam*.

Twinstead (hamlet, Essex): 'double homestead'. OE *twinn*, 'double' (modern English *twin*), + *stede*, 'place'. The DB form of the name below is garbled. DB *Tumesteda*, 1203 *Twinstede*.

Twitchen (village, Devon): '(place at the) crossroads'. OE *twicen*, 'crossroads', 'fork in a road'. 1442 *Twechon*.

Twycross (village, Leics): '(place with) two crosses'. OE *twī-*, 'two', + *cros*, 'cross'. The reference could be to a signpost with four arms at a crossroads. DB *Tvicros*.

Twyford (village, Bucks): '(place by the) double ford'. OE *twī-fyrde* (from *twī-*, 'two', + *ford*, 'ford'). A 'double ford' is either one with two parallel tracks or two fords close together over different rivers. The old road running north to Cowley crosses two streams here at Twyford Mill. DB *Tuiforde*.

Twyford (village, Hants): '(place by the) double ford'. OE *twī-fyrde* (see TWYFORD, Bucks). The river Itchen runs in two channels here to form a 'double ford'. c.970 *Tuifyrde*, DB *Tviforde*.

Twyford (town, Wokingham): '(place by the) double ford'. OE *twī-fyrde* (see TWYFORD, Bucks). The two rivers involved in the 'double ford' here are the Loddon and the Thames. 1170 *Tuiford*.

Twyning (village, Glos): '(settlement of the) dwellers between the rivers'. OE *-ingas*, 'dwellers at'. The first part of the name is a contracted form of the original name, meaning '(place) between the rivers' (OE *betwēonan*, 'between', + *ēa*, 'river'). The rivers concerned are the Avon and Severn. 814 *Bituinæum*, DB *Tveninge*.

Twywell (village, Northants): '(place by the) double stream'. OE *twī*, 'two', + *wella*, 'spring', 'stream'. There is a double stream to the east of the village. 1013 *Twiwel*, DB *Tuiwella*.

Tyburn. See MARYLEBONE.

Tyddewi. See ST DAVID'S.

Tydd St Giles (village, Cambs): '(place among) shrubs with St Giles' church'. OE *tydd*, 'shrubs', 'brushwood'. The church dedication distinguishes the village from nearby *Tydd St Mary*, Lincs. The main name in each case could also represent OE *titt*, 'teat', referring to a slight hill. DB *Tid*.

Tyldesley (town, Wigan): 'Tilwald's woodland clearing'. OE *lēah*, 'wood', 'clearing'. c.1210 *Tildesleia*.

Tyndyrn. See TINTERN ABBEY.

Tyne (river). See TYNEMOUTH.

Tynedale. See TYNEMOUTH.

Tyneham (village, Dorset): 'enclosure where goats are kept'. OE *tige*, 'goat', + *hamm*, 'enclosure'. DB *Tigeham*.

Tynemouth (resort town, N Tyneside): 'mouth of the (river) Tyne'. OE *mūtha*, 'mouth'. The Tyne has a Celtic or pre-Celtic name meaning simply 'river', while *Tynedale* ('valley of the Tyne') is the name of the council district in western Northumberland. 792 *Tinanmuthe*.

Tytherington (district of Macclesfield, Cheshire): 'estate associated with Tydre'. OE *-ing-*, 'associated with', + *tūn*, 'farmstead', 'estate'. c.1245 *Tidderington*. SO ALSO: *Tytherington*, S Glos, Wilts.

Tytherleigh (hamlet, Devon): '(place by the) young wood'. OE *tiedre*, 'weak', 'fragile', + *lēah*, 'wood', 'clearing'. The reference would be to new growth. 12C *Tiderlege*.

Tytherton Lucas. See EAST TYTHERTON.

Tywardreath (village, Cornwall): 'house on the strand'. Cornish *chi* (earlier *ti*), 'house', + *war*, 'upon', + *treth*, 'strand'. The village is immediately north of Par Sands, on the coast. DB *Tywardrai*.

Tywi Valley (river valley, Carm): 'valley of the (river) Tywi'. The river, often still known as the Towy, has a Celtic name that may mean 'rocky one'. The Romans knew it as *Tovius*.

Tywyn (resort town, Gwynedd): '(place by the) seashore'. Welsh *tywyn*, 'sandy shore'. The resort was formerly familiar as *Towyn*, an anglicized form of the name. 1254 *Thewyn*, 1291 *Tewyn*.

U

Ubbeston (hamlet, Suffolk): 'Ubbi's farmstead'. OE *tūn*, 'farmstead', 'village'. The personal name is Scandinavian. DB *Upbestuna*.

Ubley (village, Bath & NE Somerset): 'Ubba's woodland clearing'. OE *lēah*, 'wood', 'clearing'. The DB form of the name below is garbled. Late 10C *Hubbanlege*, DB *Tumbeli*.

Uckerby (hamlet, N Yorks): 'Úkyrri's or Útkári's farmstead'. OS *bý*, 'farmstead', 'village'. The personal names are Scandinavian. 1198 *Ukerby*.

Uckfield (town, E Sussex): 'Ucca's open land'. OE *feld*, 'open land' (modern English *field*). 1220 *Uckefeld*.

Uckington (village, Glos): 'estate associated with Ucca'. OE *-ing-*, 'associated with', + *tūn*, 'farmstead', 'estate'. DB *Hochinton*.

Uddingston (town, S Lanarks): 'Odda's farm'. OE *tūn*, 'farmstead'. The '-ing-' of the name does not seem to be organic. 1296 *Odistoun*, 1475 *Odingstoune*.

Udimore (village, E Sussex): '(place by the) wooded pond'. OE *wudig*, 'wooded', + *mere*, 'pond'. The first part of the DB form of the name below is corrupt. DB *Dodimere*, 12C *Odumer*.

Uffculme (village, Devon): 'Uffa's estate on the river) Culm'. For the river name, see CULLOMPTON. DB *Offecoma*.

Uffington (village, Lincs): 'estate associated with Uffa'. OE *-ing-*, 'associated with', + *tūn*, 'farmstead', 'estate'. DB *Offintone*. SO ALSO: *Uffington*, Shropshire.

Uffington (village, Oxon): 'Uffa's estate'. OE *tūn*, 'farmstead', 'estate'. The genitive ending *-n* on the personal name gave the present '-ing-'. 10C *Uffentune*, DB *Offentone*.

Ufford (village, Suffolk): 'Uffa's enclosure'. OE *worth*, 'enclosure'. DB *Uffeworda*. SO ALSO: *Ufford*, Peterborough.

Ufton (village, Warwicks): 'farmstead with a shed'. OE *huluc*, 'shed', 'hut' (related modern English *hull*), + *tūn*, 'farmstead'. 1043 *Hulhtune*, DB *Ulchetone*.

Ugborough (village, Devon): '(place by) Ugga's hill'. OE *beorg*, 'hill', 'mound'. The DB form of the name below has an extraneous *l*. DB *Ulgeberge*, 1200 *Uggeberge*.

Uggeshall (hamlet, Suffolk): 'Uggeca's corner of land'. OE *halh*, 'nook', 'corner of land'. DB *Uggiceheala*.

Ugglebarnby (village, N Yorks): 'Uglubárthr's farmstead'. OS *bý*, 'farmstead', 'village'. The personal name (a nickname meaning 'Owl Beard') is Scandinavian. DB *Ugleberdesbi*.

Ugley (village, Essex): 'Ugga's woodland clearing'. OE *lēah*, 'wood', 'clearing'. A variant form *Oakley* was at one time current, on the basis that the present name is a corruption of the original, which was said to translate Latin *Quercetum*, from *quercus*, 'oak'. This origin also avoided the undesirable associations of the true name. '*Oakley* is a modern euphemism for which there is no etymological justification' (P. H. Reaney, *The Place-Names of Essex*, 1935). c.1041 *Uggele*, DB *Ugghelea*, 1303 *Oggeley*, 1898 *Ugley, or Oakley*.

Ugthorpe (village, N Yorks): 'Uggi's outlying farmstead'. OS *thorp*, 'outlying farmstead'. The personal name is Scandinavian. DB *Ughetorp*.

Uist (island, W Isles): 'inner abode'. OS *í*, 'in', + *vist*, 'dwelling'. This is the traditional interpretation of the name of the two islands North Uist and South Uist, but it may well be pre-Scandinavian. 1282 *Iuist*, 1373 *Ouiste*.

Ulceby (village, Lincs): 'Ulfr's farmstead'. OS *bý*, 'farmstead', 'village'. The personal name is Scandinavian. DB *Ulesbi*. SO ALSO: *Ulceby*, N Lincs.

Ulcombe (village, Kent): '(place in the) valley where owls are heard'. OE *ūle*, 'owl', + *cumb*, 'valley'. 946 *Ulancumbe*, DB *Olecumbe*.

Uldale (village, Cumbria): 'Ulfr's valley'. OS *dalr*, 'valley'. The personal name is Scandinavian. The name could also mean 'valley where wolves are seen' (os *ulfr*, 'wolf', + *dalr*) . 1216 *Ulvesdal*.

Uley (village, Glos): 'wood or clearing where yew trees grow'. OE *īw*, 'yew', + *lēah*, 'wood', 'clearing'. DB *Euuelege*.

Ulgham (village, Northd): '(place in the) corner of land where owls are heard'. OE *ūle*, 'owl', + *hwamm*, 'corner', 'angle'. 1139 *Wlacam*, 1242 *Ulweham*.

Ullapool (town and port, Highland): 'Olaf's dwelling'. OS *bólstathr*, 'dwelling'. The personal name is Scandinavian. The second part of the os word has disappeared from the name. 1610 *Ullabill*.

Ullenhall (village, Warwicks): 'Ulla's corner of land'. OE *halh*, 'nook', 'corner of land'. The same personal name is seen in nearby OLDBER-ROW, and it is likely the same man was involved. DB *Holehale*.

Ulleskelf (village, N Yorks): 'Ulfr's shelf'. OS *skjalf* or OE *scelf*, 'shelf', 'bank'. The personal name is Scandinavian. The 'shelf' is probably land rising from the river Wharfe here. The DB form of the name below is corrupt. DB *Oleschel*, 1170 *Ulfskelf*.

Ullesthorpe (village, Leics): 'Ulfr's outlying farmstead'. OS *thorp*, 'outlying farmstead'. The personal name is Scandinavian. DB *Ulestorp*.

Ulley (village, Rotherham): 'woodland clearing where owls are heard'. OE *ūle*, 'owl', + *lēah*, 'wood', 'clearing'. DB *Ollei*.

Ullingswick (village, Herefords): 'dairy farm associated with Ulla'. OE *-ing-*, 'associated with', + *wīc*, 'dwelling', 'dairy farm'. DB *Ullingwic*.

Ullock (hamlet, Cumbria): 'place where wolves play'. OS *ulfr*, 'wolf', + *leikr*, 'play'. 1279 *Uluelaik*.

Ullswater (lake, Cumbria): 'Ulfr's lake'. OE *wæter*, 'water'. The personal name is Scandinavian. *c.*1230 *Ulueswater*.

Ulpha (village, Cumbria): 'hill where wolves are seen'. OS *ulfr*, 'wolf', + *haugr*, 'hill'. 1279 *Wolfhou*.

Ulrome (village, E Yorks): 'Wulfhere's or Wulfwaru's homestead'. OE *hām*, 'homestead', 'village'. The personal names are respectively those of a man and a woman. DB *Ulfram*.

Ulverston (town, Cumbria): 'Wulfhere's or Ulfarr's farmstead'. OE *tūn*, 'farmstead', 'village'. The personal names are respectively OE and Scandinavian. DB *Ulureston*.

Umberleigh (village, Devon): 'woodland clearing by the meadow stream'. OE *winn*, 'meadow', + *burna*, 'stream', + *lēah*, 'wood', 'clearing'. DB *Umberlei*, 1270 *Wumberlegh*.

Underbarrow (village, Cumbria): '(place) under the hill'. OE *under*, 'under', + *beorg*, 'hill'. The hill in question would be one of those forming the long ridge between Underbarrow Beck and the river Kent. 1517 *Underbarroe*.

Unst (island, Shetland): 'abode of eagles'. OS *orn*, 'eagle', + *vist*, 'abode'. *c.*1200 *Ornyst*.

Unstone (village, Derbys): 'Ōn's farmstead'. OE *tūn*, 'farmstead', 'village'. DB *Onestune*.

Unthank (hamlet, Cumbria): '(place held) without consent'. OE *unthanc*, 'ill will'. The allusion is to land held 'against the will' of the lawful owner, i.e. a squatter's holding. The name is common in Cumbria and Northumberland. The form below relates to Unthank near Gamblesby. 1254 *Unthank*.

Upavon (village, Wilts): '(place) higher up the (river) Avon'. OE *upp*, 'higher up'. Upavon is 4 miles further up the Avon than *Netheravon*, '(place) lower down the Avon' (OE *neotherra*, 'lower', 'nether'). For the river name, see AVON-MOUTH. DB *Oppavrene*.

Up Cerne (hamlet, Dorset): '(place) higher up the (river) Cerne'. OE *upp*, 'higher up'. Up Cerne is 4 miles further up the Cerne, which rises here, than *Nether Cerne*. For the river name, see CERNE ABBAS. DB *Obcerne*.

Upchurch (village, Kent): 'church high up'. OE *upp*, 'high up', + *cirice*, 'church'. The church and village are on a hill, the church formerly serving as a landmark for ships navigating the Medway estuary. *c.*1100 *Upcyrcean*.

Up Exe (village, Devon): '(place) higher up the (river) Exe'. OE *upp*, 'higher up'. For the river name, see EXETER. The village is further up the Exe than nearby *Nether Exe*. The DB form of the name below is garbled. DB *Ulpesse*, 1238 *Uphexe*.

Up Hatherley. See DOWN HATHERLEY.

Uphill (suburb of Weston-super-Mare, Somerset): '(place) above the tidal creek'. OE *uppan*, 'upon', + *pyll*, 'pool', 'creek'. Uphill stands near the mouth of the river Axe. DB *Opopille*.

Up Holland (suburb of Skelmersdale, Lancs): 'higher cultivated land by a hill spur'. OE *upp*, 'higher up', + *hōh*, 'hill spur', + *land*, 'cultivated land'. Up Holland is on a hillside, the name itself contrasting with that of *Dalton*, 'farmstead in a valley' (OE *dæl*, 'valley', + *tūn*, 'farmstead'), 3 miles to the northwest. DB *Hoiland*.

Upleadon (village, Glos): '(place) higher up the (river) Leadon'. OE *upp*, 'higher up'. For the river name, see LEDBURY. The village is further up the valley than *Highleadon*, '(estate on the) Leadon belonging to a religious community' (OE *hīwan*, 'household'), in this case, to the monks of St Peter's, Gloucester, to whom the estate was granted in 1239. DB *Ledene*, 1253 *Upleden*.

Upleatham (village, Redcar & Clev): '(place on the) upper slopes'. OE *upp*, 'higher up', + *hlith*, 'slope'. The meaning could equally have been given by the OS equivalent (*upp* + *hlith*), the latter word in either case being in a dative plural form. (The DB form of the name below represents OS *hlith* in a nominative plural form.) The first part of the name distinguishes the place from KIRKLEATHAM, 3 miles to the north-west. DB *Upelider*, *c.*1150 *Uplithum*.

Uplowman (village, Devon): '(place) higher up the (river) Loman'. OE *upp*, 'higher up'. The place is further up the river than Tiverton. The river name is Celtic in origin and means 'elm river'. DB *Oppaluma*.

Uplyme (village, Devon): '(place) higher up the (river) Lim'. OE *upp*, 'higher up'. The village is further up the river than LYME REGIS, at its mouth. DB *Lim*, 1238 *Uplim*.

Up Marden. See EAST MARDEN.

Upminster (town, Havering): 'higher church'. OE *upp*, 'upper', 'higher', + *mynster*, 'monastery', 'large church'. Upminster is on slightly rising ground in a generally flat landscape. DB *Upmunstra*.

Upottery. See OTTERY ST MARY.

Upper Arley (village, Worcs): 'higher wood or clearing where eagles are seen'. OE *earn*, 'eagle', + *lēah*, 'wood', 'clearing'. The first word of the name distinguishes the village from ARELEY KINGS, formerly known as *Nether Arley*, 7 miles to the south. 996 *Earnleie*, DB *Ernlege*.

Upper Arncott (hamlet, Oxon): 'higher cottage associated with Earn'. OE *-ing-*, 'associated with', + *cot*, 'cottage'. The first word of the name distinguishes this Arncott from nearby *Lower Arncott*. 983 *Earnigcote*, DB *Ernicote*.

Upper Beeding (village, W Sussex): 'higher (settlement of) Bēada's people'. OE *-ingas*, 'people of'. The first word of the name distinguishes the village from *Lower Beeding*, 12 miles to the north. The respective first words are unexpected, as Lower Beeding is on higher ground and further upcountry than Upper Beeding. 'Upper' may thus mean 'more important'. *c.*880 *Beadingum*, DB *Bedinges*.

Upper Benefield (village, Northants): 'upper open land of Bera's people'. OE *-inga-*, 'of the

people of', + *feld*, 'open land' (modern English *field*). Upper Benefield lies above *Lower Bene-field*. 10C *Beringafeld*, DB *Benefeld*.

Upper Boddington (village, Northants): 'higher (place by) Bōta's hill'. OE *dūn*, 'hill'. The first word of the name contrasts the village with nearby *Lower Boddington*. DB *Botendon*.

Upper Brailes (village, Warwicks): 'higher (place by the) tumulus'. OE *brægels*, 'burial place', 'tumulus'. The basic name could also be Celtic in origin, meaning 'hill court', from words related to modern Welsh *bre*, 'hill', and *llys*, 'court'. The first word distinguishes the village from nearby *Lower Brailes*. DB *Brailes*.

Upper Broadheath (village, Worcs): 'upper (place by the) broad heath'. Modern English *broad*, + OE *hæth*, 'heath'. The first word of the name distinguishes the village from nearby *Lower Broadheath*. 1240 *Hethe*, 1646 *Broad Heath*.

Upper Chute (village, Wilts): 'higher (place called) Chute'. The basic name is of Celtic origin and means 'woodland', from a word related to modern Welsh *coed*, 'wood'. Hence *Chute Forest* as the name of the entire forest here and as that of the modern parish containing the village of *Upper Chute*, the hamlets of *Chute Cadley* and *Chute Standen*, and part of the hamlet of *Lower Chute*. The forms of the name below refer to Chute Forest. DB *Cetum*, 1178 *Ceit*, 1252 *Chut*.

Upper Cumberworth. See LOWER CUMBER-WORTH.

Upper Denby. See DENBY DALE.

Upper Dicker. See LOWER DICKER.

Upper Dunsforth. See LOWER DUNSFORTH.

Upper Farringdon (hamlet, Hants): 'higher (place on the) fern-covered hill'. OE *fearn*, 'fern', + *dūn*, 'hill'. The first word of the name distinguishes this Farringdon from nearby *Lower Farringdon*. DB *Ferendone*.

Upper Hambleton (village, Rutland): 'higher (place on the) flat-topped hill'. OE *hamel*, 'mis-shapen', 'flat-topped', + *dūn*, 'hill'. The first word of the name distinguished the village from *Middle Hambleton* and *Lower Hambleton*, now both submerged in Rutland Water. DB *Hameldun*.

Upper Heaton. See KIRKHEATON (Kirklees).

Upper Helmsley. See GATE HELMSLEY.

Upper Heyford (village, Northants): 'higher (place by the) ford used at haymaking time'. OE *hēg*, 'hay', + *ford*, 'ford'. The river here is the Nene. The first word of the name distinguishes the village from nearby *Nether Heyford*, further downstream. DB *Heiforde*.

Upper Heyford (village, Oxon): 'higher (place by the) ford used at haymaking time'. OE *hēg*, 'hay', + *ford*, 'ford'. The river here is the Cherwell. The first word of the name distinguishes the village from nearby *Lower Heyford*, further downstream. DB *Hegford*.

Upper Langwith. See NETHER LANGWITH.

Upper Lye (hamlet, Herefords): 'higher (place at the) wood or clearing'. OE *lēah*, 'wood', 'clearing'. The first word of the name distinguishes the place from nearby *Lower Lye*. DB *Lege*.

Upper Mitton (district of Stourport-on-Severn, Worcs): 'higher farmstead at the river confluence'. OE *mȳthe*, 'confluence' (related modern English *mouth*), + *tūn*, 'farmstead'. The farm stood at the junction of the rivers Stour and Severn. The first word distinguishes it from nearby *Lower Mitton*. 841 *Myttun*, DB *Mettune*.

Upper Poppleton. See NETHER POPPLETON.

Upper Quinton. See LOWER QUINTON.

Upper Rochford (village, Worcs): 'higher (place by the) ford used by hunting dogs'. OE *rœcc*, 'hunting dog', + *ford*, 'ford'. The village is on higher ground than nearby *Lower Rochford*, on the river Teme. DB *Recesford*.

Upper Sapey (village, Herefords): 'higher (place by) Sapey Brook'. The stream here has a name meaning 'sappy', 'juicy' (OE *sæpig*). The first word of the name distinguishes the village from *Lower Sapey*, Worcs, 2 miles to the southeast. 781 *Sapian*, DB *Sapie*.

Upper Seagry (village, Wilts): 'higher (place by the) stream where sedge grows'. OE *secg*, 'sedge', + *rīth*, 'stream'. This meaning has been disputed on the grounds that sedge would be unlikely to grow in the small stream here and that the OE words would have been expected to produce a name 'Sedgery'. The first word of the name distinguishes the village from nearby *Lower Seagry*. DB *Segrete*.

Upper Slaughter (village, Glos): 'higher muddy place'. OE *slōhtre*, 'muddy place'. OE *slōhtre* is related to modern German *Schlucht*, 'ravine', and this might be a better sense, referring to the stream valley here. The first word distinguishes the village from nearby *Lower Slaughter*. DB *Sclostre*.

Upper Somborne. See KING'S SOMBORNE.

Upper Swell (village, Glos): 'higher (place on the) rising ground'. OE *swelle*, 'rising ground', 'hill' (related modern English *swell*). The first word of the name distinguishes the village from nearby *Lower Swell*. 706 *Swelle*, DB *Svelle*.

Upper Tean (village, Staffs): 'higher (place on the river) Tean'. The river name is of Celtic origin and probably means simply 'stream'. The first word of the name distinguishes the village from nearby *Lower Tean*. DB *Tene*.

Upperthong. See NETHERTHONG.

Upper Thurnham (hamlet, Lancs): 'higher (place by the) thorn bushes'. OE *thyrne*, 'thorn bush'. The second word of the name represents OE *thyrnum*, the dative plural form of *thyrne*. The first word distinguishes this Thurnham from nearby *Lower Thurnham*. The DB form of the name below is corrupt. DB *Tiernun*, 1160 *Thurnum*.

Upper Tysoe (village, Warwicks): 'higher (place by the) hill spur of Tīw'. OE *hōh*, 'hill spur'. The personal name is that of the pagan god of war who gave the name of Tuesday. The first word of the name distinguishes the village from nearby *Middle Tysoe* and *Lower Tysoe*. DB *Tiheshoche*.

Upper Winchendon (village, Bucks): 'higher (place by the) hill at a bend'. OE *wince*, 'bend', 'corner' (modern English *winch*), + *dūn*, 'hill'. The first word of the name distinguishes the village from *Lower Winchendon*, also known as *Nether Winchendon*, 1½ miles to the southwest. 1004 *Wincandone*, DB *Wichendone*.

Upper Wootton. See WOOTTON ST LAWRENCE.

Uppingham (town, Rutland): 'homestead of the hill dwellers'. OE *yppe*, 'raised place', 'upper place', + *-inga-*, 'of the dwellers at', + *hām*, 'homestead', 'village'. The homestead in question was probably on Castle Hill, to the west of the town, serving as a good vantage point. 1067 *Yppingeham*.

Uppington (village, Shropshire): 'estate associated with Uppa'. OE *-ing-*, 'associated with', + *tūn*, 'farmstead', 'estate'. DB *Opetone*, 1195 *Oppinton*.

Upsall (village, N Yorks): 'higher dwellings'. OS *upp*, 'higher up', + *salr*, 'hall', 'dwelling'. DB *Upsale*.

Upton (suburb of Poole, Dorset): 'higher farmstead'. OE *upp*, 'higher up', + *tūn*, 'farmstead'. 1463 *Upton*. SO ALSO: *Upton*, Cheshire, Slough.

Upton Cressett (village, Shropshire): 'Cressett's upper farmstead'. OE *upp*, 'higher up', + *tūn*, 'farmstead'. The Cressett family held land here in the 13C. The DB form of the name below has *l* for *p*. DB *Ultone*, 1535 *Hopton Cressett*.

Upton Grey (village, Hants): 'de Grey's higher farmstead'. OE *upp*, 'higher up', + *tūn*, 'farmstead'. The de Grey family held the manor here in the 13C. It is hard to see why the village is 'higher', as if anything it is lower than surrounding places. 1202 *Upton*, 1281 *Upton Grey*.

Upton Hellions (village, Devon): 'de Helihun's higher farmstead'. OE *upp*, 'higher up', + *tūn*, 'farmstead'. The de Helihun family held the manor here in the 13C, their name distinguishing this Upton from *Upton Pyne*, 5 miles to the southeast, where the manor was held by the de Pyn family. 1270 *Uppetone Hyliun*.

Upton Lovell (village, Wilts): 'Lovell's (estate at) Ubba's farmstead'. OE *tūn*, 'farmstead', 'village'. The Lovell family held the manor here in the 15C. 957 *Ubbantun*, 1476 *Ubbedon Lovell*.

Upton Magna (village, Shropshire): 'greater higher farmstead'. OE *upp*, 'higher up', + *tūn*, 'farmstead', + Latin *magna*, 'great'. The second word of the name distinguishes this Upton from WATERS UPTON, 7 miles to the northeast. DB *Uptune*, 1535 *Upton Magna*.

Upton Scudamore (village, Wilts): 'de Skydemore's higher farmstead'. OE *upp*, 'higher up', + *tūn*, 'farmstead'. The de Skydemore family held the manor here in the 13C. *c*.990 *Uptune*, DB *Uptone*, 1275 *Upton Squydemor*.

Upton Snodsbury (village, Worcs): 'higher farmstead by Snodsbury'. OE *upp*, 'higher up', + *tūn*, 'farmstead'. The names were originally those of two separate places, the second meaning 'Snodd's stronghold' (OE *burh*, 'fortified place'). 972 *Snoddesbyrie*, DB *Snodesbyrie*, 1280 *Upton juxta Snodebure*.

Upton St Leonards (village, Glos): 'higher farmstead with St Leonard's church'. OE *upp*, 'higher up', + *tūn*, 'farmstead'. The church here is dedicated to St Leonard. DB *Optune*, 1287 *Upton Sancti Leonardi*.

Upton upon Severn (village, Worcs): 'higher farmstead on the (river) Severn'. OE *upp*, 'higher up', + *tūn*, 'farmstead'. The village is higher up the Severn than Ripple, of which it at one time formed part. For the river name, see SEVERN STOKE. 897 *Uptune*, DB *Uptun*.

Upton Warren (village, Worcs): 'fitz Warin's higher farmstead'. OE *upp*, 'higher up', + *tūn*, 'farmstead'. The village is on low ground, and the farmstead may have been called 'up' from its position on the river Salwarpe in relation to Droitwich. William fitz Warin held the manor here in 1254. 716 *Upton*, DB *Uptune*, 1290 *Opton Warini*.

Upwaltham (hamlet, W Sussex): 'higher homestead in a forest'. OE *upp*, 'higher up', + *weald*, 'forest', + *hām*, 'homestead', 'village'. Upwaltham is on higher ground than *Cold-waltham* ('bleak homestead in a forest'), 6 miles to the east. DB *Waltham*, 1371 *Up Waltham*.

Upwell (village, Norfolk): '(place) higher up the stream'. OE *upp*, 'higher up', + *wella*, 'spring', 'stream'. The first part of the name distinguishes the village from OUTWELL, immediately to the northeast, which is further down the (original course of the) river Nene. 963 *Wellan*, 1221 *Upwell*.

Upwey (village, Dorset): '(place) higher up the (river) Wey'. OE *upp*, 'higher up'. The river Wey rises at Upwey, so that the village is by definition higher than any other place on it, and in particular WEYMOUTH. DB *Wai*, 1241 *Uppeweie*.

Urchfont (village, Wilts): '(place by) Eohrīc's spring'. OE *funta*, 'spring'. The spring in question is at Urchfont Bottom, southeast of the church. DB *Ierchesfonte*.

Ure (river). See JERVAULX ABBEY.

Urishay (hamlet, Herefords): 'Wulfrīc's enclosure'. OE *hæg*, 'enclosure' (related modern English *hedge*). 1242 *Haya Hurri*.

Urmston (town, Trafford): 'Wyrm's or Urm's farmstead'. OE *tūn*, 'farmstead', 'village'. The personal names are respectively OE and Scandinavian. 1194 *Wermeston*.

Ushaw Moor (village, Durham): 'moor by the wood where wolves are seen'. OE *wulf*, 'wolf', + *sceaga*, 'wood'. The initial *w*- of OE *wulf* has been lost under the influence of the OS equivalent, *ulfr*. 12C *Ulveskahe*.

Usk (town, Mon): '(place on the river) Usk'. The river has a Celtic name probably meaning 'abounding in fish', although it could also mean simply 'water'. The Welsh name of Usk is *Brynbuga*, 'Buga's hill' (Welsh *bryn*, 'hill'). The identity of Buga is unknown. The Roman name of the river was *Isca* (cp. EXETER). 1100 *Uscha*, 1150 *Uisc*.

Usselby (hamlet, Lincs): 'Ōswulf's farmstead'. OS *bý*, 'farmstead', 'village'. *c*.1115 *Osoluebi*.

Utterby (village, Lincs): 'Ūhtrēd's farmstead'. OS *bý*, 'farmstead', 'village'. 1150 *Uthterby*.

Uttlesford (council district, Essex): 'Ūdel's ford'. OE *ford*. The name is that of a former hundred here, referring to a ford over a tributary of the Cam at Uttlesford Bridge in Wendens Ambo. The meeting place of the hundred was at nearby Mutlow Hill. DB *Udelesforda*.

Uttoxeter (town, Staffs): 'Wuttuc's heath'. OE *hǣddre*, 'heather', 'heath'. The suggestion of a *ceaster* name, as for EXETER or WROXETER, is misleading. DB *Wotocheshede*.

Uxbridge (town, Hillingdon): '(place by the) bridge of the Wixan'. OE *brycg*, 'bridge'. The Wixan were a people who came to settle here from some other part of England, possibly the Midlands. The bridge would have been over the river Colne. *c.*1145 *Wixebrug*, 1200 *Uxebrigg*.

Uxelodunum. See STANWIX.

Uzmaston (village, Pemb): 'Ōsmund's farm'. OE *tūn*, 'farm'. 1230 *Villa Osmundi*.

V

Vale of Catmose. See CATMOSE, VALE OF.

Vale of Glamorgan. See GLAMORGAN.

Vale of Taunton Deane. See TAUNTON DEANE.

Vale of White Horse (valley, Oxon): 'valley of the white horse'. The name, now also that of the local council district, comes from the prehistoric figure of a horse cut into the chalk on Whitehorse Hill, south of Uffington. 1368 *The vale of Whithors*.

Vale Royal (council district, Cheshire): 'royal valley'. OE *val*, 'valley', + *roial*, 'royal'. The name is that of the site of St Mary's monastery, 4 miles southwest of Northwich, founded in the 13C by Edward I, who himself gave it the first (Latin) form of the name below. 1277 *Vallis Regalis*, 1357 *le Valroyal*.

Valley (village, Anglesey): 'the valley'. The name refers to the valley-like cutting from which rubble was extracted to build the Stanley Embankment from mainland Anglesey to Holy Island in the 1820s. An inn here was called The Valley, and this helped to establish the name. The Welsh form of the name is *Y Fali*, from the original English.

Vange (district of Basildon, Essex): '(place in a) marshy district'. OE *fenn*, 'marsh', 'fen', + *gē*, 'district'. Vange lies beside Vange Marshes and Vange Creek, which flows south into the Thames. 963 *Fengge*, DB *Phenge*.

Vauxhall (district, Birmingham). The former Duddeston Hall here, belonging to Sir Liston Holte, was opened as a public resort in 1759 and named after VAUXHALL, its London equivalent. It was demolished in 1850 but the name remained for the district. 'In the days of its prime, before ... Birmingham pushed up to its walls, it ranked as one of the finest places of amusement anywhere out of London' (Walter Showell, *Dictionary of Birmingham*, 1885).

Vauxhall (district, Westminster): 'Falkes' hall'. OE *hall*, 'hall', 'manor'. The OF personal name is that of Falkes de Breauté, who was granted the manor here in 1233. The famous 18C amusement gardens here gave the name of VAUXHALL, Birmingham. 1279 *Faukeshale*.

Vectis. See WIGHT, ISLE OF.

Venantodunum. See HUNTINGDON.

Venn Ottery. See OTTERY ST MARY.

Venta Belgarum. See WINCHESTER.

Venta Icenorum. See CAISTOR ST EDMUND.

Venta Silurum. See CAERWENT.

Ventnor (resort town, IoW): '(farm of) Vintner'. A family named Vintner must have held the manor here. The former name of Ventnor was *Holloway* (see HOLLOWAY), referring to the road running north out of Ventnor between Rew Down and St Boniface Down. The present town arose in the 19C. 1591 *Vintner*, 1607 *Vyntnor*.

Verbeia. See ILKLEY.

Vercovicium. See HOUSESTEADS.

Verlucio. See SANDY LANE.

Vernemetum. See WILLOUGHBY-ON-THE-WOLDS.

Vernham Dean (village, Hants): 'valley of the enclosure where ferns grow'. OE *fearn*, 'fern', + *hamm*, 'enclosure', + *denu*, 'valley'. The second word of the name distinguishes the village from nearby *Vernham Street*. The initial 'V-' (instead of expected 'F-') represents a southern dialect pronunciation (cp. VERWOOD). 1210 *Ferneham*, 1410 *Farnhamsdene*.

Verteris. See BROUGH (Cumbria).

Vertis. See WORCESTER.

Verulamium. See ST ALBANS.

Verwood (village, Dorset): '(place by the) beautiful wood'. OE *fæger*, 'fair', + *wudu*, 'wood'. The initial 'V-' results from southern dialect pronunciation, as for VERNHAM DEAN. The first name below represents the OF equivalent (*beu*, 'beautiful', + *bois*, 'wood'). 1288 *Beuboys*, 1329 *Fairwood*, 1868 *Verwood, or Fairwood*.

Veryan (village, Cornwall): '(church of) St Symphorian'. The church here is dedicated to Symphorian, a Gaulish martyr of the late 2C or early 3C. The first syllable of his name was taken to represent 'St', as for ST LEVAN, and was accordingly dropped. 1281 *Sanctus Symphorianus*.

Vickerstown (town, Cumbria). The firm of Vickers, Sons and Co. built a model town here on Walney Island in 1896 following their purchase of the Barrow shipyard and gave it their name.

Victoria (hamlet, Cornwall). The hamlet arose in the 19C by the Victoria Inn, named for Queen Victoria. 1888 *Victoria*.

Victoria (planned county, E England): '(county of Queen) Victoria'. The name was intended for a new county between Lincolnshire and Norfolk to be formed from land reclaimed from The Wash in the mid-19C. In the event the reclamation was never realized and the county never created.

Victoria (former district, London): '(district of Queen) Victoria'. The name existed in the 19C for the district between Bow, Hackney and Bethnal Green, corresponding approximately to the present borough of Tower Hamlets. The name survives in Victoria Park, opened in 1845. This Victoria was thus quite distinct from the present area of Victoria, centring on Victoria Station, to the south by the Thames. The station took its name from Victoria Street, built in the 1840s and 1850s, and it spread from there to the surrounding district.

Vigo Village (village, Kent). The village arose in modern times and was apparently named commemoratively for the British capture of the Spanish port of Vigo in 1719.

Vindocladia. See BADBURY RINGS.

Vindolanda. See CHESTERHOLM.

Vindomora. See EBCHESTER.

Vinovia. See BINCHESTER.

Virginia Water (residential district, Surrey). The name was originally that of the artificial lake created here in 1746 by William Augustus, Duke of Cumberland, itself punningly so called because planned as a pioneering venture in a 'virgin land', as was Virginia in America in 1607. 'The name was a forecast of the forest wilds, the broad waters, and tranquil solitudes that were to be called forth by the waving of the magician's wand' (James Thorne, *Handbook to the Environs of London*, 1876).

Virginstow (village, Devon): 'holy place of the Virgin'. OE *stōw*, 'holy place'. The name derives from the dedication of the church to St Bridget, who according to some legends was a personification of the Virgin Mary. c.1180 *Virginestowe*.

Viriconium. See WROXETER.

Viroconium. See WROXETER.

Vobster (hamlet, Somerset): 'Fobb's rocky hill'. OE *torr*, 'tor', 'rocky hill'. 1234 *Fobbestor*.

Vowchurch (village, Herefords): 'coloured church'. OE *fāh*, 'variegated', 'multicoloured', + *cirice*, 'church'. 1291 *Fowchirche*.

Vulcan Village (suburb of Newton-le-Willows, St Helens). The village was named after the Vulcan Works, a factory founded here in 1830 by Robert Stephenson and Charles Tayleur.

Vyrnwy. See LAKE VYRNWY.

Wackerfield (hamlet, Durham): 'open land where osiers grow'. OE *wācor*, 'osier' (related modern English *wicker*), + *feld*, 'open land' (modern English *field*). *c.*1050 *Wacarfeld*.

Wacton (village, Norfolk): 'Waca's farmstead'. OE *tūn*, 'farmstead', 'village'. DB *Waketuna*.

Wadborough (village, Worcs): 'hills where woad is grown'. OE *wād*, 'woad', + *beorg*, 'hill'. The name shows that woad, usually associated with the Ancient Britons, was cultivated in Anglo-Saxon times. The first form of the name below is in the plural. 972 *Wadbeorgas*, DB *Wadberge*.

Waddesdon (village, Bucks): '(place by) Weott's hill'. OE *dūn*, 'hill'. DB *Votesdone*.

Waddingham (village, Lincs): 'homestead of Wada's people'. OE *-inga-*, 'of the people of', + *hām*, 'homestead'. DB *Wadingeham*.

Waddington (village, Lincs): 'estate associated with Wada'. OE *-ing-*, 'associated with', + *tūn*, 'farmstead', 'estate'. DB *Wadintune*. SO ALSO: *Waddington*, Lancs.

Waddon (district, Croydon): 'hill where woad grows'. OE *wād*, 'woad', + *dūn*, 'hill'. 12C *Waddone*.

Wadebridge (town, Cornwall): '(place by a) ford with a bridge'. OE *wæd*, 'ford' (related modern English *wade*), + *brycg*, 'bridge'. The second part of the name was added when the original ford over the river Camel here was bridged in the 15C. 1358 *Wade*, 1478 *Wadebrygge*.

Wadenhoe (village, Northants): 'Wada's hill spur'. OE *hōh*, 'hill spur'. DB *Wadenho*.

Wadhurst (village, E Sussex): 'Wada's wooded hill'. OE *hyrst*, 'wooded hill'. 1253 *Wadehurst*.

Wadworth (village, Doncaster): 'Wada's enclosure'. OE *worth*, 'enclosure'. DB *Wadewrde*.

Wainfleet All Saints (town, Lincs): '(place on the) wagon stream with All Saints church'. OE *wægn*, 'wagon', + *flēot*, 'creek', 'stream'. A 'wagon stream', here the Wainfleet Haven or Steeping River, is one that can be crossed with a wagon. The church dedication distinguishes this place from nearby *Wainfleet St Mary*. DB *Wenflet*, 1291 *Weynflet Omnium Sanctorum*.

Waitby (hamlet, Cumbria): 'wet farmstead'. OS *vátr*, 'wet', + *bý*, 'farmstead'. *c.*1170 *Watebi*.

Wakefield (city, Wakefield): 'open land where wakes are held'. OE *wacu*, 'wake', + *feld*, 'open land' (modern English *field*). 'Wakes' here are festivities, as in the 'wakes weeks' still held in some north of England towns. Wakefield would have been an ideal site for these, with 'open land' available between the river Calder in the south and the extensive wood of Outwood in the north. Significantly, Wakefield later became associated with the famous cycle of mystery plays known as the Wakefield or Towneley plays, presented regularly here in medieval times. DB *Wachefeld*.

Wakerley (village, Northants): 'woodland clearing of the watchful people'. OE *wacor*, 'watchful' (related modern English *wake*, *watch*), + *lēah*, 'wood', 'clearing'. The name could also mean 'woodland clearing where osiers grow' (OE *wācor*, 'osier', + *lēah*). DB *Wacherlei*.

Wakes Colne. See COLNE ENGAINE.

Walberswick (village, Suffolk): 'Walbert's dairy farm'. OE *wīc*, 'dwelling', 'specialized farm'. The personal name is Old German. 1199 *Walberdeswike*.

Walberton (village, W Sussex): 'Wealdburh's or Waldburg's farmstead'. OE *tūn*, 'farmstead', 'village'. The personal names, respectively OE and Old German, are those of women. DB *Walburgetone*.

Walcot (village, Lincs): 'cottage of the Britons'. OE *walh*, '(Ancient) Briton', 'Welshman' (see WALES), + *cot*, 'cottage'. DB *Walecote*.

Walcote (village, Leics): 'cottage of the Britons'. OE *walh*, 'foreigner', '(Ancient) Briton',

'Welshman' (see WALES), + *cot*, 'cottage'. DB *Walecote*.

Walden (hamlet, N Yorks): '(place in the) valley of the Britons'. OE *walh*, '(Ancient) Briton', 'Welshman' (see WALES), + *denu*, 'valley'. 1270 *Waldene*.

Walden Stubbs (village, N Yorks): 'Walding's (estate by the) tree stumps'. OE *stubb*, 'stump'. One Walding held the manor here in the 12C, his name distinguishing the village from *Cridling Stubbs*, 4 miles to the northwest, held by one Cridela. The DB form of the name below is the result of the Norman clerk's attempt to render *stubb*, *c*.1180 *Stubbis*, 1280 *Stubbes Walding*.

Walderslade (suburb of Chatham, Kent): 'valley in a forest'. OE *weald*, 'forest' (cp. WEALD), + *slæd*, 'valley'. Walderslade is at the head of a long, narrow valley. 1190 *Waldeslade*.

Walderton (village, W Sussex): 'Wealdhere's farmstead'. OE *tūn*, 'farmstead'. 1168 *Walderton*.

Walditch (village, Dorset): '(place by the) ditch with a wall'. OE *weall* or *wall*, 'wall', 'embankment', + *dīc*, 'ditch', 'dyke'. DB *Waldic*.

Waldridge (village, Durham): '(place on the) ridge by a wall'. OE *wall*, 'wall', + *hrycg*, 'ridge'. 1297 *Walrigge*.

Waldringfield (village, Suffolk): 'open land of Waldhere's people'. OE *-inga-*, 'of the people of', + *feld*, 'open land' (modern English *field*). *c*.950 *Waldringfeld*, DB *Waldringafelda*.

Waldron (village, E Sussex): 'house in the forest'. OE *wald*, 'forest', + *ærn*, 'building', 'house'. DB *Waldrene*.

Wales (principality, W Britain): '(land of the) foreigners'. OE *walh*, 'foreigner', '(Ancient) Briton', 'Welshman'. The name was used by the Anglo-Saxons of the Celts, whom they saw as 'alien', with a different language and a different social structure. (The Celts could well have applied an equivalent term to the Anglo-Saxons, who were patently 'strangers' in their land.) The name represents OE *walas*, the plural form of *walh*. The Welsh name of Wales is *Cymru*, from a Celtic word meaning 'compatriot', 'fellow countryman'. Cp. CAMBRIAN MOUNTAINS, CUMBRIA.

Wales (village, Rotherham): '(settlement of the) Britons'. OE *walh*, 'Welshman', '(Ancient) Briton'. The name represents OE *walas*, the plural form of *walh*, and is thus identical in origin to that of the principality of WALES. There was presumably an isolated community of Welshmen or serfs here. DB *Wales*.

Walesby (village, Lincs): 'Valr's farmstead'. OS *bȳ*, 'farmstead', 'village'. The personal name is Scandinavian. DB *Walesbi*. SO ALSO: *Walesby*, Notts.

Walford (village, Herefords): '(place by the) ford of the Britons'. OE *walh*, '(Ancient) Briton', + *ford*, 'ford'. The village is on the river Wye. DB *Walecford*.

Walford (village, Herefords): '(place at a) ford by a spring'. OE *wælla*, 'spring', + *ford*, 'ford'. The ford in question would have been over a tributary of the river Teme here. DB *Waliforde*.

Walford (hamlet, Shropshire): '(place at a) ford by a spring'. OE *wælla*, 'spring', + *ford*, 'ford'. DB *Waleford*.

Walgherton (hamlet, Cheshire): 'Walhhere's farmstead'. OE *tūn*, 'farmstead', 'village'. DB *Walcretune*.

Walgrave (village, Northants): '(place by the) grove belonging to Old'. OE *grāf*, 'grove'. Walgrave is just over a mile southeast of OLD. DB *Waldgrave*.

Walkden (district, Salford): 'Walca's valley'. OE *denu*, 'valley'. 1325 *Walkeden*.

Walkerburn (village, Borders): '(place by the) fullers' stream'. OE *walcere*, 'fuller', + *burna*, 'stream'. The name refers to the 'walking' (fulling or dressing of cloth) that took place in the waters of a stream that flows into the Tweed here.

Walkeringham (village, Notts): 'homestead of Walhhere's people'. OE *-inga-*, 'of the people of', + *hām*, 'homestead'. DB *Wacheringeham*.

Walkern (village, Herts): 'building where cloth is fulled'. OE *walc*, 'fulling', + *ærn*, 'building'. The DB form of the name below is corrupt. DB *Walchra*, 1222 *Walkern*.

Walkhampton (village, Devon): 'farmstead of the dwellers on the (river) Wealce'. OE *hǣme*, 'dwellers' (related modern English *home*), + *tūn*, 'farmstead'. The river name means 'rolling one', from OE *wealcan*, 'to roll' (modern English *walk*). The Wealce is now the *Walkham*, named after the village. The first part of the DB form of the name below is corrupt. 1084 *Walchentone*, DB *Wachetona*.

Walkington (village, E Yorks): 'estate associated with Walca'. OE *-ing-*, 'associated with', + *tūn*, 'farmstead', 'estate'. DB *Walchinton*.

Wall (village, Northd): '(place by the) wall'. OE *wall*, 'wall'. The village is on the southern side of Hadrian's Wall. 1166 *Wal*.

Wall (village, Staffs): '(place by the) wall'. OE *wall*, 'wall'. The village arose by the walls of the

Roman town of *Letocetum*, 'grey wood', from Celtic words related to modern Welsh *llwyd*, 'grey', and *coed*, 'wood'. It was this Roman name that gave the original name of nearby LICHFIELD. 1167 *Walla*.

Wallasey (town, Wirral): 'island of Waley'. OE *ēg*, 'island'. *Waley*, a name originally applied to the whole region here, which in former times became an 'island' at high tide and during floods, means 'island of the Britons' (OE *walh*, 'Welshman', '(Ancient) Briton', + *ēg*, 'island'). A second OE *ēg* was added to this when the sense of the original was lost. DB *Walea*, 1351 *Waleyesegh*.

Wallingford (town, Oxon): '(place by the) ford of Wealh's people'. OE *-inga-*, 'of the people of', + *ford*, 'ford'. The ford would have been over the Thames here. *c*.895 *Welingaforda*, DB *Walingeford*.

Wallington (village, Herts): 'farmstead of Wændel's people'. OE *-inga-*, 'of the people of', + *tūn*, 'farmstead'. The DB form of the name below has contracted the personal name. DB *Wallingtone*, 1280 *Wandelingetona*.

Wallington (district, Sutton): 'farmstead of the Britons'. OE *walh*, 'foreigner', '(Ancient) Briton', + *tūn*, 'farmstead', 'village'. The name was originally *Walton*, but *-ing-* was then apparently introduced to distinguish this place from WALTON-ON-THAMES. DB *Waletone*, 1713 *Wallington alias Waleton*. SO ALSO: *Wallington*, Hants.

Wallops, The. See NETHER WALLOP.

Wallsend (town, N Tyneside): '(place at the) end of the wall'. OE *wall*, 'wall', + *ende*, 'end'. Wallsend lies at the eastern end of Hadrian's Wall. The Roman fort here was *Segedunum*, a name of Celtic origin meaning 'strong fort'. *c*.1085 *Wallesende*.

Walmer (district of Deal, Kent): 'pool of the Britons'. OE *walh*, 'foreigner', '(Ancient) Briton', + *mere*, 'pool', 'lake'. There is no lake at Walmer now, but the one formerly here must have been used more or less exclusively by the Britons when farming the Anglo-Saxon settlements. 1087 *Walemere*.

Walmersley (district, Bury): 'Waldmǣr's or Walhmǣr's woodland clearing'. OE *lēah*, 'wood', 'clearing'. 1262 *Walmeresley*.

Walney Island (island, Cumbria): 'island of the killer whale'. OS *vǫgn*, 'grampus', + *ey*, 'island'. The sense is hard to rationalize, and a better origin may lie in OE *wagen*, 'quaking sands', + *ēg*, 'island'. The second word of the name is essentially superfluous. 1127 *Wagneia*.

Walpole (village, Suffolk): '(place by the) pool of the Britons'. OE *walh*, 'foreigner', '(Ancient) Briton', 'Welshman', + *pōl*, 'pool'. At times of flood a large pool appears in the river Blyth here. DB *Walepola*.

Walpole St Andrew (village, Norfolk): '(place by the) pool at the wall with St Andrew's church'. OE *wall*, 'wall', + *pōl*, 'pool'. There is no pool here now as the marshland has been drained. The church dedication distinguishes this Walpole from nearby *Walpole St Peter*, and both villages are on the Roman sea wall by The Wash. DB *Walpola*.

Walsall (town, Walsall): 'Walh's corner of land'. OE *halh*, 'nook', 'corner of land'. The first part of the name could also represent OE *walh*, 'foreigner', '(Ancient) Briton', 'Welshman'. 1163 *Waleshale*.

Walsden (village, Calderdale): 'Walsa's valley'. OE *denu*, 'valley'. 1235 *Walseden*.

Walsgrave on Sowe (district, Coventry): 'grove by a forest on the (river) Sowe'. OE *wald*, 'forest', + *grāf*, 'grove'. The river name, originally used for the place itself, is pre-English and of unknown meaning. DB *Sowa*, 1411 *Woldegrove*, 1576 *Walgrove*.

Walsham le Willows (village, Suffolk): 'Walh's homestead among the willow trees'. OE *hām*, 'homestead'. DB *Walsam*.

Walsingham (village, Norfolk): 'homestead of Wæls' people'. OE *-inga-*, 'of the people of', + *hām*, 'homestead'. The name is historically that of *Great Walsingham*, as distinct from nearby *Little Walsingham*, although the latter is now larger than the former through its fame as a place of pilgrimage. It is Little Walsingham that thus holds the shrine of Our Lady of Walsingham. DB *Walsingaham*.

Walsoken (district of Wisbech, Norfolk): 'jurisdictional district by the wall'. OE *wall*, 'wall', + *sōcn*, 'soke', 'jurisdictional district'. The 'wall' is a Roman embankment here. 974 *Walsocne*, DB *Walsoca*.

Walterstone (hamlet, Herefords): 'Walter's estate'. OE *tūn*, 'manor', 'estate'. Walter de Lacy held the manor here in the late 11C. 1249 *Walterestun*.

Waltham (suburb of Grimsby, NE Lincs): 'forest estate'. OE *wald-hām* (from *wald*, 'forest', + *hām*, 'homestead', 'estate'). DB *Waltham*.

Waltham Abbey (town, Essex): 'abbey of Waltham'. The name *Waltham*, meaning 'forest estate' (OE *wald-hām*, from *wald*, 'forest', + *hām*, 'homestead', 'estate'), is found for a number of places in this region, the 'forest' being what remains of *Waltham Forest*, itself now the name of a Greater London borough. The abbey was built here in the 12C by Henry II. DB *Waltham*.

Waltham Cross (district of Cheshunt, Herts): 'cross near Waltham (Abbey)'. The cross is the 'Eleanor Cross' set up here in 1290 by Edward I in memory of Queen Eleanor (1245–90). For the main name, see WALTHAM ABBEY. 1365 *Walthamcros*.

Waltham Forest. See WALTHAM ABBEY.

Waltham on the Wolds (village, Leics): 'forest estate on the Wolds'. OE *wald-hām* (from *wald*, 'forest', + *hām*, 'homestead', 'estate'). The village is in an elevated position in the region sometimes known as the *Leicestershire Wolds* (see WOLDS). DB *Waltham*.

Waltham St Lawrence (village, Windsor & Maid): 'forest estate with St Lawrence's church'. OE *wald-hām* (from *wald*, 'forest', + *hām*, 'homestead', 'estate'). The church dedication distinguishes the village from *White Waltham*, 2 miles to the northeast, so named from the chalky soil there. 940 *Wealtham*, DB *Waltham*, 1225 *Waltamia Sancti Laurencii*.

Walthamstow (district, Waltham F): 'place where guests are welcome'. OE *wilcuma*, 'guest' (related modern English *welcome*), + *stōw*, 'place'. The name could also mean 'Wilcume's place', with a female personal name. Either way, OE *stōw* would have the sense 'holy place', so that the first meaning would refer to a religious house that welcomes guests. The present form of the name has been influenced by the name of WALTHAM ABBEY, 8 miles to the north. *c.*1075 *Wilcumestowe*, DB *Wilcumestou*.

Walton (village, Cumbria): 'farmstead by the wall'. OE *wall*, 'wall', + *tūn*, 'farmstead'. Walton lies by Hadrian's Wall. 1169 *Walton*.

Walton (hamlet, Derbys): 'farmstead of the Britons'. OE *walh*, 'Welshman', '(Ancient) Briton', + *tūn*, 'farmstead'. DB *Waletune*. SO ALSO: *Walton*, Suffolk.

Walton Cardiff (village, Glos): 'de Cardif's (estate at the) farmstead of the Britons'. OE *walh*, 'Welshman', '(Ancient) Briton', + *tūn*, 'farmstead'. The name could also mean 'farmstead by the wall' (OE *wall*, 'wall', + *tūn*), referring to a local embankment. The manor here was held from the 12C by the de Cardif family. DB *Waltone*, 1292 *Walton Kardif*.

Walton-in-Gordano (village, N Somerset): 'farmstead in a forest in Gordano'. OE *weald*, 'forest', + *tūn*, 'farmstead'. The main name could also mean 'farmstead with a wall' (OE *weall*, 'wall', + *tūn*). For the district name, see EASTON-IN-GORDANO. DB *Waltona*.

Walton-le-Dale (district of Preston, Lancs): 'farmstead of the Britons in the valley'. OE *walh*, 'foreigner', '(Ancient) Briton', 'Welshman', + *tūn*, 'farmstead', + OF *le*, 'the', + OS *dalr*, 'valley'. The distinguishing addition locates this Walton in *Ribblesdale*, the valley of the river Ribble. DB *Waletune*, 1304 *Walton in La Dale*.

Walton-on-Thames (town, Surrey): 'farmstead of the Britons on the (river) Thames'. OE *walh*, 'foreigner', '(Ancient) Briton', 'Welshman', + *tūn*, 'farmstead', 'village'. The river name (see THAMES DITTON) was added to distinguish this Walton from others. Cp. WALLINGTON (Sutton). DB *Waletona*.

Walton on the Hill (village, Surrey): 'farmstead in a forest on a hill'. OE *weald*, 'forest', + *tūn*, 'farmstead'. The first element of the name may represent OE *wall*, 'wall', giving a sense 'farmstead enclosed by a wall'. The second part of the name, denoting the location of the village on Epsom Downs, distinguishes it from WALTON-ON-THAMES, 12 miles to the northwest. DB *Waltone*.

Walton on the Naze (resort village, Essex): 'farmstead of the Britons on the Naze'. OE *walh*, 'foreigner', '(Ancient) Briton', 'Welshman', + *tūn*, 'farmstead'. The village was formerly also known as *Walton-le-Soken*, from the soke (OE *sōcn*) that also included *Kirby-le-Soken* and THORPE-LE-SOKEN. The second part of the name locates Walton on The NAZE. 11C *Walentonie*, 1545 *Walton at the Naase*.

Walton-on-Trent (village, Derbys): 'farmstead of the Britons on the (river) Trent'. OE *walh*, 'foreigner', '(Ancient) Briton', + *tūn*, 'farmstead'. For the river name, see STOKE-ON-TRENT. 942 *Waletune*, DB *Waletune*.

Walworth (district, Southwark): 'enclosure of the Britons'. OE *walh*, 'foreigner', '(Ancient) Briton', + *worth*, 'enclosure'. The first part of the name represents OE *wala*, the genitive plural form of *walh*. 1001 *Wealawyrth*, DB *Waleorde*. SO ALSO: *Walworth*, Darlington.

Wambrook (village, Somerset): '(place by the) winding brook'. OE *wōh*, 'winding', + *brōc*, 'brook'. The first part of the name represents OE *wōn*, the dative form of *wōh*. 1280 *Wambrook*.

Wanborough (village, Swindon): '(place by the) wen-shaped mounds'. OE *wenn*, 'wen', 'tumour', + *beorg*, 'mound'. The mounds in question are a group of barrows on nearby Sugar Hill. The Roman fort at Nythe Farm here was *Durocornovium*, 'fort of the Cornovii', the latter being the people who gave the name of CORN-WALL. 854 *Wænbeorgon*, DB *Wemberge*.

Wandsworth (borough, Greater London): 'Wændel's enclosure'. OE *worth*, 'enclosure'. Wandsworth gave the name of the river Wandle here. IIC *Wendleswurthe*, DB *Wandelesorde*.

Wangford (village, Suffolk): '(place at the) ford by the open fields'. OE *wang*, 'plain', 'open field', + *ford*, 'ford'. The ford would have been over the river Wang here, its own name coming from that of the village. DB *Wankeforda*.

Wanlip (village, Leics): 'lonely place'. OE *ānlīepe*, 'solitary'. DB *Anlepe*.

Wansbeck (council district, Northd): '(district of the river) Wansbeck'. The river name is of uncertain origin. The second half of the name was subsequently associated with *beck* (OS *bekkr*, 'stream'). 1137 *Wenspic*.

Wansdyke (ancient earthwork, Bath & NE Somerset): 'dyke associated with Wōden'. OE *dīc*, 'ditch', 'dyke'. The name is that of the heathen god of war, who was believed either to have actually built the earthwork or to 'preside' over it. Cp. WEDNESBURY, WEDNESFIELD. 903 *Wodnes dic*.

Wansford (village, E Yorks): '(place by) Wand's or Wandel's ford'. OE *ford*, 'ford'. The river here is the Hull. 1176 *Wandesford*.

Wansford (village, Peterborough): '(place at the) ford by a spring'. OE *wylm*, 'spring', + *ford*, 'ford'. The first part of the name could also represent OE *wælm*, 'whirlpool'. Either way, the ford would have been over the river Nene here, perhaps where the old arched bridge crosses it. 972 *Wylmesforda*.

Wanstead (district, Redbridge): 'place by a hillock'. OE *wænn*, 'tumour-shaped mound' (related modern English *wen*), + *stede*, 'place'. Wanstead lies on rising ground by the river Roding. Another possible meaning is 'place where wagons are kept', with the first part of the name representing OE *wǣn*, 'wagon' (modern English *wain*). c.1055 *Wænstede*, DB *Wenesteda*.

Wanstrow (village, Somerset): 'Wand's or Wandel's tree'. OE *trēow*, 'tree'. DB *Wandestreu*.

Wantage (town, Oxon): '(place on the river) Wantage'. The former name of Letcombe Brook that now flows through Wantage as a tributary of the river Ock was *Wantage*, meaning 'diminishing one', from a form of OE *wanian*, 'to decrease' (modern English *wane*). The name implies a stream that flows irregularly, or that sometimes almost dries up. c.880 *Waneting*, DB *Wanetinz*.

Wapley (hamlet, S Glos): 'woodland clearing by the spring'. OE *wapol*, 'bubble', 'spring', + *lēah*, 'wood', 'clearing'. DB *Wapelei*.

Wappenbury (village, Warwicks): 'Wæppa's stronghold'. OE *burh*, 'fortified place'. Remains of the 'stronghold' exist as the large rectangular entrenchment that surrounds the village. DB *Wapeberie*.

Wappenham (village, Northants): 'Wæppa's homestead or enclosure'. OE *hām*, 'homestead', or *hamm*, 'enclosure'. DB *Wapeham*.

Wapping (district, Tower Hamlets): '(settlement of) Wæppa's people'. OE *-ingas*, 'people of'. The name could also mean 'Wæppa's place' (OE *-ing*, 'place belonging to'). c.1220 *Wapping*.

Warbleton (hamlet, E Sussex): 'Wǣrburh's farmstead'. OE *tūn*, 'farmstead', 'village'. The personal name is that of a woman. DB *Warborgetone*.

Warblington (hamlet, Hants): 'farmstead associated with Wǣrblīth'. OE *-ing-*, 'associated with', + *tūn*, 'farmstead', 'village'. The personal name is that of a woman. DB *Warblitetone*, 1186 *Werblinton*.

Warborough (village, Oxon): '(place by the) lookout hill'. OE *weard*, 'watch', 'lookout' (modern English *ward*), + *beorg*, 'hill'. The hill in question is nearby Town Hill. 1200 *Wardeberg*.

Warboys (village, Cambs): '(place by) Wearda's bush'. OE *busc*, 'bush'. The first part of the name could also represent OE *weard*, 'watch', 'protection' (modern English *ward*). 974 *Weardebusc*.

Warbstow (village, Cornwall): 'holy place of St Wǣrburh'. OE *stōw*, 'holy place'. The church here is dedicated to the Anglo-Saxon saint Wǣrburh (Werburgh), daughter of King Wulfhere of Mercia. 1282 *Sancta Werburga*, 1309 *Warberstowe*.

Warburton (village, Trafford): 'Wǣrburh's farmstead'. OE *tūn*, 'farmstead', 'village'. The personal name is that of a woman. DB *Wareburgetune*.

Warcop (village, Cumbria): '(place by the) lookout hill'. OS *varthr*, 'lookout', + OE *copp*, 'hill'. The first part of the name could also represent OE *vartha*, 'cairn', giving a sense 'hill with a cairn'. The hill is the large ridge here with a crest affording wide views. 1199 *Warthecopp*.

Warden (hamlet, Northd): '(place by the) lookout hill'. OE *weard*, 'lookout' (modern English *ward*), + *dūn*, 'hill'. c.1175 *Waredun*. SO ALSO: *Warden*, Kent.

Wardington (village, Oxon): 'estate associated with Wearda or Wǣrheard'. OE *-ing-*, 'associated with', + *tūn*, 'farmstead', 'estate'. *c*.1180 *Wardinton*.

Wardle (town, Rochdale): '(place by the) lookout hill'. OE *weard*, 'watch', 'lookout' (modern English *ward*), + *hyll*, 'hill'. The name probably refers to Brown Wardle Hill, northwest of the town. *c*.1193 *Wardhul*. SO ALSO: *Wardle*, Cheshire.

Wardley (village, Rutland): '(place by the) woodland clearing'. OE *lēah*, 'wood', 'clearing'. The first part of the name is of uncertain origin. It may represent OE *weard*, 'watch', 'protection', although *d* does not appear in the earliest records of the name. Wardley stands on a hillside with good views. 1067 *Werlea*, 1241 *Wardel*.

Wardlow (village, Derbys): '(place by the) lookout hill'. OE *weard*, 'watch', + *hlāw*, 'hill'. The hill in question is nearby Wardlow Hay Cop. 1258 *Wardelawe*.

Wardour Castle (country house, Wilts): '(place by the) lookout bank'. OE *weard*, 'watch', + *ōra*, 'bank'. The reference is to a lookout post on the banks of the river Nadder nearby. DB *Werdore*.

Ware (town, Herts): '(place by the) weirs'. OE *wær*, 'weir'. The name probably refers to frequent former blockages on the river Lea here, as mentioned by Thomas Fuller in his *History of the Worthies of England* (1662): '*Weare* is the proper name of that *Town* (so *called* anciently from the *Stoppages*, which there obstruct the River)'. DB *Waras*.

Wareham (town, Dorset): 'homestead by a weir'. OE *wær*, 'weir', + *hām*, 'homestead'. There was a fishery above the weir on the river Frome here as early as the 14C. Alternatively, the name could mean 'river meadow by a weir', with the second part of the name representing OE *hamm*, 'enclosure', 'riverside meadow'. Wareham is on low-lying land between the rivers Piddle and Frome. Early forms of the name appear to favour the former origin. late 9C *Werham*, DB *Warham*.

Warenford (hamlet, Northd): '(place by the) ford over the Warren Burn'. OE *ford*, 'ford'. The river name is Celtic in origin, meaning 'stream where alders grow' (related modern Welsh *gwernen*, 'alder'). 1256 *Warneford*.

Waresley (village, Cambs): 'Wether's or Wær's woodland clearing'. OE *lēah*, 'wood', 'clearing'. The DB form of the name below has *d* for *th*. DB *Wederesle*, 1169 *Wereslea*.

Warfield (hamlet, Bracknell F): 'open land by a weir'. OE *wer*, 'weir', + *feld*, 'open land' (modern English *field*). The weir would have been constructed as a fishing enclosure across the stream here. The second part of the DB form of the name below is corrupt. DB *Warwelt*, 1171 *Warefeld*.

Wargrave (village, Wokingham): '(place by the) trench beside the weir'. OE *wer*, 'weir', + *græf*, 'pit', 'trench' (modern English *grave*). The river here is the Thames. DB *Weregrave*.

Warham All Saints (hamlet, Norfolk): 'homestead by a weir with All Saints church'. OE *wær*, 'weir', + *hām*, 'homestead'. The church dedication distinguishes this Warham from nearby *Warham St Mary*, both being on the river Stiffkey. DB *Warham*.

Wark (village, Northd): 'fortified place'. OE *geweorc*, 'fortification' (related modern English *work*). There are two villages of this name in Northumberland. The form of the name below is for the larger one, south of Bellingham, sometimes known as *Wark-on-Tyne*, but the other, near Cornhill, has a name of identical origin. 1279 *Werke*.

Warkleigh (hamlet, Devon): 'wood or clearing where spiders are seen'. OE *wæferce*, 'spider' (related modern English *weaver*), + *lēah*, 'wood', 'clearing'. 1100 *Warocle*, 1242 *Wauerkelegh*.

Warkton (village, Northants): 'estate associated with Weorc'. OE *-ing-*, 'associated with', + *tūn*, 'farmstead', 'estate'. The original *-ing-* has disappeared from the name. 946 *Wurcingtun*, DB *Werchintone*.

Warkworth (village, Northd): 'Weorca's enclosure'. OE *worth*, 'enclosure'. *c*.1050 *Werceworthe*.

Warlaby (hamlet, N Yorks): 'farmstead of the traitor'. OE *wērloga*, 'troth-breaker', + OS *bý*, 'farmstead', 'village'. DB *Werlegesbi*.

Warleggan (village, Cornwall): origin uncertain. The first part of the name may represent Cornish *gor-*, 'over-', 'very'. The rest is obscure. *c*.1250 *Wrlegan*.

Warley Town (district of Halifax, Calderdale): 'Werlāf's woodland clearing'. OE *lēah*, 'wood', 'clearing'. The second word of the name is a recent addition. DB *Werlafeslei*.

Warley Woods (district, Sandwell): 'cattle pasture in a woodland clearing'. OE *weorf*, 'draught cattle', + *lēah*, 'wood', 'clearing'. The name *Warley*, adopted in 1966 for the combined boroughs of Rowley Regis, Smethwick and Oldbury, was already current for the adjoining villages of *Warley Salop* and *Warley Wigorn*, the former being earlier in Shropshire, the latter in Worcestershire. (*Salop* is a short form of SHROPSHIRE, while *Wigorn* is from *Wigornia*, the Medieval Latin name of WORCESTER.) DB *Werwelie*.

Warlingham (town, Surrey): 'homestead of Wǣrla's people'. OE -*inga*- 'of the people of', + *hām*, 'homestead'. 1144 *Warlyngham*.

Warmfield (village, Wakefield): 'open land where wrens are seen'. OE *wærna*, 'wren', + *feld*, 'open land' (modern English *field*). The name could also mean 'open land where stallions are kept' (OE *wǣrna*, 'stallion', + *feld*). DB *Warnesfeld*.

Warmingham (village, Cheshire): 'homestead of Wǣrma's or Wǣrmund's people'. OE -*inga*-, 'of the people of', + *hām*, 'homestead'. The name could also mean 'homestead at Wǣrma's or Wǣrmund's place' (OE -*ing*, 'place belonging to', + *hām*). 1259 *Warmincham*.

Warmington (village, Northants): 'estate associated with Wyrma'. OE -*ing*-, 'associated with', + *tūn*, 'farmstead', 'estate'. *c*.980 *Wyrmingtun*, DB *Wermintone*.

Warmington (village, Warwicks): 'estate associated with Wǣrma or Wǣrmund'. OE -*ing*-, 'associated with', + *tūn*, 'farmstead', 'estate'. DB *Warmintone*.

Warminster (town, Wilts): 'church on the (river) Were'. OE *mynster*, 'monastery', 'large church'. The name of the river means 'wandering one', from OE *wōrian*, 'to wander'. The DB form of the name below has French *gu* for English *w*, as in the modern doublet French *guerre*/English *war*. *c*.912 *Worgemynster*, DB *Guerminstre*.

Warmsworth (suburb of Doncaster): 'Wǣrmi's or Wǣrmund's enclosure'. OE *worth*, 'enclosure'. The second part of the DB form of the name below is corrupt. DB *Wermesford*, *c*.1105 *Wermesworth*.

Warmwell (village, Dorset): '(place by the) warm spring'. OE *wearm*, 'warm', + *wella*, 'spring', 'stream'. The spring in question lies just north of the village. DB *Warmewelle*.

Warnham (village, W Sussex): 'Wǣrna's homestead or enclosure'. OE *hām*, 'homestead', or *hamm*, 'enclosure'. The name could also mean 'homestead or enclosure where stallions are kept' (OE *wǣrna*, 'stallion', + *hām* or *hamm*). 1166 *Werneham*.

Warningcamp (hamlet, W Sussex): 'Wǣrna's enclosure'. OE *camp*, 'enclosed piece of land' (modern English *camp*). The '-ing-' of the name appeared only in the 16C, perhaps by way of local lore which claims that the village gave 'warning' of impending attacks on Arundel Castle, across the river Arun. DB *Warnecham*.

Warninglid (village, W Sussex): 'hill slope associated with Weardel'. OE -*ing*-, 'associated with', + *hlith*, 'hill slope'. OE *hlith* can specifi-cally denote a concave hillside as here, where there is a narrow wooded hollow in the hill. 1260 *Warlingelide*.

Warrington (town, Warrington): 'farmstead by the river dam'. OE *wering*, 'river dam' (from *wer*, 'weir'), + *tūn*, 'farmstead', 'village'. The river here is the Mersey. The DB form of the name below has Norman *l* for English *r*, as for SALIS-BURY. DB *Walintune*, 1246 *Werington*.

Warsash (village, Hants): 'ash tree by the weir'. OE *wer*, 'weir', + *æsc*, 'ash'. The name could also mean 'Wǣr's ash tree', referring to such a tree on the boundary of his estate. 1272 *Weresasse*.

Warslow (village, Staffs): '(place by the) hill with a watchtower'. OE *weard-seld*, 'watch house' (from *weard*, 'watch', + *seld*, 'abode'), + *hlāw*, 'hill'. The DB form of the name below is corrupt. DB *Wereslei*, 1300 *Werselow*.

Warsop (town, Notts): 'Wǣr's valley'. OE *hop*, 'enclosed valley'. The name probably refers to the valley known as Warsop Vale, to the west of the town. DB *Wareshope*.

Warter (village, E Yorks): '(place with a) gallows'. OE *wearg-trēow*, 'gallows' (from *wearg*, 'felon', 'criminal', + *trēow*, 'tree'). DB *Wartre*.

Warthill (village, N Yorks): '(place by the) lookout hill'. OE *weard*, 'watch', + *hyll*, 'hill'. DB *Wardhilla*.

Wartling (village, E Sussex): '(settlement of) Wyrtel's people'. OE -*ingas*, 'people of'. The DB form of the name below has omitted the *t*. DB *Werlinges*, 12C *Wertlingis*.

Wartnaby (village, Leics): 'Wǣrcnōth's farmstead'. OS *bý*, 'farmstead', 'village'. DB *Worcnodebie*.

Warton (village, Lancs): 'farmstead with a lookout'. OE *weard*, 'watch', 'lookout' (modern English *ward*), + *tūn*, farmstead'. The DB form of the name below relates to Warton near Carn-forth, where the 'lookout' would probably have been on Warton Crag, but Warton near Lytham St Annes has a name of identical origin. DB *Wartun*. SO ALSO: *Warton*, Northd.

Warton (village, Warwicks): 'farmstead by a swaying tree'. OE *wæfre*, 'restless', 'unstable' (related modern English *waver*), + *tūn*, 'farm-stead'. The first part of the name could also mean 'marshy ground'. Cp. WAVERTON (Che-shire), WHARTON. *c*.1155 *Wavertune*.

Warwick (hamlet, Cumbria): 'dwelling on the bank'. OE *waroth*, 'bank', 'shore', + *wīc*, 'dwell-ing', 'farm'. Warwick is on the west bank of the river Eden. 1131 *Warthwic*.

Warwick (town, Warwicks): 'premises by the weir'. OE *wæring*, 'weir', + *wīc*, 'dwelling', 'specialized farm'. The weir would have been on the river Avon here. 1001 *Wærincwicum*, DB *Warwic*.

Warwickshire (county, central England): 'district based on Warwick'. OE *scīr*, 'shire', 'district'. See WARWICK (Warwicks). 11C *Wærincwicscir*.

Wasdale Head (hamlet, Cumbria): '(place at the) upper end of the valley of the lake'. OS *vatn*, 'water', 'lake', + *dalr*, 'valley', + OE *hēafod*, 'head', 'upper end'. The lake in question is WAST WATER. 1279 *Wastedale*, 1334 *Wascedaleheved*.

Wash, The (sea inlet, Lincs/Norfolk): 'washed (place)'. OE *wæsc*, 'sandbank washed by the sea'. The name (originally *The Washes*) applied to two sandbanks here that could be forded at low tide. The second form of the name below is from Shakespeare's *King John*. c.1545 *The Wasshes*, c.1595 *Lincolne-Washes*.

Washfield (village, Devon): 'open land by the washing place'. OE *wæsce*, 'washing place', + *feld*, 'open land' (modern English *field*). The village stands above the Exe Valley, where there would have been a place for washing sheep or clothes. DB *Wasfelte*.

Washford (village, Somerset): '(place by the) ford (on the road) to Watchet'. OE *ford*, 'ford'. Washford lies on a stream 2 miles southwest of WATCHET. c.960 *Wecetford*.

Washford Pyne (hamlet, Devon): 'de Pinu's (estate by the) ford at the washing place'. OE *wæsce*, 'washing place', + *ford*, 'ford'. The de Pinu family held the manor here in the 13C. The 'washing place', on a tributary of the river Taw, would have been used for sheep or clothes. DB *Wasforde*.

Washingborough (village, Lincs): 'stronghold of Wassa's people'. OE *-inga-*, 'of the people of', + *burh*, 'fortified place'. The first part of the name could also mean 'dwellers by the place liable to flood' (OE *wæsc*, 'flood') or 'dwellers at the place used for washing' (OE *wæsce*, 'washing place'). Washingborough is on the river Witham. DB *Washingeburh*.

Washington (town, Sunderland): 'estate associated with Wassa'. OE *-ing-*, 'associated with', + *tūn*, 'farmstead', 'estate'. 1183 *Wassyngtona*.

Washington (village, W Sussex): 'estate of Wassa's people'. OE *-inga-*, 'of the people of', + *tūn*, 'farmstead', 'estate'. 946 *Wessingatun*, DB *Wasingetune*.

Wasperton (village, Warwicks): 'pear orchard by alluvial land'. OE *wæsse*, 'alluvial land' (related modern English *wash*), + *peru*, 'pear', + *tūn*, 'enclosure', 'farmstead'. The river here is the Avon. The DB form of the name below has *m* for *p*. 1043 *Waspertune*, DB *Wasmertone*.

Wass (village, N Yorks): '(place by the) fords'. OS *vath*, 'ford'. Wass is at a point where three streams meet and where there are two fords, one to the north, the other to the west. 1541 *Wasse*.

Wast Water (lake, Cumbria): 'lake in Wasdale'. OE *wæter*, 'water'. *Wasdale* is the name of the valley here (see WASDALE HEAD), the lake in question being Wast Water itself. 1279 *Wastedale*.

Watchet (coastal town, Somerset): '(place) under the wood'. The name is Celtic in origin, based on words related to modern Welsh *gwas*, 'servant', and *coed*, 'wood'. The reference would be to the cliffs behind the town, which must at one time have been more thickly wooded than they are now. 962 *Wæcet*, DB *Wacet*.

Watchfield (village, Oxon): 'Wæcel's open land'. OE *feld*, 'open land' (modern English *field*). The present form of the name has been influenced by modern *watch*. 931 *Wæclesfeld*, DB *Wachenesfeld*.

Watendlath (hamlet, Cumbria): '(place on the) lane to the end of the lake'. OS *vatn*, 'lake', + *endi*, 'end', + OE *lane*, 'lane'. Watendlath is at the northern end of Watendlath Tarn. OS *hlatha*, 'barn', has replaced original OE *lane* as the last part of the name. late 12C *Wattendlane*.

Waterbeach (village, Cambs): '(place on a) low ridge by water'. OE *wæter*, 'water', + *bæc*, 'ridge' (modern English *back*). The first part of the name was added to distinguish this place, near the river Cam, from neighbouring LANDBEACH. The first part of the DB form of the name below represents OE *ūt*, 'outer', as Waterbeach is closer than Landbeach to the edge of the area of firm land. DB *Vtbech*, 1237 *Waterbech*.

Watercombe (hamlet, Dorset): '(place in the) wet valley'. OE *wæter*, 'water', + *cumb*, 'valley'. DB *Watrecome*.

Waterden (hamlet, Norfolk): '(place in a) wet valley'. OE *wæter*, 'water', + *denu*, 'valley'. DB *Waterdenna*.

Water Eaton (hamlet, Oxon): 'farmstead by a river in a watery place'. OE *wæter*, 'water', + *ēa*, 'river', + *tūn*, 'farmstead'. Water Eaton is on the river Cherwell. The first word of the name was added to distinguish this Eaton from nearby WOODEATON. DB *Etone*, 1227 *Water Eton*.

Waterfall (village, Staffs): '(place of the) waterfall'. OE *wæter-gefall* (from *wæter*, 'water', +

gefall, 'fall'). The reference is not to a conventional waterfall: 'The village is situated near the river Hamps, which here flows underground for about three miles to the neighbourhood of Ilam, where it joins the river Manifold' (*The National Gazetteer of Great Britain and Ireland*, 1868). 1201 *Waterfal*.

Wateringbury (village, Kent): 'stronghold of Öhthere's people'. OE *-inga-*, 'of the people of', + *burh*, 'fortified place'. 964 *Uuotryngebyri*, DB *Otringeberge*.

Waterloo (district of Crosby, Sefton). The place took its name from the Royal Waterloo Hotel here, which was founded in 1815 and named for the Battle of Waterloo that year.

Waterlooville (town, Hants): 'town of Waterloo'. French *ville*, 'town'. Waterlooville is of 19C origin and takes its name from an inn here called The Heroes of Waterloo, named for the soldiers and sailors who had disembarked at nearby Portsmouth on their return home from the Battle of Waterloo (1815).

Watermillock (hamlet, Cumbria): 'little bare hill where wethers graze'. The second part of the name is a Celtic hill name, from a word related to modern Welsh *moel*, 'bare hill', with a diminutive suffix. The first part represents OE *wether*, 'wether' (castrated ram). Early 13C *Wethermeloc*.

Water Newton (village, Cambs): 'new farmstead by the river'. OE *nīwe*, 'new', + *tūn*, 'farmstead'. The village lies by the river Nene. 937 *Niwantune*, DB *Newetone*.

Water Orton (village, Warwicks): 'farmstead by the bank in a watery place'. OE *ōfer*, 'bank', + *tūn*, 'farmstead'. The village lies by the river Tame. 1262 *Overtone*.

Waterperry (village, Oxon): '(place with) pear trees by water'. OE *wæter*, 'water', + *pirige*, 'pear tree'. The first part of the name was added for distinction from WOODPERRY, 4 miles to the northwest. Waterperry lies by the river Thame, which is liable to flood. DB *Perie*, c.1190 *Waterperi*.

Waterstock (village, Oxon): 'wet place'. OE *wæter*, 'water', + *stoc*, 'place'. The village is on the river Thame. DB *Stoch*, 1208 *Waterstokes*.

Waterston (village, Pemb): 'Walter's farm'. OE *tūn*, 'farm'. 1407 *Walterystone*.

Water Stratford (village, Bucks): '(place by the) river at a ford on a Roman road'. OE *wæter*, 'river', 'stream', + *strǣt*, 'Roman road' (modern English *street*), + *ford*, 'ford'. The Roman road from Dorchester, Oxon, to Towcester, Northants, crossed the river Ouse here. The village lies

to the west of both STONY STRATFORD and FENNY STRATFORD. Hence *West* in the second and third forms of the name below. DB *Stradford*, 1302 *Weststratforde*, 1383 *West Watrestretford*.

Waters Upton (village, Wrekin): 'Walter's upper farmstead'. OE *uppe*, 'higher up', + *tūn*, 'farmstead'. The manor here was held in the 13C by one Walter. The place was earlier known as *Upton Parva*, as distinct from UPTON MAGNA, 7 miles to the southwest. DB *Uptone*, 1346 *Upton Waters*.

Watford (town, Herts): '(place by the) ford used by hunters'. OE *wāth*, 'hunting', + *ford*, 'ford'. The ford would have been over the river Colne here. c.945 *Watford*.

Watford (village, Northants): '(place by the) ford used by hunters'. OE *wāth*, 'hunting', + *ford*, 'ford'. Nearby is the *Watford Gap*, a broad valley at the northern end of the Cotswolds through which run or ran Watling Street (the present M1), the Grand Union Canal, and a major rail route. DB *Watford*.

Wath (village, N Yorks): '(place by the) ford'. OS *vath*, 'ford'. The form of the name below relates to Wath near Ripon. OE *Wat*.

Wath upon Dearne (town, Rotherham): '(place by the) ford on the (river) Dearne'. OS *vath*, 'ford'. For the river name, see BOLTON UPON DEARNE. DB *Wade*.

Watling Street (Roman road, England): 'Roman road associated with Wacol's people'. OE *-inga-*, 'of the people of', + *strǣt*, 'Roman road' (modern English *street*). A former name for St Albans was *Wæclingaceaster*, 'Roman fort of Wacol's people' (OE *ceaster*, 'Roman station'), and the name of the road probably first applied to the stretch between St Albans and London. It was then extended to the whole length, from Dover to Wroxeter. The name was later transferred to other Roman roads. Late 9C *Wæclinga strǣt*.

Watlington (village, Norfolk): 'farmstead of Hwætel's or Wacol's people'. OE *-inga-*, 'of the people of', + *tūn*, 'farmstead'. 11C *Watlingetun*.

Watlington (town, Oxon): 'estate associated with Wæcel's people'. OE *-ing-*, 'associated with', + *tūn*, 'farmstead', 'estate'. 887 *Wæclinctune*, DB *Watelintone*.

Wattisfield (village, Suffolk): 'Wacol's or Hwætel's open land'. OE *feld*, 'open land' (modern English *field*). DB *Watlesfelda*.

Wattisham (village, Suffolk): 'Wæcci's homestead'. OE *hām*, 'homestead', 'village'. DB *Wecesham*.

Watton (village, E Yorks): '(place by the) wet hill'. OE *wǣt*, 'wet', + *dūn*, 'hill'. Watton lies on the lower slope of a hill near marshland. 731 *Uetadun*, DB *Wattune*.

Watton (village, Norfolk): 'Wada's farmstead'. OE *tūn*, 'farmstead'. DB *Wadetuna*.

Watton at Stone (village, Herts): 'farmstead where woad is grown by the stone'. OE *wād*, 'woad', + *tūn*, 'farmstead', + *stān*, 'stone'. According to J. E. Cussans, *History of Hertfordshire* (1870–81), there was an old stone under the horse trough at the Wagon and Horses inn here. 969 *Wattun*, DB *Wodtone*, 1311 *Watton atte Stone*.

Wattstown (village, Rhondda CT). The name is that of Edmund Watts, a coal owner here in the 19C.

Waun, Y. See CHIRK.

Wavendon (village, Milton K): '(place by) Wafa's hill'. OE *dūn*, 'hill'. 969 *Wafandun*, DB *Wavendone*.

Waveney Forest (woodland region, Norfolk): 'woods by the (river) Waveney'. The Waveney, forming the boundary between Norfolk and Suffolk, has a name meaning 'river by a quagmire' (OE *wagen*, 'quagmire', related to *wagian*, 'to sway' and modern English *wag*, + *ēa*, 'river'). The river name gave that of the present Suffolk council district. 1275 *Wahenhe*.

Waverley Abbey (abbey ruins, Surrey): 'woodland clearing by the marshy pool'. OE *wæfre*, 'restless', 'unstable' (related modern English *waver*), + *lēah*, 'wood', 'clearing'. A marshy or swampy pool is a fickle one. The abbey stood on a low-lying site by the river Wey. The local council district takes its name from that of the abbey. 1147 *Wauerleia*.

Waverton (village, Cheshire): 'farmstead by a swaying tree'. OE *wæfre*, 'restless', 'unstable' (related modern English *waver*), + *tūn*, 'farmstead'. Cp. WHARTON. DB *Wavretone*.

Waverton (village, Cumbria): 'farmstead by the (river) Waver'. OE *tūn*, 'farmstead'. The river name means 'winding one' (OE *wæfre*, 'restless', 'unstable', related modern English *waver*). 1183 *Wauerton*.

Wavertree (district, Liverpool): '(place by the) swaying tree'. OE *wæfre*, 'restless', 'unstable' (related modern English *waver*), + *trēow*, 'tree'. The tree in question may have been an aspen. DB *Wauretreu*.

Wawne (village, E Yorks): '(place by the) quagmire'. OE *wagen*, 'quagmire'. The name may actually be of Celtic origin, not English, but similarly meaning 'marsh', from a word related to

modern Welsh *gwaun*, 'moor'. Wawne is on low-lying ground near the river Hull. DB *Wagene*, 1868 *Wawn*, 1898 *Wawne, or Waghen*.

Waxham (coastal hamlet, Norfolk): 'Wægstān's homestead'. OE *hām*, 'homestead'. The name could also mean 'homestead by the stone where watch is kept' (OE *wacu*, 'watch', + *stān*, 'stone', + *hām*). 1044 *Waxtonesham*, DB *Wactanesham*.

Waxholme (coastal hamlet, E Yorks): 'homestead where wax is produced'. OE *weax*, 'wax', + *hām*, 'homestead'. There must have been a colony of bees here. DB *Waxham*.

Wayford (village, Somerset): '(place by the) ford on a road'. OE *weg*, 'way', 'road', + *ford*, 'ford'. The village is near the river Axe. 1206 *Waiford*.

Wayland's Smithy (prehistoric long barrow, Oxon). The barrow is named after Wayland (Wieland), the famous smith of German legend, who is said to have shoed horses in return for a groat placed on the roof slab of one of the three chambers of the megalithic tomb here. 955 *Welandes smithan*.

Weald (tract of country, E Sussex/Kent): 'woodland'. OE *weald*, 'forest'. The region bounded by the North Downs and South Downs was formerly wooded. Cp. WOLDS. The form of the name below has a dative plural ending. 1185 *Waldum*.

Wealden (council district, E Sussex): '(district of the) Weald'. The district, in the central part of the county, extends northwards to the region of the WEALD.

Wealdstone (district, Harrow): '(place by the) boundary stone of Harrow Weald'. The name probably refers to a boundary mark that separated Harrow Weald from the rest of the parish of Harrow. *Harrow Weald* takes its own name from the woodland nearby (cp. WEALD). Wealdstone itself arose only in the 19C.

Wear (river). See MONKWEARMOUTH.

Weare (village, Somerset): '(place by the) weir'. OE *wer*, 'weir'. The name relates to a fishing enclosure here on the river Axe. DB *Werre*.

Weare Giffard (village, Devon): 'Giffard's (estate by the) wear'. OE *wer*, 'wear'. The name relates to a fishing enclosure on the river Torridge here, where the manor was held in the 13C by the Giffard family. DB *Were*, 1328 *Weregiffarde*.

Wear Valley. See MONKWEARMOUTH.

Weasenham All Saints (village, Norfolk): 'Weosa's homestead with All Saints church'. OE *hām*, 'homestead', 'village'. The church dedication distinguishes this village from nearby *Weasenham St Peter*. DB *Wesenham*.

Weaver (river). See WEAVERHAM.

Weaverham (district of Northwich, Cheshire): 'homestead by the (river) Weaver'. OE *hām*, 'homestead', 'village'. The river's name is usually said to mean 'winding stream', from OE *wefer* (related modern English *weave, waver*), but a Celtic origin is also possible, from a word related to modern Welsh *gwefr*, 'amber', referring to the brownish-yellow colour of the water. DB *Wivreham*.

Weaverthorpe (village, N Yorks): 'Víthfari's outlying farmstead'. OS *thorp*, 'outlying farmstead'. The personal name is Scandinavian. DB *Wifretorp*.

Wedmore (village, Somerset): '(place in the) marsh used for hunting'. OE *wǣthe*, 'hunting', + *mōr*, 'moor', 'marsh'. Late 9C *Wethmor*, DB *Wedmore*.

Wednesbury (district, Sandwell): 'stronghold associated with Wōden'. OE *burh*, 'fortified place'. The name implies either that the pagan war god had actually made the place or that he protected it. The town was at one time popularly known as *Wedgebury*. Cp. WANSDYKE, WEDNESFIELD. DB *Wadnesberie*.

Wednesfield (district, Wolverhampton): 'Wōden's open land'. OE *feld*, 'open land' (modern English *field*). The name implies that the pagan war god favoured this land and was its 'patron'. Cp. WANSDYKE, WEDNESBURY. 996 *Wodnesfeld*, DB *Wodnesfelde*.

Weedon Bec (village, Northants): '(place by a) hill with a temple'. OE *wēoh*, 'heathen temple', + *dūn*, 'hill'. The second word of the name refers to the Abbey of Bec-Hellouin, Normandy, which held the manor here in the 12C. The name distinguishes the village from *Weedon Lois*, 9 miles to the south, with St Loy's well, although the addition could be the name of the family who held the manor. The alternative for the last form of the name below refers to the location of the village on Watling Street. 944 *Weodun*, DB *Wedone*, 1379 *Wedon Beke*, 1868 *Weedon-Beck, or Weedon-on-the-Street*.

Weeford (village, Staffs): '(place at the) ford by a heathen temple'. OE *wēoh*, 'heathen temple', + *ford*, 'ford'. Weeford lies on Watling Street (now represented by the A5) at a former ford over Black Brook. DB *Weforde*.

Weekley (village, Northants): 'wood or clearing by a Romano-British settlement'. OE *wīc*, 'Romano-British settlement', + *lēah*, 'wood', 'clearing'. 956 *Wiclea*, DB *Wiclei*.

Week St Mary (village, Cornwall): 'settlement with St Mary's church'. OE *wīc*, 'dwelling', 'settlement'. The dedication of the church here was added to distinguish this Week from PANCRAS-WEEK, Devon, 7 miles to the northeast, and GERMANSWEEK, Devon, 13 miles to the east. DB *Wich*.

Weeley (village, Essex): 'wood or clearing where willow trees grow'. OE *wilig*, 'willow', + *lēah*, 'wood', 'clearing'. 11C *Wilgelea*, DB *Wileia*.

Weeting (village, Norfolk): 'wet place'. OE *wēt*, 'wet', 'damp', + *-ing*, 'place characterized by'. Weeting is near the River Ouse. c.1050 *Watinge*, DB *Wetinge*.

Weeton (hamlet, E Yorks): 'farmstead where willow trees grow'. OE *wīthig*, 'willow' (modern English *withy*), + *tūn*, 'farmstead'. DB *Wideton*. SO ALSO: *Weeton*, Lancs, N Yorks.

Welbeck Abbey (country house, Notts): '(place by the) stream'. OE *wella*, 'stream', + *bæce*, 'stream'. The stream here was apparently originally called *Wella*, to which a further explanatory word also meaning 'stream' was added. (The addition could be OS *bekkr*.) 1179 *Wellebec*.

Welborne (village, Norfolk): '(place by the) stream fed by a spring'. OE *wella*, 'spring', + *burna*, 'stream'. DB *Walebruna*.

Welburn (village, N Yorks): '(place by the) stream fed by a spring'. OE *wella*, 'spring', + *burna*, 'stream'. DB *Wellbrune*.

Welbury (village, N Yorks): '(place on the) hill with a spring'. OE *wella*, 'spring', + *beorg*, 'hill'. DB *Welleberge*.

Welcombe (village, Devon): '(place in the) valley with a spring'. OE *wella*, 'spring', 'stream', + *cumb*, 'valley'. There are springs in the valley here, and 'outside the churchyard gate [of St Nectan's church] is an ancient Holy Well' (*Cassell's Gazetteer of Great Britain and Ireland*, 1898). DB *Walcome*.

Weldon (village, Northants): 'hill with a spring'. OE *wella*, 'spring', + *dūn*, 'hill'. OE *wella* also means 'stream', so that an alternative interpretation is 'hill by a stream'. The village is formally divided into *Great Weldon* and *Little Weldon*. DB *Weledone*.

Welford (village, Northants): '(place at the) ford by the spring'. OE *wella*, 'spring', 'stream', + *ford*, 'ford'. The river here is the Avon. DB *Wellesford*.

Welford (village, W Berks): '(place by the) ford where willow trees grow'. OE *welig*, 'willow', + *ford*, 'ford'. The river here is the Lambourn. 949 *Weligforda*, DB *Waliford*.

Welford-on-Avon (village, Warwicks): '(place at the) ford by the springs on the (river) Avon'. OE *wella*, 'spring', + *ford*, 'ford'. DB *Welleford*, 1177 *Welneford*.

Welham (village, Leics): 'homestead by the stream'. OE *wella*, 'spring', 'stream', + *hām*, 'homestead'. The name could also mean 'Wēola's homestead'. DB *Weleham*.

Well (village, N Yorks): '(place by the) spring'. OE *wella*, 'spring', 'stream'. The name refers to certain springs in the village known as *The Springs*, *St Michael's Well* and *Whitwell*. The second of these is sometimes cited as the original. 'It takes its name from a spring or well near St. Michael's hospital, founded in 1342' (*The National Gazetteer of Great Britain and Ireland*, 1868). DB *Welle*. SO ALSO: *Well*, Lincs.

Welland (village, Worcs): 'white enclosure'. The name is regarded as Celtic in origin, from words related to modern Welsh *gwyn* (feminine *gwen*), 'white', and *llan*, 'church'. 1182 *Wenelond*, 1275 *Wentland*, 1328 *Wenlone*.

Welland (river). See WESTON BY WELLAND.

Wellesbourne (village, Warwicks): '(place by the) stream with a pool'. OE *wēl*, 'pool', + *burna*, 'stream'. The 'pool' is presumably a deep place in the river Bourne here. Wellesbourne is properly divided into *Wellesbourne Hastings*, named after the de Hastanges family who held the manor here in the 14C, and *Wellesbourne Mountford*, where the de Munford family held the manor in the 12C. 840 *Welesburnan*, DB *Waleborne*.

Welling (district, Bexley): 'Welling's or Willing's (estate)'. The Welling or Willing family held land here in the early 14C. The name has been popularly interpreted as 'Well-end', referring to the safe arrival of travellers here after escaping the hazards of highwaymen on SHOOTERS HILL. 1362 *Wellyngs*.

Wellingborough (town, Northants): 'stronghold of Wændel's people'. OE *-inga-*, 'of the people of', + *burh*, 'fortified place'. The precise location of the original 'stronghold' is uncertain. DB *Wedlingeberie*, 1178 *Wendlingburch*.

Wellingham (village, Norfolk): 'homestead of the dwellers by a stream'. OE *wella*, 'spring', 'stream', + *-inga-*, 'of the dwellers at', + *hām*, 'homestead'. The DB form of the name below is clearly corrupt. DB *Walnccham*, c.1190 *Uuelingheham*.

Wellington (town, Somerset): 'estate associated with Wēola'. OE *-ing-*, 'associated with', + *tūn*, 'farmstead', 'estate'. 904 *Weolingtun*, DB *Walintone*. SO ALSO: *Wellington*, Herefords.

Wellington (town, Wrekin): 'estate associated with Wēola'. OE *-ing-*, 'associated with', + *tūn*, 'farmstead', 'estate'. DB *Walitone*, c.1145 *Welintun*.

Wellow (village, Bath & NE Somerset): '(place on the river) Wellow'. The river name is of Celtic origin and may mean 'winding one' or, more distinctively, 'pale blue' (modern Welsh *gwelw*, 'pale'). 1084 *Weleuue*.

Wellow (village, Notts): 'enclosure near a spring'. OE *wella*, 'spring', 'stream', + *haga*, 'enclosure' (related modern English *hedge*). 1207 *Welhag*.

Wells (city, Somerset): '(place at the) springs'. OE *wella*, 'spring'. The name represents OE *wella* in a plural form. The natural springs or wells here were at what is now the east end of the cathedral. The *Anglo-Saxon Chronicle* describes Wells *monasterium* in 766 as '*monasterium quod situm est juxta fontem magnum quem vocitant Wielea*' ('the monastery which is situated by the great spring that they call Wielea'). (The name is mistranscribed and should be *Wiella*.) c.1050 *Willan*, DB *Welle*.

Wells-next-the-Sea (town and port, Norfolk): '(place at the) springs by the sea'. OE *wella*, 'spring'. The second part of the name denotes the maritime location and serves as a commercial lure. The DB form of the name below has French *gu* for English *w*, as for WARMINSTER. DB *Guelle*, 1291 *Wellis*.

Welney (village, Norfolk): '(place on the) river Welle'. OE *ēa*, 'river'. The river here now is the Old Croft, but earlier it was the *Welle*, from OE *wella*, 'stream'. c.14C *Wellenhe*.

Welshampton (village, Shropshire): 'Welsh high farmstead'. OE *hēah*, 'high', + *tūn*, 'farmstead'. The first part of the name was added to the original *Hampton* to refer to the proximity to the village of a detached portion of the Welsh county of Flintshire. DB *Hantone*, 1649 *Welch Hampton*, 1898 *Welsh Hampton*.

Welsh Bicknor. See ENGLISH BICKNOR.

Welsh Frankton. See ENGLISH FRANKTON.

Welsh Newton (village, Herefords): 'Welsh new farmstead'. OE *nīwe*, 'new', + *tūn*, 'farmstead'. Although (just) on the English side of the border, the village was presumably at one time in Welsh hands. Hence the first word of the name. 1341 *Neuton*.

Welshpool (town, Powys): '(place at the) Welsh pool'. OE *welisc*, 'Welsh', + *pōl*, 'pool'. The 'pool' here, at the point where the Lledin brook joins the Severn, is only 3 miles inside the Welsh border. Hence the first word of the name, which seems to imply that there is a contrasting 'English pool', although none has been identified. (The legend persists that 'Welsh' was added to distinguish this town from English POOLE.) The Welsh name of the town is *Y Trallwng*, 'the very wet swamp' (Welsh *y*, 'the', + *tra*, 'very', + *llwng*, 'swamp', 'pool'), referring to the same pool. 1253 *Pola*, 1477 *Walshe Pole*.

Welton (village, E Yorks): 'farmstead by a spring'. OE *wella*, 'spring', 'stream', + *tūn*, 'farmstead'. There are a number of springs, including a 'St Anne's well', in or near the village. DB *Welleton*.

Welwick (village, E Yorks): 'dairy farm near a spring'. OE *wella*, 'spring', 'stream', + *wīc*, 'dwelling', 'dairy farm'. DB *Welwic*.

Welwyn (town, Herts): '(place at the) willow trees'. OE *welig*, 'willow'. The name represents the OE word in a dative plural form (*weligum*). c.945 *Welingum*, DB *Welge*.

Welwyn Garden City (town, Herts). The town was founded in 1920 as the second 'garden city' after the one at Letchworth (1903) and takes its name from WELWYN, immediately north of it. It was developed further after being designated a New Town in 1948.

Wem (town, Shropshire): 'dirty place'. OE *wemm*, 'spot', 'filth'. The name probably refers to the marshy terrain here. DB *Weme*.

Wembdon (village, Somerset): 'hill of the huntsmen'. OE *wǣthe-mann* (from *wǣthe*, 'hunting', + *mann*, 'man'), + *dūn*, 'hill'. DB *Wadmendune*.

Wembley (district, Brent): 'Wemba's woodland clearing'. OE *lēah*, 'wood', 'clearing'. 825 *Wembalea*.

Wembury (coastal village, Devon): '(particular) stronghold'. OE *burh*, 'fortified place'. The first part of the name is of uncertain origin, but may represent OE *wenn*, 'wen', 'tumour-shaped mound'. Late 12C *Wenbiria*.

Wembworthy (village, Devon): 'Wemba's enclosure'. OE *worth*, 'enclosure'. The DB form of the name below has W- miscopied as M-. DB *Mameorda*, 1207 *Wemeworth*.

Wendens Ambo (village, Essex): '(place in the) winding valley'. OE *wende*, 'winding', + *denu*, 'valley'. The second word of the name is Latin *ambo*, 'both', referring to the union of the two parishes of *Great Wenden* and *Little Wenden* in 1662. DB *Wendena*.

Wendlebury (village, Oxon): 'Wǣndla's stronghold'. OE *burh*, 'fortified place'. The DB form of the name below has omitted the *l* of the personal name. DB *Wandesberie*, c.1175 *Wendelberi*.

Wendling (village, Norfolk): '(settlement of) Wǣndel's people'. OE *-ingas*, 'people of'. DB *Wenlinga*.

Wendover (town, Bucks): '(place by the river) Wendover'. The name was originally that of the stream that flows through the town. It is Celtic in origin and means 'white waters', from words related to modern Welsh *gwyn*, 'white', and *dwfr*, 'water' (as for DOVER). c.970 *Wǣndofran*, DB *Wendoure*.

Wendron (hamlet, Cornwall): '(church of) St Wendron'. The church here is dedicated to Wendron, a female saint about whom nothing is known. 1291 *Sancta Wendrona*.

Wendy (village, Cambs): 'island at a river bend'. OE *wende*, 'bend' (related modern English *wind*), + *ēg*, 'island'. Wendy lies in a bend of the North Ditch near its confluence with the river Cam or Rhee. DB *Wandei*.

Wenhaston (village, Suffolk): 'Wynhǣth's farmstead'. OE *tūn*, 'farmstead', 'village'. DB *Wenadestuna*.

Wenlock Edge. See MUCH WENLOCK.

Wennington (district, Havering): 'estate associated with Wynna'. OE *-ing-*, 'associated with', + *tūn*, 'farmstead', 'estate'. c.1100 *Winintune*.

Wennington (village, Lancs): 'farmstead on the (river) Wenning'. OE *tūn*, 'farmstead'. The river has a name meaning 'dark stream' (OE *wann*, 'dark'). DB *Wennigetun*.

Wensley (village, Derbys): 'Wōden's grove'. OE *lēah*, 'wood', 'clearing'. The name denotes a sacred grove dedicated to the pagan war god, whose name has evolved here as for WEDNESBURY. DB *Wodnesleie*.

Wensley (village, N Yorks): 'Wǣndel's woodland clearing'. OE *lēah*, 'wood', 'clearing'. The village, on the river Ure, gave the name of WENSLEYDALE. DB *Wendreslaga*, 1203 *Wendesle*.

Wensleydale (valley, N Yorks): 'valley of Wensley'. OS *dalr*, 'valley'. The valley of the river Ure takes its name from WENSLEY, N Yorks. c.1150 *Wandesleydale*.

Wentbridge (village, Wakefield): '(place by the) bridge over the (river) Went'. OE *brycg*, 'bridge'. The river has a pre-English name of uncertain origin. 1302 *Wentbrig*.

Wentnor (village, Shropshire): 'Wonta's or Wenta's flat-topped ridge'. OE *ofer*, 'flat-topped ridge'. The village stands at the end of the ridge in question, with the church on the tip. DB *Wantenoure*, c.1200 *Wontenoure*, 1251 *Wentenour*.

Wentworth (village, Rotherham): 'Wintra's enclosure'. OE *worth*, 'enclosure'. DB *Wintreuuorde*. SO ALSO: *Wentworth*, Cambs.

Wentworth (residential district, Surrey). The name is that of Elizabeth Wentworth, who in c.1800 built a house called Wentworth House on land that she owned here. The house is now the clubhouse for Wentworth Golf Course.

Wenvoe (village, Vale of Glam): meaning uncertain. The Welsh form of the name is *Gwenfo*. 1153 *Wnfa*, c.1262 *Wenvo*.

Weobley (village, Herefords): 'Wiobba's woodland clearing'. OE *lēah*, 'wood', 'clearing'. DB *Wibelai*.

Wereham (village, Norfolk): 'homestead on the (river) Wigor'. OE *hām*, 'homestead'. The river here, now the Wissey, formerly had a Celtic name meaning 'winding one'. DB *Wigreham*.

Werrington (hamlet, Cornwall): 'estate associated with Wulfræd'. OE *-ing-*, 'associated with', + *tūn*, 'farmstead', 'estate'. DB *Ulvredintone*.

Werrington (district, Peterborough): 'estate associated with Wither'. OE *-ing-*, 'associated with', + *tūn*, 'farmstead', 'estate'. The Anglo-Saxon who gave the name of Werrington may have been the Wither who gave the name of WITTERING, 8 miles to the east. 972 *Witheringtun*, DB *Widerintone*.

Wervin (village, Cheshire): 'fen where cattle are kept'. OE *weorf*, 'draught cattle', + *fenn*, 'fen'. DB *Wivrevene*.

Wesham (village, Lancs): 'western houses'. OE *west*, 'western', + *hūs*, 'house'. The second part of the name represents the dative plural ending of OE *hūs*. The houses were 'west' with regard to nearby Kirkham. 1189 *Westhusum*.

Wessex (historic kingdom, S England): '(territory of the) West Saxons'. OE *west*, 'western', + *Seaxe*, 'Saxons'. The region was the territory of the West Saxons, as distinct from the South Saxons of SUSSEX and the East Saxons of ESSEX. See also MIDDLESEX, SURREY. The name never became that of a county, however, presumably because of the size of the region. Late 9C *West Seaxe*.

Wessington (village, Derbys): 'Wīgstān's farmstead'. OE *tūn*, 'farmstead', 'village'. DB *Wistanestune*.

West Acre. See CASTLE ACRE.

West Adderbury. See EAST ADDERBURY.

West Alvington (village, Devon): 'western estate associated with Ælf'. OE *-ing-*, 'associated with', + *tūn*, 'farmstead', 'estate'. The village is presumably 'west' with regard to ALPHINGTON. DB *Alvintone*.

West Anstey. See EAST ANSTEY.

West Appleton. See EAST APPLETON.

West Ashling. See EAST ASHLING.

West Auckland. See BISHOP AUCKLAND.

West Ayton (village, N Yorks): 'western farmstead on a river'. OE *ēa*, 'river', + *tūn*, 'farmstead'. OE *ēa* has been influenced by equivalent OS *á*. West Ayton and *East Ayton* stand opposite each other on the river Derwent. DB *Atune*.

West Bagborough (village, Somerset): 'western (place called) Bacga's hill'. OE *beorg*, 'hill'. The first word of the name distinguishes the village from nearby *East Bagborough*. 904 *Bacganbeorg*, DB *Bageberge*.

West Barming. See EAST BARMING.

West Barsham. See EAST BARSHAM.

West Beckham. See EAST BECKHAM.

West Bergholt. See EAST BERGHOLT.

West Berkshire. See BERKSHIRE.

West Bexington (coastal village, Dorset): 'western farmstead where box trees grow'. OE *byxen*, 'growing with box', + *tūn*, 'farmstead', 'village'. The first word of the name distinguishes the village from what is now nearby *East Bexington Farm*. DB *Bessintone*.

West Bilney. See EAST BILNEY.

West Blatchington. See EAST BLATCHINGTON.

Westbourne (village, W Sussex): '(place by the) western stream'. OE *burna*, 'stream'. The first part of the name was apparently added to distinguish this place from EASTBOURNE (E Sussex) almost 60 miles to the east. The village was known locally as *Bourne* until relatively recently. DB *Burne*, 1302 *Westbourne*, 1868 *West Bourne*.

West Bretton. See MONK BRETTON.

West Bridgford (town, Notts): 'western (place at the) ford by the bridge'. OE *brycg*, 'bridge', + *ford*, 'ford'. The name refers to both a ford and a bridge over the river Trent here. The first word of the name distinguishes this

Bridgford from *East Bridgford*, 7 miles to the northeast. The Roman town at East Bridgford was *Margidunum*, 'fort on the border', the latter being marked by the Trent. DB *Brigeforde*, 1572 *Westburgeforde*.

West Bromwich (town, Sandwell): 'western farm where broom grows'. OE *brōm*, 'broom', + *wīc*, 'dwelling', 'specialized farm'. The first word of the name distinguishes this Bromwich from CASTLE BROMWICH, 10 miles to the east. DB *Bromwic*, 1322 *Westbromwich*.

Westbury (town, Wilts): 'western fortified place'. OE *west*, 'western', + *burh*, 'fortified place'. The 'fortified place' is the Iron Age camp on the hill above Westbury where a white horse is carved out of the chalk. The camp was probably regarded as the 'westernmost' on Salisbury Plain. DB *Westberie*.

Westbury (village, Shropshire): 'western fortified place'. OE *west*, 'western', + *burh*, 'fortified place'. The village is presumably 'west' with regard to PONTESBURY, 4 miles to the southeast. DB *Wesberie*.

Westbury-on-Severn (village, Glos): 'western stronghold on the (river) Severn'. OE *west*, 'western', + *burh*, 'fortified place'. The village is west of Gloucester and the river Severn (see SEVERN STOKE) on the Roman road to Wales. The second part of the name distinguishes this Westbury from WESTBURY ON TRYM, 26 miles to the south. DB *Wesberie*.

Westbury on Trym (district, Bristol): 'western stronghold on the (river) Trym'. OE *west*, 'western', + *burh*, 'fortified place'. The identity of the corresponding eastern stronghold is uncertain, although the place lies west of the Roman road from Gloucester to Bristol. The addition of the river name (perhaps from OE *trum*, 'firm', 'strong') distinguishes this Westbury from WESTBURY-ON-SEVERN. The DB form of the name below may have resulted from a mishearing. 791 *Westbyrig*, DB *Hvesberie*.

West Butterwick. See EAST BUTTERWICK.

Westby (hamlet, Lancs): 'western farmstead'. OS *vestr*, 'western', + *bý*, 'farmstead'. The hamlet lies to the west of Wrea Green. DB *Westbi*.

West Camel. See QUEEN CAMEL.

West Chaldon. See CHALDON HERRING.

West Challow. See EAST CHALLOW.

West Chelborough. See EAST CHELBOR-OUGH.

West Chiltington (village, W Sussex): 'western farmstead by Cilte'. OE *-ing-*, 'associated with', + *tūn*, 'farmstead'. *Cilte* is a conjectural

Celtic hill name meaning simply 'hill slope' (as for the CHILTERN HILLS). The first word of the name distinguishes this Chiltington from the smaller *East Chiltington*, E Sussex, over 20 miles to the east. 969 *Cillingtun*, DB *Cilletone*.

West Chinnock. See EAST CHINNOCK.

West Clandon. See EAST CLANDON.

Westcliff-on-Sea (district of Southend-on-Sea, Southend): '(place by the) western cliffs by the sea'. The cliffs in question lie to the west of old Southend, while the addition to the name repeats that of its host town. (The 'sea' for both is actually the Thames estuary.) The name *Westcliff* was generally adopted in the 1880s. 'At the beginning of this Century some local landowners and estate agents sought to rename Westcliff "Kensington-on-Sea"' (*Our Town: An Encyclopaedia of Southend-on-Sea and District*, 1947). 1843 *Cliff*.

West Coker. See EAST COKER.

West Compton. See COMPTON ABBAS.

Westcote (village, Glos): 'western cottage'. OE *west*, 'western', + *cot*, 'cottage'. 1315 *Westcote*.

Westcott (village, Surrey): 'western cottages'. OE *west*, 'western', + *cot*, 'cottage'. The village lies west of Dorking. DB *Westcote*.

West Cottingwith. See EAST COTTINGWITH.

West Cranmore (village, Somerset): 'western (place by the) pool where cranes are seen'. OE *cran*, 'crane', + *mere*, 'pool'. The first word of the name distinguishes the village from nearby *East Cranmore*. The DB form of the name below is corrupt. 10C *Cranemere*, DB *Crenemelle*.

West Dean (village, Wilts): '(place in the) western valley'. OE *denu*, 'valley'. The village is 'west' in relation to *East Dean*, just across the border in Hampshire. Both are in the valley of the river Dun, a tributary of the Test. DB *Dene*.

West Dean (W Sussex). See EAST DEAN.

Westdean. See EASTDEAN.

West Deeping. See MARKET DEEPING.

West Derby (district, Liverpool): 'western farmstead where deer are kept'. OS *djúr*, 'deer', + *bý*, 'farmstead'. The first word of the name was presumably added to distinguish this Derby from DERBY, although the latter is as much as 70 miles to the southeast. DB *Derbei*, 1177 *Westderbi*.

West Dereham. See EAST DEREHAM.

West Down (village, Devon): 'western (place by the) hill'. OE *dūn*, 'hill'. The first word of the name distinguishes the village from the hamlet of *East Down*, 5 miles to the east. DB *Duna*, 1273 *Westdone*.

West Drayton (district, Hillingdon): 'western farmstead by a portage'. (See MARKET DRAYTON.) West Drayton is on the river Colne. The first word of the name distinguishes this Drayton from *Drayton Green*, Ealing, 7 miles to the east. 939 *Drægton*, DB *Draitone*, 1465 *West-drayton*.

West Drayton (Notts). See EAST DRAYTON.

West Ella. See KIRK ELLA.

West End (suburb of Southampton, Hants): '(place in the) wilderness'. OE *wēstenne*, 'waste', 'wilderness'. West End is not to the west of any place of significance (it is actually east of Southampton), so the above meaning has been proposed for it, the 'wilderness' perhaps originally being virgin woodland here. 1607 *Westend*.

Westerdale (village, N Yorks): '(place in the) more westerly valley'. OS *vestari*, 'more westerly', + *dalr*, 'valley'. Westerdale (the valley) is one of the western valleys of Eskdale. c.1165 *Westerdale*.

Westerfield (village, Suffolk): 'western open land'. OE *wester*, 'western', + *feld*, 'open land' (modern English *field*). The name could also mean 'more westerly open land' (OE *westerra*, 'more westerly', + *feld*). Westerfield may have been regarded as 'west' with respect to WALDRINGFIELD, 7 miles to the east. DB *Westrefelda*.

Westergate. See EASTERGATE.

Westerham (town, Kent): 'western homestead'. OE *wester*, 'western', + *hām*, 'homestead'. Westerham is in the extreme west of the county, near the Surrey border. The DB form of the name below shows the Norman clerk's way of rendering English *W-*. 871 *Westarham*, DB *Oistreham*. (The French town and port of *Ouistreham*, on the Channel coast at the mouth of the river Orne, has a similar Germanic name, also recorded in 1086 as *Oistreham*, but meaning 'eastern homestead', as against *Étreham*, 'western homestead', some 23 miles to the west, recorded in 1350 as *Oesterham*.)

Westerleigh (village, S Glos): 'more westerly woodland clearing'. OE *westerra*, 'more westerly', + *lēah*, 'wood', 'clearing'. 1176 *Westerlega*.

Western Isles (island group, NW Scotland): 'western islands'. The name is that of the Outer Hebrides, the most westerly island chain in Scotland. The Gaelic name of the islands is *Na h-Eileanan an Iar*, 'The Islands of the West', or in formal use, as for the unitary authority, *Eilean Siar*, 'Western Isles'.

West Farleigh. See EAST FARLEIGH.

West Farndon. See EAST FARNDON.

West Felton (village, Shropshire): 'western farmstead in open country'. OE *feld*, 'open land' (modern English *field*), + *tūn*, 'farmstead'. The village is 'west' with respect to *Felton Butler*, 7 miles to the southeast, where the manor was held by the Buteler family in the 12C. DB *Feltone*.

Westfield (village, E Sussex): 'western open land'. OE *west*, 'western', + *feld*, 'open land' (modern English *field*). The place may have been 'west' in relation to Guestling. The second part of the DB form of the name below has been influenced by *wella*, 'spring'. DB *Westewelle*, c.1115 *Westefelde*. SO ALSO: *Westfield*, Norfolk.

West Firle (village, E Sussex): 'western place where oak trees grow'. OE *fierel*, 'place growing with oaks'. There is no longer an 'East Firle' but it was probably where nearby Charleston is today. The name is also found for *Firle Beacon*, on the South Downs nearby. DB *Ferle*.

Westgate-on-Sea (district of Margate, Kent): 'western gate by the sea'. OE *west*, 'western', + *geat*, 'gate'. Westgate is to the west of Margate, while 'gate' refers to a gap in the cliffs. The second part of the name serves mainly to tempt visitors but also distinguishes the place from Margate. 1168 *Westgata*.

West Grafton. See EAST GRAFTON.

West Grimstead. See EAST GRIMSTEAD.

West Grinstead. See EAST GRINSTEAD.

West Haddlesey. See CHAPEL HADDLESEY.

West Haddon (village, Northants): 'western (place by the) hill where heather grows'. OE *hǣth*, 'heath', 'heather', + *dūn*, 'hill'. The first word of the name distinguishes the village from *East Haddon*, 3 miles to the southeast. DB *Hadone*, 12C *Westhaddon*.

West Hagbourne. See EAST HAGBOURNE.

Westhall (hamlet, Suffolk): 'western corner of land'. OE *west*, 'western', + *halh*, 'nook', 'corner of land'. 1139 *Westhala*.

West Hallam. See KIRK HALLAM.

West Halton. See EAST HALTON.

West Ham (district, Newham): 'western riverside land'. OE *west*, 'western', + *hamm*, 'enclosure', 'riverside pasture'. West Ham, beside the Thames, is the counterpart to nearby EAST HAM, and their joint name contributed to that of the borough of NEWHAM. 958 *Hamme*, DB *Hame*, 1186 *Westhamma*.

Westham (village, E Sussex): '(place on the) western promontory'. OE *west*, 'western', + *hamm*, 'enclosure', 'promontory'. The place is 'west' in relation to Pevensey. 1222 *Westham*.

Westhampnett (village, W Sussex): 'western little high farmstead'. OE *west*, 'western', + *hēah*, 'high', + *tūn*, 'farmstead', + OF diminutive suffix *-ette*. The place was originally a 'high farmstead', then a 'little high farmstead', then finally a 'western little high farmstead', the latter in relation to nearby *East Hampnett*. Cp. HAMPNETT. DB *Hentone*, c.1187 *Hamptoneta*, 1279 *Westhamptonette*.

West Hanney. See EAST HANNEY.

West Hanningfield. See EAST HANNING-FIELD.

West Harling. See EAST HARLING.

West Harlsey. See EAST HARLSEY.

West Harnham (district of Salisbury, Wilts): 'western enclosure where hares are seen'. OE *hara*, 'hare', + *hamm*, 'enclosure'. The first part of the name represents OE *harena*, the genitive plural form of *hara*. The first word distinguishes this Harnham from nearby *East Harnham*. 1115 *Harnham*.

West Harptree (village, Bath & NE Somerset): 'western tree by a highway'. OE *here-pæth*, 'highway' (from *here*, 'army', + *pæth*, 'path'), + *trēow*, 'tree'. The first word of the name distinguishes the village from nearby *East Harptree*. DB *Harpetreu*.

Westhead (hamlet, Lancs): '(place by the) western headland'. OE *west*, 'western', + *hēafod*, 'headland'. The reference is to the western part of the headland at the end of the ridge leading up to Scarth Hill. c.1190 *Westhefd*.

West Hendred. See EAST HENDRED.

West Herrington. See EAST HERRINGTON.

West Heslerton (village, N Yorks): 'western farmstead where hazels grow'. OE *hæsler*, 'hazel', + *tūn*, 'farmstead'. The first word of the name distinguishes the village from nearby *East Heslerton*. DB *Heslerton*.

Westhide (village, Herefords): 'western hide'. OE *west*, 'western', + *hīd*, 'hide'. A hide was an area of land big enough for a single family and its dependants. DB *Hide*, 1242 *Westhyde*.

West Hoathly. See EAST HOATHLY.

West Horndon. See HORNDON ON THE HILL.

Westhorpe (village, Suffolk): 'western outlying farmstead'. OS *vestr*, 'western', + *thorp*, 'outlying farmstead'. DB *Westtorp*.

West Horrington. See EAST HORRINGTON.

West Horsley. See EAST HORSLEY.

Westhoughton (town, Bolton): 'western farmstead in a corner of land'. OE *west*, 'western', + *halh*, 'nook', 'corner of land', + *tūn*, 'farmstead'. 'West' was presumably added to distinguish this Houghton from the now lost name of *Little Houghton*, near Eccles. c.1210 *Halcton*, c.1240 *Westhalcton*.

West Ilsley. See EAST ILSLEY.

West Itchenor (village, W Sussex): 'western (place called) Icca's shore'. OE *ōra*, 'shore'. The first word of the name distinguishes the village, on Chichester Channel, from the much smaller *East Itchenor*. 683 *Iccannore*, DB *Icenore*.

West Keal. See EAST KEAL.

West Kennett (village, Wilts): 'western (place on the river) Kennet'. The river has a Celtic name of uncertain meaning. The first word of the name distinguishes the village from nearby *East Kennett*. The river name is now in use for the local council district. DB *Chenete*.

West Kilbride (town, N Ayrs): 'western (place by) St Brigid's church'. The first word of name distinguishes this place from EAST KIL-BRIDE, although there are almost 30 miles between them.

West Kingsdown (village, Kent): 'western (place on the) king's hill'. OE *cyning*, 'king', + *dūn*, 'hill'. The village is presumably 'west' of the nearby hill called *Eastdown*. 1199 *Kingesdon*.

West Kington (village, Wilts): 'western royal manor'. OE *cyning*, 'king', + *tūn*, 'farmstead', 'manor'. The first word of the name distinguishes the village from KINGTON ST MICHAEL, 6 miles to the east. 1195 *Westkinton*.

West Kirby (resort town, Wirral): 'western village with a church'. OE *west*, 'western', + OS *kirkju-bý*, 'village with a church' (cp. KIRKBY). The first word of the name distinguishes this Kirkby (or Kirby) from *Kirkby* in Wallasey on the east side of the Wirral peninsula. 1081 *Cherchebia*, 1287 *Westkerkeby*.

West Knapton (hamlet, N Yorks): 'western farmstead of the servant'. OE *cnapa*, 'child', 'youth', 'servant' (related modern English *knave*), + *tūn*, 'farmstead'. The first word of the name distinguishes the place from nearby *East Knapton*. DB *Cnapetone*.

West Knighton (village, Dorset): 'western farmstead of the young retainers'. OE *cniht*, 'thane', 'retainer' (modern English *knight*), + *tūn*, 'farmstead'. The first word of the name distinguishes this Knighton from the hamlet of *East Knighton*, 5 miles to the east. DB *Chenistetone*.

West Knoyle. See EAST KNOYLE.

West Kyloe. See EAST KYLOE.

West Lambrook. See EAST LAMBROOK.

West Lavington (village, W Sussex): 'western estate associated with Lāfa'. OE *-ing-*, 'associated with', + *tūn*, 'farmstead', 'estate'. The first word of the name distinguishes the village from the hamlet of *East Lavington*, 4 miles to the southeast. DB *Levitone*.

West Lavington (Wilts). See MARKET LAVINGTON.

West Layton. See EAST LAYTON.

West Leake. See EAST LEAKE.

Westleigh (village, Devon): 'westerly wood or clearing'. OE *west*, 'western', + *lēah*, 'wood', 'clearing'. The village is 1 mile west of the hamlet of *Eastleigh*. DB *Weslega*.

Westleton (village, Suffolk): 'Westlithi's farmstead'. OE *tūn*, 'farmstead'. The personal name is Scandinavian. DB *Westledestuna*.

West Lexham. See EAST LEXHAM.

Westley (village, Suffolk): 'western wood or clearing'. OE *west*, 'western', + *lēah*, 'wood', 'clearing'. The village is 4 miles west of Bury St Edmunds. DB *Westlea*.

Westley Waterless (village, Cambs): 'western wood or clearing by the wet clearings'. OE *west*, 'western', + *lēah*, 'wood', 'clearing', + *wæter*, 'water', + *lēas*, 'clearings'. Westley Waterless is west of Dullingham Ley and southwest of Stetchworth Ley. The second word of the name emphasizes the watery nature of the locality. *c.*1045 *Westle*, DB *Weslai*, 1285 *Westle Waterles*.

West Lilling (hamlet, N Yorks): 'western (settlement of) Lilla's people'. OE *-ingas*, 'people of'. The first word of the name distinguishes the place from nearby *East Lilling*. DB *Lilinge*.

Westlinton. See KIRKLINTON.

West Linton. See EAST LINTON.

West Littleton (village, S Glos): 'western little farmstead'. OE *lȳtel*, 'little', + *tūn*, 'farmstead'. The farmstead was 'little' by comparison with Tormarton and is 'west' in relation to LITTLETON DREW, Wilts, 6 miles to the northeast. 1221 *Litlinton*.

West Lockinge. See EAST LOCKINGE.

West Lulworth. See EAST LULWORTH.

West Lydford. See EAST LYDFORD.

West Malling (village, Kent): 'western (settlement of) Mealla's people'. OE *-ingas*, 'people of'. The first word of the name distinguishes the village from the smaller *East Malling* nearby. The DB form of the name below is garbled. 942 *Meallingas*, DB *Mellingetes*.

West Malvern. See MALVERN HILLS.

West Marden. See EAST MARDEN.

West Markham. See EAST MARKHAM.

West Meon (village, Hants): 'western (place on the river) Meon'. The river has a Celtic name perhaps meaning 'swift one'. The village is 'west' with regard to *East Meon*. See also MEONSTOKE. *c.*880 *Meone*, DB *Mene*.

West Mersea (town, Essex): 'western (place in) Mersea'. The town is at the western end of MERSEA ISLAND, its name contrasting with the hamlet of *East Mersea*, to the east of it. Early 10C *Meresig*, DB *Meresai*.

Westmeston (village, E Sussex): 'most westerly farmstead'. OE *westmest*, 'westernmost', + *tūn*, 'farmstead'. The farm may have been so named by the people of Lewes with regard to Plumpton. *c.*765 *Westmæstun*, DB *Wesmestun*.

Westmill (village, Herts): 'western mill'. OE *west*, 'western', + *myln*, 'mill'. There was presumably at one time an 'eastern mill' the other side of the stream here. DB *Westmele*.

Westminster (borough, Greater London): 'western monastery'. OE *west*, 'western', + *mynster*, 'monastery'. The name relates directly to Westminster Abbey, which was built in the 13C on the site of a pre-10C monastery that lay to the west of (the City of) London. *c.*975 *Westmynster*.

West Molesey. See EAST MOLESEY.

West Monkton (village, Somerset): 'western farmstead of the monks'. OE *munuc*, 'monk', + *tūn*, 'farmstead'. DB *Monechetone*.

West Moors (village, Dorset): 'western (place by) marshy ground'. OE *mōr*, 'moor', 'marsh'. The first word of the name distinguishes the place from *East Moors Farm*, across Moors River. 1310 *La More*, 1407 *Moures*.

Westmorland (historic county, NW England): 'district of the people living west of the moors'. OE *west*, 'western', + *mōr*, 'moor', + *-inga-*, 'of the dwellers at', + *land*, 'district', 'land'. The moors referred to are those west of the North Yorkshire Pennines. The original *-ing-* has disappeared from the name. *c.*1150 *Westmoringaland*.

West Ness. See EAST NESS.

Westnewton (village, Cumbria): 'western new farmstead'. OE *nīwe*, 'new', + *tūn*, 'farmstead'. According to William Hutchinson's *The History of the County of Cumberland* (1794), Westnewton is 'so called, it is probable, in contradistinction to *Newton Arlosh*, in the parish of *Holme Cultram*, which lies to the *east*'. *c.*1187 *Neutona*, 1777 *West Newton*.

Weston (village, Herts): 'western farmstead'. OE *west*, 'western', + *tūn*, 'farmstead'. The location of any corresponding 'eastern farmstead' is unknown. DB *Westone*. SO ALSO: *Weston*, Lincs.

Westonbirt (hamlet, Glos): 'le Bret's (estate at the) western farmstead'. OE *west*, 'western', + *tūn*, 'farmstead'. The farmstead is 'west' with regard to Tetbury. The le Bret family held the manor here in the 13C. DB *Weston*, 1322 *Weston Brut*.

Weston by Welland (village, Northants): 'western farmstead by the (river) Welland'. OE *west*, 'western', + *tūn*, 'farmstead', 'village'. The river has a Celtic or pre-Celtic name of uncertain origin. A meaning 'good stream' has been tentatively proposed. DB *Westone*, 1609 *Weston by Wolland*.

Weston Favell (district of Northampton, Northants): 'Fauvell's (estate at the) western farmstead'. OE *west*, 'western', + *tūn*, 'farmstead'. The farmstead is 'west' with regard to Little Billing. The Fauvell family held the manor here in the 13C. DB *Westone*, 1376 *Weston Fauvel*.

Weston-on-the-Green (village, Oxon): 'western farmstead on the green'. OE *west*, 'western', + *tūn*, 'farmstead', 'village'. The second part of the name refers to the village green. DB *Westone*.

Weston Rhyn (village, Shropshire): 'western farmstead near Rhyn'. OE *west*, 'western', + *tūn*, 'farmstead'. The nearby settlement *Rhyn* has a name representing Welsh *rhyn*, 'peak'. DB *Westone*, 1302 *Weston Ryn*.

Weston-sub-Edge (village, Glos): 'western farmstead under the edge'. OE *west*, 'western', + *tūn*, 'farmstead', + Latin *sub*, 'under', + OE *ecg*, 'edge'. The second part of the name refers to the location of the village below the steep escarpment at the western end of the Cotswolds. The farmstead itself was 'west' with regard to nearby *Aston Subedge*. DB *Westone*, 1255 *Weston sub Egge*.

Weston-super-Mare (resort town, N Somerset): 'western farmstead on the sea'. OE *west*, 'western', + *tūn*, 'farmstead', + Latin *super*, 'on', + *mare*, 'sea'. The second part of the name distinguishes this Weston from WESTONZOYLAND, 16 miles to the south. c.1230 *Weston*, 1349 *Weston super Mare*.

Weston Turville (village, Bucks): 'de Turville's western farmstead'. OE *west*, 'western', + *tūn*, 'farmstead'. The de Turville family held the manor here in the 12C. The farmstead was 'west' with regard to nearby ASTON CLINTON. DB *Westone*, 1302 *Westone Turvile*.

Weston under Lizard (village, Staffs): 'western farmstead under Lizard Hill'. OE *west*, 'western', + *tūn*, 'farmstead'. The village, in the west of the county, is overlooked by *Lizard Hill*, Shropshire, whose name may represent Welsh *llys*, 'court', + *garth*, 'hill'. 1081 *Guestona*, DB *Westone*.

Weston under Penyard (village, Herefords): 'western farmstead under Penyard'. OE *west*, 'western', + *tūn*, 'farmstead'. The village lies below *Penyard Hill*, whose name is of the same origin as *Pennard* (see WEST PENNARD). The Roman settlement here was *Ariconium*, of uncertain meaning. DB *Westune*.

Weston under Wetherley (village, Warwicks): 'western farmstead near Wetherley'. OE *west*, 'western', + *tūn*, 'farmstead'. *Wetherley* is *Waverley Wood*, with a name perhaps meaning 'wood for hunting' (*wǣthe*, 'hunting', + *lēah*, 'wood'). DB *Westone*, 1327 *Weston juxta Wetheleye*.

Weston upon Trent. See ASTON UPON TRENT.

Westonzoyland (village, Somerset): 'western manor in the Sowi estate'. OE *west*, 'western', + *tūn*, 'farmstead', 'manor', + *land*, 'land', 'estate'. The first part of the name distinguishes the village from nearby MIDDLEZOY. DB *Sowi*, c.1245 *Westsowi*.

West Orchard (village, Dorset): 'western (place) by the wood'. The name is Celtic, from words corresponding to modern Welsh *ar*, 'on', 'over', and *coed*, 'wood'. (The common Welsh place name *Argoed* corresponds exactly to *Orchard* here.) The present form of the name has been influenced by *orchard*. The first word of the name distinguishes the village from nearby *East Orchard*. 939 *Archet*.

West Overton (village, Wilts): 'western higher farmstead'. OE *uferra*, 'higher', + *tūn*, 'farmstead'. Former *East Overton* has now been subsumed into West Overton, although the distinguishing first word of the name remains. 939 *Uferantune*, DB *Ovretone*.

Westow (village, N Yorks): 'holy place of the women'. OE *wīf*, 'woman' (modern English *wife*), + *stōw*, 'holy place'. The name could also mean 'Wīfe's holy place', with a female personal name. The reason for the name is uncertain. 12C *Wiuestou*.

West Parley (village, Dorset): 'western wood or clearing where pears grow'. OE *peru*, 'pear', + *lēah*, 'wood', 'clearing'. The first word of the name distinguishes the village from the smaller *East Parley* nearby. DB *Perlai*.

West Pennard (village, Somerset): 'western (place by a) hill'. The main name is of Celtic origin, from words corresponding to modern Welsh *pen*, 'head', 'top', and either *garth*, 'ridge', or *ardd*, 'high'. The first word distinguishes the village from *East Pennard*, 3 miles to the east. The DB form of the name below has added OE *mynster*, 'monastery', 'large church'. 681 *Pengerd*, DB *Pennarminstre*.

West Poringland. See EAST PORINGLAND.

West Portlemouth. See EAST PORTLE-MOUTH.

West Preston. See EAST PRESTON.

West Putford. See EAST PUTFORD.

West Quantoxhead. See EAST QUANTOX-HEAD.

West Rainton. See EAST RAINTON.

West Rasen. See MARKET RASEN.

Westray (island, Orkney): 'western island'. OS *vestr*, 'western', + *ey*, 'island'. Westray is the westernmost of the islands in northern Orkney (north of Westray Sound and Stronsay Firth). *c*.1260 *Vesturey*.

West Raynham. See EAST RAYNHAM.

West Riding. See EAST RIDING.

West Rounton. See EAST ROUNTON.

West Rudham. See EAST RUDHAM.

West Runton (resort village, Norfolk): 'western (place called) Rūna's or Rúni's farmstead'. OE *tūn*, 'farmstead'. The personal names are respectively OE and Scandinavian. The first word of the name distinguishes the village from nearby *East Runton*. DB *Runetune*.

West Scrafton (village, N Yorks): 'western farmstead by a hollow' OE *scræf*, 'cave', 'hollow', + *tūn*, 'farmstead'. The first word of the name distinguishes the village from nearby *East Scrafton*. DB *Scraftun*.

West Shefford. See GREAT SHEFFORD.

West Somerton. See WINTERTON-ON-SEA.

West Stafford (village, Dorset): 'western (place by the) stony ford'. OE *stān*, 'stone', + *ford*, 'ford'. The ford in question would have crossed the river Frome here. The first word of the name distinguishes the village from a now lost *East Stafford* nearby. DB *Stanford*.

West Stockwith (village, Notts): 'western landing place made of logs'. OE *stocc*, 'tree trunk', 'log', + *hýth*, 'landing place'. The village is on the river Trent, opposite *East Stockwith*, Lincs. 12C *Stochithe*.

West Stour (village, Dorset): 'western (place on the river) Stour'. For the river name, see STOURBRIDGE. The first word of the name distinguishes the village from nearby *East Stour*. DB *Sture*.

West Stourmouth. See EAST STOURMOUTH.

West Tanfield (village, N Yorks): 'western (place on) open land where shoots grow'. OE *tān*, 'twig', 'sprout', 'shoot', + *feld*, 'open land' (modern English *field*). The first word of the name distinguishes the village from nearby *East Tanfield*. DB *Tanefeld*.

West Tarring (district of Worthing, W Sussex): 'western (settlement of) Teorra's people'. OE -*ingas*, 'people of'. The first word of the name distinguishes the village from TARRING NEV-ILLE, also known as *East Tarring*, almost 30 miles to the east. 946 *Teorringas*, DB *Terringes*, 1868 *Tarring, or West Tarring*.

West Thirston. See EAST THIRSTON.

West Thorney (village, W Sussex): 'western island where thorn bushes grow'. OE *thorn*, 'thorn bush', + *ēg*, 'island'. West Thorney, on eastern THORNEY ISLAND, was 'west' in relation to *East Thorney*, now represented by *Thorney Farm*, West Wittering, across Chichester Harbour. 11C *Thorneg*, DB *Tornei*.

West Tisted. See EAST TISTED.

West Tytherton. See EAST TYTHERTON.

West Walton (village, Norfolk): 'western farmstead by the bank'. OE *wall*, 'wall', 'bank', + *tūn*, 'farmstead'. West Walton is by the former Roman sea wall here near the Wash. The first word of the name distinguishes the village from *East Walton*, 17 miles to the east. DB *Waltuna*.

Westward (hamlet, Cumbria): 'western division'. ME *west*, 'western', + *warde*, 'ward', 'division'. The name relates to the west ward or western division of Inglewood Forest. 1354 *Le Westwarde*.

Westward Ho! (resort village, Devon). The resort developed from the 1870s and was named for Charles Kingsley's novel *Westward Ho!* (1855), largely set in this region. Westward Ho! is actually on the west Devon coast, and the name aptly acts as a draw to visitors ('westward ho! to Westward Ho!').

Westwell (village, Kent): '(place by the) western spring'. OE *west*, 'western', + *wella*, 'spring', 'stream'. The name contrasts with that of *East-well*, 3 miles to the east. DB *Welle*, 1226 *Westwell*. SO ALSO: *Westwell*, Oxon.

West Wellow (village, Hants): 'western (place on the river) Wellow'. The river here now is the

Blackwater, but its earlier name is the same as that behind WELLOW. The first word of the name distinguishes the village from the smaller *East Wellow*. *c*.880 *Welewe*, DB *Weleve*.

Westwick (village, Cambs): 'western farm'. OE *west*, 'western', + *wīc*, 'dwelling', 'specialized farm'. DB *Westuuiche*. SO ALSO: *Westwick*, Durham, Norfolk.

West Wickham (district, Bromley): 'western homestead by a Romano-British settlement'. The main word of the name represents OE *wīc-hām* (*wīc*, 'special site', + *hām*, 'homestead'), used to denote a place associated with a *vicus*, or Romano-British settlement. West Wickham lies on the Roman road from the South Downs area to London, and Roman pottery has been found here. The first word of the name distinguishes this Wickham from *East Wickham*, Bexley. 973 *Wichamm*, DB *Wicheham*, 1610 *W. Wickham*.

West Winch. See EAST WINCH.

West Wittering (village, W Sussex): 'western (settlement of) Wihthere's people'. OE *-ingas*, 'people of'. The first word of the name distinguishes this Wittering from the coastal resort of *East Wittering*. The DB form of the name below is corrupt. 683 *Wihttringes*, DB *Westringes*.

West Witton. See EAST WITTON.

Westwood (village, Wilts): '(place by the) western wood'. OE *west*, 'western', + *wudu*, 'wood'. The wood was in the southwestern part of Selwood Forest. 987 *Westwuda*, DB *Westwode*.

West Worlington. See EAST WORLINGTON.

West Wratting. See GREAT WRATTING.

West Wycombe. See HIGH WYCOMBE.

Wetheral (village, Cumbria): 'corner of land where wethers are kept'. OE *wether*, 'wether' (castrated ram), + *halh*, 'nook', 'corner of land'. *c*.1100 *Wetherhala*.

Wetherby (town, Leeds): 'farmstead for wethers'. OS *vethr*, 'wether' (castrated ram), + *bý*, 'farmstead'. DB *Wedrebi*.

Wetherden (village, Suffolk): 'valley where wethers are kept'. OE *wether*, 'wether' (castrated ram), + *denu*, 'valley'. DB *Wederdena*.

Wetheringsett (village, Suffolk): 'fold of the people at Wetherden'. OE *-inga-*, 'of the people of', + *set*, 'fold'. Wetheringsett is 12 miles east of WETHERDEN. *c*.1035 *Weddreringesete*, DB *Wederingaseta*.

Wethersfield (village, Essex): 'Wihthere's or Wether's open land'. OE *feld*, 'open land' (modern English *field*). DB *Witheresfelda*.

Wettenhall (village, Cheshire): '(place in the) wet corner of land'. OE *wēt*, 'wet', + *halh*, 'nook', 'corner of land'. The first part of the name represents OE *wētan*, the dative form of *wēt*. DB *Watenhale*.

Wetwang (village, E Yorks): 'field for the trial of a legal action'. OS *véett-vangr* (from *vétti*, 'witness', 'evidence', + *vangr*, 'garden', 'field'). DB *Wetuuangha*.

Wexcombe (hamlet, Wilts): '(place in the) valley where wax is found'. OE *weax*, 'wax', + *cumb*, 'valley'. The wax would have been from bees here. 1167 *Wexcumbe*.

Wey (river). See WEYBRIDGE.

Weybourne (village, Norfolk): '(place by the) stream'. OE *burna*, 'stream'. The first part of the name is of uncertain origin. It may represent a former name of the stream here, from a pre-English word meaning 'water', or from OE *wagu*, 'quagmire', or *wær*, 'weir'. DB *Wabrune*.

Weybread (village, Suffolk): 'broad stretch of land by a road'. OE *weg*, 'way', 'road', + *brǣdu*, 'breadth'. There was a Roman road here, hence the name of the nearby hamlet of *Weybread Street*. DB *Weibrada*.

Weybridge (town, Surrey): 'bridge over the (river) Wey'. OE *brycg*, 'bridge'. The river has a pre-English name of unknown meaning. DB *Webruge*.

Weyhill (village, Hants): '(place at the) hill with a temple'. OE *wēoh*, 'idol', 'heathen temple', + modern English *hill*. The second part of the name is first recorded only in 1571. *c*.1270 *La Wou*.

Weymouth (resort town and port, Dorset): 'mouth of the (river) Wey'. OE *mūtha*, 'mouth'. The river name has an identical origin to that of the Wey that gave the name of WEYBRIDGE. 934 *Waimuthe*.

Whaddon (village, Bucks): '(place by the) hill where wheat is grown'. OE *hwǣte*, 'wheat', + *dūn*, 'hill'. 966 *Hwǣtædun*, DB *Wadone*. SO ALSO: *Whaddon*, Cambs, Wilts (near Melksham).

Whaddon (hamlet, Wilts): '(place in the) valley where wheat is grown'. OE *hwǣte*, 'wheat', + *denu*, 'valley'. This is Whaddon near Salisbury. DB *Watedene*.

Whale (hamlet, Cumbria): '(place by the) isolated round hill'. OS *hváll*, 'hill'. The hill in question is the prominent one between Whale and Lowther. 1178 *Vwal*.

Whaley Bridge (town, Derbys): 'bridge of the woodland clearing by a road'. OE *weg*, 'way', 'road', + *lēah*, 'wood', 'clearing'. The second word of the name refers to the bridge over the river Goyt here and was added to distinguish this Whaley from others locally. *c.*1250 *Weile*, *c.*1620 *Whaley-bridge*.

Whalley (town, Lancs): 'woodland clearing by a round hill'. OE *hwæl*, 'hill', + *lēah*, 'wood', 'clearing'. Whalley lies in a gap between Clerk Hill and the hill known as Whalley Nab (OS *nabbi*, 'knoll'), and the name refers to the latter. 11C *Hwælleage*, DB *Wallei*.

Whalsay (island, Shetland): 'whale island'. OS *hval*, 'whale', + *ey*, 'island'. The reference is to the shape of the island, like that of a whale. *c.*1250 *Hvalsey*.

Whalton (village, Northd): 'farmstead by a round hill'. OE *hwæl*, 'hill', + *tūn*, 'farmstead'. 1203 *Walton*.

Whaplode (village, Lincs): '(place by the) watercourse where burbots are seen'. OE *cwappa*, 'eelpout', 'burbot', + *lād*, 'watercourse'. 810 *Cappelad*, DB *Copelade*.

Wharfe (river). See BURLEY IN WHARFEDALE.

Wharles (village, Lancs): '(place by the) hills near a circle'. OE *hwerfel*, 'circle', + *hlāw*, 'mound', 'hill'. The reference is to a nearby stone circle that also gave the name of ROSEACRE. 1249 *Quarlous*.

Wharram le Street (village, N Yorks): '(place by the) kettles on the street'. OE *hwer*, 'kettle', 'cauldron'. The 'kettles' were probably some natural formation here. (The name represents the OE word in a dative plural form.) The 'street' may have been a Roman road. The second part of the name distinguishes the village from nearby *Wharram Percy*, where the manor was held early by the de Percy family. DB *Warran*, 1333 *Warrum in the Strete*.

Wharton (village, Cheshire): 'farmstead by the swaying tree'. OE *wæfre*, 'wandering', 'wavering' (related modern English *waver*), + *tūn*, 'farmstead'. OE *wæfre* could also refer to marshy ground (a 'quaking bog'). The DB form of the name below is corrupt. DB *Wanetune*, 1216 *Waverton*.

Whashton (hamlet, N Yorks): 'estate associated with Hwæssa'. OE *-ing-*, 'associated with', + *tūn*, 'farmstead', 'estate'. *c.*1160 *Whassingetun*.

Whatcombe House (mansion, Dorset): '(place in a) wet valley'. OE *wæt*, 'wet', + *cumb*, 'valley'. 1288 *Watecumbe*.

Whatcote (village, Warwicks): 'cottage where wheat is grown'. OE *hwǣte*, 'wheat', + *cot*, 'cottage'. The DB form of the name below has *qu-* to represent *hw-*. DB *Quatercote*, 1206 *Whatcote*.

Whatfield (village, Suffolk): 'open land where wheat is grown'. OE *hwǣte*, 'wheat', + *feld*, 'open land' (modern English *field*). DB *Watefelda*.

Whatley (village, Somerset): 'woodland clearing where wheat is grown'. OE *hwǣte*, 'wheat', + *lēah*, 'wood', 'clearing'. DB *Watelege*.

Whatlington (village, E Sussex): 'farmstead of Hwǣtel's people'. OE *-inga-*, 'of the people of', + *tūn*, 'farmstead'. DB *Watlingetone*.

Whatstandwell (village, Derbys): '(place of) Wat Stonewell'. Walter Stonewell had a house near the ford over the river Derwent here in the 14C. The preservation of a complete personal name (given name and surname) as a medieval place name is highly unusual. 1390 *Wattestanwell ford*.

Whatton (village, Notts): 'farmstead where wheat is grown'. OE *hwǣte*, 'wheat', + *tūn*, 'farmstead'. DB *Watone*.

Wheatacre (village, Norfolk): 'cultivated land where wheat is grown'. OE *hwǣte*, 'wheat', + *æcer*, 'plot of arable land' (modern English *acre*). DB *Hwateaker*.

Wheathampstead (village, Herts): 'homestead where wheat is grown'. OE *hwǣte*, 'wheat', + *hām-stede*, 'homestead' (see HAMPSTEAD). *c.*960 *Wathemestede*, DB *Watamestede*.

Wheatley (village, Oxon): 'clearing where wheat is grown'. OE *hwǣte*, 'wheat', + *lēah*, 'wood', 'clearing'. 1163 *Hwatelega*.

Wheaton Aston (village, Staffs): 'eastern farmstead where wheat grows'. OE *hwǣten*, 'growing with wheat', + *ēast*, 'eastern', + *tūn*, 'farmstead'. 1167 *Estona*, 1347 *Whetenaston*.

Wheddon Cross (village, Somerset): '(place in the) valley where wheat is grown'. OE *hwǣte*, 'wheat', + *denu*, 'valley'. The second word of the name refers to the crossroads here. 1243 *Wheteden*.

Wheelock (village, Cheshire): '(place on the river) Wheelock'. The river has a name of Celtic origin meaning 'winding one'. DB *Hoiloch*.

Wheelton (village, Lancs): 'farmstead with a water wheel'. OE *hwēol*, 'wheel', + *tūn*, 'farmstead'. The first part of the name could equally refer to some other circular feature here. *c.*1160 *Weltona*.

Whenby (village, N Yorks): 'farmstead of the women'. OS *kona*, 'woman', + *bý*, 'farmstead', 'village'. The first part of the name represents OS *kvenna*, the genitive plural form of *kona*. DB *Quennebi*.

Whepstead (village, Suffolk): 'place where brushwood grows'. OE *hwippe*, 'brushwood', + *stede*, 'place'. 942 *Wepstede*, DB *Huepestede*.

Wherstead (village, Suffolk): 'place by a wharf'. OE *hwearf*, 'wharf', + *stede*, 'place'. Wherstead is on the river Orwell. DB *Weruesteda*.

Wherwell (village, Hants): '(place by the) bubbling stream'. OE *hwer*, 'cauldron', + *wella*, 'stream'. The village is on the river Test, whose whirlpools are well known. 955 *Hwerwyl*.

Wheston (village, Derbys): '(place with a) whetstone'. OE *hwet-stān*, 'whetstone'. The name refers either to a single whetstone here, used as a sharpening stone, or to a place where there were small stones suitable for use as whetstones. 1251 *Whetstan*.

Whetstone (district, Barnet): '(place of the) whetstone'. OE *hwet-stān*, 'whetstone'. Cp. WHESTON. Local legend tells of a large stone here used by soldiers to sharpen their swords before the Battle of Barnet (1471). 1417 *Wheston*.

Whicham (hamlet, Cumbria): 'homestead of Hwīta's people'. OE *-inga-*, 'of the people of', + *hām*, 'homestead'. The name could also mean 'homestead at Hwīta's place' (OE *-ing*, 'place belonging to', + *hām*). The original *-inga-* has disappeared. DB *Witingham*.

Whichford (village, Warwicks): '(place by the) ford of the Hwicce'. OE *ford*, 'ford'. The Hwicce were the people who gave the name of SHIPTON UNDER WYCHWOOD. DB *Wicford*, c.1130 *Wicheforda*.

Whickham (town, Gateshead): 'homestead or enclosure with a quickset hedge'. OE *cwic*, 'quickset hedge' (one grown from cuttings), + *hām*, 'homestead' or *hamm*, 'enclosure'. 1196 *Quicham*.

Whilton (village, Northants): 'farmstead with a wheel'. OE *hwēol*, 'wheel', + *tūn*, 'farmstead'. The 'wheel' could be a waterwheel, or the circular hill on which the village stands, between two streams, or even the curving stream itself. DB *Woltone*.

Whimple (village, Devon): '(place by the river) Whimple'. The name was originally that of a stream here, meaning 'white pool', from Celtic words related to modern Welsh *gwyn*, 'white', and *pwll*, 'pool', 'stream'. Cp. WENDOVER. DB *Winple*.

Whinburgh (village, Norfolk): '(place by the) hill where gorse grows'. OS *hvin*, 'whin', 'gorse', + OE *beorg*, 'hill'. DB *Wineberga*.

Whippingham (village, IoW): 'homestead of Wippa's people'. OE *-inga-*, 'of the people of', +

hām, 'homestead'. 735 *Wippingeham*, DB *Wipingeham*.

Whipsnade (village, Beds): 'Wibba's detached piece of land'. OE *snǣd*, 'thing cut off'. The OE word usually refers to an area of woodland that has been apportioned in this way. 1202 *Wibsnede*.

Whissendine (village, Rutland): 'valley of Hwicce's or Wic's people'. OE *-inga-*, 'of the people of', + *denu*, 'valley'. The first part of the name could equally be that of the Hwicce, the people who also gave the name of SHIPTON UNDER WYCHWOOD. DB *Wichingedenu*, 1203 *Wissenden*.

Whissonsett (village, Norfolk): 'fold of Wic's people'. OE *-inga-*, 'of the people of', + *set*, 'fold' (for animals). DB *Witcingkeseta*.

Whiston (hamlet, Staffs): 'Witi's farmstead'. OE *tūn*, 'farmstead'. c.1002 *Witestun*, DB *Witestone*.

Whiston (town, Knowsley): '(place by the) white stone'. OE *hwīt*, 'white', + *stān*, 'stone'. The name refers to some local feature. The *Qu-* in the form of the name below represents the *hw-* of OE *hwīt*. (Some conservative speakers still pronounce *white* with an initial 'h' sound.) 1190 *Quistan*.

Whiston (village, Northants): 'farmstead of the Hwicce'. OE *tūn*, 'farmstead'. The tribal name also gave the name of SHIPTON UNDER WYCHWOOD. 974 *Hwiccingtune*, DB *Wicentone*.

Whiston (suburb of Rotherham): '(place by the) white stone'. OE *hwīt*, 'white', + *stān*, 'stone'. The reference is perhaps to some former landmark here. DB *Witestan*.

Whitbeck (hamlet, Cumbria): '(place by the) white stream'. OS *hvítr*, 'white', + *bekkr*, 'stream'. c.1160 *Witebec*.

Whitburn (town, S Tyneside): '(place by the) white barn'. OE *hwīt*, 'white', + *bern*, 'barn'. 1183 *Whiteberne*.

Whitby (district of Ellesmere Port, Cheshire): 'white manor house'. OE *hwīt*, 'white', + *burh*, 'fortified place', 'manor house'. The second part of the name was later replaced by OS *bý*, 'village'. c.1100 *Witeberia*, 1241 *Whiteby*.

Whitby (resort town and port, N Yorks): 'white farmstead'. OS *hvítr*, 'white', + *bý*, 'farmstead', 'village'. The first part of the name could also be the Scandinavian personal name Hvítr. DB *Witeby*.

Whitchurch (town, Hants): 'white church'. OE *hwīt*, 'white', + *cirice*, 'church'. The reference is to a church that was either built of stone, with white limestone in the fabric, or that was white-washed. 909 *Hwitancyrice.* SO ALSO: *Whitchurch,* Bath & NE Somerset.

Whitchurch (town, Shropshire): 'white church'. OE *hwīt,* 'white', + *cirice,* 'church'. A 'white church' is either one with white stone or one that was painted white. The DB name below is different and means 'western farmstead'. The second name is the Latin equivalent of the present name. The Roman town here was *Mediolanum,* '(place in the) middle of a plain'. DB *Westone,* 1199 *Album Monasterium,* 13C *Whytchyrche.*

Whitchurch Canonicorum (village, Dorset): 'white church of the canons'. OE *hwīt,* 'white', + *cirice,* 'church', + Latin *canonicorum,* 'of the canons'. The manor here was held early by the canons of Salisbury Cathedral. The church is dedicated to St Candida (Latin *candidus,* 'white'), whose name was probably suggested by the village name. DB *Witcerce,* 1262 *Whitchurch Canonicorum.*

Whitechapel (district, London): 'white chapel'. OE *hwīt,* 'white', + ME *chapele,* 'chapel'. The name refers to the original white-coloured, stone-built chapel here in the 13C. Cp. WHIT-CHURCH. 1340 *Whitechapele.*

White Colne. See COLNE ENGAINE.

Whitefield (town, Bury): 'white open land'. OE *hwīt,* 'white', + *feld,* 'open land' (modern English *field*). The exact sense of 'white' here is uncertain. It may refer to land that was unusually dry. 1292 *Whitefeld.*

Whitegate (village, Cheshire): '(place by the) white gate'. OE *hwīt,* 'white', + *geat,* 'gate'. The name refers to the outer gate of Vale Royal abbey, where the church was situated. 1540 *Whytegate.*

Whitehaven (town and port, Cumbria): 'harbour by the white headland'. OS *hvítr,* 'white', + *hofuth,* 'headland', + *hafn,* 'harbour'. The 'white headland' is the hill of white stone which forms one side of the harbour. The word for 'headland' in the original name was later dropped for ease of pronunciation. *c.*1135 *Qwithofhavene,* 1278 *Witenhauen.*

White Ladies Aston (village, Worcs): 'eastern farmstead of the White Ladies'. OE *ēast,* 'eastern', + *tūn,* 'farmstead'. Part of the manor here was held by the Cistercian nuns of Whitstones, whose name happens to reflect their popular name of 'White Ladies', referring to their white habits. The farmstead may have been seen as 'east' in relation to Low Hill. 977 *Eastune,* DB *Estun,* 1481 *Whitladyaston.*

Whiteley Village (residential estate, Surrey). The model village with almshouses was laid out here in 1911 in accordance with the will of William Whiteley (1831–1907), founder of Whiteley's Stores, London.

White Notley (village, Essex): 'white wood or clearing where nut trees grow'. OE *hwīt,* 'white', + *hnutu,* 'nut', + *lēah,* 'wood', 'clearing'. The first word of the name distinguishes the village from *Black Notley,* 2 miles to the north, the respective adjectives perhaps relating to soil colour or vegetation. 998 *Hnutlea,* DB *Nutlea,* 1235 *White Nuteleye.*

Whiteparish (village, Wilts): 'white church'. OE *hwīt,* 'white', + *cirice,* 'church'. The name refers to a white-painted church or one built of white stone. The 'church' of the name was subsequently replaced by 'parish' (ME *paroche*). 1278 *La Whytechyrch,* 1289 *Whyteparosshe.*

White Roding. See RODINGS.

Whitestaunton (village, Somerset): 'white farmstead on stony ground'. OE *stān,* 'stone', + *tūn,* 'farmstead'. The first part of the name refers to the limestone quarries here and was added to distinguish this *Stanton* from CHURCH-STANTON, 6 miles to the northwest. DB *Stantune,* 1337 *Whitestaunton.*

Whitestone (village, Devon): '(place by the) white stone'. OE *hwīt,* 'white', + *stān,* 'stone'. DB *Witestan,* *c.*1100 *Hwitastane.*

White Waltham. See WALTHAM ST LAWRENCE.

Whitfield (hamlet, Northd): 'white open land'. OE *hwīt,* 'white', + *feld,* 'open land' (modern English *field*). 1254 *Witefeld.* SO ALSO: *Whitfield,* Kent, Northants.

Whitgift (village, E Yorks): 'Hvítr's dowry'. OS *gipt,* 'gift', 'dowry'. The personal name is Scandinavian. Whitgift is so named as being former dowryland. *c.*1070 *Witegift.*

Whithorn (town, Dumfries & Gall): 'white building'. OE *hwīt,* 'white', + *ærn,* 'building'. According to Bede's *Ecclesiastical History of the English People* (731), 'the place ... is commonly known as *Candida Casa,* the White House, because he [Bishop Ninian] built the church of stone'. *c.*890 *æt Hwitan Ærne.*

Whitland (village, Carm): 'white land'. OE *hwīt,* 'white', + *land,* 'land'. The Welsh name of the village is *Hendy-gwyn,* 'old white house', from Welsh *hen,* 'old', + *tŷ,* 'house', + *gwyn,* 'white', referring to the site, later that of a Cistercian monastery, where the 10C ruler Hywel Dda is said to have promulgated the Welsh

Laws. The first two forms of the name below are Latin respectively for 'white house' and 'white land'. 1191 *Alba Domus*, 1214 *Alba Landa*, 1309 *Whitland*.

Whitley Bay (resort town, N Tyneside): '(place by) Whitley Bay'. The bay takes its name from the original settlement of *Whitley*, 'white wood' or 'white clearing' (OE *hwīt*, 'white', + *lēah*, 'wood', 'clearing'). A 'white wood' is probably a sparse and light one, as distinct from a 'black wood' (*Blackley*), which is dark and dense. 12C *Wyteleya*.

Whitminster (village, Glos): '(place on the) white wooded hill'. OE *hwīt*, 'white', + *hyrst*, 'wooded hill'. The name could also mean 'Hwīta's hill'. A white hill is a bright one. The present form of the name gradually evolved as a corruption of the original. DB *Witenhert*, 1248 *Whitenherst*, 1645 *Wheatenhurst als. Whitminster*.

Whitmore (village, Staffs): '(place on the) white moor'. OE *hwīt*, 'white', + *mōr*, 'moor', 'marsh'. DB *Witemore*.

Whitnash (suburb of Leamington, Warwicks): '(place by the) white ash tree'. OE *hwīt*, 'white', + *æsc*, 'ash'. DB *Witenas*.

Whitney-on-Wye (village, Herefords): 'white island on the (river) Wye'. OE *hwīt*, 'white', + *ēg*, 'island'. The name could also mean 'Hwīta's island'. Either way, the 'island' is raised ground by the river Wye here. For the river name, see ROSS-ON-WYE. DB *Witenie*.

Whitsbury (village, Hants): 'fortified place where wych elms grow'. OE *wice*, 'wych elm', + *burh*, 'fortified place'. The 'fortified place' is the ancient hill fort nearby known as Whitsbury Camp or Castle Ditches. c.1130 *Wiccheberia*.

Whitstable (resort town, Kent): '(place by the) white post'. OE *hwīt*, 'white', + *stapol*, 'post' (modern English *staple*). The original 'white post' could have marked either the meeting place of the local hundred or a suitable landing place. A meaning 'post of the councillors' is also possible, with the first part of the name representing OE *wita*, 'councillor'. Cp. BARNSTAPLE. DB *Witestaple*.

Whittingham (village, Northd): 'homestead of Hwīta's people'. OE *-inga-*, 'of the people of', + *hām*, 'homestead'. The name could also mean 'homestead at Hwīta's place' (OE *-ing*, 'place belonging to', + *hām*). c.1050 *Hwitincham*.

Whittingslow (hamlet, Shropshire): 'Hwittuc's burial mound'. OE *hlāw*, 'mound', 'tumulus'. DB *Witecheslawe*.

Whittington (village, Shropshire): 'estate associated with Hwīta'. OE *-ing-*, 'associated with', + *tūn*, 'farmstead', 'estate'. DB *Wititone*. SO ALSO: *Whittington*, Staffs.

Whittlebury (village, Northants): 'Witla's stronghold'. OE *burh*, 'fortified place'. c.930 *Witlanbyrig*.

Whittle-le-Woods (village, Lancs): '(place by the) white hill in the woodland'. OE *hwīt*, 'white', + *hyll*, 'hill'. The second part of the name below is Medieval Latin for 'in the wood'. c.1160 *Witul*, 1327 *Whithill in bosco*.

Whittlesey (town, Cambs): 'Wittel's island'. OE *ēg*, 'island'. The 'island' here is the raised land in fenland on which Whittlesey stands between two branches of the river Nene. c.972 *Witlesig*, DB *Witesie*.

Whittlesford (village, Cambs): '(place by) Wittel's ford'. OE *ford*, 'ford'. The river here is the Cam. DB *Witelesforde*.

Whitton (village, N Lincs): 'Hwīta's island'. OE *ēg*, 'island'. The name could also mean 'white island' (OE *hwīt*, 'white', + *ēg*). Either way, the village church stands on a distinct 'island' of land here by the river Humber. DB *Witenai*.

Whitton (hamlet, Shropshire): 'farmstead by a wood'. OE *widu*, 'wood', + *tūn*, 'farmstead'. The DB form of the name below has *b* for *d*. DB *Wibetune*, 1242 *Witton*.

Whitton (district of Ipswich, Suffolk): 'Hwīta's farmstead'. OE *tūn*, 'farmstead'. The name could also mean 'white farmstead' (OE *hwīt*, 'white', + *tūn*). The DB form of the name below is corrupt. DB *Widituna*, 1212 *Witton*.

Whittonstall (village, Northd): 'farmstead with a quickset hedge'. OE *cwic*, 'quickset hedge' (one grown from cuttings), + *tūn-stall*, 'farm site' (see TUNSTALL). 1242 *Quictunstal*.

Whitwell (village, Rutland): '(place by the) white spring'. OE *hwīt*, 'white', + *wella*, 'spring', 'stream'. A small stream has its source here. DB *Witewell*. SO ALSO: *Whitwell*, Derby, IoW.

Whitwick (hamlet, Leics): 'white dairy farm'. OE *hwīt*, 'white', + *wīc*, 'dwelling', 'dairy farm'. The name could also mean 'Hwīta's dairy farm'. DB *Witewic*.

Whitwood (suburb of Castleford, Wakefield): 'white wood'. OE *hwīt*, 'white', + *wudu*, 'wood'. A white wood is either one that has trees with white bark or blossom, or more likely one that is sparse and so light and bright. DB *Witewde*.

Whitworth (town, Lancs): 'white enclosure'. OE *hwīt*, 'white', + *worth*, 'enclosure'. 13C *White-worth*.

Whixley (village, N Yorks): 'Cwic's woodland clearing'. OE *lēah*, 'wood', 'clearing'. DB *Cucheslage*.

Whorlton (village, Durham): 'farmstead by the stream where millstones are obtained'. OE *cweorn*, 'millstone' (modern English *quern*), + *-ing*, 'stream characterized by', + *tūn*. 'farmstead'. *c*.1050 *Queorningtun*.

Whorlton (village, N Yorks): 'farmstead by the round-topped hill'. OE *hwerfel*, 'round-topped hill', + *tūn*, 'farmstead'. The reference is to nearby Whorl Hill, a high hill with a rounded top. DB *Wirveltune*.

Whyke (district of Chichester, W Sussex). The name is a shortening of *Rumboldswyke*, a nearby district that was itself originally *Whyke* (OE *wīc*, 'dairy farm') but that became associated with St Rumbold from the dedication of a church or chapel here. The earlier name is preserved in that of Rumboldswyke Church of England infant school in the city. DB *Wiche*, 1225 *Rumbaldeswic*.

Whyteleafe (district of Caterham, Surrey): '(place of) white leaves'. The mock-ME form of the name betrays its recent origin. The original name was that of a field recorded as *White Leaf Field* in 1839 and so called from the aspens that grew there.

Wibtoft (hamlet, Warwicks): 'Wibba's or Vibbi's homestead'. OS *toft*, 'homestead'. The personal names are respectively OE and Scandinavian. 1002 *Wibbetofte*, DB *Wibetot*.

Wichenford (village, Worcs): '(place at the) ford by the wych elms'. OE *wice*, 'wych elm', + *ford*, 'ford'. The '-en-' of the name represents the ending of OE *wichena*, the genitive plural form of *wice*. The ford in question must have been over one of the streams that enter a tributary of the river Severn here. 11C *Wiceneford*.

Wichling (village, Kent): '(settlement of) Wincel's people'. OE *-ingas*, 'people of'. The DB form of the name below means 'Wincel's pool' (OE *mere*) or 'Wincel's boundary' (OE *mǣre*). DB *Winchelesmere*, 1220 *Winchelinge*.

Wick (town and port, Highland): '(place by the) bay'. OS *vík*, 'bay'. The bay in question is Wick Bay, on which the town stands. 1140 *Vik*, 1455 *Weke*.

Wick (village, S Glos): 'dwelling'. OE *wīc*, 'dwelling', 'specialized farm'. 1189 *Wike*. SO ALSO: *Wick*, Worcs.

Wicken (village, Cambs): 'dwellings'. OE *wīc*, 'dwelling', 'specialized farm'. The name represents either OE *wīcum*, the dative plural form of *wīc*, or the simple ME plural *wiken*. DB *Wicha*, *c*.1200 *Wiken*.

Wicken Bonhunt (village, Essex). Originally two separate names: *Wicken*, 'dwellings' (see WICKEN), and *Bonhunt*, 'place where people were summoned for hunting'. OE *bann*, 'summons', + *hunte*, 'hunt'. DB *Wica*, 1238 *Wykes Bonhunte*.

Wickersley (suburb of Rotherham): 'Víkarr's woodland clearing'. OE *lēah*, 'wood', 'clearing'. The personal name is Scandinavian. DB *Wicresleia*.

Wickford (town, Essex): '(place at the) ford by a Romano-British settlement'. OE *wīc*, 'Romano-British settlement', + *ford*, 'ford'. The name probably refers to a *vicus* (cp. WEST WICKHAM). The river here is the Crouch. *c*.975 *Wicforda*, DB *Wicfort*.

Wickham (village, Hants): 'homestead associated with a Romano-British settlement'. OE *wīc-hām* (see WEST WICKHAM). A Roman settlement is known near the village, which is itself on a Roman road. 925 *Wicham*, DB *Wicheham*. SO ALSO: *Wickham*, W Berks.

Wickham Bishops (village, Essex): 'bishop's homestead associated with a Romano-British settlement'. OE *wīc-hām* (see WEST WICKHAM). The village is so called from its possession by the Bishop of London, whose title distinguishes it from *Wickham St Paul*, 16 miles to the north, in the possession of St Paul's Cathedral, London. DB *Wicham*, 1313 *Wykham Bishops*.

Wickhambreaux (village, Kent): 'de Brayhuse's homestead associated with a Romano-British settlement'. OE *wīc-hām* (see WEST WICKHAM). The de Brayhuse family held the manor here in the 13C. 948 *Wicham*, DB *Wicheham*, 1270 *Wykham Breuhuse*.

Wickhambrook (village, Suffolk): 'homestead associated with a Romano-British settlement by a brook'. OE *wīc-hām* (see WEST WICKHAM), + *brōc*, 'brook'. DB *Wicham*, 1254 *Wichambrok*.

Wickhamford (village, Worcs): '(place at the) ford by the lodge in the meadow'. OE *ford*, 'ford'. The first part of the name is of Celtic origin, as for CHILDSWICKHAM. The ford would have been over Badsey Brook here. 709 *Wicwona*, DB *Wiquene*, 1221 *Wikewaneford*.

Wickham Market (town, Suffolk): 'homestead associated with a Romano-British settlement with a market'. OE *wīc-hām* (see WEST WICKHAM), + ME *merket*, 'market'. The second word of the name also distinguishes the market here from the one at STOWMARKET. DB *Wikham*.

Wickhampton (village, Norfolk): 'homestead with a dairy farm'. OE *wīc*, 'dairy farm', + *hām-tūn* (from *hām*, 'homestead', + *tūn*, 'farmstead'). DB *Wichamtuna*.

Wickham Skeith (village, Suffolk): 'homestead associated with a Romano-British settlement with a racecourse'. OE *wīc-hām* (see WEST WICKHAM), + OS *skeith*, 'racecourse'. DB *Wichamm*, 1368 *Wicham Skeyth*.

Wickham St Paul. See WICKHAM BISHOPS.

Wicklewood (village, Norfolk): 'wood by the dairy-farm clearing'. OE *wīc*, 'dairy farm', + *lēah*, 'wood', 'clearing', + *wudu*, 'wood'. DB *Wikelewuda*.

Wickmere (village, Norfolk): '(place at the) pool by a dairy farm'. OE *wīc*, 'dwelling', 'dairy farm', + *mere*, 'pool'. DB *Wicmera*.

Wick Rissington. See GREAT RISSINGTON.

Wick St Lawrence (village, N Somerset): 'settlement with St Lawrence's church'. OE *wīc*, 'dwelling', 'specialized farm'. The second part of the name represents the dedication of the church. 1225 *Wike*.

Wickwar (village, S Glos): 'la Warre's specialized farm'. OE *wīc*, 'dwelling', 'specialized farm'. The first part of the name evolved from OE *æt wīcum*, 'at the dwellings'. The second part is the name of John la Warre, who held the manor here in the 13C and whose family continued to hold it to the 15C. DB *Wichen*, 13C *Wykewarre*.

Widdington (village, Essex): 'farmstead where willow trees grow'. OE *wīthign*, 'willow' (related modern English *withy*), + *tūn*, 'farmstead', 'village'. DB *Widintuna*.

Widdrington (village, Northd): 'estate associated with Widuhere'. OE -*ing*-, 'associated with', + *tūn*, 'farmstead', 'estate'. c.1160 *Vuderintuna*.

Widecombe in the Moor (village, Devon): 'valley where willow trees grow in the moor'. OE *wīthig*, 'willow' (modern English *withy*), + *cumb*, 'valley'. The second part of the name emphasizes the isolated location of the place on Dartmoor rather than distinguishing it from any other Widecombe. 12C *Widecumba*.

Widegates (village, Cornwall): '(place by the) wide gates'. The village arose in the 17C on open downland, onto which a gated road would have led. 1673 *Wide-gates*.

Widemouth Bay (resort village, Cornwall): '(place on) Widemouth Bay'. The bay here takes its name from the farms known as Widemouth, 'wide mouth' (OE *wīd*, 'wide', + *mūtha*, 'mouth'). There is no river mouth here, and the 'mouth' may be the long gap in the cliffs. The village is a recent holiday development. The first form of the name below refers to the farms, the second to the bay, and the third and fourth to the village. DB *Witemot*, 1813 *Widemouth Bay*, 1969 *Widemouth*, 1971 *Widemouth Bay*.

Widford (village, Herts): '(place by the) ford where willow trees grow'. OE *wīthig*, 'willow' (modern English *withy*), + *ford*, 'ford'. The river here is the Ash. DB *Wideford*. SO ALSO: *Widford*, Essex.

Widmerpool (village, Notts): '(place by the) wide lake pool'. OE *wīd*, 'wide', + *mere*, 'lake', + *pōl*, 'pool'. The first part of the name could also represent OE *wīthig*, 'willow tree' (modern English *withy*). DB *Wimarspol*.

Widnes (coastal town, Halton): '(place on the) wide promontory'. OE *wīd*, 'wide', + *næss*, 'promontory'. The reference is to the rounded promontory on which the town lies by the Mersey. c.1200 *Wydnes*.

Wigan (town, Wigan): 'Wigan's homestead'. The name is traditionally explained as a shortened form of an earlier Welsh name *Tref Wigan*, from Welsh *tref*, 'town', and a personal name. A more recent theory takes the name from OE *wicum*, '(place) at the dwellings', from the dative plural of *wīc*, 'dwelling' (cp. HIGH WYCOMBE), on the basis that Wigan had probably been a Romano-British *vicus* (cp. WEST WICKHAM). Celticists prefer an origin in a word related to Cornish *gwig*, 'village', as for GWEEK, with the diminutive suffix -*an*, giving a meaning 'little settlement'. 1199 *Wigan*.

Wiggenhall St Mary the Virgin (village, Norfolk): 'Wicga's corner of land with the church of St Mary the Virgin'. OE *halh*, 'nook', 'corner of land'. The church dedication distinguishes the village from three others nearby: *Wiggenhall St Mary Magdalen*, *Wiggenhall St Germans* and *Wiggenhall St Peter*. DB *Wigrehala*, 1196 *Wiggenhal*.

Wigginton (village, Herts): 'farmstead associated with Wicga'. OE -*ing*-, 'associated with', + *tūn*, 'farmstead'. The name could also mean 'Wicga's farm', with the first part representing *Wicgan*, the genitive form of the personal name. DB *Wigentone*. SO ALSO: *Wigginton*, Oxon, Staffs, York.

Wigglesworth (village, N Yorks): 'Wincel's enclosure'. OE *worth*, 'enclosure'. DB *Wincheles-uuorde*.

Wiggonby (hamlet, Cumbria): 'Wigan's farmstead'. OS *bý*, 'farmstead', 'village'. The personal name is Celtic. 1278 *Wygayneby*.

Wighill (village, N Yorks): 'corner of land with a dairy farm'. OE *wīc*, 'dairy farm', + *halh*, 'nook', 'corner of land'. The DB form of the name below is plural, with Latin *duas*, 'two'. DB *Duas Wicheles*, 1219 *Wikale*.

Wight, Isle of (island, IoW): 'island of the division'. The Isle of Wight has a Celtic name apparently related to modern Welsh *gwaith*, 'turn', 'course', referring to its location between the two arms of the Solent. The implication is that a ship heading out of Southampton Water for the English Channel will have to turn either east or west. The Roman name for the island was *Vectis*, of the same origin. DB *Wit*.

Wighton (village, Norfolk): 'farmstead with a dwelling'. OE *wīc-tūn* (from *wīc*, 'dwelling', + *tūn*, 'farmstead'). DB *Wistune*.

Wigmore (village, Herefords): '(place by the) unstable marsh'. OE *wicga*, 'unstable' (literally 'beetle', related modern English *wiggle*), + *mōr*, 'moor', 'marsh'. The reference is to the large area of unstable marsh here, where blister bogs appear and disappear. DB *Wigemore*.

Wigsley (village, Notts): 'Wicg's woodland clearing'. OE *lēah*, 'wood', 'clearing'. DB *Wigesleie*.

Wigston (town, Leics): 'Wīcing's or Vikingr's farmstead'. OE *tūn*, 'farmstead'. The personal name is either OE or Scandinavian. The town is also known as *Wigston Magna* (Latin *magna*, 'great') for distinction from *Wigston Parva* (Latin *parva*, 'small'), 11 miles to the southwest. The latter Wigston has a name of quite different origin, meaning either '(place by the) rocking stone' (OE *wigga*, 'beetle', + *stān*, 'stone') or 'Wicg's stone'. (OE *wigga*, although literally 'beetle', related to modern English *wiggle*, means 'moving' when associated with *stān*, 'stone'.) The church at Wigston Magna is dedicated to St Wistan, who more properly belongs to WISTOW. DB *Wichingestone*.

Wigtoft (village, Lincs): 'homestead by a creek'. OS *vík*, 'creek', + *toft*, 'homestead'. The creek in question is nearby Bicker Haven, at one time an arm of the sea. 1187 *Wiketoft*.

Wigton (town, Cumbria): 'Wicga's farmstead'. OE *tūn*, 'farmstead', 'village'. 1163 *Wiggeton*.

Wigtown (town, Dumfries & Gall): 'Wicga's farmstead'. OE *tūn*, 'farmstead', 'village'. 1266 *Wigeton*.

Wigwig (hamlet, Shropshire): 'Wicga's dairy farm'. OE *wīc*, 'dairy farm'. DB *Wigewic*.

Wike (village, Leeds): 'dairy farm'. OE *wīc*, 'dwelling', 'specialized farm'. DB *Wich*.

Wilbarston (village, Northants): 'Wilbeorht's farmstead'. OE *tūn*, 'farmstead', 'village'. DB *Wilbertestone*.

Wilberfoss (village, E Yorks): '(place by) Wilburh's ditch'. OE *foss*, 'ditch'. The personal name is that of a woman. 1148 *Wilburcfosa*.

Wilburton (village, Cambs): 'Wilburh's farmstead'. OE *tūn*, 'farmstead', 'village'. The personal name is that of a woman. 970 *Wilburhtun*, DB *Wilbertone*.

Wilby (hamlet, Norfolk): 'farmstead by willow trees'. OE *wilig*, 'willow', + OS *bý*, 'farmstead', 'village'. The second part of the name could also represent OE *bēag*, 'ring', giving a sense '(place by the) circle of willows'. DB *Willebeih*.

Wilby (village, Northants): 'Willa's or Villi's farmstead'. OS *bý*, 'farmstead', 'village'. The personal names are respectively OE and Scandinavian. c.1067 *Willabyg*, DB *Wilebi*.

Wilby (village, Suffolk): '(place by the) circle of willow trees'. OE *wilig*, 'willow', + *bēag*, 'ring'. DB *Wilebey*.

Wilcot (village, Wilts): 'cottages by the spring'. OE *wiella*, 'spring', 'stream', + *cot*, 'cottage'. The first form of the name below has OE *cotum*, the dative plural form of *cot*. 940 *Wilcotum*, DB *Wilcote*.

Wildboarclough (village, Cheshire): '(place in the) deep valley where wild boars are seen'. OE *wilde-bār*, 'wild boar', + *clōh*, 'deep valley'. The valley in question is that of Clough Brook. 1357 *Wildeborclogh*.

Wilden (village, Beds): '(place in the) valley where willow trees grow'. OE *wilig*, 'willow', + *denu*, 'valley'. DB *Wildene*.

Wilden (village, Worcs): 'Wifela's hill'. OE *dūn*, 'hill'. The first form of the name below is garbled. 1182 *Wineladuna*, 1299 *Wiveldon*.

Wilford (suburb of West Bridgford, Nottingham): '(place by the) ford where willow trees grow'. OE *wilig*, 'willow', + *ford*, 'ford'. The river here is the Trent. DB *Wilesford*.

Wilkesley (hamlet, Cheshire): 'Wifel's tongue of land'. OE *clēa*, 'claw', 'tongue of land'. Wilkesley lies on a tongue of land between the river Duckow and the stream that forms the county boundary nearby. The DB form of the name below has *cl* miscopied as *d*. DB *Wiuelesde*, 1230 *Wivelescle*.

Willand (village, Devon): '(place on) waste land'. OE *wilde*, 'waste', 'wild', + *land*, 'land'. The name probably implies cultivated land that has reverted to waste. DB *Willelanda*.

Willaston (village, Cheshire): 'Wīglāf's farmstead'. OE *tūn*, 'farmstead', 'village'. The form of the name below is for Willaston near Nantwich, but Willaston near Neston has a name of identical origin. DB *Wilavestune*.

Willen (village, Milton K): '(place by the) willow trees'. OE *wilig*, 'willow'. The name represents the OE word in a dative plural form in the phrase *æt thǣm wiligum*, 'at the willows'. 1189 *Wily*.

Willenhall (district, Coventry): 'corner of land where willow trees grow'. OE *wiligen*, 'growing with willows', + *halh*, 'nook', 'corner of land'. 12C *Wilenhala*.

Willenhall (district, Walsall): 'Willa's corner of land'. OE *halh*, 'nook', 'corner of land'. The '-en-' of the name represents the genitive ending of the personal name. The DB form of the name below has a miscopying of *ll* as *n*. 732 *Willanhalch*, DB *Winenhale*.

Willerby (village, N Yorks): 'Wilheard's farmstead'. OS *bý*, 'farmstead', 'village'. 1125 *Willerdebi*. SO ALSO: *Willerby*, E Yorks.

Willersey (village, Glos): 'Wilhere's or Wilheard's island'. OE *ēg*, 'island'. The 'island' would be raised ground in marshland here. 709 *Willerseye*, DB *Willersei*.

Willersley (village, Herefords): 'Wīglāf's woodland clearing'. OE *lēah*, 'wood', 'clearing'. DB *Willaveslege*.

Willesborough (suburb of Ashford, Kent): 'Wifel's hill'. OE *beorg*, 'mound', 'hill'. 863 *Wifelesberg*.

Willesden (district, Brent): '(place by the) hill with a spring'. OE *wiella*, 'spring', + *dūn*, 'hill'. One might have expected the present form of the name to be *Wilsdon*, as on the Ordnance Survey map of 1822, but the spelling was altered in *c*.1840 by the railway company to match that of neighbouring NEASDEN. 939 *Willesdone*, DB *Wellesdone*.

Willett (hamlet, Somerset): '(place on the river) Willett'. The river name is of uncertain origin. DB *Willet*.

Willey (hamlet, Shropshire): '(place by the) wood or clearing where willow trees grow'. OE *wilig*, 'willow', + *lēah*, 'wood', 'clearing'. The DB form of the name below is corrupt. DB *Wilit*, 1199 *Wilileg*. SO ALSO: *Willey*, Warwicks.

Williamscot (hamlet, Oxon): 'Wilelm's or William's cottage'. OE *cot*, 'cottage'. The personal names are Old German. 1166 *Williamescote*.

Willian (village, Herts): '(place at the) willow trees'. OE *wilig*, 'willow'. As for WELWYN, the name represents the OE word in its dative plural form (*wiligum*). DB *Wilie*.

Willingale (village, Essex): 'corner of land of Willa's people'. OE *-inga-*, 'of the people of', + *halh*, 'nook', 'corner of land'. The village is historically divided into *Willingale Doe*, where the de Ou family held the manor in the 12C, and *Willingale Spain*, where it was held by the de Ispania family from 1086. DB *Willinghehala*.

Willingdon (suburb of Eastbourne, E Sussex): '(place by) Willa's hill'. OE *dūn*, 'hill'. DB *Willendone*.

Willingham (village, Cambs): 'homestead of Wifel's people'. OE *-inga-*, 'of the people of', + *hām*, 'homestead'. *c*.1050 *Vuivlingeham*, DB *Wivelingham*.

Willington (hamlet, Warwicks): 'estate associated with Wulflāf'. OE *-ing-*, 'associated with', + *tūn*, 'farmstead', 'estate'. DB *Ullavintone*.

Willington (village, Beds): 'farmstead where willow trees grow'. OE *wilign*, 'willow', + *tūn*, 'farmstead'. DB *Welitone*. SO ALSO: *Willington*, Derbys.

Willington (town, Durham): 'estate associated with Wifel'. OE *-ing-*, 'associated with', + *tūn*, 'farmstead', 'estate'. *c*.1190 *Wyvelintun*. SO ALSO: *Willington*, N Tyneside.

Willington Corner (hamlet, Cheshire): 'Wynflæd's farmstead'. OE *tūn*, 'farmstead', 'village'. The personal name is that of a woman. The second word of the name, first recorded in the 19C, refers to a corner of Delamere Forest. DB *Winfletone*, 1831 *Willington Corner*.

Willisham (village, Suffolk): 'Wīglāf's homestead or enclosure'. OE *hām*, 'homestead', or *hamm*, 'enclosure'. *c*.1040 *Willauesham*.

Willitoft (hamlet, E Yorks): 'homestead where willow trees grow'. OE *wilig*, 'willow', + OS *toft*, 'homestead'. DB *Wilgetot*.

Williton (village, Somerset): 'farmstead on the (river) Willett'. OE *tūn*, 'farmstead', 'village'. For the river name, see WILLETT. 904 *Wilettun*, DB *Willetone*.

Willoughby (village, Warwicks): 'farmstead by willow trees'. OE *wilig*, 'willow', + OS *bý*, 'farmstead'. 956 *Wiliabyg*, DB *Wilebei*. SO ALSO: *Willoughby*, Lincs.

Willoughby-on-the-Wolds (village, Notts): 'farmstead by the willow trees in the Wolds'. OE *wilig*, 'willow', + OS *bý*, 'farmstead'. The second part of the name (see WOLDS) distinguishes this Willoughby from *Willoughby Waterleys* ('water-less'), Leics, 22 miles to the south. The Roman settlement of *Vernemetum* near Willoughby-on-the-Wolds has a Celtic name meaning 'great sacred grove'. DB *Willebi*.

Willoughton (village, Lincs): 'farmstead where willow trees grow'. OE *wilig*, 'willow', + *tūn*, 'farmstead', 'village'. DB *Wilchetone*.

Wilmcote (village, Warwicks): 'cottage associated with Wilmund'. OE *-ing-*, 'associated with', + *cot*, 'cottage'. 1016 *Wilmundigcotan*, DB *Wilmecote*.

Wilmington (village, E Sussex): 'estate associated with Wīghelm or Wilhelm'. OE *-ing-*, 'associated with', + *tūn*, 'farmstead', 'estate'. The DB form of the name below has garbled the second part. DB *Wilminte*, 1189 *Wilminton*.

Wilmington (suburb of Dartford, Kent): 'estate associated with Wīghelm'. OE *-ing-*, 'associated with', + *tūn*, 'farmstead', 'estate'. 1089 *Wilmintuna*.

Wilmslow (town, Cheshire): 'Wīghelm's mound'. OE *hlāw*, 'mound'. The name does not necessarily imply that Wīghelm was buried in the mound, and it may simply have been a mound that characterized his estate. *c.*1250 *Wilmesloe*.

Wilnecote (district of Tamworth, Staffs): 'Wilmund's cottage'. OE *cot*, 'cottage'. DB *Wilmundecote*.

Wilpshire (village, Lancs): 'Wlisp's estate'. OE *scīr*, 'district', 'estate'. The first part of the name may be a personal name meaning 'lisping one' (OE *wlisp*, 'lisping'), although Celticists prefer to derive it from a word related to modern Welsh *gwlyb*, 'wet'. Evidence of the former dampness of the region exists in the form of a reservoir to the east, testifying to heavy rainfall, and the presence of the hamlet *Clayton-le-Dale* to the west (see CLAYTON-LE-MOORS). 1246 *Wlypschyre*.

Wilsford (village, Wilts): '(place by) Wifel's ford'. OE *ford*, 'ford'. The forms of the name below are for Wilsford near Upavon, but the smaller Wilsford near Amesbury has a name of identical origin. Both places are on the river Avon. 892 *Wifelesford*, DB *Wivlesford*. SO ALSO: *Wilsford*, Lincs.

Wilsill (village, N Yorks): 'Wifel's or Vífill's corner of land'. OE *halh*, 'nook', 'corner of land'. The land in question is a small valley on a steep hillside here overlooking the river Nidd. The personal names are respectively OE and Scandinavian. *c.*1030 *Wifeleshealh*, DB *Wifleshale*.

Wilson (hamlet, Leics): 'Wifel's farmstead'. OE *tūn*, 'farmstead', 'village'. 12C *Wiuelestunia*.

Wilton (hamlet, N Yorks): 'farmstead where willow trees grow'. OE *wilig*, 'willow', + *tūn*, 'farmstead'. DB *Wiltune*. SO ALSO: *Wilton*, Redcar & Clev.

Wilton (town, Wilts): 'village on the (river) Wylye'. OE *tūn*, 'farmstead', 'village'. For the river name, see WYLYE. It was this Wilton, near Salisbury, that gave the name of WILTSHIRE. 838 *Uuiltun*, DB *Wiltune*.

Wilton (village, Wilts): 'farmstead by a spring'. OE *wiella*, 'spring', 'stream', + *tūn*, 'farmstead'. This is Wilton near Burbage. 1227 *Wulton*.

Wiltshire (county, S England): 'district based on Wilton'. OE *scīr*, 'shire', 'district'. See WILTON (Wilts, near Salisbury). 870 *Wiltunscir*, DB *Wiltescire*.

Wimbish (hamlet, Essex): 'Wine's bushy copse'. OE *bysce*, 'bushy copse' (related modern English *bush*). *c.*1040 *Wimbisc*, DB *Wimbeis*.

Wimbledon (district, Merton): 'Wynnmann's hill'. OE *dūn*, 'hill'. The present form of the name is due to the Normans, who changed the final *nn* of Wynnmann's name to *l*, then inserted a *b* between the *m* and this *l* for ease of pronunciation. Wimbledon Hill Road (the A219) here is a reminder of the hill. *c.*950 *Wunemannedune*, 1202 *Wimeldon*, 1211 *Wimbledon*.

Wimblington (village, Cambs): 'estate associated with Wynnbald'. OE *-ing-*, 'associated with', + *tūn*, 'farmstead', 'estate'. *c.*975 *Wimblingetune*.

Wimborne Minster (town, Dorset): 'monastery on the (river) Wimborne'. OE *mynster*, 'monastery'. The earlier name of the river Allen here means 'meadow stream' (OE *winn*, 'pasture', + *burna*, 'stream'). The 'monastery' was the nunnery founded here in the early 8C. Its addition to the basic name distinguishes this Wimborne from *Wimborne St Giles*, 8 miles to the north, named from the dedication of its church, and *Monkton Up Wimborne*, 'farmstead of the monks higher up the Wimborne' (OE *munuc*, 'monk', + *tūn*, 'farmstead'), northwest of Wimborne St Giles on the same river. Late 9C *Winburnan*, DB *Winburne*, 1236 *Wymburneminstre*.

Wimbotsham (village, Norfolk): 'Winebald's homestead'. OE *hām*, 'homestead'. DB *Winebotesham*.

Wimpole (village, Cambs): '(place by) Wina's pool'. OE *pōl*, 'pool'. The original pool here was converted into the ornamental lake at Wimpole Hall. DB *Winepole*.

Wimpstone (village, Warwicks): 'Wilhelm's or Wīghelm's farmstead'. OE *tūn*, 'farmstead'. 1313 *Wylmestone*.

Wincanton (town, Somerset): 'farmstead on the (river) Cale'. OE *tūn*, 'farmstead'. The river name is Celtic but of uncertain origin. In the town name it has been prefixed by the Celtic word for 'white' (modern Welsh *gwyn*). DB *Wincaletone*.

Wincham (hamlet, Cheshire): 'Wīgmund's homestead'. OE *hām*, 'homestead'. DB *Wimundisham*.

Winchcombe (town, Glos): 'valley with a bend in it'. OE *wincel*, 'corner' (related modern English *winch*), + *cumb*, 'valley'. The main valley of the river Isbourne here runs straight up to Charlton Abbots, but a side valley runs off southwest to Postlip, and Winchcombe stands at the bottom of it. *c*.810 *Wincelcumbe*.

Winchelsea (town, E Sussex): 'island by a river bend'. OE *wincel*, 'corner', + *ēg*, 'island'. The name applied to 'old' Winchelsea, much of which was swept away by the sea in the 13C. The present Winchelsea arose in the 14C on a nearby promontory. 1130 *Winceleseia*.

Winchester (city, Hants): 'Roman town of Venta'. OE *ceaster*, 'Roman station'. The Roman name of Winchester was *Venta Belgarum*, 'chief place of the Belgae', the first word of this giving the 'Win-' of the present name. The Roman city was the capital of the Belgae tribe. *c*.730 *Uintancæstir*, DB *Wincestre*.

Winchfield (village, Hants): 'open land by a corner'. OE *wincel*, 'corner', + *feld*, 'open land' (modern English *field*). 1229 *Winchelefeld*.

Winchmore Hill (district, Enfield): 'Wynsige's boundary hill'. OE *mǣre*, 'boundary', + *hyll*, 'hill'. The former hamlet lay near the southern boundary of the parish of Edmonton. 1319 *Wynsemerhull*.

Wincle (hamlet, Cheshire): '(place by) Wineca's hill'. OE *hyll*, 'hill'. The first part of the name could also represent OE *wince*, 'corner' (literally 'pulley', modern English *winch*) giving a sense 'hill with a corner'. Wincle lies in the bend of a valley. *c*.1190 *Winchul*.

Windermere (lake, Cumbria): 'Vinandr's lake'. OE *mere*, 'lake'. The middle '-er-' represents the genitive ending of the Scandinavian personal name. 12C *Winandermere*.

Winderton (village, Warwicks): 'farmstead used in winter'. OE *winter*, 'winter', + *tūn*, 'farmstead'. The village lies in a sheltered location under the ridge of Edge Hill. 1166 *Winterton*.

Windlesham (village, Surrey): 'Windel's homestead'. OE *hām*, 'homestead'. The first part of the name could also represent OE *windels*, 'windlass'. 1178 *Windesham*, 1227 *Windlesham*.

Windley (village, Derbys): 'clearing with a pasture'. OE *winn*, 'meadow', 'pasture', + *lēah*, 'clearing'. The name has been influenced by modern *wind*. 12C *Winleg*.

Windrush (village, Glos): '(place on the river) Windrush'. The river has a Celtic name probably meaning 'white marsh', from words related to modern Welsh *gwyn*, 'white', and Irish *riasc*, 'marsh'. DB *Wenric*.

Windsor (town, Windsor & Maid): '(place by the) slope with a windlass'. OE *windels*, 'windlass', + *ōra*, 'bank', 'slope'. The windlass in question was probably used for hauling carts up the muddy bank from the river Thames here rather than for actually pulling boats out of the water. Cp. BROADWINDSOR. The name, popularly interpreted as 'winding shore', originally applied to what is now the town of *Old Windsor*, as distinct from *New Windsor* (or simply *Windsor*), which grew up later around Windsor Castle. *c*.1060 *Windlesoran*, DB *Windesores*.

Winestead (village, E Yorks): 'homestead of the women'. OE *wīf*, 'woman' (modern English *wife*), + *stede*, 'place', 'homestead'. The name could also mean 'Wīfe's homestead', with a female personal name. DB *Wifestede*.

Winfarthing (village, Norfolk): 'Wina's quarter part'. OE *feorthung*, 'fourth part'. The name implies that Wina owned a quarter of an estate. DB *Wineferthinc*.

Winford (village, N Somerset): '(place on the river) Winford'. The river has a Celtic name meaning 'white stream' (modern Welsh *gwyn*, 'white', and *ffrwd*, 'stream'). *c*.1000 *Wunfrod*, DB *Wenfrod*.

Winforton (village, Herefords): 'Winefrith's farmstead'. OE *tūn*, 'farmstead', 'estate'. The DB form of the name below has corrupted the personal name. DB *Widferdestune*, 1265 *Wynfreton*.

Winfrith Newburgh (village, Dorset): 'Newburgh's (estate on the river) Winfrith'. The river name (now the Win, from the village name) is of Celtic origin and means 'white stream', from words related to modern Welsh *gwyn*, 'white', and *ffrwd*, 'stream'. The Newburgh family held the manor here in the 12C. The river also gave the name of nearby *Winfrith Heath*. DB *Winfrode*.

Wing (village, Bucks): '(settlement of) Wiwa's people'. OE *-ingas*, 'people of'. The name could also mean '(settlement of the) devotees of a temple' (OE *wīg* or *wēoh*, 'heathen temple', + *-ingas*). The first form of the name below is corrupt. 966 *Weowungum*, DB *Witehunge*.

Wing (village, Rutland): '(place at the) field'. OS *vengi*, 'field'. 12C *Wenge*.

Wingate (village, Durham): '(place in the) windswept gap'. OE *wind-geat* (from *wind*, 'wind', + *geat*, 'gate', 'gap'). The reference is to the gap between Wheatley Hill and Deaf Hill. 1071 *Windegatum*.

Wingerworth (village, Derbys): 'Winegār's enclosure'. OE *worth*, 'enclosure'. DB *Wingreurde*.

Wingfield (village, Suffolk): 'open land of Wīga's people'. OE *-inga-*, 'of the people of', + *feld*, 'open land' (modern English *field*). The first part of the name could also represent OE *wīg*, 'heathen temple'. *c.*1035 *Wingefeld*, DB *Wighefelda*.

Wingham (village, Kent): 'homestead of Wīga's people'. OE *-inga-*, 'of the people of', + *hām*, 'homestead'. The first part of the name could also represent OE *wīg*, 'heathen temple'. 834 *Uuigincggaham*, DB *Wingheham*.

Wingrave (village, Bucks): 'grove of Wiwa's people'. OE *-inga-*, 'of the people of', + *grāf*, 'grove'. The name could also mean 'grove of the worshippers at a heathen temple' (OE *wīg*, 'heathen temple', + *-inga-* + *grāf*). The DB form of the name below is corrupt. DB *Withungrave*, 1163 *Wiungraua*.

Winkburn (village, Notts): '(place by) Wineca's stream'. OE *burna*, 'stream'. The first part of the name could also represent OE *wincel*, 'bend', giving a sense '(place by the) stream with bends in it'. The '-k-' of the name is due to Scandinavian influence. The DB form of the name below has omitted the first *n*. DB *Wicheburne*, *c.*1150 *Winkeburna*.

Winkfield (village, Bracknell F): 'Wineca's open land'. OE *feld*, 'open land' (modern English *field*). The DB form of the name below is corrupt. 942 *Winecanfeld*, DB *Wenesfelle*.

Winkleigh (village, Devon): 'Wineca's woodland clearing'. OE *lēah*, 'wood', 'clearing'. DB *Wincheleia*.

Winksley (village, N Yorks): 'Winuc's woodland clearing'. OE *lēah*, 'wood', 'clearing'. DB *Wincheslaie*.

Winmarleigh (village, Lancs): 'Winemǣr's woodland clearing'. OE *lēah*, 'wood', 'clearing'. 1212 *Wynemerislega*.

Winnersh (suburb of Wokingham, Wokingham): 'ploughed field by the meadow'. OE *winn*, 'meadow', + *ersc*, 'ploughed field'. 1190 *Wenesse*.

Winnington (district of Northwich, Cheshire): 'estate associated with Wine'. OE *-ing-*, 'associated with', + *tūn*, 'farmstead'. The same personal name occurs for WINSFORD, 5 miles up the river Weaver. DB *Wenitone*.

Winscombe (village, N Somerset): '(place in) Wine's valley'. OE *cumb*, 'valley'. *c.*965 *Winescumbe*, DB *Winescome*.

Winsford (town, Cheshire): '(place by) Wine's ford'. OE *ford*, 'ford'. The ford here would have taken the road from Chester to Middlewich over the river Weaver. *c.*1334 *Wyneford*. SO ALSO: *Winsford*, Somerset.

Winsham (village, Somerset): 'Wine's homestead or enclosure'. OE *hām*, 'homestead', or *hamm*, 'enclosure'. 1046 *Winesham*, DB *Winesham*.

Winshill (district of Burton upon Trent, Staffs): '(place by) Wine's hill'. OE *hyll*, 'hill'. The DB form of the name below has garbled the second element. 1002 *Wineshylle*, DB *Wineshalle*.

Winsley (village, Wilts): 'Wine's woodland clearing'. OE *lēah*, 'wood', 'clearing'. 1242 *Winesleg*.

Winslow (town, Bucks): 'Wine's mound'. OE *hlāw*, 'mound'. Cp. WILMSLOW. 795 *Wineshlauu*, DB *Weneslai*.

Winson (village, Glos): 'Wine's farmstead'. OE *tūn*, 'farmstead', 'village'. DB *Winestune*.

Winster (village, Cumbria): '(place on the river) Winster'. The river has either a Celtic name meaning 'white stream' or a Scandinavian one meaning 'left one'. If the latter, the name would distinguish this river from the Gilpin, which flows on a parallel course to the east. 13C *Winster*.

Winster (village, Derbys): '(place by) Wine's thorn bush'. OE *thyrne*, 'thorn bush'. DB *Winsterne*.

Winston (village, Durham): 'Wine's farmstead', 'village'. OE *tūn*, 'farmstead', 'village'. 1091 *Winestona*. SO ALSO: *Winston*, Suffolk.

Winstone (village, Glos): '(place by) Wynna's stone'. OE *stān*, 'stone'. The reference is to a boundary stone here. DB *Winestan*.

Winterborne Came. See WINTERBOURNE ABBAS.

Winterborne Clenston. See WINTERBORNE ZELSTONE.

Winterborne Houghton. See WINTERBORNE ZELSTONE.

Winterborne Stickland. See WINTERBORNE ZELSTONE.

Winterborne Tomson. See WINTERBORNE ZELSTONE.

Winterborne Whitchurch. See WINTERBORNE ZELSTONE.

Winterborne Zelstone (village, Dorset): 'de Seles' (estate on the river) Winterborne'. The manor here on the river Winterborne (see WINTERBOURNE) was held in the 14C by the de Seles family. Other Winterbornes to the south and west of Blandford include *Winterborne Clenston*, where the manor was held by the Clench family, *Winterborne Houghton*, with Hugh's estate, *Winterborne Stickland*, with a steep lane (OE *sticol*, 'steep', + *lane*, 'lane'), *Winterborne Tomson*, held by one Thomas, and *Winterborne Whitchurch*, with a white church (perhaps built of stone rather than wood). DB *Wintreborne*, 1350 *Wynterbourn Selyston*.

Winterbourne (suburb of Bristol, S Glos): '(place by) Winterbourne'. The river here, now the Frome, must earlier have been the Winterbourne (OE *winter*, 'winter', + *burna*, 'stream'), a name for a stream or river that flows most fully in winter and that may dry up completely in summer. DB *Wintreborne*.

Winterbourne Abbas (village, Dorset): 'abbot's (estate by the river) Winterbourne'. The manor here on the river Winterbourne (see WINTERBOURNE) was held early by the abbey of Cerne, its name distinguishing this village from others south of Dorchester, such as *Winterborne Came*, held by the abbey of St Stephen at Caen, Normandy. DB *Wintreburne*, 1244 *Wynterburn Abbatis*.

Winterbourne Bassett (village, Wilts): 'Basset's (estate by the river) Winterbourne'. The river here now is the Kennet, but earlier it must have been the Winterbourne (see WINTERBOURNE). The manor here was held early by the Basset family, whose name distinguishes the village from *Winterbourne Monkton*, 2 miles to the south, held by the monks of Glastonbury Abbey. DB *Wintreburne*, 1242 *Winterburn Basset*.

Winterbourne Dauntsey. See WINTERBOURNE EARLS.

Winterbourne Earls (village, Wilts): 'earl's (estate by the river) Winterbourne'. The river here now is the Bourne but earlier it was the Winterbourne (see WINTERBOURNE). The manor was held early by the earls of Salisbury, their title distinguishing the village from nearby *Winterbourne Dauntsey*, held by the Danteseye family, and *Winterbourne Gunner*, held in 1249 by a lady called Gunnora. DB *Wintreburne*, 1250 *Winterburne Earls*.

Winterbourne Gunner. See WINTERBOURNE EARLS.

Winterbourne Monkton. See WINTERBOURNE BASSETT.

Winterbourne Stoke (village, Wilts): 'outlying farmstead by the (river) Winterbourne'. OE *stoc*, 'outlying farmstead'. The village preserves the earlier name (see WINTERBOURNE) of the river Till here. DB *Wintreburnestoch*.

Winteringham (village, N Lincs): 'homestead of Wintra's people'. OE *-inga-*, 'of the people of', + *hām*, 'homestead'. Winteringham is only 2 miles from WINTERTON, and both villages are probably named from the same group of settlers. DB *Wintringeham*.

Wintersett (hamlet, Wakefield): 'fold used in winter'. OE *winter*, 'winter', + *set*, 'fold' (for animals). c.1125 *Wintersete*.

Winterslow (village, Wilts): 'Winter's mound'. OE *hlǣw*, 'mound', 'tumulus'. DB *Wintreslev*.

Winterton (village, N Lincs): 'farmstead of Wintra's people'. OE *-inga-*, 'of the people of', + *tūn*, 'farmstead'. c.1067 *Wintringatun*, DB *Wintrintune*.

Winterton-on-Sea (resort village, Norfolk): 'winter farm by the sea'. OE *winter*, 'winter', + *tūn*, 'farmstead'. The farm here would have been used in winter months. A seaside site can be higher and drier than one a short distance inland, which is often low-lying and damper in winter. The name also contrasts with that of nearby *East Somerton* and *West Somerton* ('summer farm'), so that perhaps cattle were kept at Winterton in winter and taken to Somerton in the summer. 1044 *Winttertonne*, DB *Wintretuna*.

Winthorpe (hamlet, Lincs): 'Wina's outlying farmstead'. OS *thorp*, 'outlying farmstead'. The place may have been a secondary settlement of either Skegness or Ingoldmells. 12C *Winetorp*.

Winthorpe (village, Notts): 'Wīgmund's or Vígmundr's outlying farmstead'. OS *thorp*, 'outlying farmstead'. The personal names are respectively OE and Scandinavian. DB *Wimuntorp*.

Winton (district, Bournemouth). The district owes its name to Archibald William Montgomerie, 13th Earl of Eglinton (1812–61), who was created Earl of Winton in 1859. He was related to the Talbot sisters who gave the name of neighbouring TALBOT VILLAGE.

Winton (village, Cumbria): 'farmstead with pasture'. OE *winn*, 'pasture', + *tūn*, 'farmstead'. *c.*1094 *Wyntuna*.

Wintringham (village, N Yorks): 'homestead of Wintra's people'. OE *-inga-*, 'of the people of', + *hām*, 'homestead'. DB *Wentrigham*, 1169 *Wintringham*.

Winwick (village, Northants): 'Wina's farm'. OE *wīc*, 'dwelling', 'specialized farm'. 1043 *Winewican*, DB *Winewiche*. SO ALSO: *Winwick*, Cambs.

Winwick (village, Warrington): 'Wineca's farm'. OE *wīc*, 'dwelling', 'specialized farm'. 1170 *Winequic*, 1204 *Winewich*.

Wirksworth (town, Derbys): 'Weorc's enclosure'. OE *worth*, 'enclosure'. 835 *Wyrcesuuyrthe*, DB *Werchesworde*.

Wirral (peninsula, NW England): '(place in the) corner of land where bog myrtle grows'. OE *wīr*, 'bog myrtle', + *halh*, 'nook', 'corner of land'. This interpretation of the name poses problems. The Wirral is hardly a 'corner of land', and bog myrtle, as its name implies, grows in damp places, not on a mainly dry, high ridge, as here. Some other interpretation may thus be required. The name is now that of the local unitary authority. Early 10C *Wirheale*.

Wisbech (town, Cambs): '(place on the) ridge by the marshy meadow'. OE *wisse*, 'marshy meadow', + *bæc*, 'ridge' (modern English *back*). The first part of the name could alternatively come from the river *Wissey*, its name also from OE *wisse*, which rises in Norfolk some 30 miles east of Wisbech, then flows west to enter the Ouse around 10 miles southeast of the town. It is known that rivers in this fenland region have altered their course over the years, and it is not unlikely that at one time it ran further to the west to Wisbech and so gave the name of the town, today on the river Nene. The 'ridge' is the higher ground on which Wisbech stands. DB *Wisbece*.

Wisborough Green (village, W Sussex): '(place on the) hill by the marshy meadow'. OE *wisse*, 'marshy meadow', + *beorg*, 'hill'. The village, later associated with its green, lies on a small hill above a winding tributary of the river Arun. 1227 *Wisebregh*.

Wiseton (village, Notts): 'Wīsa's farmstead'. OE *tūn*, 'farmstead'. The name could also mean 'farmstead in a marshy meadow' (OE *wisc*, 'marshy meadow', + *tūn*). DB *Wisetone*.

Wishaw (town, N Lanarks): 'wood by a curved place'. OE *wiht*, 'bend', + *sceaga*, 'wood'. The 'curved place' may be the hill on which Wishaw is situated. DB *Witscaga*.

Wisley (hamlet, Surrey): '(place in the) clearing by a marshy meadow' OE *wisc*, 'marshy meadow', + *lēah*, 'wood', 'clearing'. Wisley lies low beside the river Wey and the meadows here are liable to flooding. DB *Wiselei*.

Wissett (village, Suffolk): 'Witta's fold'. OE *set*, 'fold' (for animals). DB *Wisseta*, 1165 *Witseta*.

Wissey (river). See WISBECH.

Wissington (hamlet, Suffolk): 'Wīgswīth's farmstead'. OE *tūn*, 'farmstead', 'estate'. The personal name is that of a woman. *c.*1000 *Wiswythetun*.

Wistanstow (village, Shropshire): 'Wīgstān's holy place'. OE *stōw*, 'holy place'. Wīgstān is more usually known as St Wistan, a Mercian prince murdered (perhaps here) in 850. DB *Wistanestou*.

Wistaston (village, Cheshire): 'Wīgstān's farmstead'. OE *tūn*, 'farmstead', 'village'. DB *Wistanestune*.

Wiston (village, Pemb): 'Wizo's farmstead'. OE *tūn*, 'farmstead'. Wizo was Wizo Flandrensis, 'Wizo of Flanders', who came from Flanders to set up his castle here in the 12C. Its Welsh name was *Castell Gwis*, 'Wizo's castle' (Welsh *castell*, 'castle'), which gave the present Welsh name of Wiston, *Cas-wis*. 1146 *Castellum Wiz*, 1319 *Wistune*.

Wiston (hamlet, W Sussex): 'Wīgstān's or Winestān's farmstead'. OE *tūn*, 'farmstead', 'village'. DB *Wistanestun*.

Wistow (hamlet, Leics): 'Wīgstān's holy place'. OE *stōw*, 'holy place'. The name is identical to that of WISTANSTOW, Shropshire, and the church here is dedicated to St Wistan. DB *Wistanestov*.

Wistow (village, N Yorks): 'dwelling place'. OE *wīc-stōw* (from *wīc*, 'dwelling', + *stōw*, 'place'). *c.*1030 *Wicstow*. SO ALSO: *Wistow*, Cambs.

Wiswell (village, Lancs): '(place by the) spring near a marshy meadow'. OE *wisc*, 'marshy meadow', + *wella*, 'spring', 'stream'. 1207 *Wisewell*.

Witcham (village, Cambs): '(place on the) promontory where wych elms grow'. OE *wice*, 'wych elm', + *hamm*, 'enclosure', 'promontory'. Witcham stands on a promontory jutting into the Bedford Level. 970 *Wichamme*, DB *Wiceham*.

Witchampton (village, Dorset): 'farmstead of the dwellers at (a place associated with) a Romano-British settlement'. OE *wīc*, 'Romano-British settlement', + *hǣme*, 'dwellers', + *tūn*, 'farmstead', 'village'. Extensive Roman remains have been found here, and the Roman road from Badbury Rings to Old Sarum runs nearby. DB *Wichemetune*.

Witchford (village, Cambs): '(place by the) ford where wych elms grow'. OE *wice*, 'wych elm', + *ford*, 'ford'. Witchford is only just over 2 miles from WITCHAM. DB *Wiceford*.

Witham (river). See NORTH WITHAM.

Witham (town, Essex): 'homestead by a river bend'. OE *wiht*, 'bend', + *hām*, 'homestead'. There is a bend in the river Brain to the south of Witham. DB *Witham*.

Witham Friary (village, Somerset): 'councillor's homestead'. OE *wita*, 'councillor', + *hām*, 'homestead'. The name could also mean 'Witta's homestead'. The second word of the name, first recorded in the 16C, is perhaps from Latin *fraeria*, 'guild'. DB *Witeham*.

Witham on the Hill (village, Lincs): 'homestead in a bend on the hill'. OE *wiht*, 'bend', + *hām*, 'homestead'. The second part of the name distinguishes the village from NORTH WITHAM and *South Witham*, 14 miles to the northwest. DB *Witham*.

Witheridge (village, Devon): '(place on the) ridge where willow trees grow'. OE *wīthig*, 'willow' (modern English *withy*), + *hrycg*, 'ridge'. The name could also mean '(place on the) ridge where wethers are kept' (OE *wether*, 'wether' (castrated ram), + *hrycg*). The DB form of the name below is corrupt. DB *Wiriga*, 1256 *Wytherigge*.

Witherley (village, Leics): 'Wīgthrȳth's woodland clearing'. OE *lēah*, 'wood', 'clearing'. The personal name is that of a woman. c.1204 *Wytherdele*.

Withernsea (resort village, E Yorks): 'lake (at the place) near the thorn bush'. OE *with*, 'against', 'toward' (modern English *with*), + *thorn*, 'thorn bush', + *sǣ*, 'lake' (modern English

sea). It is possible the elements of the name may be OS, not OE, but with the same individual senses. There is no lake here now. DB *Widfornessei*.

Withernwick (village, E Yorks): 'dairy farm (at the place) near the thorn bush'. OE *with*, 'against', 'toward' (modern English *with*), + *thorn*, 'thorn bush', + *wīc*, 'dairy farm'. DB *Widforneuuic*.

Withersdale Street (village, Suffolk): '(place in the) valley where wethers are kept'. OE *wether*, 'wether' (castrated ram), + *dæl*, 'valley'. The DB form of the name below has omitted a syllable. The second word of the name amounts to 'hamlet'. DB *Weresdel*, 1184 *Wideresdala*.

Withersfield (village, Suffolk): 'open land where wethers are kept'. OE *wether*, 'wether' (castrated ram), + *feld*, 'open land' (modern English *field*). DB *Wedresfelda*.

Witherslack (hamlet, Cumbria): '(place in the) valley of the wood'. OS *vithr*, 'wood', + *slakki*, 'valley'. The name could also mean '(place in the) valley of the willow tree' (OS *víth*, 'willow', + *slakki*). c.1190 *Witherslake*.

Withiel (village, Cornwall): 'wooded district'. Cornish *gwydhyel* (from *gwydh*, 'trees', + adjectival ending *-yel*). Cp. LOSTWITHIEL. The locality is not noticeably wooded today. DB *Widie*.

Withiel Florey (hamlet, Somerset): 'de Flury's (estate by the) wood or clearing where willow trees grow'. OE *wīthig*, 'willow' (modern English *withy*), + *lēah*, 'wood', 'clearing'. The de Flury family held the manor here in the 13C. 737 *Withiglea*, 1305 *Wythele Flory*.

Withington (village, Glos): '(place by) Widia's hill'. OE *dūn*, 'hill'. 737 *Wudiandun*, DB *Widindune*.

Withington (village, Herefords): 'farmstead with a willow copse'. OE *wīthign*, 'willow copse', + *tūn*, 'farmstead'. DB *Widingtune*.

Withnell (village, Lancs): '(place by the) hill where willow trees grow'. OE *wīthigen*, 'growing with willows', + *hyll*, 'hill'. c.1160 *Withinhull*.

Withybrook (village, Warwicks): '(place by the) brook where willow trees grow'. OE *wīthig*, 'willow' (modern English *withy*), + *brōc*, 'brook'. 'On the banks whereof antiently, as well as now, many Willows have grown' (William Dugdale, *The Antiquities of Warwickshire*, 1656). 12C *Wythibroc*.

Withycombe (village, Somerset): '(place in the) valley where willow trees grow'. OE *wīthig*, 'willow' (modern English *withy*), + *cumb*, 'valley'. DB *Widicumbe*.

Withycombe Raleigh (suburb of Exmouth, Devon): 'de Ralegh's (estate in the) valley where willow trees grow'. OE *wīthig*, 'willow' (modern English *withy*), + *cumb*, 'valley'. The de Ralegh family held the manor here in the early 14C. DB *Widecoma*, 1465 *Widecombe Ralegh*.

Withyham (village, E Sussex): 'enclosure where willow trees grow'. OE *wīthig*, 'willow' (modern English *withy*), + *hamm*, 'enclosure'. The 'enclosure' here is wet land hemmed in by higher ground. 1230 *Withiham*.

Withypool (village, Somerset): '(place by the) pool where willow trees grow'. OE *wīthig*, 'willow' (modern English *withy*), + *pōl*, 'pool'. Withypool is on the river Barle. DB *Widepolle*.

Witley (village, Surrey): 'woodland clearing in a bend'. OE *wiht*, 'bend', + *lēah*, 'wood', 'clearing'. The name could also mean 'Witta's woodland clearing'. DB *Witlei*.

Witnesham (village, Suffolk): 'Wittin's homestead'. OE *hām*, 'homestead'. The DB form of the name below has *d* for *n*. DB *Witdesham*, 1254 *Witnesham*.

Witney (town, Oxon): 'Witta's island'. OE *ēg*, 'island'. The 'island' is the relatively high ground on which Witney stands on the river Windrush at the point where the river divides into several branches. The town's fame for its manufacture of blankets (a word from French *blanc*, 'white') has led to the fancy that Witney takes its name from English *white*. 969 *Wyttanige*, DB *Witenie*.

Wittering (village, Peterborough): '(settlement of) Wither's people'. OE *-ingas*, 'people of'. The first form of the name below means 'island of Wither's people' (OE *-inga-*, 'of the people of', + *ēg*, 'island', referring to raised land), while the DB form means 'homestead of Wither's people' (OE *-inga-*, + *hām*, 'homestead'). The named man may be the same Wither who gave the name of WERRINGTON, 8 miles to the east. 972 *Wltheringaeige*, DB *Witheringham*, 1167 *Witeringa*.

Wittersham (village, Kent): 'Wihtrīc's promontory'. OE *hamm*, 'enclosure', 'promontory'. The village stands on high ground on the Isle of Oxney overlooking the Rother Levels. 1032 *Wihtriceshamme*.

Witton (district, Birmingham): 'farmstead by a Romano-British settlement'. OE *wīc*, 'Romano-British settlement', + *tūn*, 'farmstead'. DB *Witone*.

Witton (hamlet, Norfolk): 'farmstead by a wood'. OE *wudu*, 'wood', + *tūn*, 'farmstead'. The form of the name below is for Witton near

North Walsham, but Witton near Norwich has a name of identical origin. DB *Widituna*.

Witton Gilbert (village, Durham): 'Gilbert's farmstead by a wood'. OE *widu*, 'wood', + *tūn*, 'farmstead'. Gilbert de la Ley held the manor here in the 12C. The second word of the name is pronounced with a soft 'g', as in 'George'. 1195 *Wyton*.

Witton-le-Wear (village, Durham): 'farmstead by a wood on the (river) Wear'. OE *wudu*, 'wood', + *tūn*, 'farmstead'. For the river name, see MONKWEARMOUTH. c.1050 *Wudutun*.

Wiveliscombe (town, Somerset): 'Wifel's valley'. OE *cumb*, 'valley'. The town is in a marked valley between high hills. The first part of the name could also represent OE *wifel*, 'weevil', denoting a valley full of these beetles. 854 *Wifelescumb*, DB *Wivelescome*.

Wivelsfield (village, E Sussex): 'Wifel's open land'. OE *feld*, 'open land' (modern English *field*). The first part of the name could also represent OE *wifel*, 'weevil', giving a sense 'open land full of weevils'. c.765 *Wifelesfeld*.

Wivenhoe (town, Essex): 'Wīfe's hillspur'. OE *hōh*, 'hill spur'. The '-en-' of the name represents the genitive ending of the personal name, that of a woman. DB *Wiunhov*.

Wiveton (village, Norfolk): 'Wīfe's farmstead'. OE *tūn*, 'farmstead', 'village'. The personal name is that of a woman. DB *Wiuentona*.

Wix (village, Essex): 'dwellings'. OE *wīc*, 'dwelling', 'specialized farm'. The name represents the ME plural form *wikes*. DB *Wica*.

Wixford (village, Warwicks): '(place by) Wihtlāc's ford'. OE *ford*, 'ford'. The river here is the Alne. The DB form of the name below is garbled. 962 *Wihtlachesforde*, DB *Witelavesford*.

Wixoe (village, Suffolk): 'Widuc's hill spur'. OE *hōh*, 'hill spur'. The DB form of the name below is corrupt. DB *Witeskeou*, 1205 *Widekeshoo*.

Woburn (village, Beds): '(place by the) winding stream'. OE *wōh*, 'crooked', + *burna*, 'stream'. The name is properly that of the stream here, which also gave the name of *Woburn Sands*, Milton K, 2 miles to the northwest. DB *Woburne*.

Woking (town, Surrey): '(settlement of) Wocc's people'. OE *-ingas*, 'people of'. See also WOKINGHAM. c.712 *Wocchingas*, DB *Wochinges*.

Wokingham (town, Wokingham): 'homestead of Wocc's people'. OE *-inga-*, 'of the people of', + *hām*, 'homestead'. The same man probably gave the name of WOKING, 18 miles to the southeast. 1146 *Wokingeham*.

Woldingham (suburb of Warlingham, Surrey): 'homestead of the forest dwellers'. OE *weald*, 'forest' (see WEALD), + *-inga-*, 'of the dwellers at', + *hām*, 'homestead'. The name could also mean 'homestead of Wealda's people'. The DB form of the name below has *l* for *d*. DB *Wallingeham*, 1204 *Waldingham*.

Wold Newton (village, NE Lincs): 'new farmstead in the Wolds' OE *nīwe*, 'new', + *tūn*, 'farmstead', 'village'. The first word of the name refers to the location of the village in a dip in the Lincolnshire WOLDS. DB *Neutone*.

Wolds (upland region, Lincs): 'high woodland'. OE *wald*, 'woodland'. The *Lincolnshire Wolds* are essentially a southern continuation, across the Humber, of the *Yorkshire Wolds*, and the name itself now generally applies to high woodland that has been cleared as a result of the gradual deforestation of England. The upland region south of the Vale of Belvoir in Leicestershire and Nottinghamshire is sometimes known as the *Leicestershire Wolds*. The word is familiar as part of a distinguishing addition to a name, as FOSTON ON THE WOLDS, GARTON-ON-THE-WOLDS, etc. OE *wald* is related to WEALD.

Wolferton (village, Norfolk): 'Wulfhere's farmstead'. OE *tūn*, 'farmstead', 'village'. 1166 *Wulferton*.

Wolf Rock (rock, Cornwall). 'The rock is said to be so named from the roar of the waves dashing against it' (*Cassell's Gazetteer of Great Britain and Ireland*, 1898). It is also a danger to shipping to the west of Land's End. Hence its lighthouse. The first form of the name below apparently represents *wolf*. 1564 *The Gulfe*, 1584 *De Wolff*.

Wolfsdale (hamlet, Pemb): '(place in the) valley where wolves are seen'. OE *wulf*, 'wolf', + *dæl*, 'valley'. 1312 *Wolvedale*.

Wollaston (village, Northants): 'Wulflāf's farmstead'. OE *tūn*, 'farmstead', 'village'. The DB form of the name below has *i* for *u* in the personal name. DB *Wilavestone*, 1190 *Wullaueston*.

Wollaston (hamlet, Shropshire): 'Wīglāf's farmstead'. OE *tūn*, 'farmstead', 'village'. DB *Willavestune*.

Wollaton (district, Nottingham): 'Wulflāf's village'. OE *tūn*, 'farmstead', 'village'. DB *Olavestone*.

Wollerton (village, Shropshire): 'Wulfrūn's farmstead'. OE *tūn*, 'farmstead', 'village'. The personal name is that of a woman. DB *Ulvretone*, c.1135 *Wluruntona*.

Wolsingham (town, Durham): 'homestead at the place associated with Wulfsige'. OE *-ing*, 'place named after', + *hām*, 'homestead'. c.1150 *Wlsingham*.

Wolstanton (district of Newcastle-under-Lyme, Staffs): 'Wulfstān's farmstead'. OE *tūn*, 'farmstead'. DB *Wlstanetone*.

Wolston (village, Warwicks): 'Wulfrīc's farmstead'. OE *tūn*, 'farmstead', 'village'. DB *Ulvricetone*.

Wolvercote (district of Oxford, Oxon): 'cottage associated with Wulfgār'. OE *-ing-*, 'associated with', + *cot*, 'cottage'. DB *Ulfgarcote*.

Wolverhampton (city, Wolverhampton): 'Wulfrūn's high farmstead'. OE *hēah*, 'high', + *tūn*, 'farmstead'. The name was originally simply *Hampton*. In 985 King Ethelred granted the manor here to Wulfrun, a lady whose name was subsequently added to this for purposes of distinction from other Hamptons. Her name is also preserved in the Wulfrun Shopping Centre and in *Wulfrunian* as a modern term for a native or resident of Wolverhampton. The popular association of the name with wolves, familiar from the nickname of Wolverhampton Wanderers football club, has led to a false attribution to this animal: 'The settlement of Wolverhampton, in the middle of a forest, tells by its name of the ravages made by the wild wolves on the flocks of its first inhabitants' (Mandell Creighton, *The Story of Some English Shires*, 1897). 985 *Heantune*, c.1080 *Wolvrenehamptonia*.

Wolverley (village, Worcs): 'woodland clearing associated with Wulfweard'. OE *-ing-*, 'associated with', + *lēah*, 'wood', 'clearing'. 866 *Wulfferdinleh*, DB *Ulwardelei*.

Wolverton (town, Milton K): 'estate associated with Wulfhere'. OE *-ing-*, 'associated with', + *tūn*, 'farmstead', 'estate'. DB *Wluerintone*.

Wolvey (village, Warwicks): 'enclosure protecting against wolves'. OE *wulf*, 'wolf', + *hege* or *hæg*, 'enclosure' (related modern English *hedge*). DB *Ulveia*.

Wolviston (village, Stockton): 'Wulf's farmstead'. OE *tūn*, 'farmstead', 'village'. 1091 *Oluestona*.

Wombleton (village, N Yorks): 'Wynbald's or Winebald's farmstead'. OE *tūn*, 'farmstead'. DB *Winbeltun*.

Wombourne (town, Staffs): '(place at the) winding stream'. OE *wōh*, 'crooked', + *burna*, 'stream'. As with WOBURN, the name is actually that of the stream here. The '-m-' of the name represents the final letter of OE *wōn*, the dative form of *wōh*. DB *Wamburne*.

Wombwell (town, Barnsley): '(place at a) spring in a hollow'. OE *wamb*, 'hollow' (modern English *womb*), + *wella*, 'spring', 'stream'. The first part of the name could also represent the personal name Wamba, giving a meaning 'Wamba's (place at a) spring'. DB *Wanbuelle*.

Womenswold (village, Kent): 'forest of Wimel's people'. OE *-inga-*, 'of the people of', + *weald*, 'forest' (cp. WEALD). 824 *Wimlincgawald*.

Womersley (village, N Yorks): 'Wilmær's woodland clearing'. OE *lēah*, 'wood', 'clearing'. DB *Wilmereslege*.

Wonersh (village, Surrey): 'crooked ploughed field'. OE *wōh*, 'crooked', + *ersc*, 'ploughed field'. The first part of the name represents OE *wōgan*, a dative form of *wōh*. 1199 *Woghenhers*.

Wooburn (village, Bucks): '(place by the) crooked stream'. OE *wōh*, 'crooked', 'winding', + *burna*, 'stream'. The village lies on a curve of the river Wye before its confluence with the Thames, and this is the 'crooked stream'. Cp. WOBURN. *c.*1075 *Waburna*, DB *Waborne*, 1201 *Woburne*.

Woodbastwick (village, Norfolk): 'farm where bast is obtained by the wood'. OE *wudu*, 'wood', + *bæst*, 'bast', + *wīc*, 'farm'. Bast is limetree bark used in ropemaking. 1044 *Bastwik*, DB *Bastuuic*, 1253 *Wodbastwyk*.

Woodborough (village, Notts): 'fortified place by the wood'. OE *wudu*, 'wood', + *burh*, 'fortified place'. The 'fortified place' in question is probably the old encampment at nearby Fox Wood. DB *Udeburg*.

Woodborough (village, Wilts): '(place by the) wooded hill'. OE *wudu*, 'wood', + *beorg*, 'hill'. 1208 *Wideberghe*.

Woodbridge (town, Suffolk): '(place by the) wooden bridge'. OE *wudu*, 'wood', + *brycg*, 'bridge'. The name could also be understood as '(place by the) bridge near the wood'. Either way, the bridge would have been over the river Deben here. *c.*1050 *Oddebruge*, DB *Wudebrige*.

Woodbury (village, Devon): 'fortified place by the wood'. OE *wudu*, 'wood', + *burh*, 'fortified place'. The 'fortified place' is the ancient earthwork known as Woodbury Castle here. DB *Wodeberia*.

Woodchester (village, Glos): 'Roman camp in the wood'. OE *wudu*, 'wood', + *ceaster*,

'Roman camp'. The remains of a Roman villa lie to the north of the village. 716 *Uuduceastir*, DB *Widecestre*.

Woodchurch (village, Kent): 'wooden church'. OE *wudu*, 'wood', + *cirice*, 'church'. The name could also mean 'church by the wood'. *c.*1100 *Wuducirce*.

Woodcote (village, Oxon): 'cottage in a wood'. OE *wudu*, 'wood', + *cot*, 'cottage'. DB *Wdecote*. SO ALSO: *Woodcote*, Croydon.

Wood Dalling (hamlet, Norfolk): '(settlement of) Dalla's people in woodland'. OE *wudu*, 'wood', + *-ingas*, 'people of'. The first word of the name was added to distinguish this place from *Field Dalling*, '(settlement of) Dalla's people in the open country' (OE *feld*, 'open land'), 10 miles to the northwest. DB *Dallinga*, 1198 *Wode Dallinges*.

Woodditton. See FEN DITTON.

Woodeaton (village, Oxon): 'farmstead by a river near a wood'. OE *wudu*, 'wood', + OE *ēa*, 'river', + *tūn*, 'farmstead'. The river here is the Cherwell. The first part of the name was added for distinction from nearby WATER EATON. DB *Etone*, 1185 *Wudeetun*.

Woodend (village, Northants): '(place at the) end of the wood'. OE *wudu*, 'wood', + *ende*, 'end'. 1316 *Wodende*.

Wood Enderby. See MAVIS ENDERBY.

Woodfalls (village, Wilts): 'fold by a wood'. OE *wudu*, 'wood', + *fald*, 'fold', 'enclosure for animals'. 1258 *Wudefolde*.

Woodford (village, Northants): '(place at the) ford by a wood'. OE *wudu*, 'wood', + *ford*, 'ford'. The river here is the Nene. DB *Wodeford*. SO ALSO: *Woodford*, Cornwall, Stockport.

Woodford (village, Wilts): '(place at the) ford by a wood'. OE *wudu*, 'wood', + *ford*, 'ford'. The river here is the Avon. 972 *Wuduforda*.

Woodford Green (district, Redbridge): '(place at the) ford by a wood'. OE *wudu*, 'wood', + *ford*, 'ford'. The parish of Woodford was divided into four parts: *Woodford Green*, with a village green, to the west, *Woodford Wells*, with springs, to the north, *Woodford Bridge*, with a bridge over the river Roding, to the east, and *South Woodford*, to the south. The wood is Epping Forest. DB *Wodeforda*.

Wood Green (district, Haringey): 'green place by a wood'. OE *wudu*, 'wood', + *grēne*, 'green'. The wood involved here is Enfield Chase, and a remnant of the original 'green place' still exists in the form of Wood Green Common. 1502 *Wodegrene*.

Woodhall Spa (town, Lincs): 'spa by Woodhall'. The basic name means 'hall in the wood' (OE *wudu*, 'wood', + *hall*, 'hall'), perhaps as the place where the forest court met. The spa evolved in the 19C when a spring rich in minerals was unexpectedly discovered in an abandoned coalpit. 12C *Wudehalle*, 1824 *Woodhall Spa*.

Woodham Ferrers (village, Essex): 'de Ferrers' homestead by a wood'. OE *wudu*, 'wood', + *hām*, 'homestead'. The de Ferrers family held the manor early here, their name distinguishing this Woodham from *Woodham Mortimer*, 4 miles to the north, held by the Mortimer family, and *Woodham Walter*, 5 miles to the north, held by the Fitzwalter family. *c.*975 *Wudaham*, DB *Udeham*, 1230 *Wodeham Ferrers*.

Woodhorn (village, Northd): '(place by the) wooded horn of land'. OE *wudu*, 'wood', + *horn*, 'horn'. The 'horn' is a nearby coastal promontory. 1178 *Wudehorn*.

Woodhouse (district, Leeds): 'house by a wood'. OE *wudu*, 'wood', + *hūs*, 'house'. The name will have the same sense elsewhere. Cp. MANSFIELD WOODHOUSE. 1200 *Wdehus*.

Woodhouse Eaves (village, Leics): 'house at the edge of a wood'. OE *wudu*, 'wood', + *hūs*, 'house', + *efes*, 'edge of a wood' (modern English *eaves*). The village is on the edge of Charnwood Forest. *c.*1220 *Wodehuses*.

Woodland (hamlet, Devon): 'cultivated land by a wood'. OE *wudu*, 'wood', + *land*, 'cultivated land'. 1328 *Wodelonde*.

Woodlands (village, Dorset): 'cultivated land by a wood'. OE *wudu*, 'wood', + *land*, 'cultivated land'. 1244 *Wodelande*.

Woodleigh (village, Devon): 'clearing in a wood'. OE *wudu*, 'wood', + *lēah*, 'clearing'. *c.*1010 *Wuduleage*, DB *Odelie*.

Woodlesford (district, Rothwell, Leeds): '(place at the) ford by a thicket'. OE *wrīdels*, 'thicket', + *ford*, 'ford'. The ford in question was probably where Swillington Bridge is now, taking the Wakefield road (the present A642) over the river Aire. 12C *Wridelesford*.

Woodmancote (village, Glos): 'cottage of the woodsmen'. OE *wudu-mann* (from *wudu*, 'wood', + *mann*, 'mann'), + *cot*, 'cottage'. The form of the name below relates to Woodmancote near Cirencester, but Woodmancote near Cheltenham has a name of identical origin. 12C *Wodemancote*.

Woodmansey (village, E Yorks): '(place by the) pool of the woodman'. OE *wudu-mann*

(from *wudu*, 'wood', + *mann*, 'man'), + *sǣ*, 'pool'. 1289 *Wodemanse*.

Woodmansterne (district of Banstead, Surrey): 'thorn bush by the boundary of the wood'. OE *wudu*, 'wood', + *mǣre*, 'boundary', + *thorn*, 'thorn bush'. The name was subsequently corrupted to suggest an association with *woodman*. The DB form of the name below is similarly garbled. DB *Odemerestor*, *c.*1190 *Wudemaresthorne*.

Woodnesborough (village, Kent): '(place by the) mound associated with Wōden'. OE *beorg*, 'mound'. The name implies a place of worship dedicated to the pagan war god. The DB form of the name below has garbled the god name. DB *Wanesberge*, *c.*1100 *Wodnesbeorge*.

Woodnewton (village, Northants): 'new farmstead in woodland'. OE *wudu*, 'wood', + *nīwe*, 'new', + *tūn*, 'farmstead'. The original 'new farmstead' was distinguished from other Newtons by its location in Cliffe Forest, part of Rockingham Forest. DB *Niwetone*, 1255 *Wodeneuton*.

Woodperry (hamlet, Oxon): '(place with) pear trees by a wood'. OE *wudu*, 'wood', + *pirige*, 'pear tree'. The first part of the name was added for distinction from WATERPERRY, 4 miles to the southeast. DB *Perie*, 1120 *Wdeperie*.

Woodplumpton (village, Lancs): 'farmstead where plum trees grow in woodland'. OE *wudu*, 'wood', + *plūme*, 'plum tree', + *tūn*, 'farmstead'. DB *Pluntun*, 1327 *Wodeplumpton*.

Woodrising (hamlet, Norfolk): '(settlement of) Risa's people by the wood'. OE *-ingas*, 'people of'. DB *Risinga*, 1291 *Woderisingg*.

Woodsetts (village, Rotherham): 'folds in the wood'. OE *wudu*, 'wood', + *set*, 'fold' (for animals). 1324 *Wodesete*.

Woodsford (village, Dorset): '(place by) Weard's ford'. OE *ford*, 'ford'. The ford in question would have been over the river Frome here. DB *Wardesford*.

Woodstock (town, Oxon): 'place in the woods'. OE *wudu*, 'wood', + *stoc*, 'place'. *c.*1000 *Wudestoce*, DB *Wodestoch*.

Woodthorpe (hamlet, Derbys): 'outlying farmstead in woodland'. OE *wudu*, 'wood', + OS *thorp*, 'outlying farmstead'. 1258 *Wodethorpe*. SO ALSO: *Woodthorpe*, Lincs.

Woodton (village, Norfolk): 'farmstead by a wood'. OE *wudu*, 'wood', + *tūn*, 'farmstead'. DB *Wodetuna*.

Woodville (village, Derbys). 'A populous village of potters has sprung up in its [Butt

House's] neighbourhood by the names of "Wooden-Box", or more commonly "The Box" derived, as is well known, from a hut set up there for a person to sit in to receive the toll at the turnpike. The *Historical Collector* may add that this wooden box was originally a port wine butt from Drakelow Hall. In 1845 the name of the place was changed from Wooden-Box to Woodville, and formed into "The consolidated Chapelry of Woodville" by an order of the Queen in Council, June 17th, 1847.—See *The London Gazette* of July 6th, 1847' (*The Midland Counties Historical Collector*, vol. II, no. 26, 1 September, 1856).

Woodyates (hamlet, Dorset): '(place at the) gap in the wood'. OE *wudu*, 'wood', + *geat*, 'gate', 'gap'. 9C *Wdegeate*, DB *Odiete*.

Woofferton (village, Shropshire): 'Wulfhere's or Wulffrith's farmstead'. OE *tūn*, 'farmstead'. 1221 *Wulfreton*.

Wookey (village, Somerset): '(place by the) trap for animals'. OE *wōcig*, 'snare' (related to OE *wōh* in WOBURN). The original 'animal trap' may have been set in the cave here known as *Wookey Hole* (OE *hol*, 'ravine'). 1065 *Woky*.

Wool (village, Dorset): '(place by the) springs'. OE *wiella*, 'spring', 'stream'. The springs in question are just south of the village, and their presence is implicit in local names such as Spring Street, Springfield Cottage and Well Head Close. DB *Welle*.

Woolacombe (village resort, Devon): 'valley with a stream'. OE *wiella*, 'spring', 'stream', + *cumb*, 'valley'. Woolacombe lies in a typical West Country 'coomb'. DB *Wellecome*.

Woolaston (village, Glos): 'Wulflāf's farmstead'. OE *tūn*, 'farmstead'. DB *Odelaweston*.

Woolbeding (hamlet, W Sussex): 'place associated with Wulfbeald'. OE *-ing*, 'place associated with'. DB *Welbedlinge*.

Wooler (town, Northd): '(place on the) ridge with a spring'. OE *wella*, 'spring', + *ofer*, 'ridge'. The 'ridge' here is probably the highish ground on which the town lies overlooking the river Till. 1187 *Wulloure*.

Woolfardisworthy (village, Devon): 'Wulfheard's enclosure'. OE *worthig*, 'enclosure'. There are two Devon villages of this name, of identical origin. The one near Clovelly now usually has the abbreviated form *Woolsery*, as on Ordnance Survey maps and in press reports ('Residents of Woolsery ... threatened to resort to direct action', *The Times*, 18 May 2001). The forms of the name below are for Woolfardisworthy near Crediton, the DB

form representing the noble effort of the Norman scribe. DB *Ulfaldeshodes*, 1264 *Wolfardesworthi*, 1825 *Woolfardisworthy otherwise Woolsworthy*.

Woolhampton (village, W Berks): 'estate associated with Wulflāf'. OE *-ing-*, 'associated with', + *tūn*, 'farmstead', 'estate'. The second part of the name has become wrongly associated with OE *hām-tūn*, 'home farm', as in ROEHAMPTON. DB *Ollavintone*.

Woolhope (village, Herefords): 'Wulfgifu's (estate in the) valley'. OE *hop*, 'valley'. The personal name is that of the lady who gave the manor here to Hereford Cathedral in the 11C. DB *Hope*, 1234 *Wulvivehop*.

Woolland (village, Dorset): 'estate with a pasture'. OE *wynn*, 'meadow', 'pasture', + *land*, 'cultivated land', 'estate'. 934 *Wonlonde*, DB *Winlande*.

Woolley (village, Wakefield): 'wood or clearing where wolves are seen'. OE *wulf*, 'wolf', + *lēah*, 'wood', 'clearing'. DB *Wiluelai*. SO ALSO: *Woolley*, Cambs.

Woolpit (village, Suffolk): '(place by the) pit for trapping wolves'. OE *wulf-pytt* (from *wulf*, 'wolf', + *pytt*, 'pit'). 10C *Wlpit*, DB *Wlfpeta*.

Woolscott (hamlet, Warwicks): 'Wulfsige's cottage'. OE *cot*, 'cottage'. *c.*1235 *Wulscote*.

Woolsery. See WOOLFARDISWORTHY.

Woolstaston (village, Shropshire): 'Wulfstān's farmstead'. OE *tūn*, 'farmstead'. DB *Ulestanestune*.

Woolsthorpe by Belvoir (village, Lincs): 'Wulfstān's secondary settlement near Belvoir'. OS *thorp*, 'secondary settlement'. The second part of the name (see BELVOIR) distinguishes this Woolsthorpe, by the Leicestershire border, from WOOLSTHORPE BY COLSTERWORTH. DB *Ulestanestorp*.

Woolsthorpe by Colsterworth (village, Lincs): 'Wulflāf's secondary settlement near Colsterworth'. OS *thorp*, 'secondary settlement'. (It is likely that Colsterworth itself was the main settlement.) The second part of the name (see COLSTERWORTH) distinguishes this Woolsthorpe from WOOLSTHORPE BY BELVOIR. 1185 *Wolestorp*.

Woolston (hamlet, Shropshire): 'Ōswulf's farmstead'. OE *tūn*, 'farmstead'. This is Woolston near Oswestry. DB *Osulvestune*.

Woolston (hamlet, Shropshire): 'Wulfhere's farmstead'. OE *tūn*, 'farmstead'. This is Woolston near Craven Arms. The DB form of the name below probably resulted from confusion with nearby WISTANSTOW. DB *Wistanestune*, 1208 *Wlureston*.

Woolston (district, Southampton): 'Wulf's farmstead'. OE *tūn*, 'farmstead'. DB *Olvestune*.

Woolston (district, Warrington): 'Wulfsige's farmstead'. OE *tūn*, 'farmstead'. 1142 *Ulfitona*. SO ALSO: *Woolston*, Devon.

Woolstone (village, Glos): 'Wulfsige's farmstead'. OE *tūn*, 'farmstead'. DB *Olsendone*.

Woolton (district, Liverpool): 'Wulfa's farmstead'. OE *tūn*, 'farmstead'. DB *Uluentune*.

Woolverstone (village, Suffolk): 'Wulfhere's farmstead'. OE *tūn*, 'farmstead'. DB *Uluerestuna*.

Woolverton (village, Somerset): 'estate associated with Wulfhere'. OE *-ing-*, 'associated with', + *tūn*, 'farmstead', 'estate'. 1196 *Wulfrinton*.

Woolwich (district, Greenwich): 'port for wool'. OE *wull*, 'wool', + *wīc*, 'trading settlement', 'port'. Wool would have been loaded onto or off boats on the Thames here. The DB form of the name below is corrupt. 918 *Uuluuich*, DB *Hulviz*.

Woore (village, Shropshire): '(place by the) swaying tree'. OE *wæfre*, 'unstable' (related modern English *waver*). The name may have applied to the appearance of trees on the ridge here. DB *Wavre*.

Wootton (village, N Lincs): 'farmstead by a wood'. OE *wudu*, 'wood', + *tūn*, 'farmstead'. DB *Udetone*. SO ALSO: *Wootton*, Northants, Oxon (near Abingdon).

Wootton Bassett (town, Wilts): 'Basset's farmstead by a wood'. OE *wudu*, 'wood', + *tūn*, 'farmstead'. The manor here was held by the Basset family in the 13C, their name distinguishing this Wootton from *Wootton Rivers*, 15 miles to the southeast, where it was held by the de Rivere family. The Basset name recurs in this part of Wiltshire for BERWICK BASSETT, COMPTON BASSETT and WINTERBOURNE BASSETT. 680 *Wdetun*, DB *Wodetone*, 1272 *Wotton Basset*.

Wootton Glanville. See GLANVILLES WOOTTON.

Wootton Rivers. See WOOTTON BASSETT.

Wootton St Lawrence (village, Hants): 'farmstead by a wood with St Lawrence's church'. OE *wudu*, 'wood', + *tūn*, 'farmstead'. The church dedication distinguishes this village from nearby *Upper Wootton*. 990 *Wudatune*, DB *Odetone*.

Wootton Wawen (village, Warwicks): 'Wagen's farmstead by a wood'. OE *wudu*, 'wood', + *tūn*, 'farmstead'. A Scandinavian named Wagen held the manor here in the 11C. 'As for the name, there is no question but that it was originally occasioned from the situation, being amongst woods: and so, for the facility of pronunciation called *Wootton* instead of *Wootton* [sic], having the addition of *Wawen* in regard that [i.e. because] one *Wagen* (commonly called *Wawen*) Lord thereof before the Norman Conquest, had his seat here' (William Dugdale, *The Antiquities of Warwickshire*, 1656). 716 *Uuidutuun*, DB *Wotone*, c.1142 *Wageneswitona*.

Worcester (city, Worcs): 'Roman town of the Weogora'. OE *ceaster*, 'Roman station'. The tribal name (which also gave that of WYRE FOREST) is pre-English in origin and probably comes from a Celtic river name meaning 'winding river'. Worcester is on the Severn, but this is not necessarily the river in question. The name of the Roman town here is uncertain, but may have been something like *Vertis*. 691 *Weogorna civitas*, 717 *Wigranceastre*, DB *Wirecestre*.

Worcester Park (district, Sutton). The name comes from Worcester House formerly here, the residence of Edward Somerset, 4th Earl of Worcester (1553–1628), who was keeper of the great park of Nonsuch Palace in the early 17C. 1819 *Worcester Park*.

Worcestershire (county, W central England): 'district based on Worcester'. OE *scīr*, 'shire', 'district'. See WORCESTER. 11C *Wireceastrescir*.

Wordsley (district, Dudley): 'Wulfweard's woodland clearing'. OE *lēah*, 'wood', 'clearing'. 12C *Wuluardeslea*.

Worfield (village, Shropshire): 'open land on the (river) Worfe'. OE *feld*, 'open land' (modern English *field*). The river name means 'winding', from an OE verb related to modern English *worry*. DB *Wrfeld*.

Workington (town and port, Cumbria): 'estate associated with Weorc'. OE *-ing-*, 'associated with', + *tūn*, 'farmstead', 'estate'. c.1125 *Wirkynton*.

Worksop (town, Notts): 'Weorc's valley'. OE *hop*, 'enclosed valley'. It is not certain which particular valley is meant, and the valley of the river Ryton in which Worksop lies is hardly 'enclosed'. DB *Werchesope*.

Worlaby (village, N Lincs): 'Wulfrīc's farmstead'. OS *bȳ*, 'farmstead', 'village'. DB *Uluricebi*.

Worle (suburb of Weston-super-Mare, N Somerset): 'wood or clearing where woodpeckers are seen'. OE *wōr*, 'woodpecker', + *lēah*, 'wood', 'clearing'. DB *Worle*.

Worleston (hamlet, Cheshire): 'farmstead at the cattle pasture'. OE *weorf*, 'cattle', + *lēah*, 'clearing', 'pasture', + *tūn*, 'farmstead'. The DB form of the name below is corrupt. DB *Werblestune*, *c*.1100 *Weruelestona*.

Worlingham (village, Suffolk): 'homestead of Wērel's people'. OE -*inga*-, 'of the people of', + *hām*, 'homestead'. DB *Werlingaham*.

Worlington (village, Suffolk): 'farmstead by the winding stream'. OE *wride*, 'winding', + *wella*, 'stream', + -*ing*-, 'associated with', + *tūn*, 'farmstead'. The river here is the Lark. DB *Wirilintona*, 1201 *Wridelingeton*.

Worlingworth (village, Suffolk): 'enclosure of Wilhere's people'. OE -*inga*-, 'of the people of', + *worth*, 'enclosure'. *c*.1035 *Wilrincgawertha*, DB *Wyrlingwortha*.

Wormbridge (village, Herefords): '(place by the) bridge over Worm Brook'. OE *brycg*, 'bridge'. The river name is Celtic in origin and means 'dark stream'. 1207 *Wermebrig*.

Wormegay (village, Norfolk): 'island of Wyrma's people'. OE -*inga*-, 'of the people of', + *ēg*, 'island'. The 'island' is raised ground by the river Nar here. DB *Wermegai*.

Wormhill (village, Derbys): 'Wyrma's hill'. OE *hyll*, 'hill'. The DB form of the name below is garbled. DB *Wruenele*, *c*.1105 *Wermehull*.

Wormingford (village, Essex): '(place by) Withermund's ford'. OE *ford*, 'ford'. The river here is the Stour. DB *Widemondefort*.

Worminghall (village, Bucks): 'Wyrma's corner of land'. OE *halh*, 'nook', 'corner of land'. The DB form of the name below has omitted a syllable. DB *Wermelle*, *c*.1218 *Wirmenhale*.

Wormington (village, Glos): 'estate associated with Wyrma'. OE -*ing*-, 'associated with', + *tūn*, 'farmstead', 'estate'. DB *Wermetune*.

Wormleighton (village, Warwicks): 'Wilma's herb garden'. OE *lēac-tūn*, 'herb garden' (from *lēac*, 'leek', + *tūn*, 'enclosure'). 956 *Wilmanlehttune*, DB *Wimelestone*.

Wormley (suburb of Cheshunt, Herts): 'woodland clearing full of snakes'. OE *wyrm*, 'snake' (modern English *worm*), + *lēah*, 'wood', 'clearing'. *c*.1060 *Wrmeleia*, DB *Wermelai*.

Worms Head (headland, Swansea): 'snake's head'. OE *wyrm*, 'snake', 'dragon' (modern English *worm*), + *hēafod*, 'head'. The name alludes to the shape of the rock ridges and has its exact parallel in GREAT ORMES HEAD at the opposite (northern) end of Wales. The Welsh name of Worms Head is *Penrhyn Gŵyr*, 'Gower promontory', referring to its location at the western extremity of the GOWER Peninsula.

Wormshill (village, Kent): 'Wōden's hill'. OE *hyll*, 'hill'. The name implies a place dedicated to the pagan war god Woden. The DB form of the name below is either a misrendering or a deliberate alteration of the name by the Christian Normans to mean 'God's hill' (or 'god's hill'). But early forms also suggest a meaning 'shelter for a herd of pigs' (OE *weorn*, 'band', 'herd', + *sell*, 'shelter for animals', a word used for pig pastures). DB *Godeselle*, *c*.1225 *Wotnesell*, 1254 *Worneshelle*.

Wormsley (village, Herefords): 'Wyrm's woodland clearing'. OE *lēah*, 'wood', 'clearing'. The name could also mean 'woodland clearing full of snakes' (OE *wyrm*, 'snake', + *lēah*). DB *Wermeslai*.

Wormwood Scrubs (district, Hammersmith & Ful): 'scrubland by the wood full of snakes'. OE *wyrm*, 'snake' (modern English *worm*), + *holt*, 'wood', + *scrubb*, 'scrubland'. The present form of the name has been influenced by *wormwood*, the plant, which probably explains the addition of the second word, as if the name as a whole meant 'scrubland where wormwood grows'. The original name has been preserved in Wormholt Park, south of Wormwood Scrubs prison. 1200 *Wermeholte*, 1437 *Wormoltwode*, 1819 *Wormholt Scrubbs*, *c*.1865 *Wormwood Scrubbs*.

Worplesdon (village, Surrey): '(place by the) hill with a path'. OE *werpels*, 'path', + *dūn*, 'hill'. The reference is probably to a bridle path here. DB *Werpesdune*.

Worrall (village, Sheffield): 'corner of land where bog myrtle grows'. OE *wīr*, 'bog myrtle', + *halh*, 'nook', 'corner of land'. Cp. WIRRAL. There was probably a secluded piece of land by the river Don here. DB *Wihale*, 1218 *Wirhal*.

Worsbrough (district, Barnsley): 'Wyrc's stronghold'. OE *burh*, 'fortified place'. DB *Wircesburg*.

Worsley (town, Salford): 'Weorcgȳth's or Weorchæth's woodland clearing'. OE *lēah*, 'wood', 'clearing'. There is some doubt about the personal names. The first is that of a woman, the second of a man. 1196 *Werkesleia*, 1246 *Wyrkitheley*.

Worstead (village, Norfolk): 'site of an enclosure'. OE *worth*, 'enclosure', + *stede*, 'site'. The reference is to an enclosed farm here. 1044 *Wrthestede*, DB *Wrdestedam*.

Worsthorne (village, Lancs): 'Weorth's thorn bush'. OE *thorn*, 'thorn bush'. 1202 *Worthesthorn*.

Worston (hamlet, Lancs): 'Weorth's farmstead'. OE *tūn*, 'farmstead'. 1212 *Wrtheston*.

Worth (hamlet, W Sussex): 'enclosure'. OE *worth*, 'enclosure', 'enclosed settlement'. DB *Orde*. SO ALSO: *Worth*, Kent.

Wortham (village, Suffolk): 'homestead with an enclosure'. OE *worth*, 'enclosure', + *hām*, 'homestead'. *c.*950 *Wrtham*, DB *Wortham*.

Worthen (village, Shropshire): 'enclosure'. OE *worthign*, 'enclosure'. DB *Wrdine*.

Worthing (hamlet, Norfolk): '(settlement of) Weorth's people'. OE *-ingas*, 'people of'. 1282 *Worthing*.

Worthing (resort town, W Sussex): '(settlement of) Weorth's people'. OE *-ingas*, 'people of'. DB *Ordinges*.

Worthington (village, Leics): 'estate associated with Weorth'. OE *-ing-*, 'associated with', + *tūn*, 'farmstead', 'estate'. DB *Werditone*.

Worth Matravers. See LANGTON MATRAVERS.

Worting (suburb of Basingstoke, Hants): '(place with) herb gardens'. OE *wyrting* (from *wyrt*, 'herb', 'vegetable', modern English *wort*). The forms of the name below are in the plural. 960 *Wyrtingas*, DB *Wortinges*, 1195 *Wertinges*.

Wortley (village, Barnsley): 'woodland clearing where vegetables are grown'. OE *wyrt*, 'herb', 'vegetable' (modern English *wort*), + *lēah*, 'wood', 'clearing'. DB *Wirtleie*.

Worton (village, Wilts): '(place with a) vegetable garden'. OE *wyrt-tūn* (from *wyrt*, 'herb', 'vegetable', modern English *wort*, + *tūn*, 'enclosure'). 1173 *Wrton*.

Wotherton (hamlet, Shropshire): 'farmstead by the woodland ford'. OE *wudu*, 'wood', + *ford*, 'ford', + *tūn*, 'farmstead'. The road crosses a small stream here. DB *Udevertune*.

Wothorpe (hamlet, Peterborough): 'outlying farmstead by the thicket'. OE *wrīth*, 'thicket', + OS *thorp*, 'outlying farmstead'. DB *Wridtorpe*.

Wotton (hamlet, Surrey): 'farmstead by a wood'. OE *wudu*, 'wood', + *tūn*, 'farmstead'. DB *Wodetone*.

Wotton St Mary. See WOTTON-UNDER-EDGE.

Wotton-under-Edge (town, Glos): 'farmstead by a wood under a hill'. OE *wudu*, 'wood', + *tūn*, 'farmstead'. The second part of the name locates the town under the Cotswold escarpment and distinguishes it from *Wotton St Mary*, 17 miles to the north, now (as simply *Wotton*) a district of Gloucester. 940 *Wudutune*, DB *Vutune*, 1466 *Wotton under Egge*.

Wotton Underwood (village, Bucks): 'farmstead by a wood near the forest'. OE *wudu*, 'wood', + *tūn*, 'farmstead'. The apparently tautologous name refers to the location of Wotton by or even in the former Bernwood forest. The DB form of the name below is corrupt. 848 *Wudotun*, DB *Oltone*, 1415 *Wotton-under-Bernewode*, 1868 *Wootton Underwood, or Wootton-under-Bernwood*.

Woughton on the Green (village, Milton K): 'Wēoca's farmstead on the green'. OE *tūn*, 'farmstead'. The second part of the name alludes to the development of the village round a large central green. The DB form of the name below is corrupt. DB *Ulchetone*, 1163 *Wocheton*.

Wouldham (village, Kent): 'Wulda's homestead'. OE *hām*, 'homestead'. 811 *Uuldaham*, DB *Oldeham*.

Wrabness (village, Essex): 'Wrabba's headland'. OE *næss*, 'headland'. The village lies on a headland on the estuary of the river Stour. DB *Wrabenasa*.

Wragby (town, Lincs): 'Wraggi's farmstead'. OS *bý*, 'farmstead'. The personal name is Scandinavian. DB *Waragebi*.

Wramplingham (village, Norfolk): '(place with a) homestead'. OE *hām*, 'homestead'. The first part of the name is of uncertain origin. It may represent a personal or tribal name. DB *Wranplincham*.

Wrangle (village, Lincs): 'crooked place'. OE *wrǣngel* or OS *vrengill*, 'crooked place'. The name may relate to a crooked stream here. DB *Werangle*.

Wrantage (village, Somerset): 'pasture for stallions'. OE *wrǣna*, 'stallion', + *etisc*, 'pasture'. 1199 *Wrentis*.

Wrath, Cape. See CAPE WRATH.

Wrawby (village, N Lincs): 'Wraghi's farmstead'. OS *bý*, 'farmstead', 'village'. The personal name is Scandinavian. DB *Waragebi*.

Wraxall (village, N Somerset): 'corner of land where buzzards are seen'. OE *wrocc*, 'buzzard', + *halh*, 'nook', 'corner of land'. OE *wrocc* could also name some other bird of prey. DB *Werocosale*. SO ALSO: *Wraxall*, Dorset.

Wray (village, Lancs): '(place in the) corner of land'. OS *vrá*, 'nook', 'corner of land'. 1227 *Wra*.

Wraysbury (village, Windsor & Maid): 'Wīgrēd's stronghold'. OE *burh*, 'fortified place'. The DB form of the name below has *c* for *d* in the personal name. DB *Wirecesberie*, 1195 *Wiredesbur*, 1274 *Wyrardebury*, 1868 *Wraysbury*, or *Wyrardisbury*.

Wreay (village, Cumbria): '(place in the) corner of land'. OS *vrá*, 'nook', 'corner of land'. The form of the name below contains the name of the river Petteril, itself of uncertain origin. 1272 *Petrelwra*.

Wrecclesham (district of Farnham, Surrey): 'Wrecel's homestead or enclosure'. OE *hām*, 'homestead', or *hamm*, 'enclosure'. 1225 *Wrecclesham*.

Wrecsam. See WREXHAM.

Wrekin, The. See WROXETER.

Wrelton (village, N Yorks): 'farmstead by the hill where criminals are hanged'. OE *wearg*, 'felon', 'criminal', + *hyll*, 'hill', + *tūn*, 'farmstead'. DB *Wereltun*.

Wrenbury (village, Cheshire): 'Wrenna's stronghold'. OE *burh*, 'fortified place'. DB *Wareneberie*.

Wreningham (village, Norfolk): 'homestead of Wrenna's people'. OE *-inga-*, 'of the people of', + *hām*, 'homestead'. The DB form of the name below has garbled the personal name. c.1060 *Wreningham*, DB *Urnincham*.

Wrentham (village, Suffolk): 'Wrenta's homestead'. OE *hām*, 'homestead'. The DB form of the name below has omitted the *n* of the personal name. DB *Wretham*, 1228 *Wrentham*.

Wressle (village, E Yorks): '(place with) something twisted'. OE *wrǣsel*, 'twisted thing' (related modern English *wrestle*). The name may refer to a winding stream or broken ground. The DB form of the name below has omitted the *l*. DB *Weresa*, 1183 *Wresel*.

Wrestlingworth (village, Beds): 'enclosure of Wrǣstel's people'. OE *-inga-*, 'of the people of', + *worth*, 'enclosure'. c.1150 *Wrastlingewrd*.

Wretton (village, Norfolk): 'farmstead where crosswort grows'. OE *wrætt*, 'crosswort', + *tūn*, 'farmstead'. Crosswort (*Crucianella*) is a

medicinal plant related to the bedstraws. 1198 *Wretton*.

Wrexham (town, Wrexham): 'Wryhtel's water meadow'. OE *hamm*, 'enclosure', 'riverside meadow'. The water meadows are those beside the rivers Gwenfro and Clywedog. The Welsh form of the town's name is *Wrecsam*, a version of the English original. 1161 *Wristlesham*, 1291 *Gwregsam*.

Wribbenhall (hamlet, Worcs): 'Wrybba's corner of land'. OE *halh*, 'nook', 'corner of land'. The first part of the DB form of the name below is garbled. DB *Gurberhale*, c.1160 *Wrubbenhale*.

Wrightington (hamlet, Lancs): 'farmstead of the wrights'. OE *wyrhta*, 'wright', + *tūn*, 'farmstead'. A 'wright' is a carpenter or worker in wood. The first part of the name represents OE *wyrhtena*, the genitive plural form of *wyrhta*. 1202 *Wrichtington*.

Wrinehill (village, Staffs): '(place by the) hill'. OE *hyll*, 'hill'. The first part of the name is of uncertain origin. It may represent a district name meaning 'river bend', a stream name, or the name of the hill itself. 1225 *Wrinehull*.

Wrington (village, N Somerset): 'farmstead on the (river) Wring'. OE *tūn*, 'farmstead'. The river here now is the Yeo, but its earlier name probably means 'winding stream', from an OE word related to modern English *wry*. The DB form of the name below is corrupt. 926 *Wringtone*, DB *Weritone*.

Writtle (suburb of Chelmsford, Essex): '(place on the river) Writtle'. The river here now is the Wid, but its earlier name means 'babbling one' (OE *writol*, 'babbling'). 1066 *Writele*, DB *Writelam*.

Wrockwardine (village, Wrekin): 'enclosure by the Wrekin'. OE *worthign*, 'enclosure'. The village lies 2½ miles north of The Wrekin (see WROXETER). DB *Recordine*, 1196 *Wrocwurthin*.

Wrotham (village, Kent): 'Wrōta's homestead'. OE *hām*, 'homestead'. The initial *B-* in the DB form of the name below presumably resulted from a mishearing. 788 *Uurotaham*, DB *Broteham*.

Wroughton (village, Swindon): 'farmstead on the (river) Worf'. OE *tūn*, 'farmstead'. The river here now is the Ray. Its earlier name is of Celtic origin and means 'winding stream'. DB *Wervetone*.

Wroxall (village, IoW): 'corner of land where buzzards are seen'. OE *wrocc*, 'buzzard', + *halh*, 'nook', 'corner of land'. OE *wrocc* may also name some other bird of prey. Cp. WRAXALL. 1038 *Wroccesheale*, DB *Warochesselle*.

Wroxeter (village, Shropshire): 'Roman fort at Viriconium'. OE *ceaster*, 'Roman fort'. The name of the Roman city here is of Celtic origin and refers to the fort on the nearby craggy hill known as *The Wrekin*. The meaning of this name is uncertain, but 'Virico's town' has been suggested. The spelling *Viroconium* also occurs, while another form is *Uriconio* or *Uricon*, as in A. E. Housman's *A Shropshire Lad*: 'To-day the Roman and his trouble / Are ashes under Uricon'. DB *Rochecestre*.

Wroxham (village, Norfolk): 'homestead or enclosure where buzzards are seen'. OE *wrocc*, 'buzzard', + *hām*, 'homestead' or *hamm*, 'enclosure'. The name could also mean 'Wrocc's homestead or enclosure'. DB *Vrochesham*.

Wroxton (village, Oxon): '(place by the) stone where buzzards are seen'. OE *wrocc*, 'buzzard', + *stān*, 'stone'. OE *wrocc* could also name some other bird of prey. DB *Werochestan*.

Wybunbury (village, Cheshire): 'Wīgbeorn's stronghold'. OE *burh*, 'fortified place', 'manor'. DB *Wimeberie*, c.1210 *Wybbunberi*.

Wychavon (council district, Worcs). The name was devised for the administrative district set up in 1974. It combines *Wych* as an early form of the name of DROITWICH with the name of the river AVON. Droitwich is in the north of the district, the Avon in the south.

Wychbold (village, Worcs): 'dwelling near the trading place'. OE *wīc*, 'trading place', + *bold*, 'special house', 'dwelling'. 692 *Uuicbold*, DB *Wicelbold*.

Wyck Rissington. See GREAT RISSINGTON.

Wycliffe (hamlet, Durham): '(place on the) white bank'. OE *hwīt*, 'white', + *clif*, 'cliff', 'bank'. Wycliffe stands on a bank overlooking the river Tees. DB *Witcliue*.

Wycomb (hamlet, Leics): '(place at the) dwellings'. OE *wīc*, 'dwelling'. The name could represent OE *wīcum*, the dative plural form of *wīc*, as for HIGH WYCOMBE, but is perhaps more likely to represent OE *wīc-hām*, 'homestead by a Romano-British settlement', as for WEST WICKHAM. DB *Wiche*.

Wycombe. See HIGH WYCOMBE.

Wyddfa, Yr. See SNOWDON.

Wyddgrug, Yr. See MOLD.

Wyddial (village, Herts): 'corner of land where willow trees grow'. OE *wīthig*, 'willow' (modern English *withy*), + *halh*, 'nook', 'corner of land'. DB *Widihale*.

Wye (town, Kent): '(place at the) heathen temple'. OE *wīg*, 'heathen shrine'. 839 *Uuiæ*, DB *Wi*.

Wye (river). See ROSS-ON-WYE.

Wykeham (village, N Yorks): 'homestead associated with a Romano-British settlement'. OE *wīc-hām* (see WEST WICKHAM). DB *Wicham*.

Wyken (district, Coventry): 'dairy farms'. OE *wīc*, 'dairy farm'. The name represents OE *wīcum*, the dative plural form of *wīc*. 1249 *Wyken*.

Wyke Regis (district of Weymouth, Dorset): 'royal farm'. OE *wīc*, 'dwelling', 'specialized farm', + Latin *regis*, 'of the king'. The place was a royal manor. 984 *Wike*, 1242 *Kingeswik*.

Wylam (village, Northd): '(place by the) fish traps'. OE *wīl*, 'trick' (modern English *wile*). Fish traps were presumably set up on the river Tyne here. The name represents OE *wīlum*, the dative plural form of *wīl*. 12C *Wylum*.

Wylye (village, Wilts): '(place on the river) Wylye'. The river name is pre-English and may mean 'tricky stream', i.e. one liable to flood. (It has no connection with modern *wily*.) 901 *Wilig*, DB *Wili*.

Wymeswold (village, Leics): 'Wīgmund's forest'. OE *wald*, 'forest'. DB *Wimundeswald*.

Wymington (village, Beds): 'Wīdmund's farmstead'. OE *tūn*, 'farmstead'. DB *Wimentone*.

Wymondham (town, Norfolk): 'Wīgmund's homestead'. OE *hām*, 'homestead'. DB *Wimundham*. SO ALSO: *Wymondham*, Leics.

Wynford Eagle (hamlet, Dorset): 'del Egle's (estate on the) white stream'. The first word of the name represents the name of the river here, from Celtic words related to modern Welsh *gwyn*, 'white', and *ffrwd*, 'stream'. The del Egle family held the manor here in the 13C. DB *Wenfrot*, 1288 *Wynfrod Egle*.

Wyre (council district, Lancs): '(district of the river) Wyre'. The river name has the same origin as that of the Wyre behind WYRE FOREST.

Wyre Forest (wooded region, Worcs/Shropshire): '(place by the) winding river'. The name is of Celtic origin and was probably that of a river here. Its identity is uncertain, but it may be the Avon, which follows a winding course before joining the Severn at Tewkesbury. The name is probably related to that of the Weogora people who gave the name of WORCESTER. *Wyre*

Forest is now also the name of a Worcestershire council district. *c.*1080 *Wyre*.

Wyre Piddle (village, Worcs): '(place on the river) Piddle'. The river name represents OE *pidele*, 'marsh', 'fen'. The first word of the name distinguishes the village from *North Piddle*, 4 miles to the north on the same river, and presumably refers to WYRE FOREST, although it is some way south of it. DB *Pidele*, 1208 *Wyre Pidele*.

Wysall (village, Notts): '(place on the) hill spur with a temple'. OE *wīg*, 'heathen temple', + *hōh*, 'hill spur'. DB *Wisoc*.

Wytham (village, Oxon): 'homestead in a river bend'. OE *wiht*, 'bend', + *hām*, 'homestead', 'village'. Wytham lies in a sharp curve of the Thames. The DB form of the name below has *n* as a scribal error for *h*. *c.*957 *Wihtham*, DB *Winteham*.

Wythenshawe (district, Manchester): '(place by the) willow copse'. OE *wīthign*, 'willow', + *sceaga*, 'copse'. *c.*1290 *Witenscawe*.

Wyton (village, Cambs): 'farmstead with a dwelling'. OE *wīc-tūn* (from *wīc*, 'dwelling', + *tūn*, 'farmstead'). DB *Witune*, 1253 *Wictun*.

Y

Y. For Welsh names beginnning thus, see the next word, e.g. for *Y Fenni*, see FENNI, Y. (Such names are in turn often cross-referred to an English form or more familiar spelling.)

Yafforth (village, N Yorks): '(place at the) ford over the river'. OE *ēa*, 'river', + *ford*, 'ford'. The river here is the Wiske. DB *Iaforde*.

Yalding (village, Kent): '(settlement of) Ealda's people'. OE *-ingas*, 'people of'. DB *Hallinges*, 1207 *Ealding*.

Yanworth (village, Glos): 'enclosure used for lambs'. OE *ēan*, 'lamb', + *worth*, 'enclosure'. The name could also mean 'Gæna's enclosure'. The DB form of the name below has *I-* miscopied as *T-*. *c.*1050 *Janeworth*, DB *Teneurde*.

Yapham (village, E Yorks): '(place by the) steep slopes'. OE *gēap*, 'steep (place)'. The name represents OE *gēapum*, the dative plural form of *gēap*. The village stands high on the slope of a fairly steep hill. DB *Iapun*.

Yapton (village, W Sussex): 'estate associated with Eabba'. OE *-ing-*, 'associated with', + *tūn*, 'farmstead', 'estate'. *c.*1187 *Abbiton*.

Yarburgh (village, Lincs): '(place by the) earthwork'. OE *eorth-burh* (from *eorth*, 'earth', + *burh*, 'fortified place'.). The site of the earthwork in question is not known. DB *Gereburg*.

Yarcombe (village, Devon): '(place in the) valley of the (river) Yarty'. OE *cumb*, 'valley'. The river name is of uncertain origin. 10C *Ercecombe*, DB *Erticoma*.

Yardley (district, Birmingham): 'wood or clearing where rods are obtained'. OE *gyrd*, 'rod', 'spar', + *lēah*, 'wood', 'clearing'. 972 *Gyrdleah*, DB *Gerlei*.

Yardley Gobion (village, Northants): 'Gubyun's (estate by the) wood or clearing where rods are obtained'. OE *gyrd*, 'rod', 'spar', + *lēah*, 'wood', 'clearing'. The Gubyun family held the manor here in the 13C, their name distinguishing this Yardley from *Yardley Hastings*, 10 miles

to the northeast, held by the de Hastinges family. DB *Gerdeslai*, 1353 *Yerdele Gobioun*.

Yarkhill (village, Herefords): 'kiln with a yard'. OE *geard*, 'yard', 'enclosure', + *cyln*, 'kiln'. 811 *Geardcylle*, DB *Archel*.

Yarlet (hamlet, Staffs): '(place on a) gravelly slope'. OE *ēar*, 'gravel', + *hlith*, 'slope'. The name could also mean 'slope where eagles are seen' (OE *earn*, 'eagle', + *hlith*). DB *Erlide*.

Yarlington (village, Somerset): 'farmstead of Gerla's people'. OE *-inga-*, 'of the people of', + *tūn*, 'farmstead'. DB *Gerlincgetuna*.

Yarm (town, Stockton): '(place at the) fish weirs'. OE *gear*, 'dam'. Yarm lies in a loop of the river Tees, an ideal location for trapping fish. The name represents OE *gearum*, the dative plural form of *gear*. DB *Iarun*.

Yarmouth (resort town, IoW): '(place by the) gravelly estuary'. OE *ēaren*, 'gravelly', + *mūtha*, 'river mouth', 'estuary'. The estuary in question is that of the river Yar, which takes its name from that of the town. DB *Ermud*, 1223 *Ernemuth*.

Yarmouth (resort town and port, Norfolk): 'mouth of the (river) Yare'. OE *mūtha*, 'mouth'. The river has a Celtic name perhaps meaning something like 'babbling stream'. The town is officially known as *Great Yarmouth* for distinction from *Little Yarmouth*, now a southern district of Yarmouth itself. (Today this district, to the west of the Yare, is more familiar as *Southtown*.) DB *Gernemwa*.

Yarnfield (village, Staffs): 'open land where eagles are seen'. OE *earn*, 'eagle', + *feld*, 'open land' (modern English *field*). 1266 *Ernefeld*.

Yarnscombe (village, Devon): '(place in the) valley where eagles are seen'. OE *earn*, 'eagle', + *cumb*, 'valley'. DB *Hernescome*.

Yarnton (village, Oxon): 'estate associated with Earda'. OE *-ing-*, 'associated with', + *tūn*, 'farmstead', 'estate'. 1005 *Ærdintune*, DB *Hardintone*.

Yarpole (village, Herefords): '(place by the) pool with a weir'. OE *gear*, 'weir', + *pōl*, 'pool'. The 'weir' would probably have been a dam for catching fish on the stream here. DB *Iarpol*.

Yarwell (village, Northants): '(place at the) spring by the weir'. OE *gear*, 'weir', 'dam', + *wella*, 'spring', 'stream'. The spring in question was probably by a fishing pool on the river Nene nearby. 1166 *Jarewelle*.

Yate (village, S Glos): '(place by the) gap'. OE *geat*, 'gate', 'gap'. There is no obvious gap here, so the name may have referred to an actual gate. 779 *Geate*, DB *Giete*.

Yateley (village, Hants): 'woodland clearing by a gap'. OE *geat*, 'gate', 'gap', + *lēah*, 'wood', 'clearing'. There is no obvious gap here, so the meaning may be 'gate'. The village is close to the river Blackwater, which here forms the boundary between Hampshire and Berkshire, and Yateley may have been seen as a 'gateway' to the latter county. 1248 *Yatele*.

Yatesbury (village, Wilts): 'Gēat's stronghold'. OE *burh*, 'fortified place'. DB *Etesberie*.

Yattendon (village, W Berks): '(place by the) valley of Gēat's people'. OE *-inga-*, 'of the people of', + *denu*, 'valley'. The valley referred to is probably the one that rises from the river Pang to the higher ground just west of the village. DB *Etingedene*.

Yatton (hamlet, Herefords): 'farmstead by a gap'. OE *geat*, 'gate', 'gap', + *tūn*, 'farmstead'. DB *Getune*.

Yatton (village, N Somerset): 'farmstead by a river'. OE *ēa*, 'river', + *tūn*, 'farmstead'. The river here is the Yeo. DB *Iatune*.

Yatton Keynell (village, Wilts): 'Caynel's farmstead by a gap'. OE *geat*, 'gate', 'gap', + *tūn*, 'farmstead'. The 'gap' is the head of the valley to the west of the village. The Caynel family held the manor here in the 13C. DB *Getone*, 1289 *Yatton Kaynel*.

Yaverland (village, IoW): 'cultivated land where boars are kept'. OE *eofor*, 'boar', + *land*, 'cultivated land'. 683 *Ewerelande*, DB *Evreland*.

Yaxham (village, Norfolk): 'homestead or enclosure where cuckoos are heard'. OE *gēac*, 'cuckoo' (modern English dialect *gowk*), + *hām*, 'homestead', or *hamm*, 'enclosure'. The name could also mean 'Gēac's homestead or enclosure'. DB *Jachesham*.

Yaxley (village, Cambs): 'wood or clearing where cuckoos are heard'. OE *gēac*, 'cuckoo' (modern English dialect *gowk*), + *lēah*, 'wood', 'clearing'. 963 *Geaceslea*, DB *Iacheslei*. SO ALSO: *Yaxley*, Suffolk.

Yazor (village, Herefords): 'Iago's ridge'. OE *ofer*, 'ridge'. The personal name is Welsh. DB *Iavesovre*, 1242 *Iagesoure*.

Yeading (district, Hillingdon): '(settlement of) Geddi's people'. OE *-ingas*, 'people of'. 757 *Geddinges*.

Yeadon (town, Leeds): '(place at the) steep hill'. OE *gǣh*, 'steep', + *dūn*, 'hill'. The 'steep hill' would be the spur of the hill ridge known as The Chevin on which Yeadon is situated. DB *Iadun*.

Yealand Conyers (village, Lancs): 'de Conyers' (estate on the) high cultivated land'. OE *hēah*, 'high', + *land*, 'cultivated land'. The manor here was held early by the de Conyers family, their name distinguishing this village from nearby *Yealand Redmayne*, where it was held by the Redeman family. DB *Jalant*, 1301 *Yeland Coygners*.

Yealmpton (village, Devon): 'farmstead on the (river) Yealm'. OE *tūn*, 'farmstead'. The river has a Celtic or pre-Celtic name of obscure origin. DB *Elintona*.

Yearsley (hamlet, N Yorks): 'wood or clearing where wild boars are seen'. OE *eofor*, 'boar', + *lēah*, 'wood', 'clearing'. The name could also mean 'Eofor's wood or clearing'. DB *Eureslage*.

Yeaton (hamlet, Shropshire): 'farmstead by a river'. OE *ēa*, 'river', + *tūn*, 'farmstead'. The river here is the Perry. DB *Aitone*, 1327 *Eton*.

Yeaveley (village, Derbys): 'Geofa's woodland clearing'. OE *lēah*, 'wood', 'clearing'. DB *Gheveli*.

Yedingham (village, N Yorks): 'homestead of Ēada's people'. OE *-inga-*, 'of the people of', + *hām*, 'homestead'. 1170 *Edingham*.

Yelden (village, Beds): '(place in the) valley of the Gifle'. OE *denu*, 'valley'. The tribal name derives from the river Ivel here. Its own name is Celtic in origin and means 'forked stream'. DB *Giveldene*.

Yelford (hamlet, Oxon): '(place by) Ægel's ford'. OE *ford*, 'ford'. DB *Aieleforde*.

Yell (island, Shetland): 'barren place'. OS *geldr*, 'barren' (related modern English *gelding*). *c*.1250 *Yala*.

Yelling (village, Cambs): '(settlement of) Giella's people'. OE *-ingas*, 'people of'. 974 *Gillinge*, DB *Gellinge*.

Yelvertoft (village, Northants): 'Geldfrith's homestead'. OS *toft*, 'homestead'. The first part of the name could also mean 'ford by a pool' (OE *gēol*, 'pool', + *ford*, 'ford'). The DB form of the name below, if reliable, seems to indicate that the second part of the name was originally OE *cot*, 'cottage'. DB *Gelvrecote*, 12C *Gelvertoft*.

Yelverton (town, Devon): 'village by the elder-tree ford'. OE *ellen*, 'elder tree', + *ford*, 'ford', + *tūn*, 'farmstead', 'village'. The name today would probably be 'Elverton' if the Great Western Railway had not respelt it with an initial *Y-* in 1859 to reflect the local pronunciation. 1291 *Elleford*, 1765 *Elverton*, 1809 *Elfordtown*.

Yeo (river). See YEOVIL.

Yeolmbridge (village, Cornwall): '(place at the) bridge by the river meadow'. OE *ēa*, 'river', + *hamm*, 'enclosure', 'river meadow', + *brycg*, 'bridge'. The letter *l* was added to the name only in the 16C, perhaps by analogy with *Yealmbridge*, Devon, named after the river Yealm (see YEALMPTON). 13C *Yambrigge*.

Yeovil (town, Somerset): '(place on the river) Ivel'. The town takes its name from the river here, formerly the Ivel (*Gifl*) but now the Yeo. Its name is of Celtic origin and means 'forked river'. Cp. SOUTHILL. The present form of the river name, which gave the current town name, has been influenced by OE *ēa*, 'river'. *c*.880 *Gifle*, DB *Givele*.

Yeovilton (village, Somerset): 'farmstead on the (river) Gifl'. OE *tūn*, 'farmstead'. Yeovilton is on the same river as YEOVIL, and its name has evolved similarly. DB *Geveltone*.

Yes Tor (hill, Devon): 'eagle's hill'. OE *earn*, 'eagle', + *torr*, 'hill', 'tor'. The '-s' of the first word is possessive. 1240 *Ernestorre*.

Yetminster (village, Dorset): 'Ēata's church'. OE *mynster*, 'monastery', 'large church'. DB *Etiminstre*.

Yiewsley (district, Hillingdon): 'Wifel's woodland clearing'. OE *lēah*, 'wood', 'clearing'. The original name was the equivalent of 'Wiewsley'. 1235 *Wiuesleg*, 1406 *Wyvesle*, 1593 *Wewesley*, 1819 *Yewsley*.

Ynys Bŷr. See CALDY ISLAND.

Ynys Dewi. See RAMSEY ISLAND.

Ynys Enlli. See BARDSEY ISLAND.

Ynysoedd y Moelrhoniaid. See SKERRIES.

Ynys Seiriol. See PUFFIN ISLAND.

Yockleton (hamlet, Shropshire): '(place by a) hill'. OE *hyll*, 'hill'. The first part of the name is of uncertain origin. It may represent OE *geocled*, 'small manor' (from *geoc*, 'yoke'), a term mainly found in Kent. OE *tūn* replaced *hyll* in the 14C. DB *Ioclehuile*, 1316 *Yekelton*.

Yokefleet (village, E Yorks): '(place by) Jókell's stream'. OE *flēot*, 'creek', 'stream'. The personal name is Scandinavian. Yokefleet lies by the river Ouse. DB *Iucufled*.

York (city, York): 'place of Eburos'. The Celtic name has undergone various mutations to reach its present form. The personal name means literally 'yew man', and it is possible that the original name may actually be 'yew tree' itself. The fourth form of the name below has been influenced by OE *eofor*, 'boar', while the forms themselves are respectively Greek, Latin, OS, OE, Norman and ME. (The OS name was adopted for the city's Jorvik Viking Centre.) *c*.150 *Eborakon*, 4C *Eboracum*, 9C *Jórvík*, *c*.1060 *Eoforwic*, DB *Euruic*, 13C *York*.

Yorkshire (historic county, N England): 'district based on York'. OE *scīr*, 'shire', 'district'. See YORK. The county was divided into ridings, of which the EAST RIDING survives. 11C *Eoferwicscire*.

York Town (district of Camberley, Surrey). York Town arose in the early 19C and takes its name from Frederick Augustus, Duke of York (1763–1827), who founded the Royal Military College, Sandhurst (originally at High Wycombe), in 1799.

Yorton (hamlet, Shropshire): 'farmstead with a yard'. OE *geard*, 'yard', + *tūn*, 'farmstead'. DB *Iartune*.

Youlgreave (village, Derbys): '(place by the) yellow grove'. OE *geolu*, 'yellow', + *grǣfe*, 'grove'. The name could also mean '(place by the) yellow pit' (OE *grǣf*, 'pit', 'trench', modern English *grave*). The colour would be that of the trees of the grove or the soil of the pit. DB *Giolgrave*.

Youlthorpe (hamlet, E Yorks): 'Eyjulfr's or Jól's outlying farmstead'. OS *thorp*, 'outlying farmstead'. The personal names are Scandinavian. DB *Aiulftorp*, 1166 *Joletorp*.

Youlton (hamlet, N Yorks): 'Jóli's farmstead'. OE *tūn*, 'farmstead'. The personal name is Scandinavian. DB *Ioletun*.

Yoxall (village, Staffs): '(place in the) corner of land comprising a yoke'. OE *geoc*, 'yoke', + *halh*, 'nook', 'corner of land'. A 'yoke' was a measure of land based on the area ploughed by a pair of yoked oxen in a day. DB *Iocheshale*.

Yoxford (village, Suffolk): 'ford where a yoke of oxen can pass'. OE *geoc*, 'yoke', + *ford*, 'ford'. The name implies that the ford was wide enough to be crossed by a pair of oxen yoked together. The ford would have been over the river Yox here, itself named after the village. DB *Gokesford*.

Yr. For Welsh names beginning thus, see the next word, e.g. for *Yr Wyddgrug*, see WYDD-GRUG, YR. (Such names are in turn often cross-referred to an English form or more familiar spelling.)

Ystumllwynarth. See OYSTERMOUTH.

Z

Zeal Monachorum (village, Devon): 'monks' (estate by the) willow tree'. OE *sealh*, 'sallow', 'willow', + Latin *monachorum*, 'of the monks'. The manor here, on the river Yeo, was held early by the monks of Buckfast Abbey. *956 Seale, 1275 Sele Monachorum*.

Zeals (village, Wilts): '(place by the) willow trees'. OE *sealh*, 'sallow', 'willow'. Zeals is not far from *Selwood Forest*, Somerset, 'wood where willows grow' (*sealh + wudu*, 'wood'). The name reflects Wiltshire *z* for *s* (as *zider* for *cider*). DB *Sele*, 1176 *Seles*.

Zelah (village, Cornwall): 'dwelling'. OE *sele*, 'dwelling', 'house', 'hall'. *1311 Sele, 1613 Zela*.

Zennor (village, Cornwall): '(church of) St Sinar'. The church here is dedicated to Sinar, a female saint about whom nothing is known and whose name is not recorded anywhere else in Cornwall. *c.1170 Sanctus Sinar, 1235 Sancta Sinara, 1522 Senar, 1582 Zenar*.

Zetland. See SHETLAND.